University Casebook Series

November, 1987

ACCOUNTING AND THE LAW, Fourth Edition (1978), with Problems Pamphlet (Successor to Dohr, Phillips, Thompson & Warren)

George C. Thompson, Professor, Columbia University Graduate School of Business.
Robert Whitman, Professor of Law, University of Connecticut.
Ellis L. Phillips, Jr., Member of the New York Bar.
William C. Warren, Professor of Law Emeritus, Columbia University.

ACCOUNTING FOR LAWYERS, MATERIALS ON (1980)

David R. Herwitz, Professor of Law, Harvard University.

ADMINISTRATIVE LAW, Eighth Edition (1987), with 1983 Problems Supplement (Supplement edited in association with Paul R. Verkuil, Dean and Professor of Law, Tulane University)

Walter Gellhorn, University Professor Emeritus, Columbia University.
Clark Byse, Professor of Law, Harvard University.
Peter L. Strauss, Professor of Law, Columbia University.
Todd D. Rakoff, Professor of Law, Harvard University.
Roy A. Schotland, Professor of Law, Georgetown University.

ADMIRALTY, Third Edition (1987), with Statute and Rule Supplement

Jo Desha Lucas, Professor of Law, University of Chicago.

ADVOCACY, see also Lawyering Process

AGENCY, see also Enterprise Organization

AGENCY—PARTNERSHIPS, Fourth Edition (1987)

Abridgement from Conard, Knauss & Siegel's Enterprise Organization, Third Edition.

AGENCY AND PARTNERSHIPS (1987)

Melvin A. Eisenberg, Professor of Law, University of California, Berkeley.

ANTITRUST: FREE ENTERPRISE AND ECONOMIC ORGANIZATION, Sixth Edition (1983), with 1983 Problems in Antitrust Supplement and 1987 Case Supplement

Louis B. Schwartz, Professor of Law, University of Pennsylvania.
John J. Flynn, Professor of Law, University of Utah.
Harry First, Professor of Law, New York University.

BANKRUPTCY (1985)

Robert L. Jordan, Professor of Law, University of California, Los Angeles.
William D. Warren, Professor of Law, University of California, Los Angeles.

BUSINESS ORGANIZATION, see also Enterprise Organization

BUSINESS PLANNING, Temporary Second Edition (1984)

David R. Herwitz, Professor of Law, Harvard University.

BUSINESS TORTS (1972)

Milton Handler, Professor of Law Emeritus, Columbia University.

CHILDREN IN THE LEGAL SYSTEM (1983) with 1988 Supplement

Walter Wadlington, Professor of Law, University of Virginia.
Charles H. Whitebread, Professor of Law, University of Southern California.
Samuel Davis, Professor of Law, University of Georgia.

CIVIL PROCEDURE, see Procedure

CLINIC, see also Lawyering Process

COMMERCIAL LAW, Second Edition (1987)

Robert L. Jordan, Professor of Law, University of California, Los Angeles.
William D. Warren, Professor of Law, University of California, Los Angeles.

COMMERCIAL LAW, CASES & MATERIALS ON, Fourth Edition (1985)

E. Allan Farnsworth, Professor of Law, Columbia University.
John Honnold, Professor of Law, University of Pennsylvania.

COMMERCIAL PAPER, Third Edition (1984)

E. Allan Farnsworth, Professor of Law, Columbia University.

COMMERCIAL PAPER, Second Edition (1987) (Reprinted from COMMERCIAL LAW, Second Edition (1987))

Robert L. Jordan, Professor of Law, University of California, Los Angeles.
William D. Warren, Professor of Law, University of California, Los Angeles.

COMMERCIAL PAPER AND BANK DEPOSITS AND COLLECTIONS (1967), with Statutory Supplement

William D. Hawkland, Professor of Law, University of Illinois.

COMMERCIAL TRANSACTIONS—Principles and Policies (1982)

Alan Schwartz, Professor of Law, University of Southern California.
Robert E. Scott, Professor of Law, University of Virginia.

COMPARATIVE LAW, Fifth Edition (1988)

Rudolf B. Schlesinger, Professor of Law, Hastings College of Law.
Hans W. Baade, Professor of Law, University of Texas.
Peter E. Herzog, Professor of Law, Syracuse University.
Mirjan P. Damaska, Professor of Law, Yale Law School.

COMPETITIVE PROCESS, LEGAL REGULATION OF THE, Third Edition (1986), with 1987 Selected Statutes Supplement

Edmund W. Kitch, Professor of Law, University of Virginia.
Harvey S. Perlman, Dean of the Law School, University of Nebraska.

CONFLICT OF LAWS, Eighth Edition (1984), with 1987 Case Supplement

Willis L. M. Reese, Professor of Law, Columbia University.
Maurice Rosenberg, Professor of Law, Columbia University.

CONSTITUTIONAL LAW, Seventh Edition (1985), with 1987 Supplement

Edward L. Barrett, Jr., Professor of Law, University of California, Davis.
William Cohen, Professor of Law, Stanford University.

CONSTITUTIONAL LAW, CIVIL LIBERTY AND INDIVIDUAL RIGHTS, Second Edition (1982), with 1987 Supplement

William Cohen, Professor of Law, Stanford University.
John Kaplan, Professor of Law, Stanford University.

CONSTITUTIONAL LAW, Eleventh Edition (1985), with 1987 Supplement (Supplement edited in association with Frederick F. Schauer, Professor of Law, University of Michigan)

Gerald Gunther, Professor of Law, Stanford University.

CONSTITUTIONAL LAW, INDIVIDUAL RIGHTS IN, Fourth Edition (1986), (Reprinted from CONSTITUTIONAL LAW, Eleventh Edition), with 1987 Supplement (Supplement edited in association with Frederick F. Schauer, Professor of Law, University of Michigan)

Gerald Gunther, Professor of Law, Stanford University.

CONSUMER TRANSACTIONS (1983), with Selected Statutes and Regulations Supplement and 1987 Case Supplement

Michael M. Greenfield, Professor of Law, Washington University.

CONTRACT LAW AND ITS APPLICATION, Third Edition (1983)

The late Addison Mueller, Professor of Law, University of California, Los Angeles.
Arthur I. Rosett, Professor of Law, University of California, Los Angeles.
Gerald P. Lopez, Professor of Law, University of California, Los Angeles.

CONTRACT LAW, STUDIES IN, Third Edition (1984)

Edward J. Murphy, Professor of Law, University of Notre Dame.
Richard E. Speidel, Professor of Law, Northwestern University.

CONTRACTS, Fifth Edition (1987)

John P. Dawson, Professor of Law Emeritus, Harvard University.
William Burnett Harvey, Professor of Law and Political Science, Boston University.
Stanley D. Henderson, Professor of Law, University of Virginia.

CONTRACTS, Third Edition (1980), with Statutory Supplement

E. Allan Farnsworth, Professor of Law, Columbia University.
William F. Young, Professor of Law, Columbia University.

CONTRACTS, Second Edition (1978), with Statutory and Administrative Law Supplement (1978)

Ian R. Macneil, Professor of Law, Cornell University.

COPYRIGHT, PATENTS AND TRADEMARKS, see also Competitive Process; see also Selected Statutes and International Agreements

COPYRIGHT, PATENT, TRADEMARK AND RELATED STATE DOCTRINES, Second Edition (1981), with 1985 Case Supplement, 1987 Selected Statutes Supplement and 1981 Problem Supplement

Paul Goldstein, Professor of Law, Stanford University.

COPYRIGHT, Unfair Competition, and Other Topics Bearing on the Protection of Literary, Musical, and Artistic Works, Fourth Edition (1985), with 1985 Statutory Supplement

Ralph S. Brown, Jr., Professor of Law, Yale University.
Robert C. Denicola, Professor of Law, University of Nebraska.

CORPORATE ACQUISITIONS, The Law and Finance of (1986), with 1987 Supplement

Ronald J. Gilson, Professor of Law, Stanford University.

CORPORATE FINANCE, Third Edition (1987)

Victor Brudney, Professor of Law, Harvard University.
Marvin A. Chirelstein, Professor of Law, Columbia University.

UNIVERSITY CASEBOOK SERIES—Continued

CORPORATE READJUSTMENTS AND REORGANIZATIONS (1976)

Walter J. Blum, Professor of Law, University of Chicago.
Stanley A. Kaplan, Professor of Law, University of Chicago.

CORPORATION LAW, BASIC, Second Edition (1979), with 1983 Case and Documentary Supplement

Detlev F. Vagts, Professor of Law, Harvard University.

CORPORATIONS, see also Enterprise Organization

CORPORATIONS, Fifth Edition—Unabridged (1980), with 1987 Supplement

The late William L. Cary, Professor of Law, Columbia University.
Melvin Aron Eisenberg, Professor of Law, University of California, Berkeley.

CORPORATIONS, Fifth Edition—Abridged (1980), with 1987 Supplement

The late William L. Cary, Professor of Law, Columbia University.
Melvin Aron Eisenberg, Professor of Law, University of California, Berkeley.

CORPORATIONS COURSE GAME PLAN (1975)

David R. Herwitz, Professor of Law, Harvard University.

CORRECTIONS, SEE SENTENCING

CREDITORS' RIGHTS, see also Debtor-Creditor Law

CRIMINAL JUSTICE ADMINISTRATION, Third Edition (1986), with 1987 Case Supplement

Frank W. Miller, Professor of Law, Washington University.
Robert O. Dawson, Professor of Law, University of Texas.
George E. Dix, Professor of Law, University of Texas.
Raymond I. Parnas, Professor of Law, University of California, Davis.

CRIMINAL LAW, Fourth Edition (1987)

Fred E. Inbau, Professor of Law Emeritus, Northwestern University.
Andre A. Moenssens, Professor of Law, University of Richmond.
James R. Thompson, Professor of Law Emeritus, Northwestern University.

CRIMINAL LAW AND APPROACHES TO THE STUDY OF LAW (1986)

John M. Brumbaugh, Professor of Law, University of Maryland.

CRIMINAL LAW, Second Edition (1986)

Peter W. Low, Professor of Law, University of Virginia.
John C. Jeffries, Jr., Professor of Law, University of Virginia.
Richard C. Bonnie, Professor of Law, University of Virginia.

CRIMINAL LAW, Fourth Edition (1986)

Lloyd L. Weinreb, Professor of Law, Harvard University.

CRIMINAL LAW AND PROCEDURE, Sixth Edition (1984)

Rollin M. Perkins, Professor of Law Emeritus, University of California, Hastings College of the Law.
Ronald N. Boyce, Professor of Law, University of Utah.

CRIMINAL PROCEDURE, Third Edition (1987), with 1987 Supplement

James B. Haddad, Professor of Law, Northwestern University.
James B. Zagel, Chief, Criminal Justice Division, Office of Attorney General of Illinois.
Gary L. Starkman, Assistant U. S. Attorney, Northern District of Illinois.
William J. Bauer, Chief Judge of the U.S. Court of Appeals, Seventh Circuit.

UNIVERSITY CASEBOOK SERIES—Continued

ETHICS, see Legal Profession, and Professional Responsibility

ETHICS AND PROFESSIONAL RESPONSIBILITY (1981) (Reprinted from THE LAWYERING PROCESS)

Gary Bellow, Professor of Law, Harvard University.
Bea Moulton, Legal Services Corporation.

EVIDENCE, Sixth Edition (1987)

John Kaplan, Professor of Law, Stanford University.
Jon R. Waltz, Professor of Law, Northwestern University.

EVIDENCE, Seventh Edition (1983) with Rules, Statute and Case Supplement (1987)

Jack B. Weinstein, Chief Judge, United States District Court.
John H. Mansfield, Professor of Law, Harvard University.
Norman Abrams, Professor of Law, University of California, Los Angeles.
Margaret Berger, Professor of Law, Brooklyn Law School.

FAMILY LAW, see also Domestic Relations

FAMILY LAW Second Edition (1985)

Judith C. Areen, Professor of Law, Georgetown University.

FAMILY LAW AND CHILDREN IN THE LEGAL SYSTEM, STATUTORY MATERIALS (1981)

Walter Wadlington, Professor of Law, University of Virginia.

FEDERAL COURTS, Seventh Edition (1982), with 1987 Supplement

Charles T. McCormick, late Professor of Law, University of Texas.
James H. Chadbourn, late Professor of Law, Harvard University.
Charles Alan Wright, Professor of Law, University of Texas.

FEDERAL COURTS AND THE FEDERAL SYSTEM, Hart and Wechsler's Second Edition (1973), with 1981 Supplement

Paul M. Bator, Professor of Law, Harvard University.
Paul J. Mishkin, Professor of Law, University of California, Berkeley.
David L. Shapiro, Professor of Law, Harvard University.
Herbert Wechsler, Professor of Law, Columbia University.

FEDERAL COURTS AND THE LAW OF FEDERAL–STATE RELATIONS (1987), with 1987 Supplement

Peter W. Low, Professor of Law, University of Virginia.
John C. Jeffries, Jr., Professor of Law, University of Virginia.

FEDERAL PUBLIC LAND AND RESOURCES LAW, Second Edition (1987), with 1984 Statutory Supplement

George C. Coggins, Professor of Law, University of Kansas.
Charles F. Wilkinson, Professor of Law, University of Oregon.

FEDERAL RULES OF CIVIL PROCEDURE, 1987 Edition

FEDERAL TAXATION, see Taxation

FOOD AND DRUG LAW (1980), with Statutory Supplement

Richard A. Merrill, Dean of the School of Law, University of Virginia.
Peter Barton Hutt, Esq.

FUTURE INTERESTS (1958)

Philip Mechem, late Professor of Law Emeritus, University of Pennsylvania.

UNIVERSITY CASEBOOK SERIES—Continued

FUTURE INTERESTS (1970)

Howard R. Williams, Professor of Law, Stanford University.

FUTURE INTERESTS AND ESTATE PLANNING (1961), with 1962 Supplement

W. Barton Leach, late Professor of Law, Harvard University.
James K. Logan, formerly Dean of the Law School, University of Kansas.

GOVERNMENT CONTRACTS, FEDERAL, Successor Edition (1985)

John W. Whelan, Professor of Law, Hastings College of the Law.

**GOVERNMENT REGULATION: FREE ENTERPRISE AND ECONOMIC ORGANI-
ZATION, Sixth Edition (1985)**

Louis B. Schwartz, Professor of Law, Hastings College of the Law.
John J. Flynn, Professor of Law, University of Utah.
Harry First, Professor of Law, New York University.

**HINCKLEY JOHN W., TRIAL OF: A Case Study of the Insanity Defense
(1986)**

Peter W. Low, Professor of Law, University of Virginia.
John C. Jeffries, Jr., Professor of Law, University of Virginia.
Richard C. Bonnie, Professor of Law, University of Virginia.

INJUNCTIONS, Second Edition (1984)

Owen M. Fiss, Professor of Law, Yale University.
Doug Rendleman, Professor of Law, College of William and Mary.

INSTITUTIONAL INVESTORS, (1978)

David L. Ratner, Professor of Law, Cornell University.

INSURANCE, Second Edition (1985)

William F. Young, Professor of Law, Columbia University.
Eric M. Holmes, Professor of Law, University of Georgia.

**INTERNATIONAL LAW, see also Transnational Legal Problems, Transnational
Business Problems, and United Nations Law**

**INTERNATIONAL LAW IN CONTEMPORARY PERSPECTIVE (1981), with Essay
Supplement**

Myres S. McDougal, Professor of Law, Yale University.
W. Michael Reisman, Professor of Law, Yale University.

**INTERNATIONAL LEGAL SYSTEM, Second Edition (1981), with Documentary
Supplement**

Joseph Modeste Sweeney, Professor of Law, Tulane University.
Covey T. Oliver, Professor of Law, University of Pennsylvania.
Noyes E. Leech, Professor of Law, University of Pennsylvania.

**INTRODUCTION TO LAW, see also Legal Method, On Law in Courts, and
Dynamics of American Law**

INTRODUCTION TO THE STUDY OF LAW (1970)

E. Wayne Thode, late Professor of Law, University of Utah.
Leon Lebowitz, Professor of Law, University of Texas.
Lester J. Mazor, Professor of Law, University of Utah.

**JUDICIAL CODE and Rules of Procedure in the Federal Courts with Excerpts
from the Criminal Code, 1984 Edition**

Henry M. Hart, Jr., late Professor of Law, Harvard University.
Herbert Wechsler, Professor of Law, Columbia University.

UNIVERSITY CASEBOOK SERIES—Continued

JURISPRUDENCE (Temporary Edition Hardbound) (1949)

Lon L. Fuller, late Professor of Law, Harvard University.

JUVENILE, see also Children

JUVENILE JUSTICE PROCESS, Third Edition (1985)

Frank W. Miller, Professor of Law, Washington University.
Robert O. Dawson, Professor of Law, University of Texas.
George E. Dix, Professor of Law, University of Texas.
Raymond I. Parnas, Professor of Law, University of California, Davis.

LABOR LAW, Tenth Edition (1986), with 1986 Statutory Supplement

Archibald Cox, Professor of Law, Harvard University.
Derek C. Bok, President, Harvard University.
Robert A. Gorman, Professor of Law, University of Pennsylvania.

LABOR LAW, Second Edition (1982), with Statutory Supplement

Clyde W. Summers, Professor of Law, University of Pennsylvania.
Harry H. Wellington, Dean of the Law School, Yale University.
Alan Hyde, Professor of Law, Rutgers University.

LAND FINANCING, Third Edition (1985)

The late Norman Penney, Professor of Law, Cornell University.
Richard F. Broude, Member of the California Bar.
Roger Cunningham, Professor of Law, University of Michigan.

LAW AND MEDICINE (1980)

Walter Wadlington, Professor of Law and Professor of Legal Medicine, University of Virginia.
Jon R. Waltz, Professor of Law, Northwestern University.
Roger B. Dworkin, Professor of Law, Indiana University, and Professor of Biomedical History, University of Washington.

LAW, LANGUAGE AND ETHICS (1972)

William R. Bishin, Professor of Law, University of Southern California.
Christopher D. Stone, Professor of Law, University of Southern California.

LAW, SCIENCE AND MEDICINE (1984), with 1987 Supplement

Judith C. Areen, Professor of Law, Georgetown University.
Patricia A. King, Professor of Law, Georgetown University.
Steven P. Goldberg, Professor of Law, Georgetown University.
Alexander M. Capron, Professor of Law, University of Southern California.

LAWYERING PROCESS (1978), with Civil Problem Supplement and Criminal Problem Supplement

Gary Bellow, Professor of Law, Harvard University.
Bea Moulton, Professor of Law, Arizona State University.

LEGAL METHOD (1980)

Harry W. Jones, Professor of Law Emeritus, Columbia University.
John M. Kernochan, Professor of Law, Columbia University.
Arthur W. Murphy, Professor of Law, Columbia University.

LEGAL METHODS (1969)

Robert N. Covington, Professor of Law, Vanderbilt University.
E. Blythe Stason, late Professor of Law, Vanderbilt University.
John W. Wade, Professor of Law, Vanderbilt University.
Elliott E. Cheatham, late Professor of Law, Vanderbilt University.
Theodore A. Smedley, Professor of Law, Vanderbilt University.

UNIVERSITY CASEBOOK SERIES—Continued

LEGAL PROFESSION, THE, Responsibility and Regulation (1985)

Geoffrey C. Hazard, Jr., Professor of Law, Yale University.
Deborah L. Rhode, Professor of Law, Stanford University.

LEGISLATION, Fourth Edition (1982) (by Fordham)

Horace E. Read, late Vice President, Dalhousie University.
John W. MacDonald, Professor of Law Emeritus, Cornell Law School.
Jefferson B. Fordham, Professor of Law, University of Utah.
William J. Pierce, Professor of Law, University of Michigan.

LEGISLATIVE AND ADMINISTRATIVE PROCESSES, Second Edition (1981)

Hans A. Linde, Judge, Supreme Court of Oregon.
George Bunn, Professor of Law, University of Wisconsin.
Fredericka Paff, Professor of Law, University of Wisconsin.
W. Lawrence Church, Professor of Law, University of Wisconsin.

LOCAL GOVERNMENT LAW, Second Revised Edition (1986)

Jefferson B. Fordham, Professor of Law, University of Utah.

MASS MEDIA LAW, Third Edition (1987)

Marc A. Franklin, Professor of Law, Stanford University.

MENTAL HEALTH PROCESS, Second Edition (1976), with 1981 Supplement

Frank W. Miller, Professor of Law, Washington University.
Robert O. Dawson, Professor of Law, University of Texas.
George E. Dix, Professor of Law, University of Texas.
Raymond I. Parnas, Professor of Law, University of California, Davis.

MUNICIPAL CORPORATIONS, see Local Government Law

NEGOTIABLE INSTRUMENTS, see Commercial Paper

NEGOTIATION (1981) (Reprinted from THE LAWYERING PROCESS)

Gary Bellow, Professor of Law, Harvard Law School.
Bea Moulton, Legal Services Corporation.

NEW YORK PRACTICE, Fourth Edition (1978)

Herbert Peterfreund, Professor of Law, New York University.
Joseph M. McLaughlin, Dean of the Law School, Fordham University.

OIL AND GAS, Fifth Edition (1987)

Howard R. Williams, Professor of Law, Stanford University.
Richard C. Maxwell, Professor of Law, University of California, Los Angeles.
Charles J. Meyers, Dean of the Law School, Stanford University.
Stephen F. Williams, Judge of the United States Court of Appeals.

ON LAW IN COURTS (1965)

Paul J. Mishkin, Professor of Law, University of California, Berkeley.
Clarence Morris, Professor of Law Emeritus, University of Pennsylvania.

PATENTS AND ANTITRUST (Pamphlet) (1983)

Milton Handler, Professor of Law Emeritus, Columbia University.
Harlan M. Blake, Professor of Law, Columbia University.
Robert Pitofsky, Professor of Law, Georgetown University.
Harvey J. Goldschmid, Professor of Law, Columbia University.

PERSPECTIVES ON THE LAWYER AS PLANNER (Reprint of Chapters One through Five of Planning by Lawyers) (1978)

Louis M. Brown, Professor of Law, University of Southern California.
Edward A. Dauer, Professor of Law, Yale University.

PLANNING BY LAWYERS, MATERIALS ON A NONADVERSARIAL LEGAL PROCESS (1978)

Louis M. Brown, Professor of Law, University of Southern California.
Edward A. Dauer, Professor of Law, Yale University.

PLEADING AND PROCEDURE, see Procedure, Civil

POLICE FUNCTION, Fourth Edition (1986), with 1987 Case Supplement

Reprint of Chapters 1–10 of Miller, Dawson, Dix and Parnas's CRIMINAL JUSTICE ADMINISTRATION, Third Edition.

PREPARING AND PRESENTING THE CASE (1981) (Reprinted from THE LAW-YERING PROCESS)

Gary Bellow, Professor of Law, Harvard Law School.
Bea Moulton, Legal Services Corporation.

PREVENTIVE LAW, see also Planning by Lawyers

PROCEDURE (1988)

Robert M. Cover, Late Professor of Law, Yale Law School.
Owen M. Fiss, professor of Law, Yale Law School.
Judith Resnik, Professor of Law, University of Southern California Law Center.

PROCEDURE—CIVIL PROCEDURE, Second Edition (1974), with 1979 Supplement

The late James H. Chadbourn, Professor of Law, Harvard University.
A. Leo Levin, Professor of Law, University of Pennsylvania.
Philip Shuchman, Professor of Law, Cornell University.

PROCEDURE—CIVIL PROCEDURE, Fifth Edition (1984), with 1987 Supplement

Richard H. Field, late Professor of Law, Harvard University.
Benjamin Kaplan, Professor of Law Emeritus, Harvard University.
Kevin M. Clermont, Professor of Law, Cornell University.

PROCEDURE—CIVIL PROCEDURE, Fourth Edition (1985), with 1987 Supplement

Maurice Rosenberg, Professor of Law, Columbia University.
Hans Smit, Professor of Law, Columbia University.
Harold L. Korn, Professor of Law, Columbia University.

PROCEDURE—PLEADING AND PROCEDURE: State and Federal, Fifth Edition (1983), with 1987 Supplement

David W. Louisell, late Professor of Law, University of California, Berkeley.
Geoffrey C. Hazard, Jr., Professor of Law, Yale University.
Colin C. Tait, Professor of Law, University of Connecticut.

PROCEDURE—FEDERAL RULES OF CIVIL PROCEDURE, 1987 Edition

PRODUCTS LIABILITY (1980)

Marshall S. Shapo, Professor of Law, Northwestern University.

UNIVERSITY CASEBOOK SERIES—Continued

PRODUCTS LIABILITY AND SAFETY (1980), with 1985 Case and Documentary Supplement

W. Page Keeton, Professor of Law, University of Texas.
David G. Owen, Professor of Law, University of South Carolina.
John E. Montgomery, Professor of Law, University of South Carolina.

PROFESSIONAL RESPONSIBILITY, Fourth Edition (1987), with 1988 Selected National Standards Supplement

Thomas D. Morgan, Dean of the Law School, Emory University.
Ronald D. Rotunda, Professor of Law, University of Illinois.

PROPERTY, Fifth Edition (1984)

John E. Cribbet, Professor of Law, University of Illinois.
Corwin W. Johnson, Professor of Law, University of Texas.

PROPERTY—PERSONAL (1953)

S. Kenneth Skolfield, late Professor of Law Emeritus, Boston University.

PROPERTY—PERSONAL, Third Edition (1954)

Everett Fraser, late Dean of the Law School Emeritus, University of Minnesota.
Third Edition by Charles W. Taintor, late Professor of Law, University of Pittsburgh.

PROPERTY—INTRODUCTION, TO REAL PROPERTY, Third Edition (1954)

Everett Fraser, late Dean of the Law School Emeritus, University of Minnesota.

PROPERTY—REAL AND PERSONAL, Combined Edition (1954)

Everett Fraser, late Dean of the Law School Emeritus, University of Minnesota.
Third Edition of Personal Property by Charles W. Taintor, late Professor of Law, University of Pittsburgh.

PROPERTY—FUNDAMENTALS OF MODERN REAL PROPERTY, Second Edition (1982), with 1985 Supplement

Edward H. Rabin, Professor of Law, University of California, Davis.

PROPERTY—PROBLEMS IN REAL PROPERTY (Pamphlet) (1969)

Edward H. Rabin, Professor of Law, University of California, Davis.

PROPERTY, REAL (1984)

Paul Goldstein, Professor of Law, Stanford University.

PROSECUTION AND ADJUDICATION, Third Edition (1986), with 1987 Case Supplement

Reprint of Chapters 11–26 of Miller, Dawson, Dix and Parnas's CRIMINAL JUSTICE ADMINISTRATION, Third Edition.

PSYCHIATRY AND LAW, see Mental Health, see also Hinckley, Trial of

PUBLIC REGULATION OF DANGEROUS PRODUCTS (paperback) (1980)

Marshall S. Shapo, Professor of Law, Northwestern University.

PUBLIC UTILITY LAW, see Free Enterprise, also Regulated Industries

REAL ESTATE PLANNING, Second Edition (1980), with 1980 Problems, Statutes and New Materials Supplement

Norton L. Steuben, Professor of Law, University of Colorado.

UNIVERSITY CASEBOOK SERIES—Continued

TAXES AND FINANCE—STATE AND LOCAL (1974)

Oliver Oldman, Professor of Law, Harvard University.
Ferdinand P. Schoettle, Professor of Law, University of Minnesota.

TORT LAW AND ALTERNATIVES, Fourth Edition (1987)

Marc A. Franklin, Professor of Law, Stanford University.
Robert L. Rabin, Professor of Law, Stanford University.

TORTS, Seventh Edition (1982)

William L. Prosser, late Professor of Law, University of California, Hastings
    College.
John W. Wade, Professor of Law, Vanderbilt University.
Victor E. Schwartz, Professor of Law, American University.

TORTS, Third Edition (1976)

Harry Shulman, late Dean of the Law School, Yale University.
Fleming James, Jr., Professor of Law Emeritus, Yale University.
Oscar S. Gray, Professor of Law, University of Maryland.

TRADE REGULATION, Second Edition (1983), with 1987 Supplement

Milton Handler, Professor of Law Emeritus, Columbia University.
Harlan M. Blake, Professor of Law, Columbia University.
Robert Pitofsky, Professor of Law, Georgetown University.
Harvey J. Goldschmid, Professor of Law, Columbia University.

TRADE REGULATION, see Antitrust

TRANSNATIONAL BUSINESS PROBLEMS (1986)

Detlev F. Vagts, Professor of Law, Harvard University.

**TRANSNATIONAL LEGAL PROBLEMS, Third Edition (1986) with Documentary
    Supplement**

Henry J. Steiner, Professor of Law, Harvard University.
Detlev F. Vagts, Professor of Law, Harvard University.

**TRIAL, see also Evidence, Making the Record, Lawyering Process and Pre-
    paring and Presenting the Case**

TRIAL ADVOCACY (1968)

A. Leo Levin, Professor of Law, University of Pennsylvania.
Harold Cramer, of the Pennsylvania Bar.
Maurice Rosenberg, Professor of Law, Columbia University, Consultant.

TRUSTS, Fifth Edition (1978)

George G. Bogert, late Professor of Law Emeritus, University of Chicago.
Dallin H. Oaks, President, Brigham Young University.

TRUSTS AND SUCCESSION (Palmer's), Fourth Edition (1983)

Richard V. Wellman, Professor of Law, University of Georgia.
Lawrence W. Waggoner, Professor of Law, University of Michigan.
Olin L. Browder, Jr., Professor of Law, University of Michigan.

UNFAIR COMPETITION, see Competitive Process and Business Torts

**UNITED NATIONS LAW, Second Edition (1967), with Documentary Supple-
    ment (1968)**

Louis B. Sohn, Professor of Law, Harvard University.

UNIVERSITY CASEBOOK SERIES—Continued

WATER RESOURCE MANAGEMENT, Third Edition (1988)

Charles J. Meyers, Esq., Denver, Colorado, formerly Dean, Stanford University Law School.

A. Dan Tarlock, Professor of Law, ITT Chicago-Kent College of Law.

James N. Corbridge, Jr., Chancellor, University of Colorado at Boulder, and Professor of Law, University of Colorado School of Law.

David H. Getches, Professor of Law, University of Colorado School of Law.

WILLS AND ADMINISTRATION, Fifth Edition (1961)

Philip Mechem, late Professor of Law, University of Pennsylvania.

Thomas E. Atkinson, late Professor of Law, New York University.

WORLD LAW, see United Nations Law

University Casebook Series

THE COURTHOUSE ON THE ISLAND OF TOBAGO*

"Can the Island of Tobago pass a law to bind the rights of the whole world?"
per Lord Ellenborough in Buchanan v. Rucker, page 42, infra.

* This is the courthouse referred to by Lord Ellenborough. It has been replaced by a modern building.

CASES AND MATERIALS

ON

CONFLICT OF LAWS

By

WILLIS L. M. REESE

Charles Evans Hughes Professor Emeritus of Law,
Columbia University
Reporter, Restatement of Conflict of Laws, Second

MAURICE ROSENBERG

Harold R. Medina Professor of Procedural Jurisprudence,
Columbia University

EIGHTH EDITION

(Continuing series edited by Cheatham, Griswold et al.)

Mineola, New York
THE FOUNDATION PRESS, INC.
1984

Library of Congress Cataloging in Publication Data

Reese, Willis L. M.
  Cases and materials on conflict of laws.

  (University casebook series)
  Bibliography: p.
  Includes index.
  1. Conflict of laws—United States—Cases. I. Rosen-
berg, Maurice, 1919–   . II. Title. III. Series.
KF410.R44 1984   340.9   84–6097

ISBN 0–88277–176–0

  Reese & Rosenberg Cs. Conflict Laws 8th Ed. UCB

  3rd Reprint—1986

To
Elliott E. Cheatham
and
Erwin N. Griswold,

great teachers and men of law,
who, throughout, have been
and ever will be our mentors.

*

PREFACE

The overall arrangement that this book adopted two editions ago remains intact. We are convinced that the present plan contributes to the student's grasp of the materials. Once a student understands when and why a court may hear a case that has only tenuous connections to a state; appreciates that a court with a valid basis for hearing a case may nonetheless decline to do so; and is aware of the dramatic effects the full faith and credit principle gives a sister-state judgment, choice-of-law issues take on added meaning. Also, it aids understanding to deal in one place with the main aspects of the substance-procedure dichotomy even though the once bright line of demarcation between these concepts has continued to fade. After the student has studied the cases in chapter 7 dealing with the substance-procedure classification, the implications of applying the interests analysis to issues traditionally deemed automatically subject to the forum's procedural rules become clearer.

We also adhere to the approach of bringing together in two comprehensive chapters diverse choice-of-law problems drawn from a variety of substantive areas. This approach seems to us an effective compromise between, on the one hand, dealing with choice of law problems wholly in terms of substantive categories of cases and on the other hand scrapping all classifications.

This edition tracks recent judicial responses to the modern approaches to choice of law, such as interests analysis, the use of "choice-influencing considerations," and the Second Restatement's methodology. Newer decisions have revealed no major shift toward interests analysis or other anti-rule approaches, except possibly in the field of time limitations where the traditional "procedural" characterization of the statute of limitations has been replaced in a number of states by an interest-oriented approach.

At the constitutional level the main definitive activity since the Seventh Edition has been in the field of judicial jurisdiction. First came two jurisdiction-restricting decisions—*World-Wide Volkswagen* v. *Woodson* and *Rush* v. *Savchuk*—that gave the impression the Supreme Court intended that the states desist from efforts to extend long-arm jurisdiction over nonresidents having only tenuous contacts with the forum. However, early in 1984 the Court decided *Keeton* v. *Hustler*, suggesting a relaxation of widely-sensed restrictions on state jurisdiction over national media, flowing from First Amendent policies. Reconciliation of the somewhat inconsistent signals emanating from the judicial jurisdiction cases will be a challenging task.

In the fields of judgments and choice of law the Justices were often unable to achieve positions attracting a majority vote of the Court. Thus the long-term effects of *Thomas* v. *Washington Gaslight Co.* and *Allstate Ins. Co.* v. *Hague* are less than clear. In the judgments field it does seem plain that the courts will have numerous opportunities to grapple with the res judicata effect of state decisions on subsequent federal civil rights actions.

One of the topics that receives new emphasis in this edition is child custody in the interstate setting. Recent statutory changes in the custody field are highlighted, including the complex interaction between the Uniform Child Custody Jurisdiction Act and the federal Parental Kidnaping Prevention Act of 1980.

The decade of the 1970's was a period of consolidation in conflict of laws. At about the midway mark in the 1980's the same phenomenon is apparent. In the consolidation process, yesterday's solutions have a tendency to become today's problems.

WILLIS L. M. REESE
MAURICE ROSENBERG

April 1984

SUMMARY OF CONTENTS

SUMMARY OF CONTENTS

SUMMARY OF CONTENTS

*

TABLE OF CONTENTS

TABLE OF CONTENTS

TABLE OF CONTENTS

TABLE OF CONTENTS

TABLE OF CONTENTS

TABLE OF CONTENTS

TABLE OF CONTENTS

xxxviii

*

TABLE OF CASES

The principal cases are in italic type. Cases cited or discussed are in roman. References are to Pages.

1

liv

TABLE OF CASES

TABLE OF CASES

TABLE OF BOOKS AND ARTICLES

Books are listed first in italics.   Articles follow in chronological order.

TABLE OF BOOKS AND ARTICLES

*

CASES AND MATERIALS
ON
CONFLICT OF LAWS

*

Chapter 1

INTRODUCTION

1. *The Subject Matter*

In a basic respect laymen and lawyers are doubtless alike when they think about legal problems. They are conscious that many transactions—business, social, personal; planned and unplanned—cut across state boundaries, yet they do not instinctively turn their minds to the possible legal complications these multistate contacts may generate. This seems true for judges and legislators as well as for ordinary citizens. All of us are inured to the territorial system and are accustomed to think primarily of our own territorial unit and its laws. The uncertainties of local laws regarding familiar legal problems, such as highway accidents and making wills and contracts, keep citizens and their lawyers amply puzzled; they have no need to speculate about conflicts complexities, such as what difference it makes that the matter at hand straddles state lines or national boundaries.

In contrast to the normal instinct for one-state legal thinking, the watchword of conflict of laws is "think spatially." At all events, it was the dominant motif in this field of legal learning during most of our history. For many lawyers it still is the most helpful approach. In their view, the world is a legal checkerboard, divided into a growing number of nations, each with its own set of laws and institutions for the administration of justice. There are already about 170 independent sovereign states and the number keeps increasing.

Some of the nations are not unitary legal systems, but like the United States, federations of smaller states that possess substantial areas of sovereignty in definite spheres, making and enforcing their own laws, maintaining their own courts, insisting on their own procedures, and jealous of their own powers or prerogatives.

Because of the multitude of diverse systems of law and the increasing tendency for people to move, act, transact and make contact with legal matters in disregard of state or national boundaries, questions increasingly arise as to how to dispose of their legal conflicts when these touch more than one state.*

After studying law for a year or more, one scarcely needs to be reminded of the ramifications of a multistate system, especially if one is studying at an out-of-state school. Yet a simple illustration may

---

* The term "state" may refer either to one of the fifty states of the United States (or similar subdivisions of other countries) or to a nation-state.

1

underline the pervasiveness and diversity that results when such transactions occur.

A couple marries in State X. After several years and two children their marriage fails and they contemplate divorce. The wife is concerned for the children and their support. The wife and husband are unable to agree on terms they think important and in time he departs for State Y, intending a sojourn of limited duration. He is aware that in State Y marriages can be ended for reasons that do not suffice in State X; and, specifically, for the kinds of reasons he has, or cares to assert, to obtain a divorce.

The wife is not inclined to be cooperative, believing the husband's behavior has been reprehensible and that in the matter of providing support and other financial benefits, he has been stingy.

Conflict of laws problems pervade this everyday scenario. Will State Y's courts assume power over the marital status of a wife who has never set foot on State Y soil, driven on its highways, or even flown over its territory in a plane? Suppose they do take jurisdiction of the case on the basis of the husband's six-week residence in State Y: Will they be able to render a decree validly divorcing this pair who have spent their whole married lives in State X? If the answers thus far are affirmative, we come to the grounds for decreeing divorce. May the State Y divorce court use alleged temperamental unsuitability or incompatibility or some other formula betokening personal frictions as adequate grounds for dissolving a marriage of many years' duration—and one celebrated, consummated and domesticated in a state that may insist on serious "fault" (e.g., physical cruelty, adultery) by the respondent spouse as the only proper basis for divorcing her? If the answer is again yes and the divorce is granted to the husband and he returns to State X to take up an unwed life, will he be as legally free of obligations to support his former wife and the children as the State Y decree may provide? Or will State X compel support in a manner the local law deems just, if the wife insists?

Indeed, will State X pay any attention at all to the State Y divorce decree? Must it? On what grounds, if any, may State X permit the wife to upset or disregard the State Y divorce? Is it conceivable that State X will be compelled to recognize the divorce as a valid dissolution of the marriage, but not as a valid termination of the husband-father's duty to provide financial support for his family?

The first question—whether the wife can be compelled to go to State Y and to defend the husband's divorce suit or lose by default—involves the problem of *judicial jurisdiction*. The question of what grounds State Y would use, or be free to use, as a basis for granting a divorce is an example of a *choice of law* problem. The effect of a State Y decree of divorce (whether it would command recognition and enforcement in State X or other states) involves the third main topic in conflict of laws—*judgments*.

Questions of these kinds daily arise in countless legal contexts and they form the subject matter of conflict of laws, speaking generally and over-simply.

2. *The Functions of Conflicts as a Body of Law*

What use are all the esoteric concepts, theories, principles, rules and methods this body of learning is supposed to embrace? Would the world be a poorer place if man had not devised the dark and elaborate science of conflicts? The answer is obviously yes for the conflicts teacher, but we are not speaking so narrowly. Even those with less pointed stakes in the subject agree that conflict of laws is a necessary corpus of legal thought. They recognize that as the problems of societies grow more complex, proper intermeshing and easy accommodation of multistate diversities grow more difficult and more necessary. Conflict of laws provides insights that may help to manage the multifarious legal problems that arise from the constant crisscrossing of people and their affairs among territorially organized legal systems.

Beyond its practical potential in the world community, the subject of conflict of laws has a special educational value for law professionals. It offers a distinctive window on the legal world, through which students of the law may have an unsurpassed view of how rules of law arise, function, interact and, at times, compete with one another. It analyzes the ways in which judges attempt to resolve disputes justly and lawfully when there is added to the usual unknowns of legal controversy the extra puzzle as to which rules of decision are the proper ones to apply. Conflict of laws tries to afford insights by asking questions, suggesting guidelines, and exploring approaches regarding all those challenging problems.

3. *History*

This may be one of the rare legal subjects about which a page of history is worth less than a blank sheet. That harsh judgment by some conflicts specialists flows from their impression that history— particularly an exaggerated reverence for an ancient body of concepts and dogmas—may be in large part responsible for contemporary difficulties. They argue that the orthodox ideas and theories based on "vested rights," "*obligatio*" and territorial imperatives impede sound thinking in the modern setting. Still, Holmes' epigram about the life of the law does not down easily. History and experience count for something in dealing with today's problems. Accordingly, whether it sheds light or darkness to take a brief excursion into the historical antecedents of this subject, to do so seems proper.

Our debt to England is here not as large as in other fields, for conflict of laws had an arrested development in English jurisprudence. The early centralization of power in the king and the establishment of a common law for the whole realm put an end to the conflicting laws inside the kingdom and eliminated the intra-national conflict of laws which elsewhere stimulated the development of the subject. International conflict of laws cases were kept out of the common law courts by a principle of venue; for, since the trial was to be by a jury of the vicinage, the courts felt themselves unable to try cases arising in other countries. International cases had to go into special courts—the merchants courts and the court of admiralty. In time the difficulty of venue was surmounted in the common law courts by a fiction: the facts were treated as having occurred in England. But the idea persisted that a case must be determined under the ordinary law of the court in which it was tried and not any other. Not until the nineteenth and twentieth centuries did England develop a coherent body of doctrines of conflict of laws and by that time developments on this side of the ocean had taken their own course.

On the continent of Europe, the need for principles of conflict of laws had become apparent very early, at first in Italy and later in France. The development of the principles of conflict of laws began in the Italian universities in the 1200's and 1300's during the revival of the study of Roman law. The conditions demanded it. Northern Italy was divided into a number of city states. While they were a part of the Holy Roman Empire and regarded Roman law as a common law applicable to all of them, each had its local laws governing many matters. Trade was brisk between them and conflicts between their local laws arose with some frequency. A Bologna-Padua case or a Florence-Perugia case was apt to involve conflicting laws; in time, principles were developed to settle these conflicts. The local laws of the city states were called "statuta." The basic method or theory of the emerging system concerning the choice of the law to be applied to a case came to be called the statuta or statute theory. It is discussed in some American cases.

Afterwards, France and then the Netherlands developed conflicts theories that were in a sense intra-national, reflecting the diversity of legal systems among their constituent provinces. The writings of a Dutch jurist, Huber, proved highly influential in America, for his conception of territorial sovereignty made a deep impact on a great, early theorist in American conflicts law, Justice Joseph Story. In 1834 Story published his Commentaries on the Conflict of Laws, the first comprehensive treatment in English on the subject. For his general views he relied on continental theorists, particularly Huber, and Huber's dedication to the idea of territorial sovereignty as the foundation of thinking about the subject.

The course of growth in the next century was heavily influenced by the Story-Huber approach. This was embraced in its main parts by Professor Joseph H. Beale, who had an enormous influence through his teachings, commentaries, and, ultimately, his work as Reporter for the American Law Institute's first Restatement of Conflict of Laws, published in 1934.

4. *Recent Changes*

The social and doctrinal movements of recent decades have not neglected this subject. Conflicts thinking in the present generation bears little relationship to conflicts ideas of a half century ago.

With regard to the three main branches of the subject, the effect of the changed perspectives can be summarized in a few words. New ideas have infused the judicial jurisdiction branch of the subject, have revamped it to a considerable extent, and have challenged such established concepts as the distinction between in rem and in personam jurisdiction. The subject of judgments has reflected to some extent the expanded use of res judicata and other litigation-precluding doctrines. The topic of choice of law has been reshaped in a revolutionary way.

Judicial jurisdiction in the early part of the century was characterized by stern dogmas, implacable doctrines and impermeable conceptual compartments. For example, jurisdiction was believed to exist in three distinct and mutually exclusive species: in rem, quasi-in-rem, and in personam. "Power" over the "thing" in suit or the person of the defendant was thought to be the *sine qua non* of the capacity of courts to affect legal interests. Depending on whether jurisdiction was asserted over a thing or the defendant's person, inexorable consequences followed. These had to do with the required form of notice and the scope and effect of the judgment that resulted. The old conceptualism has given way in large measure to a more pragmatic approach.

In the field of judgments, where doctrine and theory have not undergone a revision comparable in scale to that in the jurisdiction field, the great divide still is that between sister state and other intra-national judgments on the one hand and international judgments on the other. Of course, the difference results from the fact that the former are by constitutional command due full faith and credit in this country and the latter are due some lesser level of respect.

But it is particularly the choice-of-law branch of conflicts that recent explosive ideas have reduced to jurisprudential rubble. Although other areas of law have moved rapidly to abandon old rules and embrace new ones that are often more plastic, result-oriented and fluid in operation, in the choice-of-law process, the upheaval has gone far beyond shaking and loosening the hard-and-fast prescriptions that once purported to tell courts which legal system to select to govern each conflicts case. The changes have been volcanic. Many influential modern conflicts authorities have urged, with some success, that revising and revamping the rules is not enough—that we must totally dismantle the apparatus of choice of law and discard its underlying premises. In lieu of the old systematics that were oriented to rules, they have argued for the substitution of a type of reasoning, a mode of analysis, an approach—in a word, a "method"—for the resolution of choice-of-law problems. The methodology has no patience with the old-time yearning for broad and simple choice-of-law rules. Indeed, some modernists reject the view that any *a priori* rule can provide a just, usable and rational means of resolving choice-of-law questions. The great scholarly battles over the best way to deal with choice-of-law questions continue.

5. *The Future of Conflicts*

In the years ahead the world seems destined to hear more, not less, about this sector of the law. All over the globe, law teachers, lawmakers and law practitioners are ever more aware of the existence of conflicts problems and of the need to deal with them as more than the crumbs of more significant legal fare. International groups have formed to deal with problems of "private international law," as the conflicts subject is called abroad. Treaties, conventions and protocols increasingly devote much energy and attention to conflicts problems.

Within the United States, awareness of the special demands made by multistate legal problems is also growing rapidly. As the states of the union persist in exercising their right to go their own ways and treat common problems diversely, their legislatures are becoming more conscious of the possible spill-over effects of the home state's rules in other states—especially when home state residents travel across country. Conversely, courts, legislatures and lawyers are becoming more conscious of the impact of other states' divergent rules and laws upon home state citizens.

Of course, being aware of a problem is not tantamount to seeing a solution for it. Courts and legislatures that deal only sporadically with these complex matters cannot be expected to share a single view of how to resolve them when the specialists are themselves in such gross and profound disagreement about first principles.

In many branches of the subject, there is room for federal action, both at the legislative and judicial levels. Despite a few recent attempts, the Supreme Court has not yet responded effectively to the pleas of litigants, the lower courts and academics for constitutional guidance in the judgments and choice-of-law fields. As for Congress, it has not found the interest or imagination to devise legislative solutions, either by prescribing nationwide substantive rules or mandatory choice-of-law rules. Obviously, in areas of interstate activities, soundly-designed Congressional action puts to rest uncertainties over the applicable rules of decision. But present signs do not portend an end of turbulence in this field in consequence of action at the national level. The subject of conflict of laws and the need for wisdom in dealing with it will be with us as far ahead as one can see.

Chapter 2

DOMICILE: THE CHOSEN POINT OF ENTRY

Introductory Note. Domicile affords a useful point of entry to the study of conflict of laws. It plays a significant role in many areas of the subject, such as choice of law, judicial jurisdiction (including jurisdiction to divorce) and governmental benefits and burdens, including the power to tax. Accordingly, it is desirable that the student gain a general understanding of the concept at the beginning of the course.

In this chapter, domicile is also used as a means to introduce a number of important matters that will be considered at greater length in subsequent portions of this book. In addition to choice of law and judicial jurisdiction, these matters include constitutional control, characterization and renvoi. Brief consideration of all of these matters at this stage should serve to facilitate comprehension of the problems dealt with later.

The identification made in this chapter of the various forms of domicile and the analysis of their constituent elements should not mislead anyone into supposing that the subject can be reduced to hard-and-fast rules. Rather, the effort should be to search for the core of the concept of domicile and for the basic principles on which the courts rely in deciding particular cases.

WHITE v. TENNANT

Supreme Court of Appeals of West Virginia, 1888.
31 W.Va. 790, 8 S.E. 596, 13 Am.St.Rep. 896.

SNYDER, JUDGE. This is a suit brought December, 1886, in the Circuit Court of Monongalia county by William L. White and others against Emrod Tennant, administrator of Michael White deceased and Lucinda White, the widow of said Michael White, to set aside the settlement and distribution made by the administrator of the personal estate of said decedent, and to have the same settled and distributed according to the laws of the State of Pennsylvania, which State it is claimed was the domicile of said decedent at the time of his death. The plaintiffs are the brothers and sisters of the decedent, who died in this State intestate. On October 28, 1887, the court entered a decree dismissing the plaintiffs' bill, and they have appealed.

The sole question presented for our determination is, whether the said Michael White at the time of his death, in May, 1885, had his legal domicile in this State or in the State of Pennsylvania. It is admitted to be the settled law, that the law of the State, in which the decedent had his domicile at the time of his death, will control the

7

succession and distribution of his personal estate. Before referring
to the facts proved in this cause, we shall endeavor to determine what
in law is meant by "domicile."

Dr. Wharton says: " 'Domicile' is a residence acquired as a final
abode. To constitute it there must be (1) residence, actual or inchoate; (2) the non-existence of any intention to make a domicile elsewhere." Whart.Confl.Law, sec. 21. . . . Two things must concur
to establish domicile,—the fact of residence, and the intention of remaining. These two must exist, or must have existed, in combination. There must have been an actual residence. The character of
the residence is of no importance; and, if domicile has once existed,
mere temporary absence will not destroy it, however long continued.
Munro v. Munro, 7 Cl. & Fin. 842. The original domicile continues
until it is fairly changed for another. It is a legal maxim that every
person must have a domicile somewhere; and he can have but one at
a time for the same purpose. From this it follows that one can not be
lost or extinguished until another is acquired. Baird v. Byrne, 3
Wall.Jr. 1. When one domicile is definitely abandoned and a new one
selected and entered upon, length of time is not important; one day
will be sufficient, provided the animus exists. Even when the point
of destination is not reached, domicile may shift in itinere, if the abandonment of the old domicile and the setting out for the new are plainly shown.[1] Munroe v. Douglass, 5 Madd. 405. Thus a constructive
residence seems to be sufficient to give domicile, though an actual
residence may not have begun. Whart.Confl.Law, sec. 58. A change
of domicile does not depend so much upon the intention to remain in
the new place for a definite or indefinite period as upon its being
without an intention to return. An intention to return however at a
remote or indefinite period to the former place of actual residence
will not control, if the other facts, which constitute domicile, all give
the new residence the character of a permanent home or place of
abode. The intention and actual fact of residence must concur, where
such residence is not in its nature temporary. . . .

The material facts in the case at bar are as follows: Joseph S.
White, the father of the plaintiffs and Michael White, died intestate in
Monongalia county seized of a tract of about 240 acres of land, of
which about forty acres lay in Greene county, Pa., the whole constituting but one tract or farm. The mansion-house in which the father
resided was located on the West Virginia side of the farm, and there
was also a dwelling-house generally occupied by tenants on the Pennsylvania part of the farm. After the death of the father, his widow
and the plaintiffs remained together and occupied the home-farm, residing in the mansion-house in West Virginia. Michael White, several
years before his death married the defendant, Lucinda White, a
daughter of the defendant, Emrod Tennant, and about that time pur-

1. Query whether this dictum is
sound. It is disapproved in Scoles and
Hay, Conflict of Laws § 4.19 (1982).—Ed.

chased a farm on Day's run, in Monongalia county, some fifteen miles from the home-place, to which he moved, and at which he and his wife resided. It is conceded, that Michael was born and had his domicile in West Virginia all his life, until about April 1, 1885.

In the winter of 1884–85, Michael sold his Day's run farm, and then rented or made an arrangement with his mother and brothers and sisters, the plaintiffs, to occupy the forty acres of the home-farm, in which he still had an undivided interest, and to live in the house on said forty acres in Greene county, Pa. He was to give to the purchaser the possession of his Day's run farm on April 1, 1885, and to have possession of the Pennsylvania house and forty acres at the same time. In March, 1885, he moved part of his household-goods into the Pennsylvania house, and put them into one of the rooms by permission of the tenant, who then occupied it, and who did not vacate it until between the middle and last of March, 1885. About the same time he moved an organ and some grain to the old homestead, until he could get possession of the Pennsylvania house.

On the morning of April 2, 1885, he finally left the Day's run house with the remainder of his goods and his wife, he having no children, with the declared intent and purpose of making the Pennsylvania house his home that evening. He with his team, wife and goods and live-stock passed into the State of Pennsylvania several miles before he reached said house and continued in said State thence to said Pennsylvania house, where they arrived that evening about sundown, and then and there unloaded their goods and put them in the house, setting up one bed and turning the fowls and other live-stock loose at the house.

The said house had been vacated for several days. It was a damp, cool day, and the house was found to be damp and uncomfortable. The wife was complaining of feeling unwell, and in consequence of that fact and the uncomfortable condition of the house, on the invitation of her brother-in-law and others of the family who then resided at the mansion-house, but a short distance therefrom, the said Michael and his wife went to the mansion-house in West Virginia to stay all night and return in the morning. Before leaving the Pennsylvania house the wife had gotten out of the buggy at the house, and the said Michael after putting into it his household-goods locked the door and took the key with him. On the following morning, the wife still feeling unwell, and the brother who was to return the team, which they had used in moving their goods, having taken sick, the wife after going to the Pennsylvania house to milk returned to the mansion-house, and Michael took the team back to Day's run.

On the return of Michael from this trip he found his wife so sick with typhoid fever, that it was impossible to move her, in consequence of which both he and she remained at the mansion-house,— she because she was unable to get away, and he to wait on her,—but he went daily over to the Pennsylvania house to look after it, and to feed his stock there, calling it his "home." In ten or fifteen days, and before the wife had sufficiently recovered to leave her bed, Michael was attacked with typhoid fever, and about ten days thereafter died intestate in the same house. The wife recovered, and the defendant, Emrod Tennant, her father administered on the estate of Michael, taking out letters of administration in Monongalia county, W.Va. The administrator settled his accounts before a commissioner of said county, and distributed the estate according to the laws of West Virginia; that is, by paying over to the widow the whole personal estate remaining after the payment of the debts of the decedent. It is admitted, that, if the distribution had been according to the laws of the State of Pennsylvania, the wife would have been entitled to the one half only of said estate, and the plaintiffs would have been entitled to the other half.

As the law of the State, in which the decedent had his domicile at the time of his death, must govern the distribution of his estate, the important question is, where, according to the foregoing facts, was the domicile of Michael at the time of his death? It is unquestionable, that prior to the 2d day of April, 1885, his domicile was and had been in the State of West Virginia. Did he on that day or at any subsequent day change his domicile to the State of Pennsylvania? According to the authorities hereinbefore cited, if it is shown, that a person has entirely abandoned his former domicile in one State with the intention of making his home at a fixed place in another State with no intention of returning to his former domicile and then establishes a residence in the new place for any period of time, however brief, that will be in law a change of domicile, and the latter will remain his domicile until changed in like manner.

The facts in this case conclusively prove, that Michael White, the decedent, abandoned his residence in West Virginia with the intention and purpose not only of not returning to it, but for the expressed purpose of making a fixed place in the State of Pennsylvania his home for an indefinite time. This fact is shown by all the circumstances as well as by his declarations and acts. . . . At the time he left his former home on that morning, and while he was on the way to his new home, his declared purpose and intention were to make that his home from that very day, and to occupy it that night. He arrived in Pennsylvania and at his new home with that intention; and it was only after he arrived there and for reasons not before known, which had no effect to change his purpose of making that his future home, that he failed to remain there from that time. There was no change in his purpose, except that after he arrived at his new home and unloaded and left his property there, he concluded on account of the condition of the house and the illness of his wife, that it would be better to go with his wife to remain one night with his relatives and return the next morning.

When he left his former home without any intention of returning and in pursuance of that intention did in fact move with his family and effects to his new home with the intention of making it his residence for an indefinite time, it is my opinion, that, when he and his wife arrived at his new home, it became eo instanti his domicile, and that his leaving there under the circumstances with the intention of returning the next day did not change the fact. The concurrence of his intention to make the Pennsylvania house his permanent residence with the fact, that he had actually abandoned his former residence and moved to and put his goods in the new one made the latter his domicile. According to the authorities hereinbefore referred to he must of necessity have had a domicile somewhere. If he did not have one in Pennsylvania, where did he have one? The fact, that he left the Pennsylvania house, after he had moved to it with his family and goods, to spend the night, did not revive his domicile at his former residence on Day's run, because he had sold that, and left it without any purpose of returning there. By going from his new home to the house of his relatives to spend the night he certainly did not make the house thus visited his domicile; therefore, unless the Pennsylvania house was on the evening of April 2, 1885, his domicile, he was in the anomalous position of being without a domicile anywhere, which, as we have seen, is a legal impossibility; and, that house having become his domicile, there is nothing in this case to show that he ever did in fact change or intend to change it or to establish a domicile elsewhere.

It follows, therefore, that that house remained his domicile up to and at the time of his death; and, that house being in the State of Pennsylvania, the laws of that State must control the distribution of his personal estate notwithstanding the fact that he died in the State of West Virginia.

For these reasons the decree of the Circuit Court must be reversed, and the cause must be remanded to that court to be there further proceeded in according to the principles announced in this opinion and the rules of courts of equity.

NOTES

(1) Beyond any dispute, Michael and Lucinda White had spent virtually all their lives in West Virginia, had married and lived there together for years, and had not had any contact with Pennsylvania except briefly and sporadically in the closing weeks of Michael's life. West Virginia was also the state where Michael's brothers and sisters made their home. What justification can there be in those circumstances for the court's decision to determine the right to take Michael's personal property under the rules of Pennsylvania law rather than under the West Virginia rules? Was this an unwise result? If so, did it result from a misapplication by the Supreme Court of Appeals of West Virginia of the rules of domicile, or from a defect in these rules, or from the use of the concept of domicile as the pivotal factor in selecting the law that governed the issue of intestate succession to Michael

White's movable property? See Weintraub, An Inquiry into the Utility of "Domicile" as a Concept in Conflicts Analysis, 63 Mich.L.Rev. 961 (1965).

If the dispute between the widow and her in-laws had resulted from contrary interpretations of the laws of West Virginia, without Pennsylvania laws being implicated at all, what factors and considerations would have been operative in the court's effort to arrive at a just decision? Should the fact that Michael and Lucinda White made their ill-fated brief trip to the Pennsylvania homestead alter the court's approach to the problem? Should there be rules that tell courts in advance whether to apply the Pennsylvania laws of distribution of movables on intestate succession rather than the West Virginia laws? Or should the matter be left to the court to decide in the same way it would if the issue was presented in an all-West Virginia context?

Those questions suggest some of the most prominent and pervasive issues raised throughout these materials.

(2) Experience has shown that some traditional rules of domicile are of questionable soundness. One example is the rule applied in White v. Tennant that being in a place for even a moment of time satisfies the requirement of physical presence there.

(3) It is commonly said that there are three kinds of domicile.

(a) Domicile of origin, which is the domicile the law assigns to each person at birth,

(b) Domicile of choice, which can be acquired by any person having the requisite legal capacity. As demonstrated by White v. Tennant, acquisition of such a domicile is usually said to require both physical presence in the place and a particular attitude of mind toward the place.

(c) Domicile by operation of law, which is a domicile derived from that of a third person and is possessed by persons incapable of acquiring a domicile of choice.

(4) The English courts give particular significance to the domicile of origin. They apply, for example, the reverter doctrine under which a domicile of origin is regained as soon as a person leaves a domicile of choice with the intention either of returning to the domicile of origin or of acquiring a new domicile of choice. Udney v. Udney, L.R. 1 H.L. (Sc.) 441 (1869).

(5) The English presumption against a change of domicile is stronger when the change is from the domicile of origin. See 1 Dicey and Morris, Conflict of Laws 109 (10th ed. 1980). The rigidity of the English rules has not escaped criticism from English writers. See Wade, The English Concept of Domicile, 21 Netherlands Int.L.Rev. 265 (1974).

(6) Under English law, the necessary attitude of mind for the acquisition of a domicile of choice in a place is the intention to reside there permanently. How strictly this rule is applied is evidenced by Inland Revenue Commission v. Bullock (1976) 1 W.L.R. 1178 (Court of Appeal) where a man, whose domicile of origin was Canada but who had lived in England since 1932, was held not to have acquired a domicile of choice in England since it had always been his intention to return to Canada to live if his English wife should predecease him.

(7) *"Nationality" as a connecting factor.* In many continental countries, nationality rather than domicile is used as the basis, or "connecting factor," for determining the governing law for certain personal rights. For

a consideration of the relative advantages and disadvantages of nationality and domicile for this purpose, see Scoles and Hay, Conflict of Laws §§ 4.11–4.12 (1982). There is an extensive discussion in 1 Rabel, The Conflict of Laws: A Comparative Study c. 4 (2d ed. 1958).

(8) *Residence.* Residence, rather than domicile, is the connecting factor usually found in statutes. In most contexts, "residence" is used as a synonym for "domicile" but at times the words convey different meanings; for example, "residence" has been held to differ from "domicile" in referring more narrowly to physical presence. Given the many differing contexts in which it appears, the word "residence" must be examined very carefully when it appears in a legal context, and given a meaning which fits the particular situation where it is encountered. For a thorough discussion, see Reese and Green, That Elusive Word, "Residence," 6 Vand.L.Rev. 561 (1953). See also Scoles and Hay, Conflict of Laws §§ 4.13–4.14 (1982); Restatement, Second, Conflict of Laws § 11, Comment k.

Following the divorce of his parents, a child spent weekends with his father and the rest of the time with his mother. He was held to be a resident of the "household" of each parent and hence covered by each parent's "homeowner policy." Accordingly, each insurer was held liable for the damage caused by a fire that had been set by the child. The court declared that "[w]hile a person may have only one true domicile, he may have more than one residence." Miller v. United States Fidelity and Guaranty Co., 127 N.J. Super. 37, 316 A.2d 51 (1974).

Habitual residence. The Hague Conference on Private International Law normally uses "habitual residence" rather than "domicile" in its conventions. This is partly because domicile bears different meanings in English and American law. For a discussion of "habitual residence" and whether it might have a useful role to play in American law, see Cavers, "Habitual Residence": A Useful Concept? 21 Am.U.L.Rev. 475 (1972).

(9) The impropriety of a person's motive in coming to a place does not prevent his acquisition there of a domicile of choice. In Gasper v. Wales, 223 App.Div. 89, 227 N.Y.S. 421 (1st Dep't 1928), the court had the problem of a man with two places of abode. The family home was in Connecticut. Relations with his wife were exceedingly strained. The court concluded that his real home was in New York where he had lived with another woman for many years. Proskauer, J., said: "While the furtiveness of this New York home is one of the facts to be considered in deciding whether he intended it to be his legal domicil, it is not controlling. . . . The [trial judge] seems to have assumed that Beach could not have a legal residence for an illegal purpose. Legal residence, however, does not depend upon the legality of the object of the residence; it rests upon physical presence in a dwelling coupled with an intent to make that dwelling one's home."

BANGS v. INHABITANTS OF BREWSTER

Supreme Judicial Court of Massachusetts, 1873.
111 Mass. 382.

Contract to recover the amount of a tax assessed by the defendants on the plaintiff, for the year 1869, and paid by him under protest. . . .

MORTON, J. The question at the trial was whether the plaintiff
had on May 1, 1869, acquired a domicil in Orleans. There is no doubt
as to the rule of law that the plaintiff's domicil of origin in Brewster
adhered to him until he had acquired a domicil somewhere else.
. . .

. . . The plaintiff was a shipmaster, most of whose time was
spent at sea. He went to sea in November, 1867, taking his wife with
him, and in December 1868 he sent his wife to Orleans, and she arrived there in February 1869. He did not arrive at Orleans until July
1869, so that he was not personally present in Orleans on May 1,
1869. The special findings of the jury settle conclusively that when
he went to sea in November 1867 he had the definite intent to make
Orleans his home, and that in December 1868 he sent his wife to Orleans in pursuance of that intent. . . .

By sending his wife to Orleans with the intent to make it his
home, he thereby changed his domicil. The fact of removal and the
intent concurred. Although he was not personally present, he established his home there from the time of his wife's arrival. . . .

Exceptions overruled.

NOTES

(1) McIntosh v. Maricopa County, 73 Ariz. 366, 241 P.2d 801, 31 A.L.R.2d
770 (1952), involved a man who had been domiciled with his wife in Wyoming
when he left for military service. In March, 1945, the wife went to Arizona
for medical reasons. This was done with the husband's approval, and they
both intended to change their domicile to Arizona. The husband went to the
home in Arizona immediately on his discharge from military service in November, 1945. The court refused to follow Bangs v. Inhabitants of Brewster, and held that the husband was not domiciled in Arizona on September 1,
1945, a date made determinative by a tax exemption statute. But see to the
contrary Lea v. Lea, 18 N.J. 1, 112 A.2d 540 (1955), which is discussed in 17
U.Pitt.L.Rev. 97 (1955), and Restatement, Second, Conflict of Laws § 16,
comment *f*.

(2) Bangs v. Brewster is not strictly a conflict of laws case, since it involves no interstate element. Often, however, it becomes necessary to determine a person's connection with some particular subdivision of a state. In
addition to matters of taxation, questions of process and venue, "settlement"
(responsibility for poor persons), school privileges, and voting often turn on
issues of this sort—sometimes phrased in terms of residence and sometimes
in terms of domicile.

1. EFFECT OF INTENTIONS IN
SELECTING A DOMICILE

An important question is the effect of a person's desires with respect to the location of his domicile. Such desires did not carry the
day in In re Dorrance's Estate, 309 Pa. 151, 163 A. 303 (1932). That
case involved the claim of Pennsylvania that Dr. Dorrance, the former head of the Campbell Soup Company, had died domiciled in the

state and that accordingly it was entitled to impose an inheritance tax upon his large estate. Dorrance had initially been reluctant to purchase a house in Pennsylvania because of his desire for tax reasons to remain domiciled in New Jersey. He eventually did buy the house upon the assurance of his lawyer that retaining his New Jersey domicile "was largely a matter of intention." To make clear his intention, Dorrance executed an agreement with his wife that their residence should remain in New Jersey and that both would continue to vote only in that state. He referred to himself as a New Jersey resident in various formal documents. Also, he continued to maintain his business office in New Jersey; he retained his association with a New Jersey church; was politically active in New Jersey but not in Pennsylvania; served for a number of years on a New Jersey commission; and registered his motor vehicles and obtained his driver's licenses in New Jersey. On the other hand, he and his family spent most of their time on the Pennsylvania estate and centered their social activities there. Stating that "a person's expression of desire may not supersede the effect of his conduct," the Pennsylvania court found that Dorrance had died domiciled in Pennsylvania and that the tax was due. Subsequently, the New Jersey court, relying primarily upon Dorrance's desire to remain domiciled in New Jersey and upon the previously mentioned contacts found that he had died domiciled in that state and that his estate was subject to the New Jersey inheritance tax. In re Dorrance's Estate, 115 N.J.Eq. 268, 170 A. 601 (1934). As a result, the estate was subjected to double inheritance taxation.

The Dorrance cases should be contrasted with Matter of Newcomb, 192 N.Y. 238, 84 N.E. 950 (1908). In that case, Mrs. Newcomb, a wealthy woman, who was then domiciled in New York, decided to leave substantially all her property to Tulane University in New Orleans. Fearing that her will might be contested by relatives, she sought the advice of a New Orleans lawyer who advised her to change her domicile to Louisiana. Acting upon his advice, she executed several formal declarations in which she stated that she had elected to "make the City of New Orleans my place of domicile and permanent home." These declarations were sent to various persons. Shortly thereafter, she made the will in question. Whereas in the four years preceding her formal declaration of domicile, she had spent more time in Louisiana than in New York, she spent considerably more time in New York than in Louisiana in the period between the date of the declaration and her death. Following her death, Mrs. Newcomb's heirs brought a proceeding in New York to establish that Mrs. Newcomb had died domiciled in New York and that her will was invalid on the grounds of incompetency and undue influence. The Surrogate found that Mrs. Newcomb had died domiciled in Louisiana and dismissed the proceeding. On appeal, held affirmed. ". . . in discussing those principles [of domicile] we shall consider them simply with reference to the rules relating to succession. . . . The subject [of domicile] is under the absolute control of every person of full age and sound mind who is free from restraint, unless it may be that the domicile of a wife is controlled by that of her husband as long as she lives with him. . . . Motives are immaterial, except as they indicate intention . . . a person may select and make his own domicile . . . . He may elect between his winter and summer residence and may make a domicile of either. The right to choose implies the right to declare one's choice, formally or informally as he prefers, and even for the sole purpose of making evidence to prove what his choice was. Such declarations are not self-serving in an improper sense, unless they are made with intent to deceive. . . . Mrs. Newcomb, for many years domiciled in New York, had the absolute right to change her domicile to New Orleans. As she resided a part of the time in each city, she could select either as her domicile, provided she acted in good faith. She could make the change because she preferred the people, the climate or the laws of Louisiana to those of New York, or even because she wished to have her will proved and her estate settled there. . . . The good faith of her declarations, as well as the weight to be given them, was for the referee and surrogate, but they were competent as evidence. While acts speak louder than words, the words are to be heard for what they are worth."

Why was effect given to the desires of Mrs. Newcomb with respect to the place of her domicile while effect was denied to the similar desires of Dr. Dorrance by the Pennsylvania court? Should the fact that the issue was different be sufficient?

NOTES

(1) By seeking to locate their domiciles in a particular state by means of massing contacts there, the testators in Dorrance and Newcomb were, in effect, attempting to choose the applicable law. The power of a person to choose the law that will govern the legal effect of a transaction is a question that arises in other areas of the law, particularly in the case of contracts (see pp. 573–596, infra) and trusts (see pp. 631–640, infra).

(2) The opinions in the Dorrance cases provide excellent discussion of the types of evidence which may be relevant in domicile cases, and the relative importance of acts as compared with declarations.

(3) The problem of double domicile in tax cases has been a troublesome one.

(a) In a few cases it has been possible to get the taxing authorities of one state to consent to the jurisdiction of the courts of the other state. See Matter of Trowbridge, 266 N.Y. 283, 194 N.E. 756 (1935), where the state of Connecticut petitioned for and was granted leave to intervene in the New York proceedings. The ultimate decision was that the decedent was domiciled in Connecticut. See also Curry v. McCanless, 307 U.S. 357 (1939).

(b) Under the Federal Interpleader Act, now found in 28 U.S.C.A. §§ 1335, 1397, and 2361 the district courts of the United States have nationwide jurisdiction in interpleader proceedings. An effort was made to solve the double domicile problem under this statute through a proceeding under which the taxing officials of both states were joined as parties. It was argued that such a suit was not contrary to the Eleventh Amendment, since the officers of one of the states were acting illegally, and therefore without the authority of the state; thus, an injunction against them would not enjoin the action of the state. Cf. Ex parte Young, 209 U.S. 123 (1908). The Supreme Court held, however, that the state officials were not acting illegally when all they did was to submit the question to a proper state tribunal for decision, and held that the Eleventh Amendment foreclosed the use of the Interpleader Act as a means of getting both sides of the controversy into the same court. Worcester County Trust Co. v. Riley, 302 U.S. 292 (1937). The Supreme Court has recently reaffirmed this position in Cory v. White, 457 U.S. 85 (1982).

(c) In one spectacular case, the problem was solved, but in a manner which offers little hope of relief to the ordinary executor. In State of Texas v. State of Florida, 306 U.S. 398 (1939), involving the estate of Col. E. H. R. Green, four states were claiming taxes by reason of the decedent's domicile. It appeared that the aggregate amount of taxes claimed exceeded the total value of the estate. Though the executors were unable to act themselves, in some way the state of Texas was moved to file an original bill in the Supreme Court of the United States, against the states of Florida, New York and Massachusetts. The Supreme Court found jurisdiction because of the excess of the tax claims over the value of the estate. The Court then determined that the decedent was domiciled in Massachusetts, and this determination doubtless binds all of the states concerned.

A similar problem has now arisen in connection with the estate of the late Howard Hughes. Both California and Texas claim Hughes as their domiciliary and the aggregate amount of their tax claims exceed the total value of the estate. The Supreme Court has permitted California to invoke the Court's original jurisdiction to determine whether Hughes died domiciled in Texas or in California. California v. Texas, 457 U.S. 164 (1982).

(d) The danger that intangibles will be subjected to multiple taxation has been eased considerably by the enactment in some 20 states of legislation authorizing state tax officials to compromise or submit to arbitration disputes relating to the location of the deceased's domicile. See Uniform Act on Interstate Compromise of Death Taxes and Uniform Act on Interstate Arbitration of Death Taxes. 8 Uniform Laws Annotated 255, 271.

In cases such as Texas v. Florida and California v. Texas, stated above, what law controls in determining the issue of domicile? Suppose the laws of the states involved differ in the requirements they impose with respect to the attitude of mind needed for the acquisition in a place of a domicile of choice. Should the case be governed by some sort of "federal" rule as to domicile, since it is a suit between States? If so, what is the source of that rule?

2. SPECIAL SITUATIONS

Refugees. The domicile of refugees is likely to raise peculiar problems.

An example is Roboz v. Kennedy, 219 F.Supp. 892 (D.D.C.1963) which involved a suit for the return of property vested in the Attorney General under the International Claims Settlement Act (22 U.S.C.

§ 1631 (1964)). By the terms of the Act, the vesting of plaintiffs' property would have been proper if the plaintiffs had been "domiciled" in Hungary after March 13, 1941. The plaintiffs were mother and son. They and the father were nationals of Hungary and, so far as appears, had lived in that country all of their lives up to the crucial date. At that time, they were all in Hungary, the father in a Nazi prison and the mother engaged in seeking his release. "In view of the increasing Nazi orientation of the Hungarian Government," the plaintiffs and the father had planned to leave Hungary since 1939. In 1940, the plaintiffs obtained United States visas. They did not leave at that time because of the imprisonment of the father and only reached the United States in 1947 "resolved never to return to Hungary under any circumstances." Held for the plaintiffs. "The facts . . . demonstrate conclusively that plaintiffs had a firm and continuing intent to leave Hungary forever before March 13, 1941 . . . Clearly, they were involuntarily in Hungary. They therefore cannot be considered . . . domiciled in . . . Hungary" within the meaning of the statute. "Congress could not have intended so inequitable a result. . . . "

NOTES

(1) There are a number of cases where a person has been found to have a domicile in the United States although he was here on a temporary basis or after his visa had expired. Rzeszotarski v. Rzeszotarski, 296 A.2d 431 (D.C. App.1972) (expired temporary visa—divorce); Seren v. Douglas, 30 Colo.App. 110, 489 P.2d 601 (1971) (expired student visa—in-state tuition benefits); Williams v. Williams, 328 F.Supp. 1380 (D.C.V.I.1971) (temporary worker visa—divorce and adoption); Bustamante v. Bustamante, 645 P.2d 40 (Utah 1982) (tourist visa—divorce). Contra: Gosschalk v. Gosschalk, 48 N.J.Super. 566, 138 A.2d 774 (1958), affirmed 28 N.J. 73, 145 A.2d 327 (1958) (alien on temporary visa held incapable of acquiring domicile for divorce).

(2) *Illegal entrants.* In Cabral v. State Board of Control, 112 Cal.App.3d 1012, 169 Cal.Rptr. 604 (1980), aliens who had entered the United States illegally were held capable of acquiring a domicile in California for purposes of recovering under that state's Victims of Violent Crimes Act. However, in Buscema v. Buscema, 20 N.J.Super. 114, 89 A.2d 279 (1952), an alien who was released on his own recognizance while awaiting a deportation hearing for having illegally entered the United States was held incapable of acquiring a domicile for divorce purposes.

(3) The Constitution has been held to require a state to apply its ordinary rules of domicile in determining whether an alien is eligible for state entitlements. Elkins v. Moreno, 435 U.S. 647 (1979); Toll v. Moreno, 458 U.S. 1 (1982) (eligibility for reduced tuition at state university). The conditions imposed on an alien's entry into the United States may, however, cast light upon whether the alien bears the proper attitude of mind towards the place where he claims domicile. Toll v. Moreno, 284 Md. 425, 397 A.2d 1009 (1979).

Students. A student will usually be held not to have acquired a domicile of choice in the place where the school or college is located. The tendency of most students to continue to regard their parents' dwelling as "home" and the relative shortness of the intended stay at the school or college work against regarding the school's situs as home.

The situation is different if the student has abandoned the parental home and has struck out to make an independent life, particularly if the student has married. It then becomes far more likely that the court will accept the claim that the location of the institution of learning is the student's "home" and constitutes a domicile of choice. See Matter of Robbins v. Chamberlain, 297 N.Y. 108, 75 N.E.2d 617 (1947).

NOTES

(1) The United States Constitution has been held to limit the power of a state to impose rules that make it difficult for certain classes of persons, such as servicemen and students, to acquire a local domicile for purposes of voting. In Carrington v. Rash, 380 U.S. 89 (1965), the Supreme Court struck down a Texas constitutional provision which precluded servicemen stationed in the state from acquiring a domicile there for voting purposes. Speaking of students, Judge Friendly said in Ramey v. Rockefeller, 348 F.Supp. 780 (E.D.N.Y.1972) that, although a state may insist that all applicants for the vote fulfill the requirements of bona fide residence,

"The only constitutionally permissible test is one which focuses on the individual's present intention and does not require him to pledge allegiance for an indefinite future. The objective is to determine the place which is the center of the individual's life now, the locus of his primary concern. The determination must be based on *all* relevant factors; it is not enough that a student, or any other former nondomiciliary, would find that the place of his presence is more convenient for voting or would enable him to take a more active part in political life. The state may insist on other indicia, including the important one of abandonment of a former home.

We think therefore that, in determining bona fide residence for a person physically present, the state cannot constitutionally go further than the test set out in the Restatement (Second) of the Conflict of Laws § 18 (1971), namely, that he 'must intend to make that place his home for the time at least.'"

In Newburger v. Peterson, 344 F.Supp. 559 (D.N.H.1972), the plaintiff, a Dartmouth student, complained of a New Hampshire statute which disqualified a person from voting in a town if he had a firm intention of leaving that town at a fixed time in the future. The statute was held unconstitutional. The court said:

"In this day of widespread planning for change of scene and occupation we cannot see that a requirement of permanent or indefinite intention to stay in one place is relevant to responsible citizenship. . . .

We are sensitive to the compelling need 'to preserve the basic conception of a political community'. . . . But the challenged New Hampshire law forces persons who are in every meaningful sense members of New Hampshire political communities to vote in communities elsewhere which they have long departed and with whose affairs they are no longer

concerned, if indeed the former community still recognizes the right.
. . ."

(2) Any minor over eighteen years of age has the capacity to acquire a domicile of choice for voting purposes, and his capacity is not impaired by living in a college dormitory and receiving parental support. Hershkoff v. Board of Registrars of Voters of Worcester, 366 Mass. 570, 321 N.E.2d 656 (1974). See also Paulson v. Forest City Community School District, 238 N.W.2d 344 (Iowa 1976).

(3) Wurfel: Jet Age Domicil: The Semi-Demise of Durational Residence Requirements, 11 Wake Forest L.Rev. 349 (1975) discusses the recent decisions, including those of the Supreme Court, on the use of domicile for voting, tuition, welfare, occupational qualification, and divorce purposes. The author concludes that although durational residence requirements are constitutionally suspect, domicile "continue[s] to be the legal test of individual rights and duties."

RESTATEMENT, SECOND, CONFLICT OF LAWS * :

§ 17. Presence under Compulsion

A person does not acquire a domicil of choice by his presence in a place under physical or legal compulsion.

. . .

c. *Inmates of jails.* Under the rule of this Section, it is impossible for a person to acquire a domicil in the jail in which he is incarcerated. To enter jail, one must first be legally committed and thereby lose all power of choice over the place of one's abode.

d. *Soldiers and sailors.* A soldier or sailor, if he is ordered to a station to which he must go and live in quarters assigned to him, will probably not acquire a domicil there though he lives in the assigned quarters with his family. He must obey orders and cannot choose to go elsewhere. On the other hand, if he is allowed to live with his family where he pleases provided it is near enough to his post to enable him to perform his duties, he retains some power of choice over the place of his abode and may acquire a domicil. To do so, however, he must regard the place where he lives as his home. Such an attitude on his part may be difficult to establish in view of the nomadic character of military life and particularly if he intends, upon the termination of his service, to move to some other place.

NOTES

(1) The uncompromising tone of the quoted comment to Section 17 of the Restatement, Second needs to be softened. In Stifel v. Hopkins, 477 F.2d 1116 (6th Cir. 1973), a person sent to a Pennsylvania prison under life sentence was held capable of claiming to be a Pennsylvania citizen for the pur-

pose of bringing a diversity action. He had refused a transfer to an Indiana jail and said in an affidavit that he considered Pennsylvania his home and intended to remain there indefinitely.

In Dane v. Board of Registrars, 374 Mass. 152, 371 N.E.2d 1358 (1978), the court held that persons incarcerated in Massachusetts jails had the capacity "to form the requisite intent to make . . . the place of their incarceration their domicile for voting purposes." It said that "We think that prisoners, like servicemen or students, should be able to 'rebut' the presumption that by reason of their involuntary presence at the place of incarceration, they have retained their former domicile."

Would the result in these two cases have been the same if the issue had involved either succession or taxation?

(2) Where the serviceman lives off the base and shows a clear intention to make his home where he lives, he may acquire a domicile there. See Sasse v. Sasse, 41 Wash.2d 363, 249 P.2d 380 (1952). A serviceman was found to be domiciled in the state in Slade v. Slade, 122 N.W.2d 160 (N.D.1963), even without such evidence. For a typical case refusing to find a soldier domiciled for purposes of divorce jurisdiction in the place where he was stationed, although he had testified that he intended to make that place his home following his discharge from the Army, see Hammerstein v. Hammerstein, 269 S.W.2d 591 (Tex.Civ.App.1954).

(3) More than a dozen states have statutes providing that a serviceman living in the state for a specified period shall be deemed a resident for purposes of divorce suits. See, e.g., Miss.Code Ann. § 93–5–5 (Supp.1982); N.C. Gen.Stat. § 50–18 (1966); Ariz.Rev.Stat. § 25–312 (Supp.1982); Me.Rev.Stat. Ann. Tit. 19, § 691 (Supp.1969); see generally Leflar, Conflict of Laws and Family Law, 14 Ark.L.R. 47, 49 (1960).

RESTATEMENT, SECOND, CONFLICT OF LAWS *:

§ 21. Domicil of Wife

A wife who lives with her husband has the same domicil as his unless the special circumstances of the wife make such a result unreasonable.

Comment:

a. The common law rule. At common law a married woman had no capacity to acquire a domicil of choice and was assigned that of her husband by operation of law. . . .

b. Special circumstances of wife. In the vast majority of situations, husband and wife will have but a single home and this home will be in the place of their domicil. Only in rare situations will the wife have close ties, as the ownership of a place of abode, with a state which is not the state of the husband's domicil. . . .

NOTES

(1) The recent cases hold that a wife, although living with her husband, may have a domicile apart from his. Mas v. Perry, 489 F.2d 1396 (5th Cir. 1974) (diversity jurisdiction); Napletana v. Hillsdale College, 385 F.2d 871 (6th Cir. 1967) (diversity jurisdiction); Samuel v. University of Pittsburgh, 375 F.Supp. 1119 (W.D.Pa.1974), app. dism. on other grounds, 506 F.2d 355 (3d Cir. 1974) (holding unconstitutional the presumption that wife's domicile is that of her husband for purposes of determining amount of tuition); McCormick v. United States, 57 Treas.Dec. 117 (1930) (basis for assessing customs duties); Martin v. Hefley, 259 Ark. 484, 533 S.W.2d 521 (1976) (eligibility to vote); Bowers v. Bowers, 287 So.2d 722 (Fla.D.Ct.App.1973) (diversity jurisdiction); Gladwin v. Power, 21 A.D.2d 665, 249 N.Y.S.2d 980 (1st Dep't 1964) (eligibility to hold public office); Commonwealth v. Rutherford, 160 Va. 524, 169 S.E. 909 (1933) (basis for assessing property taxes).

(2) New York has now provided by statute that a married person's domicile "shall be established for all purposes without regard to sex." N.Y.Dom. Rel.Law § 61.

(3) By the Domicile and Matrimonial Proceedings Act 1973, England adopted the rule that a married woman living with her husband can acquire a domicile of choice in the same circumstances as any other person.

Previously English law had consistently adhered to the view that a married woman could not acquire a domicile different from that of her husband under any circumstances. See Attorney General of Alberta v. Cook, [1926] A.C. 444; H. v. H. [1928] P. 206; Herd v. Herd, [1936] P. 205.

(4) Canada has provided that "the domicile of a married woman shall be determined as if she were unmarried" for the purposes of determining the jurisdiction of a court to grant a divorce. Canadian Divorce Act of 1968, sec. 6(1) (Stat.Can., 1968, c. 24).

Domicile of infants. The domicile of an infant is, under ordinary circumstances, the same as that of his father. See Restatement, Second, Conflict of Laws § 22. But there are many circumstances which are not ordinary. The child may be illegitimate, or adopted, or abandoned, or emancipated, or the parents may be separated or divorced, with custody awarded to the mother. The child may be present in a state without having domicile there. A court appointed guardian may have power to change the domicile of his ward. First Trust & Deposit Co. v. Goodrich, 3 N.Y.2d 410, 144 N.E.2d 396 (1957).

These questions are discussed in Scoles and Hay, Conflict of Laws §§ 4.37–4.44 (1982).

Domicile of weak-minded and insane persons. As to the domicile of persons non compos mentis, see Restatement, Second, Conflict of Laws § 23; Scoles and Hay, Conflict of Laws § 4.45 (1982).

Persons in hospitals or sanitariums. In Perri v. Kisselbach, 58 N.J.Super. 532, 156 A.2d 747 (1959), the court refused to allow inmates of a tuberculosis sanitarium to vote. One of the patients had been cured of the disease, but chose to remain because he was too old and infirm to care for himself. The court reached the same result as to him, pointing out that the superintendent could put him out at any time. Cf. Application of People of the State of N. Y. ex rel. Singer, 137 N.Y.S.2d 61 (Sup.Ct.1954), allowing a patient to establish domicile in a hospital for voting purposes.

BERGNER & ENGEL BREWING CO. v. DREYFUS, 172 Mass. 154, 51 N.E. 531 (1898): [The defendant had received a discharge in proceedings in Massachusetts under the latter's insolvency law. The plaintiff, a Pennsylvania corporation, doing business in Massachusetts, had not been made a party to the proceedings, and it now urges that its claim was not barred by the discharge.]

HOLMES, J. . . . The independent ground on which it is urged that the plaintiff is subject to the insolvent law in the present case is that the plaintiff is domesticated in this State, as shown by the facts above recited, of which the appointment of an attorney is only one. The word "domesticated," which was used in the argument for the defendant, presents no definite legal conception which has any bearing upon the case. We presume that it was intended to convey in a conciliatory form the notion that the plaintiff was domiciled here,— "resident," in the language of Pub.Sts. c. 157, sec. 81,[1] and therefore barred by the language and legal operation of the act. It could not be contended that the corporation was a citizen of Massachusetts. In such sense as it is a citizen of any State, it is a citizen of the State which creates it and of no other. But there are even greater objections to a double domicile than there are to double citizenship. Under the law as it has been, a man might find himself owing a double allegiance without any choice of his own. But domicile, at least for any given purpose, is single by its essence. Dicey, Confl. of Laws, 95. A corporation does not differ from a natural person in this respect. If any person, natural or artificial, as a result of choice or on technical grounds of birth or creation, has a domicile in one place, it cannot have one elsewhere, because what the law means by domicile is the one technically pre-eminent headquarters, which, as a result either of fact or of fiction, every person is compelled to have in order that by aid of it certain rights and duties which have been attached to it by the law may be determined. It is settled that a corporation has its domicile in the jurisdiction of the State which created it, and as a consequence that it has not a domicile anywhere else. . . . The so-called modifications of this rule by statutes like the act of 1884 do not modify it, because jurisdiction of the ordinary personal actions does not depend upon domicile, but only upon such presence within the jurisdiction as to make service possible. See In re Hohorst, 150 U.S. 653. But the operation of our insolvent law by its very terms may,

---

1. This statute provided that a discharge under the Massachusetts insolvency law should bar all debts founded on any contract "made within this State, to be performed within the same, or due to any person resident therein" at the time the proceedings were started.—Ed.

and in this case does, depend upon the domicile of the creditor, and as there can be no doubt either in fact or in law that the plaintiff was domiciled in Pennsylvania in such a sense that a statute like Pub.Sts. c. 157, sec. 1, would hit it there, it cannot have been domiciled here for the same purpose at the same time.

NOTE

The position is taken in Section 11, Comment *l* of the Restatement of Conflict of Laws, Second, that the concept of domicile is not properly applicable to a corporation.

Is Domicile a Unitary Concept?

As has been noted, domicile is used in three broad areas of conflict of laws: judicial jurisdiction; choice of law, particularly in matters where continuity of the application of the same law is important, such as family law and decedents' estates; and governmental benefits and burdens. A question is whether domicile has a constant meaning throughout or whether its meaning may vary somewhat from context to context. Stated in another way, the question is whether at the same time a person may have a domicile in one place for one purpose and another domicile in a second place for some other purpose.

Do the cases you have read up to now provide an answer to this question? Do you think it likely that a clear answer would be found in the cases? A famous debate on this question took place between Professors Walter Wheeler Cook and Austin Wakeman Scott at an early American Law Institute meeting. 3 The American Law Institute Proceedings 226–231 (1925). In the course of this debate, Professor Cook said:

> There is no doubt that what you might call the core of the concept is the same in all these situations; but as you get out towards what I like to call the twilight zone of the subject, I don't believe the scope remains exactly the same for all purposes.
>
> . . .
>
> The court has a concrete problem to solve. It is trying to decide whether the courts of the state should grant a divorce on constructive service; whether the man is sufficiently connected with the state to make that a reasonable thing to do. It may be reasonable to do that, but not reasonable to apply the same concept in the case involving the validity of the provisions of a will. The court has a will to consider, or a divorce, or the administration of an estate, or whatever it may be, and the exact point at which it draws the line is undoubtedly drawn with the concrete problem that they have before them in mind. . . .
>
> I do not believe we can make up our minds as to the exact scope [domicile] ought to have for a particular purpose without

having that purpose in mind, and we ought to address ourselves to the question of whether it ought to have the same exact scope for all purposes. I do not believe it should. I am not talking about a theoretical thing, but what the courts actually do. What I think the courts should do and are actually doing is, that while they use the same word as if they had a single concept, actually you will find they have not. . . .

NOTES

(1) See Reese, Does Domicile Bear a Single Meaning, 55 Colum.L.Rev. 589 (1955). Professor Cook's last word is found in Cook, Logical and Legal Bases of the Conflict of Laws 194–210 (1942).

(2) Section 5 of the Canadian Divorce Act of 1968 (Stat.Can.1968, c. 24) provides that a provincial court shall be competent to grant a divorce if the petitioner is domiciled in Canada and if either the petitioner or the respondent has been "ordinarily resident" in the province for one year prior to the filing of the petition. As a result, a person can be domiciled in Canada for divorce purposes and domiciled in a province for another purpose. Da Costa, The Canadian Divorce Law of 1968 and its Provisions on Conflicts, 17 Am.J. Comp.L. 214 (1969). A somewhat similar situation prevails in Australia. Cowen and Da Costa, The Unity of Domicile, 78 L.Q.Rev. 92 (1962).

(3) Whether a person is a citizen (or domiciliary) of a state for federal diversity purposes is determined by federal law rather than by state law. Ziady v. Curley, 396 F.2d 873 (4th Cir. 1968).

By what law is the meaning of domicile determined? The word "domicile" appears in many rules of law of many states. When the states involved in a conflicts case determine domicile by different rules, should the forum's rule always prevail or should the court look at times to the rule of the other state? A case in point is Torlonia v. Torlonia, 108 Conn. 292, 142 A. 843 (1928) where a wife sought a divorce in Connecticut from her Italian husband, claiming that she was domiciled in Connecticut and that accordingly that state had divorce jurisdiction. The husband argued that the action should be dismissed, since "as a matter of law, the plaintiff cannot have a domicile . . . other than that of her husband," because "under the law of Italy the husband is entitled to the control of the wife to the extent that she must follow him wherever he chooses to establish his residence, except as such control may be modified or affected by a decree of an Italian court of competent jurisdiction." The trial court granted the divorce and on appeal its action was affirmed. The appellate court said:

> We hold, then, that a wife separated from her husband, —. . . is not precluded from establishing an independent domicil in this State; indeed, we are convinced that this right has long been tacitly recognized and frequently given effect in divorce actions in our trial courts, although its existence has not, heretofore, been challenged on appeal.

Since domicil, as well as the other questions upon which the granting of a divorce depends, is governed by the laws of the forum in which the action is pending, the Italian law, above stated, pertaining to control of the wife by the husband, does not preclude the plaintiff from acquiring an independent domicil in Connecticut. . . .

NOTE

See Restatement, Second, Conflict of Laws § 13; Scoles and Hay, Conflict of Laws, §§ 3.3–3.12 (1982).

IN RE ANNESLEY

Chancery Division, 1926. [1926] Ch. 692.

[Summons to determine distribution of personal property in England. This turned on the validity of a will, which depended upon whether the decedent was domiciled in England or France.

The decedent was a widow over 80 years old at her death in 1924. She was married in England in 1860 to an Army officer, with whom she lived in England until 1866, and then in France until his death in 1884. She then purchased a chateau in Orthez, France, and resided there until her death, making only a few short visits back to England. After 1866 she had no place of residence in England. Two daughters survived her, but she left a will giving most of her estate to others. Under the French law she could dispose by will of only one third of her personal property. Under the English law she could dispose of all of it.]

RUSSELL, J. stated the facts and continued: The first question to be decided is whether the domicil of the testatrix was English or French. But for the fact that Mrs. Annesley took no steps to obtain a formal French domicil according to French law, and both in her will and in a codicil to it declared that it was not her intention to abandon her domicil of origin—namely, England, there could not, I conceive, be any room for doubt as to the position according to English law. She died having acquired a French domicil of choice. To use the language of Lord Westbury in Udny v. Udny, L.R. 1 H.L.Sc. 441, 458, Mrs. Annesley fixed voluntarily her sole residence in France, with an intention of continuing to reside there for an unlimited time. The domicil flows from the combination of fact and intention, the fact of residence and the intention of remaining for an unlimited time. The intention required is not an intention specifically directed to a change of domicil, but an intention of residing in a country for an unlimited time. The above recited facts in my opinion clearly establish both the necessary fact and the necessary intention.

Those who seek to establish an English domicil naturally place much reliance on the declarations in her will and codicil. They contend that we have here two statements made at different times by the lady herself, that she had never intended and did not intend to abandon her English domicil, and that in the face of these statements it is impossible for the Court to hold that a French domicil of choice had in fact or in law arisen. The contention is a tempting one to accede to in view of the fact that the finding of an English domicil would solve sundry other knotty points of difficulty which lurk in the background. But I feel unable to accede to it.

It must I think be conceded that domicil cannot depend upon mere declaration, though the fact of the declaration having been made must be one of the elements to be weighed in arriving at a conclusion on the question of domicil. But if a particular domicil clearly emerges from a consideration of the other relevant facts, a declaration of intention to retain some other domicil will not suffice to destroy the result of those facts. If (as I think she had) Mrs. Annesley had by the factum of long residence and by her animus manendi acquired before the date of her codicil a French domicil of choice, her statement that she never intended to abandon her English domicil will not prevent the acquisition of a French domicil of choice, unless weighing the statement with the other relevant facts the Court comes to the conclusion that the animus manendi had not been established. . . .

It was however contended that assuming that all the relevant facts do establish a French domicil, yet in the particular case it was according to English law impossible for Mrs. Annesley to have acquired a French domicil—because not having taken the steps prescribed by art. 13 of the Civil Code she was not and could not be a domiciled Frenchwoman in the eyes of the law of France. In other words the proposition is that no one can, according to English law, acquire a domicil of choice in a foreign country unless that person has also acquired a domicil there according to the law of the foreign country. The contention is founded upon one branch of the judgment of Farwell J. in the well known case In re Johnson, [1903] 1 Ch. 821.

Such a contention appears to me inconsistent with many decisions in the Courts of this country. In In re Martin, [1900] P. 211, 227, Lindley M. R. clearly lays it down that domicil is to be determined by English law. His judgment is no doubt a dissenting judgment, but the effect of his views upon this particular point is not weakened or affected by that fact. "The domicil . . . must be determined by the English Court . . . according to those legal principles applicable to domicil which are recognized in this country and are part of its law." If it were otherwise the question whether an individual were domiciled in France (or in any other country which requires the fulfilment of certain legal requirements before a person can be considered by the Court of that country as domiciled in that country) would be solved quite easily in every case by ascertaining whether those legal requirements had or had not been fulfilled. Yet there have been numerous cases (some of which appear in the books) in which the ques-

tion has always been considered and answered by an elaborate consideration of the various facts and circumstances in each case.
. . . .

. . . if I am free—and I think I am—to follow my own view, I
would prefer to follow what I have always considered the true view—
namely, that the question whether a person is or is not domiciled in a
foreign country is to be determined in accordance with the requirements of English law as to domicil, irrespective of the question
whether the person in question has or has not acquired a domicil in
the foreign country in the eyes of the law of that country. . . .

I accordingly decide that the domicil of the testatrix at the time of
her death was French. French law accordingly applies, but the question remains: what French law? According to French municipal law,
the law applicable in the case of a foreigner not legally domiciled in
France is the law of that person's nationality, in this case British.
But the law of that nationality refers the question back to French
law, the law of the domicil; and the question arises, will the French
law accept this reference back, or *renvoi*, and apply French municipal
law?

Upon this question arises acute conflict of expert opinion. Two
experts took the view that the *renvoi* would not be accepted, but that
a French Court would distribute the movables of the testatrix in accordance with English municipal law. One expert equally strongly
took the view that a French Court would accept the *renvoi* and distribute in accordance with French municipal law. I must come to a
conclusion as best I can upon this question of fact upon the evidence
after considering and weighing the reasons given by each side in support of their respective views. It is a case rather of views expressed
by the experts as to what the French law ought to be, than what it is.
Although there is in France no system of case law such as we understand it here—the decisions of higher Courts not being binding upon
inferior tribunals—yet I think I must pay some attention to the fact
that this question of *renvoi* has at different times come for consideration before the Cour de Cassation, the highest Court in France, and
each time with the same result—namely, the acceptance of the *renvoi*
and the application of the French municipal law. It is true that the
Cour de Cassation is quite free to take the opposite view on a future
occasion, but it has never done so. I refer to the cases which were
discussed and expounded before me—namely, the Forgo case [Clunet
(1883), 64] in 1882, and the Soulié case [Clunet (1910), 888] in 1910.
In the former case a decision of the Cour de Cassation, the *renvoi*
was accepted, and French municipal law was applied to the disposition of the estate of a Bavarian national domiciled de facto in France
(but not domiciled there according to French law), because according
to Bavarian law the law of the domicil or usual residence was applicable. The Forgo case gave rise to grave differences of opinion among
French jurists and was followed by many conflicting decisions in low-

er Courts, some favouring the "Théorie du Renvoi," others against it. The matter again came under the consideration of the branch of the Cour de Cassation entitled Chambre de Requêtes, one of whose functions is to decide whether or not an appeal to the Cour de Cassation should be allowed to proceed. That was the Soulié case, in which the Court below had held that French municipal law governed the succession to the movable property of an American subject who had died in France with a de facto domicil in that country. The Chamber declined to allow an appeal to the Cour de Cassation to proceed. This decision, coming as it did after the grave differences of opinion which resulted from the Forgo case, strikes me as of great importance. As is pointed out in a note to the report in Clunet [Clunet (1910), 888, 892] it shows that the Supreme Court persists with energy in its former view, notwithstanding the views of text writers to the contrary.

In these circumstances, and after careful consideration of the evidence of the experts called before me, I have come to the conclusion that I ought to accept the view that according to French law the French Court, in administering the movable property of a deceased foreigner who, according to the law of his country, is domiciled in France, and whose property must, according to that law, be applied in accordance with the law of the country in which he was domiciled, will apply French municipal law, and that even though the deceased had not complied with art. 13 of the Code.

The result is that as regards her English personal estate and her French movable property the testatrix in this case had power only to dispose of one-third thereof by her will.

Speaking for myself, I should like to reach the same conclusion by a much more direct route along which no question of *renvoi* need be encountered at all. When the law of England requires that the personal estate of a British subject who dies domiciled, according to the requirements of English law, in a foreign country shall be administered in accordance with the law of that country, why should this not mean in accordance with the law which that country would apply, not to the propositus, but to its own nationals legally domiciled there? In other words, when we say that French law applies to the administration of the personal estate of an Englishman who dies domiciled in France, we mean that French municipal law which France applies in the case of Frenchmen. This appears to me a simple and rational solution which avoids altogether that endless oscillation which otherwise would result from the law of the country of nationality invoking the law of the country of domicil, while the law of the country in turn invokes the law of the country of nationality, and I am glad to find that this simple solution has in fact been adopted by the Surrogates' Court of New York.[1] . . .

1. Re Tallmadge, New York Law Journal, Oct. 17, 1919, . . .: see 36 Law Quarterly Review 91.

NOTES

(1) Matter of Tallmadge, 109 Misc. 696, 181 N.Y.S. 336 (1919), cited at the end of the principal case, is the opinion of a referee in a surrogate's court. It involved the will of a United States citizen, formerly of New York, who died domiciled in France. His will, written in English in New York, left ten dollars to his brother who was his only heir. It left all of the residue of his estate to an aunt and to a cousin, share and share alike. It appeared that the cousin predeceased the testator, and the question was whether the brother took the cousin's share as intestate property according to New York law, or whether the aunt took the whole of the residue under sec. 1044 of the French Civil Code. It was held that the French internal law should be applied.

(2) In Simmons v. Simmons, 17 N.S.W.St.R. 419 (1917), the decedent was a British subject with domicile of origin in New South Wales. He died intestate in New Caledonia. According to English law, he was domiciled in New Caledonia, but, according to the French law prevailing there, he was not domiciled there, as he had never obtained official permission to live there. Under French law, his movables would be distributed according to the law of his nationality. It was held that his movable property should be distributed in accordance with the internal law of New South Wales.

(3) Suppose the conflict of laws rule of another country refers to the law of the nationality, and the nationality is United States. As will often happen, let us suppose, too, that there is no national law of the United States on the matter in question, but only the laws of the several states. To what internal law does the foreign law refer? See Scoles and Hay, Conflict of Laws §§ 4.11–4.12 (1982). Cf. In re Johnson, [1903] 1 Ch. 821; Re O'Keefe, [1940] Ch. 124 noted in 56 L.Q.Rev. 144 (1940).

IN RE SCHNEIDER'S ESTATE

Surrogate's Court of New York, New York County, 1950.
198 Misc. 1017, 96 N.Y.S.2d 652.

FRANKENTHALER, SURROGATE. This case presents a novel question in this State in the realm of the conflict of laws. Deceased, a naturalized American citizen of Swiss origin, died domiciled in New York County, leaving as an asset of his estate certain real property located in Switzerland. In his will he attempted to dispose of his property, including the parcel of Swiss realty, in a manner which is said to be contrary to the provisions of Swiss internal law. That law confers upon one's legitimate heirs a so-called *legitime*, i.e., a right to specified fractions of a decedent's property, which right cannot be divested by testamentary act. The precise issue, therefore, is whether this deceased had the power to dispose of the realty in the manner here attempted.

Ordinarily, the courts of a country not the situs of an immovable are without jurisdiction to adjudicate questions pertaining to the ownership of that property. . . . However, in this case the administratrix appointed prior to the probate of the will has liquidated the foreign realty and transmitted the proceeds to this State. She is now accounting for the assets of the estate including the fund representing that realty. As a consequence this court is called upon to direct the administration and distribution of the substituted fund and to determine the property rights therein. . . . In doing so, however, reference must be made to the law of the situs, as the question of whether the fund shall be distributed to the devisee of the realty under the terms of the will is dependent upon the validity of the original devise thereof . . .

The court is confronted at the outset with a preliminary question as to the meaning of the term "law of the situs"—whether it means only the internal or municipal law of the country in which the property is situated or whether it also includes the conflict of laws rules to which the courts of that jurisdiction would resort in making the same determination. If the latter is the proper construction to be placed upon that term, then this court must, in effect, place itself in the position of the foreign court and decide the matter as would that court in an identical case.

The meaning of the term "law of the situs" can be ascertained best from a consideration of the reasons underlying the existence of the rule which requires the application thereof. The primary reason for its existence lies in the fact that the law-making and law-enforcing agencies of the country in which land is situated have exclusive control over such land. . . . As only the courts of that country are ultimately capable of rendering enforceable judgments affecting the land, the legislative authorities thereof have the exclusive power to promulgate the law which shall regulate its ownership and transfer. . . .

Hence, the rights which were created in that land are those which existed under the whole law of the situs and as would be enforced by those courts which normally would possess exclusive judicial jurisdiction. Griswold, Renvoi Revisited, 51 Harvard L.R. 1165, 1186. . . . The purely fortuitous transfer of the problem to the courts of another state by virtue of a postmortuary conversion of the land, effected for the purpose of administering the entire estate in the country of domicile, ought not to alter the character of the legal relations which existed with respect to the land at the date of death and which continued to exist until its sale. Consequently, this court in making a determination of ownership, must ascertain the body of local law to which the courts of the situs would refer if the matter were brought before them.

It has been urged, however, that a reference to the conflict of laws rules of the situs may involve an application of the principle of *renvoi*, and if so it would place the court in a perpetually-enclosed circle from which it could never emerge and that it would never find a suitable body of substantive rules to apply to the particular case. . . . This objection is based upon the assumption that if the forum

must look to the whole law of the situs, and that law refers the matter to the law of the domicile, this latter reference must be considered
to be the whole law of the latter country also, which would refer the
matter back to the law of the situs, which process would continue
without end. That reasoning is based upon a false premise, for as
has been said by Dean Griswold, Renvoi Revisited, op. cit. supra, p.
1190: "Recognition of the foreign conflict of laws rule will not lead
us into an endless chain of references if it is clear for any reason that
the particular foreign conflicts rule (or any rule along the line of reference) is one which refers to the internal law alone . . . ." . . .

The precise question here considered, namely whether there shall
be a reference to the entire law of the situs to determine the ownership of the proceeds of foreign realty, is one of first impression in
this State. Nevertheless, the above stated principles, together with
the rule enunciated in . . . the English authorities on the subject
and in analogous cases in courts of this State and others, require us
to accept it as a part of our law and to hold that a reference to the
law of the situs necessarily entails a reference to the whole law of
that country, including its conflict of laws rule.

The rule as formulated in the Restatement is as follows: "Section
8. Rule in questions of title to land or divorce. (1) All questions of
title to land are decided in accordance with the law of the state where
the land is, including the Conflict of Laws rules of that State. (2) All
questions concerning the validity of a decree of divorce are decided in
accordance with the law of the domicile of the parties, including the
Conflict of Laws rules of that State." In all other cases the Restatement rejects the *renvoi* principle and provides that where a reference
is made to foreign law that law should be held to mean only the internal law of the foreign country. Section 7 . . . . .

The decisions in this State also indicate the applicability of the doctrine of *renvoi* in this field. In the early case of Dupuy v. Wurtz, 53
N.Y. 556, which involved personal property, there appears the first
reference to the doctrine. The Court there said by way of dictum, 53
N.Y. at page 573: "[W]hen we speak of the law of domicil as applied
to the law of succession, we mean not the general law, but the law
which the country of the domicil applies to the particular case under
consideration. . . ."

The implications of that dictum were disregarded in the celebrated
Matter of Tallmadge, Surr.Ct., New York County, 109 Misc. 696, 181
N.Y.S. 336 per Winthrop, R., where the Referee, rejecting the *renvoi*
principle completely, asserted that it "is no part of New York law."

The broad assertion in Matter of Tallmadge, supra, that the
renvoi principle is not applicable in New York is not in accord with
the earlier or later cases. The precise limits of its applicability are as
yet undefined. . . .

Thus it is now necessary to ascertain the whole of the applicable
Swiss law and apply it to this case. . . .

Concerning the actual content of Swiss law, the expert witnesses summoned by the respective parties are in agreement that the Swiss internal law would apply to the real and personal estate of a Swiss citizen domiciled in Switzerland, and that the laws of the country of domicile would, under the Swiss theory of unity of succession, apply to all of the Swiss property belonging to a foreign national. . . .

Consequently, the court holds that the testamentary plan envisaged by the testator and set out in his will is valid, even in its application to the Swiss realty. The proceeds of that realty must therefore be distributed pursuant to the directions contained in the will. . . .

Submit, on notice, decree settling the account accordingly.[1]

NOTES

(1) Matter of Zietz, 198 Misc. 77, 96 N.Y.S.2d 442 (Surr.Ct.1950), involved the estate of a national of Liechtenstein who died in Austria. It was sought to obtain ancillary administration in New York under the authority of the administrator appointed in Liechtenstein. It was alleged that there was a treaty between Austria and Liechtenstein under which it was agreed that the country of nationality should control administration when a national of one country died domiciled in the other. The court held that "If the domiciliary country, to whose law this court must refer," has determined that this matter must be governed by the law of the nationality "no reason appears why this court should not . . . accept that reference by the domicile to the law of the nationality." The court determined that evidence should be taken on the question whether the decedent was domiciled in Austria. The fact that he was not domiciled in Liechtenstein was not sufficient to deprive the Liechtenstein administrator of standing in New York.

(2) In Armitage v. Attorney General, [1906] P. 135, it appeared that a man domiciled in New York married an English woman in England. Some years later the wife started proceedings for a divorce in South Dakota. The husband answered, and a decree was granted to the wife, on a ground which would not constitute a ground for divorce in England or in New York. The court found on evidence that the divorce would be recognized in New York, the husband's domicile. It then held that the divorce must be recognized in England, since it was valid at the domicile of the parties (according to English law). Accordingly, a subsequent marriage of the wife was held valid.

(3) Richards v. United States, 369 U.S. 1 (1962), involved a suit brought in the United States District Court in Oklahoma against the United States under the Federal Tort Claims Act. 28 U.S.C.A. § 1346(b) (1964). The case arose out of an airplane accident, in which the plaintiffs' decedent was killed. The accident occurred in Missouri, which provides for limited recovery under its wrongful death statute. The flight had originated in Oklahoma, and the plaintiffs contended that the government had been negligent in Oklahoma through failure to enforce proper overhaul practices in that state. The plain-

1. There is a subsequent opinion, further discussing the Swiss law, in In re Schneider's Estate, 198 Misc. 1017, 100 N.Y.S.2d 371 (1950). The decision has been criticized on the ground the Surrogate misunderstood the Swiss law. See Falconbridge, The Renvoi in New York and Elsewhere, 6 Vanderbilt L.Rev. 708, 725-31 (1953).

tiffs argued that they should recover under the law of Oklahoma, which contains no limitation on the amount of recovery.

The Federal Tort Claims Act provides that the United States shall be liable "in accordance with the law of the place where the act or omission occurred." The Court held that this referred to "the whole law of the State where the act or omission occurred," including its conflict of laws rules. It accepted the conclusion of the lower courts that, under the Oklahoma decisions, "an action for wrongful death is based on the statute of the place where the injury occurred that caused the death." Consequently, it held that the Missouri statute, including its limitation on the amount of liability, was controlling.

RESTATEMENT, SECOND, CONFLICT OF LAWS *

§ 8. Applicability of Choice-of-Law Rules of Another State (Renvoi)

(1) When directed by its own choice-of-law rule to apply "the law" of another state, the forum applies the local law of the other state, except as stated in Subsections (2) and (3).

(2) When the objective of the particular choice-of-law rule is that the forum reach the same result on the very facts involved as would the courts of another state, the forum will apply the choice-of-law rules of the other state, subject to considerations of practicability and feasibility.

(3) When the state of the forum has no substantial relationship to the particular issue or the parties and the courts of all interested states would concur in selecting the local law rule applicable to this issue, the forum will usually apply this rule.

Comment . . .

k. *Indication of state interest.* . . .

It should be made clear that in this instance a state's choice-of-law decisions are consulted for a reason entirely different from that which gives rise to the rules of Subsections (1) and (2). In this instance, the forum consults the choice-of-law decisions of one or more other states for whatever aid these decisions may give it in determining which states have interests involved and which one of those states should be the state of the applicable law. The rules of Subsections (1) and (2) do not come into play until a later stage in the proceeding, namely, after the forum has already determined which is the state of the applicable law. These rules then provide guidance to the forum in determining whether it should apply the local law or the choice-of-law rules of the selected state.

* Quoted with the permission of the copyright owner, The American Law Institute.

Chapter 3

JURISDICTION OF COURTS

SECTION 1. INTRODUCTION AND GENERAL CONSIDERATIONS

Introductory Note: "Jurisdiction" is a concept which appears in many legal contexts and bears diverse meanings depending upon the nature or purpose of the inquiry at hand. In conflict of laws, the question of what meaning should be given the term "jurisdiction" most frequently arises in situations where it is claimed that recognition should be denied a judgment rendered in another state on the ground that the judgment is "void" because "jurisdiction" was lacking in the court which rendered the judgment. That assertion of lack of jurisdiction may seek to convey either of the following ideas:

(1) The state where the judgment was rendered did not have a proper basis upon which to go ahead to a decision. (The state, so it is said, "lacked jurisdiction over the person of the defendant" or "over the res" or "the thing in suit," tangible or intangible.)

(2) The law of the state where the judgment was rendered did not authorize the court to exercise the state's judicial power in that type of litigation or upon the jurisdictional basis that existed and was relied upon in that particular action. (The court which rendered the judgment, it is variously said, "lacked competence" or "lacked jurisdiction over the subject matter.")

The complaint of lack of jurisdiction is sometimes used also to assert that the court which rendered the judgment erred in finding that the requisite facts were present to satisfy the requirements implicit in (1) and (2), or, as it is said, the court which rendered the judgment wrongly assumed or found a "jurisdictional fact" to be present.

Other defects, which are often called "jurisdictional" by the courts on the ground that they may render the judgment "void," include lack of notice to the defendant that he has been sued and lack of an opportunity to him to be heard. Civilized states rarely deny a defendant in a court proceeding an opportunity to be heard in defense of his legal interests, so this problem does not often arise. However, the issue of lack of requisite notice frequently comes up, probably because of differences from place to place and over time in ideas about what type of notification is due a defendant as a predicate for casting him in a civil judgment or otherwise affecting his legal interests by court proceedings. We shall treat the problem of due notice in later pages of this chapter.

The meaning of the word jurisdiction that is in widest use and that has been employed in compiling this book is: the power of a state to create or affect legal interests which will be recognized as valid in other states. See Restatement, Second, Conflict of Laws § 24. Analogously, the Restatement of the Foreign Relations Law of the United States asserts (in § 6) that the term means "the capacity of a state under international law to prescribe or to enforce rules of law."

In the broad sense of those definitions, a state may exercise jurisdiction through its executive, legislative or judicial arms of government. The concern in this chapter is with the last type—the power of a state through its judicial tribunals to affect legal interests, and specifically with whether a particular judgment will be recognized as valid in other states. This deliberate emphasis on extraterritorial effects does not overlook the fact that in the home state a court's jurisdiction is determined with indifference to extraterritorial recognition and solely by the laws of the local sovereign, acting usually through its legislature. A judgment may be valid at home even if no other state would enforce it. Thus, if a court of state X in obedience to its tyrannical ruler should by decree confiscate the personal property outside X of a person who had never been a national or resident of X, the decree would surely be held unenforceable elsewhere for want of jurisdiction. Yet if the defendant or his property should ever be found in X, the decree would no doubt be upheld as jurisdictionally valid.

Among the states in the United States the subject of jurisdiction takes on a constitutional character, for even though there is no constitutional provision which in terms refers to the judicial jurisdiction of the states,* the Supreme Court has ruled that the issue is covered by the due process guarantee.

During the last generation the Supreme Court has overturned or undermined many concepts that had served as starting points for analysis in the field of jurisdiction. For example, the old ideology drew a clear line between in personam and in rem actions and caused important consequences to turn upon the distinction. Now the line has been blurred to the point where, for example, it will no longer do to say that a state can validly seize a nonresident's property simply because it is within the state, even though the state could not validly reach the nonresident; and that notice by publication will suffice in an action *because* it is "in rem" instead of "in personam." Discarding old concepts is relatively simple to do. Finding new ones to aid in analyzing novel problems is not.

---

* In specialized areas of federal authority, such as patent and copyright cases, Congress has given "exclusive" jurisdiction to the federal courts and thereby limited the jurisdiction of state courts.

CONSTITUTION OF THE UNITED STATES

Full Faith and Credit Clause—Article IV, Section 1:

Full Faith and Credit shall be given in each State to the public Acts, Records, and judicial Proceedings of every other State. And the Congress may by general Laws prescribe the Manner in which such Acts, Records and Proceedings shall be proved, and the Effect thereof.

Privileges and Immunities Clause—Article IV, Section 2:

The Citizens of each State shall be entitled to all Privileges and Immunities of Citizens in the several States.

Supremacy Clause—Article VI:

. . .

This Constitution, and the Laws of the United States which shall be made in Pursuance thereof; and all Treaties made, or which shall be made, under the Authority of the United States, shall be the supreme Law of the Land; and the Judges in every State shall be bound thereby, any Thing in the Constitution or Laws of any State to the Contrary notwithstanding. . . .

Fifth Amendment:

No person shall . . . be deprived of life, liberty, or property, without due process of law; . . .

Fourteenth Amendment:

Section 1. All persons born or naturalized in the United States, and subject to the jurisdiction thereof, are citizens of the United States and of the State wherein they reside. No State shall make or enforce any law which shall abridge the privileges or immunities of citizens of the United States; nor shall any State deprive any person of life, liberty, or property, without due process of law; nor deny to any person within its jurisdiction the equal protection of the laws.

. . .

Section 5. The Congress shall have power to enforce, by appropriate legislation, the provisions of this article.

STATUTORY PROVISIONS

TITLE 28, UNITED STATES CODE ANNOTATED, § 1738 (approved June 25, 1948):

The Acts of the legislature of any State, Territory, or Possession of the United States, or copies thereof, shall be authenticated by affixing the seal of such State, Territory or Possession thereto.

The records and judicial proceedings of any court of any such State, Territory or Possession, or copies thereof, shall be proved or admitted in other courts within the United States and its Territories and Possessions by the attestation of the clerk and seal of the court annexed, if a seal exists, together with a certificate of a judge of the court that the said attestation is in proper form.

Such Acts, records and judicial proceedings or copies thereof, so authenticated, shall have the same full faith and credit in every court within the United States and its Territories and Possessions as they have by law or usage in the courts of such State, Territory or Possession from which they are taken.

NOTE

What is now § 1738 was previously found in section 905 of the Revised Statutes, and was then included in Title 28, sec. 687, of the original United States Code. Prior to the revision in 1948, the last paragraph began: "And the said records and judicial proceedings . . .", with no reference to "Acts". The only comment of the revisers was: "This follows the language of Article IV, section 1 of the Constitution." Does the change extend the effectiveness of the statutory provision to "Acts", which had not previously been covered by the statute? The process followed in making the revision is described in Nadelmann, Full Faith and Credit to Judgments and Public Acts, 56 Mich.L.Rev. 33, 81–86 (1957).

In 1980 Congress added Section 1738(a) to the Code, one part of which calls for full faith and credit to child custody decrees in defined circumstances. Section 1738(a) is quoted below at pp. 873–874.

Jurisdiction of the district courts of the United States is prescribed in considerable detail in Title 28, United States Code, secs. 1331–1359. Provisions governing venue appear in Title 28, United States Code, secs. 1391–1406.

Service of process is governed by Rule 4 of the Federal Rules of Civil Procedure for the United States District Courts, promulgated by the Supreme Court under the authority of Title 28, United States Code, sec. 2072. Rule 4(d) prescribes how service is made on various types of persons—natural, corporate, governmental, etc. Rule 4(f) under the heading "Territorial Limits of Effective Service" provides: "All process other than a subpoena may be served anywhere within the territorial limits of the state in which the district court is held and, when authorized by a statute of the United States or by these rules, beyond the territorial limits of that state." When additional parties are brought into an action, service may be made within 100 miles of the court, even if state lines intervene.

Instances in which the district courts may have nation-wide jurisdiction include interpleader (Title 28, United States Code, sec. 1335) and certain situations under the bankruptcy act and anti-trust laws.

In American courts issues regarding jurisdiction often carry constitutional implications. To resolve them, the usual constitutional datum is the vague language of the due process clause. Because American concepts about both jurisdiction and due process evolved at common law, decisions of English courts may be helpful to understand how our concepts have developed, and how they may unfold in the future. For the same reason English statutory solutions may shed useful light. Moreover, to the extent that American rules of jurisdiction do not reflect constitutional compulsions, the English experience represents a prime source of common law authority.

BUCHANAN v. RUCKER

Court of King's Bench, 1808.
9 East 192.

The plaintiff declared in assumpsit for 2000*l.* on a foreign judgment of the Island Court in Tobago; and at the trial before Lord Ellenborough, C. J., at Guildhall, produced a copy of the proceedings and judgment, certified under the hand-writing of the Chief Justice, and the seal of the island, which were proved; which, after containing an entry of the declaration, set out a summons to the defendant, therein described as "formerly of the city of Dunkirk, and now of the city of London, merchant," to appear at the ensuing court to answer the plaintiff's action; which summons was returned, "served, etc. by nailing up a copy of the declaration at the courthouse door," etc. on which judgment was afterwards given by default. Whereupon it was objected, that the judgment was obtained against the defendant, who never appeared to have been within the limits of the island, nor to have had any attorney there; nor to have been in any other way subject to the jurisdiction of the Court at the time; and was therefore a nullity. And of this opinion was Lord Ellenborough; though it was alleged, (of which however there was no other than parol proof,) that this mode of summoning absentees was warranted by a law of the island, and was commonly practised there: and the plaintiff was thereupon nonsuited. And now

Taddy moved to set aside the nonsuit, and for a new trial, on an affidavit verifying the island law upon this subject; which stated "That every defendant against whom any action shall be entered, shall be served with a summons and an office copy of the declaration, with a copy of the account annexed, if any, at the same time by the Provost Marshal, etc. six days before the sitting of the next Court, etc.; and the Provost Marshal is required to serve the same on each defendant in person. But if such defendant cannot be found, and is not absent from the island, then it shall be deemed good service by leaving the summons, etc. at his most usual place of abode. And if the defendant be absent from the island, and hath a power of attorney recorded in the secretary's or registrar's office of Tobago, and the attorney be resident in the island, or any manager or overseer on his plantation in the island, the service shall be either upon such attorney personally, or by leaving it at his last place of abode, or upon such overseer or manager personally, or by leaving it at the house upon the defendant's plantation where the overseer or manager usually resides. But if no such attorney, overseer or manager; then the nailing up of a copy of the declaration and summons at the entrance of the court-house shall be held good service."

LORD ELLENBOROUGH, C. J. There is no foundation for this motion even upon the terms of the law disclosed in the affidavit. By persons absent from the island must necessarily be understood persons who have been present and within the jurisdiction, so as to have been subject to the process of the Court; but it can never be applied to a person who for aught appears never was present within or subject to the jurisdiction. Supposing however that the act had said in terms, that though a person sued in the island had never been present within the jurisdiction, yet that it should bind him upon proof of nailing up the summons at the court door: how could that be obligatory upon the subjects of other countries? Can the island of Tobago pass a law to bind the rights of the whole world? Would the world submit to such an assumed jurisdiction? The law itself, however, fairly construed, does not warrant such an inference: for "absent from the island" must be taken only to apply to persons who had been present there, and were subject to the jurisdiction of the Court out of which the process issued: and as nothing of that sort was in proof here to shew that the defendant was subject to the jurisdiction at the time of commencing the suit, there is no foundation for raising an assumpsit in law upon the judgment so obtained.

PER CURIAM, Rule refused.

SCHIBSBY v. WESTENHOLZ

Court of Queen's Bench, 1870. L.R. 6 Q.B. 155.

BLACKBURN, J. This was an action on a judgment of a French tribunal given against the defendants for default of appearance.

The pleas to the action were, amongst others, a plea of never indebted, and, thirdly, a special plea asserting that the defendants were not resident or domiciled in France, or in any way subject to the jurisdiction of the French court, nor did they appear; and that they were not summoned, nor had any notice or knowledge of the pending of the proceedings, or any opportunity of defending themselves there-from.   On these pleas issue was joined.

On the trial before me the evidence of a French avocat was given by which it appeared that by the law of France a French subject may sue a foreigner, though not resident in France, and that for this pur-pose an alien, if resident in France, was considered by the French law as a French subject.   The mode of citation in such a case, according to the French law, is by serving the summons on the Procureur Impé-rial.   If the foreign defendant thus cited does not within one month appear, judgment may be given against him, but he may still, at any time within two months after judgment, appear and be heard on the merits.   After that lapse of time the judgment is final and conclusive. The practice of the imperial government is, in such a case, to forward the summons thus served to the consulate of the country where the defendant is resident, with directions to intimate the summons, if practicable, to the defendant; but this, as was explained by the avo-cat, is not required by the French law, but is simply done by the impe-rial government voluntarily from a regard to fair dealing.

It appeared by other evidence that the plaintiff in this case was a Dane resident in France.   The defendants were also Danes, resident in London and carrying on business there.   A written contract had been made between the plaintiff and defendants, which was in Eng-lish, and dated in London, but no distinct evidence was given as to where it was signed.   We think, however, that, if that was material, the fair intendment from the evidence was that it was made in London.   By this contract the defendants were to ship in Sweden a cargo of Swedish oats free on board a French or Swedish vessel for Caen, in France, at a certain rate for all oats delivered at Caen.   Pay-ment was to be made on receipt of the shipping documents, but sub-ject to correction for excess or deficiency according to what might turn out to be the delivery at Caen.   From the correspondence it ap-peared that the plaintiff asserted, and the defendants denied, that the delivery at Caen was short of the quantity for which the plaintiff had paid, and that the plaintiff made some other complaints as to the con-dition of the cargo which were denied by the defendants.   The plain-tiff very plainly told the defendants that if they would not settle the claim he would sue them in the French courts.   He did issue process in the manner described, and the French consulate in London served on the defendants a copy of the citation.

The following admissions were then made, namely: that the judg-ment was regular according to French law; that it was given in fa-vour of the plaintiff, a foreigner domiciled in France, against the de-fendants, domiciled in England, and in no sense French subjects, and having no property in France. . . .

The jury found that the defendants had notice and knowledge of the summons and the pendency of the proceedings in time to have appeared and defended the action in the French court.   I then directed the verdict for the plaintiff, but reserved leave to enter the verdict for the defendants on these facts and this finding. . . .

We think that, for the reasons there given, the true principle on which the judgments of foreign tribunals are enforced in England is that stated by Parke, B., in Russell v. Smyth, 9 M. & W. at p. 819, and again repeated by him in Williams v. Jones, 13 M. & W. at p. 633, that the judgment of a court of competent jurisdiction over the defendant imposes a duty or obligation on the defendant to pay the sum for which judgment is given, which the courts in this country are bound to enforce; and consequently that anything which negatives that duty, or forms a legal excuse for not performing it, is a defence to the action.*

We were much pressed on the argument with the fact that the British legislature has, by the Common Law Procedure Act, 1852, (15 & 16 Vict. c. 76), ss. 18 and 19, conferred on our courts a power of summoning foreigners, under certain circumstances, to appear, and in case they do not, giving judgment against them by default. It was this consideration principally which induced me at the trial to entertain the opinion which I then expressed and have since changed. And we think that if the principle on which foreign judgments were enforced was that which is loosely called "comity," we could hardly decline to enforce a foreign judgment given in France against a resident in Great Britain under circumstances hardly, if at all, distinguishable from those under which we, mutatis mutandis, might give judgment against a resident in France; but it is quite different if the principle be that which we have just laid down.

Should a foreigner be sued under the provisions of the statute referred to, and then come to the courts of this country and desire to be discharged, the only question which our courts could entertain would be whether the Acts of the British legislature, rightly construed, gave us jurisdiction over this foreigner, for we must obey them. But if, judgment being given against him in our courts, an action were brought upon it in the courts of the United States (where the law as to the enforcing foreign judgments is the same as our own), a further question would be open, viz., not only whether the British legislature had given the English courts jurisdiction over the defendant, but whether he was under any obligation which the American courts could recognize to submit to the jurisdiction thus created. This is precisely the question which we have now to determine with regard

---

* This broad language was narrowed by the explanation in Godard v. Gray (1870) L.R.Q.B. 139, 149: "It must be open, therefore, to the defendant to shew that the Court which pronounced the judgment had not jurisdiction to pronounce it, either because they exceeded the jurisdiction given to them by the foreign law, or because he, the defendant, was not subject to that jurisdiction; and so far the foreign judgment must be examinable. Probably the defendant may shew that the judgment was obtained by the fraud of the plaintiff . . . and it may be that where the foreign Court has knowingly and perversely disregarded the rights given to an English subject by English law, that forms a valid excuse for disregarding the obligation thus imposed on him. . . ."

to a jurisdiction assumed by the French jurisprudence over foreigners. . . .

The question we have now to answer is, Can the empire of France pass a law to bind the whole world? We admit, with perfect candour, that in the supposed case of a judgment, obtained in this country against a foreigner under the provisions of the Common Law Procedure Act, being sued on in a court of the United States, the question for the court of the United States would be, Can the Island of Great Britain pass a law to bind the whole world? We think in each case the answer should be, No, but every country can pass laws to bind a great many persons; and therefore the further question has to be determined, whether the defendant in the particular suit was such a person as to be bound by the judgment which it is sought to enforce.

Now on this we think some things are quite clear on principle. If the defendants had been at the time of the judgment subjects of the country whose judgment is sought to be enforced against them, we think that its laws would have bound them. Again, if the defendants had been at the time when the suit was commenced resident in the country, so as to have the benefit of its laws protecting them, or, as it is sometimes expressed, owing temporary allegiance to that country, we think that its laws would have bound them.

If at the time when the obligation was contracted the defendants were within the foreign country, but left it before the suit was instituted, we should be inclined to think the laws of that country bound them; though before finally deciding this we should like to hear the question argued. But every one of those suppositions is negatived in the present case.

Again, we think it clear, upon principle, that if a person selected, as plaintiff, the tribunal of a foreign country as the one in which he would sue, he could not afterwards say that the judgment of that tribunal was not binding upon him. . . .

We think it better . . . to express no opinion as to the effect of the appearance of a defendant, where it is so far not voluntary that he only comes in to try to save some property in the hands of the foreign tribunal. But we must observe that the decision in De Cosse Brissac v. Rathbone, 6 H. & N. 301; 30 L.J. (Ex.) 238, is an authority that where the defendant voluntarily appears and takes the chance of a judgment in his favour he is bound. . . .

We think, and this is all that we need decide, that there existed nothing in the present case imposing on the defendants any duty to obey the judgment of a French tribunal.

We think, therefore, that the rule must be made absolute.

Rule absolute.

NOTES

(1) According to the Buchanan and Schibsby cases, what tests would English courts apply to determine the validity of foreign judgments in terms of jurisdiction? To what sources would the English courts turn to test jurisdiction in such cases?

(2) What standards would you suppose American courts apply in testing the jurisdictional bases of foreign country judgments? To what sources do American courts look in such cases? Will an American court always recognize a foreign country judgment as jurisdictionally sufficient if the judgment rests on a jurisdictional basis that would be sufficient in an action commenced in the American court? See pp. 315–317, infra.

For many years the basic decision on judicial jurisdiction in the United States was Pennoyer v. Neff, 95 U.S. 714 (1878) which rested squarely on the "power" theory of jurisdiction. That case involved an action in the federal court in Oregon to recover possession of a tract of Oregon land. The defense was that the defendant had acquired the land under a sheriff's deed given in execution of a judgment for lawyer's fees of less than $300 which had been recovered against the plaintiff in an Oregon state court. The plaintiff, who was a nonresident of Oregon, had been served by publication in this action and judgment had been rendered against him by default. The Supreme Court found for the plaintiff on the ground that the Oregon judgment was invalid. The Court enunciated the power theory in the strongest terms, stating that there are

". . . two well established principles of public law respecting the jurisdiction of an independent State over persons and property. . . . One of these principles is, that every State possesses exclusive jurisdiction and sovereignty over persons and property within its territory. . . . The other principle of public law referred to follows from the one mentioned; that is, that no State can exercise direct jurisdiction and authority over persons or property without its territory. . . . The several States are of equal dignity and authority, and the independence of one implies the exclusion of power from all others. And so it is laid down by jurists, as an elementary principle, that the laws of one State have no operation outside of its territory, except so far as is allowed by comity; and that no tribunal established by it can extend its process beyond that territory so as to subject either persons or property to its decisions. . . ."

The Court blended the issue of whether Oregon had a valid basis for in personam jurisdiction with the question of how the nonresident had been notified of the Oregon state court suit declaring:

"Substituted service by publication, or in any other authorized form, may be sufficient to inform parties of the object of proceedings taken where property is once brought under the control of the court by seizure or some equivalent act. The law assumes that property is always in the possession of its owner, in person or by agent; and it proceeds upon the theory that its seizure will inform him, not only that it is taken into the custody of the court, but that he must look to any proceedings authorized by law upon such seizure for its condemnation and sale. Such service may also be sufficient in cases where the object of the action is to reach and dispose of property in the State, or of some interest therein, by enforcing a contract or a lien respecting the same, or to partition it among different owners, or, when the public is a party, to condemn and appropriate it for a public purpose. In other words, such service may answer in all actions which are substantially proceedings in rem. But where the entire object of the action is to determine the personal rights and obligations of the defendants, that is, where the suit is merely in personam, constructive service in this form upon a non-resident is ineffectual for any purpose. Process from the tribunals of one State cannot run into another State, and summon parties there domiciled to leave its territory and respond to proceedings against them. Publication of process or notice within the State where the tribunal sits cannot create any greater obligation upon the non-resident to appear. Process sent to him out of the State, and process published within it, are equally unavailing in proceedings to establish his personal liability. . . .

"Except in cases affecting the personal status of the plaintiff, and cases in which that mode of service may be considered to have been assented to in advance, . . . the substituted service of process by publication, allowed by the law of Oregon and by similar laws in other States, where actions are brought against non-residents, is effectual only where, in connection with process against the person for commencing the action, property in the State is brought under the control of the court, and subjected to its disposition by process adapted to that purpose, or where the judgment is sought as a means of reaching such property or affecting some interest therein; in other words, where the action is in the nature of a proceeding in rem. . . ."

In the end the Court found that the attempt to obtain jurisdiction by attaching the property in Oregon was unavailing because the attachment had not been levied at the start of the action. Also, even though the Oregon state court judgment had been entered prior to the adoption of the Fourteenth Amendment, the Court said that the due process clause required adherence to the principles announced in its opinion.

SECTION 2.   BASES OF JUDICIAL JURISDICTION OVER NATURAL AND LEGAL PERSONS

A.   PRESENCE

The traditional basis of jurisdiction of a court over an individual at common law was the defendant's presence within the territorial limits of the state in which the court sits.   Justice Holmes stated the reason in seven categorical words: "The foundation of jurisdiction is physical power. . . ."   See McDonald v. Mabee, 243 U.S. 90 (1917). 77, infra.   Despite frequent attacks by some conflicts scholars the power theory continues to be accepted and to serve as the foundation for presence in the state as a basis for jurisdiction.   The Restatement, Second, Conflict of Laws, states in section 28: "A state has power to exercise judicial jurisdiction over an individual who is present within its territory, whether permanently or temporarily."   This rule has found application to defendants sojourning only transiently in a state.   In one well-known old case the defendant was en route by British steamer bound from Nova Scotia to New York when the vessel made for Boston harbor and was about to be moored when he was served with process.   Peabody v. Hamilton, 106 Mass. 217 (1870).   A Connecticut court upheld an English judgment based on jurisdiction obtained while the defendant was on a transient stop in a hotel, notwithstanding that the purpose of serving the defendant in England was to prevent the defendant from making his defense unless he prolonged his stay abroad indefinitely.   Fisher v. Fielding, 67 Conn. 91, 34 A. 714 (1895).

In Grace v. MacArthur, 170 F.Supp. 442 (E.D.Ark.1959), jurisdiction was upheld over a defendant who had been served with process while flying over Arkansas in a plane.

Presence, or more accurately, personal service on a person present within the state, has not proved a wholly satisfactory basis of jurisdiction.   On the one hand, it is too narrow and has had to be supplemented by other bases.   The explosive expansion of those bases is examined in the remainder of this section.   Conversely, attacks have increased upon presence itself as a basis for personal jurisdiction.   It seems clear that a person ought not be compelled to defend a civil action in whatever state he can be served with process, merely by reason of his physical presence.   The modern antidote to "transient" service has been for the court to decline to exercise jurisdiction on the ground that the plaintiff has chosen an inappropriate forum in which to bring suit.   Chapter 4 considers this and other limitations on jurisdiction, such as the effect of procuring defendant's presence in the state by the use of fraud or force.

In continental countries jurisdiction over a nonresident cannot be based on serving him during a brief sojourn. Professor Rudolph Schlesinger asserts that in those countries domicile and nationality are the most important relationships upon which jurisdiction is founded, but that jurisdiction is also acknowledged in the courts of a country where a tort was committed or a contract made, and the like. Schlesinger, Comparative Law 363–66 (4th ed. 1980). Considering recent developments in the law of jurisdiction in this country, would one be right to conclude that American states are moving closer to the civilian position? In France, under some circumstances, nationality of the *plaintiff* is a basis for judicial jurisdiction. Is jurisdiction to divorce this country's analogue? (See Chapter 12, Section 2). In Germany, the presence in the forum of property of defendant—even as trivial property as galoshes—is a basis. See Nadelmann, Jurisdictionally Improper Fora, Legal Essays in Honor of Hessel E. Yntema 321 (1961). See also de Vries and Lowenfeld, Jurisdiction in Personal Actions—A Comparison of Civil Law Views, 44 Iowa L.Rev. 306 (1959); Smit, The Terms Jurisdiction and Competence in Comparative Law, 10 Am.J.Comp.L. 164 (1961).

B.   DOMICILE, RESIDENCE AND NATIONALITY

MILLIKEN v. MEYER

Supreme Court of the United States, 1940.
311 U.S. 457, 61 S.Ct. 339, 85 L.Ed. 278, 132 A.L.R. 1357.

Suit in Colorado to enforce a Wyoming judgment against Meyer "who was asserted to be a resident of Wyoming, was personally served with process in Colorado pursuant to the Wyoming statutes; but . . . made no appearance in the Wyoming cause." The Colorado trial court found for the judgment creditor on the ground that "Meyer was domiciled in Wyoming when the Wyoming suit was commenced, that the Wyoming statutes for substituted service were constitutional, that the affidavit for constructive service on Meyer was filed in good faith, substantially conformed to the Wyoming statute and stated the truth [and] that Wyoming had jurisdiction over the person of Meyer." The Supreme Court of Colorado reversed. "It did not pass on the question of whether or not the Wyoming court had jurisdiction of the parties and subject matter. It held that the Wyoming decree was void on its face because of an irreconcilable contradiction between the findings and the decree." This was because the

Wyoming court had found that the plaintiff had validly assigned the claim on which he was nevertheless given judgment.

The Colorado judgment in turn was reversed by the Supreme Court of the United States, which, in an opinion by Mr. Justice Douglas, stated:

. . . Where a judgment rendered in one state is challenged in another, a want of jurisdiction over either the person or the subject matter is of course open to inquiry. [But, if there was jurisdiction,] the full faith and credit clause of the Constitution precludes any inquiry into the merits of the cause of action, the logic or consistency of the decision, or the validity of the legal principles on which the judgment is based. Fauntleroy v. Lum, 210 U.S. 230. . . . Whatever mistakes of law may underlie the judgment . . . it is "conclusive as to all the media concludendi." Fauntleroy v. Lum, supra, 210 U.S. at page 237.

Accordingly, if the Wyoming court had jurisdiction over Meyer, the holding by the Colorado Supreme Court that the Wyoming judgment was void because of an inconsistency between the findings and the decree was not warranted.

On the findings of the Colorado trial court, not impaired by the Colorado Supreme Court, it is clear that Wyoming had jurisdiction over Meyer in the 1931 suit. Domicile in the state is alone sufficient to bring an absent defendant within the reach of the state's jurisdiction for purposes of a personal judgment by means of appropriate substituted service. . . . Its adequacy so far as due process is concerned is dependent on whether or not the form of substituted service provided for such cases and employed is reasonably calculated to give [the defendant] actual notice of the proceedings and an opportunity to be heard. If it is, the traditional notions of fair play and substantial justice . . . implicit in due process are satisfied. Here there can be no question on that score. Meyer did not merely receive actual notice of the Wyoming proceedings. While outside the state, he was personally served in accordance with a statutory scheme which Wyoming had provided for such occasions. . . . As in case of the authority of the United States over its absent citizens (Blackmer v. United States, 284 U.S. 421), the authority of a state over one of its citizens is not terminated by the mere fact of his absence from the state. The state which accords him privileges and affords protection to him and his property by virtue of his domicile may also exact reciprocal duties. "Enjoyment of the privileges of residence within the state, and the attendant right to invoke the protection of its laws, are inseparable" from the various incidences of state citizenship. . . . The responsibilities of that citizenship arise out of the relationship to the state which domicile creates. That relationship is not dissolved by mere absence from the state. The attendant duties, like the rights and privileges incident to domicile, are not dependent on continuous presence in the state. One such incidence of domicile is amenability to suit within the state even during sojourns without the state, where the state has provided and employed a reasonable method for apprising such an absent party of the proceedings against him. . . . Here such a reasonable method was so provided and so employed.

Reversed.

NOTES

(1) Domicile may not always provide a desirable basis of jurisdiction—e.g., when the defendant's domicile is of a technical nature, as where the domicile of a child is derived from that of its parent, or when the defendant is in the process of establishing a new domicile but has not cut all connections with the present one. Cf. McDonald v. Mabee, 243 U.S. 90 (1917), summarized at p. 173, infra.

(2) To be a valid basis for jurisdiction, must the defendant be domiciled in the forum at the time the suit is commenced, or is it sufficient if the defendant had forum domicile at the time the cause of action arose and then became domiciled elsewhere? See Allen v. Superior Court, 41 Cal.2d 306, 259 P.2d 905 (1953); Owens v. Superior Court, 52 Cal.2d 822, 345 P.2d 921 (1959); Mizner v. Mizner, 84 Nev. 268, 439 P.2d 672 (1968); and Cooke v. Yarrington, 62 N.J. 123, 299 A.2d 400 (1973).

RESTATEMENT, SECOND, CONFLICT OF LAWS: *

§ 30.   Residence

A state has power to exercise judicial jurisdiction over an individual who is a resident of the state unless the individual's relationship to the state is so attenuated as to make the exercise of such jurisdiction unreasonable.

NOTES

(1) For a discussion of the distinction between "residence" and "domicile" as a basis of jurisdiction, see Restatement, Second, Conflict of Laws § 11, Comment k; Reese and Green, That Elusive Word, "Residence," 6 Vand.L. Rev. 561 (1953).

(2) Order XI, rule 1(c), of the Rules of the Supreme Court of Judicature in England reads as follows:

"1. Service out of the jurisdiction of a writ of summons or notice of a writ of summons may be allowed by the Court or a Judge whenever

. . .

"(c) Any relief is sought against any person domiciled or ordinarily resident within the jurisdiction. . . . "

---

* Quoted with the permission of the copyright owner, The American Law Institute.

RESTATEMENT, SECOND, CONFLICT OF LAWS: *

§ 31.   Nationality and Citizenship

A state has power to exercise judicial jurisdiction over an individual who is a national or citizen of the state unless the nature of the individual's relationship to the state makes the exercise of such jurisdiction unreasonable.

———

GRUBEL V. NASSAUER, 210 N.Y. 149, 103 N.E. 1113 (1913): In 1901 defendant left his home in Bavaria, Germany, became domiciled in New York, and in 1906 filed for United States citizenship. In 1907 a personal judgment was recovered against him in a Bavarian court, the only service having been by publication. The court stated the question as "how far comity should induce us to respect a foreign judgment obtained without personal service of process against a citizen, of a foreign country domiciled here at the time of recovery of the judgment." The judgment was denied enforcement, the court declaring that "a judgment for money recovered in one state without personal service of process on the defendant in that state cannot be enforced without the state." In view of Milliken v. Meyer, supra, is this decision wrong, or can it be justified on other grounds?

———

BLACKMER V. UNITED STATES, 284 U.S. 421 (1932): Blackmer, a citizen of the United States domiciled in France, was required to appear as a witness at a criminal trial in the United States under a statute authorizing the service of subpoenas for that purpose. In France a United States consul served two subpoenas on Blackmer, who however failed to appear. He was adjudged guilty of contempt and fined $30,000 and costs, to be satisfied out of his property which had been seized by order of the court. The Court rejected Blackmer's objections that his rights under the due process clause of the Fifth Amendment were violated. The Court declared that the "jurisdiction of the United States over its absent citizen, so far as the binding effect of its legislation is concerned, is a jurisdiction in personam, as he is personally bound to take notice of the laws that are applicable to him and to obey them." As "for the exercise of judicial jurisdiction in personam," the Court went on, "there must be due process, which requires appropriate notice of the judicial action and an opportunity to be heard." The case is widely viewed as establishing that nationality is a constitutionally permissible basis of both judicial and legislative jurisdiction, the theory being that citizens owe allegiance to their nation and its laws even when absent from its borders.

* Quoted with the permission of the copyright owner, The American Law Institute.

NOTES

(1) The statute involved in Blackmer v. United States, is now 28 U.S.C. § 1783. See also Federal Rules of Civil Procedure, Rule 45(e)(2) and Federal Rules of Criminal Procedure, Rule 17(e)(2). Cf. Restatement, Foreign Relations Law of the United States § 38, Reporters' Notes (1965).

The power of a state to prescribe law governing its nationals outside its territory meets sharp limits when aliens are also affected. See Restatement, Second, Foreign Relations Law of the United States § 30(2) (1965): "A state does not have jurisdiction to prescribe a rule of law attaching legal consequences to conduct of an alien outside its territory merely on the ground that the conduct affects one of its nationals."

(2) Cf. Skiriotes v. Florida, 313 U.S. 69, 61 S.Ct. 924, 85 L.Ed. 1193 (1941), affirming a state court conviction for violation of a Florida statute making it criminal to use diving suits to take commercial sponges off the coast of Florida. Skiriotes had used the forbidden apparatus outside the "three-mile limit." He was arrested within the state of Florida, so there was no question of Florida's judicial jurisdiction. The Supreme Court declared that "if the United States may control the conduct of its citizens upon the high seas, we see no reason why the State of Florida may not likewise govern the conduct of its citizens upon the high seas with respect to matters in which the State has a legitimate interest and where there is no conflict with act of Congress."

C.   APPEARANCE AND CONSENT IN ADVANCE

RESTATEMENT, SECOND, CONFLICT OF LAWS: *

§ 33.   Appearance as Defendant

A state has power to exercise judicial jurisdiction in an action over an individual who enters an appearance as defendant in that action.

§ 81.   Special Appearance

A state will not exercise judicial jurisdiction over an individual who appears in the action for the sole purpose of objecting that there is no jurisdiction over him.

NOTES

(1) Under Rule 12(b) of the Federal Rules of Civil Procedure the defense of lack of jurisdiction may be made in the pleadings or by motion. The effect is to abolish the necessity of "special appearance." Similar procedures are now provided in many of the states.

(2) Does a nonresident who starts an action in a forum that previously lacked any jurisdictional basis over him thereby become amenable to jurisdic-

tion for counterclaim purposes? In Adam v. Saenger, 303 U.S. 59, 67–68 (1938), p. 282, infra, the Supreme Court said: "The plaintiff having, by his voluntary act in demanding justice from the defendant, submitted himself to the jurisdiction of the court, there is nothing arbitrary or unreasonable in treating him as being there for all purposes for which justice to the defendant requires his presence. It is the price which the state may exact as the condition of opening its courts to the plaintiff."

RESTATEMENT, SECOND, CONFLICT OF LAWS: *

§ 32. Consent

A state has power to exercise judicial jurisdiction over an individual who has consented to the exercise of such jurisdiction.

MODEL CHOICE OF FORUM ACT †

Section 2. [*Action in This State by Agreement.*]

(a) If the parties have agreed in writing that an action on a controversy may be brought in this state and the agreement provides the only basis for the exercise of jurisdiction, a court of this state will entertain the action if

    (1) the court has power under the law of this state to entertain the action;

    (2) this state is a reasonably convenient place for the trial of the action;

    (3) the agreement as to the place of the action was not obtained by misrepresentation, duress, the abuse of economic power, or other unconscionable means; and

    (4) the defendant, if within the state, was served as required by law of this state in the case of persons within the state or, if without the state, was served either personally or by registered [or certified] mail directed to his last known address.

(b) This section does not apply [to cognovit clauses] [to arbitration clauses or] to the appointment of an agent for the service of process pursuant to statute or court order.

Comment

. . . The references to cognovit and arbitration clauses have been placed in brackets, because these clauses are regulated by statute in many states, and the special provisions regarding them may be preferred to the general provisions of this Act.

---

* Quoted with the permission of the copyright owner, The American Law Institute.

† After having been adopted in four states this model act was withdrawn in 1975 (Handbook on the Conference of Commissioners on Uniform State Laws 351 (1976)).

GROVER & BAKER SEWING MACHINE CO. V. RADCLIFFE, 137 U.S. 287 (1890). Defendant, a citizen of Maryland, signed a note in which he authorized any attorney of any state to confess judgment against him. Judgment by confession was entered against the defendant by a prothonotary (a court official) in Pennsylvania. The Maryland courts refused to enforce this judgment. The Supreme Court affirmed on the ground that the Pennsylvania judgment had not been entered in accordance with the consent. Defendant had authorized attorneys, not prothonotaries, to represent him and "he had a right to insist upon the letter of the authority conferred."

———

NATIONAL EQUIPMENT RENTAL, LIMITED V. SZUKHENT, 375 U.S. 311 (1964): Petitioner sued respondents, who were Michigan farmers, in the federal court in New York for failure to make periodic payments on a farm equipment lease. The lease was a printed form containing 18 paragraphs, the last of which read: "This agreement shall be deemed to have been made in Nassau County, New York, regardless of the order in which the signatures of the parties shall be affixed hereto, and shall be interpreted, and the rights and liabilities of the parties here determined, in accordance with the laws of the State of New York; and the Lessee hereby designates Florence Weinberg, 47–21 Forty-first Street, Long Island City, N. Y., as agent for the purpose of accepting service of any process within the State of New York."

The respondents received timely notice of the commencement of the action, but the lower courts held that the service was ineffective and should be quashed because the lease agreement had not explicitly required Florence Weinberg to send notice of suit to respondents. Reversing, the Supreme Court held (5–4) that the agency was valid and that the service was good.

"We need not and do not in this case reach the situation where no personal notice has been given to the defendant. Since the respondents did in fact receive complete and timely notice of the lawsuit pending against them, no due process claim has been made. The case before us is therefore quite different from cases where there was no actual notice. . . . Similarly, as the Court of Appeals recognized, this Court's decision in Wuchter v. Pizzutti, 276 U.S. 13, 48 S.Ct. 259, 72 L.Ed. 466, is inapposite here. . . . Wuchter dealt with the limitations imposed by the Fourteenth Amendment upon a statutory scheme by which a State attempts to subject nonresident individuals to the jurisdiction of its courts. The question presented here, on the other hand, is whether a party to a private contract may appoint an agent to receive service of process within the meaning of Federal Rule of Civil Procedure 4(d)(1), where the agent is not personally known to the party, and where the agent has not expressly undertaken to transmit notice to the party."

In a dissenting opinion, Justice Black said:

. . . This Court should reject any construction of Rule 4(d)(1) or formulation of federal standards under it to help powerful litigants to achieve by unbargained take-it-or-leave-it contracts what Congress has consistently refused to permit by legislation.

The Court's holding that these Michigan residents are compelled to go to New York to defend themselves in a New York court brings sharply into focus constitutional questions as to whether they will thereby be denied due process of law in violation of the Fifth and Fourteenth Amendments. . . .

It can of course be argued with plausibility that the Pennoyer constitutional rule has no applicability here because the process served on the Szukhents ran from a federal, not a state, court. But this case was in federal court solely because of the District Court's diversity jurisdiction. . . . Neither the Federal Constitution nor any federal statute requires that a person who could not constitutionally be compelled to submit himself to a state court's jurisdiction forfeits that constitutional right because he is sued in a Federal District Court acting for a state court solely by reason of the happenstance of diversity jurisdiction. . . .

The Court relies on the printed provision of the contract as a consent of the Szukhents to be sued in New York, making the Pennoyer rule inapplicable. In effect the Court treats the provision as a waiver of the Szukhents' constitutional right not to be compelled to go to a New York court to defend themselves against the company's claims. This printed form provision buried in a multitude of words is too weak an imitation of a genuine agreement to be treated as a waiver of so important a constitutional safeguard as is the right to be sued at home. Waivers of constitutional rights to be effective, this Court has said, must be deliberately and understandingly made and can be established only by clear, unequivocal, and unambiguous language. It strains credulity to suggest that these Michigan farmers ever read this contractual provision about Mrs. Weinberg and about "accepting service of any process within the State of New York." And it exhausts credulity to think that they or any other laymen reading these legalistic words would have known or even suspected that they amounted to an agreement of the Szukhents to let the company sue them in New York should any controversy arise. . . . The idea that there was a knowing consent of the Suzkhents to be sued in the courts of New York is no more than a fiction—not even an amiable one at that.

The Supreme Court has held in two recent cases that due process requirements are not necessarily offended by a clause in a contract in which a debtor waives notice and authorizes the confession of judgment against him. Such a clause was upheld in D. H. Overmyer Co. Inc., of Ohio v. Frick Co., 405 U.S. 174 (1972) on the ground that the Overmyer Company (against whom a confession judgment had been entered in an amount in excess of $62,000) had received good consideration and had "voluntarily and knowingly waived the rights it otherwise possessed to prejudgment notice and hearing." The Court stated that its holding would not be "controlling precedent for other facts of other cases. For example, where the contract is one of adhesion, where there is great disparity in bargaining power, and where the debtor receives nothing for the cognovit provision. . . . "

Swarb v. Lennox, 405 U.S. 191 (1972) involved an action brought on behalf of a class of Pennsylvania residents who signed documents leading, or that could have led, to confessed judgments in Philadelphia. The three-judge District Court held the Pennsylvania confession of judgment procedure unconstitutional when used against persons earning less than $10,000 annually on the ground that the judgment creditors had failed to show that this class of debtors had waived understandingly "the right to have pre-judgment notice and hearing, the right to have the burden of proof on the creditor, and the right to avoid the expenses attendant upon opening or striking a confessed judgment." The court refused to hold the Pennsylvania procedure unconstitutional with respect to other debtors. The plaintiffs, but not the defendants, appealed. In affirming the Supreme Court expressly reserved many questions of constitutionality involved in the Pennsylvania practice—e.g., the effects of disparity in bargaining power of the parties, the use by the creditor of an adhesion contract and the absence of consideration for agreement to the cognovit provision.

Section 1.201(8) of the Uniform Consumer Credit Code reads as follows:

Each of the following agreements or provisions of an agreement by a consumer who is a resident of this State at the time of a consumer credit transaction is invalid with respect to the transaction:

(a) that the law of another jurisdiction apply;

(b) that the consumer consents to be subject to the process of another jurisdiction;

(c) that the consumer appoints an agent to receive service of process;

(d) that fixes venue; and

(e) that the consumer consents to the jurisdiction of the court that does not otherwise have jurisdiction.

Suppose that this provision is in force in State X but not in State Y, and that in X an X consumer signs a contract in which he agrees to be subject to the jurisdiction of Y. Is this submission to jurisdiction valid and effective in X? In Y? And if judgment by default is obtained in Y against the X consumer, could an X court properly refuse to enforce the judgment on the ground that it had been rendered without jurisdiction? See Schlesinger, Jurisdictional Clauses in Con-

sumer Transactions: A Multifaceted Problem of Jurisdiction and Full
Faith and Credit, 29 Hast.L.J. 967 (1978).

EGLEY v. T. B. BENNETT & Co., 196 Ind. 50, 145 N.E. 830 (1924):
In Indiana, where he resided, defendant executed a cognovit note
payable to the plaintiff corporation in Flanagan, Illinois. The note
provided: "I hereby irrevocably make any attorney at law my attorney for me and in my name to appear in any court of record, in term
time or vacation, at any time hereafter to waive service of process
and confess a judgment on this note in favor of the payee, his assigns
or the legal holder, for such sum as shall then appear to be due, including an attorney fee (as stated) . . . to release all errors
. . . and to consent to immediate execution on such judgment."
Plaintiff brought suit in Illinois without notice to defendant and a
lawyer confessed judgment for the amount of the note, interest, attorney's fees and costs. The Indiana court enforced the judgment,
declaring that even though the quoted language would not have authorized confession of a valid judgment in Indiana, "no law in this
State prevents the making of such a contract to be performed in a
State where such a provision may be lawfully carried out. . . . ."
In the course of its opinion the court made clear that it believed the
validity of the Illinois judgment depended entirely on whether the
cognovit would be sustained as enforceable under the body of law
which Indiana choice of law rules would designate as authoritative on
that question. "The warrant of attorney is a matter connected with
the performance of the contract and not with its formal validity, and
since the contract can legally be performed in the place where it was
to be performed, all matters relating thereto and carried out there
must be construed according to the laws of that jurisdiction.
. . . ."

NOTES

(1) Did the Indiana court look to the right body of law to determine
whether the Illinois judgment had to be enforced? If full faith and credit
requires that F–2 enforce an F–1 judgment having a constitutionally valid
jurisdictional basis, and if F–1's jurisdiction turns on the validity of defendant's consent, how should F–2 have framed the question before it in the
principal case?

(2) A comprehensive survey of cognovit note practice reported, as of
1961, that by legislation 7 states expressly allow them, 15 outlaw them, and
23 place procedural restrictions upon their use. The other states lack pertinent statutes. Of the 7 states authorizing cognovit notes, Illinois, Pennsylvania and Ohio, which as of 1961 did not confine them in any way by type
of loan or otherwise, produced most confession judgments. Hopson, Cognovit Judgments: An Ignored Problem of Due Process and Full Faith and
Credit, 29 U. of Chi.L.Rev. 111 (1961). Ohio has since imposed restrictions
upon the use of cognovit notes. Ohio Rev.Code § 2323.13 (1973 Supp.) See

also Schuchman, Confession of Judgment as a Conflict of Laws Problem, 36 Notre Dame L.Rev. 461 (1961); Note, 34 U.Pitt.L.Rev. 103 (1972).

(3) When consent in advance is the only asserted basis for a state's jurisdiction to render a judgment on confession, a clear line of attack by the defendant is to show that his alleged "consent" was inefficacious, for example, because of forgery or fraud in the cognovit note. See Anderson v. Reconstruction Fin. Corp., 281 Ky. 531, 136 S.W.2d 741 (1940); Brone v. Golde, 267 N.Y. 284, 196 N.E. 58 (1935).

(4) In Elkin v. Austral-American Trading Corp., 10 Misc.2d 879, 170 N.Y.S.2d 131 (Sup.Ct.N.Y.Co.1957), the defendant, a foreign corporation, moved to vacate service of the summons or to dismiss for lack of jurisdiction. The plaintiff relied on the following provisions in the contract sued on:

"Both parties agree that service of process may be made by registered special delivery air mail addressed to the other party at his or its last known address and that the time to respond to such process shall be 40 days from the date of mailing thereof.

"This contract is to be construed pursuant to the laws of the State of New York and both parties agree that only the New York courts shall have jurisdiction over this contract and any controversies arising out of this contract."

Should the motion be granted? By what drafting changes might the language of the first paragraph be strengthened and clarified as a basis for jurisdiction? In the courts of other states or countries, would the provision giving New York exclusive jurisdiction be honored? See pp. 183–188 infra.

Drafting exercise: Revise the language of the first paragraph to make it clearer and stronger as a basis for jurisdiction in the New York courts.

COPIN v. ADAMSON

Court of Exchequer, 1874. L.R. 9 Exch. 345.

[Declaration by the assignee in bankruptcy of the Société de Commerce de France, Limited on a judgment for £151 15 s. recovered on the 7th of February, 1867, in France, by him against the the defendant in the Court of the Tribunal of Commerce of the Department of the Seine, being a court duly holden, and having jurisdiction in that behalf.

Plea. 3. That the suit was commenced, according to the French law, by process and summons, and that the defendant was not at any time previous to the recovery of judgment resident or domiciled within the jurisdiction of the said Court, nor is he a native of France, and he was not served with any process or summons, nor did he appear, nor had he any notice or knowledge of any process or summons, or any opportunity of defending himself.

Replication 1. That the articles of association of the French corporation in which the defendant was a stockholder provided that all disputes arising during the liquidation of the company between the shareholders and the company should be submitted to the jurisdiction of a competent tribunal of the department of the Seine, that every stockholder who should provoke a contest must elect a domicile in Paris and that, in default of such election, he would be deemed to be domiciled at the office of the imperial procurator for service of process. That, the defendant not having elected a domicile in Paris, service of process was delivered at the office of the official procurator and by the law of France this amounted to notice to the defendant.

Replication 2. The Law of France contained a similar provision.

Demurrer to the replication.]

AMPHLETT, B. An important question is raised on these replications, involving the liability of a British subject to be sued in the courts of a foreign country. As to the first replication demurred to, the Court is unanimously of opinion that the defendant is shewn upon the face of it to have contracted with the company, of which he is a shareholder, and whose representative the plaintiff is, that he would, under the circumstances disclosed, be amenable to the jurisdiction of the Court of the Tribunal of Commerce of the Department of the Seine. But as to the second replication, my brother Pigott and myself think that although the allegations are sufficient to shew that the defendant's contract is to be governed by French law, still that they do not shew that he is subject to the jurisdiction of the French Court. The contract must be interpreted by an English tribunal.

. . . I apprehend that a man may contract with others that his rights shall be determined not only by foreign law, but by a foreign tribunal, and thus by reason of his contract, and not of any allegiance absolute or qualified, would become bound by that tribunal's decision. It is upon this ground that I decide the demurrer to the first replication in the plaintiff's favour. I think that the defendant must be taken to have agreed that if he did not elect a domicile one should be elected for him; for the articles of association provide for its being done. It is said that it is not sufficiently stated that he had notice of this particular provision, but I think it must be implied that he had notice, from the fact of his becoming a shareholder in the company.

I now proceed to consider the second replication, which is silent as to the statutes or articles of association, but simply alleges that according to French law the members of the company were bound to elect a domicile; and that, according to French law, upon default a domicile would be elected for them at a public office, where process might be served, and that they would be bound thereby. I confess I cannot find a case which has gone so far as to hold a defendant liable, under such circumstances, upon a foreign judgment obtained as this was, without any knowledge on his part of the proceedings. Can it be said that an Englishman, for example, who buys a share in a foreign company on the London Stock Exchange, thereby becomes necessarily bound by any decision to which the foreign tribunal may come upon a matter affecting his interests? Suppose there had been a provision by the law of France that whenever a member neglected to elect a domicile he should pay double calls, are we to enforce his liability in an action on a judgment for such calls obtained against him without his knowledge in the foreign court?   No doubt in the present case, where the law of France is in question, the probability is that the shareholder would not be subjected to any extraordinary or unjust liabilities.   But if the principle of law is that which the plaintiff contends for, it must be applied in cases of countries where the law might be very much more open to objection than it is likely to be in a country such as France.   .   .   .

The second case relied on was Vallee v. Dumergue, 4 Ex. 290, 18 L.J. (Ex.) 398, but here again, although the decision supports the first, it fails to support the second replication.   There the defendant had become by transfer the owner of shares in a French company, and upon accepting the shares was bound, according to French law, to elect a domicile.   He actually did so, and gave notice of his election to the company.   He was, therefore, aware of what the French law was, and had complied with it.   Then, having left the country, notice of process was, as here, left at the elected domicile, but never reached the defendant against whom judgment by default was recovered.   It was held he was liable on the judgment, but upon the ground that he had done something more than become a shareholder in the company; he had so conducted himself as to warrant the inference that he had agreed to be bound by the decision of the foreign Court.   "The replication consists," says Alderson, B. (at p. 303) "of a statement of facts which shew that by the agreement to which the defendant has become a party, no actual notice need be given to him;" and again (at page 303) "It is not contrary to natural justice that a man who has agreed to receive a particular mode of notification of legal proceedings should be bound by a judgment in which that particular mode has been followed, even though he may not have had actual notice of them."

For these reasons my judgment (in which my Brother Pigott concurs) is for the plaintiff upon the demurrer to the first replication, and for the defendant upon the demurrer to the second.

Judgment accordingly.

[KELLY, C. B. dissents as to the second replication.]

NOTES

(1) The test of whether a nonresident stockholder may be held subject to some unusual duty under the laws of the state of incorporation may be different from the test of whether he may be sued there.   See, e.g., Risdon Iron and Locomotive Works v. Furness, [1906] 1 K.B. 49; Thomas v. Matthiessen, 232 U.S. 221 (1914); Converse v. Hamilton, 224 U.S. 243 (1912), p. 944, infra.

(2) In Pope v. Heckscher, 266 N.Y. 114, 194 N.E. 53 (1934), suit was brought in New York on a Canadian judgment rendered against a New York shareholder for the balance of his subscription to stock in a Canadian corporation.   The only service in the Canadian action was by mail to defendant's

address in New York but by Canadian law a stockholder of a Canadian corporation subjected himself to jurisdiction in respect to any liability incurred as a stockholder. The New York Court of Appeals refused to enforce the judgment holding that the Canadian court lacked jurisdiction. The court stated that it would have denied enforcement to a sister state judgment rendered under similar circumstances. Is this result constitutionally compelled?

D. LOCAL ACTIONS OR LOCAL EFFECTS

With the population increasingly mobile and with businesses commonly operating in several states, the traditional bases of jurisdiction proved unrealistic and inadequate. Obtaining jurisdiction over a foreign corporation which had engaged in the forum state in a transaction out of which the litigation arose was a recurring issue. The problem was complicated by dogmas regarding the territorial limits of state law and a highly legalistic view of corporate existence.

A dictum in Bank of Augusta v. Earle, 38 U.S. 519 (1839) (discussed at p. 965, infra) gave support to the notion that a corporation, being a creature of law which had force only in the incorporating state, could have no existence outside that state. It could, however, appoint agents who could enter another state, transact business for it, and sue and be sued on the corporation's behalf, provided the other state consented. Rather early the practice grew up of requiring the foreign corporation to appoint a resident agent, or to consent to service of process on a government officer in the state, such as the commissioner of corporations or the secretary of state.

The practical as well as the theoretical results were unsatisfactory. (1) Where an actual consent was filed, questions might arise with regard to the effect of the corporation's "withdrawal" of consent and recall of its designated agent from the state. (2) Similarly, questions might arise as to the scope of the consent. For example, was it applicable only to causes of action arising out of business done within the state? (3) Finally, the requirement of filing a consent was not thought to be applicable to nonresident individuals or partnerships, whom the state had no power to exclude. There were strong inducements to a corporation not to consent explicitly or "qualify" in a state in which it carried on business. The courts then began speaking of "implied consent" as a basis for jurisdiction over such corporations. This is illustrated in Lafayette Insurance Co. v. French, 18 How. 404, 15 L.Ed. 451 (1856), where the Supreme Court held that a foreign corporation transacting business in Ohio through an agent was deemed to have assented to the condition laid down by Ohio law, namely that the agent be authorized to receive process on behalf of the corporation. "Implied consent" became a much-used fiction. In due course, the "implied consent" rationale was abandoned and the courts began frankly to recognize that a state can exercise judicial jurisdiction over a foreign corporation which does business in its territory, at least with respect to causes of action arising out of that business.   Restatement, Second, Conflict of Laws § 47.

The bases for the exercise of judicial jurisdiction over foreign corporations will be examined in the material that follows.

NOTES

(1) In the United States, any corporation incorporated under the laws of a sister state or foreign country is a "foreign corporation."   Every state has fairly extensive statutory provisions dealing with foreign corporations.

The typical statute provides that no foreign corporation shall do business in the state unless it "qualifies" in the state.   See Chapter 15, section 2, infra.   In order to "qualify," it must, under the usual statutes, file an application with the Secretary of State.   In this application, it must give certain information, and it must designate an office within the state, and a registered agent.   There are then provisions for service of process.   These vary in form, but they are generally much the same in substance.   As an example, reference may be made to Section 111 of the Illinois Business Corporation Act (Ill.Stat.Ann. ch. 32, § 157.111).   This is entitled "Service of process on foreign corporation," and reads as follows:

"Service of process in any suit, action, or proceeding, or service of any notice or demand required or permitted by law to be served on a foreign corporation may be made on such corporation by service thereof on the registered agent of such corporation.   Whenever any foreign corporation authorized to transact business in this State shall fail to appoint or maintain in this State a registered agent upon whom service of legal process or service of any such notice or demand may be had, or whenever any such registered agent cannot with reasonable diligence be found at the registered office in this State of such corporation, or whenever the certificate of authority of any foreign corporation shall be revoked, then and in every such case the Secretary of State shall be irrevocably authorized as the agent and representative of such foreign corporation to accept service of any process, or service of any notice or demand required or permitted by law to be served upon such corporation.   Service on the Secretary of State of any such process, notice, or demand against any such foreign corporation shall be made by delivering to and leaving with him, or with any clerk having charge of the corporation department of his office, duplicate copies of such process, notice, or demand. In the event that any process, notice, or demand is served on the Secretary of State, he shall immediately cause a copy thereof to be forwarded by registered mail, addressed to such corporation at its principal office as the same appears in the records of the Secretary of State.   Any service so had on the Secretary of State shall be returnable in not less than thirty days. . . . "

(2) The scope of consent and its duration in the event that a foreign corporation ceases activities and "withdraws" from a state in which it has qualified are determined by the law of that state.   Washington v. Superior Court, 289 U.S. 361 (1933).

(3) In Mutual Reserve Fund Life Ass'n v. Phelps, 190 U.S. 147 (1903), the statute providing for service of process on the commissioner of insurance required that "if process is served upon the commissioner it shall be his duty

to at once send it by mail, addressed to the company at its principal office."
Is such a requirement necessary for constitutional reasons?　See Wuchter v.
Pizzutti, 276 U.S. 13 (1928) discussed in the opinion in the Szukhent case (p.
53, supra).

———

The states also desired to exercise judicial jurisdiction over foreign individuals and partnerships which conducted activities or which
caused effects within their territory.　Here likewise the "implied consent" theory was often relied upon, but it did not always meet with
success.

FLEXNER V. FARSON, 248 U.S. 289 (1918):　Suit was brought in Illinois upon a Kentucky judgment against the nonresident defendants,
who had done business in Louisville.　Service in Kentucky was made
upon an agent of the partnership.　Foreign corporation cases were
invoked as an analogy for jurisdiction over partnerships doing business within the state.　But the analogy was rejected, Mr. Justice
Holmes declaring that the consent "said to be implied in such cases is
a mere fiction, founded upon the accepted doctrine that the States
could exclude foreign corporations altogether, and therefore could establish this obligation as a condition to letting them in　.　.　.　The
State had no power to exclude the defendants, and on that ground,
without going farther, the Supreme Court of Illinois rightly held that
the analogy failed, and that the Kentucky judgment was void."

———

DOHERTY & CO. V. GOODMAN, 294 U.S. 623 (1935):　D, a New York
citizen trading as "Doherty & Co.", operated an office in Iowa for the
sale of corporate securities throughout the state.　E. A. King, in
charge of the office, was served under an Iowa statute with process
in a suit against D for damages arising out of a sale of stock in Iowa
by D's salesman.　D had never consented to service or authorized
King to be his agent for that purpose, but the statute authorized service on corporations or individuals who had an office for the "transaction of any business" within the state.　In upholding jurisdiction the
Supreme Court noted that Iowa treated as "exceptional" the business
of dealing in corporate securities and subjected it to special regulation and found support in the decisions on nonresident motorists.
Flexner v. Farson, supra, was distinguished on an obscure factual
point—that there service had been made upon one not then an agent
for the defendants.

An important breakthrough in jurisdiction over nonresident individuals came in Hess v. Pawloski, 274 U.S. 352 (1927) where the Supreme Court upheld the constitutionality of a Massachusetts statute
which provided for the exercise of judicial jurisdiction over nonresident motorists with respect to claims arising from accidents in the
state.　This statute read in part as follows:

"The acceptance by a nonresident of the rights and privileges conferred by section three or four, as evidenced by his operating a motor vehicle thereunder, or the operation by a nonresident of a motor vehicle on a public way in the commonwealth other than under said sections, shall be deemed equivalent to an appointment by such nonresident of the registrar or his successor in office, to be his true and lawful attorney upon whom may be served all lawful processes in any action or proceeding against him, growing out of any accident or collision in which said nonresident may be involved while operating a motor vehicle on such a way, and said acceptance or operation shall be a signification of his agreement that any such process against him which is so served shall be of the same legal force and validity as if served on him personally. Service of such process shall be made by leaving a copy of the process with a fee of two dollars in the hands of the registrar, or in his office, and such service shall be sufficient service upon the said nonresident: Provided, that notice of such service and a copy of the process are forthwith sent by registered mail by the plaintiff to the defendant, and the defendant's return receipt and the plaintiff's affidavit of compliance herewith are appended to the writ and entered with the declaration. The court in which the action is pending may order such continuances as may be necessary to afford the defendant reasonable opportunity to defend the action."

In sustaining the constitutionality of the statute, the Court said:

"The question is whether the Massachusetts enactment contravenes the due process clause of the Fourteenth Amendment. . . . The mere transaction of business in a state by nonresident natural persons does not imply consent to be bound by the process of its courts. Flexner v. Farson, 248 U.S. 289, 39 S.Ct. 97, 63 L.Ed. 250. The power of a State to exclude foreign corporations, although not absolute, but qualified, is the ground on which such an implication is supported as to them. Pennsylvania Fire Insurance Co. v. Gold Issue Mining Co., 243 U.S. 93, 96. But a State may not withhold from nonresident individuals the right of doing business therein. The privileges and immunities clause of the Constitution (section 2, art. 4), safeguards to the citizens of one State the right "to pass through, or to reside in any other State for purposes of trade, agriculture, professional pursuits, or otherwise. . . .

"Motor vehicles are dangerous machines, and, even when skillfully and carefully operated, their use is attended by serious dangers to persons and property. In the public interest the state may make and enforce regulations reasonably calculated to promote care on the part of all, residents and nonresidents alike, who use its highways. The measure in question operates to require a nonresident to answer for his conduct in the state where arise causes of action alleged against him, as well as to provide for a claimant a convenient method by which he may sue to enforce his rights. Under the statute the implied consent is limited to proceedings growing out of accidents or collisions on a highway in which the nonresident may be involved. It is required that he shall actually receive and receipt for notice of the service and a copy of the process. And it contemplates such continuances as may be found necessary to give reasonable time and opportunity for defense. It makes no hostile discrimination against nonresidents, but tends to put them on the same footing as residents. Literal and precise equality in respect of this matter is not attainable; it is not required. Canadian Northern Ry. Co. v. Eggen, 252 U.S. 553, 561, 562. The State's power to regulate the use of its highways extends to their use by nonresidents as well as by residents. Hendrick v. Maryland, 235 U.S. 610, 622. And, in advance of the operation of a motor vehicle on its highway by a nonresident, the State may require him to appoint one of its officials as his agent on whom process may be served in proceedings growing out of such use. Kane v. New Jersey, 242 U.S. 160, 167. That case recognizes power of the state to exclude a nonresident until the formal appointment is made. And, having the power so to exclude, the state may declare that the use of the highway by the nonresident is the equivalent of the appointment of the registrar as agent on whom process may be served. Cf. Pennsylvania Fire Insurance Co. v. Gold Issue Mining Co., [243 U.S. 93]; Lafayette Ins. Co. v. French, 18 How. 404, 407, 408. The difference between the formal and implied appointment is not substantial, so far as concerns the application of the due process clause of the Fourteenth Amendment."

NOTES

(1) The "implied consent" rationale of the principal case experienced difficulties. Did the motorist's consent survive his death in the accident so that suit could be brought against his nonresident executor or administrator? See Chapter 13, Administration of Estates, p. 909, infra. Was it not rather strained to speak of "consent" in the case of suit against a nonresident naval officer who had traveled into the state under orders, had an automobile accident, and then received process outside the state? See Hart v. Queen City Coach Co., 241 N.C. 389, 85 S.E.2d 319 (1955).

(2) Hess v. Pawloski has been a prolific authority. Not only did it support the nonresident motorist statutes, now found in all the states, but it is the foundation for similar statutes relating to travel in the air and on the sea. See e.g., Tardiff v. Bank Line, Ltd., 127 F.Supp. 945 (E.D.La.1954), sustaining the nonresident vessel owner statute.

OLBERDING V. ILLINOIS CENTRAL R. Co., 346 U.S. 338 (1953): The issue was whether driving an automobile into the state serves not only as a basis for jurisdiction but also as a waiver of the nonresident's objections to improper venue in a federal diversity suit. In ruling in the negative, the Court said: "It is true that in order to ease the process by which new decisions are fitted into pre-existing modes of analysis there has been some fictive talk to the effect that the reason why a non-resident can be subjected to a state's jurisdiction is that the non-resident has 'impliedly' consented to be sued there. In point of fact, however, jurisdiction in these cases does not rest on consent at all. The defendant may protest to high heaven his unwillingness to be sued and it avails him not. The liability rests on the inroad which the automobile has made on the decision of Pennoyer v. Neff, 95 U.S. 714, 24 L.Ed. 565, as it has on so many aspects of our social scene. The potentialities of damage by wayfaring motorists, in a population as mobile as ours, are such that those whom he injures must have opportunities of redress against the absentee motorist provided only that he is afforded an opportunity to defend himself."

———————

DUBIN V. CITY OF PHILADELPHIA, 34 Pa.D. & C. 61 (1938): A resident of New Jersey was made a third party defendant in an action against the City for damages to plaintiff when she fell on a broken sidewalk abutting property mortgaged to the third party defendant. Jurisdiction was based on a statute which provided that any "nonresident . . . owner, tenant, or user, of real estate" should be amenable to suit in Pennsylvania courts on actions arising out of injury involving such real estate. The court upheld the statute against attack on due process grounds. "This creates another exception to the rule of personal service in personal actions. Modern life is breaking down State barriers, and as it becomes easier to travel, or to do business, or to own property in other States, one must also expect the obligations arising out of such activities to follow more easily. It is just as important that nonresident owners of Philadelphia real estate should keep their property in such shape as not to injure our citizens as it is that nonresident owners of cars should drive about our streets with equal care. It is only a short step beyond this to assert that defendants in both classes of cases should be answerable in this forum. If it be argued that it would be unfair to make Philadelphians chase car owners to distant States in order to sue them, whereas Philadelphians who fall on streets can stay here and sue the city, the answer is that they are interested as taxpayers in preventing the expense incident upon the city's bringing suit against foreign property owners in foreign forums."

If the nonresident denied a requisite interest in the local property, would a default judgment based upon a contrary finding be entitled to enforcement in a sister state without further inquiry into the question? See Traynor, Is This Conflict Really Necessary?, 37 Tex.L.Rev. 657, 659–660 (1959).

NOTE

The Pennsylvania statute involved in the Dubin case was held to afford jurisdiction over nonresident defendants in an action brought to recover for injuries occasioned by the breaking of a chair located in the Pennsylvania house which the defendants were renting. Betcher v. Hay-Roe, 429 Pa. 371, 240 A.2d 501 (1968).

INTERNATIONAL SHOE CO. v. STATE OF WASHINGTON

Supreme Court of the United States, 1945.
326 U.S. 310, 66 S.Ct. 154, 90 L.Ed. 95, 161 A.L.R. 1057.

Appeal from the Supreme Court of Washington.

MR. CHIEF JUSTICE STONE delivered the opinion of the Court.

The questions for decision are (1) whether, within the limitations of the due process clause of the Fourteenth Amendment, appellant, a Delaware corporation, has by its activities in the State of Washington rendered itself amenable to proceedings in the courts of that state to recover unpaid contributions to the state unemployment compensation fund exacted by state statutes, Washington Unemployment Compensation Act, Washington Revised Statutes, § 9998—103a through § 9998—123a, 1941 Supp., and (2) whether the state can exact those contributions consistently with the due process clause of the Fourteenth Amendment.

The statutes in question set up a comprehensive scheme of unemployment compensation, the costs of which are defrayed by contributions required to be made by employers to a state unemployment compensation fund. The contributions are a specified percentage of the wages payable annually by each employer for his employees' services in the state. . . .

In this case notice of assessment for the years in question was personally served upon a sales solicitor employed by appellant in the State of Washington, and a copy of the notice was mailed by registered mail to appellant at its address in St. Louis, Missouri. Appellant appeared specially before the office of unemployment and moved to set aside the order and notice of assessment on the ground that the service upon appellant's salesman was not proper service upon appellant; that appellant was not a corporation of the State of Washington and was not doing business within the state; that it had no agent within the state upon whom service could be made; and that appellant is not an employer and does not furnish employment within the meaning of the statute.

The motion was heard on evidence and a stipulation of facts by the appeal tribunal which denied the motion and ruled that respondent Commissioner was entitled to recover the unpaid contributions. That action was affirmed by the Commissioner; both the Superior Court and the Supreme Court affirmed. 22 Wash.2d 146, 154 P.2d 801. Appellant in each of these courts assailed the statute as applied, as a violation of the due process clause of the Fourteenth Amendment, and as imposing a constitutionally prohibited burden on interstate commerce. The cause comes here on appeal under § 237(a) of the Judicial Code, 28 U.S.C. § 344(a), appellant assigning as error that the challenged statutes as applied infringe the due process clause of the Fourteenth Amendment and the commerce clause.

The facts as found by the appeal tribunal and accepted by the state Superior Court and Supreme Court, are not in dispute. Appellant is a Delaware corporation, having its principal place of business in St. Louis, Missouri, and is engaged in the manufacture and sale of shoes and other footwear. It maintains places of business in several states, other than Washington, at which its manufacturing is carried on and from which its merchandise is distributed interstate through several sales units or branches located outside the State of Washington.

Appellant has no office in Washington and makes no contracts either for sale or purchase of merchandise there. It maintains no stock of merchandise in that state and makes there no deliveries of goods in intrastate commerce. During the years from 1937 to 1940, now in question, appellant employed eleven to thirteen salesmen under direct supervision and control of sales managers located in St. Louis. These salesmen resided in Washington; their principal activities were confined to that state; and they were compensated by commissions based upon the amount of their sales. The commissions for each year totaled more than $31,000. Appellant supplies its salesmen with a line of samples, each consisting of one shoe of a pair, which they display to prospective purchasers. On occasion they rent permanent sample rooms, for exhibiting samples, in business buildings, or rent rooms in hotels or business buildings temporarily for that purpose. The cost of such rentals is reimbursed by appellant.

The authority of the salesmen is limited to exhibiting their samples and soliciting orders from prospective buyers, at prices and on terms fixed by appellant. The salesmen transmit the orders to appellant's office in St. Louis for acceptance or rejection, and when accepted the merchandise for filling the orders is shipped f.o.b. from points outside Washington to the purchasers within the state. All the merchandise shipped into Washington is invoiced at the place of shipment from which collections are made. No salesman has authority to enter into contracts or to make collections.

[Here the opinion of the State court is summarized and the contention of appellant that the statute imposes an unconstitutional burden on interstate commerce rejected.]

Appellant also insists that its activities within the state were not sufficient to manifest its "presence" there and that in its absence the state courts were without jurisdiction, that consequently it was a denial of due process for the state to subject appellant to suit. It refers to those cases in which it was said that the mere solicitation of orders for the purchase of goods within a state, to be accepted without the state and filled by shipment of the purchased goods interstate, does not render the corporation seller amenable to suit within the state.

. . . . And appellant further argues that since it was not present within the state, it is a denial of due process to subject it to taxation or other money exaction. It thus denies the power of the state to lay the tax or to subject appellant to a suit for its collection.

Historically the jurisdiction of courts to render judgment in personam is grounded on their de facto power over the defendant's person. Hence his presence within the territorial jurisdiction of a court was prerequisite to its rendition of a judgment personally binding him. Pennoyer v. Neff, 95 U.S. 714, 733. But now that the capias ad respondendum has given way to personal service of summons or other form of notice, due process requires only that in order to subject a defendant to a judgment in personam, if he be not present within the territory of the forum, he have certain minimum contacts with it such that the maintenance of the suit does not offend "traditional notions of fair play and substantial justice." Milliken v. Meyer, 311 U.S. 457, 463. See Holmes, J., in McDonald v. Mabee, 243 U.S. 90, 91. Compare Hoopeston Canning Co. v. Cullen, 318 U.S. 313, 316, 319. See Blackmer v. United States, 284 U.S. 421; Hess v. Pawloski, 274 U.S. 352; Young v. Masci, 289 U.S. 253.

Since the corporate personality is a fiction, although a fiction intended to be acted upon as though it were a fact, Klein v. Board of Tax Supervisors, 282 U.S. 19, 24, it is clear that unlike an individual its "presence" without, as well as within, the state of its origin can be manifested only by activities carried on in its behalf by those who are authorized to act for it. To say that the corporation is so far "present" there as to satisfy due process requirements, for purposes of taxation or the maintenance of suits against it in the courts of the state, is to beg the question to be decided. For the terms "present" or "presence" are used merely to symbolize those activities of the corporation's agent within the state which courts will deem to be sufficient to satisfy the demands of due process. L. Hand, J., in Hutchinson v. Chase & Gilbert, 45 F.2d 139, 141. Those demands may be met by such contacts of the corporation with the state of the forum as make it reasonable, in the context of our federal system of government, to require the corporation to defend the particular suit which is brought there. An "estimate of the inconveniences" which would result to the corporation from a trial away from its "home" or principal place of business is relevant in this connection. Hutchinson v. Chase & Gilbert, supra, 141.

"Presence" in the state in this sense has never been doubted when the activities of the corporation there have not only been continuous and systematic, but also give rise to the liabilities sued on, even though no consent to be sued or authorization to an agent to accept service of process has been given. . . . Conversely it has been generally recognized that the casual presence of the corporate agent or even his conduct of single or isolated items of activities in a state in the corporation's behalf are not enough to subject it to suit on causes of action unconnected with the activities there. . . . To require the corporation in such circumstances to defend the suit away from its home or other jurisdiction where it carries on more substantial activities has been thought to lay too great and unreasonable a burden on the corporation to comport with due process.

While it has been held in cases on which appellant relies that continuous activity of some sort within a state is not enough to support the demand that the corporation be amenable to suits unrelated to that activity, Old Wayne Mut. Life Ass'n v. McDonough [204 U.S. 8]; Green v. Chicago, Burlington & Quincy R. Co. [205 U.S. 530]; Simon v. Southern R. Co., 236 U.S. 115; People's Tobacco Co. v. American Tobacco Co. [246 U.S. 79]; cf. Davis v. Farmers' Co-operative Equity Co., 262 U.S. 312, 317, there have been instances in which the continuous corporate operations within a state were thought so substantial and of such a nature as to justify suit against it on causes of action arising from dealings entirely distinct from those activities. See Missouri, K. & T. R. Co. v. Reynolds, 255 U.S. 565; Tauza v. Susquehanna Coal Co., 220 N.Y. 259, 115 N.E. 915; cf. St. Louis S. W. R. Co. v. Alexander [227 U.S. 218].

Finally, although the commission of some single or occasional acts of the corporate agent in a state sufficient to impose an obligation or liability on the corporation has not been thought to confer upon the state authority to enforce it, Rosenberg Bros. & Co. v. Curtis Brown Co., 260 U.S. 516, other such acts, because of their nature and quality and the circumstances of their commission, may be deemed sufficient to render the corporation liable to suit. Cf. Kane v. New Jersey, 242 U.S. 160; Hess v. Pawloski, supra; Young v. Masci, supra. True, some of the decisions holding the corporation amenable to suit have been supported by resort to the legal fiction that it has given its consent to service and suit, consent being implied from its presence in the state through the acts of its authorized agents. . . . But more realistically it may be said that those authorized acts were of such a nature as to justify the fiction. Smolik v. Philadelphia & R. C. & I. Co., D.C., 222 F. 148, 151. Henderson, The Position of Foreign Corporations in American Constitutional Law, 94–95.

It is evident that the criteria by which we mark the boundary line between those activities which justify the subjection of a corporation to suit, and those which do not, cannot be simply mechanical or quantitative. The test is not merely, as has sometimes been suggested, whether the activity, which the corporation has seen fit to procure through its agents in another state, is a little more or a little less. St. Louis S. W. R. Co. v. Alexander [227 U.S. 228]; International Harvester Co. v. Kentucky [234 U.S. 587]. Whether due process is satisfied must depend rather upon the quality and nature of the activity in relation to the fair and orderly administration of the laws which it was the purpose of the due process clause to insure. That clause does not contemplate that a state may make binding a judgment in personam against an individual or corporate defendant with which the state has no contacts, ties, or relations. Cf. Pennoyer v. Neff, supra; Minnesota Commercial Men's Ass'n v. Benn, 261 U.S. 140.

But to the extent that a corporation exercises the privilege of conducting activities within a state, it enjoys the benefits and protection of the laws of that state. The exercise of that privilege may give rise to obligations; and, so far as those obligations arise out of or are connected with the activities within the state, a procedure which requires the corporation to respond to a suit brought to enforce them can, in most instances, hardly be said to be undue. . . .

Applying these standards, the activities carried on in behalf of appellant in the State of Washington were neither irregular nor casual. They were systematic and continuous throughout the years in question. They resulted in a large volume of interstate business, in the course of which appellant received the benefits and protection of the laws of the state, including the right to resort to the courts for the enforcement of its rights. The obligation which is here sued upon arose out of those very activities. It is evident that these operations establish sufficient contacts or ties with the state of the forum to make it reasonable and just according to our traditional conception of fair play and substantial justice to permit the state to enforce the obligations which appellant has incurred there. Hence we cannot say that the maintenance of the present suit in the State of Washington involves an unreasonable or undue procedure.

We are likewise unable to conclude that the service of the process within the state upon an agent whose activities establish appellant's "presence" there was not sufficient notice of the suit, or that the suit was so unrelated to those activities as to make the agent an inappropriate vehicle for communicating the notice. It is enough that appellant has established such contacts with the state that the particular form of substituted service adopted there gives reasonable assurance that the notice will be actual. . . . Nor can we say that the mailing of the notice of suit to appellant by registered mail at its home office was not reasonably calculated to apprise appellant of the suit. . . .

Only a word need be said of appellant's liability for the demanded contributions of the state unemployment fund. The Supreme Court of Washington, construing and applying the statute, has held that it imposes a tax on the privilege of employing appellant's salesmen within the state measured by a percentage of the wages, here the commissions payable to the salesmen. This construction we accept for purposes of determining the constitutional validity of the statute. The right to employ labor has been deemed an appropriate subject of taxation in this country and England, both before and since the adoption of the Constitution. Steward Machine Co. v. Davis, 301 U.S. 548, 579 et seq. And such a tax imposed upon the employer for unemployment benefits is within the constitutional power of the states. Carmichael v. Southern Coal & Coke Co., 301 U.S. 495, 508 et seq.

Appellant having rendered itself amenable to suit upon obligations arising out of the activities of its salesmen in Washington, the state may maintain the present suit in personam to collect the tax laid upon the exercise of the privilege of employing appellant's salesmen within the state. For Washington has made one of those activities, which taken together establish appellant's "presence" there for purposes of suit, the taxable event by which the state brings appellant within the reach of its taxing power. The state thus has constitutional power to lay the tax and to subject appellant to a suit to recover it. The activities which establish its "presence" subject it alike to taxation by the state and to suit to recover the tax. . . .

Affirmed.

MR. JUSTICE JACKSON took no part in the consideration or decision of this case.

MR. JUSTICE BLACK delivered the following opinion. . . .

I believe that the Federal Constitution leaves to each State, without any "ifs" or "buts", a power to tax and to open the doors of its courts for its citizens to sue corporations whose agents do business in those States. Believing that the Constitution gave the States that power, I think it a judicial deprivation to condition its exercise upon this Court's notion of "fair play", however appealing that term may be. Nor can I stretch the meaning of due process so far as to authorize this Court to deprive a State of the right to afford judicial protection to its citizens on the ground that it would be more "convenient" for the corporation to be sued somewhere else.

There is a strong emotional appeal in the words "fair play", "justice", and "reasonableness." But they were not chosen by those who wrote the original Constitution or the Fourteenth Amendment as a measuring rod for this Court to use in invalidating State or Federal laws passed by elected legislative representatives. . . . . Superimposing the natural justice concept on the Constitution's specific prohibitions could operate as a drastic abridgment of democratic safeguards they embody, such as freedom of speech, press and religion, and the right to counsel. This has already happened. Betts v. Brady, 316 U.S. 455. Compare Feldman v. United States, 322 U.S. 487, 494–503. For application of this natural law concept, whether under the terms "reasonableness", "justice", or "fair play", makes judges the supreme arbiters of the country's laws and practices. . . . This result, I believe, alters the form of government our Constitution provides. I cannot agree. . . .

NOTES

(1) The International Shoe case is a landmark in the law of judicial jurisdiction. What test or tests of jurisdiction does it announce? What factors

does it identify as determinative of whether a state's courts have jurisdiction in a given case?

(2) The Court here declares that the State's power to impose tax obligations on the International Shoe Company was established by the same factors that subjected the company to suit in Washington. Of course, that does not mean that the factors that suffice to subject a nonresident to judicial jurisdiction are always co-extensive with those that make it amenable to the State's law-making authority.

McGEE v. INTERNATIONAL LIFE INSURANCE CO.

Supreme Court of the United States, 1957.
355 U.S. 220, 78 S.Ct. 199, 2 L.Ed.2d 223.

Opinion of the Court by MR. JUSTICE BLACK, announced by MR. JUSTICE DOUGLAS.

Petitioner, Lulu B. McGee, recovered a judgment in a California state court against respondent, International Life Insurance Company, on a contract of insurance. Respondent was not served with process in California but by registered mail at its principal place of business in Texas. The California court based its jurisdiction on a state statute which subjects foreign corporations to suit in California on insurance contracts with residents of that State even though such corporations cannot be served with process within its borders.

Unable to collect the judgment in California petitioner went to Texas where she filed suit on the judgment in a Texas court. But the Texas courts refused to enforce her judgment holding it was void under the Fourteenth Amendment because service of process outside California could not give the courts of that State jurisdiction over respondent. 288 S.W.2d 579. . . . It is not controverted that if the California court properly exercised jurisdiction over respondent the Texas courts erred in refusing to give its judgment full faith and credit. 28 U.S.C. § 1738, 28 U.S.C.A. § 1738.

The material facts are relatively simple. In 1944, Lowell Franklin, a resident of California, purchased a life insurance policy from the Empire Mutual Insurance Company, an Arizona corporation. In 1948 the respondent agreed with Empire Mutual to assume its insurance obligations. Respondent then mailed a reinsurance certificate to Franklin in California offering to insure him in accordance with the terms of the policy he held with Empire Mutual. He accepted this offer and from that time until his death in 1950 paid premiums by mail from his California home to respondent's Texas office. Petitioner, Franklin's mother, was the beneficiary under the policy. She sent proofs of his death to the respondent but it refused to pay claiming that he had committed suicide. It appears that neither Empire Mutual nor respondent has ever had any office or agent in California. And so far as the record before us shows, respondent has never solicited or done any insurance business in California apart from the policy involved here.

Since Pennoyer v. Neff, 95 U.S. 714, this Court has held that the Due Process Clause of the Fourteenth Amendment places some limit on the power of state courts to enter binding judgments against persons not served with process within their boundaries. But just where this line of limitation falls has been the subject of prolific controversy, particularly with respect to foreign corporations. In a continuing process of evolution this Court accepted and then abandoned "consent," "doing business," and "presence" as the standard for measuring the extent of state judicial power over such corporations. See Henderson, The Position of Foreign Corporations in American Constitutional Law, c. V. More recently in International Shoe Co. v. State of Washington, 326 U.S. 310, the Court decided that "due process requires only that in order to subject a defendant to a judgment *in personam,* if he be not present within the territory of the forum, he have certain minimum contacts with it such that the maintenance of the suit does not offend 'traditional notions of fair play and substantial justice.' " Id., 326 U.S. at page 316.

Looking back over this long history of litigation a trend is clearly discernible toward expanding the permissible scope of state jurisdiction over foreign corporations and other nonresidents. In part this is attributable to the fundamental transformation of our national economy over the years. Today many commercial transactions touch two or more States and may involve parties separated by the full continent. With this increasing nationalization of commerce has come a great increase in the amount of business conducted by mail across state lines. At the same time modern transportation and communication have made it much less burdensome for a party sued to defend himself in a State where he engages in economic activity.

Turning to this case we think it apparent that the Due Process Clause did not preclude the California court from entering a judgment binding on respondent. It is sufficient for purposes of due process that the suit was based on a contract which had substantial connection with that State. Cf. Hess v. Pawloski, 274 U.S. 352; Henry L. Doherty & Co. v. Goodman, 294 U.S. 623; Pennoyer v. Neff, 95 U.S. 714, 735. The contract was delivered in California, the premiums were mailed from there and the insured was a resident of that State when he died. It cannot be denied that California has a manifest interest in providing effective means of redress for its residents when their insurers refuse to pay claims. These residents would be at a severe disadvantage if they were forced to follow the insurance company to a distant State in order to hold it legally accountable. When claims were small or moderate individual claimants frequently could not afford the cost of bringing an action in a foreign forum— thus in effect making the company judgment proof. Often the crucial witnesses—as here on the company's defense of suicide—will be found in the insured's locality. Of course there may be inconvenience to the insurer if it is held amenable to suit in California where it had this contract but certainly nothing which amounts to a denial of due process. Cf. Travelers Health Ass'n v. Commonwealth of Virginia ex rel. State Corporation Comm., 339 U.S. 643. There is no contention that respondent did not have adequate notice of the suit or sufficient time to prepare its defenses and appear.

The California statute became law in 1949, after respondent had entered into the agreement with Franklin to assume Empire Mutual's obligation to him. Respondent contends that application of the statute to this existing contract improperly impairs the obligation of the contract. We believe that contention is devoid of merit. The statute was remedial, in the purest sense of that term, and neither enlarged nor impaired respondent's substantive rights or obligations under the contract. It did nothing more than to provide petitioner with a California forum to enforce whatever substantive rights she might have against respondent. At the same time respondent was given a reasonable time to appear and defend on the merits after being notified of the suit. Under such circumstances it had no vested right not to be sued in California. . . .

Judgment reversed and cause remanded with directions.

NOTES

(1) On the facts of the McGee case, would Texas have had judicial jurisdiction to entertain an action brought by the insurance company against the insured for a declaratory determination that it was not liable under the policy?

(2) A Pennsylvania insurance company mailed to a resident of New York a policy insuring hotel property in New Hampshire and received a premium payment by mail from New York. Judicial jurisdiction in New York over the insurance company was upheld on the basis of that single transaction under a statute that made "delivery of contracts of insurance to residents" of New York an act "in this state" even though delivery was by mail. Zacharakis v. Bunker Hill Mut. Ins. Co., 281 App.Div. 487, 120 N.Y.S.2d 418 (1st Dep't 1953).

(3) Many observers regard the McGee decision as the high water mark in the Supreme Court's progressive expansion of the permissible bases of a state's personal jurisdiction over nonresident defendants. Is its holding confined to insurance claims? Would it support the result in Schutt v. Commercial Travelers Mutual Accident Ass'n, 229 F.2d 158 (2d Cir.), cert. denied, 351 U.S. 940 (1956)? Defendant, a New York insurance company, issued a life insurance policy to a Kentucky resident, who afterward moved to Tennessee, where he continued to pay premiums until his death. Defendant had no property, office or employees in Tennessee, but had other policy holders there and solicited business by mail in the state. A judgment on the policy was rendered against the insurance company in Tennessee. This judgment in turn was enforced as jurisdictionally valid in New York.

HANSON v. DENCKLA

Supreme Court of the United States, 1958.
357 U.S. 235, 78 S.Ct. 1228, 2 L.Ed.2d 1283.

[This case, involving due process and full faith and credit, is a contest between the appointees under an inter vivos power of appointment who won in the courts of Delaware, and residuary legatees who won in the courts of Florida.

In 1935, Mrs. Donner, domiciled in Pennsylvania, executed a deed of trust of corporate securities to a Delaware trust company as trustee and delivered the securities to it. She reserved for herself the income for life, a power of appointment of the corpus by deed or will, the power to amend or revoke the trust agreement in whole or in part and to change the trustee, and indirect control over the investments by the trustee.

In 1944, the settlor became domiciled in Florida and remained so until her death in 1952. In 1949, she executed an instrument of appointment with only one witness, under which she made small gifts to several individual beneficiaries and appointed $400,000 all told to two trusts set up by one of her daughters for the benefit of the issue of that daughter with another Delaware trust company as trustee. The same day she executed her will under which she gave the residue of her property to her executrix in trust for two other daughters.

The will was probated in Florida. In Florida the two daughters who were the beneficiaries under the residuary clause of the will filed a petition for a declaratory judgment on what property passed under that clause. Personal service was made upon the executrix, upon some but not all of the beneficiaries under the 1949 appointment, but upon neither of the Delaware trust companies who were named in the 1935 deed and the 1949 appointment.

Before the Florida court rendered a decree the executrix began a declaratory judgment action in Delaware to determine who was entitled to the trust assets in that state. All of the trust companies, beneficiaries, and legatees appeared and participated except one of the two daughters taking under the residuary clause of the will. The executrix was enjoined by the Florida court from further participation in the Delaware case, but the other parties continued to press their claims.

The decree of the Florida Chancellor came down first. He ruled that he lacked jurisdiction over the parties on whom there had been no personal service and over the trust corpus because it was outside the state. But as to the parties before the court he ruled the power of appointment was testamentary and the exercise void under the applicable Florida law, and the $400,000 in question passed under the residuary clause of the will.

The Florida decree was presented in the Delaware proceeding as res judicata. The Delaware Chancellor decided to the contrary, that the power of appointment and the inter vivos exercise were governed by Delaware law and were valid, and that the assets under the 1949 exercise were rightly paid over by one Delaware trust company to the other.

The executrix then made a motion in the Supreme Court of Florida, where the Florida case was pending on appeal, and asked that court to remand the case to the trial court with instructions to dismiss as she was bound by the Delaware decree. Denying the motion, the Supreme Court of Florida agreed with its state Chancellor that the inter vivos power of appointment and its exercise were governed by Florida law and were invalid. On the matter of jurisdiction, it went beyond the Chancellor, and its ruling, as stated by the Supreme Court of the United States, was:

"The court ruled that jurisdiction to construe the will carried with it 'substantive' jurisdiction 'over the persons of the absent defendants' even though the trust assets were not 'physically in the state.' Whether this meant jurisdiction over the person of the defendants or jurisdiction over the trust assets is open to doubt."

The Supreme Court of Delaware refused to give effect to the Florida decree.

The two cases, from Florida and Delaware, were carried to the Supreme Court of the United States.]

MR. CHIEF JUSTICE WARREN delivered the opinion of the Court. . . .

The issues for our decision, are, *first*, whether Florida erred in holding that it had jurisdiction over the nonresident defendants, and *second*, whether Delaware erred in refusing full faith and credit to the Florida decree. We need not determine whether Florida was bound to give full faith and credit to the decree of the Delaware Chancellor since the question was not seasonably presented to the Florida court. . . .

Appellants charge that this [Florida] judgment is offensive to the Due Process Clause of the Fourteenth Amendment because the Florida court was without jurisdiction. There is no suggestion that the court failed to employ a means of notice reasonably calculated to inform nonresident defendants of the pending proceedings or denied them an opportunity to be heard in defense of their interests. The alleged defect is the absence of those "affiliating circumstances" without which the courts of a State may not enter a judgment imposing obligations on persons (jurisdiction *in personam*) or affecting interests in property (jurisdiction *in rem* or *quasi in rem*). While the *in rem* and *in personam* classifications do not exhaust all the situations that give rise to jurisdiction, they are adequate to describe the affiliating circumstances suggested here, and accordingly serve as a useful means of approach to this case.

In rem jurisdiction. Founded on physical power, McDonald v. Mabee, 243 U.S. 90, 91, the *in rem* jurisdiction of a state court is limited by the extent of its power and by the coordinate authority of sister States. The basis of the jurisdiction is the presence of the subject property within the territorial jurisdiction of the forum State. . . . Tangible property poses no problem for the application of this rule, but the situs of intangibles is often a matter of controversy. In considering restrictions on the power to tax, this Court has concluded that "jurisdiction" over intangible property is not limited to a single State. State Tax Commission of Utah v. Aldrich, 316 U.S. 174; Curry v. McCanless, 307 U.S. 357. Whether the type of "jurisdiction" with which this opinion deals may be exercised by more than one State we need not decide. The parties seem to assume that the trust assets that form the subject matter of this action were located in Delaware and not in Florida. We can see nothing in the record contrary to that assumption, or sufficient to establish a situs in Florida.

The Florida court held that the presence of the subject property was not essential to its jurisdiction. Authority over the probate and construction of its domiciliary's will, under which the assets might pass, was thought sufficient to confer the requisite jurisdiction. But jurisdiction cannot be predicated upon the contingent role of this Florida will. Whatever the efficacy of a so-called *"in rem"* jurisdiction over assets admittedly passing under a local will, a State acquires no *in rem* jurisdiction to adjudicate the validity of *inter vivos* dispositions simply because its decision might augment an estate passing under a will probated in its courts. If such a basis of jurisdiction were sustained, probate courts would enjoy nationwide service of process to adjudicate interests in property with which neither the State nor the decedent could claim any affiliation. The settlor-decedent's Florida domicile is equally unavailing as a basis for jurisdiction over the trust assets. For the purpose of jurisdiction *in rem* the maxim that personalty has its situs at the domicile of its owner is a fiction of limited utility. Green v. Van Buskirk, 7 Wall. 139, 150, 19 L.Ed. 109. The maxim is no less suspect when the domicile is that of a decedent. In analogous cases, this Court has rejected the suggestion that the probate decree of the State where decedent was domiciled has an *in rem* effect on personalty outside the forum State that could render it conclusive on the interests of nonresidents over whom there was no personal jurisdiction. Riley v. New York Trust Co., 315 U.S. 343, 353; Baker v. Baker, Eccles & Co., 242 U.S. 394; Overby v. Gordon, 177 U.S. 214. The fact that the owner is or was domiciled within the forum State is not a sufficient affiliation with the property upon which to base jurisdiction *in rem*. Having concluded that Florida had no *in rem* jurisdiction, we proceed to consider whether a judgment purporting to rest on that basis is invalid in Florida and must therefore be reversed.

Prior to the Fourteenth Amendment an exercise of jurisdiction over persons or property outside the forum State was thought to be an absolute nullity, but the matter remained a question of state law over which this Court exercised no authority. With the adoption of that Amendment, any judgment purporting to bind the person of a defendant over whom the court had not acquired *in personam* jurisdiction was void within the State as well as without. Pennoyer v. Neff, 95 U.S. 714. Nearly a century has passed without this Court being called upon to apply that principle to an *in rem* judgment dealing with property outside the forum State. The invalidity of such a judgment within the forum State seems to have been assumed—and with good reason. Since a State is forbidden to enter a judgment attempting to bind a person over whom it has no jurisdiction, it has even less right to enter a judgment purporting to extinguish the interest of such a person in property over which the court has no jurisdiction.[23] Therefore, so far as it purports to rest upon jurisdiction over the trust assets, the judgment of the Florida court cannot be sustained. Sadler v. Industrial Trust Co., 327 Mass. 10, 97 N.E.2d 169.

In personam jurisdiction. Appellees' stronger argument is for *in personam* jurisdiction over the Delaware trustee. They urge that the circumstances of this case amount to sufficient affiliation with the State of Florida to empower its courts to exercise personal jurisdiction over this nonresident defendant. Principal reliance is placed upon McGee v. International Life Ins. Co., 355 U.S. 220. In *McGee* the Court noted the trend of expanding personal jurisdiction over nonresidents. . . . [T]he requirements for personal jurisdiction over nonresidents have evolved from the rigid rule of Pennoyer v. Neff, 95 U.S. 714 to the flexible standard of International Shoe Co. v. Washington, 326 U.S. 310. But it is a mistake to assume that this trend heralds the eventual demise of all restrictions on the personal jurisdiction of state courts. See Vanderbilt v. Vanderbilt, 354 U.S. 416, 418. Those restrictions are more than a guarantee of immunity from inconvenient or distant litigation. They are a consequence of territorial limitations on the power of the respective States. However minimal the burden of defending in a foreign tribunal, a defendant may not be called upon to do so unless he has had the "minimal contacts" with that State that are a prerequisite to its exercise of power over him. See International Shoe Co. v. Washington, 326 U.S. 310, 319.

We fail to find such contacts in the circumstances of this case. The defendant trust company has no office in Florida, and transacts

23. This holding was forecast in Pennoyer v. Neff, supra. When considering the effect of the Fourteenth Amendment, this Court declared that in actions against nonresidents substituted service was permissible only where *"property in* *the State* is brought under the control of the court, and subjected to its disposition by process adapted to that purpose . . . ." (Emphasis supplied.) 95 U.S. at page 733. [Footnote by the Court.]

no business there. None of the trust assets has ever been held or administered in Florida, and the record discloses no solicitation of business in that State either in person or by mail. . . .

The cause of action in this case is not one that arises out of an act done or transaction consummated in the forum State. In that respect, it differs from McGee v. International Life Ins. Co., 355 U.S. 220 (1957) and the cases there cited. In *McGee,* the nonresident defendant solicited a reinsurance agreement with a resident of California. The offer was accepted in that State, and the insurance premiums were mailed from there until the insured's death. Noting the interest California has in providing effective redress for its residents when nonresident insurers refuse to pay claims on insurance they have solicited in that State, the Court upheld jurisdiction because the suit "was based on a contract which had substantial connection with that State." In contrast, this action involves the validity of an agreement that was entered without any connection with the forum State. The agreement was executed in Delaware by a trust company incorporated in that State and a settlor domiciled in Pennsylvania. The first relationship Florida had to the agreement was years later when the settlor became domiciled there, and the trustee remitted the trust income to her in that State. From Florida Mrs. Donner carried on several bits of trust administration that may be compared to the mailing of premiums in *McGee.* But the record discloses no instance in which the *trustee* performed any acts in Florida that bear the same relationship to the agreement as the solicitation in McGee. Consequently, this suit cannot be said to be one to enforce an obligation that arose from a privilege the defendant exercised in Florida. Cf. International Shoe Co. v. Washington, 326 U.S. 310, 319. This case is also different from McGee in that there the State had enacted special legislation (Unauthorized Insurers Process Act) to exercise what *McGee* called its "manifest interest" in providing effective redress for citizens who had been injured by nonresidents engaged in an activity that the State treats as exceptional and subjects to special regulation. Cf. Travelers Health Assn. v. Virginia, 339 U.S. 643, 647–649; Doherty & Co. v. Goodman, 294 U.S. 623, 627; Hess v. Pawloski, 274 U.S. 352.

The execution in Florida of the powers of appointment under which the beneficiaries and appointees claim does not give Florida a substantial connection with the contract on which this suit is based. It is the validity of the trust agreement, not the appointment, that is at issue here. For the purpose of applying its rule that the validity of a trust is determined by the law of the State of its creation, Florida ruled that the appointment amounted to a "republication" of the original trust instrument in Florida. For choice-of-law purposes such a ruling may be justified, but we think it an insubstantial connection with the trust agreement for purposes of determining the question of personal jurisdiction over a nonresident defendant. The unilateral activity of those who claim some relationship with a nonresident defen-

dant cannot satisfy the requirement of contact with the forum State.
The application of that rule will vary with the quality and nature of
the defendant's activity, but it is essential in each case that there be
some act by which the defendant purposefully avails itself of the privilege of conducting activities within the forum State, thus invoking
the benefits and protections of its laws. . . . The settlor's execution in Florida of her power of appointment cannot remedy the absence of such an act in this case.

It is urged that because the settlor and most of the appointees and
beneficiaries were domiciled in Florida the courts of that State should
be able to exercise personal jurisdiction over the nonresident trustees.
This is a nonsequitur. With personal jurisdiction over the executor,
legatees, and appointees, there is nothing in federal law to prevent
Florida from adjudicating concerning the respective rights and liabilities of those parties. But Florida has not chosen to do so.

As we understand its law, the trustee is an indispensable party
over whom the court must acquire jurisdiction before it is empowered
to enter judgment in a proceeding affecting the validity of a trust. It
does not acquire that jurisdiction by being the "center of gravity" of
the controversy, or the most convenient location for litigation. The
issue is personal jurisdiction, not choice of law. It is resolved in this
case by considering the acts of the trustee. As we have indicated,
they are insufficient to sustain the jurisdiction.[27]

Because it sustained jurisdiction over the nonresident trustees, the
Florida Supreme Court found it unnecessary to determine whether
Florida law made those defendants indispensable parties in the circumstances of this case. Our conclusion that Florida was without
jurisdiction over the Delaware trustee, or over the trust corpus held
in that State, requires that we make that determination in the first
instance. As we have noted earlier, the Florida Supreme Court has
repeatedly held that a trustee is an indispensable party without whom
a Florida court has no power to adjudicate controversies affecting the
validity of a trust. For that reason the Florida judgment must be
reversed not only as to the nonresident trustees but also as to appellants, over whom the Florida court admittedly had jurisdiction.

No. 117, The Delaware Certiorari. The same reasons that compel reversal of the Florida judgment require affirmance of the Delaware one. Delaware is under no obligation to give full faith and
credit to a Florida judgment invalid in Florida because offensive to
the Due Process Clause of the Fourteenth Amendment. . . .
Since Delaware was entitled to conclude that Florida law made the
trust company an indispensable party, it was under no obligation to
give the Florida judgment any faith and credit—even against parties
over whom Florida's jurisdiction was unquestioned.

27. This conclusion makes unnecessary any consideration of appellants' contention that the contacts the trust agreement had with Florida were so slight that
it was a denial of due process of law to
determine its validity by Florida law.
See Home Insurance Co. v. Dick, 281 U.S.
397. [Footnote by the Court.]

It is suggested that this disposition is improper—that the Delaware case should be held while the Florida cause is remanded to give that court an opportunity to determine whether the trustee is an indispensable party in the circumstances of this case. . . .

The rule of primacy to the first final judgment is a necessary incident to the requirement of full faith and credit. Our only function is to determine whether judgments are consistent with the Federal Constitution. In determining the correctness of Delaware's judgment we look to what Delaware was entitled to conclude from the Florida authorities at the time the Delaware court's judgment was entered. To withhold affirmance of a correct Delaware judgment until Florida has had time to rule on another question would be participating in the litigation instead of adjudicating its outcome.

The judgment of the Delaware Supreme Court is affirmed and the judgment of the Florida Supreme Court is reversed and the cause is remanded for proceedings not inconsistent with this opinion.

Mr. Justice Black, whom Mr. Justice Burton and Mr. Justice Brennan join, dissenting.

I believe the courts of Florida had power to adjudicate the effectiveness of the appointment made in Florida by Mrs. Donner with respect to all those who were notified of the proceedings and given an opportunity to be heard without violating the Due Process Clause of the Fourteenth Amendment. If this is correct, it follows that the Delaware courts erred in refusing to give the prior Florida judgment full faith and credit. . . .

. . . True the question whether the law of a State can be applied to a transaction is different from the question whether the courts of that State have jurisdiction to enter a judgment, but the two are often closely related and to a substantial degree depend upon similar considerations. It seems to me that where a transaction has as much relationship to a State as Mrs. Donner's appointment had to Florida its courts ought to have power to adjudicate controversies arising out of that transaction, unless litigation there would impose such a heavy and disproportionate burden on a nonresident defendant that it would offend what this Court has referred to as "traditional notions of fair play and substantial justice." . . . So far as the nonresident defendants here are concerned I can see nothing which approaches that degree of unfairness. . . .

Mr. Justice Douglas, dissenting.

. . . Distribution of the assets of the estate could not be made without determining the validity of the power of appointment. The power of appointment, being integrated with the will, was as much subject to construction and interpretation by the Florida court as the will itself. Of course one not a party or privy to the Florida proceedings is not bound by it and can separately litigate the right to assets in other States. . . . But we have no such situation here. The trustee of the trust was in privity with the deceased. She was the

settlor; and under the trust, the trustee was to do her bidding.
. . . So far as the present controversy is concerned the trustee
was purely and simply a stakeholder or an agent holding assets of
the settlor to dispose of as she designated. It had a community of
interest with the deceased. I see no reason therefore why Florida
could not say that the deceased and her executrix may stand in judgment for the trustee so far as the disposition of the property under
the power of appointment and the will is concerned. The question in
cases of this kind is whether the procedure is fair and just, considering the interests of the parties. . . . We must remember this is
not a suit to impose liability on the Delaware trustee or on any other
absent person. It is merely a suit to determine interests in those intangibles. Cf. Mullane v. Central Hanover Trust Co., supra, 339 U.S.
at page 313. Under closely analogous facts the California Supreme
Court held in Atkinson v. Superior Court, 49 Cal.2d 338, 316 P.2d 960,
that California had jurisdiction over an absent trustee. I would hold
the same here.

———

Chief Justice Warren said in Hanson v. Denckla that the restrictions on a state's asserting personal jurisdiction "are more than a
guarantee of immunity from inconvenient or distant litigation."
"They are," he said, "a consequence of territorial limitations on the
power of the respective states." The dual requirements of avoiding
inconvenience or unfairness to the defendant on the one hand and
avoiding exercises of power that overrun the state's territorial limits
on the other are easy to state but difficult to apply. The difficulties
are clearly illustrated in the everyday case in which a nonresident
defendant has acted entirely outside the forum but in some manner
has allegedly caused injury to the plaintiff within the forum. Often
the injury results from a product the defendant designed or made
outside the forum. At other times, the injury was caused by what
the defendant said in another state, either over the airwaves, in print,
on the telephone, or in person. Applying the fairness and territoriality tests and also taking account of the plaintiff's and the forum's
needs give rise to countless problems. See, *e.g.*, Keeton v. Hustler
Magazine, Inc., ___ U.S. ___ (1984), p. 105, infra.

In Hanson v. Denckla Chief Justice Warren also observed that,
although the facts may have warranted Florida's applying its law to
the transaction, the nonresident trustee's contact was too insubstantial to warrant exercising personal jurisdiction over it. Order XI,
Rule 1(e) and (ee) of the Rules of the Supreme Court of Judicature of
England provides jurisdiction over a nonresident for breach of a contract which is "to be governed by English law." Would a judgment
in which jurisdiction was based solely on that provision be valid in the
United States?

For nearly two decades after Hanson v. Denckla the Supreme
Court of the United States had little to say about the constitutional

standards governing state court jurisdiction over nonresidents. Then, starting in 1977 with Shaffer v. Heitner, page 148, infra, the Court handed down several important decisions. The two decisions most directly pertinent at this point are set out below.

———

KULKO v. SUPERIOR COURT OF CALIFORNIA, 436 U.S. 84 (1978): The Kulkos resided in New York with their minor son and daughter until they separated in 1972. The mother moved to California and remained after obtaining a Haitian divorce that incorporated a New York separation agreement providing for the defendant's support of the children while they were in their mother's care during school vacations. The agreement called for the children to remain with their father during the school year. However, in 1973 the daughter asked to live with her mother and the father acceded, buying her a one-way plane ticket to California from New York. The mother then started an action in California against the father, seeking full custody of the two children, increased support payments and other relief. The California courts upheld personal jurisdiction. The critical factor for the California Supreme Court was the "purposeful act" of the defendant in consenting that the daughter live with her mother and sending her to California for that purpose. The Supreme Court reversed, holding California's assertion of jurisdiction unreasonable ". . . We cannot accept the proposition that appellant's acquiescence in Ilsa's desire to live with her mother conferred jurisdiction over appellant in the California courts in this action. A father who agrees, in the interests of family harmony and his children's preferences, to allow them to spend more time in California than was required under a separation agreement can hardly be said to have 'purposefully availed himself' of the 'benefits and protections' of California's laws. . . . "

———

WORLD–WIDE VOLKSWAGEN CORP. v. WOODSON, DISTRICT JUDGE OF CREEK COUNTY, OKLAHOMA

Supreme Court of the United States, 1980.
444 U.S. 286, 100 S.Ct. 559, 62 L.Ed.2d 490.

MR. JUSTICE WHITE delivered the opinion of the Court.

The issue before us is whether, consistently with the Due Process Clause of the Fourteenth Amendment, an Oklahoma court may exercise *in personam* jurisdiction over a nonresident automobile retailer and its wholesale distributor in a products liability action, when the defendants' only connection with Oklahoma is the fact that an automobile sold in New York to New York residents became involved in an accident in Oklahoma.

I

Respondents Harry and Kay Robinson purchased a new Audi automobile from petitioner Seaway Volkswagen, Inc. (Seaway) in Massena, N.Y., in 1976. The following year the Robinson family, who resided in New York, left that State for a new home in Arizona. As they passed through the State of Oklahoma, another car struck their Audi in the rear, causing a fire which severely burned Kay Robinson and her two children.[1]

The Robinsons subsequently brought a products liability action in the District Court for Creek County, Okla., claiming that their injuries resulted from defective design and placement of the Audi's gas tank and fuel system. They joined as defendants the automobile's manufacturer, Audi NSU Auto Union Aktiengesellschaft (Audi); its importer, Volkswagen of America, Inc. (Volkswagen); its regional distributor, petitioner World-Wide Volkswagen Corporation (World-Wide); and its retail dealer, petitioner Seaway. Seaway and World-Wide entered special appearances,[3] claiming that Oklahoma's exercise of jurisdiction over them would offend the limitations on the State's jurisdiction imposed by the Due Process Clause of the Fourteenth Amendment.

The facts presented to the District Court showed that World-Wide is incorporated and has its business office in New York. It distributes vehicles, parts and accessories, under contract with Volkswagen, to retail dealers in New York, New Jersey, and Connecticut. Seaway, one of these retail dealers, is incorporated and has its place of business in New York. Insofar as the record reveals, Seaway and World-Wide are fully independent corporations whose relations with each other and with Volkswagen and Audi are contractual only. Respondents adduced no evidence that either World-Wide or Seaway does any business in Oklahoma, ships or sells any products to or in that State, has an agent to receive process there, or purchases advertisements in any media calculated to reach Oklahoma. In fact, as respondents' counsel conceded at oral argument, . . . there was no showing that any automobile sold by World-Wide or Seaway has ever entered Oklahoma with the single exception of the vehicle involved in the present case.

Despite the apparent paucity of contacts between petitioners and Oklahoma, the District Court rejected their constitutional claim and reaffirmed that ruling in denying petitioners' motion for reconsideration. Petitioners then sought a writ of prohibition in the Supreme Court of Oklahoma to restrain the District Judge, respondent Charles S. Woodson, from exercising *in personam* jurisdiction over them.

1. The driver of the other automobile does not figure in the present litigation.

3. Volkswagen also entered a special appearance in the District Court, but unlike World-Wide and Seaway did not seek review in the Supreme Court of Oklahoma and is not a petitioner here. Both Volkswagen and Audi remain as defendants in the litigation pending before the District Court in Oklahoma.

They renewed their contention that because they had no "minimal contacts" . . . with the State of Oklahoma, the actions of the District Judge were in violation of their rights under the Due Process Clause.

The Supreme Court of Oklahoma denied the writ, 585 P.2d 351 (1978), holding that personal jurisdiction over petitioners was authorized by Oklahoma's "Long-Arm" Statute, Okla.Stat., Tit. 12, § 1701.3(a)(4) (1961).[7] Although the Court noted that the proper approach was to test jurisdiction against both statutory and constitutional standards, its analysis did not distinguish these questions, probably because § 1701.03(a)(4) has been interpreted as conferring jurisdiction to the limits permitted by the United States Constitution. The Court's rationale was contained in the following paragraph, 585 P.2d, at 354:

> "In the case before us, the product being sold and distributed by the petitioners is by its very design and purpose so mobile that petitioners can foresee its possible use in Oklahoma. This is especially true of the distributor, who has the exclusive right to distribute such automobile [*sic*] in New York, New Jersey and Connecticut. The evidence presented below demonstrated that goods sold and distributed by the petitioners were used in the State of Oklahoma, and under the facts we believe it reasonable to infer, given the retail value of the automobile, that the petitioners derive substantial income from automobiles which, from time to time are used in the State of Oklahoma. This being the case, we hold that under the facts presented, the trial court was justified in concluding that the petitioners derive substantial revenue from goods used or consumed in this State."

. . .

II

. . .

As has long been settled, and as we reaffirm today, a state court may exercise personal jurisdiction over a nonresident defendant only so long as there exist "minimum contacts" between the defendant and the forum State. International Shoe Co. v. Washington [p. 66, supra]. The concept of minimum contacts, in turn, can be seen to perform two related, but distinguishable, functions. It protects the defendant against the burdens of litigating in a distant or inconve-

---

7. This subsection provides:

"A court may exercise personal jurisdiction over a person, who acts directly or by an agent, as to a cause of action or claim for relief arising from the person's . . . causing tortious injury in this state by an act or omission outside this state if he regularly does or solicits business or engages in any other persistent course of conduct, or derived substantial revenue from goods used or consumed or services rendered, in this state. . . . " The State Supreme Court rejected jurisdiction based on § 1701.03(a)(3), which authorizes jurisdiction over any person "causing tortious injury in this state by an act or omission in this state." Something in addition to the infliction of tortious injury was required.

nient forum. And it acts to ensure that the States, through their courts, do not reach out beyond the limits imposed on them by their status as coequal sovereigns in a federal system.

The protection against inconvenient litigation is typically described in terms of "reasonableness" or "fairness." . . . Implicit in this emphasis on reasonableness is the understanding that the burden on the defendant, while always a primary concern, will in an appropriate case be considered in light of other relevant factors, including the forum State's interest in adjudicating the dispute, see McGee v. International Life Ins. Co. [p. 72, supra]; the plaintiff's interest in obtaining convenient and effective relief, see Kulko v. Superior Court [p. 83, supra] at least when that interest is not adequately protected by the plaintiff's power to choose the forum, cf. Shaffer v. Heitner [p. 148, infra]; the interstate judicial system's interest in obtaining the most efficient resolution of controversies; and the shared interest of the several States in furthering fundamental substantive social policies, see Kulko v. Superior Court, supra . . . . .

The limits imposed on state jurisdiction by the Due Process Clause, in its role as a guarantor against inconvenient litigation, have been substantially relaxed over the years. . . .

Nevertheless, we have never accepted the proposition that state lines are irrelevant for jurisdictional purposes, nor could we and remain faithful to the principles of interstate federalism embodied in the Constitution. The economic interdependence of the States was foreseen and desired by the Framers. In the Commerce Clause, they provided that the Nation was to be a common market, a "free trade unit" in which the States are debarred from acting as separable economic entities. H. P. Hood & Sons, Inc. v. Du Mond, 336 U.S. 525, 538 (1949). But the Framers also intended that the States retain many essential attributes of sovereignty, including, in particular, the sovereign power to try causes in their courts. The sovereignty of each State, in turn, implied a limitation on the sovereignty of all of its sister States—a limitation express or implicit in both the original scheme of the Constitution and the Fourteenth Amendment.

Hence, even while abandoning the shibboleth that "[t]he authority of every tribunal is necessarily restricted by the territorial limits of the State in which it is established," Pennoyer v. Neff [p. 44, supra], we emphasized that the reasonableness of asserting jurisdiction over the defendant must be assessed "in the context of our federal system of government," International Shoe Co. v. Washington, supra, and stressed that the Due Process Clause ensures, not only fairness, but also the "orderly administration of the laws," . . . . .

Even if the defendant would suffer minimal or no inconvenience from being forced to litigate before the tribunals of another State; even if the forum State has a strong interest in applying its law to the controversy; even if the forum State is the most convenient location for litigation, the Due Process Clause, acting as an instrument of interstate federalism, may sometimes act to divest the State of its power to render a valid judgment. Hanson v. Denckla [p. 75, supra].

III

Applying these principles to the case at hand, we find in the record before us a total absence of those affiliating circumstances that are a necessary predicate to any exercise of state-court jurisdiction. Petitioners carry on no activity whatsoever in Oklahoma. They close no sales and perform no services there. They avail themselves of none of the privileges and benefits of Oklahoma law. They solicit no business there either through salespersons or through advertising reasonably calculated to reach the State. Nor does the record show that they regularly sell cars at wholesale or retail to Oklahoma customers or residents or that they indirectly, through others, serve or seek to serve the Oklahoma market. In short, respondents seek to base jurisdiction on one, isolated occurrence and whatever inferences can be drawn therefrom: the fortuitous circumstance that a single Audi automobile, sold in New York to New York residents, happened to suffer an accident while passing through Oklahoma.

It is argued, however, that because an automobile is mobile by its very design and purpose it was "foreseeable" that the Robinsons' Audi would cause injury in Oklahoma. Yet "foreseeability" alone has never been a sufficient benchmark for personal jurisdiction under the Due Process Clause. In Hanson v. Denckla, supra, it was no doubt foreseeable that the settlor of a Delaware trust would subsequently move to Florida and seek to exercise a power of appointment there; yet we held that Florida courts could not constitutionally exercise jurisdiction over a Delaware trustee that had no other contacts with the forum State. In Kulko v. Superior Court, supra, it was surely "foreseeable" that a divorced wife would move to California from New York, the domicile of the marriage, and that a minor daughter would live with the mother. Yet we held that California could not exercise jurisdiction in a child-support action over the former husband who had remained in New York.

If foreseeability were the criterion, a local California tire retailer could be forced to defend in Pennsylvania when a blowout occurs there, see Erlanger Mills, Inc. v. Cohoes Fibre Mills, Inc., 239 F.2d 502, 507 (C.A.4 1956); a Wisconsin seller of a defective automobile jack could be haled before a distant court for damage caused in New Jersey, Reilly v. Phil Tolkan Pontiac, Inc., 372 F.Supp. 1205 (N.J. 1974); or a Florida soft drink concessionaire could be summoned to Alaska to account for injuries happening there, see Upgren v. Executive Aviation Services, Inc., 304 F.Supp. 165, 170–171 (Minn.1969). Every seller of chattels would in effect appoint the chattel his agent for service of process. His amenability to suit would travel with the chattel. We recently abandoned the outworn rule of Harris v. Balk [p. 141, infra], that the interest of a creditor in a debt could be extinguished or otherwise affected by any State having transitory jurisdiction over the debtor. Shaffer v. Heitner [p. 148, infra]. Having interred the mechanical rule that a creditor's amenability to a *quasi in rem* action travels with his debtor, we are unwilling to endorse an analogous principle in the present case.[11]

This is not to say, of course, that foreseeability is wholly irrelevant. But the foreseeability that is critical to due process analysis is not the mere likelihood that a product will find its way into the forum State. Rather, it is that the defendant's conduct and connection with the forum State are such that he should reasonably anticipate being haled into court there. . . . The Due Process Clause, by ensuring the "orderly administration of the laws," International Shoe Co. v. Washington, supra, gives a degree of predictability to the legal system that allows potential defendants to structure their primary conduct with some minimum assurance as to where that conduct will and will not render them liable to suit.

When a corporation "purposefully avails itself of the privilege of conducting activities within the forum State," Hanson v. Denckla, supra, it has clear notice that it is subject to suit there, and can act to alleviate the risk of burdensome litigation by procuring insurance, passing the expected costs on to customers, or, if the risks are too great, severing its connection with the State. Hence if the sale of a product of a manufacturer or distributor such as Audi or Volkswagen is not simply an isolated occurrence, but arises from the efforts of the manufacturer or distributor to serve, directly or indirectly, the market for its product in other States, it is not unreasonable to subject it to suit in one of those States if its allegedly defective merchandise has there been the source of injury to its owner or to others. The forum State does not exceed its powers under the Due Process Clause if it asserts personal jurisdiction over a corporation that delivers its products into the stream of commerce with the expectation that they will be purchased by consumers in the forum State. Compare Gray v. American Radiator & Standard Sanitary Corp. [p. 101, note (1), infra].

But there is no such or similar basis for Oklahoma jurisdiction over World-Wide or Seaway in this case. Seaway's sales are made in Massena, N.Y. World-Wide's market, although substantially larger, is limited to dealers in New York, New Jersey, and Connecticut.

---

11. Respondents' counsel, at oral argument, see Tr. of Oral Arg. 19–22, 29, sought to limit the reach of the foreseeability standard by suggesting that there is something unique about automobiles. It is true that automobiles are uniquely mobile, see Tyson v. Whitaker & Son, Inc., 407 A.2d 1, 6, and n. 11 (Me.1979) (McKusick, C.J.), that they did play a crucial role in the expansion of personal jurisdiction through the fiction of implied consent, e.g., Hess v. Pawloski, 274 U.S. 352 (1927), and that some of the cases have treated the automobile as a "dangerous instrumentality." But today, under the regime of *International Shoe*, we see no difference for jurisdictional purposes between an automobile and any other chattel. The "dangerous instrumentality" concept apparently was never used to support personal jurisdiction; and to the extent it has relevance today it bears not on jurisdiction but on the possible desirability of imposing substantive principles of tort law such as strict liability.

There is no evidence of record that any automobiles distributed by World-Wide are sold to retail customers outside this tri-State area. It is foreseeable that the purchasers of automobiles sold by World-Wide and Seaway may take them to Oklahoma. But the mere "unilateral activity of those who claim some relationship with a nonresident defendant cannot satisfy the requirement of contact with the forum State." Hanson v. Denckla, supra.

In a variant on the previous argument, it is contended that jurisdiction can be supported by the fact that petitioners earn substantial revenue from goods used in Oklahoma. The Oklahoma Supreme Court so found, 585 P.2d, at 354–355, drawing the inference that because one automobile sold by petitioners had been used in Oklahoma, others might have been used there also. While this inference seems less than compelling on the facts of the instant case, we need not question the Court's factual findings in order to reject its reasoning.

This argument seems to make the point that the purchase of automobiles in New York, from which the petitioners earn substantial revenue, would not occur *but for* the fact that the automobiles are capable of use in distant States like Oklahoma. Respondents observe that the very purpose of an automobile is to travel, and that travel of automobiles sold by petitioners is facilitated by an extensive chain of Volkswagen service centers throughout the Country, including some in Oklahoma.[12] However, financial benefits accruing to the defendant from a collateral relation to the forum State will not support jurisdiction if they do not stem from a constitutionally cognizable contact with that State. . . . In our view, whatever marginal revenues petitioners may receive by virtue of the fact that their products are capable of use in Oklahoma is far too attenuated a contact to justify that State's exercise of *in personam* jurisdiction over them.

. . .

Reversed.

MR. JUSTICE BRENNAN, dissenting.[*]

. . .

. . . the interest of [Oklahoma] and its connection to the litigation is strong. The automobile accident underlying the litigation occurred in Oklahoma. The plaintiffs were hospitalized in Oklahoma when they brought suit. Essential witnesses and evidence were in Oklahoma. . . . The State has a legitimate interest in enforcing its laws designed to keep its highway system safe, and the trial can proceed at least as efficiently in Oklahoma as anywhere else.

The petitioners are not unconnected with the forum. Although both sell automobiles within limited sales territories, each sold the automobile which in fact was driven to Oklahoma where it was involved

---

12. As we have noted, petitioners earn no direct revenues from these service centers. . . .

* Mr. Justice Brennan combined his dissents in World-Wide Volkswagen and Rush v. Savchuk (p. 161, infra) into a single opinion. That part of his dissent dealing with the former case is set forth here. [Footnote by the Editors.]

in an accident.[8] It may be true, as the Court suggests, that each
sincerely intended to limit its commercial impact to the limited territory, and that each intended to accept the benefits and protection of the
laws only of those States within the territory. But obviously these
were unrealistic hopes that cannot be treated as an automatic constitutional shield.[9]

An automobile simply is not a stationary item or one designed to
be used in one place. An automobile is *intended* to be moved around.
Someone in the business of selling large numbers of automobiles can
hardly plead ignorance of their mobility or pretend that the automobiles stay put after they are sold. It is not merely that a dealer in
automobiles foresees that they will move. . . . The dealer actually intends that the purchasers will use the automobiles to travel to
distant States where the dealer does not directly "do business." The
sale of an automobile does *purposefully* inject the vehicle into the
stream of interstate commerce so that it can travel to distant States.
. . . .

The Court accepts that a State may exercise jurisdiction over a
distributor which "serves" that State "indirectly" by "deliver[ing] its
products into the stream of commerce with the expectation that they
will [be] purchased by consumers in other States." . . . . It is difficult to see why the Constitution should distinguish between a case
involving goods which reach a distant State through a chain of distribution and a case involving goods which reach the same State because a consumer, using them as the dealer knew the customer
would, took them there. In each case the seller purposefully injects
the goods into the stream of commerce and those goods predictably
are used in the forum State.

Furthermore, an automobile seller derives substantial benefits
from States other than its own. A large part of the value of automobiles is the extensive, nationwide network of highways. Significant
portions of that network have been constructed by and are maintained by the individual States, including Oklahoma. The States,
through their highway programs, contribute in a very direct and important way to the value of petitioners' businesses. Additionally, a
network of other related dealerships with their service departments
operate throughout the country under the protection of the laws of
the various States, including Oklahoma, and enhance the value of petitioners' businesses by facilitating their customers' traveling. . . . .

8. On the basis of this fact the state
court inferred that the petitioners derived substantial revenue from goods
used in Oklahoma. The inference is not
without support. Certainly, were use of
goods accepted as a relevant contact, a
plaintiff would not need to have an exact
count of the number of petitioners' cars
that are used in Oklahoma.

9. Moreover, imposing liability in this
case would not so undermine certainty as
to destroy an automobile dealer's ability
to do business. According jurisdiction
does not expand liability except in the
marginal case where a plaintiff cannot
afford to bring an action except in the
plaintiff's own State. In addition, these
petitioners are represented by insurance
companies. They not only could, but did,
purchase insurance to protect them
should they stand trial and lose the case.
The costs of the insurance no doubt are
passed onto customers.

It may be that affirmance of the judgments in these cases would approach the outer limits of *International Shoe*'s jurisdictional principle. But that principle, with its almost exclusive focus on the rights of defendants, may be outdated. . . .

In answering the question whether or not it is fair and reasonable to allow a particular forum to hold a trial binding on a particular defendant, the interests of the forum State and other parties loom large in today's world and surely are entitled to as much weight as are the interests of the defendant. . . . Certainly, I cannot see how a defendant's right to due process is violated if the defendant suffers no inconvenience.

. . . Assuming that a State gives a nonresident defendant adequate notice and opportunity to defend, I do not think the Due Process Clause is offended merely because the defendant has to board a plane to get to the site of the trial. . . .

MR. JUSTICE MARSHALL, with whom MR. JUSTICE BLACKMUN joins, dissenting. . . .

To be sure, petitioners could not know in advance that this particular automobile would be driven to Oklahoma. They must have anticipated, however, that a substantial portion of the cars they sold would travel out of New York. Seaway, a local dealer in the second most populous State, and World-Wide, one of only seven regional Audi distributors in the entire country, . . . would scarcely have been surprised to learn that a car sold by them had been driven in Oklahoma on Interstate 44, a heavily traveled transcontinental highway. In the case of the distributor, in particular, the probability that some of the cars it sells will be driven in every one of the contiguous States must amount to a virtual certainty. This knowledge should alert a reasonable businessman to the likelihood that a defect in the product might manifest itself in the forum State—not because of some unpredictable, aberrant, unilateral action by a single buyer, but in the normal course of the operation of the vehicles for their intended purpose.

. . .

The majority apparently acknowledges that if a product is purchased in the forum State by a consumer, that State may assert jurisdiction over everyone in the chain of distribution. . . . With this I agree. But I cannot agree that jurisdiction is necessarily lacking if the product enters the State not through the channels of distribution but in the course of its intended use by the consumer. We have recognized the role played by the automobile in the expansion of our notions of personal jurisdiction. . . . Unlike most other chattels, which may find their way into States far from where they were purchased because their owner takes them there, the intended use of the automobile is precisely as a means of traveling from one place to another. In such a case, it is highly artificial to restrict the concept of the "stream of commerce" to the chain of distribution from the manufacturer to the ultimate consumer. . . .

[T]he "quality and nature" of commercial activity is different, for purposes of the *International Shoe* test, from actions from which a defendant obtains no economic advantage. Commercial activity is more likely to cause effects in a larger sphere, and the actor derives an economic benefit from the activity that makes it fair to require him to answer for his conduct where its effects are felt. . . .

MR. JUSTICE BLACKMUN, also dissented, emphasizing that here the instrumentality of injury was an automobile, an intentionally far-ranging product. He saw nothing unfair to hold the dealer and distributors subject to Oklahoma's jurisdiction. He saw no material distinction between foreseeable use of a product in another state and foreseeable sale of it there.

. . .

NOTES

(1) For a suggestion that concerns of federalism should play no role in a determination of whether a state has judicial jurisdiction under due process, see Redish, Due Process, Federalism, and Personal Jurisdiction: A Theoretical Evaluation, 75 Nw.U.L.Rev. 1112 (1981).

(2) See P. Kozyris, Justified Party Expectations in Choice-of-Law and Jurisdiction. Constitutional Significance or Bootstrapping? 19 San Diego L.Rev. 313 (1982).

———

(1) Realistically, can a defendant who has foreseen the likelihood of causing injury in the forum state be found not to have anticipated the likelihood of being haled into the forum state's courts? Would it be a "reasonable expectation" on the defendant's part to anticipate *not* being sued in the state where the product caused injury? Do we answer that question by inquiring whether the defendant's actual expectation was reasonable or by deciding what expectation the defendant would have been reasonable to entertain? If the former, should evidence be taken regarding what the defendant in fact expected?

(2) Should it make any difference in product liability cases of the Gray v. American Standard Radiator, (p. 101, note (1), infra, or World-Wide Volkswagen types that the nonresident defendant put the goods into interstate circulation through the consumer rather than through a distributor? In World-Wide Volkswagen Justice Brennan opined that the possible movement of an unsafe automobile to the forum was foreseeable in either case. Should it make a difference that in the distributor case it is definitely the defendant's desire and to its advantage that the goods reach the forum and be sold there; but that no similar direct advantage accrues to the defendant when a consumer takes the product to F?

(3) A New Jersey resident sued the American distributor of a German-made printing press for work injuries he sustained as a result of alleged defects in design and manufacture. The distributor invoked

long-arm jurisdiction in a third-party action against Heidelberger, the manufacturer. Heidelberger carried on no activities in the United States. It sold the printing press in Germany to the distributor, parting with title there and expecting the press would be resold in the United States but not knowing where. The New Jersey court upheld jurisdiction: "If [Heidelberger] wishes to benefit from American markets . . . it is not unreasonable or fundamentally unfair for them to be required to submit to the jurisdiction of the state whose resident has allegedly been injured by its product." Certisimo v. Heidelberg Co., 122 N.J.Super. 1, 298 A.2d 298, 305 (1972). Would World-Wide Volkswagen require a different result? Compare DeJames v. Magnificence Carriers, Inc., 654 F.2d 280 (3d Cir. 1981), p. 100, infra.

(4) Defendant, a nonresident corporation that manufactured a leveling machine in Virginia and sold it in that state to the California plaintiff's employer was held subject to California's in personam jurisdiction. The suit was for an alleged defect in the design or manufacture of the machine resulting in plaintiff's loss of five fingers while operating it. The court distinguished *World-Wide Volkswagen* as a case wherein "unilateral activity" of the product's purchaser was the only contact with the forum state. Here, however, "the manufacturer [Secrest] engaged in a number of acts in connection with the sale of the leveling machine to F & S [plaintiff's employer]. Some of these acts, such as the initial negotiations, took place outside of California. Others, such as sending an employee to assist F & S with installation of the machine, involved the physical presence of a Secrest employee in California. Still others involved communication by mail and phone between Secrest's Virginia office and F & S's California office, and the sending of drawings on spare parts for the machine to F & S." Having found requisite minimum contacts, the court went on to decide that it would be "fair and reasonable" to exercise jurisdiction, taking account of "convenience to the plaintiff, inconvenience to the defendant and the interest of California in providing a local forum. . . ." (Id., at 404). The court rejected Secrest's contention that matters relating to the convenience of California as a forum would be considered only after jurisdiction has been established, relying on Cornelison v. Chaney, p. 115, infra. Secrest Machine Corp. v. Superior Court of Los Angeles County, 33 Cal.3d 644, 190 Cal.Rptr. 175, 660 P.2d 399, 403 (1983).

INSURANCE CORP. v. COMPAGNIE DES BAUXITES DE GUINEE, 456 U.S. 694 (1982).

In a diversity action against a group of foreign insurance companies for indemnity to cover losses resulting from interruptions of plaintiff's business, defendants raised various defenses including lack of personal jurisdiction. Plaintiff initiated discovery to establish minimum contacts. Defendants failed to comply with a series of court orders for production of requested information. After due warning, the district court invoked Rule 37(b)(2) as a basis for deeming the jurisdictional facts established by reason of petitioners' failure to make the required disclosures.

The Supreme Court upheld the district court's sanction—namely, presuming that a jurisdictional basis was present on account of defendant's failure to comply with the discovery orders. Justice White for the Court reasoned that since personal jurisdiction is a waivable defense, it can be established by regarding the defendants' failure to obey procedural requirements as tantamount to waiver. However, he was troubled by the fact that the waiver theory suggests that a defendant may confer personal jurisdiction on the court in circumstances where the absence of contacts would raise a territorial-sovereignty limitation on the reach of the court's jurisdiction (456 U.S. at p. 702, n. 10):

> "It is true that we have stated that the requirement of personal jurisdiction, as applied to state courts, reflects an element of federalism and the character of state sovereignty vis-a-vis other States. . . .
>
> "The restriction on state sovereign power described in *World-Wide Volkswagen Corp.*, however, must be seen as ultimately a function of the individual liberty interest preserved by the Due Process Clause. That Clause is the only source of the personal jurisdiction requirement and the Clause itself makes no mention of federalism concerns. Furthermore, if the federalism concept operated as an independent restriction on the sovereign power of the court, it would not be possible to waive the personal jurisdiction requirement: Individual actions cannot change the powers of sovereignty, although the individual can subject himself to powers from which he may otherwise be protected."

Justice Powell saw the Court's footnote as affecting "a potentially substantial change of law. For the first time it defines personal jurisdiction solely by reference to abstract notions of fair play" (456 U.S. at p. 714). The change, according to Justice Powell, was that: "Before today . . . our cases had linked minimum contacts and fair play as *jointly* defining the 'sovereign' limits on state assertions of personal jurisdiction over unconsenting defendants. See World-Wide Volkswagen Corp. v. Woodson, supra, at 292–293; see Hanson v. Denckla, supra, at 251. The Court appears to abandon the rationale of these cases in a footnote." Footnote 10 and its doubts regarding the extent to which state sovereignty and federalism are significant in restricting judicial jurisdiction are discussed again in Keeton v. Hustler Magazine, Inc., p. 105, infra.

The *DeJames* case, infra, considers the jurisdiction problem in the international setting, where there is no federalism problem in the sense of pitting one State's interests against another.

DeJAMES v. MAGNIFICENCE CARRIERS, INC.

United States Court of Appeals, Third Circuit, 1981.
654 F.2d 280.

SEITZ, CHIEF JUDGE

I.

DeJames, a New Jersey longshoreman, was injured while working on the M.V. Magnificence Venture (the vessel) when it was moored to a pier in Camden, New Jersey. DeJames filed a complaint in the United States District Court for the District of New Jersey, alleging negligence and strict liability in tort against, *inter alia*, the charterers of the vessel and Hitachi, a Japanese corporation with its principal place of business in Japan. Hitachi had converted the vessel in Japan from a bulk carrier to an automobile carrier. DeJames alleged that Hitachi's conversion work was defective.

After the complaint was filed, process was served on Hitachi at its place of business in Japan by the Japanese Minister of Foreign Affairs apparently in accordance with the requirements of an international treaty. See Convention on the Service Abroad of Judicial and Extrajudicial Documents in Civil or Commercial Matters, 20 U.S.T. 361–367 (1969). Hitachi filed a motion to dismiss for lack of personal jurisdiction pursuant to rule 12(b)(2) of the Federal Rules of Civil Procedure. In support of this motion, Hitachi submitted an affidavit from Kiyoshi Ohno, the manager of its ship repair business department in Tokyo, Japan. According to this affidavit, Hitachi completed all work on the vessel at its Japanese shipyard and had no further contact with the vessel after it left Osaka, Japan. The affidavit also states that Hitachi does not maintain an office, have an agent of any type, or transact any business in New Jersey.

After completion of discovery, briefing, and oral argument on the question of jurisdiction, the district court dismissed the complaint against Hitachi. . . .

On appeal, DeJames makes two arguments for reversing the district court. First, he argues that Hitachi's contacts with the state of New Jersey are sufficient to support personal jurisdiction. Alternatively, he argues for the first time on appeal that service was made by wholly federal means, and thus that the district court erred in not considering Hitachi's national contacts.

II.

Because this suit arises under the district court's admiralty jurisdiction, the due process clause of the fifth amendment determines whether the district court has personal jurisdiction over Hitachi. See Fraley v. Chesapeake & Ohio Railway, 397 F.2d 1, 4 (3d Cir. 1968). However, the principle announced in diversity cases such as Interna-

tional Shoe Co. v. Washington, 326 U.S. 310 (1945), and its progeny is
also applicable to nondiversity cases. See *Fraley*, 397 F.2d at 3.
This standard provides that a defendant is subject to a forum's jurisdiction only if its contacts with the forum are such that maintenance
of the suit will not offend traditional notions of fair play and substantial justice. It is unclear whether the *Fraley* court meant that the
fifth amendment requires a defendant to have minimum contacts
with the forum state, or whether the court intended only that the *International Shoe* test be applied by analogy, so that a defendant
need only have minimum contacts with the United States as a whole.
In any event, even in nondiversity cases, if service of process must be
made pursuant to a state long-arm statute or rule of court, the defendant's amenability to suit in federal district court is limited by that
statute or rule. See Hartley v. Sioux City & New Orleans Barge
Lines, Inc., 379 F.2d 354, 357 (3d Cir. 1967).

. . . .

The New Jersey long-arm rule is intended to extend as far as is
constitutionally permissible. In enacting its long-arm rule, the state
of New Jersey is limited by the due process constraints of the fourteenth amendment. Therefore, we believe that Hitachi's amenability
to suit in the District of New Jersey must be judged by fourteenth
amendment standards. We recognize that this creates an anomalous
situation because it results in a federal court in a nondiversity case
being limited by the due process restrictions imposed on the states by
the fourteenth amendment as opposed to those imposed on the federal government by the fifth amendment. However, it would be equally anomalous to utilize a state long-arm rule to authorize service of
process on a defendant in a manner that the state body enacting the
rule could not constitutionally authorize. The anomaly of a federal
court being limited by the requirements of the fourteenth amendment
in a nondiversity case where service must be made pursuant to a
state long-arm rule could be easily rectified by congressional authorization of nationwide service of process for admiralty cases. It is not
within our province to create such authorization.

DeJames directs our attention to only one contact that Hitachi has
had with the state of New Jersey: the vessel on which Hitachi had
done conversion work was docked in Camden, New Jersey when
DeJames was injured. DeJames argues that this contact is sufficient
to support the exercise of in personam jurisdiction over Hitachi.

. . . . Recently, in Shaffer v. Heitner, 433 U.S. 186 (1977), Kulko
v. Superior Court, 436 U.S. 84 (1978), and World-Wide Volkswagen
Corp. v. Woodson, 444 U.S. 286 (1980), the Supreme Court indicated
that due process requires that the defendant have a reasonable expectation that the nature of its conduct is such that it may be "haled
before a court" in the forum state. Standing alone, the fact that the
defendant could foresee that its conduct might affect the forum
state, or that its product might find its way to the forum state, is too

attenuated to constitute such a "reasonable expectation."   See World-Wide Volkswagen, 444 U.S. at 297.

DeJames argues that the conversion work done by Hitachi on the vessel in effect makes Hitachi the "manufacturer" of the vessel, and thus distinguishes Hitachi from the local retailer and the regional distributor in *World-Wide Volkswagen*.   Because Hitachi "manufactured" a ship capable of transporting automobiles, DeJames asserts that Hitachi should be amenable to process in any port where the ship docks and injury occurs as a result of Hitachi's allegedly defective work.

In making this argument, DeJames places substantial reliance on the numerous cases adopting the "stream-of-commerce" theory as a basis for jurisdiction over a foreign manufacturer. . . .

In contrast to the manufacturers in the stream-of-commerce cases, Hitachi did not utilize the owners of the vessel it "manufactured" as distributors of its product and thus did not take advantage of an indirect marketing scheme.   Moreover, Hitachi received no economic benefit, either direct or indirect, from residents of New Jersey.   Although it could be argued that Hitachi receives some derivative benefit from the international market for Japanese cars and from the fact that the charterers of the vessel were permitted to unload cars in New Jersey, we believe that this attenuated benefit is insufficient to support the assertion of personal jurisdiction.   The only benefit that Hitachi derives from the ability of the vessel to dock in New Jersey and the international market for Japanese cars transported on the vessel is that Hitachi may do more conversion of large vessels into automobile carriers, as opposed to work on smaller ships or other kinds of ship repair.   This derivative benefit is similar to the benefit that the local retailer and the regional distributor in *World-Wide Volkswagen* derived from the fact that the cars they sold could freely travel across state lines and stop within the forum state.   The ability of the consumer to drive the car sold by the *World-Wide Volkswagen* defendants into the forum state, like the ability of the charterers of the vessel to sail the ship "manufactured" by Hitachi into the forum state, arguably increases the demand for the services performed by the defendants.   However, this derivative benefit was found insufficient to support personal jurisdiction over the defendants in *World-Wide Volkswagen*, and we likewise find it insufficient to support personal jurisdiction over Hitachi in New Jersey.

. . .   Were we to accept DeJames' foreseeability argument in this case, Hitachi would be amenable to suit in every forum where a ship on which it had done conversion work, and over which it exercised no control, could be found.

[The court rejected DeJames' argument that Hitachi's contacts with the United States as a whole should be aggregated to support jurisdiction over Hitachi.]

. . . .

The order of the district court dismissing the complaint against Hitachi will be affirmed.

GIBBONS, CIRCUIT JUDGE, dissenting:

. . . [I]t is readily apparent that Hitachi is not a local dealer. It is true that Hitachi converts bulk carriers to automobile carriers in Japan, to the order of Japanese vessel owners. It is also true that Hitachi does not control the ultimate destination of its products. But these facts do not reveal the whole story. Hitachi's ships are an integral part of the chain of international commerce in Japanese automobiles. Hitachi's ships carry Japanese automobiles to American and New Jersey ports. The Port of New York-New Jersey is this nation's largest, receiving over 185,292,125 tons of cargo per year. The New Jersey ports of Paulsboro, Camden-Glouster, and Trenton Harbor together account for another 28,533,725 tons per year. 1981 World Almanac and Book of Facts at 204. It is not "merely foreseeable," but virtually inevitable that ships Hitachi converts will dock in New Jersey.

Nor can it be said that Hitachi has no substantial interest in the destination of the ships it converts. . . . Hitachi benefits by selling its vessels to shipowners who will take them to New Jersey ports. Hitachi's ship conversion business is a vital component of the process of distribution of Japanese automobiles in the United States. The American market for Japanese cars enhances Hitachi's ship conversion business. . . .

Finally, while it is not crucial to the disposition of this case, I believe the misconception underlying the majority's statement that the fourteenth amendment governs amenability to suit on a federal claim . . . should be exposed and criticized. The fourteenth amendment due process clause does not properly apply in all its aspects to federal question claims. . . . When a court asserts personal jurisdiction over a foreign defendant on the basis of a state law claim, it must ensure that the forum state does not unduly encroach on a sister state's interests. When a court, state or federal, adjudicates a federal claim, the federalism issue is of no relevance, for the court determines the parties' rights and liabilities under uniform, national law. No state intrudes on another's interests. The only relevant interest is the national one. Thus the applicable constitutional due process provision should not be the fourteenth amendment, but the fifth amendment.

The fifth amendment requires only that the forum be a fair and reasonable place at which to compel defendant's appearance, and that he have had notice and a reasonable opportunity to be heard. See Stabilisierungsfonds fur Wein et al. v. Kaiserstuhl Wine Distributors Pty. Ltd. et al., 647 F.2d 200 (D.C.Cir.1981), at 203 & n. 4. A defendant's *national* contacts enter into the fifth amendment fairness analysis, for it would be unreasonable to subject to suit in the United States a foreign national defendant who had but one fleeting connection with this country. But it is not necessary, under the fifth amendment due process clause, that that defendant's contacts relate primarily to the particular United States location in which the claim arose. Thus, for example, it would not be unfair under the fifth amendment to subject a foreign national shipper to suit in New Jersey on the basis of an admiralty claim that arose in that state, even if the offending ship was the only one ever to dock in New Jersey, and all of defendant's other ships land in Texas. The hypothetical defendant has sufficient contacts with the United States, and the availability of witnesses points to the District of New Jersey as the most convenient forum for the litigation. Cf. Shaffer v. Heitner, 433 U.S. 186, 204 (1977) (central concern of jurisdictional inquiry is relationship among the defendant, the forum, and the litigation).

Similarly, were a state court adjudicating a federal claim, the relevant due process standard should remain the fifth amendment. The nature of the claim, not the identity of the court, should determine the appropriate due process test. . . .

NOTE

While recognizing that the Fifth Amendment rather than the Fourteenth Amendment was the source of standards governing adjudicatory jurisdiction in a suit based on commercial activities of the Federal Republic of Nigeria, the court said: "The analogy between the national and international systems may not be sufficiently exact to lead to the same result in every case, but here we see no reason to stray from our former adherence to the analysis developed under the Fourteenth Amendment." Texas Trading v. Federal Republic of Nigeria, 647 F.2d 300, 315–16, n. 37 (2d Cir. 1981).

The International Shoe, McGee, Hanson and World-Wide Volkswagen cases contain the principal statements of the Supreme Court on the constitutional requisites for in personam jurisdiction. The theme of these decisions is that the test of personal jurisdiction is whether its assertion in a particular case is "reasonable." This is another way of asking whether in the context of our federal system of government it is fair and proper to require the defendant to stand suit in the state the plaintiff has chosen. Exactly which factors determine whether the requirement of reasonableness has been met is not made clear in the Supreme Court's decisions. The next set of cases and comments illustrates how the courts have dealt with the question of when it is reasonable to assert personal jurisdiction over a nonresident. Varied types of problems are illustrated:

(1) *Product liability claims.* In some of these cases the defendant ships the product into the state—regularly, occasionally, or only once—and the product fails in the forum state causing damage to the plaintiff. In other cases the defendant parts with title to the product in another state and someone else—the plaintiff or a third party—brings it into the forum state. In still another variant of this situation, the product failure occurs somewhere other than the state in

which the plaintiff brings suit. Commonly but not invariably, this is the state of his residence.

(2) *Other long-distance torts.* Another set of cases involves not a harm-causing product but an utterance or other act that in some way is transformed into a tort against the plaintiff, again usually in the forum state. The utterance may give rise to a claim for defamation, business disparagement or medical malpractice; or the activity may consist of selling beer or liquor to someone who becomes inebriated and injures the plaintiff.

(3) *Breach of contract.* In this group of cases the nonresident and the plaintiff negotiate across state lines and enter into a sales contract or some other type of agreement that leads to plaintiff's claim for breach. The nonresident typically has had no other contact with the forum state, or at most only slight connections.

(4) *Disparate financial power; who initiated the deal?* These cases consider whether the fact that the defendant has a deep pocket is a factor properly bearing on jurisdiction; and whether it makes a difference that one party rather than the other initiated the transaction on which suit is based.

(5) *"Less-favored" categories of actions: e.g., defamation.* Suits that approach areas under the protection of the First Amendment may evoke special resistance when expansive jurisdictional outreach is attempted.

O'BRIEN v. COMSTOCK FOODS, INC.

Supreme Court of Vermont, 1963.
123 Vt. 461, 194 A.2d 568.

HOLDEN, JUSTICE. This cause has been certified here before trial to settle a jurisdictional question. The action is one of four suits instituted by the plaintiff and her husband against Comstock Foods, Inc., a New York corporation. . . . to recover for personal injuries claimed to have been sustained by the plaintiff from the presence of a piece of glass in a can of beans prepared and packed by the defendant in Newark, New York.

How the product came to be distributed in Vermont does not appear. The complaint tells us only that the commodity was "placed— in the stream of commerce" in New York state. It was purchased by the plaintiff's husband in Burlington, Vermont, where she became injured when eating part of the contents of the can. . . .

The bare allegation that the defendant at Newark, New York put its product "into the stream of commerce," without more, is insufficient to show a voluntary contract or an intentional participation in Vermont. The fact that the can of beans was ultimately purchased and consumed here does not cure the defect.

The place where the final harm is done may control for purposes of making a choice of law. But considerations important to this area of the law are sometimes insubstantial for purposes of asserting jurisdiction over a non-resident defendant. Hanson v. Denkla, supra, 357 U.S. 235.

If parts of Vermont were served directly by the defendant, or indirectly, by its customary distributors, knowledge of possible consequent injury from faulty packing, might well be imputed. But this essential jurisdictional factor cannot be supplied by speculation.
. . .

In the complaint before us, it does not appear the defendant intended this product for Vermont, nor that its present or past commercial activity was such that it should have known that faulty packaging might have potential consequences in this jurisdiction. Without any presentation in the record of these basic requirements due process is not achieved and personal jurisdiction fails. . . .

Order denying the defendant's motion to dismiss is reversed.

NOTES

(1) The Comstock case should be compared with Gray v. American Radiator & Standard Sanitary Corp., 22 Ill.2d 432, 176 N.E.2d 761 (1961). In that case, suit was brought in Illinois for personal injuries suffered in that state against the Ohio manufacturer of what was alleged to be a defective safety valve. This valve had been shipped from Ohio to a corporation in Pennsylvania which had there incorporated it into a hot water heater which "in the course of commerce" had been sold to an ultimate purchaser in Illinois. There was no evidence that the defendant had done any other business in Illinois, "either directly or indirectly." Nevertheless, jurisdiction was held to exist. The court pointed out that "defendant does not claim that the present use of its product in Illinois is an isolated instance . . . it is a reasonable inference that its commercial transactions, like those of other manufacturers, result in substantial use and consumption in this State."

The Comstock case should also be compared with Bard Bldg. Supply Co. v. United Foam Corp., 137 Vt. 125, 400 A.2d 1023 (1979), which involved suit in Vermont against a Pennsylvania manufacturer to recover damages resulting from alleged defects in a shipment of foam. The plaintiff in Vermont had placed the order by phone with the defendant in Pennsylvania. The defendant accepted the order and shipped the goods C.O.D. to the plaintiff in Vermont. The defendant had not solicited this or any other business in Vermont and did no business there "either directly or through distributors." Nevertheless, the court was held to have jurisdiction, because of the defendant's "active and intentional participation in the Vermont market." Where such participation is lacking, as was the case in Comstock, there will be no jurisdiction unless product use and consumption in Vermont is substantial.

(2) Erlanger Mills v. Cohoes Fibre Mills, 239 F.2d 502 (4th Cir. 1956) involved a North Carolina statute (N.C.Gen.Stat. § 55–145) which makes a foreign corporation subject to personal jurisdiction on claims arising out of the "production, manufacture, or distribution of goods by such corporation with the reasonable expectation that those goods are to be used or consumed in

this State and are so used or consumed . . . ." In New York, plaintiff's agent contracted to purchase yarn from defendant, f.o.b. New York, and the goods were shipped to North Carolina. Plaintiff sued for damages, claiming the yarn was defective, but the action was dismissed on the ground that the statute could not constitutionally be applied to defendant. "To illustrate the logical and not too improbable extension of the problem, let us consider the hesitancy a California dealer might feel if asked to sell a set of tires to a tourist with Pennsylvania license plates, knowing that he might be required to defend in the courts of Pennsylvania a suit for refund of the purchase price or for heavy damages in case of accident attributed to a defect in the tires."

Should the California dealer not be subject to Pennsylvania jurisdiction in the hypothetical case posed in the Erlanger opinion? Suppose on similar facts that the Pennsylvania motorist had in California given a promissory note to the dealer in payment of the tires. Would the motorist be subject to California jurisdiction in an action on the note? Should there be a wider scope of jurisdiction over a defendant with respect to conduct that is multi-state in character than with respect to conduct that is essentially local? Would it be correct to say in general that the more a defendant's activities are multistate in character the wider the scope of jurisdiction that can be exercised over him, and the less a plaintiff engages in multistate activity the narrower the scope of jurisdiction that should be exercised over the defendant in plaintiff's favor? See von Mehren and Trautman, Jurisdiction to Adjudicate: A Suggested Analysis, 79 Harv.L.Rev. 1121, 1167–1168 (1966).

(3) Should the rules of jurisdiction be more restrictive in international cases involving product liability? This question was answered in the negative in Duple Motor Bodies, Ltd. v. Hollingsworth, 417 F.2d 231 (9th Cir. 1969). In that case jurisdiction was held to exist in Hawaii in a personal injury action over the English manufacturer of a component part in a bus which had been involved in an accident in Hawaii where the defendant was aware that the bus was destined for sale. Although the defendant did no business, had no representative, and owned no property in Hawaii, the court held that it is not offensive to due process or an undue burden on foreign trade "to require a manufacturer to defend his product wherever he himself has placed it, either directly or through the normal distributive channels of trade." The dissent argued that the interstate cases dealing with jurisdiction over manufacturers should not be followed indiscriminately in international cases to avoid reprisals by foreign countries against American manufacturers.

(4) Wright v. Yackley, 459 F.2d 287 (9th Cir. 1972). While a resident of South Dakota, the plaintiff had been treated by the defendant, a South Dakota doctor, and at his direction had taken certain drugs. Plaintiff then moved to Idaho and wrote the defendant in South Dakota requesting that he confirm the prescription so that she could purchase an additional supply of the drugs. Defendant did so and plaintiff thereafter was allegedly injured by use of the drugs. She brought suit for malpractice against the defendant in the federal district court in Idaho.

Held: Idaho lacks judicial jurisdiction over the defendant.

". . . [T]he idea that tortious rendition of [personal] services is a portable tort which can be deemed to have been committed wherever the consequences foreseeably were felt is wholly inconsistent with having services of this sort generally available. Medical services, in particular, should not be proscribed by the doctor's concerns as to where the patient may carry the consequences of his treatment and in what distant lands he may be called upon to defend it. The traveling public would be ill served were the treatment of local doctors confined to so much aspirin as would get the patient into the next state. The scope of medical treatment should be defined by the patient's needs, as diagnosed by the doctor, rather than by geography . . . . [T]he forum state's [Idaho's] natural interest in the protection of its citizens is here countered by an interest in their access to medical services whenever needed."

(5) McGee v. Riekhof, 442 F.Supp. 1276 (D.Mont.1978). Having been operated on by the defendant doctor in Utah, plaintiff returned to his home in Montana. Sometime later the defendant told plaintiff's wife over the telephone that he could return to work in Montana. Allegedly as a result, the plaintiff suffered further injury. Held that the defendant was subject to the jurisdiction of the federal district court in Montana. ". . . [T]he defendant doctor did precisely what wasn't done in *Wright*, he provided a new diagnosis via telephone. This court recognizes the need to keep open the flow of medical and other personal services across state boundaries. . . . [Under the circumstances], it would be fundamentally unfair to patients to permit doctors to telephonically render services and treatment in Montana, yet shield them from suit in Montana."

(6) McBreen v. Beech Aircraft Corporation, 543 F.2d 26 (7th Cir. 1976). In answer to a question posed him in the course of a telephone call, which he received in Kansas and which he believed emanated from Massachusetts, the defendant attorney made certain allegedly defamatory remarks about the plaintiff, an Illinois corporation. In fact, the telephone call had originated in Illinois, and suit was there brought against the defendant. *Held*: The suit should be dismissed for lack of jurisdiction under due process. The court intimated, however, that its conclusion might have been different if the telephone call, which was the defendant's sole contact with Illinois, had either been solicited or initiated by him.

(7) Taylor v. Portland Paramount Corporation, 383 F.2d 634 (9th Cir. 1967). Suit brought in Oregon by a theater owner against Elizabeth Taylor claiming that his customers had been deterred from viewing the film Cleopatra by defendant's conduct with Richard Burton and by certain disparaging statements she had made about the film. Miss Taylor had no contractual relationship with the plaintiff; she did know, however, that the film would receive world wide distribution. *Held*: Action dismissed for lack of jurisdiction. The complained-of conduct did not occur in Oregon and defendant has not done "any act by which she purposely availed herself of the privilege of conducting activities within Oregon. . . . Nor does it matter that Taylor was served in the neighboring state of California, and that it is no great burden to require her to go from there to Oregon."

Contracts that involve activities in different states during their negotiation, execution or performance are fertile sources of jurisdictional issues. How much contact and what kind must a nonresident have with the forum to be amenable to suit there? Are nonresident sellers more susceptible to long-arm jurisdiction than nonresident buyers? Does the relative size or financial strength of the parties play a significant role? What importance is attached to the nonresident's dealings in the forum that are unrelated to the contract sued upon? The Supreme Court has not addressed these questions in definitive terms since the International Shoe decision, although it has had opportunities to do so. In Lakeside Bridge & Steel Co. v. Mountain State Construction Co., Inc., 445 U.S. 907 (1980), the plaintiff, a Wisconsin seller, contracted to supply structural assemblies for a dam and reservoir in Virginia. The defendant was a West Virginia corporation whose dealings with the plaintiff were conducted by mail and telephone between West Virginia and Wisconsin. The Court of Appeals for the Seventh Circuit found the defendant's contacts with Wisconsin insufficient to support jurisdiction over it in the plaintiff's suit for part of the purchase price. Justice White, joined by Justice Powell, dissented from the Supreme Court's denial of certiorari, arguing that "the issue is one of considerable importance" and that the "disarray" among the federal and state courts might be having a disruptive effect on commercial relations that place a premium on certainty.

Buyers are often treated more gently than sellers in jurisdictional cases on the theory that the buyer is more likely to be weaker financially than the seller, especially when consumer goods are involved. Thus, "with few exceptions, in those cases where jurisdiction is extended over a nonresident defendant purchaser, that purchaser has either initiated the relationship or actively participated in negotiations and plans for production (*e.g.*, design specifications)." Vacu-Maid, Inc. v. Covington, 530 P.2d 137, 141, 143 (Okla.App.1975). See also Tube Turn Div. of Chemetron v. Patterson Co., 562 S.W.2d 99 (Ky. App.1978). When the buyer is not an individual but a large and sophisticated business, jurisdiction is more likely to be sustained. Nordberg Div. of Rex Chainbelt Inc. v. Hudson Eng. Corp., 361 F.Supp. 903 (E.D.Wis.1973). The big fish-little fish approach to jurisdiction drew criticism in Vencedor Mfg. Co. Inc. v. Gougler Industries, Inc., 557 F.2d 886, 894 (1st Cir. 1977). The court said:

> . . . To vary the minimum contacts needed for jurisdiction according to the character of the suit would lead plaintiffs into disingenuous manipulation of their pleadings, and it would plunge the courts into ever more difficult refinements of the categories. They would need to decide whether a contract action involving individuals should be treated like one between corporations; whether consumers' orders from mail order catalogues should be treated like commercial contracts; whether the tort of defamation or of interference with contract is to be treated like the negligent operation of an automobile.

Some courts have made the issue of jurisdiction turn on which party took the initiative in the transaction.

CONN v. WHITMORE, 9 Utah 2d 250, 342 P.2d 871 (1959). Suit in Utah to recover on an Illinois judgment. Plaintiff, a resident of Illinois, was in the business of raising and selling Arabian horses. He mailed defendant in Utah a mimeographed sheet listing certain horses for sale. Defendant requested an Illinois friend to look at the horses and, having received a favorable report from him, wrote the plaintiff to say that he would buy two of the horses and dispatched an employee to pick them up at plaintiff's Illinois farm. Defendant, however, refused to complete payment for the horses because of plaintiff's alleged misrepresentation about one of them. The Utah court refused to enforce the Illinois judgment for lack of jurisdiction. It said:

". . . It is important to bear in mind that it was not the defendant Utah resident who took the initiative by going into Illinois to transact business, nor did he engage in any activity resulting in injury or damage there. Quite the contrary, it was the plaintiff resident of Illinois who proselyted for business in Utah, and whose proffer the defendant accepted here. He agreed to the terms offered and completed his contract of purchase in Utah by depositing his agreement together with his check to bind the bargain in the mail.

"Brief reflection will bring to mind difficulties to be encountered if the ordering of merchandise in a foreign state by mail and taking delivery through a designated carrier, whether private or common, is to be deemed "doing business" in a foreign state, which will draw one into the orbit of the jurisdiction of its courts. This would for practical purposes obliterate any protection one might have from being compelled to go to a foreign jurisdiction to defend a lawsuit. A person contemplating business in another state would have only two alternatives: either subject himself to the jurisdiction of the foreign court if any dispute arises, or refrain from doing such business. This would have a bad effect upon commerce. Mail order houses, for example, accept and fill orders from all over the country. If they could sue on their accounts in their own state where it would be highly inconvenient for out-of-state customers to defend, then forward the judgments to the jurisdictions where the customers live, demanding full faith and credit for them, this would effectively prevent the customers from presenting a meritorious defense where one existed. The ultimate result would be to dissuade customers from doing business across state lines by mail. Thus what may seem a temporary advantage to such businesses, in all likelihood would be detrimental to them and to business generally in the long run.

KEETON v. HUSTLER MAGAZINE, INC.

Supreme Court of the United States, 1984.
__ U.S. __, 104 S.Ct. 1473, 79 L.Ed.2d 790.

JUSTICE REHNQUIST delivered the opinion of the Court.

Petitioner Kathy Keeton sued respondent Hustler Magazine, Inc., and other defendants in the United States District Court for the District of New Hampshire, alleging jurisdiction over her libel complaint

π- NewHamp

by reason of diversity of citizenship. The district court dismissed her suit because it believed that the Due Process Clause of the Fourteenth Amendment to the United States Constitution forbade the application of New Hampshire's long-arm statute in order to acquire personal jurisdiction over respondent. The Court of Appeals for the First Circuit affirmed, 682 F.2d 33 (CA 1 1982), summarizing its concerns with the statement that "the New Hampshire tail is too small to wag so large an out-of-state dog." Id., at 36. We granted certiorari . . . and we now reverse.

Petitioner Keeton is a resident of New York. Her only connection with New Hampshire is the circulation there of copies of a magazine that she assists in producing. The magazine bears petitioner's name in several places crediting her with editorial and other work. Respondent Hustler Magazine, Inc., is an Ohio corporation, with its principal place of business in California. Respondent's contacts with New Hampshire consist of the sale of some 10 to 15,000 copies of *Hustler* magazine in that State each month. . . . Petitioner claims to have been libeled in five separate issues of respondent's magazine published between September, 1975, and May, 1976.[1]

The Court of Appeals, in its opinion affirming the District Court's dismissal of petitioner's complaint, held that petitioner's lack of contacts with New Hampshire rendered the State's interest in redressing the tort of libel to petitioner too attenuated for an assertion of personal jurisdiction over respondent. The Court of Appeals observed that the "single publication rule" ordinarily applicable in multistate libel cases would require it to award petitioner "damages caused in *all* states" should she prevail in her suit, even though the bulk of petitioner's alleged injuries had been sustained outside New Hampshire. 682 F.2d, at 35.[2] The court also stressed New Hampshire's unusually long (6-year) limitations period for libel actions. New Hampshire was the only State where petitioner's suit would not have been time-barred when it was filed. Under these circumstances, the Court of Appeals concluded that it would be "unfair" to assert jurisdiction over respondent. New Hampshire has a minimal interest in applying its unusual statute of limitations to, and awarding damages for, injuries to a nonresident occurring outside the State, particularly since petitioner suffered such a small proportion of her total claimed injury within the State. Id., at 35–36.

---

1. Initially, petitioner brought suit for libel and invasion of privacy in Ohio, where the magazine is published. Her libel claim, however, was dismissed as barred by the Ohio statute of limitations, and her invasion of privacy claim was dismissed as barred by the New York statute of limitations, which the Ohio court considered to be "migratory." Petitioner then filed the present action in October, 1980.

2. The "single publication rule" has been summarized as follows:

"As to any single publication, (a) only one action for damages can be maintained; (b) all damages suffered in all jurisdictions can be recovered in the one action; and (c) a judgment for or against the plaintiff upon the merits of any action for damages bars any other action for damages between the same parties in all jurisdictions." Restatement (Second) of Torts § 577A(4) (1977).

We conclude that the Court of Appeals erred when it affirmed the dismissal of petitioner's suit for lack of personal jurisdiction. Respondent's regular circulation of magazines in the forum State is sufficient to support an assertion of jurisdiction in a libel action based on the contents of the magazine. This is so even if New Hampshire courts, and thus the District Court under Klaxon Co. v. Stentor Co., 313 U.S. 450 (1941), would apply the so-called "single publication rule" to enable petitioner to recover in the New Hampshire action her damages from "publications" of the alleged libel throughout the United States.

The district court found that "[t]he general course of conduct in circulating magazines throughout the state was purposefully directed at New Hampshire, and inevitably affected persons in the state." . . . Such regular monthly sales of thousands of magazines cannot by any stretch of the imagination be characterized as random, isolated, or fortuitous. It is, therefore, unquestionable that New Hampshire jurisdiction over a complaint based on those contacts would ordinarily satisfy the requirement of the Due Process Clause that a State's assertion of personal jurisdiction over a nonresident defendant be predicated on "minimum contacts" between the defendant and the State. See World-Wide Volkswagen Corp. v. Woodson, 444 U.S. 286, 297–298 (1980); International Shoe Corp. v. Washington, 326 U.S. 310, 317 (1945). And, as the Court of Appeals acknowledged, New Hampshire has adopted a "long-arm" statute authorizing service of process on nonresident corporations whenever permitted by the Due Process Clause. . . . Thus, all the requisites for personal jurisdiction over Hustler Magazine, Inc., in New Hampshire are present.

We think that the three concerns advanced by the Court of Appeals, whether considered singly or together, are not sufficiently weighty to merit a different result. The "single publication rule," New Hampshire's unusually long statute of limitations, and plaintiff's lack of contacts with the forum State do not defeat jurisdiction otherwise proper under both New Hampshire law and the Due Process Clause.

In judging minimum contacts, a court properly focuses on "the relationship among the defendant, the forum, and the litigation." Shaffer v. Heitner, 433 U.S. 186, 204 (1977). See also Rush v. Savchuk, 444 U.S. 320, 332 (1980). Thus, it is certainly relevant to the jurisdictional inquiry that petitioner is *seeking* to recover damages suffered in all States in this one suit. The contacts between respondent and the forum must be judged in the light of that claim, rather than a claim only for damages sustained in New Hampshire. That is, the contacts between respondent and New Hampshire must be such that it is "fair" to compel respondent to defend a multistate lawsuit in New Hampshire seeking nationwide damages for all copies of the five issues in question, even though only a small portion of those copies were distributed in New Hampshire.

The Court of Appeals expressed the view that New Hampshire's "interest" in asserting jurisdiction over plaintiff's multistate claim was minimal. We agree that the "fairness" of haling respondent into a New Hampshire court depends to some extent on whether respondent's activities relating to New Hampshire are such as to give that State a legitimate interest in holding respondent answerable on a claim related to those activities. See World-Wide Volkswagen Corp. v. Woodson, 444 U.S. 286, 292 (1980); McGee v. International Life Insurance Co., 355 U.S. 220, 223 (1957). But insofar as the State's "interest" in adjudicating the dispute is a part of the Fourteenth Amendment due process equation, as a surrogate for some of the factors already mentioned, see Insurance Corp. v. Compagnie des Bauxites, 456 U.S. 694, 702–703 n. 10 (1982), we think the interest is sufficient.

The Court of Appeals acknowledged that petitioner was suing, at least in part, for damages suffered in New Hampshire. 682 F.2d, at 34. And it is beyond dispute that New Hampshire has a significant interest in redressing injuries that actually occur within the State. . . .

This interest extends to libel actions brought by nonresidents. False statements of fact harm both the subject of the falsehood *and* the readers of the statement. New Hampshire may rightly employ its libel laws to discourage the deception of its citizens. There is "no constitutional value in false statements of fact." Gertz v. Robert Welch, Inc., 418 U.S. 323, 340 (1974).

New Hampshire may also extend its concern to the injury that instate libel causes within New Hampshire to a nonresident. The tort of libel is generally held to occur wherever the offending material is circulated. Restatement (Second) of Torts § 577A, Comment a (1977). The reputation of the libel victim may suffer harm even in a state in which he has hitherto been anonymous. The communication of the libel may create a negative reputation among the residents of a jurisdiction where the plaintiff's previous reputation was, however small, as least unblemished.

New Hampshire has clearly expressed its interest in protecting such persons from libel, as well as in safeguarding its populace from falsehoods. Its criminal defamation statute bears no restriction to libels of which residents are the victim. Moreover, in 1971 New Hampshire specifically deleted from its long-arm statute the requirement that a tort be committed "against a resident of New Hampshire."

New Hampshire also has a substantial interest in cooperating with other States, through the "single publication rule," to provide a forum for efficiently litigating all issues and damage claims arising out of a libel in a unitary proceeding.[8] This rule reduces the potential

---

8. The great majority of the States now follow the "single publication rule." Restatement (Second) of Torts § 577A, Reporter's Note.

serious drain of libel cases on judicial resources. It also serves to protect defendants from harassment resulting from multiple suits. Restatement (Second) of Torts § 577A, Comment f (1977). In sum, the combination of New Hampshire's interest in redressing injuries that occur within the State and its interest in cooperating with other States in the application of the "single publication rule" demonstrate the propriety of requiring respondent to answer to a multistate libel action in New Hampshire.[9]

The Court of Appeals also thought that there was an element of due process "unfairness" arising from the fact that the statutes of limitations in every jurisdiction except New Hampshire had run on the plaintiff's claim in this case.[10] Strictly speaking, however, any potential unfairness in applying New Hampshire's statute of limitations to all aspects of this nationwide suit has nothing to do with the jurisdiction of the Court to adjudicate the claims. "The issue is personal jurisdiction, not choice of law." Hanson v. Denckla, 357 U.S. 235, 254 (1958). The question of the applicability of New Hampshire's statute of limitations to claims for out-of-state damages presents itself in the course of litigation only after jurisdiction over respondent is established, and we do not think that such choice of law concerns should complicate or distort the jurisdictional inquiry.

The chance duration of statutes of limitations in nonforum jurisdictions has nothing to do with the contacts among respondent, New Hampshire, and this multistate libel action. Whether Ohio's limitations period is six months or six years does not alter the jurisdictional calculus in New Hampshire. Petitioner's successful search for a State with a lengthy statute of limitations is no different from the litigation strategy of countless plaintiffs who seek a forum with favorable substantive or procedural rules or sympathetic local populations. Certainly Hustler Magazine, Inc., which chose to enter the New Hampshire market, can be charged with knowledge of its laws and no doubt would have claimed the benefit of them if it had a complaint against a subscriber, distributor, or other commercial partner.

9. Of course, to conclude that petitioner may properly *seek* multistate damages in this New Hampshire suit is not to conclude that such damages should, in fact, be awarded if petitioner makes out her case for libel. The actual applicability of the "single publication rule" in the peculiar circumstances of this case is a matter of substantive law, not personal jurisdiction. We conclude only that the district court has jurisdiction to *entertain* petitioner's multistate libel suit.

10. Under traditional choice of law principles, the law of the forum State governs on matters of procedure. See Restatement (Second) of Conflict of Laws § 122 (1971). In New Hampshire, statutes of limitations are considered procedural. Gordon v. Gordon, 118 N.H. 356, 360, 387 A.2d 339, 342 (1978); Barrett v. Boston & Maine R. R., 104 N.H. 70, 178 A.2d 291 (1962). There has been considerable academic criticism of the rule that permits a forum State to apply its own statute of limitations regardless of the significance of contacts between the forum State and the litigation. See, e.g., Weintraub, Commentary on the Conflict of Laws § 9.2B at 517 (2d ed. 1980); Martin, Constitutional Limitations on Choice of Law, 61 Cornell L.Rev. 185, 221 (1976); Lorenzen, The State of Limitations and The Conflict of Laws, 28 Yale L.J. 492, 496–497 (1919). But we find it unnecessary to express an opinion at this time as to whether any arguable unfairness rises to the level of a due process violation.

Finally, implicit in the Court of Appeals' analysis of New Hampshire's interest is an emphasis on the extremely limited contacts of the *plaintiff* with New Hampshire. But we have not to date required a plaintiff to have "minimum contacts" with the forum State before permitting that State to assert personal jurisdiction over a nonresident defendant. On the contrary, we have upheld the assertion of jurisdiction where such contacts were entirely lacking. . . . In Perkins v. Benguet Mining Co., 342 U.S. 437 (1952), none of the parties was a resident of the forum State; indeed, neither the plaintiff nor the subject-matter of his action had any relation to that State. Jurisdiction was based solely on the fact that the defendant corporation had been carrying on in the forum "a continuous and systematic, but limited, part of its general business." Id., at 438. In the instant case, respondent's activities in the forum may not be so substantial as to support jurisdiction over a cause of action unrelated to those activities. But respondent is carrying on a "part of its general business" in New Hampshire, and that is sufficient to support jurisdiction when the cause of action arises out of the very activity being conducted, in part, in New Hampshire.

The plaintiff's residence is not, of course, completely irrelevant to the jurisdictional inquiry. As noted, that inquiry focuses on the relations among the defendant, the forum and the litigation. Plaintiff's residence may well play an important role in determining the propriety of entertaining a suit against the defendant in the forum. That is, plaintiff's residence in the forum may, because of defendant's relationship with the plaintiff, enhance defendant's contacts with the forum. Plaintiff's residence may be the focus of the activities of the defendant out of which the suit arises. See Calder v. Jones, ___ U.S. ___, ___ (1984); McGee v. International Life Ins. Co., 355 U.S. 220 (1957). But plaintiff's residence in the forum State is not a separate requirement, and lack of residence will not defeat jurisdiction established on the basis of defendant's contacts.

It is undoubtedly true that the bulk of the harm done to petitioner occurred outside New Hampshire. But that will be true in almost every libel action brought somewhere other than the plaintiff's domicile. There is no justification for restricting libel actions to the plaintiff's home forum.[12] The victim of a libel, like the victim of any other tort, may choose to bring suit in any forum with which the defendant has "certain minimum contacts . . . such that the maintenance of the suit does not offend 'traditional notions of fair play and substantial justice.' Milliken v. Meyer, 311 U.S. 457, 463 [61 S.Ct. 339, 343, 85 L.Ed. 278]." International Shoe Co. v. Washington, 326 U.S. 310, 316, 66 S.Ct. 154, 158, 90 L.Ed. 95 (1945).

Where, as in this case, respondent Hustler Magazine, Inc., has continuously and deliberately exploited the New Hampshire market,

---

12. As noted in Calder v. Jones, [infra], we reject categorically the suggestion that invisible radiations from the First Amendment may defeat jurisdiction otherwise proper under the Due Process Clause.

it must reasonably anticipate being haled into court there in a libel action based on the contents of its magazine. World-Wide Volkswagen Corp. v. Woodson, 444 U.S. 286, 297–298, 100 S.Ct. 559, 567, 62 L.Ed.2d 490 (1980). And, since respondent can be charged with knowledge of the "single publication rule," it must anticipate that such a suit will seek nationwide damages. Respondent produces a national publication aimed at a nationwide audience. There is no unfairness in calling it to answer for the contents of that publication wherever a substantial number of copies are regularly sold and distributed.

The judgment of the Court of Appeals is reversed [13] and the cause is remanded for proceedings consistent with this opinion.

It is so ordered.

JUSTICE BRENNAN, concurring in the judgment.

I agree with the Court that "[r]espondent's regular circulation of magazines in the forum State is sufficient to support an assertion of jurisdiction in a libel action based on the contents of the magazine." . . . These contacts between the respondent and the forum State are sufficiently important and sufficiently related to the underlying cause of action to foreclose any concern that the constitutional limits of the Due Process Clause are being violated. This is so, moreover, irrespective of the state's interest in enforcing its substantive libel laws or its unique statute of limitations. Indeed, as we recently explained in Insurance Corp. v. Compagnie des Bauxites, 456 U.S. 694 (1982), these interests of the State should be relevant only to the extent that they bear upon the liberty interests of the respondent that are protected by the Fourteenth Amendment. "The restriction on state sovereign power described in World-Wide Volkswagen Corp. [v. Woodson, 444 U.S. 286, 291–292 (1980)] must be seen as ultimately a function of the individual liberty interest preserved by the Due Process Clause. That Clause is the only source of the personal jurisdiction requirement and the Clause itself makes no mention of federalism concerns." Id., at 702–703 n. 10.

13. In addition to Hustler Magazine, Inc., Larry Flynt, the publisher, editor and owner of the magazine, and L.F.P., Inc., Hustler's holding company, were named as defendants in the District Court. It does not of course follow from the fact that jurisdiction may be asserted over Hustler Magazine, Inc., that jurisdiction may also be asserted over either of the other defendants. In Calder v. Jones, [infra], we today reject the suggestion that employees who act in their offical capacity are somehow shielded from suit in their individual capacity. But jurisdiction over an employee does not automatically follow from jurisdiction over the corporation which employs him; nor does jurisdiction over a parent corporation automatically establish jurisdiction over a wholly owned subsidiary. Consol. Textile Co. v. Gregory, 289 U.S. 85, 88 (1933); Peterson v. Chicago, R.I. & P. Railway Co., 205 U.S. 364, 391 (1907). Each defendant's contacts with the forum State must be assessed individually. See Rush v. Savchuk, 444 U.S. 320, 332 (1980) ("The requirements of *International Shoe* . . . must be met as to each defendant over whom a state court exercises jurisdiction.") Because the Court of Appeals concluded that jurisdiction could not be had even against Hustler Magazine, Inc., it did not inquire into the propriety of jurisdiction over the other defendants. Such inquiry is, of course, open upon remand.

NOTES

1. In Calder v. Jones, ___ U.S. ___ (1984), decided with Keeton v. Hustler Magazine, Inc., the Supreme Court held that nonresident employees acting on behalf of their employer-defendant in distributing allegedly defamatory material are not insulated from personal jurisdiction.

2. After *Keeton* what is the role of "federalism" concerns as a limitation on the jurisdiction of state courts? Does the Supreme Court intend that in defamation actions against nationally distributed or broadcast media the defendant may be sued in every state?

3. Whether the six-year New Hampshire statute of limitations will be applied and whether, if it is applied, plaintiff will be allowed to recover damages for injury to her reputation throughout the country are questions that depend on materials examined in Chapters 7, 8 and 9, infra.

———

The closer a defendant's contacts with a state, the more likely it is that the state has judicial jurisdiction over him and the wider the scope of jurisdiction that the state may exercise. So a state may entertain in its courts suit on any and all civil claims against a defendant who is domiciled in the state and, subject to considerations of reasonableness, may do the same against a defendant who is a resident or a national of the state. For historical reasons, the same is true of a defendant who is served with process while physically present in the state.

There is some uncertainty as to the circumstances in which a state may exercise jurisdiction over a nonresident which engages in commercial activity within its territory with respect to claims that do not arise from this business. Consider in this regard the statements on this subject by Chief Justice Stone in the International Shoe case (p. 66, supra). Consider also the following cases.

———

PERKINS V. BENGUET CONSOLIDATED MINING CO., 342 U.S. 437 (1952): The president of defendant, a Philippine corporation, was served with a summons in action in personam against the corporation filed in an Ohio state court by a non-resident of Ohio. The cause of action did not arise in Ohio and did not relate to the corporation's activities there. On motion, the service was quashed by the Ohio courts. The defendant owned mining properties in the Philippine Islands, but all its operations there halted during the Japanese occupation. The main activities in Ohio were carried on by the president, who was also general manager and principal stockholder of the company, and included: maintaining the files, corresponding, paying salaries of employees out of the company's local bank accounts, holding directors' meetings, and supervising rehabilitation of the corporation after the occupation. The Supreme Court of the United States held that the due process clause of the Fourteenth Amendment did not compel Ohio to open its courts to such a case. On the other hand, it held that the activities in Ohio were sufficiently "continuous and systematic" so that Ohio could, consistently with due process, (1) entertain the cause of action if it wished to do so, even though it was unrelated to the Ohio activities, or (2) refuse to hear the case, if that was its own local rule or policy. On remand, the Supreme Court of Ohio held that its courts should exercise jurisdiction. 158 Ohio St. 145, 107 N.E.2d 203 (1952).

FISHER GOVERNOR CO. V. SUPERIOR COURT, 53 Cal.2d 222, 347 P.2d 1 (1959): An action was brought in California against the Fisher Company, a corporation of Iowa with its principal office and plants there, for wrongful death and personal injuries occurring in Idaho from allegedly defective equipment manufactured by Fisher. Fisher's products were sold in California through manufacturers' agents who sold also similar products of other manufacturers, but the California agents had no connection with the sale of the Idaho machinery. Held, the action will not lie.

TRAYNOR, J. . . . Although a foreign corporation may have sufficient contacts with a state to justify an assumption of jurisdiction over it to enforce causes of action having no relation to its activities in that state, . . . more contacts are required for the assumption of such extensive jurisdiction than sales and sales promotion within the state by independent nonexclusive sales representatives. . . . Accordingly we must look beyond defendant's sales activities in this state to determine whether jurisdiction may constitutionally be assumed. The interests of the state in providing a forum for its residents, . . . or in regulating the business involved; the relative availability of evidence and the burden of defense and prosecution in one place rather than another; . . . the ease of access to an alternative forum; the avoidance of multiplicity of suits and conflicting adjudications; and the extent to which the causes of action arose out of defendant's local activities are all relevant to this inquiry. . . .

BRYANT V. FINNISH AIRLINES, 15 N.Y.2d 426, 260 N.Y.S.2d 625, 208 N.E.2d 439 (1965): A Finnish airline was held subject to jurisdiction in a New York action by a New York resident who was injured in Paris by the alleged negligence of the airline, on the ground that it was "doing business" in New York. Defendant had not qualified in New York; had no American stockholders, directors or officers; operated no aircraft in the United States and sold no tickets in New York. Its activities in New York were unrelated to the plaintiff's cause of action, consisting of receiving reservations for travel in Europe, transmitting information and publicizing and advertising defendant's European services.

NOTES

(1) The Bryant case goes far, perhaps too far, in allowing personal jurisdiction over a foreign corporation based on unrelated activities in the forum.

Will jurisdiction be upheld on lesser contacts when an American plaintiff sues and alternative jurisdiction is a foreign country? In Centronics Data Computer Corp. v. Mannesmann, A.G., 432 F.Supp. 659 (D.N.H.1977), suit was brought against a multinational conglomerate with principal headquarters in Germany. The court held that it had jurisdiction although it admitted that this would probably not have been the case if the defendant had been incorporated in the United States. The court based its conclusion on the ground that the defendant had ample contacts with the United States as a whole and that "where an alien defendant is sued by an American plaintiff, and where there is no particular inconvenience due to the specific forum state, the fact that the defendant is an alien and that there is no other forum in which to litigate the claim should be taken into consideration for purposes of determining whether a finding of jurisdiction meets the requisite standards of fair play." But cf. DeJames v. Magnificence Carriers, Inc., supra p. 95.

(2) In Helicopteros Nacionales de Colombia, S.A. v. Hall, ___ U.S. ___, 104 S.Ct. 1868 (1984), Texas was held to lack jurisdiction over a Colombian corporation in a suit to recover for the wrongful death of American citizens in a helicopter crash in Peru. This was because the claims bore no relation to defendant's contacts with Texas. These contacts involved the purchase of about 80% of its helicopter fleet from a Texas corporation together with spare parts and accessories, the sending of prospective pilots to Texas for training, sending an officer to Texas for a contract-negotiation session and accepting into a New York bank account checks drawn on a Houston bank. There was one dissent.

RATLIFF V. COOPER LABORATORIES, INC., 444 F.2d 745 (4th Cir. 1971) cert. denied 404 U.S. 948 (1971). Suit in the federal district court of South Carolina against two drug manufacturing companies to recover damages suffered from the ingestion of allegedly defective drugs. The plaintiffs did not reside in South Carolina and had ingested the drugs in other states. They brought suit in South Carolina only because the six-year period of limitation of that state had not yet run. The period had run in all states having any connection with the claims presented. The activities of one of the defendants in South Carolina were limited to solicitation by mail. The other defendant had been given authority to do business in South Carolina and had appointed an agent there for the service of process in accordance with South Carolina law. It also maintained five "detail men" in the state to promote the sale of its products. Only rarely, however, did these men take actual purchase orders. On appeal, held, dismissed for lack of jurisdiction over both defendants. Although "South Carolina has extended its service of process laws to the outer limits allowed by *International Shoe*," jurisdiction is lacking under due process. Where a plaintiff's injury does not arise out of defendant's activity in the state, the contacts between the defendant and the state must be "fairly extensive" in order to justify requiring defendant to stand suit there. The fact that one defendant had been authorized to do business in the state is not important, since it had in fact conducted only limited activities there.

NOTE

In Lee v. Walworth Valve Company, 482 F.2d 297 (4th Cir. 1973), the same court held that the federal district court of South Carolina had jurisdiction over an out-of-state manufacturer in a suit to recover for a wrongful death on the high seas which resulted from the rupture of a steam valve on a U.S. naval vessel. The defendant manufacturer maintained no place of business in South Carolina but solicited a considerable number of orders there through traveling salesmen. The decedent and his wife were both domiciled in the state. The court said: "The difficulty . . . arises out of the fact that the cause of action did not arise out of any of [the defendant's] activity in South Carolina. The cause of action did not even arise in that State, for the injury occurred on the high seas . . . . [T]here probably are only two states in the United States with any interest in the controversy, the state of [the defendant's incorporation] and South Carolina . . . . The interest of South Carolina is substantial, however, for it has a paternal interest in the recovery by one of its citizens of appropriate compensation . . . . Our holding in *Ratliff* was dictated by the fact that South Carolina had no interest or connection with the controversy . . . and, hence, there were no countervailing considerations of fairness to be placed in the scales when weighing the substantiality of the defendant's contacts."

CORNELISON v. CHANEY

Supreme Court of California, 1976.
16 Cal.3d 143, 127 Cal.Rptr. 352, 545 P.2d 264.

[Wrongful death action by a California widow against a Nebraska resident to recover for the death of her husband in an accident that occurred in Nevada. Defendant had been engaged, for 7 years preceding the accident, in the business of hauling goods by truck in interstate commerce, making approximately 20 trips a year to California. The accident occurred near the California border while defendant was hauling goods to a manufacturer in that state. He intended to obtain cargo in California for a return shipment to an undesignated destination. The trial court dismissed the action for lack of jurisdiction. The Supreme Court of California reversed by a 4–3 vote.]

MOSK, J. The issue presented by this appeal is whether California, consistent with the due process clause of the United States Constitution, may assert jurisdiction over a nonresident individual whose essentially interstate business has a relationship to this state, but whose allegedly tortious acts occurred outside the state. . . .

Defendant was licensed to haul freight by the Public Utilities Commission of California, and had similar licenses issued by the regulatory agencies of several other states. His average cargo in any single trip to California had a value of approximately $20,000. He acted as an independent contractor for several brokerage companies engaged in shipping, one of which was in California.

A California court may exercise judicial jurisdiction over nonresidents on any basis not inconsistent with the United States Constitution or the California Constitution. (Code Civ.Proc., § 410.10.)[1]
. . .

If a nonresident defendant's activities may be described as "extensive or wide-ranging" (Buckeye Boiler Co. v. Superior Court, 71 Cal. 2d 893, 898–899 [80 Cal.Rptr. 113, 458 P.2d 57]) (1969) or "substantial . . . continuous and systematic" (Perkins v. Benguet Mining Co., 342 U.S. 437, 447–448 (1952)) (p. 112, supra), there is a constitutionally sufficient relationship to warrant jurisdiction for all causes of action asserted against him. In such circumstances, it is not necessary that the specific cause of action alleged be connected with the defendant's business relationship to the forum.

If, however, the defendant's activities in the forum are not so pervasive as to justify the exercise of general jurisdiction over him, then jurisdiction depends upon the quality and nature of his activity in the forum in relation to the particular cause of action. In such a situation, the cause of action must arise out of an act done or transaction consummated in the forum, or defendant must perform some other act by which he purposefully avails himself of the privilege of conducting activities in the forum, thereby invoking the benefits and protections of its laws. Thus, as the relationship of the defendant with the state seeking to exercise jurisdiction over him grows more tenuous, the scope of jurisdiction also retracts, and fairness is assured by limiting the circumstances under which the plaintiff can compel him to appear and defend. The crucial inquiry concerns the character of defendant's activity in the forum, whether the cause of action arises out of or has a substantial connection with that activity, and upon the balancing of the convenience of the parties and the interests of the state in assuming jurisdiction. . . .

Applying these rules to the instant case, we conclude that defendant's activities in California are not so substantial or wide-ranging as to justify general jurisdiction over him to adjudicate all matters regardless of their relevance to the cause of action alleged by plaintiff. . . .

We come, then, to an assessment of the relation between defendant's activities in California and the cause of action alleged by plaintiff. Our inquiry is directed to whether plaintiff's cause of action, based on an accident which resulted from defendant's allegedly tortious act in Nevada, arises out of or has a substantial connection with a business relationship defendant has purposefully established with California.

As we have seen, defendant has been engaged in a continuous course of conduct that has brought him into the state almost twice a

---

1. Section 410.10 provides: "A court of this state may exercise jurisdiction on any basis not inconsistent with the Constitution of this state or of the United States."

month for seven years as a trucker under a California license. The accident occurred not far from the California border, while defendant was bound for this state. He was not only bringing goods into California for a local manufacturer, but he intended to receive merchandise here for delivery elsewhere. The accident arose out of the driving of the truck, the very activity which was the essential basis of defendant's contacts with this state. These factors demonstrate, in our view, a substantial nexus between plaintiff's cause of action and defendant's activities in California.

It is true that, because the accident occurred across the state line in Nevada, the connection is not as direct as in cases such as McGee v. International Life Ins. Co., 355 U.S. 220, 223 (1958). However, we cannot overlook the fact that defendant's contacts with California, although insufficient to justify general jurisdiction over him, are far more extensive that those of the defendant in McGee. The question of jurisdiction cannot be decided by the application of some precise formula. The seminal case of Internat. Shoe Co. v. Washington, 326 U.S. 310, 319 (1945), pointed out that it is not a question whether the defendant's activity within the state "is a little more or a little less." The court there rejected a rigid test in favor of a flexible approach grounded in the quality and nature of the activity of the defendant in the state seeking to exercise jurisdiction over him, fairness to the parties, and the orderly administration of the law. Under this principle, the exercise of jurisdiction over defendant would not violate the dictates of due process if the factors of convenience discussed below weigh in plaintiff's favor.

We next consider whether it would be fair and reasonable to subject defendant to the jurisdiction of California in light of the inconvenience to him in defending an action in this state, when balanced against the interests of plaintiff in suing locally and of the state in assuming jurisdiction. . . .

In the circumstances of this case the consideration weighing most strongly in favor of a California forum is the relative burden of defense and prosecution on defendant and plaintiff. Defendant states that Nevada is a convenient forum because the witnesses to the accident reside there. While some of the witnesses who will testify at the trial reside in Nevada, plaintiff was also a witness to the accident and she is a California resident. Moreover, there is evidence in California on the amount of plaintiff's damages; and from the perspective of a Nebraska resident faced with litigation outside his state, there is little difference in the burden between defending in Nevada or California. (Cf. Fisher Governor Co. v. Superior Court, supra, 53 Cal.2d 222, 226, 1 Cal.Rptr. 1, 347 P.2d 1 (1959)). California has an interest in providing a forum since plaintiff is a California resident.

The interstate character of defendant's business is also significant in this balance. Defendant's operation, by its very nature, involves a high degree of interstate mobility and requires extensive multi-state activity. A necessary incident of that business was the foreseeable circumstance of causing injury to persons in distant forums. While the existence of an interstate business is not an independent basis of jurisdiction which, without more, allows a state to assert its jurisdiction, this element is relevant to considerations of fairness and reasonableness. The very nature of defendant's business balances in favor of requiring him to defend here. (See von Mehren & Trautman, Jurisdiction to Adjudicate (1966) 79 Harv.L.Rev. 1121, 1167–1169, note also the emphasis placed on doing a pervasive multi-state business in New York Civ. Practice Law and Rules § 302(a)(3)(ii), discussed in Homburger & Laufer, Expanding Jurisdiction (1966) 16 Buffalo L.Rev. 68, 72.)

We conclude that, under all the circumstances, it would not offend due process to subject defendant to the jurisdiction of the California courts. . . .

CLARK, J., dissenting. . . .

Whether a defendant not subject to general jurisdiction of a state may nevertheless be subject to limited jurisdiction as to a particular cause of action within the confines of due process turns essentially upon three considerations: (1) whether the cause of action "arises from" or is otherwise "connected with" defendant's forum-related activities . . . (2) the relative burdens upon the parties of trying the action in the forum state . . . and (3) the interest of the forum state in assuming jurisdiction . . . .

Applying these three considerations to the facts at issue, the majority concludes that California may constitutionally assume jurisdiction over defendant as to plaintiff's cause of action. But let's look again.

1. *Whether Plaintiff's Cause of Action "Arises From" Defendant's Forum-Related Activities*

Plaintiff's cause of action is for wrongful death to her husband. Her action alleges a specific instance of negligent conduct in the operation of a motor vehicle on a Nevada highway. Her cause of action in no sense "arises from" the fortuitous fact that defendant has been "engaged in a continuous course of conduct in California."

Defendant's continuous activity within California is relevant only to determining whether he is sufficiently "present" within the state to support an assertion of *general jurisdiction*. But the majority concedes defendant is not subject to general jurisdiction within California. The remaining issue then is whether defendant is subject to jurisdiction limited to *this cause of action*. As noted above, the appropriate test for "limited jurisdiction" focuses upon the *nexus* between the cause of action at issue and defendant's activities within the forum. The connection between plaintiff's cause of action and the fact that defendant has entered California twice a month for seven years is not shown by the majority, the latter fact being irrelevant to whether defendant was negligent in Nevada.

Equally irrelevant is the fact that "[h]e was not only bringing goods into California for a local manufacturer, but he intended to receive merchandise here for delivery elsewhere." [2]

The only conceivable connection between plaintiff's cause of action and defendant's activity inside California is that defendant was rolling toward (and plaintiff away from) its border. In this slight sense, the accident arguably "arose" from defendant's business in the state. However, the majority cites—and research has revealed—no authority supporting the conclusion that such a tenuous connection is sufficient to justify assertion of personal jurisdiction. In fact, the very decisions upon which the majority relies suggest the opposite. . . . In the case at issue, every event relevant to plaintiff's cause of action occurred in Nevada. To the extent decisions cited by the majority suggest a single rule, it is one that requires the cause of action relate in some manner to activity defendant has taken *within the forum*. The application of this rule to the facts at issue requires denial of California jurisdiction.

2. *Relative Burdens Upon the Parties in Trying the Action in the Forum State*

Excepting plaintiff herself, witnesses to the accident reside in Nevada. In addition, police and medical information as well as physical evidence repose in Nevada. Thus, trying this action in California places a heavy and expensive burden upon defendant in the presentation of his defense.

The majority claims "there is little difference in the burden between defending in Nevada or California" to a "Nebraska resident faced with litigation outside his state." This is untrue. The burden on defendant will be significantly increased if he is required to litigate in California when virtually all of the evidence relevant to his defense is located in Nevada. Further, he may be denied the ability to obtain witnesses necessary to the defense. Finally, the mere fact that a defendant who engages in "multi-state activity" may reasonably "expect litigation in distant forums" does not mean he must remain neutral as among the jurisdictions in which he may be required to litigate. Were this otherwise, such defendant would be vulnerable to artful forum shopping.

A second consideration in assessing burdens attendant to trying an action in the forum state is the ease of access to the alternative forum. . . . But the majority makes no argument that plaintiff would be burdened by having to travel to Nevada to litigate her claim. Such argument would be difficult in light of Nevada's proximity to plaintiff's residence.

2. Such fact would be relevant to determining whether California could assert limited jurisdiction in, for example, a cause of action alleging defendant's fraud in dealing with local manufacturers. It simply is not relevant to an action alleging negligent driving in Nevada.

Consideration of relative burdens upon plaintiff and defendant resulting from trying this action in California as opposed to Nevada thus clearly suggests Nevada as the more appropriate jurisdiction.

3. *California's Interest in Assuming Jurisdiction*

The majority asserts—without explanation—that "California has an interest in providing a forum since plaintiff is a California resident."

A forum's interest in assuming jurisdiction is a factor often weighed in determining whether jurisdiction may be exercised within the constraints of due process. However, a forum's interest is generally based upon much more than plaintiff's mere residence within the forum state. . . .

Plaintiff's circumstances here, and California's resultant interests in providing a forum, are manifestly distinguishable from *McGee*. Defendant did not engage in any California activity giving rise to the cause of action; rather, plaintiff voluntarily left her state and became involved in a Nevada accident. Further, plaintiff has made no showing she would be at a "severe disadvantage" if required to litigate in Nevada. Finally, the substance of plaintiff's claim *is* obviously sufficient to justify the costs of Nevada litigation.

Our busy courts should have little interest in assuring each resident who leaves the state that he may return to litigate every wrong incurred in his travels. The day of the flag following one to Tripoli has passed. . . .

NOTE

Undoubtedly the Cornelison court would have decided against jurisdiction had the plaintiff not been a California resident. Why? Does the plaintiff's residence bear on the "territoriality" limitation? on fairness? After World-Wide Volkswagen, what is the proper role of plaintiff's residence in a jurisdiction case? See Keeton v. Hustler Magazine, Inc., __ U.S. __, 104 S.Ct. 1473 (1984), p. 105 supra.

NOTE ON STATUTORY DEVELOPMENTS

The International Shoe case and its progeny made it clear that the scope of a state's long-arm jurisdiction is considerably greater than had hitherto been supposed. It remained for each state to determine the extent to which authorization would be given to its courts to operate in these new areas. There have been numerous developments.

In a few cases, the courts themselves took the initiative by greatly broadening their interpretation of the "doing business" phrase in existing jurisdiction statutes. Typical is Henry R. Jahn & Son, Inc. v. Superior Court, 49 Cal.2d 855, 323 P.2d 437 (1958) where the court held that "doing business," as used in the California statute, imposed no stricter limitation than the due process clause. See also Wanamaker v. Louis, 153 F.Supp. 195 (D.Md.1957); S. Howes, Inc. v. W.P. Milling Co., 277 P.2d 655 (Okl.1954); Note, Recent Interpretations of Doing Business Statutes, 44 Iowa L.Rev. 345 (1959).

Most developments have been statutory. One type of statute does no more than permit or direct courts to exercise jurisdiction to the extent permitted by due process. See, e.g., West's Ann.Cal.Civ.Proc. Code § 410.10 ("A Court of this state may exercise jurisdiction on any basis not inconsistent with the constitution of this state or of the United States."); R.I.Gen.Laws 1969, § 9–5–33 (jurisdiction shall be exercised over non-residents having necessary "minimum contacts" with the state "in every case not contrary to the provisions of the constitution or laws of the United States").

The great majority of long-arm jurisdiction statutes are more detailed and specific, providing more guidance with regard to the activities or contacts that will serve as jurisdictional bases. They tend to stop short of the broadest limits of jurisdiction allowed by the due process clause. An example is the Illinois statute enacted in 1955 and widely followed by other states. This statute, originally section 17 of the Civil Practice Act, now section 2–209 of the Code of Civil Procedure, as amended, provides in part:

§ 2–209. Act submitting to jurisdiction—Process. (a) Any person, whether or not a citizen or resident of this State, who in person or through an agent does any of the acts hereinafter enumerated, thereby submits such person, and, if an individual, his or her personal representative, to the jurisdiction of the courts of this State as to any cause of action arising from the doing of any of such acts:

(1) The transaction of any business within this State;

(2) The commission of a tortious act within this State;

(3) The ownership, use, or possession of any real estate situated in this State;

(4) Contracting to insure any person, property or risk located within this State at the time of contracting;

(5) With respect to actions of dissolution of marriage and legal separation, the maintenance in this State of a matrimonial domicile at the time this cause of action arose or the commission in this State of any act giving rise to the cause of action.

(b) Service of process upon any person who is subject to the jurisdiction of the courts of this State, as provided in this Section, may be made by personally serving the summons upon the defendant outside this State, as provided in this Act, with the same force and effect as though summons had been personally served within this State.

(c) Only causes of action arising from acts enumerated herein may be asserted against a defendant in an action in which jurisdiction over him or her is based upon this Section.

(d) Nothing herein contained limits or affects the right to serve any process in any other manner now or hereafter provided by law.

————

Among the problems of interpretation of the original statute, three important ones surfaced quickly: (1) May a nonresident defendant defeat the Illinois court's jurisdiction at the threshold of the action by denying commission of the act alleged to be the basis for jurisdiction? (2) Are statutory extensions of long-arm jurisdiction to be applied retroactively to causes of action arising before enactment of the new provisions? (3) When the basis for jurisdiction is "commission of a tortious act within this State," is it present when the nonresident committed an act outside Illinois (e.g., made a defective product) that failed and caused injury within Illinois? The Nelson and Gray cases decided the first question in the negative and the latter two questions in the affirmative.

————

NELSON V. MILLER, 11 Ill.2d 378, 143 N.E.2d 673 (1957): D, a Wisconsin appliance vendor, dispatched an employee to deliver a gas stove to P in Illinois. While assisting in unloading the stove P sustained an injury to his hand through the employee's negligence. Thereafter, Illinois adopted its long-arm statute subjecting non-residents to the personal jurisdiction of its courts on any cause of action arising from "commission of a tortious act" within the state. The court held that the statute (a) applied retroactively and (b) gave the court power to hear the case as soon as it was determined that the defendant was responsible for an act or omission in the state that was claimed to be tortious. In other words, a finding that the defendant had actually committed a tort was not a condition precedent to the court having power to hear the case. Both of these conclusions probably represent the view of the majority of courts in this country. As to the retroactivity question, see McGee v. International Life Ins. Co. (p. 72, supra) and Note, Retroactive Expansion of State Court Jurisdiction over Persons, 63 Colum.L.Rev. 1105 (1963).

In Gray v. American Radiator & Standard Sanitary Corp., 22 Ill.2d 432, 176 N.E.2d 761 (1961) [p. 101, note (1), supra], the Illinois Supreme Court held that the causing of tortious injury in Illinois by means of an act done elsewhere is the "commission of a tortious act within this State" within the meaning of the statute.

NOTES

(1) For a general discussion of the Illinois statute, see Currie, The Growth of the Long Arm: Eight Years of Extended Jurisdiction in Illinois, 1963 U.Ill.L.Forum 533; Cleary and Seder, Extended Jurisdictional Bases for the Illinois Courts, 50 Nw.U.L.Rev. 599 (1955).

(2) Section 8 of the Uniform Parentage Act of 1973 provides that for the purpose of an action brought under the Act to establish paternity:

> A person who has sexual intercourse in this State thereby submits to the jurisdiction of the courts of this State as to an action brought under this Act with respect to a child who may have been conceived by that act of intercourse.

Once Illinois had shown the way, long-arm statutes proliferated. In 1962 a Uniform Interstate and International Procedure Act, 13 U.L.A. 279 (1975) was promulgated. New York enacted a comprehensive statute that is notable for, among other features, expressly excluding defamation actions from its coverage. This exclusion was clearly attributable to sensitivity about First Amendment protections that might be compromised if plaintiffs could too readily assert long-arm jurisdiction over the media. See New York Times v. Sullivan, 375 U.S. 803 (1964). As embodied in the New York Civil Practice Law and Rules, the relevant provisions are:

CPLR § 301. *Jurisdiction over persons, property or status*

A court may exercise such jurisdiction over persons, property, or status as might have been exercised heretofore.

CPLR § 302. *Personal jurisdiction by acts of non-domiciliaries*

(a) Acts which are the basis of jurisdiction. A court may exercise personal jurisdiction over any non-domiciliary or his executor or administrator, as to a cause of action arising from any of the acts enumerated in this section, in the same manner as if he were a domiciliary of the state, if, in person or through an agent, he:

1. transacts any business within the state or contracts anywhere to supply goods or services in the state; or

2. commits a tortious act within the state, except as to a cause of action for defamation of character arising from the act; or

3. commits a tortious act without the state causing injury to person or property within the state, except as to a cause of action for defamation of character arising from the act, if he

(i) regularly does or solicits business, or engages in any other persistent course of conduct, or derives substantial revenue from goods used or consumed or services rendered, in the state, or

(ii) expects or should reasonably expect the act to have consequences in the state and derives substantial revenue from interstate or international commerce; or

4. owns, uses or possesses any real property situated within the state.

(b) *Personal jurisdiction over non-resident defendant.* A court in any matrimonial action or family court proceeding involving a demand for support or alimony may exercise personal jurisdiction over the respondent or defendant notwithstanding the fact that he or she no longer is a resident or domiciliary of this state, or over his or her executor or administrator, if the party seeking support is a resident of or domiciled in this state at the time such demand is made, provided that this state was the matrimonial domicile of the parties before their separation, or the defendant abandoned the plaintiff in this state, or the obligation to pay support or alimony or alimony accrued under the laws of this state or under an agreement executed in this state.

NOTES

(1) Whereas the New York courts have given § 301 an expansive interpretation (see, e.g., Bryant v. Finnish Airlines, Inc., 15 N.Y.2d 426, 208 N.E.2d 439 (1965); ABKCO Industries, Inc. v. Lennon, 52 A.D.2d 435, 384 N.Y.S.2d 781 (1st Dep't, 1976), holding Ringo Starr of the Beatles subject to personal jurisdiction on causes unrelated to his New York activities), they have tended to interpret § 302 narrowly. Thus, in interpreting the phrase "transacts any business" within the state, "the courts have tended toward an unbending insistence on the defendant's purposeful, claim-connected activities within the state, either in person or through an agent." Homburger and Laufer, Expanding Jurisdiction over Foreign Torts: The 1966 Amendment of New York's Long Arm Statute, 16 Buff.L.Rev. 67, 69 (1966); see also Homburger and Laufer, Appearance and Jurisdictional Motions in New York, 14 Buff.L.Rev. 374 (1965).

In Longines-Wittnauer Watch Co. v. Barnes & Reinecke, Inc., 15 N.Y.2d 443, 209 N.E.2d 68 (1965), the suit was for breach of warranty with regard to machinery shipped to New York by the Illinois seller after contract negotiations in both states, execution in New York of a supplementary contract and rendition of services in installing and testing the machine. The Illinois seller was held to have transacted business in New York within the meaning of CPLR § 302(a)(1) despite its argument that its preliminary and subsequent activities in New York should be disregarded since the machinery was sold f.o.b. Chicago. Other cases where a defendant was found to have transacted business in New York include George Reiner & Co. v. Schwartz, 41 N.Y.2d 648, 394 N.Y.S.2d 844, 363 N.E.2d 551 (1977) (defendant came to New York to negotiate his employment contract); Hi-Fashion Wigs, Inc. v. Peter Hammond Advertising, Inc., 32 N.Y.2d 583, 347 N.Y.S.2d 47, 300 N.E.2d 421 (1973) (defendant personally delivered in New York a document of guarantee that had been drafted elsewhere) and Parke-Bernet Galleries, Inc. v. Franklyn, 26 N.Y.2d 13, 308 N.Y.S.2d 337, 256 N.E.2d 506 (1973) (while in California, defendant received and transmitted bids over an open telephone line during an auction held in New York).

In Singer v. Walker, decided with the Longines-Wittnauer case, cert. denied sub nom. Estwing Mfg. Co. v. Singer, 382 U.S. 905 (1965), an "unbreakable" geologist's hammer, bought in New York, fragmented while being used in Connecticut and a chip injured the right eye of the boy who wielded it. Jurisdiction in New York over the defendant nonresident manufacturing company was sustained, not under the "commits a tortious act" provision, but on the ground that the defendant's shipment of substantial quantities of its products into New York as a result of selling activities there constituted "transacting business" within CPLR § 302(a)(1).

The "transacts any business" phrase has been applied to non-commercial transactions. See, e.g., Von Wagenberg v. Von Wagenberg, 241 Md. 154, 215 A.2d 812 (1966), cert. denied 385 U.S. 833 (1966) (execution of separation agreement in New York); Elman v. Belson, 32 A.D.2d 422, 302 N.Y.S.2d 961 (2d Dep't 1969) (retainer of New York attorneys to bring suit in New York).

(2) Originally, CPLR § 302(a) contained only a single tort provision (§ 302(a)(2)) which was directed to one who "commits a tortious act within the state . . . ." It will be recalled that an essentially similar phrase in the Illinois statute has been interpreted by the Illinois courts to apply to one who causes tortious injury within Illinois by means of an act done elsewhere. Gray v. American Radiator & Standard Sanitary Corp., 22 Ill.2d 432, 176 N.E.2d 761 (1961) (p. 101, note (1), supra). In Feathers v. McLucas, 15 N.Y.2d 443, 209 N.E.2d 66 (1966) (decided with Longines-Wittnauer and Singer), the New York court took a different view. In that case, the plaintiffs sued for personal and property damages from the explosion in New York of a tractor-drawn propane tank manufactured in Kansas by the defendant. The tank was mounted on wheels and sold to a Pennsylvania interstate truck carrier in that state. There was no evidence that defendant transacted in New York any of the sales of steel products that accounted for millions of dollars a year in nationwide business. Emphasizing that New York's long-arm statute conferred personal jurisdiction on a nonresident who "commits a tortious act *within* the state," the court held the Kansas manufacturer not amenable for its acts *"without* the state which [caused] injury within the state." The New York legislature then amended CPLR § 302(a) by adding present Subsection (3).

(3) CPLR § 302(a)(3) has given rise to problems of application in situations where the injury involved is non-physical in nature. A case in point is American Eutectic Welding Alloys Sales Co. v. Dytron Alloys Corp., 439 F.2d 428 (2d Cir. 1971), noted in 72 Colum.L.Rev. 191 (1972), which held that no "injury" within the meaning of this section had taken place in New York when a defendant from a point outside that state induced employees of plaintiff, a corporation whose principal place of business was in New York, to break their contract of employment with plaintiff and to "use confidential information to woo away plaintiff's customers" in Kentucky and Penn-

sylvania. To be sure, the defendant could have reasonably expected that its activities would have "consequences" in New York but, within the meaning of the statute, it did not cause "injury" there. See also Spectacular Promotions, Inc. v. Radio Station WING, 272 F.Supp. 734 (E.D.N.Y.1967), holding that in a case involving unfair competition no "injury" within the meaning of the section occurs in New York unless that was the state where the plaintiff actually lost business.

(4) An amendment to CPLR § 302(a)(1) in 1979 extended long-arm jurisdiction to nonresidents who contract outside the state to supply goods or services within the state. That abrogated the so-called "mere shipment" rule to the effect that a nonresident shipping goods into New York pursuant to a contract made outside the state was not subject to jurisdiction under the "transacts any business" language of the statute. See, e.g., Kramer v. Vogl, 17 N.Y.2d 27, 215 N.E.2d 159 (1966); McKee Electric Co., Inc. v. Rauland-Borg Corp., 20 N.Y.2d 377, 283 N.Y.S.2d 34, 229 N.E.2d 604 (1967). Also, nonresidents who wholly fail to perform contracts made outside the state that call for in-state performance become subject to long-arm jurisdiction.

Many states authorize long-arm jurisdiction on the following bases:

"Acting as a director, manager, trustee, or other officer of a corporation incorporated under the laws of, or having its principal place of business within this state." Mich.Comp.L.Ann. § 600.705.

NOTE

Could a literal application of any of these provisions lead on occasion to an unconstitutional result?

Wisconsin has enacted a most detailed and comprehensive catalogue of jurisdictional bases. Wis.Stat.Ann. § 262.05. See Foster, Expanding Jurisdiction over Non Residents, 1959 Wisc.Bar Bull. (Supp.). A few of the bases enumerated in Section 262.05 are:

(4) Local injury; foreign act. In any action claiming injury to person or property within this state arising out of an act or omission outside this state by the defendant, provided in addition that at the time of injury either:

(a) Solicitation or service activities were carried on within this state by or on behalf of the defendant; or

(b) Products, materials or things processed, serviced or manufactured by the defendant were used or consumed within this state in the ordinary course of trade.

(5) Local services, goods or contracts. In any action which:

(a) Arises out of a promise, made anywhere to the plaintiff or to some third party for the plaintiff's benefit, by the defendant to perform services within this state or to pay for services to be performed in this state by the plaintiff; or . . .

(e) Relates to goods, documents of title, or other things of value actually received by the plaintiff in this state from the defendant without regard to where delivery to carrier occurred.

(6) Local property. In any action which arises out of:

(a) A promise, made anywhere to the plaintiff or to some third party for the plaintiff's benefit, by the defendant to create in either party an interest in, or protect, acquire, dispose of, use, rent, own, control or possess by either party real property situated in this state; or . . . .

NOTES

(1) It will be observed that the statutes set out above do not in terms distinguish between natural persons and corporations in delineating the bases of personal jurisdiction. The courts adopt a similar approach. All bases for exercise of judicial jurisdiction over an individual, with the exception of presence, domicile and nationality or citizenship, will give a state judicial jurisdiction over a foreign corporation. Restatement, Second, Conflict of Laws §§ 42–52.

(2) Courts have usually held themselves without authority to exercise jurisdiction on bases not recognized at common law unless authorized to do so by statute. Restatement, Second, Conflict of Laws § 29.

(3) In a diversity action, a federal court has been held bound, within constitutional limits, to follow state standards, in determining the amenability of a defendant to in personam jurisdiction. Arrowsmith v. United Press International, 320 F.2d 219 (2d Cir. 1963), which overruled Jaftex Corporation v. Randolph Mills, Inc., 282 F.2d 508 (2d Cir. 1960), noted, 77 Harv.L.Rev. 559 (1964).

(4) Substantial treatments of the subject of jurisdiction are: D. Currie, The Growth of the Long Arm: Eight Years of Extended Jurisdiction in Illinois, 1963 U.Ill.L.F. 533, 549; Hazard, A General Theory of State-Court Jurisdiction, 1965 Supreme Court Review 241 (Kurland ed.); von Mehren and Trautman, Jurisdiction to Adjudicate: A Suggested Analysis, 79 Harv.L.Rev. 1121 (1966).

"DERIVATIVE" JURISDICTION OVER FOREIGN CORPORATIONS

A question of some importance is the extent to which a state has jurisdiction over a parent corporation by reason of the fact that it has jurisdiction over the parent's subsidiary corporation. Analytically, this question has two aspects. The first is whether ownership by the parent of the subsidiary's stock is enough to give jurisdiction over the parent to a state in which the subsidiary has taken steps to consent to jurisdiction. And the second is whether and when the activities of the subsidiary in a state will give that state jurisdiction over the parent. There is also the converse problem of the extent to which a state has jurisdiction over a subsidiary corporation by reason of the fact that it has jurisdiction over the parent.

It seems clear that mere stock ownership—even one hundred per cent stock ownership—of the subsidiary is not enough to give jurisdiction over the parent to a state which has jurisdiction over the subsidiary. Cannon Manufacturing Co. v. Cudahy Packing Co., 267 U.S. 333 (1925); O. S. C. Corporation v. Toshiba America, Inc., 491 F.2d 1064 (9th Cir. 1974); Restatement, Second, Conflict of Laws § 52, Comment *b*. On the other hand, jurisdiction over the parent will exist if the parent so controls and dominates the subsidiary as in effect to disregard the latter's separate corporate existence. Matters that the courts will consider in determining whether the separate corporate existence of the subsidiary has been adequately preserved is whether the subsidiary has its own assets, advertising, employees, payroll and accounting and whether its directors and headquarters are different from those of the parent. Vitro Electronics v. Milgray Electronics, Inc., 255 Md. 498, 258 A.2d 749 (1969); Public Administrator of the County of New York v. Royal Bank of Canada, 19 N.Y.2d 127, 224 N.E.2d 877 (1967); Taca International Airlines v. Rolls-Royce of England Limited, 15 N.Y.2d 97, 204 N.E.2d 329 (1965). Jurisdiction over the subsidiary has also been held to bring jurisdiction over the parent where the parent has no function other than owning the subsidiary's stock. United States v. Weaving & Belting Co., 155 F.Supp. 454 (S.D. N.Y.1956); cf. McPherson v. Penn Central Transportation Co., 390 F.Supp. 943 (D.Conn.1975).

Jurisdiction over the parent will frequently be found to exist even when the separate existence of the subsidiary has been faithfully maintained. This result is reached on the ground that the activities of the subsidiary in the state will provide a basis of jurisdiction over the parent if these activities (a) would provide a basis of jurisdiction over the subsidiary and (b) can be said to have been done in the course of the parent's business and in its behalf. See, e.g., Frummer v. Hilton Hotels International, Inc., 19 N.Y.2d 533, 227 N.E.2d 851 (1967). This approach is not surprising since the parent could, of course, be subjected to the jurisdiction of a state by reason of activities carried on there in its behalf and at its direction by another corporation with which the parent had no stock relationship. See, e.g., Florio v. Powder Power Tool Corp., 248 F.2d 367 (3d Cir. 1957); Kahn v. Maico Co., 216 F.2d 233 (4th Cir. 1954). Such an "agency" is indeed frequently found in the case of consignment arrangements and control of price, of merchandising or of advertising. Crucible Inc. v. Stora Kopparbergs Bergslags A B, 403 F.Supp. 9 (W.D.Pa.1975); Fielding v. Superior Court, 111 Cal.App.2d 490, 244 P.2d 968 (1952), cert. denied 244 U.S. 897 (1952); Duraladd Products Corp. v. Superior Court, 134 Cal.App.2d 226, 285 P.2d 699 (1955). It may be suspected that the courts are more likely to find an "agency" for jurisdictional purposes in a situation where the activities are those of a subsidiary rather than of a corporation in which the defendant has no stock interest. Compare Frummer v. Hilton Hotels International, Inc., supra, with Delagi v. Volkswagenwerk AG of Wolfsburg, 29 N.Y.2d 426, 328 N.Y.S.2d 653, 278 N.E.2d 895 (1972).

In the converse situation, jurisdiction over a parent corporation may give jurisdiction over a subsidiary if the separate corporate existence of each has not been adequately maintained or if the parent has acted within the state as the subsidiary's "agent." Frazier v. Alabama Motor Club, 349 F.2d 456 (5th Cir. 1965); Freeman v. Gordon & Breach, Science Publishers, 398 F.Supp. 519 (S.D.N.Y.1975); Farha v. Signal Companies, 216 Kan. 471, 532 P.2d 1330 (1975).

For a thorough discussion of the circumstances in which jurisdiction over a subsidiary corporation will give a United States court jurisdiction over a foreign multinational, see Bulova Watch Co. v. K. Hattori & Co., 508 F.Supp. 1322 (E.D.N.Y.1981). Jurisdiction over the parent Japanese multinational was found to exist. The court said:

> An important question in assessing presence for jurisdictional purposes is whether a multinational has reached a state in its evolution when it can be said that its sales and marketing subsidiaries truly have a "life of their own." C. Kindleberger, American Business Abroad, 183 . . . Sales and marketing subsidiaries generally are more likely to be controlled by the parent and less likely to develop lives of their own than those involved in manufacturing . . .

> . . . What is involved here is a series of relatively young sales and marketing subsidiaries abroad, whose purpose is to market a single product—timepieces. There is no manufacturing or product research done by any of these subsidiaries. They do not seem to have developed third-country trade except for the purpose of selling Hattori's Japanese manufactured goods . . .

> . . . The holding in this case is simply that while a subsidiary establishes and expands a parent's market position then, so long as that activity is being conducted, and with respect to those activities furthering the parent's ends, the parent is doing business in New York . . .

NOTE ON PARTNERSHIPS AND ASSOCIATIONS

Extraterritorial enforcement of in personam judgments against partnerships and other unincorporated associations raises a few special points stemming from historical oddities in local law treatment of those entities. One question, for example, is whether personal service upon a partner gives jurisdiction to bind partnership property outside the state. If the firm were owned by an individual, his presence in the state would be a sufficient basis for a valid personal judgment that could be enforced against his firm's property elsewhere. On the other hand, if the nonresident firm were incorporated, mere presence on personal business of a shareholder, officer, or director would not furnish a basis for an in personam judgment against the corporation. See Riverside & Dan River Cotton Mills v. Menefee, 237 U.S 189, 35 S.Ct. 579 (1915); Goldey v. Morning News of New Haven, 156 U.S. 518 (1895). Shall a partnership be treated as amenable in the manner of an individual, or not amenable by analogy to a corporation? Further, under what circumstances may the members of a partnership be bound as to their personal property by a judgment against the firm?

RESTATEMENT, SECOND, CONFLICT OF LAWS: *

§ 40.   Partnerships or Other Unincorporated Associations

(1) A state in which a partnership or other unincorporated association is subject to suit in the firm or common name has power to exercise judicial jurisdiction over the partnership or association if under the circumstances it could exercise judicial jurisdiction over an individual . . . ..

(2) A valid judgment rendered against a partnership or association is a binding adjudication as to the liability of the partnership or association with respect to its assets in every state.

Comment: . . .

d.   *Effect of judgment.*   A valid judgment rendered against a partnership or other unincorporated association under the circumstances stated in Subsection (1) will be recognized and enforced in other states, and, as between States of the United States, this result is required by full faith and credit. An action to enforce the judgment may be maintained against the partnership or association in another state, provided that it is subject to the judicial jurisdiction of that state and by the local law of that state may be sued in its firm or common name. If by the local law of the second state the partnership or association is not subject to suit in its firm or common name, the action to enforce the judgment may be maintained against the members individually, but recovery will be permitted to be had only out of firm, as opposed to individual, property.

NOTES

(1) In Sugg v. Thornton, 132 U.S. 524 (1889), personal service was had upon one member of a partnership and notice as provided by the state statute was sent to the other partner outside the state. The judgment rendered, purporting to be a personal judgment only against the partner personally served and a judgment against "the partnership as a distinct legal entity", was upheld against a due process attack. So far as the non-appearing part-

---

* Quoted with the permission of the
copyright owner, The American Law Institute.

ner who received only statutory service was concerned, the judgment "bound the firm assets only, and could not be proceeded on by execution against his individual property."

(2) See Kaplan, Suits Against Unincorporated Association under the Federal Rules of Civil Procedure, 53 Mich.L.Rev. 945 (1955).

E. CONTINUANCE OF JURISDICTION

RESTATEMENT, SECOND, CONFLICT OF LAWS:*

§ 26. Continuance of Jurisdiction

If a state obtains judicial jurisdiction over a party to an action, the jurisdiction continues throughout all subsequent proceedings which arise out of the original cause of action. Reasonable notice and reasonable opportunity to be heard must be given the party at each new step in the proceeding.

MICHIGAN TRUST CO. v. FERRY

Supreme Court of the United States, 1913.
228 U.S. 346, 33 S.Ct. 550, 57 L.Ed. 867.

MR. JUSTICE HOLMES delivered the opinion of the court:

These are suits brought in the Circuit Court for the District of Utah upon decrees of the Probate Court of Ottawa, Michigan. The defendant demurred to the complaints, the Circuit Court sustained the demurrers and gave judgments for the defendant, and these judgments were affirmed by the Circuit Court of Appeals. . . .

William M. Ferry died in 1867 domiciled in Ottawa County, Michigan. His will was proved, and the defendant, Edward P. Ferry, was appointed executor by the Ottawa Probate Court, qualified and entered upon his duties. In 1878 he removed to Utah and becoming incompetent was put under the guardianship of two sons, W. Mont Ferry and Edward S. Ferry, in 1892. In 1903 residuary legatees and devisees petitioned the Michigan Probate Court that the defendant be removed from his office of executor, that he be ordered to account for the unadministered residue of the estate and that the Michigan Trust Company be appointed administrator de bonis non with the will annexed. Notice of the petition and time and place of the hearing was given by publication and also was given to the defendant and his guardians personally in Utah. The guardians by order of the Utah

* Quoted with the permission of the copyright owner, The American Law Institute.

court appeared and asked for the appointment of a guardian ad litem, which was made . . . There were various proceedings the end of which was that the plaintiff was appointed administrator de bonis non . . . and it was decreed that the defendant was indebted to the estate for $1,220,473.41. The defendant being entitled to one-fourth of the above sum as residuary legatee, he was declared liable for $915,355.08 and ordered to pay it over within sixty days to the Michigan Trust Company. . . .

Ordinarily jurisdiction over a person is based on the power of the sovereign asserting it to seize that person and imprison him to await the sovereign's pleasure. But when that power exists and is asserted by service at the beginning of a cause, or if the party submits to the jurisdiction in whatever form may be required, we dispense with the necessity of maintaining the physical power and attribute the same force to the judgment or decree whether the party remain within the jurisdiction or not. This is one of the decencies of civilization that no one would dispute. . . . This is true not only of ordinary actions but of proceedings like the present. It is within the power of a State to make the whole administration of the estate a single proceeding, to provide that one who has undertaken it within the jurisdiction shall be subject to the order of the court in the matter until the administration is closed by distribution, and, on the same principle, that he shall be required to account for and distribute all that he receives, by the order of the Probate Court. . . .

It follows from what we have said that a petition to the Probate Court that the defendant be ordered to account covered all his receipts as executor and that notice of the petition was notice that the accounting would have that scope. The decree upon the account was made with full jurisdiction and . . . could be sued upon . . . and was entitled to full faith and credit elsewhere. . . .

Judgment reversed. . . .

NOTES

(1) In Fitzsimmons v. Johnson, 90 Tenn. 416, 17 S.W. 100 (1891), a decree of an Ohio court against the defendant, as executor qualified in Ohio, was enforced in Tennessee, even though the proceedings to reverse the initial judgment of the Ohio court, approving the defendant's account and discharging him, were instituted more than twenty years after the entry of that judgment, and the only service of process on the defendant, a nonresident of Ohio, was by publication. See also Blumle v. Kramer, 14 Okl. 366, 79 P. 215 (1904), involving jurisdiction to enter a judgment for a deficiency following a mortgage foreclosure, and after the defendant had moved away from the state.

(2) In Ohlquist v. Nordstrom, 143 Misc. 502, 257 N.Y.S. 711 (1932), aff'd 238 App.Div. 766, 261 N.Y.S. 1039 (1933), affirmed 262 N.Y. 696, 188 N.E. 125 (1933), A recovered a judgment in New York against B and C as joint tortfeasors, whereupon C removed his residence to Pennsylvania. B paid the entire judgment and began the present suit for contribution, serving C's at-

torneys in New York and C personally outside the state. The service was held effective. Cf. New York Life Insurance Co. v. Dunlevy, p. 144, infra.

(3) Chapman v. Chapman, 284 App.Div. 504, 132 N.Y.S.2d 707 (3d Dep't 1954), noted in 55 Colum.L.Rev. 240 (1955). Action in New York to enforce a $25,000 Vermont judgment for alimony. Initially, the wife had brought an action for separation and support in a Vermont court. The husband had been served with process in New York and had entered a personal appearance in the action by a Vermont attorney. Thereafter, the wife sought leave to amend her action to one for divorce. The court granted the wife's motion on the same day that it permitted the husband's attorney to withdraw from the case. Also on the same day the court, in the absence of the husband's attorney, proceeded to hear the case on the merits and granted the wife a divorce and a lump sum payment of $25,000. *Held:* The Vermont judgment should be denied enforcement on the ground that it had been rendered in violation of due process requirements. By amending her complaint to seek a divorce, the wife introduced a new cause of action. In Vermont, separation and divorce are dealt with in different statutes although the grounds for obtaining these two forms of relief are the same. The court also cited a New York case for the proposition that "[t]he action for absolute divorce is entirely different in every respect from an action for separation" and that amending one to the other is "changing entirely the whole scope of the action." Should the due process requirements for continuing jurisdiction depend on whether either the state of rendition of the judgment or the state of enforcement holds that the amendment proffers a "different" cause of action for some local law procedural purpose?

SECTION 3.   JURISDICTION OVER "THINGS"

RESTATEMENT, SECOND, CONFLICT OF LAWS: *

Chapter 3, Introductory Note to Topic 2:

Introductory Note: . . . every valid exercise of judicial jurisdiction affects the interests of persons. It is possible, however, to affect the interests of persons in different ways, and it is convenient to divide the subject of judicial jurisdiction into three main categories: jurisdiction over persons, jurisdiction over things and jurisdiction over status. . . . When one or more of . . . [the various bases for the exercise of judicial jurisdiction over persons] exists, a personal judgment may be rendered against the defendant. The effect of such a judgment, if it is one for money, is to make the defendant a judgment debtor of the plaintiff. This debt may be enforced against any property in the state subject to execution which the defendant then owns or subsequently acquires. An action to recover this debt may likewise be maintained against the defendant either in the same state

* Quoted with the permission of the copyright owner, The American Law Institute.

or elsewhere. A personal judgment may also take the form of an equitable decree ordering the defendant either to do something or to refrain from action. In such a case, the defendant may be punished for contempt if he fails to obey the court's order.

Even though personal jurisdiction over the defendant is lacking, the state may affect any interests he may have in things subject to its jurisdiction. A judgment rendered in such a proceeding binds only the defendant's interests in the specific thing at which it is directed and thus has a more limited effect than a judgment rendered against the defendant personally. All that a defendant risks in a proceeding directed against a particular thing, if he is at no time personally subject to the judicial jurisdiction of the state, is the loss of his interests therein. An in personam judgment, on the other hand, may be enforced against any and all of his property which is not exempt from execution.

Where a thing is subject to the judicial jurisdiction of a state, an action may be brought to affect the interests in the thing of all persons in the world. Such an action is commonly referred to as a proceeding in rem. Or, as is usually the case, the action may be brought to affect the interests in the thing of particular persons only, in which case it is commonly referred to as a proceeding quasi in rem. . . .

Proceedings quasi in rem are of two types. In the first type the plaintiff asserts an interest in a thing, and seeks to have his interest established against the claim of a designated person or persons. Of this type are actions to recover possession of land or to establish title to land, such as an action of ejectment, or one to quiet title or to remove a cloud on title, where the court has jurisdiction to give the relief asked because of its power over the land even though it has no power over the adverse claimant. Of this type also is an action to foreclose a mortgage.

In the second type of proceeding quasi in rem, the plaintiff does not assert that he has an interest in the thing, but asserts a claim against the defendant personally and seeks, by attachment or garnishment, to apply the thing to the satisfaction of his claim against the defendant. . . .

Recent decisions by the Supreme Court of the United States have seriously undermined the traditional distinctions between jurisdiction over persons and jurisdiction over things. A total merger of the concepts would be unfortunate, since the effect of a judgment still depends in important respects on whether it rests on jursidiction over the defendant's person.

A. LAND

A classic statement of the nature of a proceeding *in rem* was provided by Justice Holmes in Tyler v. Judges of the Court of Registration, 175 Mass. 71, 76, 55 N.E. 812, 814 (1900):

"If . . . [the object of the suit] is to bar indifferently all who might be minded to make an objection of any sort against the right sought to be established, and if any one in the world has a right to be heard on the strength of alleging facts which, if true, show an inconsistent interest, the proceeding is in rem. . . . All proceedings, like all rights, are really against persons. Whether they are proceedings or rights in rem depends on the number of persons affected."

The traditional concept of jurisdiction over land was based on the theory that only the state where the land was located had power to deal with it effectively; hence, only the situs state was thought to have jurisdiction to issue decrees "directly" affecting title to land. However, some courts permitted themselves to issue decrees ordering the defendant to pay damages with regard to foreign real estate, or even to convey interests in land outside the state. Penn v. Lord Baltimore, 1 Ves.Sr. 444, 27 Eng.Rep. 1132 (Ch.1750) is perhaps the most famous example of the latter remedy. The principle was approved in Massie v. Watts, 6 Cranch 148, 3 L.Ed. 181 (1810), Chief Justice Marshall declaring that where the defendant "is liable to the plaintiff, either in consequence of contract, or as trustee, or as the holder of a legal title acquired by any species of mala fides practiced on the plaintiff, the principles of equity give a court jurisdiction wherever the person may be found, and the circumstance, that a question of title may be involved in the inquiry, and may even constitute the essential point on which the case depends, does not seem sufficient to arrest that jurisdiction."

NOTES

(1) Should the fact that a great many people or "all the world" will be bound by the judgment, make it possible to utilize a more wholesale type of notification of the suit than if only one person is defendant? For the type of notice to adverse claimants, known and unknown, required by registration statutes, see McKinney's N.Y. Real Property Law § 385. Generally, as to notice, see Mullane v. Central-Hanover Bank & Trust Co., 339 U.S. 306, 70 S.Ct. 652 (1950), p. 174, infra. The Supreme Court has upheld state statutes providing that title to real property within the state may be determined in a suit in which a non-resident defendant is served only by publication. See Arndt v. Griggs, 134 U.S. 316 (1890). But such decisions seem questionable in the light of more recent cases. See p. 181, note 1, infra.

(2) A buyer of land is entitled to a decree for the conveyance of land in the state of the situs if the court has been made competent to grant such relief, even though the vendor is served outside the state. Garfein v. McInnis, 248 N.Y. 261, 162 N.E. 73 (1928).

(3) A deed to land, executed by the owner in accordance with a decree of a foreign court, will be given effect as a valid conveyance in the state where the land lies. Deschenes v. Tallman, 248 N.Y. 33, 161 N.E. 321 (1928). Where a court, having jurisdiction over the defendant, orders a conveyance of foreign land, what effect will be given to the decree in the state where the land is located, if no conveyance is actually made? See Fall v. Eastin, set out at p. 255, infra.

COMBS v. COMBS

Supreme Court of Kentucky, 1933.
249 Ky. 155, 60 S.W.2d 368, 89 A.L.R. 1095.

THOMAS, J. The appellant, A. T. Combs, who was one of the defendants below, became indebted to the appellees and plaintiffs below, in a considerable sum. A lien to secure it was created on a tract of land in Washington county, Ark. Plaintiffs were and are residents of Kentucky and of other states, and all of them were and are nonresidents of the state of Arkansas. Appellant's brother, who was a joint defendant with him, is a resident of this commonwealth, and this action was filed by plaintiffs in the Breathitt circuit court against appellant and his brother to obtain a personal judgment against them for the amount of the debt. Personal process could not [be] and was not served on appellant for a considerable time after he was proceeded against and made a defendant in the action. During that time he filed an equity action in the chancery court of Washington county, Ark., in which the land in lien was situated, against the plaintiffs in this action, and proceeded against them exclusively by constructive process in accordance with the prescribed practice of the Arkansas forum. In his petition in that court he set forth the facts creating the indebtedness, as well as the lien on his land to secure it, and stated that he had paid part of the debt, leaving a named sum as the balance due, and that the lien to secure it was a cloud on the title to his land which he desired released, and he asked that court to enter judgment fixing the amount of the balance due by him to plaintiffs in this action (but defendants in that one) and to permit him to pay that amount into that court to be followed by a decree canceling the lien on his land. The Arkansas practice for that kind of procedure was followed, and upon submission, without any of the defendants therein entering their appearance in any manner, that court adjudged that plaintiff therein, appellant herein, was indebted to the defendants in that action (plaintiffs herein) in the sum admitted in his petition, and ordered him to pay it to the master commissioner of that court which he did, and when done, that the lien on his land should be released. Appellant then procured a copy of that proceeding and filed his answer in this action relying upon the Arkansas judgment in bar of a recovery herein. The court disallowed that defense and rendered judgment against appellant for the amount it found to be due plaintiffs, and to reverse it defendant prosecutes this appeal.

The only argument made, and the only possible one that could be made, against the propriety of the judgment appealed from is that the Arkansas judgment, under the provisions of section 1 of article 4 of the Federal Constitution, is entitled to full faith and credit in this state the same as if it had been rendered by a court of competent jurisdiction in this state, and that, since it is argued that the Arkansas court had jurisdiction to render the judgment relied on as a defense herein, it is binding on plaintiffs, and that they may not impeach it in this collateral attack. In making that argument, counsel assumes the correctness of the crucial point in this case, and we think erroneously so. It is, that the Arkansas court had jurisdiction, upon constructive process alone, to finally and conclusively adjudge the amount of plaintiff's debt owed to them by defendant, and then to assume to collect it through its master commissioner, or, more appropriately, to direct plaintiff in the Arkansas judgment to discharge it by paying the amount found to be due to the court's master commissioner, and to thereby completely discharge defendant from all further liability to plaintiffs. The error in the assumption of counsel for defendant lies in their failure to appraise and comprehend the nature of the relief granted by the Arkansas judgment and relied on as a defense in this case; confusing it with the power and jurisdiction of that court to deal with and adjudicate concerning the res within its jurisdiction, which in this case was the land in lien for plaintiff's debt.

[The court first questioned, without deciding, whether, under the doctrines of equity, an appropriate case for a bill to remove a cloud on title was made out in the Arkansas proceeding, since the alleged cloud was created by the debtor himself.]

. . . [I]n this case, conceding that there was no doubt of the proper cloud upon defendant's title to his Arkansas land so as to authorize the action in that state to remove it, the judgment rendered by the Arkansas court would be obligatory on plaintiffs herein in so far as it released their lien upon the land in that state. But, when the court undertook to grant additional relief strictly in personam, it transgressed its jurisdiction so as to render such unauthorized additional relief of no force and effect whatever. That relief in this case was the adjudication that defendant herein had paid to plaintiffs herein any part of his debt and thereby discharged a part of his obligation to them, and that the court could and did fix the amount due from him to plaintiffs herein and directed its payment to the commissioner of that court. The rights so attempted to be adjudicated were and are strictly personal. It may be that the Arkansas court was vested with authority to lift the lien from the land involved, and for that purpose to incidentally determine the amount of the lien, and whether or not it had been paid, but the only binding effect of such adjudications would be that of releasing the lien as an incumbrance upon the title to the res. Such adjudications in so far as they affected the personal obligations and rights of the parties were and are not binding upon plaintiffs herein, nor do they operate as a res adjudicata estoppel in any future action. . . .

Wherefore the judgment is affirmed.

NOTES

(1) If the creditor, after the entry of the Arkansas judgment, sued the debtor in Arkansas for the balance alleged to be due, and the Arkansas court held the prior judgment to be res judicata of the plaintiff's rights, would this constitute a denial of due process? On the conclusiveness of a judgment quasi in rem, see Restatement, Second, Judgments §§ 30, 32 (1982).

(2) Freeman v. Alderson, 119 U.S. 185 (1886) determined that, in an action to try title to real estate and obtain a partition thereof against a non-resident defendant served only by publication, a personal judgment for costs could not be entered. Similarly, in State ex rel. Truitt v. District Court, 44 N.M. 16, 96 P.2d 710 (1939), a non-resident lessee of New Mexico land, sued by his sublessee for reformation of the lease, was held not subject to suit in New Mexico when notified by mail outside the state. Would there not have been jurisdiction over the non-resident in these cases under a modern statute taking advantage of all constitutionally permissible bases of personal jurisdiction, including "ownership, possession or use of real estate situated within the state?"

B. CHATTELS

RESTATEMENT, SECOND, CONFLICT OF LAWS: *

§ 60.   Judicial Jurisdiction over Chattel

A state has power to exercise judicial jurisdiction to affect interests in a chattel in the state, which is not in the course of transit in interstate or foreign commerce, although a person owning or claiming an interest in the chattel is not personally subject to the judicial jurisdiction of the state.

MARTIN v. BETTER TASTE POPCORN CO.

United States District Court, S.D.Iowa, 1950.
89 F.Supp. 754.

SWITZER, DISTRICT JUDGE.   The petition [in the Iowa state court alleged that in Fremont County, Iowa] there is situated 4¼ million

---

* Quoted with the permission of the
copyright owner, The American Law Institute.

pounds of stored popcorn, a part of which is the property of the plaintiffs, having been commingled with the remainder and unidentifiable therefrom.

Plaintiffs seek a decree determining the respective interests of each of the owners of said stored popcorn, claiming said popcorn cannot be divided or partitioned in kind; for a referee to take possession thereof, and preserve the same under order of this court, and further, that the court order an appearance and hearing and prescribe the method of notice on the defendant; for a judgment against the defendant and the popcorn, for the costs of the action and such further relief as the court may find proper. In short, this is an action to partition personal property, located in Fremont County, Iowa, in the custody of the defendant, a non-resident corporate defendant.

[After personal service pursuant to the state court's order, which allowed defendant five days to appear, defendant removed the action to the Federal court and attacked jurisdiction for "insufficiency of process and service" under state law and also for lack of "jurisdiction of the subject matter" because there were owners of interests in the popcorn who had not been joined as parties, also in violation of the requirements of state law.]

Did the five-days' notice prescribed by the State court to the defendant in this case in which to make an appearance and defend, allow a sufficient time in view of the residence of the defendant in the State of Indiana to satisfy the due process clause of the Constitution of the United States, Amend. 14 . . . ?

The real test of the sufficiency of the notice in the instant case is whether or not the defendant was informed of the claim and the nature thereof and the time and place of appearance to defend within a sufficient time to afford it an opportunity to make such defense. I believe the notice and service thereof under these tests are sufficient.

Defendant contends that the requirements of Section 616.4, Code of Iowa, 1946, I.C.A. . . . precludes the possibility of the State court obtaining jurisdiction of a nonresident defendant owning property in this State unless aided by attachment. I do not believe this reasoning to be sound. The District Court in the State of Iowa is a court of general jurisdiction. . . . Every state has uncontrolled jurisdiction over all property, real or personal, within its borders, and, as stated in Vol. 14 American Jurisprudence, Par. 189, p. 383: "Therefore, although a nonresident does not come within the territorial limits of a state, if he owns property therein the courts may acquire jurisdiction thereof which may be exercised on such property. Where property of a nonresident is thus brought within the jurisdiction of the court, notice of the proceedings may be given by publication, since the theory of the law is that the owner is always in possession of his property and that its seizure will warn him to look after his interests. . . . " See Perry v. Young, 133 Tenn. 522, 182 S.W. 577, L.R.A.1917B, 385.

Of course, no personal judgment can be rendered against such defendant and the court has jurisdiction only to the extent of adjudicating the interest in the thing itself, that is, the res or the property located within the State of Iowa. This, being an action to partition personal property in Fremont County, Iowa, is in the nature of a rem action, or, perhaps more correctly put, a "quasi-in-rem" proceeding, and the Iowa Supreme Court has . . . held valid a decree on partition predicated only upon notice by publication to non-residents and without attachment of the property itself to aid such published notice. . . .

And it is likewise true, as disclosed by the petition here itself, that all of the indispensable parties necessary to a final determination of this cause are not presently joined in this action. As such, it would not be possible or proper for this court, having assumed jurisdiction, to proceed to a final determination without first requiring that all indispensable parties be joined herein. . . .

I must therefore conclude that this court has jurisdiction of the parties hereto and of the subject matter hereof and that the Special Appearance of the defendant should be overruled in all respects; that this is an action to partition personal property located in Fremont County, Iowa, and that all persons having an interest therein or lien thereon are necessary and indispensable parties to this suit and that they should be joined as parties, plaintiffs or defendants herein.

NOTES

(1) Various parties involved in making and distributing a motion picture called "Race Track" asserted conflicting interests in the movie's negative and sound track, which had been placed in a studio in New Jersey for reproduction work. Not all the interested parties were before the court. It was held: "Where the Court of Chancery has jurisdiction, and there are conflicting equitable liens upon a chattel, and the chattel is in an incomplete and unmarketable condition, the court may, upon proper terms, permit it to be completed and sold, and the proceeds to be held in its place pending a final hearing, in order to avoid the risk of a poorer market then." Educational Studios v. Consolidated Film Industries, 112 N.J.Eq. 352, 164 A. 24 (1933). See also Cammell v. Sewell, p. 657, infra; Green v. Van Buskirk, p. 777, infra; 1 Beale, Conflict of Laws, sec. 102.1 (1935).

(2) A French court having jurisdiction in rem over an English ship in French waters ordered a sale for satisfaction of a lien levied against it. In the proceedings, the court misinterpreted the English law relating to such matters. Thereafter the original owner sought to impeach the sale on this ground. Held, that since the French court received all the evidence and acted bona fide, the action by that tribunal was conclusive despite the error in the interpretation of the English law. Castrique v. Imrie, L.R. 4 H.L. 414 (1870).

(3) State courts have been allowed to exercise jurisdiction over a chattel habitually situated in the forum even though the chattel was temporarily beyond the territorial limits of the state when the proceedings were instituted. North Carolina Land & Lumber Co. v. Boyer, 191 F. 552 (6th Cir. 1911);

1 Beale, Conflict of Laws, sec. 99.1 (1935). Has a court jurisdiction to attach or garnish chattels which the defendant, not subject to the jurisdiction of the forum, was induced by the fraudulent acts of the plaintiff to send into the forum so that they could be subjected to the jurisdiction of the forum? Even if it has jurisdiction, the court will refuse to exercise it. See Sea-Gate Tire & Rubber Co. v. Moseley, 161 Okl. 256, 18 P.2d 276 (1933).

C. INTANGIBLES

"The situs of intangibles is in truth a legal fiction, but there are times when justice or convenience requires that a legal situs be ascribed to them. The locality selected is for some purposes, the domicile of the creditor; for others, the domicile or place of business of the debtor, the place, that is to say, where the obligation was created or was meant to be discharged; for others, any place where the debtor can be found. At the root of the selection is generally a common sense appraisal of the requirements of justice and convenience in particular conditions." Cardozo, J., in Severnoe Securities Corporation v. London & Lancashire Ins. Co., Ltd., 255 N.Y. 120, 123–124, 174 N.E. 299, 300 (1931).

HARRIS v. BALK

Supreme Court of the United States, 1905.
198 U.S. 215, 25 S.Ct. 625, 49 L.Ed. 1023.

H → B– E

H → E

[Harris, a North Carolina domiciliary, was indebted to Balk, another North Carolina domiciliary, in the amount of $180. Balk in turn owed more than $300 to Epstein, who lived in Baltimore, Maryland. One day Harris came to Baltimore for a short visit and while there was served in hand by Epstein with a writ attaching the debt which Harris owed Balk. In addition, in accordance with the Maryland practice, process against Balk was delivered to a Baltimore sheriff and then placed at the court house door. Harris did not contest the garnishment action and consented to the entry against him of a payment for $180 which he paid. Thereafter in North Carolina, Balk sued Harris on his debt. A judgment in Balk's favor was affirmed by the North Carolina Supreme Court on the ground that Maryland had no jurisdiction to garnish the debt Harris owed Balk "because Harris was but temporarily in the state, and the situs of the debt was in North Carolina."]

MR. JUSTICE PECKHAM . . . delivered the opinion of the court.

. . . Attachment is the creature of the local law . . . If there be a law of the State providing for the attachment of the debt, then if the garnishee be found in that State, and process be personal-

ly served upon him therein, we think the court thereby acquires jurisdiction over him, and can garnish the debt due from him to the debtor
of the plaintiff and condemn it, provided the garnishee could himself
be sued by his creditor in that State. We do not see how the question
of jurisdiction vel non can properly be made to depend upon the so-
called original situs of the debt, or upon the character of the stay of
the garnishee, whether temporary or permanent, in the State where
the attachment is issued. Power over the person of the garnishee
confers jurisdiction on the courts of the State where the writ issues.
Blackstone v. Miller, 188 U.S. 189, 206. If, while temporarily there,
his creditor might sue him there and recover the debt, then he is liable to process of garnishment, no matter where the situs of the debt
was originally. . . . The obligation of the debtor to pay his debt
clings to and accompanies him wherever he goes. He is as much
bound to pay his debt in a foreign state when therein sued upon his
obligation by his creditor, as he was in the state where the debt was
contracted. We speak of ordinary debts, such as the one in this case.
. . . possession cannot be taken of a debt or of the obligation to
pay it, as tangible property might be taken possession of. Notice to
the debtor (garnishee) of the commencement of the suit, and notice
not to pay his creditor, is all that can be given, whether the garnishee
be a mere casual and temporary comer, or a resident of the State
where the attachment is laid. His obligation to pay to his creditor is
thereby arrested and a lien created upon the debt itself. Cahoon v.
Morgan, 38 Vermont 236; National Fire Ins. Co. v. Chambers, 53 N.J.
Eq. 468, 483. We can see no reason why the attachment could not be
thus laid, provided the creditor of the garnishee could himself sue in
that State and its laws permitted the attachment. . . .

It . . . appears that Balk could have sued Harris in Maryland
to recover his debt, notwithstanding the temporary character of Harris' stay there; it also appears that the municipal law of Maryland
permits the debtor of the principal debtor to be garnished . . .

It seems to us, therefore, that the judgment against Harris in
Maryland, condemning the $180 which he owed to Balk, was a valid
judgment, because the court had jurisdiction over the garnishee by
personal service of process within the State of Maryland.

It ought to be and it is the object of courts to prevent the payment
of any debt twice over. Thus, . . . Harris . . . should have
the right to plead his payment under the Maryland judgment. It is
objected, however, that the payment by Harris to Epstein was not
under legal compulsion. Harris in truth owed the debt to Balk, which
was attached by Epstein. He had, therefore, as we have seen, no
defense to set up against the attachment of the debt. Jurisdiction
over him personally had been obtained by the Maryland court. As he
was absolutely without defense, there was no reason why he should
not consent to a judgment impounding the debt . . . There was

no merely voluntary payment within the meaning of that phrase as applicable here.

[Justice Peckham went on to state that it is the garnishee's duty to take reasonable steps to notify his creditor of the pendency of the garnishment proceedings "so that the creditor may have the opportunity to defend himself against the claim of the person suing out the attachment." It did not appear that Harris had given Balk such notice and therefore his payment of the garnishment judgment would not under ordinary circumstances have constituted a defense to Balk's action against him. This was not true, however, in this particular case, because Balk did receive notice of the garnishment judgment shortly after its entry and under the peculiar Maryland practice had a year's time following such entry to establish that he was not indebted to Epstein in the amount claimed.]

The judgment of the Supreme Court of North Carolina must be reversed and the cause remanded for further proceedings not inconsistent with the opinion of this court.

Reversed.

MR. JUSTICE HARLAN and MR. JUSTICE DAY dissenting.

NOTES

(1) Harris v. Balk's reasoning and result were severely questioned and perhaps overruled by the United States Supreme Court in Shaffer v. Heitner, p. 148, infra, but its influence, if not its authority, endures. It gave constitutional approval to garnishment proceedings.

(2) Garnishment proceedings have been meeting with procedural as well as jurisdictional challenges. In Sniadach v. Family Finance Corp. of Bay View, 395 U.S. 337 (1969), the Supreme Court struck down as violative of due process provisions of the Wisconsin garnishment procedure under which wages are frozen when process in a garnishment action is served upon the employer of the alleged debtor and the latter "without any opportunity to be heard and to tender any defense he may have, whether it be fraud or otherwise" is thereby deprived of his earned wages until after the termination of the creditor's action against him. For essentially similar reasons the Georgia garnishment provisions were declared unconstitutional in North Georgia Finishing, Inc. v. Di Chem, Inc., 419 U.S. 601 (1975). Analogous Supreme Court decisions are Fuentes v. Shevin, 407 U.S. 67 (1972) and Mitchell v. W.T. Grant Co., 416 U.S. 600 (1974). See generally Note, Foreign Attachment after *Sniadach* and *Fuentes,* 73 Colum.L.Rev. 342 (1973); Note, Quasi in Rem Jurisdiction and Due Process Requirements, 82 Yale L.J. 1023 (1973).

(3) The United States government sued in a federal court in New York to recover income taxes allegedly owed by a Uruguayan corporation. To prevent the corporation (which had not been served with process) from withdrawing any assets that might be available to satisfy a tax liability, the government obtained a temporary injunction against the First National City Bank, restraining it from disbursing the Uruguayan's account at the Bank's branch in Montevideo. The Supreme Court sustained the injunction, holding that the Bank's obligation to the Uruguayan corporation could be reached in

New York and rejecting the argument that the debt was not a property interest in the United States. "If it were clear that the debtor [the Uruguayan] were beyond reach of the District Court as far as personal service is concerned, we would have quite a different case—one on which we intimate no opinion." United States v. First National City Bank, 379 U.S. 378, 381 (1965).

———

NEW YORK LIFE INSURANCE CO. v. DUNLEVY

Supreme Court of the United States, 1916.
241 U.S. 518, 36 S.Ct. 613, 60 L.Ed. 1140.

MR. JUSTICE McREYNOLDS delivered the opinion of the court:

Respondent, Effie J. Gould Dunlevy, instituted this suit in the superior court, Marin county, California, January 14, 1910, against petitioner and Joseph W. Gould, her father, to recover $2,479.70, the surrender value of a policy on his life which she claimed had been assigned to her in 1893, and both were duly served with process while in that state. It was removed to the United States district court, February 16, 1910, and there tried by the judge in May, 1912, a jury having been expressly waived. Judgment for amount claimed was affirmed by the circuit court of appeals. 204 F. 670, 130 C.C.A. 473, 214 F. 1.

The insurance company by an amended answer filed December 7, 1911, set up in defense (1) that no valid assignment had been made, and (2) that Mrs. Dunlevy was concluded by certain judicial proceedings in Pennsylvania wherein it had been garnished and the policy had been adjudged to be the property of Gould. Invalidity of the assignment is not now urged; but it is earnestly insisted that the Pennsylvania proceedings constituted a bar.

In 1907 Boggs & Buhl recovered a valid personal judgment by default, after domiciliary service, against Mrs. Dunlevy, in the common pleas court at Pittsburgh, where she then resided. During 1909, "the tontine dividend period" of the life policy having expired, the insurance company became liable for $2,479.70, and this sum was claimed both by Gould, a citizen of Pennsylvania, and his daughter, who had removed to California. In November, 1909, Boggs & Buhl caused issue of an execution attachment on their judgment, and both the insurance company and Gould were summoned as garnishees. He appeared, denied assignment of the policy, and claimed the full amount due thereon. On February 5, 1910,—after this suit was begun in California,—the company answered, admitted its indebtedness, set up the conflicting claims to the fund, and prayed to be advised as to its rights. At the same time it filed a petition asking for a rule upon the claimants to show cause why they should not interplead and thereby ascertain who was lawfully entitled to the proceeds, and, further, that it might be allowed to pay amount due into court for benefit of proper party. An order granted the requested rule, and directed that notice be given to Mrs. Dunlevy in California. This was done, but she made no answer and did not appear. Later the insurance company filed a second petition, and, upon leave obtained thereunder, paid $2,479.70 into court, March 21, 1910. All parties except Mrs. Dunlevy having appeared, a feigned issue was framed and tried to determine validity of alleged transfer of the policy. The jury found, October 1, 1910, there was no valid assignment, and thereupon, under an order of court, the fund was paid over to Gould.

Beyond doubt, without the necessity of further personal service of process upon Mrs. Dunlevy, the court of common pleas of Pittsburgh had ample power through garnishment proceedings to inquire whether she held a valid claim against the insurance company, and, if found to exist, then to condemn and appropriate it so far as necessary to discharge the original judgment. Although herself outside the limits of the state, such disposition of the property would have been binding on her. . . . But the interpleader initiated by the company was an altogether different matter. This was an attempt to bring about a final and conclusive adjudication of her personal rights, not merely to discover property and apply it to debts. And unless in contemplation of law she was before the court, and required to respond to that issue, its orders and judgments in respect thereto were not binding on her. . . .

Counsel maintain that having been duly summoned in the original suit instituted by Boggs & Buhl in 1907, and notwithstanding entry of final judgment therein, "Mrs. Dunlevy was in the Pennsylvania court and was bound by every order that court made, whether she remained within the jurisdiction of that court after it got jurisdiction over her person or not;" and hence, the argument is, "When the company paid the money into court where she was, it was just the same in legal effect as if it had paid it to her." This position is supposed to be supported by our opinion in Michigan Trust Co. v. Ferry, 228 U.S. 346 . . . The judgment under consideration was fairly within the reasonable anticipation of the executor when he submitted himself to the probate court. But a wholly different and intolerable condition would result from acceptance of the theory that, after final judgment, a defendant remains in court and subject to whatsoever orders may be entered under title of the cause. . . . The interpleader proceedings were not essential concomitants of the original action by Boggs & Buhl against Dunlevy, but plainly collateral; and, when summoned to respond in that action, she was not required to anticipate them. . . .

It has been affirmatively held in Pennsylvania that a judgment debtor is not a party to a garnishment proceeding to condemn a claim due him from a third person, and is not bound by a judgment discharging the garnishee (Ruff v. Ruff, 85 Pa. 333); and this is the generally accepted doctrine. . . .

We are of opinion that the proceedings in the Pennsylvania court constituted no bar to the action in California, and the judgment below is accordingly affirmed.

NOTES

(1) Are the Harris and Dunlevy cases distinguishable on a reasoned analysis—for example, by considering what values are furthered and what injuries are avoided by allowing the forum to affect the nonresident's interests?

(2) In 1963 the Federal Rules of Civil Procedure were amended in order explicitly to allow resort in original federal actions to the procedure provided by state law for commencing actions against nonresidents by attachment and garnishment. Carrington, The Modern Utility of Quasi in Rem Jurisdiction, 76 Harv.L.Rev. 303 (1962), argued prophetically against this amendment on the ground that quasi-in-rem jurisdiction is likely to be inconsistent with the reasonableness approach of International Shoe.

(3) Sanders v. Armour Fertilizer Works, 292 U.S. 190 (1934). Sanders, who was domiciled in Texas, was insured by two insurance companies against loss by fire of certain Texas property. The property was destroyed by fire and the insurance companies each admitted indebtedness to Sanders in stipulated amounts. Thereafter, garnishment proceedings seeking to attach the debts owed Sanders by the insurance companies were brought in Illinois by the Armour Fertilizer Works, a creditor of Sanders. While these proceedings were pending, the insurance companies brought an action in Texas under the Federal Interpleader Act against Sanders and Armour Fertilizer Works and paid into court the amounts owed by them under the policies. The court enjoined the Armour Fertilizer Company from proceeding further with the Illinois garnishment proceeding and, after a hearing, determined that Sanders was entitled to the sums due under the policies because these sums under Texas law were exempt from the claims of his creditors. *Held*, reversed on the ground that full faith and credit had been denied the Illinois garnishment proceedings. Under Illinois law, the commencement of a garnishment action imposes an "inchoate lien" upon the debt subject to defeat by certain subsequent events, none of which had transpired. Likewise, the Illinois courts would have rejected Sanders' claim of exemption under Texas law. "To hold that the District Court in Texas could enjoin the Fertilizer Works from proceeding further and then declare that because the last step had not been taken, Sanders, in some way, became entitled to priority, plainly would be inequitable. Moreover, it would deny to the garnishment proceedings the credit and effect accorded them in the State where taken." Four Justices dissented on the ground that under Illinois law garnishment does not create a lien upon the debt.

(4) The difficulty encountered in obtaining jurisdiction over all claimants in state proceedings led to the adoption and gradual extension of federal interpleader proceedings. The classic treatment of the development and shortcomings of interpleader proceedings in the federal courts, as well as of state interpleader proceedings, is given by Professor Zechariah Chafee in the following articles: Modernizing Interpleader, 30 Yale L.J. 814 (1921); Interstate Interpleader, 33 Yale L.J. 685 (1924); Interpleader in the United States Courts, 41 Yale L.J. 1134 (1932); The Federal Interpleader Act of 1936, 45 Yale L.J. 963 (1936); Federal Interpleader Since the Act of 1936, 49 Yale L.J. 377 (1940); Broadening the Second Stage of Interpleader, 56 Harv.L.Rev.

541, 929 (1943). It will be observed that the advantage of federal interpleader over state interpleader inheres in the fact that while the jurisdiction of a state court over persons may be limited by the boundaries of the state, the jurisdiction of the federal courts over persons may be extended throughout the whole of the United States, even in diversity cases in which the subject matter of the controversy is beyond the legislative jurisdiction of the federal government. Why should it be regarded as unfair imposition upon a nonresident defendant to be called to defend in a distant state court action, as in the Dunlevy case, supra, but entirely consistent with due process to impose the same burden upon the defendant by federal interpleader? Cf. Chapter 6, infra.

———

ATKINSON V. SUPERIOR COURT, 49 Cal.2d 338, 316 P.2d 960 (1957) appeal dismissed and cert. denied 357 U.S. 569 (1958): Groups of musicians who worked in California brought class actions attacking various agreements between their union and the California employers, companies that made movies and phonograph records. The dispute was over the allegedly improper diversion of royalties that were payable under the agreements to a trustee in New York over whom personal jurisdiction could not be obtained in California. The question was whether service of process on the trustee in New York was nevertheless sufficient under a California statute permitting service on a nonresident when the action related to "real or personal property in this State, in which [the nonresident] . . . has or claims a lien or interest . . ." That depended in turn on whether the payments due in California could be treated as being within California for purposes of in rem or quasi in rem jurisdiction. Justice Traynor said:

"The present case is not one in which an obligor has invoked the jurisdiction of a court remote from the obligee solely for the purpose of terminating his obligation . . . or sought to compel conflicting claimants to adjudicate their rights in a forum of his own choice. See, New York Life Insurance Co. v. Dunlevy, [p. 144, supra]. The obligation plaintiffs seek to enforce grows out of their employment by defendants here. The payments involved are alleged to be consideration for work performed in this state. The Federation defendant is before the court. Under these circumstances, fairness to plaintiffs demands that they be able to reach the fruits of their labors before they are removed from the state. Moreover, fairness to the defendants who are personally before the court also demands that the conflicting claims of the trustee be subject to final adjudication. . . . The evil of exposing the obligor to actions to enforce the same obligation in two jurisdictions with the attendant risk of double liability would not be obviated. It was just such double liability that was sustained in the Dunlevy case and gave impetus to the passage of federal interpleader legislation. (See, Chafee, Interstate Interpleader, 33 Yale L.J. 685, 711.) It is doubtful whether today the United States Supreme Court would deny to a state court the interstate interpleader jurisdiction that federal courts may exercise. A remedy that a federal court may provide without violating due process of law does not become unfair or unjust because it is sought in a state court instead. To sustain jurisdiction in these cases, however, we are not required to forecast the overruling of the Dunlevy case and to act on that basis. For the reasons stated above, this case is clearly distinguishable from the Dunlevy case, and the multiple contacts with this state fully sustain the jurisdiction of the superior court to exercise quasi in rem jurisdiction over the intangibles in question."

NOTES

(1) Commenting upon the Atkinson decision, the author of the court's opinion said that the "case made clear that realistic tests to determine jurisdiction to grant the specific relief sought must be applied regardless of labels," but that the court was "compelled to find a quasi-in-rem basis for jurisdiction" because of the statute. Traynor, Is This Conflict Really Necessary?, 37 Tex.L.Rev. 657 (1959). It is, generally speaking, true that the court applied "the same test in establishing quasi in rem jurisdiction over the nonresident claimant as the Supreme Court has applied for establishing in personam jurisdiction." See Note, 46 Calif.L.Rev. 637, 639 (1958).

(2) In Hartford v. Superior Court, 47 Cal.2d 447, 304 P.2d 1 (1956), plaintiff brought an action to declare that the nonresident defendant, who had been personally served in New York, was his father. He invoked California code provisions applicable to "in rem" proceedings, urging that his suit to adjudicate paternity status was of that nature, but the California Supreme Court, again speaking through Justice Traynor, rejected the contention that "because the present proceeding is concerned solely with status it must necessarily be classified as a proceeding in rem" and held that personal jurisdiction over the defendant was essential.

SHAFFER v. HEITNER

Supreme Court of the United States, 1977.
433 U.S. 186, 97 S.Ct. 2569, 53 L.Ed.2d 683.

MR. JUSTICE MARSHALL delivered the opinion of the Court.

The controversy in this case concerns the constitutionality of a Delaware statute that allows a court of that State to take jurisdiction of a lawsuit by sequestering any property of the defendant that happens to be located in Delaware. . . .

I

Appellee Heitner, a nonresident of Delaware, is the owner of one share of stock in the Greyhound Corporation, a business incorporated under the laws of Delaware with its principal place of business in Phoenix, Ariz. On May 22, 1974, he filed a shareholder's derivative suit in the Court of Chancery for New Castle County, Del., in which he named as defendants Greyhound, its wholly owned subsidiary Greyhound Lines, Inc., and 28 present or former officers or directors of one or both of the corporations. In essence, Heitner alleged that the individual defendants had violated their duties to Greyhound by causing it and its subsidiary to engage in actions that resulted in the corporations being held liable for substantial damages in a private antitrust suit and a large fine in a criminal contempt action. The activities which led to these penalties took place in Oregon.

Simultaneously with his complaint, Heitner filed a motion for an order of sequestration of the Delaware property of the individual defendants pursuant to 10 Del.C. § 366. . . . The requested sequestration order was signed the day the motion was filed. Pursuant to that order, the sequestrator "seized" approximately 82,000 shares of Greyhound common stock belonging to 19 of the defendants, and options belonging to another two defendants. . . . So far as the record shows, none of the certificates representing the seized property was physically present in Delaware. The stock was considered to be in Delaware, and so subject to seizure, by virtue of 8 Del.C. § 169, which makes Delaware the situs of ownership of all stock in Delaware corporations.

All 28 defendants were notified of the initiation of the suit by certified mail directed to their last known addresses and by publication in a New Castle County newspaper. The 21 defendants whose property was seized (hereafter referred to as appellants) responded by entering a special appearance [asserting] that under the rule of International Shoe Co. v. Washington, 326 U.S. 310 (1945), they did not have sufficient contacts with Delaware to sustain the jurisdiction of that State's courts. . . .

II

The Delaware courts rejected appellants' jurisdictional challenge by noting that this suit was brought as a *quasi in rem* proceeding. Since *quasi in rem* jurisdiction is traditionally based on attachment or seizure of property present in the jurisdiction, not on contacts between the defendant and the State, the courts considered appellants' claimed lack of contacts with Delaware to be unimportant. This categorical analysis assumes the continued soundness of the conceptual structure founded on the century-old case of Pennoyer v. Neff, 95 U.S. 714 (1877).

[Justice Marshall here discussed the *Pennoyer* case and noted that it based 'authority to adjudicate . . . on the jurisdiction's power over either persons or property.' He stated that with respect to judicial jurisdiction over persons the *Pennoyer* rule has been supplanted by the rule of *International Shoe*. He continued:]

No equally dramatic change has occurred in the law governing jurisdiction *in rem*. There have, however, been intimations that the collapse of the *in personam* wing of *Pennoyer* has not left that decision unweakened as a foundation for *in rem* jurisdiction. Well-reasoned lower court opinions have questioned the proposition that the presence of property in a State gives that State jurisdiction to adjudicate rights to the property regardless of the relationship of the underlying dispute and the property owner to the forum. See e.g., U.S. Industries v. Gregg, 540 F.2d 142 (CA3 1976), petition for cert. pending, No. 76–359; Jonnet v. Dollar Savings Bank, 530 F.2d 1123, 1130–1143 (CA3 1976) (Gibbons, J., concurring); Camire v. Scieszka, 358 A.2d 397 (NH 1976); Bekins v. Huish, 1 Ariz.App. 288, 401 P.2d 743 (1965); Atkinson v. Superior Court, 49 Cal.2d 338, 316 P.2d 960 (1955), appeal dismissed and cert. denied sub nom. Columbia Broadcasting Sys. v. Atkinson, 357 U.S. 569 (1958). The overwhelming majority of commentators have also rejected *Pennoyer's* premise that a proceeding "against" property is not a proceeding against the owners of that property. Accordingly, they urge that the "traditional notions of fair play and substantial justice" that govern a State's power to adjudicate *in personam* should also govern its power to adjudicate personal rights to property located in the State. See, e.g., . . . Von Mehren & Trautman, Jurisdiction to Adjudicate: A Suggested Analysis, 79 Harv.L.Rev. 1121 (1966); Traynor, Is This Conflict Really Necessary?, 37 Tex.L.Rev. 657 (1959); Ehrenzweig, The Transient Rule of Personal Jurisdiction: The 'Power' Myth and Forum Conveniens, 65 Yale L.J. 289 (1956) . . .

Although this Court has not addressed this argument directly, we have held that property cannot be subjected to a court's judgment unless reasonable and appropriate efforts have been made to give the property owners actual notice of the action. Schroeder v. City of New York, 371 U.S. 208 (1962); Walker v. City of Hutchinson, 352 U.S. 112 (1956); Mullane v. Central Hanover Bank & Trust Co., 339 U.S. 306 (1950). This conclusion recognizes, contrary to *Pennoyer*, that an adverse judgment *in rem* directly affects the property owner by divesting him of his rights in the property before the court. . . .

III

The case for applying to jurisdiction *in rem* the same test of "fair play and substantial justice" as governs assertions of jurisdiction *in personam* is simple and straightforward. It is premised on recognition that "[t]he phrase, 'judicial jurisdiction over a thing,' is a customary elliptical way of referring to jurisdiction over the interests of persons in a thing." Restatement (Second) of Conflict of Laws § 56, introductory note. This recognition leads to the conclusion that in order to justify an exercise of jurisdiction *in rem*, the basis for jurisdiction must be sufficient to justify exercising "jurisdiction over the interests of persons in a thing." The standard for determining whether an exercise of jurisdiction over the interests of persons is consistent with the Due Process Clause is the minimum contacts standard elucidated in *International Shoe*.

This argument, of course, does not ignore the fact that the presence of property in a State may bear on the existence of jurisdiction by providing contacts among the forum State, the defendant, and the litigation. For example, when claims to the property itself are the source of the underlying controversy between the plaintiff and the defendant, it would be unusual for the State where the property is located not to have jurisdiction. In such cases, the defendant's claim to property located in the State would normally indicate that he expected to benefit from the State's protection of his interest. The State's strong interests in assuring the marketability of property within its borders and in providing a procedure for peaceful resolution of disputes about the possession of that property would also support jurisdiction, as would the likelihood that important records and witnesses will be found in the State.[28] The presence of property may also favor jurisdiction in cases, such as suits for injury suffered on the land of an absentee owner, where the defendant's ownership of the property is conceded but the cause of action is otherwise related to rights and duties growing out of that ownership.[29]

It appears, therefore, that jurisdiction over many types of actions which now are or might be brought *in rem* would not be affected by a holding that any assertion of state court jurisdiction must satisfy the *International Shoe* standard.[30] For the type of *quasi in rem* action typified by Harris v. Balk [p. 141, supra] and the present case, however, accepting the proposed analysis would result in significant change. These are cases where the property which now serves as the basis for state court jurisdiction is completely unrelated to the plaintiff's cause of action. Thus, although the presence of the defendant's property in a State might suggest the existence of other ties among the defendant, the State, and the litigation, the presence of the property alone would not support the State's jurisdiction. If those other ties did not exist, cases over which the State is now thought to have jurisdiction could not be brought in that forum.

Since acceptance of the *International Shoe* test would most affect this class of cases, we examine the arguments against adopting that standard as they relate to this category of litigation.[31] Before doing so, however, we note that this type of case also presents the clearest illustration of the argument in favor of assessing assertions

---

28. We do not suggest that these illustrations include all the factors that may affect the decision, nor that the factors we have mentioned are necessarily decisive.

29. Cf. Dubin v. City of Philadelphia, 34 Pa.D. & C. 61 (1938). . . .

30. Smit, The Enduring Utility of In Rem Rules: A Lasting Legacy of Pennoyer v. Neff, 48 Brooklyn L.Rev. 600 (1977). We do not suggest that jurisdictional doctrines other than those discussed in text, such as the particularized rules governing adjudications of status, are inconsistent with the standard of fairness. . . .

31. Concentrating on this category of cases is also appropriate because in the other categories, to the extent that presence of property in the State indicates the existence of sufficient contacts under *International Shoe*, there is no need to rely on the property as justifying jurisdiction regardless of the existence of those contacts.

of jurisdiction by a single standard. For in cases such as *Harris* and this one, the only role played by the property is to provide the basis for bringing the defendant into court.[32] Indeed, the express purpose of the Delaware sequestration procedure is to compel the defendant to enter a personal appearance. In such cases, if a direct assertion of personal jurisdiction over the defendant would violate the Constitution, it would seem that an indirect assertion of that jurisdiction should be equally impermissible.

The primary rationale for treating the presence of property as a sufficient basis for jurisdiction to adjudicate claims over which the State would not have jurisdiction if *International Shoe* applied is that a wrongdoer "should not be able to avoid payment of his obligations by the expedient of removing his assets to a place where he is not subject to an in personam suit." Restatement (Second) of Conflicts § 66, comment a. . . . This justification, however, does not explain why jurisdiction should be recognized without regard to whether the property is present in the State because of an effort to avoid the owner's obligations. Nor does it support jurisdiction to adjudicate the underlying claim. At most, it suggests that a State in which property is located should have jurisdiction to attach that property, by use of proper procedures, as security for a judgment being sought in a forum where the litigation can be maintained consistently with *International Shoe*. . . . Moreover, we know of nothing to justify the assumption that a debtor can avoid paying his obligations by removing his property to a State in which his creditor cannot obtain personal jurisdiction over him. The Full Faith and Credit Clause, after all, makes the valid *in personam* judgment of one State enforceable in all other States.[36]

It might also be suggested that allowing *in rem* jurisdiction avoids the uncertainty inherent in the *International Shoe* standard and assures a plaintiff of a forum.[37] . . . We believe, however, that the fairness standard of *International Shoe* can be easily applied in the vast majority of cases. Moreover, when the existence of jurisdiction in a particular forum under *International Shoe* is unclear, the cost of simplifying the litigation by avoiding the jurisdictional question may be the sacrifice of "fair play and substantial justice." That cost is too high. . . .

32. The value of the property seized does serve to limit the extent of possible liability, but that limitation does not provide support for the assertion of jurisdiction. . . . In this case, appellants' potential liability under the *in rem* jurisdiction exceeds one million dollars. . . .

36. Once it has been determined by a court of competent jurisdiction that the defendant is a debtor of the plaintiff, there would seem to be no unfairness in allowing an action to realize on that debt in a State where the defendant has property, whether or not that State would have jurisdiction to determine the existence of the debt as an original matter. . . .

37. This case does not raise, and we therefore do not consider, the question whether the presence of a defendant's property in a State is a sufficient basis for jurisdiction when no other forum is available to the plaintiff.

We are left, then, to consider the significance of the long history of jurisdiction based solely on the presence of property in a State. Although the theory that territorial power is both essential to and sufficient for jurisdiction has been undermined, we have never held that the presence of property in a State does not automatically confer jurisdiction over the owner's interest in that property. This history must be considered as supporting the proposition that jurisdiction based solely on the presence of property satisfies the demands of due process, . . . but it is not decisive. . . . The fiction that an assertion of jurisdiction over property is anything but an assertion of jurisdiction over the owner of the property supports an ancient form without substantial modern justification. Its continued acceptance would serve only to allow state court jurisdiction that is fundamentally unfair to the defendant.

We therefore conclude that all assertions of state court jurisdiction must be evaluated according to the standards set forth in *International Shoe* and its progeny.[39]

IV

The Delaware courts based their assertion of jurisdiction in this case solely on the statutory presence of appellants' property in Delaware. Yet that property is not the subject matter of this litigation, nor is the underlying cause of action related to the property. Appellants' holdings in Greyhound do not, therefore, provide contacts with Delaware sufficient to support the jurisdiction of that State's courts over appellants. If it exists, that jurisdiction must have some other foundation.

Appellee Heitner did not allege and does not now claim that appellants have ever set foot in Delaware. Nor does he identify any act related to his cause of action as having taken place in Delaware. Nevertheless, he contends that appellants' positions as directors and officers of a corporation chartered in Delaware provide sufficient "contacts, ties, or relations," International Shoe Co. v. Washington, supra, at 319, with that State to give its courts jurisdiction over appellants in this stockholder's derivative action. This argument is based primarily on what Heitner asserts to be the strong interest of Delaware in supervising the management of a Delaware corporation. That interest is said to derive from the role of Delaware law in establishing the corporation and defining the obligations owed to it by its officers and directors. In order to protect this interest, appellee concludes, Delaware's courts must have jurisdiction over corporate fiduciaries such as appellants.

39. It would not be fruitful for us to re-examine the facts of cases decided on the rationales of *Pennoyer* and *Harris* to determine whether jurisdiction might have been sustained under the standard we adopt today. To the extent that prior decisions are inconsistent with this standard, they are overruled.

This argument is undercut by the failure of the Delaware Legislature to assert the state interest appellee finds so compelling. Delaware law bases jurisdiction not on appellants' status as corporate fiduciaries, but rather on the presence of their property in the State. Although the sequestration procedure used here may be most frequently used in derivative suits against officers and directors, . . . the authorizing statute evinces no specific concern with such actions. Sequestration can be used in any suit against a nonresident, . . ., and reaches corporate fiduciaries only if they happen to own interests in a Delaware corporation, or other property in the State. But as Heitner's failure to secure jurisdiction over seven of the defendants named in his complaint demonstrates, there is no necessary relationship between holding a position as a corporate fiduciary and owning stock or other interests in the corporation. If Delaware perceived its interest in securing jurisdiction over corporate fiduciaries to be as great as Heitner suggests, we would expect it to have enacted a statute more clearly designed to protect that interest.

Moreover, even if Heitner's assessment of the importance of Delaware's interest is accepted, his argument fails to demonstrate that Delaware is a fair forum for this litigation. The interest appellee has identified may support the application of Delaware law to resolve any controversy over appellants' actions in their capacities as officers and directors. But [in Hanson v. Denckla, p. 75, supra] we . . . rejected the argument that if a State's law can properly be applied to a dispute, its courts necessarily have jurisdiction over the parties to that dispute. . . .

Appellee suggests that by accepting positions as officers or directors of a Delaware corporation, appellants performed the acts required by Hanson v. Denckla. He notes that Delaware law provides substantial benefits to corporate officers and directors, and that these benefits were at least in part the incentive for appellants to assume their positions. It is, he says, "only fair and just" to require appellants, in return for these benefits, to respond in the State of Delaware when they are accused of misusing their powers. . . .

But like Heitner's first argument, this line of reasoning establishes only that it is appropriate for Delaware law to govern the obligations of appellants to Greyhound and its stockholders. It does not demonstrate that appellants have "purposefully avail[ed themselves] of the privilege of conducting activities within the forum State," Hanson v. Denckla, supra, at 253, in a way that would justify bringing them before a Delaware tribunal. Appellants have simply had nothing to do with the State of Delaware. Moreover, appellants had no reason to expect to be haled before a Delaware court. Delaware, unlike some States, has not enacted a statute that treats acceptance of a directorship as consent to jurisdiction in the State. . . . Appellants, who were not required to acquire interests in Greyhound in order to hold their positions, did not by acquiring those interests surrender their right to be brought to judgment only in States with which they had had "minimum contacts." . . .

. . . The judgment of the Delaware Supreme Court must, therefore, be reversed.

MR. JUSTICE REHNQUIST took no part in the consideration or decision of this case.

MR. JUSTICE POWELL, concurring.

I agree that the principles of International Shoe Co. v. Washington, 326 U.S. 310 (1945), should be extended to govern assertions of *in rem* as well as *in personam* jurisdiction in state court. I also agree that neither the statutory presence of appellants' stock in Delaware nor their positions as directors and officers of a Delaware corporation can provide sufficient contacts to support the Delaware courts' assertion of jurisdiction in this case.

I would explicitly reserve judgment, however, on whether the ownership of some forms of property whose situs is indisputably and permanently located within a State may, without more, provide the contacts necessary to subject a defendant to jurisdiction within the State to the extent of the value of the property. In the case of real property, in particular, preservation of the common law concept of *quasi in rem* jurisdiction arguably would avoid the uncertainty of the general *International Shoe* standard without significant cost to " 'traditional notions of fair play and substantial justice.' " . . .

Subject to that reservation, I join the opinion of the Court.

MR. JUSTICE STEVENS, concurring in the judgment.

. . . I . . . agree with the Court that on the record before us no adequate basis for jurisdiction exists and that the Delaware statute is unconstitutional on its face.

How the Court's opinion may be applied in other contexts is not entirely clear to me. I agree with Mr. Justice Powell that it should not be read to invalidate *in rem* jurisdiction where real estate is involved. . . . My uncertainty as to the reach of the opinion, and my fear that it purports to decide a great deal more than is necessary to dispose of this case, persuade me merely to concur in the judgment.

MR. JUSTICE BRENNAN, concurring and dissenting.

I join Parts I–III of the Court's opinion. I fully agree that the minimum-contacts analysis developed in International Shoe Co. v. Washington, 326 U.S. 310 (1945), represents a far more sensible construct for the exercise of state court jurisdiction than the patchwork of legal and factual fictions that has been generated from the decision in Pennoyer v. Neff, 95 U.S. 714 (1877). It is precisely because the inquiry into minimum contacts is now of such overriding importance, however, that I must respectfully dissent from Part IV of the Court's opinion. . . .

. . . I am convinced that as a general rule a state forum has jurisdiction to adjudicate a shareholder derivative action centering on the conduct and policies of the directors and officers of a corporation chartered by that State. Unlike the Court, I therefore would not foreclose Delaware from asserting jurisdiction over appellants were it persuaded to do so on the basis of minimum contacts.

It is well settled that a derivative lawsuit as presented here does not inure primarily to the benefit of the named plaintiff. Rather, the primary beneficiaries are the corporation and its owners, the shareholders. . . .

Viewed in this light, the chartering State has an unusually powerful interest in insuring the availability of a convenient forum for litigating claims involving a possible multiplicity of defendant fiduciaries and for vindicating the State's substantive policies regarding the management of its domestic corporations. I believe that our cases fairly establish that the State's valid substantive interests are important considerations in assessing whether it constitutionally may claim jurisdiction over a given cause of action. . . .

To be sure, the Court is not blind to these considerations. It notes that the State's interests "may support the application of Delaware law to resolve any controversy over appellants' actions in their capacities as officers and directors." . . . But this, the Court argues, pertains to choice of law, not jurisdiction. I recognize that the jurisdictional and choice-of-law inquiries are not identical. Hanson v. Denckla, 357 U.S. 235, 254 (1958). But I would not compartmentalize thinking in this area quite so rigidly as it seems to me the Court does today, for both inquiries "are often closely related and to a substantial degree depend upon similar considerations." Id., at 258, 78 S.Ct., at 1242 (Black, J., dissenting). In either case an important linchpin is the extent of contacts between the controversy, the parties, and the forum state. While constitutional limitations on the choice of law are by no means settled, see, e.g., Home Ins. Co. v. Dick, 281 U.S. 397 (1930), important considerations certainly include the expectancies of the parties and the fairness of governing the defendants' acts and behavior by rules of conduct created by a given jurisdiction. See, e.g., Restatement (Second) Choice of Law § 6. These same factors bear upon the propriety of a State's exercising jurisdiction over a legal dispute. At the minimum, the decision that it is fair to bind a defendant by a State's laws and rules should prove to be highly relevant to the fairness of permitting that same State to accept jurisdiction for adjudicating the controversy.

Furthermore, I believe that practical considerations argue in favor of seeking to bridge the distance between the choice-of-law and jurisdictional inquiries. . . . a court will feel less knowledgeable and comfortable in interpretation, and less interested in fostering the policies of [a] foreign jurisdiction, than would the courts established by the State that provides the applicable law. . . . Obviously,

. . . choice-of-law problems cannot entirely be avoided in a diverse legal system such as our own. Nonetheless, when a suitor seeks to lodge a suit in a State with a substantial interest in seeing its own law applied to the transaction in question, we could wisely act to minimize conflicts, confusion, and uncertainty by adopting a liberal view of jurisdiction, unless considerations of fairness or efficiency strongly point in the opposite direction.

This case is not one where, in my judgment, this preference for jurisdiction is adequately answered. Certainly nothing said by the Court persuades me that it would be unfair to subject appellants to suit in Delaware. The fact that the record does not reveal whether they "set foot" or committed "acts related to [the] cause of action" in Delaware . . . is not decisive, for jurisdiction can be based strictly on out-of-state acts having foreseeable effects in the forum state. E.g., McGee v. International Life Ins. Co., supra; Gray v. American Radiator & Standard Sanitary Corp., supra; Restatement (Second) Conflicts of Law § 37. . . .

[I] . . . would approach the minimum contacts analysis differently than does the Court. Crucial to me is the fact that appellants voluntarily associated themselves with the State of Delaware, "invoking the benefits and protections of its laws," Hanson v. Denckla, supra, at 253; International Shoe Co. v. Washington, supra, at 319, by entering into a long term and fragile relationship with one of its domestic corporations. They thereby elected to assume powers and to undertake responsibilities wholly derived from that State's rules and regulations, and to become eligible for those benefits that Delaware law makes available to its corporations' officials. . . .

———

Despite its rejection of the theoretical underpinning of Harris v. Balk, the majority in Shaffer stopped short of explicitly overruling the decision. (See footnote 39.) Perhaps the Court was aware, as Professor Andreas F. Lowenfeld has observed, that the record in the Harris case shows that both Harris and Balk were customers of Epstein and that on the facts Balk probably would be subject to jurisdiction in Maryland by today's standards. See Lowenfeld, In Search of the Intangible: A Comment on Shaffer v. Heitner, 53 N.Y.U.L.Rev. 102, 103–107 (1978).

Does the Shaffer decision spell the end of *quasi in rem* attachments for jurisdictional purposes? Since the plaintiff's judgment in an attachment-for-jurisdiction case will be limited to the value of the attached property and since the required contacts are likely to be no more exacting, the plaintiff would usually do better to use the defendant's contacts with the forum to assert *in personam* jurisdiction. (See Silberman, Shaffer v. Heitner: The End of an Era, 53 N.Y.U.L. Rev. 33, 67–68 (1978).)

In Intermeat, Inc. v. American Poultry, Inc., 575 F.2d 1017 (2d Cir. 1978), in applying the Shaffer principle to uphold jurisdiction to attach debts owing to defendant from a third party, the court relied on the nonresident buyer's contacts with the forum. The buyer had entered into at least five prior contracts for the purchase of imported meats from the New York plaintiff-importer. The contracts called for delivery to ports outside New York. On two occasions defendant-buyer signed and returned to plaintiff in New York contracts that committed it to arbitration in that state. On other occasions the defendant retained the seller's form contracts without signing them. The court said it was unnecessary to decide whether defendant was "doing business" (for general jurisdiction purposes), but only whether there were minimum contacts satisfying the International Shoe requirements. Is that correct?

A persistent question is whether a bank account maintained by a nonresident in the forum is subject to attachment. In Pennington v. Fourth National Bank, 243 U.S. 269 (1917), a nonresident husband's in-state bank account was attached by the wife in a suit for alimony. The court upheld the attachment. Does the validity of an attachment of property unrelated to the cause of action survive the Shaffer decision? An affirmative answer was given in Feder v. Turkish Airlines, 441 F.Supp. 1273 (S.D.N.Y.1977). The presence of the Turkish corporation's bank account in New York was held sufficient to supply the required jurisdictional contact. Shaffer was distinguished on the basis that the defendants there had not voluntarily associated themselves with the forum state. But the fact that a nonresident Spanish corporation sent an aircraft engine to Arizona for repair, even though there may have been some relationship between the subject matter of the contract sued upon and the engine, did not suffice to warrant quasi-in-rem-style attachment. Omni Aircraft Sales, Inc. v. Actividades Aereas Aragonesas (D.Ariz.1977) (not reported).

NOTES

(1) After the Supreme Court's decision in *Shaffer*, the Delaware Code was amended (Del.Code Title 10, § 3114) to provide that "every nonresident of [Delaware] who after September 1, 1977, accepts election or appointment as a director, trustee or member of the governing body of a [Delaware] corporation, . . . or who after June 30, 1978 serves in such capacity . . . shall, by such acceptance or by such service, be deemed thereby to have consented to the appointment of the registered agent of such corporation (or, if there is none, the Secretary of State) as his agent upon whom service of process may be made in all civil actions or proceedings brought in this state, by or on behalf of, or against such corporation, in which such director, trustee or member is a necessary or proper party, or in any action or proceeding against such director, trustee or member for violation of his duty in such capacity . . . ."

Being appointed a director of a Delaware corporation is by itself a constitutionally sufficient basis for the application of this statute to a non-resident defendant. Armstrong v. Pomerance, 423 A.2d 174 (Del.1980).

(2) Among the many articles written about Shaffer v. Heitner are: Lowenfeld, In Search of the Intangible: A Comment on Shaffer v. Heitner, 53 N.Y.U.L.Rev. 102 (1978); Riesenfeld, Shaffer v. Heitner: Holding, Implications, Forebodings, 30 Hast.L.J. 1183 (1979); Silberman, Shaffer v. Heitner, The End of an Era, 53 N.Y.U.L.Rev. 33 (1978); Slomanson, Real Property Unrelated to Claim: Due Process for Quasi in Rem Jurisdiction?, 83 Dickinson L.Rev. 51 (1978); Symposium, 1978 Wash.U.L.Q. 273; Symposium, 63 Iowa L.Rev. 991. For a helpful analysis of the effect of Shaffer v. Heitner on the interplay of principles of judicial jurisdiction and choice of law, see Hay, The Interrelations of Jurisdiction and Choice-of-Law in U.S. Conflicts Law, 28 Inter. and Comp.L.Q. 161 (1979).

(3) Judge John Gibbons had gone a considerable distance in anticipating the Shaffer decision in a concurring opinion in Jonnet v. Dollar Savings Bank of The City of New York, 530 F.2d 1123 (3d Cir. 1976), referred to by Justice Marshall in Shaffer.

SEIDER v. ROTH

Court of Appeals of New York, 1966.
17 N.Y.2d 111, 269 N.Y.S.2d 99, 216 N.E.2d 312.

DESMOND, CHIEF JUDGE. This appeal, taken by leave of the Appellate Division, brings us a question new to this court—in a personal injury action against a nonresident defendant, is defendant's liability insurer's contractual obligation to defend and indemnify defendant a "debt" owing to defendant and as such subject to attachment under CPLR 6202? Both courts below answered that question in the affirmative. We think that is the correct answer.

The two plaintiffs, husband and wife, residents of New York, were injured in an automobile accident on a highway in Vermont, allegedly through the negligence of defendant Lemiux who lives in Quebec (the other defendant, Roth, was the driver of a third car involved in the collision). The order of attachment directed the Sheriff to levy upon the contractual obligation of Hartford Accident and Indemnity Company to defend and indemnify defendant Lemiux under a policy of automobile liability issued by Hartford to Lemiux. Hartford is an insurer doing business in New York State and the attachment papers were served on it in New York State. The Hartford-Lemiux liability policy was issued in Canada. Lemiux was personally served in Quebec.

Defendant Lemiux moved to vacate the attachment and the service of the summons and complaint on Lemiux. Special Term denied the motion. . . . The controlling statutes are CPLR 5201 and 6202.* . . . The whole question, therefore, is whether Hartford's

---

* CPLR § 6202 provides in part: "Any debt or property against which a money judgment may be enforced as provided in section 5201 is subject to attachment. . . ."

contractual obligation to defendant is a debt or cause of action such as may be attached. The Hartford policy is in customary form. It requires Hartford, among other things, to defend Lemiux in any automobile negligence action and, if judgment be rendered against Lemiux, to indemnify him therefor. Thus, as soon as the accident occurred there was imposed on Hartford a contractual obligation which should be considered a "debt" within the meaning of CPLR 5201 and 6202. In fact, the policy casts on the insurer several obligations which accrue as soon as the insurer gets notice of an accident, and whether or not a suit is ever brought. For instance, under the "Insuring Agreements" and under "Additional Agreements" "No. 2", the insurer agrees upon receipt of notice of loss or damage to investigate and if expedient to negotiate or settle with the claimant. Furthermore, under "Section B" the insurer agrees to pay necessary medical and similar expenses of the insured and any other injured person. . . .

The order appealed from should be affirmed, with costs, and the certified question answered in the affirmative.

BURKE, JUDGE (dissenting). . . . The so-called "debt" which is supposed to be subject to attachment is a mere promise made to the nonresident insured by the foreign insurance carrier to *defend and indemnify* the Canadian resident *if a suit is commenced* and *if damages are awarded* against the insured. Such a promise is contingent in nature. It is exactly this type of contingent undertaking which does not fall within the definition of attachable debt contained in CPLR 5201 (subd. [a]), i.e., one which "is past due or which is yet to become due, certainly or upon demand of the judgment debtor". The bare undertaking to defend and indemnify is not an obligation "past due" and it is not certain to become due until jurisdiction over the insured is *properly* obtained. . . .

Faced with this long-established rule the plaintiffs indulge in circular ratiocination. The jurisdiction, they assert, is based upon a promise which evidently does not mature until there is jurisdiction. The existence of the policy is used as a sufficient basis for jurisdiction to start the very action necessary to activate the insurer's obligation under the policy. In other words, the promise to defend the insured is assumed to furnish the jurisdiction for a civil suit which must be validly commenced before the obligation to defend can possibly accrue. "This is a bootstrap situation." (Professor D. D. Siegel, Supplementary Commentary to CPLR 5201, McKinney's Cons. Laws of N.Y., Book 7B, 1965 Pamphlet, pp. 10–13.) It is indisputable that prior to the commencement of the suit the insurer owed no "debt" to the insured. . . .

The argument is made that several debts do accrue as soon as the insurer receives a notice of an accident. The first alleged obligation—the agreement "to investigate and if expedient to negotiate or settle with the claimant"—cannot be construed to impose a duty on the carrier which would amount to a "debt" under CPLR 5201 (subd. [a]). It is not an absolute commitment but one left solely within the discretion of the carrier as it necessarily must be because of the enormous number of notices of accident filed. The second alleged obligation under Insuring Agreement B, dealing with medical payments, has no relation to the third-party liability agreement under which these plaintiffs claim. The medical payment insuring agreement, like the collision insuring agreement, is a separate agreement and runs only in favor of the insured and the passengers in his car. It is also contingent upon submission of acceptable written proof, oftentimes required to be under oath, together with executed authorizations from each injured person to scrutinize his medical reports and permission for a personal physical examination of each person. Apart from the undeniable fact that this section of the policy has no relevance to the gravamen of plaintiffs' cause of action, the obligation to the insured is a conditional type, not absolute as specified by the statute and thus not attachable for jurisdictional purposes.

RUSH v. SAVCHUK

Supreme Court of the United States, 1980.
444 U.S. 320, 100 S.Ct. 571, 62 L.Ed.2d 516.

MR. JUSTICE MARSHALL delivered the opinion of the Court.

This appeal presents the question whether a State may constitutionally exercise *quasi in rem* jurisdiction over a defendant who has no forum contacts by attaching the contractual obligation of an insurer licensed to do business in the State to defend and indemnify him in connection with the suit.

I

On January 13, 1972, two Indiana residents were involved in a single-car accident in Elkhart, Ind. Appellee Savchuk, who was a passenger in the car driven by appellant Rush, was injured. The car, owned by Rush's father, was insured by appellant State Farm Mutual Automobile Insurance Co. (State Farm) under a liability insurance policy issued in Indiana. Indiana's guest statute would have barred a claim by Savchuk. Ind.Stat. § 9–3–3–1.

Savchuk moved with his parents to Minnesota in June 1973.[1] On May 28, 1974, he commenced an action against Rush in the Minnesota state courts.[2] As Rush had no contacts with Minnesota that would support *in personam* jurisdiction, Savchuk attempted to obtain *quasi in rem* jurisdiction by garnishing State Farm's obligation under the insurance policy to defend and indemnify Rush in connection with

---

1. Savchuk moved to Pennsylvania after this appeal was filed.

2. The suit was filed after the two-year Indiana statute of limitations had run. 272 N.W.2d 888, 891, n. 2 (1978).

such a suit. State Farm does business in Minnesota. Rush was personally served in Indiana. The complaint alleged negligence and sought $125,000 in damages.

As provided by the state garnishment statute, Savchuk moved the trial court for permission to file a supplemental complaint making the garnishee, State Farm, a party to the action after State Farm's response to the garnishment summons asserted that it owed the defendant nothing. Rush and State Farm moved to dismiss the complaint for lack of jurisdiction over the defendant. The trial court denied the motion to dismiss and granted the motion for leave to file the supplemental complaint.

On appeal, the Minnesota Supreme Court affirmed the trial court's decision. 311 Minn. 480, 245 N.W.2d 624 (1976) (*Savchuk I*). It held, first, that the obligation of an insurance company to defend and indemnify a nonresident insured under an automobile liability insurance policy is a garnishable res in Minnesota for the purpose of obtaining *quasi in rem* jurisdiction when the incident giving rise to the action occurs outside Minnesota but the plaintiff is a Minnesota resident when the suit is filed. Second, the court held that the assertion of jurisdiction over Rush was constitutional because he had notice of the suit and an opportunity to defend, his liability was limited to the amount of the policy, and the garnishment procedure may be used only by Minnesota residents. The court expressly recognized that Rush had engaged in no voluntary activity that would justify the exercise of *in personam* jurisdiction. The court found, however, that considerations of fairness supported the exercise of *quasi in rem* jurisdiction because in accident litigation the insurer controls the defense of the case, State Farm does business in and is regulated by the State, and the State has an interest in protecting its residents and providing them with a forum in which to litigate their claims.

Rush appealed to this Court. We vacated the judgment and remanded the cause for further consideration in light of Shaffer v. Heitner [p. 148, supra].

On remand, the Minnesota Supreme Court held that the assertion of *quasi in rem* jurisdiction through garnishment of an insurer's obligation to an insured complied with the due process standards enunciated in *Shaffer*. 272 N.W.2d 888 (Minn.1978) (*Savchuk II*). The court found that the garnishment statute differed from the Delaware stock sequestration procedure held unconstitutional in *Shaffer* because the garnished property was intimately related to the litigation and the garnishment procedure paralleled the asserted state interest in "facilitating recoveries for resident plaintiffs." Id., at 891. This appeal followed.

II

The Minnesota Supreme Court held that the Minnesota garnishment statute embodies the rule stated in Seider v. Roth [p. 159, supra], that the contractual obligation of an insurance company to its insured under a liability insurance policy is a debt subject to attachment under state law if the insurer does business in the State. *Seider* jurisdiction was upheld against a due process challenge in Simpson v. Loehmann, 21 N.Y.2d 305, 234 N.E.2d 669 (1967), reargument denied 21 N.Y.2d 990, 238 N.E.2d 319 (1968). The New York court relied on Harris v. Balk, 198 U.S. 215 (1905), in holding that the presence of the debt in the State was sufficient to permit *quasi in rem* jurisdiction over the absent defendant. The court also concluded that the exercise of jurisdiction was permissible under the Due Process Clause because, "[v]iewed realistically, the insurer in a case such as the present is in full control of the litigation" and "where the plaintiff is a resident of the forum state and the insurer is present in and regulated by it, the State has a substantial and continuing relation with the controversy." Simpson v. Loehmann, supra, at 311, 234 N.E.2d, at 672.

The United States Court of Appeals for the Second Circuit gave its approval to *Seider* in Minichiello v. Rosenberg, 410 F.2d 106, adhered to en banc, 410 F.2d 117 (1968), cert. denied, 396 U.S. 844 (1969), although on a slightly different rationale. Judge Friendly construed *Seider* as "in effect a judicially created direct action statute. The insurer doing business in New York is considered the real party in interest and the nonresident insured is viewed simply as a conduit, who has to be named as a defendant in order to provide a conceptual basis for getting at the insurer." 410 F.2d, at 109; see Donawitz v. Danek, 42 N.Y.2d 138, 142, 366 N.E.2d 253, 255 (1977). The court held that New York could constitutionally enact a direct action statute, and that the restriction of liability to the amount of the policy coverage made the policyholder's personal stake in the litigation so slight that the exercise of jurisdiction did not offend due process.

New York has continued to adhere to *Seider*.[10] New Hampshire follows *Seider* if the defendant resides in a *Seider* jurisdiction,[11] but not in other cases.[12] Minnesota is the only other State that has adopted *Seider*-type jurisdiction.[13] The Second Circuit recently reaf-

---

10. Baden v. Staples, 45 N.Y.2d 889, 383 N.E.2d 110 (1978). The State has declined, however, to make the attachment procedure available to nonresident plaintiffs. Donawitz v. Danek, 42 N.Y.2d 138, 366 N.E.2d 253 (1977).

11. Forbes v. Boynton, 113 N.H. 617, 313 A.2d 129 (1973).

12. Camire v. Scieszka, 116 N.H. 281, 358 A.2d 397 (1976).

13. The practice has been rejected, based on state law or constitutional grounds, in Belcher v. Government Employees Ins. Co., 282 Md. 718, 387 A.2d 770 (1978); Javorek v. Superior Court, 17 Cal.3d 629, 552 P.2d 728 (1976); Hart v. Cote, 145 N.J.Super. 420, 367 A.2d 1219 (Law Div.1976); Grinnell v. Garrett, 295 So.2d 496 (La.App.1974); Johnson v. Farmers Alliance Mutual Ins. Co., 499 P.2d 1387 (Okla.1972); State ex rel. Government Employees Ins. Co. v. Lasky, 454 S.W.2d 942 (Mo.App.1970); Howard v. Allen, 254 S.C. 455, 176 S.E.2d 127 (1970); De Rentiis v. Lewis, 106 R.I. 240, 258 A.2d 464 (1969); Housley v. Anaconda Co., 19 Utah 2d 124, 427 P.2d 390 (1967); Jardine v. Donnelly, 413 Pa. 474, 198 A.2d 513 (1964). See also Tessier v. State Farm Mutual Ins. Co., 458 F.2d 1299 (CA1 1972); Kirchman v. Mikula,

firmed its conclusion that *Seider* does not violate due process after
reconsidering the doctrine in light of Shaffer v. Heitner. O'Connor v.
Lee-Hy Paving Corp., 579 F.2d 194 (CA2), cert. denied, 439 U.S. 1034
(1978).

III

In Shaffer v. Heitner [p. 148, supra] we held that "all assertions
of state-court jurisdiction must be evaluated according to the standards set forth in *International Shoe* and its progeny." . . .

It is conceded that Rush has never had any contacts with Minnesota, and that the auto accident that is the subject of this action occurred in Indiana and also had no connection to Minnesota. The only
affiliating circumstance offered to show a relationship among Rush,
Minnesota, and this lawsuit is that Rush's insurance company does
business in the State. *Seider* constructed an ingenious jurisdictional
theory to permit a State to command a defendant to appear in its
courts on the basis of this factor alone. State Farm's contractual
obligation to defend and indemnify Rush in connection with liability
claims is treated as a debt owed by State Farm to Rush. The legal
fiction that assigns a situs to a debt, for garnishment purposes, wherever the debtor is found is combined with the legal fiction that a corporation is "present," for jurisdictional purposes, wherever it does
business to yield the conclusion that the obligation to defend and indemnify is located in the forum for purposes of the garnishment statute. The fictional presence of the policy obligation is deemed to give
the State the power to determine the policyholder's liability for the
out of state accident.

We held in *Shaffer* that the mere presence of property in a State
does not establish a sufficient relationship between the owner of the
property and the State to support the exercise of jurisdiction over an
unrelated cause of action. The ownership of property in the State is
a contact between the defendant and the forum, and it may suggest
the presence of other ties. 433 U.S., at 209. Jurisdiction is lacking,
however, unless there are sufficient contacts to satisfy the fairness
standard of *International Shoe.*

Here, the fact that the defendant's insurer does business in the
forum State suggests no further contacts between the defendant and
the forum, and the record supplies no evidence of any. State Farm's
decision to do business in Minnesota was completely adventitious as
far as Rush was concerned. He had no control over that decision,
and it is unlikely that he would have expected that by buying insurance in Indiana he had subjected himself to suit in any State to which
a potential future plaintiff might decide to move. In short, it cannot
be said that the *defendant* engaged in any purposeful activity related

443 F.2d 816 (CA5 1971); Robinson v. O.   (Conn.1975); Ricker v. LaJoie, 314
F. Shearer & Sons, 429 F.2d 83 (CA3   F.Supp. 401 (Vt.1970).
1970); Sykes v. Beal, 392 F.Supp. 1089

to the forum that would make the exercise of jurisdiction fair, just, or reasonable   . . .   merely because his insurer does business there.

Nor are there significant contacts between the litigation and the forum. The Minnesota Supreme Court was of the view that the insurance policy was so important to the litigation that it provided contacts sufficient to satisfy due process. The insurance policy is not the subject matter of the case, however, nor is it related to the operative facts of the negligence action. The contractual arrangements between the defendant and the insurer pertain only to the conduct, not the substance, of the litigation, and accordingly do not affect the court's jurisdiction unless they demonstrate ties between the defendant and the forum.

In fact, the fictitious presence of the insurer's obligation in Minnesota does not, without more, provide a basis for concluding that there is *any* contact in the *International Shoe* sense between Minnesota and the insured. To say that "a debt follows the debtor" is simply to say that intangible property has no actual situs, and a debt may be sued on wherever there is jurisdiction over the debtor. State Farm is "found," in the sense of doing business, in all 50 States and the District of Columbia. Under appellee's theory, the "debt" owed to Rush would be "present" in each of those jurisdictions simultaneously. It is apparent that such a "contact" can have no jurisdictional significance.

An alternative approach for finding minimum contacts in *Seider*-type cases, referred to with approval by the Minnesota Supreme Court, is to attribute the insurer's forum contacts to the defendant by treating the attachment procedure as the functional equivalent of a direct action against the insurer. This approach views *Seider* jurisdiction as fair both to the insurer, whose forum contacts would support *in personam* jurisdiction even for an unrelated cause of action, and to the "nominal defendant." Because liability is limited to the policy amount, the defendant incurs no personal liability, and the judgment is satisfied from the policy proceeds which are not available to the insured for any purpose other than paying accident claims, the insured is said to have such a slight stake in the litigation as a practical matter that it is not unfair to make him a "nominal defendant" in order to obtain jurisdiction over the insurance company.

Seider actions are not equivalent to direct actions, however. The State's ability to exert its power over the "nominal defendant" is analytically prerequisite to the insurer's entry into the case as a garnishee. If the Constitution forbids the assertion of jurisdiction over the insured based on the policy, then there is no conceptual basis for bringing the "garnishee" into the action. Because the party with forum contacts can only be reached through the out of state party, the question of jurisdiction over the nonresident cannot be ignored.

Moreover, the assumption that the defendant has no real stake in the litigation is far from self-evident.[20]

The Minnesota court also attempted to attribute State Farm's contacts to Rush by considering the "defending parties" together and aggregating their forum contacts in determining whether it had jurisdiction. The result was the assertion of jurisdiction over Rush based solely on the activities of State Farm. Such a result is plainly unconstitutional. Naturally, the parties' relationships with each other may be significant in evaluating their ties to the forum. The requirements of *International Shoe*, however, must be met as to each defendant over whom a state court exercises jurisdiction.

The justifications offered in support of *Seider* jurisdiction share a common characteristic: they shift the focus of the inquiry from the relationship among the defendant, the forum, and the litigation to that among the plaintiff, the forum, the insurer, and the litigation. The insurer's contacts with the forum are attributed to the defendant because the policy was taken out in anticipation of such litigation. The State's interests in providing a forum for its residents and in regulating the activities of insurance companies are substituted for its contacts with the defendant and the cause of action. This subtle shift in focus from the defendant to the plaintiff is most evident in the decisions limiting *Seider* jurisdiction to actions by forum residents on the ground that permitting nonresidents to avail themselves of the procedure would be unconstitutional.[22] In other words, the plaintiff's contacts with the forum are decisive in determining whether the defendant's due process rights are violated.

Such an approach is forbidden by *International Shoe* and its progeny. . . . The judgment of the Minnesota Supreme Court is, therefore,

Reversed.

20. A party does not extinguish his legal interest in a dispute by insuring himself against having to pay an eventual judgment out of his own pocket. Moreover, the purpose of insurance is simply to make the defendant whole for the economic costs of the lawsuit; but noneconomic factors may also be important to the defendant. Professional malpractice actions, for example, question the defendant's integrity and competence and may affect his professional standing. Cf. Donawitz v. Danek, 42 N.Y.2d 138, 366 N.E.2d 253 (1977) (medical malpractice action premised on *Seider* jurisdiction dismissed because plaintiff was a nonresident). Further, one can easily conceive of cases in which the defendant might have a substantial economic stake in *Seider* litigation—if, for example, multiple plaintiffs sued in different States for an aggregate amount in excess of the policy limits, or if a successful claim would affect the policyholder's insurability. For these reasons, the defendant's interest in the adjudication of his liability cannot reasonably be characterized as *de minimus*.

22. See, e.g., Farrell v. Piedmont Aviation, Inc., 411 F.2d 812 (CA2 1969); Rintala v. Shoemaker, 362 F.Supp. 1044 (Minn.1973); Donawitz v. Danek, 42 N.Y.2d 138, 366 N.E.2d 253 (1977); *Savchuk I.*

MR. JUSTICE STEVENS, dissenting.

. . . In this kind of case, the Minnesota statute authorizing jurisdiction is correctly characterized as the "functional equivalent" of a so-called direct action statute. The impact of the judgment is against the insurer. I believe such a direct action statute is valid as applied to a suit brought by a forum resident, . . . even if the accident giving rise to the action did not occur in the forum State, . . . so long as it is understood that the forum may exercise no power whatsoever over the individual defendant. As so understood it makes no difference whether the insurance company is sued in its own name or, as Minnesota law provides, in the guise of a suit against the individual defendant.

In this case, although appellant may have a contractual obligation to his insurer to appear in court to testify and generally to cooperate in the defense of the lawsuit, it is my understanding that Minnesota law does not compel him to do so through the contempt power or otherwise. Moreover, any judgment formally entered against the individual defendant may only be executed against the proceeds of his insurance policy. In my opinion, it would violate the Due Process Clause to make any use of such a judgment against that individual—for example, by giving the judgment collateral estoppel effect in a later action against him arising from the same accident. . . . But we are not now faced with any problem concerning use of a *quasi-in-rem* judgment against an individual defendant personally. I am therefore led to the conclusion that the Federal Constitution does not require the Minnesota courts to dismiss this action.

MR. JUSTICE BRENNAN, dissenting.*

. . . a number of considerations suggest that Minnesota is an interested and convenient forum. The action was filed by a bona fide resident of the forum. Consequently, Minnesota's interests are similar to, even if lesser than, the interests of California in *McGee*, "in providing a forum for its residents and in regulating the activities of insurance companies" doing business in the State. . . . Moreover, Minnesota has "attempted to assert [its] particularized interest in trying such cases in its courts by . . . enacting a special jurisdictional statutes." *Kulko*, page 83, supra; *McGee*, page 72, supra. As in *McGee*, a resident forced to travel to a distant State to prosecute an action against someone who has injured him could, for lack of funds, be entirely unable to bring the cause of action. The plaintiff's residence in the State makes the State one of a very few convenient fora for a personal injury case (the others usually being the defendant's home State and the State where the accident occurred).[5]

---

* Mr. Justice Brennan combined in a single opinion his dissents in Rush v. Savchuk and in World-Wide Volkswagen Corporation v. Woodson (page 89, supra). That part of his opinion dealing with Rush v. Savchuk is set forth here. [Footnote by the Editors].

5. In every *International Shoe* inquiry, the defendant, necessarily, is outside the forum State. Thus it is inevi-

In addition, the burden on the defendant is slight. . . . Here the real impact is on the defendant's insurer, which is concededly amenable to suit in the forum State. The defendant is carefully protected from financial liability because the action limits the prayer for damages to the insurance policy's liability limit. The insurer will handle the case for the defendant. The defendant is only a nominal party who need be no more active in the case than the cooperation clause of his policy requires. Because of the ease of airline transportation, he need not lose significantly more time than if the case were at home. Consequently, if the suit went forward in Minnesota, the defendant would bear almost no burden or expense beyond what he would face if the suit were in his home State. The real impact on the named defendant is the same as it is in a direct action against the insurer, which would be constitutionally permissible. . . . The only distinction is the formal, "analytical prerequisite," . . . , of making the insured a named party. Surely the mere addition of appellant's name to the complaint does not suffice to create a due process violation.

Finally, even were the relevant inquiry whether there are sufficient contacts between the forum and the named defendant, I would find that such contacts exist. The insurer's presence in Minnesota is an advantage to the defendant that may well have been a consideration in his selecting the policy he did. An insurer with offices in many States makes it easier for the insured to make claims or conduct other business that may become necessary while traveling. It is simply not true that "State Farm's decision to do business in Minnesota was completely adventitious as far as Rush was concerned." . . . By buying a State Farm policy, the defendant availed himself of the benefits he might derive from having an insurance agent in Minnesota who could, among other things, facilitate a suit for appellant against a Minnesota resident. It seems unreasonable to read the Constitution as permitting one to take advantage of his nationwide insurance network but not to be burdened by it.

In sum, I would hold that appellant is not deprived of due process by being required to submit to trial in Minnesota, first because Minnesota has a sufficient interest in and connection to this litigation and to the real and nominal defendants, and second because the burden on the nominal defendant is sufficiently slight.

NOTES

(1) Justice Marshall argued that Rush should not be bound by State Farm's decision to do business in Minnesota or Savchuk's action in moving there since he had no control over those decisions. Is there an analogy between that argument and Justice White's insistence in World-Wide Volks-

table that either the defendant or the plaintiff will be inconvenienced. The problem existing at the time of Pennoyer v. Neff, that a resident plaintiff could obtain a binding judgment against an un-

suspecting, distant defendant, has virtually disappeared in this age of instant communication and virtually instant travel.

wagen (p. 85, supra) that the nonresident defendants were not made amenable to personal jurisdiction by reason of the presence of the Audi automobile in Oklahoma, since they had not placed it in a stream of commerce that ran to Oklahoma?

(2) The Court might have taken note of a point made in Brilmayer, How Contacts Count: Due Process Limitations on State Court Jurisdiction, 1980 Supreme Court Review 77, 103 (1980), namely, that neither Minnesota nor New York allows a direct action in a non-conflicts case. Both states require that an unsatisfied judgment against the insured exist before the insurer is suable in a domestic case. Is there any good reason for the courts to dispense with the requirement in a multistate case?

(3) What is the impact of Rush v. Savchuk on statutory direct actions against insurers when the insured is not subject to personal jurisdiction in the forum? The major permutations include: (a) the state where the injury occurred provides for a direct action but the forum does not; (b) the converse; (c) the plaintiff is a forum resident; (d) the plaintiff is a nonresident. These questions are considered in Ch. 7, at p. 384, infra.

(4) In Minichiello v. Rosenberg, 410 F.2d 106 (1968), adhered to en banc, 410 F.2d 117 (1969), discussed in the Rush case, Judge Friendly in his opinion for the panel rested his argument for the constitutionality of Seider's "judicially created direct action" procedure on Watson v. Employers Liability Corp., [p. 352, infra], which the dissenters in Rush also relied upon. However, in his majority opinion for the Second Circuit en banc in Minichiello Judge Friendly shifted to reliance on Harris v. Balk, arguing that as long as it stood, the nonresident defendant's claim of unfair burden in having to defend in the forum was unpersuasive. Was reliance on Watson justified? Notice that Judge Friendly's court did not think either Watson or Minichiello would support a Seider-type proceeding brought by a nonresident plaintiff. Farrell v. Piedmont Aviation, Inc., 411 F.2d 812 (1969) cert. denied 396 U.S. 840.

(5) The demise of Seider attachments dissolved a knotty issue that had troubled the court in Minichiello: if the Seider-type action determined after trial that the nonresident defendant was at fault, would that finding bind the defendant as res judicata (collateral estoppel) in a later in personam suit in another state? That question will be considered in connection with Harnischfeger Sales Corp. v. Sternberg Dredging Co., p. 238, infra.

SECTION 4.   COMPETENCE OF COURT AND NOTICE

RESTATEMENT, SECOND, CONFLICT OF LAWS: *

§ 105. Judgment Rendered By Court Lacking Competence

A judgment rendered by a court lacking competence to render it and subject to collateral attack for that reason in the state of rendition will not be recognized or enforced in other states.

---

* Quoted with the permission of the copyright owner, The American Law Institute.

THOMPSON v. WHITMAN

Supreme Court of the United States, 1874.
85 U.S. (18 Wall.) 457, 21 L.Ed. 897.

Mr. Justice Bradley delivered the opinion of the court:

This is an action of trespass for taking and carrying away goods, originally brought in the superior court of New York City, and removed by the defendant, now plaintiff in error, into the circuit court of the United States. The declaration charges that, on the 26th of September, 1862, the defendant, with force and arms on the high seas, in the outward vicinity of the Narrows of the Port of New York, and within the southern district of New York, seized and took the sloop Ann L. Whitman, with her tackle, furniture, etc., the property of the plaintiff, and carried away and converted the same. The defendant pleaded "Not guilty" and a special plea in bar. The latter plea justified the trespass by setting up that the plaintiff, a resident of New York, on the day of seizure was raking and gathering clams with said sloop in the waters of New Jersey, to wit: within the limits of the county of Monmouth, contrary to the law of that state; and that, by virtue of said law, the defendant, who was sheriff of said county, seized the sloop within the limits thereof, and informed against her before two justices of the peace of said county, by whom she was condemned and ordered to be sold. In answer to this plea the plaintiff took issue as to the place of seizure, denying that it was within the state of New Jersey or the county of Monmouth, thus challenging the jurisdiction of the justices, as well as the right of the defendant to make the seizure. On the trial conflicting testimony was given upon this point, but the defendant produced a record of the proceedings before the justices which stated the offense as having been committed and seizure as made within the county of Monmouth, with a history of the proceedings to the condemnation and order of sale. The defendant claimed that this record was conclusive, both as to the jurisdiction of the court and the merits of the case, and that it was a bar to the action, and requested the court so to charge the jury. But this was refused, and the court charged that the said record was only prima facie evidence of the facts therein stated, and threw upon the plaintiff the burden of proving the contrary. The defendant excepted, and the jury, under the direction of the court, found for the plaintiff generally, and in answer to certain questions framed by the court found specially: first, that the seizure was made within the state of New Jersey; second, that it was not made in the county of Monmouth; third, that the plaintiff was not engaged on the day of the seizure in taking clams within the limits of the county of Monmouth. Judgment being rendered for the plaintiff, the case is brought here for review.

The main question in the cause is, whether the record produced by the defendant was conclusive of the jurisdictional facts therein contained. It stated, with due particularity, sufficient facts to give the justices jurisdiction under the law of New Jersey. Could that statement be questioned collaterally in another action brought in another State? If it could be, the ruling of the court was substantially correct. If not, there was error. . . .

Without that provision of the Constitution of the United States which declares that "full faith and credit shall be given in each State to the public acts, records, and judicial proceedings of every other State," and the act of Congress passed to carry it into effect, it is clear that the record in question would not be conclusive as to the facts necessary to give the justices of Monmouth County jurisdiction, whatever might be its effect in New Jersey. In any other State it would be regarded like any foreign judgment; and as to a foreign judgment it is perfectly well settled that the inquiry is always open, whether the court by which it was rendered had jurisdiction of the person or the thing. . . .

Justice Story, who pronounced the judgment in Mills v. Duryee [7 Cranch 484], in his Commentary on the Constitution (Sec. 1313), after stating the general doctrine established by that case with regard to the conclusive effect of judgments of one State in every other State, adds: "But this does not prevent an inquiry into the jurisdiction of the court in which the original judgment was given, to pronounce it; or the right of the State itself to exercise authority over the person or the subject-matter. The Constitution did not mean to confer [upon the States] a new power or jurisdiction, but simply to regulate the effect of the acknowledged jurisdiction over persons and things within their territory." . . .

But if it is once conceded that the validity of a judgment may be attacked collaterally by evidence showing that the court had no jurisdiction, it is not perceived how any allegation contained in the record itself, however strongly made, can affect the right so to question it. The very object of the evidence is to invalidate the paper as a record. If that can be successfully done no statements contained therein have any force. If any such statements could be used to prevent inquiry, a slight form of words might always be adopted so as effectually to nullify the right of such inquiry. Recitals of this kind must be regarded like asseverations of good faith in a deed, which avail nothing if the instrument is shown to be fraudulent. The records of the domestic tribunals of England and some of the States, it is true, are held to import absolute verity as well in relation to jurisdictional as to other facts, in all collateral proceedings. Public policy and the dignity of the courts are supposed to require that no averment shall be admitted to contradict the record. But, as we have seen, that rule has no extra-territorial force. . . .

On the whole, we think it clear that the jurisdiction of the court by which a judgment is rendered in any State may be questioned in a collateral proceeding in another State, notwithstanding the provision of the fourth article of the Constitution and the law of 1790, and not-withstanding the averments contained in the record of the judgment itself.

This is decisive of the case; for, according to the findings of the jury, the justices of Monmouth County could not have had any juris-diction to condemn the sloop in question. It is true she was seized in the waters of New Jersey; but the express finding is, that the seizure was not made within the limits of the county of Monmouth, and that no clams were raked within the county on that day. The authority to make the seizure and to entertain cognizance thereof is given by the ninth section of the act, as follows:

"It shall be the duty of all sheriffs and constables, and may be lawful for any other person or persons, to seize and secure any such canoe, flat, scow, boat, or other vessel as aforesaid, and immediately thereupon give information thereof to *two justices of the peace of the county where such seizure shall have been made*, who are hereby empowered and required to meet at such time and place as they shall appoint for the trial thereof, and hear and determine the same; and in case the same shall be condemned, it shall be sold by the order of and under the direction of the said justices, who, after deducting all legal costs and charges, shall pay one-half of the proceeds of said sale to the collector of the county in which such offense shall have been committed, and the other half to the person who shall have seized and prosecuted the same."

From this it appears that the seizure must be made in a county, and that the case can only be heard by justices of the county where it is made—"two justices of the peace of the county where such seizure shall have been made." The seizure in this case as specially found by the jury was not made in Monmouth County; but the justices who tried the case were justices of that county. Consequently the justices had no jurisdiction, and the record had no validity.

It is argued that the seizure was continuous in its character, and became a seizure in Monmouth County when the sloop was carried into that county. This position is untenable. Suppose the seizure had been made in Cumberland County, in Delaware Bay, could the sloop have been carried around to Monmouth County and there con-demned, on the ground that the seizure was continuous, and became finally a seizure in Monmouth County? This would hardly be con-tended. But it is said that the seizure was made within the State, off the county of Monmouth, and not within the limits of any county; and, hence, that Monmouth County was the first county in which the seizure took place. If this had been true (as it undoubtedly was), and the jury had so found, still it would not have helped the case. The major proposition is not correct. A seizure is a single act, and not a continuous fact. Possession, which follows seizure, is continuous. It is the seizure which must be made within the county where the vessel is to be proceeded against and condemned. The case may have been a casus omissus in the law; it is certainly not included in it.

As this disposes of all the errors which have been assigned, the judgment must be

Affirmed.

NOTES

(1) In his assertion, "the justices [of Monmouth County] had no jurisdiction," what meaning did Justice Bradley intend to convey by the word "jurisdiction"? Would "competence" have been an accurate word? Or should he have said the "venue" was incorrect? If the latter, should the New Jersey judgment have been vulnerable to collateral attack?

(2) In Pemberton v. Hughes, [1889] 1 Ch. 781, the validity of a Florida divorce decree was in question in an English court. The defendant asserted the decree was void because the return day of appearance in court was only nine days after the service of process, while under the rules of the Florida court the period should have been ten days. The court held that the divorce was valid, since the tests of "international jurisdiction" were met. What is the dividing line between a defect that can be corrected only by appeal and a defect that impairs jurisdiction?

———

MCDONALD V. MABEE, 243 U.S. 90 (1917): The case involved the validity of a previous judgment rendered against the defendant in the Texas courts. "When the former suit was begun, the defendant, Mabee, was domiciled in Texas, but had left the state with intent to establish a home elsewhere, his family, however, still residing there. He subsequently returned to Texas for a short time and later established his domicil in Missouri. The only service upon him was by publication in a newspaper once a week for four successive weeks after his final departure from the state, and he did not appear in the suit. The supreme court of the state held that this satisfied the Texas statutes, and that the judgment was a good personal judgment . . . 107 Tex. 139, 175 S.W. 676." *Held* that the judgment was void since the notice given the defendant did not comply with due process requirements. "When the former suit was begun, Mabee, although technically domiciled in Texas, had left the state, intending to establish his home elsewhere. Perhaps in view of his technical position and the actual presence of his family in the state, a summons left at his last and usual place of abode would have been enough. But it appears to us that an advertisement in a local newspaper is not sufficient notice to bind a person who has left a state, intending not to return. To dispense with personal service the substitute that is most likely to reach the defendant is the least that ought to be required if substantial justice is to be done. . . ."

———

MULLANE v. CENTRAL HANOVER BANK & TRUST CO.

Supreme Court of the United States, 1950.
339 U.S. 306, 70 S.Ct. 652, 94 L.Ed. 865.

MR. JUSTICE JACKSON delivered the opinion of the Court.

This controversy questions the constitutional sufficiency of notice to beneficiaries on judicial settlement of accounts by the trustee of a common trust fund established under the New York Banking Law. The New York Court of Appeals considered and overruled objections that the statutory notice contravenes requirements of the Fourteenth Amendment and that by allowance of the account beneficiaries were deprived of property without due process of law. . . .

Common trust fund legislation is addressed to a problem appropriate for state action. Mounting overheads have made administration of small trusts undesirable to corporate trustees. In order that donors and testators of moderately sized trusts may not be denied the service of corporate fiduciaries, the District of Columbia and some thirty states other than New York have permitted pooling small trust estates into one fund for investment administration. The income, capital gains, losses and expenses of the collective trust are shared by the constituent trusts in proportion to their contribution. By this plan, diversification of risk and economy of management can be extended to those whose capital standing alone would not obtain such advantage.

Statutory authorization for the establishment of such common trust funds is provided in the New York Banking Law, § 100–c (c. 687, L.1937, as amended by c. 602, L.1943 and c. 158, L.1944). Under this Act a trust company may, with approval of the State Banking Board, establish a common fund and, within prescribed limits, invest therein the assets of an unlimited number of estates, trusts or other funds of which it is trustee. Each participating trust shares ratably in the common fund, but exclusive management and control is in the trust company as trustee, and neither a fiduciary nor any beneficiary of a participating trust is deemed to have ownership in any particular asset or investment of this common fund. The trust company must keep fund assets separate from its own, and in its fiduciary capacity may not deal with itself or any affiliate. Provisions are made for accountings twelve to fifteen months after the establishment of a fund and triennially thereafter. The decree in each such judicial settlement of accounts is made binding and conclusive as to any matter set forth in the account upon everyone having any interest in the common fund or in any participating estate, trust or fund.

In January, 1946, Central Hanover Bank and Trust Company established a common trust fund in accordance with these provisions, and in March, 1947, it petitioned the Surrogate's Court for settlement of its first account as common trustee. During the accounting period a total of 113 trusts, approximately half *inter vivos* and half testamentary, participated in the common trust fund, the gross capital of which was nearly three million dollars. The record does not show the number or residence of the beneficiaries, but they were many and it is clear that some of them were not residents of the State of New York.

The only notice given beneficiaries of this specific application was by publication in a local newspaper in strict compliance with the minimum requirements of N.Y. Banking Law § 100–c(12): "After filing such petition (for judicial settlement of its account) the petitioner shall cause to be issued by the court in which the petition is filed and shall publish not less than once in each week for four successive weeks in a newspaper to be designated by the court a notice or citation addressed generally without naming them to all parties interested in such common trust fund and in such estates, trusts or funds mentioned in the petition, all of which may be described in the notice or citation only in the manner set forth in said petition and without setting forth the residence of any such decedent or donor of any such estate, trust or fund." Thus the only notice required, and the only one given, was by newspaper publication setting forth merely the name and address of the trust company, the name and the date of establishment of the common trust fund, and a list of all participating estates, trusts or funds.

At the time the first investment in the common fund was made on behalf of each participating estate, however, the trust company, pursuant to the requirements of § 100–c(9), had notified by mail each person of full age and sound mind whose name and address were then known to it and who was "entitled to share in the income therefrom . . . (or) . . . who would be entitled to share in the principal if the event upon which such estate, trust or fund will become distributable should have occurred at the time of sending such notice." Included in the notice was a copy of those provisions of the Act relating to the sending of the notice itself and to the judicial settlement of common trust fund accounts.

Upon the filing of the petition for the settlement of accounts, appellant was, by order of the court pursuant to § 100–c(12), appointed special guardian and attorney for all persons known or unknown not otherwise appearing who had or might thereafter have any interest in the income of the common trust fund; and appellee Vaughan was appointed to represent those similarly interested in the principal. There were no other appearances on behalf of any one interested in either interest or principal.

Appellant appeared specially, objecting that notice and the statutory provisions for notice to beneficiaries were inadequate to afford due process under the Fourteenth Amendment, and therefore that the court was without jurisdiction to render a final and binding decree. Appellant's objections were entertained and overruled, the Surrogate holding that the notice required and given was sufficient. 75

N.Y.S.2d 397. A final decree accepting the accounts has been entered, affirmed by the Appellate Division of the Supreme Court, 275 App.Div. 769, 88 N.Y.S.2d 907, and by the Court of Appeals of the State of New York, 299 N.Y. 697, 87 N.E.2d 73.

The effect of this decree, as held below, is to settle "all questions respecting the management of the common fund." We understand that every right which beneficiaries would otherwise have against the trust company, either as trustee of the common fund or as trustee of any individual trust, for improper management of the common trust fund during the period covered by the accounting is sealed and wholly terminated by the decree. . . .

We are met at the outset with a challenge to the power of the State—the right of its courts to adjudicate at all as against those beneficiaries who reside without the State of New York. It is contended that the proceeding is one *in personam* in that the decree affects neither title to nor possession of any *res*, but adjudges only personal rights of the beneficiaries to surcharge their trustee for negligence or breach of trust. Accordingly, it is said, under the strict doctrine of Pennoyer v. Neff, 95 U.S. 714, the Surrogate is without jurisdiction as to nonresidents upon whom personal service of process was not made. . . .

Judicial proceedings to settle fiduciary accounts have been sometimes termed *in rem*, or more indefinitely *quasi in rem*, or more vaguely still, "in the nature of a proceeding *in rem*." It is not readily apparent how the courts of New York did or would classify the present proceeding, which has some characteristics and is wanting in some features of proceedings both *in rem* and *in personam*. But in any event we think that the requirements of the Fourteenth Amendment to the Federal Constitution do not depend upon a classification for which the standards are so elusive and confused generally and which, being primarily for state courts to define, may and do vary from state to state. Without disparaging the usefulness of distinctions between actions *in rem* and those *in personam* in many branches of law, or on other issues, or the reasoning which underlies them, we do not rest the power of the State to resort to constructive service in this proceeding upon how its courts or this Court may regard this historic antithesis. It is sufficient to observe that, whatever the technical definition of its chosen procedure, the interest of each state in providing means to close trusts that exist by the grace of its laws and are administered under the supervision of its courts is so insistent and rooted in custom as to establish beyond doubt the right of its courts to determine the interests of all claimants, resident or nonresident, provided its procedure accords full opportunity to appear and be heard.

Quite different from the question of a state's power to discharge trustees is that of the opportunity it must give beneficiaries to contest. Many controversies have raged about the cryptic and abstract words of the Due Process Clause but there can be no doubt that at a minimum they require that deprivation of life, liberty or property by adjudication be preceded by notice and opportunity for hearing appropriate to the nature of the case.

In two ways this proceeding does or may deprive beneficiaries of property. It may cut off their rights to have the trustee answer for negligent or illegal impairments of their interests. Also, their interests are presumably subject to diminution in the proceeding by allowance of fees and expenses to one who, in their names but without their knowledge, may conduct a fruitless or uncompensatory contest. Certainly the proceeding is one in which they may be deprived of property rights and hence notice and hearing must measure up to the standards of due process.

Personal service of written notice within the jurisdiction is the classic form of notice always adequate in any type of proceeding. But the vital interest of the State in bringing any issues as to its fiduciaries to a final settlement can be served only if interests or claims of individuals who are outside of the State can somehow be determined. A construction of the Due Process Clause which would place impossible or impractical obstacles in the way could not be justified.

Against this interest of the State we must balance the individual interest sought to be protected by the Fourteenth Amendment. This is defined by our holding that "The fundamental requisite of due process of law is the opportunity to be heard." Grannis v. Ordean, 234 U.S. 385, 394. This right to be heard has little reality or worth unless one is informed that the matter is pending and can choose for himself whether to appear or default, acquiesce or contest.

The Court has not committed itself to any formula achieving a balance between these interests in a particular proceeding or determining when constructive notice may be utilized or what test it must meet. Personal service has not in all circumstances been regarded as indispensable to the process due to residents, and it has more often been held unnecessary as to nonresidents. We disturb none of the established rules on these subjects. No decision constitutes a controlling or even a very illuminating precedent for the case before us. But a few general principles stand out in the books.

An elementary and fundamental requirement of due process in any proceeding which is to be accorded finality is notice reasonably calculated, under all the circumstances, to apprise interested parties of the pendency of the action and afford them an opportunity to present their objections. . . . The notice must be of such nature as reasonably to convey the required information . . . and it must afford a reasonable time for those interested to make their appearance. . . . But if with due regard for the practicalities and peculiarities of the case these conditions are reasonably met, the constitutional requirements are satisfied. "The criterion is not the possibility of conceivable injury but the just and reasonable character of the requirements, having reference to the subject with which the statute deals." American Land Co. v. Zeiss, 219 U.S. 47, 67; and see Blinn v. Nelson, 222 U.S. 1, 7.

But when notice is a person's due, process which is a mere gesture is not due process. The means employed must be such as one desirous of actually informing the absentee might reasonably adopt to accomplish it. The reasonableness and hence the constitutional validity of any chosen method may be defended on the ground that it is in itself reasonably certain to inform those affected, compare Hess v. Pawloski, 274 U.S. 352, with Wuchter v. Pizzutti, 276 U.S. 13,* or, where conditions do not reasonably permit such notice, that the form chosen is not substantially less likely to bring home notice than other of the feasible and customary substitutes.

It would be idle to pretend that publication alone, as prescribed here, is a reliable means of acquainting interested parties of the fact that their rights are before the courts. It is not an accident that the greater number of cases reaching this Court on the question of adequacy of notice have been concerned with actions founded on process constructively served through local newspapers. Chance alone brings to the attention of even a local resident an advertisement in small type inserted in the back pages of a newspaper, and if he makes his home outside the area of the newspaper's normal circulation the odds that the information will never reach him are large indeed. The chance of actual notice is further reduced when, as here, the notice required does not even name those whose attention it is supposed to attract, and does not inform acquaintances who might call it to attention. In weighing its sufficiency on the basis of equivalence with actual notice, we are unable to regard this as more than a feint.

Nor is publication here reinforced by steps likely to attract the parties' attention to the proceeding. It is true that publication traditionally has been acceptable as notification supplemental to other action which in itself may reasonably be expected to convey a warning. The ways of an owner with tangible property are such that he usually arranges means to learn of any direct attack upon his possessory or proprietary rights. Hence, libel of a ship, attachment of a chattel or entry upon real estate in the name of law may reasonably be expected to come promptly to the owner's attention. When the state within which the owner has located such property seizes it for some reason, publication or posting affords an additional measure of notification. . . .

---

* In Wuchter v. Pizzutti, the defendant had received notice by personal service outside the state but was nevertheless allowed to attack successfully the New Jersey nonresident motorist statute on the ground that it did not require that anyone inform defendant of the commencement of suit in a way making it "reasonably probable" that he would receive actual notice. [Footnote by the Editors.]

This Court has not hesitated to approve of resort to publication as a customary substitute in another class of cases where it is not reasonably possible or practicable to give more adequate warning. Thus it has been recognized that, in the case of persons missing or unknown, employment of an indirect and even a probably futile means of notification is all that the situation permits and creates no constitutional bar to a final decree foreclosing their rights. . . .

Those beneficiaries represented by appellant whose interests or whereabouts could not with due diligence be ascertained come clearly within this category. As to them the statutory notice is sufficient. However great the odds that publication will never reach the eyes of such unknown parties, it is not in the typical case much more likely to fail than any of the choices open to legislators endeavoring to prescribe the best notice practicable.

Nor do we consider it unreasonable for the State to dispense with more certain notice to those beneficiaries whose interests are either conjectural or future or, although they could be discovered upon investigation, do not in due course of business come to knowledge of the common trustee. Whatever searches might be required in another situation under ordinary standards of diligence, in view of the character of the proceedings and the nature of the interests here involved we think them unnecessary. We recognize the practical difficulties and costs that would be attendant on frequent investigations into the status of great numbers of beneficiaries, many of whose interests in the common fund are so remote as to be ephemeral; and we have no doubt that such impracticable and extended searches are not required in the name of due process. The expense of keeping informed from day to day of substitutions among even current income beneficiaries and presumptive remaindermen, to say nothing of the far greater number of contingent beneficiaries, would impose a severe burden on the plan, and would likely dissipate its advantages. These are practical matters in which we should be reluctant to disturb the judgment of the state authorities.

Accordingly we overrule appellant's constitutional objections to published notice insofar as they are urged on behalf of any beneficiaries whose interests or addresses are unknown to the trustee.

As to known present beneficiaries of known place of residence, however, notice by publication stands on a different footing. Exceptions in the name of necessity do not sweep away the rule that within the limits of practicability notice must be such as is reasonably calculated to reach interested parties. Where the names and postoffice addresses of those affected by a proceeding are at hand, the reasons disappear for resort to means less likely than the mails to apprise them of its pendency.

The trustee has on its books the names and addresses of the income beneficiaries represented by appellant, and we find no tenable ground for dispensing with a serious effort to inform them personally of the accounting, at least by ordinary mail to the record addresses. Cf. Wuchter v. Pizzutti, supra. Certainly sending them a copy of the statute months and perhaps years in advance does not answer this purpose. The trustee periodically remits their income to them, and we think that they might reasonably expect that with or apart from their remittances word might come to them personally that steps were being taken affecting their interests.

We need not weigh contentions that a requirement of personal service of citation on even the large number of known resident or non-resident beneficiaries would, by reasons of delay if not of expense, seriously interfere with the proper administration of the fund. Of course personal service even without the jurisdiction of the issuing authority serves the end of actual and personal notice, whatever power of compulsion it might lack. However, no such service is required under the circumstances. This type of trust presupposes a large number of small interests. The individual interest does not stand alone but is identical with that of a class. The rights of each in the integrity of the fund and the fidelity of the trustee are shared by many other beneficiaries. Therefore notice reasonably certain to reach most of those interested in objecting is likely to safeguard the interests of all, since any objection sustained would inure to the benefit of all. We think that under such circumstances reasonable risks that notice might not actually reach every benficiary are justifiable. . . . .

The statutory notice to known beneficiaries is inadequate, not because in fact it fails to reach everyone, but because under the circumstances it is not reasonably calculated to reach those who could easily be informed by other means at hand. However it may have been in former times, the mails today are recognized as an efficient and inexpensive means of communication. Moreover, the fact that the trust company has been able to give mailed notice to known beneficiaries at the time the common trust fund was established is persuasive that postal notification at the time of accounting would not seriously burden the plan.

In some situations the law requires greater precautions in its proceedings than the business world accepts for its own purposes. In few, if any, will it be satisfied with less. Certainly it is instructive, in determining the reasonableness of the impersonal broadcast notification here used, to ask whether it would satisfy a prudent man of business, counting his pennies but finding it in his interest to convey information to many persons whose names and addresses are in his files. We are not satisfied that it would. Publication may theoretically be available for all the world to see, but it is too much in our day to suppose that each or any individual beneficiary does or could examine all that is published to see if something may be tucked away in it that affects his property interests. We have before indicated in reference to notice by publication that, "Great caution should be used not to let fiction deny the fair play that can be secured only by a pretty close adhesion to fact." McDonald v. Mabee, 243 U.S. 90, 91.

We hold that the notice of judicial settlement of accounts required by the New York Banking Law § 100–c(12) is incompatible with the requirements of the Fourteenth Amendment as a basis for adjudication depriving known persons whose whereabouts are also known of substantial property rights. Accordingly the judgment is reversed and the cause remanded for further proceedings not inconsistent with this opinion.

Reversed.

[A dissenting memorandum by MR. JUSTICE BURTON is omitted.]

NOTES

(1) In a series of cases the Supreme Court has held that publication in a newspaper, with or without posted notice, is insufficient to comply with the Mullane standards of due process. In Mennonite Board of Missions v. Adams, ___ U.S. ___, 103 S.Ct. 2706 (1983), a notice of tax sale was posted in the county courthouse and published once a week for three weeks. This was held inadequate notice to a mortgagee of the property despite the dissenters' argument that the notification satisfied Mullane's "balancing" test. Cf. Schroeder v. City of New York, 371 U.S. 208 (1962) and Walker v. City of Hutchinson, 352 U.S. 112 (1965), invalidating newspaper and posted notices in condemnation cases where the owner's address was known to the city. In Greene v. Lindsey, 456 U.S. 444 (1982), the court held that posting a summons on the tenant's apartment door was inadequate notice for a forcible entry and detainer.

(2) The common forms of notice in an action in personam are: handing the process to the person to be served; leaving it at his place of residence (with a person of a described class or affixed to the door, etc.); sending it by registered mail after service on a designated statutory agent, such as a registrar. Should registered mail alone always be sufficient?

(3) Is in-state service upon a local agent or designated governmental official a necessary element of due notice to a nonresident defendant not served within the state? See Wis.Stat.Ann. § 262.06; Hopson, Cognovit Judgments: An Ignored Problem of Due Process and Full Faith and Credit, 29 U. of Chi.L.Rev. 111, 140 (1961). Would the United States Supreme Court today hold that a defendant who has received actual notice may avoid jurisdiction by showing that the long-arm statute did not require constitutionally sufficient type of notification? Cf. National Equipment Rental, Ltd. v. Szukhent, 375 U.S. 311 (1964); Wuchter v. Pizzutti, 276 U.S. 13 (1928), p. 53, supra.

(4) Dobkin v. Chapman, 21 N.Y.2d 490, 236 N.E.2d 451 (1968). Involved were three cases arising from automobile accidents in New York. In two of the cases, defendants were domiciled in New York while in the third they were domiciled in another state. In each case, the defendants' whereabouts were unknown and it was therefore impossible to give them actual notice. Nevertheless in each case the plaintiff was permitted to proceed after having given notice in a form prescribed by the court, in one case by publishing the summons and order in a local newspaper and in another by mailing the process and order to defendants' last known address from which they were

known to have moved. Held affirmed. The plaintiffs should not be deprived of their rights after having done all that they reasonably could to inform the defendants. These are "situations in which insistence on actual notice, or even on the high probability of actual notice, would be both unfair to plaintiffs and harmful to the public interest."

Chapter 4

LIMITATIONS ON THE EXERCISE OF JURISDICTION

Introductory Note: This chapter examines situations where states choose not to exercise judicial jurisdiction they undoubtedly have. This may result because of an agreement between the parties purporting to give exclusive jurisdiction to the courts of another state or because the court deems itself to be an inconvenient forum for the trial of the action or to be incapable of granting appropriate relief. Another question treated in this chapter is whether, when a state seeks by statute to restrict to its own courts jurisdiction to entertain particular actions, the courts of other states will give effect to the former state's desires. On some occasions, a state which has judicial jurisdiction in the due process sense may be required by other provisions of the United States Constitution either to hear or to refrain from hearing a case.

SECTION 1. LIMITATIONS IMPOSED BY CONTRACT

Will a court refrain from exercising jurisdiction it possesses because the parties have entered into an agreement that they will bring their disputes exclusively before the courts of a state or states other than that of the forum? In the past, agreements of this kind were usually disregarded by American courts. Of late, effect has usually been given to these agreements except when it would be "unfair or unreasonable" to do so. Restatement, Second, Conflict of Laws § 80.

Section 3 of the Model Choice of Forum Act † states more precisely the circumstances making it "unfair or unreasonable" to give effect to the parties' agreement.

Section 3. [*Action in Another Place by Agreement.*] If the parties have agreed in writing that an action shall on a controversy be

† After having been adopted in four states, this model act was withdrawn in 1975. (Handbook of the Conference of Commissioners on Uniform State Laws 351 (1976).

183

brought only in another state and it is brought in a court of this state, the court will dismiss or stay the action, as appropriate, unless

(1) the court is required by statute to entertain the action;

(2) the plaintiff cannot secure effective relief in the other state, for reasons other than delay in bringing the action;

(3) the other state would be a substantially less convenient place for the trial of the action than this state;

(4) the agreement as to the place of the action was obtained by misrepresentation, duress, the abuse of economic power, or other unconscionable means; or

(5) it would for some other reason be unfair or unreasonable to enforce the agreement.

Comment

. . .

Clause (4): A significant factor to be considered in determining whether there was an "abuse of economic power or other unconscionable means" is whether the choice of forum agreement was contained in an adhesion, or "take-it-or-leave-it," contract.

The most recent Supreme Court decision in point is The Bremen v. Zapata Off-Shore Co., 407 U.S. 1 (1972). That case arose out of a contract in which the defendant, a German corporation, agreed to tow a drilling rig of Zapata, an American corporation, from Louisiana to a point off Ravenna, Italy. The contract provided that "any dispute arising must be treated before the London Court of Justice" and also contained two clauses purporting to exculpate the defendant from liability for damages to the rig. These latter provisions were valid under English law, and, according to the uncontradicted testimony of a British legal expert, would have been applied to exonerate the defendant if suit had been brought in England. On the other hand, these latter provisions were invalid under the law of the United States. The rig was damaged while being towed in the Gulf of Mexico. Suit to recover for this damage was brought in a federal district court in Florida. The lower courts refused to dismiss the action despite the fact that it had been brought in violation of the choice-of-forum clause. The Supreme Court, reversed and by Chief Justice Burger, said:

". . . The expansion of American business and industry will hardly be encouraged if, notwithstanding solemn contracts, we insist on a parochial concept that all disputes must be resolved under our laws and in our courts. . . .

"Forum-selection clauses have historically not been favored by American courts. Many courts, federal and state, have declined to enforce such clauses on the ground that they were 'contrary to public policy,' or that their effect was to 'oust the jurisdiction' of the court. Although this view apparently still has considerable acceptance, other courts are tending to adopt a more hospitable attitude toward forum-selection clauses. This view . . . is that such clauses are prima facie valid and should be enforced unless enforcement is shown by the resisting party to be 'unreasonable' under the circumstances. We believe this is the correct doctrine to be followed by federal district courts sitting in admiralty. . . . This approach is substantially that followed in other common-law countries including England. . . . It accords with ancient concepts of freedom of contract and reflects an appreciation of the expanding horizons of American contractors who seek business in all parts of the world. Not surprisingly, foreign businessmen prefer, as do we, to have disputes resolved in their own courts, but if that choice is not available, then in a neutral forum with expertise in the subject matter. Plainly, the courts of England meet the standards of neutrality and long experience in admiralty litigation. The choice of that forum was made in an arms-length negotiation by experienced and sophisticated businessmen, and absent some compelling and countervailing reason it should be honored by the parties and enforced by the courts.

"The argument that such clauses are improper because they tend to 'oust' a court of jurisdiction is hardly more than a vestigial legal fiction. It appears to rest at core on historical judicial resistance to any attempt to reduce the power and business of a particular court and has little place in an era when all courts are overloaded and when businesses once essentially local now operate in world markets. It reflects something of a provincial attitude regarding the fairness of other tribunals. No one seriously contends in this case that the forum-selection clause 'ousted' the District Court of jurisdiction over Zapata's action. The threshold question is whether that court should have exercised its jurisdiction to do more than give effect to the legitimate expectations of the parties, manifested in their freely negotiated agreement, by specifically enforcing the forum clause.

"There are compelling reasons why a freely negotiated private international agreement, unaffected by fraud, undue influence, or overweening bargaining power, such as that involved here, should be given full effect. . . . Manifestly much uncertainty and possibly great inconvenience to both parties could arise if a suit could be maintained in any jurisdiction in which an accident might occur or if jurisdiction were left to any place where the *Bremen* or Unterweser might happen to be found. The elimination of all such uncertainties by agreeing in advance on a forum acceptable to both parties is an indispensable element in international trade, commerce, and contracting.

". . . [I]t seems reasonably clear that the District Court and the Court of Appeals placed the burden on Unterweser to show that London would be a more convenient forum than Tampa, although the

contract expressly resolved that issue. The correct approach would
have been to enforce the forum clause specifically unless Zapata
could clearly show that enforcement would be unreasonable and unjust, or that the clause was invalid for such reasons as fraud or over-
reaching. Accordingly, the case must be remanded for reconsideration.

"We note, however, that there is nothing in the record presently
before us that would support a refusal to enforce the forum clause.
The Court of Appeals suggested that enforcement would be contrary
to the public policy of the forum under Bisso v. Inland Waterways
Corp., 349 U.S. 85 (1955), because of the prospect that the English
courts would enforce the clauses of the towage contract purporting
to exculpate Unterweser from liability for damages to the [rig]. A
contractual choice-of-forum clause should be held unenforceable if enforcement would contravene a strong public policy of the forum in
which suit is brought, whether declared by statute or by judicial decision. . . . It is clear, however, that whatever the proper scope of
the policy expressed in *Bisso*, it does not reach this case. *Bisso*
rested on considerations with respect to the towage business strictly
in American waters, and those considerations are not controlling in
an international commercial agreement. . . .

"Courts have also suggested that a forum clause, even though it
is freely bargained for and contravenes no important public policy of
the forum, may nevertheless be 'unreasonable' and unenforceable if
the chosen forum is *seriously* inconvenient for the trial of the action.
Of course, where it can be said with reasonable assurance that at the
time they entered the contract, the parties to a freely negotiated private international commercial agreement contemplated the claimed
inconvenience, it is difficult to see why any such claim of inconvenience should be heard to render the forum clause unenforceable.
. . . selection of a remote forum to apply differing foreign law to
an essentially American controversy might contravene an important
public policy of the forum. For example, so long as *Bisso* governs
American courts with respect to the towage business in American waters, it would quite arguably be improper to permit an American tower to avoid that policy by providing a foreign forum for resolution of
his disputes with an American towee.

"This case, however, involves a freely negotiated international
commercial transaction between a German and an American corporation for towage of a vessel from the Gulf of Mexico to the Adriatic
Sea. . . .

". . . [T]o allow Zapata opportunity to carry its heavy burden
of showing not only that the balance of convenience is strongly in
favor of trial in Tampa (that is, that it will be far more inconvenient
for Zapata to litigate in London than it will be for Unterweser to litigate in Tampa), but also that a London trial will be so manifestly and

gravely inconvenient to Zapata that it will be effectively deprived of a meaningful day in court, we remand for further proceedings."

[MR. JUSTICE DOUGLAS dissented primarily on the ground that the parties should not be permitted to escape the strong policy expressed in the *Bisso* case by means of a choice-of-forum clause.]

NOTES

(1) So far as appears, England had no contact in the Zapata case with the parties or the transaction. Under these circumstances, would a choice-of-law clause calling for application of English law have been given effect? See cases at pp. 573–596, infra. Can the parties by means of a choice-of-forum clause obtain application of a law which could not have been made applicable by a choice-of-law clause?

(2) Among the many articles discussing the Zapata case are Juenger, Supreme Court Validation of Forum-Selection Clauses, 19 Wayne L.Rev. 49 (1972); Nadelmann, Choice-of-Court Clauses in the United States: The Road to Zapata, 21 Am.J.Comp.L. 124 (1973); Reese, The Supreme Court Supports Enforcement of Choice-of-Forum Clauses, 7 Int. Lawyer 530 (1973).

(3) The needs of international trade were also emphasized in Scherk v. Alberto-Culver Co., 417 U.S. 506, 94 S.Ct. 2449, 41 L.Ed.2d 270 (1974), where the Supreme Court enforced an arbitration clause in a contract calling for the purchase by an American manufacturer of foreign enterprises owned by a German citizen. This was done despite the fact that the Court had previously held that an arbitration clause in an analogous agreement with only United States contacts was unenforceable by reason of the Securities and Exchange Act. Zapata was cited as an important precedent in the Alberto-Culver opinion.

(4) Cases in which the action was dismissed by reason of a choice-of-forum clause include Bense v. Interstate Battery System of America, 683 F.2d 718 (2d Cir. 1982); Republic International Corp. v. Amco Engineers, Inc., 516 F.2d 161 (9th Cir. 1975); Central Contracting Co. v. Maryland Casualty Co., 367 F.2d 341 (3d Cir. 1966); Smith, Valentino & Smith, Inc. v. Superior Court of Los Angeles County, 131 Cal.Rptr. 374, 551 P.2d 1206 (1976); Export Insurance Co. v. Mitsui Steamship Co., 26 A.D.2d 436, 274 N.Y.S.2d 977 (1st Dep't. 1966); Central Contracting Co. v. C. E. Youngdahl & Co., 418 Pa. 122, 209 A.2d 810 (1965); Reeves v. Chem Industrial Co., 262 Or. 95, 495 P.2d 729 (1971).

(5) Choice-of-forum agreements have sometimes been denied effect in modern cases. On the ground that it was "clearly and palpably unreasonable," the court in Calzavara v. Biehl & Co., 181 So.2d 809 (La.App.1966) ignored a provision purporting to give an Italian court exclusive jurisdiction over any action on a ticket for transportation from New Orleans to Italy. Plaintiff was a Louisiana resident and the defendant a Louisiana corporation. See also Kolendo v. Jerrell, Inc., 489 F.Supp. 983 (S.D.W.Va.1980); Lulling v. Barnaby's Family Inns, Inc., 482 F.Supp. 318 (E.D.Wis.1980); Leasewell Limited v. Jake Shelton Ford, Inc., 423 F.Supp. 1011 (S.D.W.Va.1977).

(6) Choice-of-forum clauses frequently appear in maritime and other transportation contracts. Their use in maritime contracts appears, however, to have been severely limited by Indussa Corp. v. S. S. Ranborg, 377 F.2d 200 (2d Cir. 1967), which held that Section 3(8) of the Carriage of Goods by Sea

Act (46 U.S.C.A. § 1303(8)) invalidates such clauses in bills of lading involving commerce with the United States. To similar effect, and holding that Indussa has not been superseded by Zapata, see Union Insurance Society of Canton, Limited v. S.S. Elikon, 642 F.2d 721 (4th Cir. 1981).

(7) A choice-of-forum clause providing for suit in the courts of a certain state has been held to bar a diversity action in a federal court sitting in the same jurisdiction. Spatz v. Nascone, 364 F.Supp. 967 (W.D.Pa.1973).

(8) For general discussion of the effect given choice-of-forum clauses in the United States and in other countries, see Gruson, Forum-Selection Clauses in International and Interstate Commercial Agreements, 1982 U.Ill. L.Rev. 133; Gilbert, Choice of Forum Clauses in International and Interstate Contracts, 65 Ky.L.J. 1 (1977); The Validity of Forum Selecting Clauses, 13 Am.J.Comp.L. 157–192 (1964).

SECTION 2.   FRAUD, FORCE AND PRIVILEGE *

TERLIZZI v. BRODIE

Supreme Court, Appellate Division, Second Department, 1972.
38 A.D.2d 762, 329 N.Y.S.2d 589.

MEMORANDUM BY THE COURT. . . .

. . .

In May or June, 1968 defendants, New Jersey residents, were in an automobile collision in New Jersey which caused plaintiffs, New York residents, to sustain injuries. In February, 1971 defendants were called at home and told that they had been chosen to receive two tickets to a Broadway show as a promotional venture to get their opinion on a questionnaire of the new 7:30 P.M. curtain time. After the performance and while still in the theatre, defendants were served with a summons in this action by a man who had been sitting behind them. No questionnaire had been given them. Plaintiffs have presented no facts concerning the service to refute defendants' claim and have not submitted an affidavit of the investigator retained to effect service.

It has long been held that where a defendant has been lured into this jurisdiction by fraud or deceit in order that he may be served, the service so effected is invalid . . .

In our opinion, the service was invalid and the [defendants'] motion [to vacate service of process] should have been granted.

---

* See Restatement, Second, Conflict of Laws §§ 82–83.

NOTES

(1) Where the defendant's presence in the state was obtained by fraudulent use of extradition procedure, it has been held that service on him is not effective to support a civil judgment against him. Klaiber v. Frank, 9 N.J. 1, 86 A.2d 679 (1952). However, the mere fact that the defendant is a nonresident and is under arrest for a criminal charge does not make him immune from the valid service of civil process. State ex rel. Sivnksty v. Duffield, 137 W.Va. 112, 71 S.E.2d 113 (1952).

(2) Suppose the defendant is kidnapped and brought into the state by force. If he is then served with civil process, does the state get jurisdiction over him? See Restatement, Second, Conflict of Laws, § 82, Comments *e–f.*

(3) The Uniform Criminal Extradition Act, now enacted in over 45 states (see 11 Uniform Laws Ann. 51) provides (in § 25) that where a person is brought into a state on extradition, or after waiver of extradition he shall not be subject to service of process "in civil actions arising out of the same facts as the criminal proceedings . . . until he has been convicted in the criminal proceeding, or if acquitted, until he has had reasonable opportunity to return to the state from which he was extradited." In Bubar v. Dizdar, 240 Minn. 26, 60 N.W.2d 77 (1953), the defendant waived extradition, came into the state, and pleaded guilty. Later the same day, but before sentence was imposed, he was served with process. It was held that this was after conviction, and valid.

(4) In criminal cases, the jurisdiction of the court over the defendant is usually held not to be impaired by the fact that he was unlawfully extradited, or brought in by force. State v. Waitus, 226 S.C. 44, 83 S.E.2d 629 (1954). The Supreme Court has held that a state may prosecute a person brought into the state by force even though this was a violation of the Federal Kidnapping Act. Frisbie v. Collins, 342 U.S. 519 (1952). See Scott, Criminal Jurisdiction of a State over a Defendant Based upon Presence Secured by Force or Fraud, 37 Minn.L.Rev. 91 (1953).

The question of criminal jurisdiction based on removing a person by force arose in dramatic form in the Eichmann case in Israel, with a result which is now history. There was extensive discussion. See, e.g., Woetzel, The Eichmann Case in International Law, 1962 Crim.L.Rev. 671; International Law: Jurisdiction over Extraterritorial Crime, 46 Cornell L.Q. 326 (1961).

A number of recent cases have involved persons who were brought by force from foreign countries to the United States to stand trial on criminal charges. In these cases, jurisdiction to try the defendant was ultimately upheld even though it was alleged that the defendant had been forcefully abducted at the instigation of agents of the United States. United States v. Lira, 515 F.2d 68 (2d Cir. 1975); United States v. Gengler, 510 F.2d 62 (2d Cir. 1975); United States v. Cotten, 471 F.2d 744 (2d Cir. 1975); United States v. Marzano, 388 F.Supp. 906 (N.D.Ill.1975); see Annotation, 28 A.L.R. Fed. 685 (1976). In United States v. Toscanino, 500 F.2d 267 (2d Cir. 1974), the court held that jurisdiction would be lacking and the defendant's conviction void if he could establish that he had not only been kidnapped but also tortured and interrogated abroad by U. S. agents and that the United States attorney was at all times aware of these activities. The court said that Frisbie v. Collins must be read in the light of such supervening Supreme Court decisions as Mapp, Miranda, etc. which hold that "due process not only requires a fair trial but also protects the accused against pretrial illegality by denying to the government the fruits of its exploitation of any deliberate and unnecessary lawlessness on its part." After remand to the District Court, however, Toscanino failed to establish that United States officials had participated in his abduction or torture. Accordingly, his motion to vacate his judgment of conviction was denied. United States v. Toscanino, 398 F.Supp. 916 (E.D.N.Y.1975).

(5) Privilege and Immunity. A foreign sovereign is immune from service of process. Similarly, representatives of a foreign sovereign, such as ambassadors, are often said not to be subject to the jurisdiction of the court, and are at least privileged from service of process in ordinary circumstances. See Restatement, Second, Conflict of Laws, § 83, Comment a.

(6) "It is customary for a state to grant immunity from service of process to non-residents whose presence it deems necessary for the proper conduct of a judicial proceeding. Such immunity is usually granted to witnesses and to lawyers and in some states to parties as well. The immunity ceases when the need for protection ends. It is lost, for example, when the person fails to leave the state within a reasonable time after his presence there has ceased to be necessary." Restatement, Second, Conflict of Laws § 83, Comment b.

(7) Immunity from service of process in a civil action is usually granted to persons who enter the state, either voluntarily or under subpoena, for the purpose of appearing as a witness in a state or federal proceeding. See, e.g., Celanese Corporation v. Duplan Corporation, 502 F.2d 188 (4th Cir. 1974); Northumberland Ins. Co. v. Wolfson, 251 A.2d 194 (Del.1969); Lyf Alum Inc. v. C & M Aluminum Supply Corp., 29 Wis.2d 593, 139 N.W.2d 601 (1966).

In Youpe v. Strasser, 113 F.Supp. 289 (D.D.C.1953), it was held that a witness subpoenaed to appear before a Congressional investigating committee was immune from service in a civil suit.

(8) The cases are divided on the question whether a similar immunity should be granted nonresident parties to a civil action who enter the state for the purpose of attending the trial. See, e.g., Chase Nat. Bank v. Turner, 269 N.Y. 397, 199 N.E. 636 (1936) (granting immunity); Wangler v. Harvey, 41 N.J. 277, 196 A.2d 513 (1963) (denying immunity), noted in 77 Harv.L.Rev. 1346 (1964).

(9) Nonresidents who enter the state, while not in custody, to answer criminal charges are usually granted immunity from service of process in a civil action while they are in the state for the purposes of the criminal trial. See, e.g., Thermoid Co. v. Fabel, 4 N.Y.2d 494, 151 N.E.2d 883 (1953); contra, Santos v. Figueroa, 87 N.J.Super. 227, 208 A.2d 810 (1967).

SECTION 3. FORUM NON CONVENIENS

Frequently, a plaintiff will have a wide choice of forums in which to sue. For example, in Anglo-American law, an individual is subject to the jurisdiction of any state where he can be personally served. He may be served far from his home while transient in a state. The cause of action may have nothing to do with the state where service is made and the plaintiff may be a non-resident of that state. Similarly, suit may be brought against a foreign corporation in a state where the corporation "does business" although the particular cause of action bears no relation to this business.

This situation provides a considerable opportunity for "shopping around" for a forum. The plaintiff may make the choice to harass the defendant, thus perhaps hoping to get a better settlement; or he may bring the suit in a place where it is felt that jury verdicts tend to be larger than elsewhere. He may, of course, have wholly legitimate reasons for his choice of forum, such as convenience of witnesses.

The present century has witnessed widespread adoption of the doctrine of forum non conveniens under which a court has discretion to dismiss the action in situations where there is no substantial or legitimate basis for the plaintiff's choice of forum.

GULF OIL CORP. v. GILBERT

Supreme Court of the United States, 1947.
330 U.S. 501, 67 S.Ct. 839, 91 L.Ed. 1055.

[A resident of Virginia brought an action in a federal district court in New York against a Pennsylvania corporation. The cause of action was based on a fire in Virginia alleged to have resulted from the defendant's negligence. The defendant was qualified to do business in Virginia, and could have been sued there. The defendant moved to dismiss on grounds of forum non conveniens.

The opinion of the Court, by Mr. Justice Jackson, contains the following passages:]

I.

It is conceded that the venue statutes of the United States permitted the plaintiff to commence his action in the Southern District of New York and empower that court to entertain it. But that does not settle the question whether it must do so. Indeed the doctrine of *forum non conveniens* can never apply if there is absence of jurisdiction or mistake of venue. . . . In all cases in which the doctrine of *forum non conveniens* comes into play, it presupposes at least two forums in which the defendant is amenable to process; the doctrine furnishes criteria for choice between them.

II.

The principle of *forum non conveniens* is simply that a court may resist imposition upon its jurisdiction even when jurisdiction is authorized by the letter of a general venue statute. These statutes are drawn with a necessary generality and usually give a plaintiff a choice of courts, so that he may be quite sure of some place in which to pursue his remedy. But the open door may admit those who seek not simply justice but perhaps justice blended with some harassment. A plaintiff sometimes is under temptation to resort to a strategy of forcing the trial at a most inconvenient place for an adversary, even at some inconvenience to himself.

Many of the states have met misuse of venue by investing courts with a discretion to change the place of trial on various grounds, such as the convenience of witnesses and the ends of justice. The federal law contains no such express criteria to guide the district court in exercising its power. But the problem is a very old one affecting the administration of the courts as well as the rights of litigants, and both in England and in this country the common law worked out techniques and criteria for dealing with it.

Wisely, it has not been attempted to catalogue the circumstances which will justify or require either grant or denial of remedy. The doctrine leaves much to the discretion of the court to which plaintiff resorts, and experience has not shown a judicial tendency to renounce one's own jurisdiction so strong as to result in many abuses.

If the combination and weight of factors requisite to given results are difficult to forecast or state, those to be considered are not difficult to name. An interest to be considered, and the one likely to be most pressed, is the private interest of the litigant. Important considerations are the relative ease of access to sources of proof; availability of compulsory process for attendance of unwilling, and the cost of obtaining attendance of willing, witnesses; possibility of view of premises, if view would be appropriate to the action; and all other practical problems that make trial of a case easy, expeditious and inexpensive. There may also be questions as to the enforceability of a judgment if one is obtained. The court will weigh relative advantages and obstacles to fair trial. It is often said that the plaintiff may not, by choice of an inconvenient forum, "vex," "harass," or "oppress" the defendant by inflicting upon him expense or trouble not necessary to his own right to pursue his remedy. But unless the balance is strongly in favor of the defendant, the plaintiff's choice of forum should rarely be disturbed.

Factors of public interest also have place in applying the doctrine. Administrative difficulties follow for courts when litigation is piled up in congested centers instead of being handled at its origin. Jury duty is a burden that ought not to be imposed upon the people of a community which has no relation to the litigation. In cases which touch the affairs of many persons, there is reason for holding the trial in their view and reach rather than in remote parts of the country where they can learn of it by report only. There is a local interest in having localized controversies decided at home. There is an appropriateness, too, in having the trial of a diversity case in a forum that is at home with the state law that must govern the case, rather than having a court in some other forum untangle problems in conflict of laws, and in law foreign to itself.

The law of New York as to the discretion of a court to apply the doctrine of *forum non conveniens*, and as to the standards that guide discretion is, so far as here involved, the same as the federal rule. . . .

[The Court held that the district court had acted properly in dismissing the suit.]

———

PIPER AIRCRAFT CO. v. REYNO, 454 U.S. 235 (1981).　Action in a Pennsylvania federal district court against the manufacturers of an aircraft and its propellers to recover for the wrongful death of persons killed in an airplane crash in Scotland.　At the time, the plane was registered in Great Britain and was being operated by a Scottish air taxi service.　All of the decedents were Scottish subjects and residents.　As plaintiff, the appointed administratrix of the decedents' estates was frank to admit, the suit had been brought in the United States because its laws regarding liability, capacity to sue and damages were more favorable to her cause than those of Scotland.　Held: The action should be dismissed on forum non conveniens grounds. "The possibility of a change in substantive law should ordinarily not be given conclusive or even substantial weight in the *forum non conveniens* inquiry　.　.　. [Otherwise] American courts, which are already extremely attractive to foreign plaintiffs, would become even more attractive.　The flow of litigation into the United States would increase and further congest already crowded courts　.　.　. Of course, if the remedy provided by the alternative forum is so clearly inadequate or unsatisfactory that it is no remedy at all, the unfavorable change in law may be given substantial weight."

———

A number of long-arm statutes expressly authorize the court to dismiss the case on forum non conveniens grounds.　An example is Wis.Stat.Ann. § 262.19(1).　It makes "substantial justice" the standard for the exercise of the court's discretion in the area.　It expressly provides that forum non conveniens may be invoked even where the defendant would not have been subject to compulsory service in the more convenient forum, provided that the moving party (1) stipulates consent to jurisdiction in the new forum, and (2) waives any statute of limitations that may have run therein.　§ 262.19(3) lists four criteria to be followed by the court: (a) amenability of the parties to personal jurisdiction in this and the other forum;　(b) convenience of witnesses;　(c) differences in conflict of laws rules;　and (d) "any other factors having substantial bearing upon the selection of a convenient, reasonable, and fair place of trial."

NOTES

(1) Where the forum is "inconvenient," the court will frequently impose conditions upon its refusal to exercise jurisdiction. For example, in Aetna Insurance Co. v. Creole Petroleum Corp., 23 N.Y.2d 717, 244 N.E.2d 56 (1968), the dismissal was "on condition that, within 10 days after entry of the order, the defendant should stipulate to consent to jurisdiction of the courts of Venezuela, to accept service of process in Venezuela and appear in an action to be commenced in Venezuela courts for the same relief, and that in any action commenced in Venezuela it would not challenge plaintiff's capacity to sue in the Venezuela courts, and that it would not plead the statute of limitations, and that, in event of dismissal of any action instituted in Venezuela . . . the plaintiff could reinstitute suit in New York courts within six-month period of limitations . . . ."

(2) In recent years, suits have often been dismissed on forum non conveniens grounds in situations where the more convenient forum was a foreign country. See, e.g., Vaz Borralho v. Keydril Co., 696 F.2d 379 (5th Cir. 1983); Panama Processes, S.A. v. Cities Service Co., 650 F.2d 408 (2d Cir. 1981); Dahl v. United Technologies Corp., 632 F.2d 1027 (3d Cir. 1980); In re Richardson-Merrell, Inc., 545 F.Supp. 1130 (S.D. Ohio 1982).

Dismissals have been ordered even when the plaintiff was a United States citizen. See, e.g., Pain v. United Technologies Corp., 637 F.2d 775 (D.C.Cir. 1980); Alcoa Steamship Co. v. M/V Nordic Regent, 654 F.2d 165 (2d Cir. 1979). It has been said, however, that the presumption in favor of the plaintiff's chosen forum is "even stronger" when the plaintiff is an American citizen and the alternative forum is a foreign country. Olympic Corp. v. Societe Generale, 462 F.2d 376, 378 (2d Cir. 1972).

Dismissals on forum non conveniens grounds have been denied in a variety of circumstances. Lake v. Richardson-Merrell, Inc., 538 F.Supp. 262 (N.D. Ohio 1982) (court believed that action would be dismissed in Quebec on the ground of prescription, a defense that, under Quebec law, could not be waived by the defendant); In re Air Crash Disaster Near Bombay, etc., 531 F.Supp. 1175 (W.D.Wash.1982) (statute of limitations had run in India and there was a substantial possibility that the Bombay court would not accept defendant's waiver of the statute); Canadian Overseas Ores, Limited v. Compania, etc., 528 F.Supp. 1337 (S.D.N.Y.1982) (court feared that fair trial could not be had in Chile).

(3) Factors which militate against dismissal of a case on forum non conveniens grounds include (a) the forum is in the only state where jurisdiction can be obtained over all defendants (Varkonyi v. S. A. Empresa de Viacao A. R. G., 22 N.Y.2d 333, 239 N.E.2d 542 (1968) and (b) in addition to having some relationship with the parties, the forum provides procedural remedies such as pre-trial discovery that would not be available in the other state. Mobil Tankers Co. v. Mene Grande Oil Co., 363 F.2d 611 (3d Cir. 1966). See Morley, Forum Non Conveniens, 68 Nw.U.L.Rev. 24 (1973).

(4) New York now permits dismissal of a case on forum non conveniens grounds even though either the plaintiff or defendant is domiciled in New York. Silver v. Great American Insurance Co., 29 N.Y.2d 356, 328 N.Y.S.2d 398, 278 N.E.2d 619 (1972). This case overturned a rule which prevented dismissal of a suit on a claim arising in a foreign country between foreign

parties merely because the claim had been assigned to a New Yorker. Wagner v. Braunsberg, 5 A.D.2d 564, 173 N.Y.S.2d 525 (1st Dep't 1958).

(5) *Trespass to foreign land.* The traditional rule is that a court will not take jurisdiction of a case arising out of a trespass upon land in another state. See, e.g., Ellenwood v. Marietta Chair Co., 158 U.S. 105 (1895). A few courts have taken jurisdiction in these circumstances. A notable decision refusing to follow the traditional rule is Reasor-Hill Corp. v. Harrison, 220 Ark. 521, 249 S.W.2d 994 (1952).

The decision in the Reasor-Hill case has the support of Restatement Second, Conflict of Laws § 87. See also Looper, Jurisdiction over Immovables: The Little Case Revisited after Sixty Years, 40 Minn.L.Rev. 191 (1956).

TRANSFER OF JURISDICTION IN FEDERAL COURTS

In 1948, Congress adopted a revision of the Judicial Code, known as Title 28, United States Code. Section 1404(a) of this Act provides, with respect to the Federal district courts: *reasons*

"For the convenience of parties and witnesses, in the interest of justice, a district court may transfer any civil action to any other district or division where it might have been brought."

This provision has been before the Supreme Court in a number of cases. In Norwood v. Kirkpatrick, 349 U.S. 29 (1955), the Court observed that under section 1404(a) the district court has "broader discretion in the application of the statute than under the doctrine of *forum non conveniens.*" It pointed out that a transfer under section 1404(a) does not involve a dismissal of the proceeding, and it held that Congress, by enacting the transfer statute, "intended to permit courts to grant transfers on a lesser showing of inconvenience." In Ex parte Collett, 337 U.S. 55 (1949), the Court held that a case brought under the Federal Employers' Liability Act could be transferred under § 1404(a) even though the original forum was appropriate under the special venue provision of the Act and dismissal would not be appropriate under the local state rule of forum non conveniens.

In Hoffman v. Blaski, 363 U.S. 335 (1960), the Court held that a civil action may be transferred only to a district where the plaintiff could have brought it without the consent of the defendant, that is, ordinarily, in a district where the defendant could have been served, and where venue lies.

NOTES

(1) A federal court may not dismiss under forum non conveniens if there is a convenient district to which the case may be transferred under § 1404(a). Headrick v. Atchison, Topeka & Santa Fe Railroad Co., 182 F.2d 305 (10th Cir. 1950). As a result, dismissals on forum non conveniens grounds will almost invariably be impermissible unless the only convenient forum is in a foreign country or is a state court. See e.g., Vanity Fair Mills, Inc. v. T.

Eaton Co., 234 F.2d 633 (2d Cir. 1956), cert. denied 352 U.S. 871; Yerostathis v. A. Luisi, Limited, 380 F.2d 377 (9th Cir. 1967).

In Gross v. Owen, 221 F.2d 94 (App.D.C.1955) dismissal under forum non conveniens was held justified because a federal court sitting in the convenient state would not have had jurisdiction to hear the case by reason of lack of diversity.

(2) The prevailing view appears to be that a plaintiff may obtain a transfer under § 1404(a) if, after bringing the action, he discovers good reason for the transfer. EMI Film Distributors, Limited v. L. D. S. Film Co., 404 F.Supp. 204 (S.D.N.Y.1975); Philip Carey Manufacturing Co. v. Taylor, 286 F.2d 782 (6th Cir. 1961), cert. denied 366 U.S. 948 (1961).

Many of the problems arising out of transfer of jurisdiction under sec. 1404(a) were resolved by the Supreme Court in Van Dusen v. Barrack, 376 U.S. 612 (1964). That case arose out of an airplane accident which occurred in Boston, Massachusetts. The plane was scheduled to fly from Boston to Philadelphia. As a result more than 100 actions were brought against various defendants in the United States District Court for the District of Massachusetts, and more than 45 actions were brought in the United States District Court for the Eastern District of Pennsylvania. Most of the latter actions were brought by executors and administrators appointed in Pennsylvania, who were not qualified to act in Massachusetts.

The defendants moved in the Pennsylvania court that most of the actions be transferred to Massachusetts under sec. 1404(a). The Court of Appeals for the Third Circuit held that the proceedings could not be transferred. It relied on the fact that since the plaintiffs in Pennsylvania were not qualified to act in Massachusetts, the actions were not ones which "might have been brought" in Massachusetts. Barrack v. Van Dusen, 309 F.2d 953, noted in 76 Harv.L.Rev. 1679 (1963).

The Supreme Court reversed this decision, and remanded the case to the District Court in Pennsylvania for further consideration. It held that the phrase "might have been brought" related to the suability of the defendant, and not to the capacity of the plaintiff. It also held, that, "where the defendants seek transfer, the transferee district court must be obligated to apply the state law that would have been applied if there had been no change of venue. A change of venue under § 1404(a) generally should be, with respect to state law, but a change of courtrooms." The Court added:

> . . . we do not and need not consider whether in all cases § 1404(a) would require the application of the law of the transferror, as opposed to the transferee, State. We do not attempt to determine whether, for example, the same considerations would govern if a plaintiff sought transfer under § 1404(a) or if it was contended that the transferor State would simply have dismissed the action on the ground of *forum non conveniens*. . . .

The case was remanded to the District Court to determine whether on the actual facts a transfer to Massachusetts could be justified on the grounds of "convenience and fairness." On this point, the Supreme Court noted:

> . . . it has long been recognized that: "There is an appropriateness . . . in having the trial of a diversity case in a forum that is at home with the state law that must govern the case, rather than having a court in some other forum untangle problems in conflict of laws, and in law foreign to itself." Gulf Oil Corp. v. Gilbert, 330 U.S. 501, 509. Thus, to the extent that Pennsylvania laws are difficult or unclear and might not defer to Massachusetts laws, it may be advantageous to retain the actions in Pennsylvania where the judges possess a more ready familiarity with the local laws. . . . We do not suggest that elements of uncertainty in transferor state law would alone justify a denial of transfer; but we do think that the uncertainty is one factor, among others, to be considered in assessing the desirability of transfer. . . .

Thus if a case were transferred from Pennsylvania to Massachusetts, the Massachusetts District Court, subject perhaps to a few rare exceptions, would sit as if it were a federal court in Pennsylvania. Under Erie Railroad v. Tompkins, 304 U.S. 64 (1938), it would be required to apply the law of Pennsylvania, including the conflict of laws of Pennsylvania. Klaxon Co. v. Stentor Electric Manufacturing Co., Inc., 313 U.S. 487 (1941). This would mean that it would apply the Pennsylvania law to determine the qualification of the plaintiff, and thus the Pennsylvania executors and administrators would be competent to sue in the case transferred to Massachusetts. Whether the conflict of laws of Pennsylvania would refer to the law of Massachusetts for the substantive rules applicable to the accident would have to be determined by the Massachusetts District Court sitting as if it were a District Court in Pennsylvania, and applying Pennsylvania law.

NOTES

(1) The rule of the Barrack case—that the law of the transferor forum should be applied—is a complicating factor in situations where a number of cases originally brought in various Federal districts in several states are consolidated for trial in a single district court. See, e.g., In Re Paris Air Crash of March 3, 1974, 399 F.Supp. 732 (C.D.Cal.1975); In Re Air Crash Disaster at Boston, Mass., July 31, 1973, 399 F.Supp. 1106 (D.Mass.1975); Note, Consolidation and Transfer in the Federal Courts, 22 Hastings L.Rev. 1289 (1971).

(2) Prominent among the articles discussing § 1404(a) and written prior to the Barrack case are Currie, Change of Venue and the Conflict of Laws, 22 U.Chi.L.Rev. 405 (1955), and Currie, Change of Venue and the Conflict of Laws: A Retraction, 27 U.Chi.L.Rev. 341 (1960). The latter article is reprinted in Currie, Selected Essays on the Conflict of Laws (1963), Chapter 9, p. 431.

(3) Courts and commentators are divided over what law should be applied after the plaintiff has obtained a transfer under § 1404(a). The American Law Institute advocates application of the law of the transferee forum. American Law Institute, Study of the Division of Jurisdiction between State and Federal Courts § 1306(c) (1969). On the other hand, application of the law of the transferor forum is suggested in Note, 63 Corn.L.Rev. 149 (1977). See generally Wright, Federal Courts § 44 (4th ed. 1983).

Where the case is initially brought in a court lacking proper venue, the case is governed by 28 U.S.C. § 1406(a), which provides that the district court "shall dismiss, or if it be in the interest of justice, transfer such case to any district in which it could have been brought." The courts are agreed that where the transferor forum lacks either jurisdiction or proper venue, the law of the transferee forum will be applied regardless of whether the plaintiff or the defendant sought the transfer. Nelson v. International Paint Co., 716 F.2d 640 (9th Cir. 1983); Roofing & Sheet Metal Services v. La Quinta Motor Inns, 689 F.2d 982 (11th Cir. 1982); Ellis v. Great Southwestern Corp., 646 F.2d 1099 (5th Cir. 1981); Geehan v. Monahan, 382 F.2d 111 (7th Cir. 1967).

INTERNAL AFFAIRS OF A CORPORATION

At one time, there was a fairly strong doctrine to the effect that the courts of one state would not interfere with the internal affairs of a corporation of another state. On this basis, courts often dismissed suits brought against foreign corporations by resident stockholders, when the stockholder was affected solely in his capacity as a member of the corporation. Perhaps the high water mark of this rule in the federal courts was reached in Rogers v. Guaranty Trust Co., 288 U.S. 123 (1933).

The demise of this approach was foreshadowed in Williams v. Green Bay & Western Railroad Co., 326 U.S. 549 (1946). And in Koster v. Lumbermens Mutual Casualty Co., 330 U.S. 518 (1947), the Supreme Court held, in effect, that the "internal affairs" rule should not be followed, and that the whole problem should be governed only by the general principles of forum non conveniens. This is the position of the Restatement, Second, Conflict of Laws § 84, Comment *d*. For discussion of the factors involved, see Hoffman v. Goberman, 420 F.2d 423 (3d Cir. 1970); Burton v. Exxon Corp., 536 F.Supp. 617 (S.D. N.Y.1982); Note, Forum Non Conveniens as a Substitute for the Internal Affairs Rule, 58 Colum.L.Rev. 234 (1958).

SECTION 4. OTHER LIMITATIONS
IMPOSED BY THE FORUM

———

RESTATEMENT, SECOND, CONFLICT OF LAWS: *

§ 53. Decree to Be Carried Out in Another State

b. *When jurisdiction exercised.* A person will be ordered to do an act in another state when this relief is required by the demands of justice and convenience. The reluctance of the courts to issue such orders stems primarily from (1) the fear of interfering unduly with the affairs of the other state and (2) the possible difficulty of enforcing obedience to an order that the defendant do an act in a place beyond the effective control of the court. Because of the first factor, the defendant will not, except on extremely rare occasions, be ordered to do an act which violates the law of the other state . . . there is greater likelihood of the defendant's being ordered to do an act in another state if the court has some means at its disposal of insuring compliance with the decree, such as by requiring the defendant to post a bond or to act in the other state through the medium of an agent. . . .

———

UNITED STATES v. FIRST NATIONAL CITY BANK

United States Court of Appeals, Second Circuit, 1968.

396 F.2d 897.

[In aid of a grand jury investigation of suspected antitrust violations, a subpoena was served upon the First National City Bank requiring it to produce all documents in its office in Frankfurt, Germany, which involved certain of its customers. The Bank refused to comply on the ground that production of these documents would subject it to civil liability to these customers under German law. The District Court held the Bank liable for contempt, and it appealed.]

KAUFMAN, CIRCUIT JUDGE. . . . It is no longer open to doubt that a federal court has the power to require the production of documents located in foreign countries if the court has *in personam* jurisdiction of the person in possession or control of the material. . . . Thus, the task before us, as Citibank concedes, is not one of defining power but of developing rules governing the proper exercise of power. . . . This problem is particularly acute where the documents are sought by an arm of a foreign government. The complexities of the world being what they are, it is not surprising to discover nations

———

having diametrically opposed positions with respect to the disclosure of a wide range of information. It is not too difficult, therefore, to empathize with the party or witness subject to the jurisdiction of two sovereigns and confronted with conflicting commands. . . .

. . . Where, as here, the burden of resolution ultimately falls upon the federal courts, the difficulties are manifold because the courts must take care not to impinge upon the prerogatives and responsibilities of the political branches of the government in the extremely sensitive and delicate area of foreign affairs. . . . Mechanical or overbroad rules of thumb are of little value; what is required is a careful balancing of the interests involved and a precise understanding of the facts and circumstances of the particular case.

With these principles in mind, we turn to the specific issues presented by this appeal. Citibank concedes, as it must, that compliance with the subpoena does not require the violation of the criminal law of a foreign power . . . or risk the imposition of sanctions that are the substantial equivalent of criminal penalties . . . or even conflict with the public policy of a foreign state as expressed in legislation . . . Instead, all that remains, as we see it, is a possible prospective civil liability flowing from an implied contractual obligation between Citibank and its customers that, we are informed, is considered implicit in the bank's license to do business in Germany.

. . . In the instant use, the obvious, albeit troublesome, requirement for us is to balance the national interests of the United States and Germany and to give appropriate weight to the hardship, if any, Citibank will suffer.

The important interest of the United States in the enforcement of the subpoena warrants little discussion. . . . [T]he antitrust laws . . . have long been considered cornerstones of this nation's economic policies, have been vigorously enforced and the subject of frequent interpretation by our Supreme Court. We would have great reluctance, therefore, to countenance any device that would place relevant information beyond the reach of this duly impaneled Grand Jury or impede or delay its proceedings. . . .

We examine the importance of bank secrecy within the framework of German public policy with full recognition that it is often a subtle and difficult undertaking to determine the nature and scope of the law of a foreign jurisdiction. There is little merit, however, in Citibank's suggestion that the mere existence of a bank secrecy doctrine requires us to accept on its face the bank's assertion that compliance with the subpoena would violate an important public policy of Germany. . . . While we certainly do not intend to deprecate the importance of bank secrecy in the German scheme of things, neither can we blind ourselves to the doctrine's severe limitations as disclosed by the expert testimony. We have already made the assumption that the absence of criminal sanctions is not the whole answer to or finally determinative of the problem. But, it is surely of considerable significance that Germany considers bank secrecy simply a privilege that can be waived by the customer and is content to leave the matter of enforcement to the vagaries of private litigation. Indeed, bank secrecy is not even required by statute. . . . [Likewise, the Bank could not assert bank secrecy in a criminal investigation in Germany.]

In addition, it is noteworthy that neither the Department of State nor the German Government has expressed any view on this case or indicated that, under the circumstances present here, enforcement of the subpoena would violate German public policy or embarrass German-American relations. . . .

[Finally, the court turned to the hardship, if any, which the Bank would suffer if it complied with the subpoena. The Court found little merit in the contention that compliance by the Bank would result in the loss of foreign business or in economic reprisals by its customers. The Court further found that the chance of the Bank being held liable for civil damages under German law was "slight and speculative."]

Affirmed.

NOTES

(1) In SEC v. Minas de Artemisa, S. A., 150 F.2d 215 (9th Cir. 1945), the Securities and Exchange Commission sought enforcement of a subpoena to a Mexican corporation to compel it to produce its books and records concerning the sale of securities. Service was made on the corporation's president in Arizona. The district court dismissed the suit on the ground that it required acts outside the jurisdiction. This was reversed by the Circuit Court of Appeals.

To an objection that it might be impossible to remove the material from Mexico, the court suggested that the lower court try the following remedies: (a) require defendant to apply to Mexican authorities for permission to remove the books for inspection, (b) if permission is not granted, the defendant is to permit the SEC to inspect the books in Mexico, or (c) defendant is to produce authenticated copies of the material.

(2) On occasion, courts in this country have ordered a person to testify or to bring documents from a foreign country even though compliance with the order would violate the law of that country. In re Grand Jury Proceedings, 694 F.2d 1256 (11th Cir. 1982) (attorney-client privilege); In re Grand Jury Proceedings, 691 F.2d 1384 (11th Cir. 1982) (bank secrecy law); In re Grand Jury Proceedings, 532 F.2d 404 (5th Cir. 1976) (bank secrecy law); cf. Civil Aeronautics Board v. Deutsche Lufthansa Aktiengesellschaft, 591 F.2d 951 (D.C.Cir.1979) (defendant ordered to use all good faith efforts to obtain government permission for release of documents).

On other occasions, the courts have refused to issue an order that would require violation of the law of a foreign country. In re Westinghouse Electric Corp. Uranium, etc., 563 F.2d 992 (10th Cir. 1977) interests of the foreign country held to be more seriously involved than those of the United States); Application of Chase Manhattan Bank, 297 F.2d 611 (2d Cir. 1962).

For a general discussion of the problem, see Note, Extraterritorial Discovery: An Analysis Based on Good Faith, 83 Colum.L.Rev. 1320 (1983).

(3) A court of equity will be less reluctant to issue a decree affecting property outside the state when the act ordered may be performed without the party leaving the state. See authorities set forth on p. 258, note (2), infra, and Weesner v. Weesner, p. 259, note (4), infra.

(4) For a discussion of the factors that should be considered by a court in a situation where two or more states have power to require a person to engage in inconsistent courses of conduct, see Restatement, Foreign Relations Law of the United States (Revised) § 403 (Tentative Draft No. 2, 1981).

SLATER v. MEXICAN NATIONAL R. CO.

Supreme Court of the United States, 1904.
194 U.S. 120, 24 S.Ct. 581, 48 L.Ed. 900.

MR. JUSTICE HOLMES delivered the opinion of the court.

This is an action brought in the United States Circuit Court for the Northern District of Texas by citizens and residents of Texas against a Colorado corporation operating a railroad from Texas to the City of Mexico. The plaintiffs are the widow and children of William H. Slater, who was employed by the defendant as a switchman on its road and was killed through the defendant's negligence while coupling two freight cars at Nuevo Laredo, in Mexico. This action is to recover damages for the death. The laws of Mexico were set forth in the plaintiffs' petition, and the defendant demurred on the ground that the cause of action given by the Mexican laws was not transitory, for reasons sufficiently stated. The demurrer was overruled, and the defendant excepted. A similar objection was taken also by plea setting forth additional sections of the Mexican statutes. A demurrer to this plea was sustained, subject to exception. The same point was raised again at the trial by a request to direct a verdict for the defendant. The judge who tried the case instructed the jury that the damages to be recovered, if any, were to be measured by the money value of the life of the deceased to the widow and children, and the jury returned a verdict for a lump sum, apportioned to the several plaintiffs. The judge and jury in this regard acted as prescribed by the Texas Rev.Stat. Art. 3027. The case then was taken to the Circuit Court of Appeals, where the judgment was reversed and the action ordered to be dismissed. 115 F. 593, 53 C.C.A. 239.

There is no need to encumber the reports with all the statutes in the record. . . . We assume for the moment that it was sufficiently alleged and proved that the killing of Slater was a negligent crime within the definition of Article 11 of the Penal Code, and, therefore, if the above sections were the only law bearing on the matter, that they created a civil liability to make reparation to any one whose rights were infringed.

As Texas has statutes which give an action for wrongfully causing death, of course there is no general objection of policy to enforcing such a liability there, although it arose in another jurisdiction. Stewart v. Baltimore & Ohio R. R., 168 U.S. 445. But when such a liability is enforced in a jurisdiction foreign to the place of the wrongful act, obviously that does not mean that the act in any degree is subject to the lex fori, with regard to either its quality or its consequences. On the other hand, it equally little means that the law of the place of the act is operative outside its own territory. The theory of the foreign suit is that although the act complained of was subject to no law having force in the forum, it gave rise to an obligation, an *obligatio*, which, like other obligations, follows the person, and may be enforced wherever the person may be found. Stout v. Wood, 1 Blackf. (Ind.) 71; Dennick v. Railroad Co., 103 U.S. 11, 18. But as the only source of this obligation is the law of the place of the act, it follows that the law determines not merely the existence of the obligation, Smith v. Condry, 1 How. 28, but equally determines its extent. It seems to us unjust to allow a plaintiff to come here absolutely depending on the foreign law for the foundation of his case, and yet to deny the defendant the benefit of whatever limitations on his liability that law would impose. In Northern Pacific R. R. v. Babcock, 154 U.S. 190, 199, an action was brought in the District of Minnesota for a death caused in Montana, and it was held that the damages were to be assessed in accordance with the Montana statute. Therefore we may lay on one side as quite inadmissible the notion that the law of the place of the act may be resorted to so far as to show that the act was a tort, and then may be abandoned, leaving the consequences to be determined according to the accident of the place where the defendant may happen to be caught. . . . We are aware that expressions of a different tendency may be found in some English cases. But they do not cover the question before this court, and our opinion is based . . . as it seems to us upon the only theory by which actions fairly can be allowed to be maintained for foreign torts. As the cause of action relied upon is one which is supposed to have arisen in Mexico under Mexican laws, the place of the death and the domicile of the parties have no bearing upon the case.

The application of these considerations now is to be shown. . . . By Article 318 [of the Penal Code of Mexico] civil responsibility for a wrongful homicide includes, besides the expenses of medical attendance and burial and damages to the property of the deceased, the expenses "of the support not only of the widow, descendants and ascendants of the deceased, who were being supported by him, he being under legal obligations to do so, but also to the posthumous descendants that he may leave." Then, by Art. 319, the obligation to support shall last during the time that the deceased might have lived, calculated by a given life table, but taking the state of his health before the homicide into consideration, but "the obligation shall cease: 1. At whatever time it shall not be absolutely necessary for the subsistence of those entitled to receive it. 2. When those beneficiaries get married. 3. When the minor children become of age. 4. In any other case in which, according to law, the deceased, if alive, would not be required to continue the support." It is unnecessary to set forth the detailed provisions as to support in other parts of the statutes. It is sufficiently obvious from what has been quoted that the decree contemplated by the Mexican law is a decree analogous to a decree for alimony in divorce proceedings—a decree which contemplates periodical payments and which is subject to modification from time to time as the circumstances change. See, also, Arts. 1376, 1377, of the Code of Procedure, and Penal Code, Bk. 2, Art. 363.

The present action is a suit at common law and the court has no power to make a decree of this kind contemplated by the Mexican statutes. What the Circuit Court did was to disregard the principles of the Mexican statute altogether and to follow the Texas statute. This clearly was wrong and was excepted to specifically. But we are of opinion further that justice to the defendant would not permit the substitution of a lump sum, however estimated, for the periodical payments which the Mexican statute required. The marriage of beneficiaries, the cessation of the absolute necessity for the payments, the arising of other circumstances in which, according to law, the deceased would not have been required to continue the support, all are contingencies the chance of which cannot be estimated by any table of probabilities. It would be going far to give a lump sum in place of an annuity for life, the probable value of which could be fixed by averages based on statistics. But to reduce a liability conditioned as this was to a lump sum would be to leave the whole matter to a mere guess. We may add that by Art. 225, concerning alimony, the right cannot be renounced, nor can it be subject to compromise between the parties. There seems to be no possibility in Mexico of capitalizing the liability. Evidently the Texas courts would deem the dissimilarities between the local law and that of Mexico too great to permit an action in the Texas state courts. Mexican National Ry. v. Jackson, 89 Tex. 107; St. Louis, Iron Mountain & Southern Ry. v. McCormick, 73 Tex. 660. The case is not one demanding extreme measures like those where a tort is committed in an uncivilized country. The defendant always can be found in Mexico, on the other side of the river, and it is to be presumed that the courts there are open to the plaintiffs, if the statute conferred a right upon them notwithstanding their absence from the jurisdiction, as we assume that it did, for the purposes of this part of the case. See Mulhall v. Fallon, 176 Mass. 266.

. . .

Judgment affirmed.

MR. CHIEF JUSTICE FULLER dissented in an opinion, in which MR. JUSTICE HARLAN and MR. JUSTICE PECKHAM concurred.

NOTES

(1) For a case dismissing a suit because of unwillingness to apply "the unfamiliar remedial provisions of Mexican tort law" see Ramirez v. Autobuses Blancos Flecha Roja S. A. de C. V., 486 F.2d 493 (5th Cir. 1973).

(2) Phrantzes v. Argenti, [1960] 2 Q.B. 19, [1960] 1 All Eng.L.R. 778, was a suit brought by a daughter, under Greek law, claiming a dowry from her father. The court refused to entertain the suit, saying that the Greek "machinery by way of remedies" was entirely different from the English machinery.

CONSTITUTIONAL LIMITATIONS ON POWER OF STATE TO REFUSE TO ENTERTAIN CASE

DOUGLAS v. NEW YORK, NEW HAVEN & HARTFORD RAILROAD CO., 279 U.S. 377 (1929): The plaintiff, a resident of Connecticut, brought suit in a state court in New York for injuries sustained in Connecticut. The defendant was a Connecticut corporation, although doing business in New York as well. The state court dismissed the proceeding under the forum non conveniens doctrine. The plaintiff argued in the Supreme Court that this action violated Article IV, sec. 2, of the Constitution of the United States, which provides that: "The Citizens of each State shall be entitled to all Privileges and Immunities of Citizens in the several States."

The Supreme Court sustained the dismissal. It rejected the argument based on the privileges and immunities clause on the ground that New York's refusal to entertain the suit was not based on citizenship but on residence. It said that the New York rule "applied to citizens of New York as well as to others and puts them on the same footing."

In the same case it was contended that New York was required to entertain the suit, since the action was under the Federal Employers' Liability Act and that statute provided that suits might be brought where the defendant did business. The Court held that the statute "does not purport to require State Courts to entertain suits arising under it but only to empower them to do so, so far as the authority of the United States is concerned."

MISSOURI EX REL. SOUTHERN RAILWAY CO. v. MAYFIELD, 340 U.S. 1 (1950): A Missouri state court was held free to apply the forum non conveniens doctrine to a Federal Employers' Liability Act case brought before it where the plaintiff and defendant were nonresidents, and the accident had occurred in another state.[1]

------

1. But, on remand, the Missouri state court held that it did not apply the forum non conveniens rule and, hence refused to dismiss the case. State ex rel. South-

BALTIMORE & OHIO RAILROAD CO. v. KEPNER, 314 U.S. 44 (1941): Held that an Ohio state court could not enjoin a plaintiff from bringing suit under the FELA in the Eastern District of New York, where the railroad was doing business, though the plaintiff resided in Ohio, and the accident occurred in Ohio.

———

MILES v. ILLINOIS CENTRAL RAILROAD CO., 315 U.S. 698 (1942): Held that a Tennessee state court could not enjoin the bringing of a suit in a state court in Missouri, when the accident occurred in Tennessee, under the FELA and the decedent and his administratrix were residents of Tennessee.[2]

MONDOU v. NEW YORK, NEW HAVEN & HARTFORD RAILROAD CO., 223 U.S. 1 (1912): An action was brought in a Connecticut state court by the personal representative of an employee who was killed in Connecticut in the course of his employment in interstate commerce. The action was brought under the Federal Employers' Liability Act which increased the liabilities of employers by abolishing certain common law defenses. It also provided that the jurisdiction of the courts of the United States and of the states should be concurrent under the Act. The defendant demurred to the complaint, and this was sustained by the Connecticut state court on the ground, among others, that the Act, in so extending liability, was contrary to the public policy of Connecticut.

The Supreme Court of the United States reversed. After holding the Act constitutional, the Court stated that federal action within its sphere is paramount to and supersedes state law. Consequently, the Act established a policy binding on all states, and if the court in which the action is brought is otherwise competent, it is under a duty to exercise its jurisdiction.

———

McKNETT v. ST. LOUIS & SAN FRANCISCO RAILROAD CO., 292 U.S. 230 (1934): Held that Alabama could not refuse to enforce Federal Employers' Liability Act claims when it would entertain suits based on wrongful death statutes of other states under similar circumstances.

———

TESTA v. KATT, 330 U.S. 386 (1947): A suit was brought in a state court in Rhode Island to recover triple damages for an overcharge on the sale of goods, contrary to the Emergency Price Control Act. Sec. 205(e) of that Act authorized a suit "in any court of competent jurisdiction," and sec. 205(c) provided that federal district courts should have jurisdiction of such suits "concurrently with State and Territorial courts."

ern Railway Co. v. Mayfield, 362 Mo. 101, 240 S.W.2d 106 (1951).

2. Pope v. Atlantic Coast Line Railroad Co., 345 U.S. 379 (1953), is similar.

The Supreme Court of Rhode Island held that the statute allowing recovery of treble damages was a penal statute, and could not be enforced in the Rhode Island courts. This was reversed by the Supreme Court of the United States, which said that "the State courts are not free to refuse enforcement of petitioners' claim."

Query, are there any circumstances in which a state may refrain from enforcing a Federal cause of action?[3] Suppose, for example, it enforces no wrongful death actions, either arising in its own state or in other states. Could it refuse to entertain an action for death brought under the Federal Employers' Liability Act?

CHAMBERS v. BALTIMORE & OHIO RAILROAD CO., 207 U.S. 142 (1907): A Pennsylvania citizen sued in Ohio for the wrongful death in Pennsylvania of her husband, also a Pennsylvania citizen. The Ohio courts ruled that action for wrongful death outside Ohio existed only by virtue of an Ohio statute which permitted such suits only if the *deceased* were a citizen of Ohio and that accordingly this action would not lie. Despite plaintiff's contention that this construction of the statute violated the privileges and immunities clause relating to state citizenship the Supreme Court affirmed the judgment on the grounds that the Ohio law had not been influenced by *her* citizenship, for "she would have been denied hearing on the same cause for the same reason if she had been a citizen of Ohio." The court left open the question whether the same result would obtain if the Pennsylvania statute giving the cause of action for the wrongful death had, instead of giving it originally to the survivors, given it to the deceased, "at the instant when he was vivus et mortus, and made to survive and pass to his representatives." In such a case the Ohio "denial would be based upon the citizenship of that person in whom the right of action originally vested." Cf. the Supreme Court's footnote 3, to Broderick v. Rosner, p. 947, infra: "Chambers v. Baltimore & Ohio Railroad Co., 207 U.S. 142, is not to the contrary; there no claim was made under the full faith and credit clause."

See Hughes v. Fetter, p. 322, infra.

NOTE

See Brilmayer and Underhill, Congressional Obligation to Provide a Forum for Constitutional Claims: Discriminatory Jurisdictional Rules and the Conflict of Laws, 39 Va.L.Rev. 819 (1983).

---

3. See Note, State Remedies for Federally-Created Rights, 47 Minn.L.Rev. 815 (1963).

SECTION 5.   LIMITATIONS IMPOSED BY THE STATE OF THE TRANSACTION*

BUTTRON v. EL PASO NORTHEASTERN RY. CO.

Court of Civil Appeals of Texas, 1906.

93 S.W. 676.

Action by Louis Buttron against the El Paso Northeastern Railway Co. and others.   From a judgment for defendants, plaintiff appeals.

JAMES, C. J.   This action was brought by Buttron in the district court of El Paso county, Tex., against the above-named appellee and two other railway companies, to recover damages for injury alleged to have been caused him by their negligence.   The court directed the jury to find for defendants, stating as its reason for so doing that defendants had introduced in evidence a valid and subsisting judgment of the Sixth judicial district court of the territory of New Mexico, adjudicating the issues involved.   The said territorial judgment was rendered in a proceeding begun and prosecuted by the defendants herein against Buttron, under the provisions of the second and fourth sections of the following act of the Legislature Assembly of the said territory (Laws 1903, p. 51, c. 33) . . .

There are peculiar and radical features in this law, which appellant says affect its validity.[1]   These are stated by appellant to be: (1) It provides that no suit for personal injuries incurred within the territory shall be brought in another jurisdiction, provided the defendant can be served within the territory.   (2) The right of action is taken away from the claimant, unless within ninety days after the injury, and thirty days before commencing his action he shall serve upon his adversary a sworn statement giving the details of his case and the names and addresses of his witnesses.   (3) The suit must be brought in one year after the injury.   (4) The party who has inflicted the injury can compel the one he has injured to come into the court for the district in which the wrongdoer lives and set up his claim there, and, in case he does not do it, then the court will try the case on the statement of the wrongdoer, and upon that statement of the claim render judgment, which shall be final.   (5) On its appearing to the court that any such suit has been begun in a court outside the territory, the court in the territory where an action is pending, under the act, may try the latter case upon such short notice as the court may direct, and compel the parties to plead on such short day as the court may fix,

* See Restatement, Second, Conflict of Laws § 91.

1. The text of the carefully drawn Act, which was included in full in the opinion, is omitted.   It was "disapproved and declared null and of no effect" by an Act of Congress.   Act of May 13, 1908, 35 Stat. 573, 575.

and the institution of such suit outside the territory shall be construed by the court as a waiver of a jury in the case pending in the territorial court. (6) On showing made that a party injured contemplates bringing suit outside the territory, or has already instituted such a suit, the court may perpetually enjoin the claimant from prosecuting or maintaining his suit outside the territory . . .

The Court gave effect to a judgment of the territorial court rendered under the provisions of section 2 of the act. . . . Section 2 allows the person or corporation inflicting the injury, or causing the death, to commence a proceeding against the injured party, in the district court for the county in the territory where it has its principal office, if a corporation, and requires the injured party to appear and litigate his claim. The defendants in the case resorted to such a proceeding, and plaintiff, a resident of the territory, was personally served with the prescribed summons. He failed to appear, and, the court proceeding in the prescribed manner, judgment was rendered against him in favor of these defendants on his cause of action, upon the hearing required by the act. The only point of objection which we perceive possible in reference to section 2 is that it gives to one who is accustomed to figure as a defendant, and who has heretofore invariably occupied that attitude in the courts, the right to anticipate the ordinary action, and to himself begin a proceeding requiring the injured party to appear and submit his cause of action to adjudication. Why is this not due exercise of power vested in a legislative body? It consisted in giving the person or corporation charged with committing a wrong remedy which it otherwise would not have had. Ordinarily such party would have had to await the bringing of the action by the claimant at his convenience, within the period of limitations. Such delay, it can readily be conceived, might often work a hardship on the former, by the loss of testimony. It is true there generally are statutes enabling a party to perpetuate testimony, but it is well known that written testimony is not always as effective as oral, which might not be obtainable in the course of time. Viewing the matter abstractly, what justice is there, after all, in forcing a party interested in the settlement of a controversy to await the pleasure of his adversary as to the time of its adjudication? Why should they not have equal right and opportunity to bring the matter to issue in the courts? There may be reasons of a substantial nature for such legislation. If they were sufficient in the minds of the legislators to dictate the wisdom of policy of a statute conferring on a prospective defendant such a remedy, it is for the courts to give effect to the will of the people thus expressed, though the wisdom and policy may be doubted by some. There is no obstacle of a constitutional nature, to the adoption of such a rule. It concerns merely procedure which is a proper subject of legislative action. Our courts are required to give full faith and credit to the judgment of the territorial court. Therefore we think the judgment appealed from should be affirmed.

Affirmed.

NOTES

(1) Compare Atchison, Topeka & Santa Fe Railway Co. v. Sowers, 213 U.S. 55 (1909), which involved Sec. 1 of the same New Mexico statute and is outlined in the opinion of the court in Tennessee Coal, Iron & Railroad Co. v. George, infra.

(2) A considerable number of states have adopted declaratory judgment acts. See 12 Uniform Laws Annotated 109 (1975). See also 28 U.S.C. § 2201. May the declaratory judgments acts be utilized by the alleged obligor to have a controversy tried (a) in the normal forum, or (b) in any forum selected by him that has jurisdiction over the alleged obligee? Will the courts exercise the same type of discretion in taking jurisdiction to render a declaratory judgment as they have done in other cases?

TENNESSEE COAL, IRON & RAILROAD CO. v. GEORGE

Supreme Court of the United States, 1914.
233 U.S. 354, 34 S.Ct. 587, 58 L.Ed. 997.

MR. JUSTICE LAMAR delivered the opinion of the court.

Wiley George, the defendant in error, was an engineer employed by the Tennessee Coal, Iron and Railroad Company at its steel plant in Jefferson County, Alabama. While he was under a locomotive repairing the brakes, a defective throttle allowed steam to leak into the cylinder causing the engine to move forward automatically in consequence of which he was seriously injured. He brought suit by attachment, in the City Court of Atlanta, Georgia, founding his action on sec. 3910 of the Alabama Code of 1907, which makes the master liable to the employe when the injury is "caused by reason of any defect in the condition of the ways, works, machinery or plant connected with or used in the business of the master or employer."

The defendant filed a plea in abatement in which it was set out that sec. 6115 of that Code also provided that "all actions under said section 3910 must be brought in a court of competent jurisdiction within the State of Alabama and not elsewhere." The defendant thereupon prayed that the action be abated because "to continue said case on said statutory cause of action given by the statutes of Alabama and restricted by said statutes to the courts of Alabama, . . . would be a denial so far as the rights of this defendant are concerned, of full faith and credit to said public acts of the State of Alabama in the State of Georgia, contrary to the provisions of Art. 4, sec. 1 of the Constitution of the United States." A demurrer to the plea in abatement was sustained and the judgment for the plaintiff thereafter entered was affirmed by the Court of Appeals. The case was then brought to this court.

The record raises the single question as to whether the full faith and credit clause of the Constitution prohibited the courts of Georgia from enforcing a cause of action given by the Alabama Code, to the servant against the master, for injuries occasioned by defective machinery, when another section of the same Code provided that suits to enforce such liability "must be brought in a court of competent jurisdiction within the State of Alabama *and not elsewhere.*"

There are many cases where right and remedy are so united that the right cannot be enforced except in the manner and before the tribunal designated by the act. For the rule is well settled that "where the provision for the liability is coupled with a provision for a special remedy, that remedy, and that alone, must be employed." Pollard v. Bailey, 20 Wall. 520, 527 . . . .

But that rule has no application to a case arising under the Alabama Code relating to suits for injuries caused by defective machinery. For, whether the statute be treated as prohibiting certain defenses, as removing common law restrictions or as imposing upon the master a new and larger liability, it is in either event evident that the place of bringing the suit is not part of the cause of action,—the right and the remedy are not so inseparably united as to make the right dependent upon its being enforced in a particular tribunal. The cause of action is transitory and like any other transitory action can be enforced "in any court of competent jurisdiction within the State of Alabama. . . ." But the owner of the defective machinery causing the injury may have removed from the State and it would be a deprivation of a fixed right if the plaintiff could not sue the defendant in Alabama because he had left the State nor sue him where the defendant or his property could be found because the statute did not permit a suit elsewhere than in Alabama. The injured plaintiff may likewise have moved from Alabama and for that, or other, reason may have found it to his interest to bring suit by attachment or in personam in a State other than where the injury was inflicted.

The courts of the sister State trying the case would be bound to give such faith and credit to all those substantial provisions of the statute which inhered in the cause of action or which name conditions on which the right to sue depend. But venue is no part of the right; and a State cannot create a transitory cause of action and at the same time destroy the right to sue on that transitory cause of action in any court having jurisdiction. That jurisdiction is to be determined by the law of the court's creation and cannot be defeated by the extraterritorial operation of a statute of another State, even though it created the right of action.

The case here is controlled by the decision of this court in Atchison &c. Ry. v. Sowers, 213 U.S. 55, 59, 70, where the New Mexico statute, giving a right of action for personal injuries and providing that suits should be brought after certain form of notice in a particular district, was preceded by the recital that "it has become customary for persons claiming damages for personal injuries received in this Territory to institute and maintain suits for the recovery thereof in other States and Territories to the increased cost and annoyance and manifest injury and oppression of the business interests of this Territory and in derogation of the dignity of the courts thereof." Despite this statement of the public policy of the Territory, the judgment obtained by the plaintiff in Texas was affirmed by this court in an opinion wherein it was said that where an action is brought in "another jurisdiction based upon common law principles, although having certain statutory restrictions, such as are found in this [territorial] act as to the making of an affidavit and limiting the time of prosecuting the suit, full faith and credit is given to the law, when the recovery is permitted, subject to the restrictions upon the right of action imposed in the Territory enacting the statute. . . . When it is shown that the court in the other jurisdiction observed such conditions, and that a recovery was permitted after such conditions had been complied with, the jurisdiction thus invoked is not defeated because of the provision of the statute" requiring the suit to be brought in the district where the plaintiff resides or where the defendant, if a corporation, has its principal place of business.

It is claimed, however, that the decision in the Sowers Case is not in point because the plaintiff was there seeking to enforce a common law liability, while here he is asserting a new and statutory cause of action. But that distinction marks no difference between the two cases because in New Mexico, common law liability is statutory liability—the adopting statute (Complied Laws sec. 1823) providing that "the common law as recognized in the United States of America shall be the rule of practice and decision."

The decision in the Sowers Case, however, was not put upon the fact that the suit was based on a common law liability. The court there announced the general rule that a transitory cause of action can be maintained in another State even though the statute creating the cause of action provides that the action must be brought in local domestic courts.

In the present case the Georgia court gave full faith and credit to the Alabama act and its judgment is

Affirmed.

Mr. Justice Holmes dissents.

NOTES

(1) If in the principal case the Georgia court had refused to entertain the plaintiff's action, would its refusal have been in violation of any provision of the Constitution? Would the Constitution require that the plaintiff's action be entertained in Georgia despite the wishes of both Alabama and Georgia, the only two states of interest? Compare Hughes v. Fetter, p. 322, infra.

(2) Note Justice Lamar's statement in the George case that "[t]he courts of the sister state trying the case would be bound to give such faith and credit to all those substantial provisions of the statute which inhered in the

cause of action or which name conditions on which the right to sue depend." In connection with this statement, consider the following:

In Pearson v. Northeast Airlines, Inc., 309 F.2d 553 (2d Cir. 1962), a majority of the court, sitting en banc, held it constitutional for a state to apply the wrongful death statute of a sister state to determine whether the defendant was liable for the death and at the same time refuse to apply the limitation contained in that statute as to the amount of recovery. Speaking for a minority of three, Judge Friendly wrote a dissent in which he said:

"An important reason why a forum state may not do this is that it thereby interferes with the proper freedom of action of the legislature of the sister state. The terms and conditions of a claim created by statute inevitably reflect the legislature's balancing of those considerations that favor and of those that oppose the imposition of liability. The legislature may be quite unwilling to create the claim on terms allowing it to be enforced without limit of amount as most common law rights can be, or for a period bounded only by statutes of limitations ordinarily applicable. The Full Faith and Credit Clause insures that, in making its choice, the legislature creating the claim need not have to weigh the risk that the courts of sister states looking to its 'public acts' as a source of rights will disregard substantial conditions which it has imposed . . .. This consideration is inapplicable to instances where the forum, looking solely to its own substantive law, wholly disregards that of the sister state. . . . True, conduct in the enacting state has been given consequences different from what the legislators of that state desired; but that is the inevitable result of the duplicate law-making jurisdiction that can never be wholly avoided even in our federal system. . . ."

Crider v. Zurich Insurance Co., 380 U.S. 39 (1965) involved an action brought in an Alabama court by a resident of that state to recover under the Georgia Workmen's Compensation Act for injuries suffered in Alabama. Georgia decisions had previously held that the remedy provided by the Georgia act is "an exclusive one which can be afforded only" by the Georgia Compensation Board. Nevertheless, the Supreme Court held that Alabama was not prohibited from entertaining the action. In the course of his majority opinion, Justice Douglas stated that the rule of the George case "has been eroded" to the extent that it would limit the courts of a second state to the award of a "special remedy" that is "coupled" with the provision for liability on which the action is based.

The Crider case is discussed in Greenspan, Crider v. Zurich Insurance Co.: Decline of Conceptualism in Conflict of Laws, 27 U.Pitt.L.Rev. 49 (1965). The question of whether it is a denial of full faith and credit to rely on a sister-state law as the basis for enforcing a claim while at the same time rejecting a limitation provided in that law is considered in Chapter 6, infra.

JAMES v. GRAND TRUNK WESTERN RAILROAD CO.

Supreme Court of Illinois, 1958.
14 Ill.2d 356, 152 N.E.2d 858.

[The case involved a Michigan injunction and an Illinois counter-injunction. A resident of Michigan was killed in that state by the defendant railroad company. His widow, appointed administratrix in Michigan, brought an action in Illinois under the Michigan wrongful death statute, alleging the death was caused by the negligence of the railroad.

In Michigan, where the administratrix resided, the defendant obtained a temporary injunction restraining her from proceeding with the action in Illinois.

The administratrix then filed a supplemental complaint in the Illinois court, which alleged she believed she could not obtain a fair trial in the county in Michigan where she resided, and the railroad's injunction suit in Michigan was for the purpose of preventing her from obtaining a fair trial in Illinois and of forcing her into an unjust settlement to her irreparable injury. She moved for an injunction restraining the enforcement of the Michigan injunction. The motion was denied by the Illinois trial court and the Appellate Court, and their action is the subject of the present appeal to the Supreme Court of Illinois.

In the meantime maneuvers continued, as, the arrest of the administratrix in Michigan for violation of the Michigan restraining order, a letter from her to her Illinois attorney discharging him and directing him to withdraw the Illinois case, a repudiation of the letter by her and the expression of her desire that he press the case; a second suit by the railroad in Michigan for injunction and the grant of the injunction; the issuance of an order by a justice of the Supreme Court of Illinois restraining the railroad company from taking further action in the Michigan injunction suit or in any other suit until the Supreme Court of Illinois heard the appeal in the Illinois case; the revocation of the widow's appointment as administratrix on a petition by the railroad's counsel in Michigan, the appointment of an elderly court bailiff as administrator, and shortly the appointment of still a third person as personal representative; the charge that the railroad's counsel had made arrangements for another lawyer to represent the estate in the claim against the railroad.]

BRISTOW, JUSTICE. . . . The issues are essentially whether the Illinois court, having prior jurisdiction of a wrongful death action instituted by a nonresident plaintiff, must recognize an out-of-State injunction restraining the plaintiff from proceeding with that action; and whether the Illinois court, to protect its jurisdiction of the wrongful death action, may issue a counterinjunction restraining defendant from enforcing its injunction against plaintiff in the State of her residence. . . .

In the instant case it is uncontroverted that the Illinois trial court had proper jurisdiction of the parties . . . Moreover, it is the undisputed policy of this State to keep its courts open to residents and nonresidents alike.

. . . Where, however, suits by nonresidents have no connection whatever with this jurisdiction, and the selection of this forum is purely vexatious the doctrine of *forum non conveniens* may be invoked to dismiss such cases (Cotton v. Louisville & Nashville Railroad Co., 14 Ill.2d 144, 152 N.E.2d 385). In the instant case, however, no such defense of *forum non conveniens* was interposed by defendant. Instead, it sought to remove the case from the Illinois court by enjoining plaintiff in the State of her residence from prosecuting the Illinois action.

With reference to the Michigan injunction, while we quite agree with defendant's repeated assertion that a court of equity has power to restrain persons within its jurisdiction from instituting or proceeding with foreign actions (Cole v. Cunningham, 133 U.S. 107, 6 A.L.R.2d 896), we note that the exercise of such power by equity courts has been deemed a matter of great delicacy, invoked with great restraint to avoid distressing conflicts and reciprocal interference with jurisdiction. . . .

Conversely, where other States have enjoined litigants from proceeding with a previously instituted Illinois action, this jurisdiction has followed the overwhelming judicial opinion that neither the full-faith-and-credit clause nor rules of comity require compulsory recognition of such injunctions so as to abate or preclude the disposition of the pending case. . . .

If statutes prohibiting or circumscribing the export of causes of action may not be given extraterritorial effect, it is hard to see why an equity decree should be entitled to any greater recognition. A court should be subject to the same limitations. . . .

Therefore, it is evident that legal consistency, as well as the weight of authority, do not require us to recognize the Michigan injunction, and we may retain jurisdiction and proceed with plaintiff's wrongful death action. Such a course, however, is not practicable in the instant case, unless plaintiff, who is subject to imprisonment and other coercive tactics if she fails to dismiss her Illinois action, is protected by enjoining defendant from enforcing the Michigan injunction by contempt proceedings. A plaintiff cannot be expected or required to risk imprisonment so that the court may retain jurisdiction of a cause.

This brings us to the ultimate issue in this case: whether the court which first acquires jurisdiction of the parties and of the merits of the cause can issue a counterinjunction restraining a party before it from enforcing an out-of-State injunction which requires the dismissal of the local cause and ousts the forum of jurisdiction. . . .

. . . we cannot close our eyes to the fact that the intended effect of the Michigan injunction, though directed at the parties and not at this court, is to prevent the Illinois court from adjudicating a cause of action of which it had proper jurisdiction. For it is patent that if the litigants are coerced to dismiss the Illinois action, it is our rightfully acquired jurisdiction that is thereby destroyed. Therefore, the

Michigan injunction was in everything but form an order restraining the Illinois court and determining the cases, it may properly try.

. . . this court need not, and will not, countenance having its right to try cases, of which it has proper jurisdiction, determined by the courts of other States, through their injunctive process. We are not only free to disregard such out-of-State injunctions, and to adjudicate the merits of the pending action, but we can protect our jurisdiction from such usurpation by the issuance of a counterinjunction restraining the enforcement of the out-of-State injunction. . . .

Reversed and remanded, with directions.

SCHAEFER, JUSTICE (dissenting). . . .

So far as I have been able to ascertain, no court has as yet held that such an injunction is entitled to full faith and credit in the sense that the action toward which the injunction is directed must be abated. When such injunctions have been recognized, it has been because the State in which the action is pending has chosen to do so as a matter of comity, and not because it was required to do so by constitutional command. . . .

In part this view appears to rest upon the ground that to recognize the injunction is to recognize the claim of the enjoining State to exclusive cognizance of a transitory cause of action, which might abridge constitutional privileges. . . . In part it appears to rest upon the ground that to recognize the injunction would "mean in effect that the courts of one State can control what goes on in another." . . . For these reasons I agree with the majority that the Michigan injunction is not entitled to full faith and credit.

But the question in this case goes a step beyond the issue as to full faith and credit. What is here sought is a counter-injunction to restrain the railroad from enforcing the injunction entered by the Michigan court. . . . Just as the first injunction sired the second, so the second might sire a third. The ultimate end is not foreseeable.

The place to stop this unseemly kind of judicial disorder is where it begins. The peculiar preference of one State for a particular venue in a single class of cases does not, it seems to me, afford a basis for indirect interference with litigation pending in another jurisdiction. The salutary power of a court of equity to restrain the prosecution of inequitable actions in a foreign court originated and developed upon more substantial considerations. But we are not called upon to review the propriety of the Michigan injunction. Plaintiff did not seek to review it in the Michigan courts. . . . Illinois has no connection whatever with the occurrences out of which the administrator's claim arose. The policy of Illinois with respect to the maintenance of foreign wrongful death actions was expressed in section 2 of the Injuries Act (Ill.Rev.Stat.1955, chap. 70, par. 2) which prohibited them. While it is true that this prohibition is no longer effective, the policy that it expressed is also of significance in determining whether or not a counter-injunction should have been issued.

I think that the trial court and the Appellate Court were right, and so I would affirm.

NOTES

(1) Arpels v. Arpels, 8 N.Y.2d 339, 170 N.E. 670 (1960). A wife had been granted a judgment of separation and support by a New York Court. Four years later the husband began an action in France for divorce on grounds that included adultery. The wife then brought the present action to restrain the prosecution of the French action. Held, the action will not lie. Fuld, J.: ". . . where a foreign divorce is sought, our courts will intrude, even if a serious impropriety would be involved in its procurement, only when the ensuing decree would be entitled to full faith and credit in this State. . . . Since the decree which the defendant husband seeks in France in this case would not be entitled to full faith and credit, it follows that an injunction does not lie."

(2) Pound, The Progress of the Law—Equity, 33 Harv.L.Rev. 420, 426–427 (1920): "Three types of cases may be distinguished in which courts have enjoined litigation in foreign jurisdictions. In one the foreign court had no jurisdiction, but the threatened foreign judgment would embarrass plaintiff in the assertion of his rights, the legal remedy of collateral attack on the judgment when set up against plaintiff involved danger of impairment of the evidence by which its invalidity could be made to appear, and to compel plaintiff to go to the foreign state to defend or attack the threatened judgment directly involved compelling him to litigate abroad with a wrongdoer whom he could reach at home. In a second type concurrent litigation between the same parties over the same subject matter was in progress or was threatened. In some of the cases of this type there was simply a vexatious multiplicity of actions. Here courts were cautious about interposing. In others, one court was not in as good a position to do complete justice as another. In still others, the defendant was seeking to obtain an inequitable advantage over other creditors by means of concurrent litigation abroad. In a third type there was an attempt of domestic creditors to reach exempt property of a domestic debtor by means of an action outside of the state. To these some courts are adding a fourth: Cases where the foreign court has jurisdiction, in which there is no concurrent litigation or vexatious multiplicity of actions, and in which there is no attempt to reach anything which the policy of the local legislation seeks to secure to the plaintiff, but in which a domestic creditor seeks to sue a domestic debtor, as he has full legal power to do, in another state, where the latter has property, because of more favorable procedure or more favorable views as to what is a defense in the latter jurisdiction. In these cases it cannot be said that plaintiff (in equity) has a legal right only to be sued at home, nor may he claim a legal interest in the procedure or substantive law of his domicile. Doctrines of Conflict of Laws may sometimes require the court in the other state to judge the cause by the laws of the jurisdiction where the parties are domiciled. But that is a matter for that court to consider and does not give to the latter jurisdiction any claim to exclusive cognizance of the cause nor to its citizens any legal claim to make their defense solely at their domicile. As between a plaintiff and a defen-

dant, each seeking the tribunal more favorable to him, why should not equity leave the matter to the law? . . . "

(3) The Supreme Court has not yet had occasion to determine whether an injunction against suit in another state is entitled to full faith and credit. It has generally been assumed, however, that this is not the case. Usually, the courts have disregarded the sister state injunction and have permitted the action to proceed. See Dumbauld, Judicial Interference with Litigation in Other Courts, 74 Dick.L.Rev. 369 (1970); Reese, Full Faith and Credit to Foreign Equity Decrees, 42 Iowa L.Rev. 183 (1957), Comment, 29 U.Chi.L.Rev. 740 (1962).

(4) The unwillingness manifested by a court having jurisdiction of the parties to an action to give effect to a foreign decree enjoining the institution or maintenance of that action has its counterpart in the reluctance to treat the pendency of a foreign action on the same cause of action as a defense. A plea in abatement based on the pendency of a prior personal action in another state has generally been held to be ineffective. Fitch v. Whaples, 220 A.2d 170 (Me.1966). However, since the granting of a stay does not have the effect of sustaining a plea in abatement in terminating the action, a stay may be allowed when a plea in abatement would be unavailable. See Restatement, Second, Conflict of Laws § 86.

SECTION 6.   EFFECT OF INTERSTATE COMMERCE

For many years, in a variety of circumstances, the Supreme Court has held that the States cannot unreasonably "burden" interstate commerce. Many of these decisions are in the general field of constitutional law, and they are not dealt with here. In some cases, however, the question arises with respect to the jurisdiction of the state courts. See Restatement, Second, Conflict of Laws § 84, Comment *i* (1971).

An example may be found in Sioux Remedy Co. v. Cope, 235 U.S. 197 (1914). This was an action by an Iowa corporation brought in a South Dakota court. It arose out of a contract made in South Dakota for goods to be shipped by the plaintiff from Iowa to South Dakota. The plaintiff had not "qualified" to do business in South Dakota, and a statute of the latter state provided that if a foreign corporation did business in the state without qualifying (which included the appointment of an agent for the service of process on any and all claims), the foreign corporation could not maintain any action in the South Dakota courts.

The Supreme Court held that this statute, requiring a general consent to the jurisdiction of the South Dakota courts, was unreasonable and an undue burden on interstate commerce. It held that the South Dakota courts must entertain the action.

Suppose the South Dakota statute had required the filing of a consent limited to suits arising out of the business done in South Dakota? Would that have been valid? Would a requirement of filing a consent in such a case be necessary? Would the decision in the Sioux Remedy Co. case have been different if the plaintiff had been transacting all or a substantial part of its business in South Dakota? Compare Union Brokerage Co. v. Jensen, which is set forth at p. 977, infra.

Another problem was presented in Davis v. Farmers' Co-op. Equity Co., 262 U.S. 312 (1923). The Atchison, Topeka and Santa Fe Railroad is a Kansas corporation. It does not operate any railroad in Minnesota, but does maintain there an agent for the solicitation of traffic. A Minnesota statute provided that when a railroad maintained such an agent it could be served by delivering a summons to the agent. Acting under this statute, the plaintiff, a Kansas corporation, brought suit against the railroad in Minnesota. The cause of action arose over a bill of lading for the shipment of grain from one point in Kansas to another point in the same state. After extensive consideration, the Court held that the Minnesota statute, as applied to these facts, violated the commerce clause of the Constitution. The Court said "It may be that a statute like that here assailed would be valid, although applied to suits in which the cause of action arose elsewhere, if the transaction out of which it arose had been entered upon within the State, or if the plaintiff was, when it arose, a resident of the State. . . . But orderly effective administration of justice clearly does not require that a foreign carrier shall submit to a suit in a State in which the cause of action did not arise, in which the transaction giving rise to it was not entered upon, in which the carrier neither owns nor operates a railroad, and in which the plaintiff does not reside."

This was soon followed by Atchison, Topeka & Santa Fe Railway Co. v. Wells, 265 U.S. 101 (1924), which was a suit in a federal court in Texas to enjoin the enforcement of a judgment obtained in a Texas state court. The plaintiff in the original action, a resident of Colorado, had been injured in New Mexico while in the employ of the defendant, a Kansas corporation which neither did business nor had an agent in Texas. Unable to secure personal service on the defendant in Texas the plaintiff garnisheed traffic balances due the defendant and attached rolling stock in the possession of a Texas railroad. Judgment for the plaintiff was rendered by default, the defendant not having entered an appearance. On certiorari from a decree dismissing the bill for an injunction, held, reversed. "The writ of garnishment is void because of the purpose for which it was invoked. . . . Seizure of the rolling stock and credits for the purpose of compelling the Santa Fe to submit to the jurisdiction of the court in the Wells (original) suit interfered unreasonably with interstate commerce."

———

INTERNATIONAL MILLING CO. v. COLUMBIA TRANSPORTATION CO., 292 U.S. 511 (1934): The plaintiff and the defendant were both Delaware corporations. The plaintiff's principal place of business was in Minnesota, the defendant's in Ohio. The defendant was an interstate and foreign carrier by water. When one of its ships was unloading in Minnesota, it was attached by the plaintiff, on account of damage which had been sustained to a shipment previously made by the plaintiff. This damage had occurred somewhere between Chicago and Buffalo.

The defendant moved to vacate the attachment on the ground that prosecution of the action in Minnesota "would impose a serious burden upon interstate commerce, in contravention of Article I, Section 8, of the Constitution of the United States." This was granted by the state courts.

On appeal, the Supreme Court reversed this judgment. The court held that the defendant was regularly engaged in business in Minnesota. Its ships were often there. The court said: "Viewing all of these circumstances together, we find ourselves unable to conclude that by the prosecution of this suit there has been laid upon the carrier a burden so heavy and so unnecessary as to be oppressive and unreasonable. . . . Such a suit may be a burden, but oppressive and unreasonable it is not."

NOTES

(1) Does the commerce clause objection go to the judicial jurisdiction of the state? If so, will the objection be deemed to have been waived, if not seasonably made? Cf. Atchison, Topeka & Santa Fe Railway Co. v. Wells, p. 219, supra, and Baldwin v. Iowa State Traveling Men's Association, p. 285, infra.

(2) Later cases have given little effect to any commerce clause limitation on the exercise of jurisdiction. In Baltimore & Ohio Railroad Co. v. Kepner, 314 U.S. 44 (1941), briefed at p. 206, supra, the following statement appears: "Davis v. Farmers Co-operative Co., 262 U.S. 312, is limited to its particular facts, 292 U.S. 511 at 517; . . . ." The citation is to the International Milling case, where it is stated that the Davis "decision was confined narrowly within the bounds of its own facts." For a more recent case taking a similar view, see Scanapico v. Richmond, Fredericksburg & Potomac Railroad Co., 439 F.2d 17 (2d Cir. 1970).

(3) A federal district court in North Carolina dismissed a suit against a Georgia motel, in part because exercise of jurisdiction over the motel would constitute unreasonable interference with the interstate commerce in which the motel was engaged. Bryson v. Northlake Hilton, 407 F.Supp. 73 (M.D. N.C.1976). This is a most unusual application of the commerce clause, which has almost invariably been restricted to preventing burdensome suits against common carriers.

Chapter 5

FOREIGN JUDGMENTS

SECTION 1. POLICIES UNDERLYING THE RECOGNITION AND ENFORCEMENT OF FOREIGN JUDGMENTS

"Public policy dictates that there be an end of litigation; that those who have contested an issue shall be bound by the result of the contest, and that matters once tried shall be considered forever settled as between the parties." [1] This policy, embodied in the doctrine of res judicata, prevents the parties from relitigating issues that have been determined between them by a valid local judgment. It also forms the basis for the firmly established principle of Anglo-American law that foreign judgments, subject to only a few exceptions, are not open to reexamination on the merits when placed in issue before a local court. This latter principle, however, is frequently explained by the courts in terms other than that of res judicata. Thus, in cases which do not fall within the constitutional mandate of full faith and credit, the American courts have often talked in terms of "comity," [2] while those of England usually phrase their opinions in terms of the "legal obligation of foreign judgments." [3] These modes of expression merely state but do not explain the arrived-at result; they should not be permitted to obscure the underlying policy involved.

In this country, an express constitutional mandate calls for the extraterritorial recognition and enforcement of sister state and federal judgments. This mandate is embodied in the full faith and credit clause and its implementing statute, which, in the words of Chief Justice Stone, were designed to

". . . establish throughout the federal system the salutary principle of the common law that a litigation once pursued to judgment shall be as conclusive of the rights of the parties in every other court as in that where the judgment was rendered. . . . The full faith and credit clause like the commerce clause thus became a nationally unifying force. It altered the status of the several states as independent foreign sovereignties, each free to ignore rights and obligations created under the laws or established by the judicial proceedings of the others, by making each an integral part of a single nation, in which rights judicially established in any part are given nation-

1. Roberts, J., in Baldwin v. Iowa State Travelling Men's Association, 283 U.S. 522, 525 (1931).

2. See, e.g., Hilton v. Guyot, infra.

3. See, e.g., Godard v. Gray, L.R. 6 Q.B. 139 (1870).

221

wide application. . . . Because there is a full faith and credit
clause a defendant may not a second time challenge the validity of
plaintiff's right which has ripened into a judgment and a plaintiff
may not for his single cause of action secure a second or a greater
recovery. . . . "⁴

NOTES

(1) The full faith and credit clause and its implementing statute are quoted
at pp. 37–38, supra.

For general consideration of the problems of this Chapter, see Scoles and
Hay, Conflict of Laws 916–987 (1982); Leflar, American Conflicts Law 143–
171 (3d ed. 1977).

(2) Are all questions relating to the extraterritorial respect owed to federal and state judgments governed by the full faith and credit clause and its
implementing statute? Or is there still room in this field for the occasional
application by the states of their individual conflict of laws rules? See, for
example, pp. 296–298, infra.

(3) Is the implementing statute constitutional? Note that whereas the
full faith and credit clause only requires extraterritorial respect for the acts,
records and judicial proceedings of the several states, the statute also includes within its scope those of every "Territory, or Possession of the United
States." From what source, if any, did Congress derive power so to enact?
See Embry v. Palmer, 107 U.S. 3 (1883).

It is now established that federal court judgments are entitled to the
same full faith and credit as those of the state courts. Stoll v. Gottlieb, 305
U.S. 165 (1938); Hancock National Bank v. Farnum, 176 U.S. 640 (1900);
Metcalf v. City of Watertown, 153 U.S. 671 (1894). Can such a requirement
be spelled out of the language of the implementing statute?

(4) Federal courts are required by the implementing statute to give full
faith and credit to the judgments of state and territorial courts. Huron
Holding Corp. v. Lincoln Mine Operating Co., 312 U.S. 183 (1941); Davis v.
Davis, 305 U.S. 32 (1938). A Puerto Rican judgment is covered by the imple-
menting statute. Americana of Puerto Rico, Inc. v. Kaplus, 368 F.2d 431 (3d
Cir. 1966).

(5) As to proof of non-judicial records, see 28 U.S.C.A. § 1739 (1964).

(6) For discussions of the history and development of the concept of full
faith and credit, see Nadelmann, Full Faith and Credit to Judgments and
Public Acts, 56 Mich.L.Rev. 33 (1957); Sumner, The Full Faith and Credit
Clause—Its History and Purpose, 34 Ore.L.Rev. 224 (1955); Whitten, The
Constitutional Limitations on State Choice of Law: Full Faith and Credit, 12
Memphis State U.L.Rev. 1 (1981).

---

4. Magnolia Petroleum Co. v. Hunt,
320 U.S. 430, 439–40 (1943).

HILTON v. GUYOT

Supreme Court of the United States, 1895.
159 U.S. 113, 16 S.Ct. 139, 40 L.Ed. 95.

[Action in a circuit court of the United States upon a judgment of a French court against citizens of the United States, and in favor of a French firm, the plaintiffs in the French proceeding. The answer, setting forth the original dealings between the parties, alleged that the defendants were not indebted to the plaintiffs. The defendants also contended that the French judgment should not be enforced without an examination of the merits of the case, since the courts of France would examine anew the merits of a controversy if an American judgment against a French national were sued on in France. Other objections of the defendants are specified in the court's opinion. The circuit court entered a judgment and a decree for the French firm without examining the merits.]

MR. JUSTICE GRAY, after stating the case, delivered the opinion of the court. . . .

No law has any effect, of its own force, beyond the limits of the sovereignty from which its authority is derived. The extent to which the law of one nation, as put in force within its territory, whether by executive order, by legislative act, or by judicial decree, shall be allowed to operate within the dominion of another nation, depends upon what our greatest jurists have been content to call "the comity of nations." Although the phrase has been often criticised, no satisfactory substitute has been suggested.

"Comity," in the legal sense, is neither a matter of absolute obligation, on the one hand, nor of mere courtesy and good will, upon the other. But it is the recognition which one nation allows within its territory to the legislative, executive or judicial acts of another nation, having due regard both to international duty and convenience, and to the rights of its own citizens or of other persons who are under the protection of its laws. . . .

In order to appreciate the weight of the various authorities cited at the bar, it is important to distinguish different kinds of judgments. Every foreign judgment, of whatever nature, in order to be entitled to any effect, must have been rendered by a court having jurisdiction of the cause, and upon regular proceedings and due notice. In alluding to different kinds of judgments, therefore, such jurisdiction, proceedings and notice will be assumed. It will also be assumed that they are untainted by fraud, the effect of which will be considered later.

A judgment in rem, adjudicating the title to a ship or other movable property within the custody of the court, is treated as valid everywhere. . . . The most common illustrations of this are decrees of courts of admiralty and prize, which proceed upon principles of international law. . . . But the same rule applies to judgments in rem under municipal law.

A judgment affecting the status of persons, such as a decree confirming or dissolving a marriage, is recognized as valid in every country, unless contrary to the policy of its own law. . . .

Other judgments, not strictly in rem, under which a person has been compelled to pay money, are so far conclusive that the justice of the payment cannot be impeached in another country, so as to compel him to pay it again. For instance a judgment in foreign attachment is conclusive, as between the parties, of the right to the property or money attached. Story on Conflict of Laws (2d ed.), sec. 592a. . . .

The extraterritorial effect of judgments in personam, at law or in equity, may differ, according to the parties to the cause. A judgment of that kind between two citizens or residents of the country, and thereby subject to the jurisdiction, in which it is rendered, may be held conclusive as between them everywhere. So, if a foreigner invokes the jurisdiction by bringing an action against a citizen, both may be held bound by a judgment in favor of either. And if a citizen sues a foreigner, and judgment is rendered in favor of the latter, both may be held equally bound. . . .

The effect to which a judgment purely executory, rendered in favor of a citizen or resident of the country, in a suit there brought by him against a foreigner, may be entitled in an action thereon against the latter in his own country—as is the case now before us— presents a more difficult question, upon which there has been some diversity of opinion. . . . [The court reviewed the common-law cases.]

In view of all the authorities upon the subject, and of the trend of judicial opinion in this country and in England, following the lead of Kent and Story, we are satisfied that, where there has been opportunity for a full and fair trial abroad before a court of competent jurisdiction, conducting the trial upon regular proceedings, after due citation or voluntary appearance of the defendant, and under a system of jurisprudence likely to secure an impartial administration of justice between the citizens of its own country and those of other countries, and there is nothing to show either prejudice in the court or in the system of laws under which it was sitting, or fraud in procuring the judgment, or any other special reason why the comity of this nation should not allow it full effect, the merits of the case should not, in an action brought in this country upon the judgment, be tried afresh, as on a new trial or an appeal, upon the mere assertion of the party that the judgment was erroneous in law or in fact. The defendants, therefore, cannot be permitted, upon that general ground, to contest the validity or the effect of the judgment sued on.

But they have sought to impeach that judgment upon several other grounds, which require separate consideration.

It is objected that the appearance and litigation of the defendants in the French tribunals were not voluntary, but by legal compulsion, and therefore that the French courts never acquired such jurisdiction over the defendants, that they should be held bound by the judgment. . . . [The court found that the French court had acquired jurisdiction of the person of the defendants.]

It is next objected that in those courts one of the plaintiffs was permitted to testify not under oath, and was not subjected to cross-examination by the opposite party, and that the defendants were, therefore, deprived of safeguards which are by our law considered essential to secure honesty and to detect fraud in a witness; and also that documents and papers were admitted in evidence, with which the defendants had no connection, and which would not be admissible under our own system of jurisprudence. But it having been shown by the plaintiffs, and hardly denied by the defendants, that the practice followed and the method of examining witnesses were according to the laws of France, we are not prepared to hold that the fact that the procedure in these respects differed from that of our own courts is, of itself, a sufficient ground for impeaching the foreign judgment. . . .

When an action is brought in a court of this country, by a citizen of a foreign country against one of our own citizens, to recover a sum of money adjudged by a court of that country to be due from the defendant to the plaintiff, and the foreign judgment appears to have been rendered by a competent court, having jurisdiction of the cause and of the parties, and upon due allegations and proofs, and opportunity to defend against them, and its proceedings are according to the course of a civilized jurisprudence, and are stated in a clear and formal record, the judgment is prima facie evidence, at least, of the truth of the matter adjudged; and it should be held conclusive upon the merits tried in the foreign court, unless some special ground is shown for impeaching the judgment, as by showing that it was affected by fraud or prejudice, or that, by the principles of international law, and by the comity of our own country, it should not be given full credit and effect.

There is no doubt that both in this country, as appears by the authorities already cited, and in England, a foreign judgment may be impeached for fraud. . . .

But whether those decisions can be followed in regard to foreign judgments, consistently with our own decisions as to impeaching domestic judgments for fraud, it is unnecessary in this case to determine, because there is a distinct and independent ground upon which we are satisfied that the comity of our nation does not require us to give conclusive effect to the judgments of the courts of France; and that ground is, the want of reciprocity, on the part of France, as to the effect to be given to the judgments of this and other foreign countries. . . . [The court quoted the French statutes as to the effect of foreign judgments.]

The defendants, in their answer, cited the above provisions of the statutes of France, and alleged, and at the trial offered to prove, that, by the construction given to these statutes by the judicial tribunals of France, when the judgments of tribunals of foreign countries against the citizens of France are sued upon in the courts of France, the merits of the controversies upon which those judgments are based are examined anew, unless a treaty to the contrary effect exists between the Republic of France and the country in which such judgment is obtained, (which is not the case between the Republic of France and the United States,) and that the tribunals of the Republic of France give no force and effect, within the jurisdiction of that country, to the judgments duly rendered by courts of competent jurisdiction of the United States against citizens of France after proper personal service of the process of those courts has been made thereon in this country. We are of opinion that this evidence should have been admitted. . . . [The court's lengthy review of the laws of many countries as to the enforcement of foreign judgments is omitted.]

It appears, therefore, that there is hardly a civilized nation on either continent, which, by its general law, allows conclusive effect to an executory foreign judgment for the recovery of money.   In France, and in a few smaller States—Norway, Portugal, Greece, Monaco, and Haiti—the merits of the controversy are reviewed, as of course, allowing to the foreign judgment, at the most, no more effect than of being prima facie evidence of the justice of the claim.   In the great majority of the countries on the continent of Europe—in Belgium, Holland, Denmark, Sweden, Germany, in many cantons of Switzerland, in Russia and Poland, in Roumania, in Austria and Hungary, (perhaps in Italy,) and in Spain—as well as in Egypt, in Mexico, and in a great part of South America, the judgment rendered in a foreign country is allowed the same effect only as the courts of that country allow to the judgments of the country in which the judgment in question is sought to be executed.

. . . the rule of reciprocity has worked itself firmly into the structure of international jurisprudence.

The reasonable, if not the necessary, conclusion appears to us to be that judgments rendered in France, or in any other foreign country, by the laws of which our own judgments are reviewable upon the merits, are not entitled to full credit and conclusive effect when sued upon in this country, but are prima facie evidence only of the justice of the plaintiff's claim.

In holding such a judgment, for want of reciprocity, not to be conclusive evidence of the merits of the claim, we do not proceed upon any theory of retaliation upon one person by reason of injustice done to another; but upon the broad ground that international law is founded upon mutuality and reciprocity, and that by the principles of

international law recognized in most civilized nations, and by the comity of our own country, which it is our judicial duty to know and to declare, the judgment is not entitled to be considered conclusive.
. . . .

[The judgment and the decree were reversed.]

MR. CHIEF JUSTICE FULLER, with whom concurred MR. JUSTICE HARLAN, MR. JUSTICE BREWER, and MR. JUSTICE JACKSON, dissenting.

I cannot yield my assent to the proposition that because by legislation and judicial decision in France that effect is not there given to judgments recovered in this country which, according to our jurisprudence, we think should be given to judgments wherever recovered, (subject, of course, to the recognized exceptions,) therefore we should pursue the same line of conduct as respects the judgments of French tribunals. The application of the doctrine of res judicata does not rest in discretion; and it is for the government, and not for its courts, to adopt the principle of retorsion, if deemed under any circumstances desirable or necessary.

As the court expressly abstains from deciding whether the judgment is impeachable on the ground of fraud, I refrain from any observations on that branch of the case.

NOTES

(1) Apart from the question of reciprocity, what defenses, according to the principal case, can be raised in this country to a suit seeking the enforcement of a foreign country judgment?

(2) In Ritchie v. McMullen, 159 U.S. 235 (1895), decided the same day as Hilton v. Guyot, the Supreme Court held that an Ontario judgment should be enforced without an examination of its merits, as Canada would give conclusive effect to a judgment rendered by a court in the United States.

(3) It appears that the doctrine or rule of *révision au fond* has been abandoned in France. In Munzer v. Dame Munzer-Jacoby, decided by the Cour de Cassation on January 7, 1964, it was held that no such right exists. See Nadelmann, French Courts Recognize Foreign Money-Judgments: One Down and More to Go, 13 Am.J.Comp.L. 1 (1964).

For discussions of recognition of foreign judgments within the Common Market community, see Nadelmann, Jurisdictionally Improper Fora in Treaties on Recognition of Judgments: The Common Market Draft, 67 Colum.L. Rev. 995 (1967); Hay, The Common Market Preliminary Draft Convention on the Recognition and Enforcement of Judgments—Some Considerations of Policy and Interpretation, 16 Am.J.Comp.L. 149 (1968); Herzog, The Common Market Convention on Jurisdiction and the Enforcement of Judgments: An Interim Update, 17 Va.J.Int.L. 417 (1977).

(4) A proposed U.K.–U.S. convention on the reciprocal recognition and enforcement of their judgments was prepared during the 1970's. See Hay and Walker, The Proposed Recognition-of-Judgments Convention between the United States and the United Kingdom, 11 Texas Int.L.J. 421 (1976); North, Draft U.K./U.S. Judgments Convention: A British Viewpoint, 1 N.W.J. Int.

L. & Bus. 219 (1979). It seems unlikely that this convention will ever come into force.

(5) Application of the law of a foreign state is rarely limited, if ever, by any requirement of reciprocity. What is the justification for a stricter attitude toward the enforcement of foreign judgments than toward the application of foreign law?

(6) The defense of lack of reciprocity has today been widely discarded. See, e. g., Somportex, Limited v. Philadelphia Chewing Gum Corp., 453 F.2d 435 (3d Cir. 1971); Royal Bank of Canada v. Trentham Corp., 491 F.Supp. 404 (S.D.Tex.1980); Nicol v. Tanner, 310 Minn. 68, 256 N.W.2d 796 (1976).

COWANS V. TICONDEROGA PULP & PAPER CO., 219 App.Div. 120, 219 N.Y.S. 284 (1927), affirmed on opinion below 246 N.Y. 603, 159 N.E. 669 (1927): Action brought in a New York court to enforce a money judgment recovered in the Province of Quebec, Canada. Plaintiffs appealed from an order of the trial court denying their motion for judgment on the pleadings. Held, reversed. Van Kirk, J. . . . "The question presented here is whether this Quebec judgment is in our court merely prima facie proof of liability, against which any defense which could have been used at the trial in the Quebec court is available to defeat recovery here, or is it conclusive, subject only to the recognized exceptions. The respondent's proposition is that the judgment is only prima facie evidence, because, under the Quebec law (Code Civ.Proc. of Quebec § 210): 'Any defense which was or might have been set up to the original action may be pleaded to an action brought upon a judgment rendered out of Canada' . . . ."

"The force and effect which is to be given to a foreign judgment is for each sovereign power to determine for itself. . . . The general rule in this State is settled as follows: A judgment recovered in a foreign country, when sued upon in the courts of this State, is conclusive so far as to preclude a retrial of the merits of the case, subject, however, to certain well-recognized exceptions, namely, where the judgment is tainted with fraud, or with an offense against the public policy of the State, or the foreign court had not jurisdiction.

. . . The respondent does not question the general rule as above stated, but urges that the denial of reciprocity in the Province of Quebec furnishes a further exception to the general rule. It rests its contention confidently on the decision in Hilton v. Guyot. . . ."

". . . Our Court of Appeals [in Johnston v. Compagnie Generale Transatlantique, 242 N.Y. 381, 152 N.E. 121 (1926)] has we think definitely refused to accept that holding as the policy of this State; and, without reciprocity, would give to the foreign judgment the full effect to which its persuasiveness entitles it. The decision in the Hilton case would deprive a party of the private rights he has acquired by reason of a foreign judgment because the country in whose courts that jugment was rendered has a rule of evidence different from that which we have and does not give the same effect as this State gives to a foreign judgment.

"We think the general rule as above stated must be applied to this case, and that the proposition which the respondent would maintain is in conflict with the policy and law of this State. . . . "

NOTES

(1) What law determines the effect to be given the judgments of foreign countries by American courts? Is this a question of national law or one to be decided by the conflict of laws rules of the individual states? The consensus today is that state law controls. Somportex, Limited v. Philadelphia Chewing Gum Corp., 453 F.2d 435 (3d Cir. 1971), cert. denied 405 U.S. 1017; Toronto-Dominion Bank v. Hall, 367 F.Supp. 1009 (E.D.Ark.1973). Accordingly, if the question presented in the Hilton case were to arise today in a federal court sitting in New York, the court would presumably follow Cowans v. Ticonderoga Pulp and Paper Co. rather than Hilton. Consider, however, Banco National de Cuba v. Sabbatino, 376 U.S. 398 (1964) (p. 747, infra); see generally Ginsburg, Recognition and Enforcement of Foreign Civil Judgments, 4 Int'l. Lawyer 720 (1970); Homburger, Recognition and Enforcement of Foreign Judgments, 18 Am.J.Comp.L. 367, 385–390 (1970); Kulzer, Recognition of Foreign Country Judgments in New York: The Uniform Foreign Money-Judgments Recognition Act, 18 Buff.L.Rev. 1 (1969).

(2) For a comparison of the effects accorded in this country to sister state and foreign country judgments, see pp. 315–317, infra. See Wurfel, Recognition of Foreign Judgments, 50 N.Car.L.Rev. 21 (1971).

(3) For a general discussion of the recognition and enforcement of foreign country judgments, see Scoles and Hay, Conflict of Laws 961–981 (1982).

SECTION 2.   GENERAL RECOGNITION AND ENFORCEMENT

In this section and the one immediately succeeding, we examine the effects which a state or federal judgment carries in the state of rendition and those which under full faith and credit must be accorded it in other states. Here, consideration is given to a judgment's basic effects as res judicata and to methods of enforcing a foreign judgment. In Section 3 attention is directed to other questions relating to the parties and issues concluded by a judgment and to various special matters.

A. IN PERSONAM JUDGMENTS

In the state of rendition, an in personam judgment for a sum certain can normally be enforced by a levy of execution against any local property of the defendant. All in personam judgments also have one or more of the following effects: (1) *Merger*, by which the plaintiff's original claim (cause of action) is merged in a judgment for a sum certain, so that the original claim is extinguished and a claim on the judgment takes its place.[1] (2) *Bar*, by which a judgment for the defendant extinguishes the original claim. (3) *Issue preclusion*,[2] by which issues of fact and perhaps of law actually litigated in the action are conclusively determined in subsequent proceedings in which the same issues arise, even though the claim may be different. If the subsequent proceedings are on the same claim, this is sometimes known as direct estoppel. If the question arises in connection with another claim, this has commonly been called collateral estoppel. Further reference to the problem of issue preclusion is made in Section 3B, infra.

The rule was concisely put in Mendez v. Bowie, 118 F.2d 435 (1st Cir.1941), at p. 440, as follows:

"The effect of a judgment or decree as res judicata depends upon whether the second action or suit is upon the same or a different cause of action. If upon the same cause of action, the judgment or decree upon the merits in the first case is an absolute bar to the subsequent action or suit between the same parties or those in privity with them, not only in respect of every matter which was actually offered and received to sustain the demand or to make out a defense, but also as to every ground of recovery or defense which might have been presented. . . . But if the second case be upon a different cause of action, the prior judgment or decree operates as an estoppel only as to matters actually in issue or points controverted, upon the determination of which the judgment or decree was rendered, and not as to matters or points which might have been litigated and determined."

Obviously, much depends on whether the term "claim" (cause of action) is given a broad or a narrow definition. See Restatement, Second, Judgments §§ 24–26 (1982); James and Hazard, Civil Procedure 541–563 (2d ed. 1977); Rosenberg, Collateral Estoppel in New York, 44 St. John's L.Rev. 165 (1969). The broader the definition, the

---

1. It has been held, however, that the rule of merger does not apply to a judgment of a foreign country. Eastern Townships Bank v. H. S. Beebe & Co., 53 Vt. 177 (1880). The English rule is also to the effect that the underlying cause of action is not merged in the judgment of a foreign country. Borm-Reid, Recognition and Enforcement of Foreign Judgments, 3 Int. & Comp.L.Q. 49, 50 (1954).

2. This is the terminology adopted by the Restatement, Second, Judgments § 17.

more will a plaintiff be required to seek relief in a single action for his various complaints against the defendant.

An important problem is whether the definition of claim is to be sought in the law of F–1 or of F–2. Should a distinction be made in this connection between a judgment rendered in a state of the United States and one rendered in a foreign country?

LYNDE v. LYNDE

Supreme Court of the United States, 1901.
181 U.S. 183, 21 S.Ct. 555, 45 L.Ed. 810.

[In 1892 Mrs. Lynde filed a bill in New Jersey asking for a divorce on the ground of desertion and for reasonable alimony. Service was had by publication. The decree of divorce was granted but no provision for alimony was made. In 1896 Mrs. Lynde asked that the decree be amended to provide for alimony, alleging an oversight on the part of her attorney in failing to include such a provision in the original decree. In the interim her divorced husband had married again in New York but he now appeared generally in the proceeding and contested the alimony request. The court, however, awarded the wife $7,840 back alimony and further alimony at the rate of $80 a week. A receiver of the husband's New Jersey property was appointed but was able to find no property in New Jersey. The second New Jersey decree also provided for security, which the husband failed to give, and for an injunction against disposal of property to evade the decree. (Lynde v. Lynde, 54 N.J.Eq. 473.)

The wife then brought suit in New York asking for past due alimony, counsel fees, and $80 weekly as allowed her by the New Jersey court. She also asked that her ex-husband be directed to give security, and that the order provide for sequestration, receivership, and an injunction. The New York court (Lynde v. Lynde, 162 N.Y. 405) conceded the New Jersey court's jurisdiction to grant an in personam decree against the husband for alimony because of his general appearance in the later New Jersey proceedings. The judgment was enforced only as to counsel fees and past due alimony; since future alimony remained subject to modification in the discretion of the New Jersey chancellor, the judgment on that point was not final and could not be enforced in New York. The collateral means of enforcement provided in the New Jersey decree and asked for by the plaintiff were also denied since the Constitution does not require such action to be taken, being a mode of effectuating the decree and not part of the decree itself.

Each party to the New York proceeding then sued out a writ of error from the Supreme Court of the United States, which rendered the following opinion.]

GRAY, J. The husband, as the record shows, having appeared generally in answer to the petition for alimony in the Court of Chancery in New Jersey, the decree of that court for alimony was binding upon him. . . . The court of New York having so ruled, thereby deciding in favor of the full faith and credit claimed for that decree under the Constitution and laws of the United States, its judgment on that question cannot be reviewed by this court on writ of error. . . . The husband having appeared and been heard in the proceeding for alimony, there is no color for his present contention that he was deprived of his property without due process of law. . . . His writ of error, therefore, must be dismissed.

By the Constitution and the act of Congress, requiring the faith and credit to be given to a judgment of the court of another State that it has in the State where it was rendered, it was long ago declared by this court: "The judgment is made a debt of record, not examinable upon its merits; but it does not carry with it, into another State, the efficacy of a judgment upon property or persons, to be enforced by execution. To give it the force of a judgment in another State, it must be made a judgment there; and can only be executed in the latter as its laws may permit." McElmoyle v. Cohen, 13 Pet. 312, 325; Thompson v. Whitman, 18 Wall. 457, 463. . . .

The decree of the Court of Chancery of New Jersey, on which this suit is brought, provides, first, for the payment of $7840 for alimony already due, and $1000 counsel fee; second, for the payment of alimony since the date of the decree at the rate of $80 per week; and third, for the giving of a bond to secure the payment of these sums, and, on default of payment or of giving bond, for leave to apply for a writ of sequestration, or a receiver and injunction.

The decree for the payment of $8840 was for a fixed sum already due, and the judgment of the court below was properly restricted to that. The provision of the payment for alimony in the future was subject to the discretion of the Court of Chancery of New Jersey, which might at any time alter it, and was not a final judgment for a fixed sum. The provisions for bond, sequestration, receiver and injunction, being in the nature of execution, and not of judgment, could have no extraterritorial operation; but the action of the courts of New York in these respects depended on the local statutes and practice of the State, and involved no Federal question.

On the writ of error of the wife, therefore, the judgment is affirmed.

EMERY v. HOVEY

Supreme Court of New Hampshire, 1931.
84 N.H. 499, 153 A. 322.

Assumpsit, for attorney's fees and disbursements. The defendant pleaded a former adjudication in the supreme judicial court for the state of Maine.

At a trial before Young, J., the plaintiff put in evidence a Maine statute to the effect that one not admitted to practice there cannot recover "any remuneration for his professional services rendered in this state," and that at the trial of his cause in Maine the defendant's motion for a directed verdict, based upon the statute, was granted. The services in question were rendered partly in Maine and partly in this state.

In the present suit, the court ordered judgment for the defendant on her plea, and allowed the plaintiff's bill of exceptions.

PEASLEE, C. J.   The record shows that the plaintiff had previously sued the same cause of action in the supreme judicial court of the state of Maine, that a trial by jury was had, that upon direction of the presiding justice the jury returned a verdict for the defendant and that judgment was entered upon the verdict. This judgment was pleaded in bar of the present action. The ruling that the plea stated a good defense was correct. Const. of U.S., Art. IV, sec. 1.

Whatever error there may have been in the ruling of the justice presiding at the trial in the Maine suit was correctible only in the Maine courts. The ruling having been submitted to and a final judgment having been entered in accordance therewith, the whole subject is foreclosed in the courts of any other state. The historic case, Kittredge v. Emerson, 15 N.H. 227, established in this jurisdiction the doctrine that the judgment of a court of record, having jurisdiction of the parties and the cause, is conclusive in the courts of every other state and of the United States, no matter how erroneous in law or in fact that judgment may be. . . .

There is no suggestion that the Maine judgment is not a complete bar to any further action in that state. It is equally effective here. "Thus and thus only can the full faith and credit prescribed by the Constitution of the United States and the act of Congress be secured." Hancock National Bank v. Farnum, 176 U.S. 640. . . .

Exception overruled.

———

NOTE ON METHODS OF ENFORCEMENT

In this country, the original, and still prevailing method of enforcing an F-1 judgment is to bring an action in the nature of debt upon the judgment in F-2. Only after a new judgment has been obtained in F–2 can execution there be had against the property of the defendant. This requirement is time-consuming; it also results in the efficacy of a judgment being greatly decreased when enforcement is sought in other states. For example, although a foreign judgment, since it establishes the existence of a debt, may be filed as a claim against an insolvent estate, it does not have the priority over simple contract debts in the distribution of assets which it had in F–1 or which F–2 gives to domestic judgments. Trionics Research Sales Corp. v. Nautec Corp., 21 N.Y.2d 574, 237 N.E.2d 68 (1968). To acquire such a priority, the judgment creditor must obtain a new judgment in F–2 in the manner set forth above.

To some extent, the problems and burdens presented by this method of enforcement are mitigated by the availability in the great majority of states of summary judgment procedures for the enforcement of foreign judgments. Leflar, The New Uniform Foreign Judgments Act, 24 N.Y.U.L.Q. 336 (1949).

In 1948, Congress made provision for the registration in any federal district court of a judgment rendered in any other district. This statute (28 U.S.C.A. § 1963) reads as follows:

"A judgment in any action for the recovery of money or property in any district court which has become final by appeal or expiration of time for appeal may be registered in any other district by filing therein a certified copy of such judgment. A judgment so registered shall have the same effect as a judgment of the district court of the district where registered and may be enforced in like manner.

"A certified copy of the satisfaction of any judgment in whole or in part may be registered in like manner in any district in which the judgment is a lien."

Congress has likewise provided that a judgment entered in the Court of Claims in favor of the United States may be registered and enforced in any district court. 28 U.S.C.A. § 2508 (1964).

NOTES

(1) Section 1963 applies only to judgments in "an action for the recovery of money or property." In Stiller v. Hardman, 324 F.2d 626 (2d Cir.1963), the court held that a judgment for money could be registered, even though it was rendered on a counterclaim in a suit originally brought for a declaratory judgment. The court also held that the judgment could not be registered 'insofar as it involved an injunction. It pointed out that "The mandate of an injunction issued by a Federal district court runs throughout the United States. Leman v. Krentler-Arnold Co., 284 U.S. 448 (1932)." Thus there is no need to register judgments of district courts in so far as they involve injunctions.

(2) A judgment registered in a second federal district under § 1963 becomes in effect a new F–2 judgment subject to the rules of F–2. So the judgment will be subject to the F–2 statute of limitations rather than to that of F–1. Matanuska Valley Lines, Inc., v. Molitor, 365 F.2d 358 (9th Cir.1966);

Stanford v. Utley, 341 F.2d 265 (8th Cir.1965). Similarly, the law of F–2 will be applied to determine the circumstances under which the judgment may be stayed.   United States, etc. v. Home Indemnity Co., 549 F.2d 10 (7th Cir. 1977).

UNIFORM ENFORCEMENT OF FOREIGN JUDGMENTS ACT (REVISED 1964 ACT)

13 Uniform Laws Ann. 173 (1980).

§ 1.. Definition. In this Act "foreign judgment" means any judgment, decree, or order of a court of the United States or of any other court which is entitled to full faith and credit in this state.

§ 2.   Filing and Status of Foreign Judgments. A copy of any foreign judgment authenticated in accordance with the act of Congress or the statutes of this state may be filed in the office of the Clerk of any [District Court of any city or county] of this state. The Clerk shall treat the foreign judgment in the same manner as a judgment of the [District Court of any city or county] of this state. A judgment so filed has the same effect and is subject to the same procedures, defenses and proceedings for reopening, vacating, or staying as a judgment of a [District Court of any city or county] of this state and may be enforced or satisfied in like manner.

§ 3.   Notice of Filing. (a) At the time of the filing of the foreign judgment, the judgment creditor or his lawyer shall make and file with the Clerk of Court an affidavit setting forth the name and last known post office address of the judgment debtor, and the judgment creditor.

(b) Promptly upon the filing of the foreign judgment and the affidavit, the Clerk shall mail notice of the filing of the foreign judgment to the judgment debtor at the address given and shall make a note of the mailing in the docket. The notice shall include the name and post office address of the judgment creditor and the judgment creditor's lawyer, if any, in this state. In addition, the judgment creditor may mail a notice of the filing of the judgment to the judgment debtor and may file proof of mailing with the Clerk. Lack of mailing notice of filing by the Clerk shall not affect the enforcement proceedings if proof of mailing by the judgment creditor has been filed.

[(c) No execution or other process for enforcement of a foreign judgment filed hereunder shall issue until [   ] days after the date the judgment is filed.]

§ 4.   Stay. (a) If the judgment debtor shows the [District Court of any city or county] that an appeal from the foreign judgment is pending or will be taken, or that a stay of execution has been granted, the court shall stay enforcement of the foreign judgment until the appeal is concluded, the time for appeal expires, or the stay of execution expires or is vacated, upon proof that the judgment debtor has furnished the security for the satisfaction of the judgment required by the state in which it was rendered.

(b) If the judgment debtor shows the [District Court of any city or county] any ground upon which enforcement of a judgment of any [District Court of any city or county] of this state would be stayed, the court shall stay enforcement of the foreign judgment for an appropriate period, upon requiring the same security for satisfaction of the judgment which is required in this state.

. . .

§ 6. Optional Procedure. The right of a judgment creditor to bring an action to enforce his judgment instead of proceeding under this Act remains unimpaired.

. . .

NOTES

(1) To date, the 1964 Revision of the Uniform Act has been adopted in over 20 states. It is discussed in Homburger, Recognition and Enforcement of Foreign Judgments, 18 Am.J.Comp.L. 367 (1970).

(2) Does not Congress have power to provide in the case of sister state judgments for a system of registration under which a duly registered judgment could be enforced just like a domestic judgment? See Note, Constitutionality of a Uniform Reciprocal Registration of Judgments Statute, 36 N.Y. U.L.Rev. 488 (1961); Cook, The Powers of Congress under the Full Faith and Credit Clause, 28 Yale L.J. 421 (1919).

(3) Australia, which has a federal system much like our own, has provided by an act of its Parliament for the registration throughout the Commonwealth of local state judgments. This act applies not only to judgments for money but also to those which order or forbid the doing of acts. Service and Execution of Process Act, 1901–1963 (11 Commonwealth Acts 359 (1901–1963)). In the United Kingdom, statutes provide for a similar system of registration in the case of judgments rendered in any division of the United Kingdom and also, where the court thinks it "just and convenient," in the case of those rendered in Commonwealth countries. Judgments Extension Act, 1868, 31 & 32 Vict., c. 54; Administration of Justice Act, 1920, 10 & 11 Geo. 5, c. 81. Moreover, the Foreign Judgments (Reciprocal Enforcement) Act, 1933, 23 Geo. 5, c. 13, authorizes the extension by Order in Council of the registration system to money judgments rendered in foreign countries which are prepared to give substantial reciprocity of treatment to judgments originally handed down in the United Kingdom.[1] Thus, the enforcement of intra-empire and, in some cases, of international judgments in the United Kingdom is easier than the method that generally prevails in this country for the enforcement of sister state judgments.

For a discussion of the British statutory system of registration, see Cheshire, Private International Law 534–546 (7th ed. 1965); Graveson, Con-

---

1. To date, conventions providing for such reciprocity have been concluded by the United Kingdom with a number of countries, including Austria, Belgium, France, West Germany, India, Israel, Ita- ly, The Netherlands and Norway. The provisions of the Foreign Judgments Act, 1933, have been extended to apply to judgments of the superior courts of these countries.

flict of Laws 235–245 (7th ed. 1974); 2 Dicey and Morris Conflict of Laws 1106–1111 (10th ed. 1980); Read, Recognition and Enforcement of Foreign Judgments in the Common Law Units of the British Commonwealth (1938).

B. JUDGMENTS BASED ON JURISDICTION OVER THINGS OR OVER STATUS

Judgments of this sort do not impose a personal obligation upon the defendant and hence, unlike in personam judgments, cannot be enforced by action in other states. Their basic effects in the state of rendition are set forth in the Restatement, Second, Judgments:

§ 30. Judgments Based on Jurisdiction to Determine Interests in Things*

A valid and final judgment in an action based only on jurisdiction to determine interests in a thing:

(1) Is conclusive as to those interests with regard to all persons, if the judgment purports to have that effect (traditionally described as "in rem"), or with regard to the named parties, if the judgment purports to have that effect (traditionally described as "quasi in rem"); and

(2) Does not bind anyone with respect to a personal liability; and

(3) Is conclusive between parties, in accordance with the rules of issue preclusion, as to any issues actually litigated by them and determined in the action.

Sec. 31 states an analogous rule with respect to judgments determining status.

These being the basic effects of such judgments in F–1, to what extent, if at all, do they differ when the judgment is placed in issue in F–2?

COMBS v. COMBS

Supreme Court of Kentucky, 1933.
249 Ky. 155, 60 S.W.2d 368.

[The case appears supra, p. 136]

---

* Quoted with the permission of the copyright owner, The American Law Institute.

HARNISCHFEGER SALES CORP. v.
STERNBERG DREDGING CO.

Supreme Court of Mississippi, 1939.
189 Miss. 73, 191 So. 94.

[Harnischfeger Sales Corporation sold a dredge to Sternberg Dredging Company, taking notes secured by a chattel mortgage for a part of the purchase price. Thereafter, Harnischfeger started a suit in Louisiana to enforce the chattel mortgage, and prayed a personal judgment for $16,000 on the notes. Sternberg appeared and moved to dismiss for want of jurisdiction. This plea was overruled. Sternberg then pleaded that the dredge was defective and did not meet warranties which were given at the time of sale. The trial court in Louisiana, after a full trial on the merits of this question, entered a decree that the machine be sold and also rendered a personal judgment against Sternberg for the amount due on the notes. The Supreme Court of Louisiana affirmed the judgment enforcing the lien of the chattel mortgage, but held that the trial court did not have jurisdiction to enter a personal judgment and reversed that part of its judgment. See Harnischfeger Sales Corp. v. Sternberg Dredging Co., 179 La. 317, 154 So. 10 (1934).

Harnischfeger then started the present suit in Mississippi, where it obtained personal jurisdiction over Sternberg. The suit in Mississippi was to recover the balance due on the notes after making allowance for the amount obtained through the sale of the dredge in the Louisiana proceedings. Sternberg defended on the ground of breach of warranty and fraud, and Harnischfeger replied that that issue was res judicata as a result of the Louisiana judgment. The trial court struck out the plea of res judicata, and on the merits held in favor of Sternberg on the defense of breach of warranty. Harnischfeger then appealed.]

McGOWAN, JUSTICE. . . . At the outset we will state that the effect of the estoppel by the final decree of the Supreme Court of Louisiana is to be determined by the laws of that state where the decree was rendered, and this seems to be an accepted and universal rule. . . .

. . . The ultimate facts as to whether or not a debt existed that would authorize the enforcement of a lien are the same in both the Louisiana and the Mississippi courts. The litigation was between the same parties, the same subject, the only difference in the pleas and proof in the two courts being a change in the name of the pleading. The same cause of action was alleged in the Louisiana Court as was interposed and allowed by the lower court in this state, and that cause of action was, when the case is stripped to the bone, that the machine delivered would not and did not carry a two-yard bucket, and by this we understand it to mean that the machine was not capacitated to be filled with two yards of earth and successfully dumped therefrom. . . .

It is said that the Louisiana decree cannot operate as res adjudicata or estoppel because the Supreme Court held that the proceeding was in rem. 179 La. 317, 154 So. 10. The appellant, Harnischfeger Sales Corporation, is not seeking here to bring a suit on the contention that the Louisiana judgment and action of that court, on the defense thereto, operated as a judgment which concluded the parties as to the amount of the judgment. The contention of the appellant is, as we understand it, that the Sternberg Dredging Company interposed the same defense in the Louisiana court as it interposed in the case at bar, and as to that defense the doctrine of res adjudicata is interposed and effective to conclude it, even though the proceedings in Louisiana to enforce a chattel mortgage on the thing mortgaged in that state were in rem. The appellee had its option to stand on the want of jurisdiction of the Court, but it did not do so. It appeared there. Sternberg, the main witness in both trials, testified to the same salient facts as to this defense in the Louisiana Court as was testified by him in the Mississippi Court in the case at bar. We are of the opinion that the defense was adjudged and concluded as to that defense and that every court everywhere would be bound to so hold. . . .

When the Sternberg Dredging Company decided and elected to resist the entry of any decree in rem against the machine and to interpose the breach-of-warranty defense, it thereby concluded itself irrevocably. Suppose the Louisiana Court had taken the opposite view and had determined in the court of last resort that the defense was valid in that it extinguished the debt? By that decree it would have retained the machine free from the lien; and, certainly where both parties appeared and contested the issue, debt or no debt, because of a breach of warranty, that decree would be final and conclusive on that issue actually litigated, and we think under the statute controlling in Louisiana would be res adjudicata. Such statute is as follows: "The authority of the thing adjudged takes place only with respect to what was the object of the judgment. The thing demanded must be the same; the demand must be founded on the same cause of action; the demand must be between the same parties, and formed by them against each other in the same quality." Art. 2286, Louisiana Civil Code. . . .

We are, therefore, of the opinion that the court below erred in striking the plea of res adjudicata and declining to allow it as an estoppel to the defense here involved. . . .

Reversed, and judgment for appellant.

NOTES

(1) In a further opinion in 189 Miss. 73, 195 So. 322 (1940), the court refused to modify this opinion against the contention that the issue raised in the Louisiana proceeding was breach of warranty, while in the Mississippi

suit the defendant relied on fraud. The court held that the same evidence bore on the questions of fraud and breach of warranty, and that the two defenses were really the same though "here the name given the counterclaim is different from that given it in the Louisiana court."

(2) What accounts for the different effect given the judgment of F–1 (Arkansas) in the Combs case, p. 136 supra, and the judgment of F–1 (Louisiana) in the Harnischfeger case?

(3) The defendant is faced with a dilemma when suit is brought in a state whose sole basis of jurisdiction is the presence there of the defendant's property. If the defendant does not appear and defend on the merits, he stands a strong risk of losing the property. He will not be bound, however, under principles of res judicata by any finding of fact that the court may have made. On the other hand, if he enters a defense on the merits, he runs the risk that the findings made by the court will be binding upon him everywhere. It has been argued that to place the defendant in such a position is so unfair as to violate due process. Taintor, Foreign Judgments in Rem: Full Faith and Credit v. Res Judicata *in Personam*, 8 U.Pitt.L.Rev. 223, 226 (1942).

In order to mitigate this problem, a fair number of courts permit the defendant to make a so-called limited appearance. By means of this device, the defendant can appear and resist on the merits and yet be protected from the entry of a personal judgment against him. In some states, he may further be protected from being collaterally bound as to issues actually litigated. It seems probable that the practical significance of a limited appearance has been diminished substantially by the ruling of the Supreme Court in Shaffer v. Heitner, 433 U.S. 186 (1977), p. 148, supra. This is because the property owner may now invoke the principles of International Shoe (p. 66, supra) in an attempt to have the action wholly terminated. Restatement, Second, Judgments § 8, Comment *g*.

SECTION 3. PARTICULAR EFFECTS

A. PERSONS AFFECTED*

SOVEREIGN CAMP v. BOLIN

Supreme Court of the United States, 1938.
305 U.S. 66, 59 S.Ct. 35, 83 L.Ed. 45, 119 A.L.R. 478.

MR. JUSTICE ROBERTS delivered the opinion of the Court.

We granted certiorari because of the claim that the judgment of the court below failed to accord full faith and credit to the public acts, records, and judicial proceedings of the State of Nebraska as required by Article IV, Section 1 of the Constitution.

---

* See generally Restatement, Judgments Second §§ 34–63.

The petitioner is a fraternal beneficiary association organized under the laws of Nebraska, having a lodge system, a ritualistic form of work, and a representative form of government. It has no capital stock, and transacts its affairs without profit and solely for the mutual benefit of its members and their beneficiaries. It makes provision for the payment of death benefits by assessments upon its members and issues to members certificates assuring payment of such benefits.

In 1895 the petitioner adopted a by-law authorizing the issue of life membership certificates. Under this by-law a member entering the order at an age greater than 43 years was entitled to life membership without the payment of further dues and assessments when the certificate had been outstanding 20 years. In June 1896, while the by-law remained unrepealed, Pleasant Bolin, who was over 43 years of age, joined a Missouri lodge of the petitioner and received a certificate of membership which recited that while in good standing he would be entitled to participate in the beneficial fund to the amount of $1,000 payable to his beneficiaries and to the sum of $100 for placing a monument at his grave. The certificate recited that it was issued subject to all the conditions named in the constitution and laws of the fraternity and was endorsed with the words "Payments to cease after 20 years."

After Bolin's death, the respondents, as beneficiaries, brought action to recover upon the certificate. The petitioner's answer set up that Bolin had ceased to pay the required dues and assessments in July 1916, and his certificate had therefore become void; that the by-law making the certificate fully paid after twenty years was *ultra vires* the association and had been so declared by the Supreme Court of Nebraska in a class suit brought by one Trapp, the holder of a certificate similar to that of Bolin [Trapp v. Sovereign Camp of the Woodmen of the World, 102 Neb. 562, 162 N.W. 191]; that, under Article IV, Section 1, of the Constitution, full faith and credit must be given by the courts of Missouri to this decision of the Supreme Court of Nebraska. The respondents replied that the contract was made and delivered in Missouri and was to be construed and enforced according to Missouri law; that, at the date of its consummation, the petitioner had no license or authority to transact business in Missouri as a corporation or otherwise, and the certificate was therefore to be considered as issued pursuant to, and governed by, the general insurance laws of Missouri; that Bolin having fully performed in accordance with the terms of the certificate, the petitioner was estopped to plead *ultra vires;* and that in truth the contract was not *ultra vires* the petitioner. . . .

[The Missouri courts found for the respondents. They] refused to give force or effect to the decision of the Supreme Court of Nebraska in Trapp v. Woodmen, supra, saying that . . . the contract being a Missouri contract its *ultra vires* character must be adjudged by the local law irrespective of what the courts of the domicile had held; that the respondents in the present case relied on an estoppel of the petitioner to plead *ultra vires*, whereas no such issue was presented or decided in the Trapp case.

We hold that the judgment denied full faith and credit to the public acts, records, and judicial proceedings of the State of Nebraska.

First. The beneficiary certificate was not a mere contract to be construed and enforced according to the laws of the state where it was delivered. Entry into membership of an incorporated beneficiary society is more than a contract; it is entering into a complex and abiding relation and the rights of membership are governed by the law of the state of incorporation. Another state, wherein the certificate of membership was issued, cannot attach to membership rights against the society which are refused by the law of the domicile.[1]

Second. . . .

The court below was not at liberty to disregard the fundamental law of the petitioner and turn a membership beneficiary certificate into an old line policy to be construed and enforced according to the law of the forum. The decision that the principle of *ultra vires* contracts was to be applied as if the petitioner were a Missouri old line life insurance company was erroneous in the light of the decisions of this court which have uniformly held that the rights of members of such associations are governed by the definition of the society's powers by the courts of its domicile.[2]

Third. The doctrine of estoppel was erroneously invoked to avoid the force and effect of the Nebraska judgment. The court below was of the opinion that, as the petitioner had issued a "payments to cease after 20 years" certificate, and as Bolin had fully performed on his part by paying all dues and assessments over the named period, the petitioner was estopped to plead its lack of power to issue such a certificate. This again was on the theory that whatever might be the nature of the petitioner's organization in Nebraska, for the purposes of this action it must be treated as an old line insurance company in Missouri. It was further held that no question of estoppel was decided in the Trapp case.

As to the first of these positions, it need only be said that the Trapp case was a class suit in which it was determined that the petitioner lacked power, under the law of Nebraska, to issue such certificates. In such a suit the association represents all its members and stands in judgment for them, and even though the suit had a different object than the instant one it is conclusive upon all the members

1. Modern Woodmen v. Mixer, 267 U.S. 544, 551; Royal Arcanum v. Green, 237 U.S. 531, 542.

2. Hartford Life Insurance Company v. Ibs, 237 U.S. 662; Hartford Life Insur-ance Co. v. Barber, 245 U.S. 146; Royal Arcanum v. Green, 237 U.S. 531; Modern Woodmen v. Mixer, 267 U.S. 544.

of the association with respect to all rights, questions, or facts therein determined.[3]

With respect to the second position, it appears from the record that Trapp, in the suit in Nebraska, pleaded that the association was estopped to deny its power to issue the form of certificate in question and the opinion of the Nebraska court, by reference to a case decided on the same day, clearly indicates that the issue of estoppel was considered and determined adversely to the plaintiff.

Fourth. Under our uniform holdings the court below failed to give full faith and credit to the petitioner's charter embodied in the statutes of Nebraska as interpreted by its highest court.[4]

The judgment is reversed and the cause is remanded for further proceedings not inconsistent with this opinion.

NOTES

(1) Was the doctrine of class suits properly invoked in the principal case? The Trapp case cited in the opinion was an ordinary action brought by a single claimant under another certificate.

(2) How does the court get jurisdiction to affect the rights of non-residents in so-called class or representative suits? Cf. Hansberry v. Lee, 311 U.S. 32 (1940), involving a suit brought to enjoin the breach of a restrictive covenant against selling land to black persons. The covenant by its terms was not effective unless it had been signed by the owners of 95 per cent of the frontage within the area. The defense was that the required 95 per cent had not signed. This was answered with a plea of res judicata based on an earlier suit. The defendants were not parties in this suit, but the Supreme Court of Illinois held that the earlier suit was a "class" or "representative" suit, and that all members of the class were bound by the decree. The Supreme Court of the United States reversed, holding that under the facts of the case there was not a "class" since all persons concerned did not have the same interest. It recognized, however, the possibility of binding absent parties in a class suit. It said (pp. 40–41):

"It is a principle of general application in Anglo-American jurisprudence that one is not bound by a judgment *in personam* in a litigation in which he is not designated as a party or to which he has not been made a party by service of process. . . .

"To these general rules there is a recognized exception that, to an extent not precisely defined by judicial opinion, the judgment in a 'class' or 'representative' suit, to which some members of the class are parties, may bind members of the class or those represented who were not made parties to it.

". . . there is scope within the framework of the Constitution for holding in appropriate cases that a judgment rendered in a class suit is *res judicata* as to members of the class who are not formal parties to the suit. . . . With a proper regard for divergent local institutions and interests,

3. Hartford Life Insurance Company v. Ibs, supra, [footnote 2 at] p. 673.

4. Royal Arcanum v. Green, supra, pp. 540, 543, 546; Hartford Life Ins. Co. v. Ibs, supra, [footnote 2 at] p. 669; Hartford Life Insurance Co. v. Barber, supra, [footnote 2 at] p. 151; Modern Woodmen v. Mixer, supra, [footnote 2 at] p. 551. [The footnotes to the case are from the Court's opinion.]

. . ., the Court is justified in saying that there has been a failure of due process only in those cases where it cannot be said that the procedure adopted, fairly insures the protection of the interests of absent parties who are to be bound by it . . . "

Can a class action properly be maintained in situations where members of the asserted class who have not joined in the action reside outside the forum and whose rights are subject to rules prescribed by other states laws? The problem is considered in Note, 32 Drake L.J. 441 (1983).

(3) As to the requirements of a class action, see Restatement, Second, Judgments §§ 41–42; Frankel, Some Preliminary Observations Concerning Civil Rule 23, 43 F.R.D. 39 (1968).

RILEY v. NEW YORK TRUST CO.

Supreme Court of the United States, 1941.
315 U.S. 343, 62 S.Ct. 608, 86 L.Ed. 885.

Certiorari to the Supreme Court of Delaware.

MR. JUSTICE REED delivered the opinion of the Court.

Coca-Cola International Corporation, incorporated in Delaware, filed a bill of interpleader in a Delaware Court of Chancery against Julian Riley and Hughes Spalding, petitioners here, the Executors of Mrs. Julia M. Hungerford, with letters testamentary issued by the Court of Ordinary of Fulton County, Georgia, and against the New York Trust Company, the respondent, a New York corporation, as temporary administrator (afterward administrator c.t.a.) of the same decedent, appointed by the Surrogate's Court for New York County, New York.

The Georgia executors and the New York administrator each claim the right to have transferred to them, in their representative capacity, stock in the Coca-Cola Corporation now on its books in the name of the decedent. The outstanding certificates are in Georgia, in the hands of the Georgia executors. The parties are agreed, and it is therefore assumed, that Delaware is the situs of the stock. In accordance with the prayer of the bill, the Delaware court directed the adversary claimants to interplead between themselves as to their respective claims.

The Georgia executors assert that original domiciliary probate of Mrs. Hungerford's will in solemn form was obtained by them in Georgia, with all beneficiaries and heirs at law of testatrix, including her husband, Robert Hungerford, actual parties by personal service. These, it is conceded, were all the parties under the law of Georgia entitled to be heard on the probate of the will. The respondent administrator c.t.a. was not a party. The record of probate includes a determination by special finding, over the objection of the caveator, the husband, that the testatrix was domiciled in Georgia. The special finding was specifically approved as an essential fact to determine the jurisdiction of the Court of Ordinary by the highest court of Georgia in its affirmance of the probate. Hungerford v. Spalding, 183 Ga. 547, 189 S.E. 2. . . .

From the facts alleged, petitioners inferred the conclusive establishment of the place for domiciliary distribution against "all persons," and prayed the issue to them of new certificates. An offer was made to pay all Delaware taxes or charges on the stock.

Respondent admitted that all parties entitled under the law of Georgia to be heard in opposition to probate were actually before the Georgia courts. It denied that Mrs. Hungerford was domiciled in Georgia or that the Georgia judgment of domicile and probate was binding on it, and averred testatrix's domicile at death was New York. It further averred that there were New York creditors of the estate interested in the proper and lawful administration of the estate, and that New York had certain claims for inheritance and estate taxes. Its own subsequent appointment by the Surrogate's Court of New York County, New York, on the suggestion of testatrix's husband and the State Tax Commission, was pleaded with applicable provisions of New York probate and estate tax law. By stipulation it was established that petitioners and the heirs and beneficiaries of testatrix, except her husband, who was an actual party, were notified of the New York proceedings for probate only by publication or substituted service of the citation in Georgia, and did not appear. As a domiciliary administrator c.t.a., the respondent prayed the issue to it of new certificates for the stock in controversy.

The trial court concluded from the evidence adduced at the hearings that the testatrix was domiciled in Georgia. It was therefore, as the court stated, unnecessary for it to consider the binding effect of the Georgia judgment. The Supreme Court of Delaware reversed this finding of fact, determined that New York was testatrix's domicile and denied petitioners' contention that Article IV, § 1, of the Constitution required the award of the certificates of stock to the Georgia executors. The Coca-Cola Corporation was directed to issue its stock certificate to the respondent, the New York administrator c.t.a. New York Trust Co. v. Riley, 16 A.2d 772. . . .

The constitutional effect of the Georgia decree on a claim in his own name in another state by a party to the Georgia proceedings is not here involved. The question we are to decide is whether this Georgia judgment on domicile conclusively establishes the right of the Georgia executors to demand delivery to them of personal assets of their testatrix which another state is willing to surrender to the domiciliary personal representative, when another representative, appointed by a third state, asserts a similar domiciliary right. For the purpose of this review, the conclusion of Delaware that the testatrix was in fact domiciled in New York is accepted. The answer to the question lies in the extent to which Article IV, § 1, of the Constitution, as made applicable by R.S. § 905, nevertheless controls Delaware's action.

This clause of the Constitution brings to our Union a useful means for ending litigation. Matters once decided between adverse parties in any state or territory are at rest. Were it not for this full faith and credit provision, so far as the Constitution controls the matter, adversaries could wage again their legal battles whenever they met in other jurisdictions. Each state could control its own courts but itself could not project the effect of its decisions beyond its own boundaries. Cf. Pennoyer v. Neff, 95 U.S. 714, 722. That clause compels that controversies be stilled, so that, where a state court has jurisdiction of the parties and subject matter, its judgment controls in other states to the same extent as it does in the state where rendered. Roche v. McDonald, 275 U.S. 449, 451. . . . By the Constitutional provision for full faith and credit, the local doctrines of *res judicata*, speaking generally, become a part of national jurisprudence, and therefore federal questions cognizable here.

. . . The full faith and credit clause allows Delaware, in disposing of local assets, to determine the question of domicile anew for any interested party who is not bound by participation in the Georgia proceeding [Citing cases.] It must be admitted that this re-examination may result in conflicting decisions upon domicile, but that is an inevitable consequence of the existing federal system, which endows its citizens with the freedom to choose the state or states within which they desire to carry on business, enjoy their leisure or establish their residences. Worcester County Co. v. Riley, 302 U.S. 292, 299. But, while allowing Delaware to determine domicile for itself, where any interested party is not bound by the Georgia proceedings, the full faith and credit clause and R.S. § 905, do require that Delaware shall give Georgia judgments such faith and credit "as they have by law or usage" in Georgia. . . .

We find nothing in [Tant v. Wigfall, 65 Ga. 412, and Wash v. Dickson, 147 Ga. 540, 94 S.E. 1009] which would lead to the conclusion that, in Georgia, the New York administrator c.t.a. was in privity, so far as the sequestration of assets for the payment of death taxes or indebtedness of decedent or her estate is concerned, with any parties before the Georgia court, or that the New York representative could not take steps in Georgia courts which might result in its getting possession of any assets which under the Georgia law of administration would be properly deliverable to a foreign domiciliary administrator. . . . Hence, if the Georgia judgment is to bind the New York administrator, it can be considered to do so only *in rem*.

. . . It may be assumed that the judgment of probate and domicile is a judgment *in rem* . . . But this does not bar litigation anew by a stranger, of facts upon which the decree *in rem* is based. . . . While the Georgia judgment is to have the same faith and credit in Delaware as it does in Georgia, that requirement does not give the Georgia judgment extra-territorial effect upon assets in other states. So far as the assets in Georgia are concerned, the Georgia judgment of probate is *in rem;* so far as it affects personalty beyond the state, it is *in personam* and can bind only parties thereto or their privies. This is the result of the ruling in Baker v. Baker, Eccles & Co., 242 U.S. 394, 400.[1] Phrased somewhat differently, if the effect of a probate decree in Georgia *in personam* was to bar a stranger to the decree from later asserting his rights, such a holding would deny procedural due process.

It seems quite obvious that the administrator c.t.a., appears in Delaware as an agency of the State of New York, and not as the *alter ego* of the beneficiaries of the Hungerford estate. In its answer to the petitioners' statement of claim, it established its status by alleging that not merely the beneficiaries but creditors residing in New York and the State of New York were interested in the estate, that its appointment as temporary administrator had been sought by the New York Tax Commissioner "to protect the claim of the State of New York to inheritance and succession taxes," that the State of New York was asserting such claims in substantial amount on the theory that the domicile was New York . . . .

Georgia and New York might each assert its right to administer the estates of its domiciliaries to protect its sovereign interests, and Delaware was free to decide for itself which claimant is entitled to receive the portion of Mrs. Hungerford's personalty within Delaware's borders.

Affirmed.

MR. CHIEF JUSTICE STONE: I concur upon the single ground that the New York administrator was not bound by the Georgia judgment. He was not a party to the Georgia proceedings, nor was he represented by any of those who were parties. As administrator appointed under the New York statutes, he was charged with the duty of administering the estate of the decedent and paying inheritance taxes upon it. His interest so far as he owes duties to the state is therefore adverse to that of the husband and the next of kin, who alone

---

1. Illustrative state cases.

A will is admitted to original domiciliary probate in state A. Thereafter an ancillary proceeding is commenced in state B based upon the domiciliary determination of A. At that point a beneficiary, a stranger to the proceeding in A, appears and asserts that the decedent was domiciled in B. The determination of domicile by state A will not be recognized by state B, but state B will take evidence and re-determine the issue of domicile. Estate of Clark, 148 Cal. 108, 82 P. 760 . . . .

If the objector was privy to the proceeding in state A, state B will not redetermine the issue of domicile. Willetts' Appeal, 50 Conn. 330 . . . .

Where the proceeding in state B is by a stranger to the proceedings for original domiciliary probate in state A upon the theory that the domicile is actually B, state B will determine domicile for itself. Scripps v. Wayne Probate Judge, 131 Mich. 265, 90 N.W. 1061 . . . .

Where the person seeking to establish domicile in state B, and to have original domiciliary probate there, was a party to the proceeding in state A, state B will not redetermine domicile. Hopper v. Nicholas, 106 Ohio 292, 140 N.E. 186 . . . . [Footnote by the Court. Other footnotes omitted.]

were parties to the Georgia proceeding. To have bound him by representation of those so adverse in interest would have been a denial of due process. Hansberry v. Lee, 311 U.S. 32. A judgment so obtained is not entitled to full faith and credit with respect to those not parties. . . . Any other conclusion would foreclose New York from litigating its right to collect taxes lawfully due, by the simple expedient of a probate by the next of kin of the will of the decedent as the domiciled resident of another state, without notice to any representative of New York or opportunity to be heard.

It is unnecessary to consider the other questions discussed by the opinion.

MR. JUSTICE FRANKFURTER and MR. JUSTICE JACKSON concur in this opinion.

NOTES

(1) RESTATEMENT, SECOND, CONFLICT OF LAWS:[*]

§ 94. Persons Affected

What persons are bound by a valid judgment is determined, subject to constitutional limitations, by the local law of the State where the judgment was rendered.

Comment:

. . .

d. *Privies.* Subject to constitutional limitations (see Comment b), the local law of the State where the judgment was rendered determines which persons are in privity with the parties to the action and hence are bound by and entitled to the benefits of the rules of res judicata. This law determines whether the judgment was rendered in a class action and, if so, which persons are members of the class and the extent to which the interests of these persons are affected by the judgment. This law likewise determines, for example, whether the term "privies" includes those who control an action although not parties to it, those whose interests are represented by a party to the action and those who are successors in interest to a party to the action.

. . .

(2) The various situations where privity is commonly found to exist in local law are set forth in Restatement, Second, Judgments c. 4.

KREMER v. CHEMICAL CONSTRUCTION CORP.

Supreme Court of the United States, 1982.
456 U.S. 461, 102 S.Ct. 1883, 72 L.Ed.2d 262.

[The plaintiff filed a complaint with the Equal Employment Opportunity Commission (EEOC) under Title VII of the Civil Rights Act of

[*] Quoted with the permission of the copyright owner, The American Law Institute.

1964, complaining that his discharge from employment had been caused by illegal discrimination. As required by the Civil Rights Act, the Commission referred the charge to the New York State Division of Human Rights (NYHRD), the agency charged with enforcing the New York law against discrimination. The NYHRD rejected the claim as meritless and, on appeal to the New York Appellate Division, this decision was unanimously affirmed. The plaintiff then brought a Title VII action in a federal district court which dismissed the complaint on res judicata grounds and the Court of Appeals affirmed. This decision was in turn affirmed by the Supreme Court with four Justices dissenting.]

JUSTICE WHITE delivered the opinion of the Court.

. . . Section 1738 [printed on p. 37, supra] requires federal courts to give the same preclusive effect to state court judgments that those judgments would be given in the courts of the state from which the judgments emerged. Here the Appellate Division of the New York Supreme Court has issued a judgment affirming the decision of the NYHRD Appeals Board that the discharge and failure to rehire Kremer were not the product of the discrimination that he had alleged. There is no question that this judicial determination precludes Kremer from bringing "any other action, civil or criminal, based upon the same grievance" in the New York courts. N.Y.Exec. Law § 300 (McKinney 1972). By its terms, therefore, § 1738 would appear to preclude Kremer from relitigating the same question in federal court.

Kremer . . . suggests that in Title VII cases Congress intended that federal courts be relieved of their usual obligation to grant finality to state court decisions. . . .

. . . The petitioner . . . contends that the judgment should not bar his Title VII action because the New York courts did not resolve the issue that the District Court must hear under Title VII—whether Kremer had suffered discriminatory treatment—and because the procedures provided were inadequate. Neither contention is persuasive. Although the claims presented to the NYHRD and subsequently reviewed by the Appellate Division were necessarily based on New York law, the alleged discriminatory acts are prohibited by both federal and state laws. The elements of a successful employment discrimination claim are virtually identical; petitioner could not succeed on a Title VII claim consistently with the judgment of the NYHRD that there is no reason to believe he was terminated or not rehired because of national origin or religion. The Appellate Division's affirmance of the NYHRD's dismissal necessarily decided that petitioner's claim under New York law was meritless, and thus it also decided that a Title VII claim arising from the same events would be equally meritless. . . .

Our previous decisions have not specified the source or defined the content of the requirement that the first adjudication offer a full and fair opportunity to litigate. But for present purposes, where we are bound by the statutory directive of § 1738, state proceedings need do no more than satisfy the minimum procedural requirements of the Fourteenth Amendment's Due Process Clause in order to qualify for the full-faith-and-credit guaranteed by federal law. It has long been established that § 1738 does not allow federal courts to employ their own rules of res judicata in determining the effect of state judgments. Rather, it . . . commands a federal court to accept the rules chosen by the state from which the judgment is taken. . . .

The State must, however, satisfy the applicable requirements of the Due Process Clause. A state may not grant preclusive effect in its own courts to a constitutionally infirm judgment and other state and federal courts are not required to accord full-faith-and-credit to such a judgment. Section 1738 does not suggest otherwise; other state and federal courts would still be providing a state court judgment with the "same" preclusive effect as the courts of the state from which the judgment emerged. In such a case, there could be no constitutionally recognizable preclusion at all.

We have little doubt that Kremer received all the process that was constitutionally required in rejecting his claim that he had been discriminatorily discharged contrary to the statute. . . .

In our system of jurisprudence the usual rule is that merits of a legal claim once decided in a court of competent jurisdiction are not subject to redetermination in another forum. Such a fundamental departure from traditional rules of preclusion, enacted into federal law, can be justified only if plainly stated by Congress. Because there is no "affirmative showing" of a "clear and manifest" legislative purpose in Title VII to deny res judicata or collateral estoppel effect to a state court judgment affirming that a claim of employment discrimination is unproven, and because the procedures provided in New York for the determination of such claims offer a full and fair opportunity to litigate the merits, the judgment of the Court of Appeals is

Affirmed.

[The dissenters' position was that the New York courts had decided only that the NYHRC's finding of no discrimination was a rational conclusion, not that it was correct in fact. Hence, they said, there was no judicial determination of the issue in the instant proceeding, and Section 1738 does not bar a federal district court from adjudicating the issue.]

NOTES

(1) All of the Justices, including the dissenters, were apparently agreed that the obligation of the federal courts to respect state court decisions is based on Section 1738. Does this mean that they thought that the federal courts are not bound by the full faith and credit clause itself (Article IV, Section 1) and that Congress would be free to limit the conclusive effect of state court judgments in such cases?

(2) In the eyes of the dissenting Justices, would a judicial affirmance of an administrative decision ever be entitled to full faith and credit?

(3) In Davis v. United States Steel Supply, Etc., 688 F.2d 166 (3d Cir. 1982), the facts were much the same as in the Kremer case, except that it was the defendant rather than the plaintiff who appealed from the administrative decision to a state court. It was held that once the state court had decided the appeal, the plaintiff was barred from seeking relief in a federal court. There were dissents.

(4) Allen v. McCurry, 449 U.S. 90 (1980) (en banc). At his trial in a state court for possession of heroin and assault with intent to kill, McCurry sought to suppress evidence that he claimed had been obtained by an illegal search and seizure. This motion was denied, and McCurry was convicted. He later brought a damage suit in a federal court against the officers who had entered his home and seized the evidence. The federal court granted summary judgment against McCurry on the ground that collateral estoppel prevented him from relitigating the search and seizure question that had been decided against him in the criminal trial. On writ of certiorari, this decision was affirmed by the Supreme Court since McCurry had received a "full and fair hearing" on the issue of illegal search and seizure in the state court. The dissent, written by Justice Blackmun and joined by Justices Brennan and Marshall, concluded that "The criminal defendant is an involuntary litigant in the state trial. . . . To force him to a choice between forgoing either a potential defense or a federal forum for hearing his constitutional civil claim is fundamentally unfair."

B. ISSUES AFFECTED

RESTATEMENT, SECOND, CONFLICT OF LAWS: *

§ 95. Issues Affected

What issues are determined by a valid judgment is determined, subject to constitutional limitations, by the local law of the State where the judgment was rendered.

NOTES

(1) Section 95 is in line with opinions of the Supreme Court. See, e.g., Magnolia Petroleum Co. v. Hunt, p. 267, infra; Riley v. New York Trust Co., p. 244, supra. See also, as to splitting a cause of action, Cheatham, Res Judicata and the Full Faith and Credit Clause: Magnolia Petroleum Co. v. Hunt, 44 Colum.L.Rev. 330, 346–348 (1944). And as to collateral estoppel, United States v. Silliman, 167 F.2d 607 (3d Cir.1948), cert. denied 335 U.S. 825 (1948).

* Quoted with the permission of the copyright owner, The American Law Institute.

(2) When F–1 is a foreign country, what will be the res judicata or collateral estoppel effect in this country of the F–1's determination? See pp. 315–317, infra.

(3) Compulsory counterclaims. DeGroot, Kalliel, Traint & Conklin v. Camarota, 169 N.J.Super. 338, 404 A.2d 1211 (1979). Suit by Michigan attorneys to enforce a default judgment obtained in Michigan for professional services rendered. Defendant counterclaimed for legal malpractice in connection with these services. Held that the counterclaim was properly dismissed. Under the Michigan compulsory joinder rule, the claim for malpractice should have been asserted by way of defense or counterclaim. Since the malpractice claim could no longer be asserted in Michigan, it could not, under full faith and credit, be asserted in New Jersey.

Compare Chapman v. Aetna Finance Co., 615 F.2d 361 (5th Cir.1980), where the question was whether plaintiffs' claims under the federal Truth-in-Lending law should be dismissed because of failure to assert them as compulsory counterclaims in prior Georgia state court foreclosure proceedings. Under Georgia law the unasserted claims would have been barred, but the court held that they were not precluded from relitigation by the full faith and credit clause. After noting that the purpose of the Georgia rule was to promote judicial economy and thus was "local in scope," the court said: "We think that Georgia's compulsory counterclaim, for full faith and credit purposes, is more properly analyzed as a legislative act than as an element of that state's judicial proceedings." Is that a justifiable distinction?

Mutuality of Estoppel

A question of increasing importance is the impact of full faith and credit in situations where F–1 and F–2 have different rules with respect to the collateral estoppel effect of a judgment in a later action between a party to the judgment and a stranger. A case in point is Hart v. American Airlines, Inc., 61 Misc.2d 41, 304 N.Y.S.2d 810 (1969). That case arose out of a crash in Kentucky of an American Airlines plane in which most of the passengers were killed. Of the various actions involving the crash, the first to go to judgment was an action brought in Texas. The crash was found to have been caused by the negligence of American Airlines and accordingly a judgment was rendered for the plaintiff. Thereafter, in a New York action involving different passengers, the plaintiffs contended that under principles of collateral estoppel American Airlines was precluded by the Texas judgment from denying that its negligence had caused the accident. This was the New York rule of collateral estoppel but not the Texas rule which imposed the requirement of mutuality, namely that one party is not collaterally estopped by a former adjudication if the other party would not have been estopped by a contrary outcome in the earlier suit. The court upheld the plaintiffs' contention, stating that New York's "superior interest in the issue of collateral estoppel" was established by the fact that the plaintiffs and their decedents were New York domiciliaries. The court continued that the defendant's reliance on full faith and credit was "misplaced", since this was not an action to enforce the Texas judgment and that what was here involved was New York's policy determination that "one who has had his day in court should not be permitted to relitigate the question anew."

Suppose that the New York judgment had been the first to be handed down. Some cases suggest that in this situation Texas would have been required to apply the New York rule of collateral estoppel and hold American Airlines barred from relitigating the question of its negligence although the Airline would have been free to do so under the Texas rule of mutuality. United States v. United Air Lines, Inc., 216 F.Supp. 709 (E.D.Wash., D.Nev.1962), affirmed as to issue of mutuality of collateral estoppel sub nom. United Air Lines, Inc. v. Wiener, 335 F.2d 379 (9th Cir.1964); Cummings v. Dresher, 18 N.Y.2d 105, 218 N.E.2d 688 (1966).

Can the Hart decision be sustained on the reasoning that the New York court gave the Texas judgment greater, rather than less, effect than it would have in Texas and thereby accorded it more full faith and credit, not less? Similar questions can be raised as to the preclusive effect of an F–1 judgment with respect to splitting a cause of action.

Besides the question of just what full faith requires of F–2 when its rules of res judicata (and collateral estoppel) differ from those of F–1, there are the following issues: (1) If F–1 is a federal diversity court, is the res judicata effect of its judgment determined pursuant to federal law or pursuant to the rules of the state that created the underlying claim? (2) If F–2 is a federal diversity court, is it obliged to give the same effect to the F–1 judgment that would be given in the state in which it sits? In Degnan, Federalized Res Judicata, 85 Yale L.J. 741, 773 (1976), the author asserts that the emerging principle of the res judicata scope of full faith and credit is that

"A valid judgment rendered in any judicial system within the United States must be recognized by all other judicial systems within the United States . . . [T]he claims and issues precluded by that judgment, and the parties bound thereby, are determined by the law of the system which rendered the judgment."

In accord, see Stovall v. Price Waterhouse Co., 652 F.2d 537 (5th Cir. 1981) holding that federal law should be applied to determine the res judicata effect of a judgment rendered by a federal court.

On the full-faith, Erie and choice-of-law aspects of the problem when different doctrines of mutuality of collateral estoppel prevail in the concerned jurisdictions, see Note, Collateral Estoppel: The Changing Role of the Mutuality Rule, 41 Mo.L.Rev. 521, 538–42 (1976).

NOTE

See generally Carrington, Collateral Estoppel and Foreign Judgments, 24 Ohio St.L.J. 381 (1963); Lewis, Mutuality in Conflict—Flexibility and Full Faith and Credit, 23 Drake L.Rev. 364 (1974); Overton, The Restatement of Judgments, Collateral Estoppel and the Conflict of Laws, 44 Tenn.L.Rev. 927 (1977); Rosenberg, Collateral Estoppel in New York, 44 St. John's L.Rev. 165 (1969); Note, Collateral Estoppel in Multistate Litigation, 68 Colum.L.Rev. 1590 (1968).

WARNER V. BUFFALO DRYDOCK CO., 67 F.2d 540 (2d Cir.1933), cert. denied 291 U.S. 678 (1934): Action in a federal court in New York to recover for damages to plaintiffs' steamer caused by defendant's servants. One of the defendant's pleas in bar was that prior to the commencement of this action plaintiffs had filed a libel in a federal court in Ohio based upon the same cause of action, and that the libel had been dismissed "because of laches on the part of libellants in pursuing the alleged claim." Augustus N. Hand, J. "The decisions of the Supreme Court and the English cases all indicate that the judgment of the court of a foreign state which dismisses a cause of action because of the statute of limitations of the forum is not a decision upon the merits and is not a bar to a new action upon the identical claim in the courts of another state. . . . All the court in Ohio decided was that the remedy was barred there because of laches. . . . The Ohio decree does not fail to bar the remedy in the present action because it is not res judicata as to everything which it decided, but because it did not decide that the plaintiffs' claim was extinguished, but only that they could not sue in Ohio on account of the local statute of limitations. . . . In our opinion, the dismissal of the libel by the Ohio court was not a bar to the present action."

NOTES

(1) Would not the Ohio decree have effectively barred the plaintiffs from again suing the defendant in that state on the same cause of action? How then can the result reached in the principal case be reconciled with the statutory command that F–2 must accord F–1 judicial proceedings "such faith and credit . . . as they have by law or usage in the courts" of F–1?

(2) Would an F–1 judgment dismissing plaintiff's suit on the ground of public policy be binding in F–2 whose public policy was different? If not, why should not F–2 also be permitted to apply its own rule as to collateral estoppel and the splitting of a cause of action? Compare Mertz v. Mertz, p. 388, infra.

(3) Does a judgment dismissing plaintiff's suit on the ground that it is barred by the forum's statute of limitations occupy, of necessity, the same status as one basing the dismissal upon the forum's public policy? Is a judgment of the latter type more likely to go to the merits of the cause of action?

See Paulsen and Sovern, "Public Policy" in the Conflict of Laws, 56 Colum.L. Rev. 969, 1010–1012 (1956); Restatement, Second Judgments §§ 19–20.

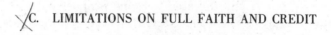

C. LIMITATIONS ON FULL FAITH AND CREDIT

FALL v. EASTIN

Supreme Court of the United States, 1909.
215 U.S. 1, 30 S.Ct. 3, 54 L.Ed. 65, 23 L.R.A.,N.S., 924, 17 Ann.Cas. 853.

MR. JUSTICE MCKENNA delivered the opinion of the Court:

The question in this case is whether a deed to land situate in Nebraska, made by a commissioner under the decree of a court of the state of Washington in an action for divorce, must be recognized in Nebraska under the due faith and credit clause of the Constitution of the United States.

[The plaintiff and E. W. Fall were married in Indiana in 1876 and subsequently moved to Nebraska, where E. W. Fall acquired title to the land in controversy. In 1889 they moved to Washington, where in 1895 the plaintiff obtained a divorce on a cross-petition filed by her. The divorce decree, in accordance with a Washington statute concerning the property of divorced parties, was accompanied by a decree awarding plaintiff the Nebraska land and ordering her husband to convey that portion to her. E. W. Fall did not comply with the decree, but a commissioner appointed by the Washington court executed to her a deed to the land. Thereafter, E. W. Fall executed to third parties, W. H. Fall and Elizabeth Eastin, a mortgage on the land and a deed to the land. Plaintiff then brought the present suit in the state court of Nebraska to quiet her title to the land and to cancel the mortgage and the deed executed by E. W. Fall. She set up the Washington decree and the commissioner's deed, and contended that Fall's conveyances were ineffective to impair the rights she claimed under that decree and the deed. E. W. Fall was never served personally in the Nebraska proceedings and did not appear, though his conveyees were duly served. The trial court gave a decree in favor of the plaintiff. The Supreme Court of Nebraska first affirmed (75 Neb. 104, 106 N.W. 412), but on rehearing, it reversed the decree of the trial court (75 Neb. 120, 113 N.W. 175).]

. . . Plaintiff urges the equities which arose between her and her husband, on account of their relation as husband and wife, in the state of Washington, and under the laws of that state. The defendant urges the policy of the state of Nebraska, and the inability of the court of Washington, by its decree alone or the deed executed through the commissioner, to convey the land situate in Nebraska.

. . . .

. . . The supreme court of the state concedes, as we understand its opinion, the jurisdiction in the Washington court to render the decree. The court said:

"We think there can be no doubt, where a court of chancery has, by its decree, ordered and directed persons properly within its jurisdiction to do or refrain from doing a certain act, it may compel obedience to this decree by appropriate proceedings, and that any action taken by reason of such compulsion is valid and effectual wherever it may be assailed. In the instant case, if Fall had obeyed the order of the Washington court, and made a deed of conveyance to his wife of the Nebraska land, even under the threat of contempt proceedings, or after duress by imprisonment, the title thereby conveyed to Mrs. Fall would have been of equal weight and dignity with that which he himself possessed at the time of the execution of the deed."

But Fall, not having executed a deed, the court's conclusion was, to quote its language, that "neither the decree nor the commissioner's deed conferred any right or title upon her. . . . The decree is inoperative to affect the title to the Nebraska land . . . it remained in E. W. Fall until devested by operation of law or by his voluntary act. He has parted with it to Elizabeth Eastin; and whether any consideration was ever paid for it or not is immaterial so far as the plaintiff is concerned, for she is in no position to question the transaction, whatever a creditor of Fall might be able to do." . . .

The territorial limitation of the jurisdiction of courts of a state over property in another state has a limited exception in the jurisdiction of a court of equity, but it is an exception well defined. A court of equity, having authority to act upon the person, may indirectly act upon real estate in another state, through the instrumentality of this authority over the person. . . .

Whether the doctrine that a decree of a court rendered in consummation of equities, or the deed of a master under it, will not convey title, and that the deed of a party coerced by the decree will have such effect, is illogical or inconsequent, we need not inquire, nor consider whether the other view would not more completely fulfil the Constitution of the United States. . . .

But, however plausibly the contrary view may be sustained, we think that the doctrine that the court, not having jurisdiction of the res, cannot affect it by its decree, nor by a deed made by a master in accordance with the decree, is firmly established. . . .

This doctrine is entirely consistent with the provision of the Constitution of the United States, which requires a judgment in any state to be given full faith and credit in the courts of every other state. This provision does not extend the jurisdiction of the courts of one state to property situated in another, but only makes the judgment rendered conclusive on the merits of the claim or subject-matter of the suit. . . .

Plaintiff seems to contend for a greater efficacy for a decree in equity affecting real property than is given to a judgment at law for the recovery of money simply. The case of Burnley v. Stevenson, 24 Ohio St. 474, in a sense sustains her. . . . [In that case, action was brought in an Ohio court to recover possession of local realty. By way of defense, the defendant relied upon a deed executed by a master commissioner in Kentucky in pursuance of a decree for specific performance rendered by a court of the latter state. The court found for the defendant, holding that, although the commissioner's deed must "be regarded as a nullity," it would recognize the validity of the actual decree "in so far as it determined the equitable rights of the parties in the land in controversy. In our judgment, the parties, and those holding under them with notice are still bound thereby."]

. . . There is . . . much temptation in the facts of this case to follow the ruling of the supreme court of Ohio . . . but, as the ruling of the [Nebraska] court, that the decree in Washington gave no such equities as could be recognized in Nebraska as justifying an action to quiet title, does not offend the Constitution of the United States, we are constrained to affirm its judgment.

So ordered.

MR. JUSTICE HARLAN and MR. JUSTICE BREWER dissent.

MR. JUSTICE HOLMES, concurring specially:

I am not prepared to dissent from the judgment of the court, but my reasons are different from those that have been stated.

The real question concerns the effect of the Washington decree. As between the parties to it, that decree established in Washington a personal obligation of the husband to convey to his former wife. A personal obligation goes with the person. If the husband had made a contract, valid by the law of Washington, to do the same thing, I think there is no doubt that the contract would have been binding in Nebraska. Ex parte Pollard, 4 Deacon, Bankr. 27, 40; Polson v. Stewart, 167 Mass. 211. So I conceive that a Washington decree for the specific performance of such a contract would be entitled to full faith and credit as between the parties in Nebraska. But it does not matter to its constitutional effect what the ground of the decree may be, whether a contract or something else. Fauntleroy v. Lum, 210 U.S. 230. (In this case it may have been that the wife contributed equally to the accumulation of the property, and so had an equitable claim.) A personal decree is equally within the jurisdiction of a court having the person within its power, whatever its ground and whatever it orders the defendant to do. Therefore I think that this decree was entitled to full faith and credit in Nebraska.

But the Nebraska court carefully avoids saying that the decree would not be binding between the original parties, had the husband been before the court. The ground on which it goes is that to allow the judgment to affect the conscience of purchasers would be giving

it an effect in rem. It treats the case as standing on the same footing as that of an innocent purchaser. Now, if the court saw fit to
deny the effect of a judgment upon privies in title, or if it considered
the defendant an innocent purchaser, I do not see what we have to do
with its decision, however wrong. I do not see why it is not within
the power of the state to do away with equity or with the equitable
doctrine as to purchasers with notice if it sees fit. Still less do I see
how a mistake as to notice could give us jurisdiction. If the judgment binds the defendant, it is not by its own operation, even with
the Constitution behind it, but by the obligation imposed by equity
upon a purchaser with notice. The ground of decision below was that
there was no such obligation. The decision, even if wrong, did not
deny to the Washington decree its full effect. Bagley v. General Fire
Extinguisher Co., 212 U.S. 477, 480.

NOTES

(1) Does the majority opinion hold that that part of the Washington decree which ordered Fall to convey the Nebraska land to the plaintiff was
entirely without extraterritorial effect? Or can the decision be explained on
the ground that the plaintiff had misconceived her remedy?

(2) Suppose that the defendant Fall had executed a conveyance to the Nebraska land in order to avoid punishment for contempt at the hands of the
Washington court. Such deeds have generally been held effective in passing
title to the land. Phillips v. Phillips, 224 Ark. 225, 272 S.W.2d 433 (1954)
(defendant signed deed in order to be released from jail); Deschenes v. Toll-
man, 248 N.Y. 33, 161 N.E. 321 (1928); Leflar, American Conflicts Law 357
(3d ed. 1977); Scoles & Hay, Conflict of Laws 344 (1982). Why should a title
deed rendered under duress be valid if the court that exercised the duress
could not itself have transferred title?

(3) Restatement, Second, Conflict of Laws § 102, Comment *b** reads:

b. Recognition. A valid foreign judgment that orders the doing of an
act other than the payment of money or that enjoins the doing of an act will
be given the same degree of recognition as any other judgment (see §§ 93–
97). This means that such a judgment will be given the same res judicata
effect with respect to the persons, the subject matter of the action and the
issues involved that it has in the state of rendition. . . . So, if a court of
State X finds that the defendant has broken his contract to convey land in
State Y and orders the defendant to make the conveyance, a court of State
Y, where the enforcement of the X judgment is sought, must give conclusive
effect to the finding of the X court that the defendant has been guilty of
breach of contract. Similarly if a court of State X finds that the defendant
has procured a judgment in State Y by fraud and enjoins its enforcement, a
court of State Y must give conclusive effect to the finding of the X court
that the judgment was procured by fraud.

(4) *Enforcement.* The great majority of cases dealing with the enforcement of equity decrees that order the doing of an act other than the payment of money have involved an order to convey land in F–2. At one time it was generally believed that such decrees would not be enforced extraterritorially. This conclusion was based on the ground either that (a) since equity decrees are discretionary in nature, F–2 could not be required to accept the relief that F–1 had found appropriate and (b) in any event no action was available for the enforcement of a foreign judgment other than one in the nature of debt. These notions were found baseless in Currie, Full Faith and Credit to Foreign Land Decrees, 21 U.Chi.L.Rev. 620 (1964). He concluded that an action could be brought in F–2 to establish the F–1 decree as one of F–2 or for a judgment declaring the interests of the parties in the F–2 land in light of the F–1 decree or, if neither of these alternatives was available, an action on the original claim with the F–2 court being required to give res judicata effect to the findings made in F–1.

Most of the recent cases have enforced foreign equity decrees ordering the conveyance of local land. Sometimes, the opinions make clear that this result was achieved by establishing the F–1 decree as one of F–2. Varone v. Varone, 359 F.2d 769 (7th Cir.1966); Cuevas v. Cuevas, 191 So.2d 843 (Miss. 1966); Higgenbotham v. Higgenbotham, 92 N.J.Super. 18, 222 A.2d 126 (1966). Frequently, the opinions leave obscure the exact basis adopted for enforcing the F–1 decree. See Phelps v. Williams, 192 A.2d 805 (D.C.App. 1963). In Weesner v. Weesner, 168 Neb. 346, 95 N.W.2d 682 (1959), the Nebraska court did what it had refused to do in Fall v. Eastin, namely, it entertained a cross-petition to quiet title to Nebraska land on the basis of an F–1 decree that ordered conveyance of this land. The F–1 defendant was subjected to the personal jurisdiction of the court in F–2. See also Day v. Wiswall, 11 Ariz.App. 306, 464 P.2d 626 (1970).

(5) Compare Lyle Cashion Co. v. McKendrick, 227 Miss. 894, 87 So.2d 289 (1956). Defendant originally brought suit in a federal court in Louisiana to obtain a declaratory judgment that plaintiff had no interest in certain Mississippi oil leases. In return, the plaintiff claimed in his pleadings that he was entitled to a one-half interest in these leases under a contract previously made with the defendant. The federal court found for the plaintiff and entered a judgment declaring him to have an undivided one-half interest in these leases. Plaintiff thereupon brought the present action in the Mississippi courts for confirmation of title of his interest in the oil leases. Held for the plaintiff. The federal court had personal jurisdiction over both parties. Its judgment "does not operate directly on the property, but on the party; it does not vest or divest title, but is conclusive of the legal rights under the contract, insofar as those rights were determined and as such may be used to establish title in the State where the land is situated."

(6) See generally Leflar, American Conflicts Law 164–166 (3d ed. 1977); Scoles and Hay, Conflict of Laws 930–933 (1982).

YARBOROUGH v. YARBOROUGH

Supreme Court of the United States, 1933.
290 U.S. 202, 54 S.Ct. 181, 78 L.Ed. 269, 90 A.L.R. 924.

MR. JUSTICE BRANDEIS delivered the opinion of the Court.

On August 10, 1930, Sadie Yarborough, then 16 years of age, was living with her maternal grandfather, R. D. Blowers, at Spartanburg, South Carolina. Suing by him as guardian ad litem, she brought this action in a court of that State to require her father, W. A. Yarborough, a resident of Atlanta, Georgia, to make provision for her education and maintenance. She alleged "that she is now ready for college and is without funds and, unless the defendant makes provision for her, will be denied the necessities of life and an education, and will be dependent upon the charity of others." Jurisdiction was obtained by attachment of defendant's property. Later he was served personally within South Carolina.

In bar of the action, W. A. Yarborough set up, among other defences, a judgment entered in 1929 by the Superior Court of Fulton County, Georgia, in a suit for divorce brought by him against Sadie's mother. He alleged that by the judgment the amount thereafter to be paid by him for Sadie's education and maintenance had been determined; that the sum so fixed had been paid; and that the judgment had been fully satisfied by him. He claimed that in Georgia the judgment was conclusive of the matter here in controversy; that having been satisfied, it relieved him, under the Georgia law, of all obligation to provide for the education and maintenance of their minor child; and that the full faith and credit clause of the Federal Constitution (Art. 4, sec. 1) required the South Carolina court to give to that judgment the same effect in this proceeding which it has, and would have in Georgia. The trial court denied the claim; ordered W. A. Yarborough to pay to the grandfather, as trustee, fifty dollars monthly for Sadie's education and support; and to pay $300 as fees of her counsel. It directed that the property held under the attachment be transferred to R. D. Blowers, trustee, as security for the performance of the order. The judgment was affirmed by the Supreme Court of South Carolina. A petition for rehearing was denied, with opinion. 168 S.C. 46, 166 S.E. 877. This Court granted certiorari. 289 U.S. 718.

For sometime prior to June, 1927, W. A. Yarborough, his wife and their daughter Sadie had lived together at Atlanta, Georgia, where he then was, and ever since has been, domiciled. In that month, Sadie's mother left Atlanta for Hendersonville, N. C., where she remained during the summer. Sadie joined her there, after a short stay at a camp. In September, 1927, while they were at Hendersonville, W. A. Yarborough brought in the Superior Court for Fulton County, at Atlanta, suit against his wife for a total divorce on the ground of mental and physical cruelty. . . . An order, several times modified, awarded to the wife the custody of Sadie and as temporary alimony, sums "for the support and maintenance of herself and her minor daughter Sadie." Hearings were held from time to time at Atlanta. At some of these, Sadie (and also her grandfather) was personally present. But she was not formally made a party to the litigation; she was not served with process; and no guardian ad litem was appointed for her therein.

"Two concurring verdicts favoring a total divorce to plaintiff having been rendered," a decree of total divorce, with the right in each to remarry, was entered on June 7, 1929; the wife was ordered to pay the costs; and jurisdiction of the case "was retained for the purpose of further enforcement of the orders of the court theretofore passed." Among such orders, was the provision for the maintenance and education of Sadie here relied upon as res judicata. . . .

W. A. Yarborough complied fully with this order.

By the law of Georgia, it is the duty of the father to provide for the maintenance and education of his child until maturity. . . . In case of total divorce, the court is authorized to make, by its decree, final or permanent provision for the maintenance and education of children during minority, and thus fix the extent of the father's obligation. But even if the decree for total divorce fails to include a provision for the support of minor children, they cannot maintain in their own names, or by guardian ad litem, or by next friend, an independent suit for an allowance for education and maintenance. . . .

[The court found, first, that the Georgia decree was "intended to relieve the father from all further liability to support Sadie"; second, that the decree conformed to Georgia law; and, third that the failure to make the child a formal party to the divorce suit did not destroy the effectiveness of the decree as to her.]

Fourth. It is contended that the order for permanent alimony is not binding upon Sadie because she was not a resident of Georgia at the time it was entered. Being a minor, Sadie's domicile was Georgia, that of her father; and her domicile continued to be in Georgia until entry of the judgment in question. She was not capable by her own act of changing her domicile. Neither the temporary residence in North Carolina at the time the divorce suit was begun, nor her removal with her mother to South Carolina before entry of the judgment, effected a change of Sadie's domicile. . . .

Fifth. The fact that Sadie has become a resident of South Carolina does not impair the finality of the judgment. South Carolina thereby acquired the jurisdiction to determine her status and the incidents of that status. Upon residents of that State it could impose duties for her benefit. Doubtless, it might have imposed upon her grandfather who was resident there a duty to support Sadie. But the mere fact of Sadie's residence in South Carolina does not give that State the power to impose such a duty upon the father who is not a resident and who long has been domiciled in Georgia. He has ful-

filled the duty which he owes her by the law of his domicile and the
judgment of its court. Upon that judgment he is entitled to rely. It
was settled by Sistare v. Sistare, 218 U.S. 1, that the full faith and
credit clause applies to an unalterable decree of alimony for a divorced wife. The clause applies, likewise, to an unalterable decree of
alimony for a minor child. We need not consider whether South Carolina would have power to require the father, if he were domiciled
there, to make further provision for the support, maintenance, or education of his daughter.

Reversed.

Mr. Justice Stone, dissenting.

I think the judgment should be affirmed.

The divorce decree of the Georgia court purported to adjudicate
finally, both for the present and for the future, the right of a minor
child of the marriage to support and maintenance, by directing her
father to make a lump sum payment for that purpose. More than
two years later, after the minor had become a domiciled resident of
South Carolina, and after the sum paid had been exhausted, a court
of that State, on the basis of her need as then shown, has rendered a
judgment directing further payments for her support out of property
of the father in South Carolina, in addition to that already command-
ed by the Georgia judgment.

For the present purposes we may take it that the Georgia decree,
as the statutes and decisions of the State declare, is unalterable and,
as pronounced, is effective to govern the rights of the parties in Georgia. But there is nothing in the decree itself, or in the history of the
proceedings which led to it to suggest that it was rendered with any
purpose or intent to regulate or control the relationship of parent and
child, or the duties which flow from it, in places outside the State of
Georgia where they might later come to reside. . . . But if we
are to read the decree as though it contained a clause, in terms, restricting the power of any other state, in which the minor might come
to reside, to make provision for her support, then, in the absence of
some law of Congress requiring it, I am not persuaded that the full
faith and credit clause gives sanction to such control by one state of
the internal affairs of another.[1] . . .

Between the prohibition of the due process clause, acting upon the
courts of the state from which such proceedings may be taken, and
the mandate of the full faith and credit clause, acting upon the state
to which they may be taken, there is an area which federal authority
has not occupied. As this Court has often recognized, there are
many judgments which need not be given the same force and effect
abroad which they have at home, and there are some, though valid in

1. It may be assumed for present purposes that the child was sufficiently rep-
resented in the Georgia proceedings.   But the point is doubtful. . . . [Foot-
notes 1–4 by Mr. Justice Stone. The oth-
er footnotes have been omitted.]

the state where rendered, to which the full faith and credit clause gives no force elsewhere. In the assertion of rights, defined by a judgment of one state, within the territory of another there is often an inescapable conflict of interest of the two states, and there comes a point beyond which the imposition of the will of one state beyond its own borders involves a forbidden infringement of some legitimate domestic interest of the other. That point may vary with the circumstances of the case, and in the absence of provisions more specific than the general terms of the congressional enactment [2] this Court must determine for itself the extent to which one state may qualify or deny rights claimed under proceedings or records of other states.

. . .

[MR. JUSTICE STONE enumerated the situations in which the Supreme Court had held that the full faith and credit clause does not compel recognition by one state of the public acts, records, and judicial proceedings of a sister state.]

Just as due process of law will not permit a state by its judgment to inflict parties "with a perpetual contractual paralysis" which will prevent them from altering outside the state their contracts or ordinary business relations entered into within it, New York L. Ins. Co. v. Head, supra (234 U.S. 161), so full faith and credit does not command that the obligations attached to a status, because once appropriately imposed by one state, shall be forever placed beyond the control of every other state, without regard to the interest in it and the power of control which the other may later acquire. See Bradford Electric Light Co. v. Clapper, 286 U.S. 145, 157, note 7. Whatever difference there may be between holding that a judgment is invalid under the Fourteenth Amendment because it is "extraterritorial," and in holding that it is not entitled to full faith and credit although it does not infringe the Fourteenth Amendment, is one of degree, or of a difference in circumstances which may prevent the operation of the latter provision of the Constitution. The Georgia judgment with which we are now concerned does not infringe the Fourteenth Amendment, for

---

2. The mandatory force of the full faith and credit clause as defined by this Court may be, in some degree not yet fully defined, expanded or contracted by Congress. Much of the confusion and procedural deficiencies which the constitutional provision alone has not avoided may be remedied by legislation. Cook, "Powers of Congress under the Full Faith and Credit Clause," 28 Yale L.J. 421; Corwin, "The Full Faith and Credit Clause," 81 University of Pa.L.Rev. 371; cf. 33 Columbia L.Rev. 854, 866. The constitutional provision giving Congress power to prescribe the effect to be given to acts, records and proceedings would have been quite unnecessary had it not been intended that Congress should have a latitude broader than that given the courts by the full faith and credit clause alone. It was remarked on the floor of the Constitutional Convention that without the extension of power in the legislature, the provision "would amount to nothing more than what now takes place among all Independent Nations." Hunt and Scott, Madison's Reports of the Debates in the Federal Convention of 1787, p. 503. The play which has been afforded for the recognition of local public policy in cases where there is called in question only a statute of another state, as to the effect of which Congress has not legislated, compared with the more restricted scope for local policy where there is a judicial proceeding, as to which Congress has legislated, suggests the Congressional power.

Georgia had "jurisdiction" of the parties and subject matter at the time its judgment was rendered. The possibility of conflict of the Georgia judgment with the interest of South Carolina first arose when the minor transferred her domicile to South Carolina, long after the Georgia judgment was given.

The question presented here is whether the support and maintenance of a minor child, domiciled in South Carolina, is so peculiarly a subject of domestic concern that Georgia law can not impair South Carolina's authority. . . . The maintenance and support of children domiciled within a state, like their education and custody, is a subject in which government itself is deemed to have a peculiar interest and concern. . . . The states very generally make some provision from their own resources for the maintenance and support of orphans or destitute children, but in order that children may not become public charges the duty of maintenance is one imposed primarily upon the parents, according to the needs of the child and their ability to meet those needs. . . . Hence, it is no answer in such a suit that at some earlier time provision was made for the child, which is no longer available or suitable because of his greater needs, or because of the increased financial ability of the parent to provide for them, or that the child may be maintained from other sources. . . .

Even though the Constitution does not deny to Georgia the power to indulge in such a policy for itself, it by no means follows that it gives to Georgia the privilege of prescribing that policy for other states in which the child comes to live.[3] South Carolina has adopted a different policy. It imposes on the father or his property located within the state the duty to support his minor child domiciled there. It enforces the duty by criminal prosecution and also permits suit by the minor child maintained by guardian ad litem. The measure of the duty is the present need of the child and the ability of the parent to provide for it. . . .

The opinion of this Court leaves it uncertain whether it is thought that the Constitution commands that the duty of support prescribed by Georgia, the domicile of the father, shall be dominant over that enjoined by South Carolina, the domicile of the child, in any event, or only after the duty has been defined by a judgment of Georgia.[4] It is attested by eminent authority that the Fourteenth Amendment, at least, does not prevent the state of the child's domicile from imposing the duty . . . a view confirmed by the uniform rulings that the father is liable to the criminal process of the state of the child's residence, though before, and at all times during his failure to conform to

3. In the custody cases a very similar situation is presented. As conventionally stated the rule has been that the most the full faith and credit clause can require is that the prior ruling shall be deemed conclusive in the absence of an asserted change in circumstances. . . . [Originally footnote 19.]

4. Cf. Home Ins. Co. v. Dick, 281 U.S. 397, with Kryger v. Wilson, 242 U.S. 171. [Originally footnote 21.]

the duty demanded by that state, he has been domiciled elsewhere. [Citing cases.] The Fourteenth Amendment does not enable a father by the expedient of choosing a domicile other than the state where the child is rightfully domiciled, to avoid the duty which that state may impose for support of his child. The reason seems plain. The locality of the child's residence must see to his welfare. . . . The conclusion must be the same when the issue is that of the credit to be given the prior Georgia judgment. . . .

. . . . Here the Georgia decree did not end the relationship of parent and child, as a decree of divorce may end the marriage relationship. Had the infant continued to reside in Georgia, and had she sought in the courts of South Carolina to compel the application of property of her father, found there, to her further maintenance and support, full faith and credit to the Georgia decree applied to its own domiciled resident might have required the denial of any relief. [Citing cases.] But when she became a domiciled resident of South Carolina a new interest came into being, the interest of the State of South Carolina as a measure of self preservation to secure the adequate protection and maintenance of helpless members of its own community and its prospective citizens. That interest was distinct from any which Georgia could conclusively regulate or control by its judgment even though rendered while the child was domiciled in Georgia. The present decision extends the operation of the full faith and credit clause beyond its proper function of affording protection to the domestic interests of Georgia and makes it an instrument for encroachment by Georgia upon the domestic concerns of South Carolina.

MR. JUSTICE CARDOZO concurs in this opinion.

NOTES

(1) Elkind v. Byck, 68 Cal.2d 453, 439 P.2d 316 (1968). In that case, the parties had been divorced in Georgia pursuant to a decree under which the husband paid a lump sum for the maintenance and support of his wife and child. Under the Georgia law, his payment was in full satisfaction of the husband's obligation and no further liability could be imposed upon him. Following the divorce, the wife made her home in New York and the husband moved to California. Thereafter, the wife sought additional support from the husband, and it was held that the California court had power to grant her request. Yarborough was said not to stand in the way "[s]ince that decision was based upon the father's continued domicile and residence in Georgia." In this case, the husband's "substantial relationship" with California "justifies the application of its law of support." The court concluded that the facts of the case served to demonstrate "why the divorce state should not be permitted to determine the welfare of the child for all time and in all states. More than ten years following the divorce, none of the parties appears to have any connection at all with Georgia: the mother and child reside in New York and the father resides in California."

(2) Restatement, Second, Conflict of Laws:*

§ 103. Limitations on Full Faith and Credit

A judgment rendered in one State of the United States need not be recognized or enforced in a sister State if such recognition or enforcement is not required by the national policy of full faith and credit because it would involve an improper interference with important interests of the sister State.

(3) Section 103 was approved in Thompson v. Thompson, 645 S.W.2d 79 (Mo.App.1982). In that case, a divorce decree rendered by a Kansas court had ordered the husband to provide child support. By Kansas statute, a parent's obligation to support a child ceases when the child attains eighteen years. Thereafter, all parties moved to Missouri and there the wife sought to compel the husband to support a son who was then over eighteen years old. The Missouri court found for the wife, holding that an exception should be made to the normal command of full faith and credit in order to protect Missouri's "overriding domestic interests." It relied upon Justice Stone's dissent in Yarborough, upon Elkind v. Byck, and upon § 103. Was it necessary for the court to rely upon an exception to full faith and credit to reach the desired result?

(4) See generally Reese and Johnson, The Scope of Full Faith and Credit to Judgments, 49 Colum.L.Rev. 153 (1949).

Kubon v. Kubon, 51 Cal.2d 229, 331 P.2d 636 (1958): A controversy between parents over children began in a Nevada proceeding in which the court, with jurisdiction over both parents, gave custody of the two children to the mother, ordered the father to pay $100 a month for child support, and reserved jurisdiction to make further orders as to custody and support. The Nevada court modified its order so as to allow the husband physical custody during the summer vacation. During the vacation while the children were with the father in California, he filed a petition in California seeking appointment of himself as guardian, and the California court issued a temporary restraining order restraining the mother from taking the children from the father's home or custody pending the hearing of the guardianship petition. Nevertheless, the mother took the children from the father's home and carried them back to Nevada with her. The Nevada court then modified its order again, taking away from the father the right to the summer custody of the children but giving him the right of reasonable visitation in Nevada. The father ceased his payments for support when he secured the California restraining order. Ten months later the mother sought a judgment in Nevada for the accrued installments for support, and the Nevada court after notice by mail to the father in California entered a judgment for the accrued installments of $1,000 and attorney's fees. The mother sued on the Nevada judgment in California. She was met by the defense that in taking the children from California she had violat-

* Quoted with the permission of the copyright owner, The American Law Institute.

ed the California restraining order and so was in contempt of the court from which she sought relief. The majority of the Supreme Court of California upheld the defense. A minority were of the opinion the defense was bad.

TRAYNOR, J. (dissenting). "It is my opinion that recognition of such defense violates the full faith and credit clause . . . The United States Supreme Court has repeatedly held that a state may not vindicate its own policy by refusing enforcement of a sister state judgment for the payment of money on the ground that its recognition would violate the policy of the state where enforcement is sought . . . Accordingly, . . . we cannot invoke that policy as a rule of procedure to sustain a plea in abatement to a suit on that judgment. . . . even had the California order such dignity as to compel its recognition in Nevada under the full faith and credit clause, a final judgment entered in disregard of it could not now be denied enforcement here. . . . Even if we were not constitutionally compelled to reject defendant's plea in abatement based on plaintiff's contempt of the temporary restraining order, we should reject it on its own merits. . . . The Nevada court did not err in placing the welfare of the children above the desirability of compelling plaintiff to respect the order of the California court."

NOTE

As to the status of custody decrees under full faith and credit, see pp. 867–881, infra.

 MAGNOLIA PETROLEUM CO. v. HUNT

Supreme Court of the United States, 1943.
320 U.S. 430, 64 S.Ct. 208, 88 L.Ed. 149, 150 A.L.R. 413.

Certiorari to the Court of Appeal, First Circuit, of Louisiana.

MR. CHIEF JUSTICE STONE delivered the opinion of the Court.

The question for decision is whether, under the full faith and credit clause, Art. IV, § 1 of the Constitution of the United States, an award of compensation for personal injury under the Texas Workmen's Compensation Law, Title 130 of the Revised Civil Statutes of Texas, bars a further recovery of compensation for the same injury under the Louisiana Workmen's Compensation Law, Title 34, Chapter 15 of the Louisiana General Statutes.

Magnolia Petroleum Company, petitioner here, employed respondent in Louisiana as a laborer in connection with the drilling of oil wells. In the course of his employment respondent, a Louisiana resident, went from Louisiana to Texas, and while working there for petitioner on an oil well, he was injured by a falling drill stem. He sought and procured in Texas an award of compensation for his injury under its Workmen's Compensation Law, and petitioner's insurer made payments of compensation as required by the statute and the award. The award became final in accordance with the terms of the Texas statute.

Respondent then brought the present proceeding in the Louisiana District Court to recover compensation for his injury under the Louisiana Workmen's Compensation Law. Petitioner filed exceptions to respondent's petition on the ground that the recovery sought was barred as res judicata by the Texas award which, by virtue of the constitutional command, was entitled in the Louisiana courts to full faith and credit. The District Court overruled the exceptions and gave judgment for the amount of the compensation fixed by the Louisiana statute, after deducting the amount of the Texas payments. The Louisiana Court of Appeal affirmed 10 So.2d 109, and the Supreme Court of Louisiana refused writs of certiorari and review for the reason that it found "no error of law in the judgment complained." . . .

In Texas a compensation award against the employer's insurer . . . is explicitly made by statute in lieu of any other recovery for injury to the employee, since Art. 8306, § 3 provides that employees subject to the Act "shall have no right of action against their employer or against any agent, servant or employé of said employer for damages for personal injuries . . . but such employés . . . shall look for compensation solely to the association [the insurer]." A compensation award which has become final "is entitled to the same faith and credit as a judgment of a court." . . .

It does not appear, nor is it contended, that Louisiana more than Texas allows in its own courts a second recovery of compensation for a single injury. The contention is that since Louisiana is better satisfied with the measure of recovery allowed by its own laws, it may deny full faith and credit to the Texas award, which respondent has procured by his election to pursue his remedy in that state. In thus refusing, on the basis of state law and policy, to give effect to the Texas award as a final adjudication of respondent's claim for compensation for his injury suffered in Texas, the Louisiana court ignored the distinction, long recognized and applied by this Court . . . between the faith and credit required to be given to judgments and that to which local common and statutory law is entitled under the Constitution and laws of the United States.

In the case of local law, since each of the states of the Union has constitutional authority to make its own law with respect to persons and events within its borders the full faith and credit clause does not ordinarily require it to substitute for its own law the conflicting law of another state, even though that law is of controlling force in the courts of that state with respect to the same persons and events. . . . It was for this reason that we held that the state of the employer and employee is free to apply its own compensation law to the injury of the employee rather than the law of another state where the injury occurred. Alaska Packers Assn. v. Industrial Accident Comm'n, [294 U.S. 532 at] 544–550. And for like reasons we held also that the state of the place of injury is free to apply its own law to the exclusion of the law of the state of the employer and employee. Pacific Employers Ins. Co. v. Industrial Accident Comm'n, [306 U.S. 493 at] 502–505.

But it does not follow that the employee who has sought and recovered an award of compensation in either state may then have recourse to the laws and courts of the other to recover a second or additional award for the same injury. Where a court must make choice of one of two conflicting statutes of different states and apply it to a cause of action which has not been previously litigated, there can be no plea of res judicata. But when the employee who has recovered compensation for his injury in one state seeks a second recovery in another he may be met by the plea that full faith and credit requires that his demand, which has become res judicata in one state, must be recognized as such in every other.

The full faith and credit clause and the Act of Congress implementing it have, for most purposes, placed a judgment on a different footing from a statute of one state, judicial recognition of which is sought in another. . . .

These consequences flow from the clear purpose of the full faith and credit clause to establish throughout the federal system the salutary principle of the common law that a litigation once pursued to judgment shall be as conclusive of the rights of the parties in every other court as in that where the judgment was rendered, so that a cause of action merged in a judgment in one state is likewise merged in every other. The full faith and credit clause like the commerce clause thus became a nationally unifying force. It altered the status of the several states as independent foreign sovereignties, each free to ignore rights and obligations created under the laws or established by the judicial proceedings of the others, by making each an integral part of a single nation, in which rights judicially established in any part are given nation-wide application. . . . Because there is a full faith and credit clause a defendant may not a second time challenge the validity of the plaintiff's right which has ripened into a judgment and a plaintiff may not for his single cause of action secure a second or a greater recovery. . . .

We have no occasion to consider what effect would be required to be given to the Texas award if the Texas courts held that an award of compensation in another state would not bar an award in Texas, for . . . Texas does not allow such a second recovery. And if the award of compensation in Texas were not res judicata there, full faith and credit would, of course, be no bar to the recovery of an award in another state. Chicago, R. I. & P. R. Co. v. Elder, 270 U.S. 611, 622–623.

Whether the proceeding before the State Industrial Accident Board in Texas be regarded as a "judicial proceeding," or its award as a "record" within the meaning of the full faith and credit clause and the Act of Congress, the result is the same. For judicial proceedings and records of the state are both required to have "such faith and credit given to them in every court within the United States as they have by law or usage in the courts of the State from which they are taken."

The decision of the state court is not supported by the suggestion that the Texas award is not res judicata in Louisiana because respondent's suit there was on a different cause of action. When a state court refuses credit to the judgment of a sister state because of its opinion of the nature of the cause of action or the judgment in which it is merged, an asserted federal right is denied and the sufficiency of the grounds of denial are for this Court to decide. . . . Respondent's injury in Texas did not give rise to two causes of action merely because recovery in each state is under a different statute, or because each affords a different measure of recovery. . . . The grounds of recovery are the same in one state as in the other—the injury to the employee in the course of his employment. . . . Respondent was free to pursue his remedy in either state but, having chosen to seek it in Texas, where the award was res judicata, the full faith and credit clause precludes him from again seeking a remedy in Louisiana upon the same grounds. . . . *

Mr. Justice Douglas, dissenting.

. . . We are dealing here with . . . a clash between the policies of two sovereign States. The question is not which policy we prefer; it is whether the two conflicting policies can somehow be accommodated. The command of the full faith and credit clause frequently makes a reconciliation of the two interests impossible. One must give way in the larger interest of the federal union. The question in each case is whether as a practical matter there is room for adjustment, consistent with the requirements of full faith and credit. . . .

. . . If the Texas award had undertaken to adjudicate the rights and duties of the parties under the Louisiana contract of employment, which we are told carries the right to compensation under the Louisiana Act (10 So.2d 109, 112), the result would be quite different. Then the judgment, . . . would undertake to regulate the relationship of the parties, or their rights and duties which flow from it, as respects their undertakings in another State. . . . But there is nothing in the Texas proceeding or in the Texas award to indicate that that was either intended or done. The most charitable construction is that Texas undertook to adjust the rights and duties of the

---

* A concurring opinion by Mr. Justice Jackson is omitted.

parties and to regulate their relationship only so long as they remained subject to the jurisdiction of Texas.

. . . But even if the Texas award were less clear than I think it is, I would resolve all doubts against an inference that rights under the Louisiana contract were adjudicated in Texas. Such a course seems to me essential so that the greatest possible accommodations of the interests of the two States, consistent with the requirements of full faith and credit, may be had whether the matter be divorce, workmen's compensation or any other subject on which state policies differ. . . .

MR. JUSTICE MURPHY joins in this dissent.

MR. JUSTICE BLACK, dissenting:

The respondent Hunt is a resident of Louisiana, employed in that state by the petitioner and sent by the petitioner to do work in Texas. While in Texas he was seriously injured in the course of his employment. Confined to a hospital he was told that he could not recover compensation unless he signed two forms presented to him. As found by the Louisiana trial judge there was printed on each of the forms "in small type" the designation "Industrial Accident Board, Austin, Texas." To get his compensation Hunt signed the forms and the Texas insurer began to pay. Returning to his home in Louisiana Hunt apparently discovered that his interest would be more fully protected under Louisiana law and notified the insurer of an intention to claim under the statute of that state. The insurer immediately stopped payment to him and notified the Texas Board to that effect. Four days later, without any request from Hunt, the Board notified him at his Louisiana home that a hearing would be held in Texas within two and a half weeks "to determine the liability of the insurance company" under Texas law. Hunt did not participate in that proceeding. The Texas Board thereafter made an award to him which, under the law of Texas, was equivalent to a judgment against the insurer. Before the Texas award became final, Hunt, who had declined to accept any money under it, filed suit against his employer in the courts of Louisiana under the Workmen's Compensation Law of Louisiana. He recovered a judgment for a substantially larger sum than had been allowed him under the Texas award, from which the Louisiana court deducted the sum he had already received from the Texas insurer. . . .

As I see it, this case properly involves two separate legal questions: (1) Did Texas intend the award of its Industrial Accident Board against the insurer to bar the right granted the employee by the Louisiana Workmen's Compensation Law to collect from his employer for the same injury the difference between the compensation allowed by Texas and the more generous compensation allowed by Louisiana? (2) Assuming the Texas award was intended to constitute such a bar, does the interest of Louisiana in regulating the employment contracts of its residents nevertheless permit it to grant that larger measure of compensation which as a matter of local policy it believes necessary? The decision of the Court on both of these issues appears to me to be wrong.

Where a state court refuses to recognize the judgment of a sister state as a bar to an asserted cause of action, the full faith and credit clause cannot raise a federal question unless the judgment would have been a bar to a similar suit in that sister state. . . . Whether Texas intended that its award should bar the employee here from recovering compensation under the Louisiana law is an issue upon which Texas courts have not spoken. In fact, they absolutely refuse to entertain any suits at all based on the Louisiana Workmen's Compensation Law. . . .

In the absence of compelling language this Court should not construe the statutes of Texas in such a manner that grave questions of their constitutionality are raised. Cf. Yarborough v. Yarborough, [290 U.S. at] 213, 214. It is extremely doubtful whether Texas has the power, by any legal device, to preclude a sister state from granting to its own residents employed within its own borders that measure of compensation for occupational injuries which it deems advisable. . . . I "am not persuaded that the full faith and credit clause gives sanction to such control by one state of the internal affairs of another." Yarborough v. Yarborough, supra, 214.

It is apparently conceded that Louisiana would not have been required to apply the Texas statute had there not been a judgment in the particular case by the Texas tribunal. This freedom of the state to apply its own policy in workmen's compensation cases despite a conflicting statute in the state in which the accident occurs rests on the theory that the state where the workman is hired or is domiciled has a genuine and special interest in the outcome of the litigation. . . . The argument of state interest is hardly less compelling when Louisiana chooses to reject as decisive of the issues of the case a foreign judgment than when it rejects a foreign statute.

The interest of Texas in providing compensation for an injured employee who like respondent was only temporarily employed in the state is not the same as that of Louisiana where the respondent was domiciled and where the contract of employment was made. Someone has to take care of an individual who has received, as has respondent, an injury which permanently disables him from performance of his work. . . . If it chooses to be more generous to injured workmen than Texas, no Constitutional issue is presented. . . .

Today's decision is flatly in conflict with accepted law and practice. The Restatement of Conflict of Laws, sec. 403 states categorically that an "award already had under the Workmen's Compensation Act of another state will not bar a proceeding under an Applicable Act, but the amount paid on a prior award in another state will be credited on the second award," and one of the foremost studies of workmen's compensation states the same rule.

. . . There should be no Constitutional barrier preventing a state in effect from increasing the workmen's compensation award of another state in a case in which it has jurisdiction over the participants and the social responsibility for the results. Where two states both have a legitimate interest in the outcome of workmen's compensation litigation, the question of whether the second state which considers the case should abide by the decision of the first is a question of policy which should be decided by the state legislatures and courts. . . . State laws vary, and uniformity is not the highest value in the law of workmen's compensation. . . .

Mr. Justice Douglas, Mr. Justice Murphy, and Mr. Justice Rutledge concur in this opinion.

INDUSTRIAL COMMISSION OF WISCONSIN v. McCARTIN

Supreme Court of the United States, 1947.
330 U.S. 622, 67 S.Ct. 886, 91 L.Ed. 1140, 169 A.L.R. 1179.

[Kopp and McCartin were both Illinois residents. Pursuant to a contract made in Illinois, Kopp worked for McCartin on a building job in Wisconsin and there suffered an eye injury in the course of his employment. Kopp sought workmen's compensation in both Illinois and Wisconsin. The Illinois award, which was the first to be handed down, provided that it "does not affect any rights" which Kopp might have under the Workmen's Compensation Statute of Wisconsin. Thereafter, the Wisconsin Commission gave Kopp an additional award but on appeal the Wisconsin courts set aside the award on the authority of the Magnolia decision. The Supreme Court granted certiorari.]

Mr. Justice Murphy delivered the opinion of the Court. . . .

If it were apparent that the Illinois award was intended to be final and conclusive of all the employee's rights against the employer and the insurer growing out of the injury, the decision in the Magnolia Petroleum Co. case would be controlling here. . . .

But there is nothing in the [Illinois award or in the underlying] statute or in the decisions thereunder to indicate that it was designed to preclude any recovery by proceedings brought in another state for injuries received there in the course of an Illinois employment. . . . And in light of the rule that workmen's compensation laws are to be liberally construed in furtherance of the purpose for which they were enacted . . . we should not readily interpret such a statute so as to cut off an employee's right to sue under other legislation passed for his benefit. Only some unmistakable language by a state legislature or judiciary would warrant our accepting such a construction . . .

We need not rest our decision, however, solely upon the absence of any provision or construction of the Illinois Workmen's Compensation Act forbidding an employee from seeking alternative or additional relief under the laws of another state. There is even stronger evidence that the employee is free to ask for additional compensation in Wisconsin. . . .

Here the employer and the employee entered into a settlement contract fixing the amount of compensation to which the employee was entitled under the Illinois statute . . .

One of the provisions in the settlement contract which became the award was the statement that "This settlement does not affect any rights that applicant may have under the Workmen's Compensation Act of the State of Wisconsin." That statement was made a part of the contract at the request of the employee, who had been informed by the Wisconsin Commission that he was entitled to claim an additional amount of compensation in Wisconsin after recovering in Illinois. . . .

This contract provision saving the rights of the employee in Wisconsin thus became part of the Illinois award. . . . [And] when the reservation in this award is read against the background of the Illinois Workmen's Compensation Act, it becomes clear that the reservation spells out what we believe to be implicit in that Act—namely, that an Illinois workmen's compensation award of the type here involved does not foreclose in additional award under the laws of another state. . . .

Since this Illinois award is final and conclusive only as to rights arising in Illinois, Wisconsin is free under the full faith and credit clause to grant an award of compensation in accord with its own laws. Magnolia Petroleum Co. v. Hunt, supra, thus does not control this case.

Reversed.

MR. JUSTICE RUTLEDGE concurs in the result.

NOTES

(1) Suppose that a contract made in State X is by its terms to be performed in State Y. Under their respective conflict of laws rules, the courts of State X look to the law of the place of making to determine the validity of a contract, those of State Y to that of the place of performance; the particular contract in question would be invalid under the local law of State X but valid under that of State Y. Suppose further that the plaintiff, domiciled in State Y, brings suit for breach of the contract in State X and loses. Does the existence of this judgment preclude him from thereafter pressing his claim in State Y even though he would almost certainly have won if he had originally brought suit in that state? If the answer to this question is in the affirmative, does it also follow that the result reached by the majority in the Magnolia case was correct?

(2) Semler v. Psychiatric Institute of Washington, D.C., 575 F.2d 922 (D.C.Cir.1978). The plaintiff's decedent had been murdered in Virginia by a person who had been placed by the defendant Psychiatric Institute in a generally unsupervised outpatient program. The plaintiff initially brought suit in Virginia and recovered $25,000 under that state's wrongful death act. She then sought recovery in the District of Columbia under the District's survival act. Held that full faith and credit required that the second suit be barred by the Virginia judgment. "Under District of Columbia law, negligent conduct resulting in death gives rise to two independent rights of action, one under the Wrongful Death Act and the other under the Survival Act." On the other hand, the Virginia Wrongful Death Act provides the "exclusive right of action in wrongful death cases" and "exists in lieu of an action based on the survival of the deceased's original claim." The court concluded that initially the plaintiff could have brought her action in either Virginia or the District of Columbia and that presumably a greater recovery for the death could have been obtained under District of Columbia law than under that of Virginia. "Either state could have properly applied its law in the first instance. But having elected to seek her remedy in Virginia, where the [effect of the judgment was to bar any further recovery for the wrongful death], the full faith and credit clause precludes her from again seeking a remedy in the District of Columbia upon the same grounds."

(3) Compare Ellis v. Garwood, 168 Ohio St. 241, 152 N.E.2d 100 (1958), where the decedent employee resided and was employed in New York. While driving in Ohio on business, with the defendant, another employee, the decedent was killed. The plaintiff, his wife, received workmen's compensation benefits under the New York statute, which, under New York law, precludes any recovery against a fellow employee. The Ohio court held that the action in Ohio could be maintained. The court relied heavily on the fact that the injury occurred in Ohio, and was thus subject to Ohio law.

✕ THOMAS v. WASHINGTON GAS LIGHT CO.

Supreme Court of the United States, 1980.
448 U.S. 261, 100 S.Ct. 2647, 65 L.Ed.2d 757.

MR. JUSTICE STEVENS announced the judgment of the Court and delivered an opinion in which MR. JUSTICE BRENNAN, MR. JUSTICE STEWART, and MR. JUSTICE BLACKMUN join. . . .

Petitioner is a resident of the District of Columbia and was hired by respondent in the District of Columbia. During the year that he was employed by respondent, he worked primarily in the District but also worked in Virginia and Maryland. He sustained a back injury while at work in Arlington, Va., on January 22, 1971. Two weeks later he entered into an "Industrial Commission of Virginia Memorandum of Agreement as to Payment of Compensation" providing for benefits of $62 per week. . . .

In 1974, petitioner notified the Department of Labor of his intention to seek compensation under the District of Columbia Act. Respondent opposed the claim primarily on the ground that since, as a matter of Virginia law, the Virginia award excluded any other recovery "at common law or otherwise" on account of the injury in Virginia, the District of Columbia's obligation to give that award full faith and credit precluded a second, supplemental award in the District.

[A second award granted the petitioner in administrative proceedings in the District of Columbia was reversed by the United States Court of Appeals. This judgment, however, was reversed by the Supreme Court.]

I

Respondent contends that the District of Columbia was without power to award petitioner additional compensation because of the Full Faith and Credit Clause of the Constitution or, more precisely, because of the federal statute implementing that Clause. An analysis of this contention must begin with two decisions from the 1940's that are almost directly on point: Magnolia Petroleum Co. v. Hunt and Industrial Commission of Wisconsin v. McCartin.

[Justice Stevens here reviewed the Magnolia and McCartin decisions]

[In its *McCartin*] opinion, the Court . . . stated that "[o]nly some unmistakable language by a state legislature or judiciary would warrant our accepting . . . a construction" that a workmen's compensation statute "is designed to preclude any recovery by proceedings brought in another state." Id., at 627–628. . . .

The Virginia Workmen's Compensation Act . . . contains no "unmistakable language" directed at precluding a supplemental compensation award in another State . . .. Consequently, *McCartin* by its terms, rather than the earlier *Magnolia* decision, is controlling as between the two precedents. . . .

II

We cannot fail to observe that, in the Court's haste to retreat from *Magnolia*, it fashioned a rule that clashes with normally accepted full faith and credit principles. It has long been the law that "the judgment of a state court should have the same credit, validity, and effect, in every other court in the United States, which it had in the state where it was pronounced." Hampton v. McConnel, 3 Wheat. 234, 235 (Marshall, C.J.). . . . .

The *McCartin* rule, however, focusing as it does on the extraterritorial intent of the rendering State, is fundamentally different. It authorizes a State, by drafting or construing its legislation in "unmistakable language," directly to determine the extraterritorial effect of its workmen's compensation awards. . . .

[This] rule represents an unwarranted delegation to the States of this Court's responsibility for the final arbitration of full faith and credit questions.[15] . . . To vest the power of determining the extraterritorial effect of a State's own laws and judgments in the State itself risks the very kind of parochial entrenchment on the interests of other States that it was the purpose of the Full Faith and Credit Clause and other provisions of Art. IV of the Constitution to prevent. . . .

Thus, a re-examination of *McCartin's* unmistakable language test reinforces our tentative conclusion that it does not provide an acceptable basis on which to distinguish *Magnolia*. But if we reject that test, we must decide whether to overrule either *Magnolia* or *McCartin*. . . .

III

. . . It is . . . appropriate to begin the inquiry by considering whether a rule that permits, or a rule that forecloses, successive workmen's compensation awards is more consistent with settled practice. The answer to this question is pellucidly clear.

It should first be noted that *Magnolia*, by only the slimmest majority, . . . effected a dramatic change in the law that had previously prevailed throughout the United States. . . . Of greater importance is the fact that as a practical matter the "unmistakable language" rule of construction announced in *McCartin* left only the narrowest area in which *Magnolia* could have any further precedential value. For the exclusivity language in the Illinois Act construed in *McCartin* was typical of most state workmen's compensation laws. Consequently, it was immediately recognized that *Magnolia* no longer had any significant practical impact. Moreover, since a state legislature seldom focuses on the extraterritorial effect of its enactments,[21] and since a state court has even less occasion to consider whether an award under its State's law is intended to preclude a sup-

---

15. See . . . Reese and Johnson. The Scope of Full Faith and Credit to Judgment, 49 Colum.L.Rev. 153, 161–162 (1949) (hereinafter Reese and Johnson):

"Full faith and credit is a national policy, not a state policy. Its purpose is not merely to demand respect from one state for another, but rather to give us the benefits of a unified nation by altering the status of otherwise 'independent, sovereign states.' Hence it is for federal law, not state law, to prescribe the measure of credit which one state shall give to another's judgment. In this regard, it is interesting to note that in dealing with full faith and credit to statutes the Supreme Court in recent years has accorded no weight to language which purported to give a particular statute extraterritorial effect. There is every reason why a similar attitude should be taken with respect to judgments."

. . .

21. Apparently only Nevada's workmen's compensation act contains the unmistakable language required under the *McCartin* rule. Nev.Rev.Stat. § 616.525 (1979) provides in part:

". . . [I]f an employee who has been hired or is regularly employed in this state receives personal injury by accident arising out of and in the course of such employment outside this state, and he . . . accepts any compensation or benefits under the provisions of this chapter, the acceptance of such compensation shall constitute a waiver by such employee . . . of all rights and remedies against the employer at common law *or given under the laws of any other state*, and shall further constitute a full and complete release of such employer from any and all liability arising from such injury . . . ." (Emphasis added.) . . .

plemental award under another State's workmen's compensation act, the probability that any State would thereafter announce a new rule against supplemental awards in other States was extremely remote. As a matter of fact, subsequent cases in the state courts have overwhelmingly followed *McCartin* and permitted successive state workmen's compensation awards. . . .

IV

Three different state interests are affected by the potential conflict between Virginia and the District of Columbia. Virginia has a valid interest in placing a limit on the potential liability of companies that transact business within its borders. Both jurisdictions have a valid interest in the welfare of the injured employee—Virginia because the injury occurred within that State, and the District because the injured party was employed and resided there. And finally, Virginia has an interest in having the integrity of its formal determinations of contested issues respected by other sovereigns.

. . .

It is . . . perfectly clear that petitioner could have sought a compensation award in the first instance either in Virginia, the State in which the injury occurred . . . or in the District of Columbia, where petitioner resided, his employer was principally located and the employment relation was formed . . . Thus . . . respondent and its insurer would have had to measure their potential liability exposure by the more generous of the two workmen's compensation schemes in any event. It follows that a State's interest in limiting the potential liability of businesses within the State is not of controlling importance.

It is also manifest that the interest in providing adequate compensation to the injured worker would be fully served by the allowance of successive awards. In this respect the two jurisdictions share a common interest and there is no danger of significant conflict.

The ultimate issue, therefore, is whether Virginia's interest in the integrity of its tribunal's determinations forecloses a second proceeding to obtain a supplemental award in the District of Columbia. . . .

We are . . . persuaded that . . . the proposition [set forth in *Magnolia*] that workmen's compensation awards stand on the same footing as court judgments was unwarranted. To be sure . . . the factfindings of state administrative tribunals are entitled to the same res judicata effect in the second State as findings by a court. But the critical differences between a court of general jurisdiction and an administrative agency with limited statutory authority forecloses the conclusion that constitutional rules applicable to court judgments are necessarily applicable to workmen's compensation awards.

A final judgment entered by a court of general jurisdiction normally establishes not only the measure of the plaintiff's rights but also the limits of the defendant's liability. A traditional application of res judicata principles enables either party to claim the benefit of the judgment insofar as it resolved issues the court had jurisdiction to decide. Although a Virginia court is free to recognize the perhaps paramount interests of another State by choosing to apply that State's law in a particular case, the Industrial Commission of Virginia does not have that power. Its jurisdiction is limited to questions arising under the Virginia Workmen's Compensation Act. . . . Typically, a workmen's compensation tribunal may only apply its own State's law. . . . The Virginia Commission could and did establish the full measure of petitioner's rights under Virginia law, but it neither could nor purported to determine his rights under the law of the District of Columbia. Full faith and credit must be given to the determination that the Virginia Commission had the authority to make; but by a parity of reasoning, full faith and credit need not be given to determinations that it had no power to make. Since it was not requested, and had no authority, to pass on petitioner's rights under District of Columbia law, there can be no constitutional objection to a fresh adjudication of those rights. . . .

. . . whether or not the worker has sought an award from the less generous jurisdiction in the first instance, the vindication of that State's interest in placing a ceiling on employers' liability would inevitably impinge upon the substantial interests of the second jurisdiction in the welfare and subsistence of disabled workers—interests that a court of general jurisdiction might consider, but which must be ignored by the Virginia Industrial Commission. . . .

We simply conclude that the substantial interests of the second State in these circumstances should not be overridden by another State through an unnecessarily aggressive application of the Full Faith and Credit Clause, as was implicitly recognized at the time of *McCartin*.

. . . The Full Faith and Credit Clause should not be construed to preclude successive workmen's compensation awards. Accordingly, Magnolia Petroleum Co. v. Hunt should be overruled.

The judgment of the Court of Appeals is reversed.

Mr. Justice White, with whom The Chief Justice and Mr. Justice Powell join, concurring in the judgment.

. . . Although the plurality argues strenuously that the rule of today's decision is limited to awards by state workmen's compensation boards, it seems to me that the underlying rationale goes much further. . . .

The plurality contends that unlike courts of general jurisdiction, workmen's compensation tribunals generally have no power to apply the law of another State and thus cannot determine the rights of the parties thereunder. . . . Yet I see no reason why a judgment should not be entitled to full res judicata effect under the Full Faith and Credit Clause merely because the rendering tribunal was obligated to apply the law of the forum—provided, of course, as was certainly the case here, that the forum could constitutionally apply its law. The plurality's analysis seems to grant state legislatures the power to delimit the scope of a cause of action for federal full faith and credit purposes merely by enacting choice of law rules binding on the State's workmen's compensation tribunals. . . .

As a matter of logic, the plurality's analysis would seemingly apply to many everyday tort actions. I see no difference for full faith and credit purposes between a statute which lays down a forum-favoring choice of law rule and a common-law doctrine stating the same principle. Hence when a court, having power in the abstract to apply the law of another State, determines by application of the forum's choice of law rules to apply the substantive law of the forum, I would think that under the plurality's analysis the judgment would not determine rights arising under the law of some other State. Suppose, for example, that in a wrongful death action the court enters judgment on liability against the defendant, and determines to apply the law of the forum which sets a limit on the recovery allowed. The plurality's analysis would seem to permit the plaintiff to obtain a subsequent judgment in a second forum for damages exceeding the first forum's liability limit. . . .

Perhaps the major purpose of the Full Faith and Credit Clause is to act as a nationally unifying force. . . . The plurality's rationale would substantially undercut that function. When a former judgment is set up as a defense under the Full Faith and Credit Clause, the court would be obliged to balance the various state interests involved. But the State of the second forum is not a neutral party to this balance. There seems to be a substantial danger—not presented by the firmer rule of res judicata—that the court in evaluating a full faith and credit defense would give controlling weight to its own parochial interests in concluding that the judgment of the first forum is not res judicata in the subsequent suit. . . .

[Justice White concluded that he would not overrule either *Magnolia* or *McCartin*, although, in his opinion, "*Magnolia* states the sounder doctrine" and *McCartin* rests "on questionable foundations." *McCartin*, however, had been on the books for over thirty years and had been widely interpreted as substantially limiting *Magnolia*. *McCartin* would clearly permit a second award in the instant case, because the Virginia Workmen's Compensation Act lacked the "unmistakable language" which *McCartin* requires if a workers' compensation award is to preclude a further award in a second state.]

MR. JUSTICE REHNQUIST, with whom MR. JUSTICE MARSHALL joins, dissenting. . . .

. . . .

One might suppose that, having destroyed *McCartin's ratio decidendi*, the plurality would return to the eminently defensible position adopted in *Magnolia*. But such is not the case. . . .

[Justice Rehnquist concluded that a balancing of state interests as done by Justice Stevens in his plurality opinion could not properly be used in determining the respect owed under full faith and credit to sister-state judgments. Such a balancing would, however, be appropriate in determining questions of constitutional control of choice of law.]

NOTES

(1) Pettus v. American Airlines, Inc., 587 F.2d 627 (4th Cir. 1979). Pettus, an employee of American Airlines, sustained injury in Virginia while acting in the scope of his employment. He was awarded benefits under the Virginia Workmen's Compensation Act, but these benefits were terminated following a finding that he had unjustifiably refused to undergo surgery in order to correct his ailment. Pettus then sought and was awarded compensation for the same injury under the District of Columbia Workmen's Compensation Act. On appeal, this latter award was reversed on grounds of full faith and credit and res judicata. The District of Columbia also provides for the termination of benefits if the employee unreasonably refuses to undergo surgery. Should the outcome have been different if the District of Columbia Act had not contained that provision? Would a different result be reached today in the light of the Thomas case?

(2) For a discussion of whether a balancing of state interests is appropriate in the case of full faith and credit to judgments, see Sterk, Full Faith and Credit, More or Less, to Judgments: Doubts About Washington Gas Light Co. v. Thomas, 69 Geo.L.J. 1329 (1981).

SECTION 4. DEFENSES

A. NATURE OF THE ORIGINAL PROCEEDINGS

A prerequisite to recognition of a judgment both at common law and under the full faith and credit clause is that it be rendered in the course of proper judicial proceedings. Such proceedings may be said to comprehend all action taken in the name of a state by a duly authorized representative or representatives in the settlement of an individual controversy. However, it has been held that a judgment obtained by confession under a warrant of attorney is not a "judicial proceeding" within the meaning of full faith and credit. Atlas Credit Corporation v. Ezrine, 25 N.Y.2d 219, 250 N.E.2d 474 (1969). Although a state ordinarily exercises judicial jurisdiction through its courts, it may also do so, if it sees fit, through its legislature and its executive and administrative bodies as well. A decision rendered by an administrative tribunal in the course of its judicial functions is entitled to full faith and credit (Magnolia Petroleum Co. v. Hunt, p. 267, supra; City of New York v. Shapiro, p. 313, note (1), infra, and so too is an arbitration award which is dignified in the state of rendition with the status of a judgment. Wernway v. Pawling, 5 G. & J. 500 (Md.1833). A divorce granted by the Danish king personally to two of his subjects has also been recognized as a judgment in this country. Sorenson v. Sorenson, 122 Misc. 196, 202 N.Y.S. 620 (1924), affirmed 219 App.Div. 344, 220 N.Y.S. 242 (1927). See Note, 53 Minn.L. Rev. 612 (1969).

On the other hand, the mere fact that something is termed a "judgment" by the state of rendition does not entitle it to full faith and credit as such. Thus, for example, the constitutional protection was denied to a commissioner's report appraising the value of property for probate purposes even though the state in which the report was filed denominated it as a judgment and treated it as binding unless appealed from (Taylor v. Barron, 30 N.H. 78 (1855)) and to a bond given in stay of execution which under the law of F–1 had the effect of a judgment confessed if forfeited. Foote v. Newell, 29 Mo. 400 (1860).

The fact that the rendering court committed error, either of fact or of law, is not an adequate reason for a failure to recognize the judgment either under full faith and credit or at common law. See in this regard Milliken v. Meyer, 311 U.S. 457 (1940) (p. 47, supra) where a Colorado judgment was reversed for failure to give full faith and credit to a Wyoming decree despite the unrebutted contention that there was "an irreconcilable contradiction between the findings [of the Wyoming court] and the decree." Likewise an English court has enforced a French judgment even though the latter was based upon a misinterpretation of English law. Godard v. Gray, L.R. 6 Q.B. 139 (1870).

A judgment, of course, is not entitled to recognition or enforcement either under full faith and credit or at common law if the rendering court lacked jurisdiction or if the defendant was not given reasonable notice and a reasonable opportunity to be heard. Schibsby v. Westenholz, L.R. 6 Q.B. 155 (1870) (p. 40, supra); Pennoyer v. Neff, 95 U.S. 714 (1878) (p. 44, supra); cf. Mullane v. Central Hanover Bank & Trust Co., 339 U.S. 306 (1950) (p. 174, supra).

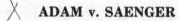

ADAM v. SAENGER

Supreme Court of the United States, 1938.
303 U.S. 59, 58 S.Ct. 454, 82 L.Ed. 649.

MR. JUSTICE STONE delivered the opinion of the Court.

The question for decision is whether the action, in this case, of the Texas state courts, in dismissing a suit founded upon a judgment of the Supreme Court of California, denied to the judgment the faith and credit which the Constitution, article 4, § 1, commands.

Petitioner, as assignee of a California judgment against the Beaumont Export & Import Company, a Texas corporation, brought the present suit in the Texas state district court against respondents, directors of the corporation acting as its trustees in dissolution, and against its stockholders as transferees of corporate assets, to collect the judgment. . . .

It appears that the corporation brought suit in the superior court of California, a court of general jurisdiction, against Montes, petitioner's predecessor in interest, to recover a money judgment for goods sold and delivered. Thereupon Montes, following what is alleged to be the California practice, with leave of the court brought a cross-action against the corporation, by service of a cross-complaint upon the corporation's attorney of record in the pending suit, to recover for the conversion of chattels. Judgment in the cross-action, taken by default, was followed by dismissal of the corporation's suit and is the judgment which is the subject of the present suit. . . .

The trial court sustained a general demurrer to the complaint and gave judgment dismissing the cause, which the Texas Court of Civil Appeals affirmed, 101 S.W.2d 1046. Petition to the Texas Supreme Court for a writ of error was denied for want of jurisdiction. . . .

The Texas Court of Civil Appeals rested its decision on a single ground, want of jurisdiction of the California court over the corporation in the cross-action in which the judgment was rendered. Construing the California statutes and decisions which the complaint set out, it concluded that they did not authorize service of the complaint in the cross-action upon the plaintiff's attorney of record. It held further that in any case as the corporation was not present within the state no jurisdiction could be acquired over it by the substituted service, and the California judgment was consequently without due process and a nullity beyond the protection of the full faith and credit clause. To review these rulings we brought the case here. . . .

Congress has not prescribed the manner in which the legal effect of the judgment and the proceedings on which it is founded in the state where rendered are to be ascertained by the courts of another state. It has left that to the applicable procedure of the courts in which they are drawn in question. Where they are in issue this Court, in the exercise of its appellate jurisdiction to review cases coming to it from state courts, takes judicial notice of the law of the several states to the same extent that such notice is taken by the court from which the appeal is taken. . . .

In the present suit petitioner, in conformity to the state procedure, has set out in his complaint the California statutes and the citations of the decisions of California courts which he contends establish the law of that state that a cross-action in a pending suit may be begun by service of a cross-complaint upon the plaintiff's attorney. The question thus raised upon demurrer for decision by the court is the legal effect in California of the service, and hence of the judgment founded upon it.

Whether the question be regarded as one of fact or more precisely and accurately as a question of law to be determined as are other questions of law . . . it is one arising under the Constitution and a statute of the United States which commands that such faith and credit shall be given by every court to the California proceedings "as they have by law or usage" of that state. And since the existence of the federal right turns on the meaning and effect of the California statute, the decision of the Texas court on that point, whether of law or of fact, is reviewable here. . . .

While this Court re-examines such an issue with deference after its determination by a state court, it cannot, if the laws and Constitution of the United States are to be observed, accept as final the decision of the state tribunal as to matters alleged to give rise to the asserted federal right. This is especially the case where the decision is rested, not on local law or matters of fact of the usual type, which are peculiarly within the cognizance of the local courts, but upon the law of another state, as readily determined here as in a state court.

. . . .

In ruling that the service in the California suit was unauthorized, the Texas Court of Civil Appeals said: "The cross-action was not an ancillary proceeding, but an independent suit in which a final judgment could be rendered without awaiting a decision in the original suit. Farrar v. Steenbergh, 173 Cal. 94, 159 P. 707. It is well settled in this state that a cross-action occupies the attitude of an independent suit and requires service of the cross-action upon the cross-defendant. Harris v. Schlinke, 95 Tex. 88, 65 S.W. 172. This being so, in the absence of a waiver of service, or an appearance by the cross-defendant, personal service on the cross-defendant must be had to confer jurisdiction upon the court to determine the matter and render judgment in the case."

But the question presented by the pleadings is the status of a cross-action under the California statutes, not under those of Texas. We think its status is adequately disclosed by the California statutes and decisions pleaded by petitioner, and is that for which he contends.

[The Court then reviewed the pertinent California statutes.]

There is nothing in the Fourteenth Amendment to prevent a state from adopting a procedure by which a judgment in personam may be rendered in a cross-action against a plaintiff in its courts, upon service of process or of appropriate pleading upon his attorney of record. The plaintiff having, by his voluntary act in demanding justice from the defendant, submitted himself to the jurisdiction of the court, there is nothing arbitrary or unreasonable in treating him as being there for all purposes for which justice to the defendant requires his presence. It is the price which the state may exact as the condition of opening its courts to the plaintiff. . . .

[Reversed.]

NOTE

The full faith and credit clause does not compel F–2 to take judicial notice of F–1 law in determining the effect of a judgment. Treinies v. Sunshine Mining Co., p. 289, infra.

THOMPSON v. WHITMAN

Supreme Court of the United States, 1874.
85 U.S. (18 Wall.) 457, 21 L.Ed. 897.

[The case appears supra, p. 170.]

NOTES

(1) Does the opinion in Thompson v. Whitman proceed on the basis that, since the New Jersey court exceeded the power accorded it by local law, the judgment condemning the sloop was legally ineffective? If so, did the Supreme Court ascertain that the judgment did in fact have no binding effect under New Jersey law? Or is there some other explanation for the result reached? See Restatement, Second, Judgments § 30, quoted p. 237, supra.

(2) Consider the following elements of the F–1 proceedings or judgment to determine whether any of them will preclude F–2 from examining into the jurisdiction of the F–1 court:

(a) Recital of jurisdiction.

(b) Recital of the jurisdictional facts on which the jurisdiction was based.

(c) Recital of a hearing on the jurisdictional facts.

(d) Opportunity to litigate the jurisdictional facts in F–1.

(e) Actual contest and litigation of the jurisdictional facts.

BALDWIN v. IOWA STATE TRAVELING MEN'S ASSOCIATION, 283 U.S. 522 (1931): Suit in the federal District Court for Southern Iowa to enforce a judgment rendered in the federal District Court for Western Missouri. The defendant had made a special appearance in the Missouri proceedings to claim that the court lacked in personam jurisdiction. This claim was rejected and judgment on the merits rendered in the plaintiff's favor. In defense of the enforcement proceeding in Iowa, the defendant contended that the Missouri judgment had been rendered without jurisdiction. The lower federal courts found for the defendant on this issue, but, on certiorari, the Supreme Court reversed. In the course of his opinion, Mr. Justice Roberts said:

The [plaintiff] suggests that Article IV, Section 1 of the Constitution forbade the retrial of the question determined on respondent's motion in the Missouri District Court; but the full faith and credit required by that clause is not involved since neither of the courts concerned was a state court. . . .

The substantial matter for determination is whether the judgment amounts to res judicata on the question of the jurisdiction of the court which rendered it over the person of the respondent. It is of no moment that the appearance was a special one expressly saving any submission to such jurisdiction. The fact would be important upon appeal from a judgment, and would save the question of the propriety of the court's decision on the matter even though after the motion had been overruled the respondent had proceeded, subject to a reserved objection and exception, to a trial on the merits. . . . The special appearance gives point to the fact that the respondent entered the Missouri court for the very purpose of litigating the question of jurisdiction over its person. It had the election not to appear at all. If, in the absence of appearance, the court had proceeded to judgment and the present suit had been brought thereon, respondent could have raised and tried out the issue in the present action, because it would never have had its day in court with respect to jurisdiction. . . . It had also the right to appeal from the decision of the Missouri District Court. . . . It elected to follow neither of those courses, but, after having been defeated upon full hearing in its contention as to jurisdiction, it took no further steps, and the judgment in question resulted.

Public policy dictates that there be an end of litigation; that those who have contested an issue shall be bound by the result of the contest, and that matters once tried shall be considered forever settled as between the parties. We see no reason why this doctrine should not apply in every case where one voluntarily appears, presents his case and is fully heard, and why he should not, in the absence of fraud, be thereafter concluded by the judgment of the tribunal to which he has submitted his cause. . . .

NOTE

A decision of a state court in a proceeding begun by a motion to set aside a judgment for lack of jurisdiction over the parties is res judicata and is entitled to full faith and credit in a federal court where the defeated movant sought an injunction against enforcement of the judgment of the state court. American Surety Co. v. Baldwin, 287 U.S. 156 (1932).

———

In DURFEE V. DUKE, 375 U.S. 106 (1963), there was first a suit to quiet title in Nebraska with both parties before the court. The land involved lay in the Missouri River, and the question of title turned on the question whether the land was in Nebraska or in Missouri. This depended on whether a shift in the river's course was a result of avulsion or accretion. The Nebraska Court decided that the land was in Nebraska, and quieted title in the Nebraska claimant. This was affirmed on appeal by the Nebraska Supreme Court.

Then the Missouri claimant started a suit in Missouri, which was removed to the Federal Court. The United States Court of Appeals for the Eighth Circuit held that the land was in Missouri, and that the Nebraska decree need not be given full faith and credit, since the Nebraska Court did not have jurisdiction over the subject matter.

On certiorari to the Supreme Court, this decision was reversed. The Supreme Court held that the issue had been litigated by the parties in Nebraska, both of whom were before the Nebraska Court, and that the Nebraska decision was res judicata between them. Speaking through Mr. Justice Stewart, the Court said:

> Full faith and credit thus generally requires every State to give to a judgment at least the *res judicata* effect which the judgment would be accorded in the State which rendered it. . . .

> It is argued that an exception to this rule of jurisdictional finality should be made with respect to cases involving real property because of this Court's emphatic expressions of the doctrine that courts of one State are completely without jurisdiction directly to affect title to land in other States. This argument is wide of the mark. Courts of one State are equally without jurisdiction to dissolve the marriages of those domiciled in other States. But the location of land, like the domicile of a party to a divorce action, is a matter "to be resolved by judicial determination." Sherrer v. Sherrer, 334 U.S., at 349. The question remains whether, once the matter has been fully litigated and judicially determined, it can be retried in another State in litigation between the same parties. Upon the reason and authority of the cases we have discussed, it is clear that the answer must be in the negative.

> It is to be emphasized that all that was ultimately determined in the Nebraska litigation was title to the land in question as between the parties to the litigation there. Nothing there decided, and nothing that could be decided in litigation between the same parties or their privies in Missouri, could bind either Missouri or Nebraska with respect to any controversy they might have, now or in the future, as to the location of the boundary between them, or as to their respective sovereignty over the land in question. . . . Either State may at any time protect its interest by initiating independent judicial proceedings here. Cf. Missouri v. Nebraska, 196 U.S. 23.

Mr. Justice Black concurred in a brief opinion, which reads as follows:

"Petitioners and respondent dispute the ownership of a tract of land adjacent to the Missouri River, which is the boundary between Nebraska and Missouri. Resolution of this question turns on whether the land is in Nebraska or Missouri. Neither State, of course, has power to make a determination binding on the other as to which State the land is in. U.S. Const. Art. III, § 2; 28 U.S.C. § 1251(a). However, in a private action brought by these Nebraska petitioners, the Nebraska Supreme Court has held that the disputed tract is in Nebraska. In the present suit, brought by this Missouri respondent in Missouri, the United States Court of Appeals has refused to be bound by the Nebraska court's judgment. I concur in today's reversal of the Court of Appeals' judgment, but with the understanding that we are not deciding the question whether the respondent would continue to be bound by the Nebraska judgment should it later be authoritatively decided, either in an original proceeding between the States in this Court or by a compact between the two States under Art. I, § 10, that the disputed tract is in Missouri."

NOTES

(1) Suppose that a court, having jurisdiction over the parties, goes ahead and decides the case. Does this constitute an adjudication that the court had jurisdiction of the subject matter so that the question cannot be reopened in a later case?. It was so held in Chicot County Drainage District v. Baxter State Bank, 308 U.S. 371 (1940), but not in Kalb v. Feuerstein, 308 U.S. 433 (1940). For cases raising the question in a conflict of laws setting, see Sherrer v. Sherrer, p. 835, infra; Coe v. Coe, p. 839, infra; cf. Davis v. Davis, p. 835, infra.

(2) In Hodge v. Hodge, 621 F.2d 590 (3d Cir. 1980), the Court said in the course of its opinion:

"Reflecting the heightened concern for finality of judgments in post-*Chicot* developments in the law, the Second Restatement of Judgments replaced the First Restatement's simple listing of factors to be considered in weighing finality against validity with a presumption of finality followed by limited, enumerated exceptions. A party is foreclosed from litigating subject matter jurisdiction in a subsequent lawsuit except if the lack of jurisdiction was so clear that its assumption 'was a manifest abuse of authority,' the challenged judgment 'would substantially infringe the authority of another tribunal or [governmental] agency,' or the rendering court was incapable of making an adequately informed assessment of its own jurisdiction."

(3) For a discussion of Durfee v. Duke, see B. Currie, Full Faith and Credit, Chiefly to Judgments: A Role for Congress, 1964 Sup.Ct.Rev. 89, 105.

(4) See Dobbs, The Validity of Void Judgments: The Bootstrap Principle, 53 Va.L.Rev. 1003, 1241 (1967).

(5) See generally Boskey and Braucher, Jurisdiction and Collateral Attack: October Term, 1939, 40 Colum.L.Rev. 1006 (1940); Restatement, Second, Conflict of Laws § 97.

✕ TREINIES v. SUNSHINE MINING CO.

Supreme Court of the United States, 1939.
308 U.S. 66, 60 S.Ct. 44, 84 L.Ed. 85.

[This case involved a dispute between Mrs. Mason and Evelyn Treinies, and her assignor John Pelkes, with respect to the ownership of a block of Sunshine Mining Company stock which had originally formed part of the estate of Pelke's wife. The first step in the complicated proceedings was an action brought by Mrs. Mason against Pelkes and Treinies in an Idaho state court in which she sought to have the stock awarded to her. Before the Idaho court had rendered judgment, Mrs. Mason filed a petition in the probate proceedings in Washington seeking to have Pelkes removed as executor of his wife's estate. Pelkes by cross-petition claimed the stock and despite the protests of Mrs. Mason that it lacked jurisdiction, the Washington court held that Pelkes was the owner. In the meantime, the Idaho litigation continued and, after an appeal to the Supreme Court of Idaho, a final judgment in Mrs. Mason's favor was handed down more than a year after the contrary decision of the Washington court. Pelkes and Treinies thereupon filed suit against Mrs. Mason in the Washington court claiming that the Idaho judgment was void for lack of jurisdiction. At this point, the Sunshine Mining Company took the initiative and brought an interpleader proceeding under the Federal Interpleader Act against all of the contestants in a federal court in Idaho. This court found in favor of Mrs. Mason and its judgment was affirmed by the federal Court of Appeals and by the Supreme Court.]

MR. JUSTICE REED delivered the opinion of the Court. . . .

On the merits petitioner's [Treinies'] objection to the decree below is that it fails to consider and give effect to the Washington judgment . . . awarding the property in question to Pelkes, petitioner's assignor. It is petitioner's claim that the Washington judgment must be considered as effective in this litigation because the question of the jurisdiction of the Washington court was actually litigated before the Supreme Court of Washington and determined favorably to petitioner by the refusal to grant a writ of prohibition against the exercise of jurisdiction by the Washington Superior Court in probate. This failure to give effect to the judgment is said to infringe the full faith and credit clause of the Constitution. The decree of the Court of Appeals is based upon the doctrine of *res judicata*. The applicability of that doctrine arises from a determination of pertinent matters by the Supreme Court of Idaho. . . .

The [federal] Court of Appeals held that the Idaho suit settled that the stock was distributed in 1923 and that therefore the Idaho court had jurisdiction to determine rights under the alleged oral trust. It was further of the view that the Idaho court's invalidation of the Washington judgment and its decree upholding Mrs. Mason's claim to the disputed property were *res judicata* in this action. Petitioner's only ground for objection to the conclusion that the Idaho decree is *res judicata* rests on the argument that by such ruling below the "judgment of the courts of the State of Washington affecting the same subject matter and parties" is ignored.

In the Idaho proceeding the Washington judgment awarding the stock and dividends to Pelkes was pleaded in bar to Mrs. Mason's suit to recover the stock. The effectiveness of the Washington judgment as a bar depended upon whether the court which rendered it had jurisdiction, after an order of distribution, to deal with settlements of distributees with respect to the assets of an estate. On consideration it was determined in the Idaho proceeding that the Washington court did not have this jurisdiction and that the stock of the Mining Company became the property of Mrs. Mason. In declining to give effect to the Washington decree for lack of jurisdiction over the subject matter, the Idaho court determined also the basic question raised by petitioner in the interpleader action. The contention of petitioner in the interpleader proceedings that the Idaho court did not have jurisdiction of the stock controversy because that controversy was in the exclusive jurisdiction of the Washington probate court must fall, because of the Idaho decision that the Washington probate court did not have exclusive jurisdiction. This is true even though the question of the Washington jurisdiction had been actually litigated and decided in favor of Pelkes in the Washington proceedings. If decided erroneously in the Idaho proceedings, the right to review that error was in those (the Idaho) proceedings. While petitioner sought review from the decree of the Supreme Court of Idaho by petition for certiorari to this Court, which was denied, no review was sought from the final decree of the Idaho District Court of August 18, 1936, on new findings of fact and conclusions of law on remittitur from the Supreme Court of Idaho.[1]

The [federal] Court of Appeals correctly determined that the issue of jurisdiction *vel non* of the Washington court could not be relitigat-

---

1. It is unnecessary to consider whether the Idaho determination as to the jurisdiction of the Washington court was properly made. As the procedure by which a state court examines into the question of the jurisdiction of the court of a sister state is a matter within the control of the respective states (Adam v. Saenger, 303 U.S. 59, 63), it need only be added that such procedure is subject to question only on direct appeal.

It was stipulated by all parties to the Idaho cause that the Idaho courts might take judicial notice of the statutes and decisions of Washington. Some constitutional and statutory provisions relating to the jurisdiction of the Superior Court were pleaded and admitted. It has long been the rule in Idaho that its courts do not take judicial notice of the laws of another state and that without allegation and evidence it will be assumed the laws are the same as those of Idaho. [Citing cases.] While none of these cases involved a stipulation, the decision of the Supreme of Idaho (57 Idaho 10) declares the law of that jurisdiction. It follows from the Idaho court's refusal to look into the statutes of Washington that the jurisdiction of the Washington court was presumed to the governed by Idaho law. Under proper proof, the Idaho court would have been compelled to examine the jurisdiction of the Washington court under Washington law.

ed in this interpleader. As the Idaho District Court was a court of general jurisdiction, its conclusions are unassailable collaterally except for fraud or lack of jurisdiction. The holding by the Idaho court of no jurisdiction in Washington necessarily determined the question raised here as to the Idaho jurisdiction against Miss Treinies' contention. She is bound by that judgment.

The power of the Idaho court to examine into the jurisdiction of the Washington court is beyond question.[2] Even where the decision against the validity of the original judgment is erroneous, it is a valid exercise of judicial power by the second court.[3]

One trial of an issue is enough.[4] "The principles of *res judicata* apply to questions of jurisdiction as well as to other issues,"[5] as well to jurisdiction of the subject matter as of the parties.[6]

Decree affirmed.

NOTES

(1) RESTATEMENT, SECOND, CONFLICT OF LAWS:*

§ 114. Inconsistent Judgments

A judgment rendered in a State of the United States will not be recognized or enforced in sister States if an inconsistent, but valid, judgment is subsequently rendered in another action between the parties and if the earlier judgment is superseded by the later judgment under the local law of the State where the later judgment was rendered.

(2) It has been suggested that the Treinies rule with respect to inconsistent judgments should not be applied in situations where it is not possible to obtain review by the Supreme Court of the second inconsistent judgment. Ginsburg, Judgments in Search of Full Faith and Credit: The Last-in-Time Rule for Conflicting Judgments, 82 Harv.L.Rev. 798 (1969). This would be true where the second judgment is that of a foreign country or where the Supreme Court denies certiorari.

(3) For a case applying the Treinies rule to inconsistent judgments of foreign countries, see Ambatiales v. Foundation Co., 203 Misc. 470, 116 N.Y.S.2d 641 (1952).

(4) Colby v. Colby, 78 Nev. 150, 369 P.2d 1019 (1962), cert. denied 371 U.S. 888 (1962). W obtained an ex parte divorce in Nevada after H had been served with process in Washington, D.C. but did not appear. Thereafter, H

2. Old Wayne Life Ass'n v. McDonough, 204 U.S. 8, 15; Thompson v. Whitman, 18 Wall. 457, 468; Adam v. Saenger, 303 U.S. 59, 62.

3. Chicago Life Ins. Co. v. Cherry, 244 U.S. 25, 30; Stoll v. Gottlieb, 305 U.S. 165, 172; Roche v. McDonald, 275 U.S. 449, 454.

4. Baldwin v. Traveling Men's Ass'n, 283 U.S. 522, 525.

5. American Surety Co. v. Baldwin, 287 U.S. 156, 166.

6. Stoll v. Gottlieb, supra, Note 3, 172.

No decision or statute relative to the reexamination of the decree or judgment of an Idaho court on a contested issue of jurisdiction has been found or called to our attention. It is concluded that the rule here expressed states too the law of Idaho.

* Quoted with the permission of the copyright owner, The American Law Institute.

was awarded a separation in Maryland. W appeared in this action and contended that the relief sought could not be granted because of the Nevada divorce. The Maryland court found, however, that W had not been domiciled in Nevada and that therefore the Nevada divorce was not entitled to full faith and credit. H then brought an action in Nevada to have the divorce set aside. Held for W. The divorce decree is still valid in Nevada. A divorce that is not entitled to full faith and credit may nevertheless have satisfied due process requirements and be valid in the state of rendition. Can this result be reconciled with Treinies v. Sunshine Mining Co., p. 289, supra and Sutton v. Leib, p. 860, infra? See Rodgers and Rodgers, The Disparity between Due Process and Full Faith and Credit: The Problem of the Somewhere Wife, 67 Colum.L.Rev. 1363 (1967), Note, 55 Tex.L.Rev. 127 (1976).

RESTATEMENT, SECOND, CONFLICT OF LAWS: *

§ 112. Vacated Judgment

.   .   .

b.   Proceedings on appeal. Whether proceedings on appeal or error vacate a judgment is determined by the local law of the state of rendition. At common law, a pending writ of error does not vacate a judgment, while an appeal in equity vacates a decree. In the United States, the rule has frequently been changed by statute. If appellate proceedings do not, by the local law of the state of rendition, vacate the judgment, suit to enforce the judgment may be brought in another state. Usually, however, the courts of the state in which enforcement of the judgment is sought will either stay their judgment, or stay execution thereof, pending the determination of the appeal (see § 107, Comment *e*). As between States of the United States, full faith and credit does not prevent in such circumstances either stay of the judgment, or stay of execution, pending determination of the appeal.

NOTES

(1) For cases applying this rule, see Maner v. Maner, 412 F.2d 449 (5th Cir. 1969); Nowell v. Nowell, 157 Conn. 470, 254 A.2d 889 (1969); Fehr v. McHugh, 413 A.2d 1285 (D.C.App.1980).

(2) See generally on the question of the finality of judgments, Restatement, Second, Conflict of Laws § 107.

(3) With respect to the stay of an action in deference to another pending action, see Developments in the Law—Res Judicata, 65 Harv.L.Rev. 818–836 (1952).

---

* Quoted with the permission of the copyright owner, The American Law Institute.

LYNDE v. LYNDE

Supreme Court of the United States, 1901.
181 U.S. 183, 21 S.Ct. 555, 45 L.Ed. 810.

[The case appears supra, p. 231.]

BARBER v. BARBER

Supreme Court of the United States, 1944.
323 U.S. 77, 65 S.Ct. 137, 89 L.Ed. 82.

MR. CHIEF JUSTICE STONE delivered the opinion of the Court.

The question for decision is whether the Supreme Court of Tennessee, in a suit brought upon a North Carolina judgment for arrears of alimony, rightly denied full faith and credit to the judgment, on the ground that it lacks finality because, by the law of North Carolina, it is subject to modification or recall by the court which entered it.

In 1920 petitioner secured in the Superior Court of North Carolina for Buncombe County, a court of general jurisdiction, a judgment of separation from respondent, her husband. The judgment directed payment to petitioner of $200 per month alimony, later reduced to $160 per month. In 1932 respondent stopped paying the prescribed alimony. In 1940, on petitioner's motion in the separation suit for a judgment for the amount of the alimony accrued and unpaid under the earlier order, the Superior Court of North Carolina gave judgment in her favor. It adjudged that respondent was indebted to petitioner in the sum of $19,707.20, under its former order, that petitioner have and recover of respondent that amount, and "that execution issue therefor".

Petitioner then brought the present suit in the Tennessee Chancery Court to recover on the judgment thus obtained. Respondent, by his answer, put in issue the finality, under North Carolina law, of the judgment sued upon. . . .

The Tennessee Chancery Court held the judgment sued upon to be entitled to full faith and credit, and gave judgment for petitioner accordingly. The Supreme Court of Tennessee reversed on the ground that the judgment was without the finality entitling it to credit under the full faith and credit clause of the Constitution, Art. IV, § 1. 180 Tenn. 353, 175 S.W.2d 324. We granted certiorari because of an asserted conflict with Sistare v. Sistare, 218 U.S. 1, . . .

In Sistare v. Sistare, supra, this Court considered whether a decree for future alimony, brought to a sister state, was entitled to full faith and credit as to installments which had accrued, but which had not been reduced to a further judgment. The Court held that a decree for future alimony is, under the Constitution and the statute, entitled to credit as to past due installments, if the right to them is "absolute and vested," even though the decree might be modified prospectively by future orders of the court. See also Barber v. Barber, 21 How. 582. The Sistare case also decided that such a decree was not final, and therefore not entitled to credit, if the past due installments were subject retroactively to modification or recall by the court after their accrual. . . .

The Sistare case considered the applicability of the full faith and credit clause, only as to decrees for future alimony some of the installments of which had accrued. The present suit was not brought upon a decree of that nature, but upon a money judgment for alimony already due and owing to the petitioner, as to which execution was ordered to issue. The Supreme Court of Tennessee applied to this money judgment the distinction taken in the Sistare case as to decrees for future alimony. It concluded that by the law of North Carolina the judgment for the specific amount of alimony already accrued, was subject to modification by the court which awarded it, that it was not a final judgment under the rule of the Sistare case, and therefore was not entitled to full faith and credit.

As we are of opinion that the Tennessee Supreme Court erroneously construed the law of North Carolina as to the finality of the judgment sued upon here, it is unnecessary to consider whether the rule of the Sistare case as to decrees for future alimony is also applicable to judgments subsequently entered for arrears of alimony. . . . For the same reason, it is unnecessary to consider whether a decree or judgment for alimony already accrued, which is subject to modification or recall in the forum which granted it, but is not yet so modified, is entitled to full faith and credit until such time as it is modified. . . .

We assume for present purposes that petitioner's judgment for accrued alimony is not entitled to full faith and credit, if by the law of North Carolina it is subject to modification. . . .

. . . Our examination of the North Carolina law on this subject must be in the light of the admonition of Sistare v. Sistare, supra, 218 U.S. 22, that "every reasonable implication must be resorted to against the existence of" a power to modify or revoke installments of alimony already accrued "in the absence of clear language manifesting an intention to confer it." The admonition is none the less to be heeded when the debt has been reduced to a judgment upon which execution has been directed to issue.

[The Court then considered the relevant North Carolina statutes and decisions.]

Upon full consideration of the law of North Carolina we conclude that respondent has not overcome the prima facie validity and finality of the judgment sued upon. We cannot say that the statutory authority to modify or recall an order providing for future allowances

of installments of alimony extends to a judgment for overdue installments or that such a judgment is not entitled to full faith and credit.

Reversed.

MR. JUSTICE JACKSON, concurring.

I concur in the result, but I think that the judgment of the North
Carolina court was entitled to faith and credit in Tennessee even if it
was not a final one. On this assumption I do not find it necessary or
relevant to examine North Carolina law as to whether its judgment
might under some hypothetical circumstances be modified.

Neither the full faith and credit clause of the Constitution nor the
Act of Congress implementing it says anything about final judgments
or, for that matter, about any judgments. Both require that full
faith and credit be given to "judicial proceedings" without limitation
as to finality. Upon recognition of the broad meaning of that term
much may some day depend.

Whatever else this North Carolina document might be, no one denies that it is a step in a judicial proceeding, instituted validly under
the strictest standards of due process. On its face it is final and by
its terms it awards a money judgment in a liquidated amount, presently collectible, and provides "that execution issue therefor." Tennessee should have rendered substantially the same judgment that it
received from the courts of North Carolina. If later a decree is made
in North Carolina which modifies or amends its judgment, that modification or amendment will also be entitled to faith and credit in Tennessee.

Of course a judgment is entitled to faith and credit for just what it
is, and no more. But its own terms constitute a determination by the
rendering court as to what it is, and an enforcing court may not
search the laws of the state to see whether the judgment terms are
erroneous. Of course, if a judgment by its terms reserves power to
modify or states conditions, a judgment entered upon it could appropriately make like reservations or conditions. No such appear in this
judgment unless they are to be annexed to it by a study of the law of
North Carolina. Any application for such relief should be addressed
to the North Carolina court and not to the Tennessee court nor to this
one. The purpose of the full faith and credit clause is to lengthen the
arm of the state court and to eliminate state lines as a shelter from
judicial proceedings. . . .

NOTE

Is not Mr. Justice Jackson correct? How can it be consistent with the
mandate of full faith and credit for F-2 to refuse to enforce an F-1 decree
merely because it remains subject to modification at the hands of the F-1
court? Such action certainly does not accord the judgment the same effect
that it enjoys by "law or usage" in F-1. But, on the other hand, if the F-2
court were to enforce the F-1 decree without question, might it not thereby

accord the judgment creditor a greater recovery than he would have obtained in F–1? Such a result could be thought inconsistent with full faith and credit (see Abbot, Res Judicata as a Federal Question, 25 Harv.L.Rev. 443 (1912)) and, in any event, might raise due process objections. Cf. Cantwell v. Connecticut, 310 U.S. 296 (1940) and American Federation of Labor v. Swing, 312 U.S. 321 (1941).

WORTHLEY v. WORTHLEY

Supreme Court of California, 1955.
44 Cal.2d 465, 283 P.2d 19.

[Suit by a wife against her husband to recover accrued arrearages under a New Jersey decree for separate maintenance and to have the New Jersey decree "established as a California decree" and the husband ordered to pay her $9 a week (the amount specified in the New Jersey decree) until further order of the court. The trial court entered judgment for the husband and the wife appealed to the Supreme Court of California.]

TRAYNOR, JUSTICE. . . . Since the New Jersey decree is both prospectively and retroactively modifiable, N.J.S.A. § 2A:34–23, we are not constitutionally bound to enforce defendant's obligations under it. Sistare v. Sistare, 218 U.S. 1 . . . Nor are we bound *not* to enforce them. People of State of New York ex rel. Halvey v. Halvey, 330 U.S. 610, 615 . . . . The United States Supreme Court has held, however, that if such obligations are enforced in this state, at least as to accrued arrearages, due process requires that the defendant be afforded an opportunity to litigate the question of modification. Griffin v. Griffin, 327 U.S. 220, 233–234 . . . . It has also clearly indicated that as to either prospective or retroactive enforcement of such obligations, this state "has at least as much leeway to disregard the judgment, to qualify it, or to depart from it as does the State where it was rendered." People of State of New York ex rel. Halvey v. Halvey, supra . . . . .

In Biewend v. Biewend, 17 Cal.2d 108, 113–114, 109 P.2d 701, 704 . . . it was held that the California courts will recognize and give prospective enforcement to a foreign alimony decree, even though it is subject to modification under the law of the state where it was originally rendered, by establishing it "as the decree of the California court with the same force and effect as if it had been entered in this state, including punishment for contempt if the defendant fails to comply. . . ." Similar holdings in reference to both alimony and support decrees have repeatedly been made by the District Courts of Appeal . . . and by the courts of other states . . . . .

Although the question of retroactive modification has been seldom litigated . . . . there is no valid reason, in a case in which both parties are before the court, why the California courts should refuse to hear a plaintiff's prayer for enforcement of a modifiable sister-state decree and the defendant's plea for modification of his obligations thereunder. If the accrued installments are modified retroactively, the judgment for a liquidated sum entered after such modification will be final and thus will be entitled to full faith and credit in all other states. . . . If the installments are modified prospectively, the issues thus determined will be res judicata so long as the circumstances of the parties remain unchanged. . . . Moreover, the interests of neither party would be served by requiring the plaintiff to return to the state of rendition and reduce her claim for accrued installments to a money judgment. . . . Repeated suits for arrearages would have to be brought in New Jersey as installments accrued, to be followed by repeated actions in California to enforce the New Jersey judgments for accrued installments, with the net result that the costs of litigation and the dilatoriness of the recovery would substantially reduce the value of the support to which plaintiff is entitled.

Furthermore, there is no merit to the contention that as a matter of practical convenience the issue of modification should be tried in the courts of the state where the support decree was originally rendered [proof of changed circumstances can be presented to the California court]. Moreover, in most states the problem of modification is dealt with according to general equitable principles, and the law of the state in which the support obligation originated can be judicially noticed, Code Civ.Proc. § 1875, and applied by the California courts.

Accordingly, we hold that foreign-created alimony and support obligations are enforceable in this state. In an action to enforce a modifiable support obligation, either party may tender and litigate any plea for modification that could be presented to the courts of the state where the alimony or support decree was originally rendered.

The judgment is reversed.

. . .

SPENCE, JUSTICE, I dissent. . . . the New Jersey judgment which plaintiff seeks to enforce in California is modifiable retroactively, as well as prospectively, under the law of New Jersey; but the majority opinion nevertheless requires its enforcement and modification by the courts of this state. This will result in confusion worse confounded, as the courts of each of several states, including New Jersey, might be called upon to modify the same decree, both retroactively as well as prospectively. In my opinion, the New Jersey decree, until made final by the courts of that state, is based upon shifting sands, which furnish no firm foundation upon which to predicate a judgment in any other jurisdiction. . . .

_____

LIGHT v. LIGHT, 12 Ill.2d 502, 147 N.E.2d 35 (1957): Proceeding in Illinois to register, under the Uniform Enforcement of Foreign Judgments Act, a divorce decree of Missouri, which ordered the defendant husband to pay alimony in gross and thereafter to pay $100 and $50 a month for alimony and for support of the child. The trial court gave a decree for past due installments only, and "the plaintiff contends [on appeal] . . . that the decree is entitled to full faith and credit as to future installments." Held, the decree is entitled to the protection the plaintiff seeks.

SCHAEFER, J. . . . Policy considerations argue strongly that such decrees are entitled to full faith and credit. Unless they receive interstate recognition, the insulated judicial systems of the several States may become sanctuaries within which obligations that have been fully and fairly adjudicated in another jurisdiction may be escaped. These policy considerations have found expression in the decisions of many State courts which, on the grounds of comity, have given full effect, . . . Strong as are the considerations of policy, the argument that derives from the language of the constitution itself is at least as strong. . . . We hold, therefore, that the decree is entitled to full faith and credit as to future payments. . . .

NOTES

(1) The majority of the recent cases follow the approach taken in Worthley v. Worthley with respect to foreign alimony decrees that are subject to modification in the state of rendition. That is to say, the courts will enforce such decrees as to past-due installments after having considered whether the decree should be modified in the light of changed circumstances. They will also, again after having considered the question of modification, order the defendant to pay future installments as they come due. See, e.g., Keating v. Keating, 542 F.2d 910 (4th Cir. 1976); Barrell v. Barrell, 288 Md. 19, 415 A.2d 579 (Md.1980). Contra: Dorey v. Dorey, 609 F.2d 1128 (5th Cir. 1980). Such decrees will be enforced with the same equitable sanctions as are available for enforcement of local decrees. See, e.g., Baker v. Baker, 243 Ga. 689, 256 S.E.2d 370 (1979).

(2) See, generally, Foster & Freed, Modification, Recognition and Enforcement of Foreign Alimony Orders, 11 Cal.W.L.Rev. 280 (1975); Scoles, Enforcement of Foreign "Non-Final" Alimony and Support Orders, 53 Colum.L.Rev. 817 (1953).

(3) The Supreme Court of the United States has not yet passed upon the relationship of the full faith and credit clause to installments of alimony that have not yet accrued in the extremely rare situation where these installments are not subject to modification in the state of rendition.

(4) The special problems of recognition and enforcement raised by sister-state custody decrees are considered at pp. 867–881 infra.

X LEVIN v. GLADSTEIN

Supreme Court of North Carolina, 1906.
*142 N.C. 482, 55 S.E. 371, 32 L.R.A.,N.S., 905, 115 Am.St.Rep. 747.

This was a suit upon a judgment obtained in the Superior Court of Baltimore City, Maryland. . . . At the beginning of the trial . . . counsel for defendant stated he admitted the regularity of the judgment sued upon and withdrew all pleas and defenses to said action, save . . . that the judgment . . . was procured by a fraud practiced by plaintiffs upon the defendant . . . . [Defendant] testified . . . that he knew Philip Levin and Simon Levin, and had bought goods of them. That some time prior to his going to Baltimore he bought a bill of goods of plaintiffs, but had shipped some of them back to Baltimore because they were not up to sample. That plaintiffs had refused to take the goods out of the depot in Baltimore. That upon his visit to Baltimore summons was served upon him in the action brought there by the plaintiffs; but after said summons was served upon him, and before the return day, he saw one of the plaintiffs [who] agreed . . . to withdraw said suit and return the goods to him at Durham, provided he would, upon their receipt pay the plaintiffs a sum of money which they agreed upon, to-wit, $133, and freight and storage not to exceed $3. That relying upon his agreement he returned to Durham and made no defense to the action. Plaintiffs never returned the goods to him at Durham. That the first time he knew of the judgment was when called upon by attorneys for plaintiffs to pay said judgment.

There was testimony contradicting defendant. After hearing testimony from both parties, the Court submitted the following issue to the jury: "Was the alleged judgment . . . obtained by the fraud of plaintiffs?" To which the jury responded "Yes." Judgment was thereupon rendered that the plaintiffs take nothing by their action, and that the defendant go without day, etc. Plaintiffs excepted and appealed.

CONNOR, J., after stating the case: . . . The plaintiffs, relying upon the provision of the Constitution of the United States, Article IV, section 1, that "Full faith and credit shall be given in each State to the public acts, records and judicial proceedings of every other State," earnestly contend that the defense is not open to the courts of this State. That the remedy for the fraud in procuring the judgment, if any, must be sought in the courts of Maryland. . . .

In Allison v. Chapman, 19 Fed.Rep. 488, Nixon, J. says: ". . . the allegation, *in a plea*, that a judgment was procured through fraud, is not a good common law defense to a suit brought upon it in the same or a sister State." This conclusion is fully supported by all of the authorities. . . . Notwithstanding the well-settled rule that the judgment when sued upon in another State cannot be impeached or attacked for fraud by any plea known to the common law system of pleading, it is equally clear that upon sufficient allegation and proof defendant is entitled, in a court of equity, to enjoin the plaintiff from suing upon or enforcing his judgment. . . .

The underlying principle is that the judgment of a sister State will be given the *same faith* and credit which is given domestic judgments. It is contended, however, and with force, that the "faith and credit" to be given such judgment is measured by the law of the State in which it is rendered. We find upon examining the decisions made by the Maryland Court that in that State a court of equity will enjoin the enforcement of a judgment obtained by fraud. . . . It is thus apparent that the judgment obtained by the fraud of plaintiffs . . . would be open to attack in the courts of Maryland . . . and in giving the defendant relief we are giving the judgment the same "faith and credit" which it has in that State. . . .

The plaintiff says, however this may be, the defendant can have this relief only in Maryland; that he must go into that State and attack the judgment or enjoin the plaintiff. Mr. Freeman says: "If the judgment was procured under circumstances requiring its enforcement to be enjoined in equity, the question will arise whether these circumstances may be interposed as a defense to an action on the judgment in another State. Notwithstanding expressions to the contrary, we apprehend that in bringing an action in another State, the judgment creditor must submit to the law of the forum, and must meet the charge of fraud in its procurement, when presented in any form in which fraud might be urged in an action on a domestic judgment. If, in the State in which the action is pending, fraud can be pleaded to an action on a domestic judgment, it is equally available and equally efficient in actions on judgments of other States. . . ."

[Affirmed.]

NOTES

(1) Accord: Leflar, American Conflicts Law 161–162 (3d ed. 1977); Scoles and Hay, Conflict of Laws 941–942 (1982).

(2) See Pryles, Impeachment of Sister State Judgment for Fraud, 25 Sw. L.J. 697 (1971).

(3) The various situations wherein local law affords equitable relief against enforcement of a judgment on the ground of fraud in its procurement are discussed in Restatement Second, Judgments § 70.

B.   NATURE OF ORIGINAL CAUSE OF ACTION

HUNTINGTON v. ATTRILL

Supreme Court of the United States, 1892.
146 U.S. 657, 13 S.Ct. 224, 36 L.Ed. 1123.

MR. JUSTICE GRAY delivered the opinion of the court.

This was a bill in equity, filed March 21, 1888, in the Circuit Court of Baltimore City, by Collis P. Huntington, a resident of New York, against the Equitable Gas Light Company of Baltimore, a corporation of Maryland, and against Henry Y. Attrill, his wife and three daughters, all residents of Canada, to set aside a transfer of stock in that company, made by him for their benefit and in fraud of his creditors, and to charge that stock with the payment of a judgment recovered by the plaintiff against him in the State of New York, upon his liability as a director in a New York corporation, under the statute of New York of 1875, c. 611, . . .

The bill alleged that on June 15, 1886, the plaintiff recovered, in the Supreme Court of the State of New York, in an action brought by him against Attrill on March 21, 1883, a judgment for the sum of $100,240, which had not been paid, secured or satisfied; and that the cause of action on which that judgment was recovered was as follows: On February 29, 1880, the Rockaway Beach Improvement Company, Limited, of which Attrill was an incorporator and a director, became a corporation under the law of New York, with a capital stock of $700,000. On June 15, 1880, the plaintiff lent that company the sum of $100,000 to be repaid on demand. On February 26, 1880, Attrill was elected one of the directors of the Company, and accepted the office, and continued to act as a director until after January 29, 1881. On June 30, 1880, Attrill, as a director of the company, signed and made oath to, and caused to be recorded, as required by the law of New York, a certificate, which he knew to be false, stating that the whole of the capital stock of the corporation had been paid in, whereas in truth no part had been paid in; and by making such false certificate became liable, by the law of New York, for all the debts of the company contracted before January 29, 1881, including its debt to the plaintiff. On March 8, 1882, by proceedings in a court of New York, the corporation was declared to be insolvent and to have been so since July, 1880, and was dissolved. A duly exemplified copy of the record of that judgment was annexed to and made part of the bill.

. . .

[The bill further alleged that Attrill was insolvent, and that he had transferred the shares of stock to himself as trustee for his wife and daughters in order to hinder, delay, and defraud the plaintiff and other creditors.]

One of the daughters demurred to the bill, because it showed that the plaintiff's claim was for the recovery of a penalty against Attrill arising under a statute of the State of New York . . . .

The Circuit Court of Baltimore City overruled the demurrer. On appeal to the Court of Appeals of the State of Maryland, the order was reversed, and the bill dismissed. 70 Maryland 191. . . .

The question whether due faith and credit were thereby denied to the judgment rendered in another State is a Federal question, of which this court has jurisdiction on this writ of error. . . .

In order to determine this question, it will be necessary, in the first place, to consider the true scope and meaning of the fundamental maxim of international law, stated by Chief Justice Marshall in the fewest possible words: "The courts of no country execute the penal laws of another." The Antelope, 10 Wheat. 66, 123. In interpreting this maxim, there is danger of being misled by the different shades of meaning allowed to the word "penal" in our language.

In the municipal law of England and America, the words "penal" and "penalty" have been used in various senses. Strictly and primarily, they denote punishment, whether corporal or pecuniary, imposed and enforced by the State, for a crime or offence against its laws. . . . But they are also commonly used as including any extraordinary liability to which the law subjects a wrongdoer in favor of the person wronged, not limited to the damages suffered. They are so elastic in meaning as even to be familiarly applied to cases of private contracts, wholly independent of statutes, as when we speak of the "penal sum" or "penalty" of a bond. . . .

The test whether a law is penal, in the strict and primary sense, is whether the wrong sought to be redressed is a wrong to the public, or a wrong to the individual. . . .

The question whether a statute of one State, which in some aspects may be called penal, is a penal law in the international sense, so that it cannot be enforced in the courts of another State, depends upon the question whether its purpose is to punish an offence against the public justice of the State, or to afford a private remedy to a person injured by the wrongful act. . . .

The provision of the statute of New York, now in question, making the officers of a corporation, who sign and record a false certificate of the amount of its capital stock, liable for all its debts, is in no sense a criminal or quasi criminal law. The statute, while it enables persons complying with its provisions to do business as a corporation, without being subject to the liability of general partners, takes pains to secure and maintain a proper corporate fund for the payment of the corporate debts. With this aim, it makes the stockholders individually liable for the debts of the corporation until the capital stock is paid in and a certificate of the payment made by the officers; and makes the officers liable for any false and material representation in that certificate. The individual liability of the stockholders takes the place of a corporate fund, until that fund has been duly created; and the individual liability of the officers takes the place of the fund, in case their statement that it has been duly created is false. If the officers do not truly state and record the facts which exempt them from liability, they are made liable directly to every creditor of the company, who by reason of their wrongful acts has not the security, for the payment of his debt out of the corporate property, on which he had a right to rely. As the statute imposes a burdensome liability on the officers for their wrongful act, it may well be considered penal, in the sense that it should be strictly construed. But as it gives a civil remedy, at the private suit of the creditor only, and measured by the amount of his debt, it is as to him clearly remedial. To maintain such a suit is not to administer a punishment imposed upon an offender against the State, but simply to enforce a private right secured under its laws to an individual. We can see no just ground, on principle, for holding such a statute to be a penal law, in the sense that it cannot be enforced in a foreign state or country.

The decisions of the Court of Appeals of New York, so far as they have been brought to our notice, fall short of holding that the liability imposed upon the officers of the corporation by such statutes is a punishment or penalty which cannot be enforced in another State.

In Garrison v. Howe, the court held that the statute was so far penal that it must be construed strictly, and therefore the officers could not be charged with a debt of the corporation, which was neither contracted nor existing during a default in making the report required by the statute; . . .

The other cases in that court, cited in the opinion of the Court of Appeals of Maryland in the present case, adjudged only the following points: Within the meaning of a statute of limitations applicable to private actions only, the action against an officer is not "upon a liability created by statute, other than a penalty or forfeiture," which would be barred in six years, but is barred in three years as "an action upon a statute for a penalty or forfeiture where action is given to the party aggrieved," because the provisions in question, said the court, "impose a penalty, or a liability in that nature." Merchants' Bank v. Bliss, 35 N.Y. 412, 417. A count against a person as an officer for not filing a report cannot be joined with one against him as a stockholder for debts contracted before a report is filed, that being "an action on contract." Wiles v. Suydam, 64 N.Y. 173, 176. The action against an officer is an action ex delicto, and therefore does not survive against his personal representatives. Stokes v. Stickney, 96 N.Y. 323.

In a later case than any of these, the court, in affirming the very judgment now sued on, and adjudging the statute of 1875 to be constitutional and valid, said that "while liability within the provision in question is in some sense penal in its character, it may have been intended for the protection of creditors of corporations created pursuant to that statute." Huntington v. Attrill, 118 N.Y. 365, 378. . . .

We do not refer to these decisions as evidence in this case of the law of New York, because in the courts of Maryland that law could only be proved as a fact, and was hardly open to proof on the demurrer, and, if not proved in those courts, could not be taken judicial notice of by this court on this writ of error. . . . Nor, for reasons to be stated presently, could those decisions, in any view, be regarded as concluding the courts of Maryland, or this court, upon the question whether this statute is a penal law in the international sense. But they are entitled to great consideration, because made by a court of high authority, construing the terms of a statute with which it was peculiarly familiar; and it is satisfactory to find no adjudication of that court inconsistent with the view which we take of the liability in question. . . .

The true limits of the international rule are well stated in the decision of the Judicial Committee of the Privy Council of England, upon an appeal from Canada, in an action brought by the present plaintiff against Attrill in the Province of Ontario upon the judgment to enforce which the present suit was brought. . . .[1]

In the Privy Council, Lord Watson, speaking for Lord Chancellor Halsbury and other judges, as well as for himself, delivered an opinion in favor of reversing the judgment below, and entering a decree for the appellant, upon the ground that the action "was not, in the sense of international law, penal, or, in other words, an action on behalf of the government or community of the State of New York for punishment of an offence against their municipal law." . . .

He had already, in an earlier part of the opinion, observed: "Their lordships could not assent to the proposition that, in considering whether the present action was penal in such sense as to oust their jurisdiction, the courts of Ontario were bound to pay absolute deference to any interpretation which might have been put upon the statute of 1875 in the State of New York. They had to construe and apply an international rule. . . . The court appealed to must determine for itself, in the first place, the substance of the right sought to be enforced, and, in the second place, whether its enforcement would, either directly or indirectly, involve the execution of the penal law of another State. Were any other principle to guide its decision, a court might find itself in the position of giving effect in one case, and denying effect in another, to suits of the same character, in consequence of the causes of action having arisen in different countries; or in the predicament of being constrained to give effect to laws which were, in its own judgment, strictly penal."

In this view that the question is not one of local, but of international, law, we fully concur. The test is not by what name the stat-

---

1. [Huntington v. Attrill, [1893] A.C. 150.]

ute is called by the legislature or the courts of the State in which it was passed, but whether it appears to the tribunal which is called upon to enforce it to be, in its essential character and effect, a punishment of an offence against the public, or a grant of a civil right to a private person.

. . . if the original liability has passed into judgment in one State, the courts of another State, when asked to enforce it, are bound by the Constitution and laws of the United States to give full faith and credit to that judgment, and if they do not, their decision, as said at the outset of this opinion, may be reviewed and reversed by this court on writ of error. . . .

If a suit to enforce a judgment rendered in one State . . . is brought in the courts of another State, this court, in order to determine, on writ of error, whether the highest court of the latter State has given full faith and credit to the judgment, must determine for itself whether the original cause of action is penal in the international sense. . . .

The Court of Appeals of Maryland, therefore, in deciding this case against the plaintiff, upon the ground that the judgment was not one which it was bound in any manner to enforce, denied to the judgment the full faith, credit and effect to which it was entitled under the Constitution and laws of the United States.

[Judgment reversed.]

NOTES

(1) In City of Philadelphia v. Austin, 86 N.J. 55, 429 A.2d 568 (1981), the New Jersey Supreme Court held that full faith and credit required enforcement of a Pennsylvania judgment for a fine for failure to file tax returns required by the Philadelphia Wage Tax Ordinance. The Court noted that the United States Supreme Court has never decided whether sister state money judgments on penal claims were entitled to full faith and credit. It reserved the question whether full faith and credit was owed to all sister state money judgments for violations other than tax laws.

(2) The fact that the plaintiff is a sovereign state does not of itself make the action one for a penalty. The action is not penal where it is brought by the state to vindicate its proprietary interests, and a judgment rendered in such an action is entitled to full faith and credit. Connolly v. Bell, 286 App. Div. 220, 141 N.Y.S.2d 753 (1st Dep't 1955), affirmed 309 N.Y. 581, 132 N.E.2d 852 (1956).

(3) For a discussion of the problems involved when the suit is on the original liability created by a foreign statute alleged to be penal, see pp. 384–388, infra.

✕ **FAUNTLEROY v. LUM**

Supreme Court of the United States, 1908.
210 U.S. 230, 28 S.Ct. 641, 52 L.Ed. 1039.

By law the State of Mississippi prohibited certain forms of gambling in futures, and inhibited its courts from giving effect to any contract or dealing made in violation of the prohibitive statute. In addition, it was made criminal to do any of the forbidden acts. With the statutes in force two citizens and residents of Mississippi made contracts in that State which were performed therein, and which were in violation of both the civil and criminal statutes referred to. One of the parties asserting that the other was indebted to him because of the contracts, both parties, in the State of Mississippi, submitted their differences to arbitration, and on an award being made in that State the one in whose favor it was made sued in a state court in Mississippi to recover thereon. In that suit, on the attention of the court being called to the prohibited and criminal nature of the transactions, the plaintiff dismissed the case. Subsequently, in a court of the State of Missouri the citizen of Mississippi, in whose favor the award had been made, brought an action on the award, and succeeded in getting personal service upon the other citizen of Mississippi, the latter being temporarily in the State of Missouri. The action was put at issue. Rejecting evidence offered by the defendant to show the nature of the transactions, and that under the laws of Mississippi the same were illegal and criminal, the Missouri court submitted the cause to a jury, with an instruction to find for the plaintiff if they believed that the award had been made as alleged. A verdict and judgment went in favor of the plaintiff. Thereupon the judgment so obtained was assigned by the plaintiff to his attorney, who sued upon the same in a court of Mississippi, where the facts upon which the transaction depended were set up and the prohibitory statutes of the State were pleaded as a defense. Ultimately the case went to the Supreme Court of the State of Mississippi, where it was decided that the Missouri judgment was not required, under the due faith and credit clause, to be enforced in Mississippi, as it concerned transactions which had taken place exclusively in Mississippi, between residents of that State, which were in violation of laws embodying the public policy of that State, and to give effect to which would be enforcing transactions which the courts of Mississippi had no authority to enforce.*

MR. JUSTICE HOLMES delivered the opinion of the court. . . .

The main argument urged by the defendant to sustain the judgment below is addressed to the jurisdiction of the Mississippi courts.

The laws of Mississippi make dealing in futures a misdemeanor, and provide that contracts of that sort, made without intent to deliver the commodity or to pay the price, "shall not be enforced by any

---

* The statement of the facts is taken
from the dissenting opinion.

court." Annotated Code of 1892, secs. 1120, 1121, 2117. The defendant contends that this language deprives the Mississippi courts of jurisdiction, and that the case is like Anglo-American Provision Co. v. Davis Provision Co. No. 1, 191 U.S. 373. There the New York statutes refused to provide a court into which a foreign corporation could come, except upon causes of action arising within the State, etc., and it was held that the State of New York was under no constitutional obligation to give jurisdiction to its Supreme Court against its will. One question is whether that decision is in point.

No doubt it sometimes may be difficult to decide whether certain words in a statute are directed to jurisdiction or to merits, but the distinction between the two is plain. One goes to the power, the other only to the duty of the court. Under the common law it is the duty of a court of general jurisdiction not to enter a judgment upon a parol promise made without consideration; but it has power to do it, and, if it does, the judgment is unimpeachable, unless reversed. Yet a statute could be framed that would make the power, that is, the jurisdiction of the court dependent upon whether there was a consideration or not. Whether a given statute is intended simply to establish a rule of substantive law, and thus to define the duty of the court, or is meant to limit its power, is a question of construction and common sense. When it affects a court of general jurisdiction and deals with a matter upon which that court must pass, we naturally are slow to read ambiguous words, as meaning to leave the judgment open to dispute, or as intended to do more than to fix the rule by which the court should decide.

The case quoted concerned a statute plainly dealing with the authority and jurisdiction of the New York court. The statute now before us seems to us only to lay down a rule of decision. The Mississippi court in which this action was brought is a court of general jurisdiction and would have to decide upon the validity of the bar if the suit upon the award or upon the original cause of action had been brought there. The words "shall not be enforced by any court" are simply another, possibly less emphatic, way of saying that an action shall not be brought to enforce such contracts. . . . We regard this question as open under the decisions below, and we have expressed our opinion upon it independent of the effect of the judgment, although it might be that, even if jurisdiction of the original cause of action was withdrawn, it remained with regard to a suit upon a judgment based upon an award, whether the judgment or award was conclusive or not. But it might be held that the law as to jurisdiction in one case followed the law in the other, and therefore we proceed at once to the further question, whether the illegality of the original cause of action in Mississippi can be relied upon there as a ground for denying a recovery upon a judgment of another State.

The doctrine laid down by Chief Justice Marshall was "that the judgment of a state court should have the same credit, validity, and effect in every other court in the United States, which it had in the State where it was pronounced, and that whatever pleas would be good to a suit thereon in such State, and none others, could be pleaded in any other court of the United States." Hampton v. McConnel, 3 Wheat. 234. . . .

Whether the award would or would not have been conclusive, and whether the ruling of the Missouri court upon that matter was right or wrong, there can be no question that the judgment was conclusive in Missouri on the validity of the cause of action. . . . A judgment is conclusive as to all the media concludendi, United States v. California & Oregon Land Co., 192 U.S. 355; and it needs no authority to show that it cannot be impeached either in or out of the State by showing that it was based upon a mistake of law. Of course a want of jurisdiction over either the person or the subject-matter might be shown. . . . But as the jurisdiction of the Missouri court is not open to dispute the judgment cannot be impeached in Mississippi even if it went upon a misapprehension of the Mississippi law. . . .

We feel no apprehensions that painful or humiliating consequences will follow upon our decision. No court would give judgment for a plaintiff unless it believed that the facts were a cause of action by the law determining their effect. Mistakes will be rare. In this case the Missouri court no doubt supposed that the award was binding by the law of Mississippi. If it was mistaken it made a natural mistake. The validity of its judgment, even in Mississippi, is, as we believe, the result of the Constitution as it always has been understood, and is not a matter to arouse the susceptibilities of the States, all of which are equally concerned in the question and equally on both sides.

Judgment reversed.

MR. JUSTICE WHITE, with whom concurred MR. JUSTICE HARLAN, MR. JUSTICE MCKENNA and MR. JUSTICE DAY, dissenting.

. . . Although not wishing in the slightest degree to weaken the operation of the due faith and credit clause as interpreted and applied from the beginning, it to me seems that this ruling so enlarges that clause as to cause it to obliterate all state lines, since the effect will be to endow each State with authority to overthrow the public policy and criminal statutes of the others, thereby depriving all of their lawful authority. . . . The whole theory upon which the Constitution was framed, and by which alone, it seems to me, it can continue, is the recognition of the fact that different conditions may exist in the different States, rendering necessary the enactment of regulations of a particular subject in one State when such subject may not in another be deemed to require regulation; in other words, that in Massachusetts, owing to conditions which may there prevail, the legislature may deem it necessary to make police regulations on a particular subject, although like regulations may not obtain in other States. . . .

. . . Now it cannot be denied that under the rules of comity recognized at the time of the adoption of the Constitution, and which at this time universally prevail, no sovereignty was or is under the slightest moral obligation to give effect to a judgment of a court of another sovereignty, when to do so would compel the State in which the judgment was sought to be executed to enforce an illegal and prohibited contract, when both the contract and all the acts done in connection with its performance had taken place in the latter State. This seems to me conclusive of this case, since both in treatises of authoritative writers (Story, Conflict of Law, sec. 609), and by repeated adjudications of this court it has been settled that the purpose of the due faith and credit clause was not to confer any new power, but simply to make obligatory that duty which, when the Constitution was adopted rested, as has been said, in comity alone. . . .

NOTES

(1) If an appeal to the Supreme Court of the United States had been taken from the decision of the Missouri court (assuming the decision of the Missouri trial court had been affirmed by the Supreme Court of Missouri), would the decision of that court have been reversed on constitutional grounds? See p. 329 et seq., infra.

(2) For a discussion of the doctrine that a court will refuse to assume jurisdiction of a suit on an original cause of action because the action is opposed to the public policy of the forum, see pp. 384–399, infra.

ROCHE v. McDONALD, 275 U.S. 449 (1928): Action in Washington to enforce an Oregon judgment. The Oregon judgment was based on a prior Washington judgment and was rendered after the expiration of the Washington period of limitation. The Washington court, relying on the Washington statute which provided that "No suit, action, or other proceeding shall ever be had on any judgment rendered in this state by which . . . the duration of such judgment . . . shall be extended or continued in force for any greater or longer period than six years from the date of the entry of the original judgment," refused to enforce the Oregon judgment. On appeal, held, reversed. "The Oregon judgment, being valid and conclusive between the parties in that state, was equally conclusive in the courts of Washington, and under the full faith and credit clause should have been enforced by them."

NOTES

(1) Union National Bank of Wichita, Kansas v. Lamb, 337 U.S. 38 (1949). Suit in Missouri to enforce a Colorado judgment obtained in 1927 and revived in 1945, in accordance with the Colorado practice, on personal service upon the defendant in Missouri. Enforcement was refused by the Missouri courts because of their local statute of limitations which (a) limited the effective life of a judgment to ten years and (b) provided that no judgment could be re-

vived after ten years from its rendition. Held, reversed. "Roche v. McDonald is dispositive of the merits. . . . In this case it is the 1945 Colorado judgment that claims full faith and credit in Missouri. No Missouri statute of limitations is tendered to cut off a cause of action based on judgments of that vintage." The dissenting opinion contended that the judgment should be vacated and the cause remanded to the Missouri court for an initial determination whether the revival proceedings had "created a new Colorado judgment, or whether they merely had the effect of extending the Colorado statute of limitations on the old judgment. Only in the former case would Roche v. McDonald be 'dispositive of the merits'; in the latter case it is equally clear that McElmoyle for Use of Bailey v. Cohen, supra, 13 Pet. 312 . . . would be controlling." See Note, Revival Judgments under the Full Faith and Credit Clause, 17 U.Chi.L.Rev. 520 (1950). A modern application of the point is Johnson Brothers Wholesale Liquor v. Clemmons, 233 Kan. 405, 661 P.2d 1242 (1983).

(2) McElmoyle for Use of Bailey v. Cohen, 13 Pet. 312 (1839) held it consistent with full faith and credit for F–2 to refuse to enforce an F–1 judgment on the ground that suit was barred under the F–2 statute of limitations applicable to judgments even though the judgment would still have been enforceable in F–1.

WATKINS v. CONWAY

Supreme Court of the United States, 1966.
385 U.S. 188, 87 S.Ct. 357, 17 L.Ed.2d 286.

PER CURIAM. This litigation began when appellant Watkins brought a tort action against Conway in a circuit court of Florida. On October 5, 1955, that court rendered a $25,000 judgment for appellant. Five years and one day later, appellant sued upon this judgment in a superior court of Georgia. Appellee raised § 3–701 of the Georgia Code as a bar to the proceeding:

"Suits upon foreign judgments.—All suits upon judgments obtained out of this State shall be brought within five years after such judgments shall have been obtained."

The Georgia trial court gave summary judgment for appellee. In so doing, it rejected appellant's contention that § 3–701, when read against the longer limitation period on domestic judgments set forth in Ga. Code §§ 110–1001, 1002 (1933), was inconsistent with the Full Faith and Credit and Equal Protection Clauses of the Federal Constitution. The Georgia Supreme Court affirmed, also rejecting appellant's constitutional challenge to § 3–701. 221 Ga. 374, 144 S.E.2d 721 (1965). . . .

Although appellant lays his claim under two constitutional provisions, in reality his complaint is simply that Georgia has drawn an impermissible distinction between foreign and domestic judgments. He argues that the statute is understandable solely as a reflection of Georgia's desire to handicap out-of-state judgment creditors. If appellant's analysis of the purpose and effect of the statute were correct, we might well agree that it violates the Federal Constitution. For the decisions of this Court which appellee relies upon do not justify the discriminatory application of a statute of limitations to foreign actions.[1]

But the interpretation which the Georgia courts have given § 3–701 convinces us that appellant has misconstrued it. The statute bars suits on foreign judgments only if the plaintiff cannot revive his judgment in the State where it was originally obtained. For the relevant date in applying § 3–701 is not the date of the original judgment, but rather it is the date of the latest revival of the judgment. Fagan v. Bently, 32 Ga. 534 (1861); Baty v. Holston, 108 Ga.App. 359, 133 S.E.2d 107 (1963). In the case at bar, for example, all appellant need do is return to Florida and revive his judgment.[2] He can then come back to Georgia within five years and file suit free of the limitations of § 3–701.

It can be seen, therefore, that the Georgia statute has not discriminated against the judgment from Florida. Instead, it has focused on the law of that State. If Florida had a statute of limitations of five years or less on its own judgments, the appellant would not be able to recover here. But this disability would flow from the conclusion of the Florida Legislature that suits on Florida judgments should be barred after that period. Georgia's construction of § 3–701 would merely honor and give effect to that conclusion. Thus, full faith and credit is insured, rather than denied, the law of the judgment State. Similarly, there is no denial of equal protection in a scheme that relies upon the judgment State's view of the validity of its own judgments. Such a scheme hardly reflects invidious discrimination.

Affirmed.

In MILWAUKEE COUNTY V. M. E. WHITE CO., 296 U.S. 268 (1935), the Supreme Court held that a sister state judgment for taxes must be enforced under full faith and credit. In the course of his opinion, Mr. Justice Stone said:

. . . Such exception as there may be to [the] all-inclusive command [of full faith and credit] is one which is implied from the nature of our dual system of government, and recognizes that consistently with the full-faith and credit clause there may be limits to the extent

1. The case most directly on point, McElmoyle for Use of Bailey v. Cohen, 13 Pet. 312, upheld the Georgia statute with which we deal today. But the parties in that case did not argue the statute's shorter limitation for foreign judgments as the ground of its invalidity. Instead, the issue presented to this Court concerned the power of the States to impose any statute of limitations upon foreign judgments. See argument for plaintiff, 13 Pet., at 313–320. . . .

2. The Florida statute of limitations on domestic judgments is 20 years. Fla. Stat.Ann. § 95.11(1) (1960). Thus, it appears that appellant still has ample time to revive his judgment and bring it back to Georgia. . . .

to which the policy of one state, in many respects sovereign, may be subordinated to the policy of another. That there are exceptions has often been pointed out. . . . and in some instances decided. See Haddock v. Haddock, 201 U.S. 562; Maynard v. Hill, 125 U.S. 190; Hood v. McGehee, 237 U.S. 611; Olmsted v. Olmsted, 216 U.S. 386; Fall v. Eastin, 215 U.S. 1. Without attempting to say what their limits may be, we assume for present purposes that the command of the Constitution and of the statute is not all-embracing, and direct our inquiry to the question whether a state to which a judgment for taxes is taken may have a policy against its enforcement meriting recognition as a permissible limitation upon the full-faith and credit clause. Of that question this court is the final arbiter. . . .

Whether one state must enforce the revenue laws of another remains an open question in this court. See Moore v. Mitchell, 281 U.S. 18. . . .

A cause of action on a judgment is different from that upon which the judgment was entered. In a suit upon a money judgment for a civil cause of action, the validity of the claim upon which it was founded is not open to inquiry, whatever its genesis. . . .

We can perceive no greater possibility of embarrassment in litigating the validity of a judgment for taxes and enforcing it than any other for the payment of money. The very purpose of the full-faith and credit clause was to alter the status of the several states as independent foreign sovereignties, each free to ignore obligations created under the laws or by the judicial proceedings of the others, and to make them integral parts of a single nation throughout which a remedy upon a just obligation might be demanded as of right, irrespective of the state of its origin. That purpose ought not lightly to be set aside out of deference to a local policy which, if it exists, would seem to be too trivial to merit serious consideration when weighed against the policy of the constitutional provision and the interest of the state whose judgment is challenged. In the circumstances here disclosed, no state can be said to have a legitimate policy against payment of its neighbor's taxes, the obligation of which has been judicially established by courts to whose judgments in practically every other instance it must give full faith and credit. . . .

We conclude that a judgment is not to be denied full faith and credit in state and federal courts merely because it is for taxes.

We intimate no opinion whether a suit upon a judgment for an obligation created by a penal law, in the international sense, see Huntington v. Attrill, supra, 146 U.S. 657, 677, is within the jurisdiction of the federal District Courts, or whether full faith and credit must be given to such a judgment even though a suit for the penalty before reduced to judgment could not be maintained outside of the state where imposed. See Wisconsin v. Pelican Insurance Co., [127 U.S. 265 (1888)]. . . .

NOTES

(1) City of New York v. Shapiro, 129 F.Supp. 149 (D.Mass.1954). Action by the City of New York to recover a sum assessed by the City Comptroller against the defendants for unpaid use and business taxes, penalties and interest. Held: this administrative determination is entitled to full faith and credit. There is no "reason of policy for distinguishing between a State's duty to give effect to a sister State's court judgment for taxes and its duty to give effect to a sister State's binding administrative determination of taxes." To similar effect, see State of Ohio v. Kleitch Brothers, Inc., 357 Mich. 504, 98 N.W.2d 636 (1959).

(2) On the question of the enforcement of foreign tax claims, not reduced to judgment, see p. 396, infra.

(3) In United States v. Harden, [1963] S.C.R. 366, 41 D.L.R.2d 721 (1963), the Supreme Court of Canada refused to enforce a United States judgment for taxes, relying primarily on British authority holding that "It is perfectly elementary that a foreign government cannot come here" to enforce its tax claims even when reduced to judgment.

Her Majesty the Queen in right of the Province of British Columbia v. Gilbertson, 433 F.Supp. 410 (D.Or.1977), affirmed 597 F.2d 1161 (9th Cir.). Suit by the Province of British Columbia to enforce a judgment for taxes obtained in its courts against certain citizens of Oregon. Enforcement of the judgment was refused. The court said "Apparently this is the first time in American legal history that a foreign government has sought enforcement of a tax judgment in a court of the United States. The best explanation for this seems to be that the 'well established rule' that it cannot be done has deterred all attempts."

For a thorough discussion of the enforcement of foreign country tax judgments, see Note, The Nonrecognition of Foreign Tax Judgments, International Tax Evasion, (1981) U. of Ill.L.Rev. 241.

(4) In Titus v. Wallick, 306 U.S. 282 (1939), suit was brought in Ohio on a judgment obtained in New York by an assignee of a cause of action. The Ohio suit was defended on the ground that the judgment creditor was not the real party in interest, and that in procuring the judgment, he had suppressed and withheld that fact from the defendant and the New York courts. The Ohio court sustained this defense on the ground that the New York judgment was impeachable there for fraud and was to the same extent impeachable in Ohio. The Supreme Court of the United States reversed, holding that the judgment creditor was entitled to maintain the suit under the law of New York. It also held that the Ohio court must recognize the judgment creditor as the real party in interest, since he held the judgment, even though he might not have been the real party in interest if he had sued in Ohio on the original cause of action.

C. LACK OF A COMPETENT COURT

KENNEY v. SUPREME LODGE OF THE WORLD, LOYAL ORDER OF MOOSE

Supreme Court of the United States, 1920.
252 U.S. 411, 40 S.Ct. 371, 64 L.Ed. 638, 10 A.L.R. 716.

MR. JUSTICE HOLMES delivered the opinion of the court.

This is an action of debt brought in Illinois upon a judgment recovered in Alabama. The defendant pleaded to the jurisdiction that the judgment was for negligently causing the death of the plaintiff's intestate in Alabama. The plaintiff demurred to the plea, setting up Article IV, secs. 1 and 2 of the Constitution of the United States. A statute of Illinois provided that no action should be brought or prosecuted in that State for damages occasioned by death occurring in another State in consequence of wrongful conduct. The Supreme Court of Illinois held that as by the terms of the statute the original action could not have been brought there, the Illinois Courts had no jurisdiction of a suit upon the judgment. The Circuit Court of Kane County having ordered that the demurrer be quashed its judgment was affirmed. 285 Ill. 188.

In the court below and in the argument before us reliance was placed upon Anglo-American Provision Co. v. Davis Provision Co., No. 1, 191 U.S. 373, and language in Wisconsin v. Pelican Insurance Co., 127 U.S. 265, the former as showing that the clause requiring full faith and credit to be given to judgments of other States does not require a State to furnish a court, and the latter as sanctioning an inquiry into the nature of the original cause of action in order to determine the jurisdiction of a court to enforce a foreign judgment founded upon it. But we are of opinion that the conclusion sought to be built upon these premises in the present case cannot be sustained.

Anglo-American Provision Co. v. Davis Provision Co. was a suit by a foreign corporation on a foreign judgment against a foreign corporation. The decision is sufficiently explained without more by the views about foreign corporations that had prevailed unquestioned since Bank of Augusta v. Earle, 13 Pet. 519, 589–591, cited 191 U.S. 375. Moreover, no doubt there is truth in the proposition that the Constitution does not require the State to furnish a court. But it also is true that there are limits to the power of exclusion and to the power to consider the nature of the cause of action before the foreign judgment based upon it is given effect.

In Fauntleroy v. Lum, 210 U.S. 230, it was held that the courts of Mississippi were bound to enforce a judgment rendered in Missouri upon a cause of action arising in Mississippi and illegal and void there. The policy of Mississippi was more actively contravened in that case than the policy of Illinois is in this. Therefore the fact that here the original cause of action could not have been maintained in Illinois is not an answer to a suit upon the judgment. See Christmas v. Russell, 5 Wall. 290; Converse v. Hamilton, 224 U.S. 243. But this being true, it is plain that a State cannot escape its constitutional obligations by the simple device of denying jurisdiction in such cases to courts otherwise competent. . . . the Illinois statute . . . read as [the Illinois courts] read it . . . attempted to achieve a result that the Constitution of the United States forbade. . . .

Judgment reversed.*

NOTE

Does the principal case in effect overrule Anglo-American Provision Co. v. Davis Provision Co., 191 U.S. 373 (1903)? Cf. Weidman v. Weidman, 274 Mass. 118, 174 N.E. 206 (1931). In that case a wife got a judgment against her husband in New York for alimony in an unsuccessful annulment suit. She then sued the husband on the judgment in Massachusetts where she was denied recovery. The court stated that it had no jurisdiction to entertain the case since Massachusetts law did not allow suit between spouses.

D. FOREIGN COUNTRY JUDGMENTS

We have now considered the various defenses that can be raised under full faith and credit to the recognition and enforcement of a sister state judgment. How do these defenses differ from those that are available when the judgment of a foreign country is involved? Consider in this connection the discussion of defenses to the enforcement of foreign country judgments in Schibsby v. Westenholz (p. 40, supra); Hilton v. Guyot (p. 223, supra) and Cowans v. Ticonderoga Pulp & Paper Co. (p. 228, supra). See also Restatement, Second, Conflict of Laws § 98.

Consider also § 4 of the Uniform Foreign Money-Judgments Recognition Act.

Section 4. [*Grounds for Non-Recognition.*]

(a) A foreign judgment is not conclusive if

(1) the judgment was rendered under a system which does not provide impartial tribunals or procedures compatible with the requirements of due process of law;

---

* "I also had a case in which Illinois tried to dodge the Constitutional requirement of due faith and aids to judgments in other states by denying jurisdiction to Courts otherwise competent. They laid hold of a statement of mine in an earlier case that the Constitution did not oblige States to furnish a Court, but we said the dodge wouldn't do." Letter from O. W. Holmes to Sir Frederick Pollock, April 25, 1920, in 2 Holmes-Pollock Letters (1941) 41.

(2) the foreign court did not have personal jurisdiction over the defendant; or

(3) the foreign court did not have jurisdiction over the subject matter.

(b) A foreign judgment need not be recognized if

(1) the defendant in the proceedings in the foreign court did not receive notice of the proceedings in sufficient time to enable him to defend;

(2) the judgment was obtained by fraud;

(3) the [cause of action] [claim for relief] on which the judgment is based is repugnant to the public policy of this state;

(4) the judgment conflicts with another final and conclusive judgment;

(5) the proceeding in the foreign court was contrary to an agreement between the parties under which the dispute in question was to be settled otherwise than by proceedings in that court; or

(6) in the case of jurisdiction based only on personal service, the foreign court was a seriously inconvenient forum for the trial of the action.

Which of the defenses listed in Section 4(a), above, would be effective against a sister state judgment?

NOTES

(1) As of 1983 the Uniform Foreign Money-Judgments Recognition Act had been adopted by twelve states. The Act is discussed in Homburger, Recognition and Enforcement of Foreign Judgments, 18 Am.J.Comp.L. 367 (1970); Kulzer, Recognition of Foreign Country Judgments in New York: The Uniform Foreign Money-Judgments Recognition Act, 18 Buff.L.Rev. 1 (1969).

The recognition and enforcement of foreign country judgments are discussed in §§ 491–496 of the Restatement, Foreign Relations Law of the United States (Revised) (Tent. Draft No. 4, 1983).

(2) Expanding notions of jurisdiction in this country have led American courts to take a more tolerant view of assertions of jurisdiction by foreign-country courts. Compare in this regard Ross v. Ostrander, 192 Misc. 140, 79 N.Y.S.2d 706 (Sup.Ct.1948) with Porisini v. Petricca, 90 App.Div.2d 949, 456 N.Y.S.2d 888 (1982). Both cases involved attempts to enforce in New York English judgments obtained by default against defendants who had engaged in transactions in England. Enforcement was refused in Ross because the "requirement of jurisdiction according to the laws of this forum" had not been met. On the other hand, enforcement was granted in Porisini. By that time New York law had been amended (CPLR § 302) to permit New York courts to entertain an action in similar circumstances. Is it correct to make decision as to the jurisdiction of a foreign court depend upon local rules of competence?

(3) A foreign country judgment in an action for alienation of affections and criminal conversation has been enforced by a state which gives no right of action for such matters under its local law. Neporany v. Kir, 5 A.D.2d 438, 173 N.Y.S.2d 146 (1st Dep't 1958) (Canadian judgment).

(4) See generally Scoles and Aarnas, The Recognition and Enforcement of Foreign Nations' Judgments: California, Oregon and Washington, 57 Ore. L.Rev. 377 (1978).

A question that remains relatively unexplored by the courts is the extent to which a foreign-country judgment will be given a lesser res judicata or collateral estoppel effect in this country than that to which a sister state judgment would be entitled under full faith and credit. The question has been much discussed in the law reviews. Some writers believe that the difference in treatment should be quite marked. See Smit, International Res Judicata and Collateral Estoppel in the United States, 9 U.C.L.A.Rev. 44 (1962); von Mehren and Trautman, Recognition of Foreign Adjudications: A Survey and Suggested Approach, 81 Harv.L.Rev. 1601 (1968). See also Kulzer, Some Aspects of Enforceability of Foreign Judgments, 16 Buff.L.Rev. 84 (1966); Reese, The Status in this Country of Judgments Rendered Abroad, 50 Colum.L.Rev. 783 (1950); Nadelmann, Enforcement of Foreign Judgments in Canada, 38 Can.Bar Rev. 68 (1960).

NOTES

(1) Recent cases in which an American court has given collateral estoppel effect to the judgment of a foreign country include Clarkson Co., Limited v. Shaheen, 544 F.2d 624 (2d Cir. 1976); Fairchild, Arabatzis & Smith, Inc. v. Prometco (Produce & Metals) Co., Limited, 470 F.Supp. 610 (S.D.N.Y.1979); Leo Feist, Inc. v. Debmar Publishing Co., 232 F.Supp. 623 (E.D.Pa.1964). The opinions normally are silent on whether they are applying American rules of collateral estoppel or those of the state of rendition. See Peterson, Foreign Country Judgments and the Second Restatement of Conflict of Laws, 72 Colum.L.Rev. 220, 259–64 (1972).

What reasons can be advanced that would justify an American court in giving a foreign country judgment either greater or less collateral estoppel effect than it would have in the state of rendition?

(2) For a discussion of the obstacles that would stand in the way of any attempt to achieve by agreement the reciprocal enforcement of United States judgments and those of some foreign country, see Nadelmann, Non-Recognition of American Money Judgments Abroad and What to Do About It, 42 Iowa L.Rev. 236 (1957); Nadelmann, The United States of America and Agreements on Reciprocal Enforcement of Foreign Judgments, 1 Netherlands Int.L.Rev. 156 (1953); Nadelmann, Reprisals against American Judgments, 65 Harv.L.Rev. 1184 (1952).

E. MATTERS SUBSEQUENT TO F–1 JUDGMENT

A judgment's effectiveness as an enforceable obligation can be affected or destroyed by events which take place thereafter. One obvious example is the running of the forum's statutory period of limitations. McElmoyle for Use of Bailey v. Cohen, p. 310, note (2), supra. Here we consider the consequences of other supervening occurrences; namely (1) payment or other discharge, (2) the rendition of a second judgment which may either be consistent or inconsistent with the first and (3) the effect on a judgment of the reversal of an earlier one upon which it was based.

a. *Payment or other discharge*

Payment, release and accord and satisfaction are, of course, valid defenses to the enforcement of a judgment. And where a second judgment has been rendered upon the first, discharge of the obligation created by either of these judgments in one of the foregoing ways, will also operate to extinguish that created by the other. Restatement, Second, Conflict of Laws § 116. This latter principle has been applied to a situation where payment of the second judgment was made in depreciated currency. Matter of James' Will, 248 N.Y. 1, 161 N.E. 201 (1928). In that case, suit to enforce a New York judgment in the amount of $65,000 was brought in France, and, according to the French procedure, an exequatur was issued which directed the payment of some 2,300,000 francs, the equivalent of the dollar judgment at the date the French proceeding was begun in 1922. This sum of francs was paid in 1925, and the judgment debtor then moved to have the New York judgment discharged as paid. This was opposed on the ground that, since the value of the franc vis-a-vis the dollar had declined in the intervening years, the francs received in 1925 were not worth $65,000. It was therefore argued that the francs should be valued as of the date of payment and treated only as a payment on account. The court held (4 to 3, with Chief Judge Cardozo dissenting) that the New York judgment was discharged. Is such a result either necessary or desirable? For a discussion of the problem, see Reese, The Status in this Country of Judgments Rendered Abroad, 50 Colum.L.Rev. 783, 798–99 (1950).

b. *Successive judgments*

A second judgment, in the sense here used, can be handed down in any one of four situations: (1) in a suit brought to enforce the first judgment, or (2) but less frequently, in one based upon the underlying cause of action,* or (3) where the first judgment was for the de-

* Such an eventuality might occur in a case where the first judgment was rendered in a foreign country (Eastern Townships Bank v. H. S. Beebe & Co., 53

fendant and constituted a bar to the prosecution of the second action, or (4) where under the principles of collateral estoppel the first judgment has already determined one or more of the relevant issues involved. Such a judgment may either be consistent or inconsistent with the first. It is consistent so long as it accords the first judgment the same res judicata effect (either by way of merger, bar or collateral estoppel) that the latter would enjoy at home, or, even if it fails to do this, where it reaches the same result with respect to the particular issue involved. It is inconsistent with the first judgment in all other situations. Common examples of the latter sort are where the second court refuses to enforce the first judgment on the ground that it was rendered without jurisdiction or where it permits the issues to be relitigated afresh and then determines them differently.

Where the second judgment is consistent with the first, the legal effectiveness of the latter remains unaffected. The doctrine of merger is inapplicable to judgments, so that the first judgment, even after it has been reduced to a second judgment in another state, continues in full force and effect and can be used, if the judgment creditor so elects, as the basis for a suit in a third state. The first judgment also retains all of its original effect as res judicata. Restatement, Second, Judgments § 18, comment *j*.

The converse is true, however, in situations where the second court hands down an inconsistent judgment. Here the second judgment—assuming always that the court had jurisdiction and that review by the Supreme Court was available—is controlling and destroys the legal effectiveness of the first judgment, so long as it remains unreversed and to the extent that it is inconsistent with the latter. Thus, the plaintiff can no longer maintain an action, or otherwise rely, upon a judgment rendered in his favor once it has been denied enforcement in a second state because of lack of jurisdiction on the part of the original court. And this is true even though the second court violated the mandate of full faith and credit; its finding of no jurisdiction is nevertheless res judicata and binding upon the parties. Plaintiff's remedy in such a case is by way of appeal from the second judgment. Treinies v. Sunshine Mining Co., p. 289, supra; Restatement, Second, Conflict of Laws § 114.

c. *Reversal of earlier judgment*

What is the effect on the second judgment of a subsequent reversal of the earlier one upon which it was based? Assuming that the second court had jurisdiction its judgment was a valid exercise of judicial power and remains res judicata of the issues involved despite the reversal of the other. Reed v. Allen, 286 U.S. 191 (1932). The judgment debtor, however, is not remediless. Dependent upon the

Vt. 177 (1880)), or where the first judgment was not drawn to the attention of the court in the second action.

particular law of the second state, he can in that state either have the second judgment vacated or reversed on appeal or else have its enforcement enjoined by means of an independent action in equity. Restatement, Second, Judgments § 16. As to the debtor's right to restitution on account of any benefits conferred in compliance with a judgment that has subsequently been reversed, see Restatement, Restitution § 74 (1937).

Suppose now that the second judgment is sought to be enforced, or is otherwise placed in issue, in the courts of a third state and that, while these proceedings are pending, the first judgment is reversed. What is the status of the second judgment in F–3 upon the happening of this event? Presumably, it cannot under full faith and credit be treated as a nullity so long as it remains valid and effective in F–2. But so long as it is subject to impeachment in F–2 on account of the F–1 reversal, it should likewise be subject to attack on this ground in F–3. And by analogy to the rule prevailing in the case of judgments procured by fraud (Levin v. Gladstein, p. 299, supra), F–3 law would presumably govern the particular method of attack—*i.e.*, whether the issue could be raised by way of defense to the plaintiff's action or only in an independent proceeding in equity for an injunction against the enforcement of the F–2 judgment. Cf. Ellis v. Delafield, 153 App. Div. 26, 137 N.Y.S. 1029 (1st Dep't 1912).

Chapter 6

THE IMPACT OF THE CONSTITUTION

Introductory Note. The bulk of this course, and particularly the material that follows, is devoted to problems in choice of law. However, before plunging into that subject, we shall pause to examine the boundaries, limitations, and compulsions that may deprive state courts of the options a common law court would normally enjoy in ruling on certain conflicts problems.

The constraints and compulsions that may literally override state court conflicts policies flow from the United States Constitution, directly or indirectly. The most important Constitutional provisions in this regard appear at page 37, supra. First comes the Supremacy Clause (Art. VI), compelling state law to give way to the United States Constitution and valid national statutes, treaties, etc. In addition, controls are exerted by the Full Faith and Credit Clause (Article IV, § 1), the Privileges and Immunities Clause (Article IV, § 2), the Due Process Clauses of the Fifth and Fourteenth Amendments and the Equal Protection Clause of the Fourteenth Amendment. The Interstate Commerce Clause (Article I, § 8), also warrants mention even though it rarely influences decision in conflicts cases.

Sometimes the Constitution compels a state to provide a forum for suit on the claim arising in a sister state. On occasion it prohibits a state from applying its own rule of decision on a substantive matter, for the reason that the state does not have adequate ties, relations, concerns, or interests in the issue and its resolution to warrant applying its own rule of decision. The same prohibition may prevent application of the rule of decision of some other state, equally unconcerned or removed from legitimate interest in the outcome of the disputed issue. On rare occasions the Constitution may affirmatively mandate that the law of a particular state be applied to decide the issue presented. Less rarely, a state will be constitutionally prohibited from discriminating unreasonably against citizens of sister states or from dealing unequally with persons in its jurisdiction who are similarly situated.

321

SECTION 1.   THE OBLIGATION TO PROVIDE OR
TO REFUSE A FORUM

HUGHES v. FETTER

Supreme Court of the United States, 1951.
341 U.S. 609, 71 S.Ct. 980, 95 L.Ed. 1212.

Mr. Justice Black delivered the opinion of the Court.

Basing his complaint on the Illinois wrongful death statute, appellant administrator brought this action in the Wisconsin state court to recover damages for the death of Harold Hughes, who was fatally injured in an automobile accident in Illinois.   The allegedly negligent driver and an insurance company were named as defendants.   On their motion the trial court entered summary judgment "dismissing the complaint on the merits."   It held that a Wisconsin statute, which creates a right of action only for deaths caused in that state, establishes a local public policy against Wisconsin's entertaining suits brought under the wrongful death acts of other states.[1]   The Wisconsin Supreme Court affirmed,* notwithstanding the contention that the local statute so construed violated the Full Faith and Credit Clause of Art. IV, § 1 of the Constitution.   The case is properly here on appeal under 28 U.S.C. § 1257.

We are called upon to decide the narrow question whether Wisconsin, over the objection raised, can close the doors of its courts to the cause of action created by the Illinois wrongful death act.   Prior decisions have established that the Illinois statute is a "public act" within the provision of Art. IV, § 1 that "Full Faith and Credit shall be given in each State to the public Acts . . . of every other State."   It is also settled that Wisconsin cannot escape this constitutional obligation to enforce the rights and duties validly created under the laws of other states by the simple device of removing jurisdiction from courts otherwise competent.   We have recognized, however, that full faith and credit does not automatically compel a forum state to subordinate its own statutory policy to a conflicting public act of another state; rather, it is for this Court to choose in each case between the

---

1.   Wis.Stat., 1949, § 331.03.   This section contains language typically found in wrongful death acts but concludes as follows: "provided, that such action shall be brought for a death caused in this state." [Some footnotes have been omitted; others have been renumbered.   Eds.]

   * The Wisconsin court stated in Hughes v. Fetter, 257 Wis. 35, 42 N.W.2d 452 (1950): "It has been repeatedly declared to be the law that it was not intended by the provisions of the Federal Constitution referred to [the full faith and credit clause and the privileges and immunities clause] to give to the laws of one state any operation in other states except by permission, express or implied, by those states. . . . The statute in another state cannot be made the basis of furnishing a remedy for action in Wisconsin whose maintenance would be wholly inconsistent with the public policy of our state as declared by the legislature." [Footnote by the editors.]

competing public policies involved. The clash of interests in cases of this type has usually been described as a conflict between the public policies of two or more states. The more basic conflict involved in the present appeal, however, is as follows: On the one hand is the strong unifying principle embodied in the Full Faith and Credit Clause looking toward maximum enforcement in each state of the obligations or rights created or recognized by the statutes of sister states;[2] on the other hand is the policy of Wisconsin, as interpreted by its highest court, against permitting Wisconsin courts to entertain this wrongful death action.[3]

We hold that Wisconsin's policy must give way. That state has no real feeling of antagonism against wrongful death suits in general. To the contrary, a forum is regularly provided for cases of this nature, the exclusionary rule extending only so far as to bar actions for death not caused locally. The Wisconsin policy, moreover, cannot be considered as an application of the *forum non conveniens* doctrine, whatever effect that doctrine might be given if its use resulted in denying enforcement to public acts of other states. Even if we assume that Wisconsin could refuse, by reason of particular circumstances, to hear foreign controversies to which nonresidents were parties, the present case is not one lacking a close relationship with the state. For not only were appellant, the decedent and the individual defendant all residents of Wisconsin, but also appellant was appointed administrator and the corporate defendant was created under Wisconsin laws. We also think it relevant, although not crucial here, that Wisconsin may well be the only jurisdiction in which service could be had as an original matter on the insurance company defendant. And while in the present case jurisdiction over the individual defendant apparently could be had in Illinois by substituted service, in other cases Wisconsin's exclusionary statute might amount to a deprivation of all opportunity to enforce valid death claims created by another state.

Under these circumstances, we conclude that Wisconsin's statutory policy which excludes this Illinois cause of action is forbidden by the national policy of the Full Faith and Credit Clause.[4] The judg-

2. This clause "altered the status of the several states as independent foreign sovereignties, each free to ignore rights and obligations created under the laws or established by the judicial proceedings of the others, by making each an integral part of a single nation. . . ." Magnolia Petroleum Co. v. Hunt, 320 U.S. 430, 439. See also Milwaukee County v. White, 296 U.S. 268, 276–277; Order of Travelers v. Wolfe, 331 U.S. 586. [Court's footnote].

3. The present case is not one where Wisconsin, having entertained appellant's lawsuit, chose to apply its own instead of Illinois' statute to measure the substan-

tive rights involved. This distinguishes the present case from those where we have said that "*Prima facie* every state is entitled to enforce in its own courts its own statutes, lawfully enacted." Alaska Packers Ass'n v. Industrial Acc. Commission, 294 U.S. 532; see, also, Williams v. State of North Carolina, 317 U.S. 287, 295–296.

4. In certain previous cases, e.g., Pacific Employers Ins. Co. v. Industrial Acc. Commission, 306 U.S. 493, 502; Alaska Packers Ass'n v. Industrial Accident Commission, 294 U.S. 532, 547, this Court suggested that under the Full Faith and Credit Clause a forum state might make

ment is reversed and the cause is remanded to the Supreme Court of Wisconsin for proceedings not inconsistent with this opinion.

Reversed and remanded.

MR. JUSTICE FRANKFURTER, with whom MR. JUSTICE REED, MR. JUSTICE JACKSON, and MR. JUSTICE MINTON join, dissenting.

. . . In the present case, the decedent, the plaintiff, and the individual defendant were residents of Wisconsin. The corporate defendant was created under Wisconsin law. The suit was brought in Wisconsin. No reason is apparent—and none is vouchsafed in the opinion of the Court—why the interest of Illinois is so great that it can force the courts of Wisconsin to grant relief in defiance of their own law.

Finally, it may be noted that there is no conflict here in the policies underlying the statute of Wisconsin and that of Illinois. The Illinois wrongful death statute has a proviso that "no action shall be brought or prosecuted in this State to recover damages for a death occurring outside of this State where a right of action for such death exists under the laws of the place where such death occurred and service of process in such suit may be had upon the defendant in such place." . . . Thus, in the converse of the case at bar—if Hughes had been killed in Wisconsin and suit had been brought in Illinois—the Illinois courts would apparently have dismissed the suit. There is no need to be "more Roman than the Romans."

NOTES

(1) For a full discussion of the principal case, see Reese, Full Faith and Credit to Statutes: The Defense of Public Policy, 19 U.Chi.L.Rev. 339 (1952). To what did the Wisconsin court fail to give full faith and credit? Note in this connection Justice Black's intimation in the third footnote—that the Wisconsin court would not have violated full faith and credit if it had decided the "substantive rights" of the parties by application of the Wisconsin wrongful death statute. Professor Brainerd Currie has suggested that the proper basis for the decision was the equal protection clause of the Fourteenth Amendment in that the Wisconsin statute discriminated unreasonably between Wisconsin citizens killed in Wisconsin and those killed in other states. In his view, Wisconsin could not constitutionally have denied plaintiff a forum if, the facts otherwise being the same, the Wisconsin decedent had met his death in a foreign country rather than in a sister state. Currie, The Constitution and the "Transitory" Cause of Action, 73 Harv.L.Rev. 36, 268 (1959), reprinted in Currie, Selected Essays on the Conflict of Laws, Chap. 6

a distinction between statutes and judgments of sister states because of Congress' failure to prescribe the extra-state effect to be accorded public acts. Subsequent to these decisions the Judicial Code was revised so as to provide: "Such Acts [of the legislature of any state] . . . and judicial proceedings . . . shall have the same full faith and credit in every court within the United States . . . as they have . . . in the courts of such State . . . from which they are taken." (Italics added.) 28 U.S.C. (1946 ed., Supp. III), § 1738. In deciding the present appeal, however, we have found it unnecessary to rely on any changes accomplished by the Judicial Code revision.

(1963). See also Chief Justice Vinson's explanation of the Hughes decision in
Wells v. Simonds Abrasive Co., below. In support of the court's rationale, is
the argument sound that the full faith and credit clause, as a basic instrument of federalism, may be given a non-literal meaning to require that a
state under certain circumstances must make its courts available for the enforcement of claims arising in sister states?

(2) First National Bank of Chicago v. United Air Lines, 342 U.S. 396
(1952) was an action in the Federal court in Illinois for wrongful death in an
airplane crash in Utah. An Illinois statute (quoted in Justice Frankfurter's
dissent in Hughes v. Fetter, supra) was similar to the Wisconsin statute but
applied only when the defendant was subject to suit in the place where the
death occurred. The majority of the court held the Illinois statute could not
bar the action. Black, J.: "Nor is it crucial here that Illinois only excludes
cases that can be tried in other states. We hold again that the Full Faith
and Credit Clause forbids such exclusion."

(3) Assuming Hughes v. Fetter was properly based on full faith and credit, may it lead to decisions by the Supreme Court that there are constitutional limitations upon the power of a state to refuse to entertain suit on a claim
arising in a sister state on the ground of forum non conveniens; or because
the state considers the claim to be penal or contrary to its public policy?
Does the Constitution limit the power of a state to refuse to entertain suit on
a claim that arose in a sister state by reason of congestion in the local
courts?

(4) As to the power of a state to refuse to entertain a suit on forum non
conveniens grounds, see Missouri ex rel. Southern Railway Co. v. Mayfield,
340 U.S. 1 (1950), p. 205, supra, and Douglas v. New York, New Haven &
Hartford Railroad Co., 279 U.S. 377 (1929), p. 205, supra.

(5) In Broderick v. Rosner, 294 U.S. 629 (1935), p. 947, infra, New Jersey
was held to have violated full faith and credit by imposing unreasonable procedural restrictions upon the ability of the New York Superintendent of
Banks to recover assessments against New Jersey shareholders of an insolvent New York bank.

(6) By reason of the Supremacy Clause (Article VI), a state cannot discriminate against claims arising under federal law. McKnett v. St. Louis &
San Francisco Railway Co., 292 U.S. 230 (1934), p. 206, supra. Likewise, a
state cannot refuse to entertain suit on a federal claim on the ground that it
is penal (Testa v. Klatt, 330 U.S. 386 (1947), p. 206, supra), or is contrary to
the state's public policy, Mondou v. New York, New Haven & Hartford Railroad Co., 223 U.S. 1 (1912), p. 206, supra.

WELLS v. SIMONDS ABRASIVE CO.

Supreme Court of the United States, 1953.
345 U.S. 514, 73 S.Ct. 856, 97 L.Ed. 1211.

[A resident of Alabama while at work with a grinding wheel in the
state was killed by the bursting of the wheel. The wheel was manufactured by respondent, a Pennsylvania corporation, with its principal
place of business in Pennsylvania. The administratrix of the decedent, finding it impossible to serve process on the respondent in Ala-

bama, brought an action for the death under the wrongful death statute of Alabama in the federal court in Pennsylvania. The action was brought more than one year, but less than two years, after the death. The Alabama wrongful death statute permitted the action to be brought within two years from the death, but the Pennsylvania death statute required the action be brought within one year. The Pennsylvania conflict of laws rule called for the application of its own period of limitation. The district judge, deeming himself bound by the Pennsylvania conflicts rule, gave summary judgment for the defendant, and the Court of Appeals affirmed.]

MR. CHIEF JUSTICE VINSON delivered the opinion of the Court.

We granted certiorari limited to the question whether this Pennsylvania conflicts rule violates the Full Faith and Credit Clause of the Federal Constitution.

. . . The Full Faith and Credit Clause does not compel a state to adopt any particular set of rules of conflict of laws; it merely sets certain minimum requirements which each state must observe when asked to apply the law of a sister state.

Long ago, we held that applying the statute of limitations of the forum to a foreign substantive right did not deny full faith and credit, . . . Recently we referred to ". . . the well established principle of conflict of laws that 'If action is barred by the statute of limitations of the forum, no action can be maintained though action is not barred in the state where the cause of action arose.' Restatement, Conflict of Laws, § 603 (1934)." . . .

The rule that the limitations of the forum apply (which this Court has said meets the requirements of full faith and credit) is the usual conflicts rule of the states. However, there have been divergent views when a foreign statutory right unknown to the common law has a period of limitation included in the section creating the right. The Alabama statute here involved creates such a right and contains a built-in limitation. The view is held in some jurisdictions that such a limitation is so intimately connected with the right that it must be enforced in the forum state along with the substantive right.

. . . Our prevailing rule is that the Full Faith and Credit Clause does not compel the forum state to use the period of limitation of a foreign state. We see no reason in the present situation to graft an exception onto it. Differences based upon whether the foreign right was known to the common law or upon the arrangement of the code of the foreign state are too unsubstantial to form the basis for constitutional distinctions under the Full Faith and Credit Clause.

. . .

Our decisions in Hughes v. Fetter, 1951, 341 U.S. 609, and First National Bank v. United Air Lines, 1952, 342 U.S. 396, do not call for a change in the well-established rule that the forum state is permitted to apply its own period of limitation. The crucial factor in those two cases was that the forum laid an uneven hand on causes of action arising within and without the forum state. Causes of action arising in sister states were discriminated against. Here Pennsylvania applies her one-year limitation to all wrongful death actions wherever they may arise. The judgment is affirmed.

Affirmed.

.   .   .

MR. JUSTICE JACKSON, with whom MR. JUSTICE BLACK and MR. JUSTICE MINTON join, dissenting.

.   .   .   I believe the United States District Court, though sitting in Pennsylvania should apply the law of Alabama, both as to liability and as to limitation.

The respondent relies upon the line of cases that began with Erie R. Co. v. Tompkins, 304 U.S. 64. A careful reading of the Erie decision will show that, so far as it applies at all, it is authority for the plaintiff's and not the defendant's position. The Erie injury occurred in Pennsylvania, but the action was brought in a United States District Court in New York. Although the trial court sat in New York, this Court held that it must decide liability by Pennsylvania law, that is, by the law of the state of injury, not that of the forum state, which holding, if applied here, would require that this case be adjudged by the law of Alabama even though it is brought in a federal court sitting in another state. That opinion, by Mr. Justice Brandeis, will be searched in vain for any hint that this result depended on the New York law of conflicts, which is not even paid the respect of mention. Erie R. Co. v. Tompkins held that there is no federal common law of torts and that federal courts must not improvise one of their own but must follow that state's law *which is applicable to the case.*

That the applicable state law was that of Pennsylvania, instead of that of the forum, was assumed without discussion of the reason because it was pursuant to what is probably the best-settled rule of conflicts in tort cases. .   .   .

[The opinion reviews cases in which the law of the place of the tort was used and in which the federal court followed the conflict of laws rule of the forum state.]

Most of these decisions are actuated by a laudable but undiscriminating yen for uniformity within the forum state. Thus, "Otherwise the accident of diversity of citizenship would constantly disturb equal administration of justice in coordinate state and federal courts sitting side by side." Klaxon Co. v. Stentor Electric Mfg. Co., supra, 313 U.S. [487] at page 496, citing the Erie case; and the Court's opinion here refers to it as a "crucial factor" that "the forum laid an uneven hand on causes of action arising within and without the forum state."

But the essence of the Full Faith and Credit Clause of the Constitution is that uniformities other than just those within the state are to be observed in a federal system. The whole purpose and the only need for requiring full faith and credit to foreign law is that it does differ from that of the forum. But that disparity does not cause the type of evil aimed at in Erie R. Co. v. Tompkins, supra, namely, that the same event may be judged by two different laws, depending upon whether a state court or a federal forum within that state is available. Application of the Full Faith and Credit Clause prevents this disparity by requiring that the law where the cause of action arose will follow the cause of action in whatever forum it is pursued.

. . .

This case is in United States Court, not by grace of Pennsylvania, but by authority of Congress, and what I said in First National Bank of Chicago v. United Air Lines, 342 U.S. 396, 398, seems to me applicable here. I had supposed, before Hughes v. Fetter, 341 U.S. 609, that the Commonwealth of Pennsylvania could close its courts to trial of this case. But no one would have questioned, I should think, that if the cause were entertained it must be tried in accordance with the law of the place of the wrong. . . .

Whether the principle of full faith and credit and of the law of conflicts will carry a general statute of limitations into the state of the forum along with the right is a more difficult question in the light of our precedents. McElmoyle v. Cohen, 13 Pet. 312.

. . .

But whatever may be the argument concerning general statutes of limitations as applied to common-law causes, this Court long ago recognized a distinction as to limitations on the action created by statutes in the pattern of the Lord Campbell Act. This Court early held such an action in federal court to be barred by the limitation contained in the applicable state statute. The reasoning of Mr. Chief Justice Waite is just as valid when it leads to a contrary result.

. . .

. . .

The Supreme Court of Alabama has held the same doctrine applicable to the very statute in question, saying, "This is not a statute of limitations, but of the essence of the cause of action, to be disclosed by averment and proof." Parker v. Fies & Sons, 243 Ala. 348, 350, 10 So.2d 13, 15. The doctrine is well recognized in the literature of the law of conflicts.

. . .

We think that the better view of the case before us would be that it is Alabama law which giveth and only Alabama law that taketh away.

NOTES

(1) Would Pennsylvania have been equally free to apply its statute of limitations if it had provided for a longer period than the Alabama statute? What policy or purpose of Pennsylvania would be served by application of its statute of limitations in such a case? The policies and purposes of statutes of limitations are treated in Chapter 7, Section 3D, infra.

(2) See generally Currie, The Constitution and the "Transitory" Cause of Action, 73 Harv.L.Rev. 36, 268 (1959), reprinted in Currie, Selected Essays on the Conflict of Laws, Chap. 6 (1963).

(3) On the history of the full faith and credit clause, especially as it is directed to public acts, see Nadelmann, Full Faith and Credit to Judgments and Public Acts, 56 Mich.L.Rev. 33 (1957).

SECTION 2. CHOICE OF LAW

HOME INSURANCE CO. v. DICK

Supreme Court of the United States, 1930.
281 U.S. 397, 50 S.Ct. 338, 74 L.Ed. 926, 74 A.L.R. 701.

Appeal from the Supreme Court of Texas.

MR. JUSTICE BRANDEIS delivered the opinion of the Court.

Dick, a citizen of Texas, brought this action in a court of that State against Compania General Anglo-Mexicana de Seguros S.A., a Mexican corporation, to recover on a policy of fire insurance for the total loss of a tug. Jurisdiction was asserted in rem through garnishment, by ancillary writs issued against the Home Insurance Company and Franklin Fire Insurance Company, which reinsured, by contracts with the Mexican corporation, parts of the risk which it had assumed. The garnishees are New York corporations. Upon them, service was effected by serving their local agents in Texas. . . .

. . .

Their defense rests upon the following facts: This suit was not commenced till more than one year after the date of the loss. The policy provided: "It is understood and agreed that no judicial suit or demand shall be entered before any tribunal for the collection of any claim under this policy, unless such suits or demands are filed within one year counted as from the date on which such damage occurs." This provision was in accord with the Mexican law to which the policy was expressly made subject. It was issued by the Mexican company in Mexico to one Bonner, of Tampico, Mexico, and was there duly assigned to Dick prior to the loss. It covered the vessel only in certain Mexican waters. The premium was paid in Mexico; and the loss was "payable in the City of Mexico in current funds of the United States of Mexico, or their equivalent elsewhere." At the time the policy was issued, when it was assigned to him, and until after the loss, Dick actually resided in Mexico, although his permanent residence was in Texas. The contracts of reinsurance were effected by correspondence between the Mexican company in Mexico and the New York companies in New York. Nothing thereunder was to be done, or was in fact done, in Texas.

.   .   . To this defense Dick demurred, on the ground that article 5545 of the Texas Revised Civil Statutes (1925) provides: "No person, firm, corporation, association or combination of whatsoever kind shall enter into any stipulation, contract, or agreement, by reason whereof the time in which to sue thereon is limited to a shorter period than two years. And no stipulation, contract, or agreement for any such shorter limitation in which to sue shall ever be valid in this State."

The trial court sustained Dick's contention and entered judgment against the garnishees. On appeal, both in the Court of Civil Appeals (8 S.W.2d 354) and in the Supreme Court of the state (15 S.W.2d 1028), the garnishees asserted that, as construed and applied, the Texas statute violated the due process clause of the Fourteenth Amendment and the contract clause. Both courts treated the policy provision as equivalent to a foreign statute of limitation; held that article 5545 related to the remedy available in Texas courts; concluded that it was validly applicable to the case at bar; and affirmed the judgment of the trial court. The garnishees appealed to this Court on the ground that the statute, as construed and applied, violated their rights under the Federal Constitution. Dick moved to dismiss the appeal for want of jurisdiction. Then the garnishees filed, also, a petition for a writ of certiorari. Consideration of the jurisdiction of this Court on the appeal, and of the petition for certiorari, was postponed to the hearing of the case on the merits.

First. Dick contends that this Court lacks jurisdiction of the action, because the errors assigned involve only questions of local law and of conflict of laws. The argument is that, while a provision requiring notice of loss within a fixed period is substantive because it is a condition precedent to the existence of the cause of action, the provision for liability only in case suit is brought within the year is not substantive because it relates only to the remedy after accrual of the cause of action; that, while the validity, interpretation, and performance of the substantive provisions of a contract are determined by the law of the place where it is made and is to be performed, matters which relate only to the remedy are unquestionably governed by the lex fori; and that, even if the Texas court erred in holding the statute applicable to this contract, the error is one of state law or of the interpretation of the contract, and is not reviewable here.

The contention is unsound. There is no dispute as to the meaning of the provision in the policy. It is that the insurer shall not be liable unless suit is brought within one year of the loss. . . . Nor are we concerned with the question whether the provision is properly described as relating to remedy or to substance. However characterized, it is an express term in the contract of the parties by which the right of the insured and the correlative obligation of the insurer are defined. If effect is given to the clause, Dick cannot recover from the Mexican corporation, and the garnishees cannot be compelled to pay. If, on the other hand, the statute is applied to the contract, it admittedly abrogates a contractual right and imposes liability, although the parties have agreed that there should be none.

The statute is not simply one of limitation. It does not merely fix the time in which the aid of the Texas courts may be invoked. Nor does it govern only the remedies available in the Texas courts. It deals with the powers and capacities of persons and corporations. It expressly prohibits the making of certain contracts. As construed, it also directs the disregard in Texas of contractual rights and obligations wherever created and assumed; and it commands the enforcement of obligations in excess of those contracted for. Therefore, the objection that, as applied to contracts made and to be performed outside of Texas, the statute violates the Federal Constitution, raises federal questions of substance; and the existence of the federal claim is not disproved by saying that the statute, or the one-year provision in the policy, relates to the remedy and not to the substance.

. . . The case is properly here on appeal. The motion to dismiss the appeal is overruled; and the petition for certiorari is therefore denied.

Second. The Texas statute as here construed and applied deprives the garnishees of property without due process of law. A state may, of course, prohibit and declare invalid the making of certain contracts within its borders. Ordinarily, it may prohibit performance within its borders, even of contracts validly made elsewhere, if they are required to be performed within the state and their performance would violate its laws. But, in the case at bar, nothing in any way relating to the policy sued on, or to the contracts of reinsurance, was ever done or required to be done in Texas. All acts relating to the making of the policy were done in Mexico. All in relation to the making of the contracts of reinsurance were done there or in New York. And, likewise, all things in regard to performance were to be done outside of Texas. Neither the Texas laws nor the Texas courts were invoked for any purpose, except by Dick in the bringing of this suit. The fact that Dick's permanent residence was in Texas is without significance. At all times here material he was physically present and acting in Mexico. Texas was therefore without power to affect the terms of contracts so made. Its attempt to impose a greater obligation than that agreed upon and to seize property in payment of the imposed obligation violates the guaranty against deprivation of property without due process of law. Compania General De Tabacos v. Collector of Internal Revenue, 275 U.S. 87; Aetna Life Ins. Co. v. Dunken, 266 U.S. 389; New York Life Ins. Co. v. Dodge, 246 U.S. 357. Compare Modern Woodmen of America v. Mixer, 267 U.S. 544, 551.[1]

The cases relied upon, in which it was held that a state may lengthen its statute of limitations, are not in point. See Atchafalaya Land Co. v. Williams Cypress Co., 258 U.S. 190; National Surety Co. v. Architectural Decorating Co., 226 U.S. 276; Vance v. Vance, 108 U.S. 514. In those cases, the parties had not stipulated a time limit for the enforcement of their obligations. It is true that a state may extend the time within which suit may be brought in its own courts, if, in doing so, it violates no agreement of the parties. And, in the absence of a contractual provision, the local statute of limitation may be applied to a right created in another jurisdiction even where the remedy in the latter is barred.[2] In such cases, the rights and obligations of the parties are not varied. When, however, the parties have expressly agreed upon a time limit on their obligation, a statute which invalidates the agreement and directs enforcement of the contract after the time has expired increases their obligation and imposes a burden not contracted for.

. . .

Third. Dick urges that article 5545 of the Texas law is a declaration of its public policy; and that a state may properly refuse to recognize foreign rights which violate its declared policy. Doubtless, a state may prohibit the enjoyment by persons within its borders of rights acquired elsewhere which violate its laws or public policy; and under some circumstances, it may refuse to aid in the enforcement of such rights. Bothwell v. Buckbee, Mears Co., 275 U.S. 274, 277, 279; Union Trust Co. v. Grosman, 245 U.S. 412; compare Fauntleroy v. Lum, 210 U.S. 230. But the Mexican corporation never was in Texas; and neither it nor the garnishees invoked the aid of the Texas courts or the Texas laws. The Mexican corporation was not before the court. The garnishees were brought in by compulsory process. Neither has asked favors. They ask only to be let alone. We need

1. The division of this court in the Tabacos and Dodge Cases was not on the principle here stated, but on the question of fact whether there were in those cases things done within the state of which the state could properly lay hold as the basis of the regulations there imposed. Compare Bothwell v. Buckbee, Mears Co., 275 U.S. 274; Palmetto Fire Ins. Co. v. Conn, 272 U.S. 295. In the absence of any such things, as in this case, the Court was agreed that a state is without power to impose either public or private obligations on contracts made outside of the state and not to be performed there. Compare Mutual Life Insurance Co. of New York v. Liebing, 259 U.S. 209; E. Merrick Dodd, Jr., "The Power of the Supreme Court to Review State Decisions in the Field of Conflict of Laws," 39 Harv.L.Rev. (1926) 533, 548. [Footnote by the Court.]

2. Whether a distinction is to be drawn between statutes of limitation which extinguish or limit the right and those which merely bar the remedy, we need not now determine. Compare Davis v. Mills, 194 U.S. 451, and Texas Portland Cement Co. v. McCord, 233 U.S. 157, with Canadian Pac. Ry. Co. v. Johnston, 61 F. 738. [Footnote by the Court.]

not consider how far the state may go in imposing restrictions on the conduct of its own residents, and of foreign corporations which have received permission to do business within its borders; or how far it may go in refusing to lend the aid of its courts to the enforcement of rights acquired outside its borders. It may not abrogate the rights of parties beyond its borders having no relation to anything done or to be done within them.

Fourth. Finally, it is urged that the Federal Constitution does not require the states to recognize and protect rights derived from the laws of foreign countries—that as to them the full faith and credit clause has no application. See Aetna Life Ins. Co. v. Tremblay, 223 U.S. 185. The claims here asserted are not based upon the full faith and credit clause. Compare Royal Arcanum v. Green, 237 U.S. 531; Modern Woodmen of America v. Mixer, 267 U.S. 544. They rest upon the Fourteenth Amendment. Its protection extends to aliens. Moreover, the parties in interest here are American companies. The defense asserted is based on the provision of the policy and on their contracts of reinsurance. The courts of the state confused this defense with that based on the Mexican Code. They held that, even if the effect of the foreign statute was to extinguish the right, Dick's removal to Texas prior to the bar of the foreign statute removed the cause of action from Mexico, and subjected it to the Texas statute of limitation. And they applied the same rule to the provision in the policy. Whether or not that is a sufficient answer to the defense based on the foreign law we may not consider; for no issue under the full faith and credit clause was raised. But in Texas, as elsewhere, the contract was subject to its own limitations.

Fifth. . . . Since we hold that the Texas statute, as construed and applied, violates the due process clause, we have no occasion to consider [the contract clause] contention. . . .

Reversed.

NOTE ON HOME INSURANCE CO. v. DICK

Home Insurance Co. v. Dick is a landmark. It stands as a warning that at some point the due process clause prevents a state deciding a multistate case from making whatever choice of law it is minded to. When is that point reached? That question requires identifying the critical factors in the Dick case. Was the nearly total absence of connections to Texas decisive? Or was it the fact that the parties had fixed by a stipulation in their contract the time within which suit had to be brought? Or that Texas purported to prevent parties from making agreements shortening the time-to-sue period to less than two years? Or was it a combination of these and perhaps other factors?

The Dick case is sometimes said to stand for the proposition that a naked forum may not apply its own rules of decision to a multistate case. However, Professor Russell J. Weintraub has pointed out that although the policy was issued to Bonner of Tampico, Mexico, the loss was payable to a firm in Texas and Dick, as their interests might appear; and many years before the boat burned the policy was assigned to Dick with defendant's written consent. See R. Weintraub, Commentary on the Conflict of Laws (2d ed. 1980), pp. 502–503. By today's standards, do those facts sufficiently clothe Texas with connections with the case to give it constitutional basis for applying the statute in question?

Consider Justice Brandeis's statement that in the absence of a contrary agreement by the parties, a state may extend the time within which suit may be brought in its own courts even when the right is created in another jurisdiction. Are the implications that (a) a state may never extend the time when the parties have made an agreement for a shorter time? (b) a state may always extend the time to sue in tort cases, where there are practically never agreements as to time-to-sue limits? (c) a state may always extend the time to sue in contract cases if the only time limits applicable are those supplied by the law of another state rather than the agreement of the parties? Cf. Clay v. Sun Insurance Office, Limited, 377 U.S. 179 (1964), p. 355 infra.

Under Shaffer v. Heitner, p. 148 supra, and Rush v. Savchuk, p. 161 supra, would there be judicial jurisdiction today on the facts of the Dick case?

NOTES

(1) The Supreme Court continues to cite the Dick case approvingly, but it has not in recent years reversed a state court decision for violating due process by a choice-of-law decision. However, in Confederation Life Insurance Co. v. de Lara, 257 So.2d 44 (Fla.1971), cert. denied 409 U.S. 953 (1972), Justice Brennan, joined by Justice Douglas, relied on the Dick decision in opposing the Court's denial of certiorari. The case upheld the constitutionality of applying Florida's substantive law to determine the obligations of a Canadian life insurer to a beneficiary residing in Florida. The policy had been issued in Cuba in 1938 to insure the life of a Cuban citizen and resident who died there in 1962. The policy was written in Spanish, conformed to Cuban law and required payment and performance in Havana. The opposite result was reached—i.e., Cuban law was held applicable—in an earlier case based on similar facts. Santovenia v. Confederation Life Insurance Association, 460 F.2d 805 (5th Cir. 1972).

(2) For an excellent discussion of the relevant Supreme Court cases, see Currie, The Constitution and Choice of Law, 26 U.Chi.L.Rev. 9 (1958), reprinted in Currie, Selected Essays on the Conflict of Laws, Chap. 5 (1963). See also Restatement, Second, Conflict of Laws § 9; Reese, Legislative Jurisdiction, 78 Colum.L.Rev. 1587 (1978).

JOHN HANCOCK MUTUAL LIFE INSURANCE CO. v. YATES, 299 U.S. 178 (1936): Suit upon a life insurance policy which had been applied for and issued in New York. The insured was a New York domiciliary who was being treated for cancer at the time. In his insurance application, the insured stated that he had not recently been under medical care. Under the law of New York this false statement constituted a material misrepresentation that voided the policy. Following the insured's death, his widow moved to Georgia and there brought suit on the policy. She recovered judgment by application of the Georgia rule that a false statement in an insurance policy is not material if the agent who solicited the policy was aware of the facts. Application of the Georgia rule was justified by the Georgia courts on the ground that the jury had found that the insurance agent knew that the insured was suffering from cancer and that it is for forum law to determine as a question of procedure whether the materiality of a misrepresentation is a question of fact to be decided by the jury. The Supreme Court reversed, holding that the Georgia courts had denied full faith and credit to the laws of New York and that "there was no occurrence, nothing done, to which the law of Georgia could apply." The Court also said (299 U.S., at 183):

". . . Because the statute is a 'public act,' faith and credit must be given to its provisions as fully as if the materiality of this specific misrepresentation in the application, and the consequent non-existence of liability, had been declared by a judgment of a New York court. . . ."

NEW YORK LIFE INSURANCE CO. v. DODGE

Supreme Court of the United States, 1918.
246 U.S. 357, 38 S.Ct. 337, 62 L.Ed. 772, Ann.Cas.1918E, 593.

Error to the Springfield Court of Appeals of Missouri.

MR. JUSTICE MCREYNOLDS delivered the opinion of the Court:

Defendant in error brought suit January 27, 1915, in circuit court, Phelps county, Missouri, upon a policy dated October 20, 1900, on life of her husband Josiah B. Dodge, who died February 12, 1912. She alleged: That plaintiff in error, a New York corporation, had long maintained local offices and carried on the business of life insurance in Missouri, where she and her husband resided; that in 1900, at St. Louis, he applied for and received the policy, she being named as beneficiary; that premiums were paid to October 20, 1907, when the policy lapsed, having then a net value, three-fourths of which less "indebtedness to the company given on account of past premium payments," applied as required by the Missouri nonforfeiture statute (section 7897), sufficed to extend it beyond assured's death. Further, that upon application by assured and herself, presented at St. Louis, the company there made him loans amounting, October 20, 1907, to

$1,350, but of this only $599.65 had been applied to premiums. She asked judgment for full amount of policy less loan, unpaid premiums, interest, etc.

Answering the company admitted issuance of policy, but denied liability because assured borrowed of it, November 1906, at its home office, New York City, $1,350, hypothecating the policy there as security, and then failed to pay premium due October 20, 1907, whereupon, in strict compliance with New York law and agreements made there, the entire reserve was appropriated to satisfy the loan, and all obligations ceased. The assured, being duly notified, offered no objection. It further set up that as the loan, pledge, and foreclosure were within New York, the Federal Constitution protected them against inhibition or modification by a Missouri statute; and, if intended to produce such result, section 7897, Mo.Rev.Stat.1899, lacked validity. .

In reply, defendant in error denied assent to alleged settlement; maintained all transactions in question took place in Missouri; and asserted validity of its applicable statutes.

The Springfield court of appeals affirmed a judgment for $2,233.45,—amount due after deducting loan, unpaid premiums, etc. Mo.App., 189 S.W. 609. It declared former opinions of the state supreme court conclusively settled the constitutionality of section 7897 and that the reserve, after paying advances for premiums, was thereby appropriated to purchasing term insurance, notwithstanding any contrary agreement. Burridge v. New York L. Ins. Co., 211 Mo. 158, 109 S.W. 560; Smith v. Mutual Ben. L. Ins. Co., 173 Mo. 329, 72 S.W. 935. Effort to secure a review by the supreme court failed.

Section 7897, Mo.Rev.Stat.1899, in effect until amended in 1903, provides: "No policies of insurance on life hereafter issued by any life insurance company authorized to do business in this state, . . . shall, after payment upon it of three annual payments, be forfeited or become void, by reason of nonpayment of premiums thereof, but it shall be subject to the following rules of commutation, to wit: The net value of the policy when the premium becomes due, and is not paid, shall be computed . . . and after deducting from three-fourths of such net value any notes or other evidence of indebtedness to the company, given on account of past premium payments on said policies, issued to the insured, which indebtedness shall be then canceled, the balance shall be taken as a net single premium for temporary insurance for the full amount written in the policy; . . ."

Both defendant in error and her husband, the assured, at all times here material, resided in Missouri. Being duly licensed by that state, plaintiff in error, responding to an application signed by Josiah B. Dodge, at St. Louis, issued and delivered to him there a five-thousand-dollar-twenty-year endowment policy upon his life, dated October 20, 1900, naming his wife beneficiary, but reserving the right to designate another. Among other things, it stipulated: "Cash loans can be obtained by the insured on the sole security of this policy on demand at any time after this policy has been in force two full years, if premiums have been duly paid to the anniversary of the insurance next succeeding the date when the loan is made. Application for any loan must be made in writing to the home office of the company, and the loan will be subject to the terms of the company's loan agreement. The amount of loan available at any time is stated below, and includes any previous loan then unpaid. Interest will be at the rate of 5 per cent per annum in advance. . . . If any premium is not paid on or before the day when due, or within the month of grace, the liability of the company shall be only as hereinbefore provided for such case." "Any indebtedness to the company, including any balance of the premium for the insurance year remaining unpaid, will be deducted in any settlement of this policy or of any benefit thereunder."

By an application addressed to the company at New York, accompanied by a loan agreement, both signed at St. Louis and "forwarded from Missouri Clearing House, branch office, August 29, 1903," together with pledge of the policy,—all received and accepted at the home office in New York City,—the assured obtained from the company a loan of $490. Its check for the proceeds, drawn on a New York bank and payable to his order, was sent to him at St. Louis by mail. Annually thereafter the outstanding loan was settled and a larger one negotiated,—all in substantial accord with plan just described. The avails were applied partly to premiums; the balance went directly to assured by the company's check on a New York bank.

[The court then outlined the terms of the loan agreement and application:] That the application for said loan was made to said company at his home office in the city of New York, was accepted, the money paid by it, and this agreement made and delivered there; that said principal and interest are payable at said home office; and that this contract is made under and pursuant to the laws of the state of New York, the place of said contract being said home office of said company. . . .

That the policy, when issued to Dodge, became a Missouri contract, subject to its statutes, so far as valid and applicable, is undisputed and clear. . . . Here the controversy concerns effect of the state statute upon agreements between the parties made long after date of the policy, and action taken thereunder; their essential fairness and accordance with New York laws are not challenged.

Considering the circumstances recited above, we think competent parties consummated the loan contract now relied upon in New York, where it was to be performed. And, moreover, that it is one of a kind which ordinarily no state by direct action may prohibit a citizen within her borders from making outside of them. It should be noted that the clause in the policy providing "cash loans can be obtained by the insured on the sole security of this policy on demand, etc.," certainly imposed no obligation upon the company to make such a loan if the Missouri statute applied and inhibited valid hypothecation of the reserve as security therefor, as defendant in error maintains. She cannot, therefore, claim anything upon the theory that the loan contract actually consummated was one which the company had legally obligated itself to make upon demand.

[The court outlined and quoted from Allgeyer v. Louisiana, 165 U.S. 578, and New York Life Ins. Co. v. Head, 234 U.S. 149.]

Under the laws of New York, where the parties made the loan agreement now before us, it was valid; also it was one which the Missouri legislature could not destroy or prevent a citizen within its borders from making beyond them by direct inhibition; and applying the principles accepted and enforced in New York L. Ins. Co. v. Head, we think the necessary conclusion is that such a contract could not be indirectly brought into subjection to statutes of the state and rendered ineffective through a license authorizng the insurance company there to do business. As construed and applied by the Springfield court of appeals, section 7897 transcends the power of the state. To hold otherwise would permit destruction of the right—often of great value—freely to borrow money upon a policy from the issuing company at its home office, and would, moreover, sanction the impairment of that liberty of contract guaranteed to all by the Fourteenth Amendment.

Reversed.

MR. JUSTICE BRANDEIS, dissenting: . . .

First: Was the loan agreement in fact made in New York?

The policy was confessedly a Missouri contract. Dodge, so far as appears, was never out of Missouri. Physically every act done by Dodge and the beneficiary in connection with the loan agreement, as with the policy, was done in Missouri: . . .

Nothing was done in New York, then, except this: The papers received from the Missouri Clearing House, branch office, were examined and filed in the home office, and certain calculations and appropriate entries in the books and on the papers were made there. No money was paid then to Dodge. The nominal advance was less than the amount, including accrued premium, then due by him to the company; and Dodge balanced the account by paying in Missouri $116.40. . . . Under the 1903 agreement the policy was delivered to the company and it had remained in the company's possession at the home office. But when the loan agreement here in question was made, nothing was done in New York except to examine and file the papers and to make the calculations and entries. No discretion was exercised there by the company's official. By the terms of the policy the company had already assented to the amount nominally advanced as a loan and to the rate of interest to be charged. The functions exercised by the officials at New York were limited to determining whether the calculations were correct and whether papers were properly executed and filed.

These acts so done by the company at its home office in connection with the loan agreement were similar in character to those performed when the policy was written. . . . But such acts did not prevent the policy being held to be a Missouri contract. . . . Even if the loan agreement be treated as an independent contract, it should, if facts are allowed to control, be held to have been made in Missouri. But the loan agreement was not an independent contract; nor is it to be treated as a modification of the original contract. It was an act contemplated by the policy and was subsidiary to it, as an incident thereof. What was done by the officials at the home office was not making a New York contract, but performing acts under a Missouri contract.

Second: What is the effect of the provision in the loan agreement that it shall be deemed to have been made in New York? [The provision was held inoperative.]

Third: Even if the rules ordinarily applied in determining the place of a contract required this court to hold, as a matter of general law, that the loan agreement was made in New York, it would not necessarily follow that the Missouri statute was unconstitutional, because it prohibited giving effect in part to the loan agreement. There is no constitutional limitation by virtue of which a statute enacted by a state in the exercise of the police power is necessarily void, if, in its operation, contracts made in another state may be affected. . . . The test of constitutionality to be applied here is that commonly applied when the validity of a statute limiting the right of contract is questioned, namely: Is the subject-matter within the reasonable scope of regulation? Is the end legitimate? Are the means appropriate to the end sought to be obtained? If so, the act must be sustained, unless the court is satisfied that it is clearly an arbitrary and unnecessary interference with the right of the individual to his personal liberty. Here the subject is insurance; a subject long recognized as being within the sphere of regulation of contracts. The specific end to be attained was the protection of the net value of insurance policies by prohibiting provisions for forfeiture; an incident of the insurance contract long recognized as requiring regulation. The means adopted was to prescribe the limits within which the parties might agree to dispose of the net value of the policy otherwise than by commutation into extended insurance; a means commonly adopted in nonforfeiture laws, only the specific limitation in question being unusual. The insurance policy sought to be protected was a contract made within the state, between a citizen of the state and a foreign corporation also resident or present there. The protection was to be afforded while the parties so remained subject to the jurisdiction of the state. The protection was accomplished by refusing to permit the courts of the state to give to acts done within it by such residents (Dodge did no act elsewhere) the effect of nullifying in part that nonforfeiture provision which the legislature deemed necessary for the welfare of the citizens of the state and for their protection against acts of insuring corporations. The statute does not invalidate any part of the loan; it leaves intact the ordinary remedies for collecting debts. The statute merely prohibits satisfying a part of the debt out of the reserve in a manner deemed by the legislature destructive of the protection devised against forfeiture.   . . .

Mr. Justice Day, Mr. Justice Pitney, and Mr. Justice Clarke concur in this dissent.

———

Mutual Life Insurance Co. v. Liebing, 259 U.S. 209 (1922): [The issues and the facts in this case were almost precisely parallel to those in the Dodge case next above, except for a difference in the wording of the loan provision in the insurance policy. The Supreme Court of the United States unanimously affirmed a judgment of the Missouri court in favor of the beneficiary against the insurance company.]

Holmes, J.   . . .   In New York L. Ins. Co. v. Dodge, supra, it was held that when the later transaction was consummated in New York, Missouri could not prohibit a citizen within her borders from executing it. But if the later contract was made in Missouri, then by the present and earlier decisions, notwithstanding any contrary agreement, the statute does govern the case. See 246 U.S. 366.

The policy now sued upon contained a positive promise to make the loan if asked, whereas, in the one last mentioned, it might be held that some discretion was reserved to the company. For here the language is, "the company will . . . loan amounts within the limits of the cash surrender value," etc., where as there it was, "cash loans can be obtained." On this distinction the Missouri court seems to have held that, as soon as the application was delivered to a representative of the company in Missouri, the offer in the policy was accepted and the new contract complete, and therefore subject to Missouri law. If, however, the application should be regarded as only an offer, the effective acceptance of it did not take place until the check was delivered to Blees, which again was in Missouri, where he lived. In whichever way regarded, the facts lead to the same conclusion; and although the circumstances may present some temptation to seek a different one by ingenuity, the Constitution and the first principles of legal thinking allow the law of the place where a contract is made to determine the validity and the consequences of the act.

———

Hartford Accident & Indemnity Co. v. Delta & Pine Land Co., 292 U.S. 143 (1934): An action was brought in a Mississippi court on a fidelity bond covering the insured's employees in any position and anywhere they worked, of course including Mississippi. The bond was issued in Tennessee. The defalcation which was the subject of the action occurred in Mississippi. The bond had a provision that claim under it must be made within fifteen months from the termination of the suretyship on the defaulting employee, and the claim sued on was not made within that period. The provision was valid under the law of Tennessee. A Mississippi statute provided "All contracts of insurance on property, lives or interests in this state shall be deemed to be made therein". Another statute struck down the kind of limitation contained in the bond. The courts of Mississippi applied the Mississippi statutes and gave judgment for the plaintiff. The Supreme Court of the United States reversed the judgment, saying "A state may limit or prohibit the making of certain contracts within its own territory . . . but it cannot extend the effect of its laws beyond its borders so as to destroy or impair the rights of citizens of other states to make a contract not operative within its jurisdiction and lawful where made. . . . it may not, on grounds of policy, ignore a right which has lawfully vested elsewhere, if, as here, the interest of the forum has but slight connection with the substance of the contract obligations. A legislative policy which attempts to draw to the state of the forum control over the obligations of contracts elsewhere validly consummated and to convert them for all purposes into contracts of the forum, regardless of the relative importance of the interests of the forum as contrasted with those created at the place of the contract, conflicts with the guaranties of the Fourteenth Amendment." The Court said it was unnecessary to reach the defendant's arguments based on the full faith and credit and contract clauses.

NOTES

(1) The principal case has had a checkered career in the Supreme Court. Its current status must be diagnosed on the basis of close reading of the Justices' opinions in Clay v. Sun Insurance Office, Limited, p. 355 infra and Allstate Insurance Co. v. Hague, p. 358 infra.

(2) What factors might argue for a different standard in determining the constitutionality of assertions of legislative power in the international context compared with the interstate? See Jones, An Interest Analysis Approach to Extraterritorial Application of Rule 10b–5, 52 Tex.L.Rev. 983 (1974); Comment, 12 Houston L.Rev. 924 (1975).

ORDER OF UNITED COMMERCIAL TRAVELERS v. WOLFE

Supreme Court of the United States, 1947.
331 U.S. 586, 67 S.Ct. 1355, 91 L.Ed. 1687, 173 A.L.R. 1107.

MR. JUSTICE BURTON delivered the opinion of the Court.

This is an action in a circuit court of the State of South Dakota, brought by an Ohio citizen against a fraternal benefit society incorporated in Ohio, to recover benefits claimed to have arisen under the constitution of that society as a result of the death of an insured member who had been a citizen of South Dakota throughout his membership. The case presents the question whether the full faith and credit clause of the Constitution of the United States required the court of the forum, South Dakota, to give effect to a provision of the constitution of the society prohibiting the bringing of an action on such a claim more than six months after the disallowance of the claim by the Supreme Executive Committee of the society, when that provision was valid under the law of the state of the society's incorporation, Ohio, but when the time prescribed generally by South Dakota for commencing actions on contracts was six years and when another statute of South Dakota declared that—

"Every stipulation or condition in a contract, by which any party thereto is restricted from enforcing his rights under the contract by the usual legal proceedings in the ordinary tribunals, or which limits the time within which he may thus enforce his rights, is void."

We hold that, under such circumstances, South Dakota, as the state of the forum, was required, by the Constitution of the United States, to give full faith and credit to the public acts of Ohio under which the fraternal benefit society was incorporated, and that the claimant was bound by the six-month limitation upon bringing suit to recover death benefits based upon membership rights of a decedent under the constitution of the society. This has been the consistent view of this Court. [Citing, in a footnote Royal Arcanum v. Green, 237 U.S. 531; Modern Woodmen v. Mixer, 267 U.S. 544; Broderick v. Rosner, 294 U.S. 629; Sovereign Camp v. Bolin, 305 U.S. 66; Pink v. A.A.A. Highway Express, 314 U.S. 201.]

. . .

. . . These public acts have created and regulated the society and the rights and obligations of its members. They are reflected in its articles of incorporation, constitution and by-laws. They make possible uniformity of rights and obligations among all members throughout the country, provided full faith and credit are given also to the constitution and by-laws of the society insofar as they are valid under the law of the state of incorporation. If full faith and credit are not given to these provisions, the mutual rights and obligations of the members of such societies are left subject to the control of each state. They become unpredictable and almost inevitably unequal.

. . .

The relationship thus established between a member and his fraternal benefit society differs from the ordinary contractual relationship between a policyholder and a separately owned corporate or "stock" insurance company. It differs also from that between an insured member of the usual business form of a mutual insurance company and that company. The fact of membership in the Ohio fraternal benefit society is the controlling and central feature of the relationship. . . . The foundation of the society is the law of Ohio. It provides the unifying control over the rights and obligations of its members. . . .

The decisions passing upon this comparatively narrow issue are to be distinguished from those which deal only with the well established principle of conflict of laws that "If action is barred by the statute of limitations of the forum, no action can be maintained though action is not barred in the state where the cause of action arose." Restatement, Conflict of Laws § 603 (1934). . . .

. . .

Accepting the view . . . , that this Court should not give what Mr. Justice Stone called a mere "automatic effect to the full faith and credit clause," [Alaska Packers Assn. v. Comm'n, 294 U.S. 532, at page 547], this Court consistently has upheld, on the basis of evaluated public policy, the law of the state of incorporation of a fraternal benefit society as the law that should control the validity of the terms of membership in that corporation. The weight of public policy behind the general statute of South Dakota, which seeks to avoid certain provisions in ordinary contracts, does not equal that which makes necessary the recognition of the same terms of membership for members of fraternal benefit societies wherever their beneficiaries may be. . . .

Reversed.

MR. JUSTICE BLACK, with whom MR. JUSTICE DOUGLAS, MR. JUSTICE MURPHY, and MR. JUSTICE RUTLEDGE join, dissenting.

. . .

Until today I had never conceived of the Federal Constitution as requiring the forty-eight states to give full faith and credit to the laws of private corporations on the theory that a policyholder-member's ability to protect himself through intra-corporate politics makes state protection of him unnecessary and unconstitutional. . . .

. . .

. . . Hereafter, if today's doctrine should be carried to its logical end, the state in which the most powerful corporations are concentrated, or those corporations themselves, might well be able to pass laws which would govern contracts made by the people in all of the other states.

NOTE

The Wolfe case has remained a rare instance of the use of the full faith and credit clause to strike down a choice of the forum's rule in preference to a sister state's.

ALASKA PACKERS ASSOCIATION V. INDUSTRIAL ACCIDENT COMMISSION OF CALIFORNIA, 294 U.S. 532 (1935): A non-resident alien executed in California a written contract of employment under which he agreed to work for his employer in Alaska during the salmon canning season. The employer agreed to transport him to and from Alaska and to pay him his stipulated wages in California on his return. The contract recited that the employee had elected to be bound by the Alaska Workmen's Compensation Law. The employee was injured in Alaska and on his return to California he sought an award under that state's compensation act and was granted it. The employer attacked the award as made in violation of the due process and full faith and credit clauses. The Supreme Court of the United States upheld the award.

Mr. Justice Stone: "The probability is slight that injured workmen, once returned to California, would be able to retrace their steps to Alaska, and there successfully prosecute their claims for compensation. Without a remedy in California, they would be remediless, and there was the danger that they might become public charges, both matters of grave public concern to the state.

"California, therefore, had a legitimate public interest in controlling and regulating this employer-employee relationship. . . .

". . . [T]he conflict is to be resolved, not by giving automatic effect to the full faith and credit clause, compelling the courts of each state to subordinate its own statutes to those of the other, but by appraising the governmental interests of each jurisdiction, and turning the scale of decision according to their weight.

". . . [O]nly if it appears that, in the conflict of interests which have found expression in the conflicting statutes, the interest of Alaska is superior to that of California, is there rational basis for denying to the courts of California the right to apply the laws of their own state."

PACIFIC EMPLOYERS INSURANCE CO. v. INDUSTRIAL ACCIDENT COMMISSION

Supreme Court of the United States, 1939.
306 U.S. 493, 59 S.Ct. 629, 83 L.Ed. 940.

MR. JUSTICE STONE delivered the opinion of the Court.

The question is whether the full faith and credit which the Constitution requires to be given to a Massachusetts workmen's compensation statute precludes California from applying its own workmen's compensation act in the case of an injury suffered by a Massachusetts employee of a Massachusetts employer while in California in the course of his employment.

. . .

The injured employee, a resident of Massachusetts, . . . instituted the present proceeding before the California Commission for the award of compensation under the California Act . . . , naming petitioner as insurance carrier under that Act . . . . The California Commission directed petitioner to pay the compensation prescribed by the California Act, including the amounts of lien claims filed in the proceeding for medical, hospital and nursing services and certain further amounts necessary for such services in the future.

By the applicable Massachusetts statute, sections 24, 26, c. 152, Mass.Gen.Laws (Ter.Ed.1932), an employee of a person insured under the Act, as was the employer in this case, is deemed to waive his "right of action at common law or under the law of any other jurisdiction" to recover for personal injuries unless he shall have given appropriate notice to the employer in writing that he elects to retain such rights. Section 26 directs that without the notice his right to recover be restricted to the compensation provided by the Act for injuries received in the course of his employment, "whether within or without the commonwealth." . . .

. . . Section 27(a) [of California's Workmen's Compensation Act] provides that "No contract, rule, or regulation shall exempt the employer from liability for the compensation fixed by this act." And section 58 provides that the commission shall have jurisdiction over claims for compensation for injuries suffered outside the state when the employee's contract of hire was entered into within the state. . . . The California Act is compulsory. Section 6(a). The Massachusetts Act is similarly effective unless the employee gives notice not to be bound by it, which in this case he did not do. Section 24.

Petitioner, which as insurance carrier has assumed the liability of the employer under the California Act, relies on the provisions of the Massachusetts Act that the compensation shall be that prescribed for injuries suffered in the course of the employment, whether within or without the state. It insists that since the contract of employment was entered into in Massachusetts and the employee consented to be bound by the Massachusetts Act, that, and not the California statute, fixes the employee's right to compensation whether the injuries were received within or without the state, and that the Massachusetts statute is constitutionally entitled to full faith and credit in the courts of California.

We may assume that these provisions are controlling upon the parties in Massachusetts, and that since they are applicable to a Massachusetts contract of employment between a Massachusetts employer and employee, they do not infringe due process. . . . Similarly the constitutionality of the provisions of the California statute awarding compensation for injuries to an employee occurring within its borders, ... is not open to question. . . .

While in the circumstances now presented, either state, if its system for administering workmen's compensation permitted, would be free to adopt and enforce the remedy provided by the statute of the other, here each has provided for itself an exclusive remedy for a liability which it was constitutionally authorized to impose. But neither is bound, apart from the compulsion of the full faith and credit clause, to enforce the laws of the other . . . .

To the extent that California is required to give full faith and credit to the conflicting Massachusetts statute it must be denied the right to apply in its own courts its own statute, constitutionally enacted in pursuance of its policy to provide compensation for employees injured in their employment within the state. . . . We cannot say that the full faith and credit clause goes so far.

While the purpose of that provision was to preserve rights acquired or confirmed under the public acts and judicial proceedings of one state by requiring recognition of their validity in other states, the very nature of the federal union of states, to which are reserved some of the attributes of sovereignty, precludes resort to the full faith and credit clause as the means for compelling a state to substitute the statutes of other states for its own statutes dealing with a subject matter concerning which it is competent to legislate. As was pointed out in Alaska Packers Assn. v. Industrial Accident Comm'n, [294 U.S. 532, 547]: "A rigid and literal enforcement of the full faith and credit clause, without regard to the statute of the forum, would lead to the absurd result that, wherever the conflict arises, the statute of each state must be enforced in the courts of the other, but cannot be in its own." And in cases like the present it would create an impasse which would often leave the employee remediless. Full faith and credit would deny to California the right to apply its own remedy, and its administrative machinery may well not be adapted to giving the remedy afforded by Massachusetts. . . .

. . .

This Court must determine for itself how far the full faith and credit clause compels the qualification or denial of rights asserted under the laws of one state, that of the forum, by the statute of another state. . . . But there would seem to be little room for the exercise of that function when the statute of the forum is the expression of domestic policy, in terms declared to be exclusive in its application to persons and events within the state. Although Massachusetts has an interest in safeguarding the compensation of Massachusetts employees while temporarily abroad in the course of their employment, and may adopt that policy for itself, that could hardly be thought to support an application of the full faith and credit clause which would override the constitutional authority of another state to legislate for the bodily safety and economic protection of employees injured within it. Few matters could be deemed more appropriately the concern of the state in which the injury occurs or more completely within its power. . . .

Bradford Electric Light Co. v. Clapper [286 U.S. 145 (1932)], on which petitioner relies, fully recognized this limitation on the full faith and credit clause. It was there held that a federal court in New Hampshire, in a suit brought against a Vermont employer by his Vermont employee to recover for an injury suffered in the course of his employment while temporarily in New Hampshire, was bound to apply the Vermont Compensation Act rather than the provision of the New Hampshire Compensation Act which permitted the employee, at his election, to enforce his common law remedy. But the Court was careful to point out that there was nothing in the New Hampshire statute, the decisions of its courts, or in the circumstances of the case, to suggest that reliance on the provisions of the Vermont statute, as a defense to the New Hampshire suit, was obnoxious to the policy of New Hampshire. The Clapper case cannot be said to have decided more than that a state statute applicable to employer and employee within the state, which by its terms provides compensation for the employee if he is injured in the course of his employment while temporarily in another state, will be given full faith and credit in the latter when not obnoxious to its policy. See Bradford Electric Light Co. v. Clapper, supra, 161.

Here, California legislation . . . expressly provides, . . . that "No contract, rule or regulation shall exempt the employer from liability for the compensation fixed by this Act." The Supreme Court of California has declared in its opinion in this case that . . . "It would be obnoxious to [the policy of the California Act] to deny persons who have been injured in this state the right to apply for compensation when to do so might require physicians and hospitals to go to another state to collect charges for medical care and treatment given to such persons."

Full faith and credit does not here enable one state to legislate for the other or to project its laws across state lines so as to preclude the other from prescribing for itself the legal consequences of acts within it.

Affirmed.

NOTES

(1) In the Pacific Employers case Justice Stone seemingly shifted away from the interest—appraising and—weighing approach to full faith and credit that he asserted so forcefully in Alaska Packers. Instead, he advanced a view based on reading Bradford Electric v. Clapper to mean that the full faith and credit clause does not require the forum state to apply another state's laws if it finds them "obnoxious" to the forum law's policy. Since the forum court presumably will not often balk at applying sister-state law that is congenial to its own, does this approach in effect read full faith and credit out of the picture? Notice what happens to the interest-weighing and "obnoxious" tests in later Supreme Court decisions, such as Carroll v. Lanza and Watson.

(2) Does the full faith and credit command add anything to the due process requirement in choice of law? If so, what? These questions thread through the remaining cases in this section.

———

CARROLL v. LANZA

Supreme Court of the United States, 1955.
349 U.S. 408, 75 S.Ct. 804, 99 L.Ed. 1183.

Mr. Justice Douglas delivered the opinion of the Court.

Carroll, the petitioner, was an employee of Hogan, an intervenor, who in turn was a subcontractor doing work for the respondent Lanza, the general contractor. Carroll and Hogan were residents of Missouri; and Carroll's employment contract with Hogan was made in Missouri. The work, however, was done in Arkansas; and it was there that the injury occurred.

Carroll, not aware that he had remedies under the Arkansas law, received 34 weekly payments for the injury under the Missouri Compensation Act.

[The Missouri workmen's compensation act, so the Court found, was applicable to injuries received outside the state if the employment contract was made in the state, as here, and the act in terms excluded "all other rights and remedies . . . at common law or otherwise" on account of an injury or death. The Arkansas workmen's compensation act also purported to provide the exclusive remedy of the employee against the employer but not against a third party as the general contractor, Lanza.

While receiving weekly payments under the Missouri act Carroll sued Lanza for common law damages in an Arkansas state court, and on removal to the federal court recovered a judgment. The Court of Appeals, while agreeing with the District Court that the judgment was sustainable as a matter of Arkansas law, reversed on the ground the Full Faith and Credit Clause of the Constitution barred recovery. The Supreme Court of the United States granted certiorari because of doubts raised by the Pacific Employers Insurance Co. case, p. 344, supra.]

The Pacific Employers Insurance Co. case allowed the Compensation Act of the place of the injury to override the Compensation Act of the home State. Here it is a common-law action that is asserted against the exclusiveness of the remedy of the home State; and that is seized on as marking a difference. That is not in our judgment a material difference. Whatever deprives the remedy of the home State of its exclusive character qualifies or contravenes the policy of that State and denies it full faith and credit, if full faith and credit is due. But the Pacific Employers Insurance Co. case teaches that in these personal injury cases the State where the injury occurs need not be a vassal to the home State and allow only that remedy which the home State has marked as the exclusive one. . . . Her interests are large and considerable and are to be weighed not only in the light of the facts of this case but by the kind of situation presented. For we write not only for this case and this day alone, but for this type of case. The State where the tort occurs certainly has a concern in the problems following in the wake of the injury. The problems of medical care and of possible dependents are among these . . . Arkansas therefore has a legitimate interest in opening her courts to suits of this nature, even though in this case Carroll's injury may have cast no burden on her or on her institutions.

. . . Arkansas, the State of the forum, is not adopting any policy of hostility to the public Acts of Missouri. It is choosing to apply its own rule of law to give affirmative relief for an action arising within its borders.

. . . Were it otherwise, the State where the injury occurred would be powerless to provide any remedies or safeguards to nonresident employees working within its borders. We do not think the Full Faith and Credit Clause demands that subserviency from the State of the injury.

Reversed.

MR. JUSTICE FRANKFURTER, whom MR. JUSTICE BURTON and MR. JUSTICE HARLAN join, dissenting.

In order to place the problems presented by this case in the proper context for adjudication, it has seemed to me desirable to examine the course of the Court's decisions touching the constitutional requirement for giving full faith and credit to statutes of a sister State.

The cases fall into three main groups:

(1) Those in which the forum was called upon to give effect to a sister-state statute and declined to do so.

. . . From these cases it appears that, the forum cannot, by statute or otherwise, refuse to enforce a sister-state statute giving a transitory cause of action, whether in contract or tort. E.g., Broderick v. Rosner, [294 U.S. 629 (1935)]; Hughes v. Fetter, [341 U.S. 609 (1951)]. Indeed, the forum may permissibly go a step in the other direction and disregard the venue provisions of an out-of-state statute which would have prevented the forum from enforcing the right. Tennessee Coal, Iron & R. Co. v. George, [233 U.S. 354 (1914)]. The forum may, however, apply its own more restrictive statute of limitations to an outside wrongful death action, Wells v. Simonds Abrasive Co., [345 U.S. 514 (1953)] and dicta indicate that it may refuse to enforce a penal law, a law found antagonistic to the forum's public policy, or a law which requires specialized proceedings or remedies not available in the forum, . . .

(2) Those in which the forum applied its own statute rather than that of a sister State because the latter was not of limiting exclusive-

ness, or in which the forum applied the sister-state statute because the forum's was not exclusive. . . .

These cases prove that where the statute of either the forum or the outside State is not found to be exclusive regarding remedies or rights elsewhere, the statute need not be accorded exclusive effect. Further, the Court has stated that, in the area of workmen's compensation, "unmistakable language" is required before exclusiveness will be attributed. See Industrial Commission of Wisconsin v. McCartin, 330 U.S. at page 628.

(3) Those in which the forum applied its own substantive law, statutory or judicial, when clearly in conflict with the out-of-state statute. [The opinion here cites twenty-one cases.]

These cases have arisen in three principal fields: (a) commercial law; (b) insurance; and (c) workmen's compensation. As a statistical matter, in 21 cases of direct conflict the Court held for the forum 10 times and for the sister State 11 times.

(a) In commercial law a number of cases have involved statutory assessment against out-of-state shareholders under the laws of the State of incorporation of an insolvent corporation. The Court's consistent position has been that the law of the incorporating State must be given effect by the forum. . . .

(b) The insurance cases reflect considerations similar to those in the commercial cases. The Court has found in fraternal benefit societies an "indivisible unity" among the members and a resultant need for uniform construction of rights and duties in the common fund.
. . .

As to ordinary insurance contracts, the forum has had a much wider scope. The Court has balanced the interests of the competing jurisdictions, including factors such as the residence of the insured, where premiums were paid or payable, where the policy was applied for and delivered, where the insured died, what law the policy itself provided should govern, and whether loan agreements and new policies were ancillary to the initial policy. The forum has been permitted to protect its residents against insurance companies, but the Court has required the forum to have more than a casual interest.
. . .

(c) In workmen's compensation cases the Court has likewise adopted an interests-weighing approach. . . .

In applying to the immediate situation the fair guidance offered by the past decisions of the Court regarding full faith and credit, a number of considerations become apparent: (1) Unlike the other workmen's compensation cases—or, for that matter, any of the cases in which the forum has prevailed in a conflict between the forum and the outside law—the interest of the forum here is solely dependent on the occurrence of the injury within its borders. No rights of Arkansas residents are involved, since none of the parties is an Arkansan;

the workman was removed immediately to a Missouri hospital and has, so far as appears, remained in Missouri. What might be regarded as the societal interest of Arkansas in the protection of the bodily safety of workers within its borders is an interest equally true of any jurisdiction where a workman is injured and exactly the sort of interest which New Hampshire had in Clapper. [Bradford Electric Light Co. v. Clapper, 286 U.S. 145 (1932).] (2) Thus, the Court is squarely faced with the Clapper problem. To make the interest of Arkansas prevail over the interest of Missouri on the basis of the Full Faith and Credit Clause would require that Clapper be explicitly overruled and that, in the area of workmen's compensation law, the place of injury be decisive. And if Clapper is to be overruled, on which I and those who join me express no opinion, it should be done with reasons making manifest why Mr. Justice Brandeis' long-matured, weighty opinion in that case was ill-founded. It should not be cast aside on the presupposition that full faith and credit need not be given to a sister-state workmen's compensation statute if the law of the forum happens to be more favorable to the claimant. (3) Furthermore, the new provision of 28 U.S.C. § 1738, cannot be disregarded. In 1948 Congress for the first time dealt with the full faith and credit effect to be given statutes. The absence of such a provision was used by Mr. Justice Stone to buttress the Court's opinions both in Alaska Packers, 294 U.S. at page 547, and Pacific Employers, 306 U.S. at page 502. Hence, if § 1738 has any effect, it would seem to tend toward respecting Missouri's legislation. See Reese, Full Faith and Credit to Statutes: The Defense of Public Policy, 19 U. of Chi.L.Rev. 339, 343 et seq.

There is, however, a readily available alternative short of overruling Clapper, which dispenses with the difficulties inherent in applying the Full Faith and Credit Clause.

[The alternative preferred in the dissent was that the Missouri law itself might not bar a right of action against the general contractor, and the case should be remanded to the Court of Appeals for a determination of the Missouri law on this matter.]

NOTES

(1) Bradford Electric v. Clapper seemed to have identified the place where the employment was entered into and centered as *the* critical factor selected by full faith and credit in implementing workmen's compensation laws. Is there anything left of that implication—or of the holding in Clapper—after Carroll v. Lanza?

(2) In Posnak, Choice of Law: A Very Well-Curried Leflar Approach, 34 Mercer L.Rev. 731 (1983), the author argues that the Carroll case may go over the edge constitutionally because it seems to allow a state with no actual interest in the aftermath of an injury (or any other element of the transaction) to apply its own rule in derogation of the contrary law of a state with strong interests in the case.

(3) How should former law professor Frankfurter's opinion be graded as an exposition of the command of full faith and credit to sister-state law as of 1955?

WATSON v. EMPLOYERS LIABILITY ASSURANCE CORP., LIMITED

Supreme Court of the United States, 1954.
348 U.S. 66, 75 S.Ct. 166, 99 L.Ed. 74.

MR. JUSTICE BLACK delivered the opinion of the Court.

Louisiana has an insurance code which comprehensively regulates the business of insurance in all its phases. This case brings to us challenges to the constitutionality of certain provisions of that code allowing injured persons to bring direct actions against liability insurance companies that have issued policies contracting to pay liabilities imposed on persons who inflict injury. Cf. Lumbermen's Mutual Casualty Co. v. Elbert, 348 U.S. 48. This is such a direct action brought by the appellants, Mr. and Mrs. Watson, in a Louisiana state court claiming damages against the appellee, Employers Liability Assurance Corporation, Ltd., on account of alleged personal injuries suffered by Mrs. Watson. The complaint charged that the injuries occurred in Louisiana when Mrs. Watson bought and used in that State "Toni Home Permanent" a hair-waving product alleged to have contained a highly dangerous latent ingredient put there by its manufacturer. The manufacturer is the Toni Company of Illinois, a subsidiary of the Gillette Safety Razor Company which has its headquarters in Massachusetts.

The particular problem presented with reference to enforcing the Louisiana statute in this case arises because the insurance policy sued on was negotiated and issued in Massachusetts and delivered in Massachusetts and Illinois. This Massachusetts-negotiated contract contains a clause, recognized as binding and enforceable under Massachusetts and Illinois law, which prohibits direct actions against the insurance company until *after* final determination of the Toni Company's obligation to pay personal injury damages either by judgment or agreement. Contrary to this contractual "no action" clause, the challenged statutory provisions permit injured persons to sue an insurance company *before* such final determination. As to injuries occurring in Louisiana, one provision of the State's direct action statute makes it applicable, even though, as here, an insurance contract is made in another state and contains a clause forbidding such direct actions. Another Louisiana statutory provision, with which Employers long ago complied, compels foreign insurance companies to consent to such direct suits in order to get a certificate to do business in the State. The basic issue raised by the attack on both these provisions is whether the Federal Constitution forbids Louisiana to apply its own law and compels it to apply the law of Massachusetts or Illinois.

. . .

[The defendant contended the two Louisiana provisions contravened the Equal Protection, Contract, Due Process and Full Faith and Credit clauses of the Constitution. The United States District Court, to which the case had been removed, dismissed the case, holding the statutory provisions unconstitutional under the Due Process Clause as to policies written and delivered outside Louisiana. The Court of Appeals affirmed the dismissal and the plaintiff appealed.]

Some contracts made locally, affecting nothing but local affairs, may well justify a denial to other states of power to alter those contracts. But, as this case illustrates, a vast part of the business affairs of this Nation does not present such simple local situations. Although this insurance contract was issued in Massachusetts, it was to protect Gillette and its Illinois subsidiary against damages on account of personal injuries that might be suffered by users of Toni Home Permanents anywhere in the United States, its territories, or in Canada. As a consequence of the modern practice of conducting widespread business activities throughout the entire United States, this Court has in a series of cases held that more states than one may seize hold of local activities which are part of multistate transactions and may regulate to protect interests of its own people, even though other phases of the same transactions might justify regulatory legislation in other states. . . .

Louisiana's direct action statute is not a mere intermeddling in affairs beyond her boundaries which are no concern of hers. Persons injured or killed in Louisiana are most likely to be Louisiana residents, and even if not, Louisiana may have to care for them. Serious injuries may require treatment in Louisiana homes or hospitals by Louisiana doctors. The injured may be destitute. They may be compelled to call upon friends, relatives, or the public for help. Louisiana has manifested its natural interest in the injured by providing remedies for recovery of damages. It has a similar interest in policies of insurance which are designed to assure ultimate payment of such damages. Moreover, Louisiana courts in most instances provide the most convenient forum for trial of these cases. But modern transportation and business methods have made it more difficult to serve process on wrongdoers who live or do business in other states. In this case efforts to serve the Gillette Company were answered by a motion to dismiss on the ground that Gillette had no Louisiana agent on whom process could be served. If this motion is granted, Mrs. Watson, but for the direct action law, could not get her case tried without going to Massachusetts or Illinois although she lives in Louisiana and her claim is for injuries from a product bought and used there. What has been said is enough to show Louisiana's legitimate interest in safeguarding the rights of persons injured there. In view of that interest, the direct action provisions here challenged do not violate due process.

What we have said above goes far toward answering the Full Faith and Credit Clause contention. That clause does not automatically compel a state to subordinate its own contract laws to the laws of another state in which a contract happens to have been formally executed. Where, as here, a contract affects the people of several states, each may have interests that leave it free to enforce its own contract policies. . . . We have already pointed to the vital interests of Louisiana in liability insurance that covers injuries to people in that State. Of course Massachusetts also has some interest in the policy sued on in this case. The insurance contract was formally executed in that State and Gillette has an office there. But plainly these interests cannot outweigh the interest of Louisiana in taking care of those injured in Louisiana. Since this is true, the Full Faith and Credit Clause does not compel Louisiana to subordinate its direct action provisions to Massachusetts contract rules. . . .

Reversed.

[Mr. Justice Frankfurter concurred in a separate opinion in which he relied on "the practically arbitrary power of a State in dealing with the desire of a foreign corporation not privileged to do so by federal authority to do business within its bounds."]

NOTES

(1) "Since," the Court said, Massachusetts' interests "cannot outweigh the interests of Louisiana in taking care of those injured in Louisiana," full faith does not compel Louisiana to enforce the no action clause of the "Massachusetts contract." The clear implication is that the full faith and credit clause would come into play if the forum state's interests were outweighed by the other state's interests. On the other hand, the position taken in the Pacific Employers case before Watson and the Carroll case after Watson was that there is no need for interest weighing; a state is privileged to apply its own law under full faith and credit provided only it has power to do so under due process.

(2) In the years since the Watson case was decided, long-arm jurisdiction has expanded so greatly it is no longer necessary to use the direct action statute as a jurisdictional device, except in circumstances dealt with by the Seider procedure. With the invalidation of that procedure by Rush v. Savchuk, p. 161, supra, the question is what contacts the forum state must have in order to permit a direct action against an insurer when the insurance contract contains a no action clause that is valid in the state where the contract was made.

(3) In Hoopeston Canning Co. v. Cullen, 318 U.S. 313 (1942), the Court held that Illinois reciprocal insurance associations could be made subject to the laws of New York as a condition of insuring property in that state against fire and related risks. The insurance contracts were completed in Illinois, and the associations contended that under the due process clause New York could not make them subject to the laws of New York. Justice

Black responded that a state other than the state where the contract was made could have a substantial interest, "measured by highly realistic considerations such as the protection of the citizen insured or the protection of the state from the incidents of loss."

(4) The usual rule is that the forum will apply its own law in determining whether or not to grant a divorce. Can this rule constitutionally be applied in a situation where neither spouse has a close relationship to the forum state? This question is discussed by Judge Hastie in his dissenting opinion in Alton v. Alton, 207 F.2d 667 (3d Cir. 1953), p. 813, infra.

Are the tests of judicial jurisdiction and of legislative jurisdiction the same or different? See, in this connection, the following statement in Leflar, American Conflicts Law 106 (3d ed. 1977):

Contacts sufficient to satisfy "fair play and substantial justice" for judicial jurisdiction under the due process clause will often satisfy whatever test (perhaps the same test) the same clause prescribes for legislative jurisdiction. It cannot be concluded, however, that identical *facts* automatically mark the outer limits of "fair play and substantial justice" for *both* constitutional purposes. The "fairness" and "justice" which the due process clause requires depend upon the purposes and functions of the law's operation in each specific separated context. Fairness and justice are relative things, not absolutes. The questions of what law may govern and what court may act are similar though not the same. The lines that delineate the answers to the questions seem to be converging but they have not merged. (Italics as in original text.)*

CLAY v. SUN INSURANCE OFFICE, LIMITED

Supreme Court of the United States, 1964.
377 U.S. 179, 84 S.Ct. 1197, 12 L.Ed. 2d 229.

MR. JUSTICE DOUGLAS delivered the opinion of the Court.

This case, which invoked the diversity jurisdiction of the Federal District Court in a suit to recover damages under an insurance policy, was here before. 363 U.S. 207. The initial question then as now is whether the 12-month-suit clause in the policy governs, in which event the claim is barred, or whether Florida's statutes nullifying such clauses if they require suit to be filed in less than five years are applicable and valid, in which event the suit is timely. The policy was purchased by petitioner in Illinois while he was a citizen and resident of that State. Respondent, a British company, is licensed to do business in Illinois, Florida, and several other States.

* Quoted with the permission of the copyright owner, The Bobbs-Merrill Company, Inc.

A few months after purchasing the policy, petitioner moved to Florida and became a citizen and resident of that State; and it was in Florida that the loss occurred two years later. When the case reached here, the majority view was that the underlying constitutional question—whether consistently with due process, Florida could apply its five-year statute to this Illinois contract—should not be reached until the Florida Supreme Court, through its certificate procedure, had construed that statute and resolved another local law question. On remand the Court of Appeals certified the two questions to the Florida Supreme Court, which answered both questions in petitioner's favor. 133 So.2d 735. Thereafter the Court of Appeals held that it was not compatible with due process for Florida to apply its five-year statute to this contract and that judgment should be entered for respondent. 319 F.2d 505. We again granted certiorari.

. . . .

While there are Illinois cases indicating that parties may contract—as here—for a shorter period of limitations than is provided by the Illinois statute, we are referred to no Illinois decision extending that rule into other States whenever claims on Illinois contracts are sought to be enforced there. We see no difficulty whatever under either the Full Faith and Credit Clause or the Due Process Clause. We deal with an ambulatory contract on which suit might be brought in any one of several States. Normally, as the Court held in Pacific Employers Ins. Co. v. Industrial Accident Comm'n, 306 U.S. 493, 502, a State having jurisdiction over a claim deriving from an out-of-state employment contract need not substitute the conflicting statute of the other State (workmen's compensation) for its own statute (workmen's compensation)—where the employee was injured in the course of his employment while temporarily in the latter State. . . .

The Court of Appeals relied in the main on Hartford Accident & Indemnity Co. v. Delta & Pine Land Co., 292 U.S. 143, and Home Ins. Co. v. Dick, 281 U.S. 397. Those were cases where the activities in the State of the forum were thought to be too slight and too casual, as in the Delta & Pine Land Co. case . . . to make the application of local law consistent with due process, or wholly lacking, as in the Dick case. No deficiency of that order is present here. As Mr. Justice Black, dissenting, said when this case was here before:

"Insurance companies, like other contractors, do not confine their contractual activities and obligations within state boundaries. They sell to customers who are promised protection in States far away from the place where the contract is made. In this very case the policy was sold to Clay with knowledge that he could take his property anywhere in the world he saw fit without losing the protection of his insurance. In fact, his contract was described on its face as a 'Personal Property Floater Policy (World Wide)'. The contract did not even attempt to provide that the law of Illinois would govern when suits were filed anywhere else in the country. Shortly after the contract was made, Clay moved to Florida and there he lived for several years. His insured property was there all that time. The company knew this fact. Particularly since the company was licensed to do business in Florida, it must have known it might be sued there . . . ." 363 U.S. at 221.

. . .

Reversed.

NOTES

(1) Were all of the Florida contacts mentioned by Justice Douglas necessary to give Florida legislative jurisdiction? Note in this connection that the policy had been issued at a time when neither the insured nor his property had any contact with Florida.

(2) Can the Clay decision be satisfactorily distinguished from John Hancock Mutual Life Insurance Co. v. Yates, p. 335, supra? Would the decision have been different in Yates if, following the issuance of the policy, the insured had moved to Georgia and had died while domiciled there?

(3) What if the insured risk is immovable? In Burger King Corp. v. Continental Insurance Co., 359 F.Supp. 184 (W.D.Pa.1973), suit was brought in Florida on a casualty policy for property loss and loss of income as a result of damage to a fast-food restaurant because of earth movement. The insured was a Florida corporation, while the defendant was a New York corporation which wrote the insurance policy in New York on property owned by plaintiff in Pennsylvania. The policy provided that no action could be brought on it more than 12 months after the loss. This suit was commenced in Florida approximately 18 months after the loss and transferred to the Pennsylvania federal court. In denying defendant's motion for summary judgment the court applied the Florida statute that declared contractual provisions "illegal and void" as contrary to Florida's public policy if they fixed the period for suit at less than the state's five-year statute of limitations.

The court noted that the constitutionality of the Florida rule had been upheld by the Supreme Court in the Clay case. It stressed that in contrast to Quarty v. Insurance Company of North America, 244 So.2d 181 (Fla.App. 1971), denying applicability of the Florida rule to a suit for loss by burglary in New York on a policy issued in New York by a New York insurer to a New York resident who became a Florida resident within the 12-month policy claim period but did not sue until later, Burger King was a Florida corporation, with its principal place of business in Florida and at the time of the transaction defendant had a licensed agent in Florida. If the instant decision had been reviewed on appeal, should it have been reversed?

_____

NEVADA V. HALL, 440 U.S. 410 (1979): Suit brought by California residents in the courts of that state to recover for injuries sustained in California in a collision with an automobile owned by the state of Nevada and being driven on state business. Nevada interposed two defenses: sovereign immunity and that full faith and credit was owed to a Nevada statute limiting recovery against the state to $25,000. The California courts rejected both defenses and plaintiffs were awarded judgment of $1,150,000. The Supreme Court granted certiorari and, in an opinion by Justice Stevens, affirmed. On the subject of full faith and credit, Justice Stevens said:

". . . this Court's decision in Pacific Insurance Company v. Industrial Accident Commission [supra p. 344] clearly establishes that the Full Faith and Credit Clause does not require a State to apply another State's law in violation of its own legitimate public policy.

". . . In this case, California's interest is the closely related and . . . substantial one of providing 'full protection to those who are injured on its highways through the negligence of both residents and nonresidents.' Hall v. University of Nevada (appendix to petition at 7). To effectuate this interest, California has provided by statute for jurisdiction in its courts over residents and nonresidents alike to allow those injured on its highways through the negligence of others to secure full compensation for their injuries in the California courts.

"In further implementation of that policy, California has unequivocally waived its own immunity from liability for the torts committed by its own agents and authorized full recovery even against the sovereign. As the California courts have found, to require California either to surrender jurisdiction or to limit respondents' recovery to the $25,000 maximum of the Nevada statute would be obnoxious to its statutorily based policies of jurisdiction over nonresident motorists and full recovery. The Full Faith and Credit Clause does not require this result.[1]"

[Three Justices dissented with respect to the denial of Nevada's claim to sovereign immunity.]

ALLSTATE INSURANCE CO. v. HAGUE

Supreme Court of the United States, 1981.
449 U.S. 302, 101 S.Ct. 633, 66 L.Ed.2d 521.

JUSTICE BRENNAN announced the judgment of the Court and an opinion in which JUSTICE WHITE, JUSTICE MARSHALL, and JUSTICE BLACKMUN join.

This Court granted certiorari to determine whether the Due Process Clause of the Fourteenth Amendment or the Full Faith and Credit Clause of Art. 4, § 1, of the United States Constitution bars the Minnesota Supreme Court's choice of substantive Minnesota law

1. California's exercise of jurisdiction in this case poses no substantial threat to our constitutional system of cooperative federalism. Suits involving traffic accidents occurring outside of Nevada could hardly interfere with Nevada's capacity to fulfill its own sovereign responsibilities. We have no occasion, in this case, to consider whether different state policies, either of California or of Nevada, might require a different analysis or a different result. [Footnote renumbered; other footnotes omitted.]

to govern the effect of a provision in an insurance policy issued to respondent's decedent. . . .

I

Respondent's late husband, Ralph Hague, died of injuries suffered when a motorcycle on which he was a passenger was struck from behind by an automobile. The accident occurred in Pierce County, Wis., which is immediately across the Minnesota border from Red Wing, Minn. The operators of both vehicles were Wisconsin residents, as was the decedent who, at the time of the accident, resided with respondent in Hager City, Wis., which is one and one-half miles from Red Wing. Mr. Hague had been employed in Red Wing for the 15 years immediately preceding his death and had commuted daily from Wisconsin to his place of employment.

Neither the operator of the motorcycle nor the operator of the automobile carried valid insurance. However, the decedent held a policy issued by petitioner Allstate Insurance Company covering three automobiles owned by him and containing an uninsured motorist clause insuring him against loss incurred from accidents with uninsured motorists. The uninsured motorist coverage was limited to $15,000 for each automobile.[3]

After the accident, but prior to the initiation of this lawsuit, respondent moved to Red Wing. Subsequently, she married a Minnesota resident and established residence with her new husband in Savage, Minn. At approximately the same time, a Minnesota Registrar of Probate appointed respondent personal representative of her deceased husband's estate. Following her appointment, she brought this action in Minnesota District Court seeking a declaration under Minnesota law that the $15,000 uninsured motorist coverage on each of her late husband's three automobiles could be "stacked" to provide total coverage of $45,000. Petitioner defended on the ground that whether the three uninsured motorist coverages could be stacked should be determined by Wisconsin law, since the insurance policy was delivered in Wisconsin, the accident occurred in Wisconsin, and all persons involved were Wisconsin residents at the time of the accident.

The Minnesota Supreme Court, sitting en banc, affirmed the District Court [and], . . . interpreting Wisconsin law to prohibit stacking, applied Minnesota law after analyzing the relevant Minnesota contacts and interests within the analytical framework developed by Professor Leflar. See Leflar, Choice-Influencing Considerations in Conflicts Law, 41 N.Y.U.L.Rev. 267 (1966). [Professor Leflar's analytical approach, discussed at p. 479, infra, focuses on five considerations as the key factors in choice of law. The Minnesota Supreme Court determined that the fifth consideration—"applying the better

---

3. Ralph Hague paid a separate premium for each automobile including an additional separate premium for each uninsured motorist coverage.

rule of law"—called for use of Minnesota's stacking law. The court stressed that most states allow stacking, recent court decisions favor it, and the practice works well by spreading accident costs more broadly. Since insurance companies know that automobiles move freely across state lines, applying the Minnesota rule would not offend due process as too arbitrary or unreasonable.]

II

It is not for this Court to say whether the choice-of-law analysis suggested by Professor Leflar is to be preferred or whether we would make the same choice-of-law decision if sitting as the Minnesota Supreme Court. Our sole function is to determine whether the Minnesota Supreme Court's choice of its own substantive law in this case exceeded federal constitutional limitations. Implicit in this inquiry is the recognition, long accepted by this Court, that a set of facts giving rise to a lawsuit, or a particular issue within a lawsuit, may justify, in constitutional terms, application of the law of more than one jurisdiction. . . . As a result, the forum State may have to select one law from among the laws of several jurisdictions having some contact with the controversy.

In deciding constitutional choice-of-law questions, whether under the Due Process Clause or the Full Faith and Credit Clause,[10] this Court has traditionally examined the contacts of the State, whose law was applied, with the parties and with the occurrence or transaction giving rise to the litigation. . . . In order to ensure that the choice of law is neither arbitrary nor fundamentally unfair, . . . the Court has invalidated the choice of law of a State which has had no significant contact or significant aggregation of contacts, creating state interests, with the parties and the occurrence or transaction.[11]

10. This Court has taken a similar approach in deciding choice-of-law cases under both the Due Process Clause and the Full Faith and Credit Clause. In each instance, the Court has examined the relevant contacts and resulting interests of the State whose law was applied. See, e.g., Nevada v. Hall, 440 U.S. 410, 424 (1979). Although at one time the Court required a more exacting standard under the Full Faith and Credit Clause than under the Due Process Clause for evaluating the constitutionality of choice-of-law decisions, see Alaska Packers Assn. v. Industrial Accident Comm'n, 294 U.S. 532, 549–550 (1935) (interest of State whose law was applied was no less than interest of State whose law was rejected), the Court has since abandoned the weighing of interests requirement. Carroll v. Lanza, 349 U.S. 408 (1955); see Nevada v. Hall, supra; Weintraub, Due Process and Full Faith and Credit Limitations on a State's Choice of Law, 44 Iowa L.Rev.

449 (1959). Different considerations are of course at issue when full faith and credit is to be accorded to acts, records and proceedings outside the choice-of-law area, such as in the case of sister state court judgments.

11. Prior to the advent of interest analysis in the state courts as the "dominant mode of analysis in modern choice of law theory," Silberman, Shaffer v. Heitner: The End of an Era, 53 N.Y.U.L. Rev. 33, 80, n. 259 (1978) . . . , the prevailing choice of law methodology focused on the jurisdiction where a particular event occurred. See, e.g., Restatment of the Law, Conflict of Laws (1934) (hereinafter cited as "Restatement First"). . . .

Hartford Accident and Indemnity Co. v. Delta & Pine Land Co., 292 U.S. 143 (1934), . . . has scant relevance for today. It implied a choice-of-law analysis which, for all intents and purposes, gave

Two instructive examples of such invalidation are Home Insurance Company v. Dick [p. 329, supra] and John Hancock Mutual Life Insurance Co. v. Yates [p. 335, supra]. In both cases, the selection of forum law rested exclusively on the presence of one nonsignificant forum contact.

. . . [Justice Brennan here reviewed the Dick and Yates decisions.]

Dick and *Yates* stand for the proposition that if a State has only an insignificant contact with the parties and the occurrence or transaction, application of its law is unconstitutional. *Dick* concluded that nominal residence—standing alone—was inadequate; *Yates* held that a postoccurrence change of residence to the forum State—standing alone—was insufficient to justify application of forum law. Although instructive as extreme examples of selection of forum law, neither *Dick* nor *Yates* governs this case. For in contrast to those decisions, here the Minnesota contacts with the parties and the occurrence are obviously significant. Thus, this case is like *Alaska Packers*, [p. 344, supra] Cardillo v. Liberty Mutual Insurance Co., 330 U.S. 469 (1947), and *Clay II* [p. 355, supra]—cases where this Court sustained choice-of-law decisions based on the contacts of the State, whose law was applied, with the parties and occurrence.

In *Alaska Packers*, the Court . . . held that the choice of California law was not "so arbitrary or unreasonable as to amount to a denial of due process," 294 U.S., at 542, because "without a remedy in California, [he] would be remediless," ibid., and because of California's interest that the worker not become a public charge, ibid.[15]
. . .

The lesson from *Dick* and *Yates*, which found insufficient forum contacts to apply forum law, and from *Alaska Packers, Cardillo,* and *Clay II*, which found adequate contacts to sustain the choice of forum law, is that for a State's substantive law to be selected in a constitutionally permissible manner, that State must have a significant contact or significant aggregation of contacts, creating state interests, such that choice of its law is neither arbitrary nor fundamentally unfair. Application of this principle to the facts of this case persuades us that the Minnesota Supreme Court's choice of its own law did not offend the Federal Constitution.

an isolated event—the writing of the bond in Tennessee—controlling constitutional significance, even though there might have been contacts with another State (there Mississippi) which would make application of its law neither unfair nor unexpected. See Martin, Personal Jurisdiction and Choice of Law, 78 Mich. L.Rev. 872, 874, and n. 11 (1980).

15. The Court found no violation of the Full Faith and Credit Clause, since California's interest was considered to be no less than Alaska's, Alaska Packers Assn. v. Industrial Accident Comm'n, supra, 294 U.S. at 547–548, 549–550, even though the injury occurred in Alaska while the employee was performing his contract obligations there. While *Alaska Packers* balanced the interests of California and Alaska to determine the full faith and credit issue, such balancing is no longer required. See Nevada v. Hall, supra, 440 U.S. at 424; n. 10, supra.

III

Minnesota has three contacts with the parties and the occurrence giving rise to the litigation. In the aggregate, these contacts permit selection by the Minnesota Supreme Court of Minnesota law allowing the stacking of Mr. Hague's uninsured motorist coverages.

First, and for our purposes a very important contact, Mr. Hague was a member of Minnesota's workforce, having been employed by a Red Wing, Minn., enterprise for the 15 years preceding his death. While employment status may implicate a state interest less substantial than does resident status, that interest is nevertheless important. The State of employment has police power responsibilities towards the nonresident employee that are analogous, if somewhat less profound, than towards residents. Thus, such employees use state services and amenities and may call upon state facilities in appropriate circumstances.

In addition, Mr. Hague commuted to work in Minnesota, a contact which was important in Cardillo v. Liberty Mutual Co., supra, . . . (daily commute between residence in District of Columbia and workplace in Virginia), and was presumably covered by his uninsured motorist coverage during the commute. The State's interest in its commuting nonresident employees reflects a state concern for the safety and well-being of its workforce and the concomitant effect on Minnesota employers.

That Mr. Hague was not killed while commuting to work or while in Minnesota does not dictate a different result. To hold that the Minnesota Supreme Court's choice of Minnesota law violated the Constitution for that reason would require too narrow a view of Minnesota's relationship with the parties and the occurrence giving rise to the litigation. An automobile accident need not occur within a particular jurisdiction for that jurisdiction to be connected to the occurrence. Similarly, the occurrence of a crash fatal to a Minnesota employee in another State is a Minnesota contact. If Mr. Hague had only been injured and missed work for a few weeks the effect on the Minnesota employer would have been palpable and Minnesota's interest in having its employee made whole would be evident. Mr. Hague's death affects Minnesota's interest still more acutely, even though Mr. Hague will not return to the Minnesota workforce. Minnesota's workforce is surely affected by the level of protection the State extends to it, either directly or indirectly. Vindication of the rights of the estate of a Minnesota employee, therefore, is an important state concern.

Mr. Hague's residence in Wisconsin does not—as Allstate seems to argue—constitutionally mandate application of Wisconsin law to the exclusion of forum law. If, in the instant case, the accident had occurred in Minnesota between Mr. Hague and an uninsured Minnesota motorist, if the insurance contract had been executed in Minnesota covering a Minnesota registered company automobile which Mr. Hague was permitted to drive, and if a Wisconsin court sought to apply Wisconsin law, certainly Mr. Hague's residence in Wisconsin, his commute between Wisconsin and Minnesota, and the insurer's presence in Wisconsin should be adequate to apply Wisconsin's law.[22] . . . Employment status is not a sufficiently less important status than residence . . . when combined with Mr. Hague's daily commute across state lines and the other Minnesota contacts present, to prohibit the choice-of-law result in this case on constitutional grounds.

Second, Allstate was at all times present and doing business in Minnesota.[23] By virtue of its presence, Allstate can hardly claim unfamiliarity with the laws of the host jurisdiction and surprise that the state courts might apply forum law to litigation in which the company is involved. "Particularly since the company was licensed to do business in [the forum], it must have known it might be sued there, and that [the forum] courts would feel bound by [forum] law."[24] Clay v. Sun Insurance Office Limited, 363 U.S. 207, 221 (1960) (Black, J., dissenting). Moreover, Allstate's presence in Minnesota gave Minnesota an interest in regulating the company's insurance obligations insofar as they affected both a Minnesota resident and court appointed representative—respondent—and a longstanding member of Minnesota's workforce—Mr. Hague. . . .

Third, respondent became a Minnesota resident prior to institution of this litigation. The stipulated facts reveal that she first settled in Red Wing, Minn., the town in which her late husband had worked.

---

22. Of course Allstate could not be certain that Wisconsin law would necessarily govern any accident which occurred in Wisconsin, whether brought in the Wisconsin courts or elsewhere. Such an expectation would give controlling significance to the wooden *lex loci delicti* doctrine. While the place of the accident is a factor to be considered in choice-of-law analysis, to apply blindly the traditional, but now largely abandoned, doctrine, Silberman, supra, 53 N.Y.U.L.Rev., at 80, n. 259; see n. 11, supra, would fail to distinguish between the relative importance of various legal issues involved in a lawsuit as well as the relationship of other jurisdictions to the parties and the occurrence or transaction. . . .

23. The Court has recognized that examination of a State's contacts may result in divergent conclusions for jurisdiction and choice-of-law purposes. See Kulko v. Superior Court, 436 U.S. 84, 98 (1978); Shaffer v. Heitner, supra, 433 U.S., at 215; cf. Hanson v. Denckla, 357 U.S. 235, 254, and n. 27 (no jurisdiction in Florida; the "issue is personal jurisdic-

tion, not choice of law," an issue which the Court found no need to decide). Nevertheless, "both inquiries 'are often closely related and to a substantial degree depend upon similar considerations.' " 433 U.S., at 224–225 (Brennan, J., concurring in part and dissenting in part). . . .

24. There is no element of unfair surprise or frustration of legitimate expectations as a result of Minnesota's choice of its law. Because Allstate was doing business in Minnesota and was undoubtedly aware that Mr. Hague was a Minnesota employee, it had to have anticipated that Minnesota law might apply to an accident in which Mr. Hague was involved. . . . Indeed, Allstate specifically anticipated that Mr. Hague might suffer an accident either in Minnesota or elsewhere in the United States, outside of Wisconsin, since the policy it issued offered continental coverage. . . . At the same time, Allstate did not seek to control construction of the contract since the policy contained no choice-of-law clause dictating application of Wisconsin law. . . .

She subsequently moved to Savage, Minn., after marrying a Minnesota resident who operated an automobile service station in Bloomington, Minn. Her move to Savage occurred "almost concurrently," 289 N.W.2d, at 45, with the initiation of the instant case. There is no suggestion that Mrs. Hague moved to Minnesota in anticipation of this litigation or for the purpose of finding a legal climate especially hospitable to her claim. The stipulated facts, sparse as they are, negate any such inference.

While John Hancock Mutual Life Insurance Company v. Yates, supra, held that a postoccurrence change of residence to the forum State was insufficient in and of itself to confer power on the forum State to choose its law, that case did not hold that such a change of residence was irrelevant. Here, of course, respondent's bona fide residence in Minnesota was not the sole contact Minnesota had with this litigation. And in connection with her residence in Minnesota, respondent was appointed personal representative of Mr. Hague's estate by the Registrar of Probate for the County of Goodhue, Minn. Respondent's residence and subsequent appointment in Minnesota as personal representative of her late husband's estate constitute a Minnesota contact which gives Minnesota an interest in respondent's recovery, an interest which the court below identified as full compensation for "resident accident victims" to keep them "off welfare rolls" and able "to meet financial obligations." 289 N.W.2d, at 49.

In sum, Minnesota had a significant aggregation[29] of contacts with the parties and the occurrence, creating state interests, such that application of its law was neither arbitrary nor fundamentally unfair. Accordingly, the choice of Minnesota law by the Minnesota Supreme Court did not violate the Due Process Clause or the Full Faith and Credit Clause.

Affirmed.

JUSTICE STEWART took no part in the consideration or decision of this case.

JUSTICE STEVENS, concurring in the judgment.

As I view this unusual case—in which neither precedent nor constitutional language provides sure guidance—two separate questions must be answered. First, does the Full Faith and Credit Clause *require* Minnesota, the forum State, to apply Wisconsin law? Second, does the Due Process Clause of the Fourteenth Amendment *prevent* Minnesota from applying its own law? The first inquiry implicates the federal interest in ensuring that Minnesota respect the sovereignty of the State of Wisconsin; the second implicates the litigants' interests in a fair adjudication of their rights.

---

29. We express no view whether the first two contacts, either together or separately, would have sufficed to sustain the choice of Minnesota law made by the Minnesota Supreme Court.

I realize that both this Court's analysis of choice-of-law questions[4] and scholarly criticism of those decisions have treated these two inquiries as though they were indistinguishable. Nevertheless, I am persuaded that the two constitutional provisions protect different interests and that proper analysis requires separate consideration of each.

I

The Full Faith and Credit Clause is one of several provisions in the Federal Constitution designed to transform the several States from independent sovereignties into a single, unified Nation. . . . The Full Faith and Credit Clause implements this design by directing that a State, when acting as the forum for litigation having multistate aspects or implications, respect the legitimate interests of other States and avoid infringement upon their sovereignty. The Clause does not, however, rigidly require the forum State to apply foreign law whenever another State has a valid interest in the litigation. . . . On the contrary, in view of the fact that the forum State is also a sovereign in its own right, in appropriate cases it may attach paramount importance to its own legitimate interests. Accordingly, the fact that a choice-of-law decision may be unsound as a matter of conflicts law does not necessarily implicate the federal concerns embodied in the Full Faith and Credit Clause. Rather in my opinion, the Clause should not invalidate a state court's choice of forum law unless that choice threatens the federal interest in national unity by unjustifiably infringing upon the legitimate interests of another State.

In this case, I think the Minnesota courts' decision to apply Minnesota law was plainly unsound as a matter of normal conflicts law. Both the execution of the insurance contract and the accident giving rise to the litigation took place in Wisconsin. Moreover, when both of those events occurred the plaintiff, the decedent, and the operators of both vehicles were all residents of Wisconsin. Nevertheless, I do not believe that any threat to national unity or Wisconsin's sovereignty ensues from allowing the substantive question presented by this case to be determined by the law of another State.

. . . Since the policy provided coverage for accidents that might occur in other States, it was obvious to the parties at the time of contracting that it might give rise to the application of the law of States other than Wisconsin. Therefore, while Wisconsin may have an interest in ensuring that contracts formed in Wisconsin in reliance upon Wisconsin law are interpreted in accordance with that law, that interest is not implicated in this case.

4. Although the Court has struck down a state court's choice of forum law on both due process, see e.g., Home Insurance Co. v. Dick, 281 U.S. 397 (1930), and full faith and credit grounds, see e.g., John Hancock Insurance Co. v. Yates, 299 U.S. 178 (1936), no clear analytical distinction between the two constitutional provisions has emerged. . . .

Petitioner has failed to establish that Minnesota's refusal to apply Wisconsin law poses any direct or indirect threat to Wisconsin's sovereignty. In the absence of any such threat, I find it unnecessary to evaluate the forum State's interest in the litigation in order to reach the conclusion that the Full Faith and Credit Clause does not require the Minnesota courts to apply Wisconsin law to the question of contract interpretation presented in this case.

II

It may be assumed that a choice-of-law decision would violate the Due Process Clause if it were totally arbitrary or if it were fundamentally unfair to either litigant. I question whether a judge's decision to apply the law of his own State could ever be described as wholly irrational. For judges are presumably familiar with their own state law and may find it difficult and time consuming to discover and apply correctly the law of another State. The forum State's interest in the fair and efficient administration of justice is therefore sufficient, in my judgment, to attach a presumption of validity to a forum State's decision to apply its own law to a dispute over which it has jurisdiction.

The forum State's interest in the efficient operation of its judicial system is clearly not sufficient, however, to justify the application of a rule of law that is fundamentally unfair to one of the litigants. Arguably, a litigant could demonstrate such unfairness in a variety of ways. Concern about the fairness of the forum's choice of its own rule might arise if that rule favored residents over nonresidents, if it represented a dramatic departure from the rule that obtains in most American jurisdictions, or if the rule itself was unfair on its face or as applied.

The application of an otherwise acceptable rule of law may result in unfairness to the litigants if, in engaging in the activity which is the subject of the litigation, they could not reasonably have anticipated that their actions would later be judged by this rule of law. A choice-of-law decision that frustrates the justifiable expectations of the parties can be fundamentally unfair. This desire to prevent unfair surprise to a litigant has been the central concern in this Court's review of choice-of-law decisions under the Due Process Clause.

Neither the "stacking" rule itself, nor Minnesota's application of that rule to these litigants, raises any serious question of fairness. As the plurality observes, "[s]tacking was the rule in most States at the time the policy was issued." . . . Moreover, the rule is consistent with the economics of a contractual relationship in which the policyholder paid three separate premiums for insurance coverage for three automobiles, including a separate premium for each uninsured motorist coverage. . . . Nor am I persuaded that the decision of the Minnesota courts to apply the "stacking" rule in this case can be said to violate due process because that decision frustrates the reasonable expectations of the contracting parties. . . .

. . . [T]he decision of the Minnesota courts to apply the law of the forum in this case does not frustrate the reasonable expectations of the contracting parties, and I can find no fundamental unfairness in that decision requiring the attention of this Court.

In terms of fundamental fairness, it seems to me that two factors relied upon by the plurality—the plaintiff's post-accident move to Minnesota and the decedent's Minnesota employment—are either irrelevant to or possibly even tend to undermine the plurality's conclusion. When the expectations of the parties at the time of contracting are the central due process concern, as they are in this case, an unanticipated post-accident occurrence is clearly irrelevant for due process purposes. . . .

III

Although I regard the Minnesota courts' decision to apply forum law as unsound as a matter of conflicts law, and there is little in this record other than the presumption in favor of the forum's own law to support that decision, I concur in the plurality's judgment. It is not this Court's function to establish and impose upon state courts a federal choice-of-law rule, nor is it our function to ensure that state courts correctly apply whatever choice-of-law rules they have themselves adopted. Our authority may be exercised in the choice-of-law area only to prevent a violation of the Full Faith and Credit or the Due Process Clause. For the reasons stated above, I find no such violation in this case.

JUSTICE POWELL, with whom THE CHIEF JUSTICE and JUSTICE REHNQUIST join, dissenting.

My disagreement with the majority is narrow. I accept with few reservations Part II of the majority opinion, which sets forth the basic principles that guide us in reviewing state choice-of-law decisions under the Constitution. The Court should invalidate a forum State's decision to apply its own law only when there are no significant contacts between the State and the litigation. This modest check on state power is mandated by the Due Process Clause of the Fourteenth Amendment and the Full Faith and Credit Clause of Art. 4, § 1. I do not believe, however, that the Court adequately analyzes the policies such review must serve. In consequence, it has found significant what appear to me to be trivial contacts between the forum State and the litigation.

I

. . . The significance of asserted contacts must be evaluated in light of the constitutional policies that oversight by this Court should serve. Two enduring policies emerge from our cases.

First, the contacts between the forum State and the litigation should not be so "slight and casual" that it would be fundamentally unfair to a litigant for the forum to apply its own State's law. Clay v. Sun Ins. Office, Ltd. [p. 355, supra]. The touchstone here is the reasonable expectation of the parties. See Weintraub, Due Process and Full Faith and Credit Limitations on a State's Choice of Law, 44 Iowa L.Rev. 449, 445–457 (1959).

Second, the forum State must have a legitimate interest in the outcome of the litigation before it. Pacific Ins. Co. v. Industrial Accident Comm'n [p. 344, supra]. The Full Faith and Credit Clause addresses the accommodation of sovereign power among the various States. Under limited circumstances, it requires one State to give effect to the statutory law of another State. Nevada v. Hall, 440 U.S. 410, 423 (1979). To be sure, a forum State need not give effect to another State's law if that law is in "violation of its own legitimate public policy." Id., at 624. Nonetheless, for a forum State to further its legitimate public policy by applying its own law to a controversy, there must be some connection between the facts giving rise to the litigation and the scope of the State's lawmaking jurisdiction.

Both the Due Process and Full Faith and Credit Clauses ensure that the States do not "reach out beyond the limits imposed on them by their status as coequal sovereigns in a federal system." World-Wide Volkswagen Corp. v. Woodson, 444 U.S. 286, 292 (1980) (addressing Fourteenth Amendment limitations on state court jurisdiction). . . .

In summary, the significance of the contacts between a forum State and the litigation must be assessed in light of these two important constitutional policies. A contact, or a pattern of contacts, satisfies the Constitution when it protects the litigants from being unfairly surprised if the forum State applies its own law, and when the application of the forum's law reasonably can be understood to further a legitimate public policy of the forum State.

II

Recognition of the complexity of the constitutional inquiry requires that this Court apply these principles with restraint. Applying these principles to the facts of this case, I do not believe, however, that Minnesota had sufficient contacts with the "persons and events" in this litigation to apply its rule permitting stacking. I would agree that no reasonable expectations of the parties were frustrated. The risk insured by petitioner was not geographically limited. . . .

The more doubtful question in this case is whether application of Minnesota's substantive law reasonably furthers a legitimate state interest. The Court attempts to give substance to the tenuous contacts between Minnesota and this litigation. Upon examination, however, these contacts are either trivial or irrelevant to the furthering of any public policy in Minnesota.

First, the post-accident residence of the plaintiff-beneficiary is constitutionally irrelevant to the choice-of-law question. John Hancock Mut. Life Ins. Co. v. Yates, supra. . . . Any possible ambiguity in the Court's view of the significance of a post-occurrence change of residence is dispelled by Home Ins. Co. v. Dick, supra, cited by the *Yates* Court, where it was held squarely that Dick's post-accident move to the forum State was "without significance." . . .

This rule is sound. If a plaintiff could choose the substantive rules to be applied to an action by moving to a hospitable forum, the invitation to forum shopping would be irresistible. Moreover, it would permit the defendant's reasonable expectations at the time the cause of action accrues to be frustrated, because it would permit the choice-of-law question to turn on a post-accrual circumstance. Finally, post-accrual residence has nothing to do with facts to which the forum State proposes to apply its rule; it is unrelated to the substantive legal issues presented by the litigation.

Second, the Court finds it significant that the insurer does business in the forum State. . . . The State does have a legitimate interest in regulating the practices of such an insurer. But this argument proves too much. The insurer here does business in all 50 States. The forum State has no interest in regulating that conduct of the insurer unrelated to property, persons or contracts executed within in the forum State. . . . The Court recognizes this flaw and attempts to bolster the significance of the local presence of the insurer by combining it with the other factors deemed significant: the presence of the plaintiff and the fact that the deceased worked in the forum State. This merely restates the basic question in the case.

Third, the Court emphasizes particularly that the insured worked in the forum State. . . . The insured's place of employment is not, however, significant in this case. Neither the nature of the insurance policy, the events related to the accident, nor the immediate question of stacking coverage are in any way affected or implicated by the insured's employment status. The Court's opinion is understandably vague in explaining how trebling the benefits to be paid to the estate of a nonresident employee furthers any substantial state interest relating to employment. Minnesota does not wish its workers to die in automobile accidents, but permitting stacking will not further this interest. The substantive issue here is solely one of compensation, and whether the compensation provided by this policy is increased or not will have no relation to the State's employment policies or police power. . . .

Neither taken separately nor in the aggregate do the contacts asserted by the Court today indicate that Minnesota's application of its substantive rule in this case will further any legitimate state interest.[6] The Court focuses only on physical contacts *vel non*, and in

6. The concurring opinion of Justice Stevens supports my view that the forum State's application of its own law to this case cannot be justified by the existence

doing so pays scant attention to the more fundamental reasons why our precedents require reasonable policy-related contacts in choice-of-law cases. Therefore, I dissent.

After Allstate v. Hague, what is the impact of due process and full faith and credit on choice of law? Perhaps it is not realistic to view full faith as retaining any significant function in this context considering that the Supreme Court, despite frequent reference to the full faith command has not since 1947 struck down a choice of law for violating that command. This suggests that the only serious test is due process. Once due process is satisfied the full-faith requirement fades away. But there is a possibility, is there not, that the forum's choice might be the equivalent of a "forbidden infringement" on a sister state's interests of the kind that Justice Stone referred to in the judgments area. If so, what are the indicia of such an infringement? Is using part of a sister state statute while rejecting an unmistakably interrelated part an example of a forbidden infringement?

The law reviews have published floods of commentary on Allstate v. Hague. A major collection is Symposium: Choice of Law Theory After Allstate Insurance Co. v. Hague, 10 Hofstra L.Rev. 1 (1981), containing comments by Cavers, Davies, Leflar, Martin, Reese, Sedler, Silberman, Trautman, Twerski, von Mehren, and Weintraub.

Among other useful commentaries are Hay, Full Faith and Credit and Federalism in Choice of Law, 34 Mercer L.Rev. 709 (1983); Hill, Choice of Law and Jurisdiction in the Supreme Court, 81 Colum.L. Rev. 960 (1981); Kozyris, Reflections on Allstate—The Lessening of Due Process in Choice of Law, 14 U.C.D.L.Rev. 889 (1981); Weinberg, Choice of Law and Minimal Scrutiny, 49 U.Chi.L.Rev. 440 (1982); Note, Legislative Jurisdiction, State Policies and Post-Occurrence Contacts in Allstate Insurance Co. v. Hague, 81 Colum.L.Rev. 1134 (1981).

The Restatment, Second, Conflict of Laws, Section 9, reads:

§ 9. Limitations on Choice of Law

A court may not apply the local law of its own state to determine a particular issue unless application of this law would be rea-

---

of relevant minimum contacts. As Justice Stevens observes, the principal factors relied on by the Court are "either irrelevant or possibly even tend to undermine the [Court's] conclusion." . . . . The interesting analysis he proposes to uphold the State's judgment is, however, difficult to reconcile with our prior decisions and may create more problems than it solves. For example, it seems questionable to measure the interest of a State in a controversy by the degree of conscious reliance on that State's law by private parties to a contract. . . . Moreover, scrutinizing the strength of the interests of a nonforum State may draw this Court back into the discredited practice of weighing the relative interests of various States in a particular controversy. . . .

sonable in the light of the relationship of the state to the issue and to the person, thing or occurrence involved.

Is that as accurate and precise a statement of the law as we can make after Allstate v. Hague?

NOTES

(1) McCluney v. Joseph Schlitz Brewing Co., 649 F.2d 578 (8th Cir. 1981), aff'd 454 U.S. 1071, 102 S.Ct. 624. The plaintiff was originally employed by the defendant to work in Missouri. Thereafter, he was transferred to a number of states and finally five years later, while working in Wisconsin, he was discharged. He requested a "service letter" in the form provided for in a Missouri statute, but the defendant refused to supply one. Plaintiff then moved to Missouri and there brought suit against the defendant under Missouri law. Held on appeal that the Missouri statute could not be applied under due process for lack of any significant contact with the parties and the contract of employment. The "significant contacts" analysis of the Supreme Court in the Hague case "addresses the traditional concerns of due process: preventing unfairness to the parties and promoting interstate relations." The defendant performs no manufacturing or processing operations in Missouri although some of its distributors are located there. Missouri's "one relevant contact" is that the plaintiff moved there after his discharge. This contact is not of itself sufficient to permit application of Missouri law. The dissenting judge emphasized that defendant was doing business in Missouri through it distributors and there was nothing to indicate that plaintiff had moved to Missouri in order to obtain application of Missouri law. He also pointed to the fact that plaintiff's original contract of employment had called for application of Missouri law and "no later agreement expressly modified that arrangement." The dissenting judge concluded that he knew of no Supreme Court case "more recent than 1936 striking down a state's choice of law under the federal Constitution." What about Commercial Travelers v. Wolfe in 1947, p. 341, supra?

(2) See Reese, Legislative Jurisdiction, 78 Colum.L.Rev. 1587 (1978); Müller-Freienfels, Conflicts of Law and Constitutional Law, 45 U.Chi.L.Rev. 598 (1978). As to federal control of choice of law, Justice Robert H. Jackson, in The Supreme Court in the American System of Government 41–44 (1955), said: "It seems to me that disagreement as to which of conflicting or competing state laws applies raises a federal question under the Full Faith and Credit Clause and that our hope for a better general legal system would be well served by wider application of that clause." Is that the best path in light of Allstate v. Hague?

(3) Professor Martin contends that full faith and credit provides a better constitutional basis than due process to rationalize the *Dick* line of cases. Martin, Constitutional Limitations on Choice of Law, 61 Cornell L.Rev. 185 (1976); Kirgis, The Roles of Due Process and Full Faith and Credit in Choice of Law, 62 Cornell L.Rev. 94 (1976). What arguments can be marshaled for and against that contention?

The Control of Choice of Law by Federal Statutes

The Constitution of the United States gives to the Congress wide powers over conflict of laws. This is done in the clearest form by the words of the full faith and credit clause: "And the Congress may by General Laws prescribe the Manner in which such Acts, Records and Proceedings shall be proved, and the Effect thereof." Perhaps, similar power is also conferred by other parts of the Constitution, as, the interstate and foreign commerce clause and the due process clauses.

This power has been sweepingly exercised by the Congress in the field of state judgments, as shown in Chapter 5, supra.

Until 1948 there seems to have been no similar federal statute on choice of law. The statute enacted in 1790 under the full faith and credit clause had dealt with the protection of "records" and "judicial proceedings", but not with "acts". In 1948 the provision was amended, as shown on p. 38, supra, to include "acts" within the scope of its protection.

The Supreme Court has not yet determined the effect, if any, of the amendment. Note, in this connection, that the Court adverted to the question, but did not decide it, in Hughes v. Fetter, p. 322, supra. Note also Justice Frankfurter's statement in his dissent in Carroll v. Lanza, p. 348, supra, that the amendment "cannot be disregarded."

SECTION 3.   UNREASONABLE DISCRIMINATION

By reason of the privileges and immunities clause (Art. IV, § 2) and the equal protection clause of the Fourteenth Amendment, a state cannot discriminate unreasonably against citizens of sister states or against persons within its jurisdiction. Up to this point we have seen the problem raised in Douglas v. New York, New Haven & Hartford Railroad Co., 279 U.S. 377 (1929), p. 205, supra, where it was held that a state does not violate the privileges and immunities clause by dismissing on a forum non conveniens grounds a suit between residents of sister states that is based on a foreign occurrence. Other cases in the book that raise problems of privileges and immunities or of equal protection are Canadian Northern Railway Co. v. Eggen, 252 U.S. 553 (1920), p. 434, infra; Blake v. McClung, 172 U.S. 239 (1898), p. 933, infra, and Kentucky Finance Corp. v. Paramount Auto Exchange, 262 U.S. 544 (1923), p. 979, infra.

It has also come to be recognized that some of the more recent approaches to choice of law reveal a tendency to extend the protection of forum law to forum residents and not to do so for nonresidents, thereby giving rise to privileges and immunities and equal protection problems. For example, suppose that the owner and driver of an automobile, who is domiciled in state X, is involved in an accident in state Y and thereafter is sued in X by two injured guest passengers, one of whom is domiciled in X and the other in Y. Would it be appropriate in these circumstances for the X court to apply X law to determine the rights of the X passenger in a favorable way, but refuse to apply X law to determine the Y passenger's rights on the ground that a state has no interest in favorable treatment of a nonresident but, on the ground that it has no interest in him, to apply Y law to determine the rights of the Y passenger? Problems of this kind are considered (particularly at pp. 495–502) in the chapters which follow. The field is intensively discussed in two articles by Professors Currie and Schreter, Unconstitutional Discrimination in the Conflict of Laws: Privileges and Immunities, 69 Yale L.J. 1323 (1960), and Unconstitutional Discrimination in The Conflict of Laws: Equal Protection, 28 U.Chi.L.Rev. 1 (1960). These articles are reprinted in Currie, Selected Essays on the Conflict of Laws, Chs. 11, 12 (1963). See also Note, Unconstitutional Discrimination in Choice of Law, 77 Colum.L.Rev. 272 (1977).

SECTION 4. GOVERNMENT SEIZURE

SECURITY SAVINGS BANK V. CALIFORNIA, 263 U.S. 282 (1923). Suit was brought by the State of California under a statute transferring to it certain deposits in the defendant bank which were unclaimed for more than twenty years, to have the deposits declared escheat. The depositors were served by publication, and the bank personally. Only the latter appeared. It defended on the ground that the judgment would not protect it, as the depositors, if they later appear, would not be bound by the judgment. Held, judgment in favor of the State affirmed.

BRANDEIS, J.: "The proceeding is not one in personam—at least, not so far as concerns the depositor. The State does not seek to enforce any claim against him. It seeks to have the deposit transferred. The suit determines the custody (and perhaps the ownership) of the deposit. The state court likened the proceeding to garnishment, and thought that it should be described as quasi in rem. In form it resembles garnishment. In substance it is like proceedings in escheat . . ., for confiscation . . ., for forfeiture . . ., for condemnation, and libels for possession brought by the Alien Property Custodian. These are generally considered proceedings strictly in rem. But whether the proceeding should be described as being in rem or as being quasi in rem is not of legal significance in this connection. In either case the essentials of jurisdiction over the deposits are that there be seizure of the res at the commencement of the suit; and reasonable notice and opportunity to be heard. . . . These requirements are satisfied by the procedure prescribed in the statutes of California. There is a seizure or its equivalent. . . . Moreover, there is no constitutional objection to considering the proceeding as in personam, so far as concerns the bank; as quasi in rem, so far as concerns the depositors; and as strictly in rem, so far as concerns other claimants. Seizure of the deposit is effected by personal service made upon the bank. . . . Thereby the res is subjected to the jurisdiction of the court. . . . The fact that the claim of the State to the deposit may be defeated by the appearance of the debtor or other claimant does not, as argued, prove that the deposit was not seized. An attachment of real estate is a seizure, although it may be dissolved by bankruptcy or otherwise."

WESTERN UNION TELEGRAPH CO. v. COMMONWEALTH OF PENNSYLVANIA

Supreme Court of the United States, 1961.
368 U.S. 71, 82 S.Ct. 199, 7 L.Ed.2d 139.

MR. JUSTICE BLACK delivered the opinion of the Court.

Pennsylvania law provides that "any real or personal property within or subject to the control of this Commonwealth . . . shall escheat to the Commonwealth" whenever it "shall be without a rightful or lawful owner," "remain unclaimed for the period of seven successive years" or "the whereabouts of such owner . . . shall be and remain unknown for the period of seven successive years." These proceedings were begun under that law in a Pennsylvania state court to escheat certain obligations of the Western Union Telegraph Company—alleged to be "property within" Pennsylvania—to pay sums of money owing to various people who had left the monies unclaimed for more than seven years and whose whereabouts were unknown. The facts were stipulated.

Western Union is a corporation chartered under New York law with its principal place of business in that State. It also does business and has offices in all the other States except Alaska and Hawaii, in the District of Columbia, and in foreign countries, and was from 1916 to 1934 subject to regulation by the I.C.C. and since then by the F.C.C. In addition to sending telegraphic messages throughout its world-wide system, it carries on a telegraphic money order business which commonly works like this. A sender goes to a Western Union office, fills out an application and gives it to the company clerk who waits on him together with the money to be sent and the charges for sending it. A receipt is given the sender and a telegraph message is transmitted to the company's office nearest to the payee directing that office to pay the money order to the payee. The payee is then notified and upon properly identifying himself is given a negotiable draft, which he can either endorse and cash at once or keep for use in the future. If the payee cannot be located for delivery of the notice, or fails to call for the draft within 72 hours, the office of destination notifies the sending office. This office then notifies the original sender of the failure to deliver and makes a refund, as it makes payments to payees, by way of a negotiable draft which may be either cashed immediately or kept for use in the future.

In the thousands of money order transactions carried on by the company, it sometimes happens that it can neither make payment to the payee nor make a refund to the sender. Similarly payees and senders who accept drafts as payment or refund sometimes fail to cash them. For this reason large sums of money due from Western Union for undelivered money orders and unpaid drafts accumulate over the years in the company's offices and bank accounts throughout the country. It is an accumulation of this kind that Pennsylvania seeks to escheat here—specifically, the amount of undisbursed money held by Western Union arising out of money orders bought in Pennsylvania offices to be transmitted to payees in Pennsylvania and other States, chiefly other States.

Western Union, while not claiming these monies for itself, challenged Pennsylvania's right to take ownership of them for itself.[1] Among other grounds the company urged that a judgment of escheat for Pennsylvania in its courts would not protect the company from multiple liability either in Pennsylvania or in other States. Its argument in this respect was that senders of money orders and holders of drafts would not be bound by the Pennsylvania judgment because the service by publication did not, for two reasons, give the state court jurisdiction: (1) that under the doctrine of *Pennoyer v. Neff*, 95 U.S. 714, the presence of property, called a "res," within the State is a prerequisite for service by publication and that these obligations did not constitute such property within Pennsylvania, and (2) that the notice by publication given in this case did not give sufficient information or afford sufficient likelihood of actual notice to meet due process requirements. In addition, Western Union urged that there might be escheats claimed by other States which would not be bound by the Pennsylvania judgment because they were not and could not be made parties to this Pennsylvania proceeding. Western Union's apprehensions that other States might later escheat the same funds were buttressed by the Pennsylvania court's finding that New York had already seized and escheated a part of the very funds here claimed by Pennsylvania. With reference to this the Pennsylvania Court of Common Pleas said: "We take this opportunity of stating that we do not recognize New York's authority to escheat that mon-

1. In its answer Western Union did claim these monies, but it has since abandoned this ground. [Court's footnote renumbered.]

ey, but since it has been done we have no jurisdiction over this sum." 73 Dauphin County Rep. 160, 173. Both the Pennsylvania trial court and the State Supreme Court rejected the contentions of Western Union and declared the unclaimed obligations escheated. 73 Dauphin County Rep. 160; 74 Dauphin County Rep. 49; 400 Pa. 337, 162 A.2d 617. Since the record showed substantial questions as to the jurisdiction of the Pennsylvania courts over the individual owners of the unclaimed monies and as to the power of the State of Pennsylvania to enter a binding judgment that would protect Western Union against subsequent liability to other States, we noted probable jurisdiction. 365 U.S. 801.

We find it unnecessary to decide any of Western Union's contentions as to the adequacy of notice to and validity of service on the individual claimants by publication. For as we view these proceedings, there is a far more important question raised by this record— whether Pennsylvania had power at all to render a judgment of escheat which would bar New York or any other State from escheating this same property.

Pennsylvania does not claim and could not claim that the same debts or demands could be escheated by two states. See Standard Oil Co. v. State of New Jersey, 341 U.S. 428, 443. And our prior opinions have recognized that when a state court's jurisdiction purports to be based, as here, on the presence of property within the State, the holder of such property is deprived of due process of law if he is compelled to relinquish it without assurance that he will not be held liable again in another jurisdiction or in a suit brought by a claimant who is not bound by the first judgment. Anderson National Bank v. Luckett, 321 U.S. 233, 242–243; Security Savings Bank v. People of State of California, 263 U.S. 282, 286–290. Applying that principle, there can be no doubt that Western Union has been denied due process by the Pennsylvania judgment here unless the Pennsylvania courts had power to protect Western Union from any other claim, including the claim of the State of New York that these obligations are property "within" New York and are therefore subject to escheat under its laws. But New York was not a party to this proceeding and could not have been made a party, and, of course, New York's claims could not be cut off where New York was not heard as a party. Moreover, the potential multi-state claims to the "property" which is the subject of this escheat make it not unlikely that various States will claim *in rem* jurisdiction over it. Therefore, Western Union was not protected by the Pennsylvania judgment, for a state court judgment need not be given full faith and credit by other States as to parties or property not subject to the jurisdiction of the court that rendered it. Pennoyer v. Neff, 95 U.S. 714; Riley v. New York Trust Co., 315 U.S. 343.

. . .

The claims of New York are particularly aggressive, not merely potential, but actual, active and persistent—best shown by the fact that New York has already escheated part of the very funds originally claimed by Pennsylvania. These claims of New York were presented to us in both the brief and oral argument of that State as *amicus curiae.* In presenting its claims New York also called our attention to the potential claims of other States for escheat based on their contacts with the separate phases of the multi-state transactions out of which these unclaimed funds arose, including: the State of residence of the payee, the State of the sender, the State where the money order was delivered, and the State where the fiscal agent on which the money order was drawn is located. Arguments more than merely plausible can doubtless be made to support claims of all these and other States to escheat all or parts of all unclaimed funds held by Western Union. And the large area of the company's business makes it entirely possible that *every State* may now or later claim a right to participate in these funds. But even if, as seems unlikely, no other State will assert such a claim, the active controversy between New York and Pennsylvania is enough in itself to justify Western Union's contention that to require it to pay this money to Pennsylvania before New York has had its full day in court might force Western Union to pay a single debt more than once and thus take its property without due process of law.

Our Constitution has wisely provided a way in which controversies between States can be settled without subjecting individuals and companies affected by those controversies to a deprivation of their right to due process of law. Article III, § 2 of the Constitution gives this Court original jurisdiction of cases in which a State is a party. The situation here is in all material respects like that which caused us to take jurisdiction in State of Texas v. State of Florida, 306 U.S. 398. There four States sought to collect death taxes out of an estate. The tax depended upon the domicile of the decedent, and this Court said that "By the law of each state a decedent can have only a single domicile for purposes of death taxes . . . ." Id., at 408. Thus, there was only one tax due to only one State. The estate was sufficient to pay the tax of any one State, but the total of the claims of the four States greatly exceeded the net value of the estate. For this reason, as we said, the risk of loss to the state of domicile was real and substantial, unless we exercised our jurisdiction. Under these circumstances we exercised our original jurisdiction to avoid "the risk of loss ensuing from the demands in separate suits of rival claimants to the same debt or legal duty." Id., at 405. The rival state claimants here, as in State of Texas v. State of Florida, can invoke our original jurisdiction.

While we have previously decided some escheat cases where it was apparent that rival state claims were in the offing, we have not in any of them closed the door to the exercise of our jurisdiction. In Connecticut Mutual Life Ins. Co. v. Moore, 333 U.S. 541 we sustained the power of New York to take custody as a conservator of unclaimed funds due persons insured by that company through policies issued for delivery in New York to persons then resident in New York. In doing so we rejected an argument that the State of domicile of the insurance companies involved alone had jurisdiction to escheat. But there we were careful to point out that "The problem of what another state than New York may do is not before us. That question is not passed upon." Id., at 548. Even though this reservation was made and New York only took custody of the funds, leaving the way clear for all claimants to bring action to recover them at any time, there were dissents urging that a way should be then found for the conflicting claims of States to be determined. Several years later a divided Court in Standard Oil Co. v. State of New Jersey, 341 U.S. 428, upheld the right of New Jersey to escheat certain unclaimed shares of stock and dividends due stockholders and employees of the Standard Oil Company. In that case New Jersey's jurisdiction to escheat was rested, at least in part, on the fact that Standard Oil was a domiciliary of that State. Again, however, the Court justified its conclusion by saying as to claims of other States: "The claim of no other state to this property is before us and, of course, determination of any right of a claimant state against New Jersey for the property escheated by New Jersey must await presentation here." Id., at 443. Later New York sought leave to file an original action here against New Jersey, alleging a controversy between the two states over jurisdiction to take custody of monies arising out of unclaimed travelers checks, outstanding for more than 15 years, issued by American Express Company, a joint stock company organized under New York law with its principal office in New York. Answering, New Jersey pointed out that under New York's then controlling law it disclaimed any purpose to escheat property claimed for escheat by any other State. In this state of the New York law, we refused to take jurisdiction. State of New York v. State of New Jersey, 358 U.S. 924. By an act effective March 29, 1960, New York amended its law eliminating the disclaimer and now strongly asserts its claim to these funds under its new law.

The rapidly multiplying state escheat laws, originally applying only to land and other tangible things but recently moving into the elusive and wide-ranging field of intangible transactions have presented problems of great importance to the States and persons whose rights will be adversely affected by escheats.[2] This makes it imperative

2. The magnitude of the problem involved is illustrated by the fact that, since 1946, at least 20 States have enacted legislation to bring or enlarge the coverage of intangible transactions under their escheat laws. . . . Of these, 10 . . . have adopted the Uniform Disposition of Unclaimed Property Act promulgated by the National Conference of Commissioners on Uniform State Laws in 1955. In addition legislation has been under consideration by other States. For discussion of this and a general description of the growing importance of these laws, see Ely, Escheats: Perils and Precautions, 15 Bus.Law 791.

The record in this very case shows that Massachusetts is laying claim to funds of Western Union on precisely the same

that controversies between different States over their right to escheat intangibles be settled in a forum where all the States that want to do so can present their claims for consideration and final authoritative determination. Our Court has jurisdiction to do that. Whether and under what circumstances we will exercise our jurisdiction to hear and decide these controversies ourselves in particular cases, and whether we might under some circumstances refer them to United States District Courts, we need not now determine. Cf. Commonwealth of Massachusetts v. State of Missouri, 308 U.S. 1, 18–20. Nor need we, at this time, attempt to decide the difficult legal questions presented when many different States claim power to escheat intangibles involved in transactions taking place in part in many States. It will be time enough to consider those complicated problems when all interested States—along with all other claimants—can be afforded a full hearing and a final authoritative determination.[3] It is plain that Pennsylvania courts, with no power to bring other States before them, cannot give such hearings. They have not done so here; they have not attempted to do so. As a result, their judgments, which cannot, with the assurance that comes only from a full trial with all necessary parties present, protect Western Union from having to pay the same single obligation twice, cannot stand. When this situation developed the Pennsylvania courts should have dismissed the case.

Accordingly, the judgment of the Supreme Court of Pennsylvania is reversed, and the cause is remanded to that Court for further proceedings not inconsistent with this opinion. It is so ordered.

Reversed and remanded.

Memorandum of MR. JUSTICE STEWART.

The appellant is a New York corporation with its principal office in that State. The funds representing these unpaid money orders are located there. I think only New York has power to escheat the property involved in this case. For that reason, while disagreeing with the Court's opinion, which for me creates more problems than it solves, I join in the judgment of reversal.*

A definitive answer to the escheat problem was provided by the Supreme Court in Texas v. New Jersey, 379 U.S. 674, 85 S.Ct. 626, 13 L.Ed. 596 (1965). In that case, Texas, invoking the Supreme Court's original jurisdiction, brought an action against several sister states

ground that Pennsylvania asserted here, thus bringing Massachusetts into conflict with New York's claims too. [Court's footnote renumbered.]

3. In State of Texas v. State of Florida, 306 U.S. 398, 405, we held that individual claimants "whose presence is necessary or proper for the determination of the case or controversy between the states are properly made parties . . . ." [Court's footnote renumbered.]

* The principal case is discussed in 18 Bus.Law 311 (1962); 50 Calif.L.Rev. 735 (1962); 62 Colum.L.Rev. 708 (1962); 11 DePaul L.Rev. 337 (1962); 76 Harv.L. Rev. 132 (1962); 57 Nw.U.L.Rev. 484 (1962).

and the Sun Oil Company to determine which state could escheat small debts totaling about $26,500 which the Sun Oil Company owed to approximately 1,730 creditors. Texas contended that the state with the "most significant contacts" with the debt should be allowed to escheat it. This contention was rejected by the Court on the ground that

> . . . the rule . . . would serve only to leave in permanent turmoil a question which should be settled once and for all by a clear rule which will govern all types of intangible obligations like these and to which all States may refer with confidence. The issue before us is not whether a defendant has had sufficient contact with a State to make him or his property rights subject to the jurisdiction of its courts, a jurisdiction which need not be exclusive. . . . Since this Court has held in Western Union Tel. Co. v. Com. of Pennsylvania, . . . that the same property cannot constitutionally be escheated by more than one State, we are faced here with the very different problem of deciding which State's claim to escheat is superior to all others. The "contacts" test as applied in this field is not really any workable test at all— it is simply a phrase suggesting that this Court should examine the circumstances surrounding each particular item of escheatable property on its own peculiar facts and then try to make a difficult, often quite subjective, decision as to which State's claim to those pennies or dollars seems stronger than another's. . . . The uncertainty of any test which would require us in effect either to decide each escheat case on the basis of its particular facts or to devise new rules of law to apply to ever-developing new categories of facts, might in the end create so much uncertainty and threaten so much expensive litigation that the States might find that they would lose more in litigation expenses than they might gain in escheats. . . .

The Court likewise rejected arguments favoring the state of the debtor's incorporation or that where its principal offices were located and concluded:

> . . . since a debt is property of the creditor, not of the debtor, fairness among the States requires that the right and power to escheat the debt should be accorded to the State of the creditor's last known address as shown by the debtor's books and records. Such a solution would be in line with one group of cases dealing with intangible property for other purposes in other areas of the law. Adoption of such a rule involves a factual issue simple and easy to resolve, and leaves no legal issue to be decided. It takes account of the fact that if the creditor instead of perhaps leaving behind an uncashed check had negotiated the check and left behind the cash, this State would have been the sole possible escheat claimant; in other words, the rule recognizes that the debt was an asset of the creditor. The rule . . . will tend to distribute es-

cheats among the States in the proportion of the commercial activities of their residents. And by using a standard of last known address, rather than technical legal concepts of residence and domicile, administration and application of escheat laws should be simplified. It may well be that some addresses left by vanished creditors will be in States other than those in which they lived at the time the obligation arose or at the time of the escheat. But such situations probably will be the exception, and any errors thus created, if indeed they could be called errors, probably will tend to a large extent to cancel each other out. . . .

The Court finally held that debts owed persons whose address is unknown to the debtor or is in a state which does not provide for escheat should be subject to escheat by the state of the debtor's incorporation "provided that another State could later escheat upon proof that the last known address of the creditor was within its borders."

MR. JUSTICE STEWART dissented. In his view, only the state of the debtor's incorporation should have power to escheat.

The sequel to Western Union Telegraph Co. v. Commonwealth of Pennsylvania was Pennsylvania v. New York, 407 U.S. 206 (1972). Following Justice Black's suggestion, Pennsylvania filed an original action in the Supreme Court to which Arizona, California, Connecticut, Florida, Indiana and New York became parties. New Jersey filed a brief as amicus curiae in support of Pennsylvania's position. In its argument before the Special Master, Pennsylvania pointed out "that Western Union's money order records do not identify any one as a 'creditor' of the Company and in many instances do not list an address for either the sender or the payee;" therefore strict application of the Texas v. New Jersey rule would result in the escheat of almost all of the funds to New York, the state of incorporation. To avoid this result, Pennsylvania proposed that the state where the money order was purchased should be allowed to escheat the funds. Nevertheless, the Special Master recommended that the Texas v. New Jersey rule should be applied and the Supreme Court adopted this recommendation by a 6 to 3 vote. Writing for the majority, Justice Brennan recognized that "[b]ecause Western Union does not regularly record the addresses of its money order creditors, it is likely that the corporate domicile will receive a much larger share of the unclaimed funds here than in the case of other obligations . . . where such records are kept as a matter of business practice." Nevertheless, "to vary the application of the *Texas* rule according to the adequacy of the debtor's records would require this Court to do precisely what [in Texas v. New Jersey] we said should be avoided," namely, to decide each escheat case on an *ad hoc* basis. The dissent written by Justice Powell and joined by Justices Blackmun and Rehnquist contended that on the particular facts "the State where the debtor-creditor relationship was established" should be the one permitted to escheat. Such a solution would preserve "the equitable foundation of the Texas v. New Jersey rule" by dividing the fund "in a proportion approximating the volume of the transactions accruing in each State" and thus denying a "windfall" to the state of incorporation. Likewise, "[t]he place of purchase and the office of destination are reflected in Western Union's ledger books and it would, therefore, be unnecessary to examine the innumerable application forms themselves. Since the ledgers are more readily available, the allocation of the fund would be effected at less expense than would be required by the majority's resolution."

NOTES

(1) In New Jersey v. Armsted Industries, 48 N.J. 544, 226 A.2d 715 (1967), New Jersey claimed that as the state of incorporation it should be permitted to escheat amounts owed creditors residing in states where jurisdiction could not be obtained over the corporate debtor. This argument was rejected on the ground that escheat claims are not penal and hence the New Jersey courts would be open to a suit by the claimant states against the corporate debtor.

(2) A United States statute, which provides that a veteran's personal property shall vest in the United States when he dies without a will or legal heirs in a veterans' hospital, overrides a state statute of escheat. United States, Trustee v. Oregon, 366 U.S. 643 (1961). Accord as to federal war pension funds, Matter of Hammond, 3 N.Y.2d 567, 147 N.E.2d 777 (1958).

(3) See generally Lake, Escheat, Federalism and State Boundaries, 24 Ohio St.L.J. 322 (1963); Santell, Escheat, Unclaimed Property and the Supreme Court, 17 West.Res.L.Rev. 50 (1965); Note, 16 Sw.L.J. 660 (1962).

UNITED STATES BREWERS ASSOCIATION, INC. v. HEALY, 692 F.2d 275 (2d Cir. 1982): In 1981 Connecticut amended its comprehensive statute regulating the sale and distribution of liquors in an effort to lower the retail price of beer. The historically higher beer prices in Connecticut had led its residents to buy their beer in contiguous states, costing Connecticut tax revenues. Under the amended statute manufacturers and importers of beer were required to file a sworn affirmation that prices charged Connecticut wholesalers were no higher than prices for comparable units of beer in any bordering state. The court upheld the brewers' attack on the beer price affirmation provisions for violating the Commerce Clause of the United States Constitution (p. 281):

> Notwithstanding the greater scope permitted to the states for regulation of traffic in intoxicating beverages, nothing in the Twenty-first Amendment suggests that a state may regulate the sale of liquor outside of its own territory. The Amendment itself speaks only of the "transportation or importation *into* any State . . . for delivery or use *therein*." (Emphasis added.) . . . We are aware of no authority to the effect that the Twenty-first

Amendment modifies the traditional Commerce Clause principles that bar a state from regulating the transport, sale, or use of products outside of its own territory.

Compare the decisions of the Supreme Court in Skiriotes v. Florida, p. 51, supra, and Steele v. Bulova Watch Co., p. 470, infra. Is their distinguishing feature the fact that the "extraterritorial" application of the forum's law in those cases did not collide with the law of any other state?

Chapter 7

THRESHOLD PROBLEMS OF THE FORUM
IN CHOICE OF LAW

SECTION 1. ADMITTING OR REJECTING THE
ACTION OR DEFENSE

LOUCKS v. STANDARD OIL CO. OF NEW YORK

Court of Appeals of New York, 1918.
224 N.Y. 99, 120 N.E. 198.

CARDOZO, J. The action is brought to recover damages for injuries resulting in death. The plaintiffs are the administrators of the estate of Everett A. Loucks. Their intestate, while traveling on a highway in the state of Massachusetts, was run down and killed through the negligence of the defendant's servants then engaged in its business. He left a wife and two children, residents of New York. A statute of Massachusetts (R.L. ch. 171, sec. 2, as amended by L.1907, ch. 375) provides that "if a person or corporation by his or its negligence, or by the negligence of his or its agents and servants while engaged in his or its business, causes the death of a person who is in the exercise of due care, and not in his or its employment or service, he or it shall be liable in damages in the sum of not less than $500, nor more than $10,000, to be assessed with reference to the degree of his or its culpability, or that of his or its servants, to be recovered in an action of tort commenced within two years after the injury which caused the death by the executor or administrator of the deceased; one-half thereof to the use of the widow and one-half to the use of the children of the deceased, or if there are no children, the whole to the use of the widow, or if there is no widow, the whole to the use of the next of kin." The question is whether a right of action under that statute may be enforced in our courts.

"The courts of no country execute the penal laws of another" (The Antelope, 10 Wheat. 66, 123, 6 L.Ed. 268). The defendant invokes that principle as applicable here. Penal in one sense, the statute indisputably is. The damages are not limited to compensation; they are proportioned to the offender's guilt. A minimum recovery of $500 is allowed in every case. But the question is not whether the statute is penal in some sense. The question is whether it is penal

384

within the rules of private international law. A statute penal in that sense is one that awards a penalty to the state, or to a public officer in its behalf, or to a member of the public, suing in the interest of the whole community to redress a public wrong. . . . The purpose must be, not reparation to one aggrieved, but vindication of the public justice (Huntington v. Attrill [p. 301, supra]; Brady v. Daly, [175 U.S. 148, 20 S.Ct. 62, 44 L.Ed. 109]). The Massachusetts statute has been classified in some jurisdictions as penal, and in others as remedial. . . . The courts of Massachusetts have said that the question is still an open one (Boott Mills v. B. & M. R. R., 218 Mass. 582, 592, 106 N.E. 680). No matter how they may have characterized the act as penal, they have not meant to hold that it is penal for every purpose (218 Mass. 592, 106 N.E. 680). . . .

We think the better reason is with those cases which hold that the statute is not penal in the international sense. On that branch of the controversy, indeed, there is no division of opinion among us. It is true that the offender is punished, but the purpose of the punishment is reparation to those aggrieved by his offense (Comm. v. B. & A. R. R. Co., 121 Mass. 36, 37; Comm. v. Eastern R. R. Co., 5 Gray, 473, 474). The common law did not give a cause of acton to surviving relatives. . . . In the light of modern legislation, its rule is an anachronism. Nearly everywhere, the principle is now embodied in statute that the next of kin are wronged by the killing of their kinsman. . . . They sue to redress an outrage peculiar to themselves.

We cannot fail to see in the history of the Massachusetts statutes a developing expression of this policy and purpose. The statutes have their distant beginnings in the criminal law. To some extent the vestiges of criminal forms survive. But the old forms have been filled with a new content. The purpose which informs and vitalizes them is the protection of the survivors. . . .

Through all this legislation there runs a common purpose (Boott Mills v. B. & M. R. R. Co., supra, 586; Brown v. Thayer, 212 Mass. 392, 99 N.E. 237). It is penal in one element and one only: the damages are punitive. . . . But the punishment of the wrongdoer is not designed as atonement for a crime; it is solace to the individual who has suffered a private wrong. This is seen in many tokens. The employer may be innocent himself. . . . The executor or administrator who sues under this statute is not the champion of the peace and order and public justice of the commonwealth of Massachusetts. He is the representative of the outraged family. He vindicates a private right.

Another question remains. Even though the statute is not penal, it differs from our own. We must determine whether the difference is a sufficient reason for declining jurisdiction.

A tort committed in one state creates a right of action that may be sued upon in another unless public policy forbids. That is the generally accepted rule in the United States. . . . The question is

whether the enforcement of a right of action for tort under the statutes of another state is to be conditioned upon the existence of a kin-
dred statute here. . . .

A foreign statute is not law in this state, but it gives rise to an
obligation, which, if transitory, "follows the person and may be enforced wherever the person may be found". . . . "No law can exist as such except the law of the land; but . . . it is a principle of
every civilized law that vested rights shall be protected" (Beale, Conflict of Laws, sec. 51). The plaintiff owns something, and we help
him to get it. . . . We do this unless some sound reason of public
policy makes it unwise for us to lend our aid. "The law of the forum
is material only as setting a limit of policy beyond which such obligations will not be enforced there" (Cuba R. R. Co. v. Crosby, [222 U.S.
473–478]). . . . If aid is to be withheld here, it must be because
the cause of action in its nature offends our sense of justice or
menaces the public welfare. . . . Our own scheme of legislation
may be different. We may even have no legislation on the subject.
That is not enough to show that public policy forbids us to enforce
the foreign right. A right of action is property. If a foreign statute
gives the right, the mere fact that we do not give a like right is no
reason for refusing to help the plaintiff in getting what belongs to
him. We are not so provincial as to say that every solution of a problem is wrong because we deal with it otherwise at home. Similarity
of legislation has indeed this importance: its presence shows beyond
question that the foreign statute does not offend the local policy.
But its absence does not prove the contrary. It is not to be exalted
into an indispensable condition. The misleading word "comity" has
been responsible for much of the trouble. It has been fertile in suggesting a discretion unregulated by general principles (Beale, Conflict
of Laws, sec. 71). . . . The courts are not free to refuse to enforce a foreign right at the pleasure of the judges, to suit the individual notion of expediency or fairness. They do not close their doors
unless help would violate some fundamental principle of justice, some
prevalent conception of good morals, some deep-rooted tradition of
the common weal.

This test applied, there is nothing in the Massachusetts statute
that outrages the public policy of New York. We have a statute
which gives a civil remedy where death is caused in our own state.
We have thought it so important that we have now embedded it in the
Constitution (Const. art. 1, sec. 18). The fundamental policy is that
there shall be some atonement for the wrong. Through the defendant's negligence, a resident of New York has been killed in Massachusetts. He has left a widow and children who are also residents.
The law of Massachusetts gives them a recompense for his death. It
cannot be that public policy forbids our courts to help in collecting
what belongs to them. We cannot give them the same judgment that
our law would give if the wrong had been done here. Very likely we
cannot give them as much. But that is no reason for refusing to give

them what we can. We shall not make things better by sending them to another state, where the defendant may not be found, and where suit may be impossible. Nor is there anything to shock our sense of justice in the possibility of a punitive recovery. The penalty is not extravagant. . . . We shall not feel the pricks of conscience if the offender pays the survivors in proportion to the measure of his offense. We have no public policy that prohibits exemplary damages or civil penalties. We give them for many wrongs. To exclude all penal actions would be to wipe out the distinction between the penalties of public justice and the remedies of private law. . . .

We hold, then, that public policy does not prohibit the assumption of jurisdiction by our courts, and that this being so, mere differences of remedy do not count. . . . We must apply the same rules that are applicable to other torts; and the tendency of those rules today is toward a larger comity, if we must cling to the traditional term (Walsh v. B. & M. R. R., 201 Mass. 527, 533, 88 N.E. 12). The fundamental public policy is perceived to be that rights lawfully vested shall be everywhere maintained. At least, that is so among the states of the Union (Walsh v. N. Y. & N. E. R. R. Co., 160 Mass. 571, 573, 36 N.E. 584, 39 Am.St.Rep. 514; Walsh v. B. & M. R. R., supra; Beach, Uniform Interstate Enforcement of Vested Rights, 27 Yale Law Journal, 656). There is a growing conviction that only exceptional circumstances should lead one of the states to refuse to enforce a right acquired in another. . . . The test of similarity has been abandoned there. If it has ever been accepted here, we think it should be abandoned now.

The judgment of the Appellate Division should be reversed, and the order of the Special Term affirmed, with costs in the Appellate Division and in this court.

NOTES

(1) In the course of deciding whether the Massachusetts statute was "penal" in the international sense, Judge Cardozo made only passing reference to Huntington v. Attrill, p. 301, supra, clearly not treating it as binding or dispositive in the Loucks case. Why not? After all, the Supreme Court in the Huntington case addressed precisely the question "whether a statute of one State, which in some aspects may be called penal, is a penal law in the international sense." What was there about the situation in Loucks that freed the New York court to decide the question in such an independent way? For a thorough discussion of the concept of penality in a conflict-of-laws sense, see Kutner, Judicial Identification of "Penal Laws" in the Conflict of Laws, 31 Okla.L.Rev. 590 (1978).

(2) In Doggrell v. Southern Box Co., 208 F.2d 310 (6th Cir. 1953), the court affirmed a judgment of the federal district court in Tennessee imposing on a stockholder of an Arkansas corporation liability for the price of goods sold to the corporation. The ground was failure of the defendant and others to comply with the corporate organization laws of Arkansas. Soon after, the Supreme Court of Tennessee held in another case that the Arkan-

sas statute should not be applied in a Tennessee action because it was a "penal" statute. Thereupon the federal court of appeals withdrew its ruling and reversed the district court, in part because it believed the doctrine of Erie R. Co. v. Tompkins, p. 683 infra, compelled a Federal court in Tennessee wielding diversity jurisdiction to apply the ruling of the state's Supreme Court. The Doggrell case is set out, p. 711, infra.

(3) When, if ever, does a court's refusal to enforce a claim resting on sister-state law on grounds of "penality" or for contravening the forum's public policy violate the United States Constitution? Does Hughes v. Fetter, p. 322, supra, shed any light on that question?

(4) Is there any inconsistency between the position that the dissimilarity of the law of a sister state is not a ground for refusing to entertain a claim based on that law and the position that the dissimilar rule should not be applied to decide the case?

———

MERTZ v. MERTZ

Court of Appeals of New York, 1936.
271 N.Y. 466, 3 N.E.2d 597, 108 A.L.R. 1120.

LEHMAN, JUDGE. The plaintiff has brought an action in this state against her husband to recover damages for personal injuries which, she alleges, she sustained in the state of Connecticut through her husband's negligent operation of an automobile, owned and controlled by him. Under the law of New York the rule is well established that a husband is not liable to his wife for personal injuries caused by his negligence. . . . The complaint alleges that under the law of the state of Connecticut a husband is liable for such injuries. The parties are residents of the state of New York. The problem presented upon this appeal is whether a wife residing here may resort to the courts of this state to enforce liability for a wrong committed outside of the state, though under the laws of this state a husband is immune from such liability. . . .

The Legislature of Connecticut has chosen to remove the common-law disability. There a wife may maintain an action against her husband for damages caused by his wrong, and no exception has been engrafted there upon the general rule that "illegality established, liability ensues." . . . A cause of action for personal injuries is transitory. Liability follows the person and may be enforced wherever the person may be found. Nonetheless, a cause of action arising in one state may be enforced in another state only by the use of remedies afforded by the law of the forum where enforcement is sought. The courts of the state of New York are not concerned with the wisdom of the law of Connecticut or of the internal policy back of that law. They must enforce a transitory cause of action arising elsewhere, unless enforcement is contrary to the law of this state.
. . .

"The term 'public policy' is frequently used in a very vague, loose or inaccurate sense. The courts have often found it necessary to define its juridical meaning, and have held that a state can have no public policy except what is to be found in its Constitution and laws. . . . Therefore, when we speak of the public policy of the state, we mean the law of the state whether found in the Constitution, the statutes or judicial records." (People v. Hawkins, 157 N.Y. 1, 12, 51 N.E. 257.) * . . . There is nothing in the opinion in Loucks v. Standard Oil Co. of New York supra, which could indicate that in the field of conflict of laws the "juridical meaning" of the vague concept of public policy is different.

In that case the administrator of a resident of this state who was killed in Massachusetts sued here to recover the damages caused by his death. . . . This court then held only that in such case the courts may not read into the law a limitation created by a supposed public policy, founded on its own notion of expediency and justice. It did not hold that the courts might disregard a limitation, contained in the law of the state, established by authority and tradition, because the court could not discern a sound public policy back of the law.

The law of the forum determines the jurisdiction of the courts, the capacity of parties to sue or to be sued, the remedies which are available to suitors and the procedure of the courts. Where a party seeks in this state enforcement of a cause of action created by foreign law, he can avail himself only of the remedies provided by our law, and is subject to the general limitations which are part of our law. . . . The law of this state attaches to the marriage status a reciprocal disability which precludes a suit by one spouse against the other for personal injuries. It recognizes the wrong, but denies remedy for such wrong by attaching to the person of the spouse a disability to sue. No other state can, outside of its own territorial limits, remove that disability or provide by its law a remedy available in our courts which our law denies to other suitors. So we said in Herzog v. Stern, 264 N.Y. 379, 191 N.E. 23. A disability to sue which arises solely from the marital status and which has no relation to a definition of wrong or the quality of an act from which liability would otherwise spring may perhaps be an anachronistic survival of a common-law rule. Even then the courts should not transform an anachrony into an anomaly, and a disability to sue attached by our law to the person of a wife becomes an anomaly if another state can confer upon a

---

* In People v. Hawkins there was an indictment for offering for sale a scrub brush which was convict-made but not so labeled, in violation of a state statute which required the label. The brush had been made in an Ohio prison and shipped to New York. The Court of Appeals struck down the statute as in violation of the interstate commerce clause of the United States Constitution. Does the quotation on "public policy" given in this context, guide or control its meaning for conflict of laws purposes?

wife, even though residing here, capacity to sue in our courts upon a cause of action arising there.

The judgment should be affirmed with costs.

CROUCH, JUDGE (dissenting). . . . The Appellate Division affirmed a judgment dismissing the complaint for insufficiency and lack of jurisdiction. It was held that "the cause of action asserted offends our public policy to so great an extent that the court is without jurisdiction to entertain it." 247 App.Div. 713, 285 N.Y.S. 590.

Without pausing to inquire whether the word "jurisdiction" was accurately used, we accept it as a convenient symbol applying to a refusal to enforce a claim created by a foreign law. In approaching the question whether the refusal was justified, certain general principles may be dogmatically stated. The cause of action rests primarily upon the law of Connecticut. If we entertain it, whether we say we are enforcing the original foreign law or a copy of it incorporated in our own rule of conflicts, is immaterial as a practical matter. It is not penal; it is transitory; and our courts will enforce it according to the substantive law of Connecticut unless it "is contrary to the strong public policy" of our own state. Restatement of Law of Conflict of Laws, section 612. We are left, then, to determine whether the law of Connecticut, which permits a wife to sue a husband for personal injuries, is contrary to some strong public policy of New York.

The public policy concept is a vague and variable phenomenon. When we find it necessary, in a general way, to embody it in words, we are apt to . . . say . . . "we mean the law of the state, whether found in the Constitution, the statutes or judicial records." We go further, sometimes, and in explanation say that the law so found evidences "the will of the Legislature," Straus & Co. v. Canadian Pacific Ry. Co., 254 N.Y. 407, 413, 173 N.E. 564, 566, and so, perhaps, represents an inarticulate public opinion on the specific matter involved. In that broad sense it may be true to say that back of every law there is something which is conventionally referred to as public policy. Obviously, however, the bulk of public policy, so defined, relates to "minor morals of expediency and debatable questions of internal policy." Hence the difference between our own public policy and that of our sister states is for the most part disregarded by our own law of conflict of laws. . . .

It may be freely conceded that back of the New York rule which withholds from the wife the right to sue the husband for personal injuries is a public policy of the kind which is back of every other rule of law. But neither in the history of the rule nor in its operation is there anything to indicate that that policy is founded upon a definite view—or even upon some vague feeling—that justice or the public welfare would be affected by a contrary rule. . . . It is enough to say that the rule exists merely as a product of judicial interpretation, is vestigial in character, and embodies no tenable policy of morals or of social welfare. To urge that it survives because it is an aid to conjugal peace disregards reality.   Conjugal peace would be as seriously jarred by an action for breach of contract, or on a promissory note, or for an injury to property, real or personal, all of which the law permits, as by one for personal injury.   In short, even though we assume that there is some shadowy element of policy back of the rule, it should give way to "the controlling public policy . . . that the courts of each State shall give effect to all valid causes of action created by the laws of another State except possibly in extreme cases."   Hubbs, J., in Herzog v. Stern, 264 N.Y. 379, 387, 191 N.E. 23, 26. . . .

CRANE, C.J., and O'BRIEN, HUBBS, and LOUGHRAN, JJ. concur with LEHMAN, J.

CROUCH, J., dissents in opinion, in which FINCH, J., concurs.

Judgment affirmed.

NOTES

(1) Does Judge Lehman's definition of public policy and its sources contradict Judge Cardozo's assertion in the Loucks case that "similarity" is not a valid test of the enforceability in New York of claims based on the law of other states?   Consider the following quotation:

"The defendant's position is that the policy of the state—the forum of the action—is to be found in its laws; and when a law of the locus of the action differs from and therefore (she says) contravenes a corresponding law of the forum, the law of the former state will not be enforced. . . .   If this were strictly true there would be no question on the subject, for then the courts of one state would, aside from considerations of comity, never enforce different laws of another state, when as a matter of fact, the books are full of cases where state courts have, without regard to their own laws, enforced contracts and permitted recovery for torts according to the laws of the state where the contracts were made and the torts committed."   Curtis v. Campbell, 76 F.2d 84, 85 (3d Cir. 1935).

(2) D held a contract franchise from P in the business of providing temporary help.   In the contract the parties stipulated that Wisconsin law was to govern.   D covenanted not to compete with P in the business for two years after termination of the franchise.   P sued in a federal court in Florida to enforce the covenant.   Rejecting the defense that enforcement of the restriction would violate Florida's statute banning "[e]very contract" in restraint of trade, the court said that failure of the Florida statute to expressly except from the ban a covenant like the one in suit did not mean it therefore contravened Florida's public policy.   Wilkinson v. Manpower, Inc., 531 F.2d 712 (5th Cir. 1976).

(3) In the *Mertz* case the dissenting opinion states that the trial court dismissed the complaint "for [1] insufficiency and [2] lack of jurisdiction".   What difference would it make for res judicata purposes in a later action in the same or a different state that the decision went on one or the other of the two grounds?   When it is unclear whether a dismissal of an action was "on the merits" for res judicata purposes, what factors and circumstances are persuasive one way or the other?   Compare Davis v. Furlong, 328

N.W.2d 150 (Minn.1983), p. 413, infra; Angel v. Bullington, p. 714, infra, and Warner v. Buffalo Drydock Co., p. 254, supra.

INTERCONTINENTAL HOTELS CORP. (PUERTO RICO) v. GOLDEN

Court of Appeals of New York, 1964.
15 N.Y.2d 9, 254 N.Y.S.2d 527, 203 N.E.2d 210.

BURKE, JUDGE. On this appeal by the plaintiff from a judgment dismissing the complaint, the only issue is whether the courts of this State must deny access to a party seeking to enforce obligations validly entered into in the Commonwealth of Puerto Rico and enforceable under Puerto Rican law.

Plaintiff, the owner and operator of a government-licensed gambling casino in Puerto Rico, seeks to recover the sum of $12,000 evidenced by defendant's check and I.O.U.'s given in payment of gambling debts incurred in Puerto Rico.

Once again we are faced with the question of when our courts may refuse to enforce a foreign right, though valid where acquired, on the ground that its "enforcement is contrary to [the public] policy of the forum" (Straus & Co. v. Canadian Pacific Ry. Co., 254 N.Y. 407, 414, 173 N.E. 564, 567). . . .

Substantially all of the commentators agree that foreign-based rights should be enforced unless the judicial enforcement of such a contract would be the approval of a transaction which is inherently vicious, wicked or immoral, and shocking to the prevailing moral sense. (Beach, Uniform Interstate Enforcement of Vested Rights, 27 Yale L.J. 656, 662; Goodrich, Conflict of Laws [3d ed., 1949], 305; 2 Rabel, Conflict of Laws: A Comparative Study [1947], 555–575; Paulsen and Sovern, "Public Policy" in the Conflict of Laws, 56 Col.L.Rev. 969; 3 Beale, Conflict of Laws [1935], 1649.)

Applying this test we find decisions in this State involving gambling transactions which put this reasoning into practice. Over 100 years ago this court held in Thatcher v. Morris, 11 N.Y. 437 [1854] that a contract involving lottery tickets if legal and valid without the State would be upheld though illegal in New York. In Harris v. White, 81 N.Y. 532 [1880] suit was permitted for wages earned in out-of-State horse races at a time when horse racing was illegal in the State of New York. In Ormes v. Dauchy, 82 N.Y. 443 [1880] suit was upheld for commissions earned by placing extrastate lottery advertisements in out-of-State newspapers. Thus, aware of the common-law rule which barred the enforcement of gambling contracts and conscious that they were illegal and void in almost all the States of this country, the courts of this State took the position, even in Victorian times, that there was no strong public policy to prevent the enforcement of such contracts according to the law of the place of per-

formance. There is nothing suggested by the respondent which
should persuade us that Judge CARDOZO was wrong when he said in
Loucks v. Standard Oil Co. (p. 384, supra): "The courts are not free
to refuse to enforce a foreign right at the pleasure of the judges, to
suit the individual notion of expediency or fairness. They do not
close their doors, unless help would violate some . . . prevalent
conception of good morals".

It has, however, been urged that suits on gambling debts contracted validly elsewhere are contrary to two public policies of this State,
i.e., in this jurisdiction gamblers are outlaws, and all gambling contracts made with them are void. Worthy though such considerations
be, they apply only to transactions governed by our domestic law.
. . . .

Public policy is not determinable by mere reference to the laws of
the forum alone. Strong public policy is found in prevailing social
and moral attitudes of the community. In this sophisticated season
the enforcement of the rights of the plaintiff in view of the weight of
authority would not be considered repugnant to the "public policy of
this State". It seems to us that, if we are to apply the strong public
policy test to the enforcement of the plaintiff's rights under the gambling laws of the Commonwealth of Puerto Rico, we should measure
them by the prevailing social and moral attitudes of the community
which is reflected not only in the decisions of our courts in the Victorian era, but sharply illustrated in the changing attitudes of the People of the State of New York. The legalization of pari-mutuel betting
and the operation of bingo games, as well as a strong movement for
legalized off-track betting, indicate that the New York public does
not consider authorized gambling a violation of "some prevalent conception of good morals [or] some deep-rooted tradition of the common
weal." (Loucks v. Standard Oil Co. [p. 384, supra]).

The trend in New York State demonstrates an acceptance of *licensed* gambling transactions as a morally acceptable activity, not objectionable under the prevailing standards of lawful and approved social conduct in a community. Our newspapers quote the odds on
horse races, football games, basketball games and print the names of
the winners of the Irish Sweepstakes and the New Hampshire lottery. Informed public sentiment in New York is only against unlicensed gambling, which is unsupervised, unregulated by law and
which affords no protection to customers and no assurance of fairness or honesty in the operation of the gambling devices.

In the present case there is no indication that the evils of gambling, which New York prohibits and Puerto Rico has licensed, will
spill over into our community if these debts are enforced in New
York courts. The New York constitutional provisions were adopted
with a view toward protecting the family man of meager resources
from his own imprudence at the gaming tables. (See Carter and

Stone, Proceedings and Debates of the Convention, 567 [Hosford, 1821].)

Puerto Rico has made provision for this kind of imprudence by allowing the court to reduce gambling obligations or even decline to enforce them altogether, if the court in its discretion finds that the losses are "[in an] amount [which] may exceed the customs of a good father of a family." (Laws of Puerto Rico Ann., tit. 31, § 4774.) This regulation is consistent with New York policy and would be properly considered in any case before a New York court which may be asked to enforce a Puerto Rican gambling debt.

There is nothing immoral per se in the contract before us, but injustice would result if citizens of this State were allowed to retain the benefits of the winnings in a State where such gambling is legal, but to renege if they were losers.

The cases relied on by the respondent miss the mark.

In the case of Mertz v. Mertz (p. 388, supra), Judge LEHMAN, writing for the court, said that "a disability to sue attached by our law to the person of a wife becomes an anomaly if another state can confer upon a wife, *even though residing here,* capacity to sue in our courts upon a cause of action arising there" . . . . As distinguished from the present case, in Mertz the court was faced with this State's interest in the marital status situated here. As a practical matter, all the significant contacts of the case were with New York and the language of the opinion indicates that the court was in reality there making a *choice of law* decision of the kind that this court today follows under the nominal heading of the "contacts" doctrine. . . .

We think, therefore, that this case falls within the consistent practice of enforcing rights validly created by the laws of a sister State which do not tend to disturb our local laws or corrupt the public.

Accordingly, the judgment of the Appellate Division should be reversed . . . .

DESMOND, CHIEF JUDGE (dissenting).

. . .

Plaintiff, a Delaware corporation and operator of a Commonwealth-licensed gambling room or casino in its hotel in Puerto Rico, sued defendant, a New York resident, on a $3,000 check and 13 "I. O. U.'s" totaling $9,000. The $12,000 total covered defendant's gambling losses at plaintiff's casino where defendant had been allowed to gamble on credit. . . .

The issue: are our courts open to suits by gambling house proprietors who let their customers run up debts; or do such transactions so offend our concept of good morals that our settled public policy prompts us to reject the suit? Closing our doors to such a lawsuit is in principle and under our decisions and statues the only possible

course. It is not a matter of choice of law as between the Puerto
Rican and domestic brands. We refuse the suit not because Puerto
Rico's law differs from ours but because we cannot in good conscience use our judicial processes to recognize the gamester's claim
by giving him a judgment. (Mertz v. Mertz, 271 N.Y. 466, 3 N.E.2d
597, 108 A.L.R. 1120). . . .

We are here asked to enforce a gambling contract, unenforceable
at common law (Ruckman v. Pitcher, 1 N.Y. 392; Meech v. Stoner, 19
N.Y. 26; Irwin v. Williar, 110 U.S. 499) and made void and illegal in
our State (and almost every other State, see Irwin v. Williar, supra)
under specific statutes (Penal Law, Consol.Laws, c. 40, §§ 991–996).
In truth, not one but two public policies of ours are offended when
we give judgment for plaintiff. First, operating a gambling business
(as distinguished from casual betting between individuals) was an in-
dictable public nuisance at common law, has always been held criminal conduct in New York State, and professional gamblers are "outlaws" in New York. . . . Second, from earliest times in this State
all gambling contracts and loans for gambling have been void and
denied enforcement by the professional gambler even to the extent
that the bettor-customer may sue for the amount he lost (Penal Law,
§ 994 . . . .)

The conclusion that settled New York policy bars suit on a claim
like this one is not disproved by pointing to our legalization of bingo
games and pari-mutuel betting on horse races (N.Y.Const. art. I, § 9).
The people of the State in amending their Constitution and the legislators in adopting and revising the statutes have found and acted on
important differences between those two forms of gambling and the
operation of gambling houses. That these differences are widely recognized elsewhere is evident from the fact that while pari-mutual betting is lawful in 24 States and bingo is legalized in 11 States (lottery
in one) nevertheless only one State (Nevada) licenses gambling rooms
and even in Nevada gambling-house debts are not suable in court
(Nevada Tax Comm. v. Hicks, 73 Nev. 115, 310 P.2d 852). . . .

NOTES

(1) Taken together, what do the Loucks, Mertz and Golden cases teach
with regard to (a) the definition and (b) the source of "public policy" as a
factor in denying enforcement of rights claimed to rest upon rules of law
drawn from other states?

(2) Is Judge Burke correct in his conclusion that in Mertz v. Mertz the
court made a "choice of law" decision—that is, rejected Connecticut's permissive rule and applied New York's rule that one spouse was without capacity
to sue the other—rather than that it refused access to the New York courts
for Mrs. Mertz' Connecticut-based cause of action? A refusal to entertain an
action may leave the plaintiff with the possibility of suit in a different forum,
thus serving as a dismissal without prejudice. On the other hand, a choice-
of-law decision may preclude further action anywhere.

(3) In a much-cited article, Paulsen and Sovern, "Public Policy" in the Conflict of Laws, 56 Colum.L.Rev. 969 (1956), the authors warned that the use of the concept is especially insidious and dangerous if it is invoked by a forum court that has only slight contacts with the occurrence or the parties. Often, its use in those circumstances has been for parochial reasons—to give protection to interests of residents. They cautioned that the "principal vice of the public policy concepts is that they provide a substitute for analysis."

(4) When public policy (*ordre public*) is used to deny a defense rather than to refuse to entertain a cause of action, there is no ambiguity regarding the res judicata consequences. Why? Does it follow that a disallowed defense is more likely to raise constitutional questions than a dismissed claim? See Chapter 6, especially Home Insurance Co. v. Dick, p. 329, supra.

TAX CLAIMS

Until relatively recently suits by one state to collect its taxes in another state's courts were dismissed by analogy to the ban on enforcing another state's penal laws. For nearly a century and a half the question of the enforcement by the courts of one country (or state) of the tax claims of another country (or state) was dominated by the influence of Lord Mansfield's statement in Holman v. Johnson, 1 Cowp. 341, 343 (K.B.1775), where he said: "No country ever takes notice of the revenue laws of another." In 1935, Milwaukee County v. M. E. White Co., p. 311, supra, holding full faith and credit due a sister state judgment for taxes, said it was an "open question" whether an unadjudicated tax claim was subject to similar constitutional compulsion. After a period of chipping away at the old doctrine, state courts have tended to enforce sister states' revenue claims. See, e.g., City of Detroit v. Gould, 12 Ill.2d 297, 146 N.E.2d 61 (1957) (personal property tax); State ex rel. Oklahoma Tax Commission v. Rodgers, 238 Mo.App. 1115, 193 S.W.2d 919 (1946) (income tax). See, also, Scoles, Interstate and International Distinctions in Conflict of Laws in the United States, 54 Calif.L.Rev. 1599, 1607–1608 (1966).

By 1977 some 44 states had enacted reciprocal statutes for enforcement of tax claims. See Greenberg, Extrastate Enforcement of Tax Claims and Administrative Tax Determinations Under the Full Faith and Credit Clause, 43 Bklyn.L.Rev. 630, 642 (1977). Judicial decisions in Nevada and Wyoming have enforced extrastate tax claims without statutory authority while several other states with reciprocal statutes have gone beyond their provisions in enforcing claims. Id. at 643. Is there any likelihood that the doctrine of Hughes v. Fetter, p. 322, supra, compels enforcement of sister-state tax claims in a non-discriminatory way when the forum state itself levies identical taxes?

HOLZER v. DEUTSCHE REICHSBAHN–GESELLSCHAFT

Court of Appeals of New York, 1938.
277 N.Y. 474, 14 N.E.2d 798.

PER CURIAM.   The complaint alleges two causes of action arising out of a contract between plaintiff, a German national, and Schenker & Co. G.m.b.H., a German corporation, for services to be performed by plaintiff for three years from January 1, 1932, in Germany and in other locations outside this state.   Defendants, German corporations, controlled either through stock ownership or otherwise, the transportation system known as Schenker & Co.

Both causes of action allege that the contract provides that "in the event the plaintiff should die or become unable, without fault on his part, to serve during the period of the contract the defendants would pay to him or his heirs the sum of 120,000 marks, in discharge of their obligations under the hiring aforesaid."

The first cause of action alleges that on June 21, 1933, defendants discharged plaintiff as of October 31, 1933, upon the sole ground that he is a Jew and that as the result of such discharge he was damaged in a sum upwards of $50,000.

The second cause of action alleges that in April, 1933, the German government incarcerated plaintiff in prison and in a concentration camp for about six months, that his imprisonment was not brought about by any act or fault of plaintiff but solely by reason of the policy of the government which required the elimination of all persons of Jewish blood from leading commercial, industrial and transportation enterprises, that as a result *"plaintiff became unable, without any fault on his part, to continue his services from the month of April 1933,"* and has been damaged in the sum of $50,000.

The second separate defense of defendant Deutsche Reichsbahn-Gesellschaft alleges that the contract of hiring was made and was to be performed in Germany, was terminated in Germany and is governed by the laws of Germany, that subsequent to April 7, 1933, the government of Germany adopted and promulgated certain laws, decrees, and orders which required persons of non-Aryan descent, of whom plaintiff is one, to be retired.

The Special Term granted plaintiff's motion to strike out this defense, the Appellate Division affirmed and certified these questions: "(1) Is the second separate defense contained in the answer of the defendant, Deutsche Reichsbahn-Gesellschaft, sufficient in law upon the face thereof?   (2) Does the complaint herein state facts sufficient to constitute a cause of action?"

The courts of this state are empowered to entertain jurisdiction of actions between citizens of foreign countries or other states of this Union based upon contracts between nonresidents to be performed outside this state. . . .   Under the decisions of this court and of the Supreme Court of the United States, the law of the country or state where the contract was made and was to be performed by citizens of that country or state governs. Salimoff & Co. v. Standard Oil Co. of New York, 262 N.Y. 220, 186 N.E. 679, 89 A.L.R. 345. Within its own territory every government is supreme (United States v. Belmont, 301 U.S. 324) and our courts are not competent to review its actions. Wulfsohn v. Russian Socialist Federated Soviet Republic, 234 N.Y. 372, 138 N.E. 24. We have so held, "however objectionable" we may consider the conduct of a foreign government. Dougherty v. Equitable Life Assur. Soc. of United States, 266 N.Y. 71, 83, 193 N.E. 897. "Every sovereign State is bound to respect the independence of every other sovereign State, and the courts of one country will not sit in judgment on the acts of the government of another done within its own territory." Oetjen v. Central Leather Co., 246 U.S. 297, 303. In the Dougherty Case, supra, 266 N.Y. 71, at page 90, 193 N.E. 897, 903, we have held: "It cannot be against the public policy of this State to hold nationals to the contracts which they have made in their own country to be performed there according to the laws of that country."

Therefore, in respect to the first cause of action, we are bound to decide, as a matter of pleading, that the complaint does not state facts sufficient to constitute a cause of action and that the second separate defense of the answer is sufficient in law upon its face. Defendants did not breach their contract with plaintiff. They were forced by operation of law to discharge him.

In respect to the second cause of action, the result is necessarily different. We are dealing merely with pleadings. Assuming, as alleged, that plaintiff became unable without any fault on his part to continue his services subsequent to April, 1933, that part of the agreement which is alleged to provide "that in the event the plaintiff should die *or become unable, without fault on his part,* to serve during the period of the contract the defendants would pay to him or his heirs the sum of 120,000 marks, in discharge of their obligations, under the hiring aforesaid," must be interpreted according to German law and the meaning of German words. What that law is depends upon the solution of questions of fact which must be determined on the trial. If the English words "become unable" are a correct translation of the German words employed in the contract, then they would not appear to be limited to inability caused by physical illness but might be intended to apply to any factor which might prevent his service.

The order should be modified by reversing so much thereof as grants plaintiff's motion to strike out the second separate defense in the answer as applied to the first cause of action. It should be affirmed as to the second cause of action and the certified questions answered as follows: (1) As to the first cause of action, "Yes." As to the second cause of action, "No."   (2) As to the first cause of action, "No."   As to the second cause of action, "Yes."

NOTES

(1) If Holzer had won on the basis that New York's public policy would not countenance the defense relying upon the Nazi regime's Aryan laws, would the defendant have been entitled to a reversal in the Supreme Court of the United States on the ground that its property had been taken without due process of law? Cf. Home Insurance Co. v. Dick, p. 329, supra. Would defendant's case have been strengthened by removal to a federal court?

(2) What is the relationship between the problem of the principal case and the "act of state" doctrine discussed in Banco Nacional de Cuba v. Sabbatino, 376 U.S. 398, 84 S.Ct. 923 (1964), p. 747, infra?

SECTION 2.   NOTICE AND PROOF OF FOREIGN LAW

A SURVEY OF THE FOREIGN LAW PROBLEM

Historically, common law courts have been presumed not to know the law of foreign states. It is hard to quarrel with that presumption. Thus, a party who desired to rely on foreign law for a claim or defense faced a variety of problems including when and how to give notice that he relied on the law of another jurisdiction, and the portions of it he invoked; how to establish his assertions about their contents; and what would occur if the court came to the conclusion that foreign law should provide the rule of decision, but was not able to discern the content of the foreign law. Compounding the complexity of the problem was the axiom that foreign law was a matter of fact, pleadable as such and provable as such—by evidence supplied by experts to a jury!

Glacially, progress has been made in the direction of treating foreign law questions as legal problems for the court, not the jury; in widening the possibility of judicial notice of the contents of another state's law; in prescribing realistic rules as to notice of intent to rely on law other than the forum's; and in dealing with the question of what a court ought to do if it knows that decision should turn on another state's rules of law, but it has not been made aware of their contents and has no way of informing itself. With regard to a sister state's laws, judicial notice is commonly used. Foreign country law— especially when in a foreign tongue—presents complexities not yet wholly mastered by American lawmakers and judges.

The case that follows treats the problem of proving foreign law in a way that fortunately is obsolescing, largely because of the widespread easing of the rigid requirement that foreign law be pleaded, proved and reviewed as a fact.

WALTON v. ARABIAN AMERICAN OIL CO.

United States Court of Appeals, Second Circuit, 1956.
233 F.2d 541.*

FRANK, CIRCUIT JUDGE. Plaintiff is a citizen and resident of Arkansas, who, while temporarily in Saudi Arabia, was seriously injured when an automobile he was driving collided with a truck owned by defendant, driven by one of defendant's employees. Defendant is a corporation incorporated in Delaware, licensed to do business in New York, and engaged in extensive business activities in Saudi Arabia. Plaintiff's complaint did not allege pertinent Saudi Arabian "law," nor at the trial did he prove or offer to prove it. Defendant did not, in its answer, allege such "law," and defendant did not prove or offer to prove it. There was evidence from which it might have been inferred, reasonably, that, under well-established New York decisions, defendant was negligent and therefore liable to plaintiff. The trial judge, saying he would not take judicial notice of Saudi-Arabian "law," directed a verdict in favor of the defendant and gave judgment against the plaintiff.

1. As jurisdiction here rests on diversity of citizenship, we must apply the New York rules of conflict of laws. It is well settled by the New York decisions that the "substantive law" applicable to an alleged tort is the "law" of the place where the alleged tort occurred.
. . .

It has been suggested that, where suit is brought in an American court by an American plaintiff against an American defendant, complaining of alleged tortious conduct by the defendant in a foreign country, and that conduct is tortious according to the rules of the forum, the court, in some circumstances, should apply the forum's tort rules. See Morris, The Proper Law of a Tort, 64 Harv.L.Rev. (1951) 881, criticizing, inter alia, Slater v. Mexican National Railroad, 194 U.S. 120. There, and in 12 Modern L.Rev. (1949) 248, Morris decries, as "mechanical jurisprudence," the invariable reference to the "law" of the place where the alleged tort happened. There may be much to Morris' suggestion; and a court—particularly with reference to torts where conduct in reliance on precedents is ordinarily absent—should not perpetuate a doctrine which, upon re-examination, shows up as unwise and unjust. . . . But we see no signs that the New York decisions pertinent here are obsolescent.[1]

---

* Cert. denied, 352 U.S. 872 (1956).

1. Were this not a diversity case, it might perhaps be appropriate to suggest that the Supreme Court should reconsider the accepted doctrine (as to the complete dominance of the "law" of the place where the alleged tort occurred) which seems to have been unduly influenced by

2. The general federal rule is that the "law" of a foreign country is a fact which must be proved. However, under Fed.Rules Civ.Proc. rule 43(a), 28 U.S.C.A., a federal court must receive evidence if it is admissible according to the rules of evidence of the state in which the court sits. At first glance, then, it may seem that the judge erred in refusing to take judicial notice of Saudi Arabian "law" in the light of New York Civil Practice Act, § 344–a.[2] In Siegelman v. Cunard White Star, 2 Cir., 221 F.2d 189, 196–197, applying that statute, we took judicial notice of English "law" which had been neither pleaded nor proved. Our decision, in that respect, has been criticized; but it may be justified on the ground that an American court can easily comprehend, and therefore, under the statute, take judicial notice of, English decisions, like those of any state in the United States.[3] However, where, as here, comprehension of foreign "law" is, to say the least, not easy, then, according to the somewhat narrow interpretation of the New York statute by the New York courts, a court "abuses" its discretion under that statute perhaps if it takes judicial notice of foreign "law" when it is not pleaded, and surely does so unless the party, who would otherwise have had the burden of proving that "law," has in some way adequately assisted the court in judicially learning it.

3. Plaintiff, however, argues thus: The instant case involves such rudimentary tort principles, that the judge, absent a contrary showing, should have presumed that those principles are recognized in Saudi Arabia; therefore the burden of showing the contrary was on the defendant, which did not discharge that burden.[4] But we do not agree that the applicable tort principles, necessary to establish plaintiff's claim, are "rudimentary": In countries where the common law does not prevail, our doctrines relative to negligence, and to a master's liability for his servant's acts, may well not exist or be vastly different. Consequently, here plaintiff had the burden of showing, to the trial court's satisfaction, Saudi Arabian "law."

This conclusion seems unjust for this reason: Both the parties are Americans. The plaintiff was but a transient in Saudi Arabia when the accident occurred and has not been there since that time. The defendant company engages in extensive business operations there, and is therefore in a far better position to obtain information concerning the "law" of that country. But, under the New York decisions

notions of sovereignty a la Hobbes. . . . [Footnotes renumbered; some shortened. Eds.]

2. It reads, in part:

"A. Except as otherwise expressly required by law, any trial or appellate court, in its discretion, may take judicial notice of the following matters of law:

"1. A law, statute, proclamation, edict, decree, ordinance, or the unwrit-ten or common law of a sister state, a territory or other jurisdiction of the United States, or of a foreign country or political subdivision thereof. . . .

3. An American court may go astray even in taking judicial notice of English "law." The similarity in language may be deceptive by concealing significant differences. . . .

4. Cuba R. Co. v. Crosby, 222 U.S. 473, 478 . . . . .

which we must follow, plaintiff had the burden. As he did not discharge it, a majority of the court holds that the judge correctly gave judgment for the defendant.

4. In argument, plaintiff's counsel asserted that Saudi Arabia has "no law or legal system," and no courts open to plaintiff, but only a dictatorial monarch who decides according to his whim whether a claim like plaintiff's shall be redressed, i.e., that Saudi Arabia is, in effect, "uncivilized." According to Holmes, J.—in Slater v. Mexican National R. Co., 194 U.S. 120, 129, in American Banana Co. v. United Fruit Co., 213 U.S. 347, 355–356, and in Cuba R. Co. v. Crosby, 222 U.S. 473, 478—the *lex loci* does not apply "where a tort is committed in an uncivilized country" or in one "having no law that civilized countries would recognize as adequate." If such were the case here, we think the New York courts would apply (and therefore we should) the substantive "law" of the country which is most closely connected with the parties and their conduct—in this case, American "law." But plaintiff has offered no data showing that Saudi Arabia is thus "uncivilized." We are loath to and will not believe it, absent such a showing. . . .

Since the plaintiff deliberately refrained from establishing an essential element of his case, the complaint was properly dismissed. The majority of the court thinks that, for the following reasons, it is inappropriate to remand the case so that the plaintiff may have another chance: He had abundant opportunity to supply the missing element and chose not to avail himself of it. . . . The judgment of dismissal must therefore be affirmed.

The writer of the opinion thinks we should remand for this reason: Apparently neither the trial judge nor the parties were aware of New York Civil Practice Act, § 344–a; consequently, in the interests of justice, we should remand with directions to permit the parties, if they so desire, to present material which may assist the trial judge to ascertain the applicable "law" of Saudi Arabia.

Affirmed.

NOTES

(1) See Schlesinger, A Recurrent Problem in Transnational Litigation: The Effect of a Failure to Invoke or Prove the Applicable Foreign Law, 59 Corn.L.Rev. 1 (1973). Requiring English law to be proved as fact, see Byrne v. Cooper, 11 Wn.App. 549, 523 P.2d 1216 (1974); but cf. Frummer v. Hilton Hotels International, Inc., p. 480, infra (English law judicially noticed). See Currie, On the Displacement of the Law of the Forum, 58 Colum.L.Rev. 964 (1958), reprinted in B. Currie, Selected Essays on the Conflict of Laws, Chap. 1 (1963), which considers closely the Walton case and its problems.

(2) Helpful treatments of this subject are: Pollack, Proof of Foreign Law, 26 Am.J.Comp.L. 470 (1978); Alexander, The Application and Avoidance of Foreign Law in the Law of Conflicts, 70 Nw.L.Rev. 602 (1975); Mill-

er, Federal Rule 44.1 and the "Fact" Approach to Determining Foreign Law, 65 Mich.L.Rev. 613 (1967).

LEARY v. GLEDHILL

Supreme Court of New Jersey, 1951.
8 N.J. 260, 84 A.2d 725.

[This is an action between two Americans based on an alleged loan of money which was made in France and which, so it was assumed, was governed by the law of France. At the trial the defendant moved that the action be dismissed because the law of France was neither pleaded nor proved. The action of the trial court in denying the motion was affirmed on appeal.]

VANDERBILT, C. J. . . . Under the common law of England as adopted in this country, . . . the law of other countries, including sister states, would not be . . . noticed and applied by a court, but it was deemed an issue of fact to be pleaded and proved as other material facts had to be . . .

The courts, however, were reluctant to dismiss an action for a failure to plead and prove the applicable foreign law as they would have dismissed it for a failure to prove other material facts necessary to establish a cause of action or a defense. Accordingly the courts frequently indulged in one or another of several presumptions: that the common law prevails in the foreign jurisdiction; that the law of the foreign jurisdiction is the same as the law of the forum, be it common law or statute; or that certain fundamental principles of the law exist in all civilized countries. As a fourth alternative, instead of indulging in any presumption as to the law of the foreign jurisdiction, the courts would merely apply the law of the forum as the only law before the court on the assumption that by failing to prove the foreign law the parties acquiesce in having their controversy determined by reference to the law of the forum, be it statutory or common law. By the application of these various presumptions the courts have in effect treated the common law rule that foreign law could not be noticed but must be pleaded and proved as if it were a matter of fact merely as a permissive rule whereby either party could, if it were to his advantage, plead and prove the foreign law. Thus the failure to plead and prove the foreign law has not generally been considered as fatal. . . .

In the instant case the transaction occurred in France. Our courts may properly take judicial knowledge that France is not a common law, but rather a civil jurisdiction. It would, therefore, be inappropriate and indeed contrary to elementary knowledge to presume that the principles of the common law prevail there. This does not mean, however, that the plaintiff must fail in his cause of action because of the absence of any proof at the trial as to the applicable law of France. In these circumstances any one of the other three presumptions may be indulged in, i.e., that the law of France is the same as the law of the forum; that the law of France, like all civilized countries, recognizes certain fundamental principles, as, e.g., that the taking of a loan creates an obligation upon the borrower to make repayment; that the parties by failing to prove the law of France have acquiesced in having their dispute determined by the law of the forum.

The court below based its decision upon the presumption that the law of France in common with that of other civilized countries recognizes a liability to make repayment under the facts here present, and its decision is not without substantial merit in reason and support in the authorities . . . The utilization of this presumption has decided limitations, however, for in many cases it would be difficult to determine whether or not the question presented was of such a fundamental nature as reasonably to warrant the assumption that it would be similarly treated by the laws of all civilized countries. The presumption that in the absence of proof the parties acquiesce in the application of the law of the forum, be it statutory law or common law, does not present any such difficulties for it may be universally applied regardless of the nature of the controversy. . . . We are of the opinion, therefore, that in the instant case the rights of the parties are to be determined by the law of New Jersey which unquestionably permits recovery on the facts proven.

NOTES

(1) Would any legal obstacle have stood in the way of the Walton court's adopting an approach and reaching a conclusion like that in Leary v. Gledhill? In Cavic v. Grand Bahama Development Co., Limited, 701 F.2d 879 (11th Cir. 1983), plaintiffs claimed they had been defrauded in a land sale deal in the Bahamas. Although the land was situated there and the misrepresentations were made there, Bahamian law was not relied on by any of the parties, each of whom "seems to have assumed that Florida [forum] law governs." The court ruled that the law of Florida would be applied. New Jersey has resolved the problem by legislation:

"In the absence of an adequate basis for taking judicial notice of the law of any jurisdiction other than this State, and the United States, the judge shall apply the law of this State." N.J.Stat.Ann. § 2A:84A–16R.9(3) (1976).

(2) In an action arising out of an intersection collision in Nuremberg, Germany, both sides agreed that New York law would be applied. The plaintiff asked the district court to charge the jury that the New York Vehicle and Traffic Law required the defendant to slow down when approaching an intersection. The court refused and the court of appeals affirmed, stating: "It is unlikely . . . in a case arising out of an accident in Germany, that the courts would add the statutory refinements to the standard of care to include the apparent slight extra duty of care in approaching intersections. Although New York law may be applicable in the absence of proof of German law, strict statutory refinements in New York should not be held binding as

the standard of care for operation of a vehicle in Germany." Loebig v. Larucci, 572 F.2d 81 (2d Cir. 1978).

(3) In a contest in the New York courts over succession to funds in a New York joint bank account opened by a husband and wife domiciled in France, the issue turned on the res judicata effects of a prior French judgment involving the same underlying controversy. Neither side pleaded or offered to rely on the French rules of res judicata, either assuming or agreeing that the preclusive effect of the judgment in France would be the same as a similar New York judgment would enjoy at home. In ascribing "New York" effect to the judgment, the court explained its acceptance of the litigants' submission on the basis that "under modern principles a failure to raise or prove foreign law, without objection, should not automatically, in the absence of a manifest injustice, prevent the application of forum law on the theory that the parties have consented that the forum law be applied to the controversy." Watts v. Swiss Bank Corp., 27 N.Y.2d 270, 265 N.E.2d 739 (1970). Can a court know whether "manifest injustice" results from acquiescence in applying forum law without determining on a prima facie basis what the foreign law provides?

RESTATEMENT, SECOND, CONFLICT OF LAWS:*

§ 136.   Notice and Proof of Foreign Law

(1) The local law of the forum determines the need to give notice of reliance on foreign law, the form of notice and the effect of a failure to give such notice.

(2) The local law of the forum determines how the content of foreign law is to be shown and the effect of a failure to show such content.

UNIFORM INTERSTATE AND INTERNATIONAL PROCEDURE ACT. ARTICLE IV, DETERMINATION OF FOREIGN LAW.**

Section 4.01 [Notice.]   A party who intends to raise an issue concerning the law of any jurisdiction or governmental unit thereof outside this state shall give notice in his pleadings or other reasonable written notice.

Section 4.02   [Materials to be Considered.]   In determining the law of any jurisdiction or governmental unit thereof outside this state, the court may consider any relevant material or source, including testimony, whether or not submitted by a party or admissible under the rules of evidence.

Section 4.03   [Court Decision and Review.]   The court, not jury, shall determine the law of any governmental unit outside this state

---

and its determination shall be subject to review on appeal as a ruling on a question of law.

Section 4.04 [Other Provisions of Law Unaffected.] This Article does not repeal or modify any other law of this state permitting another procedure for the determination of foreign law.

NOTES

(1) Article IV is an improved version of the Uniform Judicial Notice of Foreign Law Act, which has been enacted in more than half the states. See Smit, The Uniform Interstate and International Procedure Act Approved by the National Conference of Commissioners on Uniform State Laws: A New Era Commences, 11 Am.Jour.Comp.L. 415, 416 (1962). Are Section 136 of the Restatement and Article IV on sound ground in failing to refer explicitly to judicial notice? Is there any utility in encouraging courts to do their own research in order to learn the contents of foreign-country or sister-state law?

(2) Rule 44.1, Fed.Rules Civ.Proc., effective in 1966 is an even shorter rendering of the basic provisions of a useful rule on this subject. See Miller, Federal Rule 44.1 and the "Fact" Approach to Determining Foreign Law: Death Knell for a Die-Hard Doctrine, 65 Mich.L.Rev. 613 (1967). For a criticism of the prolix and lengthy provisions of New York CPLR Rules 3016 and 4511, see Smit, Report of the Adm. Board of the N.Y.Jud.Conf. 170–181 (1967).

(3) Professor Rudolph B. Schlesinger summed up the situation in 1980 with regard to judicial notice of foreign law as follows:

> More than half of the states, including all of those in which transnational litigation occurs with some frequency, have enacted statutes or Rules [sic] either providing for "judicial notice" of foreign-country law or in other ways authorizing the court, in determining foreign law, to consider any relevant material or source, regardless of admissibility under technical rules of evidence, and regardless also of whether or not such material was submitted by a party. These judicial notice statutes, it should be emphasized at the outset, have not displaced the common-law doctrines

> . . . .

> . . . [S]ituations frequently arise in which the court either lacks the power to take judicial notice, or as a matter of discretion will refuse to do so. In every case of this sort, the judicial notice statute in effect becomes inoperative; and just as in the old common-law days, the court is then faced with the question of how it should react to the parties' failure to invoke or prove the foreign law. Most of the statutes are silent on this point. To find an answer, the court must turn to decisional rules—the same rules which would govern in the absence of a judicial notice statute.

R. Schlesinger, Comparative Law 109–111 (4th ed. 1980).

(4) Florida has a statute which empowers the state supreme court to answer questions of Florida law certified to it by the Supreme Court or any Court of Appeals of the United States in a case pending before the federal court. The Supreme Court of the United States certified such questions in Clay v. Sun Insurance Office, Limited, 363 U.S. 207 (1960), set forth at p. 355, supra. See also Aldrich v. Aldrich, 375 U.S. 75, 84 S.Ct. 184 (1963).

SECTION 3.   USE OF THE FORUM'S "PROCEDURAL" RULES

A. INTRODUCTION

RESTATEMENT, SECOND, CONFLICT OF LAWS:*

TOPIC 1.   THE GENERAL PRINCIPLE

§ 122.   Issues Relating to Judicial Administration

A court usually applies its own local law rules prescribing how litigation shall be conducted even when it applies the local law rules of another state to resolve other issues in the case.

Comment:

   a. Rationale. Each state has local law rules prescribing the procedure by which controversies are brought into its courts and by which the trial of these controversies is conducted. These rules for conducting lawsuits and administering the courts' processes vary from state to state. The forum has compelling reasons for applying its own rules to decide such issues, even if the case has foreign contacts and even if many issues in the case will be decided by reference to the local law of another state. The forum is more concerned with how its judicial machinery functions and how its court processes are administered than is any other state. Also, in matters of judicial administration, it would often be disruptive or difficult for the forum to apply the local law rules of another state. The difficulties involved in doing so would not be repaid by a furtherance of the values that the application of another state's local law is designed to promote.

   Parties do not usually give thought to matters of judicial administration before they enter into legal transactions. They do not usually place reliance on the applicability of the rules of a particular state to issues that would arise only if litigation should become necessary. Accordingly, the parties have no expectations as to such eventualities, and there is no danger of unfairly disappointing their hopes by applying the forum's rules in such matters.

   Enormous burdens are avoided when a court applies its own rules, rather than the rules of another state, to issues relating to judicial administration, such as the proper form of action, service of process, pleading, rules of discovery, mode of trial and execution and costs.

   * Quoted with the permission of the copyright owner, The American Law Institute.

Furthermore, the burdens the court spares itself would have been wasted effort in most instances, because usually the decision in the case would not be altered by applying the other state's rules of judicial administration. Even if the outcome would be altered, however, the forum will usually apply its own rule if the issue primarily concerns judicial administration. The statute of limitations is a striking example of such an issue (see § 142).

The sections that follow deal separately with various issues relating to judicial administration that commonly arise in Conflict of Laws cases. As to many of them it is possible to state categorically that the local law of the forum will be applied. Other issues, as, for example, which side bears the burden of proof (see § 133) and which side bears the burden of going forward with the evidence (see § 134), fall into a gray area between issues relating primarily to judicial administration and those concerned primarily with the rights and liabilities of the parties. Such issues cannot be the subject of categorical rules, but the factors that may influence the court to apply forum local law rather than the local law of another state can usefully be stated.

One factor is whether the issue is one to which the parties are likely to have given thought in the course of entering into the transaction. If they probably shaped their actions with reference to the local law of a certain state, this is a weighty reason for applying that law rather than the local law of the forum the plaintiff has chanced to select. Another factor is whether the issue is one whose resolution would be likely to affect the ultimate result of the case. If so, the otherwise applicable law should be applied unless application of the local law of the forum is required by the dominant interest of the forum state in the decision of the particular issue. A third factor is whether the precedents have tended consistently to classify the issue as "procedural" or "substantive" for choice of law purposes. If so, the settled classification should not be discarded without good reason. Lastly, there is the question whether an effort to apply the rules of the judicial administration of another state would impose an undue burden upon the forum. If so, this is a further reason why the local law of the forum should be applied.

b. Substance—procedure dichotomy. The courts have traditionally approached issues falling within the scope of the rule of this Section by determining whether the particular issue was "procedural" and *therefore* to be decided in accordance with the forum's local law rule, or "substantive" and *therefore* to be decided by reference to the otherwise applicable law. These characterizations, while harmless in themselves, have led some courts into unthinking adherence to precedents that have classified a given issue as "procedural" or "substantive", regardless of what purposes were involved in the earlier classifications. Thus, for example, a decision classifying burden of proof as "procedural" for local law purposes, such as in determining the constitutionality of a statute that retroactively shifted the burden, might mistakenly be held controlling on the question whether burden of proof is "procedural" for choice-of-law purposes. To avoid encouraging errors of that sort, the rules stated in this Chapter do not attempt to classify issues as "procedural" or "substantive". Instead they face directly the question whether the forum's rule should be applied.

NOE v. UNITED STATES FIDELITY & GUARANTY CO.*

Supreme Court of Missouri, Division No. 2, 1966.
406 S.W.2d 666.

STOCKARD, COMMISSIONER. The issue here presented is whether an action may be maintained in the courts of this State under a Louisiana statute which gives a right of direct action by an injured person against a liability insurer for the damages he has sustained, irrespective of whether or not a judgment has been first obtained against the insured.

The Louisiana statute (La.Rev.Stat. 22:655), in its parts here material, provides that an "injured person . . . shall have a right of direct action against the insurer within the terms and limits of the policy; and such action may be brought against the insurer alone, or against both the insured and insurer jointly and in solido, in the parish in which the accident or injury occurred or in the parish in which an action could be brought against either the insured or the insurer under the general rules of venue prescribed by Art. 42, Code of Civil Procedure. This right of direct action shall exist whether the policy of insurance sued upon was written or delivered in the State of Louisiana or not and whether or not such policy contains a provision forbidding such direct action, provided the accident or injury occurred within the State of Louisiana."

Plaintiffs' petition is in two counts. The first is on behalf of Jerry L. Noe who alleged that he was injured in the State of Louisiana as the result of the negligence of Dr. Hugh Lamensdorf who was insured by a policy of liability insurance issued by defendant. The second count is on behalf of Shirley Ann Noe, wife of Jerry, for loss of consortium. Defendant contends that no action by a wife for loss of consortium exists under the Law of Louisiana, but we need not rule that question. . . .

There is no statute in Missouri comparable to the direct action statute of Louisiana, and there is no contention that plaintiffs are entitled to maintain this suit in this State except on the basis of the Louisiana statute. Plaintiffs contend that the statute is substantive, and that pursuant to the full faith and credit provision of the federal

---

* Footnotes omitted. Eds.

Constitution they are entitled to maintain in this State this direct action against the alleged tort-feasor's liability insurer. Defendant, on the other hand, contends that the statute is procedural only and has no extra-territorial effect.

It is the general rule that the court at the forum determines, according to its own rules as to conflict of laws, whether a given foreign law is substantive or procedural, but in making this determination it will give consideration to the interpretation of the foreign law by the courts of that state. Hopkins v. Kurn, 351 Mo. 41, 171 S.W.2d 625, 149 A.L.R. 762; Restatement, Conflict of Laws, § 584. In our examination of the Louisiana direct action statute, we are immediately impressed with the fact that it does not in express terms impose liability on or create a new cause of action against the insurer. Instead, it purports to create a method or procedure for enforcing in the courts of that State the cause of action which came into being by the tortious act of the insured. Following the provisions of the statute quoted above, it is further provided that it is the "intent" of the statute that "all liability policies within their terms and limits are executed for the benefit of all injured persons, his or her survivors or heirs, to whom the insured is liable". Thus it recognizes that the cause of action is based on the liability of the insured, and that the statute is designed to afford a procedural remedy to enforce that liability. In addition, the language of the statute creating the right of action directly against the insurer to enforce the liability of the insured to the injured person expressly provides where the remedy there authorized may be exercised, and it limits that right to the courts of Louisiana in certain designated parishes. Although the direct action statute, by amendment, now provides that the action may be brought in additional parishes in Louisiana than previously authorized, the effect of such a limitation contained in the statute creating the right of action was expressly recognized in Morton v. Maryland Casualty Company, 1 A.D.2d 116, 148 N.Y.S.2d 524, affirmed 4 N.Y.2d 488, 176 N.Y.S.2d 329, 151 N.E.2d 881; Pearson v. Globe Indemnity Company, 5 Cir., 311 F.2d 517; and Oltarsh v. Aetna Insurance Company, 15 N.Y.2d 111, 256 N.Y.S.2d 577, 204 N.E.2d 622. In the Morton case it was held that "the right and the remedy are so united that the right cannot be enforced except in the manner and before the tribunal designated by the act."

We shall consider now what the courts of Louisiana have had to say concerning the rights created by this direct action statute. In Finn v. Employers' Liability Assurance Corporation, La.App., 141 So. 2d 852, the court said this: "Nor do we find any merit in the contention that the direct-action statute created separate and distinct causes of action, one against the insurer alone and another against the insurer and the insured. The statute is remedial in character, rather than substantive, and does not create causes of action." [Citations omitted.] We have found no court of appeal decision to the contrary. In Burke v. Massachusetts Bonding & Insurance Co., 209 La. 495, 24 So.

2d 875, the Supreme Court of Louisiana had the issue squarely before it. There the plaintiff was injured in Mississippi as the result of the negligence of her husband, and under the law of Mississippi one spouse had no cause of action against the other for tort, and Mississippi had no direct action statute. The Louisiana Supreme Court said this: "It is conceded that Act 55 of 1930 [the direct action statute] is procedural and not substantive, and it is only by virtue of the statute that plaintiff brought her suit in Louisiana. Plaintiff insists that since the statute creates no substantive right, the case must be governed by the law of the place where the remedy is sought. But the statute merely gives a claimant a direct right of action against the liability insurer when he has a cause of action against the insured, or where the insured would be liable but for immunity personal to him. The statute does not give plaintiff any more rights than she has under the law of Mississippi. It only furnishes her with a method to enforce in Louisiana whatever rights she has in Mississippi. Since she has no cause of action under the law of Mississippi, necessarily Act 55 of 1930 confers upon her no cause of action in Louisiana. The mere fact that under the statute plaintiff was able to obtain jurisdiction against her husband's liability insurer in a direct action in this State does not create, as against her husband, or as against his insurer, a substantive cause of action that does not exist under the law of the State where the wrongful act occurred." . . .

Courts of other jurisdictions have held the Louisiana direct action statute to be procedural. See . . . Goodin v. Gulf Coast Oil Company, 241 Miss. 862, 133 So.2d 623; Penny v. Powell, 162 Tex. 497, 347 S.W.2d 601; and Pearson v. Globe Indemnity Company, 5 Cir., 311 F.2d 517.

The only basis for any different view concerning the Louisiana statute is West v. Monroe Bakery, 217 La. 189, 46 So.2d 122. In that case the insurer was sued in Louisiana for an injury occurring in Louisiana, and the insurer claimed it was released from its liability under the terms of its policy of insurance because the insured had failed to comply with the cooperation clause. The court said this: "An analysis of our jurisprudence considered by the Appellate Court [which had sustained the contention of the insurer] in reaching its conclusion discloses that with two exceptions Act 55 of 1930 has been treated consistently as conferring *substantive rights* on third parties to contracts of public liability insurance, which become vested at the moment of the accident in which they are injured," subject only to such defenses as the tort-feasor himself may legally interpose. The two cases referred to, Howard v. Rowan, La.App., 154 So. 382, and State Farm Mut. Automobile Ins. Co. v. Grimmer, D.C., 47 F.Supp. 458, held that under the facts of each case the failure of the insured to notify the insurer of the accident, as was required by the terms of the policy, relieved the insurer from liability on its contract. When we read the West case, we conclude that it dealt only with the question of whether the failure of the insured to give reasonable notice to his insurer resulted in the injured person being denied the right granted by the direct action statute to enforce directly his cause of action for his injuries against the insurer. The court held in the West case that it would be contrary to the public policy of that State as set forth in the direct action statute for the existence of that right to depend upon the actions of another. While the opinion referred to "substantive rights," we agree with the statement in Penny v. Powell, supra, that the "case did not involve a conflict of laws" issue, and we also agree with the conclusion in Morton v. Maryland Casualty Company, 1 A.D.2d 116, 148 N.Y.S.2d 524, that the vesting of the right to bring the action at the moment of the accident, as held in the West case, "was the vesting of a right to bring the action in the parishes named." Whether the creating of an additional remedy to enforce an otherwise existing cause of action creates a right that has "vested," or creates something which may in one sense be classified as "substantive" is a matter of the use of words. In any event, the fact remains that neither in the West case nor in any other Louisiana case have the Louisiana courts ruled that the direct action statute creates a separate cause of action against the insurer, as distinguished from a right to invoke the authorized procedure in Louisiana to enforce the cause of action which arose by reason of the tortious act of the insured. We note in the West case the court did not overrule the numerous previous cases which had expressly held that the direct action statute did not affect substantive rights but provided only a procedure to enforce an existing cause of action. . . . [S]ubsequent to the West case in Home Insurance Co. v. Highway Insurance Underwriters [222 La. 540, 62 So.2d 828], the Louisiana Supreme Court, without overruling, criticising or distinguishing the West case, expressly held that the direct action statute "is purely remedial." . . .

Plaintiffs cite numerous cases, but rely principally, according to the statement in their brief, on two: Collins v. American Automobile Insurance Company of St. Louis, 2 Cir., 230 F.2d 416, and Oltarsh v. Aetna Insurance Company, 15 N.Y.2d 111, 256 N.Y.S.2d 577, 204 N.E.2d 622. [T]he Collins case refused to follow the applicable New York law . . . and relied on a statement in Lumbermen's Mutual Casualty Co. v. Elbert, 348 U.S. 48, that "The Louisiana courts have characterized the statute as creating a separate and distinct cause of action against the insurer which an injured party may elect *in lieu* of his action against the tort feasor." . . .

We do not consider the Collins case to be persuasive authority that the Louisiana direct action statute is entitled to enforcement by the courts of Missouri.

The Oltarsh case construed the direct action statute of Puerto Rico and held it to be substantive and entitled to enforcement in New York. However, in doing so it distinguished the Puerto Rican statute from the Louisiana statute this way: "Unlike the Louisiana statute

. . . the statute before us contains no built-in venue provision, no clause even remotely resembling the 'localizing' provision in the Louisiana statute, or any other language which could possibly be read as a limitation restricting to the courts of Puerto Rico the direct action it authorizes." In this manner the Oltarsh case re-affirms the result of the Morton case, and in fact supports the conclusion we have reached.

We do not rule [on] defendant's contention that to enforce the Louisiana statute would be contrary to the public policy of this State, but by not doing so we do not discredit it. The position we have taken makes such ruling unnecessary.

We conclude that the direct action statute of Louisiana does not create a separate and distinct cause of action against the liability insurer which may be enforced in the courts of this State, but in accord with what we consider to constitute a proper construction of the language of the statute and the numerous pronouncements of the Louisiana courts, it provides a separate remedy available in that State alone to enforce the cause of action against the insurer which arose by reason of tortious conduct of the insured. For that reason the statute is what is termed procedural, as distinguished from substantive, and is not enforceable in the courts of this State.

The judgment is affirmed.

NOTES

(1) In Romero v. State Farm Mutual Automobile Insurance Co., 277 So.2d 649 (La.1973), the Louisiana direct action statute was held to be available in Louisiana to a plaintiff injured in an automobile accident in Texas. That case relied on a similar result in Webb v. Zurich Insurance Co., 251 La. 558, 205 So.2d 398 (1968), a wrongful death action in Louisiana based upon the fatal crash of an airplane in Michigan, to which the plane had flown from Baton Rouge, La. The insurance contracts were made in Louisiana.

(2) Would a suit in Louisiana be barred by res judicata if the plaintiff previously had sued the insurance company in the state of the accident and suffered a dismissal? No, according to McNeal v. State Farm Mutual Automobile Insurance Co., 278 So.2d 108 (La.1973), in which the dismissal in the first suit had also been put on the ground that the family immunity doctrine of the lex loci prevented the mother and child from suing for the husband-father's tort. Cf. Mertz v. Mertz, p. 388, supra.

(3) In Oltarsh v. Aetna Insurance Co., 15 N.Y.2d 111, 256 N.Y.S.2d 577, 204 N.E.2d 622 (1965), the Puerto Rican direct action statute (Laws of Puerto Rico, tit. 26, §§ 2001, 2003) was held a sufficient basis for a New York resident's direct suit against the liability insurer of Puerto Rican premises in which Mrs. Oltarsh was injured in a fall. The court said the direct action statute "went beyond merely providing a procedural shortcut" by allowing immediate suit against the insurer, and created a "separate and distinct right of action against the insurer where no such right had previously existed." Compare Davis v. Furlong, 328 N.W.2d 150 (Minn.1983), involving a similar fact pattern: automobile accident in Wisconsin, which permits direct actions; suit in Minnesota by Minnesota resident. The court held, 5–4, that forum law should be applied since the issue of whether a direct action lay was pro-

cedural. The dissenters favored applying the same methodology as Minnesota employs in resolving substantive choice-of-law issues. This would in their view have permitted the direct action to be maintained. By contrast the Illinois Supreme Court characterized the Wisconsin direct action statute as substantive, but refused to enforce it as contrary to the forum's public policy. Marchlik v. Coronet Insurance Co., 40 Ill.2d 327, 239 N.E.2d 799 (1968).

(4) Does the principal case convincingly distinguish Oltarsh as a decision that dealt with a statute containing (at that time) no venue-limiting provisions? Are venue-restricting provisions in direct action statutes valid under Tennessee Coal, Iron & Railroad Co. v. George, 233 U.S. 354, p. 210, supra?

(5) In permitting a victim of allegedly negligent operation of a motor vehicle to sue the car owner's liability insurer as a third party beneficiary of the insurance contract, a court creates a judicially sanctioned direct action. See, e.g., Shingleton v. Bussey, 223 So.2d 713 (Fla.1969). Is there any doubt that the remedy is "exportable" in the sense of permitting direct suits in other jurisdictions based upon Florida highway accidents? What is the significance of the point noted in Davidson v. Garden Properties, Inc., 386 F.Supp. 900 (N.D.Fla.1975) that "Florida decisions . . . hold that the [Shingleton decision] effected no change in the substantive law of Florida," but merely brought about a procedural change. What of direct actions for injuries resulting from alleged negligence on public premises? See Barrios v. Dade County, 310 F.Supp. 744 (S.D.N.Y.1970). After two unsuccessful tries the Florida legislature passed a statute overruling the Shingleton decision that the state's Supreme Court has upheld as valid. See Vanbibber v. Hartford Casualty Insurance Corp., 439 So.2d 880 (Fla.1983).

B. PRESUMPTIONS AND BURDEN OF PROOF

LEVY v. STEIGER

Supreme Judicial Court of Massachusetts, 1919.
233 Mass. 600, 124 N.E. 477.

DE COURCY, J. The plaintiffs were injured in a collision between an automobile, in which they were riding as guests, and a car driven by the defendant. Although the parties are residents of this Commonwealth, the accident occurred in the town of East Providence in the State of Rhode Island. The judge of the Superior Court ruled that the Massachusetts St.1914, c. 553, was applicable to the cases on trial; and accordingly instructed the jury that the defendant had the burden of showing contributory negligence on the part of the plaintiffs. The defendant's exception to this ruling and instruction raises the single question before us.

It is elementary that the law of the place where the injury was received determines whether a right of action exists; and that the law of the place where the action is brought regulates the remedy and its incidents, such as pleading, evidence and practice. Davis v.

New York & New England Railroad, 143 Mass. 301. Hoadley v. Northern Transportation Co., 115 Mass. 304. While there may be cases where it is difficult to decide whether a particular enactment relates to procedure or to substantive rights, it was settled in Duggan v. Bay State Street Railway, 230 Mass. 370, where its construction and constitutionality were in question, that this "due care" statute, so called, is one of procedure. As the court expressly said, in construing the statute, with a view to determining its constitutionality (page 377): "These two parts of the statute do not undertake to change the substantive law of negligence in any respect. The tribunal hearing the case must still be satisfied on all the evidence that the plaintiff was in the exercise of due care and did not by his own acts of omission or commission help to produce his injury, and that the defendant was negligent." And again (page 380): "The present statute simply affects procedure and the burden of proof. It does not work any modification of fundamental rights." . . . In Lemieux v. Boston & Maine Railroad, 219 Mass. 399, 106 N.E. 992, relied on by the defendant, it was expressly stated: "By the common law of Vermont, as proved at the trial, an employee assumes not only the risks ordinarily incident to his employment but such unusual and extraordinary risks as he knows and comprehends. And the burden is on him to prove as part of his case that he did not know and comprehend the danger. [Citing cases.] This affects the right of action, and does not relate merely to the matter of evidence or procedure. . . ."

Exceptions overruled.

NOTES

(1) Duggan v. Bay State Street Railway Co., 230 Mass. 370, 119 N.E. 757 (1918), relied on in the principal case, was a nonconflicts case in which the court held that a statute, creating a presumption of due care on the part of the plaintiff in a negligence action and shifting the burden of proving contributory negligence to the defendant, could be applied retroactively without infringing due process since it "simply affects procedure and burden of proof. It does not work any modification of fundamental rights." Has the Duggan decision any bearing on the question in the principal case?

(2) Applying the standards proposed in the Comment to Restatement, Second, Conflict of Laws § 122, supra, is the presumption of due care procedural or substantive in the Levy case? The extent to which a decision characterizing an issue as procedural for a local law purpose is material in a conflicts case is one to which we return after studying the "interests analysis" and other methods of resolving choice-of-law problems by attempting to advance policies that are perceived to underlie the colliding rules of decision. See Chapter 8, infra.

(3) The substance-procedure dichotomy arises in federal-state as well as state-state contexts. See Chapter 10, infra. Is there any relationship between the standards applicable in the two types of problems? Cf. Sedler, The Erie Outcome Test as a Guide to Substance and Procedure in the Conflict of Laws, 37 N.Y.U.L.Rev. 813 (1962).

NOTE ON BURDEN OF PROOF

The term "burden of proof" sometimes refers to the burden of coming forward with, or producing, sufficient evidence to avoid a directed verdict. More commonly in the conflicts context it refers to the burden of persuasion. This is the burden cast on one side to persuade the jury to the required level of conviction on one or more issues. That level is frequently cast in terms like the following (N.Y. Pattern Jury Instructions 1:23):

PJI 1:23.   Burden of Proof.

The burden of proof rests on the plaintiff. That means that it must be established by a fair preponderance of the credible evidence that the claim plaintiff makes is true. The credible evidence means the testimony or exhibits that you find to be worthy to be believed. A preponderance means the greater part of such evidence. That does not mean the greater number of witnesses or the greater length of time taken by either side. The phrase refers to the quality of the evidence, that is, its convincing quality, the weight and the effect that it has on your minds. The law requires that, in order for the plaintiff to prevail, the evidence that supports his claim must appeal to you as more nearly representing what took place than that opposed to his claim. If it does not, or if it weighs so evenly that you are unable to say that there is a preponderance on either side, then you must resolve the question in favor of the defendant. It is only if the evidence favoring the plaintiff's claim outweighs the evidence opposed to it that you can find in favor of plaintiff.

FITZPATRICK V. INTERNATIONAL RAILWAY CO., 252 N.Y. 127, 169 N.E. 112 (1929): Plaintiff was hurt in Ontario while working for the Niagara Gorge Railway Company, a New York corporation. He relied on the Ontario comparative fault statute that reduced plaintiff's recovery for defendant's negligence by the degree his own fault contributed to his injuries. The jury found the plaintiff 10 per cent negligent. Defendant claimed error in the trial judge's instruction that it had the burden of proving contributory negligence, relying on the New York rule that in personal injury actions plaintiffs have the burden of proving freedom from contributory negligence. Defendant argued that the burden of proof rule was procedural, but the Court of Appeals disagreed, saying:

The Contributory Negligence Act of Ontario does more than touch or affect a matter of procedure; it goes beyond directing who shall first proceed to prove that the act of the defendant was *solely* responsible for the act or the damage. The act gives a right to recover not recognized by the common law. It provides that even if the plaintiff be guilty of contributory negligence he may yet recover, if the defendant were more negligent, the recovery, however, being limited to the surplus degree of negligence, as figured out by a jury. The law of the State of New York has no application under such circumstances; it is impossible of application. If the Ontario act had merely dealt with this order of proof or burden of proof, and provided that the defendant, in common-law actions for negligence, had the burden of proving the plaintiff's contributory negligence, we would have another question. There would then be the same substantial right as at common law, the change merely being in the procedure at the trial or in the burden of proof. Under such circumstances our courts might feel called upon to apply our own rule.

The appellant suggests that as this act does not refer to the burden of proof, the plaintiff, under our form of procedure, should have the burden of proving either freedom from contributing negligence or else the degree to which his own negligence contributed. We have no such law in this State. To follow the appellant's suggestion would still require our courts to adopt a portion of the Ontario statute. If we are to adopt a part we must apply it as a whole, because it affects the substantial rights of the parties. Under our rule, it would be impossible for the plaintiff to prove his own contributing neglect, without proving himself out of court, as we have no comparative negligence rule for actions at common law. As has been stated more than once, this action is under the Ontario statute.

NOTES

(1) By what instruction could the court have explained to the jurors how they were to apply the New York burden of proof rule in determining the degree of plaintiff's contributory fault? Does the New York instruction on burden of proof do anything more than tell the jurors that the party with the burden is to lose if the jury cannot decide which side's evidence is more convincing? If the instruction meant that defendant had to prove the degree of plaintiff's fault by a preponderance of the evidence or the jury would be obliged to find a lesser degree of fault on plaintiff's part, in what sense was that a "substantive" matter?

(2) Reaching a similar result without getting involved in burdens of proof or resorting to the substance-procedure characterization is Frummer v. Hilton Hotels International, Inc., 60 Misc.2d 840, 304 N.Y.S.2d 335, 344 (Sup. Ct.1969). At the time New York still had the contributory negligence rule but England had comparative negligence. The court said: "England's interest is . . . greater than New York's, which certainly has no interest in applying its own law and probably has an interest in seeing England's rule used as the rule of decision." (Plaintiff had slipped and fallen in the defendant's London hotel while taking a shower.)

(3) The traditional view of presumptions as procedural was simplistic, considering how widely presumptions differ in their substantive or evidentiary effects. Conclusive presumptions are rules of substantive law. Even rebuttable presumptions may play outcome determinative roles so consistently that they should be regarded as substantive. Among these are the presump-

tions against suicide in life insurance cases; of death after 7 years' unexplained absence from the state; of the validity of marriage; and of the legitimacy of children born in wedlock. Violations of statutory standards raise presumptions of varying degrees of conclusiveness. If the presumption of negligence from violating a standard is easily refuted, it can be properly regarded as procedural. If it is difficult or nearly impossible to refute, it is more substantive.

Minor infractions of the traffic laws raise weak presumptions. Other infractions, such as greatly exceeding the speed limit or driving while intoxicated, raise strong presumptions. On this test, should the presumption of the decedent's due care in a wrongful death action be regarded as substantive or procedural?

C.   RULES OF EVIDENCE: PRIVILEGE

Rules on the admissibility of evidence are among the most arcane and diverse of any of the rules that differentiate the way litigation is conducted from forum to forum. The variations from one country to another in the rules for gathering and presenting proof are understandably great. But even among States of the Union the variations are immense and thus far the differences have not been effectively harmonized by wide adoption of a uniform system, such as has occurred in other areas of litigation management by adoption in most states of large portions of the Federal Rules of Civil Procedure.

In the interests of efficiency and convenience, the local law of the forum is usually applied to determine admissibility of evidence. Familiarity of lawyers and judges with their local rules permits them to deal with evidentiary issues with some measure of assurance, a necessary capability, if trials are to proceed swiftly and smoothly. These considerations undoubtedly apply to issues of hearsay, "best evidence," establishing authenticity of documents; and to limitations on leading or cross-examining a witness on the stand, among other matters. Those issues may influence the outcome of a trial in some cases, but they are not as deeply affected by values of the substantive law as issues of relevance and materiality. Certainly, they do not raise policy considerations as deep as those involved in creating areas of privileged communication and preventing disclosure under compulsion of matter learned in confidence.

RULES OF EVIDENCE FOR UNITED STATES
COURTS AND MAGISTRATES *

ARTICLE V. PRIVILEGES

Rule 501

. . .

General Rule

Except as otherwise required by the Constitution of the United States or provided by the Act of Congress or in rules prescribed by the Supreme Court pursuant to statutory authority, the privilege of a witness, person, government, State, or political subdivision thereof shall be governed by the principles of the common law as they may be interpreted by the courts of the United States in the light of reason and experience. However, in civil actions and proceedings, with respect to an element of a claim or defense as to which State law supplies the rule of decision, the privilege of a witness, person, government, State, or political subdivision thereof shall be determined in accordance with State law.

SAMUELSON v. SUSEN

United States Court of Appeals, Third Circuit, 1978.
576 F.2d 546.

SEITZ, CHIEF JUDGE.

. . .

Plaintiff, Dr. Gene H. Samuelson, a resident of Steubenville, Ohio, and a neurosurgeon, asserted a claim based upon defamation and tortious interference with business and professional relationships. He alleged that defendants, Drs. Anthony F. Susen and Peter J. Jannetta, published defamatory statements, either by mail, orally or both, to certain physicians at Ohio Valley Hospital, and other persons, including physicians at St. John Medical Center and Harrison Community Hospital (all in the Steubenville area) and at Weirton General Hospital, Weirton, West Virginia. He seeks damages based on his claim that defendants' conduct has resulted in his being refused privileges at two Ohio hospitals and his staff privileges severely limited at the remaining hospitals.

During the course of discovery, plaintiff sought to depose six physicians and administrators of two Steubenville, Ohio hospitals. All of the proposed deponents (appellees) filed motions for protective orders, which were granted by the district court on the basis of Ohio Revised Code § 2305.251, which provides:

* Effective July 1, 1975.

Proceedings and records of all review committees described in section 2305.25 of the Revised Code [1] shall be held in confidence and shall not be subject to discovery or introduction in evidence in any civil action against a health care professional or institution arising out of matters which are the subject of evaluation and review by such committee. No person within attendance at a meeting of such committee shall be permitted or required to testify in any civil action as to any evidence or other matters produced or presented during the proceedings of such committee or as to any finding, recommendation, evaluation, opinion or other action of such committee or member thereof. Information, documents, or records otherwise available from original sources are not to be construed as being unavailable for discovery or for use in any civil action merely because they were presented during proceedings of such committee nor should any person testifying before such committee or who is any member of such committee be prevented from testifying as to matters within his knowledge, but the witness cannot be asked about his testimony before such committee or opinion formed by him as a result of such committee hearing.

[The district court entered an order designating four questions as controlling questions of law pursuant to 28 U.S.C. § 1292(b), the first of which is relevant]:

(1) Do conflicts of law principles require the application of Ohio law to the instant matter? . . .

I.

. . . We turn . . . to Rule 501 of the Federal Rules of Evidence, which was applied by the district court. Plaintiff first argues that Rule 501 is not applicable since the statute enacting it was to take effect on July 1, 1975, subsequent to the initiation of this action. However, the statute enacting the Federal Rules of Evidence states that the Rules [including 501] should apply to pending cases where practicable and not unjust. P.L. 93–545, § 1, Jan. 2, 1975, 88 Stat. 1926. The application of Rule 501 to these proceedings is clearly feasible. Its application in our view, would work no injustice, since the same result would likely have obtained under evidentiary principles formerly applied by the federal courts. They required these courts to use "the rules of evidence applied in the courts of general jurisdiction of the state in which the United States court is held." Former Fed.R.

---

1. Section 2305.25 provides in pertinent part:

No member or employee of a utilization review committee . . . shall be deemed liable in damages to any person for any action taken or recommendation made within the scope of the functions of such committee . . . .

This section shall also apply to any member or employee of a . . . hospital board or committee reviewing professional qualifications or activities of its medical staff or applicants for admission thereto. [Some footnotes have been omitted. Eds.]

Civ.P. 43(a).   We therefore conclude that Rule 501 is applicable to this case.

Rule 501 provides that with respect to state issues in "civil actions and proceedings" any privilege "shall be determined in accordance with State law." However, that Rule provides no explicit guidance as to which state's law regarding privilege is to be applied in a diversity case.

Plaintiff argues that under Rule 501 a federal court must apply the privilege law of the forum, whether or not state courts of the forum would apply their own privilege law. We cannot agree. We believe Rule 501 requires a district court exercising diversity jurisdiction to apply the law of privilege which would be applied by the courts of the state in which it sits.

[The court's reasoning in deciding to apply the privilege rule that would be applied by a Pennsylvania state court in this case appears in Chapter 10.]

We thus look to Pennsylvania's conflict-of-laws rules to determine whether Ohio's or Pennsylvania's privilege law applies. We do so even though, it might be argued that the law, of the two jurisdictions, controlling the resolution of the privilege question is essentially the same.

There are no precise Pennsylvania precedents to guide us as to how Pennsylvania courts would rule with respect to the questions before us: consequently, we must predict how Pennsylvania courts would rule. We do know that Pennsylvania has, generally speaking, adopted the "interest analysis" approach to conflict-of-law questions. Griffith v. United Air Lines, 416 Pa. 1, 203 A.2d 796 (1964); Cipolla v. Shaposka, 439 Pa. 563, 267 A.2d 854 (1970). Under that approach "we should apply the law of the predominantly concerned jurisdiction, measuring the depth and breadth of that concern by the relevant contacts each affected jurisdiction had with . . . 'the policies and interests underlying the particular issue before the court.' " Suchomajcz v. Hummel Chemical Company, 524 F.2d 19, 23 (3d Cir. 1975).

Here the review committee proceedings were held in Ohio. The participants were Ohio residents. The proceedings were those of an Ohio body seeking to effectuate policies respecting an Ohio physician's use of Ohio medical facilities. Presumably, the proceedings were for the protection of Ohio residents. Under all these circumstances, it seems clear that the district court was justified in concluding that Ohio had the more "significant relationship" to the dispute. It was therefore warranted in prophesying that the Pennsylvania courts would apply Ohio law to the resolution of the conflicts ques-

tion, particularly since both states have adopted a non-disclosure policy with respect to medical review committee proceedings.[4]

The approach of applying the law of the jurisdiction with the more
significant relationship to the dispute is also consistent with that of
the Restatement 2d, Conflict of Laws § 139(2).

II.

The district court, concluding that Ohio law should apply, granted
deponents' motions for protective orders under O.R.C. § 2305.251.
Plaintiff contends that it was erroneous to apply O.R.C. § 2305.251 in
this litigation because it did not take effect until July 28, 1975, subsequent to plaintiff's February 21, 1975 filing of his complaint in this
action.

Article II, Section 28 of the Ohio Constitution denies to the General Assembly the power to enact retroactive legislation. Ohio courts,
however, have held that this inhibition applies only to statutes affecting substantive rights, and has no reference to laws of a remedial or
procedural nature. . . .

In the context of these proceedings, § 2305.251 works to keep possibly relevant and otherwise admissible evidence from the trier of
facts, and is thus clearly procedural. It does not impair the substantive law of defamation, or the substantive right of the plaintiff to
bring a cause of action thereon. Therefore, it may be invoked by
these deponents even though this action was commenced prior to the
effective date of the statute.

[The court considered and rejected plaintiff's contentions that the
statute was intended to apply only in malpractice actions and that its
application here would abridge federal due process.]

The protective order of the district court dated November 3, 1976,
interpreted in its memorandum order denying a motion for reconsideration will be affirmed.

ARMOUR INTERNATIONAL CO. v. WORLDWIDE COSMETICS, INC., 689
F.2d 134 (7th Cir. 1982): In a diversity action in a federal court in
Illinois to enforce a contract obligating defendant to purchase the
shares of a corporation in Japan, the defense was misrepresentation
of the financial condition of the Japanese business. Defendant obtained a subpoena duces tecum requiring Touche Ross & Co., the accounting firm that audited the Japanese corporation, to produce relevant papers. Touche Ross resisted compliance on the basis of the
accountants' privilege created by The Illinois Public Accountants Act,
1943 Ill.Laws 999, § 27, providing for examinations, registration and
rules of conduct. The privilege provision declares: "A public ac-

---

4. Compare O.R.C. § 2305.251 with
Pennsylvania Peer Review Protection
Act, 63 P.S. & 425.1 *et seq.*

countant shall not be required by any court to divulge information or evidence which has been obtained by him in his confidential capacity as a public accountant." Japanese law did not recognize an accountant's privilege. The court denied the claim of privilege, describing the Illinois statute as one that "protects citizens and business from unqualified accountants and questionable accounting practices" and along with those protections,

> . . . Illinois grants confidential information given to accountants an immunity from the inquiries of the judicial process. But accountants not subject to and in compliance with Illinois protective regulation can be considered not similarly deserving of that special privileged status. The same assumptions about the qualifications and methods of those accountants cannot be made and, consequently, the conclusion that those accountants have the same need for privileged information is unfounded. The balance between the search for truth and the attempt to improve the audit accuracy of Illinois accountants swings to the former and, therefore, to the side of full disclosure. The Illinois courts need not be impeded in their attempts to gather information useful—in this case possibly essential—to the fair resolution of the pending dispute. In sum, the context of the privilege indicates that the privilege is intended to apply to accountants registered to practice under and subject to the other provisions of the Illinois Act. . . .

NOTE

See Application of Cepeda, 233 F.Supp. 465 (S.D.N.Y.1964) for an analysis of the journalists' privilege in a conflicts setting in a federal diversity suit before the adoption in 1975 of the Federal Rules of Evidence, including Rule 501.

RESTATEMENT, SECOND, CONFLICT OF LAWS: *

§ 139.   Privileged Communications

(1) Evidence that is not privileged under the local law of the state which has the most significant relationship with the communication will be admitted, even though it would be privileged under the local law of the forum, unless the admission of such evidence would be contrary to the strong public policy of the forum.

(2) Evidence that is privileged under the local law of the state which has the most significant relationship with the communication but which is not privileged under the local law of the forum will be admitted unless there is some special reason why the forum policy favoring admission should not be given effect.

NOTES

(1) In considering which state has the "most significant relationship" with the issue of privileged communication, some of the factors to be considered are: where the disclosure took place; where the communicator resides; where the recipient practices; alternative sources of the evidence; where the deposition or testimony is to be given and used. See generally Reese and Leiwant, Testimonial Privileges and Conflict of Laws, 41 Law & Contemp. Prob. 85 (1977); Sterk, Testimonial Privileges: An Analysis of Horizontal Choice of Law Problems, 61 Minn.L.Rev. 461 (1977).

(2) In state X, suit is brought for benefits under a life insurance policy issued in X where the insured resided. The insurance company contests on the ground of alleged material misrepresentation in the application for the insurance policy. Under the Restatement rule, may a doctor in Y testify in a deposition in Y regarding emergency cardiac treatment he gave to the insured prior to the application, there being a statutory physician-patient privilege in X but not in Y? Cf. Levy v. Mutual Life Insurance Co., 56 N.Y.S.2d 32 (Sup.Ct., N.Y.Co.1945), in which the doctor was allowed to testify under analogous circumstances.

(3) In another suit for proceeds of a life insurance policy, issued to a resident of Y in favor of a beneficiary residing in Y, suit is brought in Y, which does not have the physician-patient privilege. A doctor in state X, who treated the insured in state X, could supply material evidence if permitted to depose in X, which has a physician-patient privilege. Under the reasoning of the Samuelson decision or under Restatement, Second, Conflict of Laws § 139 should the doctor be permitted to testify? If the doctor is called as a witness at the trial in Y, will he be permitted to testify to patient's communications that would have been privileged in X? Will it be decisive that the only sources of material evidence are privileged under the law of X? That the privilege is widely recognized, rather than confined to a few states?

(4) If the principal rights and duties under a contract between the litigants are to be determined by the law of state X rather than Y, will it improperly modify the rights and duties thus prescribed if Y's rule of admission or exclusion of a crucial communication is applied? See generally Weinstein, Recognition in the United States of the Privileges of Another Jurisdiction, 56 Colum.L.Rev. 535 (1956); Sedler, The Erie Outcome Test as a Guide to Substance and Procedure in the Conflict of Laws, 37 N.Y.U.L.Rev. 813, 870 (1962).

BURGE v. STATE, 443 S.W.2d 720 (Tex.Cr.App.1969): Prosecution in Texas for burglary of a home with intent to rape. The victim testified to a struggle with the defendant, during which she managed to "bite him and spit out a piece of the sweater he was wearing." The piece of material was recovered at the scene. Defendant's wife agreed to allow police officers to search their Oklahoma residence without a search warrant. The search uncovered a sweater belonging to Burge, from which a piece of material was missing. It matched the scrap found in the victim's home and was admitted at the Texas trial, which resulted in conviction.

Burge complained that the Oklahoma rule giving each spouse a separate and independent right to insist that a warrant be obtained before search of the home should have been applied to bar the incriminating evidence. The Texas court overruled the objection, holding the issue "procedural," hence governed by the forum's rule even though the search occurred in Oklahoma.

NOTES

(1) Under the rules and criteria earlier discussed, is Texas the state of "most significant relationship" to the question of privilege asserted by Burge? See Leflar, Choice of Law in Criminal Cases, 25 Case Wes.L.Rev. 44 (1974).

(2) In People v. Saiken, 49 Ill.2d 504, 275 N.E.2d 381 (1971), the police in Indiana learned that a body was buried on defendant's farm, obtained a search warrant from an Indiana judge, searched the farm and found the body. The warrant was based on hearsay information and conclusions that were insufficient under Indiana law although adequate in Illinois, the forum state. The Illinois Supreme Court upheld the defendant's conviction for conspiracy to obstruct justice by concealing the body. Burge was cited by the court en route to holding that Illinois had the significant relationship for choice-of-law purposes.

(3) Defendant was accused of murder in New York. He fled, leaving items of evidence in New Jersey and Florida. In an interesting opinion the court ruled that New York state had the greatest interest in the case, "including the New Jersey searches, the Florida arrest, searches and confessions or admissions." The interests of the other two states were said to pale before the "overwhelming New York interests in prosecution of such heinous crimes as here committed against its own residents on its own soil." People v. Graham, 90 Misc.2d 1019, 396 N.Y.S.2d 966, 974 (Co.Ct.Sullivan Co. 1977).

D. TIME LIMITATION

"[A]ll general statutes of limitation [have as their purpose] to encourage promptness in the prosecution of actions and thus avoid injustice that would result from the assertion of claims after evidence has been lost, memories have faded and witnesses have disappeared." Lillegraven v. Tengs, 375 P.2d 139 (Alaska 1962).

At common law statutes of limitations were treated as procedural in conflicts cases; accordingly, forum statutes of limitations generally applied. This was true whether the forum statute was shorter or longer than that of another state to which the action was related. Dissatisfaction with the results of this approach when the forum's statute of limitations was longer prompted two exceptions to the usual approach, one judge-made, and the other statutory. The cases that follow illustrate these exceptions. In recent years there has been a tendency to resolve statute of limitations cases by modern choice of law methods, particularly when the traditional procedural characterization would result in applying the forum's longer statute of limitations. This tendency toward the modern "interests analysis" is examined at the end of the chapter.

BOURNIAS v. ATLANTIC MARITIME CO., LIMITED

United States Court of Appeals, Second Circuit, 1955.
220 F.2d 152.

HARLAN, CIRCUIT JUDGE. Libelant, a seaman, was employed on respondents' vessel at the time she was changed from Panamanian to Honduran registry. As originally filed the libel contained two causes of action. The first was based on several Articles of the Panama Labor Code, under which the libelant claimed an extra three-months' wages payable to seaman upon change of registry, and other amounts for vacation, overtime and holiday pay. The second was for penalties under 46 U.S.C.A. § 596 for failure to pay these amounts promptly. [The district court ruled that the one-year Panama statute of limitations barred all the claims under the Labor Code.]

Article 623 of the Labor Code of Panama, applicable to Articles 127, 154, 166 and 170 of the Code, upon which the libelant based his first cause of action, reads:

> "Actions and rights arising from labor contracts not enumerated in Article 621 shall prescribe [i.e., shall be barred by the Statute of Limitations] in a year from the happening of the events from which arise or are derived the said actions and rights."

The libelant's employment terminated on December 27, 1950, and since his libel was not filed until December 29, 1952, his first cause of action would be barred by Article 623 if it is controlling in this action.

In actions where the rights of the parties are grounded upon the law of jurisdictions other than the forum, it is a well-settled conflict-of-laws rule that the forum will apply the foreign substantive law, but will follow its own rules of procedure. . . . While it might be desirable, in order to eliminate "forum-shopping," for the forum to apply the entire foreign law, substantive and procedural—or at least, as much of the procedural law as might significantly affect the choice of forum, it has been recognized that to do so involves an unreasonable burden on the judicial machinery of the forum . . . and perhaps more significantly, on the local lawyers involved . . . .

The general rule appears established that for the purpose of deciding whether to apply local law or foreign law, statutes of limitations are classified as "procedural." . . . Hence the law of the forum controls. . . . This rule has been criticized as inconsistent with the rationale expressed above, since the foreign statute, unlike evidentiary and procedural details, is generally readily discovered and applied, and a difference in periods of limitation would often be expected to influence the choice of forum. . . .

But as might be expected, some legislatures and courts, perhaps recognizing that in light of the rationale of the underlying conflict-of-laws doctrine it is anomalous to classify across-the-board statutes of limitation as "procedural," have created exceptions to the rule so categorizing such statutes. A legislative example are the so-called "borrowing statutes" which require the courts of the forum to apply the statute of limitations of another jurisdiction, often that where the cause of action arose, when the forum's statute has been tolled. . . . A court-made exception, and the one with which we are concerned here, is that where the foreign statute of limitations is regarded as barring the foreign right sued upon, and not merely the remedy, it will be treated as conditioning that right and will be enforced by our courts as part of the foreign "substantive" law. . . .

It is not always easy to determine whether a foreign statute of limitations should be regarded as "substantive" or "procedural," for the tests applied by the courts are far from precise. In The Harrisburg, 1886, 119 U.S. 199, the Supreme Court held "substantive" a limitation period contained in a wrongful death statute, emphasizing that "the liability and the remedy are created by the same statutes, and the limitations of the remedy are therefore to be treated as limitations of the right." 119 U.S. at page 214. . . . The rule was also carried a step further in Davis v. Mills, 1904, 194 U.S. 451. Suggesting that in the instances where courts have found some statutes of limitation to be "substantive" they were seeking a "reasonable distinction" for escaping from the anomaly of the rule that limitations are generally to be regarded as "procedural," Mr. Justice Holmes continued, "The common case [where limitations are treated as 'substantive'] is where a statute creates a new liability, and in the same section or in the same act limits the time within which it can be enforced, whether using words of condition or not. The Harrisburg, 119 U.S. 199. But the fact that the limitation is contained in the same section or the same statute is material only as bearing on construction. It is merely a ground for saying that the limitation goes to the right created, and accompanies the obligation everywhere. The same conclusion would be reached if the limitation was in a different statute, provided it was directed to the newly created liability so specifically as to warrant saying that it qualified the right." . . .

Two other approaches to the problem were suggested in our opinion in Wood & Selick, Inc., v. Compagnie Generale Transatlantique, 2 Cir., 1930, 43 F.2d 941. First, that the foreign law might be examined to see if the defense possessed the attributes which the forum would classify as "procedural" or "substantive"; that is, for example, whether the defense need be pleaded, as a "substantive" period of limitations need not be in this country. Second, the foreign law might be examined to see if the operation of limitation completely extinguished the right, in which case limitation would be regarded as "substantive." Still other tests are suggested by Goodwin v. Townsend, 3 Cir., 1952, 197 F.2d 970—namely, whether the foreign limitation is regarded as "procedural" or "substantive" by the courts of the foreign state concerned, and possibly whether the limitation is cast in language commonly regarded as "procedural."

Which, then, of these various tests should be applied here? It appears to us that it should be the one which Davis v. Mills, 1904, 194 U.S. 451, suggests for use where the right and its limitation period are contained in separate statutes, viz.: Was the limitation "directed to the newly created liability so *specifically* as to warrant saying that it qualified the right"? 194 U.S., at page 454, 24 S.Ct. at page 694, italics supplied. . . .

Even though the limitation period here is contained in the same statute as enacts the right sought to be enforced, The Harrisburg, supra, still, as noted later, because of the breadth of the Panama Labor Code, as contrasted with the limited scope of the statute involved in The Harrisburg, the limitation period should not automatically be regarded as "substantive." Nor would it be appropriate to make this case turn on the fact that the right sued upon was unknown at common law . . . when we are dealing with the statutes of a country where the common law does not exist. And we do not think that it should matter whether the foreign court has interpreted its statute as being "procedural" or "substantive" for some other purpose, which may have happened in Goodwin, supra, or whether the foreign practice requires that limitation be pleaded, Wood & Selick, supra. "The tendency to assume that a word which appears in two or more legal rules, and so in connection with more than one purpose, has and should have precisely the same scope in all of them, runs all through legal discussions. It has all the tenacity of original sin and must constantly be guarded against." Cook, Substance and Procedure in the Conflict of Laws, 42 Yale L.J. 333, 337 (1933). No more should it matter whether the foreign right is extinguished altogether by the mere passage of time, or is instead only repressed into a dormant state, subject to "revival" if the defense of limitation is waived or renounced, Wood & Selick, supra. Such a distinction would generally be difficult to apply, and might also lead to results out of the pattern of the precedents; that is, if the defense could be waived under foreign law, a limitation period might be considered "procedural" even though it was contained in a specific statute giving a remedy for wrongful death. . . . And whether the wording of the limitation period seems more like "procedural" or "substantive" language, Goodwin, supra, does not appear to have been generally considered important.

It is true that the test we prefer leaves much to be desired. It permits the existence of a substantial gray area between the black and the white. But it at least furnishes a practical means of mitigating what is at best an artificial rule in the conflict of laws, without exposing us to the pitfalls inherent in prolonged excursions into foreign law; and it permits us to avoid the short-comings discussed above. We conclude, therefore, that the "specificity" test is the proper one to be applied in a case of this type, without deciding, of course, whether the same test would also be controlling in cases involving domestic or other kinds of foreign statutes of limitations.

Applying that test here it appears to us that the libelant is entitled to succeed, for the respondents have failed to satisfy us that the Panamanian period of limitation in question was specifically aimed against the particular rights which the libelant seeks to enforce. The Panama Labor Code is a statute having broad objectives, viz.: "The present Code regulates the relations between capital and labor, placing them on a basis of social justice, so that, without injuring any of the parties, there may be guaranteed for labor the necessary conditions for a normal life and to capital an equitable return for its investment." In pursuance of these objectives the Code gives laborers various rights against their employers. Article 623 establishes the period of limitation for *all* such rights, except certain ones which are enumerated in Article 621. And there is nothing in the record to indicate that the Panamanian legislature gave special consideration to the impact of Article 623 upon the particular rights sought to be enforced here, as distinguished from the other rights to which that Article is also applicable. Were we confronted with the question of whether the limitation period of Article 621 (which carves out particular rights to be governed by a shorter limitation period) is to be regarded as "substantive" or "procedural" under the rule of "specificity" we might have a different case; but here on the surface of things we appear to be dealing with a "broad," and not a "specific," statute of limitations. .   .   .

We therefore conclude that under the proper test the respondents have not made out their defense. In so holding we reach the same result as we did in the similar situation involved in Wood & Selick, 1930, 43 F.2d 941. .   .   .

Reversed.

Many states have enacted borrowing statutes providing that an action cannot be maintained in the forum even if timely there if it is barred by the statute of limitations of the state to which the statute refers. These statutes do not all use the same criteria to identify the other state. Some refer to the state where the cause of action "arose" or "accrued" or to the state in which the defendant was domiciled or resided during a period subsequent to the transaction on which the claim is based. In applying the statute of limitations of the state to which its borrowing statute refers, the forum typically applies the local law rules of the other state that bear upon whether the foreign statutory period has run but not the choice-of-law rules.

NOTES

(1) In Dindo v. Whitney, 429 F.2d 25 (1st Cir. 1970), on remand, 52 F.R.D. 194, vacated 451 F.2d 1, reviewing the United States District Court for New Hampshire in a personal injury suit arising out of an automobile accident in Quebec, the court refused to apply Quebec's one-year statute of limitations against a Vermont resident in favor of a New Hampshire defendant. The court attached no weight to the fact that the Quebec statute in terms "extinguished" the cause of action after one year.

(2) Do the rules discussed in the Bournias case apply only to non-consensual transactions, such as torts, or do they also apply to actions based upon out-of-state contracts, including those that expressly fix time limits? Compare Home Insurance Co. v. Dick, supra p. 329, with Clay v. Sun Insurance Co., p. 355, supra.

(4) Is a tolling provision inoperative if the defendant, though a nonresident of the state of the forum, is subject to suit there, as under a nonresident motorist's statute, or if he has property in the state which could be reached by attachment? Upholding the constitutionally of applying the tolling statute to a nonresident corporation amenable to long-arm service is G. D. Searle Co. v. Cohn, 455 U.S. 404 (1982); see also Hopkins v. Kelsey-Hayes, Inc., 628 F.2d 801 (3d Cir. 1980).

GEORGE v. DOUGLAS AIRCRAFT CO.

United States Court of Appeals, Second Circuit, 1964.

332 F.2d 73.*

FRIENDLY, CIRCUIT JUDGE. Plaintiffs, members of the crew of a DC–7C sold by Douglas Aircraft Co. to Braniff Airways in 1957, were injured when the airplane crashed in Florida in the early morning of March 25, 1958, as the result of an engine failure shortly after taking off from Miami on a flight to South America. They brought this action against Douglas in the Southern District of New York on March 25, 1963, predicating federal jurisdiction on plaintiffs' citizenship in Texas and defendant's Delaware incorporation. The complaint alleged that Douglas had "impliedly and expressly represented and warranted" that the aircraft sold by it to Braniff and the Curtiss-Wright engines installed therein "were of good and merchantable quality, free from defects, and fit for the purposes of commercial carriage for hire for which said aircraft and model engines were intended." Douglas moved for summary judgment "on the ground that the statute of limitations has expired"—more particularly the limitations

* Cert. denied 379 U.S. 904 (1964).

statute of California, where the airplane was made and delivered, or of Florida, one or the other of which was considered to be made applicable by New York's "borrowing" statute, Civil Practice Act, § 13. Plaintiffs denied that the action was barred under the Florida statute of limitations, which they claimed to be the pertinent one. The judge ruled for Douglas. . . .

New York's borrowing statute as it stood on March 25, 1963, Civil Practice Act, § 13, forbade the bringing of an action by a non-resident to enforce a cause of action "arising" outside New York "after the expiration of the time limited by the laws . . . of the state or country where the cause of action arose, for bringing an action upon the cause of action . . . ." If the New York courts would hold that plaintiffs' "cause of action arose" in California, where the contract of sale was executed and the airplane was manufactured and delivered, that would end the matter since § 340(3) of the California Code of Civil Procedure establishes a one-year period of limitations for personal injury actions, and this has been held to apply whether the action sounds in contract or in tort. Rubino v. Utah Canning Co., 123 Cal.App.2d 18, 26, 266 P.2d 163, 168 (Dist.Ct.App.1954). . . .

. . . [W]e think New York would look to the law of the place of injury, here Florida, rather than to the law of the place of manufacture or of delivery to determine whether liability existed. . . . The interest protected by the imposition of strict liability on a manufacturer is, as Dean Pound pointed out, the interest in maintaining "the general security." Introduction to the Philosophy of Law 87 (1953 ed.). An accident caused by a defective product threatens the "general security" of the state where the injury occurs rather than of the state of delivery, which is often determined by tax or other considerations wholly extraneous to the instant problem, or even of the state of manufacture. In the typical cases of strict products liability—the trichinous pork, the inflammable garment, the exploding bottle, the defective steering gear, or the noxious cosmetic—the victim will generally be resident in the state where injured. While this will less frequently be true of airplane crashes, that state is likely to incur the burden of hospitalization and care of residents and non-residents alike. Moreover, one could hardly support application of a different choice of law rule for airplanes than for automobiles, and it would seem quite irrational that the victim's recovery on a theory of strict liability should depend upon whether or not the state where the plane was manufactured had chosen so to provide with respect to accidents as to which it had primary concern. Extra-state manufacturers are not entitled to have their goods enter a state on easier terms as to liability than the state establishes generally; they are as able as the intra-state manufacturer to provide for their own protection by insurance or self-insurance. Even more clearly if a state has decided in general that persons injured within its borders by a particular kind of defective chattel should not be allowed to recover against the manufacturer except for negligence, there would be little reason to accord a greater degree of protection because the chattel causing the injury was made in another state which has shown a broader concern for the general welfare of its citizens by imposing strict liability.

Although we travel thus far down the road with appellants, we cannot accept their conclusion that this necessarily means that New York would consider their cause of action to be one "arising" in Florida for the purpose of making Florida's limitation period the controlling one under § 13. As a matter of the ordinary meaning of language it seems equally possible to say that the cause of action "arose" in California where defendant's allegedly wrongful act was done or in Florida where plaintiffs were injured by it—and this even though Florida be regarded as furnishing the normative rule. In predicting which choice the New York Court of Appeals would make, we must give weight to the purpose of the borrowing statute. It has been said that such additions to the statute of limitations "were necessitated by the rule [e.g., New York Civil Practice Act, § 19] that the period is interrupted by absence of the defendant from the forum whether the cause of action arose in the forum or in a foreign jurisdiction against a nonresident defendant. In the absence of a borrowing statute, this rule would permit actions which have long since been barred by the *lex loci* and by the statutes of the state where the defendant resided and which would have been barred by the forum had the defendant resided there since the cause of action arose." Note, Developments in the Law: Statutes of Limitations, 63 Harv.L.Rev. 1177, 1262–63 (1950). . . . New York's policy for nearly a century has been to protect a non-resident defendant against an action in New York, which was timely because of the tolling provision of § 19 of the Civil Practice Act, but had become barred elsewhere. . . . This being the principal evil with which the New York Legislature sought to deal, a court required to choose between two linguistically permissible decisions as to where a cause of action "arose" ought to lean to the reading more likely to achieve the underlying policy against prolonging the period of limitations because of the defendant's absence from a jurisdiction where there was no reason to expect him to be present. . . . In personal injury actions against a manufacturer, the latter's amenability to suit in the place of injury would be fortuitious, at least in the absence of a considerable extenstion of "long-arm" statutes, . . . and the usual tolling statute in that state might indefinitely prolong the limitations period. On the other hand, the manufacturer would always be suable in the state of manufacture and generally in that of delivery, the two latter being identical in the instant case. As indicated above, we perceive no obstacle to predicting that the New York Court of Appeals would consider a cause of action as "arising" for the purposes of the borrowing statute in a state different from the one whose substantive law would determine liability. . . . Sharing Professor Ehrenzweig's view that the place-of-accrual test is "ambiguous" if not "entirely unworkable," Conflict of Laws 430 (1962), and despite general statements that a

tort action inevitably "arises" where the last act necessary to establish liability occurred, we predict that New York would hold that
plaintiffs' cause of action here "arose" in California, whose one year
statute would be a bar. . . .

[The court finally determined that the action would also be barred
under the Florida statute of limitations.]

Affirmed.

NOTES

(1) With Judge Friendly's statement as to the purpose of the New York
borrowing statute in the George case, compare his statement in Sack v. Low,
478 F.2d 360 (2d Cir. 1973): "[T]he policy behind the borrowing statute is to
protect New York resident-defendants from suits in New York that would be
barred by shorter statutes of limitations in other states where non-resident-
plaintiffs could have brought suit." The result of implementing this policy is
that plaintiffs do not succeed in getting a longer statute of limitations applied by suing in the New York courts on a claim centered in a state with a
short limitations period.

(2) For a thorough study of the privileges and immunities clause in con-
flict of laws, see Currie, Unconstitutional Discrimination in the Conflict of
Laws: Privileges and Immunities, 69 Yale L.J. 1323 (1960), reprinted in B.
Currie, Selected Essays on the Conflict of Laws 445 (1963).

EPILOGUE ON SUBSTANCE AND PROCEDURE

The upheaval in choice-of-law thinking with regard to concededly
"substantive" issues has spread to issues once regarded as "procedural" and "therefore" treated as automatically governed by forum
law, such as time limitations. Even as late as the end of the 1960's,
courts with few exceptions viewed statute of limitations questions in
substance-procedure terms and usually characterized them as procedural. The Restatement, Second, Conflict of Laws § 142 reflected
the prevailing view by declaring that an action will not be maintained
if it is not timely under the forum's law, including its borrowing statute; and that it will be maintained if timely by forum standards even
if it would be barred elsewhere, with one exception. It will not be
entertained despite its timeliness by forum standards if it is barred
"in the state of the otherwise applicable law by a statute of limitations which bars the right and not merely the remedy." (Id., § 143.)
See Ester, Borrowing Statutes of Limitation and Conflict of Laws, 15
U.Fla.L.Rev. 33 (1962). See Wurfel, Statutes of Limitation in the
Conflict of Laws, 52 N.C.L.Rev. 489 (1974).

A major shift has occurred in the courts' view of the problem,
with New Jersey blazing the trail in Heavner v. Uniroyal, Inc., 63
N.J. 130, 305 A.2d 412 (1973). The plaintiff was a North Carolina
resident who brought a product liability action against the manufacturer of an allegedly defective truck tire that caused a highway acci-

dent in North Carolina. Suit was filed in New Jersey more than
three years after the accident and after the action was barred by time
limitations in North Carolina. The court rejected the traditional rule
by relying on concepts drawn from modern approaches that are often
used in resolving conflicts between concededly substantive rules (305
A.2d 418):

> "We are convinced the time has come, for the reasons previously
> outlined, to discard the mechanical rule that the limitations of the
> law of this state must be employed in every suit on a foreign
> cause of action. We need go no further now than to say that
> when the cause of action arises in another state, the parties are all
> present in and amenable to the jurisdiction of that state, New
> Jersey has no substantial interest in the matter, the substantive
> law of the foreign state is to be applied, and its limitation period
> has expired at the time suit is commenced here, New Jersey will
> hold the suit barred. In essence, we will 'borrow' the limitations
> law of the foreign state. . . ."

In subsequent conflicts cases involving the statute of limitations a
growing number of courts have followed the approach in Heavner,
rejecting automatic application of forum law via a procedural characterization. See Henry v. Richardson-Merrell, Inc., 508 F.2d 28 (3d
Cir. 1975); Allen v. Volkswagen of America, Inc., 555 F.2d 361 (3d
Cir. 1977); Schum v. Bailey, 578 F.2d 493 (3d Cir. 1978); Thompson v.
Yue, 426 F.Supp. 853 (D.N.J.1977). See also Tomlin v. Boeing Co.,
650 F.2d 1065 (9th Cir. 1981); Myers v. Cessna Aircraft Corp., 275 Or.
501, 553 P.2d 355 (1976); Central Mutual Insurance Co. v. H.O. Inc.,
63 Wis.2d 54, 216 N.W.2d 239 (1974). See Grossman, Statutes of
Limitation and the Conflict of Laws: Modern Analysis, 1980 Ariz.St.
L.J. 1; Milhollin, Interest Analysis and Conflicts Between Statutes of
Limitations, 27 Hast.L.J. 1 (1975).

PRIVILEGES AND IMMUNITIES

The question of disparate treatment of nonresidents for limitations purposes was addressed in Canadian Northern Railway Co. v.
Eggen, 252 U.S. 553 (1920). The Court declared that the privileges
and immunities clause, while it protects rights which are in their nature fundamental, including the right of a citizen of one state to bring
actions in the courts of another, does not require that the nonresident
be given access on the same terms as to time limits as are accorded to
resident citizens (p. 562):

> The principle on which this holding rests is that the constitu-
> tional requirement is satisfied if the non-resident is given access
> to the courts of the State upon terms which in themselves are rea-
> sonable and adequate for the enforcing of any rights he may have,

even though they may not be technically and precisely the same in extent as those accorded to resident citizens.

Conceding that it had never attempted to formulate a comprehensive list of the rights included within the privileges and immunities clause, the Court said (p. 560) that it "has repeatedly approved as authoritative the statement by Mr. Justice Washington, in 1823, in Corfield v. Coryell, 4 Wash.C.C. 371, 380 . . . 'We feel no hesitation in confining these expressions to those privileges and immunities which are, in their nature, fundamental.'" At this point the Court also cited the Slaughter-House Cases, 83 U.S. 36, 76 (1800); Blake v. McClung, 172 U.S. 239, 248 (1898); Chambers v. Baltimore & Ohio Railroad Co., 207 U.S. 142, 155 (1907).

A recent pronouncement by the Supreme Court on the scope of the privileges and immunities clause is Baldwin v. Montana Fish and Game Commission, 436 U.S. 371 (1978). The case holds that the privileges and immunities clause does not assure access by nonresidents to recreational big game hunting in Montana as an activity within the category of rights protected by privileges and immunities. The Court went on to say that only with respect to privileges and immunities bearing upon the vitality of the nation as a single entity must a state treat nonresidents equally with residents. Montana elk do not raise that problem.

———

Chapter 8

THE PROBLEM OF CHOOSING THE RULE
OF DECISION

SECTION 1. THE RECEIVED SYSTEM AND TRADITION

A. TERRITORIALITY AND THE JURISDICTION–SELECTING PROCESS

RESTATEMENT, SECOND, CONFLICT OF LAWS: *

1. *The Position Taken by the Original Restatement*

The original Restatement stated that, with minor exceptions, all substantive questions relating to the existence of a tort claim are governed by the local law of the "place of wrong." This was described (in Section 377) as "the state where the last event necessary to make an actor liable for an alleged tort takes place." Since a tort is the product of wrongful conduct and of resulting injury and since the injury follows the conduct, the state of the "last event" is the state where the injury occurred. This rule of the original Restatement was derived from the vested rights doctrine which called for the enforcement everywhere of rights that had been lawfully created under the local law of a state. In effect, the doctrine provided for the application of the local law of the state in which had occurred the last act necessary to bring a legal obligation into existence. In the case of torts, the state of the last act, for reasons stated above, was the state where the injury had occurred. In the case of contracts, it was the state where the contract was made. . . .

"The theory . . . is that, although the act complained of was subject to no law having force in the forum, it gave rise to an obligation, an *obligatio*, which, like other obligations, follows the person, and may be enforced wherever the person may be found. . . . But as the only source of this obligation is the law of the place of the act, it follows that that law determines not merely the existence of

---

* Quoted with the permission of the copyright owner, The American Law Institute.

436

the obligation, . . . but equally determines its extent." Justice Holmes in Slater v. Mexican National Railroad Co., 194 U.S. 120, 126 (1904), which is set forth at p. 202, supra.

———

"It would be as unjust to apply a different law as it would be to determine the rights of the parties by a different transaction." Story, Conflict of Laws 38 (8th ed. 1883).

———

CAVERS, THE CHOICE–OF–LAW PROCESS (1965), pp. 5–9: *

In Anglo-American jurisdictions, the development of choice-of-law doctrine has been greatly influenced by the works of the English scholar and jurist, A.V. Dicey, and the American law professor, Joseph H. Beale. Dicey adopted the theory that the task of the court in a choice-of-law case was the enforcement of vested rights. Professor Beale coupled this with the territorial concepts that Story had drawn from Huber and thereby organized a system of choice-of-law rules, simple in structure, which could be applied without regard to the content of the particular laws between which choice had to be made. This theory dominated the American Law Institute's *Restatement of Conflict of Laws* for which Professor Beale served as Reporter.

Professor Beale confronted the welter of conflicting conflicts decisions with bland determination. "Most of the statements in this work will be dogmatic," he wrote at the start of his treatise and then asked—rhetorically: "Does not the Bar desire dogmatic statements?" I need quote only two propositions from the treatise to convey the character of his doctrine and his thought. Thus, at the outset of his discussion of the choice of law as to contracts, he declared: "The question whether a contract is valid . . . can on general principles be determined by no other law than that which applies to the acts [of the parties], that is, by the law of the place of contracting. . . . If . . . the law of the place where the agreement is made annexes no legal obligation to it, *there is no other law which has power to do so.*"

And in expounding choice of law as to torts, Professor Beale explained, "It is impossible for a plaintiff to recover in tort unless he has been given by some law a cause of action in tort; and *this cause of action can be given only by the law of the place where the tort was committed.* That is the place where the injurious event occurs, and its law is the law *therefore* which applies to it."

While the *Conflicts Restatement* was still in gestation, Beale's basic conceptions came under attack by what he termed "an ephemeral school" of "self-styled realists." Among these Professor Ernest Lorenzen and Professor Walter Wheeler Cook were the foremost. Pro-

———

fessor Charles Wesley Hohfeld, famed for his analysis of jural relations, had also been a dissenter from conflicts orthodoxy of his day, and Professor Lorenzen has credited him with the origin of the "local law" theory that, particularly as championed by Professor Cook, became the principal rival of Professor Beale's "vested rights" theory. These critics challenged the logic of the vested rights theory which they found question-begging, but they also challenged its practicality. They complained of its failure to reflect social and economic needs and policies, though they were seldom specific in identifying these. . . .

. . . Though I joined them in asking, in Professor Lorenzen's words: "What are the demands of justice in the particular situation; what is the controlling policy?" I insisted, nevertheless, that these questions could not be answered as long as the questioners continued to seek what I termed "a jurisdiction-selecting" rule,[1] that is, a rule indicating the source of the law to be applied without regard to the law's content. Without taking the content of the conflicting laws into account, how could one know what would satisfy the demands of justice or the requirements of policy?

B. EXAMPLES OF THE SYSTEM IN OPERATION

1. *The Forum Applies Its Own Rule of Decision*

TORLONIA v. TORLONIA

Supreme Court of Errors of Connecticut, 1928.
108 Conn. 292, 142 A. 843.

[This case is summarized at p. 25, supra.]

". . . the rule is well established that the courts of the State of the domicil may grant a divorce for any cause allowed by its laws, without regard to the place of the commission of the offense for which it is granted or to whether such offense constitutes a ground for divorce in the state in which it was committed. . . ."

---

1. Cavers, A Critique of the Choice-of-Law Problem, 47 Harv.L.Rev. 173, 194 (1933): This concept, launched in the article cited, is gradually becoming current. The jurisdiction-selecting rule makes a *state* the object of choice; in theory it is only after the rule has selected the governing state by reference to the "contact" prescribed in the rule that the court ascertains the content of the state's law. . . .

WORKERS' COMPENSATION

RESTATEMENT, SECOND, CONFLICT OF LAWS *

CHAPTER 7—TOPIC 3

Introductory Note. A workmen's compensation statute, as the term is used in this Topic, is a statute which makes an employer, and sometimes other persons as well, liable without regard to any question of fault for injuries suffered by an employee in the course of his employment . . . .

A peculiarity of this area is that usually relief under a particular statute may be obtained only in the state of its enactment. This is because the statutes normally provide for their enforcement by special administrative tribunals and such tribunals do not consider themselves competent to give relief under any statute but their own. Hence the principal problem in this area is not one of choice of law but rather what range of application to persons and things without the state will be given by a state to its own workmen's compensation statute . . . .

———

Problems posed by workers' compensation laws are considered at greater length at pp. 640–644, infra.

———

PEOPLE v. OLAH

Court of Appeals of New York, 1949.
300 N.Y. 96, 89 N.E.2d 329.

FULD, JUDGE. . . . Section 1941 of the Penal Law, Consol. Laws, c. 40, provides that a defendant, convicted of a felony in New York, is to be punished as a second felony offender if he was "previously" *convicted* . . . under the laws of any other state . . . *of a crime* which, if committed within this state, would be a felony. (Emphasis supplied.) . . .

In the present case, Olah was convicted in New Jersey following his plea of guilty to an indictment accusing him of having stolen a watch and a wallet containing $200, "all of the value of over Twenty Dollars." He was given a suspended sentence and placed on probation.

. . . To ascertain [the] "crime" [of which he was convicted], we must of necessity consider the statute which created and defined it and upon which the indictment was based.

———

* Quoted with the permission of the copyright owner, The American Law Institute.

The indictment was founded upon a New Jersey statute which, creating the "crime" of larceny as "a high misdemeanor", defined it as the theft of "Money, or personal goods" having a "value . . . of or above twenty dollars" (N.J.Stat.Ann. 2:145–2). Since section 1941 of the Penal Law renders vital the "crime" of which a defendant was convicted and since the "crime" in New Jersey was that of stealing $20 of more, it follows that such a crime would not have been a felony in this State—for it is the theft of more than $100 that is here denominated a felony. Penal Law, §§ 1296, 1299. . . .

. . .

. . . [S]ection 1941 of the Penal Law does not provide that a defendant should be treated as a second felony offender if he did something in another State which might furnish the basis for a felony prosecution in New York or—relating the problem to larceny cases—if he stole an amount which might justify a prosecution for grand larceny in this State. . . .

The orders should be reversed and the matter remitted to the Court of General Sessions, with directions to vacate and set aside the judgment of conviction and to take such further proceedings as may be necessary, not inconsistent with this opinion.

NOTES

(1) Is People v. Olah a choice-of-law case? Was the question whether the law of New York or of New Jersey should be applied to determine the nature of Olah's crime? Or was it clear that only the law of New York was applicable and that the law of New Jersey was considered solely for the purpose of determining whether Olah had committed a felony within the meaning of New York law? Under this latter view, New Jersey's penal law was referred to as a "datum" to give meaning to the New York statute. Cf. B. Currie, p. 477, infra.

(2) Section 1941 of the New York Penal Law has been held to require second offender sentence for a defendant convicted of larceny of $150 in a state that punishes a larceny of that amount as only a misdemeanor. People v. Evans, 20 A.D.2d 671, 246 N.Y.S.2d 953 (2d Dept. 1964).

(3) A potential choice-of-law problem evaporates if there is no essential difference in the relevant rules of decision of the interested states. An example is Pahmer v. The Hertz Corp., 32 N.Y.2d 119, 296 N.E.2d 243 (1973). In that case, Mrs. Pahmer sued for injuries she sustained in a California accident while being driven by her fellow employee, Cullen, in an automobile he had rented from the Hertz Corporation. Among the defenses was the California guest statute. After the appeal to the New York Court of Appeals on that issue had been "extensively briefed and argued . . . on choice of law principles," the Supreme Court of California declared the guest statute unconstitutional as a denial of the equal protection clauses of the California and United States constitutions. Brown v. Merlo, 8 Cal.3d 855, 106 Cal.Rptr. 388, 506 P.2d 212 (1973). The New York Court of Appeals held that, having been held unconstitutional, the California guest statute could not serve as a defense to the passenger's suit.

"PROCEDURAL" RULES

In the classical choice-of-law system, as the discussion in chapter 7 has shown, the forum applied its own rules of procedure, even when it conceived that the claim in question was governed as to substantive matters by the law of another state. Since the dividing line between procedural and substantive issues is unclear, the principle that the "forum always applies its own rules of procedure" was less absolute than it portended. In practice it gave abundant opportunities for a court to manipulate the choice-of-law process by classifying matters as procedural or substantive in order to arrive at the desired result. This gambit was but one of many that provided play in the joints for a mechanism that outwardly appeared stiff and unbending. The section directly following illustrates how mechanistically the system might operate. Then come several cases that exemplify the ways the courts managed to escape the seemingly deterministic process by in effect picking as they pleased the particular choice-of-law rule they were "bound" to follow.

---

2.   *Hard-and-Fast Choice-of-Law Rules*

ALABAMA GREAT SOUTHERN RAILROAD CO. v. CARROLL

Supreme Court of Alabama, 1892.
97 Ala. 126, 11 So. 803, 18 L.R.A. 433, 38 Am.St.Rep. 163.

[Plaintiff was a brakeman on defendant's railroad. Both parties were residents of Alabama and plaintiff was hired there. Plaintiff was injured in Mississippi due to a break in a defective car link. The evidence showed negligence on the part of railroad employees who had a duty to inspect the links at various places in Alabama.]

McClellan, J. . . . This was the negligence not of the master, the defendant, but of fellow-servants of the plaintiff, for which at common-law the defendant is not liable. . . . We feel entirely safe in declaring that plaintiff has shown no cause of action under the common-law as it is understood and applied both here and in Mississippi.

It is, however, further contended that the plaintiff . . . has made out a case for the recovery sought under the Employer's Liability Act of Alabama, it being clearly shown that there is no such . . . law . . . in the State of Mississippi. Considering this position in the abstract, that is dissociated from the facts of this particular case which are supposed to exert an important influence upon it, there cannot be two opinions as to its being unsound and untenable.

So looked at, we do not understand appellee's counsel even to deny either the proposition or its application to this case, that there can be no recovery in one State for injuries to the person sustained in another unless the infliction of the injuries is actionable under the law of the State in which they were received. Certainly this is the well established rule of law subject in some jurisdictions to the qualification that the infliction of the injuries would also support an action in the State where the suit is brought, had they been received within that State. . . .

But it is claimed that the facts of this case take it out of the general rule . . . and authorize the courts of Alabama to subject the defendant to the payment of damages under section 2590 of the Code, although the injuries counted on were sustained in Mississippi under circumstances which involved no liability on the defendant by the laws of that State.

This insistence is in the first instance based on that aspect of the evidence which goes to show that the negligence which produced the casualty transpired in Alabama, and the theory that wherever the consequence of that negligence manifested itself, a recovery can be had in Alabama. We are referred to no authority in support of this proposition, and exhaustive investigation on our part has failed to disclose any. . . .

It is admitted, or at least cannot be denied, that negligence of duty unproductive of damnifying results will not authorize or support a recovery. Up to the time this train passed out of Alabama no injury had resulted. For all that occurred in Alabama, therefore, no cause of action whatever arose. The fact which created the right to sue, the injury without which confessedly no action would lie anywhere, transpired in the State of Mississippi. It was in that State, therefore, necessarily that the cause of action, if any, arose; and whether a cause of action arose and existed at all or not must in all reason be determined by the law which obtained at the time and place when and where the fact which is relied on to justify a recovery transpired. Section 2590 of the Code of Alabama had no efficiency beyond the lines of Alabama. . . . Section 2590 of the Code, in other words, is to be interpreted in the light of universally recognized principles of private international or interstate law, as if its operation had been expressly limited to this State and as if its first line read as follows: "When a personal injury is *received in Alabama* by a servant or employee," &c., &c. . . . We have not been inattentive to the suggestions of counsel in this connection, which are based upon that rule of the statutory and common criminal law under which a murderer is punishable where the fatal blow is delivered, regardless of the place where death ensues.—Green v. State, 66 Ala. 40. This principle is patently without application here. There would be some analogy if the plaintiff had been stricken in Alabama and suffered in Mississippi, which is not the fact. There is, however, an analogy which is afforded by the criminal law, but which points away from the conclusion appellee's counsel desire us to reach. This is found in that well established doctrine of criminal law, that where the unlawful act is committed in one jurisdiction or State and takes effect—produces the result which it is the purpose of the law to prevent, or, it having ensued, punish for—in another jurisdiction or State, the crime is deemed to have been committed and is punished in that jurisdiction or State in which the result is manifested, and not where the act was committed. . . .

[Plaintiff argued that since the contract of employment was entered into in Alabama between Alabama citizens the Alabama Employer's Liability Act became a part of the contract and the defendant was under a contractual duty to the plaintiff. On this point the court said, inter alia, . . . "that the duties and liabilities incident to the relation between the plaintiff and the defendant which are involved in this case, are not imposed by and do not rest in or spring from the contract between the parties. The only office of the contract, under section 2590 of the Code, is the establishment of a relation between them, that of master and servant; and it is upon that relation, that incident or consequence of the contract, and not upon the rights of the parties under the contract, that our statute operates. The law is not concerned with the contractual stipulations, except in so far as to determine from them that the relation upon which it is to operate exists. Finding this relation the statute imposes certain duties and liabilities on the parties to it wholly regardless of the stipulations of the contract as to the rights of the parties under it, and, it may be, in the teeth of such stipulations."]

For the error in refusing to instruct the jury to find for the defendant if they believed the evidence, the judgment is reversed and the cause will be remanded.

NOTES

(1) What if the train in Carroll's case had been negligently coupled in Mississippi and his injury had occurred in Alabama? Presumably, on these facts, the Alabama court would have applied the law of Alabama. But should a simple shift in the location of conduct and injury lead to such a total reversal of result? Yet, what would be the alternative if simple, uniform, forum-proof, even-handed answers are to be reached in multistate cases? Was there a better choice-of-law rule than "place of the wrong"?

(2) D's dog strayed from Massachusetts to New Hampshire and there bit P. By New Hampshire law, D was liable only upon proof that he knew his dog was accustomed to bite (there was no such proof). By statute in Massachusetts, D was absolutely liable. P was denied recovery. LeForest v. Tolman, 117 Mass. 109 (1875). Assume identical canine behavior, but switch the rules in the two states. Cf. Fischl v. Chubb, 30 Pa.D. & C. 40 (1937), where the turnabout case arose and P was allowed to recover.

In Siegmann v. Meyer, 100 F.2d 367 (2d Cir. 1938), plaintiff was assaulted by defendant's wife in Florida, where she had gone without the defendant.

He, indeed, had never been in Florida, which, unlike defendant's New York domicile, held a husband liable for his wife's torts. Defendant was held not liable. Is the case different in principle from the dog-bite case?

(3) In Dallas v. Whitney, 118 W.Va. 106, 188 S.E. 766 (1936), plate glass stored by P in Ohio was shattered by the force of an explosion caused by D's blasting in West Virginia. The West Virginia court determined D's liability by reference to Ohio law, which imposed liability without fault. Suppose that by West Virginia law D would have been liable only if he had been negligent. Should West Virginia law then have been considered?

In Hunter v. Derby Foods, 110 F.2d 970 (2d Cir. 1940), an action for wrongful death was brought in the federal district court in New York. The deceased died in Ohio as a result of eating unwholesome canned meat which he had purchased and eaten in Ohio. The defendant, a New York distributor, has secured the meat from a concern which had processed and canned it in South America. The defendant sold it to a wholesaler in Ohio who in turn sold it to the grocer from whom the deceased purchased it. An Ohio statute made it negligence per se to sell unwholesome food without disclosure of that fact to the buyer. Held: P may recover on a showing of a violation of the statute and need not prove lack of due care.

————

PHYSICAL INJURY CASES WITH MULTISTATE CONTACTS

The Carroll case raises problems of decision in the all too common context of death or injury in interstate travel. What arguments can be made for and against the result entirely apart from the route by which it was reached? Does the outcome in the case seem particularly shocking? Exceedingly wise?

Should the rules of liability or damage give way and change according to the citizenship, residence, destination, etc., of the victim, or according to the forum in which suit is brought? A resounding negative was the answer of the traditional common law jurisprudence as epitomized by the American Law Institute's Restatement, Conflict of Laws (1934). This remarkably self-confident work was dominated by Professor Joseph H. Beale's philosophy of the nature and purposes of the systematics of choice of law. Holmes, Cardozo, Brandeis, Learned Hand and many other leaders of American legal thinking wholeheartedly shared Beale's approach, although sometimes they differed about how to explain or rationalize some of its features.

NOTES

(1) The place of injury will usually be easily identifiable in the case of personal injuries or of damage to tangible property. When, however, the tort involves fraud, defamation, invasion of privacy, alienation of affections, or other forms of non-physical injury, difficult or impossible to localize, the last event approach may prove an unsatisfactory connecting factor. Where, for example, is the place of injury when defendant's misrepresentations induce the plaintiff to (a) enter into a contract in state X to purchase the defendant's horse, (b) pay the stipulated purchase price in state Y and (c) take

possession of the horse in state Z? See Note, Conflict of Laws in Multistate Fraud and Deceit, 3 Vand.L.Rev. 767 (1950).

See also Continental Oil Co. v. General American Transportation Corp., 409 F.Supp. 288 (S.D.Texas 1976), which involved an action for breach of warranty brought by the buyer against the seller of 46 railroad tank cars. The cars had been manufactured in Ohio but the defects developed in Texas, Pennsylvania, and Ohio. The court held that Ohio was the state of injury and hence that its law was applicable.

When the injuries are not physical, the courts' answers differ widely regarding which state is the place of injury. This means that even if all states have adopted the place of injury rule they will not come to uniform decisions.

(2) Consider the following excerpt from the opinion of Wyzanski, J., in Greenberg v. Panama Transport Co., 185 F.Supp. 320 (D.Mass.1960):

". . . It is usually assumed that in connection with the tort of interfering with advantageous contractual relations, as in connection with torts generally, the governing law is supplied by the law of the place where the tort occurs. . . . But the grounds of logic, history, convenience and policy which support the doctrine in many cases, particularly cases of physical injury, are not appropriately involved in every type of case. Different torts may be governed by different principles of conflict of laws. . . . And the conflict of laws rules governing even the particular tort of interference with advantageous contractual relations may depend upon what type of contractual relationship is said to have been impeded."

(3) The Federal Tort Claims Act provides for liability on the part of the United States "where the United States, if a private person, would be liable to the claimant in accordance with the law of the place where the act or omission occurred." 28 U.S.C.A. § 1346(b). In Richards v. United States, 369 U.S. 1 (1962), the Supreme Court held that the reference under the Act is to "the whole law" (namely, both the local and conflicts law) of the state where the act or omission occurred. A federal court, in other words, must apply the same local law and reach the same ultimate result as would the courts of that state had the case involved an individual defendant. The Court said: ". . . the flexibility inherent in our interpretation" will be more in step with "a tendency" on the part of some states to apply the law of the state "having significant contact with the parties to the litigation."

(4) In England, a tort committed abroad had to satisfy two conditions in order to be actionable: "In the first place, the wrong must be of such a character that it would have been actionable if committed in England; and secondly, the act must not have been justifiable by the law of the place where it was committed." Carr v. Fracis Times & Co., [1902] A.C. 176, 182. See Hancock, Torts in the Conflict of Laws, The First Rule in Phillips v. Eyre, 3 U.Toronto L.J. 400 (1940); Hancock, Torts Problems in Conflict of Laws Resolved by Statutory Construction: The Halley and Other Older Cases Revisited, 18 U.Toronto L.J. 331 (1968).

A modern English case is Chaplin v. Boys, [1969] 3 W.L.R. 322; [1969] 2 All.E.R. 1085. (English soldiers were adversaries as a result of a motor accident in Malta, which did not allow damages for pain and suffering as England does. The five Law Lords agreed that the English rule of damages should be applied, but each wrote a separate opinion. The resulting "rule" does not summarize readily.)

THE CLASSICAL CHOICE–OF–LAW METHODOLOGY
IN CONTRACT CASES

The rules of the game in multistate contracts cases were animated by the same underlying philosophy that prevailed in the torts field. Once the matter had been categorized as a contracts case, the next step was to find the connecting factor and follow it to the state of governing law. The first Restatement distinguished (with uncharacteristic dubiety) between issues of validity, which were said to be determined by the local law of the place of contracting (Section 332) and issues of performance, which were referred to the local law of the place of performance (Section 358).

Efforts to reduce the choice-of-law process to few and simple rules in the contracts field raised even greater difficulties than in the area of torts. The variety and complexity of issues present troubles enough, but they are immeasurably complicated by differences in local law rules and in the difficulty of determining such questions as where a contract was made when the parties negotiate through the mails or over the telephone, crossing state lines again and again in their dealings, or where default has occurred. The contract rules of offer and acceptance, performance, discharge and the like are not concerned with "where" the operative events occur and therefore do little to aid a court intent on resolving a problem by locating the critical place where something allegedly occurred. Without the aid of so relatively unambiguous a "last event" as injurious impact of a physical kind, a choice-of-law system wedded to vested rights theorizing was likely to encourage a large amount of result-conscious manipulation. That is what happened.

MILLIKEN v. PRATT

Supreme Judicial Court of Massachusetts, 1878.
125 Mass. 374, 28 Am.Rep. 241.

Contract to recover $500 and interest from January 6, 1872. Writ dated June 30, 1875. The case was submitted to the Superior Court on agreed facts, in substance as follows:

The plaintiffs are partners doing business in Portland, Maine, under the firm name of Deering, Milliken & Co. The defendant is and has been since 1850, the wife of Daniel Pratt, and both have always resided in Massachusetts. In 1870, Daniel, who was then doing business in Massachusetts, applied to the plaintiffs at Portland for credit, and they required of him, as a condition of granting the same a guaranty from the defendant to the amount of five hundred dollars, and accordingly he procured from his wife the following instrument:

"Portland, January 29, 1870. In consideration of one dollar paid by Deering, Milliken & Co., receipt of which is hereby acknowledged,

I guarantee the payment to them by Daniel Pratt of the sum of five hundred dollars, from time to time as he may want—this to be a continuing guaranty. Sarah A. Pratt."

This instrument was executed by the defendant two or three days after its date, at her home in Massachusetts, and there delivered by her to her husband, who sent it by mail from Massachusetts to the plaintiffs in Portland; and the plaintiffs received it from the post-office in Portland early in February, 1870.

The plaintiffs subsequently sold and delivered goods to Daniel from time to time until October 7, 1871, and charged the same to him, and, if competent, it may be taken to be true, that in so doing they relied upon the guaranty. . . . This action is brought for goods sold from September 1, 1871, to October 7, 1871, inclusive, amounting to $860.12, upon which he paid $300, leaving a balance due of $560.12. The one dollar mentioned in the guaranty was not paid, and the only consideration moving to the defendant therefor was the giving of credit by the plaintiffs to her husband. Some of the goods were selected personally by Daniel at the plaintiffs' store in Portland, others were ordered by letters mailed by Daniel from Massachusetts to the plaintiffs at Portland, and all were sent by the plaintiffs by express from Portland to Daniel in Massachusetts, who paid all express charges. . . .

Payment was duly demanded of the defendant before the date of the writ, and was refused by her.

The Superior Court ordered judgment for the defendant; and the plaintiffs appealed to this court.

GRAY, C.J. The general rule is that the validity of a contract is to be determined by the law of the state in which it is made; if it is valid there, it is deemed valid everywhere, and will sustain an action in the courts of a state whose laws do not permit such a contract. Scudder v. Union National Bank, 91 U.S. 406. Even a contract expressly prohibited by the statutes of the state in which the suit is brought, if not in itself immoral, is not necessarily nor usually deemed so invalid that the comity of the state, as administered by its courts, will refuse to entertain an action on such a contract made by one of its own citizens abroad in a state the laws of which permit it. Greenwood v. Curtis, 6 Mass. 358. M'Intyre v. Parks, 3 Metc. 207.

If the contract is completed in another state, it makes no difference in principle whether the citizen of this state goes in person, or sends an agent, or writes a letter across the boundary line between the two states. . . . So if a person residing in this state signs and transmits, either by a messenger or through the post-office, to a person in another state, a written contract, which requires no special forms or solemnities in its execution, and no signature of the person to whom it is addressed, and is assented to and acted on by him there, the contract is made there, just as if the writer personally took the

executed contract into the other state, or wrote and signed it there.
. . .

. . . The sales of the goods ordered by him from the plaintiffs at Portland, and there delivered by them to him in person or to a carrier for him, were made in the State of Maine. . . . The contract between the defendant and the plaintiffs was complete when the guaranty had been received and acted on by them at Portland, and not before. Jordan v. Dobbins, 122 Mass. 168. It must therefore be treated as made and to be performed in the State of Maine.

The law of Maine authorized a married woman to bind herself by any contract as if she were unmarried. St. of Maine of 1866, c. 52. Mayo v. Hutchinson, 57 Maine 546. The law of Massachusetts, as then existing, did not allow her to enter into a contract as surety or for the accommodation of her husband or of any third person. Gen. Sts. c. 108, sec. 3. Nourse v. Henshaw, 123 Mass. 96. . . .

The question therefore is, whether a contract made in another state by a married woman domiciled here, which a married woman was not at the time capable of making under the law of this Commonwealth, but was then allowed by the law of that state to make, and which she could now lawfully make in this Commonwealth, will sustain an action against her in our courts.

It has been often stated by commentators that the law of the domicil, regulating the capacity of a person, accompanies and governs the person everywhere. But this statement, in modern times at least, is subject to many qualifications; and the opinions of foreign jurists upon the subject . . . are too varying and contradictory to control the general current of the English and American authorities in favor of holding that a contract, which by the law of the place is recognized as lawfully made by a capable person, is valid everywhere, although the person would not, under the law of his domicil, be deemed capable of making it. . . .

In Pearl v. Hansborough, 9 Humph. 426, the rule was carried so far as to hold that where a married woman domiciled with her husband in the State of Mississippi, by the law of which a purchase by a married woman was valid and the property purchased went to her separate use, bought personal property in Tennessee, by the law of which married women were incapable of contracting, the contract of purchase was void and could not be enforced in Tennessee. Some authorities, on the other hand, would uphold a contract made by a party capable by the law of his domicil, though incapable by the law of the place of the contract. In re Hellmann's Will [L.R. 2 Eq. 363], and Saul v. His Creditors [17 Martin (La.) 569], above cited. But that alternative is not here presented.

The principal reasons on which continental jurists have maintained that personal laws of the domicil, affecting the status and capacity of all inhabitants of a particular class, bind them wherever they may go, appear to have been that each state has the rightful power of regulating the status and condition of its subjects . . . that laws limiting the capacity of infants or of married women are intended for their protection, and cannot therefore be dispensed with by their agreement; that all civilized states recognize the incapacity of infants and married women; and that a person, dealing with either, ordinarily has notice, by the apparent age or sex, that the person is likely to be of a class whom the laws protect, and is thus put upon inquiry how far, by the law of the domicil of the person, the protection extends.

. . .

In the great majority of cases, especially in this country, where it is so common to travel, or to transact business through agents, or to correspond by letter, from one state to another, it is more just, as well as more convenient, to have regard to the law of the place of the contract, as a uniform rule operating on all contracts of the same kind, and which the contracting parties may be presumed to have in contemplation when making their contracts, than to require them at their peril to know the domicil of those with whom they deal, and to ascertain the law of that domicil, however remote, which in many cases could not be done without such delay as would greatly cripple the power of contracting abroad at all. . . .

It is possible also that in a state where the common law prevailed in full force, by which a married woman was deemed incapable of binding herself by any contract whatever, it might be inferred that such an utter incapacity, lasting throughout the joint lives of husband and wife, must be considered as so fixed by the settled policy of the state, for the protection of its own citizens, that it could not be held by the courts of that state to yield to the law of another state in which she might undertake to contract.

But it is not true at the present day that all civilized states recognize the absolute incapacity of married women to make contracts. The tendency of modern legislation is to enlarge their capacity in this respect, and in many states they have nearly or quite the same powers as if unmarried. In Massachusetts, even at the time of the making of the contract in question, a married woman was vested by statute with a very extensive power to carry on business by herself, and to bind herself by contracts with regard to her own property, business and earnings; and, before the bringing of the present action, the power had been extended so as to include the making of all kinds of contracts, with any person but her husband, as if she were unmarried. There is therefore no reason of public policy which should prevent the maintenance of this action.

Judgment for the plaintiffs.

NOTES

(1) Under the reasoning of the court in the principal case, would the decision have been different if the seller had delivered the goods by the seller's

own wagon or truck to the buyer in Massachusetts? Did the change in Massachusetts law affect the outcome? Should it?

(2) Are the rules of contract law with respect to the time *when* a contract is made to be deemed determinative of the question *where* the contract was made, and therefore controlling on the choice-of-law problem as to the law governing the various elements of an interstate contract? What policies underlie contract rules as to the point in time when an agreement becomes obligatory?

(3) Why did the Milliken court feel that the problem involved in Pearl v. Hansborough was different and more difficult than the one it faced? Is it clear that the Milliken court was firmly wedded to the "place of contract" rule?

(4) If domicile is also an unsatisfactory connecting factor for the reasons urged by Chief Justice Gray, what choice-of-law rule would be fair and acceptable?

(5) In New York P telephoned D in Pennsylvania accepting an offer to enter into a reinsurance contract for which the New York Statute of Frauds required a writing because it was not to be performed in a year. Under the law of Pennsylvania the oral agreement was enforceable. The court acknowledged that the sounder view in contract law theory was Williston's position that "the place of contracting is where the acceptance is heard," but ruled that it would promote "uniformity" and discourage "forum-shopping" to "hold that acceptance by telephone of an offer takes place where the words are spoken." Linn v. Employer Reinsurance Corp., 392 Pa. 58, 139 A.2d 638 (1958).

(6) Union National Bank v. Chapman, 169 N.Y. 538, 62 N.E. 672 (1902). Defendant wife, a resident of Alabama, signed in that state a note as surety for the firm of which her husband was a member. The note was subsequently discounted by the plaintiff bank in Illinois. It was found at the trial that "while it was the intention of the firm that the note should be negotiated and discounted in the state of Illinois she [the defendant] did not know of such intention. . . . " Under the law of Alabama, the defendant had no capacity to make the contract in question, but the law of Illinois was otherwise, and the plaintiff contended that this latter law should be applied since the note had "no legal inception" until it was discounted in Illinois. Held for the defendant. ". . . it seems clear that the capacity of Mrs. Chapman to contract must be determined by the law of the state where the contract was executed unless it can fairly be said that she . . . clearly understood and intended that it should be governed by the laws of another state."

In Chemical National Bank v. Kellogg, 183 N.Y. 92, 75 N.E. 1103 (1905), the defendant wife was held liable on facts analogous to those in the Chapman case on the ground that "since the defendant's endorsement gave no notice which would put a purchaser on guard, she is estopped from claiming that her endorsement was a New Jersey contract and therefore void."

(7) For a discussion of some of the factors of policy involved in the choice of the law governing capacity, see Cook, Logical and Legal Bases of the Conflict of Laws, Ch. XVI (1942); Currie, Married Women's Contracts: A Study in Conflict-of-Laws Method, 25 U.Chi.L.Rev. 227 (1958); Currie, The Verdict

of Quiescent Years: Mr. Hill and the Conflict of Laws, 28 U.Chi.L.Rev. 258 (1961).

SECTION 2.   ESCAPE DEVICES

A.   CHARACTERIZATION

1. *Substance vs. Procedure*

NOE v. UNITED STATES FIDELITY & GUARANTY CO.

Supreme Court of Missouri Division No. 2, 1960.
406 S.W.2d 666.

[This case appears at p. 409, supra.]

---

2. *Nature of the Action*

HAUMSCHILD v. CONTINENTAL CASUALTY CO.

Supreme Court of Wisconsin, 1959.
7 Wis.2d 130, 95 N.W.2d 814.

[A woman brought this action against her husband for personal injuries sustained through his negligence in a California motor accident. The couple were domiciled in Wisconsin. The trial court dismissed the action because under the local law of California the plaintiff could not recover. The plaintiff appealed.]

CURRIE, JUSTICE. This appeal presents a conflict of laws problem with respect to interspousal liability for tort growing out of an automobile accident. Which law controls, that of the state of the forum, the state of the place of wrong, or the state of domicile? Wisconsin is both the state of the forum and of the domicile while California is the state where the alleged wrong was committed. Under Wisconsin law a wife may sue her husband in tort. Under California law she cannot. . . .

This court was first faced with this question in Buckeye v. Buckeye, 1931, 203 Wis. 248, 234 N.W. 342. . . .

The principle enunciated in the Buckeye case and followed in subsequent Wisconsin cases, that the law of the place of wrong controls as to whether one spouse is immune from suit in tort by the other, is

the prevailing view in the majority of jurisdictions in this country.
. . .

[The court refers to the writings of Messrs. Cook, Rheinstein, Rabel and Ford, and outlines and quotes from Emery v. Emery, 45 Cal.2d 421, 289 P.2d 218 [1955], "the first case to break the ice", and Koplik v. C.P. Trucking Corp., 27 N.J. 1, 141 A.2d 34.]

. . . it is our considered judgment that this court should adopt the rule that, whenever the courts of this state are confronted with a conflict of laws problem as to which law governs the capacity of one spouse to sue the other in tort, the law to be applied is that of the state of domicile. We, therefore, expressly overrule the cases of Buckeye v. Buckeye, supra; . . . the instant decision should not be interpreted as a rejection by this court of the general rule that ordinarily the substantive rights of parties to an action in tort are to be determined in the light of the law of the place of wrong. This decision merely holds that incapacity to sue because of marital status presents a question of family law rather than tort law. . . .

. . . While the appellant's counsel did not request that we over-rule Buckeye v. Buckeye, supra, and the subsequent Wisconsin cases dealing with this particular conflict of laws problem, he did specifical-ly seek to have this court apply California's conflict of laws principle, that the law of the domicile is determinative of interspousal capacity to sue, to this particular case. . . .

Wisconsin certainly should not adopt the much criticized renvoi principle in order not to overrule the Buckeye v. Buckeye line of cases, and still permit the plaintiff to recover. Such a result we be-lieve would contribute far more to produce chaos in the field of con-flict of laws than to overrule the Buckeye v. Buckeye line of cases and adopt a principle the soundness of which has been commended by so many reputable authorities.

Judgment reversed and cause remanded for further proceedings not inconsistent with this opinion.

Fairchild, Justice (concurring). I concur in the reversal of the judgment, but do not find it necessary to re-examine settled Wiscon-sin law in order to do so. . . .

1. *Solution of this case without overruling previous decisions.*
. . . . It has been the rule in Wisconsin that the existence or nonex-istence of immunity because of family relationship is substantive and not merely procedural, and is to be determined by the law of the lo-cus state. The law of California is that the existence or nonexistence of immunity is a substantive matter, but that it is an element of the law of status, not of tort. . . . Thus it makes no difference under the facts of this case whether we look directly to the law of Wiscon-sin to determine that immunity is not available as a defense or look to the law of Wisconsin only because California, having no general tort

principle as to immunity, classifies immunity as a matter of status.
. . .

I would dispose of the present case upon the theory that California law governs the existence of the alleged cause of action and that in California the immunity question can not be decided by resort to the law of torts but rather the law of status. I would leave to a later case the consideration of whether the Wisconsin rule of choice of law as to the defense of family immunity should remain as heretofore or, if it is to be changed, which rule will be best.

NOTES

(1) It will be noted that the Haumschild case would invariably call for application of the law of the state of the couple's domicile to determine issues of interspousal immunity. Is that rule overly broad? Should a distinction be drawn between a situation where, as in the Haumschild case, there is no immunity under the law of the state of domicile but immunity under the law of the state of injury and the converse situation? What would be the rationale of such a distinction? Most of the later cases have applied the domicile's rule even in a case where there was immunity under the law of the domicile. See, e. g., Zurzola v. General Motors Corp., 503 F.2d 403 (3d Cir. 1974); Wartell v. Formusa, 34 Ill.2d 57, 213 N.E.2d 544 (1966); Balts v. Balts, 273 Minn. 419, 142 N.W.2d 66 (1966); Gordon v. Gordon, 118 N.H. 356, 387 A.2d 339 (1978); McSwain v. McSwain, 420 Pa. 86, 215 A.2d 677 (1966); but cf. Purcell v. Kapelski, 444 F.2d 380 (3d Cir. 1971).

(2) In Haynie v. Hanson, 16 Wis.2d 299, 114 N.W.2d 443 (1962), the wife was injured in Wisconsin as a result of a collision between automobiles driven by her husband and by one Hanson. The wife brought suit against Hanson and he sought contribution from the husband's liability insurer. Hanson's cross-complaint was dismissed on the ground that under the law of Illinois, where the spouses were domiciled, one spouse has no capacity to sue the other spouse in tort.

Haynie was in effect overruled *sub silentio* in Zelinger v. State Sand and Gravel Co., 38 Wis.2d 98, 156 N.W.2d 466 (1968) where the court applied an interests analysis.

(3) See, Jayme, Interspousal Immunity: Revolution and Counter-revolution in American Tort Conflicts, 40 S.Cal.L.Rev. 307 (1967).

(4) Similar problems of intrafamily immunity arise in tort suits between parents and children. See Emery v. Emery, 45 Cal.2d 421, 289 P.2d 218 (1955); Aurora National Bank v. Anderson, 132 Ill.App.2d 217, 268 N.E.2d 552 (1971); Ehrenzweig, Parental Immunity in the Conflict of Laws, 23 U.Chi.L.Rev. 474 (1956).

———

LEVY v. DANIELS' U–DRIVE AUTO RENTING CO., 108 Conn. 333, 143 A. 163, 61 A.L.R. 646 (1928): Defendant, a Connecticut automobile rental agency, rented a car in that state. The Connecticut lessee's negligent driving in Massachusetts caused injury to plaintiff, his guest, who was also a Connecticut resident. Plaintiff sued under a

Connecticut statute which made the lessor of a motor vehicle "liable for any damage to any person or property caused by the operation of such motor vehicle while so rented or leased." Judgment for the plaintiff was affirmed.

WHEELER, C.J. . . . It is the defendant's contention . . . that the action set forth in the complaint is one of tort and since Massachusetts has no statute like, or substantially like, the Connecticut Act it must be determined by the common law of that State, under which the plaintiff must prove, to prevail, the negligence of the defendant in renting a defective motor vehicle and in failing to disclose the defect. If this were the true theory of the complaint, the conclusion thus reached must have followed. . . . The plaintiff concedes the correctness of this. His counsel, however, construe the complaint as one in its <u>nature contractual</u>. . . .

. . . The statute gives, in terms, the injured person a right of action against the defendant which rented the automobile to Sack, though the injury occurred in Massachusetts. It was a right which the statute gave directly, not derivatively, to the injured person as a consequence of the contract of hiring. The purpose of the statute was not primarily to give the injured person a right of recovery against the tortious operator of the car, but to protect the safety of traffic upon highways by providing an incentive to him who rented motor vehicles to rent them to competent and careful operators by making him liable for damage resulting from the tortious operation of the rented vehicles. . . . The rental of motor vehicles to any but competent and careful operators, or to persons of unknown responsibility, would be liable to result in injury to the public upon or near highways, and this imminent danger justified, as a reasonable exercise of the police power, this statute, which requires all who engage in this business to become responsible for any injury inflicted upon the public by the tortious operation of the rented motor vehicle. . . . The statute made the liability of the person renting motor vehicles a part of every contract of hiring of a motor vehicle in Connecticut. . . .

If the liability of this defendant under this statute is contractual, no question can arise as to the plaintiff's right to enforce this contract, provided the obligation imposed upon this defendant was for the "direct, sole and exclusive benefit" of the plaintiff. The contract was made in Connecticut; at the instant of its making the statute made a part of the contract of hiring the liability of the defendant which the plaintiff seeks to enforce. The law inserted in the contract this provision. The statute did not create the liability; it imposed it in case the defendant voluntarily rented the automobile. . . . The right of the plaintiff as a beneficiary of this contract to maintain this action is no longer an open question in this State. . . . The contract was made for him and every other member of the public.

NOTES

(1) Suppose Connecticut law had allowed the rental agency to sue the driver-lessee for indemnity and he had pleaded as a defense that under Massachusetts law he would not have been liable to his guest passenger because of a defense given by the Massachusetts guest statute. Would the defense be allowable in the Connecticut third-party action? Cf. Haynie v. Hanson, 16 Wis.2d 299, 114 N.W.2d 443 (1962), p. 453, note 2, supra.

(2) As the court analyzed the problem in Levy, would it have made any difference if the plaintiff had been a Massachusetts resident? Should it make a difference?

GRANT v. McAULIFFE

Supreme Court of California, 1953.
41 Cal.2d 859, 264 P.2d 944, 42 A.L.R.2d 1162.

[Pullen died shortly after and as a result of an Arizona automobile accident. After his death, plaintiffs sued the California administrator of Pullen's estate for injuries sustained as a result of Pullen's alleged negligence which caused the accident. All parties were residents of California.

Under Arizona law tort actions do not survive the tortfeasor's death; under California law they do. The court below granted a motion to abate the suits on the ground that Arizona law applied and the causes of action did not survive.]

TRAYNOR, JUSTICE. . . . the answer to the question whether the causes of action against Pullen survived and are maintainable against his estate depends on whether Arizona or California law applies. In actions on torts occurring abroad, the courts of this state determine the substantive matters inherent in the cause of action by adopting as their own the law of the place where the tortious acts occurred, unless it is contrary to the public policy of this state. . . . "[N]o court can enforce any law but that of its own sovereign, and, when a suitor comes to a jurisdiction foreign to the place of the tort, he can only invoke an obligation recognized by that sovereign. A foreign sovereign under civilized law imposes an obligation of its own as nearly homologous as possible to that arising in the place where the tort occurs." Learned Hand, J., in Guinness v. Miller, D.C., 291 F. 769, 770. But the forum does not adopt as its own the procedural law of the place where the tortious acts occur. It must, therefore, be determined whether survival of causes of action is procedural or substantive for conflict of laws purposes.

This question is one of first impression in this state. The precedents in other jurisdictions are conflicting. . . . Before his death, the injured person himself has a separate and distinct cause of action and, if it survives, the same cause of action can be enforced by the personal representative of the deceased against the tortfeasor. The survival statutes do not create a new cause of action, as do the wrongful death statutes. . . . They merely prevent the abatement of the cause of action of the injured person, and provide for its enforcement by or against the personal representative of the deceased. They are analogous to statutes of limitation, which are procedural for conflict of laws purposes and are governed by the domestic law of the forum. . . .

Defendant contends, however, that the characterization of survival of causes of action as substantive or procedural is foreclosed by Cort v. Steen, 36 Cal.2d 437, 442, 224 P.2d 723, where it was held that the California survival statutes were substantive and therefore did not apply retroactively. The problem in the present proceeding, however, is not whether the survival statutes apply retroactively, but whether they are substantive or procedural for purposes of conflict of laws. " 'Substance' and 'procedure,' . . . are not legal concepts of invariant content." . . . and a statute or other rule of law will be characterized as substantive or procedural according to the nature of the problem for which a characterization must be made. . . .

Defendant also contends that a distinction must be drawn between survival of causes of action and revival of actions, and that the former are substantive but the latter procedural. . . . The distinction urged by defendant is not a valid one. . . . in most "revival" statutes, substitution of a personal representative in place of a deceased party is expressly conditioned on the survival of the cause of action itself. . . .

Since we find no compelling weight of authority for either alternative, we are free to make a choice on the merits. We have concluded that survival of causes of action should be governed by the law of the forum. Survival is not an essential part of the cause of action itself but relates to the procedures available for the enforcement of the legal claim for damages. Basically the question is one of the administration of decedents' estate, which is a purely local proceeding. The problem here is whether the causes of action that these plaintiffs had against Pullen before his death survive as liabilities of his estate. . . . Decedent's estate is located in this state, and letters of administration were issued to defendant by the courts of this state. The responsibilities of defendant, as administrator of Pullen's estate, for injuries inflicted by Pullen before his death are governed by the laws of this state. . . . Today, tort liabilities of the sort involved in these actions are regarded as compensatory. When, as in the present case, all of the parties were residents of this state, and the estate of the deceased tortfeasor is being administered in this state, plaintiffs' right to prosecute their causes of action is governed by the laws of this state relating to administration of estates. . . .

SCHAUER, JUSTICE. I dissent. . . . [E]ven more regrettable than the failure to either follow or unequivocally overrule the cited cases . . . is the character of the "rule" which is now promulgated: the majority assert that henceforth "a statute or other rule of law will be characterized as substantive or procedural according to the nature of the problem for which a characterization must be made," thus suggesting that the court will no longer be bound to consistent enforcement or uniform application of "a statute or other rule of law" but will instead apply one "rule" or another as the untrammeled whimsy of the majority may from time to time dictate, "according to the nature of the problem" as they view it in a given case. This concept of the majority strikes deeply at what has been our proud boast that ours was a government of laws rather than of men.

Although any administration of an estate in the courts of this State is local in a procedural sense, the rights and claims both in favor of and against such an estate are substantive in nature, and vest irrevocably at the date of death. . . .

NOTES

(1) Justice Traynor said the dispositive question in the case was "whether survival of causes of action is procedural or substantive for conflict of laws purposes." Did his opinion answer the question? If so, in what words? On the basis of the materials in Chapter 7, what are the best arguments pro and con?

(2) If Pullen had been a resident of Arizona instead of California and all else had been the same (with ancillary administration of the Pullen estate permitted in California), should the result have been different? What if suit had been brought in Arizona? If not Pullen, but the plaintiffs, had been Arizona residents, what result in each state? The survival rule of the place of injury has generally been applied in the cases, despite the steady waning of the non-survival rule. See Nelson v. Eckert, 231 Ark. 348, 329 S.W.2d 426 (1959); Allen v. Nessler, 247 Minn. 230, 76 N.W.2d 793 (1956); Tice v. E. I. DuPont de Nemours & Co., 144 W.Va. 24, 106 S.E.2d 107 (1958).

(3) "It may not be amiss to add a postscript that although the opinion [Grant v. McAuliffe] is my own, I do not regard it as ideally articulated, developed as it had to be against the brooding background of a petrified forest. Yet I would make no more apology for it than that in reaching a rational result it was less deft than it might have been to quit itself of the familiar speech of choice of law." Traynor, Is This Conflict Really Necessary?, 37 Texas L.Rev. 657, 670 (1959). How could the opinion have been made more "deft"? Consider the opinion by the same judge in Bernkrant v. Fowler, p. 609, infra.

3. *Other Ploys Involving Characterization and Definition*

The hard-and-fast rules could be manipulated without re-characterizing the issue as lying in one substantive area rather than another. For example, the court might concede that as presented the issue was a matter of contract law but then find an alternate formulation of the issue, implicating a new connecting factor, and thus bring into play State Y's law instead of State X's. Thus, characterizing a contract issue as one involving the validity of the bargain or the scope of the obligation instead of one involving the adequacy of performance or the justifiability of discharge of a promisor might have the desired effect of bringing the disputed issue under a different rule of decision from the one that would have been arrived at by using the choice-of-law rule triggered by another characterization.

If re-characterization of the issue was not feasible, another option was to play with the meaning of a key term, such as the place of contracting, in an agreed-upon choice-of-law rule—to achieve palatable, if at times unexpected, results.

LOUIS–DREYFUS v. PATERSON STEAMSHIPS, LIMITED

United States Circuit Court of Appeals, Second Circuit, 1930.
43 F.2d 824.

Appeal from the District Court of the United States for the Western District of New York.

Libel by Louis-Dreyfus and another doing business under the firm name and style of Louis-Dreyfus & Company, against Paterson Steamships, Limited. The libel was dismissed (35 F.2d 353), and libellants appeal.

L. HAND, CIRCUIT JUDGE. The libellants at Duluth shipped a parcel of wheat upon two ships of the respondent and received in exchange bills of lading, Duluth to Montreal, "with transshipment at Port Colbourne, Ontario." These contained an exception for "dangers of navigation, fire and collision," but nothing further which is here relevant. The respondent exercised its right of reshipment, unladed the wheat at Port Colbourne, stored it in an elevator, and reladed thirty-five thousand bushels in another ship, the Advance, belonging to one Webb, chartered by the respondent's agent, the Hall Shipping Company, for that purpose. This ship safely carried her cargo until she reached the entrance to the Cornwall Canal in the St. Lawrence River, where she took the ground, stove in her bottom and sank. The suit is for the resulting damage to the wheat.

The respondent . . . relied upon the Harter Act (46 U.S.C.A. secs. 190–195) and the Canadian Water-Carriage of Goods Act (9–10 Edward VII, Chap. 81), which covers among other ships those "carrying goods from any port in Canada to any other port in Canada" (section 3). . . .

We shall assume arguendo that section three of the Harter Act (46 U.S.C.A. sec. 192) did not cover the case; verbally it only includes "vessels transporting merchandise or property to or from any port in the United States." . . .

The important question is whether we should look to Canadian law at all. Here is a contract of carriage, made in Minnesota without any relevant exceptions, to be performed partly in the United States and partly in Canada; the carrier fails in performing that part of it which is to take place in Canada; he does not safely transport the grain from the entrance of the canal to Montreal. The law of the place of that performance excuses him for those faults in navigation which have caused the loss. Does that law control? Liverpool & G. W. S. Co. v. Phenix Ins. Co., 129 U.S. 397, decided that the validity of a provision in a contract of carriage, limiting the carrier's common-law duty, was to be determined by the law of the place where the contract was made, and this is well-settled law . . . .. It is of course only an instance of the usual rule that the law of the place where promises are made determines whether they create a contract . . . ; that law alone attaches any legal consequences to acts within its territory.

On the other hand, it is always said that as to matters of performance the law of the place of performance controls. Andrews v. Pond, 13 Pet. 65, 78; Scudder v. Union National Bank, 91 U.S. 408; Pritchard v. Norton, 106 U.S. 124; Hall v. Cordell, 142 U.S. 116, though in application the boundaries of this doctrine are not easy to find, as the last two cases cited illustrate very well. An exchange of mutual promises, or whatever other acts may create a contract for future performance, do not put the obligor under any immediate constraint, except so far as the doctrine of anticipatory breach demands. A present obligation arises only in the sense that it is then determined that when the time for performance arrives, his conduct shall not be open to his choice. For the present nothing is required of him; he can commit no fault and incur no liability. When the time comes for him to perform, if he fails, the law requires him to give the equivalent of the neglected performance; that compulsion is the sanction imposed by the state and the measure of the obligation. The default must indeed be at the place of performance, but the promisor need not himself be there, nor may he there have any property to respond. In such cases it is impossible to say that any liability arises under the law of that place; yet it would be exceedingly inconvenient to hold that it depended upon the law of the place where the promisor chanced to be at the time of performance, especially if such a doctrine were extended to all places where he has any property. In the interest of certainty and uniformity there must be some definite place fixed whose law shall control, wherever the suit arises. Whether the place of performance is chosen because of the likelihood that the obligor will be there present at the time of performance, or—what is nearly the same thing—because the agreement presupposes that he shall be, is not important. All we need say here is that the same law which determines what liabilities shall arise upon nonperformance, must determine any excuses for nonperformance, which are no more than exceptions to those liabilities.

The authorities in general support this view; as, for example, in the case of a moratorium (Rouquette v. Overmann, L.R. 10 Q.B. 525); of payment upon a forged indorsement (Kessler v. Armstrong Cork Co., 158 F. 744 (C.C.A.2); Belestin v. First National Bank, 177 Mo. App. 300, 164 N.Y.S. 160); of the delivery of a note as payment (Tarbox v. Childs, 165 Mass. 408, 43 N.E. 124) . . . In the case at bar, the Canadian law says that performance of the contract of carriage, as respects navigation, shall be excused if the owner uses due care to examine his ship and make her fit for her voyage, to man and victual her and the like. The conduct so specified is thus made an excuse for his failure to carry the goods safely to their destination as he has promised to do. That is exactly like any other excuse for such failure; delay is as much a breach as default; payment not specified is no payment; delivery to another, no delivery. . . .

We conclude that if the Advance was in fact seaworthy, the respondent was excused by virtue of the Canadian statute, and in that event we need not consider the issue of due diligence. . . .

[The court found there was an issue of fact as to defect in construction, which called for new proof.]

Decree reversed; cause remanded to be reheard upon the issue above mentioned.

NOTES

(1) Would Judge Hand have held that American law governed in the Louis-Dreyfus case if the ship had sunk in American waters?

(2) It is generally recognized that the law of the place of performance regulates matters involving the mode of performance, as, for example, the proper medium of payment and in the case of negotiable instruments the time and form of presentment, protest and notice. For other examples, see Restatement, Second, Conflict of Laws § 206 (1971).

B. RENVOI

UNIVERSITY OF CHICAGO v. DATER

Supreme Court of Michigan, 1936.
277 Mich. 658, 270 N.W. 175.

In November, 1928, negotiations were commenced to secure a loan in the sum of $75,000 on a piece of property in Chicago. The property was owned by George R. Dater and John R. Price of Benton Harbor, Mich. . . . Plaintiff agreed to make the loan if it could be assured that the title was good. A trust deed and certain promissory notes were drawn up with George R. Dater and Nellie E. Dater, his wife, and John R. Price and Clara A. Price, his wife, as parties of the first part, and the Chicago Title & Trust Company, as trustee, and as party of the second part. The notes were payable in the city of Chicago and at such place as the legal holder might appoint. The trust mortgage and notes were sent by mail to the Benton Harbor State Bank for the signature of the parties involved. The papers were signed in Benton Harbor, Mich., about December 8, 1928, and mailed to plaintiff's agent in the city of Chicago where the trust deed was placed on record, then it was found that there were some objections to certain delinquent taxes of 1927. Further negotiations followed, and finally on January 3, 1929, and after the tax objections were cleared in the title, the loan was actually made and the money paid over by check made payable to Mr. and Mrs. Dater and Mr. and Mrs. Price and cashed in Chicago, Ill.

January 29, 1929, John R. Price died, and it is conceded that Mrs. Price became the actual and record owner of at least one-half of the property after the death of her husband. Subsequent to December 1, 1933, foreclosure proceedings were commenced on the property and the property purchased at chancery sale. Suit was filed in Michigan . . . and on June 18, 1935, judgment was rendered in favor of plaintiff against George R. Dater in the amount of $15,536.32 and from which no appeal has been taken. On the same date judgment was entered in favor of Clara Price of no cause for action, from which judgment plaintiff appeals.*

WIEST, JUSTICE. . . . The instant case does not involve conflict of laws relative to the construction, force, and effect of the instruments, signed or executed in one state to be performed in another, but that of capacity of Mrs. Price to enter into such an obligation in this state. . . .

It must be agreed that this case is governed by the law of Michigan or of Illinois. If by the law of Michigan, it is clear, and is not disputed that defendant has no personal liability on the note, recoverable from her separate estate.

Assuming, however, that by the Michigan law of the forum the case is governed by the law of Illinois, it presents the unique situation in the realm of conflict of laws that by the law of Illinois, Burr v. Beckler, 264 Ill. 230, 106 N.E. 206, the case is governed by the law of Michigan.

In Burr v. Beckler, the wife, a resident of Illinois, was sojourning temporarily in Florida. Her husband owed a concern in Illinois, of which he was treasurer, on an overdraft. He informed his wife that he could borrow the necessary money to pay the overdraft from an estate of which he was trustee. The wife executed a note and trust deed in Florida and mailed them to her husband, as trustee, at Chicago, Ill., as he had directed her to do. The husband also signed the trust deed, but the opinion does not state when. The court held that delivery of the note and trust deed by the wife was complete in Flori-

---

* This statement of facts is from the
dissenting opinion of Sharpe, J.

da, the law of that state governed her capacity to contract, and, because she was not competent to enter into a contract under the law of Florida, her note and trust deed were void.

The question is not whether the decision is in harmony with the law of Michigan, but whether it governs this case. Here, manual delivery was as complete as in the Burr Case because it was made to a bank which had been designated by the mortgagee for that purpose.

In neither case had there been a binding engagement by the mortgagee to make the loan prior to the delivery. In neither case had the money been paid in advance of the delivery or contemporaneously therewith. There is nothing in the Burr Case to indicate that the mortgagee could not have refused to make the loan or that the mortgagors could not have refused to take the money or could not have abandoned the matter after the wife deposited the papers in the mail. The Burr opinion indicates no circumstance fixing the effect of the manual delivery which is not present here. The Burr Case is directly applicable, and, consequently, under the law of Illinois, it must be held that the capacity of defendant Clara A. Price is governed by the law of Michigan. Under the law of Michigan, a married woman cannot bind her separate estate through personal engagement for the benefit of others. Defendant Price is not liable.

Affirmed, with costs to defendant Price.

SHARPE, JUSTICE (dissenting). It is conceded that under the law of Illinois a married woman is as free to contract as a man, while in Michigan a married woman has not the legal capacity to bind herself or her separate estate by signing these notes. 3 Comp.Laws 1929, sec. 13057.

The plaintiff contends that the contract was an Illinois contract; that the signing of the notes in Michigan was not the final act in the making of the contract, but rather a preliminary step, the delivery of the note being conditional upon defendant's producing a satisfactory title, the approval of the title in Illinois was the last act necessary to make a legal delivery.

The general rule is well stated in John A. Tolman Co. v. Reed, 115 Mich. 71, 72 N.W. 1104, where the court said:

"The law is well settled that contracts must be construed and their validity determined by the law of the country where they were made, unless the contracting parties clearly appear to have had some other law in view." . . .

In the case at bar all of the negotiations for the loan occurred in Chicago, the property upon which the mortgage was placed was located in Chicago, and no money was to be paid by plaintiff until such time as the defendants could show good title to the property. . . . The final act in the making of the loan was the payment of the money in Chicago. This concluded the negotiations and made it an Illinois contract. . . .

BUSHNELL, J., concurred with SHARPE, J.

BUTZEL, JUSTICE (dissenting). I concur in the result reached by JUSTICE SHARPE. The place of contracting controls the question of the capacity of the parties to contract. . . .

We do not believe that the case of Burr v. Beckler, 264 Ill. 230, 106 N.E. 206, should in any way be controlling on this court in determining the lex loci contractus. The problem in the instant case is termed by the authorities as one of "qualifications." The prevailing view in answer to the problem is that the law of the forum should control on the question of lex loci contractus. . . .

Were we not to be controlled by our own law and obliged each time to ascertain what a foreign state would have held under similar circumstances, our decisions would be in hopeless confusion, and it would be necessary each time to examine the decisions of other states in determining the lex loci contractus. . . .

The judgment should be reversed, with costs to plaintiff.

BUSHNELL, J., concurred with BUTZEL, J.

NOTES

(1) In the third quoted paragraph of Justice Wiest's opinion, the word "law" appears four times. What meaning does the word bear in each instance? See Cook, The Logical and Legal Bases of the Conflict of Laws, 33 Yale L.J. 457, 471–473 (1924).

(2) In House v. Lefebvre, 303 Mich. 207, 6 N.W.2d 487 (1942), which involved a factual situation similar to that in University of Chicago v. Dater, the Supreme Court of Michigan determined the capacity of the defendant wife solely with reference to the internal law of Ohio where the note was delivered to the creditor. No consideration was given to the Ohio choice-of-law rule.

USING THE CONFLICTS RULES OF THE "STATE OF APPLICABLE LAW"

The use by a forum directed by its choice-of-law rule to apply the "law" of another state afforded a means of avoiding the undesirable results seemingly dictated by a particular choice-of-law rule. This practice—unhelpfully called *renvoi*—was viewed as respectable in determining interests in land, as illustrated by In re Schneider's Estate (p. 30, supra); In re the Duke of Wellington, [1947] Ch. 506, aff'd [1948] Ch. 118. It was also acceptable when the validity of decree of divorce was in question, as in Armitage v. Attorney General, [1906] p. 33, n. 2, supra. Otherwise, as Surrogate Frankenthaler observed in the Schneider case, the first Restatement rejected the renvoi approach by laying down the principle that whenever reference was made to foreign law, the internal rules of law of the foreign state were to be applied, not the conflicts rules.

Yet a broader use of the referent state's conflicts rules at times offered a way of escaping from its unattractive internal rule in a particular case. In Haumschild, p. 451, infra, the blandishment was resisted by the majority; in University of Chicago v. Dater, supra, however, it was not resisted.

NOTES

(1) Until the dawn of the new era in choice of law with the advent of "interests" analysis and policy-centered approaches, renvoi had few champions. An exception was Professor Erwin N. Griswold, who thought the utility of the doctrine had been underestimated. Griswold, Renvoi Revisited, 51 Harv.L.Rev. 1165 (1938).

(2) One of the rare examples of the use of renvoi in a torts case occurred in applying the Federal Tort Claims Act, 28 U.S.C.A. § 1346(b). See Richards v. United States, 369 U.S. 1 (1962) which is discussed at p. 445, note 3, supra.

(3) For discussion of modern approaches to renvoi, see Pfau v. Trent Aluminum Co., p. 556, infra; Restatement, Second, Conflict of Laws § 8, Comment *k* (1971).

C. PUBLIC POLICY

KILBERG v. NORTHEAST AIRLINES, INC.

Court of Appeals of New York, 1961.
9 N.Y.2d 34, 172 N.E.2d 526.

[Kilberg, a New York domiciliary, purchased in New York a ticket from the defendant airline, which was incorporated in Massachusetts, for transportation from New York to Nantucket, Massachusetts. The airplane crashed in Nantucket and Kilberg was killed. Both Massachusetts and New York have wrongful death statutes. The Massachusetts statute limited recovery against a common carrier to not less than $2,000 or more than $15,000. By way of contrast, the New York Constitution forbade any limitation on the amount of recovery. Kilberg's administrator brought suit in New York for the death. Two of the three causes of action pleaded in the complaint were considered on appeal. The first was a cause of action under the Massachusetts wrongful death statute; the second was a cause of action for breach of an alleged contract of safe carriage asking for $150,000 in damages. The trial court denied a motion to dismiss the second cause of action on the ground that, as it was in contract, the law of New York, the place of contracting, governed. The Appellate Division reversed and dismissed the second cause of action because, however labeled, it was in tort for negligently causing death and was subject to the Massachusetts limitation. The Court of Appeals unanimously affirmed the dismissal of the second cause of action, but a majority of the court stated that the first cause of action for wrongful death was not subject to the Massachusetts limitation of damages.]

DESMOND, C.J. . . . If the alleged contract breach had caused injuries not resulting in death, a New York-governed contract suit would, we will assume, be available. . . . But it is law long settled that wrongful death actions, being unknown to the common law, derive from statutes only and that the statute which governs such an action is that of the place of wrong. . . .

This does not mean, however, that for the alleged wrong plaintiff cannot possibly recover more than the $15,000 maximum specified in the Massachusetts act. Modern conditions make it unjust and anomalous to subject the traveling citizen of this State to the varying laws of other States through and over which they move. The number of States limiting death case damages has become smaller over the years but there are still 14 of them. . . . An air traveler from New York may in a flight of a few hours' duration pass through several of those commonwealths. His plane may meet with disaster in a State he never intended to cross but into which the plane has flown because of bad weather or other unexpected developments, or an airplane's catastrophic descent may begin in one State and end in another. The place of injury becomes entirely fortuitous. Our courts should if possible provide protection for our own State's people against unfair and anachronistic treatment of the lawsuits which result from these disasters. . . .

Since both Massachusetts . . . and New York . . . authorize wrongful death suits against common carriers, the only controversy is as to amount of damages recoverable. New York's public policy prohibiting the imposition of limits on such damages is strong, clear and old. Since the Constitution of 1894, our basic law has been (N.Y.Const., art. I, § 16; N.Y.Const. [1894], art. I, § 18) that "The right of action now existing to recover damages for injuries resulting in death, shall never be abrogated; and the amount recoverable shall not be subject to any statutory limitation." Each later revision of the State Constitution has included this same prohibition against limitations of death action damages. . . . We will still require plaintiff to sue on the Massachusetts statute but we refuse on public policy grounds to enforce one of its provisions as to damages. . . .

As to conflict of law rules it is of course settled that the law of the forum is usually in control as to procedures including remedies . . . . As to whether the measure of damages should be treated as a procedural or a substantive matter in wrongful death cases, there is

. . . no controlling New York decision . . . It is open to us, therefore, particularly in view of our own strong public policy as to death action damages, to treat the measure of damages in this case as being a procedural or remedial question controlled by our own State policies. . . .

From all of this it follows that while plaintiff's second or contract cause of action is demurrable, his first count declaring under the Massachusetts wrongful death action is not only sustainable but can be enforced, if the proof so justifies, without regard to the $15,000 limit. Plaintiff, therefore, may apply if he be so advised for leave to amend his first cause of action accordingly. . . .*

FULD, J., concurred in the decision on the second count. He felt foreclosed by earlier decisions, though if the matter were of first impression New York might be deemed the jurisdiction having "the most significant contact or contacts".

FROESSEL, JUDGE (concurring). We concur for affirmance of the judgment appealed from, dismissing plaintiff's second cause of action. We should reach no other question. . . .

Plaintiff's right to maintain this action must . . . stem from the provisions of the Massachusetts statute (Mass.Gen.Stat., ch. 229, § 2). That statute, however, expressly limits the extent of the right given, and declares that the damages assessed thereunder shall not be more than $15,000. . . . The majority, by giving extraterritorial effect to our prohibition against the limitation of recovery in such actions, would permit plaintiff to recover on the basis of the foreign law, and yet not be bound by its express limitation. . . .

No sound reason appears why our courts, in enforcing such a right at all, should not enforce it in its entirety. . . .

The position adopted by the majority may result in the situation where, in a single airplane crash in which numerous passengers from various States are killed, a different law will be applied in each action resulting therefrom. . . .

NOTES

(1) In Davenport v. Webb, 11 N.Y.2d 17, 183 N.E.2d 902 (1962), the court retracted the "procedural" basis of the Kilberg decision. That case involved an action for the wrongful death of persons domiciled in New York in an automobile collision in Maryland. A New York statute provided that a judgment for the plaintiff in a wrongful death action should include interest from the date of death. Maryland law did not authorize prejudgment interest. The Court of Appeals held that the New York statute could not properly be applied to provide for the inclusion of interest in the judgment, and that the Kilberg decision "must be held merely to express this State's strong public policy with respect to limitations in wrongful death actions."

---

* Kilberg's administrator ultimately settled for less than $15,000 and did not seek leave to amend his first cause of action. Presumably, this was because he did not believe he could prove greater damages. [Footnote by the editors.]

(2) Kilberg was followed in Pearson v. Northeast Airlines, Inc., 309 F.2d 553 (2d Cir. 1962; en banc opinion), overturning the decision of the panel, 307 F.2d 131 (1962). Erie Railroad Co. v. Tompkins, p. 683, infra, and its conflicts progeny were thought to compel the Federal court to echo the New York court's view of the wrongful death damage ceiling question, but no enthusiasm was registered for Chief Judge Desmond's sledgehammer use of the "public policy" argument. Judge Friendly's dissent from the en banc opinion is excerpted at p. 213, note 2, supra.

(3) The issue of applying ceilings on damages recoverable for wrongful death has been a prolific source of choice-of-law decisions. Not all the decisions are reconcilable, to put it mildly. See the cases collected in Section 4 of this chapter, infra.

(4) Criminal law. There seems to be universal agreement that if a court takes jurisdiction in a criminal case it will apply only its own penal law. Hence criminal law cases do not involve choice-of-law questions in the ordinary sense. However, there is the question whether the court will construe its own law as applicable to activities outside the state that cause criminal consequences within it, and to activities within the state that cause criminal consequences outside it. With rare exceptions, such as section 103 of the Model Penal Code, criminal law statutes do not deal explicitly with the question of their extraterritorial application. Generally speaking, the courts have purported to apply a strict territorial test in interpreting these statutes, but, in point of fact, they have often mitigated the rigidity of this test by resort to a variety of devices. So, for example, a defendant who shot a bullet into the state was said, in contemplation of law, to have accompanied the bullet on its flight. Simpson v. State, 92 Ga. 41, 17 S.E. 984 (1893). And a defendant who brought stolen goods into the state of the forum has been said to have engaged in a continuing theft and therefore to be guilty of larceny under that state's criminal law. Worthington v. State, 58 Md. 403 (1882). See generally Leflar, Conflict of Laws: Choice of Law in Criminal Cases, 25 Case Western Reserve L.Rev. 44 (1974).

RETROSPECTIVE ON DEVICES USED TO ESCAPE THE TRADITIONAL CHOICE–OF–LAW SYSTEM

Resort to characterization, renvoi and even a brute force type of public policy argument to convert hard-and-fast choice-of-law rules into more pliable ones showed that the courts were commendably sensitive to the value of tempering the rules with justice. However, in avoiding slot-machine, automatic application of the received choice-of-law rules, they surrendered some of the aspects of simplicity, certainty, and forum-proof uniformity that had been the pride of the vested rights era.

To many judges there was serious hypocrisy in giving the appearance of following inexorable commands in deciding multistate cases while actually adjudicating them by a process of result-selective subjectivity. The subjectivity came into the picture because of the many options confronting the judges as they deliberately chose the "inexorable" rule they wanted to be bound by. Many were restive about the illusory game they were playing. Starting in the 1950's several courts began to try to break free of the "Ice Age" of choice-of-law systematics. In their search for new approaches they leaned heavily on a profusion of theories that had been fermenting in the scholarly vats for decades. The transition was speeded by the American Law Institute's project, launched in 1951, to produce a second Restatement of Conflict of Laws to replace the predecessor volume published in 1934 under the influence of the vested rights ideology which Beale and other leading scholars so fully embraced.

SECTION 3. TRANSITION: THE SEARCH FOR NEW APPROACHES

A. EARLY GROPINGS

SCHMIDT v. DRISCOLL HOTEL, INC.

Minnesota Supreme Court, 1957.
249 Minn. 376, 82 N.W.2d 365.

GALLAGHER, JUSTICE. Plaintiff, Herbert G. Schmidt . . . instituted this action against the Driscoll Hotel, Inc., doing business as The Hook-Em-Cow Bar and Cafe in South St. Paul . . .

The complaint alleged that defendant illegally sold intoxicating liquors to Sorrenson to the extent of causing him to become intoxicated in defendant's establishment in South St. Paul so that shortly thereafter, as a proximate result thereof, plaintiff sustained injuries when an automobile driven by Sorrenson, in which plaintiff was a passenger, was caused to turn over near Prescott, Wisconsin.

Defendant . . . moved to dismiss the action on the ground that the pleadings failed to state a claim against the defendant . . .

On April 28, 1956, the trial court made its order granting defendant's motion . . . [on the ground] that "No penalty by way of collecting damages arose under M.S.A 340.95 [Civil Damage Act] . . . unless the illegal sale in the state was followed by an injury in the state. . . ."

This is an appeal from the judgment entered pursuant to the foregoing order.

1. . . . M.S.A. 340.95, commonly known as the Civil Damage Act, provides that: "Every * * * person who is injured in person or property, * * * by any intoxicated person, or by the intoxica-

tion of any person, has a right of action, in his own name, against any person who, by illegally selling, bartering or giving intoxicating liquors, caused the intoxication of such person, for all damages, sustained; * * *." . . .

2. It is defendant's position that the action is governed by the law of torts and that, since the last act in the series of events for which plaintiff instituted his action occurred in Wisconsin, which has no Civil Damage Act similar to § 340.95, the latter can have no application in determining plaintiff's rights or defendant's liability. In support thereof defendant cites Restatement, Conflict of Laws, § 377, which states:

"The place of wrong is in the state where the last event necessary to make an actor liable for an alleged tort takes place."

And § 378, which states:

"The law of the place of wrong determines whether a person has sustained a legal injury."

3. . . . plaintiff's damages are the result of two distinct wrongs—one committed by defendant in Minnesota when it sold Sorrenson intoxicating liquors in violation of M.S.A. 340.14, subd. 1; and one committed by Sorrenson in Wisconsin when his negligence caused the car in which plaintiff was riding to turn over. It cannot be disputed that, had plaintiff's action been against Sorrenson for his negligence, his rights would be governed by the law of Wisconsin applicable in tort actions of this kind. . . . But, even if at the time of the accident there had been in effect in Wisconsin a statute similar to § 340.95, it is doubtful if it could be applied to ascertain plaintiff's rights against defendant since there is nothing here to support a claim that defendant ever consented to be bound by Wisconsin law.
. . .

4. . . .

5. We feel that the principles in Restatement, Conflict of Laws, §§ 377 and 378, should not be held applicable to fact situations such as the present to bring about the result described and that a determination to the opposite effect would be more in conformity with principles of equity and justice. Here all parties involved were residents of Minnesota. Defendant was licensed under its laws and required to operate its establishment in compliance therewith. Its violation of the Minnesota statutes occurred here, and its wrongful conduct was complete within Minnesota when, as a result thereof, Sorrenson became intoxicated before leaving its establishment. The consequential harm to plaintiff, a Minnesota citizen, accordingly should be compensated for under M.S.A. 340.95 which furnishes him a remedy against defendant for its wrongful acts. By this construction, no greater burden is placed upon defendant than was intended by § 340.95.

6. In arriving at this conclusion, we have in mind decisions of a number of jurisdictions which have reached similar results in situa-

tions, which, though not involving civil damage acts, presented factual circumstances comparable to those here. Gordon v. Parker, D.C.D. Mass., 83 F.Supp. 40. . . .

In Gordon v. Parker, supra, an action for alienation of affections was instituted in Massachusetts by plaintiff, who, with his wife, was domiciled in Pennsylvania. Therein it appeared that defendant's wrongful acts had taken place in Massachusetts, and accordingly plaintiff sought the application of a Massachusetts statute relating to alienation of affections. Defendant contended that, since the matrimonial domicile of the parties was in Pennsylvania, which accordingly was the place where the ultimate wrong was done to plaintiff, only Pennsylvania law could be applied. [A Pennsylvania statute had abolished the tort of alienation of affections.] In denying this contention and applying the Massachusetts statute, the court stated, 83 F.Supp. 42:

"This is not a situation in which the interests of Pennsylvania plainly outweigh those of Massachusetts. The social order of each is implicated. As the place of matrimonial domicil, Pennsylvania has an interest in whether conduct in any part of the world is held to affect adversely the marriage relationship between its domiciliaries. But, as the place where the alleged . . . wrongdoer lives, Massachusetts also has an interest. She is concerned with conduct within her borders which in her view lowers the standards of the community where they occur. She also is concerned when her citizens intermeddle with other people's marriages." . . .

Reversed.

———

Can any choice-of-law rule be derived from the court's decision in the Schmidt case? What if either the plaintiff or Sorrenson had been Wisconsin residents?

Is the Minnesota court right that even if Wisconsin had had a Dram Shop Act paralleling Minnesota's, it probably would not have given Schmidt a right to sue the Minnesota defendant? Cf. Bernhard v. Harrah's Club, which is set forth at p. 538, infra.

In Steele v. Bulova Watch Co., 344 U.S. 280 (1952), Bulova sued Steele, an American citizen residing in Texas, for trademark infringement and unfair competition because Steele ran a watch business in Mexico City which involved stamping "Bulova" on watches he assembled and sold there. Steele argued that the United States could not project its laws into Mexico to enjoin or penalize conduct proper there. Steele lost. The Court declared that the United States is not barred by international law from governing the conduct of its citizens on the high seas or in foreign countries if the rights of other nations or their nationals are not infringed. The Court also pointed out that the Lanham Act could be construed to cover Steele's activities because he did not confine his operations to Mexico, but bought component parts in the United States and his spurious "Bulovas" found their way back into the United States, causing complaints from retail jewelers whose customers brought in defective "Bulovas" for repair.

Would the Steele case support the constitutionality of a Dram Shop Act that is construed to impose liability on saloon-keepers who, in some other state, sell drink to drivers who then cause injury in the state of enactment?

Would it be possible to draft black-letter rules that preserved the essence of Sections 377 and 378 of the first Restatement of Conflict of Laws and also ratified the result of Schmidt v. Driscoll Hotel, Inc.? Is the effort to sensitize the first Restatement's sweeping rules by breaking them down into narrower rules a useful enterprise?

NOTES

(1) Blamey v. Brown, 270 N.W.2d 884 (Minn.1978).   Plaintiff, a resident of Minnesota, started an evening attending a beer party in Minnesota.   After the beer had run out, plaintiff and a number of others drove to defendant's bar in Wisconsin which is located close to the Wisconsin-Minnesota border. More beer was purchased there and, some hours later, plaintiff was injured in an automobile accident in Minnesota.   Held for the plaintiff.   Recovery could not be based on the Minnesota Civil Damage Act referred to in the *Schmidt* case since this Act is applicable only to Minnesota barkeepers. However, defendant would be liable to plaintiff under the Minnesota common law rules of negligence, but not under those of Wisconsin.   In holding the Minnesota law applicable, the Court relied on Professor Leflar's "Choice-Influencing Considerations" which are discussed on pp. 479–480, infra.

(2) Does a decision by a court of F that restricts the protection of admonitory or conduct-prescribing rules to F's own citizens run afoul of Federal constitutional guarantees—the equal protection clause of the Fourteenth Amendment or the privileges and immunities clause in Article IV, section 2? See Currie and Schreter, Unconstitutional Discrimination in the Conflict of Laws: Equal Protection, 28 U.Chi.L.Rev. 1 (1960); Currie and Schreter, Unconstitutional Discrimination in the Conflict of Laws: Privileges and Immunities, 69 Yale L.J. 1323 (1960).

(3) For a case bearing on extraterritorial application of United States law in a labor dispute setting, see Windward Shipping (London) Ltd. v. American Radio Association, 415 U.S. 104, 94 S.Ct. 959, 39 L.Ed.2d 195 (1974).

See also the discussion at pp. 667–668, infra.

AUTEN v. AUTEN

Court of Appeals of New York, 1954.
308 N.Y. 155, 124 N.E.2d 99.

[This is an action by Mrs. Auten against Mr. Auten to recover installments owing under a separation agreement executed in New York in 1933.

The parties, married in England in 1917, continued to live there with their two children until 1931, when he deserted her and came to the United States. He obtained a Mexican divorce and married another woman. In 1933 Mrs. Auten came to New York to make some arrangement with the defendant, and there they executed a separation agreement under which he promised to pay 50 pounds a month for the support of herself and the children. In addition the agreement provided that the parties would continue to live apart, that neither should sue "in any action relating to their separation" and that the wife should not "cause any complaint to be lodged against . . . [the husband], in any jurisdiction by reason of the said alleged divorce or remarriage". The plaintiff immediately returned to England where she has continued to live with her children.

The defendant failed to live up to the agreement, making only a few payments. In 1934 the plaintiff filed a petition for separation in an English court, charging the defendant with adultery, and in 1938 an order was entered against him to pay alimony. The English action was instituted upon the advice of English counsel that it was the plaintiff's only means of obtaining support.

Having realized nothing through the English action, the plaintiff in 1947 instituted the present suit to recover the amounts alleged to be due under the 1933 separation agreement. The defendant claimed that the institution of the English suit was a repudiation of the agreement and ended plaintiff's right to payments under it. The trial court, agreeing with the defense, dismissed the complaint, and the Appellate Division affirmed the dismissal.]

FULD, J. . . . Both of the courts below, concluding that New York law was to be applied, held that under such law plaintiff's commencement of the English action and the award of temporary alimony constituted a rescission and repudiation of the separation agreement, requiring dismissal of the complaint. Whether that is the law of this state, or whether something more must be shown to effect a repudiation of the agreement . . . need not detain us, since in our view it is the law of England, not that of New York which is here controlling.

Choosing the law to be applied to a contractual transaction with elements in different jurisdictions is a matter not free from difficulty. The New York decisions evidence a number of different approaches to the question. See, e.g., Jones v. Metropolitan Life Ins. Co., 158 Misc. 466, 286 N.Y.S. 4.*

---

* The opinion in the Jones case stated: "The cases in New York take various positions on the question of which law governs the validity of a contract. In some, the place where the contract was made is said to be determinative. . . .

"Other cases maintain that the contract is governed by the law of the place of performance. . . . Still other cases rely on the intention of the parties to determine which law governs the contract. . . . The last position that the cases take is the one which assumes that it is the grouping of the various elements which have gone to make up the contract that determines which law governs."

Most of the cases rely upon the generally accepted rules that " 'All matters bearing upon the execution, the interpretation and the validity of contracts . . . are determined by the law of the place where the contract is made' ", while " 'all matters connected with its performance . . . are regulated by the law of the place where the contract, by its terms, is to be performed.' " . . . What constitutes a breach of the contract and what circumstances excuse a breach are considered matters of performance, governable, within this rule, by the law of the place of performance. . . .

Many cases appear to treat these rules as conclusive. Others consider controlling the intention of the parties and treat the general rules merely as presumptions or guideposts, to be considered along with all the other circumstances. . . . And still other decisions, including the most recent one in this court, have resorted to a method—first employed to rationalize the results achieved by the courts in decided cases, see Barber Co. v. Hughes, 223 Ind. 570, 586, 63 N.E.2d 417,—which has come to be called the "center of gravity" or the "grouping of contacts" theory of the conflict of laws. Under this theory, the courts, instead of regarding as conclusive the parties' intention or the place of making or performance, lay emphasis rather upon the law of the place "which has the most significant contacts with the matter in dispute". Rubin v. Irving Trust Co., 305 N.Y. 288, 305, 113 N.E.2d 424, 431 . . .

Although this "grouping of contacts" theory may, perhaps, afford less certainty and predictability than the rigid general rules . . . , the merit of its approach is that it gives to the place "having the most interest in the problem" paramount control over the legal issues arising out of a particular factual context, thus allowing the forum to apply the policy of the jurisdiction "most intimately concerned with the outcome of [the] particular litigation". 3 Utah L.Rev., pp. 498–499. Moreover, by stressing the significant contacts, it enables the court, not only to reflect the relative interests of the several jurisdictions involved . . . , but also to give effect to the probable intention of the parties and consideration to "whether one rule or the other produces the best practical result". Swift & Co. v. Bankers Trust Co., supra, 280 N.Y. 135, 141, 19 N.E.2d 992, 995; . . .

Turning to the case before us, examination of the respective contacts with New York and England compels the conclusion that it is English law which must be applied to determine the impact and effect to be given the wife's institution of the separation suit. It hardly needs stating that it is England which has all the truly significant contacts, while this state's sole nexus with the matter in dispute— entirely fortuitous, at that—is that it is the place where the agreement was made and where the trustee, to whom the moneys were in the first instance to be paid, had his office. The agreement effected a separation between British subjects, who had been married in England, had children there and lived there as a family for fourteen years. . . .

In short, then, the agreement determined and fixed the marital responsibilities of an English husband and father and provided for the support and maintenance of the allegedly abandoned wife and children who were to remain in England. It merely substituted the arrangements arrived at by voluntary agreement of the parties for the duties and responsibilities of support that would otherwise attach by English law. There is no question that England has the greatest concern in prescribing and governing those obligations, and in securing to the wife and children essential support and maintenance. . . .

It is, perhaps, not inappropriate to note that, even if we were not to place our emphasis on the law of the place with the most significant contacts, but were instead simply to apply the rule that matters of performance and breach are governed by the law of the place of performance, the same result would follow. Whether or not there was a repudiation, essentially a form of breach . . . , is also to be determined by the law of the place of performance, cf. Wester v. Casein Co. of America, 206 N.Y. 506, 100 N.E. 488; Restatement, Conflict of Laws, § 370, Caveat, and that place, so far as the wife's performance is concerned, is England. Whatever she had to do under the agreement—"live separate and apart from" her husband, "maintain, educate and support" the children and refrain from bringing "any action relating to [the] separation"—was to be done in England. True, the husband's payments were to be made to a New York trustee for forwarding to plaintiff in England, but that is of no consequence in this case. It might be if the question before us involved the manner or effect of payment to the trustee, but that is not the problem; we are here concerned only with the effect of the wife's performance. . . .

Since, then, the law of England must be applied, and since, at the very least, an issue exists as to whether the courts of that country treat the commencement of a separation action as a repudiation of an earlier-made separation agreement, summary judgment should not have been granted. . . .

Judgments reversed, etc.*

NOTES

(1) It will be noted that Judge Fuld detoured the issue of whether a correct construction of New York's contract law rules would have produced the same result as applying the English rule. Does by-passing that issue put the cart before the horse by treating as a choice-of-law problem an issue to which the supposedly "conflicting" rules may in fact give a single answer?

* The principal case is discussed in M. Traynor, Conflict of Laws: Professor Currie's Restrained and Enlightened Forum, 49 Calif.L.Rev. 845 (1961); Reese, Chief Judge Fuld and Choice of Law, 71 Colum.L.Rev. 548 (1971).

(2) Did Judge Fuld intend to say that if the "center of gravity" or "grouping of contacts" made English law governing and if by that law the wife had effectively repudiated the agreement, she would have lost the appeal, even if there had not been a repudiation under New York's law of contracts?

(3) By what tests did the court determine which contacts were "significant" or which state had the greatest "interest" or the most "intimate concern" in Auten v. Auten?

(4) In Haag v. Barnes, 9 N.Y.2d 554, 216 N.Y.S.2d 65, 175 N.E.2d 441 (1961), an unwed mother sued to establish paternity and support for her child. The putative father set up an Illinois agreement which provided support and which was valid under Illinois law, where it was executed, defendant resided, the child was born and payments were made. The agreement provided that it was to be governed by Illinois law. Purporting to follow Auten, the court, per Fuld, J., upheld the agreement under Illinois law even though under New York local law it would have been ineffective because it had not been approved by a court. For critical comment on the decision, see Ehrenzweig, The "Bastard" in the Conflict of Laws—A National Disgrace, 29 U.Chi.L.Rev. 498 (1962); Currie, Conflict, Crisis and Confusion in New York, 1963 Duke L.J. 1, reprinted in B. Currie, Selected Essays on the Conflict of Laws, Ch. 14, at pp. 727–739 (1963).

B. SCHOLARLY CAMPS

THE UNDERLYING CONSIDERATIONS

Two themes have run through the upheaval of recent decades concerning choice of law. One is the question of whether *any rules*, formulated *a priori*, can usefully and justly be applied to determine which substantive norm shall be the basis of decision in a multistate case, when one of the competing norms is found in the corpus juris of one state and the other (or others) in the body of substantive law of another state. The opposing thesis is that all that can be hoped for is a *method* of solving or approaching a solution to the choice of which of vying norms shall control a disputed issue in a multistate case. Adherents of this view generally assert for various—and sometimes inconsistent—reasons that choice-of-law rules serve no constructive purpose; that they are unsound in theory and foolish in practice for they purport to bind a court to decide a case on the basis of a "governing law" whose contents and relation to the issue in dispute may make its application in the particular instance an exercise in futility or a positive injustice.

A second pervasive theme comes to the fore if it is once conceded that choice-of-law rules are needed and are draftable. The question then becomes: What type of rules? Broad or narrow? Rigid or flexible? Dependent upon the contents of the particular competing norms or independent of them? An English conflicts scholar, as far back as 1951, put the first part of this question in cogent terms: "[I]t seems extraordinary that there should be so . . . much uncritical acceptance of the rule that tort liability is governed by the law of the place of wrong." He thought it not probable that courts will reach "socially desirable results if they apply the same conflicts rule to liability for automobile negligence, radio defamation, escaping animals, the seduction of women, economic conspiracies, and conversion." See Morris, The Proper Law of a Tort, 64 Harv.L.Rev. 881, 883 (1951). In his view the "proper law" would often not be the traditional "place of wrong." At about the same time, a more comprehensive analysis was ventured by two Columbia Law School conflicts teachers.

ELLIOTT E. CHEATHAM AND WILLIS L.M. REESE, "CHOICE OF THE APPLICABLE LAW," 52 Colum.L.Rev. 959 (1952).

When an occurrence has substantial elements in two or more states having different local laws, it is necessary to determine which of these laws shall govern the rights of the parties. The problem of choice thus presented is the most difficult one in conflict of laws. This difficulty is primarily a consequence of the youth and fluidity of the subject. Not only is precedent relatively sparse in this area; that which exists is frequently misleading. Guidance therefore cannot be sought, as in many other branches of the law, from an accepted body of settled rules. Rather the judge frequently finds himself forced to pursue the inquiry into basic questions of policy and value. . . .

The . . . policies, [that are] of significance in the great majority of cases where there is no express legislative direction on the subject of choice of law are discussed in what is conceived to be the order of their relative importance—subject to the constant warning that in large part this latter question depends on the facts of the particular case.

I. THE NEEDS OF THE INTERSTATE AND INTERNATIONAL SYSTEMS

Except in the comparatively rare situation where a court must follow the explicit directions of its legislature, the smooth functioning of the interstate and international systems in private law matters should be the basic consideration in the decision of every choice of law case. In no country are the needs of the interstate system more important than in the United States where business and social activities almost ignore state lines. . . .

Of necessity, this overriding policy is so vaguely worded as to be difficult of application. Frequently, it is well-nigh impossible to determine whether the needs of the interstate or international system would best be served by the resolution of a given dispute one way or the other. . . .

[In the rest of their article the authors listed in order of importance the policies they thought salient. A court should: apply its own local law, with which it is more familiar and adept, unless impelled by good reason not to; try to advance its local law purposes in deciding the choice-of-law question; try to advance certainty, predictability and uniformity of result; try to protect justified expectations; try to advance the policies of the state of dominant interest in the case; try to formulate rules of choice of law that will be easy for the court to apply; try to implement the broader local law substantive values involved; and try to achieve justice in the individual case.]

Currie: *The Governmental Interest Methodology*

One of the most influential conflicts scholars of the mid-20th century was the late Professor Brainerd Currie. He developed the governmental interests analysis, postulating that a choice-of-law case confronts a court with the problem of analyzing the policies that are in competition in the local law rules vying for application. His work fired the imagination and interest of many of the oncoming generation of conflicts scholars and attracted the support of a number of courts. For the 1964 edition of this book,* he prepared a succinct statement of his theory, the substance of which follows:

Currie begins by observing that a court may refer to foreign law for quite different purposes. One purpose is to find the "rule of decision"—the answer to such questions as: Is this a valid contract? Does this injury constitute an actionable wrong? On what principle is the estate of this decedent to be distributed? Another purpose is to find some "datum" made relevant by a known rule of decision [see, e.g., People v. Olah, p. 439, supra]. Thus a case otherwise wholly domestic may involve mistake of foreign law. The rule of decision is unquestionably supplied by the law of the forum, but it is necessary to refer to foreign law to establish the fact of mistake. Putting aside for further study all such references to foreign law for other purposes, Currie concentrates on the problem of reference to the foreign law as the source of the rule of decision. In this context he finds choice-of-law rules of the traditional type unacceptable, and suggests as a substitute for all such rules the following guides:

1.   When a court is asked to apply the law of a foreign state different from the law of the forum, it should inquire into the policies expressed in the respective laws, and into the circumstances in which it is reasonable for the respective states to assert an interest in the application of those policies. In making these determinations the court should employ the ordinary processes of construction and interpretation.

---

* Currie originally set out his theories in an article, Currie, Notes on Methods and Objectives in the Conflict of Laws, 1959 Duke L.J. 171, 178. These he modified quite quickly in a series of articles and statements, culminating in the present statement. See also B. Currie, Selected Essays on the Conflict of Laws (1963).

2. If the court finds that one state has an interest in the application of its policy in the circumstances of the case and the other has none, it should apply the law of the only interested state.

3. If the court finds an apparent conflict between the interests of the two states it should reconsider. A more moderate and restrained interpretation of the policy or interest of one state or the other may avoid conflict.

4. If, upon reconsideration, the court finds that a conflict between the legitimate interests of the two states is unavoidable, it should apply the law of the forum.

5. If the forum is disinterested, but an unavoidable conflict exists between the interests of two other states, and the court cannot with justice decline to adjudicate the case, it should apply the law of the forum, at least if that law corresponds with the law of one of the other states. Alternatively, the court might decide the case by a candid exercise of legislative discretion, resolving the conflict as it believes it would be resolved by a supreme legislative body having power to determine which interest should be required to yield.

6. The conflict of interest between states will result in different dispositions of the same problem, depending on where the action is brought. If with respect to a particular problem this appears seriously to infringe a strong national interest in uniformity of decision, the court should not attempt to improvise a solution sacrificing the legitimate interest of its own state, but should leave to Congress, exercising its powers under the full faith and credit clause, the determination of which interest shall be required to yield.*

Step 2, above, in Professor Currie's methodology has become known as the technique of identifying "false conflicts" and eliminating the spurious issues they involve. This proved to be one of the most attractive features of Currie's methodology. However, analysis of the "false conflict" concept has persuaded some writers that it is a misbegotten idea. Professor Leflar has said that it confuses cases of no conflict with cases in which opposed rules of internal law appear to by vying for application, but where the claim of one of the rules to being invoked is so slender that the conflict is easily resolved in favor of the other rule. A more trenchant attack has been mounted by a student writer, who pointed out that the term has at least a half-dozen meanings which shift from case to case and from user to user. See Comment, False Conflicts, 55 Calif.L.Rev. 74 (1967). Perhaps the principal notion of "false conflicts" can be put in one sentence. When rules of two or more states are phrased in terms that literally construed would lead to opposed results, they pose a gratuitous con-

* For comments on Professor Currie's writings, see Hill, Governmental Interest and the Conflict of Laws—a Reply to Professor Currie, 27 U.Chi.L.Rev. 463 (1960); M. Traynor, Professor Currie's Restrained and Enlightened Forum, 49 Calif.L.Rev. 845 (1961).

flict if, on according them their intended scope, the rules would produce the same decision on the issue presented.

A serious criticism of the Currie approach is that it fails to take account of the need for system-coordination in a highly mobile society in which multistate transactions are commonplace. It addresses itself to the problem of giving effect to underlying substantive law interests on a case-by-case basis without ascribing value to the need to avoid elaborate investigation of cases inundating the judicial process. Currie did not deny that there are choice-of law rules and that these rest on policies, but he deprecated their value compared to substantive concerns:

"A choice-of-law rule does express a policy, but it is not of the same order as the social and economic policies which are normally developed by a state in the pursuit of its governmental interests and the interests of its people. . . .

"[T]he policy is that the state, as a member of the community of states, will join in a fairly general movement that imposes a degree of restraint upon its sovereignty and upon the pursuit of its selfish interests . . . . This is but a mild, tentative, and self-denying policy." B. Currie, Selected Essays on the Conflict of Laws 52–53 (1963).

Policy-interest theorists fill the void of non-existent legislative intent as to territorial scope of enacted rules by consulting their own intuitions. See Reese, Conflict of Laws and the Restatement, Second, 28 Law & Contemp.Prob. 679, 686 (1963); Juenger, Choice of Law in Interstate Torts, 118 U.Pa.L.Rev. 202, 209 (1969). There is a very strong presumption in Currie's position favoring the forum's rule. With expanding bases of jurisdiction, this gives strong inducement to select a forum with a desired substantive rule on a key issue. Parochialism becomes a magnet that attracts case filings when the local rule favors the plaintiff.

NOTES

(1) For an interesting article which espouses the Currie approach, subject to rather substantial limitations, see Traynor, War and Peace in the Conflict of Laws, 25 Int. and Comp.L.Q. 121 (1976).

(2) For criticism of Professor Currie's interest analysis approach, see Brilmayer, Interest Analysis and the Myth of Legislative Intent, 78 Mich.L. Rev. 392 (1980); Juenger, Conflict of Law: A Critique on Interest Analysis, 32 Am.J.Comp.L. 1 (1984); Rosenberg, The Comeback of Choice-of-Law Rules, 81 Colum.L.Rev. 946 (1981).

Leflar: *Choice-Influencing Considerations*

An important entrant in the ideological derby is Professor Robert A. Leflar's analysis listing five "choice-influencing considerations" as the underlying tugs and thrusts which propel courts toward choice-of-law decisions, whatever rhetorical window-dressing they employ. The factors he lists suggest a shortened group similar to those developed by Cheatham and Reese in their 1952 article, Choice of the Applicable Law, 52 Colum.L.Rev. 959 (1952), supra, with priorities somewhat altered. They resemble also the list of factors of Restatement, Second, Conflict of Laws, Section 6 (p. 485, infra). In the order he names them, they are: (1) predictability of results; (2) maintenance of interstate and international order; (3) simplification of the judicial task; (4) advancement of the forum's governmental interests; and (5) application of the better rule of law. R. Leflar, American Conflicts Law 193–195 (3d ed. 1977). He does not offer these factors as rules of thumb, but as values that will guide courts to wiser decisions based on more thoughtful analysis. (Id. at 259). He concedes overlap and some indefiniteness, but argues that the five considerations will assure a "continuing re-examination of precedents, a readiness to lay aside old mechanical rules" that are out of harmony with the sound factors he lists, and "a reaffirmation of old rules, or at least of old results" that are in line with the considerations. (Ibid.)

Courts have revealed an unmistakable affinity for Leflar's formulation. Shown the way by Chief Justice Kenison's finely articulated opinion in Clark v. Clark, 107 N.H. 351, 222 A.2d 205 (1966), other courts have fallen into line. See, e.g., Satchwill v. Vollrath Co., 293 F.Supp. 533 (E.D.Wis.1968); Schneider v. Nichols, 280 Minn. 139, 158 N.W.2d 254 (1968); Mitchell v. Craft, 211 So.2d 509 (Miss.1968); Tiernan v. Westext Transport, Inc., 205 F.Supp. 1256 (D.R.I.1969); Conklin v. Horner, 38 Wis.2d 468, 157 N.W.2d 579 (1968).

Professor Leflar's "better rule of law" factor has come under heavy fire from commentators as but a sly way out for judges who want to apply their own notions of justice in the case, unrestrained by rules. In defense he argues:

". . . Common law courts have always, when they had to choose between two competing rules of law proposed for application to a given case, tried to choose the sounder rule. They have done this openly when the competing rules were urged within a single jurisdiction. This was not a 'free law' jurisprudence; it is the common law tradition. The only new idea that is proposed is that it is permissible to do the same thing in choice-of-law cases. . . . " *

NOTES

(1) Courts that engage in a search for the "better rule of law" usually end by applying their own local rule in the decision of the case. A notable exception is Frummer v. Hilton Hotels International Inc., 60 Misc.2d 840, 304 N.Y.S.2d 335 (Sup.Ct., Kings Co. 1969), which involved an action brought by a New York resident to recover for personal injuries suffered when he slipped and fell while showering in a London hotel. Using an interest analy-

---

* Leflar, True "False Conflicts," Et Alia, 48 B.U.L.Rev. 164, 168 (1968).

sis approach, the court rejected its local contributory negligence rule in favor of the lex loci's comparative negligence rule.

(2) Ought a common law court have more latitude to reject a statutory rule or binding judicial precedent of the forum in a multistate case than in a local case? Does a case such as Frummer indicate that it has?

(3) In Wallis v. Mrs. Smith's Pie Co., 261 Ark. 622, 550 S.W.2d 453 (1977), two Arkansas residents on their way home from a trip to Ohio were involved in a collision with the Pennsylvania defendant's trailer truck in Missouri. The accident happened when the defendant's rig rear-ended the plaintiff's car in the left lane of the interstate highway, where the car was traveling in apparent violation of a Missouri statute which required vehicles to keep to the right. Arkansas' standard of care was comparative negligence; Missouri's, the common law rule making contributory negligence a total defense. *Held:* The Arkansas comparative negligence rule should have been applied, not the Missouri contributory negligence rule. "The only contact either party had with the State of Missouri was traveling the interstate highway there en route to a destination in another state." (550 S.W.2d, at p. 456.) The court concluded (id., at p. 458):

> This State's government interest in its citizens is best served by application of our comparative fault statute rather than Missouri's contributory negligence law. . . .
>
> We therefore find this State has a predominate interest in applying its comparative fault statutes to its own citizens and those who seek relief in its courts. . . . For equally compelling reasons we find Missouri rules of the road are applicable to questions of alleged negligence in the actual driving of the vehicle.

The following year the court ruled on the converse situation in Williams v. Carr, 263 Ark. 326, 565 S.W.2d 400 (1978), where the occupants of both vehicles were Tennessee residents and the crash occurred in Arkansas. Again, in issue was whether the Arkansas comparative negligence rule or the other state's contributory negligence rule should apply and which state's driving rules were binding. The court said (565 S.W.2d, at p. 404):

> . . . Under *Wallis*, the substantive law of Tennessee is applicable, but Arkansas' rules of the road are applicable in the instant case.

Is the *Williams* decision a correct application of the interest analysis? of Leflar's choice-influencing considerations?

---

von Mehren & Trautman: *The Functional Analysis*

The "functional" approach of Professors Arthur T. von Mehren and Donald T. Trautman is a subtle and sophisticated variation on the theme of interest analysis. It focuses on the contents and purposes of the rules in competition and then goes on to a series of analytical steps that probably are too demanding to catch the fancy of the judges:

(1) The court identifies the issue and determines which of the states ostensibly related to the case has a rule that rests upon a poli-

cy that would be advanced by application here. Such a state has an "interest" and is a "concerned jurisdiction."

(2) However, the ostensible concern may yield—in appreciation of the multistate character of the case—and give way to a special rule, unlike the state's rule for a domestic case raising the same issue. This is the "regulating rule" for the issue presented in its multistate aspects.

(3) If all "concerned" states have an identical "regulating rule" for the issue at hand, the problem is solved. If they do not, the concerns of each will have to be evaluated more precisely to determine the state of strongest, most significant concern.

(4) A rare case will survive even the foregoing steps and then will have to be resolved in a fashion that goes to still more rarified levels of analysis.

The functional approach is not a sport for dullards. A serious question is whether it plumbs deeper than all but a few judges and lawyers are prepared to dig or follow. For those who can keep pace, the analysis is intellectual stimulation of a high order. Adding to or subtracting from its usefulness is a set of new terms, some of which have been quoted above. (For a very helpful analysis, see Gorman, Book Review, The Law of Multistate Problems, 115 U.Pa.L.Rev. 288 (1966).)

Cavers: *Principles of Preference*

On the eve of publication of the first Restatement of Conflict of Laws, Professor David F. Cavers wrote a penetrating critique of the whole conceptual apparatus of the choice-of-law system the American Law Institute was to embrace. See Cavers, A Critique of the Choice-of-Law Problem, 47 Harv.L.Rev. 173 (1933). His shaft went home, but the message reached the brain of the monster only after years and years and scores and scores of tortured choice-of-law decisions. The single message was that the traditional rules were bent on "juris-diction-selecting"—choosing a body of governing law or a legal sys-tem—instead of on choosing the decisional norm whereby to resolve the issue presented.

He argued that choice-of-law rules should not be oblivious to the contents of the rules of decision whose application they dictated and urged a revised body of choice-of-law rules. As time went on, he faced the task of producing rules and found himself unable to draft particularized ones that would advance justice as the facts of the cases varied and shifted locales. In 1965, he presented a limited set of "principles of preference" that he had carefully worked out on the basis of diverse fact-law multistate combinations and that he pro-posed as guidelines for courts concerned with reaching principled decisions that were neither completely result-selectively ad hoc nor yet blind to consequences.

One example will suffice to illustrate his appreciation of the problem and the path to solution. In his words, the "problem we face today is not how to exorcise choice-of-law rules and principles but how to develop them." D. Cavers, The Choice-of-Law Process 113 (1965). Using tort cases as his chief subjects, he offered the following as an example of principles of preference (p. 138):

"1. Where the liability laws of the state of injury set a *higher* standard of conduct or of financial protection against injury than do the laws of the state where the person causing the injury has acted or had his home, the laws of the state of injury should determine the standard and the protection applicable to the case, at least where the person injured was not so related to the person causing the injury that the question should be relegated to the law governing their relationship."

Professor Cavers has admitted to greater confidence in the idea that principles of preference are necessary than in the particular formulations he has advanced. He is satisfied that as courts consciously strive for principled decisions and as precedents accumulate, better principles and a more just choice-of-law process will evolve.

Weintraub: *A Pragmatic Approach*

Another influential writer in the field is Professor Russell Weintraub of the University of Texas School of Law. The second edition of his Commentary or Choice of Law appeared in 1980. In it he proposes the following as an approach to choice of law in torts (p. 346):

1. "False conflict" cases: If, in the light of its contacts with the parties or the transaction, only one state will have the policies underlying its tort rule advanced, apply the law of that state.

2. "True conflict" cases: If two or more states having contacts with the parties or the transaction will have the policies underlying their different tort rules advanced, apply the law that will favor the plaintiff unless one or both of the following factors is present:

   a. That law is anachronistic or aberrational.

   b. The state with that law does not have sufficient contact with the defendant or the defendant's actual or intended course of conduct to make application of its law reasonable.

3. "No interest" cases: If none of the states having contacts with the parties or the transaction will have the policies underlying its tort rule advanced, apply the law that will favor the plaintiff unless one or both of the following factors is present:

   a. That law is anachronistic or aberrational.

b. The state with that law does not have sufficient contact with the defendant or the defendant's actual or intended course of conduct to make application of its law reasonable.

These rules are sympathetically, but critically, discussed in Seidelson, Interest Analysis: The Quest for Perfection and the Frailties of Man, 19 Duq.L.Rev. 207 (1981).

NOTE

See also Weintraub, The Future of Choice of Law for Torts: What Principles Should be Preferred?, 1977 Law and Contemp.Prob. 146.

A prolific author of conflicts articles is Professor Robert A. Sedler, whose work has been strongly influenced by the late Brainerd Currie's writings. He has not been content to leave the Currie methodology as he found it, even though he endorses it warmly as "the approach that . . . has found the greatest favor with courts committed to a policy-centered view of choice of law . . . [and] has produced sound and fair results." See Sedler, The Governmental Interest Approach to Choice of Law: An Analysis and a Reformulation, 25 U.C.L.A.L.Rev. 181, 243 (1977). See also Sedler, Rules of Choice of Law Versus Choice-of-Law Rules: Judicial Method in Conflicts Torts Cases, 44 Tenn.L.Rev. 975 (1977); Sedler, Choice of Law in Michigan: Judicial Method and the Policy-Centered Conflict of Laws, 29 Wayne L.Rev. 1193 (1983).

The torts cases best illustrate the difficulties in the policy-interest approach to solving choice-of-law problems. In Wright v. Standard Oil Co., Inc., 470 F.2d 1280 (5th Cir. 1972), the issue was whether the negligence of the father of a five-year-old boy (who was rendered paraplegic when hit by the defendant's truck) was imputable to the mother. The family's home was Indiana, which by statute vested the boy's right of action in his father, excluding the mother. The father's negligence in leaving the child unattended occurred in Mississippi, which permitted the mother to sue. The federal diversity court, in following Mississippi law, showed how susceptible the policy-analysis approach is to the influence of the forum: ". . . While [application of the Indiana] statute may advance Indiana policies when Indiana is the forum, those policies would not be furthered by applying the statute in a Mississippi forum. For this reason, Mississippi would look solely to forum law. . . ." (470 F.2d, at p. 1285).

RESTATEMENT, SECOND, CONFLICT OF LAWS

Since 1960 or thereabouts the basic approach of the Restatement Second in contracts choice of law has been to locate the state with the "most significant relationship" to the matter under consideration. During the preliminary draft stages, the approach was embodied in Section 332 (Restatement, Second, Conflict of Laws, Tentative Draft No. 6, 1960), and in that form was said to be "roughly synonymous" with the center of gravity approach of the *Auten* case. See Baffin Land Corp. v. Monticello Motor Inn, Inc., 70 Wn.2d 893, 425 P.2d 623, 625 n. 1 (1967).

The original and final versions of the Restatement Second provisions on the law governing contracts are set forth at pp. 586–589, infra.

In the field of torts, original Section 379 of the Restatement Second asserted in part as "The General Principle": "The local law of the state which has the most significant relationship with the occurrence and with the parties determines their rights and liabilities in tort." (Tentative Draft No. 8, 1963; Tentative Draft No. 9, 1964.)

The basic section on choice of law principles in general (§ 6) and the introductory section on torts (§ 145) of the Restatement Second are set forth below:

§ 6.   Choice-of-Law Principles*

(1) A court, subject to constitutional restrictions, will follow a statutory directive of its own state on choice of law.

(2) When there is no such directive, the factors relevant to the choice of the applicable rule of law include

(a) the needs of the interstate and international systems,

(b) the relevant policies of the forum,

(c) the relevant policies of other interested states and the relative interests of those states in the determination of the particular issue,

(d) the protection of justified expectations,

(e) the basic policies underlying the particular field of law,

(f) certainty, predictability and uniformity of result, and

(g) ease in the determination and application of the law to be applied.

---

§ 145.   The General Principle

(1) The rights and liabilities of the parties with respect to an issue in tort are determined by the local law of the state which, with respect to that issue, has the most significant relationship to the occurrence and the parties under the principles stated in § 6.

* Quoted with the permission of the copyright owner, The American Law Institute.

(2) Contacts to be taken into account in applying the principles of § 6 to determine the law applicable to an issue include:

  (a) the place where the injury occurred,

  (b) the place where the conduct causing the injury occurred,

  (c) the domicil, residence, nationality, place of incorporation and place of business of the parties, and

  (d) the place where the relationship, if any, between the parties is centered.

These contacts are to be evaluated according to their relative importance with respect to the particular issue.

———

". . . Although it is printed in black letters, section 145 is not much of a rule since it fails to offer a definition of the central word 'significant.'* Thus, the Restatement provisions on tort choice of law appear to be programmatic rather than normative. . . ." Juenger, Choice of Law in Interstate Torts, 118 U.Pa.L.Rev. 202, 212 (1969). With regard to the latter sentence, Professor Juenger quotes from the Reporter for the Second Restatement this observation: "This rule of most significant relationship, at the very least, will not stand in the way of progress." Reese, Conflict of Laws and the Restatement Second, 28 Law & Contemp.Prob. 679, 697 (1963).

———

If we grant that the "most significant relationship" doctrine is not part of the problem, does that mean it is part of the solution? An affirmative answer is suggested on the ground that the Restatement's provisions direct attention to the right questions. Although they do not for the most part supply firm answers to these questions, they may set the stage for decisions that in time can be synthesized into workable rules that take account of the significant underlying considerations.

———

* Do the references in the Restatement's black-letter rules to the choice-of- law factors listed in section 6 provide definitional guidance?

SECTION 4.   THE NEW ERA

A.   THE COURTS AT WORK

BABCOCK v. JACKSON

Court of Appeals of New York, 1963.
12 N.Y.2d 473, 240 N.Y.S.2d 743, 191 N.E.2d 279.

FULD, JUDGE.   On Friday, September 16, 1960, Miss Georgia Babcock and her friends, Mr. and Mrs. William Jackson, all residents of Rochester, left that city in Mr. Jackson's automobile, Miss Babcock as guest, for a week-end trip to Canada.   Some hours later, as Mr. Jackson was driving in the Province of Ontario, he apparently lost control of the car; it went off the highway into an adjacent stone wall, and Miss Babcock was seriously injured.   Upon her return to this State, she brought the present action against William Jackson, alleging negligence on his part in operating his automobile.

At the time of the accident, there was in force in Ontario a statute providing that "the owner or driver of a motor vehicle, other than a vehicle operated in the business of carrying passengers for compensation, is not liable for any loss or damage resulting from bodily injury to, or the death of any person being carried in . . . the motor vehicle" (Highway Traffic Act of Province of Ontario [Ontario Rev. Stat. (1960), ch. 172], § 105, subd. [2]).   Even though no such bar is recognized under this State's substantive law of torts . . . the defendant moved to dismiss the complaint on the ground that the law of the place where the accident occurred governs and that Ontario's guest statute bars recovery.   The court at Special Term, agreeing with the defendant, granted the motion and the Appellate Division . . . affirmed the judgment of dismissal without opinion.

The question presented is simply drawn.   Shall the law of the place of the tort [2] *invariably* govern the availability of relief for the tort or shall the applicable choice of law rule also reflect a consideration of other factors which are relevant to the purposes served by the enforcement or denial of the remedy?

The traditional choice of law rule, embodied in the original Restatement of Conflict of Laws (§ 384), and until recently unquestioningly followed in this court . . . has been that the substantive

---

2. In this case, as in nearly all such cases, the conduct causing injury and the injury itself occurred in the same jurisdiction.   The phrase "place of the tort," as distinguished from "place of wrong" and "place of injury," is used herein to designate the place where both the wrong and the injury took place. [Footnote by the Court.]

rights and liabilities arising out of a tortious occurrence are determinable by the law of the place of the tort. . . . It had its conceptual foundation in the vested rights doctrine, namely, that a right to recover for a foreign tort owes its creation to the law of the jurisdiction where the injury occurred and depends for its existence and extent solely on such law. . . . [T]he vested rights doctrine has long since been discredited . . .. More particularly, as applied to torts, the theory ignores the interest which jurisdictions other than that where the tort occurred may have in the resolution of particular issues. It is for this very reason that, despite the advantages of certainty, ease of application and predictability which it affords . . . there has in recent years been increasing criticism of the traditional rule by commentators and a judicial trend towards its abandonment or modification.

. . . .

In Auten v. Auten, 308 N.Y. 155, 124 N.E.2d 99, . . . this court . . . applied what has been termed the "center of gravity" or "grouping of contacts" theory of the conflict of laws. "Under this theory," we declared in the Auten case, "the courts, instead of regarding as conclusive the parties' intention or the place of making or performance, lay emphasis rather upon the law of the place 'which has the most significant contacts with the matter in dispute' " (308 N.Y., at p. 160, 124 N.E.2d, at pp. 101–102). . . .

The "center of gravity" or "grouping of contacts" doctrine adopted by this court in conflicts cases involving contracts impresses us as likewise affording the appropriate approach for accommodating the competing interests in tort cases with multi-State contacts. Justice, fairness and "the best practical result" (Swift & Co. v. Bankers Trust Co., 280 N.Y. 135, 141, 19 N.E.2d 992, 995 . . .) may best be achieved by giving controlling effect to the law of the jurisdiction which, because of its relationship or contact with the occurrence or the parties, has the greatest concern with the specific issue raised in the litigation. . . .

Comparison of the relative "contacts" and "interests" of New York and Ontario in this litigation, vis-a-vis the issue here presented, makes it clear that the concern of New York is unquestionably the greater and more direct and that the interest of Ontario is at best minimal. The present action involves injuries sustained by a New York guest as the result of the negligence of a New York host in the operation of an automobile, garaged, licensed and undoubtedly insured in New York, in the course of a week-end journey which began and was to end there. In sharp contrast, Ontario's sole relationship with the occurrence is the purely adventitious circumstance that the accident occurred there.

New York's policy of requiring a tort-feasor to compensate his guest for injuries caused by his negligence cannot be doubted—as attested by the fact that the Legislature of this State has repeatedly refused to enact a statute denying or limiting recovery in such cases (see, e.g., 1930 Sen.Int.No. 339, Pr.No. 349; 1935 Sen.Int.No. 168, Pr. No. 170; 1960 Sen.Int.No. 3662, Pr.No. 3967)—and our courts have neither reason nor warrant for departing from that policy simply because the accident, solely affecting New York residents and arising out of the operation of a New York based automobile, happened beyond its borders. Per contra, Ontario has no conceivable interest in denying a remedy to a New York guest against his New York host for injuries suffered in Ontario by reason of conduct which was tortious under Ontario law. The object of Ontario's guest statute, it has been said, is "to prevent the fraudulent assertion of claims by passengers, in collusion with the drivers, against insurance companies" (Survey of Canadian Legislation, 1 U.Toronto L.J. 358, 366) and, quite obviously, the fraudulent claims intended to be prevented by the statute are those asserted against Ontario defendants and their insurance carriers, not New York defendants and their insurance carriers. Whether New York defendants are imposed upon or their insurers defrauded by a New York plaintiff is scarcely a valid legislative concern of Ontario simply because the accident occurred there, any more so than if the accident had happened in some other jurisdiction.

It is hardly necessary to say that Ontario's interest is quite different from what it would have been had the issue related to the manner in which the defendant had been driving his car at the time of the accident. Where the defendant's exercise of due care in the operation of his automobile is in issue, the jurisdiction in which the allegedly wrongful conduct occurred will usually have a predominant, if not exclusive, concern. In such a case, it is appropriate to look to the law of the place of the tort so as to give effect to that jurisdiction's interest in regulating conduct within its borders, and it would be almost unthinkable to seek the applicable rule in the law of some other place.

The issue here, however, is not whether the defendant offended against a rule of the road prescribed by Ontario for motorists generally or whether he violated some standard of conduct imposed by that jurisdiction, but rather whether the plaintiff, because she was a guest in the defendant's automobile, is barred from recovering damages for a wrong concededly committed. As to that issue, it is New York, the place where the parties resided, where their guest-host relationship arose and where the trip began and was to end, rather than Ontario, the place of the fortuitous occurrence of the accident, which has the dominant contacts and the superior claim for application of its law. Although the rightness or wrongness of defendant's conduct may depend upon the law of the particular jurisdiction through which the automobile passes, the rights and liabilities of the parties which stem from their guest-host relationship should remain constant and not vary and shift as the automobile proceeds from place to place. Indeed, such a result, we note, accords with "the interests of the host in procuring liability insurance adequate under the applicable law, and the interests of his insurer in reasonable calculability of the premium." (Ehrenzweig, Guest Statutes in the Conflict of Laws, 69 Yale L.J. 595, 603.)

Although the traditional rule has in the past been applied by this court in giving controlling effect to the guest statute of the foreign jurisdiction in which the accident occurred . . . it is not amiss to point out that the question here posed was neither raised nor considered in those cases and that the question has never been presented in so stark a manner as in the case before us with a statute so unique as Ontario's. Be that as it may, however, reconsideration of the inflexible traditional rule persuades us, as already indicated, that, in failing to take into account essential policy considerations and objectives, its application may lead to unjust and anomalous results. This being so, the rule, formulated as it was by the courts, should be discarded. . . .

In conclusion, then, there is no reason why all issues arising out of a tort claim must be resolved by reference to the law of the same jurisdiction. Where the issue involves standards of conduct, it is more than likely that it is the law of the place of the tort which will be controlling but the disposition of other issues must turn, as does the issue of the standard of conduct itself, on the law of the jurisdiction which has the strongest interest in the resolution of the particular issue presented.

The judgment appealed from should be reversed, with costs, and the motion to dismiss the complaint denied.

Van Voorhis, Judge (dissenting). The decision about to be made of this appeal changes the established law of this State . . . . The decision in Auten v. Auten rationalized and rendered more workable the existing law of contracts. . . . The difference between the present case and Auten v. Auten is that Auten did not materially change the law, but sought to formulate what had previously been decided. The present case makes substantial changes in the law of torts. . . .

In my view there is no overriding consideration of public policy which justifies or directs this change in the established rule or renders necessary or advisable the confusion which such a change will introduce. . . .

NOTES

(1) Is Judge Fuld's opinion internally consistent? Can a court consistently call for application of the law of the state that has the greatest interest in the issue to be decided and yet say that "the rights and liabilities of the parties which stem from the guest-host relationship should . . . not vary and shift as the automobile proceeds from place to place"?

(2) The principal case produced a torrent of commentary, mostly approving, starting with a symposium, Comments on Babcock v. Jackson, 63 Colum. L.Rev. 1212 (1963). Professors Cavers, Cheatham, Currie, Leflar and Reese

all found the result pleasing, but they gave different reasons for doing so. Each tended to find in the opinion support for his own theories.

DYM v. GORDON

Court of Appeals of New York, 1965.
16 N.Y.2d 120, 262 N.Y.S.2d 463, 209 N.E.2d 792.

[Plaintiff and defendant, New York residents, attended summer school at the University of Colorado in Boulder, Colorado. Defendant offered plaintiff a ride to a nearby town in Colorado and en route collided with another car, injuring plaintiff and, possibly, others. The Appellate Division ruled that ordinary negligence was not a sufficient basis for recovery, since the Colorado guest statute applied, requiring "willful and wanton disregard" of the passenger's safety.]

BURKE, J. . . . Following our approach in Babcock, it is necessary first to isolate the issue, next to identify the policies embraced in the laws in conflict, and finally to examine the contacts of the respective jurisdictions to ascertain which has a superior connection with the occurrence and thus would have a superior interest in having its policy or law applied. The issue here is simply whether in an automobile host-guest relationship a negligent driver should be liable to his injured passenger. The New York law finds nothing in the host-guest relationship which warrants a digression from the usual negligence rule of ordinary care. In Colorado, however, this relationship is treated specially and, while ordinary negligence is usually enough for recovery in that state, injuries arising out of this relationship are compensable only if they result from "willful and wanton" conduct. Contrary to the narrow view advanced by plaintiff, the policy underlying Colorado's law is threefold: the protection of Colorado drivers and their insurance carriers against fraudulent claims, the prevention of suits by "ungrateful guests", and the priority of injured parties in other cars in the assets of the negligent defendant. Examining Colorado's interest in light of its public policy we find that over and above the usual interest which Colorado may bring to bear on all conduct occurring within its boundaries, Colorado has an interest in seeing that the negligent defendant's assets are not dissipated in order that the persons in the car of the blameless driver will not have their right to recovery diminished by the present suit.

Finally we come to the question of which state has the more significant contacts with the case such that its interest should be upheld. In this regard, the factual distinctions between this case and Babcock do have considerable influence. Babcock did not involve a collision between two cars; thus only New Yorkers were involved and it was unnecessary for us to consider the interest of Ontario in the rights of those in a car of a nonnegligent driver. In Babcock we pointed out that the host-guest relationship was seated in New York and that the place of the accident was "entirely fortuitous". In this case the parties were dwelling in Colorado when the relationship was formed and the accident arose out of Colorado based activity; therefore, the fact that the accident occurred in Colorado could in no sense be termed fortuitous. Thus it is that in this case where Colorado has such significant contacts with the *relationship itself* and the *basis of its formation* the application of its law and underlying policy are clearly warranted.

Of compelling importance in this case is the fact that here the parties had come to rest in the State of Colorado and had thus chosen to live their daily lives under the protective arm of Colorado law. Having accepted the benefits of that law for such a prolonged period, it is spurious to maintain that Colorado has no interest in a relationship which was formed there. In Babcock the New Yorkers at all times were *in transitu* and we were impressed with the fundamental unfairness of subjecting them to a law which they in no sense had adopted.

To say that this relationship was formed in Colorado implies that the parties had acquired so sufficient a nexus with that jurisdiction that relationships formed there were in the real sense Colorado relationships. In other words, it is neither the physical situs where the relationship was created nor the time of its creation which is controlling but rather these factors in conjunction with the general intent of the parties as inferred from their actions.   .   .   .

The alleged contacts referred to by plaintiff may be classified under the heading of domicile. Certainly it is merely a long-handed method of reciting that the parties were domiciled in New York to state that the car was registered here and that the insurance was written here. These and many other factors may usually be presumed from the fact of domicile; they have no independent significance as regards the host-guest relationship apart from their inclusion as natural incidents of domicile.

Judicial hostility to "guest" statutes and a preoccupation with New York social welfare problems and the relative liability of insurers should not be treated as "contacts" which are found then to outweigh the factual contacts.   .   .   .

Here, necessarily, the only valid competing consideration bearing on the host-guest relationship is that of domicile. However appealing it might seem to give effect to our own public policy on this issue, merely because the negligent driver of the car in the collision, and his guest, are domiciled here, to do so would be to totally neglect the interests of the jurisdiction where the accident occurred, where the relationship arose and where the parties were dwelling . . . . To give domicile or an alleged public policy such a preferred status is to substitute a conflicts rule every bit as inflexible and arbitrary as its *lex loci* predecessor. Such was not our intention in Babcock. It is suggested that New York has a dominant governmental interest in seeing that the plaintiff receives compensation because it is this State that she will look to for welfare payments should she become a public charge as a result of her injuries. Such an argument is hardly a legal one. Were we to give our attention to such considerations we might just as well speculate about the possibility that the New York defendant could become a public charge if the plaintiff were to be given recovery. There is no guarantee that the recovery will not far exceed the insurance coverage in this or in any other case. A reflection on the import of this argument gives one the feeling that a preference for whatever law will compensate the New York tort plaintiff lurks in the background. The suggestion that our courts should apply this State's policy of compensation for innocent tort victims to all cases of returning domiciliaries is tantamount to saying that different rules or interests of other jurisdictions should be denied application in a New York forum on the ground of their not suiting our public policy. The principles justifying our refusal to apply foreign law on the ground of public policy are well defined, and a mere difference between the foreign rule and our own will not warrant such refusal.

Public policy, per se, plays no part in a *choice* of law problem. . . .

The present decision represents no departure from the rule announced in Babcock; merely an example of its application. . . .

Accordingly, the order of the Appellate Division should be affirmed, without costs.

FULD, JUDGE (dissenting).

. . .

The [Babcock] rule is not, and does not profess to be, a talisman of legal certainty, nor does it of itself provide a formulary means for resolving conflicts problems. What it does provide is a method, a conceptual framework, for the disposition of tort cases having contacts with more than one jurisdiction. Although the majority in this case reaffirms Babcock's abandonment of the prior inflexible rule of *lex loci delicti*, its decision, nevertheless, in essence, reflects the adoption of an equally mechanical and arbitrary rule that, in litigation involving a special relationship, controlling effect must be given to the law of the jurisdiction in which the relationship originated, notwithstanding that that jurisdiction may not have the slightest concern with the specific issue raised or that some other state's relationship or contact with the occurrence or the parties may be such as to give it the predominant interest in the resolution of that issue.

There is, indeed, no material distinction between the factual situation here presented and that in the Babcock case . . .

. . . Under the circumstances of the present case, then, Colorado, to paraphrase what we wrote in Babcock, "has no conceivable interest in denying a remedy to a New York guest against his New York host for injuries suffered in [Colorado] by reason of conduct which was tortious under [Colorado] law" (12 N.Y.2d, at p. 482, 240 N.Y.S.2d, at p. 750, 191 N.E.2d, at p. 284).

Nor is the majority's position advanced by its further suggestion . . . that the Colorado statute also reflects (1) an antipathy on the part of Colorado to suits by "ungrateful" guests (see Dobbs v. Sugioka, 117 Colo. 218, 220, 185 P.2d 784,) and (2) a policy to assure "the priority of injured parties in other cars in the assets of the negligent defendant." Indeed, as regards the latter asserted policy, there does not appear to be any Colorado pronouncement even to intimate that the Colorado Legislature was motivated by any such objective. In any event, though, Colorado would be legitimately concerned with the application of these alleged policies only in relation to matters within its legislative competence, such as the burdens of the Colorado courts, the regulation of the affairs and relationships of Colorado citizens or the protection of Colorado claimants or insurers. . . .

CHIEF JUDGE DESMOND (dissenting). . . . What we did in the [Babcock, p. 487, supra and Kilberg, p. 464, supra] decisions was to announce for New York a modern public policy which abandoned the old sweeping rule that the law to be applied in every tort case was the law of the place of the wrong. Babcock and Kilberg (supra) together should be the law of this present case.

. . .

No guides satisfactory to me are found in the concepts currently favored by teachers and writers on conflict of laws, such as "significant contacts", "center of gravity", and "interests of the respective states". . . . Counting up "contacts" or locating the "center of gravity" or weighing the respective "interests" of two states can never be a satisfactory way of deciding actual lawsuits. . . .

NOTES

(1) Is Judge Burke's opinion internally consistent? Does the fact that the parties' relationship was centered in Colorado have any relevance in determining the degree of Colorado's interest in the application of its guest-passenger statute? On the other hand, emphasis upon the place where the parties' relationship is centered would obviate the risk of drawing invidious distinctions between the parties based upon their different domiciles. This problem did not arise in the Babcock and Dym cases because all of the parties involved were from New York. This problem would, however, have arisen in Dym if there had been two guest passengers, one from Colorado and one from New York. Compare Neumeier v. Kuehner, p. 503, infra. See von Mehren, Recent Trends in Choice-of-Law Methodology, 60 Corn.L.Rev. 927, 946–952 (1975).

(2) In Macey v. Rozbicki, 18 N.Y.2d 289, 274 N.Y.S.2d 591, 221 N.E.2d 380 (1966), the facts fell between the Babcock and Dym patterns. The host and guest were sisters who lived in Buffalo, New York; the accident occurred in Ontario; but the guest sister had gone to visit with her host sister and brother-in-law at the latters' Ontario summer home; the trip was intended to be an all-Ontario round trip to church, when the accident occurred. De-

spite the Ontario guest statute, the Court of Appeals held the plaintiff could recover on common law negligence, saying that "the relationship of two sisters living permanently in New York was not affected or changed by their temporary meeting" in Ontario. Concurring, Judge Keating argued for overruling Dym on the ground that the place where the guest-host relationship is centered has only minor importance. He said that the only facts significant in guest statute choice-of-law cases are the parties' residence and the place where the auto is insured and garaged. His views prevailed in Tooker v. Lopez, infra.

(3) Meanwhile, a case that was a perfect mirror-image reversal of Babcock on the facts was in litigation, but did not reach the Court of Appeals. In Kell v. Henderson, 26 A.D.2d 595, 270 N.Y.S.2d 552 (3d Dep't 1966), Ontario motorists, with a car registered there, set out on a short holiday trip to New York, planning to return home to Ontario. In New York the guest-passenger was injured when the auto left the highway and struck a bridge. Despite the Ontario guest statute, the guest recovered. The court was of the view that Babcock had not intended to change the New York law that a guest has a cause of action for personal injuries sustained in an accident in New York! Comments on the case appear in 67 Colum.L.Rev. 459, 465 (1967), by Professors Rosenberg and Trautman, Two Views on Kell v. Henderson. The former complained in a mythical opinion by "Neanderthal, J." for the New York Court of Appeals that after Babcock and Dym, "A New York lawyer with a guest statute case has more need of an ouija board . . . than a copy of Shepard's citations." (Kell was extinguished by the court that decided it in Arbuthnot v. Allbright, 316 N.Y.S.2d 391 (3d Dep't 1970), which explained away Kell on a procedural point.)

In accord with Kell are Milkovich v. Saari, 295 Minn. 155, 203 N.W.2d 408 (1973), and Conklin v. Horner, 38 Wis.2d 468, 157 N.W.2d 579 (1968); but cf. Vick v. Cochran, 316 So.2d 242 (Miss.1975) (holding Alabama guest statute applicable to determine liability of (1) owner of truck and (2) driver; accident took place in Mississippi while truck was passing through a corner of that state).

TOOKER v. LOPEZ

Court of Appeals of New York, 1969.
24 N.Y.2d 569, 301 N.Y.S.2d 519, 249 N.E.2d 394.

KEATING, JUDGE. On October 16, 1964, Catharina Tooker, a 20-year-old coed at Michigan State University, was killed when the Japanese sports car in which she was a passenger overturned after the driver had lost control of the vehicle while attempting to pass another car. The accident also took the life of the driver of the vehicle, Marcia Lopez, and seriously injured another passenger, Susan Silk. The two girls were classmates of Catharina Tooker at Michigan State University and lived in the same dormitory. They were en route from the University to Detroit, Michigan, to spend the weekend.

Catharina Tooker and Marcia Lopez were both New York domiciliaries. The automobile which Miss Lopez was driving belonged to her father who resided in New York, where the sports car he had given his daughter was registered and insured.

This action for wrongful death was commenced by Oliver P. Tooker, Jr., the father of Catharina Tooker, as the administrator of her estate. The defendant asserted as an affirmative defense the Michigan "guest statute" (C.L.S. § 257.401 [Stat.Ann.1960, § 9.2101]) which permits recovery by guests only by showing willful misconduct or gross negligence of the driver. The plaintiff moved to dismiss the affirmative defense on the ground that under the governing choice-of-law rules it was New York law rather than Michigan law which applied. The motion was granted by the Special Term Justice who concluded that: "New York State 'has the greatest concern with the specific issue raised in the litigation' and New York law should apply." The Appellate Division (Third Department) agreed with "the cogent argument advanced by Special Term" but felt "constrained" by the holding in Dym v. Gordon, 16 N.Y.2d 120, 262 N.Y.S.2d 463, 209 N.E.2d 792 [1965] to apply the Michigan guest statute.

We are presented here with a choice-of-law problem which we have had occasion to consider in several cases since our decision in Babcock v. Jackson, 12 N.Y.2d 473, 240 N.Y.S.2d 743, 191 N.E.2d 279, 95 A.L.R.2d 1 [1963] rejected the traditional rule which looked invariably to the law of the place of the wrong. Unfortunately, as we recently had occasion to observe, our decisions subsequent to rejection of the *lex loci delictus* rule "have lacked a precise consistency" (Miller v. Miller, 22 N.Y.2d 12, 15, 290 N.Y.S.2d 734, 736, 237 N.E.2d 877, 878 [1968]; see, also, D. Currie, Comments on Reich v. Purcell, 15 U.C.L.A.L.Rev., 595–598). This case gives us the opportunity to resolve those inconsistencies in a class of cases which have been particularly troublesome.

. . .

The decision in Dym v. Gordon, upon which the Appellate Division relied in the instant case, is clearly distinguishable from the facts here. There is here no third-party "non-guest" who was injured and there is no question of denying such a party priority in the assets of the negligent defendant. We cannot, however, in candor rest our decision on this basis in light of a subsequent decision which refused to apply the Ontario guest statute in a case indistinguishable from Dym v. Gordon (supra). (See Macey v. Rozbicki, 18 N.Y.2d 289, 274 N.Y.S. 2d 591, 221 N.E.2d 380 [1966].)

. . .

The teleological argument advanced by some (see Cavers, Choice-of-Law Process, p. 298) that the guest statute was intended to assure the priority of injured nonguests in the assets of a negligent host, in addition to the prevention of fraudulent claims, overlooks not only the statutory history but the fact that the statute permits recovery by guests who can establish that the accident was due to the gross negligence of the driver. If the purpose of the statute is to protect the rights of the injured "non-guest", as opposed to the owner or his insurance carrier, we fail to perceive any rational basis for predicating that protection on the degree of negligence which the guest is able to establish. The only justification for discrimination between injured guests which can withstand logical as well as constitutional scrutiny . . . is that the legitimate purpose of the statute—prevention of fraudulent claims against local insurers or the protection of local automobile owners—is furthered by increasing the guest's burden of proof. This purpose can never be vindicated when the insurer is a New York carrier and the defendant is sued in the courts of this State. Under such circumstances, the jurisdiction enacting such a guest statute has absolutely no interest in the application of its law.

. . .

. . . [T]he instant case is one of the simplest in the choice-of-law area. If the facts are examined in light of the policy considerations which underlie the ostensibly conflicting laws it is clear that New York has the only real interest in whether recovery should be granted and that the application of Michigan law "would defeat a legitimate interest of the forum State without serving a legitimate interest of any other State" (Intercontinental Planning v. Daystrom, Inc., [24 N.Y.2d 372, 300 N.Y.S.2d 817, 248 N.E.2d 576 (1969)].

The policy of this State with respect to all those injured in automobile accidents is reflected in the legislative declaration which prefaces New York's compulsory insurance law: "The legislature is concerned over the rising toll of motor vehicle accidents and the suffering and loss thereby inflicted. The legislature determines that it is a matter of grave concern that motorists shall be financially able to respond in damages for their negligent acts, so that innocent victims of motor vehicle accidents may be recompensed for the injury and financial loss inflicted upon them." (Vehicle and Traffic Law, Consol. Laws, c. 71, § 310.)

Neither this declaration of policy nor the standard required provisions for an auto liability insurance policy make any distinction between guests, pedestrians or other insured parties.

New York's "grave concern" in affording recovery for the injuries suffered by Catharina Tooker, a New York domiciliary, and the loss suffered by her family as a result of her wrongful death, is evident merely in stating the policy which our law reflects. On the other hand, Michigan has no interest in whether a New York plaintiff is denied recovery against a New York defendant where the car is insured here.[1] The fact that the deceased guest and driver were in

1. The Michigan courts have suggested that the purpose of their guest statute is to protect the owner of the vehicle (Castle v. McKeown, 327 Mich. 518, 42 N.W.2d 733 [1950]; Hunter v. Baldwin, 268 Mich. 106, 255 N.W. 431 [1934].) It is no longer clear that a Michigan court would apply Michigan law here (see Abendschein v. Farrell, 11 Mich.App. 662, 162 N.W.2d 165 [1968]; House v. Gibbs, 4 Mich.App. 519, 145 N.W.2d 248 [1966]).

Michigan for an extended period of time is plainly irrelevant. Indeed, the Legislature, in requiring that insurance policies cover liability for injuries regardless of where the accident takes place (Vehicle & Traffic Law, § 311, subd. 4) has evinced commendable concern not only for residents of this State, but residents of other States who may be injured as a result of the activities of New York residents. Under these circumstances we cannot be concerned with whether Miss Tooker or Miss Lopez were in Michigan for a summer session or for a full college education (see Baade, Counter-Revolution or Alliance for Progress? Reflections on Reading Cavers, The Choice-of-Law Process, 46 Texas L.Rev. 141, 168–170).

The argument that the choice of law in tort cases should be governed by the fictional expectation of the parties has been rejected unequivocally by this court. . . .

Moreover, when the Legislature has chosen to compel an owner of an automobile to provide a fund for recovery for those who will be injured, and thus taken the element of choice and expectation out of the question, it seems unreasonable to look to that factor as a basis for a choice of law. And, even if we were to engage in such fictions as the expectations of the parties, it seems only fair to infer that the owner of the vehicle by purchasing a New York insurance policy which provided for the specific liability "intended to protect [the] passenger against negligent injury, as well as to secure indemnity for liability, in whatever state an accident might occur" (Kopp v. Rechtzigel, 273 Minn. 441, 443, 141 N.W.2d 526, 528 [1966]).

⌐   . . .

The dissent is, of course, correct that it was "adventitious" that Miss Tooker was a guest in an automobile registered and insured in New York. For all we know, her decision to go to Michigan State University as opposed to New York University may have been "adventitious". Indeed, her decision to go to Detroit on the weekend in question instead of staying on campus and studying may equally have been "adventitious". The fact is, however, that Miss Tooker went to Michigan State University; that she decided to go to Detroit on October 16, 1964; that she was a passenger in a vehicle registered and insured in New York; and that as a result of all these "adventitious" occurrences, she is dead and we have a case to decide. Why we should be concerned with what might have been is unclear.

. . .

We rejected the *lex loci delictus* rule because it placed controlling reliance upon one factor totally unrelated to the policies reflected by the ostensibly conflicting laws. The only fact less relevant to those policies in guest statute cases is whether the presence of the guest in the particular automobile was "adventitious."[2]

2. Similar reasons compel the rejection of the rule suggested by the Restatement, 2d, Conflict of Laws, P.O.D., pt. II, § 159, upon which the dissent relies. Where the guest-host relationship "arose" or is "centered" is wholly irrele-

. . . . Applying the choice-of-law rule which we have adopted, it is not an "implicit consequence" that the Michigan passenger injured along with Miss Lopez should be denied recovery. Under the reasoning adopted here, it is not at all clear that Michigan law would govern (Gaither v. Myers, 404 F.2d 216, 224 [D.C.Cir.1968]). We do not, however, find it necessary or desirable to conclusively resolve a question which is not now before us. It suffices to note that any anomaly resulting from the application of Michigan law to bar an action brought by Miss Silk is "the implicit consequence" of a Federal system which, at a time when we have truly become one nation, permits a citizen of one State to recover for injuries sustained in an automobile accident and denies a citizen of another State the right to recover for injuries sustained in a similar accident. The anomaly does not arise from any choice-of-law rule.

. . .

The order of the Appellate Division should be reversed, with costs, and the order of Special Term reinstated.

FULD, CHIEF JUDGE (concurring).

The time has come . . . to endeavor to minimize what some have characterized as an *ad hoc* case-by-case approach by laying down guidelines as well as we can for the solution of guest-host conflicts problems. [Chief Judge Fuld then advanced three principles, which, in Neumeier v. Kuehner, p. 503, infra, were accepted by a majority of the judges of the Court of Appeals.]

Guidelines of the sort suggested will not always be easy of application, nor will they furnish guidance to litigants and lower courts in all cases. They are proffered as a beginning, not as an end, to the problems of sound and fair adjudication in the troubled world of the automobile guest statute.

BURKE, JUDGE (concurring).

. . .

From all that has been written, it is apparent that our decision in *Dym* is overruled. . . . It is evident that the philosophy of the court has changed since *Dym* and, as a result of this transformation, we have firmly embarked upon an interest analysis approach to a conflicts problem. . . . [T]his approach . . . does not, I feel, remove all future problems from the [guest-passenger] area. Reference to the status of Miss Silk illustrates this point.

It is not at all clear whether the majority would conclude that she too, although not a New York resident, could recover should she bring an action against this defendant. Logically, the majority might

vant to policies reflected by the laws in conflict. Any language in our earlier opinions lending support to a contrary view has, as Judge Burke notes in his concurring opinion . . . , been over- ruled. We would note that there is some question as to whether the portion of the Restatement, relied upon by the dissent, is applicable to the precise facts present here.

declare, as they have in this case . . ., that "the Legislature, in requiring that insurance policies cover liability for injuries regardless of where the accident takes place . . . has evinced commendable concern not only for residents of this State, but residents of other States who may be injured as a result of the activities of New York residents." The dissenters, however, intimate that since Miss Silk could not recover in Michigan, she would presumably be barred from a recovery in this court.

I am not now prepared to decide that question nor am I ready to suggest what this State's interest would be in the present situation if the car were not insured in New York. I merely refer to these situations to illustrate the difficulty which we shall encounter in future guest statute cases even under the standard adopted by the majority today. . . . For this reason, and because of the nature of automotive traffic today, I view the entire matter as one of national concern which cannot be settled by any rule this court might proffer. As the matter is of Federal dimension, only Federal legislation will ultimately succeed in resolving these continuing controversies in a rational and equitable manner. . . .

BREITEL, JUDGE (dissenting).

. . .

Except for the facts that plaintiff and the deceased were New York residents, that defendant's deceased daughter had a New York operator's license, that the registered owner of the car was a New York resident, and that the car was registered and insured in New York, every other facet of the accident was based in Michigan and was as localized as it could be in that State. The students were in residence at the university, were not in sojourn for short courses or interim sessions, or on tour. The trip was intrinsically and exclusively a Michigan trip, concerned only with Michigan places, roads, and conditions.

The registration and ownership of the car and the residence of its driver, as well as that of plaintiff's deceased daughter, were adventitious so far as this trip was concerned. The same trip with the same purposes with some automobile would have or could have taken place among a similar group of students from other States or Michigan, or by the same students, even if the States of residence and automobile ownership and insurance were changed. Indeed, defendant might have chosen to have the automobile registered and insured in either Michigan or New York, and in his daughter's name, since the car, as a matter of family arrangements, was really hers rather than his.

In this highly mobile and automotive Nation the slight admixture of multi-state contacts as occurred here is now very frequent, and is becoming increasingly so. Unless conflicts rules move over to substitute a completely personal law for the territorial system that infuses Anglo-American jurisprudence and underlies the understanding and expectations of Americans, it is still true that the law of a territory governs the conduct and qualifiedly the status of persons, resident and nonresident, within it, except in the extraordinary situation where the localization of persons and conduct is adventitious. At least this has been true until quite recently. . . .

The converse occurred in this case. The incidental registration and ownership of the car, and the domicile of these Michigan students, did not influence their conduct or the establishment or nature of the relationship among them. Regardless of these facts they would undoubtedly have entered into the same relationship, made the same trip, and behaved the same way. These facts were, therefore, extrinsic or adventitious.

On this view, Dym v. Gordon, 16 N.Y.2d 120, 262 N.Y.S.2d 463, 209 N.E.2d 792 was soundly decided, and this case, which is even stronger on its intrinsic facts because of the young women's being students in residence, as that term is used in the academic world, should be decided the same way (Cavers, Choice-of-Law Process, pp. 300–304). . . .

Intra-mural speculation on the policies of other States has obvious limitations because of restricted information and wisdom. It is difficult enough to interpret the statutes and decisional rules of one's own State. To be sure, there is no total escape from considering the policies of other States. But this necessity should not be extended to produce anomalies of results out of the same accident, with unpredictability, and lack of consistency in determinations. Thus, it is hard to accept the implicit consequence that Miss Silk, the Michigan resident injured in the accident, should not be able to recover in Michigan (and presumably in New York) but a recovery can be had for her deceased fellow-passenger in the very same accident.

If the trend continues uninterruptedly, the shift to a personal law approach in conflicts law, especially in the torts field, will continue apace (see Cavers, Choice-of-Law Process, supra, pp. 150–156). . . .

NOTES

(1) Is it correct, as Judge Keating assumed, that New York's law "that insurance policies cover liability for injuries regardless of where the accident takes place" shows that New York liability rules are to apply with co-extensive territorial reach? Is the "declaration of policy" he perceived in the compulsory insurance law—to assure compensation for victims by obliging motorists to provide a source of reimbursement—a policy that requires that New Yorkers be liable, wherever they travel, under the New York law of tort? Compare Cavers, *Cipolla* and Conflicts Justice, 9 Duquesne L.Rev. 360, 371 (1971); Johnson v. The Hertz Corporation, 315 F.Supp. 302 (S.D. N.Y.1970).

(2) With regard to the Michigan girl, Susan Silk, does New York have an "interest" in providing recovery for an out-of-state resident against a New

Yorker that the plaintiff's own state legislature has not seen fit to allow? Does Michigan have an interest in disregarding its guest-host policy in the case of a Michigan guest hurt in a Michigan accident when to do so would apparently bring money into Michigan from New York? If Michigan does have such an interest, from what source—statutory or otherwise—is this interest derived?

(3) As Judge Keating saw the hypothetical Susan Silk claim, would it not be a "false" conflict? New York would have an interest in mulcting an insured New Yorker in favor of a Michigan girl, as a result of its outreaching objective of providing insurance coverage; and Michigan would have a parallel interest in seeing its citizen bring money home. Thus, both states might agree on the nonapplicability of the guest statute. But what if Miss Silk's damages exceeded the insurance limits? Would New York acquire a new and opposed interest?

HEPP v. IRELAND, United States District Court, S.D.N.Y. (66 Civ. 2128, Frankel, J., 1970, unreported). In an automobile guest case the plaintiff passenger was a resident of Illinois who attended Colorado College. Fellow student William Ireland, a resident of New York, was allegedly driving when the accident occurred in Colorado. They were in a car borrowed from another student, David Christian, of Kansas, where the car was registered and insured.

Two New York insurers defended the action on behalf of Ireland, pleading the guest statute of Colorado as a defense. Illinois and Kansas have similar guest statutes; New York has the common law rule. A Kansas insurance carrier had written liability insurance on the Kansas vehicle, but disclaimed coverage because of a dispute over who was at the wheel when the car crashed.

The New York insurers had issued coverage on four vehicles owned by Ireland's father. These were registered and garaged in New York. An "omnibus" clause in the New York policies covered members of Ireland Sr.'s family, even when operating other vehicles. But the New York insurers raised the argument that the Kansas policy provided "primary" coverage and the New York insurance had force only as excess insurance should the Kansas policy prove insufficient. The District Court held that the New York common law rule applied, relying heavily on Tooker v. Lopez (set forth above), especially Judge Keating's argument that the New York compulsory liability laws showed a purpose to extend protection to victims of insured motorists, wherever the accidents occurred and whatever the state of residence of the victim. Should the result be different and the guest statute be held applicable to the extent the damages claimed exceed the coverage of the defendant's policy?

NOTES

(1) Tooker dealt with the lack of governmental interest flowing from the policies underlying Michigan's guest statutes when applied to determine the guest-host rights of New York citizens who met with an accident in Michigan

during an intrastate trip while sojourning there as college students. Have Tooker's pronouncements on the inapplicability of Michigan's interest any bearing on the issue of Colorado's interest in an Illinois guest and a New York host?

(2) Should the court have considered the relative interests of Illinois and Kansas? See Cavers, *Cipolla* and Conflicts of Justice, 9 Duquesne L.Rev. 360, 368–69 (1971). Could Kansas' interests be properly evaluated without determining whether any recovery would ultimately fall upon a Kansas insurer?

(3) It appears that if the driver had not been covered by the omnibus clause in the New York policies issued to his father, the results might well have been different. Should such matters be of any significance in deciding whether a guest statute applies?

(4) How would the Hepp case now be decided in view of Neumeier v. Kuehner, which appears immediately below?

NEUMEIER v. KUEHNER

Court of Appeals of New York, 1972.
31 N.Y.2d 121, 335 N.Y.S.2d 64, 286 N.E.2d 454.

FULD, CHIEF JUDGE. A domiciliary of Ontario, Canada, was killed when the automobile in which he was riding, owned and driven by a New York resident, collided with a train in Ontario. That jurisdiction has a guest statute, and the primary question posed by this appeal is whether in this action brought by the Ontario passenger's estate, Ontario law should be applied and the New York defendant permitted to rely on its guest statute as a defense.

The facts are quickly told. On May 7, 1969, Arthur Kuehner, the defendant's intestate, a resident of Buffalo, drove his automobile from that city to Fort Erie in the Province of Ontario, Canada, where he picked up Amie Neumeier, who lived in that town with his wife and their children. Their trip was to take them to Long Beach, also in Ontario, and back again to Neumeier's home in Fort Erie. However, at a railroad crossing in the Town of Sherkston—on the way to Long Beach—the auto was struck by a train of the defendant Canadian National Railway Company. Both Kuehner and his guest-passenger were instantly killed.

Neumeier's wife and administratrix, a citizen of Canada and a domiciliary of Ontario, thereupon commenced this wrongful death action in New York against both Kuehner's estate and the Canadian National Railway Company. The defendant estate pleaded, as an affirmative defense, the Ontario guest statute and the defendant railway also interposed defenses in reliance upon it. In substance, the statute provides that the owner or driver of a motor vehicle is not liable for damages resulting from injury to, or the death of, a guest-passenger unless he was guilty of gross negligence (Highway Traffic Act of Province of Ontario [Ont.Rev.Stat. (1960), ch. 172], § 105, subd. [2], as amd. by Stat. of 1966, ch. 64, § 20, subd. [2]). It is worth noting, at this point, that, although our court originally considered that the sole purpose of the Ontario statute was to protect Ontario defendants and their insurers against collusive claims (see Babcock v. Jackson, 12 N.Y.2d 473, 482–483, 240 N.Y.S.2d 743, 749–750, 191 N.E.2d 279, 283–284[,]) "Further research . . . has revealed the distinct possibility that one purpose, and perhaps the only purpose, of the statute was to protect owners and drivers against ungrateful guests." (Reese, Chief Judge Fuld and Choice of Law, 71 Col.L.Rev. 548, 558; see Trautman, Two Views on Kell v. Henderson: A Comment, 67 Col.L.Rev. 465, 469.)*

The plaintiff, asserting that the Ontario statute "is not available . . . in the present action", moved, pursuant to CPLR 3211 (subd. [b]), to dismiss the affirmative defenses pleaded. The court at Special Term holding the guest statute applicable, denied the motions (63 Misc.2d 766, 313 N.Y.S.2d 468) but, on appeal, a closely divided Appellate Division reversed and directed dismissal of the defenses (37 A.D.2d 70, 322 N.Y.S.2d 867). It was the court's belief that such a result was dictated by Tooker v. Lopez, 24 N.Y.2d 569, 301 N.Y.S.2d 519, 249 N.E.2d 394.

In reaching that conclusion, the Appellate Division misread our decision in the *Tooker* case—a not unnatural result in light of the variant views expressed in the three separate opinions written on behalf of the majority. It is important to bear in mind that in *Tooker*, the guest-passenger and the host-driver were both domiciled in New York, and our decision—that New York law was controlling—was based upon, and limited to, that fact situation. Indeed [both] . . . Judge Keating (24 N.Y.2d at p. 580, 301 N.Y.S.2d at p. 528, 249 N.E.2d at p. 400) and Judge Burke (at p. 591, 301 N.Y.S.2d at p. 537, 249 N.E.2d at p. 407) expressly noted that the determination then being made left open the question whether New York law would be applicable if the plaintiff passenger happened to be a domiciliary of the very jurisdiction which had a guest statute.[1] Thus, Tooker v. Lopez did no more than hold that, when the passenger and driver are residents of the same jurisdiction and the car is there registered and insured, its law, and not the law of the place of accident, controls and determines the standard of care which the host owes to his guest.

What significantly and effectively differentiates the present case is the fact that, although the host was a domiciliary of New York, the

* Another scholar's research into the legislative history of the Ontario statute has led him to the conclusion that the statute was only intended to protect insurance companies. Baade, The Case of The Disinterested Two States: Neumeier v. Kuehner, 1 Hofstra L.Rev. 150, 152–154 (1973). [Footnote by the Editors.]

249 N.E.2d at p. 404), I wrote that in such a case—where the passenger is a resident of the state having a guest statute—"the applicable rule of decision will [normally] be that of the state where the accident occurred". [Footnote by the court.]

1. In the other concurring opinion (24 N.Y.2d at p. 585, 301 N.Y.S.2d at p. 533,

guest, for whose death recovery is sought, was domiciled in Ontario, the place of accident and the very jurisdiction which had enacted the statute designed to protect the host from liability for ordinary negligence. It is clear that although New York has a deep interest in protecting its own residents, injured in a foreign state, against unfair or anachronistic statutes of that state, it has no legitimate interest in ignoring the public policy of a foreign jurisdiction—such as Ontario—and in protecting the plaintiff guest domiciled and injured there from legislation obviously addressed, at the very least, to a resident riding in a vehicle traveling within its borders.

To distinguish *Tooker* on such a basis is not improperly discriminatory. It is quite true that, in applying the Ontario guest statute to the Ontario-domiciled passenger, we, in a sense, extend a right less generous than New York extends to a New York passenger in a New York vehicle with New York insurance. That, though, is not a consequence of invidious discrimination; it is, rather, the result of the existence of disparate rules of law in jurisdictions that have diverse and important connections with the litigants and the litigated issue.

The fact that insurance policies issued in this State on New York-based vehicles cover liability, regardless of the place of the accident (Vehicle and Traffic Law, Consol.Laws, c. 71 § 311, subd. 4), certainly does not call for the application of internal New York law in this case. The compulsory insurance requirement is designed to cover a car-owner's liability, not create it; in other words, the applicable statute was not intended to impose liability where none would otherwise exist. This being so, we may not properly look to the New York insurance requirement to dictate a choice-of-law rule which would invariably impose liability. . . .

When, in Babcock v. Jackson (12 N.Y.2d 473, 240 N.Y.S.2d 743, 191 N.E.2d 279, supra), we rejected the inexorable choice-of-law rule in personal injury cases because it failed to take account of underlying policy considerations, we were willing to sacrifice the certainty provided by the old rule for the more just, fair and practical result that may best be achieved by giving controlling effect to the law of the jurisdiction which has the greatest concern with, or interest in, the specific issue raised in the litigation. . . . In consequence of the change effected—and this was to be anticipated—our decisions in multi-state highway accident cases, particularly in those involving guest-host controversies, have, it must be acknowledged, lacked consistency. This stemmed, in part, from the circumstance that it is frequently difficult to discover the purposes or policies underlying the relevant local law rules of the respective jurisdictions involved. It is even more difficult, assuming that these purposes or policies are found to conflict, to determine on some principled basis which should be given effect at the expense of the others.

The single all-encompassing rule which called, invariably, for selection of the law of the place of injury was discarded, and wisely, because it was too broad to prove satisfactory in application. There, is, however, no reason why choice-of-law rules, more narrow than those previously devised, should not be successfully developed, in order to assure a greater degree of predictability and uniformity, on the basis of our present knowledge and experience. . . . "The time has come," I wrote in Tooker (24 N.Y.2d, at p. 584, 301 N.Y.S.2d, at p. 532, 249 N.E.2d, at p. 403), "to endeavor to minimize what some have characterized as an *ad hoc* case-by-case approach by laying down guidelines, as well as we can, for the solution of guest-host conflicts problems." *Babcock* and its progeny enable us to formulate a set of basic principles that may be profitably utilized, for they have helped us uncover the underlying values and policies which are operative in this area of the law. . . . "Now that these values and policies have been revealed, we may proceed to the next stage in the evolution of the law—the formulation of a few rules of general applicability, promising a fair level of predictability." Although it was recognized that no rule may be formulated to guarantee a satisfactory result in every case, the following principles were proposed as sound for situations involving guest statutes in conflicts settings (24 N.Y.2d, at p. 585, 301 N.Y.S.2d, at p. 532, 249 N.E.2d, at p. 404):

"1.   When the guest-passenger and the host-driver are domiciled in the same state, and the car is there registered, the law of that state should control and determine the standard of care which the host owes to his guest.

"2.   When the driver's conduct occurred in the state of his domicile and that state does not cast him in liability for that conduct, he should not be held liable by reason of the fact that liability would be imposed upon him under the tort law of the state of the victim's domicile. Conversely, when the guest was injured in the state of his own domicile and its law permits recovery, the driver who has come into that state should not—in the absence of special circumstances—be permitted to interpose the law of his state as a defense.

"3.   In other situations, when the passenger and the driver are domiciled in different states, the rule is necessarily less categorical. Normally, the applicable rule of decision will be that of the state where the accident occurred but not if it can be shown that displacing that normally applicable rule will advance the relevant substantive law purposes without impairing the smooth working of the multi-state system or producing great uncertainty for litigants. (Cf. Restatement, 2d, Conflict of Laws, P.O.D., pt. II, §§ 146, 159 [later adopted and promulgated May 23, 1969].)"

The variant views expressed not only in *Tooker* but by Special Term and the divided Appellate Division in this litigation underscore and confirm the need for these rules. Since the passenger was domiciled in Ontario and the driver in New York, the present case is covered by the third stated principle. The law to be applied is that of the jurisdiction where the accident happened unless it appears that "displacing [that] normally applicable rule will advance the relevant substantive law purposes" of the jurisdictions involved. Certainly, ignoring Ontario's policy requiring proof of gross negligence in a case which involves an Ontario-domiciled guest at the expense of a New Yorker does not further the substantive law purposes of New York. In point of fact, application of New York law would result in the exposure of this State's domiciliaries to a greater liability than that imposed upon resident users of Ontario's highways. Conversely, the failure to apply Ontario's law would "impair"—to cull from the rule set out above—"the smooth working of the multi-state system [and] produce great uncertainty for litigants" by sanctioning forum shopping and thereby allowing a party to select a forum which could give him a larger recovery than the court of his own domicile. In short, the plaintiff has failed to show that this State's connection with the controversy was sufficient to justify displacing the rule of *lex loci delictus*. . . .

In each action, the Appellate Division's order should be reversed, that of Special Term reinstated, without costs, and the questions certified answered in the negative.

BREITEL, JUDGE (concurring).

I agree that there should be a reversal, but would place the reversal on quite narrow grounds. It is undesirable to lay down prematurely major premises based on shifting ideologies in the choice of law. True, Chief Judge Fuld in his concurring opinion in the *Tooker* case . . . took the view that there had already occurred sufficient experience to lay down some rules of law which would reduce the instability and uncertainty created by the recent departures from traditional *lex loci delictus*. This case, arising so soon after, shows that the permutations in accident cases, especially automobile accident cases, is disproof that the time has come.

Problems engendered by the new departures have not gone unnoticed and they are not confined to the courts of this State (Juenger, Choice of Law in Interstate Torts, 118 U.Pa.L.Rev. 202, 214–220). They arise not merely because any new departure of necessity creates problems, but much more because the departures have been accompanied by an unprecedented competition of ideologies, largely of academic origin, to explain and reconstruct a whole field of law, each purporting or aspiring to achieve a single universal principle.

Babcock v. Jackson, 12 N.Y.2d 473, 240 N.Y.S.2d 743, 191 N.E.2d 279, an eminently correctly and justly decided case, applied the then current new doctrine of grouping of contacts. Troubles arose only when the universality of a single doctrine was assumed . . . . By the time of Miller v. Miller, 22 N.Y.2d 12, 290 N.Y.S.2d 734, 237 N.E.2d 877 and the *Tooker* case, supra, the new doctrine had been displaced by a still newer one, that of governmental interests developed most extensively by the late Brainerd Currie, and the court was deeply engaged in probing the psychological motivation of legislatures of other States in enacting statutes restricting recoveries in tort cases. Now, evidently, it is suggested that this State and other States may have less parochial concerns in enacting legislation restricting tort recoveries than had been believed only a short time ago. The trouble this case has given the courts below and now this court stems, it is suggested, more from a concern in sorting out ideologies than in applying narrow rules of law in the traditional common-law process (Juenger, op. cit., supra, at p. 233).

What the *Babcock* case, . . . taught and what modern day commentators largely agree is that *lex loci delictus* is unsoundly applied if it is done indiscriminately and without exception. It is still true, however, that the *lex loci delictus* is the normal rule, as indeed Chief Judge Fuld noted in the *Tooker* case, . . . to be rejected only when it is evident that the situs of the accident is the least of the several factors or influences to which the accident may be attributed . . . Certain it is that States are not concerned only with their own citizens or residents. They are concerned with events that occur within their territory, and are also concerned with the "stranger within the gates" (Juenger, op. cit., supra, at pp. 209–210).

In this case, none would have ever assumed that New York law should be applied just because one of the two defendants was a New York resident and his automobile was New York insured, except for the overbroad statements of Currie doctrine in the *Tooker* case . . . .

Consequently, I agree that there should be a reversal and the defenses allowed to stand. The conclusion, however, rests simply on the proposition that plaintiff has failed by her allegations to establish that the relationship to this State was sufficient to displace the normal rule that the *lex loci delictus* should be applied, the accident being associated with Ontario, from inception to tragic termination, except for adventitious facts and where the lawsuit was brought.

BERGAN, JUDGE (dissenting). . . .

There is a difference of fundamental character between justifying a departure from *lex loci delictus* because the court will not, as a matter of policy, permit a New York owner of a car licensed and insured in New York to escape a liability that would be imposed on him here; and a departure based on the fact a New York resident makes the claim for injury. The first ground of departure is justifiable as sound policy; the second is justifiable only if one is willing to treat the rights of a stranger permitted to sue in New York differently from the way a resident is treated. Neither because of "interest" nor "contact" nor any other defensible ground is it proper to say in a court of law that the rights of one man whose suit is accepted shall be adjudged differently on the merits on the basis of where he happens to live. . . .

. . . What the court is deciding today is that although it will prevent a New York car owner from asserting the defense of a protective foreign statute when a New York resident in whose rights it has an "interest" sues; it has no such "interest" when it accepts the suit in New York of a nonresident. This is an inadmissible distinction.

NOTES

(1) On occasion, Judge Fuld's principles may produce results that some may think unpalatable. See, e.g., Foster v. Leggett, 484 S.W.2d 827 (Ky. 1972). The defendant driver was legally domiciled in Ohio, which has a guest statute, but he was employed in Kentucky and spent much of his time there. He and his guest set out from Kentucky for Columbus, Ohio, intending to "have dinner, go to a show or the races" and then return to Kentucky "the night of the same day." In Ohio the car was in an accident and the passenger was killed. The Kentucky court refused to apply the Ohio guest statute and found for the plaintiff by applying Kentucky's common law standard of negligence. Judge Fuld's second principle would apparently call for application of the law of Ohio. Is an occasional questionable result an inevitable by-product of even a good rule? Foster v. Leggett is the subject of a symposium in 61 Ky.L.J. 368–428 (1973).

(2) Subsequent cases in the New York courts have apparently only been concerned with Chief Judge Fuld's third principle. Pursuant to this principle, the law of the place of injury was applied and judgment rendered in the defendant's favor in Croft v. National Car Rental, 56 N.Y.2d 989, 453 N.Y.S.2d 631, 439 N.E.2d 346 (1982) (vicarious liability of owner for negligence of driver); Towley v. Arthur Rings, Inc., 40 N.Y.2d 129, 386 N.Y.S.2d 80, 351 N.E.2d 728 (1976) (guest-passenger statute); Blais v. Deyo, 92 A.D.2d 998, 461 N.Y.S.2d 471 (3rd Dept.1983) (limit on amount of recovery); Rogers v. U-Haul Co., 41 A.D.2d 834, 342 N.Y.S.2d 158 (1973) (vicarious liability of owner for negligence of driver).

(3) The New York Court of Appeals also cited Neumeier in an opinion in which it said by way of dictum that "*lex loci delicti* remains the general rule in tort cases to be displaced only in extraordinary circumstances." Cousins v. Instrument Flyers, Inc., 44 N.Y.2d 698, 699; 376 N.E.2d 914, 915 (1978).

(4) Action by a guest-passenger to recover for injuries resulting from an automobile accident in Ohio. The plaintiff was domiciled in New Jersey and the defendant driver in New York. The automobile was registered, principally garaged and "presumably insured" in New York. *Held*: The Ohio guest-passenger statute was not available to the defendant as a defense. Chief Judge Fuld's third principle would not require application of Ohio law in this instance, since "none of the litigants reside in a state having a guest statute, nor presumably did the insurer calculate the defendants' insurance premiums with a guest statute in mind." Chila v. Owens, 348 F.Supp. 1207 (S.D.N.Y.1972).

(5) Other states have given Chief Judge Fuld's Neumeier principles a mixed reception. First National Bank in Fort Collins v. Rostek, 514 P.2d 314 (Colo.1973), adopted the first two principles; but in Labree v. Major, 306 A.2d 808 (R.I.1973). the court said:

"Where a driver is from a state which allows a passenger to recover for ordinary negligence, the plaintiff should recover, no matter what the law of his residence or the place of the accident. We adopt this rule because the only state with an interest in protecting the driver and his insurer does not do so."

Would it not have been equally logical for the court to have held in the *Major* case that a plaintiff domiciled in a state having a guest-passenger statute should have that statute applied to him on the ground that the only state with an interest in protecting him did not choose to do so?

(6) Neumeier v. Kuehner is the subject of a symposium, consisting of articles by Professors Twerski, Sedler, Baade, Shapira and King, in 1 Hofstra L.Rev. 104–182 (1973). All of the writers, with the exception of the last mentioned, criticize the decision on a variety of grounds. For a more recent criticism of the *Neumeier* decision, see Trautman, Rule or Reason in Choice of Law: A Comment on Neumeier, 1 Vt.L.Rev. 1 (1976).

(7) See generally Reese, Chief Judge Fuld and Choice of Law, 71 Colum. L.Rev. 548 (1971); Reese, Choice of Law: Rules or Approach, 57 Corn.L.Q. 315 (1972); Powers, Formalism and Nonformalism in Choice of Law Methodology, 52 Wash.L.Rev. 27 (1976); Haworth, The Mirror Image Conflicts Case, 1974 Wash.U.L.Q. 1.

CIPOLLA V. SHAPOSKA, 439 Pa. 563, 267 A.2d 854 (1970). In Delaware, D, driving a car garaged, registered and insured in Delaware where he resided, injured his guest passenger, P, who was domiciled in Pennsylvania. P sued for ordinary negligence in Pennsylvania, but lost. A majority of the court held the Delaware guest statute applicable both because "Delaware's contacts are qualitatively greater than Pennsylvania's and * * * has the greater interest in having its law applied" and because "it seems only fair to permit a defendant to rely on his home state's law when he is acting within that state."

ROBERTS, J., dissenting, saw a "true" conflict of evenly balanced interests. On one side was Delaware's policy to protect a generous host from liability for ordinary negligence; on the other, Pennsylvania's purpose to compensate the injured guest. To cut the knot, he invoked the "better rule of law approach" urged by Professor Leflar, adding that he found guest statutes regressing and weakening, especially in multistate situations. A symposium on Cipolla v. Shaposka appears in 9 Duquesne L.Rev. 360 (1971).

NOTE

See L. McDougal, The New Frontier in Choice of Law—The Need Demonstrated in Theory and in the Context of Motor Vehicle Guest-Host Controversies, 53 Tulane L.Rev. 731 (1979).

THE MODERN DILEMMA IN THE CHOICE–OF–LAW PROCESS

Babcock v. Jackson and the cases that follow exemplify the chaotic effects from the collision between the classical system of choice-of-law rules and the no-rules methodology. Without doubt, the result was to throw choice of law in New York state into a jumble, marked by a succession of confusing decisions. New York, however, is not the only state and the guest-host problem is not the only issue buffetted by the tempest of changing ideas in this field.

How to resolve the dilemma? On the one hand, the old systematics functioned either woodenly and mechanically—producing many foolish results—or erratically and trickily—with a pretense of simplicity that was false in fact. On the other hand, abandonment of rules in favor of a contents-conscious "method" of selecting the norm by which to decide the disputed issue resulted in a welter of frequently incoherent opinions and an unhealthy judicial subjectivity. Is there some way of moving off one horn of the dilemma without becoming impaled on the other? The focus now shifts to wrongful death cases, where a similar process of groping for better answers has occurred, and then to other types of problems.

REICH v. PURCELL

Supreme Court of California, 1967.
67 Cal.2d 551, 63 Cal.Rptr. 31, 432 P.2d 727.*

TRAYNOR, CHIEF JUSTICE. This wrongful death action arose out of a head-on collision of two automobiles in Missouri. One of the automobiles was owned and operated by defendant Joseph Purcell, a resident and domiciliary of California who was on his way to a vacation in Illinois. The other automobile was owned and operated by Mrs. Reich, the wife of plaintiff Lee Reich. The Reichs then resided in Ohio and Mrs. Reich and the Reichs' two children, Jay and Jeffry, were on their way to California, where the Reichs were contemplating settling. Mrs. Reich and Jay were killed in the collision, and Jeffry was injured.

Plaintiffs, Lee Reich and Jeffry Reich, are the heirs of Mrs. Reich and Lee Reich is the heir of Jay Reich. Plaintiffs moved to California and became permanent residents here after the accident. The estates of Mrs. Reich and Jay Reich are being administered in Ohio.

The parties stipulated that judgment be entered in specified amounts for the wrongful death of Jay, for the personal injuries suffered by Jeffry, and for the damages to Mrs. Reich's automobile. For the death of Mrs. Reich they stipulated that judgment be entered

---

* A symposium devoted to this case appears in Comments on Reich v. Purcell, 15 U.C.L.A.L.Rev. 551 (1968).

for $55,000 or $25,000 depending on the court's ruling on the applicability of the Missouri limitation of damages to a maximum of $25,000. (Vernon's Ann.Mo.Stats. § 537.090.) Neither Ohio nor California limit recovery in wrongful death actions. The trial court held that the Missouri limitation applied because the accident occurred there and entered judgment accordingly. Plaintiffs appeal.

For many years courts applied the law of the place of the wrong in tort actions regardless of the issues before the court, e.g., whether they involved conduct, survival of actions, applicability of a wrongful death statute, immunity from liability, or other rules determining whether a legal injury has been sustained. . . . It was assumed that the law of the place of the wrong created the cause of action and necessarily determined the extent of the liability. (Slater v. Mexican National R.R. Co., 194 U.S. 120, 126, 24 S.Ct. 581, 48 L.Ed. 900.) Aside from procedural difficulties (see Currie, Selected Essays on Conflict of Laws (1963) pp. 10–18), this theory worked well enough when all the relevant events took place in one jurisdiction, but the action was brought in another. In a complex situation involving multistate contacts, however, no single state alone can be deemed to create exclusively governing rights. . . . The forum must search to find the proper law to apply based upon the interests of the litigants and the involved states. Such complex cases elucidate what the simpler cases obscured, namely, that the forum can only apply its own law. . . . When it purports to do otherwise, it is not enforcing foreign rights but choosing a foreign rule of decision as the appropriate one to apply to the case before it. Moreover, it has now been demonstrated that a choice of law resulting from a hopeless search for a governing foreign law to create a foreign vested right may defeat the legitimate interests of the litigants and the states involved. (See generally, Cavers, The Choice of Law Process (1965); Currie, Selected Essays on Conflict of Laws, supra; Ehrenzweig, Conflict of Laws (1962).)

Accordingly, when application of the law of the place of the wrong would defeat the interests of the litigant and of the states concerned, we have not applied that law. (Grant v. McAuliffe [p. 455, supra] . . .; Emery v. Emery, 45 Cal.2d 421, 428, 289 P.2d 218.) *Grant* was an action for personal injuries arising out of an automobile accident in Arizona between California residents. The driver whose negligence caused the accident died, and the court had to choose between the California rule that allowed an action against the personal representative and the Arizona rule that did not. We held that since "all of the parties were residents of this state, and the estate of the deceased tortfeasor is being administered in this state, plaintiffs' right to prosecute their causes of action is governed by the laws of this state relating to administration of estates." Under these circumstances application of the law of the place of the wrong would not only have defeated California's interest and that of its residents but would have advanced no interest of Arizona or its residents. (Grant

v. McAuliffe, supra . . .). In *Emery* members of a California family were injured in Idaho when another member of the family who was driving lost control of the car and it went off the road. The question was whether Idaho or California law determined when one member of a family was immune from tort liability to another. We applied the law of the family domicile rather than the law of the place of the wrong. "That state has the primary responsibility for establishing and regulating the incidents of the family relationship and it is the only state in which the parties can, by participation in the legislative processes, effect a change in those incidents. Moreover, it is undesirable that the rights, duties, disabilities, and immunities conferred or imposed by the family relationship should constantly change as members of the family cross state boundaries during temporary absences from their home." (45 Cal.2d at p. 428, 289 P.2d at p. 223.)

Defendant contends, however, that there were compelling reasons in the *Grant* and *Emery* cases for departing from the law of the place of the wrong and that such reasons are not present in this case. He urges that application of that law promotes uniformity of decisions, prevents forum shopping, and avoids the uncertainties that may result from ad hoc searches for a more appropriate law in this and similar cases.

Ease of determining applicable law and uniformity of rules of decision, however, must be subordinated to the objective of proper choice of law in conflict cases, i.e., to determine the law that most appropriately applies to the issue involved (see Leflar, Choice-Influencing Considerations In Conflicts Law (1966) 41 N.Y.U.L.Rev. 267, 279–282). Moreover, as jurisdiction after jurisdiction has departed from the law of the place of the wrong as the controlling law in tort cases, regardless of the issue involved . . ., that law no longer affords even a semblance of the general application that was once thought to be its great virtue. We conclude that the law of the place of the wrong is not necessarily the applicable law for all tort actions brought in the courts of this state . . . [and] cases to the contrary are overruled.

As the forum we must consider all of the foreign and domestic elements and interests involved in this case to determine the rule applicable. Three states are involved. Ohio is where plaintiffs and their decedents resided before the accident and where the decedents' estates are being administered. Missouri is the place of the wrong. California is the place where defendant resides and is the forum. Although plaintiffs now reside in California, their residence and domicile at the time of the accident are the relevant residence and domicile. At the time of the accident the plans to change the family domicile were not definite and fixed, and if the choice of law were made to turn on events happening after the accident, forum shopping would be encouraged. (See Cavers, op. cit., supra, p. 151, fn. 16.)

Accordingly, plaintiffs' present domicile in California does not give this state any interest in applying its law, and since California has no limitation of damages, it also has no interest in applying its law on behalf of defendant. As a forum that is therefore disinterested in the only issue in dispute, we must decide whether to adopt the Ohio or the Missouri rule as the rule of decision for this case.

Missouri is concerned with conduct within her borders and as to such conduct she has the predominant interest of the states involved. Limitations of damages for wrongful death, however, have little or nothing to do with conduct. They are concerned not with how people should behave but with how survivors should be compensated. The state of the place of the wrong has little or no interest in such compensation when none of the parties reside there. Wrongful death statutes create causes of action in specified beneficiaries and distribute the proceeds to those beneficiaries. The proceeds in the hands of the beneficiaries are not distributed through the decedent's estate and, therefore, are not subject to the claims of the decedent's creditors and consequently do not provide a fund for local creditors. Accordingly, the interest of a state in a wrongful death action insofar as plaintiffs are concerned is in determining the distribution of proceeds to the beneficiaries and that interest extends only to local decedents and beneficiaries. (Currie, op. cit., supra, pp. 690, 702). Missouri's limitation on damages expresses an additional concern for defendants, however, in that it operates to avoid the imposition of excessive financial burdens on them. That concern is also primarily local and we fail to perceive any substantial interest Missouri might have in extending the benefits of its limitation of damages to travelers from states having no similar limitation. Defendant's liability should not be limited when no party to the action is from a state limiting liability and when defendant, therefore, would have secured insurance, if any, without any such limit in mind. A defendant cannot reasonably complain when compensatory damages are assessed in accordance with the law of his domicile and plaintiffs receive no more than they would have had they been injured at home. (See Cavers, op. cit., supra, pp. 153–157.) Under these circumstances giving effect to Ohio's interests in affording full recovery to injured parties does not conflict with any substantial interest of Missouri. (Cf. Bernkrant v. Fowler, 55 Cal.2d 588, 595, 12 Cal.Rptr. 266, 360 P.2d 906.) Accordingly, the Missouri limitation does not apply. . . .

The part of the judgment appealed from is reversed with directions to the trial court to enter judgment for the plaintiffs in the amount of $55,000 in accordance with the stipulations of the parties.

NOTES

(1) Does a choice-of-law rule emerge from the principal case, or does it proceed entirely on the interest analysis method? If a rule were formulated, would it be as follows: "Damages for wrongful death in an automobile acci-

dent should not be in a lesser amount than that recoverable in the respective states of domicile of the plaintiff and of the defendant."

(2) Is it of any significance that the Ohio conflicts rule required application of the Missouri death limit to the case of an Ohioan wrongfully killed in Missouri? Goranson v. Capital Airlines, Inc., 345 F.2d 750 (6th Cir.1965). Cf. Pfau v. Trent Aluminum Co., 55 N.J. 511, 263 A.2d 129 (1970) (p. 556, infra); Long v. Pan American World Airways, (p. 558, n. (2), infra).

(3) If Mrs. Reich had been killed by a driver domiciled in Missouri, would her beneficiaries have been limited to $25,000? Cf. Miller v. Miller, infra.

(4) Is Hurtado v. Superior Court of Sacramento, 11 Cal.3d 574, 114 Cal. Rptr. 106, 522 P.2d 666 (1974) consistent with Reich v. Purcell? In Hurtado, decedent and his family resided in a state of Mexico that limited recoveries for wrongful death to less than $2,000. The fatal collision in California involved a car driven and owned by California residents. The Supreme Court held that the state of plaintiffs' domicile had no interest in limiting their recovery from California defendants and allowed California damage norms for the reason in part that one purpose of California's higher measure of recovery was to deter negligent conduct. Is it probable that the court first decided upon the result it wished to reach and then attributed a policy to the California law which would call for this law's application?

If the facts were reversed—that is, if a Californian had been killed through the fault of a Mexican citizen in a Mexican state limiting damages to under $2,000—would a California court be in violation of the Home Insurance v. Dick principle if it allowed California-level damages against the Mexican defendant's insurer, assuming an attachment in California? Compare Rosenthal v. Warren, p. 519, infra.

(5) Could it not be persuasively argued that California in Hurtado had an affirmative interest in not applying its rule of unlimited recovery on the ground that to do so would tend to increase the insurance rates of all Californians? See Ratner, Choice of Law: Interest Analysis and Cost Contribution, 47 S.Cal.L.Rev. 817 (1974).

(6) See Milhollin: The Forum Preference in Choice of Law; Some Notes on Hurtado v. Superior Court, 10 U.S.F.L.Rev. 625 (1977).

MILLER v. MILLER

Court of Appeals of New York, 1968.
22 N.Y.2d 12, 290 N.Y.S.2d 734, 237 N.E.2d 877.

[Action to recover for a wrongful death resulting from an automobile accident in Maine which occurred in the course of what was intended to be a short business trip from one point in Maine to another. The defendant driver and the decedent were brothers. At the time of the accident the defendant resided in Maine while the decedent was a resident of New York. Shortly after the accident, however, the defendant moved to New York. The question presented on appeal was the applicability of a Maine statute which imposed a $20,000 limitation on recovery for wrongful death. The statute was repealed subsequent to the accident but it was assumed that the Maine courts would have continued to apply it to pre-enactment deaths.]

KEATING, JUDGE.

. . . Prior to the adoption of the [New York] Constitution of 1894, recoveries for wrongful death were limited to the sum of $5,000 (Code of Civ.Pro. [1894], § 1904). The Record of Debates of the Constitutional Convention of 1894 (Vol. 2, pp. 581–595, 651, 652, 947–962) indicates that the framers of the constitutional provision regarded the arbitrary limitation of $5,000 as absurd and unjust. . . .

Our inquiry as to the choice of an appropriate law cannot, however, stop merely in defining a New York interest—albeit a substantial one—in the application of the particular law which is the object of the conflict. We must recognize that, in addition to the interest in affording the plaintiff full recovery, there may be other more general considerations which should concern "a justice-dispensing court in a modern American state". (Leflar, Choice-Influencing Considerations in Conflicts Law, 41 N.Y.U.L.Rev. 267, 295). Among other considerations are the "fairness" of applying our law where a nonresident or even a resident has patterned his conduct upon the law of the jurisdiction in which he was acting (Babcock v. Jackson, 12 N.Y.2d 473, 483, supra) as well as the possible interest of a sister State in providing the remedy for injuries sustained as a result of conduct undertaken within its borders . . .

As we view the facts in this case, however, we perceive no substantial countervailing considerations of the kind described above which would warrant the rejection of our own law in favor of that of Maine. The Maine statute with which we are concerned here, dealing as it does with the nature of the remedy for concededly tortious conduct, is obviously not the kind of statute which regulates conduct and, therefore, is not the kind of statute upon which a person would rely in governing his conduct. The only justifiable reliance which could be present here would involve the purchase of liability insurance in light of the remedies available to an injured person. No such reliance is claimed here and, as a more careful examination of the problem reveals, this is not without good reason.

Under Maine law as it existed at the time of the accident, the defendants would have been fully liable for compensatory damages, had the decedent not been killed but merely injured and this no matter how serious his injuries. We have been advised by the Insurance Department of the State of Maine that, despite the limitation on recovery in wrongful death actions, the standard automobile liability policies issued in Maine drew no distinction between liability coverage for wrongful death and personal injuries. It would, therefore, appear that no proper claim that the defendants relied upon the limitation in purchasing insurance can be made here and, as we have noted, no such claim is made. . . .

With respect to the liability insurer—the real party in interest—a somewhat different situation obtains. The insurer may have expected that Maine's limitation on death recoveries would apply to accidents in Maine. But here in determining whether any unfairness will result by virtue of the application of New York law, we may also consider the fact that the policy in question was not and could not have been limited to affording protection only to accidents occurring in the State of Maine (Maine Rev.Stat.Ann., tit. 29, § 781 et seq.) and that, therefore, the possibility of liability in excess of $20,000 was certainly not unexpected and was insured against. Moreover, an analysis of the actuarial process as well as an inquiry to the Insurance Commission of the State of Maine reveals that the presence of the limitations had no substantial effect on insurance premiums, and a refusal to apply Maine law here will have an infinitesimal effect, if that, on insurance rates in Maine (see Morris, Enterprise Liability and the Actuarial Process—The Insignificance of Foresight, 70 Yale L.J. 554, 560–581).

. . . [W]e turn next to the question of whether the application of New York law here will unduly interfere with a legitimate interest of a sister State in regulating the rights of its citizens, at least with regard to conduct within its borders. Here again we perceive no reason to deny application of our own law. To the extent that the Maine limitation evinced a desire to protect its residents in wrongful death actions, that purpose cannot be defeated here since no judgment in this action will be entered against a Maine resident. Maine would have no concern with the nature of the recovery awarded against defendants who are no longer residents of that State and who are, therefore, no longer proper objects of its legislative concern. It is true that, at the time of the accident, the defendants were residents of Maine but they would have no vested right to the application of the law of their former residence unless it could be demonstrated that they had governed their conduct in reliance upon it . . . —a reliance which is neither present nor claimed in the case at bar. Any claim that Maine has a paternalistic interest in protecting its residents against liability for acts committed while they were in Maine, should they move to another jurisdiction, is highly speculative and ignores the fact that for the very same acts committed today Maine would now impose the same liability as New York.

There may be times where policy considerations such as a desire to prevent forum shopping would require us to ignore changes in domicile after the accident (Gore v. Northeast Airlines, [373 F.2d 717 (2d Cir.1967)]; Reich v. Purcell [p. 511, supra]). In the instant case, however, the change in domicile has nothing whatever to do with a desire to achieve a more favorable legal climate, and we see no reason to ignore the facts as they are presented at the time of the litigation. . . .

BREITEL, JUDGE (dissenting).

. . .

Infusing the old territorial rules as well as the newer theories of grouping of contacts or interest analysis is a desire to satisfy the reasonable expectations of persons participating in transactions. This is perhaps the dominant motif in the adjudication of multistate transactions, and therefore generally leads to the "justice" of the determination (see Rheinstein, Book Review, 32 U.Chi.L.Rev. 369).

Justice favors the fulfillment of expectations for two reasons. First, parties may have acted in reliance upon their assumption that courts would apply a certain rule of decision, and application of a different rule to their detriment would then be unjust. Of course, this pragmatic significance of expectations varies with the type of legal rule involved. It is undoubtedly strongest in contract cases (see, e.g., Auten v. Auten, 308 N.Y. 155; Ehrenzweig, Conflict of Laws, §§ 175–184). But it exists even in tort cases . . .

Justified expectations are also relevant in a second, more intangible, way: it is jurisprudentially significant that parties' rights be determined by the law or system of rules which they most probably believed would control their relationship. In this respect, the application of the proper law of the tort exercises an influence in "promoting an unconscious acceptance of legality and legal order" (Kegel, [The Crisis of Conflict of Laws, 112 Recueil des Cours], pp. 91, 184). Thus, in guest-statute cases, courts have applied a rule of guest-host liability which, in effect, reflects the parties' unexpressed but undoubted assumption that a single system of rules will control guest-host liability no matter where the accident happens to take place. For this reason there is much to be said for applying the rule of the seat of the relationship, or, alternatively, that of the common domicile of guest and host . . . .

NOTES

(1) Was the Court right to give weight to post-accident events in deciding a question of choice of law? A negative answer was given by Chief Justice Traynor in Reich v. Purcell, p. 511, supra, because, "if the choice of law were made to turn on events happening after the accident, forum shopping would be encouraged." On the other hand, see Note, Post Transaction or Occurrence Events in Conflict of Laws, 69 Colum.L.Rev. 843, 865 (1969), which concludes:

> The logic of interest analysis requires that governmental interests be weighed as they exist at the time of trial rather than at the time of the transaction or occurrence in issue. At the same time, . . . [c]onsiderations of fairness, predictability, and the existence of forum shopping should all be considered. Consequently, it is as wrong categorically to give effect to post occurrence events as it is categorically to deny their relevance.

(2) Cf. Tjepkema v. Kenney, 31 A.D.2d 908, 298 N.Y.S.2d 175 (1st Dep't 1969), where an intermediate New York appellate court relied on Kilberg v. Northeast Airlines, Inc., p. 464, supra as the basis for knocking out the defense of the Missouri limit on death damages in a case involving a fatal accident to a New Yorker run over while crossing a highway in Missouri by a local resident. Jurisdiction was based on an insurance attachment of the Seider v. Roth type (p. 159, supra).

(3) For a helpful and comprehensive discussion of major approaches to this problem, see Juenger, Choice of Law in Interstate Torts, 118 U.Pa.L. Rev. 202 (1969).

(4) *Conflict of laws in time.* What is the crucial time for ascertaining the content of a state's law? The time of the occurrence? The time of the trial? Some other time? In Berghammer v. Smith, 185 N.W.2d 226 (Iowa 1971), suit was brought by Minnesota plaintiffs against an Illinois defendant to recover for damages arising out of an Iowa accident. One question was whether the wife of the injured plaintiff could recover for loss of consortium. The Iowa court determined that Minnesota law governed this issue since "only Minnesota is concerned with the marital status of plaintiff and the interspousal rights and duties arising therefrom." At the time of the accident, Minnesota did not recognize a wife's cause of action for loss of consortium. By the time of the trial, however, the Minnesota courts had changed the rule to permit such an action, but had stated that the new rule should be given only a prospective application. Nevertheless, the Iowa court applied the new Minnesota rule retroactively and permitted recovery by the wife. The court justified its decision by stating that the policy which had led the Minnesota courts to make the new rule solely prospective would not be furthered by applying this limitation in the present case. The court said: "The prospective application was apparently to permit those relying on the old rule to protect themselves against enlarged liability by securing additional insurance coverage . . . . But that element is not present here. Defendant, a resident of Illinois, cannot claim either surprise or injustice about the application of a rule which his own state recognized . . . . Certainly, Minnesota's purpose was not to protect non-resident motorists who had not relied upon the old rule at the expense of its own citizens." The dissenting judge thought it wrong to apply the new Minnesota rule without at the same time adhering to its provisions as to prospectivity and retroactivity.

ROSENTHAL v. WARREN

United States Circuit Court of Appeals, Second Circuit, 1973.
475 F.2d 438.

OAKES, CIRCUIT JUDGE: This appeal in a diversity case raises the question whether New York would apply a Massachusetts damage limitation to the death of a New York domiciliary occurring in Massachusetts. The appeal, taken before final judgment pursuant to 28 U.S.C. § 1292(b), is from an order of the district court granting partial summary judgment in favor of the plaintiff in an action for wrongful death. The partial summary judgment struck the affirmative defense based upon the Massachusetts wrongful death statute limiting recoverable damages to ". . . not less than Five Thousand Dollars nor more than Fifty Thousand Dollars, to be assessed with reference to the degree of [the tortfeasor's] culpability . . . ."[1] The district court held that New York law was applicable. That law places no fixed value on wrongful death or limitation upon the damages in a wrongful death action. N.Y. Estates, Powers & Trust Law, § 5–4.3; N.Y.Const. art. 1, sec. 16. We affirm.

The relevant facts are simple, the legal issue difficult. The decedent, Dr. Martin C. Rosenthal, was a citizen of New York. Decedent and his wife, who as executrix is plaintiff here, went to Boston where he was examined and diagnosed by Dr. Warren, whom the plaintiff describes as a world-renowned physician and surgeon treating patients from all over the world. On March 27, 1969, eight days after an operation performed by Dr. Warren at the New England Baptist Hospital, decedent died in the hospital while under the care of the defendant Warren.

Suit, alleging malpractice and asking for $1,250,000 in damages, was brought in New York state court. Jurisdiction of Dr. Warren to the extent of his insurance coverage was obtained by attachment levied on the St. Paul Fire & Marine Insurance Company, a Minnesota corporation doing business in New York, the malpractice insurer of a clinic where Dr. Warren is employed.[2] Jurisdiction of New England Baptist Hospital, of which Dr. Warren is surgeon in chief, a trustee, a member of the planning committee and an officer of the corporation, was obtained by service upon another officer of the hospital while soliciting funds in New York City. Defendants removed the suit to the federal district court on the basis of diversity of citizenship.

It is undisputed that although the hospital is a Massachusetts corporation, approximately one-third of its patients in 1969 came from outside Massachusetts and approximately 8 per cent of its patients in the same year were from New York. Indeed, the hospital claimed in its 1969 annual report that it was "not a local or community hospital in the usual sense because its patients come from literally everywhere." An affidavit of the head of the casualty underwriting department of the Boston office of St. Paul Fire & Marine, which issued the liability policy under which defendant Warren was covered, indicates that a general surgeon's liability policy in Massachusetts has a basic limit premium of $192, while a New York City surgeon pays a basic limit premium of $1,139, and that one factor contributing to the difference is the "dollar exposure" in New York, which has no wrongful death limitation. Dr. Warren's policy, however, makes no reference to coverage limitation in wrongful death cases.

This being a diversity case, it is, of course, elemental that we must look to the choice of law rules of the forum state, that is, to New

1. M.G.L.A. c. 229 § 2 (1959).

2. Jurisdiction was obtained under Seider v. Roth, 17 N.Y.2d 111, 216 N.E.2d 312, 269 N.Y.S.2d 99 (1966). [p. 159, supra].

York law. [Judge Oakes here reviewed Kilberg v. Northeast Airlines, Inc. (p. 464, supra); Babcock v. Jackson (p. 487, supra); Long v. Pan American World Airways, Inc. (p. 558, infra); Miller v. Miller (p. 515, supra); Tooker v. Lopez (p. 495, supra).]

The most recent conflict of laws tort case to reach the New York Court of Appeals, Neumeier v. Kuehner [p. 503, supra], did hold the Ontario guest law applicable in a suit by an *Ontario* decedent's executrix against a New York driver's estate arising from an accident in Ontario, the court saying that New York has "no legitimate interest in ignoring the public policy of [the] foreign jurisdiction . . . and in protecting the plaintiff guest domiciled and injured there from legislation obviously addressed, at the very least, to a resident riding in a vehicle traveling within its borders." 31 N.Y.2d at 125–26, 286 N.E.2d at 456, 335 N.Y.S.2d at 68. In no way, however, did the court retreat from the position it had staked out in *Kilberg* and *Miller*, refusing to apply other states' wrongful death limitations in the case of the death of a New York domiciliary. . . .

This review of the relevant case law leaves us with the overwhelming conclusion that . . . the strong New York public policy against damage limitations has triumphed over the contrary policies of sister states in every case where a New York domiciliary has brought suit. This conclusion is particularly striking in wrongful death actions where the New York policy, embedded in a state constitutional prohibition against damage limitations, has without exception been applied in suits brought for New York decedents since *Kilberg*. One might well inquire whether it would be anomalous to permit Dr. Rosenthal's heirs to recover without damage limitation if he died in a plane crash en route to Boston's Logan International Airport (*Kilberg*) or in a taxi cab from Logan to New England Baptist (*Miller*) but not once he stepped into the hospital itself. But to do so would substitute "a domiciliary conceptualism that rested on a vested right accruing from the fact of domicile," Miller v. Miller, supra, 22 N.Y.2d at 29, 237 N.E.2d at 887, 290 N.Y.S.2d at 748 (dissenting opinion), for New York's sophisticated "interest analysis" approach to choice of law problems. The New York precedents require more.

Appellants contend that Massachusetts is the situs of the events leading to this law suit and, in effect, that the intent, either actual or constructive, of the parties was for the Massachusetts limitation on damages to govern in the event of a malpractice claim. This argument fails for many reasons. Quite probably it never occurred to Dr. Rosenthal, Dr. Warren or to the New England Baptist Hospital that a choice of law problem would arise; at least one does not ordinarily think of wrongful death limitations even when undertaking surgery. This is not a case where the conduct of the Massachusetts doctor or hospital vis-a-vis the decedent was patterned upon the Massachusetts death limitation. It is therefore not unfair to apply New York's compensatory policy to them. Cf. Babcock v. Jackson, supra, 12 N.Y.2d at 483, 191 N.E.2d at 284, 240 N.Y.S.2d at 750–51. Additionally, it cannot be said that the defendants purchased insurance with the expectation Massachusetts law would govern damage recovery in this case. As in Miller v. Miller, supra, the specific insurance policy here does not distinguish between liability coverage for wrongful death and personal injuries, nor does it distinguish between medical practice on Massachusetts and out of state citizens. Finally, neither the hospital nor the doctor named here as defendants operate provincially; the doctor has a world-wide following and the hospital actively solicits funds from outside the Commonwealth of Massachusetts (including New York) and treats patients from "literally everywhere." It is thus impossible to say with any certainty what the parties' actual "expectations" as to choice of law were.

Even if expectations, real or constructive, could be hypothesized, they would be legally irrelevant. Despite the argument that looking to the expectations of the parties to solve choice of law problems promotes " 'an unconscious acceptance of legality and the legal order,' " Miller v. Miller, supra, 22 N.Y.2d at 28, 237 N.E.2d at 886, 290 N.Y.S.2d at 747 (dissenting opinion), this contractual type of approach to multistate tort problems has been "summarily rejected" by the New York Court of Appeals. Tooker v. Lopez, supra, 24 N.Y.2d at 577, 249 N.E.2d at 399, 301 N.Y.S.2d at 526; Miller v. Miller, supra, 22 N.Y.2d at 20, 237 N.E.2d at 881, 290 N.Y.S.2d at 741 . . .

Rather, as we view it, the New York courts would balance against the New York interest in protecting its domiciliaries against wrongful death limitations the interests of Massachusetts in limiting damages for wrongful deaths allegedly caused by Massachusetts citizens or occurring in Massachusetts. Consideration of Massachusetts' interests in this case should, however, be from the perspective that the damage limitation is not confined to wrongful deaths resulting from medical malpractice but applies to all wrongful deaths however caused. Thus, any interest Massachusetts has in keeping medical liability insurance premiums down so as to avoid passing the increased costs on to Massachusetts citizens in the form of higher medical fees is simply one facet of whatever larger interest it may have in limiting in death as distinguished from personal injury cases the size of damage recovery against its citizens generally.[8] . . .

8. If this case presented the converse fact situation where the decedent was a Massachusetts domiciliary and defendant doctor and hospital New York based, it is by no means clear a New York court would apply the Massachusetts wrongful death limitation. For, in addition to its interest in providing adequate compensation to those New York domiciliaries who suffer a wrongful demise, the unlimited nature of the possible recovery in New York can be said to deter resident doctors and medical facilities from acts of malpractice. Thus, New York would have an interest in regulating the conduct of the tortfeasors and "it would be almost unthinkable to seek the applicable rule in the law of some other place." Babcock v. Jackson, 12 N.Y.2d 473, 483, 191 N.E.2d 279, 284, 240 N.Y.S.2d 743, 751 (1962).

That interest we think the New York courts would say is one not based upon logic, reason or social policy, but is really the vestigial remains of the mistaken view that there was no common law action for wrongful death. We say "mistaken," for Massachusetts has only recently held precisely that, as of now, "the right to recovery for wrongful death is of common law origin . . . ," Gaudette v. Webb, 362 Mass. 60, 284 N.E.2d 222, 229 (1972) . . . . In any event, it is our considered view that the New York Court of Appeals would view the Massachusetts limitation . . . as so "absurd and unjust" that the New York policy of fully compensating the harm from wrongful death would outweigh any interest Massachusetts has in keeping down in this limited type of situation the size of verdicts (and in some cases insurance premiums). If as *Kilberg* pointed out, "The absurdity and injustice [of wrongful death recovery limitations] have become increasingly apparent [since 1894] . . . ," . . . since *Kilberg* they have become even more so. Since *Kilberg*, a number of states have repealed their wrongful death limitations or increased the amounts so that at the present time there are only seven which have an outright limit,[9] although some jurisdictions place a limit on a component of the damages [10] and various states impose a limit in suits against certain governmental bodies.[11] Indeed, Massachusetts itself recently increased its limits.[12] Our examination indicates that Massachusetts is unique, moreover, in both imposing minimum and maximum damage limitations and assessing damages in proportion to the degree of the wrongdoer's culpability.[13] Thus, the "absurdity and injustice" of death recovery limitations in general is heightened insofar as Massachusetts is concerned, because it relates damages recoverable not to the damages sustained, but to the degree of culpability, however that can be measured, on the part of the defendant. A respected, famous surgeon like Dr. Warren might well be held liable, were the Massachusetts statute applicable, for only $5,000 in damages, regardless of the damages sustained by the decedent's

9. See Colo.Rev.Stat. Ch. 41, art. 1 § 3 (1963) ($45,000 limit if decedent left no dependent relative; otherwise unlimited recovery); Kan.Stat.Anno., ch. 60, § 1903 (1970) ($50,000 limit); Mo.Rev. Stat. § 537.090 (1966) ($50,000 limit); N.H.Rev.Stat.Anno., ch. 556, § 13 (1971) ($30,000 unless decedent left a relative in which case the limit is $120,000); Va. Code, § 8–636 (1968) ($25,000 limit if no evidence of pecuniary loss to the survivors; a $75,000 limit if there is such evidence plus funeral and medical expenses of deceased); Michie's West Va.Code, ch. 55, art. 7 § 6 (1965) ($10,000 limit if no evidence of pecuniary loss to the dependent survivors; a $110,000 limit if there is such evidence).

10. E.g., Michie's Md.Code, art. 93 § 4–401(n) (1971) ($2,000 limit on recovery for funeral expenses); Wis.Stat. § 895.04 (1971) ($5,000 limit on recovery for loss of consortium).

11. E.g., S.C.Code of Laws, tit. 33, § 926 (1962) ($5,000 limit for wrongful death action against a county based on defectively maintained roads).

12. 7A Mass.Anno.Laws ch. 229, § 2 (Supp.1971) ($5,000 to $100,000 limit depending on tortfeasor's degree of culpability).

13. Alabama assesses damages in proportion to the culpability of the tortfeasor but has no limit on maximum recovery. See S. Speiser, Recovery for Wrongful Death 71 (1966). [The remainder of Judge Oakes' footnotes are omitted.]

survivors. Thus the anachronistic concept embodied in the Massachusetts act is hardly one that the New York courts can be expected to embrace in the case of the death of a New York domiciliary with whose wife and children New York is "vitally concerned . . . ." Miller v. Miller, supra, 22 N.Y.2d at 18, 237 N.E.2d at 880, 290 N.Y.S.2d at 739. . . .

The constitutional argument, skillfully set forth in the dissent, was not raised by the parties below or on this appeal. We believe that in this case . . . New York has a significant interest—its domiciliary is the one who died and his next of kin are New York's charges—and the "incident" in Massachusetts is not purely "a local one," . . . since the decedent was from out of state, and the defendant hospital is a national one in terms of its patients, its staff, its reputation and its efforts to obtain out-of-state contributions. In these circumstances, the refusal by New York to apply the Massachusetts death act's qualitative and quantitative limitations, even as it applies the remainder of the death act, is not so unreasonable as to violate the full faith and credit clause . . . .. The fact that Massachusetts was the situs of the tort and the residence of the defendant would not be sufficient to require as a matter of full faith and credit that the limitations in the Massachusetts law control, in light of the very strong New York policy against wrongful death limitations in connection with its citizens and next of kin and in light of the interstate aspects of the transaction. *Pearson* established that the Massachusetts death statute could be constitutionally sued upon in New York absent its penal quality and its damage limitations. Given a legitimate forum state interest—as is here present—we see no *constitutional* difference between death on the *Pearson* airplane, death in a taxicab on the way from the airport and death on the operating table.

We agree with the court below and affirm the judgment.

LUMBARD, CIRCUIT JUDGE—(dissenting): . . . I must dissent both because I do not agree that [the majority's] is a proper appraisal of applicable New York law and because I believe that the full faith and credit clause of the United States Constitution bars the New York courts, and federal district courts sitting in diversity, from refusing to apply the Massachusetts limitation on the facts of this case. . . .

The majority purports to decide this case on interest-analysis grounds. However, the sole interest that it has found in New York emanates from the facts of plaintiff's and decedent's New York residence. Such an analysis simply proves too much; for it is tantamount to a per se rule that the courts will not apply such foreign damage limitations when the plaintiff is a resident of the forum state. Thus, I believe the majority's approach amounts to an insupportable abandonment of interest-analysis principles with regard to foreign damage limitations.

Appellee has correctly noted that the New York courts have never honored a foreign damage limitation such as that in issue. However, it is also true that the New York courts have never considered a case in which the interests of New York, in relation to those of the foreign state, were as minimal as they are here. The incident at the root of this litigation, the alleged malpractice of Dr. Warren, does not have the inter-state flavor of the *Kilberg* facts—death caused while in transit from one state to another. Here the decedent made a deliberate choice to undergo the operation in Massachusetts at defendant hospital. Hence, he journeyed into Massachusetts and registered in defendant hospital where he was under the care of defendant, Dr. Warren. The alleged negligence that resulted in decedent's death, the operation by Dr. Warren, occurred wholly within Massachusetts under the care of Massachusetts residents and in a Massachusetts institution. New York's only connection with this occurrence was the patient's permanent residence in New York. I do not see that New York's interest in this occurrence is enhanced by the fact that this Massachusetts physician and Massachusetts institution have such an eminent reputation that a substantial number of their patients, many from New York, are not Massachusetts residents and choose to come into Massachusetts and undergo treatment there; for there is no evidence that either defendant solicited patients from outside Massachusetts—their popularity is due solely to their reputation and the choice of the individual patients.

In my opinion the Massachusetts interests and contacts with the occurrence underlying this litigation should predominate, In addition to its interest in protecting its citizens and institutions from excessive recoveries, an important consideration behind the Massachusetts limitation is its policy of keeping liability premiums as low as possible for its residents. The significant differential that the majority has noted between malpractice insurance premiums in New York and those in Massachusetts is some testimony to the success of this policy. This interest of Massachusetts is fortified by the fact that the insurance policy from which any recovery will be paid was issued in Massachusetts. The fact that the policy has no coverage limitation in wrongful death cases, as noted by the majority, is irrelevant; for the difference in premiums makes it clear that the Massachusetts damage limitation is considered by insurance companies in calculating premiums for liability insurance issued in Massachusetts. Therefore, if we are to take the New York courts at their word that they follow an interest-analysis approach to torts conflict of laws problems, I can see no escape from the conclusion that Massachusetts interests predominate here and that the New York Court would on these facts be impelled to apply the Massachusetts damage limitation. . . .

In any event, even if the majority were correct that the New York courts would refuse to apply the Massachusetts damage limitation against a New York plaintiff, I would hold that such an approach, when applied to a case in which the contacts with Massachusetts are as great as they are here, violates the full faith and credit clause of the United States Constitution. . . .

Accordingly, I would reverse the order of the district court.

NOTES

(1) Is the decision in the principal case consistent with Neumeier v. Kuehner? Are *Kilberg* and *Miller* correctly invoked for support? Is *Babcock*?

(2) Under interest analysis may a court properly refuse to apply another state's rule because it considers the rule "absurd and unjust?"

(3) Are malpractice insurance rates, provisions, or expectations material? If the insurance policy excluded out-staters from coverage should the result have been different?

(4) As noted in Judge Oakes' opinion, Dr. Rosenthal's executrix also brought suit for malpractice against the New England Baptist Hospital which raised the defense of the charitable immunity it enjoyed under Massachusetts law. The defense was stricken by the trial court on the plaintiff's motion. The court relied heavily on the Court of Appeals decision involving Dr. Warren and held that in view of New York's interest in the wellbeing of the surviving family of Dr. Rosenthal, who were New York domiciliaries, a New York court would refuse to give effect to the Massachusetts charitable immunity doctrine on the ground that "it is unfair, out of step with the times and abhorrent to [New York] public policy." The court also said that Massachusetts had no "current interest in perpetuating the charitable immunity doctrine," having abolished it by legislation after Dr. Rosenthal's death. Rosenthal v. Warren, 374 F.Supp. 522 (S.D.N.Y.1974).

(5) The New York cases on choice of law are discussed in a lengthy and scholarly article in Korn, The Choice-of-Law Revolution: A Critique, 83 Colum.L.Rev. 772 (1983).

Rosenthal was followed and applied in O'Connor v. Lee-Hy Paving Corp., 579 F.2d 194 (2d Cir. 1978). That case involved a suit by a New York widow to recover for the wrongful death of her husband as a result of his being struck by defendant's motor grader at a construction site in Virginia. Under the Virginia Workers' Compensation Law, the plaintiff would have no claim in tort against the defendant; the contrary was true under the law of New York. In finding for the plaintiff by application of New York law, the court (per Judge Friendly) said:

. . . we see no indication that the highest court of New York has wavered in its determination to afford New York tort plaintiffs the benefit of New York law more favorable than the law of the *lex loci delictus* whenever there is a fair basis for doing so.

. . .

. . . Appellants have failed to furnish us with persuasive reasons to believe that, if confronted with the problem here presented, the New York Court of Appeals would turn away from the path it has consistently followed since *Kilberg* and subject a New York resident, employed in New York by a New York employer and based in New York, to Virginia law which prevents him or his estate from suing for negligence a non-employer alleged to have negligently injured or killed him at the worksite. Accordingly we uphold the ruling of the district judge.

––––––

DO STATES HAVE "INTERESTS" IN THE RESULTS OF CIVIL SUITS?

In Miller v. Miller, Judge Breitel expressed doubt that the proponents of interest analysis have exercised sufficient restraint in plying their doctrine in multistate cases. Every substantive rule is imbedded in a context of related rules that may at times modulate, at times intensify, the strength of the policy the rule in question appears to be designed to further. Even simple rules such as those encountered in the guest-host automobile field or limiting recoveries for wrongful death do not stand alone. They are composites of thrusts and counterthrusts of diverse policies. It will be a rare case in which a state can correctly be said to have a singular and unequivocal "interest" in the application of a particular rule to a multistate fact situation. On the basis of the cases we have examined, would it be fair to say that courts frequently find that a state has an interest in having one of its local law rules applied without having first made a conscientious effort to discover whether the relevant policies, both local and multistate, call for the rule's application?

A rare example of a clear and unequivocal official state interest is found in Tramontana v. S. A. Empresa de Viacao Aerea Rio Grandense, 350 F.2d 468 (D.C.Cir.1965), cert. denied 383 U.S. 943, 86 S.Ct. 1195, 16 L.Ed.2d 206 (1966). The decedent, who was domiciled in Maryland, was killed when a United States Navy airplane in which he was traveling collided over Rio de Janeiro with an airplane owned and operated by the defendant, a Brazilian air line. It was held that the provision of the Brazilian Air Code limiting recovery to 100,000 cruzeiros (then worth $170) was applicable. The decision was based on the ground that Brazil was the state with the greatest interest in the question of the measure of recovery, the Code provision having been enacted to help the nation develop its infant air carriage enterprise.

See also Ciprari v. Servicas Aeros Cruzeiro, S. A., 245 F.Supp. 819 (S.D.N.Y.1965), aff'd 359 F.2d 855 (2d Cir. 1966), upholding the same limit (reduced in value by judgment day to only $70) to a New York passenger severely injured in the course of an airplane trip from one city in Brazil to another. Brazil was said to be the state which had the greatest interest in the decision of the particular issues.

NOTES

(1) "In an action for wrongful death, the local law of the state where the injury occurred determines the rights and liabilities of the parties unless, with respect to the particular issue, some other state has a more significant relationship to the occurrence and the parties, in which event the local law of the other state will be applied." Restatement, Second, Conflict of Laws § 175. This principle determines what defenses on the merits are open (§ 176), which persons shall share in the recovery as beneficiaries and the portions (§ 177), and the measure of damages (§ 178).

(2) In a recent article, Professor Herma Hill Kay concluded that, in whole or in part, 22 states still follow the traditional choice-of-law approach, 14 states follow the Restatement, Second, 3 states apply Professor Leflar's choice-influencing factors, and 2 states follow the interest analysis approach of Professor Currie. Kay, Theory into Practice: Choice of Law in the Courts, 34 Mercer L.Rev. 521 (1983).

(3) Even when the interest analysis is used, the plaintiff's side does not always succeed in having the more favorable rule applied. See Fabricius v. Horgen, 257 Iowa 268, 132 N.W.2d 410 (1965) (lower damages of forum-domicile of beneficiaries applied on ground of greater interest in issue); Watts v. Pioneer Corn Co., 342 F.2d 621 (7th Cir. 1965) (non-dependent survivors denied recovery upon application of law of "more significant relationship").

What role, if any, should a jury play in the determination of a choice-of-law question? This problem was presented in Marra v. Bushee, 447 F.2d 1282 (2d Cir. 1971), an action for alienation of affections. The defendant's conduct had taken place partly in Vermont and partly in New York. Following Section 154 of the Restatement, Second, Conflict of Laws, the trial judge determined that the applicable law was that of the state where the defendant's conduct had "principally occurred." The judge further decided that "a factual finding territorializing the defendant's conduct was a jurisdictional matter not within the province of the jury" and, without submitting the issue to the jury, found that Vermont was the state where the defendant's conduct had "principally occurred." On appeal, held, reversed, ". . . the defendant was entitled to the jury's finding of the facts which were determinative of the choice-of-laws principles." See also Szlinis v. Moulded Fiberglass Companies, Inc., 51 Mich.App. 620, 215 N.W.2d 777 (1974) where the court held that it was for the jury to determine in which state the injury had occurred. If these decisions are correct, would it likewise follow that a court must submit to the jury the question of which is the "state of most significant relationship?" The problem is explored in Reese, Smit and Reese, The Role of the Jury in Choice of Law, 25 Case Western Res.L.Rev. 82 (1974).

LILIENTHAL v. KAUFMAN

Supreme Court of Oregon, 1964.
239 Or. 1, 395 P.2d 543.

DENECKE, JUSTICE. This is an action to collect two promissory notes. The defense is that the defendant maker has previously been declared a spendthrift by an Oregon court and placed under a guardianship and that the guardian has declared the obligations void. The plaintiff's counter is that the notes were executed and delivered in California, that the law of California does not recognize the disability of a spendthrift, and that the Oregon court is bound to apply the law of the place of the making of the contract. The trial court rejected plaintiff's argument and held for the defendant.

This same defendant spendthrift was the prevailing party in our recent decision in Olshen v. Kaufman, 235 Or. 423, 385 P.2d 161 (1963). In that case the spendthrift and the plaintiff, an Oregon resident, had gone into a joint venture to purchase binoculars for resale. For this purpose plaintiff had advanced moneys to the spendthrift. The spendthrift had repaid plaintiff by his personal check for the amount advanced and for plaintiff's share of the profits of such venture. The check had not been paid because the spendthrift had had insufficient funds in his account. The action was for the unpaid balance of the check.

The evidence in that case showed that the plaintiff had been unaware that Kaufman was under a spendthrift guardianship. The guardian testified that he knew Kaufman was engaging in some business and had bank accounts and that he had admonished him to cease these practices; but he could not control the spendthrift.

The statute applicable in that case and in this one is ORS 126.335:

"After the appointment of a guardian for the spendthrift, all contracts, except for necessaries, and all gifts, sales and transfers of real or personal estate made by such spendthrift thereafter and before the termination of the guardianship are voidable." (Repealed 1961, ch. 344, § 109, now ORS 126.280).

We held in that case that the voiding of the contract by the guardian precluded recovery by the plaintiff and that the spendthrift and the guardian were not estopped to deny the validity of plaintiff's claim. Plaintiff does not seek to overturn the principle of that decision but contends it has no application because the law of California governs, and under California law the plaintiff's claim is valid.

The facts here are identical to those in Olshen v. Kaufman, supra, except for the California locale for portions of the transaction. The notes were for the repayment of advances to finance another joint venture to sell binoculars. The plaintiff was unaware that defendant had been declared a spendthrift and placed under guardianship. The guardian, upon demand for payment by the plaintiff, declared the notes void. The issue is solely one involving the principles of conflict of laws.

. . .

Plaintiff contends that the substantive issue of whether or not an obligation is valid and binding is governed by the law of the place of making, California. This court has repeatedly stated that the law of the place of contract "must govern as to the validity, interpretation, and construction of the contract." . . .

This principle, that *lex loci contractus* must govern, however, has been under heavy attack for years. . . .

There is no need to decide that our previous statements that the law of the place of contract governs were in error. Our purpose is to state that this portion of our decision is not founded upon that principle because of our doubt that it is correct if the *only* connection of the state whose law would govern is that it was the place of making.

In this case California had more connection with the transaction than being merely the place where the contract was executed. The defendant went to San Francisco to ask the plaintiff, a California resident, for money for the defendant's venture. The money was loaned to defendant in San Francisco, and by the terms of the note, it was to be repaid to plaintiff in San Francisco.

On these facts, apart from *lex loci contractus*, other accepted principles of conflict of laws lead to the conclusion that the law of California should be applied. Sterrett v. Stoddard Lumber Co., 150 Or. 491, 504, 46 P.2d 1023 (1935), rests, at least in part, on the proposition that the validity of a note is determined by the law of the place of payment. . . .

There is another conflict principle calling for the application of California law. Stumberg terms it the application of the law which upholds the contract. Stumberg, supra, at 237. Ehrenzweig calls it the "Rule of Validation." Ehrenzweig, Conflict of Laws, 353 (1962).

. . .

Thus far all signs have pointed to applying the law of California and holding the contract enforceable. There is, however, an obstacle to cross before this end can be logically reached. In Olshen v. Kaufman, supra, we decided that the law of Oregon, at least as applied to persons domiciled in Oregon contracting in Oregon for performance in Oregon, is that spendthrifts' contracts are voidable. Are the choice-of-law principles of conflict of laws so superior that they overcome this principle of Oregon law?

To answer this question we must determine, upon some basis, whether the interests of Oregon are so basic and important that we should not apply California law despite its several intimate connections with the transaction. The traditional method used by this court and most others is framed in the terminology of "public policy." The court decides whether or not the public policy of the forum is so

strong that the law of the forum must prevail although another jurisdiction, with different laws, has more and closer contacts with the
transaction. Included in "public policy" we must consider the economic and social interests of Oregon. When these factors are included in a consideration of whether the law of the forum should be applied this traditional approach is very similar to that advocated by
many legal scholars. This latter theory is "that choice-of-law rules
should rationally advance the policies or interests of the several
states (or of the nations in the world community)." Hill, Governmental Interest and the Conflict of Laws—A Reply to Professor Currie,
27 Chi.L.Rev. 463, 474 (1960); Currie, Selected Essays on the Conflict
of Laws, 64–72 (1963), reprint from 58 Col.L.Rev. 964 (1958). . . .

Some of the interests of Oregon in this litigation are set forth in
Olshen v. Kaufman, supra. The spendthrift's family which is to be
protected by the establishment of the guardianship is presumably an
Oregon family. The public authority which may be charged with the
expense of supporting the spendthrift or his family, if he is permitted
to go unrestrained upon his wasteful way, will probably be an Oregon
public authority. These, obviously, are interests of some substance.

Oregon has other interests and policies regarding this matter
which were not necessary to discuss in Olshen. As previously stated,
Oregon, as well as all other states, has a strong policy favoring the
validity and enforceability of contracts. This policy applies whether
the contract is made and to be performed in Oregon or elsewhere.

The defendant's conduct,—borrowing money with the belief that
the repayment of such loan could be avoided—is a species of fraud.
Oregon and all other states have a strong policy of protecting innocent persons from fraud. . . .

It is in Oregon's commercial interest to encourage citizens of other states to conduct business with Oregonians. If Oregonians acquire a reputation for not honoring their agreements, commercial in-
tercourse with Oregonians will be discouraged. If there are Oregon
laws, somewhat unique to Oregon, which permit an Oregonian to escape his otherwise binding obligations, persons may well avoid commercial dealings with Oregonians.

The substance of these commercial considerations, however, is de-
flated by the recollection that the Oregon Legislature has determined, despite the weight of these considerations, that a spendthrift's
contracts are voidable.

California's most direct interest in this transaction is having its
citizen creditor paid. . . . California probably has another, although more intangible, interest involved. It is presumably to every
state's benefit to have the reputation of being a jurisdiction in which
contracts can be made and performance be promised with the certain
knowledge that such contracts will be enforced. Both of these interests, particularly the former, are also of substance.

We have, then, two jurisdictions, each with several close connections with the transaction, and each with a substantial interest, which will be served or thwarted, depending upon which law is applied. The interests of neither jurisdiction are clearly more important than those of the other. We are of the opinion that in such a case the public policy of Oregon should prevail and the law of Oregon should be applied; we should apply that choice-of-law rule which will "advance the policies or interests of" Oregon. Hill, supra, 27 Chi.L.Rev. at 474.

Courts are instruments of state policy. The Oregon Legislature has adopted a policy to avoid possible hardship to an Oregon family of a spendthrift and to avoid possible expenditure of Oregon public funds which might occur if the spendthrift is required to pay his obligations. In litigation Oregon courts are the appropriate instrument to enforce this policy. The mechanical application of choice-of-law rules would be the only apparent reason for an Oregon court advancing the interests of California over the equally valid interests of Oregon. The present principles of conflict of laws are not favorable to such mechanical application.

We hold that the spendthrift law of Oregon is applicable and the plaintiff cannot recover.

Judgment affirmed.

O'CONNELL, JUSTICE (specially concurring). . . . .

In the Olshen case we had to choose between two competing policies; on one hand the policy of protecting the interest of persons dealing with spendthrifts, which, broadly, may be described as the interest in the security of transactions, and on the other hand the policy of protecting the interests of the spendthrift, his family and the county. It was decided that the Oregon Legislature adopted the latter policy in preference to the former.

. . . To distinguish the Olshen case it would be necessary to assume that although the legislature intended to protect the interest of the spendthrift, his family and the county when local creditors were harmed, the same protection was not intended where the transaction adversely affected foreign creditors. I see no basis for making that assumption. There is no reason to believe that our legislature intended to protect California creditors to a greater extent than our own.

GOODWIN, JUSTICE (dissenting). . . .

In the case before us, I believe that the policy of both states, Oregon and California, in favor of enforcing contracts, has been lost sight of in favor of a questionable policy in Oregon which gives special privileges to the rare spendthrift for whom a guardian has been appointed.

The majority view in the case at bar strikes me as a step backward toward the balkanization of the law of contracts. Olshen v.

Kaufman, 235 Or. 423, 385 P.2d 161 (1963), held that there was a policy in this state to help keep spendthrifts out of the almshouse. I can see nothing, however, in Oregon's policy toward spendthrifts that warrants its extension to permit the taking of captives from other states down the road to insolvency.

I would enforce the contract.

CASEY v. MANSON CONSTRUCTION AND ENGINEERING CO.

Supreme Court of Oregon, 1967.
247 Or. 274, 428 P.2d 898.

[Action by a wife to recover for the loss of her husband's consortium sustained as a result of an injury suffered by him in the State of Washington. Plaintiff and her husband were domiciled in Oregon. Manson Construction was a Washington corporation which did business in Oregon. Plaintiff's husband, a business invitee, was injured by reason of a defective road while driving a tractor on Manson's property in Washington. Washington adhered to the common law rule which denied to a wife a right of action for the loss of her husband's consortium. Oregon conferred such a right by statute. The trial court found against the wife by application of Washington law and the Supreme Court of Oregon affirmed. That court said in part:]

This court has heretofore been committed to the traditional choice-of-law rule that in tort cases the law of the place of wrong—*lex loci delicti*—governs: Nadeau v. Power Plant Engr. Co., 216 Or. 12, 20, 337 P.2d 313 (1959). In Lilienthal v. Kaufman, 239 Or. 1, 395 P.2d 543 (1964), however, we abandoned the mechanical application of the corresponding rule in contract cases—*lex loci contractus*. . . .

Careful consideration of [the] decisions, as well as of the extensive writings on the subject, persuade us that we should adopt for tort actions the rule of "most significant relationship with the occurrence and with the parties" as set forth in the Tentative Draft of the Restatement.

. . . It cannot be said, . . . that we are dealing here with an easy case. It differs in important particulars from any of those which we have examined in which the courts have refused to apply the law of the place of the wrong. There was nothing fortuitous here about the place of the accident; it could not have happened anywhere except on the negligently constructed and maintained road in the State of Washington.

As to the underlying policies involved and the interests of the respective states, it is to be presumed that the Oregon Legislature deemed it desirable that an anachronistic common law rule . . . should be removed, and a wife accorded the same right as a husband to recover for a similar injury, though not to the same extent, because, with regard to the service element of consortium, in order to prevent a double recovery, the husband's recovery would be taken into account in measuring the wife's damages. . . .   Since it must be presumed that if the wife is entitled to recover for loss of consortium the husband is also entitled to recover for his personal injury, this state's chief concern is that a wife's loss of her husband's society and affection should not go uncompensated.

Washington's policy is in one aspect rather negative than affirmative. Her highest court announced more than 13 years ago that no such action could be maintained unless the legislature provided for it and the legislature has not done so. Washington, of course, has no concern with whether an Oregon wife recovers for loss of consortium in an Oregon court, but Washington has a legitimate concern in whether she recovers against Washington residents when the wrong giving rise to the action occurs in Washington in circumstances such as those we deal with here. Washington has a legitimate concern with whether her residents engaged in a construction job there—in this case a job related to the public interest—should be disappointed in their reasonable expectation that the extent of their liability for negligent conduct in Washington be governed by the law of that state, regardless of the domicile of an injured plaintiff. It bears repetition that this case is to be distinguished from those in which the place of injury is a mere happenstance.

. . . .

While consideration should be given, we assume, to the interest of Oregon arising from the fact that the effects of the injury are experienced by the plaintiff in this state, we, nevertheless, have a case in which both conduct and injury occurred in Washington when the plaintiff's husband was a business invitee of the defendants on land in their possession and control.

We conclude that Washington has the most significant relationship with the occurrence and with the parties and that Washington's law should govern the issue presented by the demurrer to the complaint. . . .

The judgment is affirmed.

HOLMAN, JUSTICE (concurring).

After consideration of all the circumstances and the situation as a whole, it seems more logical to apply the law of the State of Washington. If it were otherwise, Washington citizens carrying on activities in Washington would have to lift their financial protection to an unaccustomed level and one which would be dependent upon the locality from which the injured party might come. Theoretically, citizens of Washington could be subjected to 49 different levels of responsibility for acts done within their state of residence, and this seems to me highly undesirable. It seems more reasonable that under the present circumstances ". . . By entering the state or nation, the visitor has exposed himself to the risks of the territory and should not expect to subject persons living there to a financial hazard that their law had not created."

At this time I am doubtful that I desire to be finally wedded to the methods of the second restatement as set forth in the majority opinion.

GOODWIN, J., concurs in this opinion.

NOTE

Are the Lilienthal and Casey decisions consistent? Is there more justice in subjecting the California lender in the former case to Oregon's unusual spendthrift trust law than in subjecting the Washington engineering firm to the increasingly common rule that negligent injury of a husband produces actionable injury to the wife deprived of his consortium? Was it a violation of due process for the court in Lilienthal to apply the Oregon spendthrift law?

FISHER v. HUCK, 50 Or. 635, 624 P.2d 177 (1981). The case involved an action by the plaintiff, a guest passenger, to recover damages against his host driver for injuries sustained in an automobile accident in British Columbia, Canada. The defendant was a resident of British Columbia and the plaintiff "was going to British Columbia for the purpose of taking prearranged employment and establishing residence there." British Columbia had repealed its guest passenger statute some years prior to the accident and the defendant relied, by way of defense, on the guest-passenger statute of Oregon. In holding for the plaintiff on the ground that the issue was governed by British Columbia law and not by that of Oregon, the court said in part:

Whether the demurrer to plaintiff's negligence count was properly sustained depends on whether Oregon law or British Columbia law governs this action. Gone are the days when the choice of law in tort cases was relatively definite and simple. Prior to Casey v. Manson Constr. Co. [p. 533, supra] the law of the place where the tort occurred controlled. *Casey* adopted the "most significant relationships" approach of the Restatement (Second) Conflict of Laws. Since then, the choice of law has been based upon somewhat amorphous considerations, the evaluation of which depends in large measure on the semantics used by the court making the particular decision. Regardless of whether that approach represents progress, it was new and different when adopted, and is now with us.

When any court embarks on a determination of the "relevant policies of other interested states and the relative interests of those states in the determination of the particular issue" (Restatement, . . . § 6), the endeavor, in many instances, is like skeet shooting with a bow and arrow: a direct hit is likely to be a rarity, if not pure luck. With that chance of success in mind, we nock the arrow and draw the string.

The efforts of the Oregon court in two cases subsequent to *Casey* help to demonstrate the problem. In Erwin v. Thomas, 264 Or. 454, 506 P.2d 494 (1973), the issue was whether Washington or Oregon law applied to determine if plaintiff, a Washington resident, could recover [against an Oregon defendant] for the loss of consortium of her husband . . . injured in Washington. Washington did not permit such actions; Oregon did. The court [granted recovery on the ground that]

> "Washington policy cannot be offended if the court of another state affords rights to a Washington woman which Washington does not afford, so long as a Washington defendant is not required to respond. The state of Washington appears to have no material or urgent policy or interest which would be offended by applying Oregon law." 264 Or. at 458–59, 506 P.2d 494.

Perhaps that analysis of the public policy of Washington is correct. But it is at least problematical whether it is any more correct than an analysis which concludes that Washington has decided that the rights of a married woman residing in Washington, whose husband is injured in Washington, may not recover for loss of consortium, it being against its public policy to recognize such rights regardless of the residency of the tortfeasor. If the *Erwin* court's analysis of the Washington policy is correct, it would seem to follow that a Washington court would permit a loss of consortium claim against a non-resident defendant. That conclusion seems highly unlikely and under the alternative analysis just suggested that conclusion would not follow. By changing the semantics of the analysis only slightly, a different choice of law might result.

The court in *Erwin*, having analyzed the policy of Washington as it did, concluded that, even though Oregon's policy was to recognize those rights, this state had no compelling interest in enforcing them in favor of non-resident married women whose husbands are injured outside the state. The result, the court concluded, was a stand-off, because the policy of neither state had any significant relationship to the case. Accordingly, the court applied the law of the forum—Oregon. If Washington had been the forum state and used the same approach the Oregon court used, it would have applied Washington law. That does not seem to be a very satisfactory way of resolving the rights of the parties; consistency would lie only in that the law of the forum would be applied, but forum shopping would be encouraged.

In the most recent case involving choice of law, Tower v. Schwabe, 284 Or. 105, 585 P.2d 662 (1978), the issue was whether British Columbia or Oregon law applied where both the guest-passenger plaintiff and host-driver defendant were Oregon residents, and the accident occurred in British Columbia. At that time, British Columbia had repealed its guest-passenger statute, but Oregon had not. If the "most significant relationships" approach has any merit in tort cases, as opposed to the *lex loci delicti, Tower* appears to be an example of such a case. Both plaintiff and defendant were Oregon residents who were on a trip to British Columbia; at the time of the accident they were returning to Oregon. In other words, Oregon was the only state with any real interest: the dispute was between two Oregonians in an Oregon court concerning an accident that happened somewhere else. Unless the court were simply to revert to the pre-*Casey* rule requiring application of the *lex loci delicti*, Oregon law would have had to be applied because all significant relationships were to Oregon. Although the court did apply Oregon law, in doing so it discussed what it thought was behind British Columbia's policy in repealing its guest-passenger statute. Conceding some difficulty in that undertaking, the court concluded:

> ". . . Here, British Columbia is legitimately concerned only with the ability of its citizens to obtain compensation for their injuries. . . . " 284 Or. at 109, 585 P.2d 662.

. . . One can only surmise that British Columbia's only "legitimate concern" was with the ability of its "citizens" to obtain compensation for their injuries on the presumed premise that the British Columbia government would be required, under its social welfare programs, to take care of the uncompensated guest, if a "citizen," but that no such obligation would exist with respect to the non-citizen. However, we do not know that to be the case; but if it is, then it would seem to follow that if the guest is a British Columbia resident and is injured by an Oregon host in Oregon, British Columbia law should apply regardless of the forum. . . .

Our purpose in discussing at length the *Erwin* and *Tower* cases is to point out the hazards involved where one state attempts to enunciate the public policy of another jurisdiction. Most courts have more than enough difficulty discerning the policies of the jurisdiction in which they sit. Moreover, as we view *Tower*, it was not necessary for the court to delve into British Columbia's public policy in repealing its guest-passenger statute. All of the significant relationships militated in favor of applying Oregon law regardless of the British Columbia policy unless the place of the wrong were to control. . . .

BERNHARD v. HARRAH'S CLUB

Supreme Court of California, 1976.
16 Cal.3d 313, 128 Cal.Rptr. 215, 546 P.2d 719, cert. denied
429 U.S. 859, 97 S.Ct. 159, 50 L.Ed.2d 136.

[Action against defendant Harrah's Club, a Nevada corporation, to recover for personal injuries suffered in California. The plaintiff alleged that defendant owned and operated gambling and drinking establishments in Nevada and solicited business for such establishments in California "knowing and expecting that many California residents would use the public highways in going to and from defendant's . . . establishments." In response to defendant's advertisements, two Californians patronized one of defendant's clubs in Nevada where they were served numerous alcoholic beverages "progressively reaching a point of obvious intoxication rendering them incapable of safely driving a car." After they had entered California on their way home, the car, while being driven by one of these Californians in an intoxicated state, collided head-on with a motorcycle operated by plaintiff Bernhard, also a California domiciliary, who suffered severe injuries. Defendant demurred to the complaint on the ground that Nevada law gave no right to recover against a tavern keeper for injuries caused by the selling of alcoholic beverages to an intoxicated person and that Nevada law governed since defendant's alleged tort had been committed in Nevada. The trial court sustained the demurrer and plaintiff appealed.]

SULLIVAN, JUSTICE:

We face a problem in the choice of law governing a tort action. As we have made clear on other occasions, we no longer adhere to the rule that the law of the place of the wrong is applicable in a California forum regardless of the issues before the court. . . . Rather we have adopted in its place a rule requiring an analysis of the respective interests of the states involved—the objective of which is "to determine the law that most appropriately applies to the issue involved." (*Hurtado*, supra, at pp. 579–580, quoting from *Reich*, supra, at p. 555.) . . .

We observe at the start that the laws of the two states—California and Nevada—applicable to the issue involved are not identical. California imposes liability on tavern keepers in this state for conduct such as here alleged. In Vesely v. Sager, . . . 5 Cal.3d 153, 166, 95 Cal.Rptr. 623, 486 P.2d 151 (1971), this court [held that such liability should be imposed since not to do so would be] patently unsound and totally inconsistent with the principles of proximate cause established in other areas of negligence law. [Also] the Legislature has expressed its intention in this area with the adoption of Business and Professions Code § 25602 [making it a misdemeanor to sell to an obviously intoxicated person], a statute to which this presumption [of negligence, Evidence Code § 669] applies. . . . Nevada on the other hand refuses to impose such liability. In Hamm v. Carson City Nuggett, Inc., 85 Nev. 99, 450 P.2d 358, 359 (1969), the court held it would create neither common law liability nor liability based on the criminal statute banning sale of alcoholic beverages to a person who is drunk, because "if civil liability is to be imposed, it should be accomplished by legislative act after appropriate surveys, hearings, and investigations to ascertain the need for it and the expected consequences to follow. . . ."

Although California and Nevada, the two "involved states" . . . have different laws governing the issue presented in the case at bench, we encounter a problem in selecting the applicable rule of law only if *both* states have an interest in having their respective laws applied. . . .

Defendant contends that Nevada has a definite interest in having its rule of decision applied in this case in order to protect its resident tavern keepers like defendant from being subjected to a civil liability which Nevada has not imposed either by legislative enactment or decisional law. . . .

Plaintiff on the other hand points out that California also has an interest in applying its own rule of decision to the case at bench. California imposes on tavern keepers civil liability to third parties injured by persons to whom the tavern keeper has sold alcoholic beverages when they are obviously intoxicated "for the purpose of protecting members of the general public from injuries to person and damage to property resulting from the excessive use of intoxicating liquor." (Vesely v. Sager, supra, 5 Cal.3d 153, 165, 95 Cal.Rptr. 623, 486 P.2d 151 (1971).) California, it is urged, has a special interest in affording this protection to all California residents injured in California.

Thus, since the case at bench involves a California resident (plaintiff) injured in this state by intoxicated drivers and a Nevada resident tavern keeper (defendant) which served alcoholic beverages to them in Nevada, it is clear that each state has an interest in the application of its respective law of liability and nonliability. It goes without saying that these interests conflict. Therefore, unlike Reich v. Purcell, supra, 67 Cal.2d 551, 63 Cal.Rptr. 31, 432 P.2d 727 (1967), and Hurtado v. Superior Court, supra, 11 Cal.3d 574, 114 Cal.Rptr. 106, 522 P.2d 666 (1974), where we were faced with "false conflicts," in the instant case for the first time since applying a governmental interest analysis as a choice of law doctrine in *Reich*, we are confronted with a "true" conflicts case. We must therefore determine the appropriate rule of decision in a controversy where each of the states involved has a legitimate but conflicting interest in applying its own law in respect to the civil liability of tavern keepers.

The search for the proper resolution of a true conflicts case, while proceeding within orthodox parameters of governmental interest analysis, has generated much scholarly examination and discussion. The father of the governmental interest approach, Professor Brainerd Currie, originally took the position that in a true conflicts situation the law of the forum should always be applied. (Currie, Selected Essays on Conflicts of Laws p. 184 (1963).) However, upon further reflection, Currie suggested that when under the governmental interest approach a preliminary analysis reveals an apparent conflict of interest upon the forum's assertion of its own rule of decision, the forum should reexamine its policy to determine if a more restrained interpretation of it is more appropriate. . . . This process of reexamination . . . can be approached under principles of "comparative impairment." (Baxter, Choice of Law and the Federal System, supra, 16 Stan.L.Rev. 1–22; Horowitz, The Law of Choice of Law in California—A Restatement, supra, 21 U.C.L.A. L.Rev. 719, 748–758.)

. . . the "comparative impairment" approach to the resolution of such conflict seeks to determine which state's interest would be more impaired if its policy were subordinated to the policy of the other state. This analysis proceeds on the principle that true conflicts should be resolved by applying the law of the state whose interest would be the more impaired if its law were not applied. Exponents of this process of analysis emphasize that it is very different from a weighing process. The court does not " 'weigh' the conflicting governmental interests in the sense of determining which conflicting law manifested the 'better' or the 'worthier' social policy on the specific issue. . . .

Mindful of the above principles governing our choice of law, we proceed to reexamine the California policy underlying the imposition of civil liability upon tavern keepers. At its broadest limits this policy would afford protection to all persons injured in California by intoxicated persons who have been sold or furnished alcoholic beverages while intoxicated regardless of where such beverages were sold or furnished. Such a broad policy would naturally embrace situations where the intoxicated actor had been provided with liquor by out-of-state tavern keepers. Although the State of Nevada does not impose such *civil* liability on its tavern keepers, nevertheless they are subject to *criminal* penalties under a statute making it unlawful to sell or give intoxicating liquor to any person who is drunk or known to be an habitual drunkard. (See Nev.Rev.Stats. 202.100; see Hamm v. Carson City Nuggett, Inc., supra, 85 Nev. 99, 450 P.2d 358 (1969).)

We need not, and accordingly do not here determine the outer limits to which California's policy should be extended, for it appears clear to us that it must encompass defendant, who as alleged in the complaint, "advertis[es] for and otherwise solicit[s] in California the business of California residents at defendant HARRAH'S CLUB Nevada drinking and gambling establishments, knowing and expecting said California residents, in response to said advertising and solicitation, to use the public highways of the State of California in going and coming from defendant HARRAH'S CLUB Nevada drinking and gambling establishments." Defendant by the course of its chosen commercial practice has put itself at the heart of California's regulatory interest, namely to prevent tavern keepers from selling alcoholic beverages to obviously intoxicated persons who are likely to act in California in the intoxicated state. It seems clear that California cannot reasonably effectuate its policy if it does not extend its regulation to include out-of-state tavern keepers such as defendant who regularly and purposely sell intoxicating beverages to California residents in places and under conditions in which it is reasonably certain these residents will return to California and act therein while still in an intoxicated state. California's interest would be very significantly impaired if its policy were not applied to defendant.

Since the act of selling alcoholic beverages to obviously intoxicated persons is already proscribed in Nevada, the application of California's rule of civil liability would not impose an entirely new duty requiring the ability to distinguish between California residents and other patrons. Rather the imposition of such liability involves an increased economic exposure, which, at least for businesses which actively solicit extensive California patronage, is a foreseeable and coverable business expense. Moreover, Nevada's interest in protecting its tavern keepers from civil liability of a boundless and unrestricted nature will not be significantly impaired when as in the instant case liability is imposed only on those tavern keepers who actively solicit California business.

. . . [W]e conclude that California has an important and abiding interest in applying its rule of decision to the case at bench, that the policy of this state would be more significantly impaired if such rule were not applied and that the trial court erred in not applying California law.

Defendant argues, however, that even if California law is applied, the demurrer was nonetheless properly sustained because the tavern keeper's duty stated in Vesely v. Sager, supra, 5 Cal.3d 153, 95 Cal. Rptr. 623, 486 P.2d 151 (1971), is based on Business and Professions Code section 25602, which is a criminal statute and thus without extraterritorial effect. . . .

However, our decision in *Vesely* was much broader than defendant would have it.

. . . [O]ur opinion in *Vesely* struck down the old common law rule of nonliability constructed on the basis that the consumption, not the sale, of alcoholic beverages was the proximate cause of the injuries inflicted by the intoxicated person. Although we chose to impose liability on the *Vesely* defendant on the basis of his violating the applicable statute, the clear import of our decision was that there was no bar to civil liability under modern negligence law. . . .

The judgment is reversed and the cause is remanded to the trial court with directions to overrule the demurrer and to allow defendant a reasonable time within which to answer.

NOTES

(1) Was the court right to conclude that Nevada's policies were not impaired substantially by the imposition of civil liability on Harrah's Club? "If Nevada protects its taverns from liability to its own residents, it has an even greater interest in preventing their liability to out-of-state residents." Note, Conflict of Laws, 65 Calif.L.Rev. 290, 296 (1977). In a thoughtful article focusing on the principal case Professor Kanowitz wrote that the court's comparative-impairment method suffered from "imprecision, . . . manipulability . . . and its propensity to engage in interest-counting;" and also that it "appears to reflect natural-law premises." Kanowitz, Comparative Impairment and Better Law: Grand Illusions in the Conflict of Laws, 30 Hastings L.J. 255, 293 (1979).

(2) In 1978 the California legislature amended Cal.Bus.&Prof.Code § 25602 (West Cum.Supp.1979) to absolve bartenders and hosts at private parties from civil liability for acts of drunken patrons or guests. It remains a misdemeanor to serve a person who is obviously intoxicated. The statute overruled by name Vesely, Bernhard and a third decision of the California Supreme Court.

(3) Cable v. Sahara Tahoe Corp., 93 Cal.App. 384, 155 Cal.Rptr. 770 (1979). The issue was the same as in the Bernhard case and so too were the facts, except that the plaintiff, who was assumed to be domiciled in California, had been employed by the defendant bar in Nevada and had been injured while driving from her place of employment to a destination in Nevada. Following the accident the plaintiff returned to California and, by reason of her injuries, has become and presumably will remain a public charge. Held for the defendant. Nevada's interests would be more impaired by application of California law than would California's interests be impaired by the application of the law of Nevada. "The state with the 'predominant' interest in controlling conduct normally is the state in which such conduct occurs and is most likely to cause injury." The policy that was given effect in the Bernhard case is applicable only to injuries that occur in California. Also, by statute enacted after the occurrence of the accident in question, California has repudiated the rule that a bartender is liable for injuries caused by intoxicated patrons. "Though an existing cause of action would not be nullified by the [statute], it is obvious that the impairment of such a repudiated policy [by application of Nevada law] has a minimal effect upon California's governmental interest."

(OFFSHORE RENTAL CO. v. CONTINENTAL OIL CO.) 22 Cal.3d 157, 148 Cal.Rptr. 867, 583 P.2d 721 (1978). The case involved a suit by a California corporation to recover for the loss of services of a "key" employee who, it was alleged, had been negligently injured by the defendant in Louisiana. Recovery could be had under California law, but not under the law of Louisiana. Applying what it said to be its "comparative impairment" approach, the Supreme Court of California held that Louisiana law was applicable and affirmed a judgment for the defendant. The court said in part:

In sum, the comparative impairment approach to the resolution of true conflicts attempts to determine the relative commitment of the respective states to the laws involved. The approach incorporates several factors for consideration: the history and current status of the states' laws; the function and purpose of those laws.

Applying the comparative impairment analysis to the present case, we first probe the history and current status of the laws before us. The majority of common law states that have considered the matter do not sanction actions for harm to business employees, recognizing that even if injury to the master-servant relationship were at one time the basis for an action at common law, the radical change in the nature of that relationship since medieval times nullifies any right by a modern corporate employer to recover for negligent injury to his employees. . . . Louisiana law accords with the common law's consistent refusal generally to recognize a cause of action based on negligent, as opposed to intentional, conduct which interferes with the performance of a contract between third parties or renders its performance more expensive or burdensome. . . .

. . . We therefore conclude that the trial judge in the present case correctly applied Louisiana, rather than California, law, since California's interest in the application of its unusual and outmoded statute is comparatively less strong than Louisiana's corollary interest . . . in its "prevalent and progressive" law.

An examination of the function and purpose of the respective laws before us provides additional support for our limitation of the reach of California law in the present case. The accident in question occurred within Louisiana's borders; although the law of the place of the wrong is not necessarily the applicable law for all tort actions . . . the situs of the injury remains a relevant consideration. At the heart of Louisiana's denial of liability lies the vital interest in promoting freedom of investment and enterprise *within Louisiana's borders*, among investors incorporated both in Louisiana and elsewhere. The imposition of liability on defendant, therefore, would strike at the essence of a compelling Louisiana law.

Furthermore, in connection with our search for the proper law to apply based on the "maximum attainment of underlying purpose by all governmental entities," we note the realistic fact that insurance is available to guard against the exigencies of the present case. As one commentator has remarked, "[T]he fact that the potential [tort] victim does not usually calculate his risk and plan his insurance program accordingly, hardly detracts from the consideration that he can fairly be made to bear the consequences of not doing so." (Ehrenzweig, A Treatise on the Conflict of Laws (1962) pp. 575–576.) The present plaintiff, a business corporation, is a potential "victim" peculiarly able to calculate such risks and to plan accordingly. Plaintiff could have obtained protection against the occurrence of injury to its corporate vice-president by purchasing key employee insurance, certainly a reasonable and foreseeable business expense. By entering Louisiana, plaintiff "exposed [it]self to the risks of the territory," and should not expect to subject defendant to a financial hazard that Louisiana law had not created. (Cavers, The Choice-of-Law Process (1965) p. 147.)

Although it is equally true that defendant is a business corporation able to calculate the risks of potential tort liability and to plan accordingly, because defendant's operations in Louisiana presumably involved dealing with key employees of companies incorporated in diverse states defendant would most reasonably have anticipated a need for the protection of premises' liability insurance based on Louisiana law. Accordingly, under these circumstances, we conclude that the burden of obtaining insurance for the loss at issue here is most properly borne by the plaintiff corporation. . . .

The judgment is affirmed.

NOTE

The principal case is criticized for relying on a "better law" analysis despite the court's insistence that it was following the comparative-impairment approach in Kanowitz, Comparative Impairment and Better Law: Grand Illusions in the Conflict of Laws, 30 Hastings L.J. 255 (1979).

REYNO v. PIPER AIRCRAFT CO.

United States Circuit Court of Appeals, Third Circuit, 1980.
630 F.2d 149.

[Wrongful death action, stemming from airplane crash in Scotland against Pennsylvania plane manufacturer. The plane was owned by a Scottish air taxi service and all the passengers and crew were Scottish. The action was originally brought in California and then was transferred to the federal court in Pennsylvania under 28 U.S.C. § 1404(a). The Court of Appeals first held that under Van Dusen v. Barrack (p. 196, supra), the California choice-of-law rules should be applied in the suit against Piper, the plane manufacturer. The court then continued:]

ADAMS, CIRCUIT JUDGE.

. . . .

a. *California Conflicts Law Applied to Piper*

California was a pioneering state in the governmental interest analysis approach to choice of law that was developed by Professor Currie. . . .

Any asserted conflict between American strict liability and Scottish negligence law is, we believe, a false one. Two basic policies underlie theories of tort liability: deterrence of harm-causing conduct and compensation of persons injured by that conduct. In private tort law, in which civil rather than criminal liability is imposed, the deterrence function is accomplished by compensation of the plaintiff. The choice between holding a manufacturer liable only for negligence and holding it strictly liable for any dangerous products or design is, practically speaking, a matter both of searching for optimal deterrence of harmful conduct and of allocating the costs of injuries either to producers or consumers. A negligence standard is, broadly speaking, more protective of producers, while strict liability is more solicitous of consumers.

The perceived conflict in this case is between Scotland's interest in encouraging industry by protecting manufacturers and making it relatively more difficult for consumers to recover. Pennsylvania, by contrast, in adopting strict liability, has shifted some of the burdens of injuries from consumers to producers. By adopting this policy of increased deterrence, it seeks to make manufacturers more careful in production and design than they would be if held to a negligence standard.

Applying Pennsylvania's strict liability standard to its resident manufacturer would serve that state's interest in the regulation of manufacturing. Scotland's interest in encouraging industry within its borders would not be impaired, however, by applying a stricter standard of care on a foreign corporation which has no industrial operations in Scotland. Furthermore, Scotland would have no interest in *denying* compensation to its residents for the purpose of benefiting a foreign corporation. Finally, imposition of strict liability on Piper cannot be said to be unfair to it. Inasmuch as Pennsylvania, the state in which Piper makes its product, and the vast majority of American jurisdictions in which most of Piper's aircraft are sold and fly, have strict liability, that is the legal standard under which it plans its operations.

Pennsylvania's interest in deterring defects in products can be served without impairing any significant interest in Scotland. Application of Scotland's negligence law would only harm resident beneficiaries without any countervailing benefit to its industrial economy. We therefore conclude that, as between Pennsylvania and Scottish law on this issue, a California court would apply Pennsylvania's strict liability analysis. . . .

. . .

[This case was subsequently reversed by the Supreme Court [Piper Aircraft Co. v. Reyno, 454 U.S. 235 (1981)] on the ground that the suit should have been dismissed for forum non conveniens reasons.]

NOTE

For a more recent case applying the plaintiff-favoring rule of the state where the product was produced, see Saloomey v. Jeppesen & Co., 707 F.2d 671 (2d Cir. 1983).

TOMLIN V. BOEING CO., 650 F.2d 1065 (9th Cir. 1981).   Suit to recover for the deaths of two servicemen who were killed in a helicopter crash in Vietnam.   At the time of the crash, the servicemen were
domiciled in Alabama and Florida, respectively, and their beneficiaries continued to remain domiciled in those states.   The defendant
Boeing Co. was incorporated in Washington, but the helicopter in
question had been manufactured by a division of Boeing in Pennsylvania.   The action was barred by the statutes of limitations of Alabama, Florida and Pennsylvania.   It was not, however, barred by the
Washington statute.   In finding that Washington law applied and the
action was not time-barred, the court said in part:

The purpose of a statute of limitation is to protect courts and defendants.   By barring stale claims, such statutes conserve judicial resources and provide repose to defendants.   .   .   .   The district judge
correctly concluded that there was no conflict between the interests
of the four states with regard to conserving judicial resources.
Washington has expressed a policy of not closing its courts to wrongful death actions for three years.   If Washington chooses to allow a
case to be brought in its courts that would be time-barred in Alabama, Florida, or Pennsylvania, the judicial resources of those states
are unaffected.

The district judge also correctly determined that application of
Washington's three year statute would not frustrate any policy of Alabama or Florida to protect in-state defendants.   Although those
states would have barred the action in their courts, they are not interested in denying a recovery to their own residents where it would not
affect a resident defendant.

The conflict, then, is between Pennsylvania's former one year
statute and Washington's more plaintiff oriented three year statute.
.   .   .   By providing for a longer period of limitation, Washington
has in effect   .   .   .   expressed a policy of deterring the conduct of
tort defendants.   .   .   .

We are not persuaded that [the fact that the helicopter was manufactured in Pennsylvania] should lead to a different result.   .   .   .
We believe Washington would be interested in deterring the wrongful
conduct of its most prominent corporate citizen regardless of where
the manufacturing is performed.   This action is against the Boeing
Company, not its Vertol division.   Our attention has not been directed
to any equally strong defendant protecting policy of Pennsylvania,
other than what might be inferred from that state's shorter statute
of limitations.   .   .   .

In applying the Washington statute, we are also guided by Washington's reliance on a more general principle of law favoring the decision of cases on their merits.   This policy has been expressed by the
Washington Supreme Court which has stated that where it is "questionable which of   .   .   .   two statutes [of limitation] appl[y] the rule
is that the statute applying the longest period is generally used."

Shew v. Coon Bay Loafers, Inc., 76 Wash.2d 40, 455 P.2d 359, 366 (1969). . . .

NOTE

Notice that the Washington court has discerned a positive purpose in its state's longer statute of limitations: "deterring the conduct of tort defendants"; and ruled that this objective should be pursued even when the conduct (manufacturing helicopters) occurred outside the state. Is the length of time in which suit may be brought likely to be a consideration affecting the care a manufacturer uses in producing helicopters? Would the deterrent effect of a longer statute of limitations be reflected in insurance rates? In short, how can we learn whether time limitations play any deterrent role in the torts field?

DALE SYSTEM, INC. v. TIME, INC.

United States District Court, District of Connecticut, 1953.
116 F.Supp. 527.

HINCKS, CHIEF JUDGE. This is an action in tort. Plaintiff is a Connecticut corporation which furnishes to clients, most of which are retail stores, in Connecticut, New York, Massachusetts, Rhode Island and New Jersey, a service for testing the efficiency and honesty of the clients' employees. This is done by reports recording the experiences of plaintiff's employees, posing as ordinary customers, in making purchases at the clients' stores. Defendant Willmark is engaged in the same line of business. Both Willmark and Time are New York corporations.

The complaint alleges that the defendants caused to be published an article in Life magazine describing in detail Willmark's business and asserting falsely and maliciously that Willmark was "unique" and "the only company of its kind." The complaint also alleges that the defendants caused the Life article to be digested in the Readers Digest of September 1951, in which it was falsely and maliciously stated that Willmark is "the only company of its kind in the world"; and that the defendants caused to be broadcast over radio Station WOR a summary of the Readers Digest article with the statement that "Willmark is the only company of its kind."

The parties have stipulated as follows. The text of the Life article was prepared in New York, the plates were made in Illinois, and printing first commenced in Illinois which was followed by printing in Philadelphia and Los Angeles. The broadcast took place from a studio in New York City, but was accomplished through a transmitter located in New Jersey. The broadcast could be heard from Massachusetts to Georgia. The Readers Digest article was edited in New York; its plates were made in New Hampshire; the printing for the domestic issue was done in New Hampshire and Ohio; and foreign editions were printed in many foreign countries. And it was in New York that Willmark gave Time the information upon which the alleged publications were made.

The defendants have moved to dismiss the complaint for failure to state a claim upon which relief can be granted. . . .

Although the Connecticut courts as yet have had no occasion to discuss and pass upon the "single publication" rule which has been adopted in New York as recently restated in Gregoire v. G. P. Putnam's Sons, 298 N.Y. 119, 81 N.E.2d 45, 50, . . . the general policy of the Connecticut courts to shape the law of the State to harmonize with the realities of contemporary life, convince me that a Connecticut court if confronted with this case would adopt the "single publication rule". It would hold, I think, that the complaint purported to state at most three torts: one growing out of the publication in Life, one out of that in Readers Digest and the other out of the WOR broadcast; and that on each the Statute of Limitations began to run "when the finished product (was) released by the publisher for sale in accord with trade practice", as stated in the Gregoire opinion. . . .

But when it comes to determine the State, the law of which shall govern a case such as this of libel published in many states, there appear to be no cases in Connecticut, or New York, or indeed in other jurisdictions where the single publication rule prevails, which lay down an authoritative conflict of laws rule of general application or which even discuss the underlying problem. However, . . . the "single publication" rule fails to achieve its major objective as a needed development of the substantive law if in practice it is tied to a multiple-publication, conflict-of-laws rule. The terrifying babel of media having publications of nation-wide and international scope urgently requires the development of a conflict of laws rule which shall provide the certainty so essential for the protection of the public, an ease of application which is so helpful to judicial administration and without which justice through litigation becomes for many an unattainable luxury, and an intrinsic realism whereby the existence and incidents of a libel may be determined by the law of the place in which generally, more often than not, the libel will have done the most harm. The law of the plaintiff's domicil, I think, best meets these and any other pertinent requirements. Acting vicariously, as it were, for the Connecticut Courts I hold the Connecticut conflict of laws rule to be that the law of plaintiff's domicil is the law to be applied to a multi-state libel which has been communicated in the state of plaintiff's domicil as well as in other jurisdictions. . . .

After all, a plaintiff's repute is his character and personality in the eyes of others. It thus comprises myriad relationships in all of which the plaintiff's individuality is the focus. Thus viewed, the concept of repute, even though not involving legal relationships, is akin to the concept of status which traditionally is determined by the law of the domicil. The same compelling reasons for applying the law of the domicil to the determination of one's status require that the law of the domicil should determine one's right to his good repute: in cases of multi-state libel generally the greatest harm to repute will occur in the state of domicil.

Of course the artificial rule whereby a corporation is deemed to be domiciled in the state of its incorporation irrespective of the places of its greater activities may at times create situations in which there is substantially less harm to the corporate business by libelous publication in the state of incorporation than by publications occurring where it is more active. For this reason perhaps something could be said for a rule fixing the location of the harm to a corporation in the state of its principal office rather than its domicil. If such were the rule here, the same result would obtain: the plaintiff here is a Connecticut corporation having its principal place of business in Connecticut. However, in my opinion the certainty of domicil and its use generally to locate the law which governs many corporate relationships, commends a rule whereby the law of plaintiff's corporate domicil shall govern also questions relating to harm to its repute. . . .

If it should seem at first glance that the rule is without reasonsable relation to the subject-matter, reflection will demonstrate that no other rule—at least no other *uniform* rule—more reasonably related could be devised. . . . If we were to adopt the rule that the *place of wrong* is the place where the product was released, etc., as likely as not it might be that the place of release was not only difficult to determine but also some place completely unrelated to plaintiff's injury. For example, under the stipulation here, the "release" of the Life issue might be found to have occurred in Illinois or California where plaintiff was not known at all.

In addition to its simplicity, certainty and ease of application the rule of plaintiff's domicil has some merit for its tendency to prevent plaintiff from shopping for the most favorable out of a plurality of jurisdictions: wherever it sues the same law will apply. And surely one would not expect that future libel litigation as a plaintiff would influence the choice of the state in which to incorporate. On the other hand, somewhat less remote is the possibility that a corporation engaging in publishing as its principal business and hence peculiarly liable to libel actions, might be influenced to incorporate in a state the law of which was deemed favorable to defendants in libel suits, if the *defendant's domicil*, were deemed to be a factor in determining the choice of law.

[The court held the article was not defamatory under Connecticut law, but it stated a cause of action against Willmark for unfair competition by means of injurious falsehood.]

———

RESTATEMENT, SECOND, CONFLICT OF LAWS*

§ 149. Defamation

In an action for defamation, the local law of the state where the publication occurs determines the rights and liabilities of the parties, except as stated in § 150, unless, with respect to the particular issue, some other state under the principles stated in § 6 has a more significant relationship to the occurrence and the parties, in which event the local law of the other state will be applied.

§ 150. Multistate Defamation

(1) The rights and liabilities that arise from defamatory matter in any one edition of a book or newspaper, or any one broadcast over radio or television, exhibition of a motion picture, or similar aggregate communication are determined by the local law of the state which, with respect to the particular issue, has the most significant relationship to the occurrence and the parties under the principles stated in § 6.

(2) When a natural person claims that he has been defamed by an aggregate communication, the state of most significant relationship will usually be the state where the person was domiciled at the time, if the matter complained of was published in that state.

(3) When a corporation, or other legal person, claims that it has been defamed by an aggregate communication, the state of most significant relationship will usually be the state where the corporation, or other legal person, had its principal place of business at the time, if the matter complained of was published in that state.

NOTES

(1) Is the interest analysis desirable or feasible in deciding the applicable rule for issues in multistate defamation cases where there are aggregate communications? If the forum has the single publication rule (Restatement, Second, Torts § 577A), (cf. Zuck v. Interstate Pub. Corp., 317 F.2d 727 (2d Cir. 1963)), the possibility of effectively applying the interest methodology theoretically exists, but problems remain.

(2) Palmisano v. News Syndicate Co., 130 F.Supp. 17 (S.D.N.Y.1955), identifies nine proffered solutions to the choice of law problem: the state of plaintiff's domicile; of plaintiff's principal activity to which the defamation relates; where plaintiff in fact suffered the greatest harm; the publisher's domicile (or state of incorporation); where defendant's main publishing office is located; the state of principal circulation; of emanation; where the defamation was first published; and the law of the forum.

In Prosser, Interstate Publication, 51 Mich.L.Rev. 959 (1953), there is a similar list identifying 10 choices. See, also, Warner, Multistate Publication in Radio and Television, 23 Law & Contemp.Prob. 14 (1958); Note, 77 Harv. L.Rev. 1463 (1964).

(3) Hartmann v. Time, Inc., 166 F.2d 127 (3d Cir. 1948), cert. den. 334 U.S. 838 (1948). Plaintiff alleged that he was libeled by an issue of Life magazine which was distributed first in Illinois and later throughout the world. The court held that Pennsylvania, the situs of the court, would follow the single publication rule as a matter of internal law. However, as to injury in other states, also covered by the complaint, it was bound by Pennsylvania conflicts rules to refer to the law of each jurisdiction where the magazine was distributed. In determining the applicable statute of limitations the cause of action was held barred as to publication in all single publication jurisdictions since it was barred in Illinois, the place of first distribution. As to all common law jurisdictions, the statute of limitations of each state applied and the period ran from the last publication in that state. The rule of the Hartmann case was disapproved in Tocco v. Time, Inc., 195 F.Supp. 410 (E.D.Mich.1961) where the court held that a libel action instituted more than one year after the first public release of the offending issue of Life magazine was barred by the Michigan one-year statute of limitations.

B. DÉPEÇAGE

Dépeçage, as the term is used in this book, is the application by a court of the law of different states to govern different issues in a case. As seen from the cases in Chapter 7, it has long been customary for the courts to apply their own law to issues of procedure and the applicable foreign law to issues of substance. More recently, it has come to be recognized that there are situations where it is appropriate to apply the law of different states to different issues of substance. It can be expected that the trend in this direction will accelerate in view of the prevalence of the doctrine that choice of the applicable law should depend upon the precise issue to be determined.

There are, however, countervailing considerations. Application of the law of a number of states obviously places a greater burden upon the courts and the lawyers involved than does application of the law of a single state. There is also the question whether it is appropriate for a court to apply the law of different states to arrive at a result that could not be obtained in a local case based on identical facts by applying the decisional rules of any one of these states. Finally, and most importantly, application of the law of different states will sometimes result in frustrating the policy underlying one or more of the laws involved. Clearly, there will come a point where such application would be unsound. The general problem is explored in the cases that follow.

NELSON v. ECKERT, 231 Ark. 348, 329 S.W.2d 426 (1959). A fatal highway accident occurred in Texas, which prescribed a two-year limit for wrongful death actions. More than two years after the death, suit was brought in Arkansas, which held the action timely under its longer limitations provisions, but applied Texas' survival statute. This permitted the action to proceed, a result that would not have been possible if the suit had been a wholly Arkansas case. What justification is there for splitting the application of rules of two states to achieve a result not possible under the internal law of either state?

———

LILLEGRAVEN v. TENGS

Supreme Court of Alaska, 1962.
375 P.2d 139.

[Plaintiff was a passenger in a "share-the-expense" auto trip from Seattle to Alaska and sustained injuries when the nonowner-driven car met with an accident en route in British Columbia on October 8, 1958. She commenced an action against the owner on September 26, 1960, within Alaska's two-year statute of limitations, but beyond the one-year period prescribed by Section 80(1) of the Motor Vehicle Act of British Columbia.

Unlike Alaska, which did not hold an owner liable in these circumstances, British Columbia's Motor Vehicle Act imposed liability on the consenting owner. This statute was used as the basis of plaintiff's suit against the owner. The Supreme Court reversed a summary judgment for defendant based on the British Columbia one-year statute.]

DIMOND, J.

There is nothing in the law showing that the legislative body of the province of British Columbia gave special consideration to the impact of Section 80 upon the particular right sought to be enforced in this case, as distinguished from other rights to which the act was also applicable. Because of this, we look upon Section 80 as a broad limitation on all tort actions growing out of the operation of motor vehicles, having as its purpose that of all general statutes of limitation, which is to encourage promptness in the prosecution of actions and thus avoid injustice that would result from the assertion of claims after evidence has been lost, memories have faded, and witnesses have disappeared. What minimum period of time for commencing actions would best effect that purpose is a matter of policy of government. British Columbia has declared it to be one year. But Alaska has chosen a longer period of two years, and it is the forum in which the rights of the parties are being determined. In these circumstances, we can see no good reason why this state's policy as to limitation of tort actions should give way to the differing view of a foreign country. The trial court erred in applying the British Columbia one-year period of limitation to plaintiff's claim. . . .

NOTE

Professor Currie disapproved of the result reached in the Lillegraven case on the ground that the British Columbia limitations' period should have been considered to be a substantive limitation on the right. Cavers, The Choice-of-Law Process 38–39 (1965). On the other hand, the decision is approved in Reese, Dépeçage: A Common Phenomenon in Choice of Law, 73 Colum.L.Rev. 58, 69 (1973).

Suppose that in Babcock v. Jackson, p. 487, supra, there had been two issues for the court to decide, namely, the applicability of the Ontario guest-passenger statute and the question of the defendant's negligence. Would it have been appropriate for the court in such a case to apply the law of New York to the guest-passenger issue and, as Judge Fuld suggested, the law of Ontario to determine whether the defendant had been negligent?

FELLS V. BOWMAN, 274 So.2d 109 (Miss.1973): Action to recover for personal injuries suffered in a collision between a truck and an automobile in Louisiana. All of the parties involved were domiciled in Mississippi. *Held:* The Mississippi comparative negligence rule, rather than the contributory negligence rule of Louisiana, should be applied since this issue was of interest to Mississippi but of no "legitimate concern" to Louisiana. On the other hand, Louisiana law governed with respect to the proper placement of tail lights since "the primary concern of Louisiana was with the safety of its highways." Was the result correct even though it could not probably have been obtained by the exclusive application of either Mississippi or Louisiana law?

It will be recalled that in Kilberg v. Northeast Airlines, Inc., p. 464, supra, the New York Court of Appeals applied the Massachusetts wrongful death statute except that it disregarded the statute's provision with respect to the limitation of damages and applied the law of New York instead. By so doing, the court clearly frustrated the policy underlying the Massachusetts statute. Was the decision nevertheless correct? Would the answer be different if New York law had not had a wrongful death statute of its own?

MARYLAND CASUALTY CO. V. JACEK, 156 F.Supp. 43 (D.N.J.1957): A New Jersey couple was involved in an automobile accident in New York as a result of the husband's negligence. New Jersey law does not permit spouses to sue each other, while New York law (by amendment of the Domestic Relations Law, sec. 57, after Mertz v. Mertz, p. 388, supra) does. But at the time of the removal of interspousal immunity, the New York Insurance Law, c. 28, § 167, was amended to provide: "No policy or contract shall be deemed to insure against any liability of an insured because of death or injuries to his or her spouse . . . unless express provision . . . is included in the policy." The insurer brought a diversity action for a declaratory judgment that its policy did not cover liability for the wife's injuries. Applying New Jersey conflicts law, the court granted judgment against the insurer: New York law permits the tort liability; New Jersey law, as the place of making the insurance contract, provides the coverage.

NOTE

Would the appropriateness of this result depend upon whether the purpose of the New Jersey rule of interspousal immunity was to preserve marital harmony or to protect insurance companies against fraud? Did the court distort the policy underlying both the New Jersey and the New York rules?

BRANIFF AIRWAYS, INC. v. CURTISS-WRIGHT CORP., 424 F.2d 427 (2d Cir. 1970): Suit was brought in New York by two passengers against Curtiss-Wright, the manufacturer of the airplane, to recover for personal injuries suffered in a Florida airplane accident. The suit was brought more than three years, but less than six years, after the accident. The suit was barred by the 6-year New York statute of limitations, which started to run at the time of the sale of the engine. The suit was also barred by the 3-year Florida statute which began to run only when the party seeking recovery had discovered, or should have discovered, the defect. The plaintiffs urged, however, that the court should apply the New York 6-year statute, but hold, in accordance with Florida law, that the statutory period began to run only from the date of the accident. A majority of the court rejected this argument and found for the defendant, Curtiss-Wright. There was a dissent. Who was right?

MARIE v. GARRISON

13 Abb.N.C. 210 (N.Y.1883).

[The plaintiffs alleged that the defendant, Garrison, a large bondholder of a railroad in Missouri, had instituted a suit in Missouri to foreclose the mortgage. To induce the plaintiffs not to defend the foreclosure action, Garrison had written a letter in Missouri in which he proposed that if he bought in the property at the foreclosure sale and if they would organize a successor corporation which would reimburse him for his expenditures, he would convey the property to the successor corporation. On the faith of the letter, the plaintiffs had withdrawn their opposition to the foreclosure. The plaintiffs further alleged that after the decree of foreclosure but before the foreclosure sale they had surrendered the letter to the defendant in New York because of a modification of the agreement. Under the new agreement, the defendant had orally promised that if he were the purchaser at the foreclosure sale *he* would organize the successor company and convey the property to it. The defendant purchased at the foreclosure but refused to carry out the agreement. The defendant moved to exclude the evidence of the alleged contract. The cause was referred to Dwight, Referee, who denied the motion, saying:]

"The introduction of the letter in evidence is objected to by the defendant as not complying with the New York Statute of Frauds, on the ground that it does not 'express the consideration' . . . in the New York statute an agreement in contravention of its provisions is declared to be 'void'.* . . .

"Can it fairly be said that a contract declared 'void' by statute still subsists *as a contract,* and that the only effect of the statute is to deprive a party of a remedy? Is such a word as 'void' a mere word of *evidence?*

"I think not. I regard the word 'void' as a word of substance, and not as a mere word of procedure. In that view, the statute cannot, by accepted rules under the Conflict of Laws, be applied to contracts made in other States, and accordingly not to the present case. . . .

"I now propose to examine the point whether the Statute of Frauds of Missouri has been violated so as to affect the validity of the contract or its provability in this court.

"Considering still the subject of the real estate embraced within the letter, I find that the statute of Missouri differs from our own in important respects. . . .

"The contract for the sale of land is not made *void* in Missouri, if the statute is not complied with. It is only enacted that no 'action shall be brought,' in that case. Under the rule in Leroux v. Brown, supra, [outlined infra, p. 604] the remedy *in Missouri only* is affected by these words. . . .

"The conclusion then is that this letter, whether tested by the law of New York or Missouri, does not trench upon any provision of the Statute of Frauds. . . ."

NOTE

See Reese, Dépeçage: A Common Phenomenon in Choice of Law, 73 Colum.L.Rev. 58 (1973); Weintraub, Beyond Dépeçage: A "New Rule" Approach to Choice of Law in Consumer Credit Transactions and a Critique of the Territorial Application of the Uniform Consumer Credit Code, 25 Case

---

* The New York statute provided: "Every contract for the leasing for a longer period than one year, or for the sale of any lands or any interest in lands, shall be void unless the contract, or some note or memorandum thereof, expressing the consideration, be in writing and be subscribed by the party by whom the lease or sale is to be made."

Western Res.L.Rev. 16 (1974); Wilde, Dépeçage in the Choice of Tort Law, 41 S.Calif.L.Rev. 329 (1968).

C. RENVOI

PFAU v. TRENT ALUMINUM CO.

Supreme Court of New Jersey, 1970.
55 N.J. 511, 263 A.2d 129.

PROCTOR, J. This appeal presents a conflict of laws problem regarding a host's liability to his guest for negligence arising out of an automobile accident. Plaintiff, a Connecticut domiciliary, was injured in Iowa while a passenger in an automobile driven by a New Jersey domiciliary and owned by a New Jersey corporation. Iowa has a guest statute which provides that a host-driver is not liable to his passenger-guest for ordinary negligence. The defendants pleaded, *inter alia*, the Iowa guest statute as a defense. . . .

The facts pertinent to this appeal are undisputed. Plaintiff, Steven Pfau, a domiciliary of Connecticut, was a student at Parsons College in Iowa, and the defendant, Bruce Trent, a domiciliary of New Jersey, was a student at the same college. The boys met for the first time at Parsons.

Following the Easter vacation in 1966, the defendant, Bruce Trent, drove the automobile involved in the accident back to Iowa for his use at college. The automobile was registered in New Jersey in the name of the Trent Aluminum Company, a New Jersey corporation owned by Bruce's father. Bruce was using the car with the owner-corporation's consent. The vehicle was insured in New Jersey by a New Jersey carrier.

About a month after Bruce's return to college and several days before the accident, he agreed to drive the plaintiff to Columbia, Missouri, for a weekend visit. They never reached their destination. Shortly after leaving Parsons on April 22, 1966, and while still in Iowa, Bruce failed to negotiate a curve and the car he was operating collided with an oncoming vehicle driven by Joseph Davis. Mr. Davis and his wife and child, who were Iowa domiciliaries, were injured in the accident. Their claims have now been settled by defendants' insurance carrier. The sole question presented by this appeal is whether the Iowa guest statute is applicable to this action.

In Mellk v. Sarahson, 49 N.J. 226, 229 A.2d 625 (1967) this Court abandoned the old *lex loci delicti* rule for determining choice of law in tort cases . . . and adopted the governmental interest analysis approach. . . .

Our decision in *Mellk* followed Babcock v. Jackson, 12 N.Y.2d 473, 240 N.Y.S.2d 743, 191 N.E.2d 279, 95 A.L.R.2d 1 (1963) . . . .

In order to determine whether the Iowa guest statute should apply to this case, we must first examine its purposes as articulated by the Iowa courts. . . . These purposes are: "to cut down litigation arising from the commendable unselfish practice of sharing with others transportation in one's vehicle and protect the Good Samaritan from claims based on negligence by those invited to ride as a courtesy," Rainsbarger v. Shepherd, 254 Iowa 486, 492, 118 N.W.2d 41, 44, 1 A.L.R.3d 1074 (1962); to prevent ingratitude by guests, Knutson v. Lurie, 217 Iowa 192, 195, 251 N.W. 147, 149 (1933); to prevent suits by hitchhikers, Id.; "to prevent collusion suits by friends and relatives resulting in excessively high insurance rates," Hardwick v. Bublitz, 253 Iowa 49, 54, 111 N.W.2d 309, 312 (1961).

The above policies expressed by the Iowa courts would not appear to be relevant to the present matter. [The court followed Tooker v. Lopez, p. 495, supra and excluded in turn each of the possible Iowa policies as inapplicable to a Connecticut plaintiff and a New Jersey defendant in a New Jersey car.]

. . . .

It may well be that in this case, however, New Jersey has an interest. We are not certain that a defendant's domicile lacks an interest in seeing that its domiciliaries are held to the full measure of damages or the standard of care which that state's law provide for. A state should not only be concerned with the protection and self-interest of its citizens.

. . . Therefore, if Connecticut had a guest statute in this case, we would be forced to choose between our state's policy of holding our hosts to a duty of ordinary care and Connecticut's policy of denying a guest recovery for the ordinary negligence of his host and we might have a true conflict. But since Connecticut has the same policy of applying principles of ordinary negligence to the host-guest relationship as does New Jersey, this case presents a false conflict and it is unnecessary for us to decide whether this state has an interest sufficient to warrant application of its law. See Leflar, American Conflicts Law at 328–29.

It would appear that Connecticut's substantive law allowing a guest to recover for his host's ordinary negligence would give it a significant interest in having that law applied to this case. Defendants argue, however, that if we apply Connecticut's substantive law, we should apply its choice-of-law rule as well. In other words, they contend Connecticut's interest in its domiciliaries is identified not only by its substantive law, but by its choice-of-law rule. Connecticut adheres to *lex loci delicti* and according to its decisions would most likely apply the substantive law of Iowa in this case. E.g., Landers v. Landers, 153 Conn. 303, 216 A.2d 183 (1966). Defendants contend that plaintiff should not be allowed to recover when he could not do so in either Iowa where the accident occurred or in Connecticut where he is domiciled. We cannot agree for two reasons. First, it is not definite that plaintiff would be unable to recover in either of those states.[2] More importantly, however, we see no reason for applying Connecticut's choice-of-law rule. To do so would frustrate the very goals of governmental-interest analysis. Connecticut's choice-of-law rule does not identify that state's interest in the matter. *Lex loci delicti* was born in an effort to achieve simplicity and uniformity, and does not relate to a state's interest in having its law applied to given issues in a tort case. . . .

We conclude that since Iowa has no interest in this litigation, and since the substantive laws of Connecticut and New Jersey are the same, this case presents a false conflict and the Connecticut plaintiff should have the right to maintain an action for ordinary negligence in our courts. In this situation principles of comity, and perhaps the equal protection and privileges and immunities clauses of the Constitution, dictate that we should afford the Connecticut plaintff the same protection a New Jersey plaintiff would be given. Cavers, The Choice-of-Law Process, 144 n. 8, 299 n. 14 (1965).

For the reasons expressed the order of the Appellate Division is reversed and the order of the trial court striking the separate defense of the Iowa guest statute is reinstated.

NOTES

(1) In Griffith v. United Airlines, 416 Pa. 1, 203 A.2d 796 (1964), a Pennsylvanian died when his plane crashed in Colorado in the course of a flight from Philadelphia to Arizona. The more generous Pennsylvania survival statute was applied, with the court rejecting the place of wrong rule for one that was "more flexible" and "permits analysis of the policies and interests underlying the particular issue before the court." These pointed to the Pennsylvania rule.

(2) The following year, the New York Court of Appeals decided Long v. Pan American World Airways, 16 N.Y.2d 377, 266 N.Y.S.2d 513, 213 N.E.2d 796 (1965). En route from Puerto Rico to Pennsylvania the defendant's airplane crashed in Maryland with two Pennsylvania domiciliaries aboard. New York's only contact, apart from being the forum, was that it had incorporated the defendant. Applying interest analysis to the issue of whether the surviving relatives, ineligible to bring a claim under the Maryland lex loci delicti, could invoke Pennsylvania's law, the New York court held they could. In its decision, should the New York court have taken the Griffith case into account and applied Pennsylvania's choice-of-law rules or disregarded them? Is there anything to the view that a state's choice-of-law rules should be considered when the forum refers to a state using the interest methodology, but not when the referent state uses orthodox choice-of-law rules? See

2. . . . It is possible that Connecticut would avoid applying the Iowa guest statute to these facts. If, as defendants urge, we should look to Connecticut's whole law, i.e., both its substantive law and its choice-of-law rule, why should not Connecticut look to Iowa's whole law if suit were brought in Connecticut? If it did look to Iowa's whole law, Connecticut might well be led back to its own substantive law. See Leflar, American Conflicts Law at 215–16. See generally, Seidelson, "The Americanization of Renvoi," 7 Duquesne L.Rev. 201; Griswold, "Renvoi Revisited," 51 Harv.L.Rev. 1165, 1166–70 (1938).

Seidelson, Interest Analysis for Those Who Like It and Those Who Don't, 11 Duquesne L.Rev. 283 (1973).

D. PROBLEMS, EMERGED AND EMERGING

---

1. *Rules, No Rules, Bad Rules*

D. CAVERS, THE CHOICE-OF-LAW PROCESS (1965) pp. 20–23:

[Professor Cavers asked a group of well-known Conflict of Laws scholars to "decide" hypothetical choice-of-law cases that he posited. One of the judges was Dean Erwin N. Griswold, former Dean of the Harvard Law School and later Solicitor General of the United States.]

GRISWOLD, J. ". . . The object of our legal system, I suppose, is to provide 'equal justice under law.' This is something different from 'justice,' which is a very elusive concept, and surely as much of an unruly horse as 'public policy.' If we are to have 'equal justice under law,' there must be law, which means that there must be rules of law. Cases must be put into groups or categories, and cases which rightly fall within the same category should receive the same decision. This need not be a mechanical process. Indeed, it cannot be such a process, for the problems which arise in human relations have infinite variation. Nevertheless, we should not be deluded by the variation. We should recognize that our function is to develop rules of law so that, in so far as possible, similar cases will be similarly decided.

"This problem, which runs through the law, becomes especially acute in the field of conflict of laws. . . .

"Though a case has extra-state elements, it is still incumbent upon us to find or develop rules of law for its decision, if we are to meet our responsibility to establish, so far as possible, 'equal justice under law.' Through long experience, American courts have developed the basic rule that many problems in the law of torts are to be decided by law of the state where the tort occurred.

"The rule which has been developed in such cases was stated succinctly in Section 378 of the original *Restatement of the Conflict of Laws*. This Section reflects the great weight of authority in this country, both before and since its promulgation. . . . Section 388 of the *Restatement* specifically provides, 'If there is a defense on the merits to the plaintiff's claim by the law of the place of wrong, no recovery can be had on the claim in another state.'

"In reaching this conclusion, I am not unaware of criticisms of the 'place of tort' rule; nor have I overlooked recent ferment, both academic and judicial, in the field of conflict of laws. I do not think that the place of tort rule should be applied woodenly. For example, it may well be unwise to apply it to the question of survival of causes of action, either on the plaintiff's side or on the defendant's. This means that each problem must be considered carefully and thoughtfully. Nevertheless, in such considerations, we should never forget that what we are seeking is a rule of law. The rule that basic aspects of a tort are covered by the place of the tort is such a rule of law. I know of no other rule which shows any capacity of replacing it. The decision of each case on an *ad hoc* basis should be plainly recognized as the antithesis of a rule of law.

". . . what is the purpose or objective of the conflict of laws? It is not simply to provide a means of deciding cases, for that could be done by flipping a coin, or by always applying the domestic law of the forum. . . . If we were setting up the United States today, we would almost surely think it foolish to have different rules of law applicable every few hundred miles within its territory. But we have a Federal system, with more than fifty separate legal units. Quite apart from the function of conflict of laws in the international scene, its function within the United States is to bring order out of this chaos, and to provide some rules of law which will make it possible for states to decide cases having some external elements on a rational and reasonably consistent basis.

"Within the United States, there can very rarely be any legitimate basis for one state to apply its 'public policy' against the laws of another state. Nor should any state, in seeking 'justice,' fail to apprehend that there will be no justice unless cases are decided in accordance with law, that is, in the conflict-of-laws area, on a basis which will be accepted by other states, and will lead, in so far as humanly possible, to the same decision of a controversy no matter where the suit is brought.

"Thus, as it seems to me, to say that each state must seek the result which it regards as just under all the circumstances, including the extra-state elements and laws, is simply to deny the existence and purpose of the conflict of laws. It is as much a denial of the purpose of the conflict of laws as is the decision of each case by law of the forum, regardless of its extra-state elements. This should be apparent on its face. It is made apparent when the question of forum-shopping is considered. If each court simply decides what it regards as 'just,' or, on the other hand, if it applies only its own law, then diverse precedents will surely develop, and counsel for plaintiffs will be remiss in their duty if they do not study all the cases in all the states, and file their suit (as they often can) in a state which will give them a favorable result.

"Not only is this a denial of true justice, a denial of the purpose of the conflict of laws, but also it is a denial of law itself. It provides no opportunity for certainty in the law. It makes it difficult to plan transactions having interstate elements. Even after an injury of some sort has occurred, there is, under such a rule, no basis for advising a client as to his rights, or for settling or adjusting the dispute without litigation. All that the lawyer can say is, 'Well, it depends upon the state in which the suit is brought. We will have to see where we can serve the defendant, and then try to find the state where the prospects are best. Perhaps we should sue in three or four states, and then nurse the several cases along until we see how the precedents develop.'

"All of this is fun for lawyers, and provides much for the law professors to write about. But it is not law. It is not conflict of laws, if that term has any real and constructive meaning and objective. We will not have law in this area, we will not fulfill the objectives of the conflict of laws, unless we can provide rules for cases under which the same cases will be decided the same way no matter where the suit is brought, to the extent that this is possible within the limits of human frailty. We will not always be successful in achieving uniformity, but we will surely have more success if we constantly hold up uniformity of result as a major objective, and recognize that there can be no true justice without it."

NOTE ON BAD RULES vs. NO RULES

Afficionados of the interest-policy methodology are in no sense apologetic about the absence of *a priori* rules that point to one state as the place of the governing rule. Professor Currie did not propose to substitute new rules for the old ones he attacked, and neither do his followers. Of necessity, in their view decisions must be ad hoc, because issues, contacts, concerns, policies, interests and the other elements of the apparatus vary endlessly.

However worthy the concern of modern conflicts scholars for case-by-case justice instead of an illusory quest for uniformity, simplicity and predictability, there are clear signs that the no-rules approach has gotten out of hand. An agitated statement of that conclusion by one of the editors of this volume asserts that

"a choice-of-law rule need not achieve perfect justice every time it is invoked in order to be preferable to the no-rule approach. The idea that judges can be turned loose in the three-dimensional chess games we have made of these cases, and can be told to do hand-tailored justice, case by case, free from the constraints or guidelines of rules, is a vain and dangerous illusion. It tries to dispose of law's ancient dilemma—the one or the many?—by exhorting courts to think deeply and decide justly. It elevates local substantive law policies to complete dominance and shockingly neglects policies concerned with making the federal system function smoothly. Above all, the idea that we need only a method, not rules, overlooks the key point: the present concern [multistate highway accidents] is with high-volume problems in the *adminis-tration* of justice, not in its inspired divination." (Rosenberg, Comments on Reich v. Purcell, 15 U.C.L.A.L.Rev. 551, 644 (1968).)

Besides, is not the effort to discard rules of choice of law as un-promising as trying to throw away a boomerang? In a system based on stare decisis, will not the precedents at some stage synthesize into a principle, or perhaps even a rule? If so, is there harm in anticipat-ing, and, while retaining a good measure of flexibility, working con-sciously to develop principles and prudently narrow rules? If so, may not the Second Restatement be on the right track in supplying a half-way stage in the evolution from a free-wheeling unruliness to balanced, justice-promoting principles and rules? These will at the same time be conscious of the contents of the decisional rules chosen and of the need to coordinate a complex multistate system, which is a key element of the task of the conflicts scholar.

Soundly designed principles and rules will avoid some of the esca-lating complexities of the no-rules approaches. They will, for exam-ple, escape the illogicality of using liability insurance as a choice-in-fluencing consideration without taking evidence on whether it exists and to what extent!

----

2. *System Coordination*

STATUTORY CHOICE–OF–LAW RULES

Legislative prescriptions that mandate how courts must react to certain types of multistate conflicts situations have existed for a long time. Their presence in appreciable numbers in significant areas of the law shows that at least on occasion the legislature of a state is prepared to require a court to follow an *a priori* rule for choice of law, disallowing in such instances the ad hoc interest analysis. The legislative rules may adopt various approaches, including laying down a flat rule that the forum courts must apply the substantive law of the state where the "cause of action arose"; or where the "wrongful act, neglect or default occurred"; or an alternative reference rule, selecting one or another of the competing rules of decision in order to achieve a prescribed result.

Examples of such choice-regulating statutes are:

—The Federal Tort Claims Act, making the United States liable "in accordance wih the law of the place where the act or omission occurred." 28 U.S.C.A. § 1346(b) (West Supp. 1983).

—West's Ann.Cal. Civil Code § 1646, providing that "a contract is to be interpreted according to the law and usage of the place where it is to be performed; or, if it does not indicate a place of performance, according to the law and usage of the place where it is made."

—Maryland Code § 3–903, providing that "If the wrongful act occurred in another state, the District of Columbia or a territory of the United States, a Maryland court shall apply the substantive law of that jurisdiction."

Presumably, in a state with a choice-regulating statute like Maryland's, even a court that followed the interest-policy method espoused by the New York Court of Appeals in Miller v. Miller, p. 515, supra or by the California Supreme Court in Hurtado v. Superior Court, p. 515, note (4), supra, would be bound to follow the "jurisdiction-selecting" command. Such statutes are evidence that system-coordinating values may transcend the substantive values that underlie local law policies affecting the subject matter under concern.

For a long list of statutes containing choice-of-law provisions see Brilmayer, Interest Analysis and the Myth of Legislative Intent, 78 Mich.L.Rev. 392, 424, 425–26 nn. 100–108 (1980). Professor Leflar has called attention to the considerable flexibility these statutes permit in choosing a choice-of-law approach suited to the needs of the situation. See Leflar, American Conflicts Law § 101, pp. 202–203 (3d ed. 1977).

The Uniform Securities Act has a detailed choice-of-law section, of a character quite different from Section 1–105 of the Uniform Commercial Code. The Uniform Securities Act is specific in selecting the places of particular events as providing the governing law for particular issues. This approach is desirable for the types of transactions controlled by this act, as to which it is urgent that the exact legal consequences of acts be known at once. The practical reasons that justify mechanical rules here are similar to those that justify comparable rules in some of the exceptions to the Uniform Commercial Code's general choice-of-law provision. Good choice-of-law statutes, cleanly and wisely drafted, may employ many different approaches. Their common feature is that they are designed realistically to give practical policy-oriented answers to choice-of-law problems. They are drafted to help serve the socio-economic functions of the law of which they are a part.

NOTES

(1) Assume that a case involving a state X victim of a fatal auto accident in state Y reached the Supreme Court of Y, which decided that: (1) the lex loci rule should apply to limit damages to the ceiling prescribed in the Y wrongful death action; and (2) since the defendant was a Y driver the statute's purpose would also be advanced by limiting the damage recovery. In a later case in a Maryland court, involving a Maryland citizen killed in an automobile accident in state Y by a Maryland driver, would the Y damage ceiling be applied under the Maryland statute mentioned immediately above? What if the first case had been decided on an interest analysis?

(2) See Leflar, Choice-of-Law Statutes, 44 Tenn.L.Rev. 951 (1978).

UNIFORM PROBATE CODE

§ 2–201(b)

If a married person not domiciled in this state dies, the right, if any, of the surviving spouse to take an elective share in property in this state is governed by the law of the decedent's domicile at death.

UNIFORM WILLS ACT

Uniform Laws Annotated, Vol. 9A (1965)

§ 7. Foreign Execution. A will executed outside this state in a manner prescribed by this Act, or a written will executed outside this state in a manner prescribed by the law of the place of its execution or by the law of the testator's domicile at the time of its execution, shall have the same force and effect in this state as if executed in this state in compliance with the provisions of this Act.

This is an example of a statutory alternative reference rule to promote validation of wills.

NOTES

(1) Statutes in more than thirty states provide for alternative places of reference to determine whether a will has been executed in proper form. In the majority of these states, a will executed elsewhere, when in writing and subscribed by the testator, is legally effective if executed in the mode prescribed by the law of the forum, or by the law of the place of execution, or by the law of the testator's domicile. There are differences among the states as to whether the reference is to the testator's domicile at the time of execution of the will or at the time of death. See, for example, Model Probate Code § 50. See also, Rees, American Wills Statutes: II, 46 Va.L.Rev. 856, 905 (1960).

(2) A liberal provision providing for numerous places of alternative reference has been enacted in England, Wills Act, 1963, 11 & 12 Eliz. 2, Chapter 44. This provision is based upon the Hague Convention of 1960 which is reprinted in 9 Am.J.Comp.Law 705 (1960).

NEW YORK CIVIL PRACTICE LAW AND RULES

§ 202. Cause of action accruing without the state

An action based upon a cause of action accruing without the state cannot be commenced after the expiration of the time limited by the laws of either the state or the place without the state where the cause of action accrued, except that where the cause of action accrued in favor of a resident of the state the time limited by the laws of the state shall apply.

This appears in one aspect to be an open-ended delegation to any other state the power to set a shorter limitations period that will then be accepted as binding in New York, even though New York is not obligated by constitutional command or common law doctrine thus to subordinate its limitations policies. The delegation does not apply if a New York resident is plaintiff, for his time can never be shortened to lesser length than New York allows for the type of action he has brought. This common form of discrimination in favor of residents has been held constitutional (see Canadian Northern Railway Co. v. Eggen, 252 U.S. 553 (1920), p. 434, supra), but it seems, at best, a dubious form of parochialism.

The proposed Swiss code on private international law is particularly interesting in that it gives the plaintiff the power to choose one of several designated laws in the case of certain torts. For example, in the case of product liability, Article 131 gives the plaintiff the choice of the law of either the state of the defendant's establishment or habitual residence or of that where the plaintiff acquired the product in question. Article 134 permits a plaintiff complaining of air pollution to choose the law either of the state where the pollution originated or where the effects of the pollution were felt. Similarly in the case of defamation, Article 135 gives the plaintiff the choice of the law of the state (a) of his own habitual residence or (b) of the establishment or habitual residence of the defendant or (c) where the effects of the defamation were felt.

Provisions of this sort provide a clear rule and also further what the draftsmen believed to be the basic substantive policy involved, namely, to provide compensation for the plaintiff. Along the same lines, see Reese, The Law Governing Airplane Accidents, 39 Wash. & Lee L.Rev. 1303 (1982), which suggests that the plaintiff should be given the choice of the law of several states in suits against airplane carriers and producers.

---

3. *Problems, Disappearing and Emerging*

It will have been noted that most of the recent choice-of-law cases found in this chapter involved either guest-passenger statutes or statutes which imposed limitations on the amount recoverable for wrongful death. Both kinds of statutes have now largely disappeared. What, then, of the future? Can it be anticipated that choice-of-law cases in tort will diminish both in number and importance? This question should probably be answered in the negative because of the many areas of potential choice-of-law problems that remain. For example, there are the problems that can be expected to arise between comparative negligence and contributory negligence states. See, e.g., Fells v. Bowman, p. 553, supra; Issendorf v. Olson, 194 N.W.2d 750 (N.D.1972). There are still many significant differences among the wrongful death and survival statutes of the several states, particularly with respect to the elements of damages recoverable, the persons who will share in the recovery and statutes of limitations. Likewise, the field of product liability may engender more choice-of-law problems than it has in the past. And the same may be true of the malpractice area where there recently have been significant changes in the law of many states. Finally, mention should be made of "nofault," which is treated below and threatens to give rise to a deluge of choice-of-law cases. In the foreseeable future, as one choice-of-law problem disappears, another seems likely to take its place.

A case that gives a glimpse of some of the choice-of-law problems that may continue to bedevil us is In re Paris Air Crash of March 3, 1974, 399 F.Supp. 732 (C.D.Cal.1975). That case involved the crash in France of a Turkish Air Lines plane, in which all 346 occupants were killed. Of these, 23 were Americans from 12 different states; the remainder came from 24 foreign countries. In all, some 203 suits were filed against McDonnell Douglas Corporation, the manufacturer of the plane, and General Dynamics, a subcontractor. Both defendants are incorporated in California, which was also the state where the plane had been manufactured. Most of the suits were originally brought in the federal district court in California and others were transferred there under 28 U.S.C. § 1407 by the Judicial Panel on Multidistrict Litigation. One of the principal issues involved the basis of liability. Under California law, the defendants would be strictly liable for injuries resulting from an original defect in the plane. Under the laws of most of the foreign countries involved, proof of negligence, would be required to hold them liable. Also, the amount of damages recoverable varied widely from law to law. Recovery would be most restricted under the law of England where most of the passengers had been domiciled. It would be considerably larger under the laws of France, Turkey, Japan and California.* After lengthy discussion, the judge determined that California law should be applied to determine both the basis of liability and the measure of recovery. To be sure, California "has no interest in the distribution of proceeds to foreign beneficiaries." But application of California law was required because of that state's interest in "(1) deterring conduct of its defendants, (2) avoiding the imposition of excessive financial burdens on its resident defendants, and . . . (3) providing a uniform rule of liability and damages so that those who come under the ambit of California strict product liability law and market their product outside of California and/or in foreign countries may know

* The statements with respect to the relevant local law rules of the states and countries involved are based on Speiser, Conflict of Laws in Wrongful Death Cases, 81 Case & Comment 49 (1975).

what risks they are subject to when they make and sell their products."

NOTE

For a suggestion that federal common law rules should be developed to govern rights and liabilities arising from aircraft accidents in the United States, see Note, The Case for a Federal Common Law of Aircraft Disaster Litigation, 51 N.Y.U. L.Rev. 231 (1976).

No Fault

No fault seems destined to become a fertile field for choice-of-law problems. At the moment, approximately half of the states have enacted some form of no-fault legislation. Without question, we face a period in which some states have adopted the no-fault concept while others will continue to rely exclusively upon the rules of tort. In addition, there are wide differences among the no-fault statutes of the several states. Choice-of-law problems are therefore bound to arise between states that have adopted no-fault systems and those that have not; and also between states with divergent no-fault programs.

No-fault statutes do essentially two things: (1) they provide that the insured and some designated classes of persons can claim reimbursement without regard to fault from the insured's own insurance company for certain losses resulting from injuries sustained in a motor vehicle accident and (2) they eliminate certain negligence claims in tort unless the injuries sustained are of a defined type or result in financial loss in excess of a prescribed amount. See Keeton and O'Connell, Basic Protection for the Traffic Victim (1965); Symposium on No-Fault Automobile Insurance, 71 Colum.L.Rev. 189 et seq. (1971). Most no-fault statutes contain provisions directed to their territorial application. A very few, such as that of New York (Article 18 of the New York Insurance Law) apply only to accidents occurring within the state; the great majority of statutes provide coverage to certain persons injured outside the state. The relevant provisions of a typical statute appear below.

Presumably, most of the forthcoming choice-of-law problems will concern the extent to which the no-fault statute of one state will be given effect in another state. It will be noted, for example, that Section 5 of the Uniform Motor Vehicle Accident Reparations Act, which is set forth below, abolishes tort liability in certain circumstances in the case of accidents occurring within the state. Suppose that persons domiciled in a fault state are involved in an automobile accident in a state which has enacted the Uniform Act and that subsequently one of these persons brings suit against the other in tort in the home state. Would the court give effect to the Act by dismissing the suit? A similar problem can arise as between two no-fault states in a situation where the injured party is precluded from suing in tort under the no-fault statute of the state of injury but not under that of his home state where he brings suit. Additional choice-of-law problems of this sort can easily be brought to mind.

Provisions in no-fault statutes that are directed to their territorial application involve two important questions. One relates to the scope of applicability of their *benefits:* To whom do these apply in cases that involve multi-state elements? The other relates to *exemptions* from tort liability: When, if ever, are non-residents given exemption from tort liability by force of a no-fault statute? Do residents retain statutory exemptions when they travel outside the state? These questions raise issues of constitutionality as well as sound policy. Consider the following statutory provisions.

UNIFORM MOTOR VEHICLE ACCIDENT REPARATIONS ACT

14 U.L.A. 48 (1972)

SECTION 1. [Definitions]

(a) In ths Act:

(1) . . .

(2) "Basic reparation benefits" mean benefits providing reimbursement for net loss suffered through injury arising out of the maintenance or use of a motor vehicle. . . .

(3) "Basic reparation insured" means:

(i) a person identified by name as an insured in a contract of basic reparation insurance complying with this Act . . . ; and

(ii) while residing in the same household with a named insured, the following persons not identified by name as an insured in any other contract of basic reparation insurance complying with this Act: a spouse or other relative of a named insured; and a minor in the custody of a named insured or of a relative residing in the same household with a named insured. A person resides in the same household if he usually makes his home in the same family unit, even though he temporarily lives elsewhere.

SECTION 2. [Right to Basic Reparation Benefits]

(a) If the accident causing injury occurs in this State, every person suffering loss from injury arising out of maintenance or use of a motor vehicle has a right to basic reparation benefits.

(b) If the accident causing injury occurs outside this State, the following persons and their survivors suffering loss from injury arising out of maintenance or use of a motor vehicle have a right to basic reparation benefits:

(1) basic reparation insureds; and

(2) the driver and other occupants of a secured vehicle. . . .

COMMENT

All persons injured in motor vehicle accidents within this State are entitled to receive basic reparation benefits for the loss suffered, with two limited exceptions. Limited disqualifications are provided for some converters of motor vehicles (Section 21) and those intentionally causing injury to themselves or other persons (Section 22). . . . As to accidents occurring outside this State, basic reparation insureds and persons occupying the secured vehicle are entitled to basic reparation benefits. Non-occupants, such as pedestrians who are not basic reparation insureds, are not entitled to basic reparation benefits solely because they have been injured in an out-of-State accident involving a secured vehicle. . . .

SECTION 5. [Partial Abolition of Tort Liability]

[This section provides that tort liability for automobile accidents occurring "in this state" is abolished except if the vehicle involved is not covered by required insurance; or the harm caused is the result of a failure by a repair business; is intentional; exceeds amounts recoverable as basic reparation benefits; or if the accident causes death or severe injuries of specified kinds.]

SECTION 9. [Included Coverages]

(a) An insurance contract which purports to provide coverage for basic reparation benefits . . . has the legal effect of including all coverages required by this Act.

(b) Notwithstanding any contrary provision in it, every contract of liability insurance for injury, wherever issued, covering ownership, maintenance, or use of a motor vehicle . . . includes basic reparation benefit coverages and minimum security for tort liabilities required by this Act, while it is in this State, and qualifies as security covering the vehicle.

(c) An insurer authorized to transact or transacting business in this State may not exclude, in any contract of liability insurance for injury, wherever issued, covering ownership, maintenance, or use of a motor vehicle . . . the basic reparation benefit coverages and required minimum security for tort liabilities required by this Act, while the vehicle is in this State.

COMMENT

Subsection (a) assures that every contract purporting to do so contains the mandated basic reparation and liability coverages regardless of the language actually used in the contract.

Subsection (b) explicitly applies to an insurer even though the insured is a nonresident of this State, the insurer is not qualified to do business in this State, and the only contact of the insurer with this State is that its insured permitted operation of the insured vehicle in this State. The effect of this provision is to convert a foreign insurer's automobile or motor vehicle liability policy or contract to the coverages required under this Act if the insured vehicle is registered in this State or operated in this State with the owner's permission. Since only "liability" insurance contracts are converted, an insurance contract limited to collision and comprehensive coverages is unaffected by this provision. Given the ready ability of the owner of a motor vehicle to drive his vehicle from state to state within a few days over an interstate highway system, it is unreasonable for an insurer to argue that it could not contemplate out-of-state use of the motor vehicle, or that it could only contemplate or foresee use within a limited geographic area. Accordingly, operation of the insured vehicle within the State, standing alone, should be a sufficient contact allowing the State to impose its substantive laws upon the out-of-State insurer of an out-of-State vehicle. Cf. Clay v. Sun Insurance Office, 377 U.S. 179 (1964) [p. 355, supra].

Subsection (c) is, in part, a safety valve in the event subsection (b) were held to be unconstitutional. Without reference to where the contract is written, it requires, if the insurer is authorized to transact or is transacting business in this State, that the coverages required by this Act be included in any automobile or motor vehicle liability insurance contract if the insured vehicle is registered or operated in this State. . . .

NOTES

(1) Is there justification for having the no-fault provisions of the Act apply to accidents within the state which involve only out-of-state automobiles and in which only nonresidents are injured? Conversely, is there good reason for making these provisions inapplicable to the claims of a resident of the state who, although not himself a "basic reparation insured," is injured outside the state by an automobile that is licensed and insured in the state?

(2) Is there justification for giving some extraterritorial application to the no-fault benefits of the Act (Section 2) and for restricting exemption from tort liability to accidents within the state (Section 5)?

(3) Compare § 1009.110(c) of Chapter 40 of the Pennsylvania statutes.

(c) *Applicable law.*

(1) The basic loss benefits available to any victim or to any survivor of a deceased victim shall be determined pursuant to the provisions of the state no-fault plan for motor vehicle insurance in effect in the state of domicile of the victim on the date when the motor vehicle accident resulting in injury occurs. If there is no such state no-fault plan in effect or if the victim is not domiciled in any state, then basic loss benefits available to any victim shall be determined pursuant to the provisions of the state

no-fault plan for motor vehicle insurance, if any, in effect in the state in which the accident resulting in injury occurs.

(2) The right of a victim or of a survivor of a deceased victim to sue in tort shall be determined by the law of the state of domicile of such victim. If a victim is not domiciled in a state, such right to sue shall be determined by the law of the state in which the accident resulting in injury or damage to property occurs.

KOZYRIS, NO-FAULT AUTOMOBILE INSURANCE AND THE CONFLICT OF LAWS—CUTTING THE GORDIAN KNOT HOME-STYLE, 1972 DUKE L.J. 331, 335–336.

It is too early to predict the outcome of the no-fault versus negligence liability battle. . . . If opposition to no-fault remains strong, however, a permanent stalemate may result, with some states switching to no-fault while others retain negligence liability. In either case, a "crazy-quilt" pattern lasting for many years is quite likely to develop, and the problems of choice of law will be multiplied to an unprecedented degree.

NOTES

(1) In the above-quoted article, Professor Kozyris examined a number of no-fault laws and concluded (at page 405):

"A personal system of choice of law incorporating explicit directives based on domicil or habitual residence, adequately defined, giving to all parties the benefits of, and imposing on them the obligations under, their own home state law, with certain minor territorial exceptions for special problems, is clearly more consistent with the goals of no-fault automobile reparations than a territorial or any other presently known system."

(2) In a follow-up article, "An Interim Update," 1973 Duke L.J. 1009, Professor Kozyris defended his thesis by comparing the operation of his proposed principles in a modified hypothetical version of Tooker v. Lopez (p. 495, supra). He found that his proposed approach worked much better than choice-of-law provisions of various no-fault statutes.

(3) There have been proposals for the enactment of a federal No-Fault Motor Vehicle Insurance Act. See, e.g., S. 354 and H.R. 19000 (94th Congress). This Act would provide for a federal system of no-fault that would take effect in states which either have enacted no legislation of this sort or whose legislation does not meet federal standards. Under § 110(c) of the Act, no-fault benefits would be determined in accordance with the law of the state of the victim's domicile provided that this law satisfies federal standards. The Act was considered by a number of sessions of Congress, but has not been enacted.

(4) Choice-of-law decisions involving no-fault have begun to appear. In Juodis v. Schule, 79 Misc.2d 955, 361 N.Y.S.2d 605 (1974), the Connecticut no-fault statute was held to provide a defense to a tort action in New York. The infant plaintiff had been injured in a one car accident in Connecticut and had brought suit against the driver and owner. All of the parties were New

York residents. New York's no-fault statute did not become effective until after the date of the accident.

In Wierbinski v. State Farm Mutual Automobile Insurance Co., 477 F.Supp. 659 (W.D.Pa.1979), the plaintiff, a New York domiciliary, was injured in a one-car accident in Pennsylvania. Plaintiff's medical and rehabilitative expenses were far in excess of the basic loss coverage available under the New York No-Fault Act. The court found that Pennsylvania was the state of most significant relationship and that, accordingly, Pennsylvania law governed. The Pennsylvania no-fault statute, however, provides that the basic loss benefits shall be determined by the no-fault law of the state of the victim's domicile, in this case New York. Ultimately, however, the plaintiff was permitted to recover the larger amount provided by Pennsylvania law, since, under the New York statute, the insurance company was required to provide coverage in the amount required by the law of any state in which the covered vehicle was involved in an accident.

(5) For an example of a novel question of choice of law, see Lopata v. Bemis Co., Inc., 406 F.Supp. 521 (E.D.Pa.1975) which involved the question of what law determines whether a corporation that has purchased the assets of another corporation is liable for injuries caused by an allegedly defective machine that had been manufactured and sold by the transferor corporation prior to the transfer of assets. See Juenger and Schulman, Assets, Sales and Products Liability, 22 Wayne L.Rev. 39 (1975).

Chapter 9

CHOICE OF THE APPLICABLE LAW: FURTHER CONSIDERATIONS

SECTION 1. CONTRACTS

A. AUTONOMY

This chapter examines various choice-of-law problems that for the most part are different from those considered in Chapter 8. The materials also develop several methodological issues from diverse perspectives and survey new approaches to the field.

During the recent upheavals in choice-of-law theory, not every area of the subject has been equally affected. Some substantive areas—for example, trusts, property law (especially land law), administration of decedents' estates and corporation law—have been relatively untouched by the revolution and have retained substantially intact their traditional approach to multistate choice-of-law problems. In this chapter we glance at some of these areas, reserving in-depth treatment of them for later in the book.

B. CHOICE OR ABSENCE OF CHOICE OF LAW BY THE PARTIES

Here the concern is with multistate contractual disputes raising choice-of-law issues, sometimes unaccompanied by explicit statements of intention as to which state's law should apply, sometimes covered by express law-selecting provisions. In the former case, the courts drew on the Chinese menu of potential rules of choice in the way briefly catalogued by Judge Fuld in Auten v. Auten, supra, p. 471. It will be recalled that one of their options was to divine the presumed intention of the parties regarding which law they wanted the courts to apply to potential disputes under their contract.

PRITCHARD v. NORTON

Supreme Court of the United States, 1882.
106 U.S. 124, 1 S.Ct. 102, 27 L.Ed. 104.

[Pritchard had become surety on an appeal bond in Louisiana on behalf of a defendant railroad company against which a judgment had been rendered in Louisiana. McComb and Norton executed and delivered to Pritchard in New York an indemnity bond in which they promised to indemnify him against all losses arising from his liability on the appeal bond. McComb and Norton had not requested Pritchard to become a surety. The judgment against the railroad company was affirmed and Pritchard was compelled to satisfy the bond. Pritchard's executrix sued McComb and Norton in Louisiana on the indemnity bond. Under Louisiana law the preexisting liability of Pritchard as surety was sufficient consideration to support the promise of indemnity, although Pritchard's obligation was not incurred at the defendant's request. The law of New York was otherwise. The lower court, the Circuit Court of the United States for the District of Louisiana, accepted the defendants' contention that the law of New York governed. The plaintiff appealed.]

Mr. Justice Matthews delivered the opinion of the court. . . .

The argument in support of the judgment is simple, and may be briefly stated. It is, that New York is the place of the contract, both because it was executed and delivered there, and because no other place of performance being either designated or necessarily implied, it was to be performed there. . . .

The phrase lex loci contractus is used, in a double sense, to mean, sometimes, the law of the place where a contract is entered into; sometimes, that of the place of its performance. And when it is employed to describe the law of the seat of the obligation, it is, on that account, confusing. The law we are in search of, which is to decide upon the nature, interpretation, and validity of the engagement in question, is that which the parties have, either expressly or presumptively, incorporated into their contract as constituting its obligation. It has never been better described than it was incidentally by Mr. Chief Justice Marshall in Wayman v. Southard, 10 Wheat. 1, 48, where he defined it as a principle of universal law,—"The principle that in every forum a contract is governed by the law with a view to which it was made." . . .

So, Phillimore says: . . .

"As all the foregoing rules rest upon the presumption that the obligor has voluntarily submitted himself to a particular local law, that presumption may be rebutted, either by an express declaration to the contrary, or by the fact that the obligation is illegal by that particular law, though legal by another. The parties cannot be presumed to have contemplated a law which would defeat their engagements." 4 Int.Law, sect. DCLIV, pp. 470, 471.

This rule, if universally applicable, which perhaps it is not, . . . would be decisive of the present controversy, as conclusive of the question of the application of the law of Louisiana, by which alone the undertaking of the obligor can be upheld.

At all events, it is a circumstance, highly persuasive in its character, of the presumed intention of the parties, and entitled to prevail, unless controlled by more express and positive proofs of a contrary intent. . . .

If now we examine the terms of the bond of indemnity, and the situation and relation of the parties, we shall find conclusive corroboration of the presumption, that the obligation was entered into in view of the laws of Louisiana.

The antecedent liability of Pritchard, as surety for the railroad company on the appeal bond, was confessedly contracted in that State, according to its laws, and it was there alone that it could be performed and discharged. Its undertaking was, that Pritchard should, in certain contingencies, satisfy a judgment of its courts. That could be done only within its territory and according to its laws. The condition of the obligation, which is the basis of this action, is, that McComb and Norton, the obligors, shall hold harmless and fully indemnify Pritchard against all loss or damage arising from his liability as surety on the appeal bond. A judgment was, in fact, rendered against him on it in Louisiana. There was but one way in which the obligors in the indemnity bond could perfectly satisfy its warranty. That was, the moment the judgment was rendered against Pritchard on the appeal bond, to come forward in his stead, and, by payment, to extinguish it. He was entitled to demand this before any payment by himself, and to require that the fund should be forthcoming at the place where otherwise he could be required to pay it. Even if it should be thought that Pritchard was bound to pay the judgment recovered against himself, before his right of recourse accrued upon the bond of indemnity, nevertheless he was entitled to be reimbursed the amount of his advance at the same place where he had been required to make it. So that it is clear, beyond any doubt, that the obligation of the indemnity was to be fulfilled in Louisiana, and, consequently, is subject, in all matters affecting its construction and validity, to the law of that locality. . . .

We do not hesitate, therefore, to decide that the bond of indemnity sued on was entered into with a view to the law of Louisiana as the place for the fulfillment of its obligation; and that the question of its validity, as depending on the character and sufficiency of the consideration, should be determined by the law of Louisiana, and not that of New York. For error in its rulings on this point, consequently, the judgment of the Circuit Court is reversed, with directions to grant a new trial.

NOTES

(1) Is the search for "presumed intention" of the parties any more than an effort by the court to pick the rule it thinks should apply, regardless of whether the parties intended anything in that respect, or what they intended? Consider this quotation:

". . . the question of intent can hardly be said to involve the actual mental operations of the parties. For, as a matter of fact, they probably did not stop to consider what was the legal effect of their agreement, or whether there was any diversity in the law of the two States; and, therefore, when we speak of the 'question of intent' we are making use of what may perhaps be termed a 'legal fiction'; but, nevertheless, the law does look at the acts of the parties and the circumstances surrounding them which may possibly have exerted some influence upon their actions, and then assumes that their intention is in harmony with such acts and circumstances." Grand v. Livingston, 4 App.Div. 589, 595, 38 N.Y.S. 490, 494 (4th Dep't. 1896).

(2) Is there a "Basic Rule of Validation" of such compelling force that the courts must nearly always choose the law which upholds and enforces the parties' "engagements"? See Ehrenzweig, Contracts and the Conflict of Laws, 59 Colum.L.Rev. 973, 1171 (1959). Or is that suggestion an example of a penchant for "transmuting a tendency into a doctrine"? See Cavers, Re-Restating the Conflict of Laws: The Chapter on Contracts, XXth Century Comparative and Conflict Laws 349, 358 (1961).

———

Judge Learned Hand in E. Gerli & Co. v. Cunard Steamship Co., 48 F.2d 115 (2d Cir. 1931), declared: "People cannot by agreement substitute the law of another place; they may of course incorporate any provisions they wish into their agreements—a statute like anything else—and when they do, courts will try to make sense out of the whole, so far as they can. But an agreement is not a contract, except as the law says it shall be, and to try to make it one is to pull on one's bootstraps. Some law must impose the obligation, and the parties have nothing whatever to do with that; no more than with whether their acts are torts or crimes." Is that view sound, or may the forum provide that under its conflict of laws rules an agreement that would be ineffective under the forum's local law may be enforced if it is valid under the law of a state selected by the parties in their contract?

———

Questions of construction of a contract depend for solution upon what the parties intended. Accordingly, the courts readily give effect to a provision that a contract shall be interpreted in accordance with the law of a given state, on the reasoning that such a provision is no more than a shorthand method by which parties may express the obligations they intended to assume.

The problem becomes more difficult if the issue concerns capacity or essential validity. May a person too young to enter a binding contract in his own state vest himself with capacity to contract merely by agreeing that the contract shall be governed by the law of a state which affords such power? Similarly, may the parties escape the requirement of consideration by referring to a law under which consideration is not essential to the validity of the contract?

Besides depending upon what type of question the parties have attempted to regulate by their reference to a foreign state's law, the efficacy of their attempt may turn upon whether the transaction bears any relationship to the state whose law they selected. It may also turn on whether the choice was the result of a free process of selection by both sides. Finally, the efficacy of their attempt may turn on how sharp a contradiction exists between the rule that would have been decisive had no choice been made by the parties and the rule chosen as applicable.

REVIEW BY RHEINSTEIN OF FALCONBRIDGE, ESSAYS ON THE CONFLICT OF LAWS (1947), in 15 U.Chi.L.Rev. 478, 485–487 (1948).

. . . [T]here cannot be found any reason why a state, through its legislature or its courts, should not lay down the following rule: Whenever parties to a situation which is alleged by one to have given rise to a legally enforceable contract, have in some ascertainable way expressed the opinion that disputes which may later arise out of that relation shall be decided under the legal system of some particular state or country, such law shall be resorted to whenever such a dispute actually arises. . . . If a state adopts that rule, then the law thus determined by the parties is the proper law of the contract and it is inconsistent to say that, by their understanding, they cannot exempt their contract from the prohibitive or restrictive provisions of the proper law. The law to whose prohibitive, restrictive, and other provisions the alleged contract is subject is the law referred to by the parties, just because it is the proper law and it is the proper law simply because the choice of law rule of the forum declares it to be such.

. . . If we agree that it is one of the very basic policies of the conflict of laws to prevent the application of a legal system of which the parties could not have thought, or, to express the same idea in a positive way, if we regard it as one of the principal purposes of the conflict of laws to protect the justified expectations of the parties, then the intention of the parties rule is the one which fulfills that purpose better than any rival rule . . .

. . . opposition to the intention of the parties rule has been motivated by the fear that the rule might too easily lend itself to evasion of the law. But which law is it that the opponents fear might be evaded? All the prohibitive and restrictive provisions of the law chosen by the parties apply. . . . There are also applicable all those prohibitive and restrictive rules of . . . the forum . . . which are regarded . . . as sufficiently important to merit classification as rules of public policy. If a state thinks that a contract should not be enforced because it was made in contravention of an important prohibition of the place where the agreement was made . . . it can perfectly well do so by an appropriate exception to the general intention of the parties rule. . . . Whether we should . . . [limit] the parties' choice to those laws with which their transaction has some factual connection is not a question of logic but of legal policy. . . . The choice of some unknown law may have been imposed upon one party to the transaction by the other, especially where the latter is occupying an economically or otherwise dominant position. That danger may be guarded against however, by the application of rules against duress, undue influence, or similar abuses. . . . There also remains the practical difficulty with which the court may be faced when it is asked to ascertain and interpret some foreign, conceivably exotic, law. This effort should not be asked of the court unless there are some good, objective reasons. It ought to be considered, however, that . . . [if] parties to a transaction stipulate some law other than that of their respective places of business or domicile, they will hardly do so without cause.

NOTE

For a discussion of contractual autonomy, see Gruson, Governing Law Clauses in Commercial Agreements—New York's Approach, 18 Colum.J. Transnat'l L. 323 (1980); Prebble, Choice of Law to Determine the Validity and Effect of Contracts: A Comparison of English and American Approaches to the Conflict of Laws, 58 Cornell L.Rev. 433, 491–536 (1973); Johnston, Party Autonomy in Contracts Specifying Foreign Law, 7 Wm. & Mary L.Rev. 37 (1966).

SIEGELMAN v. CUNARD WHITE STAR, LIMITED

United States Court of Appeals, Second Circuit, 1955.
221 F.2d 189.

[This is an action by the husband of a dead woman, brought in his own right and as administrator of her estate, against a British steamship company to recover for injuries suffered by her during a trip on one of the defendant's vessels.

On September 9, 1949, an agent of the defendant company sold to the husband and wife in New York a "Contract Ticket" for a voyage from New York to Cherbourg. The printed ticket was a document about a foot long and almost as wide and on its back it contained extensive notices to passengers. On the front there was conspicuously printed a notice directing attention to the ticket's "terms and conditions". Three of its provisions were:

"10. . . . No suit, action, or proceeding against the Company or the ship, or the Agents of either, shall be maintainable for loss of life of or bodily injury to any passenger unless . . . (b) . . . the suit, action or proceeding is commenced within one year from the day when the death or injury occurred.

"11. The price of passage hereunder has been fixed partly with reference to the liability assumed by the Company as defined by this contract, and no agreement, alteration or amendment creating any other or different liability shall be valid unless made in writing and signed for the Company by its Chief Agent at the port of embarkation.

"20. All questions arising on this contract ticket shall be decided according to English Law with reference to which this contract is made."

The injuries in question were suffered on the vessel on the high seas, September 24, 1949. On August 31, 1950, the defendant made an offer of $800 in settlement. Her lawyer, noticing the requirement of suit within a year, asked Swaine, a claim agent of the defendant, whether it would be necessary to begin suit to protect his client's rights. Swaine replied, so it is testified, that suit was not necessary and there was no point in commencing it, as it appeared the chance of settlement was excellent.

Later the injured woman died. On January 4, 1951, the defendant withdrew its offer, stating it could be tendered only to the injured party. On June 7, 1951, the plaintiff was appointed administrator of his wife's estate. On December 14, 1951, the present action was begun in a New York state court. It was removed on diversity grounds to the federal district court.

As one defense, the defendant relied on the failure of the plaintiff to bring the action within a year of the date of the injury. The district court sustained the defense and dismissed the complaint, and the plaintiff appeals.]

Before CLARK, CHIEF JUDGE, and FRANK and HARLAN, CIRCUIT JUDGES.

HARLAN, CIRCUIT JUDGE. . . . Before reaching the merits of the plaintiff's claim, we must deal with a number of preliminary questions: (1) Are federal or state choice-of-laws rules to be applied here? (2) What is the applicable choice-of-law rule of the proper authority? (3) If the applicable choice-of-law rule points to the use of English law, what difference is made by the facts that English law was not pleaded or proved below, and that the plaintiff made no attempt to supply affidavits of experts on English law, after the trial Judge had offered him an opportunity to do so?

I.

This case involves a claim based on a tort, committed on the high seas, and a defense based on a contract made in New York, to be performed there, on the high seas, and abroad. Our first question, though, is not what law governs the issues involved, but rather what law, federal or New York, controls the choice of the governing law. This is not a question of choice of laws, properly speaking, but rather a question of the division of competence between federal and state authority.

[The court held that since the federal judicial power extends under the Constitution "to all Cases of admiralty and maritime Jurisdiction", and Federal statutes have implemented this power, the doctrine of Erie R.R. Co. v. Tompkins, p. 683, infra, and Klaxon v. Stentor, p. 704, infra, did not apply and the federal court sitting in New York would not have to use New York conflict of laws rules.]

. . . Instead, . . . the federal choice-of-law rule might well be binding on the state courts, if either rule is to be binding in both sets of courts. . . .

II.

Our next question is: under the federal choice-of-law rule, what law governs the issues here? We are not concerned with the law applicable to the accident. Instead we must decide what law applies to the validity and interpretation of certain provisions of the "Contract Ticket," and to the effect of Swaine's conduct upon Cunard's right to resort to the one-year limitation period in the contract.

The ticket stipulated that "All questions arising on this contract ticket shall be decided according to English Law with reference to which this contract is made." Considering, as we do, the ticket to be a contract—see Foster v. Cunard White Star, 2 Cir. 1941, 121 F.2d 12—the provision that English law should govern must be taken to represent the intention of both parties. Therefore, this provision, if effective under the federal choice-of-law rule, renders English law applicable here, even though, absent the provision, some other law would govern under the applicable federal conflicts rule. . . .

. . . since we cannot assume that the parties' choice of law will always foreclose the court from applying another law, our question is whether the contract provision here should have the effect, under federal conflicts rules, of making the English law applicable to the particular questions posed by this case. While this question may appear on the surface to be purely one of conflict of laws, we think it also involves interpretation of the contract. For it is not altogether free from doubt what is meant by the stipulation that "All questions arising on this contract ticket shall be decided according to English Law. . . ." See 40 Col.L.Rev. 518, 522–23 (1940), criticizing one interpretation of a similar provision.

Our issue, then, involves two lines of inquiry: (1) What questions did the parties intend to be controlled by English law? and (2) Will the federal conflicts rule give effect to their intention? In pursuing the first inquiry, we must examine more closely the provision of the ticket quoted above.

Three questions as to the scope of this provision arise under its language. *First*, are questions to be decided by the "whole" English law, including its conflicts rules, or just by the substantive English law? That is, are questions to be decided according to the law of England, or instead, as an English court might decide them, applying where appropriate the law of some other country? We think the provision must be read as referring to the substantive law alone, for surely the major purpose of including the provision in the ticket was to assure Cunard of a uniform result in any litigation no matter where the ticket was issued or where the litigation arose, and this result might not obtain if the "whole" law of England were referred to. *Second*, does the provision intend that questions of validity of the contract and its provisions, as well as questions of interpretation, are to be governed by English law? The language of the clause, covering "all questions," indicates that validity as well as interpretation is embraced. *Third*, is the recital meant to require the application of English law to the question of what conduct may amount to a waiver of its provisions? Although the wording of the clause—relating to questions arising "on" the contract—may indicate that such a question was not meant to be covered, it appears unnatural to hold that all questions of validity and interpretation were intended to be governed by English law but that this question was not. We therefore consider that the question of what conduct was sufficient to operate as a waiver of the ticket's provisions was also meant to be determined by English law.

We now come to the inquiry as to the extent to which this provision, so construed, is to be given effect in deciding the particular issues before us. Those issues are: (1) Is the one-year limitation period provided in the contract for the bringing of suits valid? (2) Does Swaine's conduct prevent Cunard from using the period as a defense? and (3) How is this matter affected by the clause requiring alterations of the contract to be in writing? It appears not to be contested that the ticket should be treated as a contract and that failure to bring the action within the contract limitation period would be a defense under English law—see Jones v. Oceanic Steam Navigation Co., [1924] 2 K.B. 730, but since the same result would follow under American law—see 46 U.S.C.A. § 183(b); Scheibel v. Agwilines, Inc., 2 Cir. 1946, 156 F.2d 636—we need not decide whether English law is applicable to the first of these issues. As to the second and third issues—where English and American law may differ—in the view which we take of the case, we need really only deal with applicability of English law to the second issue—viz., whether Swaine's conduct prevents Cunard from using the one-year limitations provision as a defense—although in light of what we say below we think that English law would clearly control the third issue—viz., the effect of the "alterations" clause.

As we have said, we construe the contract as establishing the intention of the parties that English law should govern both the interpretation and validity of its terms.   And we think it clear that the federal conflicts rule will give effect to the parties' intention that English law is to be applied to the *interpretation* of the contract. Stipulating the governing law for this purpose is much like stipulating that words of the contract have the meanings given in a particular dictionary.   See Cheatham, Goodrich, Griswold & Reese, Cases on Conflict of Laws 461 (1951).   On the other hand, there is much doubt that parties can stipulate the law by which the *validity* of their contract is to be judged.   Beale, Conflict of Laws, § 332.2 (1935).   To permit parties to stipulate the law which should govern the validity of their agreement would afford them an artificial device for avoiding the policies of the state which would otherwise regulate the permissibility of their agreement.   It may also be said that to give effect to the parties' stipulation would permit them to do a legislative act, for they rather than the governing law would be making their agreement into an enforceable obligation.   And it may be further argued that since courts have not always been ready to give effect to the parties' stipulation, no real uniformity is achieved by following their wishes. See Beale, op. cit. supra, at page 1085.

Here, of course, the question is neither one of interpretation nor one of validity, but instead involves the circumstances under which parties may be said to have partially rescinded their agreements or to be barred from enforcing them.   The question is, however, more closely akin to a question of validity.   .   .   .   Instead of viewing the parties as usurping the legislative function, it seems more realistic to regard them as relieving the courts of the problem of resolving a question of conflict of laws.   Their course might be expected to reduce litigation, and is to be commended as much as good draftsmanship which relieves courts of problems of resolving ambiguities.   To say that there may be no reduction in litigation because courts may not honor the provision is to reason backwards.   A tendency toward certainty in commercial transactions should be encouraged by the courts.   Furthermore, in England, where much if the litigation on these contracts might be expected to arise, the parties' stipulation would probably be respected.   Vita Food Products, Inc. v. Unus Shipping Co., Ltd., [1939] A.C. 277 (P.C.) (similar provision in bill of lading given effect; construed, however, as referring to England's whole law, including its conflicts rules).

Where the law of the parties' intention has been permitted to govern the validity of contracts, it has often been said (1) that the choice of law must be *bona fide*, and (2) that the law chosen must be that of a jurisdiction having some relation to the agreement, generally either the place of making or the place of performance.   The second of these conditions is obviously satisfied here.   The fact that a conflicts question is presented in the absence of a stipulation is some indication that the first condition is also satisfied. Furthermore, there does not appear to be an attempt here to evade American policy. . . .

This is not to suggest that English and American policies on this subject are identical. Any difference in law reflects some difference in policy. Consequently, to the extent English and American policies may differ on this question, we would consider that the parties may choose to have the English policies apply. But we express no opinion on what result would follow if we had stronger policies at stake, or if the parties had attempted a feigned rather than a genuine solution of the conflicts problem.

III.

We must next decide whether it is within our competence to apply English law, which was neither pleaded nor proved below.

Pleading the foreign law was clearly unnecessary. The Federal Rules of Civil Procedure, 28 U.S.C.A., apply here. . . .

Rule 43(a) of the Federal Rules of Civil Procedure permits the presentaion of evidence according to the most convenient method prescribed in (1) the statutes of the United States, (2) the rules of evidence formerly applied in suits in equity by federal courts, or (3) the rules of evidence applied in the courts of general jurisdiction of the state in which the federal court is held. . . .

The District Judge in this case appears to have exercised both his options under the New York law. He took notice of the English law and stated what he believed it to be. He also offered the parties an opportunity to submit affidavits of experts on English law, if it was thought that his understanding was incorrect. So far as appears, no affidavits were submitted. . . .

Finally we come to the substantive question whether Swaine's conduct prevents Cunard from successfully invoking the contractual limitation period as a defense.

[The court found Cunard could invoke the contractual time limitation.]

Affirmed.

FRANK, CIRCUIT JUDGE (dissenting). . . .

Disregarding for the moment clause 20 of the ticket (referring to "English law"), I think it clear that, under federal and New York decisions, the defendant waived (or is estopped to assert) the one-year provision (clause 10) and thereby completely abandoned it.

. . . My colleagues, in holding that there was no waiver or estoppel, rely principally . . . on clause 20 which reads: "All questions arising on this contract ticket shall be decided according to English Law with reference to which this contract is made."

I think this clause does not import "English law" concerning a waiver after the injury occurred. For, at best, as my colleagues apparently concede, the words "*on* this contract" are ambiguous, i.e., do not (to say the least) unambiguously cover the post-injury conduct, in New York, of defendant's claim agent.

Because the contract was made in New York, for a journey beginning in New York, the usual rule is that its provisions must be interpreted according to New York "law," or by the "maritime law" which, as previously noted, must (absent decisions on the subject) be learned from federal "law" as to internal transactions. What, then, of a provision, clause 20, which ambiguously refers to "English law"? Surely, in interpreting that ambiguous provision, we should not look to English decisions. Thus to consult "English law," in interpreting an American contract ambiguously referring to "English law," would indeed be a pulling-yourself-up-by-your-own-bootstraps device. Especially is this true here, since the interpretation of a clause in a contract like this involves an important internal public policy. For, since the document was a fixed printed form prepared by defendant and tendered to the passenger, clause 20, under New York and federal decisions, must be construed most strongly against defendant.
. . . .

. . . Although I think the foregoing sufficient to render "English law" inapplicable to the issue before us, the following factors are also pertinent:

. . . Consider a suit brought in this country on a contract made in England to be performed in England, and where a breach of the contract happened in England. Under the usual "conflict" rule, English "law" would be ordinarily decisive as to the interpretation of the contract. That "law" would not govern, I think, with reference to acts, in New York, asserted to be a discharge—by way of release, rescission, accord and satisfaction, or an account stated; see Restatement of Conflict of Laws, Section 373, Comments a and b. Accordingly, I think "American law" governs the legal effect, as a waiver, of the New York conduct of defendant after the injury occurred.

[Judge Frank indicated his belief that clause 20 referred "to 'English law' as a 'whole'" and not to English local law.]

. . . I call attention to another factor which, while unnecessary to my conclusion, I think supports it: The ticket is what has been called a "contract of adhesion" or a "take-it-or-leave-it" contract. In such a standardized or mass-production agreement, with one-sided control of its terms, when the one party has no real bargaining power, the usual contract rules, based on the idea of "freedom of contract," cannot be applied rationally. . . . The commentators on "adhesion" contracts do not at all suggest that all standardized contracts be stricken down, for they recognize that such contracts often serve a highly useful purpose where the parties are not markedly unequal in bargaining power (as in many "commercial" contracts).

An ordinary contract has been called a sort of private statute, mutually made by the parties and governing their relations. But in a take-it-or-leave-it contract, absent actual freedom to contract, the parties do not "legislate" by mutual agreement; the dominant party "legislates" for both. . . .

All this has special pertinence here: A party, like the passenger here, having no real choice about the matter, cannot in fairness be said to have joined in a "choice of law" merely because the carrier has inserted a provision that some particular foreign "law" shall govern; therefore it would seem that that party should not be bound by such a provision. I shall not elaborate this point, since it is amply discussed in a recent excellent article, Ehrenzweig, "Adhesion Contracts in The Conflict of Laws," 53 Col.L.Rev. (1953) 1072, where most of the authorities are cited and considered.

. . . I grant that, in this context, I am stressing the need to do justice in particular instances. I do so unashamedly. For it is generally agreed that the decisions of conflict-of-laws cases by mechanized rules, without regard to particularized justice, cannot be defended on the ground that they have promoted certainty and uniformity, since such results have not been thus achieved. Several wise commentators have urged that the element of justice should have a dominating influence.

NOTES

(1) Does Judge Frank have the better of the argument? What about his point that New York law should determine the effect of the alleged discharge, agreed to in New York, of the one-year limitation? Cf. Restatement, Second, Conflict of Laws § 212.

(2) The English view is that a contractual provision calling for arbitration in England provides a strong, but not conclusive, indication that the parties intended to have English law govern their contract. This is so even though neither the parties nor the transaction had any other contact with England. Compagnie Tunisienne de Navigation S.A. v. Compagnie d'Armement Maritime S.A., [1971] A.C. 572; Dicey and Morris, The Conflict of Laws 762 (10th ed. 1980).

(3) A steamship ticket in the English language was issued in Germany to the German plaintiff and called for application of "United States" law. The court, ruling on the defense that the claim was time barred under United States law, declared that "unilaterally imposed provisions of this nature should not be enforced unless the party urging enforcement provided the other, illiterate in the language of the contract, with knowledge of what was intended." Fricke v. Isbrandtsen Co., 151 F.Supp. 465, 468 (S.D.N.Y.1957).

For decades contracts have posed the thorniest questions in choice of law, exceeding in diversity and difficulty even the wide range of problems developing in the field of torts. First, courts and commentators have been vexed by the paradox that a party to a carefully negotiated agreement with multistate contacts runs the risk of a bad misadventure due to some erratic resolution of a choice-of-law issue.

This possibility results because the courts are free to employ a large number of options in deciding a choice-of-law issue in the contract field and no one can predict which one they will use.

The second vexation comes from awareness that the misadventure theoretically should have been avoided by an explicit contractual provision stipulating which state's rules would apply to resolve disputes that might arise under the contract.

Faced with this experience, a natural response for draftsmen of the Second Restatement was to make explicit a point to which the first Restatement had not addressed itself. They accorded contracting parties in multistate situations substantial power, which they would be expected to exercise frequently, to choose in advance the law applicable to disputes their contracts might generate.

In default of an effective choice, the Second Restatement provided a number of choices of law rules. These began with Section 188, whose key feature is an attempt to discover the state of "most significant relationship" by applying a group of broad principles set out in Section 6.

Section 188 differs in significant respects from the provisions of its predecessor, Section 332b, as promulgated in Tentative Draft No. 6 (1960). These differences are a barometer of the changing climate of the choice-of-law process, in contracts, at least, during the drafting and adoption of the Second Restatement.

_____

RESTATEMENT, SECOND, CONFLICT OF LAWS (1971):*

§ 187.   Law of the State Chosen by the Parties

(1) The law of the state chosen by the parties to govern their contractual rights and duties will be applied if the particular issue is one which the parties (could have resolved by an explicit provision) in their agreement directed to that issue.

(2) The law of the state chosen by the parties to govern their contractual rights and duties will be applied, even if the particular issue is one which the parties could not have resolved by an explicit provision in their agreement directed to that issue, unless either

(a) the chosen state has no substantial relationship to the parties or the transaction and there is no other reasonable basis for the parties' choice, or

(b) application of the law of the chosen state would be contrary to a fundamental policy of a state which has a materially greater interest than the chosen state in the determination of the particular issue and which, under the rule of § 188, would be the

* Quoted with the permission of the copyright owner, The American Law Institute.

state of the applicable law in the absence of an effective choice of law by the parties.

(3) In the absence of a contrary indication of intention, the reference is to the local law of the state of the chosen law.

---

§ 188. Law Governing in Absence of Effective Choice by the Parties $G(A$

(1) The rights and duties of the parties with respect to an issue in contract are determined by the local law of the state which, with respect to that issue, has the most significant relationship to the transaction and the parties under the principles stated in § 6.

(2) In the absence of an effective choice of law by the parties (see § 187), the contacts to be taken into account in applying the principles of § 6 to determine the law applicable to an issue include:

(a) the place of contracting,

(b) the place of negotiation of the contract,

(c) the place of performance,

(d) the location of the subject matter of the contract, and

(e) the domicil, residence, nationality, place of incorporation and place of business of the parties.

These contacts are to be evaluated according to their relative importance with respect to the particular issue.

(3) If the place of negotiating the contract and the place of performance are in the same state, the local law of this state will usually be applied, except as otherwise provided in §§ 189–199 and 203.

NOTES

(1) Are the exceptions in § 187 necessary and workable? They are extensively considered in Reese, Power of Parties to Choose Law Governing Their Contract, 1960 Proc.Am.Soc.Int'l Law 49. See also Weinberger, Party Autonomy and Choice-of-Law: The Restatement (Second), Interest Analysis, and the Search for a Methodological Synthesis, 4 Hofstra L.Rev. 605 (1976); Note, Effectiveness of Choice-of-Law Clauses in Contract Conflicts of Law: Party Autonomy or Objective Determination?, 82 Colum.L.Rev. 1659 (1982).

(2) Professor Weintraub believes that choice-of-law clauses should only control issues of construction and that, with respect to issues of validity, there should be a rebuttable presumption that the validating law will be applied unless certain factors, which he enumerates, point in a contrary direction. Among these factors are that the invalidating rule is protective of the party in the inferior bargaining position and that it differs in basic policy from the validating rule. Weintraub, Commentary on the Conflict of Laws 382, 396–297 (2d ed. 1980).

(3) The American Law Institute reports "uncertainty" as to dépeçage— whether the parties should be permitted to select the local law of two or

more states to govern different aspects of a contract. Restatement, Second, Conflict of Laws § 187, Comment *i*. What contentions might be made?

(4) What should be the result when a choice-of-law clause calls for application of a law that would invalidate a contract? Section 187, Comment *e* of the Restatement, Second, states that in such circumstances the court should disregard the choice-of-law provision and, instead, apply the law of the state which would otherwise be applicable.

RESTATEMENT, SECOND, CONFLICT OF LAWS

(Tentative Draft No. 6, 1960)*

§ 332a. Law Chosen by the Parties

(1) The validity of a contract is determined by the law chosen by the parties for this purpose, unless

(a) the choice of law was obtained by improper means or was the result of mistake, or

(b) the contract has no substantial relationship with the state of the chosen law and there is no other reasonable basis for the parties' choice, or

(c) application of the chosen law would be contrary to a fundamental policy of the state which would be the state of the governing law in the absence of an effective choice by the parties.

(2) In the absence of a contrary indication of intention, the reference is to the local law of the chosen state.

§ 332b. Law Governing in Absence of an Effective Parties' Choice

(1) In the absence of an effective choice of law by the parties, consideration will be given to the following factors, among others, in determining the state with which the contract has its most significant relationship:

(a) the place of contracting

(b) the place of negotiation of the contract

(c) the place of performance

(d) the situs of the subject matter of the contract

(e) the domicil, residence, nationality, place of incorporation and place of business of the parties

(f) the place under whose local law the contract will be most effective.

* Quoted with the permission of the copyright owner, The American Law Institute.

(2) If the place of contracting, the place of negotiating the contract and the place of performance are in the same state, the local law of this state ordinarily determines the validity of the contract, except in the case of usury (see § 334d) and as stated in §§ 346e to 346n.

NOTES

(1) What are the chief differences between Sections 187 and 188 of the Restatement, Second, which were cast in their present terms in the Proposed Official Draft, published in 1968, and Sections 332a and 332b, their predecessors, published in 1960? What developments in the intervening years probably impelled these changes?

(2) What argument can be made that the broad grant of autonomy in Section 187 will be frustrated by the need to determine as to each dispute which state's law would govern under the provisions of Section 188? In what way does Section 187(2)(b) arguably compel such a determination?

BARNES GROUP, INC. v. C & C PRODUCTS, INC.

United States Court of Appeals, Fourth Circuit, 1983.
716 F.2d 1023.

[Suit to recover damages for tortious interference with plaintiff's contracts with certain sales agents. The plaintiff was incorporated in Delaware but the agents were hired by its Bowman division which operates a nationwide business out of its headquarters in Ohio. The agents were to act as Bowman's sales representatives in Alabama, Maryland, Virginia, District of Columbia, Louisiana and South Carolina. Each agent had sent his employment application to Bowman in Ohio and Bowman had accepted these applications and executed the employment contracts in that state. The agents had also received training materials from Ohio and had attended a four-day training course there. Each of the contracts provided that it should be governed by Ohio law and that each agent after terminating his relationship with Bowman would not during a two-year period sell products similar to those sold by Bowman to any person with whom he had dealt on the behalf of Bowman. Thereafter, the agents terminated their contracts with Bowman and entered into contracts with the defendant, an Ohio corporation, which called for performance in violation of their earlier contracts with Bowman. Suit was initially brought in the federal district court of Ohio but was then transferred to the district court in South Carolina under 28 USC 1404(a). The district court found for the plaintiff by application of Ohio law and the defendant appealed.]

JAMES DICKSON PHILLIPS, CIRCUIT JUDGE: . . .

As the parties concede, a necessary element of the tort of intentional interference with contract is that the contract at issue be valid

and enforceable as between the parties to it. . . . In this case particularly, C & C's liability for tortious interference hinges almost entirely upon whether the Bowman restrictive covenants are enforceable, because the facts clearly establish all other elements of the tort.
. . .

As dictated by Van Dusen v. Barrack, 376 U.S. 612 (1964), the district court was bound, as are we, to apply here the prevailing law of the transferor forum, the District Court for the Northern District of Ohio, which in turn would apply Ohio choice-of-law principles in this diversity action, Klaxon Co. v. Stentor Electric Manufacturing Co., 313 U.S. 487 (1941).

Seeking the applicable Ohio choice-of-law rule, we have [concluded] that the Ohio courts currently apply contemporary choice-of-law doctrine based upon interest analysis, the most significant relationship, and the Restatement (Second) of Conflicts. . . .

A basic principle under contemporary choice-of-law doctrine is that parties cannot by contract override public policy limitations on contractual power applicable in a state with materially greater interests in the transaction than the state whose law is contractually chosen. See Restatement (Second) of Conflicts § 187(2)(b) (1971). While contemporary doctrine recognizes a sphere of party autonomy within which contractual choice-of-law provisions will be given effect, it also limits the extent to which deft draftsmanship will be allowed to bypass legislative judgments as to basic enforceability or validity. This is implicit in the Restatement (Second) of Conflicts § 187(2)(b), which provides that a contractual choice-of-law clause will not be given effect on matters such as "capacity, formalities and substantial validity," id. comment d, when "application of the law of the chosen state would be contrary to a fundamental policy of a state which has a materially greater interest than the chosen state in the determination of the particular issue and which . . . would be the state of the applicable law in the absence of an effective choice of law by the parties." We believe Ohio would apply this choice-of-law rule here as part of its contemporary choice-of-law doctrine. . . .

Applying the Restatement (Second) § 187 formulation we think it clear that, absent the contractual choice-of-law provision, Ohio conflicts principles would mandate application here of the substantive laws of Alabama, Louisiana, Maryland, and South Carolina—where the six salesmen whose contracts are at issue work and reside—to determine the basic enforceability of these restrictive covenants between the contracting parties. The local jurisdictions involved here have interests at two levels in applying their own law on the enforceability of restrictive covenants: to protect employee-residents from contractually abrogating their ability to earn a livelihood, and to control the degree of free competition in the local economy. These interests in regulating business relationships within the states outweigh any generalized interest Ohio might have in applying its own law to protect the interstate contracts of its domiciliary . . . and compel the conclusion that, under Ohio choice-of-law rules, the laws of these other jurisdictions would control if there were no contractual stipulation of Ohio law. . . .

The remaining and most vexing element of the Restatement (Second) formulation, in determining whether to adhere to the contractual choice-of-law provision, concerns whether application of Ohio law would be "contrary to a fundamental policy" of any or all of the jurisdictions involved, all of which undoubtedly have a "materially greater interest" than does Ohio in whether these covenants are enforceable. . . . It is apparent that there can be no clear-cut delineation of those policies that are sufficiently "fundamental," within the meaning of § 187(2)(b), to warrant overriding a contractual stipulation of controlling law. See Restatement (Second) of Conflicts § 187 comment g. Nonetheless, a few general landmarks offer some structure for this inquiry. First, not every situation where contractually chosen law diverges merely in degree from that of the state whose law would otherwise apply impinges upon the fundamental policy of that state. . . . This is seen most clearly in regard to usury statutes, where the parties' choice of law has been held to validate interest rates that would be usurious and unenforceable in the jurisdiction whose law would prevail absent the contractual stipulation of controlling law. . . . At the other extreme, it seems apparent that where the law chosen by the parties would make enforceable a contract flatly unenforceable in the state whose law would otherwise apply, to honor the choice-of-law provision would trench upon that state's "fundamental policy." . . .

. . . Under Ohio law, covenants not to compete are enforceable if reasonable . . . a test similar to that applied under the laws of South Carolina . . . Maryland . . . and Louisiana. These latter jurisdictions differ from Ohio, if at all, only in degree concerning the enforceability of convenants not to compete; hence the district court properly applied Ohio law to the covenants of the Maryland, South Carolina, and Louisiana salesmen, as stipulated by the parties, because it is not "contrary to a fundamental policy" of those states.

Under Alabama law, however, covenants not to compete, whether or not reasonable, are void as against public policy and cannot be enforced. . . . To honor the contractual choice of law would make enforceable a contract flatly unenforceable in Alabama, surely impinging upon "fundamental policy" of Alabama. It was error, therefore, for the district court to apply Ohio law to determine the enforceability of the Alabama salesmen's covenants not to compete. . . .

Affirmed in part; reversed in part; vacated in part; and remanded in part.

K. K. HALL, CIRCUIT JUDGE, concurring in part and dissenting in part.

I concur in the majority's opinion insofar as it concludes that the district court erred in applying Ohio law to determine the enforceability of the Alabama salesmen's covenant not to compete and the claim of tortious interference with respect to the Alabama and Louisiana salesmen and that, with respect to those salesmen, the judgment below must be reversed. However, I cannot agree with the majority's conclusion that the district court correctly applied Ohio law to determine the enforceability of the covenant not to compete with respect to the Louisiana, Maryland and South Carolina salesmen. I dissent in part. . . .

The majority concedes that there are no Ohio cases which address whether the enforceability or non-enforceability of a covenant not to compete involves a policy sufficiently weighty to be considered "fundamental" [under Restatement, Second, Conflict of Laws § 187(2)(b) (1971).] The majority further acknowledges that "there can be no clear-cut delineation of those policies that are sufficiently 'fundamental' . . . to warrant overriding a contractual stipulation of controlling law" and relies upon usury cases for the proposition that a state's "fundamental policy" is not impinged upon if the contractually chosen law differs only in minor respects from the law that would apply absent the choice of law. . . . I do not find usury cases to be controlling in this case which involves the enforceability of a restrictive covenant in employment contracts. In my view, the instant case is more analogous to insurance cases, where the oppressive use of superior bargaining power by the insurance company against the insured may be present, than to usury cases. See generally, Restatement (Second) of Conflicts § 187 comment g. Accordingly, I conclude that a contract which prevents an individual from earning his livelihood and which restrains competition involves "fundamental policy." Based upon the facts of this case, I further conclude that the Ohio Supreme Court would defer to the superior interest of the states where the independent contractors resided, worked, executed the contracts, and engaged in the acts about which Bowman complains. . . .

Under Ohio law, a convenant not to compete is enforceable if reasonable. . . . The majority acknowledges that this test concerning the enforceability of restrictive covenants is not the same as the tests applied under the laws of Maryland and South Carolina.

For an employee in Maryland to be covered by a restrictive covenant, he must perform "unique" services or have received valuable trade secrets. . . . In South Carolina, non-competition covenants in employment contracts are critically examined and construed against the party imposing them because they are "generally disfavored." . . . The test for enforceability is (1) reasonable duration and (2) protection of some legitimate business interest. . . . In Ohio, by contrast, these requirements of Maryland and South Carolina law are simply factors to be considered in assessing reasonableness. . . .

Accordingly, I would remand this case with respect to the Maryland and South Carolina salesmen for specific findings whether the covenant is valid and enforceable in those states.

MURNAGHAN, CIRCUIT JUDGE, concurring in part and dissenting in part:

I.

All of us agree that Ohio's choice-of-law principles should be dispositive of whether Ohio's or another state's substantive law should apply in determining the validity of the restrictive covenant at issue here. Although the point is less eminently clear, it appears that Ohio would look to the Restatement (Second) of Conflict of Laws and to the general theory of interest analysis contained therein in applying its own choice-of-law rules. Consequently, where I part ways with my panel colleagues is simply as to the proper application of those principles to the case before us.

Clearly, Ohio law should not be construed so as automatically to accept whatever law the parties contract to apply. Nevertheless, the basic premise behind the *Restatement*'s treatment of contractual statements of mutual preference as to applicable law is that giving force to the parties' choice of law is the rule rather than the exception . . . .. There is no question that here there is a clear and effective choice of Ohio law by the parties, and no challenge has been directed to the validity of the choice-of-law term in the contract.

Rather, the majority concludes that one of two limitations on the rule of *Restatement* § 187 applies here. The first limitation of § 187 is that the chosen state must have a "substantial relationship to the parties or the transaction" or there must be some other "reasonable basis for the parties' choice." *Restatement*, supra, § 187(a). Here it is not denied that Ohio has both a substantial relationship to the parties, and a very reasonable basis for being the chosen state. . . .

. . . [Restatement, Second, § 187(2)(b)] requires that two facts be shown before the parties' contractual choice of law will be disregarded: that a competing state has a materially greater interest in the issue in dispute than does the contractually chosen state, and that application of the contractually chosen law would violate a fundamental policy of that competing state.]

Taking the requirement of the contravention of a fundamental policy first, the majority rightly notes that the inquiry as to whether a fundamental policy exists is by its very nature usually devoid of readily ascertainable and quantifiable results. The opportunity, accordingly, is presented for the fundamental policy exception to the general rule of § 187 to become "an escape valve out of which all the predictability and certainty of the autonomy rule [honoring contractual choice of law] flows";[3] the exception may well threaten to swallow the rule.[4] Nevertheless, I am prepared to accept that a state statute which voids covenants not to compete, as does Alabama's statute, is an expression of a fundamental state policy.

What remains to be shown, then, is whether Alabama has a materially greater interest than does Ohio in the issue of the validity of the covenants not to compete. I do not believe the majority has shown, nor that it can be shown, that Alabama has such a materially greater interest. The crucial steps here are those of reviewing the facts of the case at bar, allotting the contacts to the various states concerned, assessing each state's interest in the resolution of the disputed issue, determining the significance of the former in light of the latter, and doing it all with an eye towards the policy ends expressed in Restatement (Second) of Conflict of Laws § 6.

Instead of performing such an analysis, however, the majority merely assumes, without initial analysis or even discussion, that Alabama's interests in the resolution of the issue of the validity of the restrictive covenants are stronger than any "generalized interest" Ohio might have, and leaves it at that. A more careful review should lead to a different result. . . .

A recitation of the contacts of the contracting parties with Ohio and Alabama, respectively, is revealing. Although Bowman's parent company, Barnes Group, Inc., is incorporated in Delaware with its principal place of business in Connecticut, Bowman's headquarters are located in Ohio. The district judge found that each of the independent contractor salespeople involved in the instant litigation had sent his or her employment applications to Bowman in Ohio, and that Bowman had accepted the applications and executed the sales agreement contracts in Ohio as well. The salespeople received all their sales and training materials from Ohio, and attended a four-day training course there. Business was continually transacted between the independent contractors and Bowman's Ohio headquarters by telephone and by mail; McGuire, the South Carolina salesman, for example, alone called Ohio more than twenty times in the eight months prior to his leaving Bowman. Letters, notes, orders and returned merchandise were frequently sent to Ohio by the salespeople, and weekly sales reports were sent there as well for as long as the salespeople worked for Bowman. Every two weeks salespeople received commission checks sent from Ohio and drawn on an Ohio bank.

3. Note, Effectiveness of Choice-of-Law Clauses in Contract Conflicts of Law: Party Autonomy or Objective Determination?, 82 Colum.L.Rev. 1659, 1673 (1982).

4. Here we have a situation where the contacts of Ohio, the mutually selected state, are numerous. That consideration counsels against the application of the fundamental policy exception unless the existence and nature of such a policy is strongly evident:

> The more closely the state of the chosen law is related to the contract and the parties, the more fundamental must be the policy of the state of the otherwise applicable law to justify denying effect to the choice-of-law provision.

Restatement, supra, § 187 comment g.

Clearly, then, Ohio would be considered the place of contracting, the place of negotiation, and the domicile of one of the parties to the contracts. Likewise, it is too limited a view to conclude that the contracts were performed only in Alabama, Louisiana, Maryland or South Carolina, where the salespeople lived and gathered customers. A bilateral contract is inherently as well as linguistically two-sided, and all of Bowman's contractual obligations were fulfilled in Ohio, in addition to the several aspects of the salespeople's performance which occurred in or involved communication with Ohio. Finally, the location of the subject matter of the contract, one to pay persons commissions for the sale of certain products, could be as easily construed to have been in Ohio, where the products and payment originated, as in the other states, where the independent contractors consummated the sales.

When the weight of the contacts is evaluated in light of their relative importance to the contractual issue in dispute, Ohio still emerges as, at the very least, a state with a material interest in the resolution of the case equally as great as that of Alabama. The larger issue here is one of contractual validity; since Ohio is, among other things, the state of execution of the contracts, and overall the state with most of the contacts once one accepts that things must be looked at from the point of view of both of the parties and not just one of them, Ohio obviously has an indefeasible interest in the resolution of the contract's validity. More narrowly, the validity of the restrictive covenant is at issue. The majority rightly recognizes that the competing states have an interest in protecting their workers and setting local economic policies, but gives short shrift to Ohio's interests in assuring its employers, as far as possible, of uniform enforcement in Ohio courts of valid contracts with out-of-state employees.

Given the strong predisposition of the *Restatement* to honor contractual choices of law wherever possible, its underlying policy goals of furthering predictability and reliability in contractual affairs, the numerous contacts with Ohio in the instant case, and the interest Ohio has in seeing that its employers can assure their employees of evenhanded treatment, the bland assumption simply does not follow that Alabama has a materially greater interest than Ohio in the transaction and dispute before us. I therefore dissent insofar as Alabama substantive law, rather than the law of Ohio, was applied here.

[The Court's discussion of whether the defendant was liable in tort for interference with the agents' contracts has been omitted.]

NOTES

(1) See also Southern International Sales Co., Inc. v. Potter & Brumfield Division, 410 F.Supp. 1339 (S.D.N.Y.1976), invalidating a clause permitting termination at will for any reason of a dealer's contract and choosing Indiana law, where the clause was enforceable and where defendant was based. Plaintiff, a Puerto Rican corporation, successfully relied on a statute of the

Commonwealth protecting against unilateral termination clauses to override the choice of law.

(2) By what criteria is a state's policy determined to be fundamental for purposes of Restatement, Second, Conflict of Laws § 187(2)(b)? Should the quantity and quality of contacts with the state have any bearing on determining whether its policy is fundamental? See Note, Effectiveness of Choice of Law Clauses in Contract Conflicts of Law: Party Autonomy or Objective Determination, 82 Colum.L.Rev. 1659 (1982).

UNIFORM COMMERCIAL CODE. *Section 1–105. Territorial Application of the Act; Parties' Power to Choose Applicable Law.**

(1) Except as provided hereafter in this section, when a transaction bears a reasonable relation to this state and also to another state or nation the parties may agree that the law either of this state or of such other state or nation shall govern their rights and duties. Failing such agreement this Act applies to transactions bearing an appropriate relation to this state.

(2) Where one of the following provisions of this Act specifies the applicable law, that provision governs and a contrary agreement is effective only to the extent permitted by the law (including the conflict of laws rules) so specified:

Rights of creditors against sold goods. Section 2–402.

Applicability of the Article on Bank Deposits and Collections. Section 4–102.

Bulk transfers subject to the Article on Bulk Transfers. Section 6–102.

Applicability of the Article on Investment Securities. Section 8–106.

Perfection provisions of the Article on Secured Transactions. Section 9–103.

NOTES

(1) With all states having adopted the Code (Louisiana with some exceptions), along with the District of Columbia, Guam and the Virgin Islands, conflicts are expected to be few and the emphasis to be on where to file to perfect security interests.

(2) The history of Section 1–105 is sketched in Braucher, The Legislative History of the Uniform Commercial Code, 58 Colum.L.Rev. 798, 810–812 (1958).

(3) In general, the universality of the Code tends to minimize the importance of party autonomy in contracts subject to its provisions. See, Tuchler, Boundaries to Party Autonomy in the Uniform Commercial Code: A Radical View, 11 St. Louis L.J. 180 (1967). See generally Siegel, The U.C.C. and Choice of Law: Forum Choice or Forum Law, 21 Am.U.L.Rev. 494 (1972).

---

* As amended in 1972.

HAINES v. MID–CENTURY INSURANCE CO.

Supreme Court of Wisconsin, 1970.
47 Wis.2d 442, 177 N.W.2d 328.

[Mrs. Haines was injured in an automobile collision in Wisconsin while a passenger in her husband's car, which was licensed and garaged in Minnesota, where the couple lived. Mr. Haines worked just across the state line in Wisconsin. Sued under the Wisconsin direct action statute, the defendant carrier, which had issued a policy of automobile liability insurance to Mr. Haines, set up the family exclusion clause, providing that the policy would not apply "(11) to the liability of any insured for bodily injury to (a) any member of the same household . . . ". The trial court granted the defendant's motion for summary judgment and Mrs. Haines appealed.]

WILKIE, JUSTICE. There is only one issue on this appeal: Does Wisconsin or Minnesota law govern the effect of the policy of insurance covering plaintiff's husband's automobile?

The parties concede that Wisconsin law governs the tort aspects of this case. The issue involved here relates solely to the contract aspects of the insurance policy issued by the respondent Mid-Century Insurance Company.

If the policy is governed by Minnesota law, the family-exclusion clause is effective to foreclose the plaintiff from recovering her damages from her husband's insurer.[1] If, on the other hand, the law to be looked to in deciding the efficacy of the family-exclusion clause of the policy is Wisconsin, then it is clear this exclusion can have no effect.[2]

Recently, this court, in Urhammer v. Olson,[3] involving a factual situation very similar to the instant one, specifically adopted the grouping-of-contacts approach for the resolution of conflicts questions pertaining to the validity and rights created by the provisions of a disputed contract. This approach had previously been suggested and discussed in several earlier cases.

Sec. 188 of the Second Restatement of Conflicts[4] is the embodiment of this approach. . . . [The Court quoted § 188 in full.]

This section, in the absence (as here) of an agreement between the parties of their choice of law, permits a functional conflicts analysis under which the method is not to count contacts but rather to consider which contacts are the most significant and to determine where

1. Minners v. State Farm Mutual Automobile Ins. Co. (1969), 284 Minn. 343, 170 N.W.2d 223; Tomlyanovich v. Tomlyanovich (1953), 239 Minn. 250, 58 N.W.2d 855. [Footnotes renumbered; some footnotes omitted. Eds.]

2. Sec. 204.34(2), Stats., makes it unlawful to include family-exclusion clauses in Wisconsin automobile liability insurance contracts.

3. (1968), 39 Wis.2d 447, 159 N.W.2d 688.

4. Restatement, Conflicts of Laws 2d, Proposed Official Draft, Part II, 200, sec. 188.

those contacts are found. It must be recognized that a contact can be considered to be significant only in terms of its relevance to a specific domestic law and the policy underlying that law.

Thus, the discussion must focus on the purpose of the Wisconsin statute, sec. 204.34(2), declaring family-exclusion clauses to be invalid as compared to the Minnesota judge-made law giving effect to this type of clause.

In Klatt v. Zera,[5] this court said that the purpose of sec. 204.34(2), Stats., is to prohibit exclusion clauses that would withdraw any coverage or protection required to be given under sec. 204.30(3), the so-called omnibus coverage statute. In essence, the purpose of both these sections read together is to provide protection to innocent third persons injured by the negligent operation of motor vehicles by others regardless of the relationship between the victim and the driver.

On the other hand, the purpose of the Minnesota policy of giving effect to the family-exclusion clause was stated in Tomlyanovich v. Tomlyanovich,[6] as follows:

". . . The obvious purpose of the clause here involved is to exempt the insurer from liability to those persons to whom the insured, on account of close family ties, would be apt to be partial in case of injury."

Thus, in essence the reason why Minnesota gives effect to a family-exclusion clause is to protect insurance companies from false claims. It should be noted that by legislative action, Minnesota has recently invalidated family-exclusion clauses.[7] However, this invalidation came about after the policy was issued and the accident occurred in this case.

With these opposing purposes in mind, we must analyze the facts of this case in detail in light of the particular contacts listed in sec. 188 of the Restatement.

Before making that analysis, it is necessary to consider the application here of the special provisions of sec. 193 of the Restatement, which concerns the validity of insurance contracts. That section provides:

"193.   Contracts of Fire, Surety or Casualty Insurance.

"The validity of a contract of fire, surety, or casualty insurance and the rights created thereby are determined by the local law of the state which the parties understood was to be the principal location of the insured risk during the term of the policy, unless, with respect to the particular issue, some other state has a more significant relation-

---

5. (1960), 11 Wis.2d 415, 105 N.W.2d 776.

6. Supra, footnote 1, 239 Minn. at page 263, 58 N.W.2d at page 862.

7. See subd. 1, 72A.1491, Minn.Stat. (Laws of 1969, ch. 474, sec. 1, effective July 1, 1969).

ship to the transaction and the parties, in which event the local law of the other state will be applied."

Respondent contends that the principal location of the insured risk is Minnesota. But as the Restatement comment to sec. 193 indicates, there may be no principal location of the insured risk in the case of moving vehicles.

". . . In such a case, the location of the risk can play little role in the determination of the applicable law. The law governing insurance contracts of this latter sort must be determined in accordance with the principles set forth in the rule of sec. 188."

It is obvious that although the Haineses' automobile was to be garaged in La Crescent, Minnesota, it was to be used a great deal in La Crosse, Wisconsin, where Mr. Haines was employed.

While in Peterson v. Warren[8] we cited the forerunner of this section when we held that Minnesota law should apply to the determination of legal-validity questions pertaining to an insurance contract covering vehicles used in a construction business, the vehicles there involved were admittedly located principally in Minnesota and we also held that whether the grouping-of-contacts test or the intention test was used, Minnesota law applied. We are not faced with such a factual situation here. The particular issue here is as to the validity of the family-exclusion provision and we are governed in the selection of the law to apply to that issue by the method of analysis embodied in the grouping-of-contacts approach of sec. 188, Restatement.

The affidavits filed in support of and in opposition to the motion for summary judgment establish the following additional facts: The insurance policy in question was obtained by the defendant who was then a resident of La Crescent, Minnesota, in Mid-Century's office in La Crosse, Wisconsin. The policy was delivered in La Crosse, premiums were paid in La Crosse, and accident reports were made in La Crosse.

La Crescent, Minnesota, is a bedroom suburb almost totally dependent upon La Crosse for its existence. . . .

The trial court concluded that all the significant contacts involved in this case were with Minnesota. Accordingly, the trial court granted the insurer's motion for summary judgment. We must respectfully disagree.

At best the significant contacts are split between the two states. The place of negotiation and the place of contracting are in Wisconsin. Wisconsin, therefore, would have an interest in seeing that its policy of protecting injured parties, regardless of their relationship to negligent drivers, would be given effect in insurance contracts negotiated and entered into in this state. The place of performance of the contract is apparently equally divided between Wisconsin and Minne-

8. 31 Wis.2d 547, 143 N.W.2d 560 (1966).

sota. Likewise, the location of the subject matter of the contract is in both states.

The domicile of the parties at the time of the accident was Minnesota. It could be argued that in that situation the Minnesota policy of discouraging collusion and fraud by its domiciliaries against insurance companies should be given controlling weight. However, this is offset by the fact that the complaint alleges that the plaintiff, at the time of the commencement of this action, was a resident of La Crosse, Wisconsin. In such a situation, Wisconsin's policy of not recognizing the family-exclusion clause becomes more important. Any fear that a plaintiff would purposefully move to this state in order to take advantage of Wisconsin's policy of nonrecognition of family-exclusion clauses is, for the most part, unfounded. It is doubtful that anyone would move from one state to another merely to take advantage of the latter's allegedly more favorable policies.

It is clear, therefore, that we are presented with a true conflicts case in that Minnesota and Wisconsin, having opposing policies, each has relatively equally significant contacts.

In deciding which law is finally to be applied in this situation, we must turn to an additional guide beyond the formulation contained in sec. 188 of the Restatement. In Heath v. Zellmer,[9] Mr. Justice Heffernan, speaking for the court, detailed the five factors to be applied in making our choice-of-law decisions with respect to true conflicts questions presented in tort cases. These are:

"Predictability of results,

"Maintenance of interstate and international order,

"Simplification of the judicial task,

"Advancement of the forum's governmental interests,

"Application of the better rule of law."

The only relevant factor here in making our choice of law is the fifth factor, namely, the "application of the better rule of law." We think the rule protecting the injured party's right to collect damages from the person or persons responsible for his injuries (even if a member of his family) and his insurer, is to be preferred over the rule preventing that recovery. Thus, we conclude that Wisconsin law applies. The argument that Wisconsin has the better rule of law received tacit confirmation by the Minnesota legislature when it enacted the statute invalidating the family-exclusion clause. Thus Minnesota law is now the same as Wisconsin.

Since Wisconsin law applies, the family-exclusion clause in the subject insurance contract is invalid and summary judgment in favor of the respondent insurance company was improperly granted.

Judgment reversed and cause remanded for further proceedings.

9. (1967), 35 Wis.2d 578, 151 N.W.2d 664.

NOTES

(1) How would this case have been decided under the first Restatement, by Professor Currie and under the somewhat different approaches adopted by Judge Fuld in Auten v. Auten (p. 471, supra) and Babcock v. Jackson (p. 487, supra)?

(2) In Peterson v. Warren, 31 Wis.2d 547, 143 N.W.2d 560 (1966), plaintiff, a Wisconsin resident, was injured in that state while a passenger in a truck driven by a Wisconsin resident who was employed by a business firm operating in Minnesota. The truck was insured in Minnesota, which unlike Wisconsin, made the insurer absolutely liable for $10,000 coverage despite lack of notice of an accident. Minnesota law laid the burden of proving failure of notice upon the carrier, again unlike Wisconsin. The Wisconsin Supreme Court, after analyzing the predecessor versions of §§ 188 and 193 (§§ 332 and 346i), held that either under the "intention" of the parties theory or "grouping of contacts," Minnesota law applied to the issue of absolute liability. Cf. Schmidt v. Driscoll Hotel, Inc., supra p. 468.

Likewise, as to the issue of burden of proof, the court held Minnesota's rule applicable, citing Restatement, Second, § 599c, predecessor to § 133, and concluding: "Since the primary purpose of the Minnesota rule . . . is to influence the decision of the issue rather than to regulate the conduct of the trial, the Minnesota rule applies even if the matter of burden of proof is held to be procedural . . . " [sic!]

WOOD BROTHERS HOMES, INC. v. WALKER ADJUSTMENT BUREAU, 198 Colo. 444, 601 P.2d 1369 (1979): Suit to recover for work done on defendant's apartment complex in New Mexico. Plaintiff's assignor was domiciled in California. Defendant, a Delaware corporation, had its principal place of business in Colorado. Negotiations leading up to the contract took place in California, Colorado and New Mexico. The defense was that the plaintiff had not obtained the necessary license from the New Mexico authorities and consequently was prohibited by a New Mexico statute from seeking compensation for work done in that state. Held for the defendant. ". . . [W]e now adopt the Restatement (Second) approach for contract actions. . . . In addition to the general principles set forth in sections 6 and 188, several sections of chapter 8 (Contracts) of the Restatement (Second) apply to specific types of contracts." Under § 196, contracts for the rendition of services should be determined by the law of the state where the services are to be rendered unless some other state has the most significant relationship with the issue to be decided under the principles set forth in § 6. "In this situation the value of protecting the parties' contractual obligations is outweighed by New Mexico's interest in applying its invalidating rule." The court also found support in § 202(2) of the Restatement (Second), which provides: "When performance is illegal in the place of performance, the contract will usually be denied enforcement."

LILIENTHAL v. KAUFMAN

Supreme Court of Oregon, 1964.
239 Or. 1, 395 P.2d 543.

[The case appears at p. 529, supra.]

RESTATEMENT, SECOND, CONFLICT OF LAWS*

CHAPTER 8

Title B. Particular Contracts

Introductory Note.   This Title deals with particular kinds of contracts. These contracts are given special attention because it is considered possible to state with respect to each that, in the absence of an effective choice of law by the parties, a particular contact plays an especially important role in the determination of the state of the applicable law.   Except in the case of insurance contracts (see §§ 192–193), a choice of law by the parties will be effective, under the circumstances stated in § 187, in the case of the contracts discussed in this Title.

NOTES

(1) The structure of each black-letter rule in Title B is to designate a presumptively decisive contact for the particular type of contract dealt with, and provide that validity and rights under the contract will be determined by the local law of the state of the contact, unless another state has a more significant relationship to the transaction and the parties, as to the issue involved.

(2) For contracts involving transfer of interests in land, situs is the key contact (§§ 189, 190); for chattels, place of seller's delivery (§ 191); life insurance, insured's domicile (§ 192); fire, surety or casualty insurance, location of the risk (§ 193); etc.

C. VALIDITY—ESPECIALLY, THE STATUTE OF FRAUDS

The law governing the validity of contracts in conflict of laws has normally been discussed by the text writers in three subdivisions: formalities, capacity, and essential validity. "Formalities" relates to such matters of form as whether a contract, to be valid, must be in writing, subscribed by the party to be charged, signed before witnesses or acknowledged before a notary public. "Capacity" concerns the power of a party to obligate himself (or herself) to be bound in contract. "Essential validity" includes issues regarding the need for

---

* Quoted with the permission of the copyright owner, The American Law Institute.

consideration, legality of the object of the contract and similar substantial questions.

MARIE v. GARRISON

13 Abb.N.C. 210 (N.Y.1883).

[This case appears at p. 554, supra.]

LAMS v. F.H. SMITH CO.

Superior Court of Delaware, 1935.
36 Del. 477, 178 A. 651, 105 A.L.R. 646.

[In an action on a written purchase agreement accompanying the sale of bonds, the declaration alleged that on December 10, 1928, the defendant's agent had sold the plaintiff some bonds in New York. Part of the written contract of sale was an agreement by the defendant's agent that at the plaintiff's option at any time after December 10, 1931, the defendant would repurchase the bonds from the plaintiff at par and accrued interest. The defendant's agent did not have written authority to make such an agreement. At the expiration of the three years, the plaintiff offered the bonds to the defendant who refused to buy them. The plaintiff also pleaded the Statute of Frauds of New York (declaring that "Every agreement is void, unless," etc.), which required that contracts not to be performed in one year must be in writing, signed by the party to be charged "or his lawful agent," and that the words "or his lawful agent" had been construed by the New York courts to permit authority to be given by parol. The defendant pleaded the Delaware Statute of Frauds which required such authority to be in writing.]

To the 5th, 6th, 7th and 8th pleas the plaintiff demurred upon the ground that as the agreement and transaction were executed in the state of New York and the statutes of that state pleaded that, therefore, the law of the state of New York and not the Statute of Frauds of Delaware was the applicable law in the case.

RODNEY, JUDGE, delivering the opinion of the Court:

The pleas of the defendant having set up the Delaware Statute of Frauds and the plaintiffs' demurrer having been directed thereto, the question presented is whether the Delaware law (the law of the forum) shall be applied in the case. The answer to this question involves the construction of the nature and character of the Delaware Act. The question is whether, on the one hand, the Act is procedural in nature, having to do with the remedy, or, more properly speaking, the process or machinery by which rights under the contract are litigated or whether, on the other hand, the Act is to be construed as affecting the substance, the formalities or the enforceable validity of the contract itself, as a contract.

The cited Delaware Act [which reads: "No action shall be brought," etc.] is almost the counterpart of the English Act. The leading case adopting the view of the procedural nature of the Statute was Leroux v. Brown [1852] 12 C.B. 801, 138 E.R. 1119. . . . [H]owever, the Delaware Act was adopted in 1752, exactly one hundred years before the decision of Leroux v. Brown, and that case is, therefore, entitled to the greatest respect but is in no sense binding on this Court.

In Leroux v. Brown, supra, an oral agreement, not to be performed within a year, had been entered into in France and was enforceable there. Suit was brought upon the contract in England and it was held that Section 4 of the Statute of Frauds applied to the procedure and that the suit could not be maintained unless the contract was in writing in conformity with the English Law. A distinction was drawn between the words of the 4th Section, "no action shall be brought," and those of the 17th Section, "no contract shall be allowed to be good." This distinction has not generally been approved either in England or America and in England the wording of the 17th Section was changed by the "Sale of Goods Act," (1893), so as to read "shall not be enforceable by action" so as to make the two Sections conform. In construing the Delaware Act we are not confronted with any variation or distinction between the language of the two Sections originally known as Section 4 and Section 17. Section 17 was not adopted in Delaware (Alderdice v. Truss, 2 Houst. 268) until its new language, as found in the English "Sale of Goods Act," was incorporated in our Law in 1933 by the approval of the Uniform Sales Law, vol. 38, Laws of Delaware, c. 158, p. 570, sec. 2644-F. It would seem that both Sections of our Law must, therefore, relate to the substance or formalities of the contract or both must simply relate to and exclude the remedy. . . .

Most of the American decisions discussing the nature and character of the Statute of Frauds, and especially in connection with the conflict of laws, may generally be divided into three groups:

(1) those that adopt the distinction laid down in Leroux v. Brown and hold the Statute remedial or procedural;

(2) those that repudiate the distinction yet still hold the Statute remedial; and

(3) those that repudiate the distinction and hold the Statute is substantive.

Some Courts in holding their Statute as procedural and as merely affecting the remedy have seized upon the title of the original English Act (1677), "An Act for prevention of Frauds and Perjuryes," and of the language of section 4, "no action shall be brought," as indicative of a legislative intent to limit the opportunities of perjury by preventing the introduction of oral testimony when the circumstances of the transaction had become dimmed by lapse of time or other circumstances require a written memorandum. While this is, of course, true, yet the Statute may have a deeper significance, viz.: that long before any questions of admissibility of oral testimony can arise—before any suit is brought—there is such an infirmity in the contract itself as will prevent its enforceability as a contract by action, and therefore, "no action shall be brought." In any event the prevention of perjury, insofar as it affects the ordinary contracts of citizens of Delaware, can as readily be accomplished by holding the Statute one of substance as one of procedure.

The Delaware Statute of Frauds requiring an agreement not to be performed within a year to be evidenced by a memorandum in writing is primarily for the benefit of the citizens of Delaware. It was the agreements or contracts of Delawareans which were mainly sought to be protected from the future uncertainties of oral testimony . . . . If the necessity of writing be procedural then while the lack of writing would prevent the enforcement of the contract in the Courts of Delaware yet the Delaware citizen would still be liable to be harassed upon the contract and to be faced by oral testimony if sued in the Courts of another State, the Statute of which had been held to be substantive. On the other hand, if the necessity of writing be construed as one of the formalities of the contract, then the absence of the writing would make the contract—not void—but unenforceable in the Courts of Delaware, and, under principle of comity and conflict of laws, unenforceable outside of the State and insure to the citizens for whose benefit the Act was passed the full measure of protection. Restatement, Conflict of Laws, sec. 334.

When Leroux v. Brown was determined the English Court did not face the same problems of Conflict of Laws which must be considered in America. In England the whole nation operated under the one Statute of Frauds which controlled all litigation. With us the Statutes of forty-eight different jurisdictions, varying somewhat in phraseology and differing widely in purpose and interpretation, require a large measure of harmony in construction.

It is a general rule of the widest acceptation that the construction and validity of a contract is governed by the law of the place where it is made. We see no reason why this principle should not apply to the formality or necessity of a written memorandum required by the Statute of Frauds. Where two people solemnly enter into a contract which is good, valid and entirely enforceable in that jurisdiction where it is made, it seems to us as an unnecessary and undesirable construction to hold the contract unenforceable in another jurisdiction where one of the parties may have taken refuge unless, indeed, the contract contravenes some rule of public policy decreed by the law of the forum.

Counsel in the present case argue that the Statute of Frauds is both procedural and also an expression of public policy prohibiting an action on a contract not to be performed within a year unless evidenced by a memorandum in writing. This argument is not basically sound and it has received but a small measure of support in other jurisdictions.

Having in mind the clear intent of the Legislature to require contracts, coming within the Statute, to be executed with certain formalities and believing that the purpose of the Statute was not only the prevention of perjuries but the deeper purpose of protection of its citizens from the effect of such perjured testimony, we believe that the greatest measure of protection should be afforded to its citizens and so hold that the statute refers to the substance or formality with which the contract must be executed.

The demurrer is sustained.

NOTES

(1) Is the exact wording of a statute significant in classifying it as substantive rather than procedural? Cf. Holmes, J., in Emery v. Burbank, infra, p. 607: "When the law involved is a statute, it is a question of construction whether the law is addressed to the necessary constituent elements, or legality, of the contract on the one hand, or to the evidence by which it shall be proved on the other." Assume a legislature enacts a statute of frauds in order to set courtroom standards of proof for certain types of agreements. Ought it not cast the statute in words that show an intention to proscribe oral and other informal types of evidence? Suppose, on the other hand, the legislature aims to deter parties from contracting in haste, seeks to induce deliberateness in their actions, and assure a simple, unchangeable record of the transaction, and to achieve those purposes, enacts the requirement that parties must write out and sign their undertakings to make them enforceable. May it not also find words appropriate to that purpose? But see Section 141, *Comment c* of the Restatement, Second, Conflict of Laws, which declares: "Unless a legislature did in fact have choice-of-law problems in mind in enacting a statute, a court should not make its decision as to the statute's application . . . to foreign facts depend upon the language in which the statute is phrased. To do so would give the words of the statute a meaning never intended by the legislature."

(2) Are not contracting parties naturally prone to try to comply with the law of the place where they execute their contract? See Restatement, Second, Conflict of Laws, Section 199, *Comment c.* But cf. A.S. Rampell, Inc. v. Hyster Co., 3 N.Y.2d 369, 165 N.Y.S.2d 475, 144 N.E.2d 371 (1967), applying the law of the state (Oregon) selected by the parties to invalidate a written provision barring oral modification of the contract's terms, an effect not countenanced in the state where apparently the contract was executed.

(3) Restatement, Second, Conflict of Laws, Sections 140 and 141 provide that both the parole evidence rule and the statute of frauds are to be treated as substantive matters governed by the choice-of-law principles set forth in the chapter on contracts. The parole evidence rule is deemed substantive because it determines the rights and duties of the parties once they have

integrated their agreement in a writing. The statute of frauds is deemed substantive, even though the Restatement concedes that good arguments can be made either way, regarding its characterization. Supporting a procedural classification is the argument that the purpose of the statute of frauds is to protect the courts by limiting possibilities of perjury and avoiding unseemly disputes as to whether the parties entered into a contract at all and if so on what terms.

EMERY v. BURBANK

Supreme Judicial Court of Massachusetts, 1895.
163 Mass. 326, 39 N.E. 1026, 28 L.R.A. 57, 47 Am.St.Rep. 456.

HOLMES, J. This is an action on an oral agreement, alleged to have been made in Maine in 1890, by the defendant's testatrix, Mrs. Rumery, to the effect that, if the plaintiff would leave Maine and take care of Mrs. Rumery, the latter would leave the plaintiff all her property at her death, and also would put four thousand dollars in a house which the plaintiff should have. At the trial evidence was introduced tending to prove the agreement as alleged. The presiding justice ruled that the action could not be maintained, and the case is here on exceptions. As we are of opinion that the ruling must be sustained under St.1888, c. 372, requiring agreements to make wills to be in writing, a fuller statement of the facts is not needful.

There is no doubt of the general principles to be applied. A contract valid where it is made is valid everywhere, but it is not necessarily enforceable everywhere. It may be contrary to the policy of the law of the forum. . . . Or again, if the law of the forum requires a certain mode of proof, the contract, although valid, cannot be enforced in that jurisdiction without the proof required there. . . . When the law involved is a statute, it is a question of construction, whether the law is addressed to the necessary constituent elements, or legality, of the contract on the one hand, or to the evidence by which it shall be proved on the other. In the former case the law affects contracts made within the jurisdiction, wherever sued, and may affect only them. . . . In the latter, it applies to all suits within the jurisdiction, wherever the contracts sued upon were made, and again may have no other effect. It is possible, however, that a statute should affect both validity and remedy by express words, and this being so, it is possible that words which in terms speak only of one should carry with them an implication also as to the other. . . .

The words of the statute before us seem in the first place, and most plainly, to deal with the validity and form of the contract. "No agreement . . . shall be binding, unless such agreement is in writing." If taken literally, they are not satisfied by a written memorandum of the contract; the contract itself must be made in writing. They are limited, too, to agreements made after the passage of the act, a limitation which perhaps would be more likely to be inserted in a law concerning the form of a contract than in one which only changed a rule of evidence. But we are of opinion that the statute ought not to be limited to its operation on the form of contracts made in this State. The generality of the words alone, "no agreement," is not conclusive. But the statute evidently embodies a fundamental policy. The ground, of course, is the prevention of fraud and perjury, which are deemed likely to be practised without this safeguard. The nature of the contract is such that it naturally would be performed or sued upon at the domicil of the promisor. If the policy of Massachusetts makes void an oral contract of this sort made within the State, the same policy forbids that Massachusetts testators should be sued here upon such contracts without written evidence, wherever they are made. . . .

In our view, the statute, whatever it expresses, implies a rule of procedure broad enough to cover this case. It is not necessary to decide exactly how broad the rule may be,—whether, for instance, if, by some unusual chance, a suit should happen to be brought here against an ancillary administrator upon a contract made in another State by one of its inhabitants, the contract would have to be in writing. The rule extends at least to contracts by Massachusetts testators. It might be possible to treat the words, "signed by the party whose executor or administrator is sought to be charged," as meaning "signed by the party whose executor or administrator is sought to be charged in Massachusetts," and to construe the whole statute as directed only to procedure. . . . Upon this question also we express no opinion. All that we decide is that the statute does apply to a case like the present.

The law of the testator's domicil is the law of the will. A contract to make a will means an effectual will, and therefore a will good by the law of the domicil. In a sense, the place of performance, as well as the forum for a suit in case of breach, is the domicil. We do not draw the conclusion that therefore the validity of all such contracts, wherever sued on, must depend on the law of the domicil. That would leave many such contracts in a state of indeterminate validity until the testator's death, as he may change his domicil so long as he can travel. But the consideration shows that the final domicil is more concerned in the policy to be insisted on than any other jurisdicion, and justifies it in framing its rules accordingly. There would be no question to be argued if the law were in terms a rule of evidence. It is equally open for a State to declare, upon the same considerations which dictate a rule of evidence, that a contract must have certain form if it is to be enforced against its inhabitants in its courts. Legislation of this kind for contracts which thus necessarily reach into the jurisdiction in their operation hardly goes as far as statutes dealing with substantive liability which would have been upheld. . . .

If the statute applies, the fact that the plaintiff has furnished the stipulated consideration will not prevent its application.

Exceptions overruled.

NOTES

(1) What are the objectives of statutes that require certain contracts to be in writing and subscribed by the party to be charged or otherwise evidenced in some formal fashion? See Fuller, Consideration and Form, 41 Colum.L.Rev. 799 (1941). Why are particular types of contractual undertakings selected and others omitted? What bearing have such questions on the applicability of the statute of frauds in multistate cases?

(2) Are the policies requiring signed writings stronger in the case of some types of contracts subject to the statute of frauds than in others? Types of contracts often subject to the statute are those: not to be performed in a year; involving the sale of goods worth more than a specified amount; involving transfer of interests in land; promising to make testamentary dispositions; designed to protect vulnerable groups, such as certain consumers, laborers, debtors, etc.

(3) Does the provision requiring written and signed agreements as a prerequisite for enforcing promises to remember a promisee in the promisor's will embody a particularly powerful policy that ought to be strictly safeguarded? For these purposes, which state has the strongest interest in such a promise—the state where the alleged promise was made, the state of the decedent's domicile at death, or some other state such as the state where the subject matter, for example, land, is located?

(4) For an excellent discussion of the general problem, see Cavers, Oral Contracts to Provide by Will and the Choice-of-Law Process, in Perspectives of Law, Essays for Austin Wakeman Scott 38 (1964).

BERNKRANT v. FOWLER

Supreme Court of California, 1961.
55 Cal.2d 588, 12 Cal.Rptr. 266, 360 P.2d 906.

[A vendor named Granrud, whose installments of deferred purchase money were secured by a second deed of trust on the Nevada land purchased, asked the purchasers to refinance their obligations and to pay a substantial part of their indebtedness before the due date. He promised orally that if the purchasers would do this he would provide by will that any part of the purchase price remaining unpaid on his death would be cancelled. In compliance with the request the purchasers arranged a new loan and paid to the vendor a substantial sum in advance on their obligation. The vendor died with about $6,000 of the purchase money unpaid, but his will made no provision for cancellation of the debt. The purchasers brought an action in California against the vendor's executor to enforce the oral agreement. Under Nevada law, so the Supreme Court of California found, the oral agreement was valid. A California statute provided: "An agreement which by its terms is not to be performed during the lifetime of the promisor, or an agreement to devise or bequeath any property, or to make any provision by will" is "invalid unless the same, or some note or memorandum thereof, is in writing, and subscribed by the party to be charged or his agent." The trial court gave judgment for the defendant and the purchasers appealed.]

TRAYNOR, J. . . . We are therefore confronted with a contract that is valid under the law of Nevada but invalid under the California statute of frauds if that statute is applicable. We have no doubt that California's interest in protecting estates being probated here from false claims based on alleged oral contracts to make wills is constitutionally sufficient to justify the Legislature's making our statute of frauds applicable to all such contracts sought to be enforced against such estates. . . . The Legislature, however, is ordinarily concerned with enacting laws to govern purely local transactions, and it has not spelled out the extent to which the statute of frauds is to apply to a contract having substantial contacts with another state. Accordingly, we must determine its scope in the light of applicable principles of the law of conflict of laws. See People v. One 1953 Ford Victoria, 48 Cal.2d 595, 598–599, 311 P.2d 480; 2 Corbin on Contracts, p. 67; Currie, Married Women's Contracts, 25 U.Chi.L.Rev. 227, 230–231; Cheatham and Reese, Choice of the Applicable Law, 52 Col.L. Rev. 959, 961.

In the present case plaintiffs were residents of Nevada, the contract was made in Nevada, and plaintiffs performed it there. If Granrud was a resident of Nevada at the time the contract was made, the California statute of frauds, in the absence of a plain legislative direction to the contrary, could not reasonably be interpreted as applying to the contract even though Granrud subsequently moved to California and died here. . . . The basic policy of upholding the expectations of the parties by enforcing contracts valid under the only law apparently applicable would preclude an interpretation of our statute of frauds that would make it apply to and thus invalidate the contract because Granrud moved to California and died here. Such a case would be analogous to People v. One 1953 Ford Victoria, 48 Cal. 2d 595, 311 P.2d 480, where we held that a Texas mortgagee of an automobile mortgaged in Texas did not forfeit his interest when the automobile was subsequently used to transport narcotics in California although he had failed to make the character investigation of the mortgagor required by California law. A mortgagee entering into a purely local transaction in another state could not reasonably be expected to take cognizance of the law of all the other jurisdictions where the property might possibly be taken, and accordingly, the California statute requiring an investigation to protect his interest could not reasonably be interpreted to apply to such out of state mortgagees. Another analogy is found in the holding that the statute of frauds did not apply to contracts to make wills entered into before the statute was enacted (Rogers v. Schlotterback, 167 Cal. 35, 45, 138

P. 728). Just as parties to local transactions cannot be expected to take cognizance of the law of other jurisdictions, they cannot be expected to anticipate a change in the local statute of frauds. Protection of rights growing out of valid contracts precludes interpreting the general language of the statute of frauds to destroy such rights whether the possible applicability of the statute arises from the movement of one or more of the parties across state lines or subsequent enactment of the statute. See Currie and Schreter, Unconstitutional Discrimination in the Conflict of Laws: Privileges and Immunities, 69 Yale L.J. 1323, 1334.

In the present case, however, there is no finding as to where Granrud was domiciled at the time the contract was made. Since he had a bank account in California at that time and died a resident here less than two years later it may be that he was domiciled here when the contract was made. Even if he was, the result should be the same. The contract was made in Nevada and performed by plaintiffs there, and it involved the refinancing of obligations arising from the sale of Nevada land and secured by interests therein. Nevada has a substantial interest in the contract and in protecting the rights of its residents who are parties thereto, and its policy is that the contract is valid and enforcible. California's policy is also to enforce lawful contracts. That policy, however, must be subordinated in the case of any contract that does not meet the requirements of an applicable statute of frauds. In determining whether the contract herein is subject to the California statute of frauds we must consider both the policy to protect the reasonable expectations of the parties and the policy of the statute of frauds. See Cheatham and Reese, Choice of the Applicable Law, 52 Col.L.Rev. 959, 978–980. It is true that if Granrud was domiciled here at the time the contract was made, plaintiffs may have been alerted to the possibility that the California statute of frauds might apply. Since California, however, would have no interest in applying its own statute of frauds unless Granrud remained here until his death, plaintiffs were not bound to know that California's statute might ultimately be invoked against them. Unless they could rely on their own law, they would have to look to the laws of all of the jurisdictions to which Granrud might move regardless of where he was domiciled when the contract was made. We conclude, therefore, that the contract herein does not fall within our statute of frauds. . . . Since there is thus no conflict between the law of California and the law of Nevada, we can give effect to the common policy of both states to enforce lawful contracts and sustain Nevada's interest in protecting its residents and their reasonable expectations growing out of a transaction substantially related to that state without subordinating any legitimate interest of this state.

The judgment is reversed.

NOTES

(1) In Rubin v. Irving Trust Co., 305 N.Y. 288, 113 N.E.2d 424 (1953), decedent was alleged to have made an oral contract in Florida to bequeath his shares of stock to his brother. Both brothers were residents of New York. The promise was enforceable under Florida law, but not under New York law. Following Emery v. Burbank, supra, the court held that the contract was invalid, New York being the testator's domicile. Is the Bernkrant case distinguishable on the ground that it involved an arms-length business transaction rather than family-related finances? See Cavers, American Law Institute, Study of the Division of Jurisdiction Between State and Federal Courts (Tentative Draft No. 1, 1963), p. 169. If the Rubin brothers had orally agreed that Florida law should apply, would the outcome of the case have been different?

(2) In the Bernkrant case, Justice Traynor said that, considering the California legislature's silence as to the reach of the statute of frauds in multi-state cases, the court was obliged to "determine its scope in the light of applicable principles of the law of conflict of laws." What are those "applicable principles"?

(3) Ehrenzweig, The Statute of Frauds in the Conflict of Laws, 59 Colum. L.Rev. 874, 876 (1959): "Contracts having foreign contacts quite generally have been upheld by American courts where such contracts have satisfied either the formality requirements of the forum, or those of another jurisdiction provided that the state of the validating law had sufficient contacts with the transaction to justify application of its law."

RESTATEMENT, SECOND, CONFLICT OF LAWS (1971)*

CHAPTER 8.   CONTRACTS

§ 199.   Requirements of a Writing—Formalities

(1) The formalities required to make a valid contract are determined by the law selected by application of the rules of §§ 187–188.

(2) Formalities which meet the requirements of the place where the parties execute the contract will usually be acceptable.

NOTES

(1) If Bernkrant v. Fowler had been decided pursuant to Restatement, Second, Conflict of Laws § 199, what might the reasoning and the result have been?

(2) See Intercontinental Planning, Limited v. Daystrom, Inc., 24 N.Y.2d 372, 300 N.Y.S.2d 817, 248 N.E2d 576 (1969), which utilized an interest analysis to grant summary judgment under New York's statute of frauds against the plaintiff who claimed that by reason of an oral agreement he was entitled to a finder's fee. The oral agreement would have been enforceable in

New Jersey where it was made and where numerous other contacts with the transaction were located.

---

1. *Assignment of Contractual Rights*

Assignment of legal interests not embodied in negotiable instruments may raise choice-of-law problems. One question is whether the right is assignable. If so, other questions concern the legal effect of the assignment on the assignor and assignee and on the obligor of the underlying obligation as well as questions of priority among successive assignees.

To a large degree the importance of formulating common law conflicts rules about assignments has been eclipsed by the nearly universal enactment of the Uniform Commercial Code, which has all but eliminated prospects of serious conflicts in this area. Assignments of future wages and of life insurance benefits have accounted for a large fraction of the cases that have come to the courts in recent years.

DOWNS V. AMERICAN MUTUAL LIABILITY INSURANCE CO., 14 N.Y. 2d 266, 251 N.Y.S.2d 19, 200 N.E.2d 204 (1964): H and W, New York residents, entered into a separation agreement by which H assigned validly, under New York, one-half his future wages to W. He moved to Massachusetts and was employed as a salesman by the Insurance Company. In New York, W sued to compel the Insurance Company to pay her half of H's wages and was met by the defense that they were not assignable under a Massachusetts statute. Even on the assumption the Massachusetts statute barred an assignment for family support, the Court of Appeals (per Fuld, J.) said:

". . . Since New York undoubtedly has the most significant relationship and contacts with the assignment and a predominant interest and concern in assuring support to a New York wife and New York children, its law is applicable. (Cf. Auten v. Auten, 308 N.Y. 155, 124 N.E.2d 99, 50 A.L.R.2d 246; Morris Plan Industrial Bank of N.Y. v. Gunning, 295 N.Y. 324, 329–330, 67 N.E.2d 510, 511–512.) The assignment of wages was made in New York by a New York husband and, quite obviously, without regard as to where he would be employed, for the protection of his family. The marital domicile of the parties was New York, the separation agreement recited that the law applicable was that of New York and the agreement and the obligations of the parties are embodied in a New York judgment. . . ."

On the ground of the manifest "paramount interest" of New York, the Court affirmed a judgment for W. How could New York law properly be applied to determine the assignability of wages paid in Massachusetts by a Massachusetts employer?

A contrary result was reached on similar facts in Freedom Finance Co., Inc. v. New Jersey Bell Telephone Co., 123 N.J.Super. 255, 302 A.2d 184, affirmed 126 N.J.Super. 375, 314 A.2d 614 (1974).

NOTES

(1) As to assignability of a contractual right, Section 208, Restatement, Second, Conflict of Laws uses its familiar formula, referring the dispute to the local law of the state with the most significant relationship to the contract and the parties with respect to the issue. See Detroit Greyhound Employees Federal Credit Union v. Aetna Life Insurance Co., 71 Mich.App. 430, 151 N.W.2d 852 (1967), involving the assignability of the benefits of a group life insurance policy.

(2) Section 209 of the Restatement, Second, uses the same formula (making allowance for the change in issue) to determine whether the assignor had capacity, observed the required formalities, needed to receive consideration, was subjected to duress, etc., and the nature of interests transferred as a result of the assignment. Thus, whether a life insurance policy is assignable is determined under Section 208; whether the assignee must have an insurable interest, by Section 209. (Id., *Comment a.*) Sections 210 and 211 treat, respectively, the law governing the effect of the assignment on the obligor of the underlying obligation and questions of priority as between two or more assignees.

(3) New England Mut. Life Insurance Co. v. Spence, 104 F.2d 665 (2d Cir. 1939). The insured took out a life insurance policy in New York, payable to his wife, at a time when the parties resided in New York. Subsequently they became domiciled in Texas, where the wife obtained a divorce. Under Texas law the divorce decree operated to pass the wife's interest in the policy to the husband. L. Hand, J.: "The question before us is whether the law of conflict of laws of New York will treat as valid an involuntary transfer of the wife's chose in action, valid by the law of the place where both parties resided. There can be no doubt that if the transfer had been voluntary, i.e. by assignment, the courts of New York would follow the law of the place where the assignment took place . . . We can see no reason to distinguish an involuntary transfer, when both parties are present within the state, where the transaction occurs; a fortiori, when they are both domiciled there. There is no magic in consent . . . this part of the law of Texas is not so repugnant to notions of justice prevalent in New York that we must reject it." Judge Clark, dissenting, stated that the Texas decree did not operate as a transfer, and that the case was not one of assignment. The peculiar Texas law was in effect merely a rule under which a divorced wife could not prove in a Texas court that she had an insurable interest under the policy. The question was solely the identity of the beneficiary under the terms of the policy, a contract question to be determined by the law of New York as the place of contracting.

For a more recent case reaching a similar result on similar reasoning, see Travelers Insurance Co. v. Fields, 451 F.2d 1292 (6th Cir. 1971).

2. *Arbitration*

Commercial Arbitration—An Atypical Conflicts Problem

A multistate contract containing a provision for submission of disputes arising under it to arbitration presents an atypical choice-of-law question if one side breaks the promise to arbitrate. Usually the problem in such cases is whether one side can compel arbitration over the objection of the other, or compel it to be conducted in a certain way, or insist that the arbitrators have or have nor particular powers.

In bygone days, the courts viewed agreements to arbitrate with hostility. As a result, they would usually entertain a suit brought in violation of an arbitration provision. This result would be justified either on the ground that it was dictated by forum public policy or on the theory that since arbitration is a procedural device, a matter of remedy, the law of the forum should control. Leflar, American Conflicts Law 319 (3d ed. 1977). Today the situation is almost the exact reverse of what it formerly was. The great majority of states have enacted statutes which make arbitration agreements enforceable. Also, according to § 219 of the Restatement, Second, Conflict of Laws, the courts will refuse to entertain a suit brought in violation of an arbitration agreement unless such a suit could be maintained under the law which governs the agreement as a contract.

NOTES

(1) Most American states provide statutory procedures for reducing awards to judgments, after which they become entitled to full faith and credit. Foreign country and sister state awards not reduced to judgment will nevertheless often be enforced. Restatement, Second, Conflict of Laws, Section 220 indicates prerequisites for enforcement of awards in the latter categories if the forum possesses jurisdiction and competence: that the award be enforceable in the state of rendition, has been rendered with due process, and does not violate the forum's strong public policy.

(2) When enforcement is sought of a sister-state arbitration award, the validity of the award is determined under the law of the state where it was rendered. Moyer v. Van-Dye-Way Corp., 126 F.2d 339 (3d Cir. 1942); Maxwell Shapiro Woolen Co., Inc. v. Amerotron Corp., 339 Mass. 252, 158 N.E.2d 875 (1959).

(3) The forum's procedures will govern the mode of enforcing an arbitration agreement, including ordering arbitration to proceed in another state. See Domke, The Law and Practice of Commercial Arbitration 256–259 (1968).

MATTER OF AMTORG TRADING CORP., 304 N.Y. 519, 109 N.E.2d 606 (1952): Camden Fibre Mills, a Pennsylvania corporation, made a contract of purchase and sale with Amtorg Trading Corporation. Amtorg is a New York corporation which is in effect an agency of the Soviet Government in carrying on trade in this country. The contract provided for the arbitration of disputes before the U.S.S.R. Chamber of Commerce Foreign Trade Arbitration Commission in Moscow, U.S.S.R. The designated arbitrator was a juridical person but it was also a public organization subject to the general supervision of the People's Commissariat for Foreign Trade. Camden brought suit in New York against Amtorg on the contract. Amtorg moved for a stay of the suit until arbitration was had before the arbitrator and at the place designated. Held, the suit should be stayed.

PER CURIAM. "Camden chose to do business with Amtorg and to accept, as one of the conditions imposed, arbitration in Russia; it may not now ask the courts to relieve it of the contractual obligation it assumed.

"It may be noted that the order of the Appellate Division does not preclude Camden from taking appropriate action should the arbitration in fact deprive it of its fundamental right to a fair and impartial determination."

NOTES

(1) The United States Arbitration Act makes "valid, irrevocable, and enforceable", subject to the defenses usually available in contracts, a written provision for arbitration "in any maritime transaction or a contract evidencing a transaction involving commerce." 43 Stat. 883 (1925), 9 U.S.C.A. § 1 (1926). The statute, being confined to "any maritime transaction" and "a transaction involving [interstate or foreign] commerce," does not settle the matter where a case is in the federal courts under the diversity of citizenship clause. Such a case was Bernhardt v. Polygraphic Co. of America, Inc., 350 U.S. 198 (1956), where a suit for damages for the discharge of plaintiff under an employment contract was removed from a Vermont state court to the federal court sitting in that state. The contract, which was made in New York between New York parties, contained a provision that in case of dispute the parties would submit the matter to arbitration under New York law by the American Arbitration Association. The defendant moved in the federal court for a stay of the proceedings so the controversy could go to arbitration in New York. A question was whether the effectiveness of the arbitration provision should be determined by the law of the federal courts or by the law of one of the states, Vermont or New York. The Supreme Court held that state law, not federal courts law, should be applied, saying: "For the remedy by arbitration, whatever its merits or shortcomings, substantially affects the cause of action created by the State". Conversely, in Southland Corp. v. Keating, —— U.S. —— (1984), the Supreme Court held that the Federal Arbitration Act forecloses states from creating exceptions to the enforcement of arbitration agreements entered into by the disputing parties. See also Chapter 10, Section 1, infra.

(2) In international business dealings, arbitration has become the favored mode of resolving disputes. An arbitration agreement allows the parties to the contract great flexibility in choosing their forum, arranging for the composition of the tribunal, the applicable procedures, and—within limits—the rules of law that will be applicable to disputes that may arise. For a treatment of a variety of legal problems in this context, see International Trade Arbitration (Domke ed. 1958).

(3) The United States has acceded to the United Nations-developed Convention on the Recognition and Enforcement of Foreign Arbitral Awards. See Aksen, American Arbitration Accession Arrives in the Age of Aquarius, 3 Sw.U.L.Rev. 1 (1971); Quigley, Convention on Foreign Arbitral Awards, 58 A.B.A.J. 821 (1972). The Convention facilitates enforcement of foreign arbitration awards in American courts. The permissible grounds for refusing enforcement of an award that is covered by the Convention are quite narrow. Section 207 of the Federal Arbitration Act provides that federal courts will confirm an award within three years after it is made, unless one of the grounds for refusing or deferring recognition or enforcement specified in the Convention exists.

(4) See generally Scoles and Hay, Conflict of Laws 982–987 (1982); Note, 47 Wash.L.Rev. 441 (1972).

PARSONS & WHITTEMORE OVERSEAS CO., INC. v. SOCIETE GENERALE DE L'INDUSTRIE DU PAPIER (RAKTA)

United States Court of Appeals, Second Circuit, 1974.
508 F.2d 969.

J. JOSEPH SMITH, CIRCUIT JUDGE:

Parsons & Whittemore Overseas Co., Inc., (Overseas), an American corporation, appeals from the entry of summary judgment . . . on the counterclaim by Societe Generale de L'Industrie du Papier (RAKTA), an Egyptian corporation, to confirm a foreign arbitral award holding Overseas liable to RAKTA for breach of contract. . . . Jurisdiction is based on 9 U.S.C. § 203, which empowers federal district courts to hear cases to recognize and enforce foreign arbitral awards, and 9 U.S.C. § 205, which authorizes the removal of such cases from state courts, as was accomplished in this instance. We affirm the district court's confirmation of the foreign award.
. . . .

In November 1962, Overseas consented by written agreement with RAKTA to construct, start up and, for one year, manage and supervise a paperboard mill in Alexandria, Egypt. The Agency for International Development (AID), a branch of the United States State Department, would finance the project . . . . Among the contract's terms was an arbitration clause, which provided a means to settle differences arising in the course of performance, and a "force majeure" clause, which excused delay in performance due to causes beyond Overseas' reasonable capacity to control.

Work proceeded as planned until May, 1967. Then, with the Arab-Israeli Six Day War on the horizon, recurrent expressions of Egyptian hostility to Americans—nationals of the principal ally of the Israeli enemy—caused the majority of the Overseas work crew to leave Egypt. On June 6, the Egyptian government broke diplomatic ties with the United States and ordered all Americans expelled from Egypt except those who would apply and qualify for a special visa.

Having abandoned the project for the present with the construction phase near completion, Overseas notified RAKTA that it regarded this postponement as excused by the force majeure clause. RAKTA disagreed and sought damages for breach of contract. Overseas refused to settle and RAKTA, already at work on completing the performance promised by Overseas, invoked the arbitration clause. Overseas responded by calling into play the clause's option to bring a dispute directly to a three-man arbitral board governed by the rules of the International Chamber of Commerce. After several sessions in 1970, the tribunal issued a preliminary award, which recognized Overseas' force majeure defense as good only during the period from May 28 to June 30, 1967. In so limiting Overseas' defense, the arbitration court emphasized that Overseas had made no more than a perfunctory effort to secure special visas and that AID's notification that it was withdrawing financial backing did not justify Overseas' unilateral decision to abandon the project. . . .

. . . The principal issues [raised by Overseas] on this appeal are derived from the express language of the applicable United Nations Convention on the Recognition and Enforcement of Foreign Arbitral Awards (Convention), 330 U.N.Treaty Ser. 38 . . .. These include: enforcement of the award would violate the public policy of the United States, the award represents an arbitration of matters not appropriately decided by arbitration; the tribunal denied Overseas an adequate opportunity to present its case; the award is predicated upon a resolution of issues outside the scope of the contractual agreement to submit to arbitration; and the award is in manifest disregard of law. . . .

In 1958 the Convention was adopted by 26 of the 45 states participating in the United Nations Conference on Commercial Arbitration held in New York. For the signatory states, the New York Convention superseded the Geneva Convention of 1927, 92 League of Nations Treaty Ser. 302. The 1958 Convention's basic thrust was to liberalize procedures for enforcing foreign arbitral awards: While the Geneva Convention placed the burden of proof on the party seeking enforcement of a foreign arbitral award and did not circumscribe the range of available defenses to those enumerated in the convention, the 1958 Convention clearly shifted the burden of proof to the party defending against enforcement and limited his defenses to seven set forth in Article V. . . . Not a signatory to any prior multilateral agreement on enforcement of arbitral awards, the United States declined to sign the 1958 Convention at the outset. The United States ultimately acceded to the Convention, however, in 1970, [1970], 3 U.S.T. 2517, T.I.A.S. No. 6997, and implemented its accession with 9 U.S.C. §§ 201–208. Under 9 U.S.C. § 208, the existing Federal Arbitration Act, 9 U.S.C. §§ 1–14, applies to the enforcement of foreign awards except to the extent to which the latter may conflict with the Convention. . . .

A. *Public Policy*

Article V(2)(b) of the Convention allows the court in which enforcement of a foreign arbitral award is sought to refuse enforcement, on the defendant's motion or *sua sponte,* if "enforcement of the award would be contrary to the public policy of [the forum] country." The legislative history of the provision offers no certain guidelines to its construction. . . .

Perhaps more probative . . . are the inferences to be drawn from the history of the Convention as a whole. The general pro-enforcement bias informing the Convention and explaining its supersession of the Geneva Convention points toward a narrow reading of the public policy defense. An expansive construction of this defense would vitiate the Convention's basic effort to remove preexisting obstacles to enforcement. . . . Additionally, considerations of reciprocity—considerations given express recognition in the Convention itself[4] —counsel courts to invoke the public policy defense with caution lest foreign courts frequently accept it as a defense to enforcement of arbitral awards rendered in the United States.

We conclude, therefore, that the Convention's public policy defense should be construed narrowly. Enforcement of foreign arbitral awards may be denied on this basis only where enforcement would violate the forum state's most basic notions of morality and justice. . . .

Under this view of the public policy provision in the Convention, Overseas' public policy defense may easily be dismissed. Overseas argues that various actions by United States officials subsequent to the severance of American-Egyptian relations—most particularly, AID's withdrawal of financial support for the Overseas-RAKTA contract—required Overseas, as a loyal American citizen, to abandon the project. Enforcement of an award predicated on the feasibility of Overseas' returning to work in defiance of these expressions of national policy would therefore allegedly contravene United States public policy. In equating "national" policy with United States "public" policy, the appellant quite plainly misses the mark. To read the public policy defense as a parochial device protective of national political interests would seriously undermine the Convention's utility. This provision was not meant to enshrine the vagaries of international politics under the rubric of "public policy." Rather, a circumscribed public policy doctrine was contemplated by the Convention's framers and every indication is that the United States, in acceding to the Convention, meant to subscribe to this supranational emphasis. . . .

To deny enforcement of this award largely because of the United States' falling out with Egypt in recent years would mean converting a defense intended to be of narrow scope into a major loophole in the

---

4. A Contracting State shall not be entitled to avail itself of the present Convention against other Contracting States except to the extent that it is itself bound to apply the Convention.

Article XIV. . . .

Convention's mechanism for enforcement. We have little hesitation, therefore, in disallowing Overseas' proposed public policy defense.

B. *Non-Arbitrability*

Article V(2)(a) authorizes a court to deny enforcement, on a defendant's or its own motion, of a foreign arbitral award when "[t]he subject matter of the difference is not capable of settlement by arbitration under the law of that [the forum] country." Under this provision, a court sitting in the United States might, for example, be expected to decline enforcement of an award involving arbitration of an antitrust claim in view of domestic arbitration cases which have held that antitrust matters are entrusted to the exclusive competence of the judiciary. . . . On the other hand, it may well be that the special considerations and policies underlying a "truly international agreement," Scherk v. Alberto-Culver Co., 417 U.S. 506, at 515, 94 S.Ct. 2449 (see p. 187, n. 3, supra) call for a narrower view of non-arbitrability in the international than the domestic context. Compare id. with Wilko v. Swan, 346 U.S. 427, 74 S.Ct. 182, 98 L.Ed. 168 (1953) (enforcement of international, but not domestic, agreement to arbitrate claim based on alleged Securities Act violations.)

Resolution of Overseas' non-arbitrability argument, however, does not require us to reach such difficult distinctions between domestic and foreign awards. For Overseas' argument, that "United States foreign policy issues can hardly be placed at the mercy of foreign arbitrators 'who are charged with the execution of no public trust' and whose loyalties are to foreign interests," . . . plainly fails to raise so substantial an issue of arbitrability. The mere fact that an issue of national interest may incidentally figure into the resolution of a breach of contract claim does not make the dispute not arbitrable. Rather, certain *categories* of claims may be non-arbitrable because of the special national interest vested in their resolution. . . . Furthermore, even were the test for non-arbitrability of an ad hoc nature, Overseas' situation would almost certainly not meet the standard, for Overseas grossly exaggerates the magnitude of the national interest involved in the resolution of its particular claim. Simply because acts of the United States are somehow implicated in a case one cannot conclude that the United States is vitally interested in its outcome. Finally, the Supreme Court's decision in favor of arbitrability in a case far more prominently displaying public features than the instant one, Scherk v. Alberto-Culver, Co., supra, compels by analogy the conclusion that the foreign award against Overseas dealt with a subject arbitrable under United States law. . . .

[The court then proceeded to reject Overseas' other defenses.]

3. *Negotiable Instruments*

RESTATEMENT, SECOND, CONFLICT OF LAWS 357–58*

CHAPTER 8. CONTRACTS

TOPIC 4. NEGOTIABLE INSTRUMENTS

Introductory Note: This Topic is directed to choice of law questions relating to negotiable drafts (bills of exchange), including checks, and notes and certificates of deposit. These instruments are covered by Article 3 of the Uniform Commercial Code. Attention is not here given to negotiable documents embodying title to a chattel, as bills of lading and warehouse receipts (see Article 7 of the Uniform Commercial Code). Cases of multistate transactions involving the contractual aspects of such documents have not yet come before the courts with sufficient frequency to make appropriate the statement of choice of law rules respecting them. Nor is consideration here given to negotiable debt securities (see Article 8 of the Uniform Commercial Code). . . .

On account of the previous widespread enactment by States of the United States of the Uniform Negotiable Instrument Law, choice of law problems relating to negotiable instruments have arisen infrequently in the interstate area. They have done so on occasion, however, because of minor differences in the statutes of certain States and because of the different judicial interpretations that a given provision has sometimes received. . . . This country's foreign commerce provides an area where choice of law problems of this sort have arisen and will continue to arise.

Negotiable instruments have both contractual and property aspects. Each of these instruments upon its effective delivery imposes contractual obligations on one or more of the original parties thereto. Furthermore, each of these instruments may give rise to a series of obligations, as those from the drawer and the acceptor to the payee of a draft, from the maker to the payee of a note, and from an indorser to an indorsee of either a draft or a note. The question therefore arises whether one law regulates all the obligations arising from a single instrument or whether each of these obligations may be governed by a separate law. By and large, the latter alternative is the one adopted by the courts. In general, the validity of each individual obligation and the rights created thereby are determined by the proper law of that obligation. . . .

. . .

---

* Quoted with the permission of the copyright owner, The American Law Institute.

§ 214.   Obligations of Makers and Acceptors

(1) The obligations of the maker of a note and of the acceptor of a draft are determined, except as stated in §§ 216–217, by the local law of the state designated in the instrument as the place of payment.

(2) In the absence of a designated place of payment, the obligations of a maker or acceptor are determined, except as stated in §§ 216–217, by the local law of the state where he delivered the instrument.   That state is presumptively the state where the instrument is dated, if such a state is indicated, and this presumption is conclusive with respect to a holder in due course.

NOTES

(1) See, e.g., Youngstown Sheet and Tube Co. v. Westcott, 147 F.Supp. 829 (W.D.Okl.1957); McCornick & Co. v. Tolmie Bros., 46 Idaho 544, 269 Pac. 96 (1928).

(2) See generally Bailey, Conflict of Laws in the Law of Bank Checks, 80 Banking L.J. 404 (1963); Johnson and Parachini, Forged Indorsements and Conflict of Laws, 82 Banking L.J. 95 (1965).

(3) As to the duties of a bank in this context, the Uniform Commercial Code provides in Section 4–102(2) that the law of the place where the bank is located determines its liability "for action or non-action with respect to any item handled by it for purposes of presentment, payment or collection."

KOECHLIN ET CIE. v. KESTENBAUM BROTHERS

Court of Appeal, 1927.
[1927] 1 K.B. 889.

The plaintiffs as indorsees of a bill of exchange for 60,000 francs, dated December 14, 1925, drawn payable to the order of M. Vigderhaus, claimed to recover 461*l*. 10*s*. thereon from the defendants as acceptors.

The bill was drawn in France by E. Vigderhaus upon the defendants in London to the order of M. Vigderhaus.   It was sent to London, was accepted by the defendants payable at a London bank, returned to Paris, indorsed there by E. Vigderhaus, and discounted by the plaintiffs.   On presentation for payment the defendants refused to meet it on the ground that it did not bear the indorsement of M. Vigderhaus, but merely the indorsement of E. Vigderhaus in his own name. . . .

The plaintiffs appealed.

BANKES, L.J. . . .   The defence is that the indorsement is not in order, because the bill being drawn in favour of the father, M. Vigderhaus, should have been indorsed by him.   The appellants' answer to that is that by French law if the son E. Vigderhaus was duly authorized, as he was, he was entitled to indorse the bill in his own name simpliciter, without adding the words "per pro"; and that being a French bill and the indorsement being good by French law the appellants are entitled to sue the acceptors in this country upon their contract of acceptance.

. . . At the trial one witness only was called on the subject, and he was called for the appellants. He said that the indorsement in question was good by French law, assuming that the son had his father's authority to indorse the bill. . . . In my opinion, the judge was justified in coming to the conclusion he did, that the witness correctly informed him as to French law. That being so we have to deal with the case on the footing that the indorsement is good according to French law.

. . . This at any rate is clear, because it was so decided by the Court of Appeal in Embiricos v. Anglo-Austrian Bank, [1905] 1 K.B. 677, long after the Bills of Exchange Act was passed, that "the rule of international law, that the validity of a transfer of movable chattels must be governed by the law of the country in which the transfer takes place, applies to the transfer of bills of exchange or cheques by indorsement." That is clear authority, if authority were required, that the ordinary rule of international law applies to this particular indorsement, and as the law applicable is French law, the appellants as indorsees have, according to French law, a perfectly good title to the bill. . . . Sect. 72 of the Bills of Exchange Act appears to me for this purpose to be exhaustive, because it provides that "where a bill drawn in one country is negotiated, accepted, or payable in another, the rights, duties and liabilities of the parties thereto"—that includes this acceptance—"are determined as follows: (1) The validity of a bill as regards requisites in form is determined by the law of the place of issue"—this bill is in form according to the law of France—"and the validity as regards requisites in form of the supervening contracts, such as acceptance, or indorsement, or acceptance supra protest, is determined by the law of the place where such contract was made."

In my opinion this appeal must be allowed.

[The concurring opinions of SARGANT, L.J., and AVORY, J., are omitted.]

NOTES

(1) Sections 216 and 217 of the Restatement, Second, Conflict of Laws, are couched in hard-and-fast terms to provide, respectively, that the local law of the state where a negotiable instrument actually was when transferred determines, in the commonest situations, whether the transferee holds the instrument in due course and has title; and that details of presentment, payment, protest and dishonor are determined by the local law of the state where these actions occur. For leading cases involving international transactions and the title problem, see United States v. Guaranty Trust Co., 293

U.S. 340 (1934); Weissman v. Banque de Bruxelles, 254 N.Y. 488, 173 N.E. 835 (1930).

(2) Duties of indorsers and drawers are dealt with in Section 215 of Restatement, Second, Conflict of Laws, which, in general, provides that their obligations are determined by the local law of the state where the indorser or drawer delivered the instrument. The state where the paper was dated, if indicated, is presumptively the state of delivery. The designated place of payment is the source of the law as to where presentment may be made.

---

4. *Usury, A Special Issue*

SEEMAN v. PHILADELPHIA WAREHOUSE CO.

Supreme Court of the United States, 1927.
274 U.S. 403, 47 S.Ct. 626, 71 L.Ed. 1123.

MR. JUSTICE STONE delivered the opinion of the court.

Respondent brought suit in the district court for Southern New York to recover for the conversion of a quantity of canned salmon pledged to it as security for a loan. The pledgor, who had fraudulently regained possession, sold the salmon to petitioners. The defense set up was that the transaction between respondent and the pledgor was usurious and therefore void under the law of New York, where the pledgor conducted its business and where petitioners contend the pledge agreement was made.

The trial court charged the jury that the New York law was applicable. The jury returned a verdict for petitioners. The judgment on the verdict was reversed by the court of appeals for the second circuit. 7 F.2d 999. This Court granted certiorari. 269 U.S. 543.

Respondent is a Pennsylvania corporation having its only office or place of business in Philadelphia. It has an established credit and for many years has engaged in a business which is carried on according to the routine followed in the present case which respondent contends, results in loans of credit and not of money. To applicants in need of funds it delivers its promissory note, payable to its own order and then endorsed. The applicant in exchange gives the required security—here warehouse receipts for the salmon—and a pledge agreement by which he undertakes to pay the amount of the note at maturity to respondent at its office in Philadelphia, and agrees that the collateral pledged shall be security for all obligations present and prospective. At the same time the applicant pays to respondent a "commission" for its "services" and for the "advance of its credit" computed at the rate of 3 per cent. per annum on the face of the note. He is then free to discount the note, and to use the proceeds. In practice, as in the present case, respondent usually, with the consent of the borrower, delivers the note to its own note broker in Philadelphia, receives from him the proceeds of the note less discount and brokerage, and pays or forwards the amount so received to the borrower. At maturity he must pay the face value of the note to respondent, or, as was the case here, renew the note by paying a new commission and the amount of the discount on the matured note. On each transaction the applicant thus pays, in addition to the amount of the proceeds of the note, the commission and the discount. Respondent, after taking up its note, retains the commission alone as the net compensation for its part in the transaction. In addition, the applicant may, as was the case here, pay the fees of the note broker and the fee or compensation of a loan broker, acting as intermediary in securing the accommodation by respondent, a total amount far exceeding 6 per cent., the legal rate of interest in New York. The commission and discount paid here varied from $8\frac{1}{2}$ to $10\frac{1}{2}$ per cent. per annum of the face amount of the notes, taking no account of fees paid to brokers.

In Pennsylvania, the exaction of interest on loans of money in excess of 6 per cent., the lawful rate, does not invalidate the entire transaction, but excess interest may be recovered by the borrower. . . . The business carried on by respondent as described, was considered and upheld by the Supreme Court of Pennsylvania as not usurious in Righter, Cowgill & Co. v. Philadelphia Warehouse Co., 99 Pa. St. 289.

To avoid the application of the Pennsylvania law . . . petitioners at the trial relied on evidence that preliminary negotiations were had in New York City between the pledgor and the agent of respondent from which it might be inferred that the agreement was in fact made there, although the formal documents were dated at Philadelphia and respondent actually executed its note and delivered it to the note broker there. Petitioners also relied on the special circumstances of the case, particularly the fact that respondent itself procured the proceeds of the note in Philadelphia and forwarded them to the borrower in New York, as ground for the inference by the jury that the real transaction was a loan of money thinly disguised as a loan or a sale of credit. . . .

. . . in the view we take, we think it immaterial whether the contract was entered into in New York or Pennsylvania, and it may be assumed for the purposes of our decision that the jury might have found that in fact the parties stipulated for a loan of money rather than of credit. . . . as we said in Andrews v. Pond, 13 Pet. 65, 77–78, "The general principle in relation to contracts made in one place, to be executed in another, is well settled. They are to be governed by the law of the place of performance, and if the interest allowed by the laws of the place of performance, is higher than that permitted at the place of contract, the parties may stipulate for the higher interest, without incurring the penalties of usury." . . .

In support of a policy of upholding contractual obligations assumed in good faith, this Court has adopted the converse of the rule quoted from Andrews v. Pond, supra. "If the rate of interest be higher at the place of contract than at the place of performance, the parties may lawfully contract in that case also for the higher rate." [Citing cases.]

A qualification of these rules, as sometimes stated, is that the parties must act in good faith, and that the form of the transaction must not "disguise its real character." . . . As thus stated, the qualification, if taken too literally, would destroy the rules themselves for they obviously are to be invoked only to save the contract from the operation of the usury laws of the one jurisdiction or the other. The effect of the qualification is merely to prevent the evasion or avoidance at will of the usury law otherwise applicable, by the parties' entering into the contract or stipulating for its performance at a place which has no normal relation to the transaction and to whose law they would not otherwise be subject. Wharton, in his Conflict of Laws, Section 510*o*, in discussing this qualification says: "Assuming that their real, bona fide intention was to fix the situs of the contract at a certain place which has a natural and vital connection with the transaction, the fact that they were actuated in so doing by an intention to obtain a higher rate of interest than is allowable by the situs of some of the other elements of the transaction does not prevent the application of the law allowing the higher rate." . . .

Here respondent, organized and conducting its business in Pennsylvania, was subject to laws of that state and had a legitimate interest in seeking their benefit. The loan contract which stipulated for repayment there and which thus chose that law as governing its validity cannot be condemned as an evasion of the law of New York which might otherwise be deemed applicable. . . .

Judgment affirmed.

GREEN v. NORTHWESTERN TRUST CO.

Supreme Court of Minnesota, 1914.
128 Minn. 30, 150 N.W. 229, L.R.A.1916D, 739.

[A contract to sell Montana land called for a purchase money mortgage and notes that were payable in Minnesota. The notes bore interest at 6 per cent, with a provision that after maturity the rate on unpaid principal and interest should rise to 8 per cent. The opinion sets forth other pertinent contacts with the two states mentioned.]

DIBELL, C. . . . . The provision for an increase of interest after maturity is valid under the Montana law. Its effect under the Minnesota law is to forfeit all interest reserved. . . .

The transaction here in question was vitally related to Montana. The Rosebud Co. was a resident of Montana. So were its officers and stockholders. The plaintiff, who was the vendee in the contract of November 23, 1911, and a promoter and incorporator and a large stockholder of the Cartersville Co., resided there. The contract of sale was signed there, and was returned there, though originally intended for a different transaction. The land conveyed was there. The mortgage was drafted there. It was for unpaid purchase money and was secured upon lands located there. The notes were negotiable in Montana and non-negotiable in Minnesota. The Cartersville Co. covenanted in the trust deed to pay the taxes and assessments levied in Montana, including irrigation taxes. It had the right by the trust deed to sell portions of the mortgaged lands at not less than specified prices, and upon payment of a certain percentage of the price received was entitled to a release of the mortgage as to the land sold. It covenanted to keep the buildings, fences, ditches and other improvements on the Montana lands in repair. It was contemplated by the November contract that the mortgage should contain, as it did, clauses usual to Montana mortgages. The connection between the transaction here involved and Montana was not artificial.

Opposed to the claim that the presumed intent was that the law of Montana should be the governing law, and supporting the contention that the Minnesota law should be presumed to be intended to be the governing law, these considerations are urged: The notes were signed, delivered and payable in Minnesota. The trust deed, and the deed of the lands except as to the signature of the secretary, were executed here. Both were delivered here. The mortgagee was a corporation of this state. The mortgagor had its principal office in Minnesota. All of the negotiations relative to the transaction were had in Minnesota.

There was no intent to evade the usury law. The Cartersville Co., the Rosebud Co., and the Trust company, had no thought of engaging in other than a lawful and honest transaction. Indeed, there was no greed for interest. If the notes had provided for interest at 8 or 10 per cent. from the beginning, instead of an advance from six to eight per cent. on principal and interest in default, more interest would have been received and the Minnesota law would not have been offended.

The courts go far in giving effect to the presumption that the parties intended their contract to be performed in the state where it could be validly performed according to its terms, rather than in a state where it would be wholly or in part invalid. . . .

Applying the rules stated we hold that the law of Montana was the proper law of the contract, and that its law, under which the transaction was involved is valid, is the governing law. . . .

Order affirmed.

NOTE

In a diversity action in Idaho by the lender to foreclose a mortgage on Idaho property, the court rejected the defense of usury (12% interest) under

Idaho law. "In the case at bar the lender did not seek out the borrower in the State of Idaho, nor sit in wait for him in that state. Rather, the borrower sought out the lender in the State of Washington." Witman v. Green, 289 F.2d 566, 568 (9th Cir. 1961).

RESTATEMENT, SECOND, CONFLICT OF LAWS:*

§ 203. Usury

The validity of a contract will be sustained against the charge of usury if it provides for a rate of interest that is permissible in a state to which the contract has a substantial relationship and is not greatly in excess of the rate permitted by the general usury law of the state of the otherwise applicable law under the rule of § 188.

NOTES

(1) O'Brien v. Shearson Hayden Stone, Inc., 90 Wash.2d 680, 586 P.2d 830 (1978). Class action against defendant stockbroker alleging that Washington residents who maintained margin accounts with the defendant were charged interest rates that were usurious under Washington law. Each margin agreement provided that it should be governed by New York law. Under Washington law, the permissible rate of interest was 12% while under the law of New York it was 25%. The actual rate of interest charged the plaintiffs, however, was only 14%. Held for the plaintiffs on the choice-of-law issue. The provision in the margin agreements that called for application of New York law should not be given effect under § 187 of the Restatement Second since the Washington rule of usury embodies a fundamental policy and Washington has a "materially greater interest" than New York in the determination of the usury issue and "under the rule of § 188, would be the state of the applicable law in the absence of an effective choice of law by the parties." To be sure, New York did have a "substantial relationship" to the transaction within the meaning of § 203 of the Restatement Second, but the New York permissible rate of 25% is "greatly in excess" of that authorized in Washington. The dissent maintained that a proper construction of § 203 would require that reference be made to the rate of interest (14%) that was in fact charged rather than that (25%) which could legally have been charged under the law of New York. This 14% rate was not greatly in excess of that permitted by Washington law.

This case is discussed at length in Davidson and Loomis, Usury, The Choice of Law in Washington, 16 Gonzaga L.Rev. 259 (1981); see also Crandall, It Is Time for a Federal Consumer Credit Code, 58 N.C.L.Rev. 1, 22–23 (1979).

(2) The Restatement provides that, in the case of general usury statutes, if a contract is usurious under the usury statutes of every state with which it has a substantial relationship, the forum will apply the usury statute of the state that imposes the lightest penalty. Restatement, Second, Conflict of

---

* Quoted with the permission of the copyright owner, The American Law Institute.

Laws § 203, Comment *d*. See, in accord, Miller v. Premier Corp., 608 F.2d 973 (4th Cir. 1979).

(3) Under certain circumstances, the lender may use a choice-of-law clause in the contract to obtain a rate of interest that would not be tolerated by the state in which the transaction is localized. In Consolidated Jewelers, Inc. v. Standard Financial Corp., 325 F.2d 31 (6th Cir. 1963), Standard in New York loaned money to Consolidated under a revolving loan agreement calling for interest up to 17¹/₂% and providing that "all transactions hereunder shall be governed and construed by the laws of" New York. The court upheld the contract against the defense of usury under the 6% statute in Kentucky, where the borrower conducted its business and generated accounts receivable which it assigned each week to the lender in return for sums loaned. "Here the parties did not stipulate a forum having no normal relation to the transaction. To the contrary, a number of vital elements of the contract were related to New York . . . ." (Id., at p. 34.) To similar effect, see Sarlot-Kantarjian v. First Pennsylvania Mortgage Trust, 599 F.2d 915 (9th Cir. 1979). Compare Brierly v. Commercial Credit Co., 43 F.2d 730 (3d Cir. 1930), where a stipulation selecting the law of X was denied effect, the principal contacts having been with States Y and Z.

(4) See generally Hawkes, The Conflict of Laws and the Florida Usury Cases, 9 Fla.State U.L.Rev. 543 (1981); Note, Usury in the Conflict of Laws, 55 Calif.L.Rev. 123 (1967).

KINNEY LOAN & FINANCE CO. v. SUMNER

Supreme Court of Nebraska, 1954.
159 Neb. 57, 65 N.W.2d 240.

[Action by a Colorado corporation against a resident of Nebraska to replevy a trailer coach. The trial court sustained a general demurrer to plaintiff's petition and entered judgment for the defendant. The plaintiff appealed.

The petition alleged that plaintiff was authorized to do business by the State of Colorado under its small loan laws which, as the petition stated, were similar in principle to the regulatory small loan laws of Nebraska. The defendant, being indebted to the plaintiff, executed and delivered in Colorado his installment promissory note for $2,712 with interest at 2% per month on unpaid balances in conformity with the laws of Colorado. On the same day the defendant executed and delivered to the plaintiff in Colorado a chattel mortgage on the trailer coach then in Nebraska, as security for payment of the note. The chattel mortgage was filed with the appropriate recording official in Nebraska and the chattel mortgage lien was entered on the certificate of title to the trailer. The defendant paid nothing on the note. So the plaintiff, as provided in the note, and mortgage, declared the whole amount due, and brought this action for the trailer.]

CHAPPELL, JUSTICE. . . . Assuming as we must upon demurrer, that such note and mortgage were not usurious under the laws of Colorado where they were made and to be performed, and that they were valid under the laws of that state, the sole question presented here for determination is whether or not they are enforceable in this state simply because they both reserved a rate of interest higher than that permitted by law in this state. The trial court concluded that they were not, but we conclude otherwise.

. . .

. . . provisions relating to "installment loans" now appear as sections 45–114 to 45–158, R.R.S.1943. Such 1943 act included section 9, page 375, now section 45–158, R.R.S.1943, which provides: "No loan, made outside this state, in the amount or of the value of one thousand dollars or less, for which a greater rate of interest, consideration or charges than is permitted by section 45–138 has been charged, contracted for or received, shall be enforced in this state and every person, in anywise participating therein in this state, shall be subject to the provisions of this act; Provided, that the foregoing shall not apply to loans legally made in any state under and in accordance with a regulatory small loan law similar in principle to this act."

. . .

[The court reviewed the Nebraska and Colorado statutes applicable to small loans. The applicable Nebraska statute fixes the maximum interest rate at 9% per annum on loans exceeding $1,000.]

To meticulously compare each section of such Colorado statutes under which the loan here involved was made with our own relating to installment loans would serve no useful purpose and unduly prolong this opinion. It is sufficient for us to say that they are not identical, but they are "similar in principle" with our own act within the meaning of section 45–158, R.R.S.1943.

. . .

. . . By use of the phrase "a regulatory small loan law similar in principle to this act" in section 45–158, R.R.S.1943, our Legislature clearly did not mean "identical" or "precisely like," or the statute would be of little use. It meant a regulatory small loan law resembling our own installment loan act in origin, purpose, and result, which licenses, controls, and regulates those engaged in lending money at conventional higher rates of interest in order to combat the reservation of extortionate and oppressive rates.

. . .

In the light of the foregoing rules and circumstances presented in this case, we conclude that the loan here involved came within the purview of the proviso and that, unless there are other defenses thereto, which are not an issue here, the public policy of this state permits its enforcement in this state. . . .

Reversed and remanded.

NOTE

In London Finance Co. v. Shattuck, 221 N.Y. 702, 117 N.E. 1075 (1917), the defendant, a resident of New York, executed at the office of the Star Finance Company in New York an application for a loan of twenty-five dollars addressed to the plaintiff in Massachusetts, a promissory note bearing interest at the rate of three per cent per month, and a confession of judgment. Shortly thereafter, the defendant received a check from the plaintiff, mailed in Massachusetts. On nonpayment judgment by confession was entered in New York for $43.70. The Special Term vacated the judgment because "it was apparent the contract was made in the state of New York and that the claim that it had been made in the state of Massachusetts was a mere subterfuge for the purpose of evading the usury laws of the state of New York." On appeal, held, affirmed.

SECTION 2.   TRUSTS

Trusts may be created by deed during the lifetime of the settlor or by will. They may at times arise by operation of law, constructively, but we deal here with express trusts. Questions involving trusts fall into three broad categories: validity, administration, and construction. Validity involves such questions as capacity of the settlor to create the trust; formalities; and essential propriety in a legal sense, e.g., whether the trust provisions violate the rules against perpetuities or accumulations. Administration of a trust concerns its management—carrying out the terms of the trust. Construction involves deciding what the terms of the trust instrument require in situations in which it is impossible to determine the meaning intended. Ordinarily, the rules for deciding all three types of issues are derived from the same state's law, but there are exceptions.

Of the many policies and purposes of choice of law and other decisions affecting trusts, one stands out as primary: to carry out the intent of the trust's creator in establishing the trust and declaring his desires. This leads strongly in the direction of validating the trust whenever a choice between a rule upholding and one upsetting the trust is presented. At times doing this will conflict with an admonitory or prohibitory policy of one of the states related to the trust—perhaps even the forum.

HUTCHISON v. ROSS

Court of Appeals of New York, 1933.
262 N.Y. 381, 187 N.E. 65, 89 A.L.R. 1007.

[Under an antenuptial agreement executed in 1902 in Quebec, where the parties to it were both domiciled, John Ross promised to establish by deed or will a trust fund of $125,000 for the benefit of his prospective wife. In 1916, after inheriting $10,000,000 from his father, Ross decided to set up a trust of $1,000,000 for the benefit of his wife and children, and he directed that some securities then in New York City be used for that purpose. The trust instrument was drawn in New York and was signed in Quebec by Ross and his wife. It was then sent back to New York City where the trustee, the Equitable Trust Company of New York, signed it and where the securities constituting the corpus of the trust were thereupon delivered to it. The trust instrument contained a clause to the effect that the $1,000,000 trust was in lieu of the $125,000 trust.

Ross had lost almost the entire fortune by 1926 when he discovered that under the law of Quebec an antenuptial agreement cannot be modified in any way and under that law the trust of $1,000,000 with respect to the wife was invalid. In consideration for a further loan, Ross promised a creditor to institute proceedings to have the trust set aside and to deliver the trust res to the creditor as collateral. Ross commenced the action and, upon his involuntary bankruptcy, his trustee in bankruptcy was substituted as party plaintiff. The trial court held that the attempted modification of the antenuptial agreement was governed by the law of Quebec, the matrimonial domicile, and, therefore, that the $1,000,000 trust was invalid. The Appellate Division reversed the trial court, and the plaintiff appealed.]

LEHMAN, J. . . . With possible limitations, not relevant to the question here presented . . . the rule is well established that the essential validity of a testamentary trust must be determined by the law of the decedent's domicile. . . . The plaintiff urges that the same rule should be applied to a conveyance in trust inter vivos, especially where such trust is established for the benefit of the wife and children of the settlor.

It cannot be gainsaid that there are expressions in the opinions of the courts of this State which support the plaintiff's contentions. In considering the effect of these expressions, we must give due weight to the circumstances under which they were made. The paucity of old judicial decisions upon conveyances in trust inter vivos, compared with the number of decisions upon testamentary trusts, shows that conveyances in trust inter vivos were comparatively rare. Thus the possible importance of drawing distinctions between the rules applicable to testamentary trusts and trusts inter vivos, was not apparent or brought to the attention of the courts. . . . Today the courts cannot close their eyes to the fact that trusts of personal property and securities are created by settlors during their lifetime for many purposes, and for the first time our court is called upon to decide directly the question whether conveyances in trust of securities made inter vivos shall be governed by the same rules as testamentary trusts or by the same rules as other conveyances inter vivos. . . .

. . . now that we are called upon to decide that question, we must weigh other considerations not then apparent to the courts which seem to point logically to the need for differentiation between the rule to be applied to testamentary trusts and the rule to be applied to trusts inter vivos.

In all the affairs of life there has been a vast increase of mobility. Residence is growing less and less the focal point of existence and its practical effect is steadily diminishing. Men living in one jurisdiction often conduct their affairs in other jurisdictions, and keep their securities there. Trusts are created in business and financial centers by settlors residing elsewhere. A settlor, regardless of residence, cannot establish a trust to be administered here which offends our public policy. If we hold that a non-resident settlor may also not establish a trust of personal property here which offends the public policy of his domicile, we shackle both the non-resident settlor and the resident trustee.

Our courts have sought whenever possible to sustain the validity even of testamentary trusts to be administered in a jurisdiction other than the domicile of the testator. . . . In regard to other conveyances or alienations of personal property situated here, they have steadfastly applied the law of the jurisdiction where the personal property is situated. . . . Where a non-resident settlor establishes here a trust of personal property intending that the trust should be governed by the law of this jurisdiction, there is little reason why the courts should defeat his intention by applying the law of another jurisdiction. . . .

. . . We may throw in the balance also expressions of public policy by the Legislature of this State. It has provided that: "Whenever a person being a citizen of the United States, or a citizen or a subject of a foreign country, wherever resident, creates a trust of personal property situated within this State at the time of the creation thereof, and declares in the instrument creating such trust that it shall be construed and regulated by the laws of this State, the validity and effect of such trust shall be determined by such laws." (Pers. Prop.Law; Const.Laws, ch. 41, sec. 12–a). It is true that the statute was enacted long after the creation of the trust now the subject of this litigation and the validity of the trust must, probably, be determined by the law as it then existed. The statute does not change retroactively a well-established rule of law. It merely establishes a definite public policy in a field where the rules of law were still fluid and undefined. When the courts are called upon to define these rules even as of an earlier date, they cannot entirely disregard this public policy. . . .

It is said that the statute establishes a public policy only where there is an express declaration of intention in the instrument that it shall be construed and regulated by the laws of this State. Here there is no express declaration of intention, but the intention is implied in every act and word of the parties. The statute makes express declaration of intention conclusive, but a construction which would deny effect to intention appearing by implication would be unreasonable. . . . It follows that the validity of a trust of personal property must be determined by the law of this State, when the property is situated here and the parties intended that it should be administered here in accordance with the laws of this State. . . .

The judgment in each action should be affirmed, with costs. . . .

[Two judges dissented.]

SHANNON v. IRVING TRUST CO.

Court of Appeals of New York, 1937.
275 N.Y. 95, 9 N.E.2d 792.

RIPPEY, JUDGE. . . . a trust indenture was duly executed in the city of New York between Joseph G. Shannon, who was . . . domiciled within the State of New Jersey, and the Irving Trust Company, a corporation organized and existing under the laws of the State of New York . . . as trustee, whereby an irrevocable trust was created for the benefit, among others, of Goewey F. Shannon, wife of the settlor, and plaintiff herein, John Shannon, the son of the settlor, both of which beneficiaries were then . . . domiciled within the State of New Jersey. . . . The trust created for the wife consisted of fixed items of income with the provision that all income in excess of the amount named should accumulate and become part of the principal of the trust. Up to December 26, 1933, when Goewey F. Shannon died, she continued to be . . . domiciled within the State of New Jersey. . . . The trust instrument provided that upon her death the trustee should thereafter pay to the son, John Shannon, monthly, an aggregate annual income of $3,000 until the son should arrive at twenty-five years of age; that thereafter the income to the son, payable in monthly installments, should aggregate $5,000 per year until the son arrived at the age of thirty years; that thereafter the income to the son should be increased to $10,000 per year until he should arrive at the age of thirty-five years, after which time he should receive the full income from the trust estate for the balance of his life. All income in excess of the amounts thus payable to the son was directed to become a part of the trust estate. The trust instrument provided that, at the death of the son, the principal and accumulated income should pass to the issue of the son, or, if the son should die without issue surviving, to the Hill School of Pottstown, Pa. At the time the trust was created, the plaintiff was a resident of and domiciled within the State of New Jersey and his domicile has continued in that state to the time of the commencement of the action. . . . the trust instrument [provided] "The Trustee shall receive for its services, its necessary expenses and the commissions allowed testamentary trustees by the laws of the State of New York instead of the laws of the State of New Jersey, but otherwise the laws of the State of New Jersey shall govern this trust indenture and any construction to be placed thereupon or interpretation thereof."

. . . the plaintiff contended that the validity of the trust is to be determined by the laws of the State of New York and, inasmuch as the provisions for accumulations of income are void under section 16 of the Personal Property Law (Consol.Laws, c. 41) of the State of New York (Laws 1909, c. 45), the accumulations should be paid over to him as the person presumptively entitled to the next eventual estate . . . while the defendants assert that the validity of the trust provisions is to be determined by the laws of the State of New Jersey, where the accumulations are valid. . . . The Appellate Division found that the trust was valid and certified to this court that a question of law was involved which ought to be here reviewed.

. . . Where the domicile of the owner of the res and the actual and business situs of the trust do not coincide, the law applicable to the interpretation, construction, and validity of the trust and the legal obligations arising out of it . . . depend upon facts involved in and circumstances surrounding the particular case. In such a situation, the express or clearly implied intent of the settlor may control. . . .

In the case at bar the execution of the trust instrument, the location of the res, the domicile of the trustee, and the place of administration of the trust are in the city of New York. The intent of the settlor that in all matters affecting the trust except remuneration of the trustee his domiciliary law shall govern is expressly stated in the body of the trust instrument. . . . The instrument should be construed and a determination of its validity made according to the law chosen by the settlor unless so to do is contrary to the public policy of this state. . . .

Consideration of the New Jersey law and our own relating to perpetuities and accumulations of income will indicate that our policy in that connection is substantially the same as that of New Jersey. . . . The general policy of New Jersey and New York to put some limitation on the absolute suspension of the power of alienation of property and the accumulation of income from trusts is the same. Difference arises only as to the ending of the period during which such power to suspend alienation and to provide for accumulation of income may be permitted.

Under the facts existing in the case at bar, . . . we find nothing in our public policy which forbids extending comity and applying the New Jersey law so as to carry out the wish of the settlor and sustain the trust. The positive direction contained in the trust instrument that the validity of the trust should be determined by the law of the settlor's domicile must prevail. Our decision here does not extend, however, beyond instances where conflict arises between the domiciliary law of the settlor and the law of the situs of the trust where the construction and validity of trusts inter vivos are involved.

Judgment affirmed.

NOTES

(1) What common principle reconciles the Hutchison and Shannon decisions?

(2) Would Shannon be differently decided if an interests analysis were applied? To what extent is the settlor's expressed choice of one applicable law to determine the trustee's reimbursement for expenses and commissions, and another to determine other aspects of the trust analogous to the problem of autonomy in contract choice of law? Is there anything wrong with the dépeçage employed here?

National Shawmut Bank v. Cumming, 325 Mass. 457, 91 N.E.2d 337 (1950). S, a Vermont resident, transferred a fund to a Massachusetts trustee to pay the income to himself for life and after his death to distribute it in equal shares among his widow, mother, brothers and sister; upon the death of the life beneficiaries, the corpus was to go to the settlor's nephews and nieces. After S's death, his widow claimed the principal of the trust contending that the trust was invalid under Vermont law since it was made for the purpose of depriving her of her inheritance rights. Held: Massachusetts law governs and under that law the trust is valid. "The general tendency of authorities . . . is away from the adoption of the law of the settlor's domicil where the property, the domicil and place of business of the trustee and the place of administration intended by the settlor are in another State."

Did not Vermont have a greater interest than Massachusetts in the decision of the particular issue? Did the court place too much weight upon the policy in favor of upholding the validity of a trust? Was the issue one when the respective policies of Massachusetts and Vermont differed markedly?

(4) See generally 5 Scott, The Law of Trusts 3766–4159 (3d ed. 1967, 1982 Supp.); Leflar, American Conflicts Law 383–396 (3d ed. 1977); Scoles and Hay, Conflict of Laws 800–821 (1982).

RESTATEMENT, SECOND, CONFLICT OF LAWS: *

§ 270. Validity of Trust of Movables Created Inter Vivos

An inter vivos trust of interests in movables is valid if valid

(a) under the local law of the state designated by the settlor to govern the validity of the trust, provided that this state has a substantial relation to the trust and that the application of its law does not violate a strong public policy of the state with which, as to the matter at issue, the trust has its most significant relationship under the principles stated in § 6, or

(b) if there is no such effective designation, under the local law of the state with which, as to the matter at issue, the trust has its most significant relationship under the principles stated in § 6.

Comment:

a. The general principle. It is desirable that a trust should be treated as a unit and, to this end, that the trust as to all of the movables included therein, no matter where they happen to be at the time of the creation of the trust, should be governed by a single law. The creation of a trust is different from an outright conveyance, which is either valid or invalid at the outset. In the case of a trust there is something more. In the first place, the creation of a trust establishes a continuing relationship between the trustee and the beneficiaries, and the state in which the trust is to be administered or which is otherwise connected with the trust may be different from the state in which the trust property is situated when the trust is created. In the second place, the trust property is ordinarily not a single movable but includes a group of movables which may be situated in different states at the time of the creation of the trust. The validity of a trust of movables, therefore, should be governed by a single law and not held valid as to some of the movables included in the trust and invalid as to others. This is true whether the movables consist of chattels, rights embodied in a document or intangibles. The rule of this Section is applicable to all these types of movables, no matter where they are situated at the time of the creation of the trust. It does not follow, however, that all questions of validity are determined by the same law. See Comment *e*.

FARMERS AND MERCHANTS BANK v. WOOLF

Supreme Court of New Mexico, 1974.
86 N.M. 320, 523 P.2d 1346.

MONTOYA, JUSTICE.

The plaintiff-trustee (trustee), Farmers and Merchants Bank of Las Cruces, New Mexico, filed this action for declaratory judgment to determine the rights of the parties involved in a trust estate. From a judgment awarding the balance of the trust estate of Mabel Evelyn Jones (testatrix) to the Alcoholics Foundation of San Antonio, Texas

(Foundation), Dale Woolf (Woolf), the administrator with will annexed of the estate of Gordon Vance Jones brings this appeal. . . .

[By will the testatrix, who died domiciled in Arizona, left her residuary estate in trust to the Farmers and Merchants Bank with the provision that following the death of her brother, the corpus of the trust should be paid to Alcoholics Anonymous of San Antonio, Texas. The trial court upheld the provision for Alcoholics Anonymous under Texas law although it would have been invalid under the law of Arizona. Woolf, the administrator of the deceased brother's estate appealed on the ground, among others, that the trial court had erred in not applying the law of Arizona, the state of the testatrix' domicil, since her estate consisted entirely of personal property.]

We first consider which law governs the disposition of the trust property. The testatrix was domiciled in Arizona and the main probate proceeding was held there. Ancillary probate proceedings were completed by the Dona Ana County Probate Court, since the funds involved in the trust were in the custody of the trustee in New Mexico. The legatee of the trust property is organized under the laws of the State of Texas, and the administration of the trust will also be in the State of Texas.

Under Restatement, Second, Conflict of Laws, Ch. 10 Trusts, § 269, at 152–153, it is stated:

"§ 269. Validity of Trust of Movables Created by Will

"The validity of a trust of interests in movables created by will is determined

"(a) as to matters that affect the validity of the will as a testamentary disposition, by the law that would be applied by the courts of the state of the testator's domicil at death, and

"(b) as to matters that affect only the validity of the trust provisions, except when the provision is invalid under the strong public policy of the state of the testator's domicil at death,

"(i) by the local law of the state designated by the testator to govern the validity of the trust, provided that this state has a substantial relation to the trust, or

"(ii) if there is no such effective designation, by the local law of the state of the testator's domicil at death, except that the local law of the state where the trust is to be administered will be applied if application of this law is necessary to sustain the validity of the trust."

Since the testatrix did not designate what law was to govern the validity of the trust, the provisions of § 269(b)(ii), supra, would apply. In the commentary to the foregoing section in Restatement, supra, the following appears in comment (h) at 157:

"h. Charitable trusts. In the case of charitable trusts, the courts have been even more ready than in the case of private trusts to uphold the trust if valid under the local law of the state of administration, even though the trust would be invalid under the local law of the testator's domicil. . . .

"When a testator bequeaths movables to be administered for charitable purposes in a state other than that of his domicil, the disposition is valid if valid under the local law of the state of administration, even though it would be invalid under the local law of the state of the testator's domicil. . . ."

In Fletcher v. Safe Deposit & Trust Co., 193 Md. 400, 410–411, 67 A.2d 386, 390 (Ct.App.1949), in considering the question of the applicable law to determine the validity of a trust estate, the court stated:

"The general rule is that the validity of a will of movables, or of a trust of movables created by will, is determined by the law of the testator's domicile. . . . 'However, where a trust is to be administered in a state other than that of the domicile, but is by the domiciliary law invalid from the outset under a rule grounded in a feeling that the administration of such a trust would be difficult or against the policy of the domicile, if such objections do not prevail at the place of administration the courts of the domicile will hold the trust valid.' [Citations omitted.]" . . .

Accordingly, we hold that the trial court did not err as claimed by Woolf under his first point. . . .

NOTES

(1) Cross v. United States Trust Co., 131 N.Y. 330, 30 N.E. 125 (1892). The will of testatrix who died domiciled in Rhode Island was admitted to probate in that state. The will created a trust of personal property to be administered in New York by a New York trust company. The provisions of the trust violated the New York rule against perpetuities but were valid under the law of Rhode Island. The court applied Rhode Island law and held the trust valid. It stated that application of Rhode Island law would not be contrary to New York public policy. "The only material difference in the law of the two states on this subject [rule against perpetuities] is that in each a different rule is adopted for measuring the period within which absolute ownership may lawfully be suspended. . . . If . . . a person desiring to make a will must not only know the law of his domicile, but also the law of every country in which his personal estate may happen to be at his death, . . . our courts would become the resort of dissatisfied heirs, or legatees, seeking to nullify wills, valid by the laws of the state where the persons who made them were domiciled. The question is not changed by the circumstance that the trustee and the trust fund is within our jurisdiction and all the beneficiaries but one are now residents of this state."

Matter of Chappell, 124 Wash. 128, 213 P. 684 (1923). By will, the testator, who died domiciled in California, established a trust covering personal property situated in Washington. The trust provisions were valid under Washington law; they were invalid under the California rule against perpetuities. Held that the validity of the trust should be sustained by application of Washington law. The trust did not contain any choice-of-law provision.

But the court reasoned that the testator had obviously intended that the trust should be valid and that his intentions should be given effect "if that be possible and lawful."

(2) Hope v. Brewer, 136 N.Y. 126, 32 N.E. 558 (1892). The will of testator, a domiciliary of New York, directed his executors to convert his New York real estate into money and to pay over the proceeds to three named Scottish trustees, in trust, for the purpose of founding and endowing an infirmary "for the care and relief of the sick and infirm of Langholm, in Dunfrieshire, Scotland." This disposition was void under New York law on the ground of indefiniteness of beneficiaries; under the law of Scotland it was valid. On appeal from a judgment, upholding the validity of the trust against attack by a legatee, held, affirmed. "I have not been able to find any well-considered case . . . where a gift to a foreign charity in trust, contained in a valid testamentary instrument, has been held void, where there was a trustee competent to take and hold, and the trust was capable of being executed and enforced, according to the law of the place to which the property was to be transmitted under the will of the donor. . . . Our law with respect to the creation and validity of trusts . . . was designed only to regulate the holding of property under our laws, and in our state, and a trust intended to take effect in another state, or in a foreign country, would not seem to be within either its letter or spirit."

(3) As to the law governing the validity of testamentary trusts of movables, see 5 Scott, Trusts §§ 588–596A (3d ed. 1967). As to the law governing powers of appointment of movables, see 5 Scott, Trusts §§ 629–642.

SECTION 3.   WORKERS' COMPENSATION

Workers' compensation statutes generally impose liability upon employers for work-related injuries to employees regardless of fault. As a quid pro quo, employers are relieved of ordinary liability in tort and wrongful death. Awards recoverable by injured employees under the compensation systems are usually limited by fixed schedules, and in each state the program is ordinarily administered by special tribunals of prescribed powers and procedures. In consequence, relief under a particular state's workers' compensation system is usually obtainable only in that state, in the manner and amounts prescribed. While this inhibition on other states is not constitutionally mandated, Crider v. Zurich Insurance Co., 380 U.S. 39 (1965) (set forth at p. 213, supra), it is so common that when suit is brought in State F for workers' compensation benefits, there is in effect no choice-of-law issue presented: F uses its own special administrative tribunals and award system even though other states could properly have applied their compensation machinery had the employee chosen to assert his claim in one of them. Thus, Restatement, Second, Conflict of Laws declares in Section 182: "Relief may be awarded under the workmen's compensation statute of a State of the United States, although the statute of a sister State is also applicable."

Yet, significant choice-of-law problems arise when multistate industrial accidents occur because of the interaction of the workers' compensation and tort law regimes. For instance, a statute of the state where the employee was hired, or of the state where he was injured, may explicitly provide that the employee's remedies under the particular workers' compensation system of the particular state are exclusive of any rights he might otherwise have under the local law of another state.

The manifold possibilities of choice-of-law problems that flow from the circumstance that many states have a sufficient relationship to apply their tort or compensation laws to industrial injuries become apparent when we consider how many of these there may be in a given case: the state where the employee was injured; where he contracted to be employed; where he lives; where he usually works; where the employer supervises his activities; where the parties have agreed he will look for compensation in the event of injury, etc. See Restatement, Second, Conflict of Laws § 181. The Reporter's Note to Section 181 collects numerous illustrative cases.

These numerous possibilities are compounded when the employment and accident circumstances are not in the simple pattern of an employee sustaining an on-the-job injury in which only his own employer is a potential source of damage benefits. The following case, Wilson v. Faull, suggests a few of the ramifications.

WILSON v. FAULL

Supreme Court of New Jersey, 1958.
27 N.J. 105, 141 A.2d 768.

[Action in tort by an employee of a subcontractor against the general contractor. The defendant, Faull, who resided and maintained his regular place of business in New Jersey, made a contract in Pennsylvania to repair a building there. In New Jersey he made a subcontract with Tragle for part of the repairs, and he agreed to erect a scaffold on which Tragle's employees would work. The plaintiff, Wilson, who resided in New Jersey as did Faull and Tragle, was hired in New Jersey by Tragle and was sent to the Pennsylvania job. While at work in Pennsylvania, Wilson fell from the scaffold that the general contractor, Faull, had erected. For the resulting injuries he obtained workers' compensation in New Jersey from Tragle, his employer. He then brought the present common law negligence action in New Jersey against the general contractor, Faull.

Faull, the general contractor, carried workers' compensation insurance for plaintiff's benefit under the Pennsylvania compensation law. The subcontractor, Tragle, carried workers' compensation insurance for plaintiff's benefit under the New Jersey act. The laws of the two states differed as to the liability of the general contractor to the employees of the subcontractor. Under the Pennsylvania statute, the general contractor was liable for the payment of compensation to the subcontractor's employees; but the general contractor was granted immunity from common law liability for negligence. Under the New Jersey law a general contractor was liable for compensation to an employee of a subcontractor only if the subcontractor had not secured workers' compensation insurance. Where the subcontractor had procured compensation insurance, as he had in the present case, the general contractor was not granted immunity from liability in negligence to the subcontractor's employee.

The trial court granted the defendant's motion for summary judgment on the ground the law of the place of injury controlled the right of action in tort. On appeal, the Appellate Division reversed, since in its view the choice-of-law problem was concerned not with tort law but with "the regulation of employment relations" and the law of New Jersey should be applied as that state had "the preponderance of significant contacts with the employment relationship involved".]

PROCTOR, J. . . . Workmen's compensation laws were designed to provide an expeditious and certain remedy for employees who sustain work injuries by the statutory imposition of absolute but limited and determinate liability upon the employer. . . . These laws generally provide that the compensation remedy is exclusive. The theory behind this exclusiveness is that the laws provide predictable compensation for any on the job injury. They represent a compromise that inures to the ultimate benefit of both employer and employee. The employee surrenders his right to seek damages in an action at law in return for swift recovery independent of proof of fault. The employer gives up common law defenses to negligence suits and assumes an absolute liability to provide compensation; in return he is granted immunity from common law negligence suits by his employees. . . .

. . . If the injured employee is seeking a compensation remedy, application by the forum of its compensation law, whether it be the state of the injury or the state of the contract or the state of the employment relation, does no violence to the basic principles of workmen's compensation. The employee is provided a prompt and certain recovery and the employer's liability is limited to that provided by the compensation law of the forum, which has a sufficient interest in the work-injury to justify the application of its own law. Nor is there any constitutional impediment to the forum's application of its own compensation law, whether the forum be the state of the injury . . . or the state of contract or employment relation . . . notwithstanding that the compensation law of another interested state purports to provide an exclusive remedy. . . .

However, where the injured employee seeks to maintain a common law tort action against his employer in one of two or more states having a legitimate interest in the work-injury, the forum has almost invariably applied the law of the state in which the employer has provided compensation insurance and whose law granted such employer immunity from common law negligence actions by the employee, and dismissed the suit. . . .   This choice of law has been made by . . . the forum, whether it was the state of the injury, . . . or the state of employment relation, ... This almost universal recognition by the forum of the compensation law of a sister state which grants immunity to an employer who has provided compensation insurance for an employee, irrespective of the interest of the state of the forum, cannot be said to be the result of an inflexible or mechanical application by the forum of "tort," "contract" or "employment relation" conflict of laws principles. Instead, the recognition of the law of a sister state in this situation reflects the basic philosophy underlying the adoption of workmen's compensation acts by the several states as the exclusive remedy for industrial accidents. . . .

The question remains whether this reasoning applies with equal force when an injured employee of a subcontractor brings a common law negligence action in the state of contract or employment relation against a general contractor, who under the compensation law of the state of the injury is substituted for the immediate employer for compensation purposes. . . .

We think . . . there is no substantial difference between an immediate employer-subcontractor who is obligated to provide compensation coverage for his employees, and a general contractor, who, under the law of the state of the injury, is substituted in the employment relation for the immediate employer and becomes primarily liable for workmen's compensation to the employees of the immediate employer. . . .

Choice of law in the situation presented here should not be governed by wholly fortuitous circumstances such as where the injury occurred, or where the contract of employment was executed, or where the parties resided or maintained their places of business, or any combination of these "contacts." Rather, it should be founded on broader considerations of basic compensation policy which the conflicting laws call into play, with a view toward achieving a certainty of result and effecting fairness between the parties within the framework of that policy. The injured workman has a prompt and practical compensation remedy in any state having a legitimate interest in his welfare. The person who provides that compensation in an interested state has a definitive liability which is predictable with some degree of accuracy and is granted an immunity from an employee's suit for damages which does not disappear whenever his enterprise chances to cross state lines and the suit is brought in another state. . . .

The judgment of the Appellate Division is reversed and the judgment of the trial court is reinstated.

[The concurring opinion of WEINTRAUB, C.J. is omitted.]

NOTES

(1) It is clear that on the facts of the principal case, New Jersey would have been constitutionally privileged to apply its own local law to hold Faull liable in tort. Carroll v. Lanza, 349 U.S. 408 (1955), set forth at p. 348, supra.

(2) Restatement, Second, Conflict of Laws § 184 provides that a defendant should not be exposed to liability in tort or wrongful death at the suit of an employee when the defendant has been declared immune from such liability by the workers' compensation statute of any state under which the employee has already obtained an award for the injury or under the statute of any one of a number of enumerated states under which the employee could obtain such an award.

(3) Approving the Restatement's position and reasoning is Elston v. Industrial Lift Truck Co., 420 Pa. 97, 216 A.2d 318 (1966). The Pennsylvania supplier of a fork-lift truck which had allegedly injured a Pennsylvanian on the job in New Jersey was sued at common law for tort damages. The supplier tried to join Elston's New Jersey employer, but failed. The court held that even though partial contribution from the employer was allowed by the Pennsylvania rule, in the interests of equitable distribution of loss from industrial accidents, the immunity given the employer by New Jersey's compensation system should prevail: "The extent to which the New Jersey program of workmen's compensation should assimilate the equities underlying contribution is a determination more appropriately to be made by that state."

For a case permitting recovery in tort in situations where such recovery would not be permitted by § 184 of the Restatement, see O'Connor v. Lee-Hy Paving Corp., 579 F.2d 194 (2d Cir. 1978).

(4) Are Wilson v. Faull and Elston v. Industrial Lift Truck Co. examples of cases where the forum subordinates its own policies and interests to what it deems to be the basic policy underlying the substantive field involved?

(5) In Gentry v. Jett, 235 Ark. 20, 356 S.W.2d 736 (1962), an Arkansas employee, who had been injured in Oklahoma, obtained recovery in tort in an Arkansas court against the tortfeasor by application of Oklahoma law. When the employee subsequently sought workers' compensation against his employer in Arkansas, he was met with the defense that under Oklahoma law a workers' compensation award is barred after there has been recovery in tort from a third-party tortfeasor. Held for the employee. Full faith and credit does not prevent Arkansas from giving relief under its own workers' compensation act in these circumstances.

(6) To what extent, if any, does full faith and credit preclude an employee who has obtained a workers' compensation award in one state from obtaining a second award for the same injury in another state? Thomas v. Washington Gas Light Co., p. 275, supra.

SECTION 4.   MARRIAGE

IN RE MAY'S ESTATE

Court of Appeals of New York, 1953.
305 N.Y. 486, 114 N.E.2d 4.

LEWIS, CHIEF JUDGE. In this proceeding, involving the administration of the estate of Fannie May, deceased, we are to determine
whether the marriage in 1913 between the respondent Sam May and
the decedent, who was his niece by the half blood—which marriage
was celebrated in Rhode Island, where concededly such marriage is
valid—is to be given legal effect in New York where statute law declares incestuous and void a marriage between uncle and niece. Domestic Relations Law, § 5, subd. 3, McK.Consol.Laws.

The question thus presented arises from proof of the following
facts: The petitioner Alice May Greenberg, one of six children born
of the Rhode Island marriage of Sam and Fannie May, petitioned in
1951 for letters of administration of the estate of her mother Fannie
May, who had died in 1945. Thereupon, the respondent Sam May,
who asserts the validity of his marriage to the decedent, filed an objection to the issuance to petitioner of such letters of administration
upon the ground that he is the surviving husband of the decedent and
accordingly under section 118 of the Surrogate's Court Act, he has
the paramount right to administer her estate. . . .

The record shows that for a period of more than five years prior
to his marriage to decedent the respondent Sam May had resided in
Portage, Wisconsin; that he came to New York in December, 1912,
and within a month thereafter he and the decedent—both of whom
were adherents of the Jewish faith—went to Providence, Rhode Island, where, on January 21, 1913, they entered into a ceremonial marriage performed by and at the home of a Jewish rabbi. The certificate issued upon that marriage gave the age of each party as twenty-
six years and the residence of each as "New York, N.Y." Two weeks
after their marriage in Rhode Island the respondent May and the decedent returned to Ulster County, New York, where they lived as
man and wife for thirty-two years until the decedent's death in 1945.
Meantime the six children were born who are parties to this proceeding. . . .

In Surrogate's Court, where letters of administration were granted to the petitioner, the Surrogate ruled that although the marriage
of Sam May and the decedent in Rhode Island in 1913 was valid in
that State, such marriage was not only void in New York as opposed
to natural law but is contrary to the provisions of subdivision 3 of
section 5 of the Domestic Relations Law. . . .

At the Appellate Division the order of the Surrogate was reversed on the law and the proceeding was remitted to Surrogate's Court with direction that letters of administration upon decedent's estate be granted to Sam May who was held to be the surviving spouse of the decedent. . . .

We regard the law as settled that, subject to two exceptions presently to be considered and in the absence of a statute expressly regulating within the domiciliary State marriages solemnized abroad, the legality of a marriage between persons *sui juris* is to be determined by the law of the place where it is celebrated. . . .

The statute of New York upon which the appellants rely is subdivision 3 of section 5 of the Domestic Relations Law which, insofar as relevant to our problem, provides:

"§ 5. *Incestuous and void marriages*

"A marriage is incestuous and void whether the relatives are legitimate or illegitimate between either: . . .

"3. An uncle and niece or an aunt and nephew.

"If a marriage prohibited by the foregoing provisions of this section be solemnized it shall be void, and the parties thereto shall each be fined not less than fifty nor more than one hundred dollars and may, in the discretion of the court in addition to said fine, be imprisoned for a term not exceeding six months. Any person who shall knowingly and wilfully solemnize such marriage, or procure or aid in the solemnization of the same, shall be deemed guilty of a misdemeanor and shall be fined or imprisoned in like manner."

Although the New York statute quoted above declares to be incestuous and void a marriage between an uncle and a niece and imposes penal measures upon the parties thereto, it is important to note that the statute does not by express terms regulate a marriage solemnized in another State where, as in our present case, the marriage was concededly legal. . . .

. . . the statute's scope should not be extended by judicial construction. . . . Accordingly, as to the first exception to the general rule that a marriage valid where performed is valid everywhere, we conclude that, absent any New York statute expressing clearly the Legislature's intent to regulate within this State marriages of its domiciliaries solemnized abroad, there is no "positive law" in this jurisdiction which serves to interdict the 1913 marriage in Rhode Island of the respondent Sam May and the decedent.

As to the application of the second exception to the marriage here involved—between persons of the Jewish faith whose kinship was not in the direct ascending or descending line of consanguinity and who were not brother and sister—we conclude that such marriage, solemnized, as it was, in accord with the ritual of the Jewish faith in a State whose legislative body has declared such a marriage to be "good and valid in law", was not offensive to the public sense of morality to a degree regarded generally with abhorrence and thus was not within the inhibitions of natural law. . . .

DESMOND, JUDGE (dissenting). It is fundamental that every State has the right to determine the marital status of its own citizens [citing cases]. Exercising that right, New York has declared in section 5 of the Domestic Relations Law that a marriage between uncle and niece is incestuous, void and criminal. Such marriages, while not within the Levitical forbidden degrees of the Old Testament, have been condemned by public opinion for centuries (see 1 Bishop on Marriage, Divorce and Separation, § 738), and are void, by statute in (it would seem) forty-seven of the States of the Union (all except Georgia, see Martindale-Hubbell, Law Digests, and except, also, that Rhode Island, one of the forty-seven, exempts from its local statute "any marriage which shall be solemnized among the Jews, within the degrees of affinity or consanguinity allowed by their religion", Gen. L. of R.I., ch. 415, § 4). It is undisputed here that this uncle and niece were both domiciled in New York in 1913, when they left New York for the sole purpose of going to Rhode Island to be married there, and that they were married in that State conformably to its laws (see above) and immediately returned to New York and ever afterwards resided in this State. That Rhode Island marriage, between two New York residents, was in New York, absolutely void for any and all purposes, by positive New York law which declares a strong public policy of this State. See Penal Law, § 1110.

The general rule that "a marriage valid where solemnized is valid everywhere" (see Restatement, Conflict of Laws, § 121) does not apply. To that rule there is a proviso or exception, recognized, it would seem, by all the States, as follows: "unless contrary to the prohibitions of natural law or the express prohibitions of a statute". See Thorp v. Thorp, 90 N.Y. 602, 605. Section 132 of the Restatement of Conflict of Laws states the rule apparently followed throughout America: "A marriage which is against the law of the state of domicil of either party, though the requirements of the law of the state of celebration have been complied with, will be invalid everywhere in the following cases: . . . (b) incestuous marriage between persons so closely related that their marriage is contrary to a strong public policy of the domicil". . . .

. . . Section 5 of the Domestic Relations Law, the one we are concerned with here, lists the marriages which are "incestuous and void" in New York, as being those between parent and child, brother and sister, uncle and niece, and aunt and nephew. All such misalliances are incestuous, and all, equally, are void. The policy, language, meaning and validity of the statute are beyond dispute. It should be enforced by the courts.

. . .

Decree affirmed.

NOTES

(1) Catalano v. Catalano, 148 Conn. 288, 170 A.2d 726 (1961) involved a similar situation and reached an opposite result. In that case, an uncle and niece were married in Italy, which was then the domicile of the wife and under whose law the marriage was valid. Five years later, the wife moved to Connecticut, where the husband had been domiciled at all critical times, and resided with him in that state until his death. Her right to succeed to an interest in his estate was denied on the ground that the marriage was invalid by application of Connecticut law.

(2) What type of choice-of-law approach will serve justice best in multi-state cases involving the validity of marriage, such as the incest cases, above, and the underage bride case below? Will the interests analysis work well here? tight rules? alternative reference rules? principles of preference?

————

WILKINS v. ZELICHOWSKI

Supreme Court of New Jersey, 1958.
26 N.J. 370, 140 A.2d 65.

JACOBS, J. . . . The plaintiff and the defendant were domiciled in New Jersey as were their respective parents. They ran away from New Jersey to marry and they chose Indiana because they believed "it was the quickest place." The Indiana statutes provide that "females of the age of sixteen" are capable of marriage although they also provide that where the female is within the age of 18 the required marriage license shall not be issued without the consent of her parents. See Burns, Indiana Statutes Annotated, §§ 44–101, 44–202. After their marriage in Indiana on April 23, 1954, the plaintiff and defendant returned immediately to New Jersey where they set up their home. On February 22, 1955 the plaintiff bore the defendant's child. . . . On January 4, 1956 the plaintiff filed her annulment complaint under N.J.S. 2A:34–1(e), N.J.S.A., which provides that a judgment of nullity may be rendered on the wife's application upon a showing that she was under the age of 18 years at the time of her marriage and that the marriage has not been "confirmed by her after arriving at such age"; the statute also provides that where a child has been born there shall be no judgment of nullity unless the court is of the opinion that the judgment "will not be against the best interests of the child." . . .

The plaintiff's evidence adequately established that she was 16 years of age when she was married and that she did not confirm her marriage after she had reached 18 years of age and the Chancery Division expressly found that an annulment would be "for the best interests of the child"; nevertheless it declined to grant the relief sought by the plaintiff on the ground that the marriage was valid in Indiana and should therefore, under principles of the conflict of laws, not be nullified by a New Jersey court because of the plaintiff's nonage. In reaching the same result the Appellate Division recognized that the Chancery Division had ample power to nullify the Indiana marriage of the New Jersey domiciliaries . . . but expressed the view that comity dictated that it should not take such action unless there was an imperative New Jersey policy (which it did not find) against marriages of 16-year-old females. . . .

In 1905 the Court of Chancery had occasion to deal with an application by a New Jersey resident for annulment of an English marriage entered into when she was 14 years of age; the court expressed the view that there could be "no doubt" as to its jurisdiction. After reviewing the plaintiff's evidence of fraud and duress and pointing out that while our law is interested in the permanency and inviolability of the marriage contract "it is equally interested in having it entered into by persons of competent age and judgment," it awarded a decree of annulment. See Avakian v. Avakian, 69 N.J.Eq. 89, 100, 60 A. 521, 525 (Ch.1905, per Pitney, V.C.), affirmed 69 N.J.Eq. 834, 66 A. 1133 (E. & A.1906). In 1907 the Legislature revised the statutory provisions relating to annulments (L.1907, c. 216, p. 474); it directed that a decree of nullity could be rendered not only in the case of a bigamous or incestuous marriage (see L.1902, c. 157, p. 502) but also in any case, among others, where the wife sought the decree and established that she was under 16 at the time of the marriage and had not confirmed it after attaining such age. . . . In 1928 the Legislature strengthened its policy by increasing the wife's age requirement and providing that the wife could obtain a decree of nullification "when she was under the age of eighteen years at the time of the marriage, unless such marriage be confirmed by her after arriving at such age." See L.1928, c. 65, p. 139.

The vigor of New Jersey's policy against marriages by persons under the prescribed age is evidenced not only by the breadth of the statutory language but also by the judicial decisions. [The court discussed at this point a number of New Jersey decisions.]

It is undisputed that if the marriage between the plaintiff and the defendant had taken place here, the public policy of New Jersey would be applicable and the plaintiff would be entitled to the annulment; and it seems clear to us that if New Jersey's public policy is to remain at all meaningful it must be considered equally applicable though their marriage took place in Indiana. While that State was interested in the formal ceremonial requirements of the marriage it had no interest whatever in that marital status of the parties. Indeed, New Jersey was the only State having any interest in that status, for both parties were domiciled in New Jersey before and after the marriage and their matrimonial domicile was established here. The purpose in having the ceremony take place in Indiana was to evade New Jersey's marriage policy and we see no just or compelling reason for permitting it to succeed. . . .

. . .   We are not here concerned with a collateral attack on an Indiana marriage or with a direct attack on an Indiana marriage between domiciliaries of Indiana or some state other than New Jersey. We are concerned only with a direct and timely proceeding, authorized by the New Jersey statute (N.J.S. 2A:34–1(e), N.J.S.A.), by an underage wife for annulment of an Indiana marriage between parties who have at all times been domiciled in New Jersey. We are satisfied that at least in this situation the strong public policy of New Jersey (see Restatement, Conflict of Laws § 132(b), comment b) requires that the annulment be granted. The annulment will not render the plaintiff's child illegitimate (N.J.S. 2A:34–20, N.J.S.A.) and, as the Chancery Division found, it will be for his best interests. The annulment will also serve the plaintiff's best interests for it will tend to reduce the tragic consequences of her immature conduct and unfortunate marriage. The Legislature has clearly fixed the State's policy in her favor and has granted her the right to apply for a judgment nullifying her marriage; we know of no considerations of equity or justice or overriding principles of the law which would lead us to deprive her of the relief she seeks under the circumstances she presents.   . . .

Reversed.

NOTE

Were different issues involved in May v. May and Wilkins v. Zelichowski? Can the decisions be reconciled on this basis?

SECTION 5.   PROPERTY

The concept of property, in the sense of legally protected interests, has many dimensions in choice-of-law contexts. Property interests take varied forms and have a correspondingly varied set of terms: Immovable or real for land; movable or personal for chattels; intangible or incorporeal for choses in action, claims, expectancies, and the like. Even if the main heads of property are sufficiently distinct to avoid problems of classification among them, there is nevertheless much elasticity in the characterization process in dealing with even the tangible forms.

One example of a familiar type of characterization exercise occurs in the case of a contract executed by seller and buyer in state Y for the conveyance of land in state X. The orthodox choice-of-law rule, referring questions regarding land to the place of the situs, state X, might not even be mentioned by a court determined to look upon the problem as one involving the validity or interpretation of a contract— questions that state Y's "law" would determine, since Y was the place of contracting. Tort characterization offered another form of elasticity. Suppose a creditor claimed the contract was designed to defraud him. He would no doubt attempt to invoke a tort choice-of-law rule if that served his advantage. The following cases are illustrative.

IN RE ESTATE OF BARRIE

Supreme Court of Iowa, 1949.
240 Iowa 431, 35 N.W.2d 658.

HAYS, J.—Appeal from an order overruling a motion to strike objections to petition for probate of the alleged last will and testament of Mary E. Barrie, deceased.

Mary E. Barrie, domiciled in Whiteside County, Illinois, died owning real and personal property in Illinois and real property in Tama County, Iowa. The instrument in question was offered for probate in Whiteside County, Illinois. Although first admitted to probate, it was later denied probate after the Illinois Supreme Court had ruled that said instrument had been revoked by cancellation and that decedent died intestate.

Thereafter the instrument was offered for probate in Tama County, Iowa, by one of the beneficiaries named therein. To the petition for probate, decedent's heirs at law filed objections based upon the judgment of the Illinois Supreme Court, to the effect that the said last will and testament had been revoked. Objectors assert that this judgment is conclusive upon the Iowa courts. Proponent's motion to strike said objections for the reason that they do not constitute a valid basis for denying probate, being overruled by the trial court, this appeal was taken.

The instrument offered for probate was duly signed by decedent and witnessed by two witnesses. . . . When found, after the death of decedent, the instrument had the word "void" written across its face in at least five places, including the attestation clause. Also, upon the cover and upon the envelope containing same appears the word "void" written with the name "M. E. Barrie" and "Mary E. Barrie." The Illinois court found that the writing of the word "void" on the instrument, as above related, constituted a revocation by cancellation within the purview of the Illinois Revised Statutes, 1945, chapter 3, section 197. This statute provides for the revocation of a will ". . . (a) by burning, cancelling, tearing, or obliterating it by the testator."

No question is raised as to the due execution of the instrument either under the Illinois or the Iowa statutes. No question is raised as to the testamentary capacity of decedent, nor is it claimed by the objectors that there has been a revocation under the Iowa statute, section 633.10, Code of 1946. The question before this court for determination may be stated thus, "Is the judgment of the Illinois court, holding that said instrument had been revoked and that decedent died intestate, conclusive and binding upon the Iowa courts?" . . .

Decedent was a nonresident of the state and died owning property in Tama county which was subject to administration. Clearly the district court of Tama county has original jurisdiction to probate this instrument unless the Illinois judgment has the effect of nullifying or modifying said statute. . . . That this is in accordance with the recognized rule, see Restatement of the Law, Conflict of Laws, section 469, which states: "The will of a deceased person can be admitted to probate in a competent court of any state in which an administrator could have been appointed had the decedent died intestate", and under comment c of said provision: "Probate in a state other than at the domicil can be had although the will has not been admitted to probate in the state of the decedent's domicil." . . .

Section 633.33, Code of 1946, provides: "A will probated in any other state or country shall be admitted to probate in this state, without the notice required in the case of domestic wills, on the production of a copy thereof and of the original record of probate."

Upon the general question as to the validity, operation, effect, etc. of a will by which property is devised, there are certain well-established and generally recognized rules, and which definitely differentiate between movable (personal) and immovable (real) property. We are only concerned with immovables in the instant case.

The general rule as stated in Story on Conflict of Laws, Eighth Ed., page 651, is, "the doctrine is clearly established at the common law, that the law of the place where the property [speaking of real (immovable) property] is locally situate is to govern as to the capacity or the incapacity of the testator . . . the forms and solemnities to give the will or testament its due attestation and effect." . . . Restatement of the Law, Conflict of Laws, section 249, states: "The validity and effect of a will of an interest in land are determined by the law of the state where the land is." Upon the specific question as to revocation of a will, . . . Restatement of the Law, Conflict of Laws, section 250, says: "The effectiveness of an intended revocation of a will of an interest in land is determined by the law of the state where the land is." . . .

. . .

Under the above-stated rule Iowa courts are free to place their construction, interpretation and sanction upon the will of a nonresident of the state who dies owning real property within the state whether the will be admitted to probate under section 604.3 or section 633.33, Code of 1946, both supra, although it has been admitted to probate in the state of the domicile of testator. . . .

Does a different rule pertain where instead of being admitted to probate in the domicile state probate is denied? We think not. It is generally held that the full faith and credit provision of the Constitution of the United States, Article IV, section 1, does not render foreign decrees of probate conclusive as to the validity of a will as respects real property situated in a state other than the one in which the decree was rendered, nor does the doctrine of res adjudicata or estoppel by judgment apply. . . .

. . .

. . . To hold that an act which constitutes a revocation in one state is a revocation in another state where under the law the act does not constitute a revocation is contrary to the general rule, which is stated in 57 Am.Jur., Wills, section 493, to be, "where a statute prescribes the method and acts by which a will may be revoked, no acts other than those mentioned in the statute are to operate as a revocation, no matter how clearly appears the purpose of the testator to revoke his will and his belief that such purpose has been accomplished." . . . That the acts held to be a revocation in Illinois do not constitute such in Iowa, see section 633.10, Code of 1946. . . .

Section 633.49, Code of 1946 provides:

"A last will and testament executed without this state, in the mode prescribed by the law either of the place where executed or of the testator's domicile, shall be deemed to be legally executed, and shall be of the same force and effect as if executed in the mode prescribed by the laws of this state, provided said last will and testament is in writing and subscribed by the testator."

This statute has not been before this court, so far as the writer of this opinion can find. It is clearly a modification of the common law and should not be extended to include matters not clearly included therein. It specifically deals with the formalities in the execution of the will, and nothing more. No question of execution is here involved. That the legislature might have waived the common-law rule as applicable to revocations as well as to the formal execution, as it has done, cannot be denied. However, the legislature has not seen fit to do so. . . . The statute is not applicable.

We hold that the Illinois judgment denying probate to the will in question is not conclusive and binding upon the courts of this state in so far as the disposition of the Iowa real estate is concerned; that the objections filed to the petition do not constitute a basis for denying probate of the will and the appellant's motion to strike should have been sustained. Reversed and remanded for an order in accordance herewith.—Reversed and remanded.

SMITH, J. (dissenting)

. . .

III. It is true of course that Code section 633.49 refers to *execution* and not directly to *revocation*; and we have here a document, held in Illinois to be nontestamentary, because of *revocation* and not because of any defect in original *execution.* In other words, we have an instrument not merely "executed" but also *revoked* "without this state, in the mode prescribed by the law . . . of the testator's domicile."

But revocation is merely the converse of execution. The power to execute implies the power to revoke. A will can no longer be said to be *executed* after it has been *revoked.* Whether an instrument is a will is determined not only by the manner of its execution but also by the manner of its attempted revocation. Both acts are a part of the testamentary process. It is unthinkable that our legislature intended to require recognition of the laws of another jurisdiction in the matter of one and not of the other.

. . .

The purpose of both Code sections 633.33 and 633.49 must have been to abolish or minimize confusion and conflict between states in the matter of handling wills. Foreign ownership of property has become common. Owners of property in different jurisdictions should not be required in making and revoking their wills to do more than comply with the law of their own domiciles, or with the law of the jurisdiction where the instrument is drawn or revoked. . . .

. . .

The fundamental error in the majority opinion is in assuming that the validity of an instrument offered as a *foreign* will is to be determined by the same standard that would determine its status if offered as a *domestic* will. But the Iowa statutes establish a different standard without any differentiation between real and personal property. The lex loci rei sitae is in that respect changed. Code section 633.49 is just as effective in its field as are our general statutes prescribing the forms and solemnities for the execution and revocation of domestic wills.

NOTE

Can the decision be justified on the ground that Iowa was the state with the greater interest in the determination of the issue involved? Would application of Illinois law have made more difficult the task of searching title to Iowa land?

———

Problems of characterization must frequently be reckoned with. A provision in a contract dealing with land may be held to be contractual in character and hence governed by choice-of-law principles applicable to contracts. Mallory Associates, Inc. v. Barving Realty Co., 300 N.Y. 297, 90 N.E.2d 468 (1949) (discussed in Note (4), p. 765, infra). Even when the issue involves the specific enforcement of a contract for the conveyance of land, the court may look upon the problem as one involving the validity or interpretation of a contract and hence apply the law governing the contract rather than the law of the state of the situs. Polson v. Stewart, 167 Mass. 211, 45 N.E. 737 (1897) (set forth at p. 762, infra). Likewise, it may be claimed that a conveyance of an interest in land was tortious in character and that, accordingly, the law governing the tort should be applied to determine whether the transferee should be ordered to reconvey. Irving Trust Co. v. Maryland Casualty Co., 83 F.2d 168 (2d Cir. 1968) (set forth at p. 769, infra).

YOUSSOUPOFF v. WIDENER

Court of Appeals of New York, 1927.
246 N.Y. 174, 158 N.E. 64.

[In 1921, the plaintiff, Prince Youssoupoff, a Russian refugee in dire need of funds, entered into an arrangement for the sale or transfer of two Rembrandt portraits to the defendant, Mr. Widener of Pennsylvania, for one hundred thousand pounds. The negotiations were entered into in England. The writing evidencing the transaction was executed by the defendant in Pennsylvania and was sent to his agent in London, where it was executed by the plaintiff and duly delivered. Thereupon the portraits were delivered to the defendant's representative in London and were removed to the defendant's residence in Pennsylvania.

The writing evidencing the transaction provided: ". . . Mr. Widener grants to Prince Youssoupoff the right and privilege to be exercised on or before January 1, 1924 and not thereafter, of repurchasing these pictures at the purchase price, one hundred thousand pounds (£100,000) plus eight per cent. (8%) interest from this date to the date of repurchase; the repurchase to be made in the City of Philadelphia and the pictures to be redelivered to Prince Youssoupoff upon payment of the full purchase money.

"This privilege is a purely personal one granted to Prince Youssoupoff in recognition of his love and appreciation of these wonderful pictures. It is not assignable nor will it inure to the benefit of his heirs, assigns or representatives and Prince Youssoupoff represents that this privilege of repurchase will be exercised only in case he finds himself in the position again to keep and personally enjoy these wonderful works of art. . . ."

In 1923, the plaintiff tendered to the defendant in Pennsylvania in money of the United States the equivalent of the stipulated one hundred thousand pounds plus interest at eight per cent., and demanded the return of the portraits; but the money so tendered was borrowed by the plaintiff from a lender with whom the portraits if returned by the defendant were to be pledged as security.]

LEHMAN, J. . . . The defendant declined the tender and refused to transfer the pictures to the plaintiff. In effect the defendant's reply to the plaintiff's demand is that the defendant is the absolute owner of the pictures under the contract of sale, subject only to the right of the plaintiff to repurchase the pictures in accordance with the terms contained in the contract. That right is, by its terms, to be exercised only in case the plaintiff "finds himself in the position again to keep and personally enjoy these wonderful works of art." It may not be exercised for the purpose of enabling the plaintiff to transfer the pictures to another. . . .

The plaintiff has brought this action in equity to compel the defendant to accept the money tendered to him, and to transfer the pictures.

It is said . . . that under the law of Pennsylvania, where Mr. Widener resided, where he kept his collection of paintings and where any option to repurchase must be exercised, the contract between the parties hereto would be conclusively presumed to be a mortgage, regardless of the actual intention of the parties, and enforced only as a mortgage. The courts below have made no finding to that effect. We have not analyzed the testimony or the Pennsylvania decisions introduced in evidence to determine whether they would support such a finding. We hold that the law of England and not the law of Pennsylvania governs this transaction.

The general rule is well established that the construction and legal effect of a contract for the transfer of, or the creation of a lien upon, property situated in the jurisdiction where the contract is made is governed by the law of that jurisdiction. (Goetschius v. Brightman, 245 N.Y. 186, 156 N.E. 360.) Various grounds, however, are urged upon which it is said that this case presents an exception to the general rule. We dispose of them briefly. . . .

The fact that Mr. Widener obtained the pictures with the intention of removing them to his home, does not change the general rule. It is true that it has been held in some States that where property, transferred by contract in one jurisdiction, must be removed to another jurisdiction in order to carry out the purpose of the contract, the construction and effect of the contract may be governed, in accordance with the intention of the parties, not by the law of the jurisdiction where the contract was made and where the property was then situated, but by the law of the jurisdiction to which the property was removed thereafter and where the parties intended that it should be permanently located. (Beggs v. Bartels, 73 Conn. 132, 46 A. 874.) We need not now consider whether upon a similar state of facts we should reach a similar conclusion. If under such circumstances exception to the general rule may be created, that may be done only for the purpose of carrying out a presumed intention of the parties. Here the parties have given convincing evidence that the parties intended that the law of England should apply. . . .

Finally, it is said that since the provisions for the repurchase of the paintings in Pennsylvania were the only executory provisions of the contract, we should construe the contract according to the law of Pennsylvania where performance was to be made. (International Text Book Co. v. Connelly, 206 N.Y. 188, 99 N.E. 722.) The contract in effect is primarily a bill of sale of the paintings, and was so intended. The right to repurchase was merely an incident to the transfer. The transfer of title was completed simultaneously with the signing of the contract. The parties certainly did not intend the law of Pennsylvania should apply to the transfer of property completed in England by contract made and dated there and by delivery accepted there. Under the law of England, full ownership was then transferred to the defendant, subject only to a condition that plaintiff should have a limited right to repurchase in Pennsylvania. Since full ownership had then been transferred to the defendant, and the plaintiff no longer held an equity of redemption, he might regain the pictures only by exercising his option of repurchase in accordance with the provisions of the contract. If we assume that the parties intended that the law of Pennsylvania should apply to the provisions giving an option of repurchase, and construe those provisions accordingly (Hamlyn & Co. v. Talisker Distillery, [1894] Appeal Cases 202), we must begin construction upon the basis, fatal to plaintiff's claim, that these provisions apply to property of which the defendant is the full owner and in which the plaintiff has no equity of redemption. . . .

Judgment affirmed, etc.

NOTES

(1) When faced with the question of what law governs a consensual transaction involving movables, should a court adopt the approach ordinarily used in contracts cases, i.e., "place of making," "place of performance," or an approach based on property concepts, i.e., "title," "situs"? Which approach was used in the principal case?

(2) See Cavers, The Conditional Seller's Remedies and the Choice-of-Law Process, 35 N.Y.U.L.Rev. 1126 (1960).

CAMMELL v. SEWELL

Court of Exchequer Chamber, 1860.
5 Hurl. & N. 728.

[Action of trover for lumber, with a count for money had and received. The plaintiffs were English underwriters and the defendants were London merchants.

The lumber had been part of a cargo shipped on board a Prussian vessel from a Russian port to a firm in Hull, England, and insured with the plaintiffs.

The Prussian ship put into Norwegian waters in consequence of the shifting of the deck cargo, and was driven on rocks off the Norwegian coast. The cargo was unloaded, and the master of the ship applied to a Norwegian official to fix a day for the sale of the cargo at auction. This was done and the cargo was sold to one Clausen. The plaintiffs, having paid the Hull firm as for a total loss, instituted proceedings in Norway against the master and the purchaser of the cargo to have the action disavowed, but the court confirmed it. After the auction sale but before the judicial confirmation, the purchaser at the auction sale forwarded the lumber to the defendants in London, who refused to deliver it to the plaintiffs on demand.

The present action was thereupon instituted. After a verdict for the plaintiffs, subject to a special case, in the Court of Exchequer, the verdict for the plaintiffs was set aside and a verdict entered for the defendants. (3 Hurl. & N. 617.)

Proceedings in error were instituted in the Exchequer Chamber.]

CROMPTON, J. In this case the majority of the Court are of opinion that the judgment of the Court of Exchequer should be affirmed. At the same time we are by no means prepared to agree with the Court of Exchequer in thinking the judgment of the Diocesan Court in Norway conclusive as a judgment in rem, nor are we satisfied that the defendants in the present action were estopped by the judgment of that Court or what was relied on as a judicial proceeding at the auction. It is not, however, necessary for us to express any decided opinion on these questions, as we think that the case should be determined on the real merits as to the passing of the property.

If we are to recognize the Norwegian law, and if according to that law the property passed by the sale in Norway to Clausen as an innocent purchaser, we do not think that the subsequent bringing the property to England can alter the position of the parties. . . . it appears to us that the questions are—did the property by the law of Norway vest in him as an innocent purchaser? and are we to recognize that law? . . . The conclusion which we draw from the evidence is, that by the law of Norway the captain, under circumstances such as existed in this case, could not, as between himself and his owners, or the owners of the cargo, justify the sale, but that he remained liable and responsible to them for a sale not justified under the circumstances; whilst, on the other hand, an innocent purchaser would have a good title to the property bought by him from the agent of the owners.

It does not appear to us that there is anything so barbarous or monstrous in this state of the law as that we can say that it should not be recognized by us. . . . We think that the law on this subject was correctly stated by the Lord Chief Baron in the course of the argument in the Court below, where he says "If personal property is disposed of in a manner binding according to the law of the country where it is, that disposition is binding everywhere." And we do not think that it makes any difference that the goods were wrecked, and not intended to be sent to the country where they were sold. We do not think that the goods which were wrecked here would on that account be the less liable to our laws as to market overt, or as to the landlord's right of distress, because the owner did not foresee that they would come to England. . . .

. . . as, on the evidence before us, we cannot treat Clausen otherwise than as an innocent purchaser, and as the law of Norway appears to us, on the evidence, to give a title to an innocent purchaser, we think that the property vested in him, and in the defendants as subpurchasers from him, and that, having once so vested, it did not become devested by its being subsequently brought to this country, and, therefore, that the judgment of the Court of Exchequer should be affirmed.

BYLES, J. This alleged law of Norway . . . placing the cargo at the caprice of the master, seems to me to be a law not only of an alarming nature, but so far as I can perceive without precedent, without necessity and at variance with the general maritime law of the world, at least as understood in this country. I think the comity of nations would not recognize a law of this character . . .

I admit, if there be a judgment in rem founded on a recognized law, and pronounced by a competent tribunal of the country where a movable chattel then is, that that judgment determines and changes the property everywhere and between all persons, as in the cases of a condemnation of goods in the Exchequer, or of a ship in a lawful prize Court.

. . . I collect that the opinion of the rest of the Court is that there has been no judgment in rem, and I entirely agree with them. . . . At the time of that judgment the goods in question were not within the jurisdiction of the Diocesan Court, for they had long before arrived in England.

As to the effect of the same judgment as a judgment inter partes, I collect that both the parties to this action are not in privity with that judgment, because the defendant's title to the deals had accrued before the judgment. This is not a mere objection of form against the justice of the case. For that judgment is contended to be an estoppel, and not examinable. . . .

But as the rest of the Court are of a different opinion on the first point, the judgment of the Court of Exchequer will be affirmed.

Judgment affirmed.

NOTES

(1) Is the problem presented by the principal case essentially different from that in Youssoupoff v. Widener? If so, does it call for the application of a different choice of law rule?

(2) The principal case was not an action to determine title but a suit in trover for conversion. Where did the defendant commit the alleged exercise of dominion or refusal to return on demand? What is normally the controlling law in tort cases?

(3) For a modern case citing Cammell v. Sewell and reaching the same result, see Winkworth v. Christie, Manson and Woods, Ltd. [1980] 2 W.L.R. 937.

SECTION 6. CHANGING CHOICE–OF–LAW APPROACHES, INTERNATIONAL AND INTERSTATE

LAURITZEN v. LARSEN

Supreme Court of the United States, 1952.
345 U.S. 571, 73 S.Ct. 921, 97 L.Ed. 1254.

MR. JUSTICE JACKSON delivered the opinion of the Court.

The key issue in this case is whether statutes of the United States should be applied to this claim of maritime tort. Larsen, a Danish seaman, while temporarily in New York joined the crew of the *Randa*, a ship of Danish flag and registry, owned by petitioner, a Danish citizen. Larsen signed ship's articles, written in Danish, providing that the rights of crew members would be governed by Danish law and by the employer's contract with the Danish Seamen's Union, of which Larsen was a member. He was negligently injured aboard the *Randa* in the course of employment, while in Havana harbor.

Respondent brought suit under the Jones Act on the law side of the District Court for the Southern District of New York and demanded a jury. Petitioner contended that Danish law was applicable and that, under it, respondent had received all of the compensation to which he was entitled. [The district court ruled that American rather than Danish law applied and gave judgment for the plaintiff.] The Court of Appeals, Second Circuit, affirmed.

[The Supreme Court first conceded that taken literally the Jones Act applied, but]

. . . it has long been accepted in maritime jurisprudence that " . . . if any construction otherwise be possible, an Act will not be construed as applying to foreigners in respect to acts done by them outside the dominions of the sovereign power enacting. That is a rule based on international law, by which one sovereign power is bound to respect the subjects and the rights of all other sovereign powers outside its own territory." Lord Russell of Killowen in The Queen v. Jameson [1896], 2 Q.B. 425, 430. . . .

Congress could not have been unaware of the necessity of construction imposed upon courts by such generality of language and . . . that in the absence of more definite directions than are contained in the Jones Act it would be applied by the courts to foreign events, foreign ships and foreign seamen only in accordance with the usual doctrine and practices of maritime law.

Respondent places great stress upon the assertion that petitioner's commerce and contacts with the ports of the United States are frequent and regular . . .   But the virtue and utility of sea-borne commerce lies in its frequent and important contacts with more than one country. If, to serve some immediate interest, the courts of each were to exploit every such contact to the limit of its power, it is not difficult to see that a multiplicity of conflicting and overlapping burdens would blight international carriage by sea. . . .

Maritime law, like our municipal law, has attempted to avoid or resolve conflicts between competing laws by ascertaining and valuing points of contact between the transaction and the states or governments whose competing laws are involved. The criteria, in general, appear to be arrived at from weighing of the significance of one or more connecting factors between the shipping transaction regulated and the national interest served by the assertion of authority. . . .

  . . .   in dealing with international commerce we cannot be unmindful of the necessity for mutual forbearance if retaliations are to be avoided; nor should we forget that any contact which we hold sufficient to warrant application of our law to a foreign transaction will logically be as strong a warrant for a foreign country to apply its law to an American transaction.

In the case before us, two foreign nations can claim some connecting factor with this tort—Denmark, because, among other reasons, the ship and the seaman were Danish nationals; Cuba, because the tortious conduct occurred and caused injury in Cuban waters. The United States may also claim contacts because the seaman had been hired in and was returned to the United States, which also is the state of the forum. We therefore review the several factors which, alone or in combination, are generally conceded to influence choice of law to govern a tort claim, particularly a maritime tort claim, and the weight and significance accorded them.

1. *Place of the Wrongful Act.*—The solution most commonly accepted as to torts in our municipal and in international law is to supply the law of the place where the acts giving rise to the liability occurred, the *lex loci delicti commissi*. This rule . . . would indicate application of the law of Cuba, in whose domain the actionable wrong took place. The test of location of the wrongful act or omission, however sufficient for torts ashore, is of limited application to shipboard torts, because of the varieties of legal authority over waters she may navigate. . . .

2. *Law of the Flag.*—Perhaps the most venerable and universal rule of maritime law relevant to our problem is that which gives cardinal importance to the law of the flag. . . .

3. *Allegiance or Domicile of the Injured.* . . . the long-standing rule . . . was that the nationality of the vessel for jurisdictional purposes was attributed to all her crew. . . . Surely during service under a foreign flag some duty of allegiance is due. But, also, each nation has a legitimate interest that its nationals and permanent inhabitants be not maimed or disabled from self-support. . . . We need not, however, weigh the seaman's nationality against that of the ship, for here the two coincide without resort to fiction. . . .

4. *Allegiance of the Defendant Shipowner.*— . . . in recent years a practice has grown, particularly among American shipowners, to avoid stringent shipping laws by seeking foreign registration . . . Confronted with such operations, our courts on occasion have pressed beyond the formalities of more or less nominal foreign registration to enforce against American shipowners the obligations which our law places upon them. But here . . . it appears beyond doubt that this owner is a Dane by nationality and domicile.

5. *Place of Contract.*—Place of contract, which was New York, is the factor on which respondent chiefly relies to invoke American law. . . .

The place of contracting in this instance . . . was fortuitous. . . . The practical effect of making the *lex loci contractus* govern all tort claims during the service would be to subject a ship to a multitude of systems of law, to put some of the crew in a more advantageous position than others, and not unlikely in the long run to diminish hirings in ports of countries that take best care of their seamen.

But if contract law is nonetheless to be considered, we face the fact that this contract was explicit that the Danish law and the contract with the Danish union were to control. . . .

6. *Inaccessibility of Foreign Forum.*—It is argued . . . that justice requires adjudication under American law to save seamen expense and loss of time in returning to a foreign forum. This might be a persuasive argument for exercising a discretionary jurisdiction to adjudge a controversy; but it is not persuasive as to the law by which it shall be judged. . . .

7. *The Law of the Forum.*—It is urged that, since an American forum has perfected its jurisdiction over the parties and defendant does more or less frequent and regular business within the forum state, it should apply its own law to the controversy between them. . . . The purpose of a conflict-of-laws doctrine is to assure that a case will be treated in the same way under the appropriate law regardless of the fortuitous circumstances which often determine the forum. Jurisdiction of maritime cases in all countries is so wide and the nature of its subject matter so far-flung that there would be no justification for altering the law of a controversy just because local jurisdiction of the parties is obtainable. . . .

This review of the connecting factors which either maritime law or our municipal law of conflicts regards as significant in determining the law applicable to a claim of actionable wrong shows an overwhelming preponderance in favor of Danish law. . . . [The decision below was reversed on the theory that Danish, not American, law applied. Justice Black dissented.]

TIMBERLANE LUMBER CO. v. BANK OF AMERICA, NATIONAL TRUST & SAVINGS ASSOCIATION

United States Court of Appeals, Ninth Circuit, 1976.
549 F.2d 597.

CHOY, CIRCUIT JUDGE:

. . . This action raises important questions concerning the application of American antitrust laws to activities in another country, including actions of foreign government officials. The district court dismissed the Timberlane action under the act of state doctrine and for lack of subject matter jurisdiction. . . . We vacate . . . and remand.

I.   The Timberlane Action

The basic allegation of the Timberlane plaintiffs is that officials of the Bank of America and others located in both the United States and Honduras conspired to prevent Timberlane, through its Honduras subsidiaries, from milling lumber in Honduras and exporting it to the United States, thus maintaining control of the Honduran lumber export business in the hands of a few select individuals financed and controlled by the Bank. The intent and result of the conspiracy, they contend, was to interfere with the exportation to the United States, including Pureto Rico, of Honduran lumber for sale or use there by the plaintiffs, thus directly and substantially affecting the foreign commerce of the United States.

Procedural Background

Some of the defendants moved to dismiss the Timberlane action. After a hearing . . ., the district court granted the motion in a brief judgment entered on March 20, 1974. The court gave as its reason "that it is prohibited under the act of state doctrine from examining the acts of a foreign sovereign state; and in any event, that there is no direct and substantial effect on United States foreign commerce," . . .

. . .

It is apparent that the [act-of-state] doctrine does not bestow a blank-check immunity upon all conduct blessed with some imprimatur of a foreign government. In Continental Ore Co. v. Union Carbide &

Carbon Corp., 370 U.S. 690 (1962), the Canadian government had made a private corporation its exclusive agent for the purchase of vanadium, a material used in steel production. The Canadian corporation, acting in concert with an affiliated American company, used its position to exclude a competitor of the American affiliate from the Canadian market. The Court held that the Canadian corporation's activity was not entitled to immunity, carefully noting that the plaintiff did not question the validity of any action taken by the Canadian government and that there was no indication that any Canadian government official "approved or would have approved" of the monopolizing efforts. Id. at 706.

. . .

A corollary to the act of state doctrine in the foreign trade antitrust field is the often-recognized principle that corporate conduct which is compelled by a foreign sovereign is also protected from antitrust liability, as if it were an act of the state itself. . . .

On the other hand, mere governmental approval or foreign governmental involvement which the defendants had arranged does not necessarily provide a defense. In United States v. Sisal Sales Corp., 274 U.S. 268 (1927), the defendants were accused of conspiring to monopolize sales of sisal, a material used in making rope, from Mexico to the United States by inducing Mexican officials to recognize the conspirators as the exclusive traders and to impose discriminatory taxes on rival sellers. The Court rejected the defendants' claim to act of state protection, ruling that a conspiracy formed in the United States for the purpose of monopolizing sales to the United States was not protected simply because one element of the conspiracy involved securing favorable action by foreign officials. In *Continental Ore*, the Court indicated that it continued to accept the *Sisal* reasoning. See 370 U.S. at 705. . . .

Extraterritorial Reach of the United States Antitrust Laws

There is no doubt that American antitrust laws extend over some conduct in other nations. . . .

That American law covers some conduct beyond this nation's borders does not mean that it embraces all, however. Extraterritorial application is understandably a matter of concern for the other countries involved. Those nations have sometimes resented and protested, as excessive intrusions into their own spheres, broad assertions of authority by American courts. . . . In any event, it is evident that at some point the interests of the United States are too weak and the foreign harmony incentive for restraint too strong to justify an extraterritorial assertion of jurisdiction.

What that point is or how it is determined is not defined by international law. . . .

It is the effect on American foreign commerce which is usually cited to support extraterritorial jurisdiction. *Alcoa* [United States v. Aluminum Co. of America, 148 F.2d 416 (2d Cir. 1945)] set the course, when Judge Hand declared, id.:

> [I]t is settled law . . . that any state may impose liabilities, even upon persons not within its allegiance, for conduct outside its borders that has consequences within its borders which the state reprehends; and these liabilities other states will ordinarily recognize.

. . . Few cases have discussed the nature of the effect required for jurisdiction, perhaps because most of the litigated cases have involved relatively obvious offenses and rather significant and apparent effects on competition within the United States. . . . The effects test by itself is incomplete because it fails to consider other nations' interests. Nor does it expressly take into account the full nature of the relationship between the actors and this country. Whether the alleged offender is an American citizen, for instance, may make a big difference; applying American laws to American citizens raises fewer problems than application to foreigners. . . .

A tripartite analysis seems to be indicated. As acknowledged above, the antitrust laws require in the first instance that there be *some* effect—actual or intended—on American foreign commerce before the federal courts may legitimately exercise subject matter jurisdiction under those statutes. Second, a greater showing of burden or restraint may be necessary to demonstrate that the effect is sufficiently large to present a cognizable injury to the plaintiffs and, therefore, a civil *violation* of the antitrust laws. . . . Third, there is the additional question which is unique to the international setting of whether the interests of, and links to, the United States—including the magnitude of the effect on American foreign commerce—are sufficiently strong, vis-à-vis those of other nations, to justify an assertion of extraterritorial authority.

It is this final issue which is both obscured by undue reliance on the "substantiality" test and complicated to resolve. An effect on United States commerce, although necessary to the exercise of jurisdiction under the antitrust laws, is alone not a sufficient basis on which to determine whether American authority *should* be asserted in a given case as a matter of international comity and fairness. In some cases, the application of the direct and substantial test in the international context might open the door too widely by sanctioning jurisdiction over an action when these considerations would indicate dismissal. At other times, it may fail in the other direction, dismissing a case for which comity and fairness do not require forebearance, thus closing the jurisdictional door too tightly—for the Sherman Act does reach some restraints which do not have both a direct and substantial effect on the foreign commerce of the United

States. A more comprehensive inquiry is necessary. We believe that the field of conflict of laws presents the proper approach . . . .

The act of state doctrine discussed earlier demonstrates that the judiciary is sometimes cognizant of the possible foreign implications of its action. Similar awareness should be extended to the general problems of extraterritoriality. Such acuity is especially required in private suits, like this one, for in these cases there is no opportunity for the executive branch to weigh the foreign relations impact, nor any statement implicit in the filing of the suit that that consideration has been outweighed. . . .

. . .

The elements to be weighed include the degree of conflict with foreign law or policy, the nationality or allegiance of the parties and the locations or principal places of business of corporations, the extent to which enforcement by either state can be expected to achieve compliance, the relative significance of effects on the United States as compared with those elsewhere, the extent to which there is explicit purpose to harm or affect American commerce, the foreseeability of such effect, and the relative importance to the violations charged of conduct within the United States as compared with conduct abroad. A court evaluating these factors should identify the potential degree of conflict if American authority is asserted. A difference in law or policy is one likely sore spot, though one which may not always be present. Nationality is another; though foreign governments may have some concern for the treatment of American citizens and business residing there, they primarily care about their own nationals. Having assessed the conflict, the court should then determine whether in the face of it the contacts and interests of the United States are sufficient to support the exercise of extraterritorial jurisdiction.

We conclude, then, that the problem should be approached in three parts: Does the alleged restraint affect, or was it intended to affect, the foreign commerce of the United States? Is it of such a type and magnitude so as to be cognizable as a violation of the Sherman Act? As a matter of international comity and fairness, should the extraterritorial jurisdiction of the United States be asserted to cover it? The district court's judgment found only that the restraint involved in the instant suit did not produce a direct and substantial effect on American foreign commerce. That holding does not satisfy any of these inquiries. . . .

The comity question is more complicated. From Timberlane's complaint it is evident that there are grounds for concern as to at least a few of the defendants, for some are identified as foreign citizens: Laureano Gutierrez Falla, Michael Casanova and the Casanova firms, of Honduras, and Patrick Byrne, of Canada. Moreover, it is clear that most of the activity took place in Honduras, though the conspiracy may have been directed from San Francisco, and that the most direct economic effect was probably on Honduras. However, there has been no indication of any conflict with the law or policy of the Honduran government, nor any comprehensive analysis of the relative connections and interests of Honduras and the United States. Under these circumstances, the dismissal by the district court cannot be sustained on jurisdictional grounds.

We, therefore, vacate the dismissal and remand the Timberlane action.

NOTE

For a later case which also follows a balancing approach to determine whether the anti-trust laws should be given extraterritorial application, see Mannington Mills, Inc. v. Congoleum Corp., 595 F.2d 1287 (3d Cir. 1979).

NOTE ON EXTRATERRITORIAL APPLICATION OF UNITED STATES LAW

The extent to which United States laws may properly be applied to conduct abroad depends upon whether doing so furthers the laws' purposes and is consistent with good international relations. In the past, courts in the United States focused mainly on the first factor and evinced little concern for whether application of United States laws would impinge upon foreign interests and foreign sensitivities. Today the courts are more responsive to the international aspects of the situation when they are asked to extend extraterritorial application to American laws. The general field is covered in 402, 403, 415, 416, and 418 of the Restatement of Foreign Relations Law of the United States (Revised) (Tent. Draft No. 2, 1981) and extensive Reporter's Notes thereto.

What has been said above is particularly true of the extraterritorial application of the antitrust laws. Initially, the courts were concerned almost entirely with implementing the purposes of these laws. See, e.g., United States v. Aluminum Co. of America, 148 F.2d 416 (2d Cir. 1945); United States v. Imperial Chemical Industries, 100 F.Supp. 504 (S.D.N.Y.1951), supplemented 105 F.Supp. 215 (1952). As a result, the resentment of foreign countries was frequently aroused, and sometimes American judgments were refused recognition and enforcement. See, e.g., British Nylon Spinners, Ltd. v. Imperial Chemical Industries, Ltd. [1952], 2 All.E.R. 88. On occasion, indeed, foreign countries law enacted legislation to impede the enforcement of the antitrust laws. See Lowe, Blocking Extraterritorial Jurisdiction: The British Protection of Trading Interests Act of 1980. The Act is discussed in Lowenfeld, Sovereign Jurisdiction and Reasonableness: A Reply to A.V. Lowe, 75 Am.J.Int.Law 629 (1981). The heightened alertness of American courts to foreign interests and sensitivities is evidenced in the balancing approach adopted by the courts in the Timberlane and Mannington Mills cases, supra. See also Restatement of Foreign Relations Law of the United States (Revised) § 415 (Tent. Draft No. 2, 1981).

A similar trend can be noted in the extraterritorial application of our securities laws and of the Lanham Trade Mark Act. See Leasco Data Processing Equipment Co. v. Maxwell, 468 F.2d 1326 (2d Cir. 1972); American Rice, Inc. v. Arkansas Rice Growers, 701 F.2d 408 (5th Cir. 1983); Restatement of Foreign Relations Law of the United States (Revised), § 416 (Tent. Draft No. 2, 1981). Comment; The Transnational Reach of Rule 10b–5, 121 U.Pa.L.Rev. 1363 (1973).

The United States has also sought on occasion to prevent subsidiaries of American corporations from trading with countries considered to be hostile. Such actions have at times evoked diplomatic challenges and interference by foreign courts. See, e.g., Fruehauf Corp. v. Massardy, [1968] D.S.Jur. 147, [1965] J.C.P.II 14,000, 274 bis. (Cour d'appel, Paris); Restatement of Foreign Relations Law of the United States (Revised), § 418 (Tent. Draft No. 2, 1981).

To date, U.S. labor laws have been applied to protect American employees working abroad for an American employer on a U.S. naval base. See, e.g., Vermilya-Brown Co. v. Connell, 335 U.S. 377 (1948); cf. Foley Brothers v. Filardo, 336 U.S. 281 (1948) (labor laws not applied to American employees working for American employer in a foreign country). Relying upon what they perceived to be the intent of Congress, American courts have refused to apply our labor laws to foreign seamen on foreign ships. See, e.g., International Longshoremen's Association, Local 1416 v. Ariadne Shipping Co., 397 U.S. 195 (1970); Incres Steamship Co. v. International Maritime Workers Union, 372 U.S. 24 (1963); McCulloch v. Sociedad Nacional, 372 U.S. 10 (1963).

As to the fast-growing field of environmental control, can Congress require that United States-centered manufacturers who have branches in foreign countries install devices—for example on automobiles—to control harmful emissions in those countries? What if the legislation asserts a connection between air pollution abroad and consequent air pollution in the United States? See Note, Extraterritorial Application of United States Laws: A Conflict of Laws Approach, 28 Stan.L.Rev. 1005, 1022–24 (1976); Restatement, Foreign Relations Law of the United States (Revised) §§ 601–602, 611–612 (Tent. Draft No. 4, 1983).

———

THE COMMISSION OF THE EUROPEAN COMMUNITY

DRAFT CONVENTION ON THE LAW APPLICABLE TO
CONTRACTUAL OBLIGATIONS

PREAMBLE

The High Contracting Parties to the Treaty establishing the European Economic Community,

Anxious to continue in the field of private international law the work of unification of law which has already been done within the Community, in particular in the field of jurisdiction and enforcement of judgments,

Wishing to establish uniform rules concerning the law applicable to contractual obligations,

Have Agreed as Follows:

TITLE I

Scope of the Convention

Article 1

1. The rules of this Convention shall apply to contractual obligations in any situation involving a choice between the laws of different countries.

. . .

Article 2

Application of law of non-contracting States

Any law specified by this Convention shall be applied whether or not it is the law of a Contracting State.

TITLE II

Uniform rules

Article 3

Freedom of choice

1. A contract shall be governed by the law chosen by the parties. The choice must be express or demonstrated with reasonable certainty by the terms of the contract or the circumstances of the case. By their choice the parties can select the law applicable to the whole or a part only of the contract.

2. The parties may at any time agree to subject the contract to a law other than that which previously governed it, whether as a result of an earlier choice under this Article or of other provisions of this Convention. Any variation by the parties of the law to be applied made after the conclusion of the contract shall not prejudice its for-

mal validity under Article 9 or adversely affect the rights of third parties.

3.   The fact that the parties have chosen a foreign law, whether or not accompanied by the choice of a foreign tribunal, shall not, where all the other elements relevant to the situation at the time of the choice are connected with one country only, prejudice the application of rules of the law of that country which cannot be derogated from by contract, hereinafter called "mandatory rules".

4.   The existence and validity of the consent of the parties as to the choice of the applicable law shall be determined in accordance with the provisions of Articles 8, 9 and 11.

Article 4

Applicable law in the absence of choice

1.   To the extent that the law applicable to the contract has not been chosen in accordance with Article 3, the contract shall be governed by the law of the country with which it is most closely connected. Nevertheless, a severable part of the contract which has a closer connection with another country may by way of exception be governed by the law of that other country.

2.   Subject to the provisions of paragraph (5) of this Article, it shall be presumed that the contract is most closely connected with the country where the party who is to effect the performance which is characteristic of the contract has, at the time of conclusion of the contract, his habitual residence, or, in the case of a body corporate or unincorporate, its central administration. However, if the contract is entered into in the course of that party's trade or profession, that country shall be the country in which the principal place of business is situated or, where under the terms of the contract the performance is to be effected through a place of business other than the principal place of business, the country in which that other place of business is situated.

3.   Notwithstanding the provisions of paragraph (2) of this Article, to the extent that the subject matter of the contract is a right in immovable property or a right to use immovable property it shall be presumed that the contract is most closely connected with the country where the immovable property is situated.

4.   A contract for the carriage of goods shall not be subject to the presumption in paragraph (2). In such a contract if the country in which, at the time the contract is concluded, the carrier has his principal place of business is also the country in which the place of loading or the place of discharge or the principal place of business of the consignor is situated, it shall be presumed that the contract is most closely connected with that country. In applying this paragraph single voyage charter-parties and other contracts the main purpose of which is the carriage of goods shall be treated as contracts for the carriage of goods.

5. Paragraph (2) shall not apply if the characteristic performance cannot be determined, and the presumptions in paragraphs (2), (3) and (4) shall be disregarded if it appears from the circumstances as a whole that the contract is more closely connected with another country.

Article 5

Certain consumer contracts

1. This Article applies to a contract the object of which is the supply of goods or services to a person ("the consumer") for a purpose which can be regarded as being outside his trade or profession, or a contract for the provision of credit for that object.

2. Notwithstanding the provisions of Article 3, a choice of law made by the parties shall not have the result of depriving the consumer of the protection afforded to him by the mandatory rules of the law of the country in which he has his habitual residence:

— if in that country the conclusion of the contract was preceded by a specific invitation addressed to him or by advertising, and he had taken in that country all the steps necessary on his part for the conclusion of the contract, or

— if the other party or his agent received the consumer's order in that country, or

— if the contract is for the sale of goods and the consumer travelled from that country to another country and there gave his order, provided that the consumer's journey was arranged by the seller for the purpose of inducing the consumer to buy.

3. Notwithstanding the provisions of Article 4, a contract to which this Article applies shall, in the absence of choice in accordance with Article 3, be governed by the law of the country in which the consumer has his habitual residence if it is entered into in the circumstances described in paragraph (2) of this Article.

4. This Article shall not apply to:

(a) a contract of carriage;

(b) a contract for the supply of services where the services are to be supplied to the consumer exclusively in a country other than that in which he has his habitual residence.

5. Notwithstanding the provisions of paragraph (4), this Article shall apply to a contract which, for an inclusive price, provides for a combination of travel and accommodation.

Article 6

Individual employment contracts

1. Notwithstanding the provisions of Article 3, in a contract of employment a choice of law made by the parties shall not have the

result of depriving the employee of the protection afforded to him by the mandatory rules of the law which would be applicable under paragraph (2) in the absence of choice.

2.   Notwithstanding the provisions of Article 4, a contract of employment shall, in the absence of choice in accordance with Article 3, be governed:

> (a) by the law of the country in which the employee habitually carries out his work in performance of the contract, even if he is temporarily employed in another country; or

> (b) if the employee does not habitually carry out his work in any one country, by the law of the country in which the place of business through which he was engaged is situated;

unless it appears from the circumstances as a whole that the contract is more closely connected with another country, in which case the contract shall be governed by the law of that country.

Article 7

Mandatory rules

1.   When applying under this Convention the law of a country, effect may be given to the mandatory rules of the law of another country with which the situation has a close connection, if and insofar as, under the law of the latter country, those rules must be applied whatever the law applicable to the contract.   In considering whether to give effect to these mandatory rules, regard shall be had to their nature and purpose and to the consequences of their application or nonapplication.

2.   Nothing in this Convention shall restrict the application of the rules of the law of the forum in a situation where they are mandatory irrespective of the law otherwise applicable to the contract.

Article 8

Material validity

1.   The existence and validity of a contract, or of any term of a contract, shall be determined by the law which would govern it under this Convention if the contract or term were valid.

2.   Nevertheless a party may rely upon the law of the country in which he has his habitual residence to establish that he did not consent if it appears from the circumstances that it would not be reasonable to determine the effect of his conduct in accordance with the law specified in the preceding paragraph.

Article 9

Formal validity

1.   A contract concluded between persons who are in the same country is formally valid if it satisfies the formal requirements of the law which governs it under this Convention or of the law of the country where it is concluded.

2.   A contract concluded between persons who are in different countries is formally valid if it satisfies the formal requirements of the law which governs it under this Convention or of the law of one of those countries.

3.   Where a contract is concluded by an agent, the country in which the agent acts is the relevant country for the purposes of paragraphs (1) and (2).

4.   An act intended to have legal effect relating to an existing or contemplated contract is formally valid if it satisfies the formal requirements of the law which under this Convention governs or would govern the contract or of the law of the country where the act was done.

5.   The provisions of the preceding paragraphs shall not apply to a contract to which Article 5 applies, concluded in the circumstances described in paragraph (2) of Article 5. The formal validity of such a contract is governed by the law of the country in which the consumer has his habitual residence.

6.   Notwithstanding paragraphs (1) to (4) of this Article, a contract the subject matter of which is a right in immovable property or a right to use immovable property shall be subject to the mandatory requirements of form of the law of the country where the property is situated if by that law those requirements are imposed irrespective of the country where the contract is concluded and irrespective of the law governing the contract.

Article 10

Scope of the applicable law

1.   The law applicable to a contract by virtue of Articles 3 to 6 and 12 of this Convention shall govern in particular:

   (a) interpretation;

   (b) performance;

   (c) within the limits of the powers conferred on the court by its procedural law, the consequences of breach, including the assessment of damages insofar as it is governed by rules of law;

   (d) the various ways of extinguishing obligations, and prescription and limitation of actions;

   (e) the consequences of nullity of the contract.

2.   In relation to the manner of performance and the steps to be taken in the event of defective performance regard shall be had to the law of the country in which performance takes place.

Article 11

Incapacity

In a contract concluded between persons who are in the same country, a natural person who would have capacity under the law of that country may invoke his incapacity resulting from another law only if the other party to the contract was aware of this incapacity at the time of the conclusion of the contract or was not aware thereof as a result of negligence.

Article 12

Voluntary assignment

1.   The mutual obligations of assignor and assignee under a voluntary assignment of a right against another person ("the debtor") shall be governed by the law which under this Convention applies to the contract between the assignor and assignee.

2.   The law governing the right to which the assignment relates shall determine its assignability, the relationship between the assignee and the debtor, the conditions under which the assignment can be invoked against the debtor and any question whether the debtor's obligations have been discharged.

Article 13

Subrogation

1.   Where a person ("the creditor") has a contractual claim upon another ("the debtor"), and a third person has a duty to satisfy the creditor, or has in fact satisfied the creditor in discharge of that duty, the law which governs the third person's duty to satisfy the creditor shall determine whether the third person is entitled to exercise against the debtor the rights which the creditor had against the debtor under the law governing their relationship and, if so, whether he may do so in full or only to a limited extent.

2.   The same rule applies where several persons are subject to the same contractual claim and one of them has satisfied the creditor.

Article 14

Burden of proof, etc.

1. The law governing the contract under this Convention applies to the extent that it contains, in the law of contract, rules which raise presumptions of law or determine the burden of proof.

2. A contract or an act intended to have legal effect may be proved by any mode of proof recognized by the law of the forum or by any of the laws referred to in Article 9 under which that contract or act is formally valid, provided that such mode of proof can be administered by the forum.

Article 15

Exclusion of renvoi

The application of the law of any country specified by this Convention means the application of the rules of law in force in that country other than its rules of private international law.

Article 16

"Ordre public"

The application of a rule of the law of any country specified by this Convention may be refused only if such application is manifestly incompatible with the public policy ("ordre public") of the forum.

Article 17

No retrospective effect

This Convention shall apply in a Contracting State to contracts made after the date on which this Convention has entered into force with respect to that State.

.   .   .

Article 22

Reservations

1. Any Contracting State may, at the time of signature, ratification, acceptance or approval, reserve the right not to apply:

(a) the provisions of Article 7(1);

(b) the provisions of Article 10(1)(e).

.   .   .

The Common Market Draft Convention on the Law Applicable to Contractual Obligations provides striking evidence of the efforts that have recently been made in Europe to reduce areas of conflict of laws to statutory and conventional form. Other recent codifications are the Austrian Conflicts Code of 1978 and the all-encompassing draft of a Swiss code which is currently awaiting approval by the Swiss government. These attempts at codification have much in common. They all seek to provide for some predictability of result while at the same time giving sufficient flexibility to enable the courts to reach an appropriate result in the individual case. Flexibility is assured by the constant refrain that the more precise formulations are usually no more than guides and that the ultimate aim of the courts should be the application of the law of the state of the "closest (or strongest) connection." The obvious tensions between the goals of predictability and flexibility make clear the difficulties in attempting to regulate by statute or convention a field that is as complex and unexplored as conflict of laws. See generally Palmer, Delaume, The European Convention on the Law Applicable to Contractual Obligations: Why a Convention?, 22 Va.J. Int'l L. 105 (1981); Juenger, The European Convention on the Law Applicable to Contractual Obligations: Some Critical Observations, 22 Va.J. Int'l L. 123 (1981); Lagarde, The European Convention on the Law Applicable to Contractual Obligations: An Apologia, 22 Va.J. Int'l L. 91 (1981); see also, The Austrian Codification of Conflicts Law, 28 Am.J.Comp.L. 197 (1980); McCaffrey, The Swiss Draft Conflicts Law, 28 Am.J.Comp.L. 235 (1980).

In his 1970 lectures at The Hague Academy of International Law, Professor David F. Cavers discussed earlier European efforts to reduce conflict of laws problems to statutory or conventional form. D. Cavers, Contemporary Conflicts Law in American Perspective, 2 Recueil des Cours 77–308 (1970).

New Approaches; An Epilogue and Prologue?

From the welter of latter-day decisions, commentary and occasional legislative proposals concerning choice of law, it is possible to discern at least a half-dozen approaches to the problem of bringing the chaos under control.

(1) *Jurisdiction-selecting rules.* The orthodox rules of this type, general in sweep, intent on the search for the goals of uniformity, simplicity and certainty, have failed in substantial part. Broad choice-of-law rules in the fields of torts and contracts such as that "The law of the place of wrong determines whether a person has sustained a legal injury", (Restatement, Conflict of Laws § 378 (1934)), have few champions today. The old rules were blind to the content of the law whose selection they compelled and were prone to lead to

unfortunate results. However, narrow choice-of-law rules, based on an appreciation of the underlying purposes and policies at stake, can be useful. An example is Restatement, Second, Conflict of Laws § 217, referring details of presentment, payment, protest and notice of dishonor of negotiable instruments to the local law of the state where the activity in question occurs.

(2) *Rules that presumptively select the law of a determinate state, subject to displacement,* are another possibility. An example is Restatement, Second, Conflict of Laws § 146, dealing with personal injuries. It provides that in an action of that type, the local law of the state where the injury occurred determines the rights and liabilities of the parties *unless,* having regard for the particular *issue* involved, there is a state that has a more significant relationship to the elements of the dispute, as more fully spelled out. This sort of rule creates a defeasible presumption that points at the start to a selected state as the source of the rule of decision, but is not contents-blind in its formulation. The presumption it creates is based upon a conscious choice of applicable policy; and flexibility is built in to take care of exotic or merely unexpected patterns of fact, law and policy.

(3) *Principles of preference.* These are the creation of Professor David F. Cavers and set guidelines for courts and lawyers dealing with multistate choice of law problems in common context. Their basic design is to create presumptions favoring choices of rules of particular content when the underlying fact pattern is of a carefully defined type. A distinctive feature of these principles is that they nominate a key connecting factor, based upon the nature of the issue and an awareness of underlying policies that are deemed decisive. In common with the rules mentioned above, they would presumably apply in whatever forum the particular issue is presented.

(4) *Alternative reference rules.* Rules of this type combine an effort to select a certain state with an effort to favor a particular resolution of the substantive issue presented. Thus Restatement, Second, Conflict of Laws § 203(2) says that when usury is raised as a defense to the validity of an interest-bearing contract, the contract will be upheld if the rate charged is valid in a state with a substantial relationship to the contract and if the rate is not greatly in excess of that permitted by the state of most significant relationship as determined by the Restatement's approach in Section 188. This alternative reference rule is a contents-conscious rule, with a bias in favor of validating a contract of the type described. Other validation-favoring alternative reference rules are to be found in the areas of trusts and wills.

(5) *Special substantive rules for multistate cases.* Professor Arthur von Mehren has suggested that when two or more concerned states have domestic decisional rules that point to opposed results in the case, the proper resolution is to fashion a "special substantive

rule" for the problem. The special rule would be different from the domestic rule of any concerned state. See von Mehren, Special Substantive Rules for Multi-State Problems: Their Role and Significance in Contemporary Choice of Law Methodology, 88 Harv.L.Rev. 347 (1974). For the Neumeier case, p. 503, supra, the author suggests that a compromise between New York's full-recovery and Ontario's no-recovery rules should be effected, in "the form of allowing partial recovery by permitting the guest to recover one-half of the damage suffered." (Id., at p. 369.)

(6) *Result selective approach.* Here, there is no "rule" as such except that the validity of a marriage or of a contract or trust is to be upheld in the absence of strong reasons to the contrary, or that higher standards of liability are to be applied whenever constitutionally possible, or that the court is to apply what it conceives to be the "better" rule, or the decisional norm that is on the upswing rather than regressing, or a combination of such approaches. This view of the choice-of-law process is entirely contents conscious. It is not concerned with preventing forum shopping or variations in outcome depending on the court in which the issue is presented. Presumably, its proponents assume that most courts and judges will be prone to select the same result and that this will keep subjectivity from becoming too rampant.

(7) *Narrow choice-of-law rules based upon experience with a recurrent problem.* An example, in the field of automobile-caused wrongful death cases involving the applicability of a ceiling on collectible damages, has been proposed by one of the editors of this volume. Rosenberg, Comments on *Reich v. Purcell*, 15 U.C.L.A.L.Rev. 551, 641, 646–7:

Group 1.   Death damage limit not applicable.

Rule 1.1. A limit upon damages for wrongful death that is prescribed by the state in which the harm occurred will not be applied if no similar limit is prescribed by the law of any domiciliary state.

Rule 1.2. A limit upon damages for wrongful death that is prescribed by the state of the defendant's domicile will not be applied if no similar limit is prescribed either by the state in which the accident occurred or in which the decedent was domiciled.

Rule 1.3. A limit upon damages for wrongful death that is prescribed by the state in which the decedent was domiciled will not be applied if no similar limit is prescribed either by the state in which the accident occurred or in which the defendant was domiciled.

Group 2.   Death damage limit applicable.

Rule 2.1.   A limit upon damages for wrongful death that is prescribed by the state in which the accident occurred will be applied if either

(a) defendant is domiciled there, *or*

(b) defendant is domiciled in a state that similarly limits damages, *or*

(c) the decedent was domiciled in a state that similarly limits damages.

The premise of drafting such narrowly specific rules is to avoid litigation whenever possible in the all too common circumstances of multistate highway fatalities.

The strategy of efforts to draft rules of whatever kind, for situations where rules can function effectively, is to prevent choice of law from becoming an over-sophisticated game that leaves judges and lawyers, bewildered and confused; and that adds complex multistate litigations to the crushing caseload of busy courts.

NOTES

(1) Professor Friedrich K. Juenger has argued that applying the "simple and straightforward" German choice-of-law rules for torts would improve the decisional process in the group of well known New York cases on guest statutes and wrongful death damage limits. See Juenger, Lessons Comparison Might Teach, 23 Am.J.Comp.L. 742, 747–748 (1975):

"To illustrate, I propose to apply German tort choice-of-law rules to several New York decisions. The rules—in part statutory, in part judge-made—are simple and straightforward:

(1) If both parties have the same nationality the law of the country whose nationals they are governs;

(2) If the parties have different nationalities the law of the place of wrong governs;

(a) The term "place of wrong" refers to all jurisdictions in which any tortious conduct or any injuries occur;

(b) If there is more than one "place of wrong," the law most favorable to the injured party will prevail.

"[I shall leave aside one further statutory provision of a somewhat chauvinistic nature which the German courts have, with laudable urbanity, construed rather narrowly. It establishes the rule that German parties cannot be held liable for torts committed abroad in excess of the liability provided by German law.]

"If we substitute 'domicile' for 'nationality,' *voilà*, the whole series of Court of Appeals cases from Kilberg v. Northeast Airlines, Inc. to Neumeier v. Kuehner, (except perhaps for Miller v. Miller) fall in line, at least if the plaintiff in Kilberg could have shown sufficient conduct in the air space over New York, from where the ill-fated plane had departed. In this event the plaintiff would benefit from the German rule on long distance torts, while in the guest statute cases the victims could rely on the common-domicile rule. . . . ."

(2) For a further elaboration of the suggestion that special substantive rules should be fashioned for cases involving collisions in substantive policies in multistate situations, see von Mehren, Choice of Law and the Problem of Justice, 41 Law and Contemp. Problems 27 (1977); Twerski and Mayer, Toward a Pragmatic Solution of Choice-of-Law Problems—at the Interface of Substance and Procedure, 74 N.W.U.L.Rev. 781 (1979).

Chapter 10

CONFLICTS PROBLEMS IN FEDERAL AND INTERNATIONAL SETTINGS

SECTION 1.   SPECIAL PROBLEMS IN FEDERAL COURTS

A.   THE CONSTRAINTS AND TOLERANCES OF THE ERIE PRINCIPLE

Introductory Note. This section brings together a group of issues that have appeared episodically in earlier chapters. Their theme is a broad question: how completely are federal courts bound to follow state conflicts principles in diversity cases? As examples: May the federal diversity court entertain a suit based on state-created rights that would not be entertained in a state court of the forum? Does the *Erie* doctrine compel a diversity court to follow the choice-of-law rules or methods of the forum's state courts, and to apply at the end the same decisional rule the state judges would? As the *Erie* principle has changed shape over the years, has comparable change occurred in its influence or conflicts methodology?

Treated here also are issues regarding the scope and impact of "national" or "federal" common law—the body of law that is not spelled out in the text of the Constitution, or treaties or statutes, having been laid down by the courts to fill interstices in those sources of law. When the Constitution of the United States or a valid treaty or statute of the nation supplies the rule of decision, the determination of governing law is simple, whether the issue arises in a federal or a state court. In short, if national law supplies a governing rule, it overrides any opposed rule derived from state law; but in other cases, state conflicts rules control.

We shall take up the problem of state law in the federal courts in a broad context, tracing the movements and counter-movements in state law-federal law relations that bear on the conflicts problems that are the focus of our interest. Two of the important movements in the past half century concern only the federal courts. The third applies also to the state courts.

(1) Erie Railroad Co. v. Tompkins, infra, p. 683, sharply curtailed the growth of a general and independent body of common law, rules

681

in the federal courts. For in overruling Swift v. Tyson, 41 U.S. (16 Pet.) 1 (1842), it obliterated the century old doctrine of a separate substantive common law as to commercial matters in the federal courts. It thereby sharpened the question: from what source can the federal courts get separate rules of conflict of laws?

(2) In the same year Erie Railroad Co. v. Tompkins was decided, the area of federal courts law was much expanded by occupying the entire field of federal "procedure". For many years the Conformity Act had directed the federal district courts hearing actions at law to follow the procedure of the states in which the federal courts were sitting. But in 1938 the Federal Rules of Civil Procedure, went into effect as a uniform set of rules for litigation in the federal district courts throughout the country. By coincidence the Rules created a special law of procedure for the federal district courts at almost the same time the Erie case was ending the special body of general common law on substantive matters lying outside the ordinary sphere of national law.

(3) A third movement, affecting state and federal courts alike but more conspicuous in the federal courts, is concerned with federal law. The increasing regulation of interstate and foreign commerce and the growing activities of the federal government have brought the realization that there are areas of substantive law which are not explicitly dealt with by the federal statutes but which are nevertheless covered by a single national law. This corpus is a part of the law of the land to be applied by all courts, state or federal. Its importance for lawyers with private interstate or international cases is manifest, for in so far as the national law comes into play there is no conflict of laws.

TWO FEDERAL STATUTES

"The laws of the several States, except where the Constitution or treaties of the United States or Acts of Congress shall otherwise require or provide, shall be regarded as rules of decision in civil actions in the courts of the United States, in cases where they apply." (Rules of Decision Act, 28 U.S.C. § 1652 (1970) (corresponds to Judiciary Act of 1789, ch. 20, § 34, 1 Stat. 92)).*

"The Supreme Court shall have the power to prescribe by general rules, the forms of process, writs, pleadings, and motions, and the practice and procedure of the district courts and courts of appeals of the United States in civil actions, including admiralty and maritime cases, and appeals therein, and the practice and procedure in proceedings for the review by the courts of appeals of decisions of the Tax Court of the United States and for the judicial review or enforcement

---

* The words "civil actions" were substituted for the phrase "trials at common law" in the 1948 recodification of Title 28 of the United States Code. See 28 U.S.C. § 1652 (1970). [Eds.]

of orders of administrative agencies, boards, commissions, and officers.

"Such rules shall not abridge, enlarge or modify any substantive right and shall preserve the right of trial by jury as at common law and as declared by the Seventh Amendment to the Constitution.

"Such rules shall not take effect until they have been reported to Congress by the Chief Justice at or after the beginning of a regular session thereof but not later than the first day of May, and until the expiration of ninety days after they have been thus reported.

"All laws in conflict with such rules shall be of no further force or effect after such rules have taken effect. Nothing in this title, anything therein to the contrary notwithstanding, shall in any way limit, supersede, or repeal any such rules heretofore prescribed by the Supreme Court." (Rules Enabling Act, 28 U.S.C. § 2072 (1970) (formerly Act of June 19, 1934, ch. 651, 48 Stat. 1064).)

ERIE RAILROAD CO. v. TOMPKINS

Supreme Court of the United States, 1938.
304 U.S. 64, 58 S.Ct. 817, 82 L.Ed. 1188, 114 A.L.R. 1487.*

Certiorari to the United States Circuit Court of Appeals for the Second Circuit.

MR. JUSTICE BRANDEIS delivered the opinion of the Court.

The question for decision is whether the oft-challenged doctrine of Swift v. Tyson shall now be disapproved.

Tompkins, a citizen of Pennsylvania, was injured on a dark night by a passing freight train of the Erie Railroad Company while walking along its right of way at Hughestown in that state. He claimed that the accident occurred through negligence in the operation, or maintenance, of the train; that he was rightfully on the premises as licensee because on a commonly used beaten footpath which ran for a short distance alongside the tracks; and that he was struck by something which looked like a door projecting from one of the moving cars. To enforce that claim he brought an action in the federal court for Southern New York, which had jurisdiction because the company is a corporation of that state. It denied liability; and the case was tried by a jury.

The Erie insisted that its duty to Tompkins was no greater than that owed to a trespasser. It contended, among other things, that its duty to Tompkins, and hence its liability, should be determined in accordance with the Pennsylvania law; that under the law of Pennsylvania, as declared by its highest court, persons who use pathways along the railroad right of way—that is, a longitudinal pathway as

* Some footnotes omitted; others re-numbered. [Eds.]

distinguished from a crossing—are to be deemed trespassers; and that the railroad is not liable for injuries to undiscovered trespassers resulting from its negligence, unless it be wanton or willful. Tompkins denied that any such rule had been established by the decisions of the Pennsylvania courts; and contended that, since there was no statute of the state on the subject, the railroad's duty and liability is to be determined in federal courts as a matter of general law.

The trial judge refused to rule that the applicable law precluded recovery. The jury brought in a verdict of $30,000; and the judgment entered thereon was affirmed by the Circuit Court of Appeals, which held (2 Cir., 90 F.2d 603, 604), that it was unnecessary to consider whether the law of Pennsylvania was as contended, because the question was one not of local, but of general, law, and that "upon questions of general law the federal courts are free, in absence of a local statute, to exercise their independent judgment as to what the law is. . . ."

Because of the importance of the question whether the federal court was free to disregard the alleged rule of the Pennsylvania common law, we granted certiorari. 302 U.S. 671.

First. Swift v. Tyson, 16 Pet. 1, 18, held that federal courts exercising jurisdiction on the ground of diversity of citizenship need not, in matters of general jurisprudence, apply the unwritten law of the state as declared by its highest court; that they are free to exercise an independent judgment as to what the common law of the state is— or should be; and that, as there stated by Mr. Justice Story: "the true interpretation of the 34th section limited its application to state laws, strictly local, that is to say, to the positive statutes of the state, and the construction thereof adopted by the local tribunals, and to rights and titles to things having a permanent locality, such as the rights and titles to real estate, and other matters immovable and intraterritorial in their nature and character. It never has been supposed by us, that the section did apply, or was designed to apply, to questions of a more general nature, not at all dependent upon local statutes or local usages of a fixed and permanent operation, as, for example, to the construction of ordinary contracts or other written instruments, and especially to questions of general commercial law, where the state tribunals are called upon to perform the like functions as ourselves, that is, to ascertain, upon general reasoning and legal analogies, what is the true exposition of the contract or instrument, or what is the just rule furnished by the principles of commercial law to govern the case."

. . . The federal courts assumed, in the broad field of "general law," the power to declare rules of decision which Congress was confessedly without power to enact as statutes. Doubt was repeatedly expressed as to the correctness of the construction given section 34, and as to the soundness of the rule which it introduced. But it was the more recent research of a competent scholar, who examined the original document, which established that the construction given to it by the Court was erroneous; and that the purpose of the section was merely to make certain that, in all matters except those in which some federal law is controlling, the federal courts exercising jurisdiction in diversity of citizenship cases would apply as their rules of decision the law of the state, unwritten as well as written.[1]

Criticism of the doctrine became widespread after the decision of Black & White Taxicab & Transfer Co. v. Brown & Yellow Taxicab & Transfer Co., 276 U.S. 518. . . .

Second.   Experience in applying the doctrine of Swift v. Tyson, had revealed its defects, political and social; and the benefits expected to flow from the rule did not accrue.   Persistence of state courts in their own opinions on questions of common law prevented uniformity; and the impossibility of discovering a satisfactory line of demarcation between the province of general law and that of local law developed a new well of uncertainties.

On the other hand, the mischievous results of the doctrine had become apparent.   Diversity of citizenship jurisdiction was conferred in order to prevent apprehended discrimination in state courts against those not citizens of the state.   Swift v. Tyson introduced grave discrimination by noncitizens against citizens.   It made rights enjoyed under the unwritten "general law" vary according to whether enforcement was sought in the state or in the federal court; and the privilege of selecting the court in which the right should be determined was conferred upon the noncitizen.   Thus, the doctrine rendered impossible equal protection of the law.   In attempting to promote uniformity of law throughout the United States, the doctrine had prevented uniformity in the administration of the law of the state.

The discrimination resulting became in practice far-reaching. This resulted in part from the broad province accorded to the so-called "general law" as to which federal courts exercised an independent judgment. . . .

. . .

The injustice and confusion incident to the doctrine of Swift v. Tyson have been repeatedly urged as reasons for abolishing or limiting diversity of citizenship jurisdiction.   Other legislative relief has been proposed.   If only a question of statutory construction were involved, we should not be prepared to abandon a doctrine so widely applied throughout nearly a century.   But the unconstitutionality of the course pursued has now been made clear, and compels us to do so.

Third.   Except in matters governed by the Federal Constitution or by acts of Congress, the law to be applied in any case is the law of the state.   And whether the law of the state shall be declared by its

1. Charles Warren, New Light on the History of the Federal Judiciary Act of   1789 (1923) 37 Harv.L.Rev. 49, 51–52, 81–88, 108.

Legislature in a statute or by its highest court in a decision is not a matter of federal concern. There is no federal general common law. Congress has no power to declare substantive rules of common law applicable in a state whether they be local in their nature or "general," be they commercial law or a part of the law of torts. And no clause in the Constitution purports to confer such a power upon the federal courts. . . .

The fallacy underlying the rule declared in Swift v. Tyson is made clear by Mr. Justice Holmes.[2] The doctrine rests upon the assumption that there is "a transcendental body of law outside of any particular State but obligatory within it unless and until changed by statute," that federal courts have the power to use their judgment as to what the rules of common law are; and that in the federal courts "the parties are entitled to an independent judgment on matters of general law":

"but law in the sense in which courts speak of it today does not exist without some definite authority behind it. The common law so far as it is enforced in a State, whether called common law or not, is not the common law generally but the law of that State existing by the authority of that State without regard to what it may have been in England or anywhere else. . . .

"the authority and only authority is the State, and if that be so, the voice adopted by the State as its own [whether it be of its Legislature or of its Supreme Court] should utter the last word."

Thus, the doctrine of Swift v. Tyson is, as Mr. Justice Holmes said, "an unconstitutional assumption of powers by the Courts of the United States which no lapse of time or respectable array of opinion should make us hesitate to correct." In disapproving that doctrine we do not hold unconstitutional section 34 of the Federal Judiciary Act of 1789 or any other act of Congress. We merely declare that in applying the doctrine this Court and the lower courts have invaded rights which in our opinion are reserved by the Constitution to the several states.

. . . The Circuit Court of Appeals ruled that the question of liability is one of general law; and on that ground declined to decide the issue of state law. As we hold this was error, the judgment is reversed and the case remanded to it for further proceedings in conformity with our opinion.

Reversed.

MR. JUSTICE CARDOZO took no part in the consideration or decision of this case.

[MR. JUSTICE BUTLER dissented in an opinion in which MR. JUSTICE MCREYNOLDS concurred. The dissent urged (a) that the doctrine of Swift v. Tyson be adhered to and applied; and (b) that otherwise the

2. Kuhn v. Fairmont Coal Co., 215 U.S. 349, 370–372; Black & White Taxi- cab, etc., Co. v. Brown & Yellow Taxicab, etc., Co., 276 U.S. 518, 532–536.

case be set down for reargument, for counsel on both sides had assumed in their briefs the validity of Swift v. Tyson; so important a question as the constitutional overruling of that case should not be decided without argument.]

MR. JUSTICE REED (concurring in part).

. . .

To decide the case now before us and to "disapprove" the doctrine of Swift v. Tyson requires only that we say that the words "the laws" include in their meaning the decisions of the local tribunals. . . . It is unnecessary to go further and declare that the "course pursued" was "unconstitutional," instead of merely erroneous.

The "unconstitutional" course referred to in the majority opinion is apparently the ruling in Swift v. Tyson that the supposed omission of Congress to legislate as to the effect of decisions leaves federal courts free to interpret general law for themselves. I am not at all sure whether, in the absence of federal statutory direction, federal courts would be compelled to follow state decisions. There was sufficient doubt about the matter in 1789 to induce the first Congress to legislate. No former opinions of this Court have passed upon it. . . . If the opinion commits this Court to the position that the Congress is without power to declare what rules of substantive law shall govern the federal courts, that conclusion also seems questionable. . . .

. . . It seems preferable to overturn an established construction of an act of Congress, rather than, in the circumstances of this case, to interpret the Constitution.

NOTES

(1) A vigorous debate has raged over whether the Erie doctrine is constitutionally compelled. In the affirmative is former Chief Judge Henry J. Friendly who wrote In Praise of Erie—and of the New Federal Common Law, 39 N.Y.U.L.Rev. 383, 385–386 (1964). On the other side of the issue was the late Chief Judge Charles E. Clark whose views were set forth in State Law in the Federal Courts: The Brooding Omnipresence of Erie v. Tompkins, 55 Yale L.J. 267–278 (1946). See Wright, Federal Courts 359–364 (4th Ed. 1983).

(2) For examples of the "new federal common law" or "national common law," see the D'Oench, Duhme and Bank of America cases, pp. 722, 731, infra. Under the interstate commerce power, could Congress not enact rules determining the measure of an interstate railroad's duty to persons walking along the railroad's right of way?

For nearly two decades the sway of the Erie doctrine expanded, requiring federal courts to apply one state rule after another as "substantive." Strong impetus to the spread of substantive characterization came from Guaranty Trust v. York, which propounded a deceptively attractive test, the first of several recastings of the doctrine by the Supreme Court.

GUARANTY TRUST CO. v. YORK

Supreme Court of the United States, 1945.
326 U.S. 99, 65 S.Ct. 1464, 89 L.Ed. 2079.

[In 1942 York filed a class suit in a Federal district court in New York, charging defendant with breach of trust in connection with transactions in 1931. Defendant obtained a summary judgment on the ground the suit was time-barred under the New York rule, but this was reversed, the Court of Appeals ruling that in a diversity action brought on its equity side the district court was not bound to apply the statute of limitations as it would have been applied by a New York court. The Supreme Court granted certiorari.]

MR. JUSTICE FRANKFURTER delivered the opinion of the Court.

. . .

Our starting point must be the policy of federal jurisdiction which Erie R. Co. v. Tompkins, 304 U.S. 64, embodies. . . . .

. . .

In relation to the problem now here, the real significance of Swift v. Tyson lies in the fact that it did not enunciate novel doctrine. Nor was it restricted to its particular situation. It summed up prior attitudes and expressions in cases that had come before this Court and lower federal courts for at least thirty years, at law as well as in equity. . . .

. . .

And so this case reduces itself to the narrow question whether, when no recovery could be had in a State court because the action is barred by the statute of limitations, a federal court in equity can take cognizance of the suit because there is diversity of citizenship between the parties. Is the outlawry, according to State law, of a claim created by the States a matter of "substantive rights" to be respected by a federal court of equity when that court's jurisdiction is dependent on the fact that there is a State-created right, or is such statute of "a mere remedial character" . . . which a federal court may disregard?

Matters of "substance" and matters of "procedure" are much talked about in the books as though they defined a great divide cutting across the whole domain of law. But, of course, "substance" and "procedure" are the same key-words to very different problems. Neither "substance" nor "procedure" represents the same invariants. Each implies different variables depending upon the particular problem for which it is used. See Home Ins. Co. v. Dick, 281 U.S. 397, 409. And the different problems are only distantly related at best, for the terms are in common use in connection with situations turning on such different considerations as those that are relevant to questions pertaining to ex post facto legislation, the impairment of the obligations of contract, the enforcement of federal rights in the State courts and the multitudinous phases of the conflict of laws.

Here we are dealing with a right to recover derived not from the United States but from one of the States. When, because the plaintiff happens to be a non-resident, such a right is enforceable in a federal as well as in a State court, the forms and mode of enforcing the right may at times, naturally enough, vary because the two judicial systems are not identic. But since a federal court adjudicating a state-created right solely because of the diversity of citizenship of the parties is for that purpose, in effect, only another court of the State, it cannot afford recovery if the right to recover is made unavailable by the State nor can it substantially affect the enforcement of the right as given by the State.

And so the question is not whether a statute of limitations is deemed a matter of "procedure" in some sense. The question is whether such a statute concerns merely the manner and the means by which a right to recover, as recognized by the State, is enforced, or whether such statutory limitation is a matter of substance in the aspect that alone is relevant to our problem, namely does it significantly affect the result of a litigation for a federal court to disregard a law of a State that would be controlling in an action upon the same claim by the same parties in a State court?

It is therefore immaterial whether statutes of limitation are characterized either as "substantive" or "procedural" in State court opinions in any use of those terms unrelated to the specific issue before us. Erie R. Co. v. Tompkins was not an endeavor to formulate scientific legal terminology. It expressed a policy that touches vitally the proper distribution of judicial power between State and federal courts. In essence, the intent of that decision was to insure that, in all cases where a federal court is exercising jurisdiction solely because of the diversity of citizenship of the parties, the outcome of the litigation in the federal court should be substantially the same, so far as legal rules determine the outcome of a litigation, as it would be if tried in a State court. The nub of the policy that underlies Erie R. Co. v. Tompkins is that for the same transaction the accident of a suit by a nonresident litigant in a federal court instead of in a State court a block away, should not lead to a substantially different result. And so, putting to one side abstractions regarding "substance" and "procedure," we have held that in diversity cases the federal courts must follow the law of the State as to burden of proof, Cities Service Oil Co. v. Dunlap, 308 U.S. 208, as to conflict of laws, Klaxon Co. v. Stentor Co., 313 U.S. 487, as to contributory negligence, Palmer v. Hoffman, 318 U.S. 109, 117. And see Sampson v. Channell, 1 Cir., 110 F.2d 754. Erie R. Co. v. Tompkins has been applied with an eye alert to essentials in avoiding disregard of State law in diversity cases in the federal courts. A policy so important to our federalism must be kept free from entanglements with analytical or terminological niceties.

Plainly enough, a statute that would completely bar recovery in a suit if brought in a State court bears on a State-created right vitally and not merely formally or negligibly. As to consequences that so intimately affect recovery or nonrecovery a federal court in a diversity case should follow State law. See Morgan, Choice of Law Governing Proof (1944) 58 Harv.L.Rev. 153, 155–158. . . .

. . .

Diversity jurisdiction is founded on assurance to non-resident litigants of courts free from susceptibility to potential local bias. The Framers of the Constitution, according to Marshall, entertained "apprehensions" lest distant suitors be subjected to local bias in State courts, or, at least, viewed with "indulgence the possible fears and apprehensions" of such suitors. Bank of the United States v. Deveaux, 5 Cranch 61, 87. And so Congress afforded out-of-State litigants another tribunal, not another body of law. The operation of a double system of conflicting laws in the same State is plainly hostile to the reign of law. Certainly, the fortuitous circumstance of residence out of a State of one of the parties to a litigation ought not to give rise to a discrimination against others equally concerned but locally resident. The source of substantive rights enforced by a federal court under diversity jurisdiction, it cannot be said too often, is the law of the States. Whenever that law is authoritatively declared by a State, whether its voice be the legislature or its highest court, such law ought to govern in litigation founded on that law, whether the forum of application is a State or a federal court and whether the remedies be sought at law or may be had in equity.

. . .

The judgment is reversed and the case is remanded for proceedings not inconsistent with this opinion. . . .

MR. JUSTICE ROBERTS and MR. JUSTICE DOUGLAS took no part in the consideration or decision of this case.

[MR. JUSTICE RUTLEDGE dissented in an opinion, in which MR. JUSTICE MURPHY joined, which argued that "this case arises from what are in fact if not in law interstate transactions," involving "the rights of security holders in relation to securities which were distributed not in New York or Ohio alone but widely throughout the country."]

NOTES

(1) Since the limitations issue in the Guaranty Trust case was statutory, why was Erie apposite at all? Does the outcome-determinative test mean that even state rules undoubtedly regulating the conduct of the litigation are subject to the Erie command if they can affect the result of the action?

(2) Substance-procedure characterization has been a pervasive issue in state-state conflicts cases as Chapter 7, supra, demonstrates. It is also a recurring issue in federal court diversity suits, where a federal rule that is arguably procedural may differ significantly from a forum state rule addressed to the same problem. To what extent are similar considerations and criteria at work in the federal diversity area? See Meador, State Law and the Federal Judicial Power, 49 Va.L.Rev. 1082 (1963).

(3) In 1949 a trio of important cases accepted the broad view of Erie and made major inroads on the independence of federal diversity courts in their conduct of state-law-based litigation. In Ragan v. Merchants Transfer and Warehouse Co., 337 U.S. 530 (1949), a state rule was held to be dispositive of whether a suit had been started in time to avoid being barred by limitations. In Cohen v. Beneficial Industrial Loan Corp., 337 U.S. 541 (1949), the state security-for-costs rule was held applicable in the diversity suit. Both cases are discussed in the concurring opinion of Harlan, J., in Hanna v. Plumer, p. 696, infra. In Woods v. Interstate Realty Co., 337 U.S. 535 (1949), state law was held to prevent a corporation that qualified under federal law from suing in a diversity action because a state statute closed state courts to it.

(4) "The question of the burden of [proof in] establishing contributory negligence is a question of local law which federal courts in diversity of citizenship cases . . . must apply." See Palmer v. Hoffman, 318 U.S. 109, 117 (1943). In direct contrast is Garrett v. Moore-McCormack Co., 317 U.S. 239 (1942), involving the burden of proof as to the validity of a release in an admiralty case tried in a state court, with a federal statute governing the major rights of the parties. The court held that the federal law must be used by the state court.

BERNHARDT V. POLYGRAPHIC CO., 350 U.S. 198 (1956): Plaintiff sued in a Vermont court for damages for breach of a contract of employment. Defendant removed the action to the federal district court and moved for a stay pending arbitration, invoking a provision of the contract. The district judge refused the stay for the reason that under Vermont law an arbitration agreement is revocable at any time before award and therefore could not be enforced in a federal court. The Supreme Court agreed declaring:

". . . [The] right to recover . . . owes its existence to one of the States, not to the United States. The federal court enforces the state-created right by rules of procedure which it has acquired from the Federal Government and which therefore are not identical with those of the state courts. Yet, in spite of that difference in procedure, the federal court . . . may not 'substantially affect the enforcement of the right as given by the State.' [Guaranty Trust Co. v. York, 326 U.S. 99, 109.] If the federal court allows arbitration where the state court would disallow it, the outcome of litigation might depend on the courthouse where suit is brought. For the remedy by arbitration, whatever its merits or shortcomings, substantially affects the cause of action created by the State. The nature of the tribunal where suits are tried is an important part of the parcel of rights behind a cause of action. The change from a court of law to an arbitration panel may make a radical difference in ultimate result. Arbitration carries no right to trial by jury that is guaranteed both by the Seventh Amendment and by Ch. 1, Art. 12th, of the Vermont Constitution. Arbitrators do not have the benefit of judicial instruction on the law; they need not give their reasons for their results; the record of their proceedings is not as complete as it is in a court trial; and judicial review of an award is more limited than judicial review of a trial—all as discussed in Wilko v. Swan, 346 U.S. 427, 435–438. . . . There would in our judgment be a resultant discrimination if the parties suing on a Vermont cause of action in the federal court were remitted to arbitration, while those suing in the Vermont court could not be."

BYRD v. BLUE RIDGE ELECTRIC COOPERATIVE, INC.

Supreme Court of the United States, 1958.
356 U.S. 525, 78 S.Ct. 893, 2 L.Ed.2d 953.

[Petitioner was injured in South Carolina while working as a lineman for a firm which had a contract to erect electrical power lines for respondent. As a defense to his diversity action for damages resulting from its negligence, respondent asserted that petitioner was a statutory employee and could recover only the statutory compensation benefits. Respondent claimed further that the defense was to be decided by the court and not the jury because of a controlling South Carolina decision. The Court of Appeals reversed a judgment for petitioner entered on a jury verdict.]

Mr. Justice Brennan delivered the opinion of the Court. . . .

. . . The respondent argues on the basis of the decision of the Supreme Court of South Carolina in Adams v. Davison-Paxon Co., 230 S.C. 532, 96 S.E.2d 566, that the issue of immunity should be decided by the judge and not by the jury. That was a negligence action brought in the state trial court against a store owner by an employee of an independent contractor who operated the store's millinery department. The trial judge denied the store owner's motion for a directed verdict made upon the ground that § 72–111 [of the South Carolina Workmen's Compensation Act] barred the plaintiff's action. The jury returned a verdict for the plaintiff. The South Carolina Supreme Court reversed, holding that it was for the judge and not the jury to decide on the evidence whether the owner was a statutory employer, and that the store owner had sustained his defense. . . .

The respondent argues that this state-court decision governs the present diversity case and "divests the jury of its normal function" to decide the disputed fact question of the respondent's immunity under § 72–111. This is to contend that the federal court is bound under Erie R. Co. v. Tompkins, 304 U.S. 64, to follow the state court's holding to secure uniform enforcement of the immunity created by the State.

First. It was decided in Erie R. Co. v. Tompkins that the federal courts in diversity cases must respect the definition of state-created rights and obligations by the state courts. We must, therefore, first examine the rule in Adams v. Davison-Paxon Co. to determine whether it is bound up with these rights and obligations in such a way that its application in the federal court is required. Cities Service Oil Co. v. Dunlap, 308 U.S. 208.

The Workmen's Compensation Act is administered in South Carolina by its Industrial Commission. The South Carolina courts hold that, on judicial review of actions of the Commission under § 72–111, the question whether the claim of an injured workman is within the Commission's jurisdiction is a matter of law for decision by the court, which makes its own findings of fact relating to that jurisdiction. The South Carolina Supreme Court states no reasons in Adams v. Davison-Paxon Co. why, although the jury decides all other factual issues raised by the cause of action and defenses, the jury is displaced as to the factual issue raised by the affirmative defense under § 72–111. The decisions cited to support the holding . . . are concerned solely with defining the scope and method of judicial review of the Industrial Commission. A State may, of course, distribute the functions of its judicial machinery as it sees fit. The decisions relied upon, however, furnish no reason for selecting the judge rather than the jury to decide this single affirmative defense in the negligence action. They simply reflect a policy, cf. Crowell v. Benson, 285 U.S. 22, that administrative determination of "jurisdictional facts" should not be final but subject to judicial review. The conclusion is inescapable that the Adams holding is grounded in the practical consideration that the question had theretofore come before the South Carolina courts from the Industrial Commission and the courts had become accustomed to deciding the factual issue of immunity without the aid of juries. We find nothing to suggest that this rule was announced as an integral part of the special relationship created by the statute. Thus the requirement appears to be merely a form and mode of enforcing the immunity, Guaranty Trust Co. v. York, 326 U.S. 99, 108, and not a rule intended to be bound up with the definition of the rights and obligations of the parties. The situation is therefore not analogous to that in Dice v. Akron, C. & Y. R. Co., 342 U.S. 359, where this Court held that the right to trial by jury is so substantial a part of the cause of action created by the Federal Employers' Liability Act that the Ohio courts could not apply, in an action under that statute, the Ohio rule that the question of fraudulent release was for determination by a judge rather than by a jury.

Second. But cases following Erie have evinced a broader policy to the effect that the federal courts should conform as near as may be—in the absence of other considerations—to state rules even of form and mode where the state rules may bear substantially on the question whether the litigation would come out one way in the federal court and another way in the state court if the federal court failed to apply a particular local rule. E.g., Guaranty Trust Co. v. York, supra; Bernhardt v. Polygraphic Co., 350 U.S. 198. Concededly the nature of the tribunal which tries issues may be important in the enforcement of the parcel of rights making up a cause of action or defense, and bear significantly upon achievement of uniform enforcement of the right. It may well be that in the instant personal-injury case the outcome would be substantially affected by whether the issue of immunity is decided by a judge or a jury. Therefore, were "outcome" the only consideration, a strong case might appear for saying that the federal court should follow the state practice.

But there are affirmative countervailing considerations at work here. The federal system is an independent system for administering justice to litigants who properly invoke its jurisdiction. An essential characteristic of that system is the manner in which, in civil common-law actions, it distributes trial functions between judge and jury and, under the influence—if not the command—of the Seventh Amendment, assigns the decisions of disputed questions of fact to the jury. Jacob v. New York, 315 U.S. 752. The policy of uniform enforcement of state-created rights and obligations, see, e.g., Guaranty Trust Co. v. York, supra, cannot in every case exact compliance with a state rule—not bound up with rights and obligations—which disrupts the federal system of allocating functions between judge and jury. Herron v. Southern Pacific Co., 283 U.S. 91. Thus the inquiry here is whether the federal policy favoring jury decisions of disputed fact questions should yield to the state rule in the interest of furthering the objective that the litigation should not come out one way in the federal court and another way in the state court.

We think that in the circumstances of this case the federal court should not follow the state rule. It cannot be gainsaid that there is a strong federal policy against allowing state rules to disrupt the judge-jury relationship in the federal courts. In Herron v. Southern Pacific Co., supra, the trial judge in a personal-injury negligence action brought in the District Court for Arizona on diversity grounds directed a verdict for the defendant when it appeared as a matter of law that the plaintiff was guilty of contributory negligence. The federal judge refused to be bound by a provision of the Arizona Constitution which made the jury the sole arbiter of the question of contributory negligence. This Court sustained the action of the trial judge, holding that "state laws cannot alter the essential character or function of a federal court" because that function "is not in any sense a local matter, and state statutes which would interfere with the appropriate performance of that function are not binding upon the federal court under either the Conformity Act or the 'rules of decision' Act." Id., at 94. Perhaps even more clearly in light of the influence of the Seventh Amendment, the function assigned to the jury "is an essential factor in the process for which the Federal Constitution provides." Id., at 95.   Concededly the Herron case was decided before Erie R. Co. v. Tompkins, but even when Swift v. Tyson, 16 Pet. 1, was governing law and allowed federal courts sitting in diversity cases to disregard state decisional law, it was never thought that state statutes or constitutions were similarly to be disregarded.   Green v. Neal's Lessee, 6 Pet. 291.   Yet Herron held that state statutes and constitutional provisions could not disrupt or alter the essential character or function of a federal court.

Third.   We have discussed the problem upon the assumption that the outcome of the litigation may be substantially affected by whether the issue of immunity is decided by a judge or a jury.   But clearly there is not present here the certainty that a different result would follow, cf. Guaranty Trust Co. v. York, supra, or even the strong possibility that this would be the case, cf. Bernhardt v. Polygraphic Co., supra.   There are factors present here which might reduce that possibility.   The trial judge in the federal system has powers denied the judges of many States to comment on the weight of evidence and credibility of witnesses, and discretion to grant a new trial if the verdict appears to him to be against the weight of the evidence.   We do not think the likelihood of a different result is so strong as to require the federal practice of jury determination of disputed factual issues to yield to the state rule in the interest of uniformity of outcome.

The Court of Appeals did not consider other grounds of appeal raised by the respondent because the ground taken disposed of the case.   We accordingly remand the case to the Court of Appeals for the decision of the other questions, with instructions that, if not made unnecessary by the decision of such questions, the Court of Appeals shall remand the case to the District Court for a new trial of such issues as the Court of Appeals may direct.

Reversed and remanded.*

NOTES

(1) The principal case signalled a changed approach to the Erie doctrine: a state law need not be applied if it alters the "essential character or function of a Federal court."   See Smith, Blue Ridge and Beyond: A Byrd's-Eye View of Federalism in Diversity Litigation, 36 Tul.L.Rev. 443 (1962).

(2) Since Byrd, to what extent must the forum state's rules be followed as to: availability of a jury; power to remove cases from its determination; review of sufficiency of evidence for directed verdict or new trial purposes, and similar issues?

(a) As to the grant of trial by jury, the diversity court is not bound to follow the state view, because of the heavy involvement of the Seventh Amendment.   See Simler v. Conner, 372 U.S. 221 (1963), rejecting the state

* Mr. Justice Whittaker dissented on the issue of how integral it was to the South Carolina rule that the question of statutory immunity be decided by the judge. Justices Harlan and Frankfurter also dissented. [Footnotes omitted. Eds.]

view that trial by jury was not available on the ground the suit was in "equity."

(b) As to tests for a directed verdict and sufficiency of evidence, in pre-Byrd days, Stoner v. New York Life Insurance Co., 311 U.S. 464 (1940) was read by some courts to mean that a diversity court is bound by state rules as to the sufficiency of the evidence to go to the jury. The question was explicitly left open in Dick v. New York Life Insurance Co., 359 U.S. 437, 444–445 (1959). Wratchford v. S. J. Groves & Sons Co., 405 F.2d 1061 (4th Cir. 1969) and Planters Manufacturing Co. v. Protection Mutual Insurance Co., 380 F.2d 869 (5th Cir. 1967) held that federal, not state, law determines when the judge takes an issue from the jury for insufficiency of opposing evidence. See Wright, Federal Courts 377–387 (4th Ed. 1983).

(c) As to size of the jury in civil cases, Wilson v. Nooter Corp., 475 F.2d 497 (1st Cir. 1973) ruled that having 12 jurors is not an "integral" part of the state-created right in a diversity action, so that a six-member jury suffices even when the state forum requires 12. See also Palmer v. Ford Motor Co., 498 F.2d 952 (10th Cir. 1974). See Moore & Bendix, Congress, Evidence and Rulemaking, 84 Yale L.J. 9 (1974); Note, The Law Applied in Diversity Cases: The Rules of Decision and the *Erie* Doctrine, 85 Yale L.J. 678 (1976).

HANNA v. PLUMER

Supreme Court of the United States, 1965.
380 U.S. 460, 85 S.Ct. 1136, 14 L.Ed.2d 8.

MR. CHIEF JUSTICE WARREN delivered the opinion of the Court.

The question to be decided is whether, in a civil action where the jurisdiction of the United States district court is based upon diversity of citizenship between the parties, service of process shall be made in the manner prescribed by state law or that set forth in Rule 4(d)(1) of the Federal Rules of Civil Procedure.

On February 6, 1963, petitioner, a citizen of Ohio, filed her complaint in the District Court for the District of Massachusetts, claiming damages in excess of $10,000 for personal injuries resulting from an automobile accident in South Carolina, allegedly caused by the negligence of one Louise Plumer Osgood, a Massachusetts citizen deceased at the time of the filing of the complaint. Respondent, Mrs. Osgood's executor and also a Massachusetts citizen, was named as defendant. On February 8, service was made by leaving copies of the summons and the complaint with respondent's wife at his residence, concededly in compliance with Rule 4(d)(1). . . . Respondent filed his answer . . . alleging, *inter alia*, that the action could not be maintained because [service had not been made in accordance with the "delivery in hand"] provisions of Massachusetts General Laws (Ter.Ed.) Chapter 197, Section 9. . . . On October 17, 1963, the District Court granted respondent's motion for summary judgment, citing Ragan v. Merchants Transfer & Warehouse Co., 337 U.S. 530, and Guaranty Trust Co. of New York v. York, 326 U.S. 99,

. . . The Court of Appeals for the First Circuit, . . . unanimously affirmed. . . .

We conclude that the adoption of Rule 4(d)(1), designed to control service of process in diversity actions, neither exceeded the congressional mandate embodied in the Rules Enabling Act [quoted on pages 669–670 of the Casebook] nor transgressed constitutional bounds, and that the Rule is therefore the standard against which the District Court should have measured the adequacy of the service. Accordingly, we reverse the decision of the Court of Appeals. . . .

Respondent suggests that the Erie doctrine acts as a check on the Federal Rules of Civil Procedure . . . Reduced to essentials, the argument is: (1) Erie, as refined in York, demands that federal courts apply state law whenever application of federal law in its stead will alter the outcome of the case. (2) In this case a determination that the Massachusetts service requirements obtained will result in immediate victory for respondent. If, on the other hand, it should be held that Rule 4(d)(1) is applicable, the litigation will continue, with possible victory for petitioner. (3) Therefore, Erie demands application of the Massachusetts rule. The syllogism possesses an appealing simplicity, but is for several reasons invalid.

In the first place, it is doubtful that, even if there were no Federal Rule making it clear that in-hand service is not required in diversity actions, the Erie rule would have obligated the District Court to follow the Massachusetts procedure. "Outcome-determination" analysis was never intended to serve as a talisman. . . . Indeed, the message of *York* itself is that choices between state and federal law are to be made not by the application of any automatic, "litmus paper" criterion, but rather by reference to the policies underlying the *Erie* rule. Guaranty Trust Co. v. York, supra, at 108–112.

The Erie rule is rooted in part in a realization that it would be unfair for the character or result of a litigation materially to differ because the suit had been brought in a federal court. . . . The decision was also in part a reaction to the practice of "forum-shopping" which had grown up in response to the rule of Swift v. Tyson. . . . Not only are nonsubstantial, or trivial, variations not likely to raise the sort of equal protection problems which troubled the Court in Erie; they are also unlikely to influence the choice of a forum. The "outcome-determination" test therefore cannot be read without reference to the twin aims of the Erie rule: discouragement of forum-shopping and avoidance of inequitable administration of the laws.

The difference between the conclusion that the Massachusetts rule is applicable, and the conclusion that it is not, is of course at this point "outcome-determinative" in the sense that if we hold the state rule to apply, respondent prevails, whereas if we hold that Rule 4(d)(1) governs, the litigation will continue. But in this sense *every* procedural variation is "outcome-determinative." For example, having brought suit in a federal court, a plaintiff cannot then insist on the right to file subsequent pleadings in accord with the time limits applicable in state courts, even though enforcement of the federal timetable will, if he continues to insist that he must meet only the state time limit, result in determination of the controversy against him. So it is here. Though choice of the federal or state rule will at this point have a marked effect upon the outcome of the litigation, the difference between the two rules would be of scant, if any, relevance to the choice of a forum. Petitioner, in choosing her forum, was not presented with a situation where application of the state rule would wholly bar recovery; rather, adherence to the state rule would have resulted only in altering the way in which process was served. . . .

There is, however, a more fundamental flaw in respondent's syllogism: the incorrect assumption that the rule of Erie R. Co. v. Tompkins constitutes the appropriate test of the validity and therefore the applicability of a Federal Rule of Civil Procedure. The Erie rule has never been invoked to void a Federal Rule. . . .

. . . It is true that both the Enabling Act and the Erie rule say, roughly, that federal courts are to apply state "substantive" law and federal "procedural" law, but from that it need not follow that the tests are identical. For they were designed to control very different sorts of decisions. When a situation is covered by one of the Federal Rules, the question facing the court is a far cry from the typical, relatively unguided Erie choice: the court has been instructed to apply the Federal Rule, and can refuse to do so only if the Advisory Committee, this Court, and Congress erred in their prima facie judgment that the Rule in question transgresses neither the terms of the Enabling Act nor constitutional restrictions.

. . . [T]he opinion in Erie, which involved no Federal Rule and dealt with a question which was "substantive" in every traditional sense (whether the railroad owed a duty of care to Tompkins as a trespasser or a licensee), surely neither said nor implied that measures like Rule 4(d)(1) are unconstitutional. For the constitutional provision for a federal court system (augmented by the Necessary and Proper Clause) carries with it congressional power to make rules governing the practice and pleading in those courts, which in turn includes a power to regulate matters which, though falling within the uncertain area between substance and procedure, are rationally capable of classification as either. . . .

Erie and its offspring cast no doubt on the long-recognized power of Congress to prescribe housekeeping rules for federal courts even though some of those rules will inevitably differ from comparable state rules. . . . To hold that a Federal Rule of Civil Procedure must cease to function whenever it alters the mode of enforcing state-created rights would be to disembowel either the Constitution's grant of power over federal procedure or Congress' attempt to exercise that power in the Enabling Act.   Rule 4(d)(1) is valid and controls the instant case.

Reversed.

Mr. JUSTICE HARLAN, concurring.

It is unquestionably true that up to now Erie and the cases following it have not succeeded in articulating a workable doctrine governing choice of law in diversity actions.   I respect the Court's effort to clarify the situation in today's opinion.   However, in doing so I think it has misconceived the constitutional premises of Erie and has failed to deal adequately with those past decisions upon which the courts below relied.

Erie was something more than an opinion which worried about "forum-shopping and avoidance of inequitable administration of the laws,"   .   .   .   although to be sure these were important elements of the decision.   I have always regarded that decision as one of the modern cornerstones of our federalism, expressing policies that profoundly touch the allocation of judicial power between the state and federal systems.   Erie recognized that there should not be two conflicting systems of law controlling the primary activity of citizens, for such alternative governing authority must necessarily give rise to a debilitating uncertainty in the planning of everyday affairs.   And it recognized that the scheme of our Constitution envisions an allocation of law-making functions between state and federal legislative processes which is undercut if the federal judiciary can make substantive law affecting state affairs beyond the bounds of congressional legislative powers in this regard.   Thus, in diversity cases Erie commands that it be the state law governing primary private activity which prevails.

The shorthand formulations which have appeared in some past decisions are prone to carry untoward results that frequently arise from oversimplification.   The Court is quite right in stating that the "outcome-determinative" test of Guaranty Trust Co. of New York v. York, 326 U.S. 99, if taken literally, proves too much, for any rule, no matter how clearly "procedural," can affect the outcome of litigation if it is not obeyed.   In turning from the "outcome" test of York back to the unadorned forum-shopping rationale of Erie, however, the Court falls prey to like oversimplification, for a simple forum-shopping rule also proves too much; litigants often choose a federal forum merely to obtain what they consider the advantages of the Federal Rules of Civil Procedure or to try their cases before a supposedly more favorable judge.   To my mind the proper line of approach in determining whether to apply a state or a federal rule, whether "substantive" or "procedural," is to stay close to basic principles by inquiring if the choice of rule would substantially affect those primary decisions respecting human conduct which our constitutional system leaves to state regulation.   If so, Erie and the Constitution require that the state rule prevail, even in the face of a conflicting federal rule.

The Court weakens, if indeed it does not submerge, this basic principle by finding, in effect, a grant of substantive legislative power in the constitutional provision for a federal court system . . . , and through it, setting up the Federal Rules as a body of law inviolate. So long as a reasonable man could characterize any duly adopted federal rule as "procedural," the Court, unless I misapprehend what is said, would have it apply no matter how seriously it frustrated a State's substantive regulation of the primary conduct and affairs of its citizens. Since the members of the Advisory Committee, the Judicial Conference, and this Court who formulated the Federal Rules are presumably reasonable men, it follows that the integrity of the Federal Rules is absolute. Whereas the unadulterated outcome and forum-shopping tests may err too far toward honoring state rules, I submit that the Court's "arguably procedural, *ergo* constitutional" test moves too fast and far in the other direction.

The courts below relied upon this Court's decisions in Ragan v. Merchants Transfer & Warehouse Co., 337 U.S. 530, and Cohen v. Beneficial Indus. Loan Corp., 337 U.S. 541. Those cases deserve more attention than this Court has given them, particularly Ragan which, if still good law, would in my opinion call for affirmance of the result reached by the Court of Appeals. Further, a discussion of these two cases will serve to illuminate the "diversity" thesis I am advocating.

In Ragan a Kansas statute of limitations provided that an action was deemed commenced when service was made on the defendant. Despite Federal Rule 3 which provides that an action commences with the filing of the complaint, the Court held that for purposes of the Kansas statute of limitations a diversity tort action commenced only when service was made upon the defendant. The effect of this holding was that although the plaintiff had filed his federal complaint within the state period of limitations, his action was barred because the federal marshal did not serve a summons on the defendant until after the limitations period had run. I think that the decision was wrong. At most, application of the Federal Rule would have meant that potential Kansas tort defendants would have to defer for a few days the satisfaction of knowing that they had not been sued within the limitations period. The choice of the Federal Rule would have had no effect on the primary stages of private activity from which torts arise, and only the most minimal effect on behavior following the commission of the tort. In such circumstances the interest of the federal system in proceeding under its own rules should have prevailed.

Cohen v. Beneficial Indus. Loan Corp. held that a federal diversity court must apply a state statute requiring a small stockholder in a stockholder derivative suit to post a bond securing payment of defense costs as a condition to prosecuting an action. Such a statute is not "outcome determinative"; the plaintiff can win with or without it. . . . The proper view of Cohen is, in my opinion, that the statute was meant to inhibit small stockholders from instituting "strike suits," and thus it was designed and could be expected to have a substantial impact on private primary activity. Anyone who was at the trial bar during the period when Cohen arose can appreciate the strong state policy reflected in the statute. I think it wholly legitimate to view Federal Rule 23 as not purporting to deal with the problem. But even had the Federal Rules purported to do so, and in so doing provided a substantially less effective deterrent to strike suits, I think the state rule should still have prevailed. That is where I believe the Court's view differs from mine; for the Court attributes such overriding force to the Federal Rules that it is hard to think of a case where a conflicting state rule would be allowed to operate, even though the state rule reflected policy considerations which, under Erie, would lie within the realm of state legislative authority.

It remains to apply what has been said to the present case. The Massachusetts rule provides that an executor need not answer suits unless in-hand service was made upon him or notice of the action was filed in the proper registry of probate within one year of his giving bond. The evident intent of this statute is to permit an executor to distribute the estate which he is administering without fear that further liabilities may be outstanding for which he could be held personally liable. If the Federal District Court in Massachusetts applies Rule 4(d)(1) of the Federal Rules of Civil Procedure instead of the Massachusetts service rule, what effect would that have on the speed and assurance with which estates are distributed? As I see it, the effect would not be substantial. It would mean simply that an executor would have to check at his own house or the federal courthouse as well as the registry of probate before he could distribute the estate with impunity. As this does not seem enough to give rise to any real impingement on the vitality of the state policy which the Massachusetts rule is intended to serve, I concur in the judgment of the Court.

WALKER V. ARMCO STEEL CORP., 446 U.S. 740 (1980): In a diversity action the complaint was filed within the two year statute of limitations of the forum state, but defendant was not served with process until after the statutory period had run. The Court found these facts "indistinguishable" from those in Ragan v. Merchants Transfer & Warehouse Co., 337 U.S. 530 (1949), p. 691, supra. Contrary to petitioner's claim, Ragan was not weakened by Hanna v. Plumer because Rule 3 did not come into "direct collision" with state law by affecting the running of state statutes of limitation. The Court said,

"In contrast to Rule 3, the Oklahoma statute is a statement of a substantive decision by that State that actual service on, and accordingly actual notice by, the defendant is an integral part of the several policies served by the statute of limitations. See C & C Tile Co. v. Independent School District No. 7 of Tulsa County, 503 P.2d 554, 559 (Okl.1972). The statute of limitations establishes a deadline after which the defendant may legitimately have peace of mind; it also recognizes that after a certain period of time it is unfair to require the defendant to attempt to piece together his defense to an old claim. A requirement of actual service promotes both of those functions of the statute. See generally ibid.; Seitz v. Jones, 370 P.2d 300, 302 (Okl. 1961). See also Ely, The Irrepressible Myth of Erie, 87 Harv.L.Rev. 693, 730–731 (1974).[12] It is these policy aspects which make the service requirement an 'integral' part of the statute of limitations both in this case and in *Ragan*. As such, the service rule must be considered part and parcel of the statute of limitations."

NOTES

(1) For a treatment of Hanna and the problems it addresses, see Ely, The Irrepressible Myth of Erie, 87 Harv.L.Rev. 693 (1974). Commenting *dubitante* on Professor Ely's view that the Enabling Act furnishes a useful standard in determining whether federal law is applicable whenever the issue is covered by a Federal Rule, see Chayes, The Bead Game, 87 Harv.L.Rev. 741 (1974). After Hanna, if the Federal Rules of Civil Procedure adopt provisions fixing time limitations for diversity actions in the federal courts, will they be constitutional? If so, is Guaranty Trust Co. v. York overruled?

(2) Byrnes v. Kirby, 453 F.Supp. 1014 (D.Mass.1978). Diversity action in a federal district court in Massachusetts to recover for injuries suffered in this state as the result of alleged malpractice. Upon motion of the defendant, the court referred the case to a medical malpractice tribunal pursuant to a Massachusetts statute which provided that if the tribunal were to find that the case involved "merely an unfortunate medical result" the plaintiff could maintain the action only after filing a bond. The court said that

> reference to a medical malpractice tribunal . . . would fulfill the "twin aims of Erie," expressed in the *Hanna* case, of preventing forum shopping and avoiding unfairness in the administration of the laws. . . . It would . . . be inequitable to permit [diversity] litigants to bypass the procedure of a tribunal hearing . . . . There appears to be no federal policy, such as that favoring jury determination of factual is-

---

12. The importance of actual service, with corresponding actual notice, to the statute of limitations scheme in Oklahoma is further demonstrated by the fact that under Okla.Stat., Tit. 12, § 97 (1971) the statute of limitations must be tolled as to each defendant through individual service, unless a codefendant who is served is "united in interest" with the unserved defendant. That requirement, like the service requirement itself, does nothing to promote the general policy behind all statutes of limitations of keeping stale claims out of court. Instead, the service requirement furthers a different but related policy decision: that each defendant has a legitimate right not to be surprised by notice of a lawsuit after the period of liability has run. If the defendant is "united in interest" with a codefendant who has been served, then presumably the defendant will receive actual notice of the lawsuit through the codefendant and will not have his peace of mind disturbed when he receives official service of process. Similarly, the defendant will know that he must begin gathering his evidence while that task is still deemed by the State to be feasible.

sues . . . that would be contravened by [this] reference to a state medical malpractice tribunal.

For a discussion of the factors that should be considered by a federal court in determining whether to apply federal or state law in a situation not covered by the Rules Enabling Act, see Redish and Phillips, *Erie* and the Rules of Decision Act: In Search of the Appropriate Dilemma, 91 Harv.L. Rev. 356 (1977). See also Wellborn, The Federal Rules of Evidence and The Application of State Law in The Federal Courts, 55 Tex.L.Rev. 371 (1977).

(3) Grand Bahama Petroleum Co. v. Asiatic Petroleum, 550 F.2d 1320 (2d Cir. 1977). Diversity action brought in a federal district court in New York to compel arbitration under the United States Arbitration Act. The defense was that the action could not be maintained by reason of a New York statute which prohibited the bringing of an action in the state by a foreign corporation which was doing business there without authority. Held that the action could proceed. To hold otherwise would "frustrate the petitioner's access to a federal forum to litigate an admittedly federal matter and thereby limit the uniform and effective application of a federal statute."

(4) Despite some retraction of the scope of the Erie doctrine, it remains the law that in diversity cases state law prevails over federal on many issues crucial to the decision. To what extent do state rules of res judicata prevail over federal in determining the effect of the decision in later litigation? See Vestal, Res Judicata/Preclusion by Judgment: The Law Applied in Federal Courts, 66 Mich.L.Rev. 1723 (1968). Cf. Vestal, Res Judicata Preclusion: Expansion, 47 So.Cal.L.Rev. 357, 359 (1974); Vestal, Preclusion/Res Judicata Variables: Parties, 50 Iowa L.Rev. 27 (1964). See Chapter 5, p. 253, supra; Angel v. Bullington, p. 714, infra.

B. THE ERIE DOCTRINE AND CONFLICT OF LAWS IN DIVERSITY CASES

In Sampson v. Channell, 110 F.2d 754 (1st Cir. 1940), cert. denied 310 U.S. 650, the issue was whether a federal diversity court in Massachusetts was bound to follow state or federal law as to burden of proof of contributory negligence by plaintiff in a Maine auto accident case; and if state law, that of Maine or Massachusetts. In the view of the Court of Appeals, the questions turned on whether the burden of proof question should be classified as an issue of federal procedure, in order to implement the underlying policy of the Erie doctrine, or whether it should be viewed as substantive under a fair reading of that doctrine's criteria. In a superb opinion Judge Magruder ruled that the issue was substantive by Erie criteria and, hence, that state law was determinative; that Massachusetts would have applied its own burden rule, classifying the issue as procedural for state-state choice-of-law purposes; that this would be a constitutionally valid approach; and that consistent with the "implications" of Erie, the federal court must follow the Massachusetts conflict of laws approach, in order to promote uniformity between the federal and state courts of the forum.

Does not the Sampson decision pose the prospect of a lack of uniformity among federal courts, not only on any given issue, but even on a single issue in a single case? Thus, if suit is brought in one federal court (i.e., Maine, the site of the accident) rather than in another possible forum (i.e., Massachusetts, where one side was domiciled), the outcome changes.

In non-diversity cases, such as admiralty or other federal specialties, the federal courts are, of course, free to fashion independent choice-of-law rules. See e.g., Scott v. Eastern Airlines, 399 F.2d 14 (3d Cir. 1967), cert. denied 393 U.S. 979 (1968).

KLAXON CO. v. STENTOR ELECTRIC MANUFACTURING CO.

Supreme Court of the United States, 1941.
313 U.S. 487, 61 S.Ct. 1020, 85 L.Ed. 1477.

MR. JUSTICE REED delivered the opinion of the Court.

The principal question in this case is whether in diversity cases the federal courts must follow conflict of laws rules prevailing in the states in which they sit. We left this open in Ruhlin v. New York Life Insurance Company, 304 U.S. 202, 208, note 2. The frequent recurrence of the problem, as well as the conflict of approach to the problem between the Third Circuit's opinion here and that of the First Circuit in Sampson v. Channell, 110 F.2d 754, 759–762, 128 A.L.R. 394, led us to grant certiorari.

In 1918 respondent, a New York corporation, transferred its entire business to petitioner, a Delaware corporation. Petitioner contracted to use its best efforts to further the manufacture and sale of certain patented devices covered by the agreement, and respondent was to have a share of petitioner's profits. The agreement was executed in New York, the assets were transferred there, and petitioner began performance there although later it moved its operations to other states. Respondent was voluntarily dissolved under New York law in 1919. Ten years later it instituted this action in the United States District Court for the District of Delaware, alleging that petitioner had failed to perform its agreement to use its best efforts. Jurisdiction rested on diversity of citizenship. In 1939 respondent recovered a jury verdict of $100,000, upon which judgment was entered. Respondent then moved to correct the judgment by adding interest at the rate of six percent from June 1, 1929, the date the action had been brought. The basis of the motion was the provision in section 480 of the New York Civil Practice Act directing that in contract actions interest be added to the principal sum "whether theretofore liquidated or unliquidated." The District Court granted the motion, taking the view that the rights of the parties were governed by New

York law and that under New York law the addition of such interest was mandatory. 30 F.Supp. 425, 431. The Circuit Court of Appeals affirmed, 3 Cir., 115 F.2d 268, 275, and we granted certiorari, limited to the question whether section 480 of the New York Civil Practice Act is applicable to an action in the federal court in Delaware, 312 U.S. 674.

The Circuit Court of Appeals was of the view that under New York law the right to interest before verdict under section 480 went to the substance of the obligation, and that proper construction of the contract in suit fixed New York as the place of performance. It then concluded that section 480 was applicable to the case because "it is clear by what we think is undoubtedly the better view of the law that the rules for ascertaining the measure of damages are not a matter of procedure at all, but are matters of substance which should be settled by reference to the law of the appropriate state according to the type of case being tried in the forum. The measure of damages for breach of a contract is determined by the law of the place of performance; Restatement, Conflict of Laws, sec. 413." The court referred also to section 418 of the Restatement, which makes interest part of the damages to be determined by the law of the place of performance. Application of the New York statute apparently followed from the court's independent determination of the "better view" without regard to Delaware law, for no Delaware decision or statute was cited or discussed.

We are of opinion that the prohibition declared in Erie Railroad v. Tompkins, 304 U.S. 64, against such independent determinations by the federal courts extends to the field of conflict of laws. The conflict of laws rules to be applied by the federal court in Delaware must conform to those prevailing in Delaware's state courts. Otherwise the accident of diversity of citizenship would constantly disturb equal administration of justice in coordinate state and federal courts sitting side by side. . . . Any other ruling would do violence to the principle of uniformity within a state upon which the Tompkins decision is based. Whatever lack of uniformity this may produce between federal courts in different states is attributable to our federal system, which leaves to a state, within the limits permitted by the Constitution, the right to pursue local policies diverging from those of its neighbors. It is not for the federal courts to thwart such local policies by enforcing an independent "general law" of conflict of laws. Subject only to review by this Court on any federal question that may arise, Delaware is free to determine whether a given matter is to be governed by the law of the forum or some other law. Cf. Milwaukee County v. White Co., 296 U.S. 268, 272. This Court's views are not the decisive factor in determining the applicable conflicts rule. Cf. Funkhouser v. J.B. Preston Co., 290 U.S. 163. And the proper function of the Delaware federal court is to ascertain what the state law is, not what it ought to be. . . . [The opinion states it would be constitutional for Delaware to apply its local law in this case.]

Accordingly, the judgment is reversed and the case remanded to the Circuit Court of Appeals for decision in conformity with the law of Delaware.

NOTES

(1) On remand of the principal case the Court of Appeals found there was no Delaware statute or decision directly on the conflict of laws point. It adhered to its earlier conclusion that the Delaware conflict of laws rule was that the New York local law would govern. 125 F.2d 820 (1942). The Supreme Court denied certiorari. 316 U.S. 685 (1942).

(2) Is Klaxon v. Stentor an inevitable deduction from the logic of Erie? Should a federal court in a diversity action be any less able to prescribe its own choice of law rules than a court of State Z in a transaction solely connected with states X and Y? Cf. Cheatham, Federal Control of Conflict of Laws, 6 Vand.L.Rev. 581 (1953). For a penetrating and comprehensive discussion of the subject, see Cavers, Change in Choice-of-Law Thinking and Its Bearing on the Klaxon Problem, in the American Law Institute's Study of the Division of Jurisdiction Between State and Federal Courts (Official Draft 1969). See also Baxter, Choice of Law and the Federal System, 16 Stan.L. Rev. 1 (1963); Meador, State Law and the Federal Judicial Power, 49 Va.L. Rev. 1082 (1963); Weintraub, The Erie Doctrine and State Conflict of Laws Rules, 39 Ind.L.J. 228 (1964).

(3) The Supreme Court went out of its way in Day and Zimmerman v. Challoner, 423 U.S. 3 (1975), to reaffirm Klaxon in strong terms, declaring:

". . . A federal court in a diversity case is not free to engraft onto . . . state rules [of choice of law] exceptions or modifications which may commend themselves to the federal court, but which have not commended themselves to the State in which the federal court sits."

(4) In re Holiday Airlines Corp., 620 F.2d 731 (9th Cir. 1980). The question involved the effect that should be given in a California bankruptcy proceeding to an artisan's lien for work done in the State of Washington on a propeller assembly. The Court held that the lien was effective under the law of Washington which, being the state of most significant relationship, was the state whose law should be applied. The Court said that "the rule in diversity of citizenship cases, i.e., a mechanical application of the conflicts law of the forum State, should not be required in bankruptcy proceedings, at least in Federal Aviation Act cases."

GRIFFIN v. McCOACH, 313 U.S. 498 (1941): A policy of insurance on the life of a syndicate promoter named the members of the syndicate, who were to pay the premiums as the principal beneficiaries. The promoter was a citizen of Texas, but the policy was applied for and delivered in New York. The application was acted on in New Jersey at the home office of the Insurance company. Years later an agreement not to change beneficiaries was executed. All elements of this latter transaction occurred in either New York or New Jersey, except that the promoter insured signed the insurance forms in Texas. On the death of the insured his personal representative contended that the snydicate members could not take under the policy, for according to Texas law they had no insurable interest. The insurance company filed a bill of interpleader in the federal court in Texas to have it determined who was entitled to the proceeds of the policy. The personal representative of the insured urged that Texas law should be held to govern the transaction, but that even if the law of another state applied it was against the public policy of Texas for the syndicate members to collect the proceeds.

MR. JUSTICE REED. . . .

For the reasons given in Klaxon Co. v. Stentor Electric Manufacturing Co., 313 U.S. 487, decided today, we are of the view that the federal courts in diversity of citizenship cases are governed by the conflict of laws rules of the courts of the states in which they sit. In deciding that the changes made in the insurance contract left its governing law unaffected and that the laws of Texas could not be applied to a foreign contract in Texas courts, the federal courts were applying rules of law in a way which may or may not have been consistent with Texas decisions. Likewise it is for Texas to say whether its public policy permits a beneficiary of an insurance policy on the life of a Texas citizen to recover where no insurable interest in the decedent exists in the beneficiary. . . . The decision must be reversed and remanded to the Circuit Court of Appeals for determination of the law of Texas as applied to the circumstances of this case.

. . .

If upon examination of the Texas law it appears that the courts of Texas would refuse enforcement of an insurance contract where the beneficiaries have no insurable interest on the ground of its interference with local law, such refusal would be, in our opinion, within the constitutional power of the Texas courts. . . . [T]his Court affirmed the federal court in following Texas' decisions which refused to enforce a valid foreign contract of guarantyship against a married woman. Union Trust Co. v. Grosman, 245 U.S. 412. . . . Where this Court has required the state of the forum to apply the foreign law under the full faith and credit clause or under the Fourteenth Amendment it has recognized that a state is not required to enforce a law obnoxious to its public policy. . . .

. . . It is for the state to say whether a contract contrary to such a statute or rule of law is so offensive to its view of public welfare as to require its courts to close their doors to its enforcement.

Reversed.

MR. JUSTICE FRANKFURTER concurs in the result.

NOTES

(1) Is the Griffin case "unreasonable" in applying the law of Texas to a person from outside the state considering that Texas could not have exercised judicial jurisdiction over him? See Vestal, Erie R.R. v. Tompkins: A Projection, 48 Iowa L.Rev. 248, 269 (1963).

(2) Are the federal courts to have any share in the development of conflict of laws? See Freund, Chief Justice Stone and the Conflict of Laws, 59 Harv.L.Rev. 1210, 1236 (1946). Did the summary rejection of federally fashioned choice-of-law rules and reaffirmation of Klaxon in Day and Zimmerman, Inc. v. Challoner, 423 U.S. 3 (1975), end that speculation?

The Impact of the Interest Analysis Upon Klaxon and Griffin

Was Klaxon correct to fear that freeing a federal diversity court from the choice-of-law rules of the state forum "would do violence" to Erie's principle? Many commentators believe not. Professor Alfred Hill cogently argued that local bias—the very evil federal diversity jurisdiction was to combat—can make itself felt "particularly through arbitrary choice of law rules" which bear unevenly on out-of-state litigants. Hill, The Erie Doctrine and The Constitution, 53 Nw. U.L.Rev. 427, 544 (1958). This was true even in the days when the vested rights approach to choice of law was the norm. It is even more true in modern times, with the rise of the interest analysis and its strong forum-favoring tendencies.

As Currie taught, and as many courts and commentators agree, a state court is likely to perceive its own state's interests as more heavily implicated and its own legislature's rules as more just and deserving of vindication than competing norms derived from other legal systems. Furthermore, with the expansion of long-arm jurisdiction, the plaintiff's options in selecting a forum have multiplied, raising the odds that the court chosen is one with plaintiff-favoring rules on critical issues. Accentuating these factors is the circumstance that through the whole of the law is a rising trend to favor compensating the plaintiff for injuries suffered. Courts can be counted on to strain their ingenuity—sometimes more, sometimes less—to maximize the chances and size of claimant's recoveries. With all these forces combining through the calculus of the interest analysis to impel a state forum to make a choice of law to favor a local plaintiff, why should the federal courts ape them?

Doing so not only makes the federal courts allies of the states in indulging local bias through choice of law, but also enhances uncertainty and non-uniformity. In H. Hart and H. Wechsler, The Federal Courts and The Federal System 634–35 (1953), the argument was made that the Klaxon doctrine is directly opposed to Erie's purpose of avoiding uncertainty for persons conducting primary activities, because when the doctrine is applied results will shift with the happenstance of the forum's choice-of-law rules; and the unpredictability will apply in federal courts as much as in state courts.

Is the Erie doctrine not misapplied here for yet another reason? When multistate "interests" collide, why should the United States courts not function as federal system umpires, rather than as "ventriloquists' dummies" for the state courts of the forum? See Hart,

The Relations Between State and Federal Law, 54 Colum.L.Rev. 489 (1954); Baxter, Choice of Law and The Federal System, 16 Stan.L. Rev. 1 (1963); Horowitz, Toward a Federal Common Law of Choice of Law, 14 U.C.L.A.L.Rev. 1191 (1967).

Taking the other side of the argument, Professor Cavers, p. 706, n. 2, supra, favors the Klaxon doctrine for several reasons already noted and also on the pragmatic ground that forum-shopping as between state and federal courts in a given state is a more serious risk than the possibility of shopping across state lines. This is so because the person in control of the choice of forum is the plaintiff's lawyer, who will not want to compromise his fee by sending the case to an attorney in another state.

SAMUELSON v. SUSEN

United States Court of Appeals, Third Circuit, 1978.
576 F.2d 546.

[A portion of the opinion in this case appears in Chapter 7, supra, starting at p. 419.]

.   .   .

Prior to the enactment of Rule 501, federal court decisions had determined that in civil actions and proceedings governed by Erie R. Co. v. Tompkins, 304 U.S. 64 (1938), state created privileges conferred substantive rights beyond regulation by federal procedural rules. See Republic Gear Co. v. Borg-Warner Corp., 381 F.2d 551, 555–556 n. 2 (2d Cir. 1967). In the form originally prepared, the Federal Rules of Evidence would not have required federal courts to recognize privileges created by state law in civil actions and proceedings governed by *Erie*. Preliminary Draft of Proposed Rules of Evidence for the United States Courts and Magistrates, 46 F.R.D. 161 (1969).

The House of Representatives amended the proposed rules to require the application of state privilege law in cases governed by *Erie*. (It was the House amendment that was eventually enacted into law as Rule 501). The House supported its position with the following contentions: (1) privilege rules are and should continue to be considered substantive for *Erie* purposes; (2) privilege rules are outcome determinative; (3) where state law supplies the rule of decision, state rules of privilege should be applied because there is no federal interest substantial enough to justify departure from state policy; and (4) state policy regarding privilege should not be thwarted merely because of diversity jurisdiction, a situation which, if allowed, would encourage forum shopping. H.R.Rep.No.650, 93rd Cong., 1st Sess. 9 (1973).

A federal court's application of the law of privilege which the forum states' courts would apply in cases like the instant one, seems to us to be consistent with Congress' goal of effectuating state substantive rights, laws and policies in controversies where there is no substantial federal interest. Such an approach furthers Congress' goal of preserving the domain of state privilege law in diversity cases by achieving outcome identity between state and federal courts of the forum state on choice of law, thus discouraging forum shopping. Such an approach also takes cognizance of the fact that a forum state's choice-of-law rules may reflect important policy underpinnings of its own law and are an integral part of it. . . .

We are mindful of the fact that in *Klaxon* the Supreme Court was in effect interpreting the reference in the Rules of Decision Act to "the laws of the several states . . . in cases where they 'apply' to include a forum state's choice-of-law rules." As one commentator has pointed out, "[t]he reference in that Act to the laws of the several states . . . in cases where they apply is no less ambiguous in terms of horizontal choice of law than the references to 'State law' in the Federal Rules of Evidence." Wellborn, The Federal Rules of Evidence and the Application of State Law in Federal Courts, 55 Texas L.Rev. 371, 446 (1977).

The interpretation of "State law" urged upon us by plaintiff would prevent the application of all of a forum state's law, including its choice-of-law rules. Such a denial would be antithetical to one of the primary goals of Rule 501, the recognition that where states have created rights, the federal courts should apply the same rules of law to those rights which the states themselves would apply. Moreover, to require a federal court to ignore some of a state's choice-of-law rules, as plaintiff's interpretation of "State law" in Rule 501 would do, would obviously invite forum shopping in direct contradiction of one of the aims of Rule 501.

We believe our interpretation of the meaning of "State law" in the second sentence of Rule 501 to be the most consistent with the prevailing view of federalism on the allocation of lawmaking authority in diversity cases—a view Congress seemed intent upon preserving when it enacted the measure. . . .

FACTORS ETC., INC. v. PRO ARTS, INC., 652 F.2d 278 (2d Cir. 1981), cert. denied 456 U.S. 927 (1982): The Memphis Development Foundation was formed to erect a bronze statue of Elvis Presley in downtown Memphis. The Foundation sought to raise money by selling eight-inch pewter replicas of the proposed statue at $25 each. It sued in a federal court in Tennessee to prevent Factors from interfering with the Foundation's efforts to market the Presley statuettes. Factors claimed under an exclusive license to use Presley's name and likeness for the manufacture and sale of merchandise of all kinds. The Sixth Circuit Court of Appeals decided in favor of the Foundation, holding that under Tennessee law Presley's right of publicity did not survive his death. Memphis Development Foundation v. Factors Etc., Inc., 616 F.2d 956 (6th Cir.), cert. denied 449 U.S. 953 (1980).

Contemporaneously, Factors started a diversity action in New York to enforce its exclusive license against Pro Arts, Inc. On the question of Factors' right to enforce its license on the basis of Tennessee law, the Court of Appeals for the Second Circuit decided in the negative because it felt it was obliged to follow the holding to that effect by Tennessee's "home" circuit, the Sixth:

ative because it felt it was obliged to follow a holding to that effect
by Tennessee's "home" circuit, the Sixth:

> . . . Where, as here, the pertinent court of appeals has essayed
> its own prediction of the course of state law on a question of first
> impression within that state, the federal courts of other circuits
> should defer to that holding, perhaps always, and at least in all
> situations except the rare instance when it can be said with convic-
> tion that the pertinent court of appeals has disregarded clear sig-
> nals emanating from the state's highest court pointing toward a
> different rule. . . .

A few months after this decision a Tennessee state court held that
the right of publicity did survive. The plaintiffs were allowed to petition the Second Circuit to recall its mandate and rehear the case in
the light of the Tennessee decision. See Factors, Etc., Inc. v. Pro
Arts, Inc., 541 F.Supp. 231 (S.D.N.Y.1982).

———

DOGGRELL v. SOUTHERN BOX CO.

Court of Appeals of the United States, Sixth Circuit, 1953.
208 F.2d 310.

[An Arkansas corporation was formed with three men as the in-
corporators and stockholders, two of whom were residents of Tennessee and the third a resident of Arkansas. The statutes of Arkansas
called for the articles of incorporation to be filed with the Secretary
of State and also with the County Clerk of the county in which the
corporation had its principal place of business. Through the inadver-
tence of the Arkansas stockholder the articles were not filed with the
County Clerk until after the corporate purchase mentioned below,
though the Tennessee stockholders did not know of the failure. Under the Arkansas law the stockholders of a corporation were liable as
partners when the articles of incorporation were not filed with the
County Clerk. The Arkansas stockholder, who managed the business
of the corporation, purchased goods in Arkansas in the name of the
corporation. When the goods were not paid for, the creditor brought
suit for the purchase price against the Tennessee stockholders in the
Federal district court in Tennessee. The defense was made that the
Arkansas statute was a penal one, but the District Court rejected the
defense and gave judgment for the plaintiff. The Court of Appeals,
with the judges divided two to one, affirmed the judgment for the
plaintiff. (206 F.2d 671.) The defendant filed a petition for rehearing. During the pendency of the petition for rehearing, the Supreme
Court of Tennessee held in another case that the Arkansas statute
was a penal one and would not be enforced by the Tennessee state
courts.

Thereupon the Court of Appeals, with the same three judges sitting, withdrew their earlier ruling and reversed the judgment for the plaintiff, again by a vote of two to one.]

McALLISTER, CIRCUIT JUDGE. For the reasons stated in the dissenting opinion heretofore filed,* and because of the decisions of the Supreme Court of Tennessee in the cases of Paper Products Co. v. Doggrell, 261 S.W.2d 127 [195 Tenn. 581] as well as the decision and opinion of the Supreme Court of Tennessee on the petition for rehearing of Paper Products Co. v. Doggrell, 261 S.W.2d 130 [195 Tenn. 581, 588], all filed during the pendency of a motion for rehearing in the above entitled cause, in which it was held that the provision of the Arkansas statute in question was a penal statute and would not be enforced by the courts of Tennessee, and that appellant was a stockholder in a *de facto* corporation and, according to the law of Tennessee, would not be individually liable for the payment of the debts of the Arkansas corporation, I am of the opinion that the petition for rehearing should be granted; that the opinion heretofore filed should be set aside; and that a judgment should be entered in favor of appellant.

MILLER, CIRCUIT JUDGE. Although I am not in agreement with the recent opinion of the Supreme Court of Tennessee in the case of Paper Products Co. v. Doggrell, Tenn.Sup., 261 S.W.2d 127, rehearing denied, October 9, 1953, Tenn.Sup., 261 S.W.2d 130, I am of the opinion that under the authority of Erie R. Co. v. Tompkins, 304 U.S. 64; Vandenbark v. Owens-Illinois Glass Co., 311 U.S. 538; Klaxon Co. v. Stentor Co., 313 U.S. 487, and Guaranty Trust Co. v. York, 326 U.S. 99, 109–110, the ruling in that case is controlling in this case, with the result that the petition for rehearing should be granted and the judgment of the District Court be reversed.

MARTIN, CIRCUIT JUDGE (dissenting).

Appellant presents on petition for rehearing the opinion of the Supreme Court of Tennessee in Paper Products Co. v. Doggrell, Tenn. Sup., 261 S.W.2d 130, wherein the state court adheres to its previous decision and cites and discusses with approval the dissenting opinion of Judge McAllister in the instant case. Judge McAllister adheres to his previous views and Judge Miller, who concurred in the opinion which I wrote, while not in agreement with the conclusion reached by the Supreme Court of Tennessee, is of the opinion that the petition to rehear should be sustained, the former ruling of this court set aside, and the judgment of the district court reversed. He bases this conclusion upon what he considers to be the compelling effect of the following authorities: . . . if we had before us a simple issue of conflict in the common law between states, the Klaxon case would be controlling. . . .

* Doggrell v. Great Southern Box Co.,
206 F.2d 671 (1953).

But, in my judgment, we confront no such situations here. I think that, in the instant matter, the Supreme Court of Tennessee, contrary to the Constitution of the United States, has failed to give full faith and credit as required by the Constitution to the judgment of the highest court of Arkansas, based upon the latter court's interpretation of an Arkansas statute. The appellant in the case at bar occupies the exact status which the Supreme Court of Arkansas, in an identical case, Whitaker v. Mitchell Mfg. Co., 219 Ark. 779, 244 S.W. 2d 965, held imposed liability upon a stockholder of an Arkansas corporation which had failed to conform to the corporate organization laws of that state.

Long before the revolutionary doctrine of Erie R. Co. v. Tompkins was promulgated, it had been recognized that the interpretation of a state statute by its highest court becomes in effect a part of the statute, unless in contravention of the federal Constitution or of federal law. As pointed out in my previous writing in this case, Huntington v. Attrill, 146 U.S. 657, held that whether a state statute is penal in the sense that it cannot be enforced in another state depends upon whether the purpose of the statute is to punish an offense against the public justice or to afford a private remedy to a person injured by wrongful act; and that the Supreme Court of the United States would decide for itself whether or not a state statute is penal in the international sense. The Supreme Court of Tennessee has ignored this long-established doctrine. . . . I read nothing in Erie R. Co. v. Tompkins, or in any other Supreme Court opinion, which permits the Supreme Court of Tennessee to exercise any such authority. I refer again to the authorities cited in my original opinion for the then-majority of our court to the point that the courts of a forum state, including a federal court sitting therein, are bound to apply the pertinent statutes of a sister state as construed by the highest court of that state. Broderick v. Rosner, 294 U.S. 629, 643; Converse v. Hamilton, 224 U.S. 243, 260, 261; Hughes v. Fetter, 341 U.S. 609, 613. . . .

For the foregoing reasons, I would adhere to the former decision of this court and deny appellant's petition for rehearing.

NOTES

(1) Judge Martin cited Huntington v. Attrill, p. 301 supra (cf. Milwaukee County v. White, p. 311 supra) to support his view that "penal" characterization is a federal question, not controlled by state views. Is Huntington authority for closing federal court doors in order to vindicate state door-closing policies?

(2) Does full faith and credit receive shorter shrift in this case than it deserves?

ANGEL v. BULLINGTON

Supreme Court of the United States, 1947.
330 U.S. 183, 67 S.Ct. 657, 91 L.Ed. 832.

MR. JUSTICE FRANKFURTER delivered the opinion of the Court.

In 1940, Bullington, a citizen of Virginia, sold land in Virginia to Angel, a citizen of North Carolina. Only part of the purchase price was paid. For the balance, Angel executed a series of notes secured by a deed of trust on the land. Upon default on one of the notes, Bullington, acting upon an acceleration clause in the deed, caused all other notes to become due and called upon the trustees to sell the land. The sale was duly made in Virginia and the proceeds of the sale applied to the payment of the notes. This controversy concerns attempts to collect the deficiency.

Bullington began suit for the deficiency in the Superior Court of Macon County, North Carolina. Angel countered with a demurrer, the substance of which was that a statute of North Carolina (c. 36, Public Laws 1933, Michie's Code § 2593(f)) precluded recovery of such a deficiency judgment. This is the relevant portion of that enactment:

"In all sales of real property by mortgagees and/or trustees under powers of sale contained in any mortgage or deed of trust hereafter executed, . . . the mortgagee or trustee or holder of the notes secured by such mortgage or deed of trust shall not be entitled to a deficiency judgment on account of such mortgage, deed of trust or obligation secured by the same. . . ." The Superior Court overruled the demurrer, and an appeal to the Supreme Court of North Carolina followed. Bullington supported his Superior Court judgment on the ground that the United States Constitution precluded North Carolina from shutting the doors of its courts to him. The North Carolina Supreme Court, holding that the North Carolina Act of 1933 barred Bullington's suit against Angel, reversed the Superior Court and dismissed the action. 220 N.C. 18. Bullington did not seek to review this judgment here. Instead, he sued Angel for the deficiency in the United States District Court for the Western District of North Carolina. Angel pleaded in bar the judgment in the North Carolina action. The District Court gave judgment for Bullington and the Circuit Court of Appeals for the Fourth Circuit affirmed. 150 F.2d 679. We granted certiorari, 326 U.S. 713, because the failure to dismiss this action, on the ground that the judgment in the North Carolina court precluded the right thereafter to recover on the same cause of action in the federal court, presented an important question in the administration of justice.

1. We start with the fact that the prevailing rule as to res judicata is settled law in North Carolina. An adjudication bars future litigation between the same parties not only as to all issues actually raised and decided but also as to those which could have been raised.

. . . It is indisputable that the parties, the nature of the claim and the desired relief were precisely the same in the two actions successively brought by Bullington against Angel, first in the Superior Court of Macon County and then in the federal district court. For all practical purposes, the complaint in the present action was a carbon copy of the complaint in the State court action. . . .

2. The judgment of the Supreme Court of North Carolina would clearly bar this suit had it been brought anew in a state court. For purposes of diversity jurisdiction a federal court is "in effect, only another court of the State" [Citing cases.] Of course, Bullington could not have succeeded in the District Court for the Western District of North Carolina after an adverse judgment in the State courts, had the decision in this case involved no federal ground. That is equally true where a federal question was decided in the State courts. That the adjudication of federal questions by the North Carolina Supreme Court may have been erroneous is immaterial for purposes of res judicata. Baltimore S. S. Co. v. Phillips, 274 U.S. 316, 325. A higher court was available for an authoritative adjudication of the federal questions involved. And so the question is whether federal rights were necessarily involved and adjudicated in the litigation in the State courts.

3. For purposes of res judicata, the significance of what a court says it decides is controlled by the issues that were open for decision. What were the issues in the North Carolina litigation? Bullington sought a deficiency judgment. Angel, by demurrer, resisted on the ground that a North Carolina statute precluded a deficiency judgment. The North Carolina Supreme Court, reversing the trial court, found the North Carolina statute a bar to such a suit. It said that "the limitation created by the statute is upon the jurisdiction of the court in that it is declared that the holder of notes given to secure the purchase price of real property 'shall not be entitled to a deficiency judgment on account' thereof. This closes the courts of this state to one who seeks a deficiency judgment on a note given for the purchase price of real property. The statute operates upon the adjective law of the state, which pertains to the practice and procedure, or legal machinery by which the substantive law is made effective, and not upon the substantive law itself. It is a limitation of the jurisdiction of the courts of this state." 220 N.C. 18, 20, 16 S.E.2d 411, 412.

But the allowable "limitation of the jurisdiction of the courts" of North Carolina presents more than a question of local law for determination by the North Carolina Supreme Court. Speaking for a unanimous Court, Mr. Justice Brandeis thus expressed the subordination to the requirements of the Constitution of the power of a State to withdraw jurisdiction from its courts: "The power of a state to determine the limits of the jurisdiction of its courts and the character of the controversies which shall be heard in them is, of course, subject to the restrictions imposed by the Federal Constitution." McKnett v. St. Louis & S. F. R. Co., 292 U.S. 230, 233. . . .

4. Here, claims based on the United States Constitution were plainly and reasonably made in the North Carolina suit. The North Carolina Supreme Court met these claims. It met them by saying that the North Carolina statute did not deal with substantive matters but merely with matters regulating local procedure. But whether the claims are based on a federal right or are merely of local concern is itself a federal question on which this Court, and not the Supreme Court of North Carolina, has the last say. That Court could not put a federal claim aside, as though it were not in litigation, by the talismanic word "jurisdiction." When an asserted federal right is denied, the sufficiency of the grounds of denial is for this Court to decide. . . . Since it was open for Bullington to come here to seek reversal of the decision of the North Carolina Supreme Court shutting him out of the North Carolina courts and he chose not to do so, the decision of the North Carolina Supreme Court concluded an adjudication of a federal question even though it was not couched in those terms. For purposes of litigating the issues in controversy in the North Carolina action, the North Carolina Supreme Court was an intermediate tribunal. . . .

5. It is suggested that the North Carolina Supreme Court did not adjudicate the "merits" of the controversy. It is a misconception of res judicata to assume that the doctrine does not come into operation if a court has not passed on the "merits" in the sense of the ultimate substantive issues of a litigation. An adjudication declining to reach such ultimate substantive issues may bar a second attempt to reach them in another court of the State. Such a situation is presented when the first decision is based not on the ground that the distribution of judicial power among the various courts of the State requires the suit to be brought in another court in the State, but on the inaccessibility of all the courts of the State to such litigation. And that is the essence of the present case. . . .

The "merits" of a claim are disposed of when they are refused enforcement. If an asserted federal claim is denied enforcement on a professed local ground, but a so-called local ground which is subject to review here because it is in fact the adjudication of a federal question, then the "merits" of that claim were adjudicated in the only sense that adjudication of the "merits" is relevant to the principles of res judicata. A State court cannot sterilize federal claims by putting on the adjudication a local label.

6. The merits of this controversy were adjudicated by the North Carolina Supreme Court since that court, or this Court on appeal, might have decided that the North Carolina statute did not bar Bullington's first action. The North Carolina statute might have been found unconstitutional. Federal issues were thus involved in the adjudication by the North Carolina Supreme Court. Bullington knew

that there were federal issues in the State suit because he raised them. He was then content to drop them and let the intermediate adjudication stand. Now he wants an encore.

7. It is suggested that the North Carolina Supreme Court construed the North Carolina statute to close only the North Carolina state courts but not the federal court sitting in North Carolina. In the first place, the North Carolina Supreme Court said no such thing. It construed the statute expressive of state policy and spoke only of the jurisdiction of the state courts because it was concerned only with the state courts. Secondly, it is most incongruous to attribute to the legislature and judiciary of North Carolina the imposition of a restriction against all its citizens from suing for a deficiency judgment, while impliedly authorizing citizens of other states to secure such deficiency judgments against North Carolinians. Thirdly, a North Carolina statute, upheld by the highest court of North Carolina, is of course expressive of North Carolina policy. The essence of diversity jurisdiction is that a federal court enforces state law and state policy. If North Carolina has authoritatively announced that deficiency judgments cannot be secured within its borders, it contradicts the presuppositions of diversity jurisdiction for a federal court in that state to give such a deficiency judgment. North Carolina would hardly allow defeat of a state-wide policy through occasional suits in a federal court. What is more important, diversity jurisdiction must follow state law and policy. . . . A federal court in North Carolina, when invoked on grounds of diversity of citizenship, cannot give that which North Carolina has withheld. Availability of diversity jurisdiction which was put into the Constitution so as to prevent discrimination against outsiders is not to effect discrimination against the great body of local citizens. . . .

8. After an adverse decision against Bullington on a cause of action created by State law, Bullington wants to start all over again in another North Carolina court, albeit a federal court. The first litigation raised and adjudicated federal issues every one of which is again involved in the second suit. . . .

Judgment reversed.

MR. JUSTICE REED, dissenting.

My understanding of the Court's decision is that the doctrine of res judicata, that is a former adjudication, defeats Bullington's claim against Angel. . . .

. . .

In my view, the North Carolina court merely decided that it had no power to adjudicate the cause of action. Certainly the state court had the power to interpret its own statute. [Citing cases.] The withdrawal of jurisdiction surely does not make a judgment one upon the merits. . . .

. . .

The pith of the problem . . . consists of the question whether the North Carolina decision establishes a controlling rule of law upon the constitutionality of the state statute as tested by the federal Constitution or adjudicates that the statute merely withdraws jurisdiction from state courts over a type of action. . . .

. . .

   . . . [T]his Court's present determination that the statute is substantive for our purposes cannot change the effect in this litigation of the state's decision to the contrary. When the state court held that for its purposes the statute was remedial, it was remedial in that court. If remedial, the state judgment was not upon the merits and could not be res judicata in any court as to the right to recover on the cause of action.

If the plea of res judicata is not good and this Court should decide that the state statute is substantive law, i.e., a declaration of the policy of North Carolina against claims on deficiencies after sales of incumbered property, it would be necessary to determine the constitutionality of the North Carolina statute that declares uncollectible in North Carolina a claim on a contract that was good in Virginia. In view of this Court's present decision, I express no opinion upon this issue.

Mr. Justice Jackson and Mr. Justice Rutledge join in this opinion.

Mr. Justice Rutledge, dissenting.

This is a hard case making, I think, proverbially bad law. On the surface what seems to be decided is simply a question of res judicata. Actually the decision rests on an "and/or" hodgepodge of res judicata and Erie doctrines. In my judgment the admixture not only is unnecessary but distorts and misapplies both doctrines. . . .

. . .

Res judicata is a generally sound but by no means unlimited policy of judicial action. The doctrine is grounded in the need for putting an end to litigation. It does this by precluding the parties from showing what is or may be the truth. The sound core of the policy is that ordinarily one suit which determines or gives a full and fair chance for determining causes of action and issues between litigants should be enough. . . .

. . .

Upon the law as well as the policy, the question has been one of balancing considerations of justice and convenience between stopping litigation and stopping the showing of the truth. That balance has never been so one-sided in favor of the former that the matter is ended simply by showing that a party has had some chance however slight, in a previous litigation to secure a favorable decision. . . .

. . .

Bullington has not had such an opportunity. He has never received, and now never can receive a decision on the substantive merits of his claim, unless possibly he can catch and serve Angel in another state and after prolonged further litigation succeed in inducing this Court to hold the North Carolina bar and res judicata not operative there. . . .

. . .

The real trouble here is not with the law of res judicata, for that law has no valid application to these facts. It is that the doctrine is used as an escape from facing squarely the real question presented. This is whether North Carolina's decision made the Erie doctrine applicable. . . .

That issue is inescapable here. The Erie rule did not purport to change the law of federal jurisdiction in diversity cases, taking it out of the hands of Congress and the federal courts and putting it within the states' power to determine. It purported only to prescribe the rule federal courts should follow in applying the substantive law. If the North Carolina decision was exclusively a jurisdictional one, it had no effect on the power of the federal courts in that state to hear controversies excluded by it from the state courts . . .

From the Court's opinion I cannot say whether the question has been resolved. . . . But, if so, why speak also of res judicata? The law should not be made into such a merry-go-round. Bullington is entitled to one full day in court on the substance of his claim. This he has not had.

I hardly need add that I agree with the views expressed by MR. JUSTICE REED.

MR. JUSTICE JACKSON joins in this opinion.

NOTES

(1) Does the North Carolina statute read as if it is intended to be door-closing, rather than to define substantive entitlements? Can any other interpretation prevail after the Supreme Court of North Carolina has construed it as a "limitation . . . upon the jurisdiction of the court"?

(2) Does Mr. Justice Frankfurter tell us whether the res judicata law of North Carolina would regard the first decision as an adjudication on the merits for purposes of precluding all issues that might have been raised? Without knowing the answer to that question, can we know what the outcome would be if, as Mr. Justice Rutledge speculated, Bullington were able to "catch and serve Angel in another state"? For example, in Virginia, would Bullington be precluded from challenging the constitutionality of the North Carolina ban on deficiency judgments as applied to a Virginian who sold Virginia land and was left with a deficiency claim after a foreclosure sale?

(3) If prior to the instant action, another creditor in Bullington's position had sued and then met with the North Carolina Supreme Court's interpretation of its statute, would the outcome in the instant case have been the same? If so, as a consequence of res judicata or of Erie? If the first judg-

ment had been rendered by a federal district court, would the res judicata effect be determined under North Carolina law, Federal law, or would the answer depend on which forum was the locus for the succeeding action?

(4) A different situation would be presented, of course, if North Carolina closed its courts' doors to deficiency suits by non-residents while opening them to residents. See Szantay v. Beech Aircraft Corp., 349 F.2d 60 (4th Cir. 1965), in which a federal diversity court was held not bound by a South Carolina statute barring suits by non-residents against foreign corporations on foreign causes of action. The court was unimpressed with the argument that the statute implemented the forum state's doctrine of forum non conveniens; it spoke favorably of the full faith and credit clause's policy of abetting enforcement of rights created by sister states. Angel v. Bullington was distinguished. Should it have been? See Note, 66 Colum.L.Rev. 377 (1966).

(5) Compare Poitra v. Demarrias, 502 F.2d 23 (8th Cir. 1974), cert. denied 421 U.S. 934 (1975). The diversity litigants in a wrongful death action based on state-created rights were Indians who lived on opposite sides of the state line running through their reservation. The federal district court in North Dakota dismissed the action on the ground that in the absence of the tribe's consent, the doors of the North Dakota state courts were closed to the plaintiff; and this required the same result, according to the district judge, when federal diversity jurisdiction was invoked in that state.

Reversing, the court of appeals held that the closing of the state courts in this case was not a result of any underlying state policy, but a consequence of the Indian tribe's declining to give consent to state court jurisdiction. Accordingly, the court of appeals held, the state-created right was enforceable in the federal diversity court. Distinguished were Hot Oil Service, Inc. v. Hall, 366 F.2d 295 (9th Cir. 1966) and Littel v. Nakai, 344 F.2d 486 (9th Cir. 1965), cert. denied 382 U.S. 986, holding federal courts could not assume diversity jurisdiction in disputes arising on an Indian Reservation unless the state courts would have had subject matter jurisdiction.

SOUTHERN JAM, INC. V. ROBINSON, 675 F.2d 94 (5th Cir. 1982): In Allen v. McCurry, 499 U.S. 90 (1980), the Supreme Court held that McCurry's § 1983 claim was subject to collateral estoppel, but left open the question whether an issue the claimant might have but did not litigate is precluded in a later federal action. Held that res judicata applies to plaintiff's claim. ". . . [I]f Georgia law would bar Southern Jam from raising these issues in a suit in state court, because a state court has or could have properly and constitutionally adjudicated them already, then it is barred from raising them before the F–2 court." (P. 98.)

C. FEDERAL QUESTIONS IN RELATION TO STATE LAW

Introductory Note. Even in areas where the national power clearly reaches and the Erie doctrine clearly does not, there can be problems of interplay between federal and state law. First, in national spheres Congress may if it chooses specify the rules of decision, entirely supplanting any contrary state rules and indirectly eradicating interstate choice of law problems, as the Federal Employers Liability Act did with reference to the fellow-servant issue illustrated in Alabama Great Southern Railway Co. v. Carroll, supra, p. 429. Second, Congress may see fit to legislate directly and explicitly on the conflict of laws problem, as it did in the Federal Tort Claims Act provision making the government liable in certain circumstances "in accordance with the law of the place where the act or omission occurred" (28 U.S.C. § 1346(b)). See Richards v. United States, 369 U.S. 1 (1962); cf. Meisenhelder v. Chicago & Northwestern Railway Co., 170 Minn. 317, 213 N.W. 32 (1927), infra, p. 809, n. 2. Third, Congress may choose to incorporate state definitions of legal rights by using terms and referring to subjects as to which the states alone have well developed bodies of law. For instance, in a copyright case the question was whether the deceased author's illegitimate son came within the federal copyright statute's term "children" for the purpose of sharing in renewal rights. While the "scope of a federal right is, of course, a federal question," the Court declared, "that does not mean that its content is not to be determined by state, rather than federal law." De Sylva v. Ballentine, 351 U.S. 570, 580 (1956).

In each case not obviously ruled entirely by federal law, a federal court must decide first whether it is *bound* to apply state rules, or whether it is free to apply rules from whichever source, federal or state, the federal choice of law rule makes appropriate. Then, having decided for the federal source, the court may still have to look to state law to give content or add meaning to some terms of the federal law.

———

CLEARFIELD TRUST CO. v. UNITED STATES, 318 U.S. 363 (1943): Action by the United States to recover the amount of a check on which the payee's name had been forged. The check was drawn on the Treasurer of the United States for services rendered to the Works Progress Administration. It was cashed under the forged endorsement and then endorsed over to the defendant bank, which as agent for collection guaranteed all prior endorsements. Fifteen months after notification of the United States agents of payee's non-receipt of her check, notice of the forgery was communicated to the defendant bank in a demand for reimbursement of the Treasurer who had paid for payee's services a second time. Suit followed upon the express guaranty. The District Court held the rights of the parties to be governed by Pennsylvania law and that since the United States had delayed unreasonably in giving notice of the forgery to defendant, it was barred from recovery. On appeal from a reversal by the Circuit Court of Appeals, affirmed.

DOUGLAS, J. . . . We agree with the Circuit Court of Appeals that the rule of Erie Railroad Co. v. Tompkins, 304 U.S. 64, does not apply to this action. The rights and duties of the United States on commercial paper which it issues are governed by federal rather than local law. When the United States disburses its funds or pays its debts, it is exercising a constitutional function or power. . . . The authority to issue the check had its origin in the Constitution and the statutes of the United States and was in no way dependent on the laws of Pennsylvania or of any other state. Cf. Board of Commissioners v. United States, 308 U.S. 343; Royal Indemnity Co. v. United States, 313 U.S. 289. The duties imposed upon the United States and the rights acquired by it as a result of the issuance find their roots in the same federal sources. . . . In absence of an applicable Act of Congress it is for the federal courts to fashion the governing rule of law according to their own standards. United States v. Guaranty Trust Co., 293 U.S. 340, is not opposed to this result. That case was concerned with a conflict of laws rule as to the title acquired by a transferee in Yugoslavia under a forged endorsement. Since the payee's address was Yugoslavia, the check had "something of the quality of a foreign bill" and the law of Yugoslavia was applied to determine what title the transferee acquired.

In our choice of the applicable federal rule we have occasionally selected state law. . . . But reasons which may make state law at times the appropriate federal rule are singularly inappropriate here. The issuance of commercial paper by the United States is on a vast scale and transactions in that paper from issuance to payment will commonly occur in several states. The application of state law, even without the conflict of laws rules of the forum, would subject the rights and duties of the United States to exceptional uncertainty. It would lead to great diversity in results by making identical transactions subject to the vagaries of the laws of the several states. The desirability of a uniform rule is plain. And while the federal law merchant, developed for about a century under the regime of Swift v. Tyson, 16 Pet. 1, represented general commercial law rather than a choice of a federal rule designed to protect a federal right, it nevertheless stands as a convenient source of reference for fashioning federal rules applicable to these federal questions. . . .

D'OENCH, DUHME & CO. v. FEDERAL DEPOSIT INSURANCE CORP.

Supreme Court of the United States, 1942.
315 U.S. 447, 62 S.Ct. 676, 86 L.Ed. 956.

MR. JUSTICE DOUGLAS delivered the opinion of the Court.

Respondent instituted this suit in the United States District Court for the Eastern Division of the Eastern District of Missouri on a demand note for $5000 executed by petitioner in 1933 and payable to the Belleville Bank & Trust Co., Belleville, Illinois. Respondent insured that bank January 1, 1934; and it acquired the note in 1938 as part of the collateral securing a loan of over $1,000,000 to the bank, made in connection with the assumption of the latter's deposit liabilities by another bank. Since 1935 the note had been among the charged off assets of the bank. The note was executed by petitioner in renewal of notes which it had executed in 1926. Petitioner who was engaged in the securities business at St. Louis, Missouri, had sold the bank certain bonds which later defaulted. The original notes were executed to enable the bank to carry the notes and not show any past due bonds. Proceeds of the bonds were to be credited on the notes. The receipts for the notes contained the statement, "This note is given with the understanding it will not be called for payment. All interest payments to be repaid." Respondent had no knowledge of the existence of the receipts until after demand for payment on the renewal note was made in 1938. Certain interest payments on the notes were made prior to renewal for the purpose of keeping them "as live paper." Petitioner's president who signed the original notes knew that they were executed so that the past due bonds would not appear among the assets of the bank, and that the purpose of the interest payments was "to keep the notes alive." The original notes were signed in St. Louis, Missouri, were payable at petitioner's office there, and were delivered to the payee in Illinois. The evidence does not disclose where the note sued upon was signed, though it was dated at Belleville, Illinois, and payable to the bank there.

The main point of controversy here revolves around the question as to what law is applicable. The District Court held that Illinois law was applicable and that petitioner was liable. The Circuit Court of Appeals applied "general law" to determine that the note was an Illinois rather than a Missouri contract; and it decided that under Illinois law respondent was the equivalent of a holder in due course and entitled to recover. 117 F.2d 491. Petitioner contends that under the rule of Klaxon Company v. Stentor Electric Mfg. Co., 313 U.S. 487, a federal court sitting in Missouri must apply Missouri's conflict of law rules; that if, as was the case here, Illinois law was not pleaded or proved, a Missouri court would have ascertained Illinois law from Missouri decisions since in such a case Illinois law would be presumed to be the same as the Missouri law; and that the District Court was bound to follow that same course. We granted the petition for certiorari, because of the asserted conflict between the decision below and Klaxon Company v. Stentor Electric Mfg. Co., supra.

. . .

The jurisdiction of the District Court in this case, however, is not based on diversity of citizenship. Respondent, a federal corporation, brings this suit under an Act of Congress authorizing it to sue or be sued "in any court of law or equity, State or Federal." Sec. 12B,

Federal Reserve Act, 12 U.S.C. § 264(j), 48 Stat. 162, 168, 172, 49 Stat. 684, 692. And see 28 U.S.C. § 42, 43 Stat. 941. Whether the rule of the Klaxon case applies where federal jurisdiction is not based on diversity of citizenship, we need not decide. For we are of the view that the liability of petitioner on the note involves decision of a federal not a state question under the rule of Deitrick v. Greaney, 309 U.S. 190. . . .

Sec. 12B(s) of the Federal Reserve Act, 12 U.S.C. § 264(s), provides that "Whoever, for the purpose of obtaining any loan from the Corporation . . . or for the purpose of influencing in any way the action of the Corporation under this section, makes any statement, knowing it to be false, or willfully overvalues any security, shall be punished by a fine of not more than $5,000, or by imprisonment for not more than two years or both." Subdivision (y) of the same section provided, at the time respondent insured the Belleville bank, that such a state bank "with the approval of the authority having supervision" of the bank and on "certification" to respondent "by such authority" that the bank "is in solvent condition" shall "after examination by, and with the approval of" the respondent be entitled to insurance.

These provisions reveal a federal policy to protect respondent and the public funds which it administers against misrepresentations as to the secutities or other assets in the portfolios of the banks which respondent insures or to which it makes loans. If petitioner and the bank had arranged to use the note for the express purpose of deceiving respondent on insurance of the bank or on the making of the loan, the case would be on all fours with Deitrick v. Greaney, supra. . . . . But the reach of the rule which prevents an accommodation maker of a note from setting up the defense of no consideration against a bank or its receiver or creditors is not delimited to those instances where he has committed a statutory offense. . . .

. . .

Those principles are applicable here because of the federal policy evidenced in this Act to protect respondent, a federal corporation, from misrepresentations made to induce or influence the action of respondent, including misstatements as to the genuineness or integrity of securities in the portfolios of banks which it insures or to which it makes loans. . . .

. . .

Affirmed.

[MR. JUSTICE FRANKFURTER and THE CHIEF JUSTICE concurred on the ground that the result reached by the majority would also follow under Missouri or Illinois law and that it was unnecessary to stretch the federal statute to fit the case.]

Mr. Justice Jackson, concurring:

I think we should attempt a more explicit answer to the question whether federal or state law governs our decision in this sort of case than is found either in the opinion of the Court or in the concurring opinion of Mr. Justice Frankfurter. That question, as old as the federal judiciary, is met inescapably at the threshold of this case. . . .

. . .

Although by Congressional command this case is to be deemed one arising under the laws of the United States, no federal statute purports to define the Corporation's rights as a holder of the note in suit or the liability of the maker thereof. There arises, therefore, the question whether in deciding the case we are bound to apply the law of some particular state or whether, to put it bluntly, we may make our own law from materials found in common-law sources.

This issue has a long historical background of legal and political controversy as to the place of the common law in federal jurisprudence. . . .

I do not understand Justice Brandeis's statement in Erie R. Co. v. Tompkins, 304 U.S. 64, at 78, that "There is no federal general common law," to deny that the common law may in proper cases be an aid to or the basis of decision of federal questions. In its context it means to me only that federal courts may not apply their own notions of the common law at variance with applicable state decisions except "where the Constitution, treaties, or statutes of the United States [so] require or provide." Indeed, in a case decided on the same day as Erie R. Co. v. Tompkins, Justice Brandeis said that "whether the water of an interstate stream must be apportioned between the two States is a question of 'federal common law' upon which neither the statutes nor the decisions of either State can be conclusive." Hinderlider v. La Plata Co., 304 U.S. 92, 110.

Were we bereft of the common law, our federal system would be impotent. This follows from the recognized futility of attempting all-complete statutory codes, and is apparent from the terms of the Constitution itself.

. . .

. . . Federal law is no juridical chameleon, changing complexion to match that of each state wherein lawsuits happen to be commenced because of the accidents of service of process and of the application of the venue statutes. It is found in the federal Constitution, statutes, or common law. Federal common law implements the federal Constitution and statutes, and is conditioned by them.[1] Within these limits, federal courts are free to apply the addi-

---

1. For example, the common-law doctrines of conflict of laws worked out in a unitary system to deal with conflicts between domestic and truly foreign law may not apply unmodified in conflicts between the laws of states within our federal system which are affected by the full faith and credit or other relevant clause of the Constitution.

tional common-law technique of decision and to draw upon all the sources of the common law in cases such as the present. Board of Commissioners v. United States, 308 U.S. 343, 350.

The law which we apply to this case consists of principles of established credit in jurisprudence selected by us because they are appropriate to effectuate the policy of the governing Act. . . . That a particular state happened to have the greatest connection in the conflict of laws sense with the making of the note involved or that the subsequent conduct happened to be chiefly centered there is not enough to make us subservient to the legislative policy or the judicial views of that state.

I concur in the Court's holding because I think that the defense asserted is nowhere admissible against the Corporation and that we need not go to the law of any particular state as our authority for so holding.

. . .

UNITED STATES v. KIMBELL FOODS, INC.

Supreme Court of the United States, 1979.
440 U.S. 715, 99 S.Ct. 1448, 59 L.Ed.2d 711.

MR. JUSTICE MARSHALL delivered the opinion of the Court.

We granted certiorari in these cases to determine whether contractual liens arising from certain federal loan programs take precedence over private liens, in the absence of a federal statute setting priorities. To resolve this question, we must decide first whether federal or state law governs the controversies; and second, if federal law applies, whether this Court should fashion a uniform priority rule or incorporate state commercial law. We conclude that the source of law is federal, but that a national rule is unnecessary to protect the federal interests underlying the loan programs. Accordingly, we adopt state law as the appropriate federal rule for establishing the relative priority of these competing federal and private liens. . . .

This Court has consistently held that federal law governs questions involving the rights of the United States arising under nationwide federal programs. . . .

. . . [w]e think it clear that the priority of liens stemming from federal lending programs must be determined with reference to federal law. The SBA [Small Business Authority] and FHA [Farmers Home Administration] unquestionably perform federal functions within the meaning of *Clearfield* [p. 721, supra].

. . . [W]hen there is little need for a nationally uniform body of law, state law may be incorporated as the federal rule of decision. Apart from considerations of uniformity, we must also determine whether application of state law would frustrate specific objectives of the federal programs.   If so, we must fashion special rules solicitous of those federal interests.   Finally, our choice of law inquiry must consider the extent to which application of a federal rule would disrupt commercial relationships predicated on state law.

.   .   .   We are unpersuaded that in the circumstances presented here, nationwide standards favoring claims of the United States are necessary to ease program administration or to safeguard the federal treasury from defaulting debtors.   Because the state commercial codes "furnish convenient solutions in no way inconsistent with adequate protection of the federal interest[s]," United States v. Standard Oil Co.,   .   .   . ,   332 U.S., at 309, we decline to override intricate state laws of general applicability on which private creditors base their daily commercial transactions.

.   .   .

.   .   .   [T]he agencies' own operating practices belie their assertion that a federal rule of priority is needed to avoid the administrative burdens created by disparate state commercial rules.   The programs already conform to each State's commercial standards.   By using local lending offices and employees who are familiar with the law of their respective localities, the agencies function effectively without uniform procedures and legal rules.

.   .   .   The importance of securing adequate revenues to discharge national obligations justifies the extraordinary priority accorded federal tax liens through the choateness and first in time doctrines.   By contrast, when the United States operates as a money-lending institution under carefully circumscribed programs, its interest in recouping the limited sums advanced is of a different order.   Thus, there is less need here than in the tax lien area to invoke protective measures against defaulting debtors in a manner disruptive of existing credit markets.

.   .   .   The overriding purpose of the tax lien statute obviously is to ensure prompt revenue collection.   The same cannot be said of the SBA and FHA lending programs.   They are a form of social welfare legislation, primarily designed to assist farmers and businesses that cannot obtain funds from private lenders on reasonable terms.   We believe that had Congress intended the private commercial sector, rather than taxpayers in general, to bear the risks of default entailed by these public welfare programs, it would have established a priority scheme displacing state law.   .   .   .

.   .   .

In structuring financial transactions, businessmen depend on state commercial law to provide the stability essential for reliable evaluation of the risks involved.   Cf. National Bank of Genesee v. Whitney, 103 U.S. 99, 102 (1881).   However, subjecting federal contractual liens to the doctrines developed in the tax lien area could undermine that stability.   Creditors who justifiably rely on state law to obtain superior liens would have their expectations thwarted whenever a federal contractual security interest suddenly appeared and took precedence.

Because the ultimate consequences of altering settled commercial practices are so difficult to foresee, we hesitate to create new uncertainties, in the absence of careful legislative deliberation. Of course, formulating special rules to govern the priority of the federal consensual liens in issue here would be justified if necessary to vindicate important national interests. But neither the Government nor the Court of Appeals advanced any concrete reasons for rejecting well-established commercial rules which have proven workable over time. Thus, the prudent course is to adopt the readymade body of state law as the federal rule of decision until Congress strikes a different accommodation.

. . .

[In disposing of the two decisions under review, the court affirmed the judgment which had applied Texas law giving preference to the respondent's lien and remanded the other case for determination of lien priorities under applicable Georgia law.]

NOTES

(1) Is this decision inconsistent with Clearfield Trust Co. v. United States, p. 721, supra? See Note, Formulating a Federal Rule of Decision in Commercial Transactions after Kimbell, 66 Iowa L.Rev. 391 (1981).

(2) Federal precedent generally supplants the provisions of the UCC, according to Comment, Application of the Uniform Commercial Code to Federal Government Contracts: Doing Business on Business Terms, 16 Wm. & Mary L.Rev. 395 (1974).

(3) Vanston Bondholders Protective Committee v. Green, 329 U.S. 156 (1946) concerned a Delaware corporation with its principal place of business in Kentucky which mortgaged Kentucky property under an indenture. The indenture, executed in New York with a New York bank as trustee, provided the bonds secured by it would be paid in New York or Illinois at the option of the holder. The corporation went into an equity receivership and then into reorganization under the Bankruptcy Act, in a federal court in Kentucky. The indenture and the bonds provided for payment of interest on unpaid interest, and the validity of this provision was in issue. The District Court and the Circuit Court of Appeals treated the matter as one of conflict of laws to be governed by the law of New York. The Supreme Court in an opinion by Black, J., stated: "In determining what claims are allowable and how a debtor's assets shall be distributed, a bankruptcy court does not apply the law of the state where it sits. Erie R.R. v. Tompkins, 304 U.S. 64, has no such implication. . . . bankruptcy courts must administer and enforce the Bankruptcy Act as interpreted by this Court in accordance with authority granted by Congress to determine how and what claims shall be allowed under equitable principles. And we think an allowance of interest on interest under the circumstances shown by this case would not be in accord with the equitable principles governing bankruptcy distributions."

(4) Federal law may also determine common law tort issues. In United States v. Standard Oil Co., 332 U.S. 301 (1947), it was held that federal law determined whether the United States could obtain reimbursement from one who had negligently injured a soldier, for hospital care and pay during his disablement. The defendant was held not liable. See also Kohr v. Allegheny Airlines, Inc., 504 F.2d 400 (7th Cir. 1974), holding that federal common law determines rights of indemnity and contribution in airplane crash litigation. The argument suggested by its title is advanced in Note, The Case for a Federal Common Law of Aircraft Disaster Litigation, 51 N.Y.U.L.Rev. 232 (1976). The note writer asserts that federal courts should exercise their power to imply a federal cause of action for victims of air crashes, borrowing from the Supreme Court's decision in Cort v. Ash, 422 U.S. 66 (1975), where four factors were listed as determinative of when a federal right of action should be implied from a statute not expressly creating one.

(5) In re "Agent Orange" Product Liab. Litigation, 635 F.2d 987 (2d Cir. 1980) was a class action by Army veterans asserting a right under federal common law to recover against corporations that supplied the United States government with chemicals that were alleged to have been contaminated and to have injured the veterans. Held that veterans had no claim under federal common law. The court found that there was "no federal interest in uniformity for its own sake" since the litigation was between private parties and "no substantial rights or duties of the government hinged on its outcome." Also, the interests of the federal government were conflicting since it had an interest both in the welfare of its veterans and in that of the suppliers of its material. "The extent to which either group should be favored . . . is preeminently a policy determination of the sort reserved in the first instance for Congress." Congress has not yet determined how these two competing interests should be reconciled. ". . . before common law rules should be fashioned, the use of state law must pose a threat to an 'identifiable' federal policy. . . . In the present litigation the federal policy is not yet identifiable." The dissent emphasized that it would be unfortunate if veterans' recoveries for Agent Orange injuries were to vary from state to state "despite the fact that these soldiers fought shoulder to shoulder, without regard to state citizenship, in a national endeavor abroad." Likewise "the conclusion seems inescapable" that the United States has a greater interest in the welfare of its veterans than in that of its suppliers.

GREENBERG v. PANAMA TRANSPORT CO., 185 F.Supp. 320 (D.Mass. 1960): Suit by an attorney against two corporations for interference with advantageous contractual relations. Plaintiff claimed that his client, a seaman, had been induced to discharge plaintiff as his proctor in admiralty in a Jones Act suit for personal injury.

WYZANSKI, J. . . . Despite the fact that this case is presented as one within the diversity jurisdiction, it does not automatically follow that, in considering the validity of Greenberg's retainer, this Court must turn to the state law of Massachusetts for guidance as to the appropriate conflict of laws rules or the appropriate substantive rules. . . . The claims for which Vazquez retained Greenberg arose out of the general maritime law and out of an Act of Congress, the Jones Act. Such claims, while theoretically presentable in either a state court or a federal court, are usually presented in a federal court. And, in fact, presentation before the federal court in the Southern District of New York did occur in the case at bar.

To hold that the validity of a retainer to perform services in a federal court with respect to a federal cause of action should be determined by state law would seem highly artificial. Every policy consideration dictates that the federal courts should enunciate uniform national rules to determine the validity of contracts made by proctors in admiralty, who are officers of federal courts, to present claims to federal courts. That is, there should be "a uniform national rule of law, binding on state and federal courts alike, where the operative legal policies are federal in origin." Paul A. Freund, Federal-State Relations In The Opinions of Judge Magruder, 72 Harv.L.Rev. 1204, 1213.

Applying a national rule of law this Court concludes that the contract under which Vazquez retained Greenberg was valid. The contract was an entirely normal arrangement. It did not in the technical sense provide for a contingent fee. And the terms of compensation fall within the zone of reasonableness.

Having determined that the retainer contract is governed by federal law, and that under such law the contract is valid, the Court must next consider what law governs a claim that defendants have tortiously interfered with the contract. It is usually assumed that in connection with the tort of interfering with advantageous contract relations, as in connection with torts generally, the governing rule is supplied by the law of the place where the tort occurs. . . . But the grounds of logic, history, convenience, and policy which support this doctrine in many cases, particularly cases of physical injury, are not appropriately invoked in every type of case. Different torts may be governed by different principles of conflict of laws. Cf. Gordon v. Parker, D.C.D.Mass., 83 F.Supp. 40, affirmed sub nom. Parker v. Gordon, 1 Cir., 178 F.2d 888. See A.A. Ehrenzweig, Alienation of Affections In the Conflict of Laws, 45 Cornell Law Qu. 514, 515. And the conflict of laws rules governing even the particular tort of interference with advantageous contractual relations may depend upon what type of contract relationship is said to have been impeded.

Here we have a claim that when sued in a federal court defendants interfered with the contractual relationship between the then plaintiff who was suing them and his attorney, the present plaintiff. In determining the applicable law to decide this claim, it does not seem of the greatest importance where that interference occurred. Nor does it seem of decisive importance in what forum the claim of alleged interference is made. The controlling principles of substantive law should be enunciated on a national basis applicable to anyone who is said to have interfered with a professional relation between an officer of a national court and his client. . . .

The federal courts being free to apply a national rather than a state standard to claims that defendants have interfered with relations between federal lawyers and their clients, the federal courts would probably mould the national standard with appropriate references to Restatement, Torts, §§ 766–774. Drawing upon those sections as well as the general case law this Court concludes that in the case at bar defendants, without a privilege so to do, have induced Vazquez not to continue his professional relations with Greenberg and are therefore liable to Greenberg for the damages thereby caused to Greenberg.

BANK OF AMERICA NATIONAL TRUST & SAVINGS ASSOCIATION v. PARNELL

Supreme Court of the United States, 1956.
352 U.S. 29, 77 S.Ct. 119, 1 L.Ed.2d 93.

[An action was brought in a federal court in Pennsylvania for the conversion of bonds which had been owned by the plaintiff. The bonds were bearer bonds of Home Owners' Loan Corporation, with payment guaranteed by the United States. The bonds were originally due to mature in 1952, but pursuant to their terms they had been called for payment on or about May 1, 1944. On May 2, 1944, they disappeared, apparently having been stolen from plaintiff. In 1948 they were cashed by the defendant bank in Pennsylvania when presented to it by the individual defendant. At the trial the principal issue was the burden of establishing that the defendants took the bonds in good faith, without knowledge or notice of the defect in title. The jury brought in verdicts against both defendants and judgment was entered against them.]

MR. JUSTICE FRANKFURTER delivered the opinion of the court.

. . .

The District Court in this suit, based on diversity jurisdiction, for the conversion in Pennsylvania of pieces of paper of defined value, deemed itself a court of Pennsylvania in which, in view of the nature of the claim, Pennsylvania law would govern. See Guaranty Trust Co. of New York v. York, 326 U.S. 99, 108. But respondents claim, and the Court of Appeals sustained them, that the decision in Clearfield Trust Co. v. United States, 318 U.S. 363, 63 S.Ct. 573, 87 L.Ed. 838, compels the application of federal law to the entire case. The Court of Appeals misconceived the nature of this litigation in holding that the Clearfield Trust case controlled. . . .

Securities issued by the Government generate immediate interests of the Government. These were dealt with in Clearfield Trust and in National Metropolitan Bank v. United States, 323 U.S. 454. But they also radiate interests in transactions between private parties. The present litigation is purely between private parties and does not touch the rights and duties of the United States. The only possible interest of the United States in a situation like the one here, exclusively involving the transfer of Government paper between private persons, is that the floating of securities of the United States might somehow or other be adversely affected by the local rule of a particular State regarding the liability of a converter. This is far too speculative, far too remote a possibility to justify the application of federal law to transactions essentially of local concern.

We do not mean to imply that litigation with respect to Government paper necessarily precludes the presence of a federal interest to be governed by federal law, in all situations merely because it is a suit between private parties, or that it is beyond the range of federal legislation to deal comprehensively with Government paper. We do not of course foreclose such judicial or legislative action in appropriate situations by concluding that this controversy over burden of proof and good faith represents too essentially a private transaction not to be dealt with by the local law of Pennsylvania where the transaction took place. Federal law of course governs the interpretation of the nature of the rights and obligations created by the Government bonds themselves. A decision with respect to the "overdueness" of the bonds is therefore a matter of federal law, which, in view of our holding, we need not elucidate. . . .

Reversed and remanded.

MR. JUSTICE BLACK and MR. JUSTICE DOUGLAS, dissenting.

We believe that the "federal law merchant" which Clearfield Trust Co. v. United States, 318 U.S. 363, 367, held applicable to transactions in the commercial paper of the United States should be applicable to all transactions in that paper. . . . Not until today has a distinction been drawn between suits by the United States on that paper and suits by other parties. But the Court does not stop there. Because this is "essentially a private transaction", it is to be governed by local law. Yet the nature of the rights and obligations created by commercial paper of the United States Government is said to be controlled by federal law. Thus, federal law is to govern some portion of a dispute between private parties, while that portion of the dispute which is "essentially of local concern" is to be governed by local law. The uncertainties which inhere in such a dichotomy are obvious.

The virtue of a uniform law governing bonds, notes, and other paper issued by the United States is that it provides a certain and definite guide to the rights of all parties rather than subjecting them to the vagaries of the law of many States. . . . If the rule of the Clearfield Trust case is to be abandoned as to some parties, it should be abandoned as to all and we should start afresh on this problem.

NOTES

(1) Does the Parnell case imply that federal courts lack authority to fashion rules governing private parties' interests in government securities? See Friendly, In Praise of Erie—and of the New Federal Common Law, 19 Record of N.Y.C.B.A. 64 (1964); 39 N.Y.U.L.Rev. 383 (1964).

(2) Professor Mishkin has urged that "a decision to apply state law as a matter of federal incorporation does not necessarily carry with it the obligation to adhere to the range and techniques which have been held to govern under Erie; there remains a freedom . . . to control the extent and methods of that adoption . . . " State law may be applied to issues singly, having regard for the content of the state rule, without the need to follow state choice of law rules, and with little fear of disparity between federal and state decisions in a single forum. Mishkin, The Variousness of "Federal Law": Competence and Discretion in the Choice of National and State Rules for Decision, 105 U.Pa.L.Rev. 797, 804–10 (1957).

SECTION 2.　SPECIAL CONSTRAINTS IN INTERNATIONAL SETTINGS

With international travel, commerce and private transactions increasing by quantum leaps, the subject of "private international law" in its literal sense has grown in importance for American lawyers. All through the book we have encountered conflicts cases that cut across international boundaries. They were sprinkled, almost interchangeably, among the cases involving states of the Union. In re Annesley, Matter of Schneider, Gilbert v. Burnstine, Hilton v. Guyot, Holzer v. Deutsche-Reichsbahn Gesellschaft, Slater v. Mexican Ry. Co., Walton v. Arabian American Oil Co., Babcock v. Jackson, Home Insurance Co. v. Dick and many others made their appearance. From time to time, it was observed that international judgments, statutes and other legal affirmations differ from sister-state judgments and statutes at least in the respect that amorphous principles of comity rather than pointed commands of full faith and credit are involved in their recognition.

In Hilton v. Guyot, another type of question was raised: May the several states impose diverse, individual tests for recognition of foreign judgments, or is the problem one committed to the national government? In somewhat more dilute form, the same sort of issue lurked in the Holzer case, where the New York Court of Appeals was asked to refuse to countenance a defense based upon the Nazi government's anti-Jewish laws. In the materials that follow, questions of the effective scope of state law in the international arena are considered against the backdrop of the accepted principle that the United States, in its relations with foreign nations, should speak with a single voice, not with more than fifty voices; and that traditionally and constitutionally, for the most part, the spokesman has been the chief executive and his delegates.

ZSCHERNIG v. MILLER

Supreme Court of the United States, 1968.
389 U.S. 429, 88 S.Ct. 664, 19 L.Ed.2d 683.

[An American citizen died in Oregon, leaving property to relatives in the Soviet Zone of Germany. An Oregon statute conditioned a nonresident alien's right to inherit property in Oregon upon the existence of a reciprocal right of American citizens to inherit in the alien's country upon the same terms as citizens of that country; upon the right of American citizens to receive payment within the United States from the estates of decedents dying in that country; and upon proof that the alien heirs of the American decedent would receive the benefit, use, and control of their inheritance without confiscation. The Oregon Supreme Court affirmed the finding of the trial court that the evidence did not establish that American citizens were accorded reciprocal rights to take property from or to receive the proceeds of East German estates. However, it found that a 1923 treaty was still effective with respect to East Germany, and consequently held that under Clark v. Allen, 331 U.S. 503, the East German heirs must be permitted to take the real property despite the Oregon statute. They were not permitted to take the personal property.]*

MR. JUSTICE DOUGLAS delivered the opinion of the Court.

This case concerns the disposition of the estate of a resident of Oregon who died there intestate in 1962. Appellants are decedent's sole heirs and they are residents of East Germany. Appellees include members of the State Land Board that petitioned the Oregon probate court for the escheat of the net proceeds of the estate under the provisions of Ore.Rev.Stat. § 111.070 (1957), which provides for escheat in cases where a nonresident alien claims real or personal property unless three requirements are satisfied:

(1) the existence of a reciprocal right of a United States citizen to take property on the same terms as a citizen or inhabitant of the foreign country;

(2) the right of United States citizens to receive payment here of funds from estates in the foreign country; and

(3) the right of the foreign heirs to receive the proceeds of Oregon estates "without confiscation."

* The statement of facts is taken from the concurring opinion of Mr. Justice Harlan.

The Oregon Supreme Court held that the appellants could take the Oregon realty involved in the present case by reason of Article IV of the 1923 Treaty of Friendship, Commerce and Consular Rights with Germany (44 Stat. 2135) but that by reason of the same Article, as construed in Clark v. Allen, 331 U.S. 503, 67 S.Ct. 1431, 91 L.Ed. 1633, they could not take the personalty. . . .

. . .

We do not accept the invitation to re-examine our ruling in Clark v. Allen. For we conclude that the history and operation of this Oregon statute make clear that § 111.070 is an intrusion by the State into the field of foreign affairs which the Constitution entrusts to the President and the Congress. See Hines v. Davidowitz, 312 U.S. 52, 63. . . .

. . . It has never been seriously suggested that state courts are precluded from performing [the probate] function, although there is a possibility, albeit remote, that any holding may disturb a foreign nation—whether the matter involves commercial cases, tort cases, or some other type of controversy. At the time Clark v. Allen was decided, the case seemed to involve no more than a routine reading of foreign laws. It now appears that in this reciprocity area under inheritance statutes, the probate courts of various States have launched inquiries into the type of governments that obtain in a particular foreign nation—whether aliens under their law have enforceable rights, whether the so-called "rights" are merely dispensations turning upon the whim or caprice of government officials, whether the representation of consuls, ambassadors, and other representatives of foreign nations are credible or made in good faith, whether there is in the actual administration in the particular foreign system of law any element of confiscation.

. . .

As we read the decisions that followed in the wake of Clark v. Allen, we find that they radiate some of the attitudes of the "cold war," where the search is for the "democracy quotient" of a foreign regime as opposed to the Marxist theory. The Oregon statute introduces the concept of "confiscation," which is of course opposed to the Just Compensation Clause of the Fifth Amendment. And this has led into minute inquiries concerning the actual administration of foreign law, into the credibility of foreign diplomatic statements, and into speculation whether the fact that some received delivery of funds should "not preclude wonderment as to how many may have been denied 'the right to receive' . . . ." See State Land Board v. Kolovrat, 220 Or. 448, 461–462, 349 P.2d 255, 262, rev'd sub nom. Kolovrat v. Oregon, 366 U.S. 187 on other grounds.

That kind of state involvement in foreign affairs and international developments—matters which the Constitution entrusts solely to the Federal Government—is not sanctioned by Clark v. Allen. Yet such forbidden state activity has infected each of the three provisions of § 111.070, as applied by Oregon.

.   .   .

It seems inescapable that the type of probate law that Oregon enforces affects international relations in a persistent and subtle way. .   .   .   Reversed.

NOTES

(1) In Clark v. Allen, 331 U.S. 503 (1947), Mr. Justice Douglas wrote for the Court that a California reciprocal inheritance statute was constitutional and permitted German nationals to take as legatees of a California resident decedent's personal property in that state. (The United States Alien Property Custodian had vested in himself all interest of the German nationals in the decedent's estate, but the question of the validity of the attempted testamentary disposition remained because it was done under authority of a reciprocal statute of the type struck down in Zschernig v. Miller.) The opinion said in part:

".   .   . Rights of succession to property are determined by local law. .   .   . Those rights may be affected by an overriding federal policy, as where a treaty makes different or conflicting arrangements. .   .   . Then the state policy must give way. .   .   . But here there is no treaty governing the rights of succession to the personal property. Nor has California entered the forbidden domain of negotiating with a foreign country, United States v. Curtiss-Wright Export Corp., 299 U.S. 304, 316, 317, or making a compact with it contrary to the prohibition of Article I, Section 10 of the Constitution. What California has done will have some incidental or indirect effect in foreign countries. But that is true of many state laws which none would claim cross the forbidden line."

Was Mr. Justice Douglas consistent in the two cases?

(2) See Scoles, Interstate and International Distinctions in Conflict of Laws in the United States, 54 Calif.L.Rev. 1599 (1966); Trautman, The Role of Conflicts Thinking in Defining the International Reach of American Regulatory Legislation, 22 Ohio St.L.J. 586 (1961).

(3) The area of American conflicts law controlled by treaties is discussed generally in Scoles and Hay, Conflict of Laws § 3.56 (1982).

DOUGHERTY v. EQUITABLE LIFE ASSURANCE SOCIETY

Court of Appeals of New York, 1934.
266 N.Y. 71, 193 N.E. 897.

[Actions against the Equitable Life Assurance Society, a New York corporation, growing out of life insurance policies issued by the Society to Russian citizens in Russia before the Russian Revolution of 1917. The defendant had been licensed to do business in Russia and the policies issued by it contained the following provisions of Russian law: Russian law should govern all disputes; the Russian government could at any time cancel the defendant's right to do business in Russia, whereupon the defendant must immediately liquidate and settle its accounts with the assured in the manner that should be indicated by the Russian government; the Society was obliged to keep on deposit with the government or the state bank assets sufficient to more than meet the liabilities incurred by the policies issued; and, further, "the exact fulfilment of the obligations entered into by the Society regarding the Russian assured shall be guaranteed, besides its sums and security found in Russia, by all the property belonging to the Society."

After the Revolution the Soviet government by its decrees declared that the business of insurance should be a state monopoly; that all private companies be liquidated immediately; and that the state assumed all obligations of the Society under its Russian policies. By a later decree all existing life insurance policies were cancelled and the government established a system of social protection. The Soviet government seized and confiscated the Society's assets in Russia.

The policies were payable according to their terms in rubles. Some of the present actions were brought to recover the premiums paid, on the theory of rescission; others were brought for the face value of the matured policies. From judgment of the appellate division affirming judgments in favor of certain plaintiffs and reversing judgments in favor of defendant (238 App.Div. 696, 265 N.Y.S. 714), all the parties appeal.]

CRANE, J. . . . The question now for us to determine is, What effect these laws and decrees of an established government, binding upon the citizens of Russia in Russia, have upon this defendant's contracts, made in Russia with Russian citizens, to be determined and interpreted and given effect, if any, according to Russian law. . . .

. . . Soviet Russia, as to all the insurance policies here in question, stands in the same position as if the government of Russia had never been interrupted by revolution; its decrees have the same force and effect as if they had been issued by the imperial government. . . .

. . .

The plaintiffs seek to make a distinction between the seizure of tangible property (Salimoff and Sagor Cases) and the disposition and canceling of rights to intangible property. We can see no distinction in this instance. The right to collect money by a Russian citizen on a contract to be interpreted according to Russian law is no different in this respect than the right to tangible property in Russia or the possession thereof. Both rights are dependent upon the law of Russia.

. . .

. . .

. . . [I]t cannot be against the public policy of this state to hold nationals to the contracts which they have made in their own country to be performed there according to the laws of that country. When they have specifically stipulated that the laws of their native land shall govern their acts, we give effect to those laws after recognition by this country the same as we would give effect to the laws of any nation which had not developed out of revolution.

Our conclusion, therefore, is that, since recognition, the Soviet decree became the laws of Russia, governing the policies here in question, and that obligations thereunder were at an end.

Assuming, however, that these contracts of insurance were not terminated by these Soviet decrees, and that the plaintiffs may recover the premiums paid prior to 1918, upon the theory of repudiation by the company in 1920, we also find that the plaintiffs cannot maintain this action, for the reason that the rubles in which payment is to be made are valueless. . . .

. . .

The Soviets, in order to give to their money an exchange value, created the chervonetz bank notes, taking the chervonetz as a standard, worth ten rubles. Having placed its notes or currency on a supposed gold basis, with a reserve of gold to meet them, the ruble became worth 51 cents of our money. On the withdrawal of all other paper money, by 1924 the chervonetz bank notes and the state treasury notes became the only circulating medium or legal tender. The plaintiffs' claim, sustained by the referee, is, that all previous obligations, even those created in 1918 and before, were payable "ruble for ruble" in this new gold currency, whereas the day before its creation their obligations were worthless.

. . .

. . . The plaintiffs can only recover when they show that by the law of Soviet Russia pre-existing obligations are to be paid "ruble for ruble" in the new chervonetz gold note, or, that there is an established ratio between such gold standard and the pre-existing ruble of the obligation. It is the ruble recovery in Russia—what would they get there—which is sued for here. When established, it is translated into our money.

. . .

The judgments of the lower courts should, therefore, be reversed, and the complaints dismissed, with costs in all courts.

LEHMAN, JUDGE (concurring). . . . The primary question presented upon this appeal is whether under the law of this jurisdiction the defendant's contractual obligation has been canceled or discharged.

. . .

. . . We may assume, as the defendant contends, that the intended effect of the decree was cancellation of the obligation, so far as the Soviet government had power to cancel. Even so, the Russian government could not decree cancellation which would be effective beyond its borders, except in so far as the courts of other jurisdictions choose to give effect to such a decree.

The problem now presented would be simple if the sole situs of the defendant's obligation had been in Russia and resort was had to our courts for remedy of a wrong arising in Russia, or for vindication of property or contractual rights there. Cf. Salimoff & Co. v. Standard Oil Co. of New York, supra [262 N.Y. 220, 223, 186 N.E. 679, 681, 89 A.L.R. 345]. For some purposes the situs of the defendant's obligation was in Russia; not for all. The defendant is a domestic corporation. Seizure of its assets and termination of its privilege of doing business did not end its contractual obligations. Though with one exception, all the assured were residents or subjects of Russia at the time the policies were issued, many of them had ceased to be subjects or residents of that country at the time the Soviet government decreed cancellation of the obligations due to them. We have said in similar circumstances, "The intangible chose in action, at least when it is the result of a deposit in a bank, has for some purposes a situs at the residence or place of business of the debtor, though the creditor be far away." Sokoloff v. National City Bank of New York, 239 N.Y. 158, 169, 145 N.E. 917, 920, 37 A.L.R. 712. That is true, to at least the same degree, where the intangible chose in action is a promise to pay insurance in a foreign jurisdiction. In this case, indeed, that legal principle is fortified by the express agreement of the defendant that its assets everywhere should constitute a guaranty of the "exact fulfillment," of its obligations in Russia.

. . . We cannot hold that Russian law can relieve the defendant of an obligation for which it has received payment unless we give Russian law an extraterritorial effect which under our own law we are not required to accord to foreign law. The obligation of exact fulfillment remains in force. That obligation has been repudiated or breached. Right to restitution or damages still remains. It has not been discharged by confiscation of the obligation due to the assured, for a confiscatory foreign law offends our public policy and cannot constitute excuse for restitution or performance here. It has not been discharged by confiscation of the assets of the defendant in Russia, for the assured have the right under the policies to look to the assets of the defendant here for fulfillment of the obligation.

JUDGE CRANE'S conclusion rests, in my opinion, upon premises which are entirely fallacious. A majority of the assured, even though Russian citizens at the time the policies were issued, were not subjects of Russia domiciled there when the decrees were made. The insurer was not a Russian corporation. The obligation of the insurer followed it wherever the insurer could be found. It was, therefore, not intangible property within Russia and the Russian government did not have the same dominion over it as it had over tangible property situated there. . . .

. . .

Assuming that the plaintiff has a cause of action, the question of how recovery shall be measured still remains. . . .

The obligation of the defendant at its inception could be discharged by payment of imperial rubles. When new issues of rubles were made, the defendant's debt was payable either in imperial rubles or in rubles of the new issues. All these rubles depreciated until they were without value. The result was that the obligation to the assured by the insurer, payable in valueless rubles, was also valueless . . .

. . . That was not the result of a confiscatory decree, but of unrestrained inflation. For loss so sustained, our law furnishes no remedy. That was true before the Soviet government was recognized; it is true now.

We can measure the value of the defendant's obligation only upon the basis of the value of the currency in which it was payable. . . . Here the defendant was required to leave such equitable value [of the policy] in Russia. It has been confiscated by the Russian government, but even if it had not been confiscated, it would itself have become valueless by reason of the depreciation of the ruble. Thus, even though events have rendered performance of the defendant's obligation valueless, the same events have rendered valueless the consideration received by the defendant.

For these reasons, I concur in the reversal of the judgment.

JOHANSEN v. CONFEDERATION LIFE ASSOCIATION

United States Court of Appeals, Second Circuit, 1971.
447 F.2d 175.

LUMBARD, CHIEF JUDGE: . . .

I.

Defendant is a Canadian life insurance company with its head office in Toronto. It does business not only in Canada and in the United States, but also in twenty-two other countries including Cuba. Since 1909 it has had a branch office in Cuba; and from 1909 to 1959, when Castro took over, it issued policies to residents of Cuba. Its operations in that country have always been subject to Cuban laws and to the supervision of the Cuban government.

Turull, who was the insured of the two policies upon which plaintiffs now seek to recover, moved from his birthplace, Brooklyn, New York, to Cuba when he was a young man. He married a Cuban and had a substantial export-import business in Havana. In 1937 and 1939, he took out the two policies in question here with the defendant's Cuban office, his wife being the beneficiary of the first and his daughter the beneficiary of the second. He moved back to New York only after Castro came into power and died in New York in 1961.

Johansen, also a United States citizen born in New York, married Turull's daughter in New York in 1941 and thereafter went to work for his father-in-law in Cuba. In 1946, he took out a policy with defendant's Cuban office, and he remained in Cuba until Castro took over. Afterwards, he moved back to New York where he now resides. He seeks a declaration that defendant is obligated to accept premium payments from him in United States dollars, to make policy loans in United States dollars, and to pay proceeds upon his death in United States dollars.

Each of the three policies stated that "[a]ll sums payable or [receivable] under the policy shall be paid at . . . Havana, Republic of Cuba." Further, with respect to currency, each provided that "[a]ll sums payable or [receivable] under this policy shall be paid in lawful currency of the United States of America."

Although the latter provision might seem at first glance to solve the problem of this case, it does not do so because of the effect of the Cuban currency laws throughout the years. From 1914 to 1939, two currencies were legal tender in Cuba, the peso and the United States dollar. Theoretically they were of equal value and creditors could demand payment in whichever currency they chose. By 1939, however, the peso was actually worth less than the dollar. In an effort to bolster the peso, the Cuban government enacted a law in 1939 making the dollar and the peso interchangeable on a one-for-one basis. Each continued to be legal tender, but they could be used interchangeably, and debtors were now given the option as to which currency they wished to use in payment of their debts. Creditors were required to accept pesos in extinguishment of an obligation expressed in dollars and vice versa. Thus, it is evident that when the policies in question here stated that United States currency was to be paid, it was referring to a legal Cuban tender which after 1939 could be paid in either dollars or pesos.

In 1951, however, there was a significant change in the Cuban law. The new decree provided that henceforth pesos would be the only legal tender. United States dollars ceased to be legal tender and all obligations had to be expressed and paid in pesos. Obligations previously contracted in dollars had to be discharged in pesos at the rate of one peso for one dollar. Although a person could still own dollars in Cuba, he could not use them to pay debts. Thus, this Cuban law in effect changed the insurance contracts in question here from dollar contracts to peso contracts. The 1951 law was widely published in Cuba and defendant notified all its Cuban policyholders that all payments under policies which referred to United States currency would henceforth by payable in pesos. Neither Turull nor Johansen objected to this and both paid their premiums in pesos after

1951 as they were required to do. Indeed, even before 1951 Johansen had paid in pesos, although Turull had paid in dollars.

In 1959, when Castro took over, a new Cuban law made it a criminal offense to hold dollars and required owners of dollars to turn them in for pesos on a one-for-one basis. Since that time the peso has diminished in value in relation to dollars and today is substantially worthless in terms of dollars. This fact causes the dilemma of the instant case.

Although defendant is willing to pay plaintiffs the amounts due them in pesos and in Havana, plaintiffs seek payment of dollars in New York, because pesos are worthless to them here and they are forbidden by United States law to travel to Cuba. Defendant wants to pay in pesos because throughout the years it has invested the insurance proceeds from its Cuban policyholders in Cuban assets precisely in order to meet the obligations in pesos to those policyholders. Now, since it is forbidden by Cuban law to transfer those funds out of Cuba and since pesos are as worthless to it as to plaintiffs in terms of dollars, it has no present use for the funds which it invested in Cuba other than to pay off the Cuban policies. Hence, to require defendant to pay plaintiffs in New York dollars out of its general assets would leave it with worthless reserves of pesos on its hands.

II.

The first question arising here is one of conflict of laws, i.e., whether the applicable law governing the disposition of this case is Cuban law, New York law, or Canadian law. . . .

. . . According to plaintiffs, New York has a vital interest in determining whether or not its citizens who have fully performed insurance contracts in hard currency will receive hard currency back from the insurance company. On the other hand, they contend, Cuba has no legitimate interest in having its internal currency regulations applied to determine the outcome of this litigation.

Plaintiffs argue further that under this "greatest interest" rationale now used by New York courts, the present domicile of the parties seeking to recover is generally decisive. . . .

Finally, plaintiffs argue, Canada also has an important interest in this case—that of having insurance companies domiciled there perform their contracts according to their express terms. In plaintiffs' view, the district court's decision here frustrates that policy. . . .

. . . The cases cited by plaintiffs in this regard were either wrongful death actions where New York domiciliaries were killed in out-of-state automobile accidents . . . or actions involving property rights. . . . This case, however, is an insurance contract matter; and if domicile is to be determinative in such a case, it seems more logical to look to the domicile of the insureds themselves at the time they entered into the contracts, rather than to the domicile of the plaintiffs at the time of bringing suit. For the rights and obligations of the parties under such contracts are determined by the law of the place where the insureds lived when the contracts were made and can hardly be changed solely because the insureds or the beneficiaries subsequently changed domiciles.

. . .

In addition, the large number of contracts between the insurance contracts and Cuba cannot be ignored. . . . Judge McLean found those contacts to be overwhelming and decisive. Moreover, Turull and Johansen did not object to the 1951 notice that payments on the policies would henceforth be made in pesos; and indeed until Castro, they were clearly willing to accept Cuban law as governing those policies.

Thus, we hold that under either the "grouping of contacts" test or the test propounded by plaintiffs, Cuban law governs the disposition of this case; and under Cuban law, defendant's obligation on these policies is to pay in pesos, since the 1951 Cuban law forbade defendant to pay in dollars and changed the contracts in question here from dollar contracts to peso contracts.

III.

. . .

Plaintiffs argue that . . . there is no reason to give the Cuban law effect in New York, when both New York and Canada have stronger interests in the outcome of this case than Cuba has. According to plaintiffs, the insurance contracts imposed upon the company a general obligation to pay plaintiffs when the insureds died. . . . [H]ence the company has no right to convert its general obligation into a limited one to pay only from the assets which it had elected to invest in Cuba. This is especially true, plaintiffs contend, since the company failed to inform the insureds of the limitation which it now asserts. Thus, in plaintiffs' view, the defendant must pay its debts out of its general assets, not out of the limited reserves in Cuba.

We do not agree. As shown above, Cuban law governed these policies when they were made; that law in 1951 converted the currency of these policies to pesos; and until Castro, Turull and Johansen accepted the applicability of Cuban law and acquiesced in the shift in premiums from dollars to pesos. Neither objected to the 1951 change or to the contractual provision that all payments were to be made in Cuba until after Castro came into power—which in our view was too late. Thus . . . there is no reason or policy for a New York court not to give effect to the Cuban law, under which defendant's obligation is to pay in pesos.

. . .

IV.

Looking finally to the "equities" of the situation, they seem to us to tip the scale slightly in the defendant's favor. On the one hand, plaintiffs would have no use for pesos; and, according to them, they are entitled to payment on their policies in valuable currency since they paid their premiums in hard valuable currency. On the other hand, defendant accumulated reserves of pesos and invested in Cuba in order to meet its obligations on the Cuban policies, and those pesos are now worthless to it except to pay off the Cuban policies. . . .

Plaintiffs rely on the fact that the company was not compelled by any law to invest in Cuban assets in order to meet its obligations on the Cuban policies, but rather did so voluntarily and as part of its general policy; and they argue that therefore the company should now have to meet its obligations in currency valuable to plaintiffs. It seems to us, however, that the company's policy of investing in the country where the insured lived was a reasonable and almost necessary business decision, especially where, as here, the policy expressly provided for payment in that country. Thus, the company would not be unjustly enriched by being allowed to pay in pesos, whereas requiring it to pay in dollars would in effect be compelling it to pay twice and thereby put a burden on its general uncommitted reserves.

Affirmed.

[The concurring opinion of JUDGE SMITH is omitted.]

FEINBERG, CIRCUIT JUDGE (dissenting):

The basic issue in this case is whether the promise of an insurance company to an American citizen to pay death benefits "in lawful currency of the United States of America" should be enforced. The case would have been far different had the insurer's obligation been to pay benefits in "lawful currency" or in "legal tender" or in "lawful currency of Cuba." The first two phrases are capable of the construction defendant seeks, which the third embodies. But that is not what the policy said. The obligation instead was to pay benefits in "lawful currency of the United States." The majority concludes that this unmistakably clear promise of defendant insurance company is unenforceable even though that conclusion is inconsistent with the insurer's own selling practices and the insured's justified expectations and is contrary to the most relevant precedents. I emphatically dissent from such an inequitable and unjustified result. . . .

. . . . .

. . . It is true that ordinarily the rights created by a life insurance contract are determined by the local law of the jurisdiction (here Cuba) where the insured was domiciled at the time of application for the policy. See Restatement (Second) of Conflict of Laws § 192 (P.O.D.1969). But that rule is by no means ironclad, particularly in international cases. See Rossano v. Manufacturers' Life Insurance

Co. [1963] 2 QB 352, and other cases cited in Restatement, supra, Reporter's Note § 192 at 10. When the insured changes his domicile after the policy is issued, as concededly occurred here in 1959, the jurisdiction to which he has moved has "the dominant interest in him." Restatement, supra, Explanatory Notes § 192, comment d at 3. Moreover, in view of defendant's selling practices . . . such a move was clearly foreseeable to it. Cf. Clay v. Sun Insurance Office, Ltd., 377 U.S. 179 (1964). These practices gave rise to a justified expectation by the insured that he could count on payment of benefits in American dollars when he went back to his domicile of origin where American dollars, rather than pesos, were used. . . . When to these considerations is added the fact that the beneficiaries here are New York domiciliaries and that New York's choice of law would be influenced by its strong policy of construing insurance contracts to protect the insured. . . . I do not think that New York would apply the Cuban law in this case and render worthless the benefits under the contracts.

Defendant argues that a New York court would look to the law of the place of payment as specified in the contract to decide in which currency payment of the obligation is to be made. That may correctly state a New York conflicts principle, but it only governs "details of performance and not . . . matters which substantially affect the nature and extent of the obligations imposed by the contract." See Restatement (Second) of Conflict of Laws, Explanatory Notes § 206, comment b at 319 (P.O.D.1968). In any event, application of that rule is doubtful where the contract itself makes provision, as do the policies in this case, for the type of currency to be used. Liebeskind v. Mexican Light & Power Co., 116 F.2d 971, 974 (2d Cir. 1941). Without deciding which law applies as to where performance is to be had, it seems reasonably clear that under New York or Cuban law the duty of defendant to pay benefits should not be narrowly construed as a duty to pay only in Havana. Defendant points to no Cuban law that limits the obligation to pay money under a contract to the place named in a place of payment clause. As the district court found, it would not be illegal under Cuban law for defendant to pay dollars in New York. 312 F.Supp. at 1056. The policies themselves contemplated that payment might be made elsewhere. . . . It seems clear that the place of payment clause was inserted into the policies as a matter of convenience and not as an essential part of the bargain. In light of this and the other conflicts considerations discussed in this opinion, I do not believe that under New York law the naming of Havana as the place of payment requires that Cuban law be applied to these policies.

There are only two jurisdictions, other than New York, with any arguable interest in the outcome of this case, Cuba and Canada. I agree that Cuba has numerous contacts with the transaction, but on analysis it is apparent that Cuba has no interest in the outcome of this case. Whether or not defendant has to pay plaintiffs, neither defendant's nor plaintiffs' assets in Cuba will be removed from that country. On the other hand, insurance is a highly regulated business and Canada has a strong interest in the practices of an insurance company domiciled there. Therefore, New York courts would be influenced by a recent ruling of the Canadian Supreme Court, Imperial Life Assurance Co. v. Casteleiro y Colemnares [1967] Can.S.Ct. 443, 62 D.L.R.2d 138, which refused to apply Cuban law in a situation not fairly distinguishable from this case.

In *Imperial Life*, defendant, a Canadian insurance company, had issued life insurance to plaintiff, a Cuban national. The policies were written in Spanish, were delivered in Cuba, and were payable in United States dollars. The Canadian court reasoned that a contract is governed by the law "with which it appears to have the closest and most substantial connection." 62 D.L.R.2d at 143. Finding that the decision to "go on the risk" was made at defendant's head office in Toronto, that the policies, although in Spanish, were a standard form that complied with the law of Ontario, that the place of contracting was Ontario, and that the insured would reasonably anticipate that the law of Ontario would govern the contracts, the court held that Ontario law applied to the policies. Accordingly, defendant was required to pay in Canadian currency the equivalent of the United States dollar value of the policies.

The decision below reaches a result, therefore, that defendant could not have obtained in its home jurisdiction of Canada. When the local law of the jurisdictions with the most interest in the insured, the beneficiaries, and the insurer would allow plaintiffs to recover, a New York court would not choose Cuban law. As between the law of Canada and that of the forum, there is no conflict and New York would apply its own local law.

That defendant can no longer transfer its assets out of Cuba does not require affirmance of the district court order. Defendant's obligation to plaintiffs is a general one, payable from defendan's general assets. Defendant's unannounced policy of investing in Cuban assets enough funds to cover payment of its Cuban policies is irrelevant to its obligation to plaintiffs. On their face, there is no indication that the policies are restricted to assets held in Cuba. While perhaps it was a reasonable business practice to invest in Cuban assets, no Cuban law required defendant to do so. . . .

Finally, a word on the equities. The district court regarded as inequitable the allocation to defendant of the loss resulting, in truth, from its decision to invest in Cuban pesos its net premium income from policies issued to American citizens who resided in Cuba. . . . I fail to see how this makes great sense. It places the loss resulting directly from defendant's voluntary, if now proved to be unfortunate, decision to invest in Cuba on those who had no part in making, nor notice of, that decision and who can clearly less afford to bear it than defendant. . . .

NOTES

(1) The Castro government of Cuba adopted a series of financial measures involving Cuban holders of policies in life insurance companies in the United States. The measures included the expropriation of the Cuban property of the companies, the substitution of the Cuban state as the obligor under the policies, and a prohibition of payment of monies to Cuban nationals anywhere except in Cuba. Several Cuban holders of policies with an American company, who had escaped from Cuba after the Castro regime came to power, brought suit on the policies in the United States. The insurance companies set up the Cuban laws as a defense. This defense was rejected in Pan-American Life Insurance Co. v. Recio, 154 So.2d 197 (Fla.1963) largely on the ground that the policy provided for payments in New Orleans. In Confederation Life Insurance Co. v. deLara, 257 So.2d 42 (Fla.1971), cert. denied 409 U.S. 953 (1972), the state courts applied Florida law which called for payment in dollars rather than Cuban pesos. Two dissenting United States Supreme Court Justices would have granted certiorari to determine whether the choice of law was consistent with the Fourteenth Amendment due process protection as outlined in Home Insurance Co. v. Dick, p. 329, supra.

(2) Santovenia v. Confederation Life Association, 460 F.2d 805 (5th Cir. 1972), involved a policy which was issued in Cuba and called for payment in Cuba in Cuban pesos. By a provision in the policy the parties agreed to be bound by any change in the Cuban currency laws. It was held that the insurance company would not be ordered to make payment in dollars in the United States. In another case the defense was upheld on the ground, among others, that respect for the Cuban decrees was required by the International Monetary Fund to which Cuba and the United States had adhered. Theye Y Adjuria v. Pan American Life Insurance Co., 154 So.2d 450 (La. 1963). The extent to which the exchange systems of the two countries accord with the purposes of the Fund appear from brief surveys of the two systems in International Monetary Fund, Thirteenth Annual Report on Exchange Restrictions 89, 355 (1962).

(3) Although Restatement, Second, Conflict of Laws § 192 refers the validity of a life insurance contract and the rights it creates prima facie to the law of the state of the insured's domicil at the time of issue, in international cases, where confiscation is a factor, the courts have shied away from that result. Thus, in Blanco v. Pan-American Life Ins. Co., 221 F.Supp. 219 (S.D. Fla.1963), the court decided the effect of Cuban decrees under the law of the place of payment, which was the insurer's place of incorporation. Accord: Rossano v. Manufacturers' Life Assurance Co. [1963], 2 Q.B. 352.

BANCO NACIONAL de CUBA v. SABBATINO

Supreme Court of the United States, 1964.
376 U.S. 398, 84 S.Ct. 923, 11 L.Ed.2d 804.

[This was an action in a federal court against an American commodity broker for the alleged conversion of maritime bills of lading covering sugar which had been loaded on a ship in Cuban waters.

The sugar had been the property in Cuba of American business interests but it had been there expropriated by the Cuban government for illusory compensation in retaliation for the reduction by the American government of the Cuban sugar quota. The Cuban government characterized the American action as an act of "aggression, for political purposes." The State Department stated that the Cuban law under which the expropriation took place was "manifestly in violation of those principles of international law which have long been accepted by the free countries in the West."

In support of the legal validity of the expropriation the plaintiff relied on the act of state doctrine. The defendant urged effect should not be given to the expropriation because it was in violation of international law. The Supreme Court reversed the judgment of the Court of Appeals for the defendant and remanded the case to the District Court.

The Court considered, among other things, whether the act of state doctrine is governed by federal law or state law, and whether under the separation of powers principle the range of application of that doctrine is to be determined by the federal judiciary or by the executive.]

MR. JUSTICE HARLAN. . . . Preliminarily, we discuss the foundations on which we deem the act of state doctrine to rest, and more particularly the question of whether state or federal law governs its application in a federal diversity case.

We do not believe that this doctrine is compelled either by the inherent nature of sovereign authority . . . or by some principle of international law. . . . While historic notions of sovereign authority do bear upon the wisdom of employing the act of state doctrine, they do not dictate its existence. . . .

. . . .

. . . The text of the Constitution does not require the act of state doctrine; it does not irrevocably remove from the judiciary the capacity to review the validity of foreign acts of state.

The act of state doctrine does, however, have "constitutional" underpinnings. It arises out of the basic relationship between branches of government in a system of separation of powers. It concerns the competency of dissimilar institutions to make and implement particular kinds of decisions in the area of international relations. The doctrine as formulated in past decisions expresses the strong sense of the Judicial Branch that its engagement in the task of passing on the validity of foreign acts of state may hinder rather than further this country's pursuit of goals both for itself and for the community of nations as a whole in the international sphere. Many commentators disagree with this view. . . . Whatever considerations are thought to predominate, it is plain that the problems involved are uniquely federal in nature. If federal authority, in this instance this

Court, orders the field of judicial competence in this area for the federal courts, and the state courts are left free to formulate their own rules, the purposes behind the doctrine would be as effectively undermined as if there had been no federal pronouncement on the subject.

.　.　.

.　.　. [W]e are constrained to make it clear that an issue concerned with a basic choice regarding the competence and function of the Judiciary and the National Executive in ordering our relationships with other members of the international community must be treated exclusively as an aspect of federal law.[1] It seems fair to assume that the Court did not have rules like the act of state doctrine in mind when it decided Erie R. Co. v. Tompkins. Soon thereafter, Professor Philip C. Jessup, now a judge of the International Court of Justice, recognized the potential dangers were Erie extended to legal problems affecting international relations.[2] He cautioned that rules of international law should not be left to divergent and perhaps parochial state interpretations. His basic rationale is equally applicable to the act of state doctrine.

.　.　.

.　.　. We conclude that the scope of the act of state doctrine must be determined according to federal law.

If the act of state doctrine is a principle of decision binding on federal and state courts alike but compelled by neither international law nor the Constitution, its continuing vitality depends on its capacity to reflect the proper distribution of functions between the judicial and political branches of the Government on matters bearing upon foreign affairs. It should be apparent that the greater the degree of codification or consensus concerning a particular area of international law, the more appropriate it is for the judiciary to render decisions regarding it, since the courts can then focus on the application of an agreed principle to circumstances of fact rather than on the sensitive task of establishing a principle not inconsistent with the national interest or with international justice. .　.　. [R]ather than laying down or reaffirming an inflexible and all-encompassing rule in this case, we decide only that the Judicial Branch will not examine the validity of a taking of property within its own territory by a foreign sovereign government, extant and recognized by this country at the time of suit, in the absence of a treaty or other unambiguous agreement regarding controlling legal principles, even if the complaint alleges that the taking violates customary international law.

.　.　.

1.　At least this is true when the Court limits the scope of judicial inquiry. We need not consider whether a state court might, in certain circumstances, adhere to a more restrictive view concerning the scope of examination of foreign acts than that required by the Court. [Footnotes renumbered. Most of the footnotes have been omitted. Eds.]

2.　The Doctrine of Erie Railroad v. Tompkins Applied to International Law, 33 Am.J.Int'l.L. 740 (1939).

. . . [W]hatever way the matter is cut the possibility of conflict between the Judicial and Executive Branches could hardly be avoided.

[MR. JUSTICE WHITE dissented.]

NOTES

(1) An important sequel to the Sabbatino decision is First National City Bank v. Banco Nacional de Cuba, 406 U.S. 759 (1972). For an enlightening treatment of the main decision, see Henkin, The Foreign Affairs Power of the Federal Courts: *Sabbatino*, 64 Colum.L.Rev. 805 (1964).

(2) Following the Sabbatino decision, Congress enacted, and the President signed, the so-called Hickenlooper Amendment, (22 U.S.C.A. § 2370(e)(2)), which provides that ". . . no court in the United States shall decline on the ground of the federal act of state doctrine to make a determination on the merits giving effect to the principles of international law in a case in which a claim . . . is asserted . . . based upon . . . a confiscation or other taking after January 1, 1959 . . . [unless] the President determines that application of the act of state doctrine is required in that particular case by the foreign policy interests of the United States. . . ."

After remand, it was held that the Sabbatino case itself came under the scope of the Hickenlooper Amendment and the complaint was dismissed. Banco Nacional de Cuba v. Farr, 383 F.2d 166 (2d Cir. 1967), cert. denied 390 U.S. 956. See Paul, The Act of State Doctrine: Revived but Suspended, 113 U.Pa.L.Rev. 691 (1965).

(3) A Turkish bank raised the act-of-state doctrine unsuccessfully in trying to avoid a commitment to pay the plaintiff bank in Swiss francs in New York. The payment was due on a note executed in Turkey. The court rejected the defense that a Turkish currency regulation barred payment by the defendant in non-Turkish currency. Weston Banking Corp. v. Turkiye Garanti Bankasi A.S., 57 N.Y.2d 315, 456 N.Y.S. 684, 442 N.E.2d 1195 (1982). Could the Sabbatino doctrine have been applied in Holzer v. Deutsche-Reichsbahn Gesellschaft, p. 397, supra?

(4) For a helpful discussion of the act-of-state doctrine in the Sabbatino context, see Cheatham and Maier, Private International Law and Its Sources, 22 Vand.L.Rev. 27, 88 (1968). Its history in relation to sovereign immunity is summarized:

"The act-of-state doctrine in American law is closely related to the principle of sovereign immunity. Both stemmed, initially, from conceptions of absolute territorial sovereignty and the relationship between those conceptions and a power-oriented theory of jurisdiction which equated physical power over parties with a right to decide their disputes and lack of such power with a lack of jurisdiction. Thus, the adjudication of disputes concerning either the person or the acts of a foreign sovereign was conceived as the application of physical force against the sovereign personality. But the decision to apply force to a foreign sovereign is essentially political in nature. It is not to be made upon the accident of the presence of the sovereign, or of one claiming legal rights based upon the validity of the sovereign's acts, before a court whose even-handed justice could be enforced only by the exercise of its own sovereign's power. . . ."

———

Conflicts Problems in International Settings, Other Than as Affected by Control of Foreign Affairs

———

In examining further the differences between intranational, sister state conflicts problems and those involving transnational contacts, the influence of the United States Constitution, various federal statutes and public international law come into consideration.

The Constitution of the United States. Two of the three provisions of the Constitution that are most important in sister-state conflict of laws do not apply to international conflict of laws: the full faith and credit clause and the privileges and immunities clauses, which are limited to citizens "of each state" or of the United States. The due process clause and the equal protection clause of the Fourteenth Amendment, however, may apply in international conflicts.

Federal Statutes. In some areas the Constitution gives to the Congress the power to legislate on private international law, as, in the areas of foreign commerce and of admiralty. In cases such as injuries to seamen (Lauritzen v. Larsen, p. 660, supra); anti-trust law enforcement (Timken Roller Bearing Co. v. United States, 341 U.S. 593 (1951); British Nylon Spinners, Ltd. v. Imperial Chemical Industries, Ltd. [1952] 2 All E.R. 780); patent and trademark protection (Steele v. Bulova Watch Co., 344 U.S. 280 (1952), p. 470 supra; Vanity Fair Mills v. T. Eaton Co., 133 F.Supp. 522 (S.D.N.Y.1955), affirmed, 234 F.2d 633 (2d Cir. 1956)), the national power has been dominant.

Public International Law and Transnational Law. In some matters of international law, such as immunities of foreign representatives and jurisdiction over marginal waters, international law influences conflict of laws. But, short of treaties or conventions, choice of law is not subjected to controls set by legal principles of the international community.

Should conflicts rules affecting international cases be "segregated" from those applicable to sister-state situations? Professor Cheatham has doubted the desirability of stressing differences between international and interstate conflicts. He points out that the question of which foreign nation is involved and which underlying policies are in issue may be more significant than the simple issue of whether the case is international rather than interstate. Consider three parallel San Francisco cases on judgments or contracts, one with Seattle, another with Vancouver, a third with Peking. Surely, it would be unusual for the California court to treat the Vancouver case differently from the Seattle case. Almost certainly it would find the

Vancouver case closer to the Seattle case than to the other international case, the Peking case. Cheatham, Book Review, 45 A.B.A.J. 1190 (1959). See Restatement, Second, The Foreign Relations Law of the United States (1965).

There is no *ipso facto* warrant for treating a case differently merely because it is an international instead of an interstate one, or merely because it involves an alien instead of a citizen. The purpose of conflict of laws is to aid in making the international and the interstate systems work well when they affect multistate legal affairs of private persons. Principles must be developed to advance that fundamental purpose. Whenever there is a difference in the treatment of international and interstate cases, it should be justified by differences in the circumstances that call for differences in treatment. See Leflar, American Conflicts Law 8–9 (3d Ed. 1977).

A significant difference is in the safeguards a state sets up to assure justice. In the United States two groups of constitutional safeguards apply with full force in interstate conflicts. The first group makes any grossly unjust law or grossly unfair proceeding invalid in its own state as a denial of due process. The other group guarantees a minimum of respect (in varying degrees) by one state of the Union to the statutes, decisions and citizens of another state. In the international area, there is no assurance of comparable safeguards. This calls for closer scrutiny of international conflicts cases.

Some tentative conclusions can be drawn from the cases. Ordinarily the same rules are followed in interstate and international areas. (1) The element of alienage of one of the parties is of little or no importance. The common law employs domicile, not nationality, as an important factor in choice of law, and in increasing measure the Supreme Court of the United States has extended the equal protection of the laws clause to aliens. Sugarman v. Dougall, 413 U.S. 634 (1973); Graham v. Richardson, 403 U.S. 365 (1971). (2) Judgments of courts of foreign nations are recognized and enforced if the essentials of judicial jurisdiction and of a fair hearing were observed by the foreign court. See Chapter 5, supra. (3) Commercial arbitration agreements are respected, whether the arbitration is called for in a sister state or in a foreign country, subject again to the requirements of judicial jurisdiction and of a fair hearing, and, of course, to applicable treaties or conventions.

When Congress enacts statutes to regulate activities that are international in scope, the application of the statutes may at times raise public questions of great consequence. See McCulloch v. Sociedad Nacional de Marineros de Honduras, 372 U.S. 10, 17 (1963). For example, if a United States law is construed as prohibiting conduct abroad that is not only lawful there but positively encouraged by the laws of another country, delicate questions are presented. A court in this country should not automatically transfer the choice-of-law approaches it follows in dealing with sister state choice-of-law problems to questions involving other countries. If it does, it may give offense and provoke retaliatory action. Cf. Reese, Limitations on the Extra-territorial Application of Law, 4 Dalhousie L.J. 578 (1978); Note, Extra-territorial Discovery: An Analysis Based on Good Faith, 83 Colum.L.Rev. 1320 (1983).

Chapter 11

PROPERTY

Introductory Note

Cook, The Jurisdiction of Sovereign States and The Conflict of Laws, 31 Colum.L.Rev. 368, 381 (1931): "Since all legislation, all judicial action, creates (and destroys) the rights of persons, even though these have relation to things, there is no logical basis upon which to classify laws into those which affect persons and those which affect things."

SECTION 1. LAND *

Introductory Note

RESTATEMENT, SECOND, CONFLICT OF LAWS **

§ 223. Validity and Effect of Conveyance of Interest in Land

(1) Whether a conveyance transfers an interest in land and the nature of the interest transferred are determined by the law that would be applied by the courts of the situs.

(2) These courts would usually apply their own local law in determining such questions.

Comment:

a. Rationale. . . . The rule of this Section is derived from those principles looking to furtherance of the needs of the interstate and international systems, application of the law of the state of dominant interest, protection of justified expectations, certainty, predictability and uniformity of result and ease in the determination and application of the law to be applied.

Issues falling within the scope of the rule of this Section are the capacity of the party who conveys to make an effective conveyance, the capacity of the party to whom the conveyance is made to acquire

---

* See Restatement, Second, Conflict of Laws §§ 223–243.

** Quoted with the permission of the copyright owner, The American Law Institute.

the interest involved, the formal validity of the conveyance, the validity of the conveyance in other respects, and the nature of the interest transferred.   .   .   .

   b.   Applicable law.   .   .   .

Whether the courts of the situs would decide the case in accordance with their own local law may depend upon the precise issue involved. These courts would apply their own local law to determine issues in which the situs has the dominant interest. Examples of such issues are who may own the land, the conditions under which land may be held and the uses to which land may be put. So these courts would apply their own local law to determine what restrictions, if any, are imposed upon the ownership of land by a corporation or by an alien and the period during which the power to alienate interests in land may be suspended.   .   .   .

The courts of the situs would also frequently apply their local law to determine issues in which it might be thought that the situs does not have the dominant interest. In the normal course of events, transactions involving land are not entered into until considerable thought has been given by the parties and their lawyers to the possible consequences. This is an area where it is peculiarly important that there be certainty, predictability and uniformity of result and ease in the determination and application of the law to be applied. For these reasons, the courts of the situs would apply their local law in situations where it is likely that a person relied on the record title before entering into a transaction involving interests in local land. Likewise, considerations of convenience make it desirable that a prospective purchaser and his agents, such as draftsmen and title searchers, need consult only a single law and that the one with which they are most familiar. This latter point may be illustrated by an example. Suppose that in state X, where both A and B are domiciled, A gives B a deed to land in state Y and that thereafter the question arises before a Y court whether A had the requisite capacity to do so. It could be argued in support of application by the Y courts of X local law to determine this question of capacity that X is the state which has the dominant interest in the determination of this issue. But such a decision would complicate the task of title searchers and of other persons concerned with Y land. Thereafter, they could not always safely restrict their attention to Y local law in determining the capacity of a transferor of Y land. There would be situations, perhaps uncertain both in their nature and extent, where the local law of one or more other states would have to be consulted.   .   .   .

On the other hand, situations will arise where the courts of the situs would not apply their own local law to the decision of a particular issue.   .   .   .

Whichever law would have been applied by the courts of the situs in the decision of the particular issue will likewise so be applied by the forum.   .   .   .

NOTE

For an extensive criticism of the rule that the law of the situs should be applied to determine questions involving transfers of interests in land, see Weintraub, Commentary on the Conflict of Laws 398–445 (2d ed. 1980).

A.   SUCCESSION ON DEATH

IN RE ESTATE OF BARRIE

Supreme Court of Iowa, 1949.
240 Iowa 431, 35 N.W.2d 658.

[The case appears p. 651, supra.]

NOTES

(1) Is the rule of the principal case a desirable one? Would it not be convenient to have one law govern questions of succession to all parts of an estate? On the other hand, would problems of title search in Iowa have been increased if the Iowa court had applied the law of the testatrix's last domicile (Illinois) to determine whether her will had been effectively revoked?

(2) Why is such preeminence accorded the law of the situs? Is one reason the fact that land is within the exclusive control of the state in which it is situated, and the officials of that state are the only ones who can lawfully deal with the land physically?

(3) Statutes in more than thirty states provide for alternative places of reference to determine whether a will has been executed in proper form. In the majority of these states a will executed elsewhere, when in writing and subscribed by the testator, is legally effective if executed in the mode prescribed by the law of the forum, or by the law of the place of execution or by the law of the testator's domicile. There are differences among the states as to whether the reference is to the testator's domicile at the time of execution of the will or at the time of death. See, for example, Uniform Probate Code § 2–506. See also Rees, American Wills Statutes: II, 46 Va.L.Rev. 856, 905 (1960).

A liberal provision, recognizing numerous places of alternative reference to determine issues of testamentary formalities, is The English Wills Act 1963, 11 & 12 Eliz. 2, Chapter 44. This provision is based upon the Hague Convention of 1960, which is reprinted in 9 Am.J.Comp.Law 705 (1960).

(4) When a testator dies domiciled in one state owning land in another state, does the law of the state of domicile or of the situs determine (a) the forced share interest of the surviving spouse in the land or (b) the effect upon interests in the land of the surviving spouse's election to take against the will? See two articles by Scoles in 30 Ind.L.J. 293 (1955), and in 8 Fla.L. Rev. 151 (1955). See also the material on marital property (pp. 889 – 908, infra).

(5) Craig v. Craig, 140 Md. 322, 117 Atl. 756 (1922). The intestate died domiciled in Pennsylvania leaving a leasehold interest in Maryland land. The Maryland courts characterized this interest as one in a movable and held that it should be distributed in accordance with the Pennsylvania rules of intestacy.

(6) Uniform Probate Code:

Section 2–602. [Choice of Law as to Meaning and Effect of Wills.]

The meaning and legal effect of a disposition in a will shall be determined by the local law of a particular state selected by the testator in his instrument unless the application of that law is contrary to the public policy of this state otherwise applicable to the disposition.

COMMENT

. . . This provision . . . enables a testator to select the law of a particular state for purposes of interpreting his will without regard to the location of property covered thereby. So long as local public policy is accommodated, the section should be accepted as necessary and desirable to add to the utility of wills. . . .

DUCKWALL V. LEASE, 106 Ind.App. 664, 20 N.E.2d 204 (1939): Testatrix died domiciled in Ohio owning a farm in Indiana. In her will she gave her husband a life estate in the farm and directed that at his death the farm should be sold and the proceeds divided equally between a brother and a sister. The brother and sister predeceased the testatrix and the question was whether their legacies had lapsed. This would be so under the law of Indiana but not under the law of Ohio. The court held that Ohio law was applicable and that the legacies had not lapsed. The law of Indiana, the state of the situs was said to determine whether an equitable conversion had taken place. Under this law, the effect of the provision in the will for the sale of the farm was equitably to convert the farm into personalty. Hence the farm was treated as personal property, and its distribution and disposition held to be governed by the law of Ohio. For a more recent and similar holding by the same court, see Moore v. Livingston, 148 Ind.App. 275, 265 N.E.2d 251 (1970).

TOLEDO SOCIETY FOR CRIPPLED CHILDREN V. HICKOK, 152 Tex. 578, 261 S.W.2d 692 (1953): Mr. Hickok died domiciled in Ohio. His will left his estate in trust to some of the respondents for 20 years and then to petitioners, all charities. All of the respondents were Ohio domiciliaries and the charities were Ohio organizations. The Ohio mortmain statute, if applicable, barred the gift over to the charities but Texas had no such statute. The charities brought a suit to determine their rights under the will in certain mineral estates in Texas land. At the time of Hickok's death the mineral estates were owned by a partnership of which he was a partner. During his life, Hickok had agreed with his partner that they would form an Ohio corporation and transfer to it all of the partnership's assets in return for stock. Hickok's will incorporated the contract by reference and directed his executor to complete the exchange. The charities appealed from a decision which denied them any rights in the mineral interests, on the ground that Ohio law was applicable since the mineral interests should be deemed to have been equitably converted into personalty by reason of the provision in Hickok's will that the partnership assets should be conveyed to a corporation in return for stock.

Held: reversed. "We are disposed to agree with the majority of the text writers . . . that the fiction of equitable conversion from realty to personalty or vice versa, 'can have no place in the conflict of laws.' . . . the circumstances that the will . . . directs the contract to be carried out, does not change the fact that, on Mr. Hickok's death, what passed for the benefit of the petitioners and others was his interest in the minerals." To find that these interests had been converted into personalty for purposes of conflict of laws would "deprive the petitioners of the last remnant of benefits the testator obviously intended them to have, and, [would] enforce here a legislative policy of Ohio, which is contrary to the policy of our own Legislature." *

IN RE McDOUGAL'S WILL, 49 N.J.Super. 485, 140 A.2d 249 (1958), aff'd 55 N.J.Super. 36, 149 A.2d 801 (1959): The testatrix died domiciled in California leaving land in New Jersey. By a holographic will valid under the law of California but not under the law of New Jersey, she provided that this land should be sold and the proceeds divided among her brother's children. The court held that the will failed with respect to the New Jersey land but not as to any personal property held by the testatrix in New Jersey. In dissent Justice Schettino contended that under New Jersey law the land should be deemed to have been equitably converted into personal property with the result that it passed under the will. He emphasized the "value of upholding the will and the testator's intent" and stated that the current "trend . . . is to minimize the importance of formalities."

NOTES

(1) Does the doctrine of equitable conversion provide a useful means for determining a choice-of-law issue involving a land conveyance in a situation where application of the local law of the situs would lead to unfortunate results? See Restatement, Second, Conflict of Laws § 225.

(2) Was the Texas court right in refusing to apply the doctrine of equitable conversion in the Hickok case? The Hickok decision is criticized in Hancock, "In the Parish of St. Mary le Bow, in the Ward of Cheap," 16 Stan.L. Rev. 561 (1964).

---

* Certiorari denied 347 U.S. 936 (1954).

IN RE SCHNEIDER'S ESTATE

Surrogate's Court of New York, New York County, 1950.
198 Misc. 1017, 96 N.Y.S.2d 652.

[The case appears p. 30, supra.]

B. SECURITY TRANSACTIONS

SWANK v. HUFNAGLE

Supreme Court of Judicature of Indiana, 1887.
111 Ind. 453, 12 N.E. 303.

ELLIOTT, J. The appellant sued the appellee, Melissa Hufnagle, and her husband, upon a note and mortgage executed in Darke county, Ohio, on land situate in this State. The appellee, Melissa Hufnagle, answered that she was a married woman, and that the mortgage was executed by her as the surety of her husband, and assumed to convey land in this State owned by her. The appellant replied that the contract was made in Ohio, and that by a statute of that State a married woman had power to execute such a mortgage, but the statute of Ohio is not set forth.

The trial court did right in adjudging the reply bad. The validity of the mortgage of real property is to be determined by the law of the place where the property is situated. . . .

Under the act of 1881 a mortgage executed by a married woman as surety on land owned by her in this State is void. . . .

Judgment affirmed.

NOTES

(1) In Thomson v. Kyle, 39 Fla. 582, 23 So. 12 (1897), the defendant, a married woman, had executed in Alabama a promissory note together with her husband, and also had given a mortgage on Florida land. The note and mortgage were executed by her to secure a debt of the husband. The court enforced the mortgage against the Florida land, even though the note was void as to the defendant under the law of Alabama. "Notwithstanding Mrs. Thomson's incapacity by the laws of Alabama to execute the mortgage sought to be foreclosed here, she was capable under our laws of executing in Alabama, a mortgage upon her separate statutory real property in this State to secure her husband's debt."

(2) In Burr v. Beckler, 264 Ill. 230, 106 N.E. 206, L.R.A.1916A, 1049, Ann. Cas.1915D, 1132 (1914), a married woman domiciled in Illinois, executed and delivered in Florida a note and as security therefor a trust deed to Illinois land. Although the note would have been good if executed and delivered in Illinois, the court held that the note was void since the woman lacked capaci-

ty under Florida law. The court held that since the note was void, "the trust deed, which was incidental and intended to secure a performance of the obligation created by the note, could not be enforced." The Burr case is discussed in University of Chicago v. Dater, p. 460, supra.

———————

PROCTOR V. FROST, 89 N.H. 304, 197 A. 813 (1938): A married woman executed and delivered at her home in Massachusetts a mortgage on New Hampshire land to secure her husband's debt. The mortgage was enforceable under Massachusetts law, but a New Hampshire statute provided, "No contract or conveyance by a married woman, as surety or guarantor for her husband . . . shall be binding on her. . . " The court held that the effect of the mortgage was to be determined by New Hampshire law, but that the statute was not meant to apply to mortgages executed outside of New Hampshire. The court stated that New Hampshire had no power to regulate contracts executed elsewhere and that "The primary purpose of the statute . . . was not to regulate the transfer of New Hampshire real estate, but to protect married women in New Hampshire. . . ."

NOTES

(1) Is this decision a wise one? Undoubtedly, Massachusetts was the state with the greatest interest in the married woman's capacity. But will the decision increase the burdens of title searchers in New Hampshire? Will it require that henceforth title searchers and lawyers look to some law other than that of New Hampshire to determine whether an out-of-state married woman has capacity to give a mortgage on New Hampshire land to secure her husband's debt? Also, might the willingness of the New Hampshire court to apply in this instance the law of the domicile to determine a question of capacity impel title searchers to look henceforth in other kinds of cases to the law of the transferor's domicile, or of some other state, to determine the effectiveness of out-of-state attempts to transfer interests in New Hampshire land?

Suppose that the married woman in Proctor v. Frost had sold her land to a third person who had purchased in reliance on his belief that the mortgage which she had previously given was void by reason of the New Hampshire statute. Would the New Hampshire court in such a case, in a litigation between the purchaser and the mortgagee, hold the mortgage valid by application of Massachusetts law?

Suppose that in the actual case the respective rules of Massachusetts and New Hampshire had been reversed so that the married woman had capacity to give the mortgage under the law of New Hampshire but not under that of Massachusetts. Would the New Hampshire court have held the mortgage void for lack of the wife's capacity as against a mortgagee who had acted in reliance on the law of New Hampshire?

(2) The various effects of an encumbrance on land are governed by the law of the situs. Thus, in addition to matters relating to validity, this law determines the extent of the mortgagor's right to redemption after foreclosure and what constitutes a discharge of a mortgage. Smith v. Schlein, 79

U.S.App.D.C. 166, 144 F.2d 257 (1944); Hughes v. Winkleman, 243 Mo. 81, 147 S.W. 994 (1912); Restatement, Second, Conflict of Laws §§ 228–230.

(3) Restatement, Second, Conflict of Laws § 229.*

. . .

e. Issues collateral to foreclosure. The courts of the situs would apply their own local law to determine questions involving the foreclosure which affect interests in the land. Issues which do not affect any interest in the land, although they do relate to the foreclosure, are determined, on the other hand, by the law which governs the debt for which the mortgage was given. Examples of such latter issues are the mortgagee's right to hold the mortgagor liable for any deficiency remaining after foreclosure or to bring suit upon the underlying debt without having first proceeded against the mortgaged land. . . .

(4) Even in a situation where the note is governed by the law of the situs, certain provisions of that law may be held procedural and hence not entitled to extraterritorial effect. Such a conclusion has been reached, for example, with respect to a statute providing that a deficiency judgment can be recovered only in conjunction with the foreclosure action itself. Maxwell v. Ricks, 294 F. 255 (9th Cir. 1923).

A forum statute limiting the secured creditor's right to recover a deficiency judgment, even if not applicable under choice-of-law principles, may nevertheless be thought to embody so important a policy as to require dismissal of the action without reaching the merits. See Bullington v. Mize, 25 Utah 2d 173, 478 P.2d 500 (1970).

(5) See Currie and Lieberman, Purchase-Money Mortgages and State Lines, (1960) Duke L.J. 1.

C. CONVEYANCES AND CONTRACTS

SMITH V. INGRAM, 130 N.C. 100, 40 S.E. 984 (1902): In 1878, the plaintiff, who was then a married woman, sold land located in North Carolina for the sum of $130. Thereafter, the town of Star was built on the land and its value increased to at least $40,000. In this action, the plaintiff claimed the right to recover the land from its present owners on the ground that her deed to the original purchaser was void under North Carolina law since she had not been given a "privy examination", as required by North Carolina law, to ascertain whether she was selling the land of her own free will. No such privy examination was required by the law of South Carolina where the plaintiff was at all times domiciled. The court held, nevertheless, for the plaintiff on the ground that the validity of a conveyance of an interest in land is determined by the law of the situs. In denying a petition for rehearing (132 N.C. 959, 44 S.E. 643 (1903)), the court left

----

* Quoted with the permission of the copyright owner, The American Law Institute.

open the possibility that the dispossessed bona fide purchasers might
have an equitable remedy for the value of the improvements.

NOTE

The law of the situs is commonly said to determine the validity and effect
of a conveyance of an interest in land including the question of formalities
and of the capacity of the respective parties to convey and to receive title.
Restatement, Second, Conflict of Laws § 223. For a discussion of some possible exceptions to the rule, see Note, Choice of Law for Land Transactions,
38 Colum.L.Rev. 1049 (1938).

POLSON v. STEWART

Supreme Judicial Court of Massachusetts, 1897.
167 Mass. 211, 45 N.E. 737, 36 L.R.A. 771, 57 Am.St.Rep. 452.

Bill in Equity, filed June 6, 1895, to enforce specific performance
of a covenant executed by the defendant to his wife, Kitty T.P. Stewart, who died on December 26, 1893, intestate, and of whose estate
the plaintiff, who was her brother, was appointed administrator, he
having also acquired the rights of the other heirs in her estate.
. . .

The defendant demurred to the bill, assigning several grounds
therefor. Hearing before Knowlton, J., who, at the request of the
parties, reserved the case upon the bill and demurrer for the consideration of the full court.

HOLMES, J. This is a bill to enforce a covenant made by the defendant to his wife, the plaintiff's intestate, in North Carolina, to surrender all his marital rights in certain land of hers. The land is in
Massachusetts. The parties to the covenant were domiciled in North
Carolina. According to the bill, the wife took steps which under the
North Carolina statutes gave her the right to contract as a feme sole
with her husband as well as with others, and afterwards released her
dower in the defendant's lands. In consideration of this release, and
to induce his wife to forbear suing for divorce, for which she had just
cause, and for other adequate considerations, the defendant executed
the covenant. The defendant demurs. . . .

But it is said that the laws of the parties' domicil could not authorize a contract between them as to lands in Massachusetts. Obviously
this is not true. It is true that the laws of other States cannot render
valid conveyances of property within our borders which our laws say
are void, for the plain reason that we have exclusive power over the
res. . . . But the same reason inverted establishes that the lex rei
sitae cannot control personal covenants, not purporting to be conveyances, between persons outside the jurisdiction, although concerning
a thing within it. Whatever the covenant, the laws of North Carolina
could subject the defendant's property to seizure on execution, and

his person to imprisonment, for a failure to perform it. Therefore, on principle, the law of North Carolina determines the validity of the contract. Such precedents as there are, are on the same side. . . . Lord Cottenham stated and enforced the rule in the clearest way in Ex parte Pollard, 4 Deac. 27, 40 et seq.; S.C.Mont. & Ch. 239, 250. . . .

If valid by the law of North Carolina there is no reason why the contract should not be enforced here. The general principle is familiar. Without considering the argument addressed to us that such a contract would have been good in equity if made here . . . we see no ground of policy for an exception. The statutory limits which have been found to the power of a wife to release dower . . . do not prevent a husband from making a valid covenant that he will not claim marital rights with any person competent to receive a covenant from him. . . . The competency of the wife to receive the covenant is established by the law of her domicil and of the place of the contract. The laws of Massachusetts do not make it impossible for him specifically to perform his undertaking. He can give a release which will be good by Massachusetts law. If it be said that the rights of the administrator are only derivative from the wife, we agree, and we do not for a moment regard anyone as privy to the contract except as representing the wife. But if then it be asked whether she could have enforced the contract during her life, an answer in the affirmative is made easy by considering exactly what the defendant undertook to do. So far as occurs to us, he undertook three things: first, not to disturb his wife's enjoyment while she kept her property; secondly, to execute whatever instrument was necessary in order to release his rights if she conveyed; and thirdly, to claim no rights on her death, but to do whatever was necessary to clear the title from such rights then. All these things were as capable of performance in Massachusetts as they would have been in North Carolina. Indeed, all the purposes of the covenant could have been secured at once in the lifetime of the wife by a joint conveyance of the property to a trustee upon trusts properly limited. It will be seen that the case does not raise the question as to what the common law and the presumed law of North Carolina would be as to a North Carolina contract calling for acts in Massachusetts, or concerning property in Massachusetts, which could not be done consistently with Massachusetts law. . . .

Demurrer overruled.

FIELD, C.J. I cannot assent to the opinion of a majority of the court. . . . By our law husband and wife are under a general disability or incapacity to make contracts with each other. . . . It seems to me illogical to say that we will not permit a conveyance of Massachusetts land directly between husband and wife, wherever they may have their domicil, and yet say that they may make a contract to convey such land from one to the other which our courts will specifically enforce. It is possible to abandon the rule of lex rei sitae, but to keep it for conveyances of land and to abandon it for contracts to convey land seems to me unwarrantable.   .   .   .

It is only on the ground that the contract conveyed an equitable title that the plaintiff as heir has any standing in court. His counsel founds his argument on the distinction between a conveyance of the legal title to land and a contract to convey it.   .   .   .   On reason and authority I think it cannot be held that, although a deed between a husband and his wife, domiciled in North Carolina, of the rights of each in the lands of the other in Massachusetts, is void as a conveyance by reason of the incapacity of the parties under the law of Massachusetts to make and receive such a conveyance to and from each other, yet, if there are covenants in the deed to make a good title, the covenants can be specifically enforced by our courts, and a conveyance compelled, which, if voluntarily made between the parties, would be void.

.   .   .   Whatever may be true of contracts between husband and wife made in or when they are domicilied in other jurisdictions, so far as personal property or personal liability is concerned, I think that contracts affecting the title to real property situate within the Commonwealth should be such as are authorized by our laws. I am of opinion that the bill should be dismissed.

NOTES

(1) According to Justice Holmes, would a release by the husband of his interests in the wife's Massachusetts land have been effective? If not, is it not strange that a contract by the husband to release these interests in the land was held to be valid and enforceable?

(2) Can this decision be supported on the ground that it applied the law of the state with the dominant interest in the determination of the particular issue?

(3) In Ex parte Pollard, Mont. & C. 239 (1840), relied on by Justice Holmes in the Polson case, a borrower had deposited with an English lender title deeds to land in Scotland and a memorandum assuming to give a lien on the land. Under the law of England, an equitable security interest was thereby created, but under the law of Scotland no such interest arose. After the borrower became insolvent, the lender claimed in the English bankruptcy proceedings that his debt should be paid out of the Scottish land in preference to the claims of general creditors. The English court found for the lender and ordered execution by the borrower in the proper Scottish form of an instrument giving the creditor the requisite security interest in the land. In the course of his opinion, the Lord Chancellor said that in cases involving foreign land the English courts "act upon their own rules" in "administering equities between parties residing here" and then continued: "Bills for specific performance of contracts for the sale of lands, or respecting mortgages of estates, in the colonies and elsewhere out of the jurisdiction of this Court, are of familiar occurrence. Why then, consistently with these principles and these authorities, should the fact, that by the law of Scotland no lien or equitable mortgage was created by the deposit and memorandum in this case,

prevent the courts of this country from giving such effect to the transactions between the parties as it would have given if the land had been in England? If the contract had been to sell the lands a specific performance would have been decreed; and why is all relief to be refused because the contract is to sell, subject to a condition for redemption?"

Is this an early example of a governmental interest analysis approach?

(4) Mallory Associates, Inc. v. Barving Realty Co., 300 N.Y. 297, 90 N.E.2d 468 (1949). Lessor and lessee, both of New York, there executed a lease on Virginia property. The lessee sued to recover a deposit given pursuant to the lease as security for performance. He claimed that the lessor had converted this deposit by mingling it with other funds in violation of a New York statute providing that lessees' deposits should be held in trust. The court held the statute to be applicable although the land was in another state. "The provision in the lease for the deposit of security is a personal covenant between the contracting parties, creating rights in personam. . . . The question presented . . . relates solely to the rights and liabilities of the parties as a matter of contractual obligation. Accordingly, it is to be determined by the law governing the contract, even though the subject matter of the contract may be land in another State."

(5) Liljedahl v. Glassgow, 190 Iowa 827, 180 N.W. 870 (1921). Plaintiff held a mortgage on Colorado land which had been issued as security for a debt payable in Iowa. The mortgagor sold the land to defendant and delivered to him a deed which contained a blank space for the insertion of the name of the grantee and which recited, among other things, that the grantee assumed and agreed to pay the plaintiff's mortgage. Defendant never inserted his name as grantee and in due course delivered the deed for consideration to another. Under the law of Iowa, defendant became bound to pay the mortgage upon his acceptance of the deed, but no such liability was imposed upon him by Colorado law since he had never inserted his name as grantee in the deed. Held for the plaintiff: ". . . the assumption of the encumbrance and the agreement to pay the same are personal covenants, executed and to be performed in the state of Iowa, and therefore the legal effect thereof must be determined by the law of this state, and not by the law of Colorado."

(6) For a discussion of the conflict of laws rules as to land, and especially of the asserted difference between conveyance and contract, see Goodrich, Two States and Real Estate, 89 U.Pa.L.Rev. 417 (1941); Herzog, The Conflict of Laws in Land Transactions, 8 Syracuse L.Rev. 191 (1957); Williams, Land Contracts in the Conflict of Laws, 11 Hastings L.J. 159 (1959).

SELOVER, BATES & CO. v. WALSH, 226 U.S. 112 (1912): Action in a state court in Minnesota for damages for breach of an executory contract for the sale by the defendant to the plaintiff's assignor of land in Colorado. The contract was made and the instalments on the purchase price were to be paid in Minnesota. The contract provided time was of the essence of the contract, and upon failure to make payments punctually or to perform literally any covenant in the contract, at the option of the vendor, the contract should be terminated, the sums paid being forfeited. The vendee having defaulted in the payment of taxes, the defendant elected to exercise his option and resold the land to a third party. Plaintiff relied on a Minnesota statute which provided that a vendor could not cancel a contract for the sale of land except upon thirty days' written notice to the vendee, who would then have thirty days in which to remedy the default. The Supreme Court of Minnesota, in affirming a judgment for the plaintiff, held the Minnesota statute applicable. The defendant, contending that the application of the statute to this contract involving land in Colorado deprived it of its property without due process of law, carried the case to the Supreme Court of the United States. In overruling the defendant's contention, the Supreme Court said: "The argument to support the contention is somewhat confused, as it mingles with the right of contract simply a consideration of the state's jurisdiction over the land which was the subject of the contract. As to the contract simply, we have no doubt of the state's power over it, and the law of the state, therefore, constituted part of it. . . . Whether it had extraterritorial effect is another question . . . Courts, in many ways, through action upon or constraint of the person, affect property in other states . . ., and in the case at bar the action is strictly personal. . . . The case at bar is certainly within the principle expressed in Polson v. Stewart. The Minnesota supreme court followed the prior decision in Finnes v. Selover, Bates & Co., 102 Minn. 334, 113 N.W. 883, in which it said that, upon repudiation of a contract by the seller of land, two courses were open to the purchaser: 'He might stand by the contract, and seek to recover the land, or he could declare upon a breach of the contract, and recover the amount of his damages.' If he elected the former, it was further said, the courts of Colorado alone could give him relief; if he sought redress in damages, the courts of Minnesota were open to him. And this, it was observed, was in accordance with the principle that the law of the situs governs as to the land, and the law of contract as to the rights of the parties in the contract."

NOTES

(1) In comparing the instant case with Polson v. Stewart, p. 762, supra, consider the difference in the relief prayed for—in Polson v. Stewart, there was a suit for specific performance, while in the instant case the plaintiff was suing for damages.

(2) Kryger v. Wilson, 242 U.S. 171 (1916). By contract "made and to be performed in Minnesota," the plaintiff agreed to sell North Dakota land to the defendant. Upon the latter's default, plaintiff caused notice of cancellation to be served in accordance with the requirements of North Dakota law and then brought suit in a North Dakota court to quiet title to the land. Defendant appeared in the action and requested the court to find that the contract was still valid and subsisting since plaintiff had not taken the action prescribed by Minnesota law to entitle a vendor to cancel a contract for the sale of land. From a decree of the North Dakota courts finding that the contract had been legally cancelled and quieting title in plaintiff, defendant appealed to the Supreme Court on the ground that he had been deprived of his property without due process of law. Held affirmed. "The most that

the plaintiff in error can say is that the state court made a mistaken application of doctrines of the conflict of laws in deciding that the cancellation of a land contract is governed by the law of the situs instead of the place of making and performance. But that, being purely a question of local common law, is a matter with which this court is not concerned. . . ."

"If the contract properly interpreted or the law properly applied required that this condition [the notice of cancellation] be performed in Minnesota, steps taken by him [the defendant in error] under the North Dakota statute would be ineffective. Whether or not proper proceedings had been taken to secure cancellation could be determined only by a court having jurisdiction; and the North Dakota court had jurisdiction not only over the land but through the voluntary appearance of plaintiff in error, also over him. . . . If the plaintiff in error had not submitted himself to the jurisdiction of the court, the decree could have determined only the title to the land . . . But having come into court . . . he cannot now complain if he has been concluded altogether in the premises. The plaintiff in error relies upon Selover, Bates & Co. v. Walsh, 226 U.S. 112. That was a personal action for breach of contract and not, like the present case, an action merely to determine the title to land. . . . "

————

BEAUCHAMP V. BERTIG, 90 Ark. 351, 119 S.W. 75 (1909): Action for Arkansas land. An Oklahoma court had rendered a judgment removing the disabilities of nonage of the two minor owners of the land and had specifically authorized them to sell the land. The minors had then executed in Oklahoma a deed of the land to the defendant in which they covenanted to warrant and defend the title against all lawful claims. The deed was recorded in Arkansas. Immediately after the younger had reached his majority, the two executed a deed to the plaintiff of "all their right, title and interest in and to" the land but gave no covenants of title. Plaintiff then brought the present action to determine his interest in the land. The defendant relied on the Oklahoma judgment and the deed pursuant to it.

Held for the plaintiff. "Since immovable property is fixed forever in the State where it lies, and since no other State can have any jurisdiction over it, it follows necessarily that no right, title or interest can be finally acquired therein, unless assented to by the courts of that State, in accordance with its laws." Minor on Conflict of Laws, sec. II. . . .

It has long been the rule in this State that an infant's deed conveys title to his real estate subject to his right to disaffirm when he becomes of age. Bagley v. Fletcher, 44 Ark. 153; . . .

But appellees argue that the covenants for title are separate contracts, creating personal obligations and therefore governed by the lex loci contractus. . . . even if these covenants create obligations that would, generally speaking, be governed by the lex loci contractus, still that law would have to give way to the local policy as declared by this court.

The covenants under consideration, however, are not personal in the sense that the obligations incurred under them are governed by the law concerning movables. There are many contracts relating to real estate that are so governed. For example, covenants of seisin, of right to convey and against incumbrances, and executory contracts for deeds or other instruments containing covenants that do not run with the land. All these contracts, in the absence of statutory law or an expressed intention to the contrary, are usually governed by the law of the place where such contracts are made. Such is not the case, however, with contracts containing covenants that run with the land—as, for instance, covenants of warranty and for quiet enjoyment; or covenants that can only be performed where the land lies, as, for instance, to defend title, to pay taxes, to repair, etc. These are governed by the law of the place where the land is situated.
. . .

. . . It is unnecessary to determine whether the district court of Oklahoma had jurisdiction to render judgment removing the disabilities of the Sitterdings, for it follows from what we have said that they had the right to disaffirm, even if such judgment be valid.
. . .

NOTES

(1) Suppose that in State X, A executes and delivers to B a deed to land situated in State Y. The deed contains no express covenants and for this reason A would not be liable to B under the law of X for any defects in his title. By the law of State Y, however, the usual covenants of title would be implied by the use of the terms of bargain and sale contained in the deed. What law governs B's right to damages against A in the event of a defective title? Should the answer depend upon whether under the law of State Y the covenants are personal to the parties or run with the land in the sense that they impose duties upon the grantor in favor of a remote grantee? See Scoles and Hay, Conflict of Laws 721–723 (1982).

(2) Sun Oil Co. v. Guidry, 99 So.2d 424 (La.App.1957). Proceeding to determine ownership of mineral interests in Louisiana land. The question was whether the interest of one of the parties was barred on account of non-user. This would be so if the prescriptive period commenced running from the date when he was judicially emancipated in Texas, the state of his domicile. Held claimant's interest is barred by non-user. "The general rule is that the law of the individual's domicile determines his status of majority or minority . . ., but the law of the place where the immovable property is situated determines the effect of such status. . . . [Under] Louisiana law . . . prescription runs against the minor over the age of eighteen fully emancipated by marriage . . . or judicially. . . . Thus, in our opinion, prescription commenced running in Louisiana . . . as soon as [the minor] attained the personal status of an emancipated minor under the law of his domicile. . . ." The court distinguished Beauchamp v. Bertig on the ground that under Arkansas law "even a local decree removing the disability

of minority" would not prevent the minor from disavowing the sale after he had reached the age of twenty-one years.

IRVING TRUST CO. v. MARYLAND CASUALTY CO.

United States Circuit Court of Appeals, Second Circuit, 1936.
83 F.2d 168.*

[Suit by a trustee in bankruptcy against transferees of the bankrupt, a Delaware corporation doing business in New York, to avoid preferential transfers of land and personal property made in violation of New York law. Some of the land was in states other than New York.]

L. HAND, CIRCUIT JUDGE. . . . A more troublesome question concerns the property outside New York. Although the bill does not say where the transfers were made, the contracts required them to be delivered in [New York], and we are to assume that the parties performed as stipulated. The receipt of the deeds by the defendants was therefore a wrong, and any liabilities imposed as a remedy would be recognized and enforced elsewhere, for the law of the place where acts occur normally fixes their jural character. . . . The question here is whether it makes a difference that the wrong consisted in the conveyance of property in another state, under whose laws the conveyance might perhaps have been valid. It is in general no objection to a liability arising out of a consensual transaction that it may be determined by events happening in another jurisdiction. . . . A fortiori it is none that it may have indirect effects upon extraterritorial rights. But it might nevertheless be true that when the transaction consisted in the transfer of property situated elsewhere and would be valid by the lex rei sitae, the act of conveyance would not be a wrong where executed, though the law of that place forbade it as respects property within its own borders. The local doctrine of conflict of laws might impose that exception upon the general language of the statute. The doctrine is of course well settled, certainly as to real property, and, as we shall assume arguendo, equally at the present time as to personal, that the law of the situs absolutely determines the validity of conveyances wherever made. No title will pass and no interest will arise, save as that law prescribes. . . .

We have no doubt therefore that title passed by the deeds delivered in New York to property situated in those of the three states whose laws did not forbid such transfers; yet the law of New York might still make receipt of the deed a wrong and impose a liability upon the grantee though he got a good title. That would not trench upon the sovereignty of the state of the situs whose power over the res would remain wholly unimpaired. Nobody would question this so far as concerned the grantee's liability in damages; it would be but

* Certiorari denied 299 U.S. 571 (1936).

reasonable that he should become liable to the grantor's creditors just because his title was unimpeachable. In the case of contracts for the sale of land the lex loci contractus certainly controls. . . . True, the same doctrine might not apply to the remedy of specific restitution, or specific performance; English speaking courts have always been sensitive about land and in recent years the doctrine of the lex rei sitae has been extended to chattels. Yet in principle there ought to be no distinction between the remedies, for, as we have said, one would invade as little as the other the sovereignty of the state of the situs, which would be free to refuse any effect to the enforced conveyance, if it chose. The result of such a refusal upon a suit elsewhere might indeed by crucial, but only because, seeing that its remedy would be futile if granted, the court would decline to act at all, when, as here, there is no reason to suspect that the lex rei sitae would not recognize such conveyances as valid though made under the duress of a decree, there is no reason to hesitate.

The authorities are not indeed many . . . There are a few cases which do raise the point and they support our view. The first is Lord Cranstown v. Johnson, 3 Ves.Jr. 170, where the defendant in England beguiled the plaintiff into letting him pursue his remedies against land in St. Kitt's. The law of St. Kitt's gave the plaintiff no remedy either in equity, or at law. Yet Lord Alvanley held that the defendant's conduct in England raised a liability for which he could award specific restitution. In Ex parte Pollard, Mont. & C. 239, the defendant in England pledged to the plaintiff his title papers to land in Scotland, which would have created a valid equitable lien upon English land, but did not upon Scotch. Lord Cottenham held the defendant to be subject to an equitable obligation which could be enforced specifically in personam. . . . Some of the relief asked by the bill cannot therefore be granted; the court cannot adjudge the transfers void as to land and chattels outside the state, except as the lex rei sitae is the same as [the law of New York]. But under his general prayer the plaintiff, if he proves his case, may have a decree as to any of the property transferred directing the defendants to reconvey it, and this he can enforce in personam. Of course he may also recover damages as a substitute if he so elects.

Decree reversed; defendants to answer over.

JAMES v. POWELL

New York Court of Appeals, 1967.
19 N.Y.2d 249, 279 N.Y.S.2d 10, 225 N.E.2d 741.

FULD, CH.J.—The parties in this litigation are not strangers to our court. In July, 1964, we affirmed a libel judgment for $46,500 that had been granted to the plaintiff against the defendant, Congressman Adam Clayton Powell (14 N.Y.2d 881; see also 18 N.Y.2d 931). And now we are called upon to review an award of damages to the plaintiff against the defendant and his wife, Yvette Powell, based upon the charge that they had transferred real property owned by them in order to frustrate collection of the original libel judgment.

That judgment was entered in the office of the Clerk of the County of New York on April 5, 1963, and execution was duly issued on the same day, to be returned wholly unsatisfied two months later. On April 17, 1963, defendant Yvette Powell, "acting in her own capacity and as the holder of power of attorney from her . . . husband," transferred certain real estate which they owned in Puerto Rico to her uncle and aunt, Gonzalo and Carmen Diago. The plaintiff never docketed the libel judgment in Puerto Rico nor, since she could find no property listed in Powell's name in Puerto Rico, did she institute any proceedings for the purpose of levying execution there.

Instead, she sued the defendants . . . in New York alleging as a cause of action . . . that the conveyance of the Puerto Rican property was made without consideration and with intent to defraud the plaintiff by preventing the collection of her judgment. . . .

A Supreme Court Justice, sitting without a jury, awarded the plaintiff compensatory damages against both defendants in the sum of $75,000, inclusive of the costs of the litigation and attorney's fees, plus punitive damages in the amount of $500,000 against the defendant Powell and in the sum of $25,000 against Mrs. Powell. The Appellate Division, on appeal, . . . modified the final judgment by reducing the award of compensatory damages against both defendants to slightly less than $56,000 and the award of punitive damages against Powell to $100,000 and by entirely eliminating the punitive damages assessed against his wife.

The parties have assumed that the substantive law of New York is completely dispositive of the appeal, and the courts below have in fact decided the case under such law. In so doing, they have overlooked the applicable choice of law principle which establishes that the issue of whether the plaintiff was defrauded must be determined under the law of Puerto Rico. The rule is that the validity of a conveyance of a property interest is governed by the law of the place where the property is located. . . .

Whatever right the plaintiff had to levy execution on the land in question necessarily arose solely under the law of Puerto Rico, the jurisdiction empowered to deal with the res. Puerto Rico might have regarded the property, when it was owned by the defendants, as not being subject to attachment . . . and, if that were the case, manifestly the plaintiff could not be heard to complain about the conveyance no matter what the defendants' motives. The same would be true if the land were subject to attachment prior to its transfer and if under the law of Puerto Rico the plaintiff's right to proceed against the property were unaffected by the conveyance to the Diagos. On the other hand, it is clear that, if the plaintiff did have a right initially to proceed against the land and that right was frustrated, impaired or made more costly to enforce, her remedy, if any, must itself arise under the law of Puerto Rico. . . .

One point remains—whether there is legitimate basis for an award of punitive damages against Mr. Powell. Although it is clear that the measure of compensatory damages is determined by the same law under which the cause of action arises . . . this is not necessarily true with regard to exemplary damages. An award of compensatory damages depends upon the *existence* of wrongdoing— in this case an issue for resolution under the lex situs of the property alleged to have been fraudulently conveyed. An award of punitive damages, on the other hand, depends upon the *object or purpose* of the wrongdoing, and on this issue we should look to the "law of the jurisdiction with the strongest interest in the resolution of the particular issue presented" (Babcock v. Jackson, 12 N.Y.2d 473, 484 . . .). If the conveyance were invalid, the particular wrong which would serve as a predicate for punitive damages is the attempt to frustrate satisfaction of a New York judgment. It cannot be disputed that New York has the "strongest interest" in the protection of its judgment creditors and, accordingly, New York law should govern as to whether the judgment debtor's conduct in the case before us—if it should prove wrongful under Puerto Rican law—warranted an award of punitive damages.

We do not believe that [under the law of New York] this case involves the type of behavior for which punitive damages may be justified. . . .

To recapitualte—the Appellate Division erred in awarding compensatory damages under the law of New York, since the applicable law on that issue is the law of Puerto Rico. In view of the fact that the parties have not previously litigated the law of Puerto Rico they should be given an opportunity to do so. Under the law of New York, which is controlling on the question of punitive damages, such an award would not, in any event, be justified here. . . .

NOTES

(1) Can the Powell decision be reconciled with that in Irving Trust Co. v. Maryland Casualty Co., p. 769, supra? Which state's policies—those of New York or Puerto Rico—were most significantly involved in the question whether the Powells should be held liable for having transferred Puerto Rican land in order to prevent collection of a New York judgment? Would holding the Powells liable for damages under New York law affect title to Puerto Rican land or complicate problems of title search in Puerto Rico?

For critical comment on the Powell decision, see Ehrenzweig and Westen, Fraudulent Conveyances in the Conflict of Laws, 66 Mich.L.Rev. 1679 (1968); Comment, 67 Colum.L.Rev. 1313 (1967).

(2) What were the various reasons advanced in the preceding cases for applying the law governing the contract, or the tort, rather than the law of

the situs? Are any of them convincing? Contrariwise, what reasons can be suggested for the application in such situations of the law of the situs?

(3) In situations where there have been consensual dealings with respect to land, is it wise to distinguish for choice-of-law purposes between matters relating to title and those involving personal claims arising either in tort or contract? Should determination of the applicable law depend upon the particular relief which plaintiff seeks—e.g. ejectment, specific performance, damages for breach of contract to convey? If the law of the situs properly governs questions affecting title, should it also determine whether plaintiff is entitled to specific performance of a contract to convey, or to a constructive trust in, local realty?

(4) Would it make sense to have all such matters governed by a single law—i.e., that of the situs? On the other hand, would it be unwise to have but a single choice-of-law rule, and should the question of the applicable law depend upon the particular issue involved in the individual case—e.g. usury, capacity, etc? See Note, 38 Colum.L.Rev. 1049 (1938); Note, 111 U.Pa.L.Rev. 482 (1963).

(5) In view of the frequent uncertainty whether a given court will apply the law governing the contract or the law of the situs, what precautions can a lawyer take in planning a transaction to insure so far as possible the application of a particular law?

(6) See generally Hancock, "In the Parish of St. Mary le Bow, in the Ward of Cheap," 16 Stan.L.Rev. 561 (1964); Hancock, Equitable Conversion and the Land Taboo in Conflict of Laws, 17 Stan.L.Rev. 1095 (1965); Hancock, Full Faith and Credit to Foreign Laws and Judgments in Real Property Litigation, 18 Stan.L.Rev. 1299 (1966); Hancock, Conceptual Devices for Avoiding the Land Taboo in Conflict of Laws, 20 Stan.L.Rev. 1 (1967); Weintraub, An Inquiry into the Utility of "Situs" as a Concept in Conflicts Analysis, 52 Corn.L.Q. 1 (1966).

SECTION 2. MOVABLES, IN GENERAL *

A. SUCCESSION ON DEATH

RESTATEMENT, SECOND, CONFLICT OF LAWS **

§ 260. Intestate Succession to Movables

The devolution of interests in movables upon intestacy is determined by the law that would be applied by the courts of the state where the decedent was domiciled at the time of his death.

---

* See Restatement, Second, Conflict of Laws §§ 244–266.

** Quoted with the permission of the copyright owner, The American Law Institute.

Comment:

a. Scope of section. The rule of this Section applies to a decedent's interests in chattels, in rights embodied in a document and in rights that are not embodied in a document.

b. Rationale. . . .

It is desirable that insofar as possible an estate should be treated as a unit and, to this end, that questions of intestate succession to movables should be governed by a single law. This is the law that would be applied by the courts of the state where the decedent was domiciled at the time of his death. This state would usually have the dominant interest in the decedent at the time.

Provided that they apply the common law rules of choice of law, the courts of the state where the decedent was domiciled at the time of his death would look to their own local law to determine what categories of persons are entitled to inherit upon intestacy. . . .

Whichever law would have been applied in the ultimate decision of the case by the courts of the state where the decedent was domiciled at the time of his death will likewise be so applied by the forum. . . .

§ 263. Validity and Effect of Will of Movables

(1) Whether a will transfers an interest in movables and the nature of the interest transferred are determined by the law that would be applied by the courts of the state where the testator was domiciled at the time of his death.

(2) These courts would usually apply their own local law in determining such questions.

Comment:

a. Scope of section. The . . . law selected by application of the present rule determines the capacity of a person to make a will or to accept a legacy, the validity of a particular provision in the will, such as whether it violates the rule against perpetuities or constitutes a forbidden gift to a charity, and the nature of the estate created. Questions concerning the required form of the will and the manner of its execution also fall within the scope of the present rule. The rule applies to a decedent's interests in chattels, in rights embodied in a document and in rights that are not embodied in a document.

b. Rationale. For reasons stated in § 260, Comment *b*, questions relating to the validity of a will of movables and the rights created thereby are determined by the law that would be applied by the courts of the state where the decedent was domiciled at the time of his death. These courts would usually apply their own local law to determine such questions as the testator's capacity to make a will, the nature of the estates that can validly be created and the categories of legatees to whom the testator may leave his movables. These courts would also usually apply their own local law in determining whether a legacy for charitable purposes is invalid, in whole or in part, because of statutory restrictions on the power of a testator to make charitable dispositions by will. . . .

NOTES

(1) See White v. Tennant, p. 7, supra; In re Annesley, p. 26, supra.

(2) More than thirty states provide for alternative places of reference to determine whether a will has been executed in proper form. Ester and Scoles, Estate Planning and the Conflict of Laws, 24 Ohio St.L.J. 270 (1963). The English Wills Act 1963 (11 and 12 Eliz. 2, chapter 44) provides numerous places of alternative reference. See p. 564, note 2, supra.

(3) The law of the testator's domicile at death determines whether certain events, such as divorce or the birth of a child to the testator after execution of a will involving movables, operate to revoke the will. Restatement, Second, Conflict of Laws § 263, Comment *i*. On the other hand, the law of the situs determines whether similar circumstances operate to revoke a will involving land. In re Barrie's Estate, 240 Iowa 431, 35 N.W.2d 658 (1949), set out at p. 651, supra.

(4) *Succession to movables and the renvoi.* Application of the whole law of the situs to determine succession to tangible movables is supported by Griswold, Renvoi Revisited, 51 Harv.L.Rev. 1165, 1195 (1938); see also Briggs, The Dual Relationship of the Rules of Conflict of Laws in the Succession Field, 15 Miss.L.J. 77 (1943).

(5) Some states provide by statute that their own local law shall be applied to govern the validity and effect of the will of a non-resident testator, in so far as it affects movables located within the state, if the testator has expressed a desire in his will to have this law applied. See, e.g., 3 Ill.Ann. Stat., ch. 110½ § 7–6 (Smith-Hurd 1978); N.Y.E.P.T. Law § 3–5.1; Uniform Probate Code § 2–602. A few courts have given non-resident testators a similar power of choice in the absence of any statute. See e.g., Matter of Chappell, 124 Wash. 128, 213 Pac. 684 (1923). See generally Bright, Permitting a Non-Resident to Choose a Place of Probate, 95 Trusts and Estates 865 (1956); Lowenfeld, "Tempora Mutantur"—Wills and Trusts and the Conflicts Restatement, 72 Colum.L.Rev. 382 (1972).

(6) In Re Estate of Clark, 21 N.Y.2d 478, 288 N.Y.S.2d 993, 236 N.E.2d 152 (1968); Matter of Renard, 56 N.Y.2d 973, 453 N.Y.S.2d 625, 439 N.E.2d 341 (1982). Both cases involved a situation where a person who died domiciled outside of New York had provided, as permitted by New York statute, that his will should be governed by New York law. In each instance, the question was whether a spouse (as in Clark) or a son (as in Renard) of the decedent could claim a forced share in the New York assets as would be permitted by the law of the state where the decedent had died domiciled, but not by the law of New York. In Clark, the court found for the claimant on the ground that the New York statute, which at that time referred to "testamentary dispositions", did not cover the right to claim a forced share against a will. Hence this right continued to be governed by the law of the decedent's last domicile. By the time of Matter of Renard, the New York statute had been changed to provide that a person could provide by will to have New York law govern the "disposition of his property situated" in New York. It

was held that by reason of this change in language, the claim to a forced share should be denied.

B. INTER VIVOS TRANSACTIONS

RESTATEMENT, SECOND, CONFLICT OF LAWS [*]

TOPIC 3. MOVABLES

Introductory Note: Mention should be made at the outset of the Uniform Commercial Code. The Code states rules (principally in Articles 2, 6, 7 and 9) which determine most issues arising from the nongratuitous transfer of interests in movables, including secured transactions. By reason of the almost universal adoption of the Code by States of the United States, local law rules with respect to nongratuitous conveyances (Title A) and encumbrances (Title B) of interests in movables will henceforth be uniform in most respects throughout the United States and choice-of-law problems involving them will arise only infrequently. Such problems, however, will continue to arise on occasion. This is so because the Code does not cover all transactions or all issues involving interests in chattels. The Code does not, for example, cover gratuitous conveyances or most aspects of bailments or of liens for services or materials. Nor does the Code, by and large, regulate such issues as "capacity to contract, principal and agent, estoppel, fraud, misrepresentation, duress, coercion, mistake, bankruptcy or other validating or invalidating cause" or usury (see §§ 1–103 and 9–201) or "impair or repeal any statute regulating sales to consumers, farmers or other specified classes of buyers" (§ 2–102). Likewise, the Code has been enacted with slight variations in a number of States, and almost certainly some of its provisions will not be interpreted uniformly by the courts of all States. Choice-of-law problems, in any event, will continue to arise in the case of transactions involving foreign nations.

The Uniform Commercial Code sets forth certain provisions on choice of law. The most important of these provisions is § 1–105 [which is set forth at p. 596, supra]. . . .

§ 244. Validity and Effect of Conveyance of Interest in Chattel

(1) The validity and effect of a conveyance of an interest in a chattel as between the parties to the conveyance are determined by the local law of the state which, with respect to the particular issue, has

---

[*] Quoted with the permission of the copyright owner, The American Law Institute.

the most significant relationship to the parties, the chattel and the conveyance under the principles stated in § 6.

§ 245.   Effect of Conveyance on Pre-Existing Interests in Chattel

(1) The effect of a conveyance upon a pre-existing interest in a chattel of a person who was not a party to the conveyance will usually be determined by the law that would be applied by the courts of the state where the chattel was at the time of the conveyance.

(2) These courts would usually apply their own local law in determining such questions.

YOUSSOUPOFF v. WIDENER

Court of Appeals of New York, 1927.
246 N.Y. 174, 158 N.E. 64.

[The case appears p. 655, supra.]

CAMMELL v. SEWELL

Court of Exchequer Chamber, 1860.
5 Hurl. & N. 728.

[The case appears p. 657, supra.]

C.   SECURITY TRANSACTIONS

GREEN v. VAN BUSKIRK

Supreme Court of the United States, 1866, 1868.
5 Wall. 307, 18 L.Ed. 599; 7 Wall. 139, 19 L.Ed. 109.

[Bates, who lived in New York, executed and delivered to Van Buskirk, who lived in the same State, a chattel mortgage on certain iron safes which were then in the City of Chicago. Two days after this, Green, who was also a citizen of New York, being ignorant of the existence of the mortgage, sued out a writ of attachment in the courts of Illinois, levied on the safes, and subsequently had them sold in satisfaction of the judgment obtained in the attachment suit. There was no appearance or contest in this attachment suit, and Van Buskirk was not a party to it, although he could have made himself such party and contested the right of Green to levy on the safes, being expressly authorized by the laws of Illinois so to do. It was conceded that by the law of Illinois mortgages of personal property, until acknowledged and recorded, were void as against third persons. Subsequently Van Buskirk sued Green in New York for the value of the safes mortgaged to him by Bates, of which Green had thus received the proceeds. The courts of New York gave judgment in favor of Van Buskirk, holding that the law of New York was to govern and not the law of Illinois, although the property was situated in the latter State, and that the title passed to Van Buskirk by the execution of the mortgage. The cause was then brought to this court and first considered upon a motion to dismiss for want of jurisdiction.*]

MR. JUSTICE MILLER delivered the opinion of the Court:

. . . It is claimed by the plaintiff in error that the faith and credit which these proceedings have by law and usage in the state of Illinois, were denied to them by the decision of the courts of New York, and that in doing so, they decided against a right claimed by him under section 1, article IV of the Constitution and the act of Congress of May 26, 1790, on that subject. . . .

The record before us contains the pleadings in the case, the facts found by the court, and the conclusions of law arising thereon.

Among the latter, the court decides "that, by the law of the state of New York, the title to the property passed on the execution and delivery of the instrument under the facts found in the case, and overreached the subsequent attachment of the state of Illinois and actual prior possession under it at the suit of defendant, although he was a creditor having a valid and fair debt against Bates, and had no notice of the previous assignment and sale. And that the law of the state of New York was to govern the transaction and not the law of the state of Illinois, where the property was situated." . . .

It is said that Van Buskirk, being no party to the proceedings in Illinois, was not bound by them, but was at liberty to assert his claim to the property in any forum that might be open to him; and, strictly speaking, this is true. He was not bound by way of estoppel, as he would have been if he had appeared and submitted his claim, and contested the proceedings in attachment. He has a right to set up any title to the property which is superior to that conferred by the attachment proceedings; and he has the further right to show that the property was not liable to the attachment—a right from which he would have been barred if he had been a party to that suit. And this question of the liability of the property in controversy to that attachment is the question which was raised by the suit in New York, and which was there decided. That court said that this question must be decided by the laws of the state of New York, because that was the domicil of the owner at the time the conflicting claims to the property originated.

* The statement of facts is taken from the outline of the principal case given in Cole v. Cunningham, 133 U.S. 107, 132.

We are of opinion that the question is to be decided by the effect given by the laws of Illinois, where the property was situated, to the proceedings in the courts of that state, under which it was sold.

There is no little conflict of authority on the general question as to how far the transfer of personal property by assignment or sale, made in the country of the domicil of the owner, will be held to be valid in the courts of the country where the property is situated, when these are in different sovereignties. . . . And it may be conceded that as a question of comity, the weight of . . . authority is in favor of the proposition that such transfers will, generally, be respected by the courts of the country where the property is located, although the mode of transfer may be different from that prescribed by the local law. . . .

But, after all, this is a mere principle of comity between the courts, which must give way when the statutes of the country where property is situated, or the established policy of its laws prescribe to its courts a different rule. . . .

We do not here decide that the proceedings in the state of Illinois have there the effect which plaintiff claims for them; because that must remain to be decided after argument on the merits of the case. But we hold that the effect which these proceedings have there, by the law and usage of that state was a question necessarily decided by the New York courts, and that it was decided against the claim set up by plaintiff in error under the constitutional provision and statute referred to, and that the case is, therefore, properly here for review.

The motion to dismiss the writ of error is overruled. . . .

MR. JUSTICE NELSON, dissenting. . . . The court below decided that the instrument was to be governed by the law of the state of New York, where it was made, and which was the domicil of the parties. . . . The question here is whether, in so deciding, the court denied full faith, credit, and effect to the judgment in Illinois. In other words, did the court, in holding that the prior assignment was not fraudulent and void but valid and effectual to transfer the title, thereby discredit the Illinois judgment? The answer to the question, I think, is obvious. These assignees were not parties to the judgment. It could not bind them. They were free, therefore, to set up and insist upon this prior title to the property; and, if there was nothing else in the case, it is clear the junior attachment could not hold it. . . .

I agree, if the attachment had been levied before the assignment, and the court had given effect to this instrument over the levy, it might be said that full faith and credit had not been given to it; but, being posterior, these proceedings could not have the effect, per se, to displace the assignment as against a stranger. Another element must first be shown, namely; fraud or other defect in the instrument, to render it inoperative.

My conclusion is that the regularity of the attachment proceedings was not called in question in the court below; but, on the contrary, full force and credit were given to them, and the case should be dismissed for want of jurisdiction.

MR. JUSTICE SWAYNE concurs in this opinion.

[The case then came up for final adjudication. 7 Wall. 139 (1868).]

MR. JUSTICE DAVIS delivered the opinion of the Court:

That the controversy in this case was substantially ended when this court refused, 5 Wall. 312, to dismiss the writ of error for want of jurisdiction, is quite manifest, by the effort which the learned counsel for the defendants in error now made, to escape the force of that decision. . . .

This decision, supported as it was by reason and authority, left for consideration on the hearing of the case, the inquiry, whether the Supreme Court of New York did give to the attachment proceedings in Illinois the same effect they would have received in the courts of that State. . . .

[The court here stated the law of Illinois, and showed that under that law the purchaser at the attachment sale would prevail over the New York mortgagee.]

. . . And as the effect of the levy, judgment and sale is to protect Green if sued in the courts of Illinois, and these proceedings are produced for his own justification, it ought to require no argument to show that when sued in the court of another State for the same transaction, and he justifies in the same manner, that he is also protected. Any other rule would destroy all safety in derivative titles, and deny to a State the power to regulate the transfer of personal property within its limits and to subject such property to legal proceedings. . . .

The judgment of the Supreme Court of the State of New York is reversed, and the cause remitted to that court, with instructions to enter judgment for the plaintiff in error.

NOTES

(1) In the principal case, was full faith and credit denied to the judgment or to the law of Illinois? In any event, would the case be followed today?

(2) Does the decision in the principal case require, as a compliance with full faith and credit, that in a case involving tangible things the reference to the law of the state of the situs be to that state's conflict of laws rules?

Choice-of-law questions involving secured transactions in movables fall into two broad categories: those arising between the secured creditor and his immediate debtor and those involving the rights of the creditor against some third person, such as an attaching creditor or a transferee of the immediate debtor.

Today, such questions are governed in large measure by the Uniform Commercial Code, which has obtained almost universal enactment throughout the United States. Initially, there was some question whether the rights inter se of the secured creditor and his immediate debtor were governed exclusively by Section 1–105 (which is set forth at p. 596, supra) or also by Sections 9–102 and 9–103. This uncertainty was removed by a 1972 revision of the Code which removes all references to choice of law in Section 9–102 and amends Section 9–103 to deal exclusively with problems of perfection of security interests and the effect of perfection or non-perfection. As a result, it is now clear that choice-of-law questions arising between the secured creditor and his immediate debtor are governed by Section 1–105.

JOHN J. SHANAHAN v. GEORGE B. LANDERS CONSTRUCTION CO.

United States Court of Appeals, First Circuit, 1959.
266 F.2d 400.

[The plaintiff, a construction corporation of New Hampshire with its principal office there, entered a conditional sale contract for the purchase of a trench hoe for about $25,000 plus a finance charge f.o.b. Burlington, Vermont. The seller was John J. Shanahan, Inc., a Massachusetts corporation with its principal place of business in that state. The conditional sale contract and the accompanying promissory note were executed by the plaintiff in New Hampshire in 1953, and the conditional sale contract was signed by the seller at its place of business in Massachusetts where the note and the conditional sale contract were assigned with recourse to a finance company.

The hoe was delivered to the plaintiff in Vermont. On the completion of the construction job there, the plaintiff shipped it to New Hampshire for use on a job in that state, where it remained until it was repossessed.

The plaintiff never met any installments when they fell due, but on December 20, 1954 it paid all accrued installments, which amounted to about $17,000. The next installment due on December 28th was not met, and on January 6, 1955, an agent of the finance company repossessed the hoe in New Hampshire without the knowledge of the plaintiff and removed it to Massachusetts. There, after payment to the finance company of the balance due, the seller, Shanahan, Inc., without notice to the plaintiff, sold the hoe to Shanahan, the individual, for the balance due by plaintiff of about $8,300, and after making repairs and changes Shanahan sold it to a third party for about $15,000.

The plaintiff, the purchaser under the conditional sale contract, brought this action for the conversion of the hoe in the federal court in Massachusetts. The defendants were the seller, Shanahan, Inc., as well as Shanahan, the individual and the finance company. The District Court gave judgment for the plaintiff, and the defendants appeal.]

WOODBURY, CIRCUIT JUDGE. . . . The court below ruled and the parties concede that if the law of Massachusetts applies the plaintiff has no claim for the reason that the defendants in repossessing the hoe as they did acted in full compliance with the provisions of the Massachusetts Conditional Sales Act, Mass.G.L., c. 255 §§ 11–13H, and thus extinguished the plaintiff's right of redemption. On the other hand, it was ruled by the court below and is likewise conceded by the parties, that the opposite result would have to be reached if the law of New Hampshire applies. The reason for this is that repossession by a conditional vendor without prior notice in writing to the conditional vendee, plus immediate removal of the repossessed property from the state, violates the provisions of N.H.Rev.Stat. c. 361 §§ 18, 19 which require a conditional vendor either to give written notice to the conditional vendee not more than forty nor less than twenty days prior to retaking, or else, after retaking without such notice, to retain the property within the state for ten days after repossession, during which time on tender of the amount in default under the contract, with interest, expenses of retaking and costs of keeping and storage, the conditional vendee "may redeem the goods and become entitled to take possession of them and to continue in the performance of the contract as if no default had occurred." The District Court ruled that the law of New Hampshire applied and we agree.

The court below quite rightly recognized that it must follow the choice of law rules of the forum, Massachusetts, in deciding what law to apply. . . . Also the court below very appropriately began its study of the problem presented by the case at bar with consideration of Jewett, Inc. v. Keystone Driller Co., 1933, 282 Mass. 469, 185 N.E. 369, 371, 87 A.L.R. 1298, a case in some respects like the present, on which the appellants heavily rely.

The Jewett case, like the one at bar, was an action for conversion of . . . a gasoline powered shovel brought by a conditional vendee against a repossessing conditional vendor. The plaintiff-vendee . . . was a Massachusetts corporation with its principal office in that Commonwealth and the defendant-vendor was a Pennsylvania corporation with its principal place of business in that Commonwealth but with a sales agent in Massachusetts. The contract of conditional sale of the gasoline powered shovel was executed in Massachusetts and the purchase price was payable at a Massachusetts bank. It does not appear where the shovel actually was when the contract was signed but it was delivered as the contract required F.O.B. Manchester, New Hampshire. It was used for a short time in New Hampshire and then remained in storage in that state until, the buyer being in default, the defendant-vendor took possession of the shovel, immediately removed it to Connecticut, and there sold it, without giving notice to the plaintiff-vendee as the New Hampshire statute required.

On these basic facts a divided court held that the law of Massachusetts, rather than the law of New Hampshire, applied. Mr. Justice Crosby writing for the majority rested the conclusion that the law of Massachusetts governed on the [ground that this law governed the contract between the parties].

Mr. Justice Lummus in dissent rejected characterization of the problem as one of contract. He treated the problem instead as one of property, saying: . . . "that the right of redemption given by the New Hampshire statute applied to the shovel, either because the shovel was in New Hampshire when the interests of the parties under the conditional sale became vested . . . or on the . . . ground . . . that the law of the state in which the chattel is situated when foreclosure or redemption proceedings are begun shall govern . . . ."

From the decision in the Jewett case we may infer that the Supreme Judicial Court of the Commonwealth of Massachusetts, were it deciding the case at bar, would treat the fact that the power hoe was delivered in Vermont as "immaterial." For here, as in Jewett, the evidence warrants the inference that delivery in Vermont was only for the convenience of the purchaser in performing a single contract in that state and on completion of its work there the plaintiff-purchaser intended to remove the shovel to its headquarters in New Hampshire or to some other place, in New Hampshire or elsewhere, where it might obtain another contract. This eliminates the law of Vermont from our consideration. Furthermore, we may also infer from the Jewett case that under circumstances like the present the Massachusetts court would not concern itself with the law of the state where the shovel was when the contract for its conditional sale arose and the rights of the parties with respect to it were created. We say this because there is no reference in the majority opinion in the Jewett case to the place where the shovel was when the contract for its conditional sale was entered into. In choosing Massachusetts law as the law to apply, the majority gave controlling consideration to the place where the contract of conditional sale was entered into, and did not even mention the place where the shovel was when that contract was made. . . . Indeed, under circumstances like the present, to apply the law of the place where the chattel is at the time of contracting might well produce the incongruous result of applying the law of some state with which neither the parties nor the transaction had any substantial contacts whatever. That is to say, it might require application of the law of the state where the chattel was manufactured (we were given to understand at oral argument that the power hoe involved herein was manufactured in a middle western state), and where after shipment that chattel might never be again and where the parties neither contracted nor resided. It might even require application of the law of a state through which the chattel was only in transit from the state of its manufacture to the state of its delivery. Thus . . . it would seem that under Massachusetts law as expounded in the Jewett case there is no occasion for us to send this case back to the court below to find out where the power hoe actually was on the date of its conditional sale—whether it was still in the state of its manufacture, wherever that was, or in some other state on its way to its place of delivery in Vermont.

As we understand the law of Massachusetts our choice lies between the law of Massachusetts and the law of New Hampshire. The appellants strongly urge that the Jewett case requires us to choose the law of Massachusetts. We do not think so.

The court below distinguished Jewett on the ground that the majority of the court in that case placed emphasis on the fact that the shovel was not permanently located in New Hampshire but was only delivered in that state for the convenience of the purchaser, who was a citizen of Massachusetts, whereas in the instant case the purchaser was a New Hampshire corporation with its principal place of business in that state. On these facts the District Court thought the majority in the Jewett case might well have reached the result advocated by the dissenting justice. . . . it does seem to us . . . that the Supreme Judicial Court of Massachusetts . . . would not be disposed to extend the rule of the Jewett case to facts like those in the case at bar, where the purchaser of the chattel was not a Massachusetts corporation but a New Hampshire corporation with its headquarters in that state and where in addition the shovel was not only located in New Hampshire when it was repossessed, but also where the shovel would presumably be kept when not in use on out-of-state jobs. . . .

[The Court of Appeals concluded that the New Hampshire law governed and the statute of that state relating to conditional sales had not been complied with. But it found the District Court had erred in the amount of the award to the plaintiff, $12,500, so it remanded the case.]

NOTES

(1) The Shanahan opinion provides a good example of the reasoning that was employed by the courts prior to the adoption of the Uniform Commercial Code. Was not the result reached sensible and desirable? Could the court arrive at the same result now that Massachusetts has adopted the Code? Would the court have been required to apply Massachusetts law by reason of Section 1–105, which provides, in the absence of a choice of law between parties, for the Code's application "to transactions bearing an appropriate relationship to this state?" The Comment to § 1–105 strongly suggests that the term "appropriate relationship" should be interpreted to mean a closer contact with a state than that which would be required to make it constitu-

tional for the state to apply its own local law? On the other hand, the Comment also suggests that the term should not be interpreted so strictly as to require that the state be the one that would be selected as "the most appropriate" or, following the Restatement Second terminology, as the "state of most significant relationship," by the choice-of-law rules of the forum? Can support for the latter stricter interpretation be found in the fact that the Code has now been almost universally adopted throughout the United States?

(2) Do statutes provide the best way of handling choice-of-law problems? See the discussion of choice-of-law statutes in Ch. 8, pp. 562–565, supra.

(3) For an excellent discussion of the Shanahan case, see Cavers, The Conditional Seller's Remedies and the Choice-of-Law Process, 35 N.Y.U.L. Rev. 1126 (1960).

———

We turn now to a consideration of the law governing the rights of the secured creditor against persons other than the immediate debtor. We are concerned with a situation where a chattel has first been subjected to a security interest in state X and then is taken to state Y where it becomes involved in a transaction with a third person who is unaware of the existence of the security interest. Typically, the secured creditor is a conditional vendor or a chattel mortgagee and the third person a purchaser of the chattel or an attaching creditor. The question is whether the interests of the secured creditor or of the third person should be preferred. This question is now governed by § 9–103 of the Uniform Commercial Code.

Prior to the nearly universal adoption of the Uniform Commercial Code, the usual position of the courts was that the secured creditor would be preferred over the third person if (a) the security interest had been perfected under the law of the state (X) where the chattel was situated at the time and (b) the chattel was taken to another state (Y) without the creditor's knowledge or consent and was there dealt with by the third person before the secured creditor had become aware of the chattel's presence in the state. On the other hand, the third person would usually be preferred over the secured creditor if the security interest had not been perfected in state Y and either the chattel had been taken to Y with the creditor's knowledge and consent or the creditor had become aware of the chattel's presence in Y prior to the time that it was there dealt with by the third person.

For automobiles the rule may have been somewhat different. There was at least a tendency to prefer the interests of the third person over those of the secured creditor in all situations where a title certificate which did not show the existence of the security interest had been issued for the automobile in Y prior to the time that it was there dealt with by the third person. Restatement, Second, Conflict of Laws, §§ 252–253, 1 Gilmore, Security Interests in Personal Property 551–552, 595–632 (1965); Leary, Horse and Buggy Lien Law and Migratory Automobiles, 96 U. of Pa.L.Rev. 455 (1948); Vernon, Re-

corded Chattel Security Interests in the Conflicts of Laws, 47 Iowa
L.Rev. 346 (1962).

Significant portions of § 9–103 of the 1972 version of the Uniform
Commercial Code are set forth below:

§ 9–103.   Perfection of Security Interests in Multiple State Trans-
           actions

(1) Documents, instruments and ordinary goods.

(a) This subsection applies to documents and instruments and
to goods other than those covered by a certificate of title described in subsection (2) . . ..

(b) Except as otherwise provided in this subsection, perfection
and the effect of perfection or non-perfection of a security interest
in collateral are governed by the law of the jurisdiction where the
collateral is when the last event occurs on which is based the assertion that the security interest is perfected or unperfected.

(c) If the parties to a transaction creating a purchase money
security interest in goods in one jurisdiction understand at the
time that the security interest attaches that the goods will be kept
in another jurisdiction, then the law of the other jurisdiction governs the perfection and the effect of perfection or nonperfection
of the security interest from the time it attaches until thirty days
after the debtor receives possession of the goods and thereafter if
the goods are taken to the other jurisdiction before the end of the
thirty-day period.

(d) When collateral is brought into and kept in this state while
subject to a security interest perfected under the law of the jurisdiction from which the collateral was removed, the security interest remains perfected, but if action is required by Part 3 of this
Article to perfect the security interest,

(i) if the action is not taken before the expiration of the period of perfection in the other jurisdiction or the end of four
months after the collateral is brought into this state, whichever period first expires, the security interest becomes unperfected at the end of that period and is thereafter deemed to
have been unperfected as against a person who became a purchaser after removal;

(ii) if the action is taken before the expiration of the period
specified in subparagraph (i), the security interest continues
perfected thereafter. . . .

(2) Certificate of title.

(a) This subsection applies to goods covered by a certificate of
title issued under a statute of this state or of another jurisdiction
under the law of which indication of a security interest on the certificate is required as a condition of perfection.

(b) Except as otherwise provided in this subsection, perfection and the effect of perfection or non-perfection of the security interest are governed by the law (including the conflict of laws rules) of the jurisdiction issuing the certificate until four months after the goods are removed from that jurisdiction and thereafter until the goods are registered in another jurisdiction, but in any event not beyond surrender of the certificate. After the expiration of that period, the goods are not covered by the certificate of title within the meaning of this section.

(c) Except with respect to the rights of a buyer described in the next paragraph, a security interest, perfected in another jurisdiction otherwise than by notation on a certificate of title, in goods brought into this state and thereafter covered by a certificate of title issued by this state is subject to the rules stated in paragraph (d) of subsection (1).

(d) If goods are brought into this state while a security interest therein is perfected in any manner under the law of the jurisdiction from which the goods are removed and a certificate of title is issued by this state and the certificate does not show that the goods are subject to the security interest or that they may be subject to security interests not shown on the certificate, the security interest is subordinate to the rights of a buyer of the goods who is not in the business of selling goods of that kind to the extent that he gives value and receives delivery of the goods after issuance of the certificate and without knowledge of the security interest. . . .

NOTES

(1) For an extensive discussion of the original and amended versions of §§ 9–102 and 9–103 and of many of the leading cases, see Weintraub, Commentary on the Conflict of Laws 460–494 (2d ed. 1980). See also Adams, The 1972 Official Text of the Uniform Commercial Code: Analysis of Conflict of Laws Provision, 45 Miss.L.J. 281 (1974).

(2) The movement of motor vehicles from state to state gives rise to difficult problems involving the conflicting interests of a secured creditor and a bona fide purchaser. At the present time all, or nearly all, of the states have adopted certificate-of-title laws which provide for the notation of the security interests on the certificate. There are, however, significant differences among these laws. In some states, perfection of the security interest is completed by the notation of the interest on the certificate of title or by the issuance of a new certificate after such notation. Other states provide that perfection is complete as soon as delivery of the appropriate papers has been made by the secured creditor to the proper official, even though the interest is not noted on the certificate of title or indeed even though no certificate is ever issued. The problems are made more complex by the fact that some states retain the earlier version of the Uniform Commercial Code § 9–103 while other states have adopted the 1972 version.

The subject is given extensive treatment in Meyers, Multi-state Motor Vehicle Transactions Under the Uniform Commercial Code: An Update, 30 Okla.L.Rev. 834 (1977).

D.   FUTURE INTERESTS AND TRUSTS *

Validity—Inter Vivos Trusts

HUTCHISON v. ROSS

Court of Appeals of New York, 1933.
262 N.Y. 381, 187 N.E. 65, 89 A.L.R. 1007.

[The case appears p. 632, supra.]

SHANNON v. IRVING TRUST CO.

Court of Appeals of New York, 1937.
275 N.Y. 95, 9 N.E.2d 792.

[The case appears p. 634, supra.]

WILMINGTON TRUST CO. v. WILMINGTON TRUST CO.

Supreme Court of Delaware, 1942.
26 Del.Ch. 397, 24 A.2d 309, 139 A.L.R. 1117.

[In 1920, William Donner as settlor created a trust through the deposit of personal property with the trustee, Dora Donner. The trust instrument provided that the income was to be paid to members of the settlor's family, and gave to each of his children a power of appointment over a part of the trust property. The settlor and the trustee were domiciled in New York and the trust was created there.

Subsequent to 1920, a successor trustee was named under a power given by the trust instrument. The new trustee was a trust company of Delaware.

In 1929, Joseph W. Donner, one of the settlor's children assumed to exercise the power of appointment given him. In doing so he set up trusts which were invalid under the New York rules against perpetuities but were valid under the law of Delaware.

* See Restatement, Second, Conflict of Laws §§ 267–282.

From a decree of the Court of Chancery upholding the validity of the exercise of the power, an appeal was taken to the Supreme Court of Delaware.]*

LAYTON, CHIEF JUSTICE. . . . The power of appointment exercised by Joseph W. Donner for the benefit of his two children had its origin in the donor's deed of trust; the provisions of the deed of appointment are viewed in law as though they had been embodied in that instrument . . . . The validity of the deed of appointment and of the rights and interests assigned thereunder depend upon the law of the jurisdiction in which the trust had its seat when the power of appointment was exercised.

The diversity of judicial opinion with respect to the discovery of the jurisdiction under whose law the validity of a trust inter vivos of intangible personal property is to be determined is such that no useful purpose will be served by an attempted analysis of the decisions. Courts have variously looked to the domicile of the donor, the place of execution of the trust instrument, the situs of the trust property, the place of administration of the trust, the domicile of the trustee, the domicile of the beneficiaries, and to the intent or desire of the donor, or to a combination of some of these denominators, in deciding the troublesome question of conflict of law. . . . The place of one's residence no longer is a sure indication of one's place of business; nor is ownership of property closely tied to residence. The domicile of the donor is, of course, a circumstance to be considered in the ascertainment of the seat of the trust; but courts, today, . . . are disposed to take a more realistic and practical view of the problem; and the donor's domicile is no longer regarded as the decisive factor. The place of execution of the trust instrument and the domicile of the beneficiaries are not important indicia. The domicile of the trustee and the place of administration of the trust—quite generally the same place—are important factors; and the intent of the donor, if that can be ascertained, has been increasingly emphasized. . . .

Where the donor in a trust agreement has expressed his desire, or if it pleases, his intent to have his trust controlled by the law of a certain state, there seems to be no good reason why his intent should not be respected by the courts, if the selected jurisdiction has a material connection with the transaction. More frequently, perhaps, the trust instrument contains no expression of choice of jurisdiction; but, again, there is no sufficient reason why the donor's choice should be disregarded if his intention in this respect can be ascertained . . . provided that the same substantial connection between the transaction and the intended jurisdiction shall be found to exist. . . .

The donor was careful to provide for a change of trustee subject to his approval in his lifetime. In the event of such change he declared that the successor trustee should "hold the said trust estate

---

* The statement of facts is taken in part from the report of the case on the original hearing in the Court of Chancery, 21 Del.Ch. 102, 180 A. 597.

subject to all the conditions herein *to the same effect as though now named herein*". The italicized language either has a significance of its own or it is to be considered as no more than a superfluous or redundant phrase. . . . We are of opinion that the phrase "to the same effect as though now named herein", as applied to the power to appoint a successor trustee in another state, must be accepted as authorizing a removal of the seat of the trust from its original location, and its re-establishment under the law of another jurisdiction. . . .

There is no substantial reason why a donor, in dealing with that which is his own, may not provide for a change in the location of his trust with a consequent shifting of the controlling law. In an era of economic uncertainty, with vanishing returns from investments and with tax laws approaching confiscation, such a provision would seem to amount to no more than common foresight and prudence. The rights of beneficiaries may, it is true, be disturbed by a shift of jurisdiction, but if such change has been provided for, they have no more cause to complain that other persons who are the recipients of bounty under some condition or limitation.

The adult beneficiaries, with the donor's approval, transferred the seat of the trust from New York to Delaware. On October 9, 1929, when Joseph W. Donner availed himself of the power of appointment conferred on him by the trust agreement, the home of the trust was in this State, and, being subject then to local law, the validity and effect of his deed of appointment and of the rights and interests of the appointees thereunder are to be adjudged and determined by the law of Delaware. . . .

[Affirmed.]

NOTE

See Cavers, Trusts Inter Vivos and the Conflict of Laws, 44 Harv.L.Rev. 161 (1930); Ester and Scoles, Estate Planning and Choice of Law, 24 Ohio St. L.J. 270 (1963); Scott, What Law Governs Trusts? 99 Trusts and Estates, 186 (1960); Scott, Spendthrift Trusts and the Conflict of Laws, 77 Harv.L. Rev. 845 (1964); Comment, Choice of Law: The Validity of Trusts of Movables—Intention and Validation, 64 Nw.L.Rev. 388 (1969).

IN RE BAUER'S TRUST

New York Court of Appeals, 1964.
14 N.Y.2d 272, 251 N.Y.S.2d 23, 200 N.E.2d 207.

DESMOND, CHIEF JUDGE. In 1917 Dagmar Bauer, then a resident of New York, executed in New York City an irrevocable trust indenture which stipulated that she should receive the life income and that the remainder should go to her husband. In the event her husband predeceased her, the principal was to be distributed to such person or persons as she appointed by her will and, failing a valid disposition in her will, to the settlor's next of kin pursuant to the statutes of the State of New York. Settlor's husband predeceased her. She died a resident of London, England, in 1956. A codicil [to her will probated in England] left the trust fund to Midland Bank for the benefit of two nieces for life with the remainder to Dr. Barnardo's Homes, etc., a charitable corporation of the United Kingdom and Northern Ireland. . . .

We . . . summarize our holdings as follows:

(1) The law to be applied here is the law of New York which was the donor's domicile and where there was executed the trust agreement containing the power of appointment . . . . This rule applies where the same person is donor and donee. . . .

(2) The trust was irrevocable and created a remainder interest but no reversionary interest in Mrs. Bauer. She retained no more than a testamentary power of appointment and hers was, therefore, one of the "measuring lives". . . .

(3) The original trust plus the codicil trust thus involved three lives in being, resulting in unenforceability under the applicable former New York law . . . and thus the attempt in the will and codicil to exercise the power of appointment was ineffective. . . .

(5) Since . . . there has been no valid testamentary disposition of the trust principal it must, as directed by the indenture itself, be distributed to the settlor's next of kin pursuant to the statutes of New York.

The order appealed from should be modified accordingly, with costs to parties filing separate briefs.

[The dissenting opinion of Judge Dye is omitted.]

FULD, JUDGE (dissenting). . . .

We deal here with a testatrix (Dagmar Bauer) who died in England, where she had long been domiciled, after there executing a will in which she exercised a general power of appointment, of which she was donor as well as donee, pursuant to a trust indenture executed in New York almost 40 years earlier. The court's decision to apply New York law to test the validity of Mrs. Bauer's exercise in England (in 1954) of the power of appointment which she had reserved to herself (in 1917) strikes me as an unfortunate example of adherence to mechanical and arbitrary formulae. The same considerations which prompted a departure from the inflexible and traditional choice-of-law rules in other cases (see, e.g., Auten v. Auten, 308 N.Y. 155, 124 N.E.2d 99, 50 A.L.R.2d 246; Babcock v. Jackson, 12 N.Y.2d 473, 240 N.Y.S.2d 743, 191 N.E.2d 279), it seems to me, should move the court to re-examine the wisdom and justice of continuing to apply similarly inflexible rules, with regard to significant underlying factors, in disposing of cases such as the present one.

The traditional rule which identifies the instrument exercising the power with the instrument creating it, for the purpose of testing the validity of the exercise of the power . . . assumes that ownership of the appointive property remains at all times in the donor of the power and that the donee of the power serves merely as a conduit or agency through which the donor's intention with respect to the appointive property is realized. . . . Such an assumption is, perhaps, justified where the power created is "special" and confines the donee's exercise of the power within the limits prescribed by the instrument creating the power. However, the assumption is certainly not justified when the power created is "general" or "beneficial", whether exercisable by deed or will or by will alone, and no restrictions of any other kind are imposed on its exercise by the donee. In the latter case—and in the one before us upon the death of Mrs. Bauer's husband—it is evident that the donee is vested with the equivalence of ownership as to the appointive property. . . . And this is particularly true where the donor and donee of the general power are the same person. This being so, it runs counter to reason to assume that the donor in such a case becomes his own agent to preserve an attachment to the place where the original trust agreement was executed, even though he has abandoned that place as his residence and acquired a new domicile in another jurisdiction, to the laws of which he voluntarily subjected himself.

In exercising the general power of appointment in England 37 years after she had conferred such power upon herself, Mrs. Bauer was justified in treating the appointive property as her own, and it is reasonable to suppose that, in disposing of such property under a will executed in England by an English solicitor, designating an English institutional executor and trustee to administer the trust and conferring benefits, at least in part, upon an English charity, Mrs. Bauer (through her English solicitor) had exercised the power in the light of English, rather than New York, law. The inference is inescapable that she intended the disposition of the appointive property to be governed by the same law which would govern the disposition of her personal estate, namely, the law of her last domicile. Since no discernible New York policy or interest dictates the application of its law to invalidate the disposition by the English testatrix valid under her personal law—and, indeed, now valid under present New York law—such intention should be given effect.

I do not, of course, mean to suggest that New York law would not govern the validity and effect of the provisions of the *trust indenture.* That instrument was executed in 1917 against the background of New York law, which Mrs. Bauer at that time undoubtedly intended would control. . . . However, I reject as insupportable any suggestion . . . that the law governing the trust conclusively governs the exercise of the power of appointment in every case, even to the extent of overriding the manifest intent of the donor-donee to have the law of his last domicile apply so as to effect a valid exercise of the general power. . . .

In sum, then, I would disavow the rule requiring the inexorable application of the law governing the instrument creating the power and I would apply the law of the jurisdiction intended by the donor-donee to control—in the case before us, England which, quite obviously, has the principal, if not the sole, interest and concern with " 'the outcome of . . . [this] litigation' ". . . .

Validity—Testamentary Trusts

FARMERS AND MERCHANTS BANK v. WOOLF

Supreme Court of New Mexico, 1974.
86 N.M. 320, 523 P.2d 1346.

[The case appears p. 637, supra.]

Administration of Trusts

RESTATEMENT, SECOND, CONFLICT OF LAWS: *

§ 271.   Administration of Trust of Movables Created by Will

The administration of a trust of interests in movables created by will is governed as to matters which can be controlled by the terms of the trust

(a) by the local law of the state designated by the testator to govern the administration of the trust, or

(b) if there is no such designation, by the local law of the state of the testator's domicil at death, unless the trust is to be administered in some other state, in which case the local law of the latter state will govern.

Comment:

a. What are matters of administration. The term "administration of a trust," as it is used in the Restatement of this Subject, includes those matters which relate to the management of the trust. Matters of administration include those relating to the duties owed by the trustee to the beneficiaries. . . . They include the powers of a trustee, such as the power to lease, to sell and to pledge, the exercise of discretionary powers, the requirement of unanimity of the trustees in the exercise of powers, and the survival of powers. . . . They include the liabilities which may be incurred by the trustee for breach of trust. . . . They include questions as to what are proper trust investments. . . . They include the trustee's right to compensa-

---

* Quoted with the permission of the copyright owner, The American Law Institute.

tion. . . . They include the trustee's right to indemnity for expenses incurred by him in the administration of the trust. . . . They include the removal of the trustee and the appointment of successor trustees. . . . They include the terminability of the trust. . . .

On the other hand, where the question is as to who are beneficiaries of the trust and as to the extent of their interests, the question is one of construction rather than of administration. . . .

c. Law designated by the testator to govern administration of the trust. The testator may designate in the will a state whose local law is to govern the administration of the trust. As to the effectiveness of such designation, a distinction must be made between those matters of administration which the testator can control by provisions in the will and those which he cannot control.

As to those matters which are subject to his control, he may designate a state which has no relation to the trust. The testator can freely regulate most matters of administration. . . .

The testator may provide that different matters of administration shall be governed by different laws. Thus, he may provide that the local law of one state shall govern the compensation of the trustee, and that the local law of another state shall govern investments. . . .

h. Matters which cannot be controlled by the terms of the trust. Certain matters of administration may be such that the testator cannot regulate them by any provision in the terms of the trust. Thus, . . . under the local law of the state of the testator's domicil there may be unusually strict rules as to self-dealing. If a testator fixes the administration of a trust in a state other than that of his domicil, it is not certain whether the courts will apply the rule of the domicil or the rule of the place of administration.

§ 272. Administration of Trust of Movables Created Inter Vivos

The administration of an inter vivos trust of interests in movables is governed as to matters which can be controlled by the terms of the trust

> (a) by the local law of the state designated by the settlor to govern the administration of the trust, or

> (b) if there is no such designation, by the local law of the state to which the administration of the trust is most substantially related.

NOTES

(1) Appointment of a trust company as trustee provides persuasive evidence that the settlor of either an inter vivos or a testamentary trust intended that the trust should be administered in the state where the trust company is incorporated. Restatement, Second, Conflict of Laws §§ 271–272; see

also Boston Safe Deposit & Trust Co. v. Alfred University, 339 Mass. 82, 157 N.E.2d 662 (1959).

(2) Application of New York Trust Co., 197 Misc. 598, 87 N.Y.S.2d 787 (1949). The case involved the question whether the situs of an inter vivos trust created in New York by a resident of that state with a New York trust company as trustee could be removed to California. The trust deed appointed two trustees, an individual and a corporation, and provided that the individual trustee, who was also the life beneficiary, could "request in writing the resignation of the corporate trustee, and upon receiving such request such corporate trustee shall forthwith resign. . . ." Acting under this provision, the individual trustee, who was a resident of California, requested the resignation of the New York corporate trustee and appointed a California trust company in its stead. Held, in a proceeding brought by the New York trust company, that the situs of the trust could be removed to California and that the California trust company was qualified to act as trustee. ". . . the express provision in the clause under discussion . . . makes it perfectly clear that the grantor contemplated the substitution when she executed the trust agreement. . . . The grantor must have realized that her son might find it more convenient to have the trust administered in a place readily accessible to him and that he might request the resignation of the corporate trustee for the very purpose of bringing about this result." Neither the law nor the public policy of New York were found to be offended by such a transfer.

Would the change in the place of administration in the New York Trust Co. case result in a change in the law governing the administration of the trust?

Does a provision of the type found in this case afford a convenient and effective way of giving a beneficiary power to change the law governing the validity of a trust?

(3) The authorities are divided on the question whether allocation of the federal estate tax as between life tenant and remainderman of an inter vivos trust, which has been included in the settlor's gross estate for tax purposes, should be determined by the law governing the administration of the trust or by the law of the settlor's domicile at death. See Scoles, Apportionment of Federal Estate Taxes and Conflict of Laws, 55 Colum.L.Rev. 261 (1955); Doetsch v. Doetsch, 319 F.2d 323 (7th Cir. 1963).

MULLANE v. CENTRAL HANOVER BANK & TRUST CO.

Supreme Court of the United States, 1950.
339 U.S. 306, 70 S.Ct. 652, 94 L.Ed. 865.

[The case appears p. 174, supra]

NOTE

Jurisdiction to supervise the administration of a trust of interests in movables and, if necessary, to remove a trustee and to appoint a successor trustee is usually exercised by the court in which the trustee has qualified as trustee or by the courts of the state in which the trust is to be administered. Restatement, Second, Conflict of Laws § 267.

SECTION 3.   INTANGIBLES

MORSON v. SECOND NATIONAL BANK OF BOSTON

Supreme Court of Massachusetts, 1940.
306 Mass. 588, 29 N.E.2d 19, 131 A.L.R. 189.

QUA, JUSTICE.   This is a bill in equity by the administrator of the estate of Herbert B. Turner . . . alleging . . . that a certificate for one hundred and fifty shares of the stock of the defendant Massachusetts Mohair Plush Company, a Massachusetts corporation, had been originally issued to Herbert B. Turner, but had been delivered to the defendant bank as "transfer agent" of the plush company by the defendant Mildred Turner Copperman for transfer to her on the ground that Herbert B. Turner in his lifetime had made her a gift of the stock.   The prayers are for injunctions against the transfer of the stock and for recovery of the certificate.

The judge . . . entered a decree for the plaintiff.   The issue is whether the facts found show a valid gift of the stock, which should now be recognized by a transfer on the books of the corporation and the issuance of a new certificate to Mildred Turner Copperman.   We think that they do.

Among the facts found are these: About September 20, 1937, while Turner and Mildred Turner Copperman were travelling together in Italy, Turner handed to Mildred Turner Copperman a sealed envelope previously marked by him "Property of Mildred Turner Copperman."   As he did so he said, "These are yours."   The certificate in his name, dated October 6, 1933, was in the envelope.   He also said that he would have to sign the back of the certificate.   Two days later a notary and two witnesses came to the hotel where the parties were staying.   Mildred Turner Copperman produced the certificate, and "Turner signed his name on the back . . . and then he filled in the name of Miss Copperman and her address" and delivered the certificate to Mildred Turner Copperman, who "accepted it."   Turner's intention at that time was "to make an absolute gift to Mildred Copperman to take effect at once."

It is provided by G.L.(Ter.Ed.) c. 155, sec. 27 (Uniform Stock Transfer Act sec. 1), that title "to a certificate and to the shares represented thereby shall be transferred only—(a) By delivery of the certificate endorsed either in blank or to a specified person by the person appearing by the certificate to be the owner of the shares represented thereby; or (b) By delivery of the certificate and a separate document containing a written assignment of the certificate or a power of attorney to sell, assign or transfer the same or the shares represented thereby, signed by the person appearing by the certificate to be the owner of the shares represented thereby. . . . Plainly that which was done in Italy would have been sufficient, if it had been done in Massachusetts, to effect a transfer of legal title to the shares.

But it is argued that the validity of the transfer is to be judged by the law of Italy, and that certain formalities required by that law for the making of gifts in general were not observed. Doubtless it is true that whether or not there is a completed gift of an ordinary tangible chattel is to be determined by the law of the situs of the chattel. . . . Shares of stock, however, are not ordinary tangible chattels. A distinction has been taken between the shares and the certificate, regarded as a piece of paper which can be seen and felt, the former being said to be subject to the jurisdiction of the state of incorporation and the latter subject to the jurisdiction of the state in which it is located. . . . The shares are part of the structure of the corporation, all of which was erected and stands by virtue of the law of the state of incorporation. The law of that state determines the nature and attributes of the shares. If by the law of that state the shares devolve upon one who obtains ownership of the certificate it may be that the law of the state of a purported transfer of the certificate will indirectly determine share ownership. . . . But at the least when the state of incorporation has seen fit in creating the shares to insert in them the intrinsic attribute or quality of being assignable in a particular manner it would seem that that state, and other states as well, should recognize assignments made in the specified manner wherever they are made, even though that manner involves dealing in some way with the certificate. . . .

The final decree is reversed, and a final decree is to be entered dismissing the bill with costs to the defendant Mildred Turner Copperman.

NOTES

(1) Does the principal case establish an alternative reference rule to determine the effect of a voluntary transfer of a stock certificate which embodies the underlying share—i. e., such a transfer will be held effective so long as this result would follow by applying either the law of the state of incorporation or that of the situs of the certificate?

(2) Travelers Insurance Co. v. Fields, 451 F.2d 1292 (6th Cir. 1971). While domiciled in Kentucky with his first wife, the decedent obtained employment in Ohio. He designated his first wife as beneficiary of group insurance policies issued by Travelers and which insured the employees of the Ohio employer against accidental death. The policies expressly provided that they should be governed by Ohio law. Thereafter, the decedent was divorced by his first wife in Kentucky. In due course, the decedent remar-

ried but did not amend the provision in the policies which designated his first wife as beneficiary. He later changed his domicile to Ohio and there met an accidental death. Both the first and second wives claimed the proceeds of the policies. Held for the second wife. The divorce took place in Kentucky where the decedent and his first wife were domiciled at the time. Hence Kentucky law, under which the divorce extinguished the first wife's rights under the policy, was applicable. The first wife would have won if Ohio law had been held applicable.

SECTION 4. INTERPRETATION AND CONSTRUCTION OF DOCUMENTS

The meaning and effect of words contained in wills, trusts, deeds and other instruments of transfer may be determined in any one of three ways:

(1) *Interpretation.* This is the process used most frequently. It involves the attempt to determine the meaning which the words in question were actually intended to bear. In ascertaining the intentions of the party or parties, the court will consider the ordinary meaning of the words, the context in which they appear in the instrument, and the circumstances in which the instrument was drafted. It will consider who drafted the instrument (whether the party or parties or some third person) and whether the draftsman was probably using the language of his domicile or of the place of execution or of the situs of the land or chattel. The tribunal will also consider any other properly admissible evidence that casts light on the actual intentions of the party or parties. The question to be determined is one of fact rather than one of law. The forum will apply its own rules in determining the admissibility of evidence, and it will use its own standards in drawing conclusions from the evidence. Accordingly, interpretation does not involve choice-of-law problems.

(2) *Construction.* Sometimes it proves impossible to determine the meaning the words in an instrument were intended to bear, either because the party or parties did not give thought to the question or left no evidence of their thinking. In such cases, a rule of construction must be employed to fill what would otherwise be a gap in the instrument.

A typical problem of this sort arises when the question is whether an adopted child should be included within the scope of the word "heirs," as used in an instrument of conveyance, and there is no satisfactory evidence of what was actually intended. Here a rule of construction must be employed to provide an answer to this question.

(3) *Legal effect.* Sometimes the law ascribes definite legal consequences, irrespective of the parties' actual intent, to the use of cer-

tain words in an instrument of transfer. Here the sole inquiry is as to the legal effect of the language, and so the term "legal effect" is used to describe the process. Instances of this sort are comparatively rare and, generally speaking, are confined to transfers of interests in land. One example is the common law rule that, in order to convey a fee simple interest in land by transfer inter vivos, the words "his heirs" must appear in the deed following the name of the grantee. Another is the rule in Shelley's Case, that when an owner of land made a conveyance to a person for life and limited a remainder to the heirs of the same person, he created an estate in fee simple in that person and not a life estate in him with a remainder to his heirs.

Where the contacts are divided among two or more states, determination of the meaning and effect of the language contained in an instrument of transfer may involve the preliminary inquiry: what law governs questions of construction and legal effect, and, assuming a change in this law during the period involved, at what time did the meaning and effect of the language become fixed? The necessity of making a selection among two or more competing laws is obvious when the problem at hand relates to the "legal effect" of words, an area where the actual intention of the parties is irrelevant and hard-and-fast rules of law supreme. As has already been stated, questions of this sort are usually confined to transfers of interests in land, and as to them it is agreed that the law of the situs governs. Restatement, Second, Conflict of Laws §§ 224, 240.

"Construction" is likewise a fertile field for choice-of-law questions. Canons of construction are actual rules of law, and where the laws of the interested states differ in this regard, the problem of making a selection between them is essentially the same as that arising in any other field of choice of law.

Typical of the conflicts problems which may arise in this field is what law determines (1) the meaning of a term, such as "heirs," "issue" or "next of kin," contained in a will or conveyance inter vivos, (2) whether covenants for title will be implied from ordinary words of grant (e. g. "bargain, sell and convey") in a deed of land, (3) whether, in the absence of any provision on the point in her husband's will, a wife can take under the will and claim dower as well or whether she must make an election between the two (see 69 A.L.R.3d 1081 (1976)) and (4) assuming again that the will is silent, whether a devisee of land that is encumbered by a mortgage receives only the remaining equity or whether the mortgage must be paid from the personal property in the estate.

Effect will be given to a provision in an instrument that the instrument should be construed in accordance with the rules of construction of a particular state. It is not necessary that this state have a substantial connection with the parties or the subject-matter of the transfer. This is because construction is a process for giving meaning to an instrument in areas where the intentions of the parties would have been followed if these intentions had been made clear. Restatement, Second, Conflict of Laws § 224, Comment *e*.

In the absence of a choice-of-law provision, the cases are agreed that instruments of transfer of interests of land will be construed in accordance with the law that would be applied by the courts of the situs. When the transfer is gratuitous, as in the case of a will or trust, the transferor's intentions are particularly important. Here authority is divided as to whether the situs courts would apply the rules of construction of the situs or the rules of the state where the transferor was domiciled at the time that he made the conveyance or executed the will or trust. When the transfer is based on consideration, as in the case of a sale or lease, the intentions of both the transferor and transferee are important. Here the situs courts would presumably construe the words in accordance with their own local rules unless perhaps the transferor and transferee were both domiciled in another state or, although they were domiciled in different states, the words happened to bear the same meaning in each state of domicile. In any event, all courts will construe the words in accordance with the rules which the situs courts would have applied. Restatement, Second, Conflict of Laws §§ 224, 240.

In the absence of a choice-of-law provision, words in a will of movables will be construed in accordance with the rules of construction that would be applied by the courts of the state where the testator was domiciled at the time of his death. These courts, in the absence of controlling circumstances to the contrary, would usually construe the words in accordance with the rules of construction prevailing in the state where the testator was domiciled at the time the will was executed. Restatement, Second, Conflict of Laws § 264; Hamilton National Bank of Chattanooga v. Hutchison, 357 F.Supp. 114 (E.D. Tenn.1973); In re Sewart, 342 Mich. 491, 70 N.W.2d 732, 52 A.L.R.2d 482 (1955).

On occasion, the meaning of a term, such as "heirs" or "next of kin," has been determined by applying the law of the testator's domicile as it existed at the time of the death of the person to whose heirs or next of kin the remainder was given. Second Bank-State Street Trust Co. v. Weston, 342 Mass. 630, 174 N.E.2d 763 (1961); Matter of Battell, 286 N.Y. 97, 35 N.E.2d 913 (1941); cf. Carnegie v. First National Bank of Brunswick, 218 Ga. 585, 129 S.E.2d 780 (1963). It may be suspected that in such cases the courts frequently apply that law which they believe will achieve the fairest and most desirable result for all concerned.

Words in a trust of movables, in the absence of a choice-of-law provision, will be construed, as to matters pertaining to administration, in accordance with the rules of construction of the state whose law governs the administration of the trust and, as to other matters, in accordance with the rules of construction of the state which the testator or settlor would probably have wished to be applied. Restatement, Second, Conflict of Laws § 268.

NOTES

(1) See generally 5 Scott, Trusts §§ 575, 576, 579, 641, 648 (3d ed. 1967); Scoles and Hay, Conflict of Laws 779–783, 788–791 (1982).

(2) For other discussions of the rules governing interpretation and construction, see Note, 72 Harv.L.Rev. 1154 (1959); 2 Powell, The Law of Real Property, c. 25–27 (1950); Casner, Estate Planning—Powers of Appointment, 64 Harv.L.Rev. 185, 208–10 (1950).

(3) For discussion of the choice-of-law rules applicable to the interpretation of contracts, see Restatement, Second, Conflict of Laws § 204; Weintraub, Commentary on the Conflict of Laws 394–396 (2d ed. 1971).

Chapter 12

FAMILY LAW

RESTATEMENT, SECOND, CONFLICT OF LAWS*

CHAPTER 11

STATUS

Introductory Note: . . .

In law, a status can be viewed from two standpoints. It can be viewed as a relationship which continues as the parties move from state to state, or it can be viewed from the standpoint of the incidents that arise from it. So marriage can be viewed as a relationship, namely solely from the point of view of whether a given man and woman are husband and wife. On the other hand, marriage can be viewed from the standpoint of its incidents, such as whether the man and woman may lawfully cohabit as husband and wife, the interests which the one has in the other's assets and the right of each to inherit, or to take a forced share in, the other's estate. Similarly, legitimacy can be viewed from the standpoint of whether there is a relationship of legitimacy between a child and its parent, or it can be viewed from the standpoint of its incidents, such as whether the child is entitled to an intestate share in the parent's estate or whether, as a matter of construction, the child qualifies as "issue" of that parent under the provisions of a will.

On occasion, the courts are faced with a question of pure status, namely whether, as a general proposition, there is a marital, or a legitimate, or an adoptive relationship between the parties. For example, in the case of marriage, a question of pure status may arise in an action for an annulment, in an action for a declaratory judgment that a marriage does or does not exist or in a criminal prosecution for bigamy. It is clear, however, that questions involving the incidents of a status arise more frequently than do questions which purely involve the status as such. One problem is whether a question involving the incidents of a status can properly be decided without having made a preliminary determination of whether the status does, or does not, exist. For example, can a court properly determine that a woman may inherit from the deceased as a "surviving spouse" within the meaning of its intestacy statute without having first determined that she was validly married to him under the law governing the marriage? Or can a court properly determine that a child born before the marriage of his parents may inherit from his father under its intestacy statute without having first determined that the child is legitimate under the law governing legitimacy? By and large, the courts have acted on the assumption that a decision of questions involving the incidents of a marriage should be preceded by a determination of the validity of the marriage. On the other hand, the courts have been more inclined to decide questions of incidents involving legitimacy and adoption without having first determined whether legitimacy or adoption existed as a status. . . .

SECTION 1. MARRIAGE*

IN RE MAY'S ESTATE

Court of Appeals of New York, 1953.
305 N.Y. 486, 114 N.E.2d 4.

[The case appears p. 645, supra.]

NOTES

(1) As indicated by In re May's Estate, a marriage will usually be held valid everywhere if it is good under the law of the state of celebration. This state has an obvious interest in the manner in which the marriage is celebrated. On the other hand, this state will not, simply by reason of the fact that it is the state of celebration, be the state of most significant relationship for purposes of questions that do not relate to formalities, e.g., the capacity of the parties to marry or whether they are within one of the forbidden degrees of relationship. Application of the law of the state of celebration to uphold the validity of the marriage with respect to questions of the latter sort must therefore rest on other grounds. See Restatement, Second, Conflict of Laws § 283, Comments *f–h*; Baade, Marriage and Divorce in American Conflicts of Law, 72 Colum.L.Rev. 329 (1972); Fine, The Application of Issue-Analysis to Choice of Law Involving Family Law Matters in the United States, 26 Loyola L.Rev. 31, 295 (1980); Reese, Marriage in American Conflicts Law, 26 Int'l & Comp.L.Q. 952 (1977); Scoles and Hay, Conflict of Laws 415–446 (1982).

Does it follow that a marriage which is invalid under the law of the state of celebration must necessarily be invalid everywhere? In this connection, should a distinction be drawn between questions of formalities and questions of substance? See Restatement, Second, Conflict of Laws § 283, Comment *i*.

(2) The general rule is that the validity of a marriage celebrated on board a vessel on the high seas is governed by the law of the vessel's flag. When

---

* See Restatement, Second, Conflict of
Laws §§ 283–284.

the flag is that of the United States, this rule alone is insufficient to determine the applicable law since there is no federal law of marriage. In Fisher v. Fisher, 250 N.Y. 313, 165 N.E. 460 (1929) (an action for separation and support), the law of the shipowner's domicile was applied to validate the marriage; that of the ship's registry, which would have invalidated the marriage, being rejected. In Norman v. Norman, 121 Cal. 620, 54 P. 143 (1898) (an action seeking a judgment declaring a marriage valid), the court applied the law of the state which, at the time of marriage, was the domicile of both spouses and also the place where they intended to live thereafter to invalidate the marriage which had been celebrated on the high seas for the express purpose of evading this law. Are these two cases reconcilable?

(3) See Starkowski v. Attorney General (1953) 2 All E.R. 1272 (H.L.), which upheld a marriage celebrated in Austria by application of an Austrian statute enacted subsequent to the marriage at a time when the spouses were no longer living in Austria. The marriage was originally invalid under Austrian law because it had been celebrated by a priest rather than by the civil authorities. The validating act was held to relate to formalities. See Da Costa, The Formalities of Marriage in the Conflict of Laws, 7 Int'l & Comp. L.Q. 217 (1958).

(4) Problems arise when the validity of a second marriage depends upon the dissolution or invalidity of the first marriage. It has been said that the "generally accepted American view is that the presumption of the validity of the second marriage is 'stronger' than the presumption of the continuance of the first marriage." Headen v. Pope & Talbot, Inc., 252 F.2d 739 (3d Cir. 1958); cf. Woolery v. Metropolitan Life Insurance Co., 406 F.Supp. 641 (E.D. Va.1976).

(5) It is increasingly common for persons to live together without entering a marriage relationship. Presumably some of these relationships are intended to be permanent while others are not. It is to be expected that, in due course, the law will attach certain rights and duties to at least some of these relationships, and these developments in local law can be expected to have repercussions in the conflicts area.

WILKINS v. ZELICHOWSKI

Supreme Court of New Jersey, 1958.
26 N.J. 370, 140 A.2d 65.

[The case appears p. 648, supra.]

NOTES

(1) Statutes in a number of states expressly declare that a marriage, valid where contracted, is valid within the state. See, e.g., Cal.Civ.Code Ann. § 4104; Idaho Code Ann. § 32–209; Kan.Gen.Stat.Ann. § 23–115; Ky.Rev. Stat. § 402.040; Neb.Rev.Stat. § 42–117; N.M.Stat.Ann. § 40–1–4; N.D. Code 14–03–08 (but note exception as to its residents' contracting a marriage prohibited by North Dakota); S.D.C.L. 25–1–38; Utah Code Ann. § 30–1–4.

Section 210 of the Uniform Marriage and Divorce Act (currently in effect in eight states) carries the validation urge even further. It provides:

All marriages contracted within this State prior to the effective date of this Act, or outside this State, that were valid at the time of the contract or subsequently validated by the laws of the place in which they were contracted or by the domicil of the parties, are valid in this State.

Are general provisions of this sort desirable? Would Section 210 have required the court to reach a different result in the Wilkins case? Would it be possible to frame a general choice-of-law rule on the subject of marriage that would permit the court to give consideration to the particular issue?

(2) The Wilkins case demonstrates that a marriage which meets the requirements of the place of celebration will occasionally be held invalid under the law of another jurisdiction. With rare exceptions (see, e.g., Catalano v. Catalano, p. 648, note (1), supra), such a marriage will be invalidated only by application of the law of the state which was the domicile of either one or both parties at the time of marriage and which was also the place where they intended to live thereafter. Restatement, Second, Conflict of Laws § 283; Taintor, Marriage to a Paramour after Divorce: The Conflict of Laws, 43 Minn.L.Rev. 889 (1959). It has been suggested that the law of the state where the parties intend to make their home should have the ultimate voice in determining the validity of their marriage. See Cook, The Logical and Legal Bases of the Conflict of Laws 452–56 (1942). What objections could be advanced to the adoption of such a rule?

(3) Did the marriage in the Wilkins case represent a more objectionable union than the one upheld in In re May's Estate, p. 645, supra? In the absence of a statute expressly dealing with the problem, what criteria should guide the courts in determining whether to invalidate a marriage that meets the requirements of the state of celebration? Should decision depend upon the particular issue involved?

(4) A statute directed explicitly to out-of-state marriages is the Uniform Marriage Evasion Act.[1]

Sec. 1. If any person residing and intending to continue to reside in this state who is disabled or prohibited from contracting marriage under the laws of this state shall go into another state or country and there contract a marriage prohibited and declared void by the laws of this state, such marriage shall be null and void for all purposes in this state with the same effect as though such prohibited marriage had been entered into in this state.

Sec. 2. No marriage shall be contracted in this state by a party residing and intending to continue to reside in another state or jurisdiction if such marriage would be void if contracted in such other state or jurisdiction and every marriage celebrated in this state in violation of this provision shall be null and void.

The Commissioners on Uniform State Laws withdrew the Act in 1943 stating that it tended to produce confusion in the law because so few states had adopted it.[2]

1. The Act is currently in force in four states, Ill.Ann.Stat. ch. 40, § 216–219 (Smith-Hurd 1980); Mass.Ann.Laws ch. 207, §§ 10–13, 50 (Michie/Law Coop. 1981) (with modifications); Vt.Stat.Ann. tit. 15, § 5–6 (1974); Wis.Stat.Ann. § 765–04 (West 1981). For somewhat similar statutes, see La.Civ.Code Ann. art. 95 (West 1952); N.D.Cent.Code § 14–03–08 (1981).

2. The District of Columbia, Indiana, Maine, Mississippi, Virginia and West Virginia have evasion statutes similar in effect to section 1 of the Uniform Marriage Evasion Act. D.C.Code Ann. § 30–105 (1981); Ind. Code Ann. § 31–1–3–5

(5) At one time, statutes in the divorce states commonly imposed restrictions upon the further marriage of divorced persons. Most of these statutes have now been repealed. Even in their heyday, they were usually denied extraterritorial effect. When directed against the guilty party alone, they would frequently be denied effect in other states on the ground that they were penal in nature. When directed against both parties (e.g., by prohibiting remarriage for a certain period after divorce), they would usually be refused application against parties who did not seek to remarry until after they had acquired a domicile in another state. Even courts in the divorce state itself were reluctant to apply their local prohibitions to invalidate out-of-state marriages of local domiciliaries. Scoles and Hay, Conflict of Laws 429–434 (1982); Restatement, Second, Conflict of Laws § 283, Comment *l*.

(6) If a divorce does not become final until the termination of the period within which remarriage is prohibited, a second marriage within this period in a second state will usually be invalid under the law of the second state and, if so, will be held invalid everywhere. Marek v. Fleming, 192 F.Supp. 528 (S.D.Tex.1961); Knoll v. Knoll, 104 Wash. 110, 176 P. 22 (1918).

IN RE OMMANG'S ESTATE

Supreme Court of Minnesota, 1931.
183 Minn. 92, 235 N.W. 529.

OLSEN, J. . . .

This is a contest . . . as to who is entitled to administer the estate of one Nick Ommang, a resident of St. Louis county, in this state, who died intestate at Duluth in said county on March 13, 1929. Appellant is a half-sister of the decedent, and claims to be one of his heirs at law entitled to the estate, and to be entitled to have an administrator appointed. Respondent claims she is the widow of the deceased and his sole heir, and entitled to have an administrator appointed. The probate court of St. Louis county found against the respondent, and held she was not the lawful wife of the deceased prior

(Burns 1980) (requires an "intent to evade" the local law); Me.Rev.Stat.Ann. tit. 19 § 91 (1981) (requires an "intent to evade" the local law); Miss.Code Ann. § 93–1–3 (1973) ("any attempt to evade"); Va.Code § 20–40 (1983); W.Va.Code § 48–1–17 (1980) ("in order to evade"). The Connecticut statute states that marriages celebrated outside of the state shall be valid provided "each party would have legal capacity to contract such marriage in this state." Conn.Gen.Stat.Ann. § 46.6 (West 1978). The Arizona statute provides that marriages celebrated outside of the state by parties intending to reside at the time in Arizona shall have the same legal consequences as if solemnized in Arizona. Ariz.Rev.Stat. Ann. § 25–112 (1976). The Georgia statute is substantially the same as the Arizona statute. Ga.Code Ann. § 19–3–43 (1982). The Wyoming statute makes it the duty of the clerk to inquire whether the parties have capacity to contract by the law of the domicile, and provides that a license shall be refused if it appears that there be an impediment to marriage by that law. Wyo.Stat. § 20–1–103 (1977).

Some states make it unlawful for their residents to cohabit within the state if they have elsewhere contracted a marriage which is prohibited by the law of the state. See, e.g., Del.Code Ann. tit. 13 § 104 (1975); Ind.Code Ann. § 31–1–3–5 (Burns 1980); Miss.Code Ann. § 97–29–9 (1973); Va.Code § 20–40 (1983); W.Va. Code § 48–1–18 (1980).

and up to the time of his death. On appeal to the district court, that court reversed the probate court and held that respondent was the lawful wife of the deceased prior to and at the time of his death, his sole heir at law, and entitled to have an administrator appointed.

. . .

1. In 1907, Nick Ommang and respondent, whose name was then Mrs. Seligman, were residents of Superior, Wis. Respondent had secured a divorce from her husband on January 2, 1907. On August 7, 1907, respondent and Nick Ommang went to Duluth and were there lawfully married. They returned to Superior immediately after the marriage, and lived there together as husband and wife for about two years. They then separated, and decedent moved to Duluth late in 1909, and there resided until his death. Respondent remained in Superior for about two more years, then moved to Duluth, and resided there for three or more years. She then came to St. Paul to live with a daughter of her prior marriage, and has since resided there. After their separation, decedent met and visited the respondent from time to time, but they did not thereafter live together. After respondent moved to St. Paul, decedent visited her there many times. At one time he took her out to entertainments there. He gave her money at times. He asked her to come back and live with him. One time, at his request, respondent came to Duluth and stayed with decedent in his room overnight. He wanted her to remain, but she did not like the place or surroundings where he was living, and left the next day. This evidence, while it does not clearly prove cohabitation by the parties in this state, does show that decedent recognized the marriage relation existing between them and acknowledged respondent as his wife after both parties had become residents of this state. We do not hold that actual cohabitation in this state, under the circumstances shown, was necessary.

The marriage of the parties in this state, more than six months after respondent had obtained a divorce from her former husband, was a valid marriage under our laws. Its validity, at the time of the death of one of the parties in this state, after both parties were and had been residents of this state for many years, is now attacked. The marriage has never been set aside or adjudged invalid.

2. The general rule, that the validity of a marriage must be tested by the laws of the state or country where the marriage ceremony was performed and that a marriage valid where performed is valid everywhere, as well as the exceptions to the general rule, has been argued. The general rule is followed in this state. . . . This general rule has application when the marriage was performed in one state or country and the question of its validity arises in the courts of another state or country. The rule and the exceptions thereto would seem to have but incidental bearing upon the present case, where the marriage was performed in this state and was valid under our laws; the parties thereto were residents of this state at the time one of

them died; the survivor remains a resident here; and the validity of the marriage is challenged in a court of this state.

3. The ground urged by appellant for holding the marriage invalid is that the law of Wisconsin, wherein the parties resided at the time of the marriage, provides that it shall not be lawful for a divorced person to remarry within one year after the judgment of divorce was entered, and declares any such marriage, within the year, null and void. The Wisconsin court, in Lanham v. Lanham, 136 Wis. 360, 117 N.W. 787, 17 L.R.A.(N.S.) 804, 128 Am.St.Rep. 1085, held that this statute invalidated a marriage performed in Michigan, where the parties were residents of Wisconsin, and, for the purpose of evading the law, went to Michigan, were there married, and returned to Wisconsin to live. . . .

4. This court, as stated, has consistently followed the rule that the validity of a marriage is to be tested by the laws of the state or country where it was performed. . . .

The Meisenhelder Case [note 2, infra] was an action to recover for the death of one D'Albani, under the Federal Employers' Liability Act (45 USCA §§ 51-59). Louise D'Albani claimed to be his widow and beneficiary. The parties resided in Illinois, and decedent was there killed. The cause of action arose in that state. If Louise D'Albani was not the lawful wife of decedent, under the Illinois law, she was not a beneficiary under the act, and no cause of action existed in her favor. In other words, her status as the wife of decedent in Illinois was an essential link in the cause of action. The general rule, that a marriage valid where performed is valid everywhere, is not departed from in this case, except to the extent of holding that, where a marriage between residents of Illinois is by the laws of that state declared invalid although performed in another state where it is not invalid, the laws and decisions of Illinois, where the cause of action arose, govern the cause of action here. Had the marriage been a valid marriage performed in Illinois, it could not have been questioned here.

. . .

6. Counsel urge that the parties came to Minnesota to be married with the intention of avoiding the Wisconsin law, and therefore the marriage should be held invalid here. We are not prepared to so hold. The marriage was legal in this state, and the parties did not evade, or seek to evade, any of our laws. . . .

Order affirmed.

NOTES

(1) Would the decision have been the same if the parties had remained domiciled in Wisconsin? If not, did the originally invalid marriage become valid when the parties moved to Minnesota? Or is there some other explanation for the decision?

(2) Did the court in the principal case satisfactorily distinguish its earlier decision in Meisenhelder v. Chicago & N.W. Ry. Co., 170 Minn. 317, 213 N.W. 32 (1927)? In that case, first cousins, who were domiciled in Illinois and were prohibited by Illinois law from marrying, went to Kentucky to be married and then returned to Illinois. This marriage was void in Illinois, which had enacted the Uniform Marriage Evasion Act. Thereafter, the man was killed in Illinois in the course of his employment and the woman brought suit against his employer in Minnesota under the Federal Employees' Liability Act. Recovery was denied on the ground that she was not a "surviving widow" within the meaning of the Act. The court said that since the term "surviving widow" was not defined in the Act, its meaning must be sought in state law, "in this case the law of Illinois." The Illinois statute

"modifies the rule that marriages valid where the ceremony is performed are valid anywhere. . . .

"There is no real question but that the purpose of the decedent and Louise D'Albani in going to Kentucky and marrying was to evade the Illinois law. There is evidence that they intended moving later to Minnesota, but it is indefinite, and their removal was entirely contingent. When married they gave their residence as Illinois, they were under oath, they were in Kentucky not more than four or five days, and they returned to Illinois to live and lived there until the decedent's death in December, 1924.

"The result, following the Illinois law, is that Louise D'Albani is not the widow of the deceased and cannot take as beneficiary under the Federal Employers' Liability Act."

(3) Professor Ehrenzweig suggested that a marriage should be upheld if it is valid under the law of the state of celebration or the law of either spouse's domicile at the time of the marriage, or the law of spouses' domicile at the commencement of the suit. Ehrenzweig, Conflict of Laws 378–379 (1962). In Professor Ehrenzweig's view the validity of the marriage need not finally be determined at the time of the marriage but may depend upon the law of the state where the spouses happen to be domiciled at the time when the validity of the marriage is brought into question. Are there any practical objections to such a view? Should more attention be paid to the particular issue?

(4) Section 210 of the Uniform Marriage and Divorce Act [set forth at p. 804, note 1, supra] provides that a marriage celebrated outside of the state shall be held valid if it was valid or was "subsequently validated" by the law of the state in which the marriage was contracted or where the parties were domiciled.

IN RE ESTATE OF LENHERR

Supreme Court of Pennsylvania, 1974.
455 Pa. 225, 314 A.2d 255.

NIX, JUSTICE. The sole issue involved in this appeal is whether or not the West Virginia marriage of Sarah T. Lenherr to Leo A. Lenherr, the decedent, will be recognized in this Commonwealth for purposes of the marital exemption to the Transfer Inheritance Tax.

See, Act of June 15, 1961, P.L. 373, Art. III, § 311, 72 P.S. § 2485–311. If their marriage is so recognized, property held in their joint names will pass from the decedent to Sarah Lenherr without the imposition of a Pennsylvania inheritance tax. . . .

The pertinent facts are as follows. On October 23, 1930, the deceased, Leo A. Lenherr was divorced on the grounds of adultery from his then wife Anna Kelly Lenherr and Sarah Barney [Lenherr] was named as the co-respondent. On December 27, 1930, Sarah was divorced from her then husband William K. Barney on the grounds of adultery and Leo Lenherr was named as co-respondent.

On March 12, 1932, after the two divorce decrees were entered and while William Barney and Anna Lenherr were living, Leo Lenherr and Sarah Gillespie Barney were married in West Virginia. They returned to Pennsylvania where they lived as husband and wife until the death of Leo Lenherr in August of 1971.

At the outset, it should be noted that all parties agree that Leo and Sarah's marriage was valid under the applicable laws of West Virginia. This dispute arises because of the Act of June 17, 1971, P.L. ——, No. 16, § 1, amending, Act of March 13, 1815, P.L. 150, § 9, 48 P.S. § 169 (Supp.1973–74), which provides:

> "The husband or wife, who shall have been guilty of the crime of adultery, shall not marry the person with whom the said crime was committed during the life of the former wife or husband. . . . "
> . . . .

[Since] the laws of Pennsylvania and West Virginia are in conflict with regard to the validity of this marriage, we must next determine which law should be applied in this case. . . .

Since both Leo and Sarah were residents of Pennsylvania before and after their West Virginia marriage, we have no trouble concluding that Pennsylvania has the most significant relationship to the spouses and the marriage. It remains for us to determine whether the policy behind section 169 is so strong that it must be given extra-territorial effect in this case, thereby destroying the uniformity of result which is so desirable in a case concerning the recognition of a marriage that is valid in the state where it was contracted.

In resolving that conflict, we must realize that the strength of the policy behind section 169 depends to a significant degree upon the incident of marriage under consideration. For example, the legislature has determined that at least one incident of marriage—the legitimacy of the children—is not to be denied despite the prior adjudication of adultery. See, Act of June 17, 1971, supra. Our task therefore is to balance on the one hand the policy behind section 169, *as it relates to the marital exemption to the inheritance tax,* against the need for uniformity and predictability of result on the other.

It is apparent from the terms of section 169 that the provision is intended not so much as a penalty upon the parties who failed to recognize the sanctity of the former marriage vow as it is intended to protect the sensibilities of the injured spouse. Were it otherwise, the prohibition would not be limited to the lifetime of that spouse. . . .

While that policy may yet be quite strong with respect to cohabitation and many other incidents of marriage, . . . we are concerned here only with the marital exemption to the inheritance tax. We are not convinced that the denial of that exemption will foster the policy of section 169 to any significant extent. Such denial could do so only if it: (1) could deter either the adulterous conduct during the valid marriage or the subsequent marriage of the guilty spouse and his or her paramour; or (2) could in any way spare the aggrieved former spouse the affront caused by such marriage.

We are convinced that denying the marital exemption would be all but fruitless in achieving the above goals. Moreover, we must balance any illusory gain from such denial against the need for uniformity of result in this area and against the statutory policy that the property of two persons living as man and wife and held in their joint names with right of survivorship is in reality the product of their joint efforts and should pass to the survivor without the imposition of a tax. Both of those policies would be frustrated by applying section 169 to this marriage. On balance, we find that the degree to which the policy behind section 169 will be fostered by application in this case is significantly outweighed by countervailing policies. We therefore decline to apply Pennsylvania law to invalidate this marriage for this purpose. . . .

NOTES

(1) Does the Lenherr case suggest that marriage is not an all-purpose concept and that in effect a marriage may be valid for one purpose and yet invalid for another?

(2) The courts are frequently called upon to determine the meaning of such terms as "wife," "widow" or "surviving spouse" in local statutes. Usually, such inquiry has been held to require an investigation of whether there was a valid marriage under choice-of-law principles. See, e.g., In re May's Estate, p. 645, supra. Sometimes, however, this approach has not been followed. For example, in Borax v. Commissioner, 349 F.2d 666 (2d Cir.1965), a man and a woman with whom he had gone through a wedding ceremony following a Mexican divorce were held entitled to file joint income tax returns and deduct alimony paid to the first wife even after the first wife had obtained a New York judgment that the Mexican divorce was invalid and that she and the man were still married. In Toler v. Oakwood Smokeless Coal Corp., 173 Va. 425, 4 S.E.2d 364 (1949), W, erroneously believing her first husband dead, married H in West Virginia where a bigamous marriage is void only from the time it is so judicially decreed. A few weeks later H and W moved to Virginia where H was killed in the course of his employment. By Virginia law a bigamous marriage is void ab initio. Compensation was denied W on the ground that the marriage was void, and therefore W

was not H's widow. Can this decision be explained on the ground that the Virginia legislature intended that its own marriage law, rather than that of another jurisdiction, should be applied in determining who can qualify as a "widow" under the Virginia compensation statute? In Guevara v. Inland Steel Co., 120 Ind.App. 47, 88 N.E.2d 398 (1949), 228 Ind. 135, 90 N.E.2d 347 (1950), the Indiana Act provided that a common-law wife is entitled to compensation if the common-law relationship existed openly for not less than five years immediately preceding the death of her husband. H and W had begun their relationship in Illinois, where common-law marriages are void, and had removed to Indiana only three years before H's death. W was held entitled to recover compensation if on remand it were found that her relationship with H had existed for the required five years including the period of residence in Illinois.

See D. Currie, Suitcase Divorce in the Conflict of Laws, 34 U.Chi.L.Rev. 26, 64–77 (1967); Engdahl, Proposal for a Benign Revolution in Marriage Law and Marriage Conflicts Law, 55 Iowa L.Rev. 56 (1969); Fine, The Application of Issue-Analysis to the Choice of Law Involving Family Matters in the United States, 26 Loyola L.Rev. 31, 295 (1980); Reese, Marriage in American Conflict of Laws, 26 Int. & Comp.L.Q. 952 (1977).

IN RE DALIP SINGH BIR'S ESTATE, 83 Cal.App.2d 256, 188 P.2d 499 (Ct.App.1948): While domiciled in the Punjab Province of India, the decedent legally married two wives. Thereafter, he moved to California where he died intestate. The question was whether both women could inherit as "wives" of the decedent. Held that they could so inherit. The conclusion might be different "if the decedent had attempted to cohabit with his two wives in California." But the "public policy" of California would not be affected by dividing money equally between them.

NOTES

(1) A state will usually afford the same incidents—in the sense of resulting legal interests—to a valid foreign marriage that it gives to a marriage contracted within its territory. Restatement, Second, Conflict of Laws § 284. It will not do so, however, when it believes that doing so would be contrary to its strong public policy in the sense discussed by Judge Cardozo in Loucks v. Standard Oil Co., p. 384, supra. For this reason, marriages between persons of different races were sometimes denied recognition in what is now a bygone era. In re Takahashi's Estate, 113 Mont. 490, 123 P.2d 217 (1942) (inheritance); State v. Bell, 7 Baxt. (Tenn.) 9 (1872) (cohabitation). To be effectively invoked the "public policy" reason must, of course, be a constitutional one.

(2) The Supreme Court has declared miscegenation statutes unconstitutional as violative of the due process and equal protection clauses of the Constitution. Loving v. Virginia, 388 U.S. 1 (1967).

(3) Marriage among the American Indians according to their laws and customs, where tribal regulations and government exist, has been almost universally recognized in the United States, even though both polygamy and termination by mutual consent may be permitted. Wall v. Williamson, 8 Ala.

48 (1844); Kobogum v. Jackson Iron Co., 76 Mich. 498, 43 N.W. 602 (1899); Earl v. Godley, 42 Minn. 361, 44 N.W. 254 (1890); People ex rel. La Forte v. Rubin, 98 N.Y.S. 787 (1905); Morgan v. McGhee, 24 Tenn. 13 (1844).

(4) A difficult problem may arise when a court is required to determine what incidents should be attached to a relationship or status that is unknown to its law. A case in point is Nevarez v. Bailon, 287 S.W.2d 521 (Tex.Civ. App.1956). Appellant and the deceased had lived together in Mexico in a relationship termed "concubinage" by Mexican law but which would have constituted a common-law marriage had they lived in Texas. Her petition for a widow's allowance and to be appointed administratrix of the deceased's Texas estate was denied. "It should be said in passing that the term 'concubine' as used in Mexico does not carry with it the stigma ordinarily attached to it by the English language. It is an institution recognized by the law of Mexico, and . . . the relationship of more than half a million Mexican couples. . . . [B]ecause the relationship between appellant and deceased was entered into and existed wholly within [Mexico], it must be regulated and defined by the Code Law of that state. This Code Law . . . defines appellant as a concubine, and grants her certain rights of inheritance as such, but does not recognize her relationship as a valid, provable marriage in . . . Mexico. The Courts of Texas must therefore recognize her as do the courts of her residence, viz., as a concubine, and there is no provision in the Texas law for her to inherit as such. . . . [S]he could not claim as a common-law wife in Texas for such a relationship is nonexistent in the jurisdiction of her residence."

Was the result reached in this case wise and equitable? If not, how could if have been avoided by the court?

SECTION 2. DIVORCE*

A. CONDITIONS FOR DECREEING DIVORCE

ALTON v. ALTON

United States Court of Appeals, Third Circuit, 1953.
207 F.2d 667.

GOODRICH, CIRCUIT JUDGE. This case involves an important and novel question with regard to jurisdiction for divorce. The plaintiff, Sonia Alton, left her home in West Hartford, Connecticut, and went to the Virgin Islands, where she arrived February 10, 1953. After six weeks and one day continuous presence there she filed a suit for divorce on March 25, 1953. Her husband, David Alton, defendant, entered an appearance and waived service of summons. He did not

* See Restatement, Second, Conflict of Laws §§ 70–74.

contest the allegations of the complaint. . . . When the case came to the judge of the district court he asked for further proof on the question of domicile. This was not furnished. He thereupon denied the plaintiff the relief sought, and the case comes here on her appeal. The defendant has filed no brief and made no argument.

The core of our question is found in two acts of the Legislative Assembly of the Virgin Islands. The first is the Divorce Law of 1944, section 9 of which requires six weeks' residence in the Islands prior to commencement of a suit for divorce. In Burch v. Burch, 3 Cir., 1952, 195 F.2d 799, this court construed the words "inhabitant" and "residence" in that statute to mean "domiciliary" and "domicile." In 1953 the Legislative Assembly passed another act which must be stated in full in order to understand the specific problem involved in this case. It amends section 9 of the Divorce Law of 1944 by adding to it an additional subsection (a) which reads:

"Notwithstanding the provisions of sections 8 and 9 hereof, if the plaintiff is within the district at the time of the filing of the complaint and has been continuously for six weeks immediately prior thereto, this shall be prima facie evidence of domicile, and where the defendant has been personally served within the district or enters a general appearance in the action, then the Court shall have jurisdiction of the action and of the parties thereto without further reference to domicile or to the place where the marriage was solemnized or the cause of action arose."

. . . we think it pretty clear as a matter of construction of the English language that there are here two separable provisions. There are two rules provided and they are connected with a conjunctive "and." We think, therefore, that we must give attention to the two clauses independently.

[The Court struck down the first clause of the statute on the ground that "If domicile is really the basis for divorce jurisdiction . . . six weeks' physical presence without more is not a reasonable way to prove it."]

. . . The second part of the statute goes on to provide that the court shall have jurisdiction, after six weeks' residence by the plaintiff, where the defendant has been personally served or appeared, "without further reference to domicile." . . . The action, in other words, is to become a simple transitory action like a suit for tort or breach of contract. . . . Can divorce be turned into a simple, transitory action at the will of any legislature?

The background of divorce legislation and litigation shows that it has not been considered a simple transitory personal action. The principle said to govern is that marriage is a matter of public concern, as well as a matter of interest to the parties involved. Because it is a matter of public concern, the public, through the state, has an interest both in its formation and in its dissolution, and the state which has that interest is the state of domicile, because that is where the party "dwelleth and hath his home."

. . .

So deeply has it been thought that the responsibility for divorce was that of the domicile, that divorce litigation has been called an action in rem, the res being the marital relationship between the parties. One may question whether the analogy has not caused more confusion than clarity, but at any rate it shows the way in which the matter has been regarded in the law. It is of significance upon the importance of domicile as the foundation for jurisdiction that the Supreme Court has recently held that a divorce action at the domicile of one of the parties is entitled to full faith and credit as a matter of constitutional compulsion even without the presence of the defending spouse.[20] On the other hand, a divorce not at the domicile gives no protection against a prosecution for bigamy in the state of the domicile,[21] although if the defendant is in court he, himself, may be precluded from questioning the decree on the grounds of res judicata.[22]

We now go out beyond the place where legal trails end. The Supreme Court has never had occasion to say what would happen in a case where two parties, being personally before the court, are purportedly divorced by a state which has no domiciliary jurisdiction, and the question of the validity of the decree comes up in a second state in a prosecution for bigamy, or in a suit for necessaries by a creditor, or in some other such fashion. Granted that the parties are precluded from attacking the decree, does that immunity extend only to attacks by them or by those in privity with them?[23] Here is an unanswered question. . . .

But assume that the Virgin Islands cannot grant to a nondomiciliary a decree which will be impregnable elsewhere by the shield of full faith and credit. Can it not, if it pleases, provide for the granting of a divorce decree to any plaintiff who has a defendant in court in the Virgin Islands? If the decree is good by the law of the Islands and the parties thereto and those in privity with them cannot attack it, it may well be good enough for practical purposes in a world where divorce decrees as well as everything else may fall short of perfection. But is such a decree, which the parties might regard as good enough, one which a nondomiciliary court may grant?

. . .

20. Williams v. North Carolina (I), 1942, 317 U.S. 287.

21. Williams v. North Carolina (II), 1945, 325 U.S. 226.

22. Sherrer v. Sherrer, 1948, 334 U.S. 343; Coe v. Coe, 1948, 334 U.S. 378.

23. Following the Sherrer and Coe cases, supra, note 22, the Supreme Court has held that if a person cannot collaterally attack the decree by the law of the state which rendered it, he cannot do so in the second state. Johnson v. Muelberger, 1951, 340 U.S. 581. See also Cook v. Cook, 1951, 342 U.S. 126.

Before the days of the Fourteenth Amendment, a state could and some states did, pass rules for the exercise of jurisdiction against nonconsenting, nonresident absentee defendants. These rules were not based upon what are now considered the fundamental requisites for such jurisdiction. The judgments were not recognized in other states under the full faith and credit clause, but there was no foundation for testing their validity in the state where they were rendered. After the Fourteenth Amendment provided a way for testing the validity of these judgments in the rendering state under the due process clause, it became well settled that an attempt to give a personal judgment for money against one not subject to the state's jurisdiction was invalid at home under due process, as well as invalid abroad under full faith and credit. With regard to this type of case one can generalize and say that due process at home and full faith and credit in another state are correlative.

. . .

We think that adherence to the domiciliary requirement is necessary if our states are really to have control over the domestic relations of their citizens. The instant case would be typical. In the Virgin Islands incompatibility of temperament constitutes grounds for divorce. In Connecticut it does not. We take it that it is all very well for the Virgin Islands to provide for whatever matrimonial regime it pleases for people who live there. But the same privilege should be afforded to those who control affairs in Connecticut.

Our conclusion is that the second part of this statute conflicts with the due process clause of the Fifth Amendment. . . . Domestic relations are a matter of concern to the state where a person is domiciled. An attempt by another jurisdiction to affect the relation of a foreign domiciliary is unconstitutional even though both parties are in court and neither one raises the question. The question may well be asked as to what the lack of due process is. The defendant is not complaining. Nevertheless, if the jurisdiction for divorce continues to be based on domicile, as we think it does, we believe it to be lack of due process for one state to take to itself the readjustment of domestic relations between those domiciled elsewhere. . . .

The judgment of the district court will be affirmed.

HASTIE, CIRCUIT JUDGE (dissenting). The majority of the court think that both . . . changes [in the Virgin Islands statute] violate the Constitution of the United States. Dissenting, I think both changes are within legislative competency. . . .

[That part of Judge Hastie's opinion dealing with the first clause of the statute is omitted.]

In striking down the second amendment of the statute . . . this court now says that the Fifth Amendment requires that the exercise of legal power to grant divorce be restricted to those cases where one party at least is a local domiciliary. The agreed starting point in this phase of the case is the fact that English and American judges in recent times have refrained, in the absence of statute, from exercising their divorce power except in cases involving local domiciliaries. But what is it that raises this judicial rule of self-restraint to the status of an invariable Constitutional principle?   . . .

I can find nothing in the history of the present judge-made rule which entitles it to Constitutional sanction.   Certainly it is no ancient landmark of the common law. . . .

. . . the rule . . . is a creation of nineteenth century American judges.   It is also clear that the rule did not become settled in England . . . until the 1895 decision of the Privy Council in Le Mesurier v. Le Mesurier, [1895] A.C. 517. . . .

I do not mean to suggest that pre-revolutionary existence is essential to Constitutional protection of a doctrine. . . . I think our real question on this phase of the case is whether it is clearly arbitrary or unfair for a legislature to adopt an alternative for domicil as an appropriate foundation for divorce power.

When I get to this point I am impressed that a number of states in the British Commonwealth have by legislation made domicil unnecessary to divorce jurisdiction in various situations.   See Griswold, Divorce Jurisdiction and Recognition of Divorce Decrees—A Comparative Study, 1951, 65 Harv.L.Rev. 193, 197–208.   I find it difficult to see in what respect these abandonments of domicil as a fundamental basis of divorce are patently unfair and arbitrary, even though a particular legislature may not have been restrained by a written Constitution. . . .

Actually, the concept of domicil as a basis of jurisdiction is in practice elusive and very unsatisfactory for several reasons.   It is a highly technical concept depending upon the proof of the mental attitude of a person toward a place.   Whether in taxation or in divorce, the use of domicil as a jurisdictional base gives trouble when it is applied to people who really have no "home feeling" toward any place or, at the other end of the scale, to those who have more than one home. And . . . in the divorce field difficulties are multiplied because the estranged spouses so often establish separate homes.   Thus, when a court is asked to grant a divorce it very often finds that not one domicil but at least two—potentially more through refinements of the "marital domicil" concept—may be interested in the parties and their relationship.   In these all too familiar situations of divided domicil, the jurisdictional requirement which the majority regards as so essential to fairness that it can not be changed is a troublemaker and a potential source of injustice.

. . . it seems to me that a reasonable person can say that the domiciliary rule does not accomplish what its proponents, including the majority here, claim for it.   If it is socially justified in some circumstances, it works unfairly without social justification in others. Perhaps the trouble is that it exaggerates the theoretical interest of the technical domicil of a plaintiff at the time of suit for divorce at the expense of personal and community interests on the defendant's side. . . .

In the Virgin Islands it has seemed to the legislature that an alternative to the domiciliary rule is worth a trial. And in selecting the alternative of personal jurisdiction over both parties, the legislature has obviated that very disregard of interests on the defendant's side which is the great weakness of the domiciliary rule. In this action I can find nothing arbitrary or unfair; hence, nothing inconsistent with the Fifth Amendment.

One other matter should be mentioned. Although the court recognizes that, as concerns authoritative precedents, this case requires us to travel beyond the place "where legal trails end", the majority opinion places some reliance upon the less than pellucid body of case law which is concerned with various aspects of the problem of recognition of divorce granted in one state of the union by a sister state. For present purposes I do not find these cases very helpful. The due process question in divorce jurisdiction which we have to decide is whether it is fair for a state and its courts to adjudicate the merits of a petition for the dissolution of a particular marriage. The problem of the full faith and credit cases is to what extent a second state must subordinate its notions of policy about a marital matter in which it wants to have a voice to what a sister state has already decided. Perhaps full faith should be given to every American divorce decree which satisfies due process. But until the Supreme Court makes it clear that in this area due process and full faith are of the same dimensions, I mistrust any inversion of reasoning which would extract from the not invariant line of decisions on full faith and credit the essentials of due process in the original exercise of divorce power.

. . . it seems proper to point out that if a state proceeds upon this new basis of divorce jurisdiction another conflict of laws difficulty must be faced before the merits of the claim can be decided. That difficulty is the proper choice of the law to govern the controversy.

So long as one of the spouses has had a domiciliary relationship to the forum it has been conventional theory that the forum has sufficient connection with the domestic relation which is the subject matter of suit to justify not only the exercise of its judicial power to decide the controversy but also the application of its own substantive law of divorce as well. Stewart v. Stewart, 1919, 32 Idaho 180, 180 P. 165. It is quite possible that some of the difficulties which have arisen in this field are the result of failure to keep in view that these are distinct problems although the existence of a domiciliary relationship is thought to solve both.

But once the power to decide the case is based merely upon personal jurisdiction a court must decide as a separate question upon what basis, if any, the local substantive law of divorce can properly be applied to determine whether the plaintiff is entitled to the relief sought. In this case, if it should appear that Mr. and Mrs. Alton were both domiciled in Connecticut at the time of suit in the Virgin Islands and that their estrangement had resulted from conduct in the matrimonial home state, it may well be that under correct application of conflict of laws doctrine, and even under the due process clause, it is encumbent upon the Virgin Islands, lacking connection with the subject matter, to apply the divorce law of some state that has such connection, here Connecticut. . . .

Of course such a solution would be a novelty in divorce procedure. But the entire situation presented by this statute is very unusual. And the legislation is an innovation in a very important area. I think, therefore, that we should try to answer no more questions than the exigencies of this litigation require. . . . Accordingly, I do no more than point out that this choice of law question would have to be considered if the court's power to decide this case depended upon personal jurisdiction and that basis of jurisdiction were sustained, as I believe it should be.

. . .

I am authorized to state that CHIEF JUDGE BIGGS and CIRCUIT JUDGE KALODNER concur in the views stated in this opinion.

NOTES

(1) The Supreme Court granted certiorari in the Alton case, but then dismissed the proceeding as moot upon learning that in the meantime one of the spouses had procured a second divorce in another jurisdiction, 347 U.S. 911 (1954). In Granville-Smith v. Granville-Smith, 349 U.S. 1 (1955), the Supreme Court invalidated the Virgin Islands statute, however, without passing upon the constitutionality of the statute under the due process clause. The decision was based on the ground that in enacting the statute the Virgin Islands Legislative Assembly had exceeded the power granted it by Congress. This power was to legislate on "all subjects of local application," and this language was held not to include the granting of a divorce to non-residents.

(2) Does the opinion of Judge Hastie place as serious a road-block in the way of a non-resident seeking a divorce as does that of Judge Goodrich?

(3) How can a state violate due process by giving spouses a divorce which both desire? Apart from considerations of fairness to the individual parties, should there be some restrictions upon the power of a member state of a federal union to hear and adjudicate issues which are of far greater concern to a sister state? See Rheinstein, The Constitutional Bases of Jurisdiction, 22 U.Chi.L.Rev. 775 (1955).

(4) The Supreme Court has never had occasion to determine whether domicile of one of the spouses in the divorce state is an essential jurisdictional basis for the granting of a divorce.

Statutes in an increasing number of states permit the rendering of a divorce on some basis other than domicile. The most common type of statute is one which authorizes the granting of a divorce to military personnel who have been stationed in the state for a given period, which is frequently a

year but is only 90 days under § 302 of the Uniform Marriage and Divorce
Act.

An Arkansas statute (Ark.Stats.Ann. §§ 34–1208, 34–1208.1 (1947)) empowers the Arkansas courts to grant a divorce to one who alleges and proves
"actual presence" within the state for a three-month period. The constitutionality of this statute was upheld in Wheat v. Wheat, 229 Ark. 842, 318
S.W.2d 793 (1958).

(5) Comment *b* of § 72 of Restatement, Second, Conflict of Laws reads as
follows:

b. Relationships other than domicil. If one or both of the spouses are
domiciled in the state, the state has a sufficient interest in the marriage status to give it judicial jurisdiction to dissolve the marriage (see §§ 70–71).
The domicil of one or of both of the spouses in the state is not, however, the
only possible basis of jurisdiction. A state may have a sufficient interest in
a spouse by reason of some relationship other than domicil, to give the state
judicial jurisdiction to dissolve the marriage. In the present state of the authorities, few definite statements can be made as to what relationships with
a state, other than domicil, will suffice. Residence, as distinguished from
domicil, by one of the spouses in the state for a substantial period, such as a
year, is an adequate jurisdictional basis for the rendition of a divorce. On
the other hand, the fact that the spouses were married in the state should
not of itself provide an adequate jurisdictional basis. A distinction may ultimately be drawn between situations where both spouses are subject to the
personal jurisdiction of the divorce court and where there is jurisdiction over
only one spouse. One or more jurisdictional bases may be found adequate
for the granting of a divorce in the first situation and inadequate in the second.*

(6) Indyka v. Indyka, [1967] 3 W.L.R. 510. The case involved the status
in England of a divorce granted in Czechoslovakia. H and W were Czech
nationals who had married in Czechoslovakia. After the start of World War
II, H acquired a domicile in England. Thereafter W, who had remained in
Czechoslovakia, obtained there an ex parte divorce. H remarried in England
and, when his second wife sought a divorce, defended on the ground that
their marriage was void for bigamy, attacking the Czech divorce as invalid.
The House of Lords unanimously held that the Czech divorce was valid and
that domicile of at least one of the spouses is not the only jurisdictional basis
for divorce. Among other jurisdictional bases suggested in the five opinions
were nationality and residence. The case probably stands for no more precise a proposition than that a state will be recognized as having jurisdiction
to grant a divorce if it has a "real and substantial connection" with the plaintiff spouse. See 1 Dicey and Morris, The Conflict of Laws 344–347 (10th ed.
1980).

(7) As made clear by both opinions in the Alton case, one of the most
peculiar aspects of divorce litigation is that the law of the forum is usually
applied to determine whether there are adequate grounds for a divorce. So
if the action is brought in state X, the law of X will usually be applied even
though the complained-of conduct took place in state Y. Restatement, Second, Conflict of Laws § 285. Some states insist, however, that the acts on

---

* Quoted with the permission of the
copyright owner, The American Law Institute.

which the divorce action is based should have occurred in their territory (Nicholas v. Maddox, 52 La.Ann. 1493, 27 So. 966 (1900); Norris v. Norris, 64 N.H. 523, 15 A. 19 (1888)); or that these acts be recognized as a cause for divorce by the law of the state where the plaintiff spouse was domiciled at the time. Fitzgerald v. Fitzgerald, 66 N.J.Super. 277, 168 A.2d 851 (1961).

(8) The Supreme Court has not yet squarely passed upon the question of what sort of notice of the divorce proceedings must be given the defendant spouse. State statutes sometimes authorize the giving of notice to a nonresident spouse by some form of publication. It seems unlikely that such statutes would be upheld today by the Supreme Court. See Mullane v. Central Hanover Bank & Trust Co., p. 174, supra; p. 181, note (1), supra.

(9) Compare Hartford v. Superior Court, 47 Cal.2d 447, 304 P.2d 1 (1956). Plaintiff, domiciled in California, brought an action to have it determined that defendant was his father. Defendant was not domiciled in California and was served with process outside the state. Plaintiff contended that the California courts had jurisdiction on the ground that the proceeding to establish paternity was a proceeding in rem by analogy to ex parte divorce proceedings. Held, (Traynor, J.) California has no judicial jurisdiction over the defendant. Plaintiff's action against the defendant is in personam. "Basically the difference [between this action and an ex parte divorce action] is between the state's power to insulate its domiciliary from a relationship with one not within its jurisdiction and its lack of power to reach out and fasten a relationship upon a person over whom it has no jurisdiction." Is the distinction sound?

SOSNA v. IOWA, 419 U.S. 393 (1975): In recent years, a frequently litigated question has been whether a state may constitutionally impose a durational residence requirement for obtaining a divorce. The cases were divided. In the principal case, the Supreme Court upheld the constitutionality of the Iowa one-year residence requirement. The suit was a class action on behalf of all Iowa residents who had resided in the state for less than one year but wished to institute divorce proceedings there. For the majority, Mr. Justice Rehnquist said:

> "The imposition of a durational residency requirement for divorce is scarcely unique to Iowa, since 48 States impose such a requirement as a condition for maintaining an action for divorce.[15]

15. Louisiana and Washington are the exceptions. La.Civ.Code, Art. 10A(7) (Supp.1974). But see Art. 10B providing that "if a spouse has established and maintained a residence in a parish of this state for a period of twelve months, there shall be a rebuttable presumption that he has a domicile in this state in the parish of such residence." Wash.Laws 1973, 1st Ex.Sess., c. 157. Among the other 48 States, the durational residency requirements are of many varieties, with some applicable to all divorce actions, others only when the respondent is not domiciled in the State, and still others applicable depending on where the grounds for divorce accrued. See the 50-State compilation issued by the National Legal Aid and Defenders Association, Divorce, Annulment and Separation in the United States (1973). [Some of the Court's footnotes have been omitted.]

As might be expected, the periods vary among the States and range from six weeks[16] to two years.[17] The one-year period selected by Iowa is the most common length of time prescribed.[18]

"Appellant contends that the Iowa requirement of one year's residence is unconstitutional for two separate reasons: first, because it establishes two classes of persons and discriminates against those who have recently exercised their right to travel to Iowa . . . and, second, because it denies a litigant the opportunity to make an individualized showing of bona fide residence and therefore denies such residents access to the only method of legally dissolving their marriage. . . .

"Iowa's residency requirement may reasonably be justified on grounds other than purely budgetary considerations or administrative convenience. Cf. Kahn v. Shevin, 416 U.S. 351 (1974). . . . Both spouses are obviously interested in the proceedings, since it will affect their marital status and very likely their property rights. Where a married couple has minor children, a decree of divorce would usually include provisions for their custody and support. With consequences of such moment riding on a divorce decree issued by its courts, Iowa may insist that one seeking to initiate such a proceeding have the modicum of attachment to the State required here.

"Such a requirement additionally furthers the State's parallel interests in both avoiding officious intermeddling in matters in which another State has a paramount interest, and in minimizing the susceptibility of its own divorce decrees to collateral attack. A State such as Iowa may quite reasonably decide that it does not wish to become a divorce mill for unhappy spouses who have lived there as short a time as appellant had when she commenced her action in the state court after having long resided elsewhere. . . . Perhaps even more importantly, Iowa's interests extend beyond its borders and include the recognition of its divorce decrees by other States under the Full Faith and Credit Clause of the Constitution, Art. IV, § 1. . . . For that reason, the State asked to enter such a decree is entitled to insist that the putative divorce plaintiff satisfy something more than the bare minimum of constitutional requirements before a divorce may be granted. The State's decision to exact a one-year residency requirement as a matter of policy is therefore buttressed by a quite permissible inference that this requirement not only effectuate[s] state substantive policy but likewise provides a greater safeguard against

16. See, e.g., Idaho Code § 32-701 (1963); Nev.Rev.Stat. § 125.020 (1973).

17. See, e.g., R.I.Gen.Laws Ann. § 15-2-2 (1970); Mass.Gen.Laws Ann., c. 208, §§ 4-5 (Supp.1974).

18. More than a majority of the States impose a one-year residency requirement of some kind. Divorce, Annulment and Separation in the United States, supra, n. 15.

successful collateral attack than would a requirement of bona fide residence alone.[21] . . ."

In his dissenting opinion, MR. JUSTICE MARSHALL said:

"The Court omits altogether what should be the first inquiry: whether the right to obtain a divorce is of sufficient importance that its denial to recent immigrants constitutes a penalty on interstate travel. In my view, it clearly meets that standard. . . .

"Having determined that the interest in obtaining a divorce is of substantial social importance, I would scrutinize Iowa's durational residency requirement to determine whether it constitutes a reasonable means of furthering important interests asserted by the State. The Court, however, has not only declined to apply the 'compelling interest' test to this case, it has conjured up possible justifications for the State's restriction in a manner much more akin to the lenient standard we have in the past applied in analyzing equal protection challenges to business regulations. . . . I continue to be of the view that the 'rational basis' test has no place in equal protection analysis when important individual interests with constitutional implications are at stake . . . .

". . . Certainly the stakes in a divorce are weighty both for the individuals directly involved in the adjudication and for others immediately affected by it. The critical importance of the divorce process, however, weakens the argument for a long residence requirement rather than strengthening it. The impact of the divorce decree only underscores the necessity that the State's regulation be evenhanded.

"It is not enough to recite the State's traditionally exclusive responsibility for regulating family law matters; some tangible interference with the State's regulatory scheme must be shown. Yet in this case, I fail to see how any legitimate objective of Iowa's divorce regulations would be frustrated by granting equal access to new state residents. . . .

". . . Iowa has a legitimate interest in protecting itself against invasion by those seeking quick divorces in a forum with relatively lax divorce laws, and it may have some interest in avoiding collateral attacks on its decree in other States. These interests, however, would adequately be protected by a simple require-

21. Since the majority of States require residence for at least a year, see n. 18, supra, it is reasonable to assume that Iowa's one-year "floor" makes its decrees less susceptible to successful collateral attack in other States. As the Court of Appeals for the Fifth Circuit observed in upholding a six-month durational residency requirement imposed by Florida, an objective test may impart to a State's divorce decrees "a verity that tends to safeguard them against the suspicious eyes of other states' prosecutorial authorities, the suspicions of private counsel in other states, and the post-decree dissatisfactions of parties to the divorce who wish a second bite. Such a reputation for validity of divorce decrees is not, then, merely cosmetic."

Makres v. Askew, 500 F.2d 577, 579 (CA5 1974), aff'g 359 F.Supp. 1225 (M.D. Fla.1973).

ment of domicile—physical presence plus intent to remain—which would remove the rigid one-year barrier while permitting the State to restrict the availability of its divorce process to citizens who are genuinely its own.[6] . . . If, as the majority assumes, Iowa is interested in assuring itself that its divorce petitioners are legitimately Iowa citizens, requiring petitioners to provide convincing evidence of bona fide domicile should be more than adequate to the task.[9]"

B. EXTRATERRITORIAL RECOGNITION

Three different situations should be distinguished at the outset. In the first the divorce is handed down in a state where both spouses are domiciled. In the second the divorce state is the domicile of only one spouse, and in the third this state is the domicile of neither spouse.

Prior to the Williams decisions, the situation which gave rise to most litigation was the second one, in which a divorce had been rendered in State F–1 where one spouse was domiciled, and its effect was questioned in State F–2. Many states recognized such a divorce under their rules of conflict of laws. But some states refused to do so except as compelled by the full faith and credit requirement.

The two leading decisions on full faith and credit were Atherton v. Atherton, 181 U.S. 155 (1901) and Haddock v. Haddock, 201 U.S. 562 (1906). Both involved the second situation. In the Atherton case, a divorce granted to the husband in the state of matrimonial domicile was held entitled to full faith and credit and thus to constitute a bar to an action for separation brought by the wife in a second state.

---

6. The availability of a less restrictive alternative such as a domicile requirement weighs heavily in testing a challenged state regulation against the "compelling interest" standard. See Shapiro v. Thompson, 394 U.S., at 638; Dunn v. Blumstein, 405 U.S., at 342, 350–352; Memorial Hospital v. Maricopa County, 415 U.S., at 267; Shelton v. Tucker, 364 U.S. 479, 488 (1960). Since the Iowa courts have in effect interpreted the residence statute to require proof of domicile as well as one year's residence, see Korsrud v. Korsrud, 242 Iowa 178, 45 N.W.2d 848 (1951); Julson v. Julson, 255 Iowa 301, 122 N.W.2d 329 (1963), a shift to a "pure" domicile test would impose no new burden on the State's fact-finding process.

9. The majority argues that since most States require a year's residence for divorce, Iowa gains refuge from the risk of collateral attack in the understanding solicitude of States with similar laws. Of course, absent unusual circumstances, a judgment by this Court striking down the Iowa statute would similarly affect the other states with one- and two-year residency requirements. For the same reason, the risk of subjecting Iowa to an invasion of divorce-seekers seems minimal. If long residency requirements are held unconstitutional, Iowa will not stand conspicuously alone without a residency requirement "defense." Moreover, its 90-day conciliation period, required of all divorce petitioners in the State, would still serve to discourage peripatetic divorce-seekers who are looking for the quickest possible adjudication.

But in the Haddock case a divorce granted to the husband in a state where he was then domiciled, but which was not the state of matrimonial domicile, was denied constitutional protection in the second state where the wife brought a suit for separation and alimony. In neither case did State F-1 have personal jurisdiction over the respondent. These decisions led to the belief that a divorce at the domicile of one spouse was not entitled to full faith and credit, unless there was some additional strengthening factor, e.g., that F-1 was the matrimonial domicile or had personal jurisdiction over the respondent. Some of the earlier doctrine and the uncertainty are reflected in the opinions from the two Williams decisions which follow.

NOTE

For a brief and useful discussion of many of the problems dealt with in this Subsection, see Leflar, Conflict of Laws and Family Law, 14 Ark.L.Rev. 47 (1960).

WILLIAMS v. NORTH CAROLINA

Supreme Court of the United States, 1942.
317 U.S. 287, 63 S.Ct. 207, 87 L.Ed. 279, 143 A.L.R. 1273.

Certiorari to the Supreme Court of North Carolina.

MR. JUSTICE DOUGLAS delivered the opinion of the Court.

Petitioners were tried and convicted of bigamous cohabitation under § 4342 of the North Carolina Code, 1939, and each was sentenced for a term of years to a state prison. The judgment of conviction was affirmed by the Supreme Court of North Carolina. 220 N.C. 445, 17 S.E.2d 769. The case is here on certiorari.

Petitioner Williams was married to Carrie Wyke in 1916 in North Carolina and lived with her there until May, 1940. Petitioner Hendrix was married to Thomas Hendrix in 1920 in North Carolina and lived with him there until May, 1940. At that time petitioners went to Las Vegas, Nevada, and on June 26, 1940, each filed a divorce action in the Nevada court. The defendants in those divorce actions entered no appearance nor were they served with process in Nevada. In the case of defendant Thomas Hendrix, service by publication was had by publication of the summons in a Las Vegas newspaper and by mailing a copy of the summons and complaint to his last post-office address. In the case of defendant Carrie Williams, a North Carolina sheriff delivered to her in North Carolina a copy of the summons and complaint. A decree of divorce was granted petitioner Williams by the Nevada court on August 26, 1940, . . . the court finding that "the plaintiff has been and now is a *bona fide* and continuous resident of the County of Clark, State of Nevada, and had been such resident for more than six weeks immediately preceding the commencement of this action in the manner prescribed by law." The Ne-

vada court granted petitioner Hendrix a divorce on October 4, 1940
. . . and made the same finding as to this petitioner's *bona fide*
residence in Nevada as it made in the case of Williams. Petitioners
were married to each other in Nevada on October 4, 1940. Thereafter they returned to North Carolina where they lived together until
the indictment was returned. . . . The Supreme Court of North
Carolina in affirming the judgment held that North Carolina was not
required to recognize the Nevada decrees under the full faith and
credit clause of the Constitution (Art. IV, § 1) by reason of Haddock
v. Haddock, 201 U.S. 562. The intimation in the majority opinion (220
N.C. pp. 460–464) that the Nevada divorces were collusive suggests
that the second theory on which the State tried the case may have
been an alternative ground for the decision below, adequate to sustain the judgment under the rule of Bell v. Bell, 181 U.S. 175—a case
in which this Court held that a decree of divorce was not entitled to
full faith and credit when it had been granted on constructive service
by the courts of a state in which neither spouse was domiciled. But
. . . North Carolina does not seek to sustain the judgment below
on that ground. Moreover it admits that there probably is enough
evidence in the record to require that petitioners be considered "to
have been actually domiciled in Nevada. . . ." Accordingly, we
cannot avoid meeting the Haddock v. Haddock issue in this case
. . . on the easy assumption that petitioners' domicil in Nevada
was a sham and a fraud. Rather, we must treat the present case for
the purpose of the limited issue before us precisely the same as if
petitioners had resided in Nevada for a term of years and had long
ago acquired a permanent abode there. . . .

The Haddock case involved a suit for separation and alimony,
brought in New York by the wife on personal service of the husband.
The husband pleaded in defense a divorce decree obtained by him in
Connecticut where he had established a separate domicil. This Court
held that New York, the matrimonial domicil where the wife still resided, need not give full faith and credit to the Connecticut decree,
since it was obtained by the husband who wrongfully left his wife in
the matrimonial domicil, service on her having been obtained by publication and she not having entered an appearance in the action. But
we do not agree with the theory of the Haddock case that so far as
the marital status of the parties is concerned, a decree of divorce
granted under such circumstances by one state need not be given full
faith and credit in another. . . .

Moreover, Haddock v. Haddock is not based on the . . . theory . . . that a decree of divorce granted by the courts of one
state need not be given full faith and credit in another if the grounds
for the divorce would not be recognized by the courts of the forum.
It does not purport to challenge or disturb the rule, earlier established by Christmas v. Russell [5 Wall. 290], and subsequently fortified by Fauntleroy v. Lum [210 U.S. 230] that, even though the cause
of action could not have been entertained in the state of the forum, a

judgment obtained thereon in a sister state is entitled to full faith and credit. For the majority opinion in the Haddock case accepted both Cheever v. Wilson, 9 Wall. 108, and Atherton v. Atherton, 181 U.S. 155. Cheever v. Wilson held that a decree of divorce granted by a state in which one spouse was domiciled and which had personal jurisdiction over the other was as conclusive in other states as it was in the state where it was obtained. Atherton v. Atherton held that full faith and credit must be given a decree of divorce granted by the state of the matrimonial domicil on constructive service against the other spouse who was a non-resident of that state. The decisive difference between those cases and Haddock v. Haddock was said to be that, in the latter, the state granting the divorce had no jurisdiction over the absent spouse, since it was not the state of the matrimonial domicil, but the place where the husband had acquired a separate domicil after having wrongfully left his wife. . . . But such differences in result between Haddock v. Haddock and the cases which preceded it rest on distinctions which in our view are immaterial, so far as the full faith and credit clause and the supporting legislation are concerned.

The historical view that a proceeding for a divorce was a proceeding *in rem* (2 Bishop, Marriage & Divorce, 4th ed., § 164) was rejected by the Haddock case. We likewise agree that it does not aid in the solution of the problem presented by this case to label these proceedings as proceedings *in rem*. Such a suit, however, is not a mere *in personam* action. Domicil of the plaintiff, immaterial to jurisdiction in a personal action, is recognized in the Haddock case and elsewhere (Beale, Conflict of Laws, § 110.1) as essential in order to give the court jurisdiction which will entitle the divorce decree to extraterritorial effect, at least when the defendant has neither been personally served nor entered an appearance. The findings made in the divorce decrees in the instant case must be treated on the issue before us as meeting those requirements. For it seems clear that the provision of the Nevada statute that a plaintiff in this type of case must "reside" in the State for the required period requires him to have a domicil, as distinguished from a mere residence, in the state. . . . Hence, the decrees in this case, like other divorce decrees, are more than *in personam* judgments. They involve the marital status of the parties. Domicil creates a relationship to the state which is adequate for numerous exercises of state power. . . . Each state as a sovereign has a rightful and legitimate concern in the marital status of persons domiciled within its borders. The marriage relation creates problems of large social importance. Protection of offspring, property interests, and the enforcement of marital responsibilities are but a few of commanding problems in the field of domestic relations with which the state must deal. Thus it is plain that each state, by virtue of its command over its domiciliaries and its large interest in the institution of marriage, can alter within its own borders the marriage status of the spouse domiciled there, even though the other spouse is

absent. There is no constitutional barrier if the form and nature of
the substituted service . . . meet the requirements of due process. . . .

. . . if one is lawfully divorced and remarried in Nevada and
still married to the first spouse in North Carolina, [a] . . . complicated and serious condition would be realized. . . . Under the circumstances of this case, a man would have two wives, a wife two
husbands. The reality of a sentence to prison proves that that is no
mere play on words. Each would be a bigamist for living in one state
with the only one with whom the other state would permit him lawfully to live. Children of the second marriage would be bastards in
one state but legitimate in the other. And all that would flow from
the legalistic notion that where one spouse is wrongfully deserted he
retains power over the matrimonial domicil so that the domicil of the
other spouse follows him wherever he may go, while, if he is to
blame, he retains no such power. But such considerations are inapposite. As stated by Mr. Justice Holmes in his dissent in the Haddock case (201 U.S. p. 630), they constitute a "pure fiction, and fiction
always is a poor ground for changing substantial rights." Furthermore, the fault or wrong of one spouse in leaving the other becomes
under that view a jurisdictional fact on which this Court would ultimately have to pass. Whatever may be said as to the practical effect
which such a rule would have in clouding divorce decrees, the question as to where the fault lies has no relevancy to the existence of
state power in such circumstances. See Bingham, In the Matter of
Haddock v. Haddock, 21 Corn.L.Q. 393, 426. The existence of the
power of a state to alter the marital status of its domiciliaries, as
distinguished from the wisdom of its exercise, is not dependent on the
underlying causes of the domestic rift. . . . Moreover, so far as
state power is concerned, no distinction between a matrimonial domicil and a domicil later acquired has been suggested or is apparent.
. . . It is one thing to say as a matter of state law that jurisdiction
to grant a divorce from an absent spouse should depend on whether
by consent or by conduct the latter has subjected his interest in the
marriage status to the law of the separate domicil acquired by the
other spouse. . . . But where a state adopts, as it has the power
to do, a less strict rule, it is quite another thing to say that its decrees
affecting the marital status of its domiciliaries are not entitled to full
faith and credit in sister states. Certainly if decrees of a state altering the marital status of its domiciliaries are not valid throughout the
Union even though the requirements of procedural due process are
wholly met, a rule would be fostered which could not help but bring
"considerable disaster to innocent persons" and "bastardize children
hitherto supposed to be the offspring of lawful marriage" (Mr. Justice Holmes dissenting in Haddock v. Haddock, supra, p. 628), or else
encourage collusive divorces. Beale, Constitutional Protection of Decrees for Divorce, 19 Harv.L.Rev. 586, 596. These intensely practical
considerations emphasize for us the essential function of the full

faith and credit clause in substituting a command for the former principles of comity [Broderick v. Rosner, 294 U.S. 629 at p. 643] and in altering the "status of the several states as independent foreign sovereignties" by making them "integral parts of a single nation." Milwaukee County v. White Co. [296 U.S. 268 at p. 277].

It is objected, however, that if such divorce decrees must be given full faith and credit, a substantial dilution of the sovereignty of other states will be effected. For it is pointed out that under such a rule one state's policy of strict control over the institution of marriage could be thwarted by the decree of a more lax state. But such an objection goes to the application of the full faith and credit clause to many situations. It is an objection in varying degrees of intensity to the enforcement of a judgment of a sister state based on a cause of action which could not be enforced in the state of the forum. Mississippi's policy against gambling transactions was overridden in Fauntleroy v. Lum [210 U.S. 230], when a Missouri judgment based on such a Mississippi contract was enforced by this Court. Such is part of the price of our federal system.

This Court, of course, is the final arbiter when the question is raised as to what is a permissible limitation on the full faith and credit clause. . . . But the question . . . as to what is a permissible limitation on the full faith and credit clause does not involve a decision on our part as to which state policy on divorce is the most desirable one. . . . It is a Constitution which we are expounding—a Constitution which in no small measure brings separate sovereign states into an integrated whole through the medium of the full faith and credit clause. Within the limits of her political power North Carolina may, of course, enforce her own policy regarding the marriage relation—an institution more basic in our civilization than any other. But society also has an interest in the avoidance of polygamous marriages . . . and in the protection of innocent offspring of marriages deemed legitimate in other jurisdictions. And other states have an equally legitimate concern in the status of persons domiciled there as respects the institution of marriage. So, when a court of one state acting in accord with the requirements of procedural due process alters the marital status of one domiciled in that state by granting him a divorce from his absent spouse, we cannot say its decree should be excepted from the full faith and credit clause merely because its enforcement or recognition in another state would conflict with the policy of the latter. . . .

Haddock v. Haddock is overruled. The judgment is reversed and the cause is remanded to the Supreme Court of North Carolina for proceedings not inconsistent with this opinion.

Reversed.

Mr. Justice Frankfurter concurred in a separate opinion and Mr. Justice Murphy and Mr. Justice Jackson dissented in separate opinions.

NOTE

Was attention given in the principal case to the value of fairness to the defendant that was stressed so heavily in International Shoe Co. v. State of Washington, p. 66, supra?

Was the application in the principal case of Nevada law to determine the plaintiff spouse's right to a divorce consistent with the rule of Home Insurance Co. v. Dick, p. 329, supra?

WILLIAMS v. NORTH CAROLINA

Supreme Court of the United States, 1945.
325 U.S. 226, 65 S.Ct. 1092, 89 L.Ed. 1577, 157 A.L.R. 1366.

Certiorari to the Supreme Court of North Carolina.

MR. JUSTICE FRANKFURTER delivered the opinion of the Court.

This case is here to review judgments of the Supreme Court of North Carolina, affirming convictions for bigamous cohabitation, assailed on the ground that full faith and credit, as required by the Constitution of the United States, was not accorded divorces decreed by one of the courts of Nevada. Williams v. North Carolina, 317 U.S. 287, decided an earlier aspect of the controversy. . . . The record then before us did not present the question whether North Carolina had the power "to refuse full faith and credit to Nevada divorce decrees because, contrary to the findings of the Nevada court, North Carolina finds that no *bona fide* domicil was acquired in Nevada." Williams v. North Carolina, supra, at 302. This is the precise issue which has emerged after retrial of the cause following our reversal. Its obvious importance brought the case here. 322 U.S. 725.

. . .

Under our system of law, judicial power to grant a divorce—jurisdiction, strictly speaking—is founded on domicil. Bell v. Bell, 181 U.S. 175; Andrews v. Andrews, 188 U.S. 14. The framers of the Constitution were familiar with this jurisdictional prerequisite, and since 1789, neither this Court nor any other court in the English-speaking world has questioned it. Domicil implies a nexus between person and place of such permanence as to control the creation of legal relations and responsibilities of the utmost significance. The domicil of one spouse within a State gives power to that State, we have held, to dissolve a marriage wheresoever contracted. . . . Williams v. North Carolina, supra . . .

It is one thing to reopen an issue that has been settled after appropriate opportunity to present their contentions has been afforded to all who had an interest in its adjudication. This applies also to jurisdictional questions. After a contest these cannot be relitigated as between the parties. . . . But those not parties to a litigation ought not to be foreclosed by the interested actions of others; especially not a State which is concerned with the vindication of its own social policy and has no means, certainly no effective means, to protect that interest against the selfish action of those outside its borders. The State of domiciliary origin should not be bound by an unfounded, even if not collusive, recital in the record of a court of another State. As to the truth or existence of a fact, like that of domicil, upon which depends the power to exert judicial authority, a State not a party to the exertion of such judicial authority in another State but seriously affected by it has a right, when asserting its own unquestioned authority, to ascertain the truth or existence of that crucial fact.

These considerations of policy are equally applicable whether power was assumed by the court of the first State or claimed after inquiry. This may lead, no doubt, to conflicting determinations of what judicial power is founded upon. Such conflict is inherent in the practical application of the concept of domicil in the context of our federal system. . . . What was said in Worcester County Trust Co. v. Riley . . . is pertinent here. "Neither the Fourteenth Amendment nor the full faith and credit clause requires uniformity in the decisions of the courts of different states as to the place of domicil, where the exertion of state power is dependent upon domicil within its boundaries." 302 U.S. 292, 299. If a finding by the court of one State that domicil in another State has been abandoned were conclusive upon the old domiciliary State, the policy of each State in matters of most intimate concern could be subverted by the policy of every other State. . . .

Although it is now settled that a suit for divorce is not an ordinary adversary proceeding, it does not promote analysis, as was recently pointed out, to label divorce proceedings as actions *in rem*. Williams v. North Carolina, supra, at 297. But insofar as a divorce decree partakes of some of the characteristics of a decree *in rem*, it is misleading to say that all the world is party to a proceeding *in rem*. . . . All the world is not party to a divorce proceeding. What is true is that all the world need not be present before a court granting the decree and yet it must be respected by the other . . . States provided—and it is a big proviso—the conditions for the exercise of power by the divorce-decreeing court are validly established whenever that judgment is elsewhere called into question. In short, the decree of divorce is a conclusive adjudication of everything except the jurisdictional facts upon which it is founded, and domicil is a jurisdictional fact. To permit the necessary finding of domicil by one State to foreclose all States in the protection of their social institutions would be intolerable.

But to endow each State with controlling authority to nullify the power of a sister State to grant a divorce based upon a finding that one spouse had acquired a new domicil within the divorcing State would, in the proper functioning of our federal system, be equally indefensible. . . . The necessary accommodation between the right of one State to safeguard its interest in the family relation of its own people and the power of another State to grant divorces can be left to neither State.

The problem is to reconcile the reciprocal respect to be accorded by the members of the Union to their adjudications with due regard for another most important aspect of our federalism whereby "the domestic relations of husband and wife . . . were matters reserved to the States," Popovici v. Agler, 280 U.S. 379, 383–84 . . . The rights that belong to all the States and the obligations which membership in the Union imposes upon all, are made effective because this Court is open to consider claims . . . that the courts of one State have not given the full faith and credit of a sister State that is required by Art. IV, § 1 of the Constitution.

But the discharge of this duty does not make of this Court a court of probate and divorce. Neither a rational system of law nor hard practicality calls for our independent determination, in reviewing the judgment of a State court, of that rather elusive relation between person and place which establishes domicil. . . . The challenged judgment must, however, satisfy our scrutiny that the reciprocal duty of respect owed by the States to one another's adjudications has been fairly discharged, and has not been evaded under the guise of finding an absence of domicil and therefore a want of power in the court rendering the judgment.

What is immediately before us is the judgment of the Supreme Court of North Carolina. We have authority to upset it only if there is want of foundation for the conclusion that that Court reached. The conclusion it reached turns on its findings that the spouses who obtained the Nevada decrees were not domiciled there. The fact that the Nevada court found that they were domiciled there is entitled to respect, and more. The burden of undermining the verity which the Nevada decrees import rests heavily upon the assailant. But simply because the Nevada court found that it had power to award a divorce decree cannot, we have seen, foreclose reexamination by another State. . . . If this Court finds that proper weight was accorded to the claims of power by the court of one State in rendering a judgment the validity of which is pleaded in defense in another State, that the burden of overcoming such respect by disproof of the substratum of fact—here domicil—on which such power alone can rest was properly charged against the party challenging the legitimacy of the judgment, that such issue of fact was left for fair determination by appropriate procedure, and that a finding adverse to the necessary foundation for any valid sister-State judgment was amply supported in evidence, we cannot upset the judgment before us. And we cannot do so even if we also found in the record of the court of original judgment warrant for its finding that it had jurisdiction. If it is a matter turning on local law, great deference is owed by the courts of one State to what a court of another State has done. . . . But when we are dealing as here with an historic notion common to all English-speaking courts, that of domicil, we should not find a want of deference to a sister State on the part of a court of another State which finds an absence of domicil where such a conclusion is warranted by the record. . . .

. . . The trial judge charged that the State had the burden of proving beyond a reasonable doubt that (1) each petitioner was lawfully married to one person; (2) thereafter each petitioner contracted a second marriage with another person outside North Carolina; (3) the spouses of petitioners were living at the time of this second marriage; (4) petitioners cohabited with one another in North Carolina after the second marriage. The burden, it was charged, then devolved upon petitioners "to satisfy the trial jury, not beyond a reasonable doubt nor by the greater weight of the evidence, but simply to satisfy" the jury from all the evidence, that petitioners were domiciled in Nevada at the time they obtained their divorces. The court further charged that "the recitation" of *bona fide* domicil in the Nevada decree was "prima facie evidence" sufficient to warrant a finding of domicil in Nevada but not compelling "such an inference." If the jury found . . . that petitioners had been domiciled in North Carolina and went to Nevada "simply and solely for the purpose of obtaining divorces, intending to return to North Carolina on obtaining" them, they never lost their North Carolina domicils nor acquired new domicils in Nevada. . . .

The scales of justice must not be unfairly weighted by a State when full faith and credit is claimed for a sister-State judgment. But North Carolina has not so dealt with the Nevada decrees. She has not raised unfair barriers to their recognition. North Carolina did not fail in appreciation or application of federal standards of full faith and credit. Appropriate weight was given to the finding of domicil in the Nevada decrees, and that finding was allowed to be overturned only by relevant standards of proof. There is nothing to suggest that the issue was not fairly submitted to the jury and that it was not fairly assessed on cogent evidence. . . .

We conclude that North Carolina was not required to yield her State policy because a Nevada court found that petitioners were domiciled in Nevada when it granted them decrees of divorce. North Carolina was entitled to find, as she did, that they did not acquire domicils in Nevada and that the Nevada court was therefore without power to liberate the petitioners from amenability to the laws of North Carolina governing domestic relations. And, as was said in connection with another aspect of the Full Faith and Credit Clause, our conclusion "is not a matter to arouse the susceptibilities of the States, all of which are equally concerned in the question and equally on both sides." Fauntleroy v. Lum, 210 U.S. 230, 238.

Affirmed.

[MR. JUSTICE MURPHY wrote a concurring opinion, joined in by MR. CHIEF JUSTICE STONE and MR. JUSTICE JACKSON, which reemphasizes the jurisdictional fact rationale of the majority opinion.

MR. JUSTICE RUTLEDGE wrote a dissenting opinion questioning the entire domiciliary concept, reasoning that "jurisdictional fact" has been used to cloak "unitary domicil" so that divorce is back to the era of Haddock with respect to effects.

MR. JUSTICE BLACK wrote a dissenting opinion, joined in by MR. JUSTICE DOUGLAS, which reasons that civil liberties are endangered when a criminal offense is grounded on refusal to recognize what another state has apparently regarded as sufficient domicil, and on the further reasoning that the Constitution does not "measure the power of state courts to pass upon petitions for divorce".]

NOTES

(1) What law should the F–2 court apply in determining whether the plaintiff spouse acquired a bona fide domicile in F–1? Specifically, is it Supreme Court law, F–1 law or that of F–2? In note 7, on page 231 of the opinion in Williams II, it is said: "Since an appeal to the Full Faith and Credit Clause raises questions arising under the Constitution of the United States, the proper criteria for ascertaining domicil, should these be in dispute, become matters for federal determination. . . ." See Rice v. Rice, 336 U.S. 674 (1949), where the Supreme Court sustained the finding of a Connecticut court that a Nevada divorce was not supported by a bona fide domicile. This case is commented upon in Freund, Rice v. Rice—A Comment, 23 Conn.Bar J. 182 (1949); Rheinstein, Domicile as Jurisdictional Basis of Divorce Decrees, 23 Conn.Bar J. 280 (1949).

(2) A helpful article on the problems presented by the Williams cases is D. Currie, Suitcase Divorce in the Conflict of Laws, 34 U.Chi.L.Rev. 26 (1967).

(3) For a discussion of professional ethics problems which may arise in connection with matrimonial litigation, see Adams and Adams, Ethical Problems in Advising Migratory Divorce, 16 Hastings L.J. 60 (1964); Drinker, Problems of Professional Ethics in Matrimonial Litigation, 66 Harv.L.Rev. 443 (1953); Drinker, Legal Ethics 80, 122–128 (1953).

(4) For a study of the effect given U.S. divorces in foreign countries, see Wiesner, Recognition of American Divorce Decrees in France, Spain and Latin America, 2 Comp.Judicial Rev. 143 (1965).

C.   EXTRATERRITORIAL RECOGNITION: LIMITS ON ATTACK FOR JURISDICTIONAL DEFECTS

DAVIS V. DAVIS, 305 U.S. 32 (1938): Husband, alleging he was a Virginia domiciliary, instituted divorce action there. Wife was served personally in the District of Columbia, her domicile, and appeared in the Virginia action to contest husband's allegations as to his domicile. The court found that husband was domiciled in Virginia and granted the divorce. Husband thereafter brought suit in the District of Columbia to have a prior separation decree modified as a result of the Virginia divorce. The District of Columbia court refused to recognize the Virginia divorce on the grounds of lack of jurisdiction. Held, reversed. Both parties having appeared, and the domicile question having been fully argued, the Virginia decision is res judicata.

SHERRER v. SHERRER

Supreme Court of the United States, 1948.
334 U.S. 343, 68 S.Ct. 1087, 92 L.Ed. 1429, 1 A.L.R.2d 1355.

Certiorari to the Probate Court for Berkshire County, Massachusetts.

Mr. Chief Justice Vinson delivered the opinion of the Court.

We granted certiorari in this case and in Coe v. Coe . . . to consider the contention of petitioners that Massachusetts has failed to accord full faith and credit to decrees of divorce rendered by courts of sister States.

Petitioner Margaret E. Sherrer and the respondent, Edward C. Sherrer, were married in New Jersey in 1930, and from 1932 until April 3, 1944, lived together in Monterey, Massachusetts. Following a long period of marital discord, petitioner, accompanied by the two children of the marriage, left Massachusetts on the latter date, ostensibly for the purpose of spending a vacation in the State of Florida. Shortly after her arrival in Florida, however, petitioner informed her husband that she did not intend to return to him. . . .

On July 6, 1944, a bill of complaint for divorce was filed at petitioner's direction in the Circuit Court of the Sixth Judicial Circuit of the State of Florida. The bill alleged extreme cruelty as grounds for divorce and also alleged that petitioner was a "bona fide legal resident of the State of Florida." The respondent received notice by mail of the pendency of the divorce proceedings. He retained Florida counsel who entered a general appearance and filed an answer denying the allegations of petitioner's complaint, including the allegation as to petitioner's Florida residence.

On November 14, 1944, hearings were held in the divorce proceedings. Respondent appeared personally to testify with respect to a stipulation entered into by the parties relating to the custody of the children. Throughout the entire proceedings respondent was represented by counsel. Petitioner introduced evidence to establish her

Florida residence and testified generally to the allegations of her complaint. Counsel for respondent failed to cross-examine or to introduce evidence in rebuttal.

The Florida court on November 29, 1944, entered a decree of divorce after specifically finding that petitioner "is a bona fide resident of the State of Florida, and that this court has jurisdiction of the parties and the subject matter in said cause . . ." Respondent failed to challenge the decree by appeal to the Florida Supreme Court.

On December 1, 1944, petitioner was married in Florida to one Henry A. Phelps, whom petitioner had known while both were residing in Massachusetts and who had come to Florida shortly after petitioner's arrival in that State. Phelps and petitioner lived together as husband and wife in Florida, where they were both employed, until February 5, 1945, when they returned to Massachusetts.

In June, 1945, respondent instituted an action in the Probate Court of Berkshire County, Massachusetts, which has given rise to the issues of this case. Respondent alleged that he is the lawful husband of petitioner, that the Florida decree of divorce is invalid, and that petitioner's subsequent marriage is void. Respondent prayed that he might be permitted to convey his real estate as if he were sole and that the court declare that he was living apart from his wife for justifiable cause. Petitioner joined issue on respondent's allegations.

In the proceedings which followed, petitioner gave testimony in defense of the validity of the Florida divorce decree. The Probate Court, however, resolved the issues of fact adversely to petitioner's contentions, found that she was never domiciled in Florida, and granted respondent the relief he had requested. The Supreme Judicial Court of Massachusetts affirmed the decree on the grounds that it was supported by the evidence and that the requirements of full faith and credit did not preclude the Massachusetts courts from reexamining the finding of domicile made by the Florida court.

At the outset, it should be observed that the proceedings in the Florida court prior to the entry of the decree of divorce were in no way inconsistent with the requirements of procedural due process. We do not understand respondent to urge the contrary. The respondent personally appeared in the Florida proceedings. Through his attorney he filed pleadings denying the substantial allegations of petitioner's complaint. It is not suggested that his rights to introduce evidence and otherwise to conduct his defense were in any degree impaired; nor is it suggested that there was not available to him the right to seek review of the decree by appeal to the Florida Supreme Court. It is clear that respondent was afforded his day in court with respect to every issue involved in the litigation, including the jurisdictional issue of petitioner's domicile. Under such circumstances, there is nothing in the concept of due process which demands that a defendant be afforded a second opportunity to litigate the existence of jurisdictional facts. . . .

It should also be observed that there has been no suggestion that under the law of Florida, the decree of divorce in question is in any respect invalid or could successfully be subjected to the type of attack permitted by the Massachusetts court. The implicit assumption underlying the position taken by respondent and the Massachusetts court is that this case involves a decree of divorce valid and final in the State which rendered it; and we so assume.

That the jurisdiction of the Florida court to enter a valid decree of divorce was dependent upon petitioner's domicile in that State is not disputed. This requirement was recognized by the Florida court which rendered the divorce decree, and the principle has been given frequent application in decisions of the State Supreme Court. But whether or not petitioner was domiciled in Florida at the time the divorce was granted was a matter to be resolved by judicial determination. Here, unlike the situation presented in Williams v. North Carolina, 325 U.S. 226 (1945), the finding of the requisite jurisdictional facts was made in proceedings in which the defendant appeared and participated. The question with which we are confronted, therefore, is whether such a finding made under the circumstances presented by this case may, consistent with the requirements of full faith and credit, be subjected to collateral attack in the courts of a sister State in a suit brought by the defendant in the original proceedings.

No

The question of what effect is to be given to an adjudication by a court that it possesses requisite jurisdiction in a case, where the judgment of that court is subsequently subjected to collateral attack on jurisdictional grounds has been given frequent consideration by this Court over a period of many years. Insofar as cases originating in the federal courts are concerned, the rule has evolved that the doctrine of *res judicata* applies to adjudications relating either to jurisdiction of the person or of the subject matter where such adjudications have been made in proceedings in which those questions were in issue and in which the parties were given full <u>opportunity</u> to litigate.
. . .

H.

We believe that the decision of this Court in the Davis case [p. 835, supra] and those in related situations are clearly indicative of the result to be reached here. Those cases stand for the proposition that the requirements of full faith and credit bar a defendant from collaterally attacking a divorce decree on jurisdictional grounds in the courts of a sister State where there has been participation by the defendant in the divorce proceedings, where the defendant has been accorded full opportunity to contest the jurisdictional issues, and where the decree is not susceptible to such collateral attack in the courts of the State which rendered the decree.

Applying these principles to this case, we hold that the Massachusetts courts erred in permitting the Florida divorce decree to be subjected to attack on the ground that petitioner was not domiciled in Florida at the time the decree was entered. . . .

It is urged further, however, that because we are dealing with litigation involving the dissolution of the marital relation, a different result is demanded from that which might properly be reached if this case were concerned with other types of litigation. It is pointed out that under the Constitution the regulation and control of marital and family relationships are reserved to the States. It is urged, and properly so, that the regulation of the incidents of the marital relation involves the exercise by the States of powers of the most vital importance. Finally, it is contended that a recognition of the importance to the States of such powers demands that the requirements of full faith and credit be viewed in such a light as to permit an attack upon a divorce decree granted by a court of a sister State under the circumstances of this case even where the attack is initiated in a suit brought by the defendant in the original proceedings.

But the recognition of the importance of a State's power to determine the incidents of basic social relationships into which its domiciliaries enter does not resolve the issues of this case. This is not a situation in which a State has merely sought to exert such power over a domiciliary. This is, rather, a case involving inconsistent assertions of power by courts of two States of the Federal Union and thus presents considerations which go beyond the interests of local policy, however vital. In resolving the issues here presented, we do not conceive it to be a part of our function to weigh the relative merits of the policies of Florida and Massachusetts with respect to divorce and related matters. Nor do we understand the decisions of this Court to support the proposition that the obligation imposed by Article IV, § 1 of the Constitution and the Act of Congress passed thereunder amounts to something less than the duty to accord *full* faith and credit to decrees of divorce entered by courts of sister States. The full faith and credit clause is one of the provisions incorporated into the Constitution by its framers for the purpose of transforming an aggregation of independent, sovereign States into a nation. If in its application local policy must at times be required to give way, such "is part of the price of our federal system." Williams v. North Carolina, 317 U.S. 287, 302 (1942).

This is not to say that in no case may an area be recognized in which reasonable accommodations of interest may properly be made. But as this Court has heretofore made clear, that area is of limited extent. We believe that in permitting an attack on the Florida divorce decree which again put in issue petitioner's Florida domicile and in refusing to recognize the validity of that decree, the Massachusetts courts have asserted a power which cannot be reconciled with the requirements of due faith and credit. We believe that assurances that such a power will be exercised sparingly and wisely render it no less repugnant to the constitutional commands.

It is one thing to recognize as permissible the judicial reexamination of findings of jurisdictional fact where such findings have been made by a court of a sister State which has entered a divorce decree in *ex parte* proceedings. It is quite another thing to hold that the vital rights and interests involved in divorce litigation may be held in suspense pending the scrutiny by courts of sister States of findings of jurisdictional fact made by a competent court in proceedings conducted in a manner consistent with the highest requirements of due process and in which the defendant has participated. We do not conceive it to be in accord with the purposes of the full faith and credit requirement to hold that a judgment rendered under the circumstances of this case may be required to run the gauntlet of such collateral attack in the courts of sister States before its validity outside of the State which rendered it is established or rejected. That vital interests are involved in divorce litigation indicates to us that it is a matter of greater rather than lesser importance that there should be a place to end such litigation. And where a decree of divorce is rendered by a competent court under the circumstances of this case, the obligation of full faith and credit requires that such litigation should end in the courts of the State in which the judgment was rendered.

Reversed.

MR. JUSTICE FRANKFURTER, with whom MR. JUSTICE MURPHY concurs, dissented. In the course of the dissenting opinion, he said (334 U.S. at 368) "A divorce may satisfy due process requirements, and be valid where rendered, and still lack the jurisdictional requisites for full faith and credit to be mandatory."

NOTES

(1) In Coe v. Coe, 334 U.S. 378 (1948), decided the same day as Sherrer v. Sherrer, H after residing for six weeks in Nevada sued W for divorce. W appeared personally and through her attorney filed an answer admitting H's residence in Nevada and a cross-complaint for divorce. The Nevada court found it had jurisdiction of the parties and subject matter and entered a decree granting W a divorce. H remarried and returned to Massachusetts where W brought proceedings against him under a decree for support rendered in Massachusetts before the Nevada divorce. The Massachusetts court disregarded the Nevada divorce as void for lack of jurisdiction. Held, that Massachusetts could not under the requirements of full faith and credit subject the Nevada decree to collateral attack by readjudicating the existence of jurisdictional facts. The dissent in Sherrer v. Sherrer also encompassed Coe v. Coe. For discussion of the Sherrer and Coe cases, see Carey and MacChesney, Divorces by the Consent of the Parties and Divisible Divorce Decrees, 43 Ill.L.Rev. 608 (1948); Paulsen, Migratory Divorce: Chapters III and IV, 24 Ind.L.J. 25 (1948).

(2) There are differences among the state courts as to whether the rule of the Sherrer case applies in a situation where the defendant enters an appearance through an attorney in the divorce proceedings but is not physically present and does not contest any issues. In Boxer v. Boxer, 12 Misc.2d 205, 177 N.Y.S.2d 85 (Sup.Ct.1958), affirmed without opinion 7 N.Y.2d 781, 163

N.E.2d 149 (1959), H obtained a divorce in Alabama after having been in that state only one day. W appeared through an Alabama attorney whom she had appointed by an instrument mailed from New York. The decree was held entitled to full faith and credit. A similar result was reached in Boudreaux v. Welch, 249 La. 983, 192 So.2d 356 (1966).

On the other hand a divorce has been held subject to collateral attack when the defendant spouse did not appear personally in the divorce proceedings and (a) was represented by an attorney employed and controlled by the plaintiff spouse (Pelle v. Pelle, 229 Md. 160, 182 A.2d 37 (1962); Staedler v. Staedler, 6 N.J. 380, 78 A.2d 896 (1951)) or (b) filed in the divorce proceedings an answer admitting that plaintiff spouse was domiciled in the divorce state. Donnell v. Howell, 257 N.C. 175, 125 S.E.2d 448 (1962). Can these decisions be reconciled with Johnson v. Muelberger, which appears immediately below, and Cook v. Cook, p. 842, infra?

(3) Day v. Day, 237 Md. 229, 205 A.2d 798 (1965). H and W were domiciled in Maryland. They separated and finally after much importuning W signed at H's request a document waiving notice of divorce proceeding and consenting to the submission of the cause for final decree. H then obtained an Alabama divorce after having been there one day. Thereafter, W in Maryland sought a declaratory judgment that the Alabama decree was invalid claiming that she signed the paper on the understanding that it would not be used in court. The trial court found for W on the ground that she had not consented to her husband's use of the document. On appeal, affirmed. The validity of a document of waiver or consent to an ex parte divorce is controlled by the law of the domicile of the married parties and the situs of its execution. The case is noted in 65 Colum.L.Rev. 924 (1965).

JOHNSON v. MUELBERGER

Supreme Court of the United States, 1951.
340 U.S. 581, 71 S.Ct. 474, 95 L.Ed. 552.

MR. JUSTICE REED delivered the opinion of the Court.

The right of a daughter to attack in New York the validity of her deceased father's Florida divorce is before us. She was his legatee. The divorce was granted in Florida after the father appeared there and contested the merits. The issue turns on the effect in New York under these circumstances of the Full Faith and Credit Clause of the Federal Constitution.

Eleanor Johnson Muelberger, respondent, is the child of decedent E. Bruce Johnson's first marriage. After the death of Johnson's first wife in 1939, he married one Madoline Ham, and they established their residence in New York. In August 1942, Madoline obtained a divorce from him in a Florida proceeding, although the undisputed facts as developed in the New York Surrogate's hearing show that she did not comply with the jurisdictional ninety-day residence requirement. The New York Surrogate found that

"In the Florida court, the decedent appeared by attorney and interposed an answer denying the wrongful acts but not questioning the allegations as to residence in Florida. The record discloses that testimony was taken by the Florida court and the divorce granted Madoline Johnson. Both parties had full opportunity to contest the jurisdictional issues in that court and the decree is not subject to attack on the ground that petitioner was not domiciled in Florida."

In 1944 Mr. Johnson entered into a marriage, his third, with petitioner, Genevieve Johnson, and in 1945 he died, leaving a will in which he gave his entire estate to his daughter, Eleanor. After probate of the will, the third wife filed notice of her election to take the statutory one-third share of the estate, under § 18 of the New York Decedent's Estate Law. This election was contested by respondent daughter, and a trial was had before the Surrogate, who determined that she could not attack the third wife's status as surviving spouse, on the basis of the alleged invalidity of Madoline's divorce, because the divorce proceeding had been a contested one, and "[s]ince the decree is valid and final in the State of Florida, it is not subject to collateral attack in the courts of this state."

The Appellate Division affirmed the Surrogate's decree *per curiam*, but the New York Court of Appeals reversed. 301 N.Y. 13, 92 N.E.2d 44. . . . The Court . . . held that the Florida judgment finding jurisdiction to decree the divorce bound only the parties themselves. This followed from their previous opportunity to contest the jurisdictional issue. As the court read the Florida cases to allow Eleanor to attack the decree collaterally in Florida, it decided she should be equally free to do so in New York. The Court of Appeals reached this decision after consideration of the Full Faith and Credit Clause. Because the case involves important issues in the adjustment of the domestic-relations laws of the several states, we granted certiorari, 340 U.S. 874.

. . . There is substantially no legislative history to explain the purpose and meaning of the [full faith and credit] clause and of the [implementing] statute. From judicial experience with and interpretation of the clause, there has emerged the succinct conclusion that the Framers intended it to help weld the independent states into a nation by giving judgments within the jurisdiction of the rendering state the same faith and credit in sister states as they have in the state of the original forum. The faith and credit given is not to be niggardly but generous, full. . . .

This constitutional purpose promotes unification, not centralization. It leaves each state with power over its own courts but binds litigants, wherever they may be in the Nation, by prior orders of other courts with jurisdiction. . . .

[At this point, the Court discussed the Davis, Williams, Sherrer and Coe cases.]

It is clear from the foregoing that, under our decisions, a state by virtue of the clause must give full faith and credit to an out-of-state divorce by barring either party to that divorce who has been personally served or who has entered a personal appearance from collaterally attacking the decree. Such an attack is barred where the party attacking would not be permitted to make a collateral attack in the courts of the granting state. This rule the Court of Appeals recognized. 301 N.Y. 13, 17, 92 N.E.2d 44. It determined, however, that a "stranger to the divorce action," as the daughter was held to be in New York, may collaterally attack her father's Florida divorce in New York if she could have attacked it in Florida.

No Florida case has come to our attention holding that a child may contest in Florida its parent's divorce where the parent was barred from contesting, as here, by *res judicata*. . . . If the laws of Florida should be that a surviving child is in privity with its parent as to that parent's estate, surely the Florida doctrine of res judicata would apply to the child's collateral attack as it would to the father's. If, on the other hand, Florida holds . . . that the child of a former marriage is a stranger to the divorce proceedings, late opinions of Florida indicate that the child would not be permitted to attack the divorce, since the child had a mere expectancy at the time of the divorce. [At this point, the Court discussed certain Florida cases.]

We conclude that Florida would not permit Mrs. Muelberger to attack the Florida decree of divorce between her father and his second wife as beyond the jurisdiction of the rendering court. In that case New York cannot permit such an attack by reason of the Full Faith and Credit Clause. When a divorce cannot be attacked for lack of jurisdiction by parties actually before the court or strangers in the rendering state, it cannot be attacked by them anywhere in the Union. The Full Faith and Credit Clause forbids.

Reversed.

MR. JUSTICE FRANKFURTER dissents, substantially for the reasons given in the opinion of the New York Court of Appeals, 301 N.Y. 13, 92 N.E.2d 44, in light of the views expressed by him in Sherrer v. Sherrer and Coe v. Coe, 334 U.S. 343, 356.

MR. JUSTICE MINTON took no part in the consideration or decision of this case.

COOK v. COOK

Supreme Court of the United States, 1951.
342 U.S. 126, 72 S.Ct. 157, 96 L.Ed. 146.

[Shortly after he had gone through a marriage ceremony with W, H discovered that she was still the lawful wife of one Mann. H and W thereupon agreed to remarry after W had procured a Florida divorce from Mann. This course was followed, but after the remarriage marital difficulties developed and eventually H brought suit in Vermont to have the marriage annulled. This relief was granted by the Vermont courts on the ground that the divorce, and hence the remarriage, were void since W had never acquired a Florida domicile. The case was then taken on certiorari to the Supreme Court.]

MR. JUSTICE DOUGLAS delivered the opinion of the Court.

.   .   .

On this record we do not know what happened in the Florida divorce proceedings except that the Florida court entered a divorce decree in favor of petitioner and against Mann. So far as we know, Mann was a party to the proceedings. So far as we know, the issue of domicile was contested, litigated and resolved in petitioner's favor. If the defendant spouse appeared in the Florida proceedings and contested the issue of the wife's domicile, Sherrer v. Sherrer, 334 U.S. 343, or appeared and admitted her Florida domicile, Coe v. Coe, 334 U.S. 378, or was personally served in the divorce state, Johnson v. Muelberger, 340 U.S. 581, 587, he would be barred from attacking the decree collaterally; and so would a stranger to the Florida proceedings, such as respondent, unless Florida applies a less strict rule of *res judicata* to the second husband than it does to the first. See Johnson v. Muelberger, supra. On the other hand, if the defendant spouse had neither appeared nor been served in Florida, the Vermont court, under the ruling in Williams v. State of North Carolina, 325 U.S. 226, could reopen the issue of domicile.

.   .   .   The Vermont Supreme Court recognized that there were no findings on those issues in the present record. The Court in referring to the case of Williams v. State of North Carolina, 325 U.S. 226, said, "It was there held that the question of bona fide domicile was open to attack, notwithstanding the full faith and credit clause when the other spouse neither had appeared nor been served with process in the state. The findings here do not show either of these criteria." 116 Vt. 374, 378, 76 A.2d 593, 595. Yet it is essential that the court know what transpired in Florida before this collateral attack on the Florida decree can be resolved. For until Florida's jurisdiction is shown to be vulnerable, Vermont may not relitigate the issue of domicile on which the Florida decree rests. .   .   .

Reversed.

MR. JUSTICE FRANKFURTER dissented in a separate opinion.

NOTE

A Nevada statute bars all third-party attacks on Nevada divorce decrees that are binding on the parties to the action. Nev.Rev.Stat. § 125.185 (1967). Would this statute also have the effect of barring third-party attacks in sister states?

KRAUSE v. KRAUSE

Court of Appeals of New York, 1940.
282 N.Y. 355, 26 N.E.2d 290.

FINCH, JUDGE. This is an action for separation brought by a wife in which she seeks support. The husband seeks to avoid liability to plaintiff by alleging the invalidity of a Nevada divorce which he obtained from his first wife. May he avail himself of such a defense?

. . .

The facts presented by the defense are as follows: Defendant and his first wife domiciled in this State, were married here in 1905. There are two children by that marriage. In 1932 the present defendant, while retaining his residence in this State, made a visit to Reno, Nev., where he invoked the jurisdiction of the courts of that State and obtained a decree of divorce from his first wife, who neither entered an appearance nor was personally served in that action, and who at all times has remained a resident of this State. . . . Consequently this divorce against the first wife is not recognized by the courts of this State. . . . The subsequent marriage between plaintiff and defendant, therefore, was void for the incapacity of the defendant to marry. But none the less plaintiff and defendant participated in a complete marriage ceremony and did live together as man and wife for six years pursuant thereto, after which time defendant abandoned plaintiff, who now brings this action. Defendant entered the defense already noted, viz., that he lacked capacity to marry plaintiff because the court, which upon his petition purported to accord him a divorce from his first wife, lacked jurisdiction to act in the premises. Upon motion of plaintiff Special Term struck out the defense as insufficient in law . . . The Appellate Division affirmed by a divided court . . .

The question upon this appeal, therefore, depends upon whether defendant husband may now be heard to assert in this action, brought by his second "wife," that the judgment of divorce which he sought and obtained failed of its purpose and thereby did not give to the defendant that freedom to remarry which he appeared to possess by virtue of said judgment.

In general, a person who invokes the jurisdiction of a court will not be heard to repudiate the judgment which that court entered upon his seeking and in his favor. . . . The rule has been applied in this State in cases where property rights arising out of the marriage have been involved. . . . It is said, however, that in Stevens v. Stevens [273 N.Y. 157, 7 N.E.2d 26] we have answered the question upon which the case at bar turns. But in the Stevens case an action for separation was brought in this State by a wife against her husband who had previously secured a divorce in a Nevada court which was admittedly without jurisdiction. The husband counterclaimed for a divorce. At the trial the wife sought to defeat the counterclaim by

introducing in evidence the Nevada divorce obtained by the husband
in order to put him in a position where he could not maintain his claim
for divorce because he was no longer the husband of the wife. Upon
the facts of that case this court held that the husband was not prevented from maintaining the action for divorce despite the prior Nevada decree which he had obtained. . . . In the Stevens case the
position which the husband assumed in the proceedings in this State
was inconsistent with the decree which he had obtained in Nevada
only in the sense that as part of a cause of action for divorce it is
necessary to prove the marriage. . . . But the action which he
sought to take was parallel with that which he had previously undertaken in the Nevada proceedings in that the object of both was the
same, to wit, termination of the marriage with his wife. Such is not
the situation in the case at bar where the action which defendant
seeks to take is inconsistent with the result purportedly achieved by
the invalid Nevada decree. . . .

We come, then, to a consideration of the principle applicable in the
case at bar. We cannot lose sight of the fact that the present defendant was himself the party who had obtained the decree of divorce
which he now asserts to be invalid and repudiates in order that he
may now disown any legal obligation to support the plaintiff, whom
he purported to marry. To refuse to permit this defendant to escape
his obligation to support plaintiff does not mean that the courts of
this State recognize as valid a judgment of divorce which necessarily
is assumed to be invalid in the case at bar, but only that it is not open
to defendant in these proceedings to avoid the responsibility which he
voluntarily incurred.

It is conceded that the estoppel which is invoked against the present defendant is not a true estoppel as that term is ordinarily understood, although the effect is the same in the case at bar.

But it is urged that even though the prior authorities in this State
do not compel a contrary result, a different conclusion should be
reached as a matter of principle. It is said that public policy requires
that the interest of the State in the first marriage be protected even
though that may also give to the individual defendant an incidental
advantage to which he is not entitled in his private right. Thus defendant seeks to avoid the obligation which he has purported to undertake to support his second wife, upon the pretext that such is inconsistent with his obligations toward his first wife. Objection upon
this score is fully met by the fact that the needs of the first wife are
to be taken into account in arriving at the ability of defendant to support plaintiff in the case at bar. Defendant would altogether disavow
any obligation toward this plaintiff because of his obligation to his
first wife. The result which we reach here is the only one which
awards justice to this plaintiff, prevents her from becoming a public
charge if she should be impecunious and at the same time protects
the first wife in adequate degree. Thus there is complete observance

of not only the interest of the State in the protection of the first marriage, but also of the other interest of the State that marriage obligations shall not be lightly undertaken and lightly discarded.

Nothing in this decision should be taken to mean that because the defendant may not in these proceedings avail himself of the invalidity of his Nevada decree he is not the husband of his first wife. On the contrary, the very theory that defendant is precluded in these proceedings presupposes that the true situation is the contrary of that which he may show in the case at bar.

It follows, therefore, that the order appealed from should be affirmed, with costs, and the question certified answered in the negative.

Order affirmed, etc.

[The dissenting opinion is omitted.]

NOTES

(1) Suppose that a spouse would be estopped from attacking the divorce in F–1. Does the Constitution require in such a case that he likewise be estopped in F–2? Will the Sherrer, Coe, Johnson and Cook cases result in a narrower application of the estoppel doctrine?

(2) The estoppel principle is frequently applied to a spouse who did not obtain the divorce but who took advantage of it by remarrying. Carbulon v. Carbulon, 293 N.Y. 375, 57 N.E.2d 59 (1944). On the other hand, the principle has not been applied to the children of a spouse who would himself be estopped. So in Matter of Lindgren, 293 N.Y. 18, 55 N.E.2d 849 (1944), W–2 could not prevail over a child of H by his first marriage, H having secured a "divorce" from W–1.

D. EXTRATERRITORIAL RECOGNITION: DIVISIBLE DIVORCE

ESTIN v. ESTIN

Supreme Court of the United States, 1948.
334 U.S. 541, 68 S.Ct. 1213, 92 L.Ed. 1561, 1 A.L.R.2d 1412.

Certiorari to the Court of Appeals of New York.

Opinion of the Court by MR. JUSTICE DOUGLAS, announced by MR. JUSTICE REED.

This case, here on certiorari to the Court of Appeals of New York, presents an important question under the Full Faith and Credit Clause of the Constitution. Article IV, § 1. It is whether a New York decree awarding respondent $180 per month for her maintenance and support in a separation proceeding survived a Nevada divorce decree which subsequently was granted petitioner.

The parties were married in 1937 and lived together in New York until 1942 when the husband left the wife. There was no issue of the marriage. In 1943 she brought an action against him for a separation. He entered a general appearance. The court, finding that he had abandoned her, granted her a decree of separation and awarded her $180 per month as permanent alimony. In January 1944 he went to Nevada where in 1945 he instituted an action for divorce. She was notified of the action by constructive service but entered no appearance in it. In May, 1945, the Nevada court, finding that petitioner had been a bona fide resident of Nevada since January 30, 1944, granted him an absolute divorce "on the ground of three years continual separation, without cohabitation." The Nevada decree made no provision for alimony, though the Nevada court had been advised of the New York decree.

Prior to that time petitioner had made payments of alimony under the New York decree. After entry of the Nevada decree he ceased paying. Thereupon respondent sued in New York for a supplementary judgment for the amount of the arrears. Petitioner appeared in the action and moved to eliminate the alimony provisions of the separation decree by reason of the Nevada decree. The Supreme Court denied the motion and granted respondent judgment for the arrears. 63 N.Y.S.2d 476. The judgment was affirmed by the Appellate Division, 271 App.Div. 829, 66 N.Y.S.2d 421, and then by the Court of Appeals, 296 N.Y. 308, 73 N.E.2d 113.

We held in Williams v. North Carolina, 317 U.S. 287; 325 U.S. 226 (1) that a divorce decree granted by a State to one of its domiciliaries is entitled to full faith and credit in a bigamy prosecution brought in another State, even though the other spouse was given notice of the divorce proceeding only through constructive service; and (2) that while the finding of domicile by the court that granted the decree is entitled to *prima facie* weight, it is not conclusive in a sister State but might be relitigated there. And see Esenwein v. Esenwein, 325 U.S. 279. The latter course was followed in this case, as a consequence of which the Supreme Court of New York found, in accord with the Nevada court, that petitioner "is now and since January, 1944, has been a bona fide resident of the State of Nevada."

Petitioner's argument therefore is that the tail must go with the hide—that since by the Nevada decree, recognized in New York, he and respondent are no longer husband and wife, no legal incidence of the marriage remains.

. . . the highest court in New York has held in this case that a support order can survive divorce and that this one has survived petitioner's divorce. That conclusion is binding on us, except as it conflicts with the Full Faith and Credit Clause. . . . The only question for us is whether New York is powerless to make such a ruling in view of the Nevada decree.

We can put to one side the case where the wife was personally served or where she appeared in the divorce proceedings. . . . The only service on her in this case was by publication and she made no appearance in the Nevada proceeding. The requirements of procedural due process were satisfied and the domicile of the husband in Nevada was foundation for a decree effecting a change in the marital capacity of both parties in all the other States of the Union, as well as in Nevada. Williams v. North Carolina, 317 U.S. 287. But the fact that marital capacity was changed does not mean that every other legal incidence of the marriage was necessarily affected.

Although the point was not adjudicated in Barber v. Barber, 21 How. 582, 588, the Court in that case recognized that while a divorce decree obtained in Wisconsin by a husband from his absent wife might dissolve the *vinculum* of the marriage, it did not mean that he was freed from payment of alimony under an earlier separation decree granted by New York. An absolutist might quarrel with the result and demand a rule that once a divorce is granted, the whole of the marriage relation is dissolved, leaving no roots or tendrils of any kind. But there are few areas of the law in black and white. The greys are dominant and even among them the shades are innumerable. For the eternal problem of the law is one of making accommodations between conflicting interests. This is why most legal problems end as questions of degree. That is true of the present problem under the Full Faith and Credit Clause. . . .

Marital status involves the regularity and integrity of the marriage relation. It affects the legitimacy of the offspring of marriage. It is the basis of criminal laws, as the bigamy prosecution in Williams v. North Carolina dramatically illustrates. The State has a considerable interest in preventing bigamous marriages and in protecting the offspring of marriages from being bastardized. The interest of the State extends to its domiciliaries. The State should have the power to guard its interest in them by changing or altering their marital status and by protecting them in that changed status throughout the farthest reaches of the nation. For a person domiciled in one State should not be allowed to suffer the penalties of bigamy for living outside the State with the only one which the State of his domicile recognizes as his lawful wife. And children born of the only marriage which is lawful in the State of his domicile should not carry the stigma of bastardy when they move elsewhere. These are matters of legitimate concern to the State of the domicile. They entitle the State of the domicile to bring in the absent spouse through constructive service. In no other way could the State of the domicile have and maintain effective control of the marital status of its domiciliaries.

Those are the considerations that have long permitted the State of the matrimonial domicile to change the marital status of the parties by an *ex parte* divorce proceeding . . . considerations which in the Williams case we thought were equally applicable to any State in which one spouse had established a bona fide domicile. See 817 U.S. pp. 300–301. But those considerations have little relevancy here. In this case New York evinced a concern with this broken marriage when both parties were domiciled in New York and before Nevada had any concern with it. New York was rightly concerned lest the abandoned spouse be left impoverished and perhaps become a public charge. The problem of her livelihood and support is plainly a matter in which her community had a legitimate interest. The New York court, having jurisdiction over both parties, undertook to protect her by granting her a judgment of permanent alimony. Nevada, however, apparently follows the rule that dissolution of the marriage puts an end to a support order. . . . But the question is whether Nevada could under any circumstances adjudicate rights of respondent under the New York judgment when she was not personally served or did not appear in the proceeding.

Bassett v. Bassett, 141 F.2d 954, held that Nevada could not. We agree with that view.

The New York judgment is a property interest of respondent, created by New York in a proceeding in which both parties were present. . . . The property interest which it created was an intangible, jurisdiction over which cannot be exerted through control over a physical thing. Jurisdiction over an intangible can indeed only arise from control of power over the persons whose relationships are the source of the rights and obligations. . . .

Jurisdiction over a debtor is sufficient to give the State of his domicile some control over the debt which he owes. . . . But we are aware of no power which the State of domicile of the debtor has to determine the personal rights of the creditor in the intangible unless the creditor has been personally served or appears in the proceeding. . . .

We know of no source of power which would take the present case out of that category. The Nevada decree that is said to wipe out respondent's claim for alimony under the New York judgment is nothing less than an attempt by Nevada . . . to exercise an *in personam* jurisdiction over a person not before the court. That may not be done. Since Nevada had no power to adjudicate respondent's rights in the New York judgment, New York need not give full faith and credit to that phase of Nevada's judgment. A judgment of a court having no jurisdiction to render it is not entitled to the full faith and credit which the Constitution and statute of the United States demand. . . .

The result in this situation is to make the divorce divisible—to give effect to the Nevada decree insofar as it affects marital status and to make it ineffective on the issue of alimony. It accommodates the interests of both Nevada and New York in this broken marriage by restricting each State to the matters of her dominant concern.

Since Nevada had no jurisdiction to alter respondent's rights in the New York judgment, we do not reach the further question whether in any event that judgment would be entitled to full faith and credit in Nevada. . . . And it will be time enough to consider the effect of any discrimination shown to out-of-state *ex parte* divorces when a State makes that its policy.

Affirmed.

MR. JUSTICE FRANKFURTER and MR. JUSTICE JACKSON dissent in separate opinions.

NOTES

(1) Kreiger v. Kreiger, 334 U.S. 555 (1948), a companion case to Estin v. Estin, involved a similar situation and was resolved by the Court in the same manner. Discussion of the two cases and the problems raised may be found in Carey and MacChesney, Divorces by the Consent of the Parties and Divisible Divorce Decrees, 43 Ill.L.Rev. 608 (1948); Krauskopf, Divisible Divorce and Rights to Support, Property and Custody, 24 Ohio St.L.J. 346 (1963).

(2) Lynn v. Lynn, 302 N.Y. 193, 97 N.E.2d 748 (1951). The case involved exactly the same facts as Estin v. Estin except that the wife appeared in the Nevada divorce proceedings. The decree made no provision for alimony and recited that the wife had made no claim therefor. It was held that an earlier New York support order did not survive the divorce decree since "the Nevada court had jurisdiction of the wife's person by reason of her appearance."

Compare Portnoy v. Portnoy, 81 Nev. 235, 401 P.2d 249 (1965) where a wife, after having obtained an ex parte divorce in California, was awarded support against her husband in Nevada. The court held that under California law "a former wife [may] obtain support following the entry of an ex parte divorce. . . . We must honor California's view. . . ."

(3) Vanderbilt v. Vanderbilt, 354 U.S. 416 (1957), affirming 1 N.Y.2d 342, 135 N.E.2d 553 (1956). The spouses separated in 1952 while living in California. Thereafter, the husband became domiciled in Nevada and obtained there an ex parte divorce whose effect under Nevada law was to put an end to his duty to support the wife. The wife had moved to New York prior to the institution of the Nevada action, and, after the handing down of the decree, she sued the husband for alimony in New York under a New York statute (now Dom.Rel.L. § 236) which in terms authorizes such an action. The New York courts found for the wife and the Supreme Court affirmed on the ground that "[s]ince the wife was not subject to its jurisdiction, the Nevada divorce court had no power to extinguish any right which [the wife] had under the law of New York to financial support from her husband." There were dissents by Justices Frankfurter and Harlan. Justice Frankfurter believed that Nevada had as much power under due process to affect support rights ex parte as it had to dissolve the marriage. Justice Harlan summarized the grounds of his dissent in his concurring opinion in Simons v. Miami Beach First Nat. Bank, p. 851, infra.

Loeb v. Loeb, 4 N.Y.2d 542, 152 N.E.2d 36 (1958). The spouses originally were domiciled in Vermont. After the husband had obtained an ex parte divorce in Nevada, the wife sought alimony in Vermont but was denied this relief on the ground that the Vermont courts could not grant alimony after a valid divorce. The wife moved to New York and there sought alimony from the husband under the New York statute (now Dom.Rel.L. § 236). Relief was denied on the ground that the New York statute should not be applied to give relief to a wife who was not domiciled in New York when the husband obtained the ex parte divorce. Could the New York statute have been constitutionally applied in this case to award support to the wife? Must a state have had some contact with the spouses prior to the divorce in order to have the power to grant support to one of them? If so, what sort of contact is required?

(4) One difficulty that faces the plaintiff spouse who has not obtained a support order prior to the rendition of an ex parte divorce is the possibility that the forum will have no available remedy. In some states, alimony can only be given in connection with a divorce, and the action for separate maintenance and support will lie only between parties who are married. Stambaugh v. Stambaugh, 458 Pa. 147, 329 A.2d 483 (1974). Paulsen, Support Rights and an Out-of-State Divorce, 38 Minn.L.Rev. 709 (1954). By common law rule, the California courts may require a husband to pay alimony to his wife following the entry of an ex parte divorce. Hudson v. Hudson, 52 Cal. 2d 735, 344 P.2d 295 (1959); Weber v. Superior Court of Los Angeles County, 53 Cal.2d 403, 348 P.2d 572 (1960).

(5) Suppose that after a Nevada ex parte divorce the non-appearing spouse brings an original suit for alimony and support against the other spouse in the Nevada courts. May these courts refuse to entertain the action on the ground that, so far as Nevada is concerned, plaintiff's right to such relief was terminated by the divorce decree? This question was answered in the affirmative, with one judge dissenting, in Cavell v. Cavell, 90 Nev. 334, 526 P.2d 330 (1974).

(6) A result similar to that of the Estin case has been reached in England. Wood v. Wood, [1957] 2 All E.R. 14 (C.A.).

SIMONS v. MIAMI BEACH FIRST NATIONAL BANK

Supreme Court of the United States, 1965.
381 U.S. 81, 85 S.Ct. 1315, 14 L.Ed.2d 232.

Mr. Justice Brennan delivered the opinion of the Court.

The question to be decided in this case is whether a husband's valid Florida divorce, obtained in a proceeding wherein his nonresident wife was served by publication only and did not make a personal appearance, unconstitutionally extinguished her dower right in his Florida estate.

The petitioner and Sol Simons were domiciled in New York when, in 1946, she obtained a New York separation decree that included an award of monthly alimony. Sol Simons moved to Florida in 1951 and, a year later, obtained there a divorce in an action of which petitioner had valid constructive notice but in which she did not enter a personal appearance. After Sol Simons' death in Florida in 1960, respondent, the executor of his estate, offered his will for probate in the Probate Court of Dade County, Florida. Petitioner appeared in the proceeding and filed an election to take dower under Florida law, rather than have her rights in the estate governed by the terms of the will, which made no provision for her. The respondent opposed the dower claim, asserting that since Sol Simons had divorced petitioner she had not been his wife at his death, and consequently was not entitled to dower under Florida law. Petitioner thereupon brought the instant action in the Circuit Court for Dade County in order to set aside the divorce decree and to obtain a declaration that the divorce, even if valid to alter her marital status, did not destroy or impair her claim to dower. The action was dismissed after trial, and the Florida District Court of Appeal for the Third District affirmed. 157 So.2d 199. The Supreme Court of Florida declined to review the case, 166 So.2d 151. We granted certiorari, 379 U.S. 877. We affirm.

Petitioner's counsel advised us during oral argument that he no longer challenged the judgment below insofar as it embodied a holding that the 1952 Florida divorce was valid and terminated the marital status of the parties. We therefore proceed to the decision of the question whether the Florida courts unconstitutionally denied petitioner's dower claim.

Petitioner argues that since she had not appeared in the Florida divorce action the Florida divorce court had no power to extinguish any right which she had acquired under the New York decree. She invokes the principle of Estin v. Estin, 334 U.S. 541, where this Court decided that a Nevada divorce court, which had no personal jurisdiction over the wife, had no power to terminate a husband's obligation to provide the wife support as required by a pre-existing New York separation decree. . . .

The short answer to this contention is that the only obligation imposed on Sol Simons by the New York decree, and the only rights granted petitioner under it, concerned monthly alimony for petitioner's support. Unlike the ex-husband in Estin, Sol Simons made the support payments called for by the separate maintenance decree notwithstanding his *ex parte* divorce. . . . when he died there was consequently nothing left of the New York decree for Florida to dishonor. . . .

Insofar as petitioner argues that since she was not subject to the jurisdiction of the Florida divorce court its decree could not extinguish any dower right existing under Florida law, Vanderbilt v. Vanderbilt, 354 U.S. 416, 418, the answer is that under Florida law no dower right survived the decree. The Supreme Court of Florida has said that dower rights in Florida property, being inchoate, are extinguished by a divorce decree predicated upon substituted or constructive service. Pawley v. Pawley, 46 So.2d 464.[6]

6. In Pawley the Supreme Court of Florida distinguished the dower right from the right to support saying at 46 So.2d 464, 472–473, n. 2:

"In this, if not in every jurisdiction, right of dower can never be made the subject of a wholly independent issue in any divorce suit. It stands or falls

It follows that the Florida courts transgressed no constitutional bounds in denying petitioner dower in her ex-husband's Florida estate.

Affirmed.

MR. JUSTICE HARLAN, concurring.

I am happy to join the opinion of the Court because it makes a partial retreat from Vanderbilt v. Vanderbilt, 354 U.S. 416, a decision which I believe must eventually be rerationalized, if not entirely overruled.

The Vanderbilt case was this. The Vanderbilt couple was domiciled in California. Mr. Vanderbilt went to Nevada, established a new domicile, and obtained an *ex parte* divorce decree which did not provide for alimony payments to Mrs. Vanderbilt. In the meantime Mrs. Vanderbilt went to New York. After the Nevada decree had become final, she sued in New York for support under New York law, sequestering Mr. Vanderbilt's property located there. New York ordered support payments, rejecting full-faith-and-credit arguments based on the Nevada decree. . . .

Two rules emerged from the case, neither of which, I suggest with deference, commends itself: (1) an *ex parte* divorce can have no effect on property rights; (2) a State in which a wife subsequently establishes domicile can award support to her regardless of her connection with that State at the time of the *ex parte* divorce and regardless of the law in her former State of domicile.[2]

as a result of the decree which denies or grants divorce. It arises upon marriage, as an institution of the law. The inchoate right of dower has some of the incidents of property. It partakes of the nature of a lien or encumbrance. It is not a right which is originated by or is derived from the husband; nor is it a personal obligation to be met or fulfilled by him, but it is a creature of the law, is born at the marriage altar, cradled in the bosom of the marital status as an integral and component part thereof, survives during the life of the wife as such and finds its sepulcher in divorce. Alimony too is an institution of the law but it is a personal obligation of the husband which is based upon the duty imposed upon him by the common law to support his wife and gives rise to a personal right of the wife to insist upon, if she be entitled to, it. It has none of the incidents of, and is in no sense a lien upon or interest in, property. Consequently, the right of the wife to be heard on the question of alimony should not, indeed lawfully it cannot, be destroyed by a divorce decree sought and secured by the husband in an action wherein only constructive service of process was effected." . . .

2. The Vanderbilt result might have been proper on any of three grounds. (1) If New York was Mrs. Vanderbilt's State of domicile at the time of the *ex parte* Nevada divorce, New York law investing a wife with support rights should not be overborne by an *ex parte* decree in another State. (2) If California was Mrs. Vanderbilt's domicile at the time of the Nevada divorce and under California law support could have been awarded, New York should also be free (though not bound) to award support. (3) If Mr. Vanderbilt owned property in New York at the time of the *ex parte* divorce, New York might arguably be free to hold that ownership of New York property carries with it the obligation to support one's wife, at least to the extent of the value of that property.

The Court did not concern itself with the location of Mrs. Vanderbilt's domicile or Mr. Vanderbilt's property at the time of the Nevada divorce.

The first rule slips unobtrusively into oblivion in today's decision, for Florida is allowed to turn property rights on its *ex parte* decree. . . .

Because New York was petitioner's State of domicile at all times relevant to this case and did not purport to invest her with any rights to property beyond those she received from her husband, the second rule is not involved here. My hope is that its time will come too. . . .

MR. JUSTICE BLACK, with whom MR. JUSTICE DOUGLAS joins, concurring. . . .

I do not think that today's decision marks any "retreat" at all from the opinion or holding in Vanderbilt, . . . Vanderbilt held that a wife's right to support could not be cut off by an *ex parte* divorce. In the case before us, Mrs. Simons' Florida dower was not terminated by the *ex parte* divorce. It simply never came into existence. No one disputes that the *ex parte* divorce was effective to end the marriage, so that after it Mrs. Simons was no longer Mr. Simons' wife. Florida law, as the Court's opinion shows, grants dower only to a woman who is the legal wife of the husband when he dies. Mrs. Simons therefore had no property rights cut off by the divorce. She simply had her marriage ended by it, and for that reason was not a "widow" within the meaning of the Florida law. Unless this Court were to make the novel declaration that Florida cannot limit dower rights to widows, I see no possible way in which the Vanderbilt case, which dealt with rights which a State did give to divorced wives, could be thought to apply.

[A dissenting opinion by MR. JUSTICE STEWART, joined in by MR. JUSTICE GOLDBERG, is omitted.]

NOTES

(1) The Simons case makes clear that an absent spouse can constitutionally lose "inchoate" property interests as a result of an ex parte divorce decree. Can this case be reconciled with Estin v. Estin? See D. Currie, Suitcase Divorce in the Conflict of Laws, 34 U.Chi.L.Rev. 26 (1967).

(2) Carr v. Carr, 46 N.Y.2d 370, 413 N.Y.S.2d 305, 385 N.E.2d 1234 (1978). The issue was which of two wives was entitled to certain survivor benefits. After having become separated from her husband, the first wife settled in New York. He subsequently obtained an ex parte divorce and remarried. Then, following his death, the first wife brought an action in New York seeking a declaration that husband's divorce was invalid and that accordingly she was his lawful wife. Held: The action must be dismissed for lack of personal jurisdiction over the second wife. The dissenting judges argued that "when the first wife came to New York, she brought with her the 'res' of the marriage" and that accordingly New York had in rem jurisdiction to determine the validity of this marriage. "The majority's analysis would presumably prevent even a woman married in New York and a lifelong resident

from seeking in New York a declaration, for estate purposes, that her husband's out-of-state divorce was invalid."

NOTE ON FOREIGN COUNTRY DIVORCES

Domicile in the state by at least one of the parties is not the only jurisdictional basis for divorce under the law of most foreign countries. Indeed, "most countries do not even have a concept equivalent to our notion of domicile." Juenger, Recognition of Foreign Divorces, 20 Am.J. of Comp.L. 1, 19 (1972). To the extent that ties other than domicile in the state suffice as a jurisdictional basis for divorce in the forum state, some foreign country divorces will be entitled to recognition in the United States. Juenger, supra. On the other hand, many of the divorces that were denied recognition in this country involved situations where the divorce had been sought abroad by an American citizen in order to escape the restrictions of his state of domicile. Mexican divorces provide striking examples. In some Mexican states, a divorce could be granted for practically any reason. Sometimes there was no residence requirement, and in certain states a petitioning spouse did not even have to appear in person but could arrange by mail to have an appearance entered on his or her behalf. For these reasons, thousands of Americans sought Mexican divorces, and the question of what extraterritorial effect should be given these divorces has frequently come before American courts. Mexican "mail-order divorces"—i.e. those where neither spouse personally appears before the divorce court—have almost invariably been denied legal effect. Divorces granted upon the personal appearance of one or both spouses have also been denied recognition in most states on the ground that neither spouse had a bona fide domicile in Mexico. The New York courts, on the other hand, have given effect to Mexican divorces if one spouse was before the divorce court and the other appeared either personally or by attorney.

√ ROSENSTIEL v. ROSENSTIEL, WOOD v. WOOD, 16 N.Y.2d 64, 73, 262 N.Y.S.2d 86, 90, 209 N.E.2d 709, 712 (1965): Both of these cases involved divorces obtained in Chihuahua, Mexico, by New Yorkers. In both cases the plaintiff spouse was in Mexico for less than twenty-four hours during which time he appeared personally before the divorce court. The defendant spouse in both cases entered an appearance by an attorney but did not personally go to Mexico. Held, the divorces should be recognized in New York. "The State or county of true domicile has the closest real public interest in a marriage but, when a New York spouse goes elsewhere to establish a synthetic domicile to meet technical acceptance of a matrimonial suit, our public interest is not affected differently by a formality of one day than by a formality of six weeks. Nevada gets no closer to the real public concern with the marriage than Chihuahua."

In 1971, the Federal Government of Mexico issued a decree stating that an alien may not obtain a divorce in any Mexican state without having been present in Mexico for a period of not less than six months. See Diario Oficial (Mexico) 18, Feb. 20, 1971. As a result, "quickie" divorces are no longer obtainable in Mexico. Haiti and the Dominican Republic then entered the lists by enacting legislation similar to that of the Mexican states referred to above. It seems probable that such Haitian and Dominican Republic divorces will be recognized as freely in New York as were those of Mexico. Greschler v. Greschler, 51 N.Y.2d 368, 434 N.Y.S.2d 194, 414 N.E.2d 694 (1980).

NOTES

(1) On the subject of Mexican divorces, see D. Currie, Suitcase Divorce in the Conflict of Laws, 34 U.Chi.L.Rev. 26 (1967), Caballero, A Reexamination of Mexican "Quickie" Divorces, 4 Int.Lawyer 871 (1970).

It is said in the Reporters' Notes to § 494 of the Restatement, American Foreign Relations Law (Revised) (Tent. Draft 1983) that Connecticut, Tennessee and the Virgin Islands apply the rule of the Rosenstiel case but that in all other states, Rosenstiel type divorces are denied recognition.

(2) Suppose that in a foreign country a New Yorker gets a Rosenstiel type divorce that New York would recognize as valid. He then returns to New York and eventually moves to a sister state where he marries for a second time. Should the second state recognize the divorce as valid even though it would have held invalid a similar divorce obtained by one of its own domiciliaries? See Note, 114 U.Pa.L.Rev. 771 (1966).

(3) In Caldwell v. Caldwell, 298 N.Y. 146, 81 N.E.2d 60 (1948), a spouse who procured a "mail order" Mexican divorce was held not estopped from attacking it because "there is not even the slightest color of jurisdiction." The rule of the Caldwell case was extended somewhat in Alfaro v. Alfaro, 5 App.Div.2d 770, 169 N.Y.S.2d 943 (2d Dep't 1958), affirmed without opinion 7 N.Y.2d 949, 165 N.E.2d 880 (1960). In that case a spouse was permitted collaterally to attack an ex parte Mexican divorce which he had procured even though the decree recited that he had appeared before the court and he had testified that he had visited the court and "picked up" the decree.

On the other hand, it has been held more recently that a spouse would be held estopped if his purpose in attacking the "mail order" Mexican divorce he had procured was "primarily for the purpose of obtaining financial gain" rather than to re-establish his former marital status. Considine v. Rawl, 242 N.Y.S.2d 456 (Sup.Ct.1963).

SECTION 3. ANNULMENT*

WHEALTON v. WHEALTON

Supreme Court of California, 1967.
67 Cal.2d 656, 63 Cal.Rptr. 291, 432 P.2d 797.

TRAYNOR, CHIEF JUSTICE. Defendant appeals from a default judgment annulling her marriage to plaintiff on the ground of fraud.

Plaintiff, a petty officer on active duty with the United States Navy, married defendant at Bel Air, Maryland, on June 15, 1964. Thereafter his military duties took him from place to place on the east coast until he was assigned to the U.S.S. *Reposte* at the San Francisco Naval Shipyard. He arrived in California on July 14, 1965. Plaintiff and defendant lived together for only six or seven weeks on the east coast.

On September 3, 1965, plaintiff filed this action for annulment of the marriage. Summons was issued and an order for publication of summons was filed on the same day. Publication of the summons was accomplished as prescribed by law. Defendant received a copy of the summons by mail at her home in Maryland on September 7, 1965. . . . On October 11, 1965, the court entered her default, heard testimony in support of the complaint, and entered a judgment annulling the marriage. On October 19, 1965, defendant made a motion to set aside the default and the judgment by default and to permit the filing of an answer and a cross-complaint. The motion was denied on November 9, 1965.

[The Court first found that the judgment was void because it had been prematurely entered.]

Even if the default judgment were not premature, it would have to be reversed, for neither the pleadings nor the evidence establish that either party was a domiciliary of California. The court therefore lacked jurisdiction to award an ex parte annulment. . . .

Ex parte divorces are a striking exception to the rule that a court must have personal jurisdiction over a party before it may adjudicate his substantial rights. . . . The legal fiction that explains the exception by regarding the marital status as a res present at the permanent home of either of the spouses provides doctrinal consistency with other rules governing jurisdiction over things, but the appellation "in rem" is unnecessary to support the conclusion that jurisdiction is properly assumed. (Williams v. State of North Carolina (1945) 325 U.S. 226.) *Williams* does hold, however, that due process requires something more than mere presence of a party within a juris-

* Restatement, Second, Conflict of Laws §§ 76, 286.

diction before that party can invoke the legal process of the forum to force an absent spouse to defend her marital status in an inconvenient forum and to subvert the policies of other interested jurisdictions in preserving marriages. When the forum state is also the domicile of one of the parties, however, its interest and that of its domiciliary justify subordinating the conflicting interests of the absent spouse and of any other interested jurisdiction.

Jurisdiction to grant annulments has followed an analogous, but somewhat divergent course. An annulment differs conceptually from a divorce in that a divorce terminates a legal status, whereas an annulment establishes that a marital status never existed. The absence of a valid marriage precluded reliance on the divorce cases in formulating a theory of ex parte jurisdiction in annulment, for no res or status could be found within the state. . . . The courts, however, did not let jurisdictional concepts of in personam and in rem dictate results in annulment actions. They recognized a state's interest in providing a forum for some annulment actions even though the court lacked personal jurisdiction over one of the parties. . . . The crucial question, then, is whether there are sufficient factors to justify the court's exercising ex parte annulment jurisdiction. . . .

. . . The primary issue under the facts of this case is whether due process concepts of fairness to defendant permit plaintiff to choose a forum inconvenient to her absent personal jurisdiction over her. . . . We find no factor here that would justify an exception to the general rule requiring personal jurisdiction and thereby shift the burden of inconvenience to defendant. The marriage ceremony took place elsewhere, defendant lives elsewhere, the matrimonial domicil was elsewhere, and witnesses are likely to be located elsewhere. Although domicile of a plaintiff here would afford jurisdiction to award an ex parte annulment, plaintiff in this case did not plead or prove that he was a domiciliary of California when the default judgment was entered. The court was therefore without jurisdiction to enter the default judgment.

Since the entry of the judgment, however, defendant has appeared in the action. We must therefore determine for purposes of proceedings on retrial whether the court may award an annulment when both parties are before it, even though neither is a domiciliary of the state.

The primary basis for jurisdiction to resolve disputes between parties is their presence before the court. Plaintiff initiated this action in the only jurisdiction practically available to him because of his military service. Although defendant was not within the jurisdiction of the court when the default was erroneously entered, she voluntarily appeared while the action was before the court. Her appearance was not limited to challenging the jurisdiction of the court, but included a request for relief on the merits by way of an answer and cross-complaint for separate maintenance. . . .

Since both parties are properly before the court, we confront the questions whether we may treat the action as a transitory cause . . . and whether the interest of another state compels us to refuse to hear this cause.

The rule that domicile is a prerequisite to a valid divorce, even when the parties are before the court, may be justified by the superior interests of the domiciliary jurisdiction. Such jurisdiction is primarily concerned with the status of its domiciliaries and the application of its own law in preserving or terminating marriages in accord with its social policies. . . . When both parties to a divorce action are before the court, however, it is questionable whether domicile is an indispensable prerequisite for jurisdiction. If the moving party's mobility is greatly restricted, for instance, access to a domiciliary forum may be practically unavailable. . . . Moreover, when parties secure a divorce without the prerequisite domicile in the forum state, it may not be attacked at a later date by either of them. . . . Hence, the prerequisite of domicile may be easily avoided at the trial by parties wishing to invoke the jurisdiction of a court, with little fear in most instances that the judgment will be any less effective than if a valid domicile in fact existed. . . .

However valid the rationale for the domicile prerequisite may be in divorce actions, it does not apply to annulment actions. In divorce actions, the applicable substantive law changes as parties change their domicile, but in annulment actions courts uniformly apply the law of the state in which the marriage was contracted. . . . We conclude, therefore, that the interests of the state of celebration of the marriage or the state of domicile of either party do not preclude a court that has personal jurisdiction over both parties from entertaining an annulment action.

It does not follow that because a court may exercise that jurisdiction it must do so in all cases. In the present case plaintiff was under a special disability in terms of access to any forum other than California. Moreover, defendant was not caught inadvertently within California, and personal jurisdiction was not exercised on a territorial power theory but was obtained over defendant through her consent. Hence, we assume that no undue burdens are placed on her by the trial of the action in California. In other annulment actions where personal jurisdiction is the sole jurisdictional basis, however, the doctrine of *forum non conveniens* might well be invoked by one of the parties, or asserted by the court, to cause a discretionary dismissal when fairness and the interests of judicial administration so demand. . . .

The judgment is reversed.

WILKINS v. ZELICHOWSKI

Supreme Court of New Jersey, 1958.
26 N.J. 370, 140 A.2d 65.

[The case appears p. 648, supra.]

NOTES

(1) There is uncertainty about the bases of judicial jurisdiction for annulment. It is usually held that, at the least, a court has jurisdiction to decree an annulment if it could render a divorce. Under this view, personal jurisdiction over the defendant spouse is not necessary but suit must ordinarily be brought in the domicile of the plaintiff spouse. A few courts, on the other hand, believe that personal jurisdiction over the defendant spouse is essential. See, e.g., Owen v. Owen, 127 Colo. 359, 257 P.2d 581 (1953). Rarely, however, has this latter view been carried to the extreme of holding that an annulment action can be brought in any state where personal jurisdiction over both spouses can be obtained. A number of cases hold that the state where the marriage was celebrated has jurisdiction to annul it if both spouses are before the court. See, e.g., Feigenbaum v. Feigenbaum, 210 Ark. 186, 194 S.W.2d 1012 (1946); Sawyer v. Slade, 196 N.C. 697, 146 S.E. 864 (1929).

According to Section 76 of the Restatement, Second, a state has jurisdiction to annul a marriage (a) if it would have jurisdiction to dissolve the marriage by divorce or (b) if the respondent spouse is subject to the judicial jurisdiction of the state and either the marriage was contracted there or the validity of the marriage is determined under its law.

(2) See generally Storke, Annulment in the Conflict of Laws, 43 Minn.L. Rev. 849 (1959); Vernon, Labyrinthine Ways: Jurisdiction to Annul, 10 J.Pub.L. 47 (1961).

(3) Sutton v. Leib, 342 U.S. 402 (1952). Suit in a federal district court in Illinois to recover alimony due under an Illinois divorce decree requiring payment of alimony to plaintiff until remarriage. The plaintiff had remarried in Nevada, but thereafter this marriage was annulled by a New York court for the reason that the man plaintiff married "had another wife living at the time of said marriage." The District Court rendered summary judgment for the defendant, and the Court of Appeals affirmed on the ground that plaintiff's Nevada marriage, since it was good in that state, terminated the liability for alimony under the Illinois divorce decree. On writ of certiorari to the Supreme Court, held reversed. Since plaintiff and her second husband were before the New York court, that court's annulment decree is entitled to full faith and credit and therefore plaintiff's Nevada marriage must be held void. Illinois, however, was held "free to decide for itself the effect of New York's . . . annulment on the obligations of respondent, a stranger to the decree." As a result, the case was remanded for a determination whether under Illinois law plaintiff's invalid marriage released respondent from the obligation to pay further alimony.

SECTION 4.   JUDICIAL SEPARATION

RESTATEMENT, SECOND, CONFLICT OF LAWS*

§ 75.   Judicial Separation.

(1) A state may exercise judicial jurisdiction to grant a judicial separation under the circumstances which would give the state jurisdiction to dissolve the marriage by divorce.

(2) A state may exercise judicial jurisdiction to grant a judicial separation when both spouses are personally subject to the jurisdiction of the state.

Comment:

a.   Nature of judicial separation.   A decree of judicial separation does not affect the existence of the marriage.   It does, however, modify the incidents of the marriage relationship by relieving the spouses from the duty of living with each other.

Jurisdiction to render a decree of judicial separation and so to end the duty of the spouses to live together does not necessarily entail the jurisdiction to affect their economic rights and duties, such as by ordering one to provide for the support of the other or of the children of the marriage.   For the latter purpose, it is essential that the court have personal jurisdiction over the respondent spouse or over so much of his property as it seeks to affect by its decree . . .

Comment on Subsection (1):

b.   A state may exercise judicial jurisdiction to grant a judicial separation whenever it would have jurisdiction to dissolve the marriage by divorce . . .   Hence a state which is the domicil of both spouses, or which is the domicil of one spouse and has personal jurisdiction over the other, may exercise judicial jurisdiction to grant a judicial separation.   Under these circumstances the state also may exercise judicial jurisdiction to affect the spouses' economic rights and duties, such as by ordering one to provide for the support of the other.   As between States of the United States, such a decree is entitled to full faith and credit. . . .

A state which lacks personal jurisdiction over the respondent spouse, but which nevertheless would have judicial jurisdiction to grant a divorce, either because it is the state of domicil of the plaintiff spouse or because it has some other appropriate relationship to the plaintiff spouse . . .   may exercise judicial jurisdiction to

---

* Quoted with the permission of the copyright owner, The American Law Institute.

grant a judicial separation. As between States of the United States, such a decree is entitled to full faith and credit. . . . Under these circumstances, however, the state lacks judicial jurisdiction to affect the respondent spouse's economic rights and duties . . . except to the extent that it has jurisdiction over the respondent's property . . .

Comment on Subsection (2):

c. A state may exercise judicial jurisdiction to grant a judicial separation even though it would not have jurisdiction to grant a divorce. This is because separation is a less drastic remedy than divorce and because it is essential that a state have power to protect a spouse, who is present within its territory, from the violence or cruelty of the other. Accordingly, a state with personal jurisdiction over both spouses may exercise judicial jurisdiction to grant a judicial separation. It follows that a decree rendered with personal jurisdiction over both spouses is entitled to full faith and credit. . . .

SECTION 5. LEGITIMATION

Introductory Note: The concept of the inferior status of the "bastard" child, socially and legally, is under heavy attack and does not retain its past importance in law. The attack is based both on more humane attitudes toward out-of-wedlock offspring and on constitutional doubts about the fairness and equality of punishing a child for the parents' failure to comply with society's norms and legal rules in begetting the child.

In recent decisions the Supreme Court has declared unconstitutional some statutes favoring legitimates over illegitimates while upholding others. Compare Trimble v. Gordon, 430 U.S. 762; Weber v. Aetna Casualty & Surety Co., 406 U.S. 164 (1972); Levy v. Louisiana, 391 U.S. 68 (1968); Glona v. American Guaranty & Liability Insurance Co., 391 U.S. 73 (1968) with Lalli v. Lalli, 439 U.S. 259 (1978); Norton v. Mathews, 427 U.S. 524 (1976); Mathews v. Lucas, 427 U.S. 495 (1976); Labine v. Vincent, 401 U.S. 532 (1971).

The materials that follow must be read with awareness that fortunately the days when birth out of wedlock was burdened with both social stigma and legal disadvantages are waning.

RESTATEMENT, SECOND, CONFLICT OF LAWS*

Topic 2.   Legitimacy

Introductory Note: As stated in the Introductory Note to this Chapter, a status, such as legitimacy, can be viewed from two standpoints. It can be viewed as a relationship which continues as the parties move from state to state. Or it can be viewed from the standpoint of the incidents that arise from it. Among the incidents that may depend upon a person's legitimacy are his nationality, his right to his father's name and support and his right to share in the latter's estate. Whether a person is legitimate may also have a decisive bearing upon questions of construction, such as whether he is included within such terms as "children" or "issue" contained in a will or trust. The interests of his parents and of third persons may also be affected. If he is legitimate, his father is certain to owe him a duty of support and, conversely, may have a right to his custody and services as well as the right to inherit from him upon his intestacy. Furthermore, to the extent that a finding of legitimacy permits him to share in an estate or to take under a will, the shares of other beneficiaries are correspondingly reduced.

Questions involving legitimacy as a relationship entirely divorced from its incidents—that is as a pure status—arise infrequently. Nevertheless, it is necessary to state choice-of-law rules on the subject for the reason that the courts have often acted on the assumption that they could not properly decide questions involving the incidents of legitimacy until they had made a preliminary determination of whether legitimacy did or did not exist as a relationship under the law governing the relationship.

At common law only children born in lawful wedlock were legitimate. In most states, this rule has now been modified by statute. It is usually provided that the offspring of certain invalid marriages shall be legitimate. In addition, children, originally born illegitimate, can commonly be legitimated by events occurring after their birth, such as by the marriage of their parents or by some form of recognition on the part of one or both. Differences in the pertinent statutes of the various states give rise to choice-of-law problems. It may be possible for a child to be legitimate as to one parent and illegitimate as to the other.

It is commonly said that a person's status as legitimate or illegitimate does not vary but remains constant from state to state. The incidents which flow from his status, however, may vary, since they depend upon the law which governs the question at hand.

. . .

§ 287. Law Governing Legitimacy

. . .

(2) The child will usually be held legitimate if this would be his status under the local law of the state where either (a) the parent was domiciled when the child's status of legitimacy is claimed to have been created or (b) the child was domiciled when the parent acknowledged the child as his own.

§ 288. Incidents of Legitimacy Created by Foreign Law

A state usually gives the same incidents to a status of legitimacy created by a foreign law under the principles stated in § 287 that it gives to the status when created by its own local law.

NOTES

(1) The courts of the state of the parent's domicile at death have usually interpreted the provisions of their law to require that the legitimating act have been done at a time when the parent is domiciled in the state. See, e.g., Meekins v. Meekins, 169 Ark. 265, 275 S.W. 337 (1925); Eddie v. Eddie, 8 N.D. 376, 79 N.W. 856 (1899); In re Presley's Estate, 113 Okl. 160, 240 P. 89 (1925).

A number of cases, however, have not imposed such a requirement. Estate of Bassi, 234 Cal.App.2d 529 (1965); In re Lund's Estate, 26 Cal.2d 472, 159 P.2d 643 (1945); Colpitt v. Cheatham, 267 P.2d 1003 (Okl.1954); Rhode Island Hospital Trust Co. v. Hopkins, 93 R.I. 173, 172 A.2d 345 (1961); In re Engelhardt's Estate, 272 Wis. 275, 75 N.W.2d 631 (1956).

(2) See generally Scoles and Hay, Conflict of Laws 535–541 (1982); Ester, Illegitimate Children and the Conflict of Laws, 36 Ind.L.J. 161 (1961).

(3) Robles v. Folsom, 239 F.2d 562 (2d Cir. 1956). The case involved an illegitimate child who was born and recognized by his father in Puerto Rico while both were domiciled there. Under Puerto Rican law, this recognition would not legitimate the child but would entitle him to inherit from the father. The father subsequently died domiciled in New York. The court held (Clark, J., dissenting) that the child could not inherit from the father in New York since New York law allows only legitimate children to inherit from their father upon intestacy.

SECTION 6.   ADOPTION*

Adoption was unknown to the common law and is purely the creature of statute. In the sense here used, it is the process whereby the adoptive parent is substituted for the natural parents, and whereby in many states the child's legal relationship with the latter is severed

---

* See Restatement, Second, Conflict of Laws §§ 78, 289–290.

entirely. Some statutes, however, employ the term in a sense closely akin to legitimation, such as when provision is made for the so-called adoption by a natural parent of his illegitimate child. On rare occasions, adoption is used in a restricted sense to describe a process whereby the child becomes no more than an heir presumptive of the adopter and his relations with his natural parents remain undisturbed. Adoption, as here defined, exists by virtue of statutory enactment in the great majority of States in this country.

Adoption, like any other status, can be viewed from two standpoints. It can be viewed as a relationship which continues as the parties move from state to state. Or it can be viewed from the standpoint of the incidents which arise from it. Questions involving adoption as a relationship entirely divorced from its incidents—that is as a pure status—are most unlikely to arise. Yet the courts have often acted on the assumption that they could not properly decide questions involving the incidents of adoption, such as a child's right to inherit from another, without having first decided whether the child has been properly adopted under the local law of a state having jurisdiction to grant the adoption.

Unlike legitimation (see Section 5), adoption is usually effected by court proceedings. The two main conflicts problems in the field are the judicial jurisdiction of a state to grant an adoption and the effect which will be accorded an adoption in another state. The statutes differ rather widely in their details, particularly as to the circumstances under which a court can decree an adoption and with respect to the rights of inheritance of the adopted child. There is agreement in common law countries that in determining whether to grant the adoption, the forum will apply the local provisions of its own law and not those of some other state.

There is some uncertainty as to what jurisdictional bases must exist to enable a state to grant an adoption through its courts. It is believed that such jurisdiction exists in a state (a) which is the domicile of either the child or the adoptive parent and (b) which has personal jurisdiction over the adoptive parent and over either the adopted child or the person having legal custody of the child. Two principal questions are involved in an adoption proceeding: first, whether the child's situation is such as to make adoption advisable in his own best interests and, if so, whether the would-be adopter is a desirable person from the child's point of view. Courts sitting in either the domicile of the child or in that of the adoptive parent will normally be equally well situated to determine such issues. And the interests of the two states in the matter are of approximately equal weight.

An adoption, decreed in a state with judicial jurisdiction, will usually be given the same legal incidents in another state as the latter gives to a decree of adoption by its own courts.

Incidents arising from an adoption include such matters as the right of the adoptive parent to the custody and control of the child and the right of either the child or the adoptive parent to share in the other's estate and to recover damages for the other's wrongful death. To date, the bulk of the cases involving the effect of a foreign adoption have concerned the inheritance rights of the adopted child. According to most of the decisions, such rights are determined by the law governing succession; that is to say by the law of the situs in the case of immovables and by the law of the decedent's last domicile in the case of movables. So, if the question concerns the right of a child adopted in state X to inherit the movables of an adoptive or of a natural parent or some other relative who died domiciled in state Y, the case will be decided by Y law rather than by that of X. See, e.g., In re Youmans' Estate, 218 Minn. 172, 15 N.W.2d 537 (1944); In re Dreer's Estate, 404 Pa. 368, 173 A.2d 102 (1961). However, some courts take the position that the inheritance rights of the adopted child pertain to status itself and hence are governed by the law of the state where the adoption was granted. See, e.g., Slattery v. Hartford-Connecticut Trust Co., 115 Conn. 163, 161 A. 79 (1932).

NOTES

(1) In Anglo-American countries, the forum will look to its own law in determining whether to grant an adoption. 1 Rabel, Conflict of Laws 681 (2d ed. 1958). The courts of civil law countries, on the other hand, apply what they deem to be the proper law (frequently the state of the adoptive parent's domicile or nationality) to govern the case. Scoles and Hay, Conflict of Laws 544–545 (1982).

(2) See generally Baade, Interstate and Foreign Adoptions in North Carolina, 40 N.C.L.Rev. 691 (1962); Cowen, English and Foreign Adoptions, 12 Int'l & Comp.L.Q. 168 (1963); Kennedy, Adoption in the Conflict of Laws, 34 Can.B.Rev. 507 (1956).

(3) In Hood v. McGehee, 237 U.S. 611 (1915), the Supreme Court upheld a refusal by the Alabama courts to allow inheritance of Alabama land by children adopted in Louisiana. The Alabama courts had held that under Alabama law only children adopted in Alabama could inherit. The Supreme Court based its decision on the ground that there had been no failure to give "full credit" to the adoption, and that Alabama was free to determine the devolution of Alabama land. Was the decision consistent with Clark v. Williard, p. 942, infra?

(4) In Armstrong v. Manzo, 380 U.S. 545 (1965), no notice of the Texas adoption proceedings was given the natural father although those seeking the adoption (the mother and her new husband) "well knew his precise whereabouts in . . . Texas." It was held that, as a result of this failure to give notice, the adoption decree was constitutionally invalid.

(5) In Barry E. (Anonymous) v. Ingraham, 43 N.Y.2d 87, 400 N.Y.S.2d 772, 371 N.E.2d 492 (1977), the court refused on public policy grounds to give effect to a Mexican decree providing for the adoption by a New York couple of a child born in New York to a New York mother.

(6) In Doulgeris v. Bambacus, 203 Va. 670, 127 S.E.2d 145 (1962), inheritance rights were denied a child who had been adopted in Greece on the ground that the Greek adoption procedures, which placed primary emphasis upon the welfare of the adoptive father rather than of the adoptive child, were repugnant to Virginia public policy. The effect of the decision was to deny the child's inheritance rights from her adoptive brother. Would Virginia's public policy have been seriously contravened by permitting the child to inherit? For cases recognizing Greek adoption decrees, see Corbett v. Stergios, 257 Iowa 1387, 137 N.W.2d 266 (1965); In re Christoff's Estate, 411 Pa. 419, 192 A.2d 737 (1963).

SECTION 7.   CUSTODY OF CHILDREN

MAY v. ANDERSON

Supreme Court of the United States, 1953.
345 U.S. 528, 73 S.Ct. 840, 97 L.Ed. 1221.

Mr. Justice Burton delivered the opinion of the Court.

. . .

The parties were married in Wisconsin and, until 1947, both were domiciled there. After marital troubles developed, they agreed in December, 1946, that appellant should take their children to Lisbon, Columbiana County, Ohio, and there think over her future course. By New Year's Day, she had decided not to return to Wisconsin and by telephone, she informed her husband of that decision.

Within a few days he filed suit in Wisconsin, seeking both an absolute divorce and custody of the children. The only service of process upon appellant consisted of the delivery to her personally, in Ohio, of a copy of the Wisconsin summons and petition. . . . Appellant entered no appearance and took no part in this Wisconsin proceeding which produced not only a decree divorcing the parties from the bonds of matrimony but a decree purporting to award the custody of the children to their father, subject to a right of their mother to visit them at reasonable times. Appellant contests only the validity of the decree as to custody. . . .

Armed with a copy of the decree and accompanied by a local police officer, appellee, in Lisbon, Ohio, demanded and obtained the children from their mother. The record does not disclose what took place between 1947 and 1951, except that the children remained with their father in Wisconsin until July 1, 1951. He then brought them back to Lisbon and permitted them to visit their mother. This time, when he demanded their return, she refused to surrender them.

Relying upon the Wisconsin decree, he promptly filed in the Probate Court of Columbiana County, Ohio, the petition for a writ of habeas corpus now before us. Under Ohio procedure that writ tests only the immediate right to possession of the children. It does not open the door for the modification of any prior award of custody on a showing of changed circumstances. Nor is it available as a procedure for settling the future custody of children in the first instance.

. . .

Separated as our issue is from that of the future interests of the children, we have before us the elemental question whether a court of a state, where a mother is neither domiciled, resident nor present, may cut off her immediate right to the care, custody, management and companionship of her minor children without having jurisdiction over her *in personam*. Rights far more precious to appellant than property rights will be cut off if she is to be bound by the Wisconsin award of custody. . . .

In Estin v. Estin [page 846, supra] . . . and Kreiger v. Kreiger [p. 850, note (1), supra] . . . this Court upheld the validity of a Nevada divorce obtained *ex parte* by a husband, resident in Nevada, insofar as it dissolved the bonds of matrimony. At the same time, we held Nevada powerless to cut off, in that proceeding, a spouse's right to financial support under the prior decree of another state. In the instant case, we recognize that a mother's right to custody of her children is a personal right entitled to at least as much protection as her right to alimony.

In the instant case, the Ohio courts gave weight to appellee's contention that the Wisconsin award of custody binds appellant because, at the time it was issued, her children had a technical domicile in Wisconsin, although they were neither resident nor present there. We find it unnecessary to determine the children's legal domicile because, even if it be with their father, that does not give Wisconsin, certainly as against Ohio, the personal jurisdiction that it must have in order to deprive their mother of her personal right to their immediate possession. . . .

Reversed and remanded.

Mr. Justice Clark, not having heard oral argument, took no part in the consideration or decision of this case.

Mr. Justice Frankfurter, concurring.

The views expressed by my brother Jackson make it important that I state, in joining the Court's opinion, what I understand the Court to be deciding and what it is not deciding in this case.

What is decided—the only thing the Court decides—is that the Full Faith and Credit Clause does not require Ohio, in disposing of the custody of children in Ohio, to accept, in the circumstances before us, the disposition made by Wisconsin. The Ohio Supreme Court felt itself so bound. This Court does not decide that Ohio would be precluded from recognizing, as a matter of local law, the disposition made by the Wisconsin court. For Ohio to give respect to the Wisconsin decree would not offend the Due Process Clause. Ohio is no more precluded from doing so than a court of Ontario or Manitoba would be, were the mother to bring the children into one of these provinces.

Property, personal claims, and even the marriage status . . . generally give rise to interests different from those relevant to the discharge of a State's continuing responsibility to children within her borders. Children have a very special place in life which law should reflect. Legal theories and their phrasing in other cases readily lead to fallacious reasoning if uncritically transferred to determination of a State's duty towards children. . . . But the child's welfare in a custody case has such a claim upon the State that its responsibility is obviously not to be foreclosed by a prior adjudication reflecting another State's discharge of its responsibility at another time. Reliance on opinions regarding out-of-State adjudications of property rights, personal claims or the marital status is bound to confuse analysis when a claim to the custody of children before the courts of one State is based on an award previously made by another State. Whatever light may be had from such opinions, they cannot give conclusive answers.

Mr. Justice Jackson, whom Mr. Justice Reed, joins, dissenting.

The Court apparently is holding that the Federal Constitution prohibits Ohio from recognizing the validity of this Wisconsin divorce decree insofar as it settles custody of the couple's children. In the light of settled and unchallenged precedents of this Court, such a decision can only rest upon the proposition that Wisconsin's courts had no jurisdiction to make such a decree binding upon appellant. . . .

The Ohio courts reasoned that although personal jurisdiction over the wife was lacking, domicile of the children in Wisconsin was a sufficient jurisdictional basis to enable Wisconsin to bind all parties interested in their custody. This determination that the children were domiciled in Wisconsin has not been contested either at our bar or below. Therefore, under our precedents, it is conclusive. . . .

The Court's decision holds that the state in which a child and one parent are domiciled and which is primarily concerned about his welfare cannot constitutionally adjudicate controversies as to his guardianship. The state's power here is defeated by the absence of the other parent for a period of two months. The convenience of a leave-taking parent is placed above the welfare of the child, but neither party is greatly aided in obtaining a decision. The Wisconsin courts cannot bind the mother, and the Ohio courts cannot bind the father. A state of the law such as this, where possession apparently is not merely nine points of the law but all of them and self-help the ultimate authority, has little to commend it in legal logic or as a principle of order in a federal system. . . .

The difference between a proceeding involving the status, custody and support of children and one involving adjudication of property rights is too apparent to require elaboration. In the former, courts are no longer concerned primarily with the proprietary claims of the contestants for the *"res"* before the court, but with the welfare of the *"res"* itself. Custody is viewed not with the idea of adjudicating rights *in* the children, as if they were chattels, but rather with the idea of making the best disposition possible for the welfare of the children. To speak of a court's "cutting off" a mother's right to custody of her children, as if it raised problems similar to those involved in "cutting off" her rights in a plot of ground, is to obliterate these obvious distinctions. Personal jurisdiction of all parties to be affected by a proceeding is highly desirable, to make certain that they have had valid notice and opportunity to be heard. But the assumption that it overrides all other considerations and in its absence a state is constitutionally impotent to resolve questions of custody flies in the face of our own cases. . . .

I fear this decision will author new confusions. The interpretative concurrence, if it be a true interpretation, seems to reduce the law of custody to a rule of seize-and-run. I would affirm the decision of the Ohio courts that they should respect the judgment of the Wisconsin court, until it or some other court with equal or better claims to jurisdiction shall modify it.

[A dissenting opinion by MR. JUSTICE MINTON is omitted.]

NOTES

(1) Is Justice Burton's notion that personal jurisdiction over the defendant parent is essential to the rendition of a valid custody decree out of line with the realities of the situation? How, under these circumstances, could a custody issue be resolved in a situation where each parent is domiciled in a different state and neither proves willing to appear in the courts of the other's domicile? The general consensus has rejected Justice Burton's position in favor of Justice Frankfurter's. Weintraub, Affecting the Parent-Child Relationship Without Jurisdiction Over Both Parents, 36 Sw.L.J. 1167 (1983).

Personal jurisdiction over the defendant parent, although not essential to the rendition of a valid custody decree, is essential for the rendition against the parent of a valid judgment for support. Kumar v. Santa Clara City Superior Court, 124 Cal.App.3d 1003, 177 Cal.Rptr. 763 (1981); In Re Hudson, 434 N.E.2d 107 (Ind.App.1982). Is this sensible?

(2) In People of State of New York ex rel. Halvey v. Halvey, 330 U.S. 610 (1947), the Supreme Court held that under full faith and credit a custody decree is as subject to modification in F–2 as it is in F–1. Almost invariably, custody decrees are subject to modification in the state of their rendition on a showing of changed circumstances. Since these can usually be found, the net effect of the Halvey decision was to attenuate markedly the role of full faith and credit in the custody area. This had the disadvantage of making it possible for a parent who was displeased with a custody decision of one state to seek a fresh determination in another state. Moreover, to give the courts of that other state jurisdiction, one parent might in effect kidnap the child

and take it there. The other parent might then retaliate in kind and the custody battle might go on and on unless and until the courts of one state chose of their own volition to respect the other state's decree. The child would, of course, be the principal victim in the tug-of-war.

(3) The Supreme Court did nothing to alleviate the situation. In one typically unfortunate battle the Georgia and California courts handed down inconsistent custody decrees within the space of a few months, although, so far as appears, the merits were litigated by both parents in each state and the courts of each state were apprised of the contrary decision that had been reached by the courts of the other. The Supreme Court of the United States denied certiorari in each case. Stout v. Pate, and Pate v. Stout, 347 U.S. 968 (1954).

In Kovacs v. Brewer, 356 U.S. 604 (1958) and Ford v. Ford, 371 U.S. 187 (1962), the Court found it unnecessary to determine the "difficult and important" question whether full faith and credit requires that a custody decree be given the same effect in a sister state as it has in the state of rendition.

———

Today, the situation has drastically changed. Questions involving the recognition, enforcement and modification of sister state and foreign country decrees are now regulated in large part by statute. Nearly all of the states have adopted the Uniform Child Custody Jurisdiction Act and the recently enacted federal Parental Kidnaping Prevention Act of 1980 (28 U.S.C.A. § 1738A) entitles some custody decrees to full faith and credit. The interplay of these two statutes is illustrated by the next case.

———

QUENZER v. QUENZER

Supreme Court of Wyoming, 1982.
653 P.2d 295.

THOMAS, JUSTICE.

The task confronting our court in this case is that of reconciling, in the context of the power to enter a judgment modifying a child-custody decree, the laws of the State of Texas, the State of Wyoming, and the United States of America. . . .

The appellant, Fred August Quenzer, Jr., and the appellee, Nola Kathleen Quenzer (now Sharrard), were divorced in Texas in 1975. Primary custody of the parties' daughter was awarded to the mother pursuant to the Decree of Divorce which followed the provisions of a Property Settlement Agreement previously entered into by the parties. Not long after the divorce the mother removed herself from Texas with the result that the father could not exercise weekend visitation rights as provided for in the Decree of Divorce. . . .

In August of 1977 the father petitioned the circuit court in Oregon [to which the mother had gone] to enforce the visitation provisions of the Texas decree in accordance with Oregon's adoption of the Uniform

Child Custody Jurisdiction Act. A cross-petition by the mother sought modification of the Texas decree and also arrearages in child and spousal support payments, and an increase in the amount of monthly child support. . . . The father then filed a motion for a change in custody of the daughter. . . . Essentially the Oregon decree continued custody in the mother; . . . Although appealed, that judgment was affirmed by the Oregon Court of Appeals.

. . . In August of 1979 the mother married her present husband and the mother, daughter and the stepfather moved to . . ., Alaska, . . . In June of 1980 the daughter was sent to visit in Texas. The father was entitled to custody for a six-week period starting on the second Sunday of June of each year. During the period of this visit the mother and her husband moved from Alaska to Teton County, Wyoming, where they intended to establish a permanent residence. On July 8, 1980, which was less than a week before the scheduled visitation in Texas was to end, the father filed a motion in the Texas district court, seeking a modification in custody of the child. Process was served upon the mother in Eugene, Oregon, where she was visiting prior to returning to Wyoming.

Thereafter the mother instituted a separate habeas corpus proceeding in the Texas court, seeking enforcement of the Oregon decree returning the child to her custody. The return to her custody was ordered by the Texas court, and on August 16, 1980, the mother and daughter left Texas, and since that time they have resided in Wyoming. . . . In the meantime the modification proceeding had been held in abeyance pending a determination of the status of the mother, who had attempted to appear specially. The Texas court, by the same judge who had heard the habeas corpus proceeding, entered an order denying the mother's special appearance and ordering the case to proceed to trial on the merits. Thereafter, in January of 1981, trial was held with respect to the proceeding seeking modification of custody. On January 12, 1981, an Order of Modification in Suit Affecting Parent-Child Relationship was entered in Texas in which the court held that custody should be given to the father with visitation rights to the mother. January 26, 1981, was specified as the date for transferring possession of the child, and the Texas court did enter findings that it had jurisdiction and that the mother had not been a continuous domiciliary or resident of any state for six months preceding the filing of this action. It further found that no other court had or has continuing jurisdiction of the suit or of the daughter and that it had jurisdiction of the child because it was the most convenient forum to determine the best interest of the child.

The proceeding in Wyoming was commenced on February 23, 1981. . . . The Wyoming court found that it had jurisdiction under the Wyoming version of the Uniform Child Custody Jurisdiction Act; that the mother was the proper person to have custody of the child; and that the circumstances before the court showed that any orders of any court in the past should be modified, because of a change in circumstances, to give the mother custody of the child. While critical of the Texas proceeding, the Wyoming district court premised its authority upon the existence of jurisdiction pursuant to Wyoming statute, and it did proceed to modify the Texas modification order by restoring permanent custody to the mother; denying visitation rights in the father "at the present time unless substantial safeguards are erected in that regard" . . . The father has appealed from this order. . . .

The father argues earnestly, that the Parental Kidnaping Prevention Act of 1980, Pub.L. 96–611, 94 Stat. 3569 (1980) . . . forecloses the Wyoming court from modifying the modification decree entered by the Texas court. . . .

This legislation, if applicable, must be afforded primary consideration under the Supremacy Clauses of our federal and state constitutions. Constitution of the United States, Art. VI, Cl. 2; Constitution of the State of Wyoming, Art. 1, § 37. By this statute Congress has provided for the effect to be given to the judicial proceedings in the state originally exercising jurisdiction, and thus has defined what full faith and credit requires in such instances.[1]

Any child-custody determination made consistently with the provisions of the Parental Kidnaping Prevention Act is required to be enforced according to its terms by the courts of every other state (28 U.S.C.A. § 1738A), and the authorities of another state are not permitted to modify except as provided in subsection (f) of 28 U.S.C.A. § 1738A such a child-custody determination. Subsection (f), which is referred to, provides as follows:

"(f) A court of a State may modify a determination of the custody of the same child made by a court of another state, if—

"(1) it has jurisdiction to make a child custody determination; and

"(2) the court of the other State no longer has jurisdiction, or it has declined to exercise such jurisdiction to modify such determination." . . .

There is, however, a threshold test which must be applied . . . . . The modification order in Texas must have been made consistently with the provisions of the Parental Kidnaping Prevention Act. Subsection (c) of the Parental Kidnaping Prevention Act provides as follows:

"(c) A child custody determination made by a court of a State is consistent with the provisions of this section only if—

1. It would appear that this legislation was intended to supplement existing state legislation such as the Uniform Child Custody Jurisdiction Act to promote interstate judicial cooperation and communication, facilitate the enforcement of custody and visitation decrees of sister states, discourage interstate controversies over child custody, prevent jurisdictional competition and conflicts between state courts, and to deter parental kidnapping and forum shopping. See § 7(c), Pub.L. 96–611, 94 Stat. 3569 (1980). . . .

"(1) such court has jurisdiction under the law of such State; and

"(2) one of the following conditions is met:

"(A) such State (i) is the home State of the child on the date of the commencement of the proceeding, or (ii) had been the child's home State within six months before the date of the commencement of the proceeding and the child is absent from such State because of his removal or retention by a contestant or for other reasons, and a contestant continues to live in such State;

"(B)(i) it appears that no other State would have jurisdiction under subparagraph (A), and (ii) it is in the best interest of the child that a court of such State assume jurisdiction because (I) the child and his parents, or the child and at least one contestant, have a significant connection with such State other than mere physical presence in such State, and (II) there is available in such State substantial evidence concerning the child's present or future care, protection, training, and personal relationships;

"(C) the child is physically present in such State and (i) the child has been abandoned, or (ii) it is necessary in an emergency to protect the child because he has been subjected to or threatened with mistreatment or abuse;

"(D)(i) it appears that no other State would have jurisdiction under subparagraph (A), (B), (C), or (E), or another State has declined to exercise jurisdiction on the ground that the State whose jurisdiction is in issue is the more appropriate forum to determine the custody of the child, and (ii) it is in the best interest of the child that such court assume jurisdiction; or

"(E) The court has continuing jurisdiction pursuant to subsection (d) of this section." . . .

The Texas determination . . . was not made consistently with the second requirement of the Parental Kidnaping Prevention Act, in that its exercise of jurisdiction did not fit any of the conditions contained in 28 U.S.C.A. § 1738A(c)(2). Obviously Texas was not the home state of the child under subsection (A) of that provision. The father cannot rely upon subsection (B) of that provision because the daughter had been living in Alaska for at least six consecutive months immediately preceding the time she went to visit the father, and [therefore] Alaska would be the home state of the child as defined in 28 U.S.C.A. § 1738A(b)(4). The Texas court therefore could not, and it did not, find that no other state would have jurisdiction under subparagraph (A) of 28 U.S.C.A. § 1738A(c)(2)(A). Subsections (C), (D), and (E) of the title similarly are not applicable, and we must conclude that the jurisdiction of the district court in Wyoming was not foreclosed by the provisions of the Parental Kidnaping Prevention Act because the modification order entered in the State of Texas was not a "custody determination made consistently with the provisions of this section by a court of another State."

Having concluded that neither the Full Faith and Credit Clause nor the provisions of the Parental Kidnaping Prevention Act foreclosed the exercise of jurisdiction by the district court in Wyoming, we still must consider whether the exercise of that jurisdiction was precluded under some provision of Wyoming law. Our conclusion with respect to this proposition will also dispose of the first issue urged by the father in his appeal. Section 20–5–104, W.S.1977 [U.C. C.J.A. § 3] is the provision governing the jurisdiction of Wyoming courts in child-custody proceedings, and it provides as follows:

"(a) A court of this state competent to decide child custody matters has jurisdiction to make a child custody determination by initial decree or modification decree if:

"(i) This state is the home state of the child at the time of commencement of the proceeding, or was the child's home state within six (6) months before commencement of the proceeding and the child is absent from the state because of his removal or retention by a person claiming his custody or for other reasons, and a parent or person acting as parent continues to live in this state;

"(ii) It is the best interest of the child that a court of this state assume jurisdiction because the child and his parents, or the child and at least one (1) contestant, have a significant connection with the state and there is available in this state substantial evidence concerning the child's present or future care, protection, training and personal relationships;

"(iii) The child is physically present in this state and has been abandoned or if it is necessary in an emergency to protect the child because he has been subjected to or threatened with mistreatment or abuse or is otherwise neglected or dependent; or

"(iv) It appears that no other state would have jurisdiction under prerequisites substantially in accordance with paragraphs [subdivisions] (i), (ii) or (iii) of this subsection, or another state has declined to exercise jurisdiction on the ground that this state is the more appropriate forum to determine the custody of the child and it is in the best interest of the child that this court assume jurisdiction.

"(b) Except under paragraphs [subdivisions] (a)(iii) and (iv) of this section, physical presence in this state of the child or of the child and one (1) of the contestants is not alone sufficient to confer jurisdiction on a court of this state to make a child custody determination.

"(c) Physical presence of the child, while desirable, is not a prerequisite for jurisdiction to determine his custody."

Both subsections (a)(i) and (a)(ii) in this instance justify the exercise of jurisdiction by the courts of the State of Wyoming. In § 20–

5–103(a)(v), W.S.1977, [U.C.C.J.A. § 2] "Home state" is defined as follows:

". . . 'Home state' means the state in which the child immediately preceding the time involved has lived with his parents, a parent or a person acting as parent, for at least six (6) consecutive months, and in the case of a child less than six (6) months old the state in which the child has lived since birth with any of the persons mentioned. Periods of temporary absence of any of the names [sic] persons are counted as part of the six (6) month or other period; . . ."

The record is clear that the daughter had resided with her mother in Wyoming from the time of the conclusion of the habeas corpus proceeding in Texas until the commencement of the Wyoming proceeding, which was more than six months. It is equally apparent that there did exist in this instance a significant connection with the State of Wyoming, and that there was available in this state substantial evidence concerning the child's present or future care, protection, training and personal relationships. Friends, neighbors, school personnel, and a professional psychologist were all present to assist the court in making determinations with respect to the best interest of the child. We note by contrast that the testimony in the Texas proceeding duplicated some of this testimony, and that the Texas witnesses appeared primarily as character witnesses for the father and his second wife. Any balanced comparison of these factors results in a clear preference for the State of Wyoming as the appropriate forum. The district court [determined] that it was in the best interest of the child that it exercise its jurisdiction. The evidence present in the record sustains this determination, and in the absence of some other inhibiting factor or prohibition the district court had jurisdiction over this matter under Wyoming law.

The father, however, points to the provisions of § 20–5–107(a), W.S.1977, [U.C.C.J.A. § 6] and urges that this section prohibits the exercise of jurisdiction in Wyoming. Section 20–5–107(a), W.S.1977, provides:

"(a) A court of this state shall not exercise its jurisdiction under this act if at the time of filing the petition a proceeding concerning the custody of the same child was pending in a court of another state exercising jurisdiction substantially in conformity with this act, unless the proceeding is stayed by the court of the other state because this state is a more appropriate forum or for other reasons."

Again the record is clear that when this proceeding was commenced in the Wyoming district court the proceedings in the courts of Texas had been concluded, and become final there according to local law. Since there was no proceeding pending in Texas, § 20–5–107(a) did not interfere with the exercise of jurisdiction by the district court in Wyoming. We note in this regard that the father apparently has abandoned his claim that the district court abused its discretion by failing to decline jurisdiction as an inconvenient forum in favor of Texas under § 20–5–108, W.S.1977 [U.C.C.J.A. § 7].

Relying upon still another contention, the father argues that the district court committed error in asserting and exercising jurisdiction to determine child custody in the light of §§ 20–5–114 [U.C.C.J.A. § 13] and 20–5–115(a) [U.C.C.J.A. § 14] W.S.1977. The provisions of those statutes read as follows:

"§ 20–5–114. Recognition and enforcement of initial or modification decree made by court of another state.

"The courts of this state shall recognize and enforce an initial or modification decree of a court of another state which had assumed jurisdiction under statutory provisions substantially in accordance with this act, or which was made under factual circumstances meeting the jurisdictional standards of the act, so long as this decree has not been modified in accordance with jurisdictional standards substantially similar to those of this act."

"§ 20–5–115. Modifying custody decree made by court of another state.

"(a) If a court of another state has made a custody decree a court of this state shall not modify that decree unless it appears that the court which rendered the decree does not now have jurisdiction under jurisdictional prerequisites substantially in accordance with this act or has declined to assume jurisdiction to modify the decree, and the court of this state has jurisdiction."

The mother meets these contentions by asserting that the district court correctly refused to recognize and enforce the Texas order because the statutory provisions in Texas are not substantially in accordance with the Uniform Child Custody Jurisdiction Act, and she asserts that the factual circumstances were such that the jurisdictional standards of the Uniform Act were not met in Texas. . . . She points out that, while tit. 2, § 11.045(1)(2)(A), Tex.Fam.Code Ann. (Vernon 1975), facially is similar to § 20–5–104(a)(ii), W.S.1977, the State of Texas has no provision similar to § 20–5–109(b), W.S.1977. [U.C.C.J.A. § 8] This latter provision provides as follows:

"(b) Unless required in the interest of the child and subject to W.S. 20–5–115(a), the court shall not exercise its jurisdiction to modify a custody decree of another state if the petitioner without consent of the person entitled to custody has improperly removed the child from the physical custody of the person entitled to custody or has improperly retained the child after a visit or other temporary relinquishment of physical custody. If the petitioner has violated any other provision of a custody decree of another state the court in its discretion and subject to W.S. 20–5–115(a) may decline to exercise jurisdiction."

The record before us discloses that while the father filed his action for modification in Texas during the period that the daughter was visiting him pursuant to the provisions of the Oregon decree, his retention of custody beyond the time provided by the decree was wrongful and in derogation of the mother's rights. We agree with the mother that . . . a Wyoming court under these circumstances would not be permitted to exercise its jurisdiction to modify a custody decree.

It would appear from the circumstances that the policy of the State of Texas differs. Consequently, if the issue in this case were confined to the enforcement of the Texas order it well might be that the doctrine of res judicata, combined with the provisions of our Wyoming law and the Parental Kidnaping Prevention Act, would require the recognition and enforcement of the Texas decree. . . . Still the availability of the jurisdiction of the district court to modify the provisions of the Texas order is not foreclosed. Unless the prohibition contained in § 20–5–115(a), W.S.1977, is applicable, the district court in Wyoming had the power to act and enter its own order modifying the custody provisions upon a sufficient showing of a change in circumstances to warrant a different decree. . . .

We conclude that it is the duty of the Wyoming court to determine the applicability of § 20–5–115(a), W.S.1977, i.e., to determine whether the Texas court at the time the jurisdiction of the Wyoming court was exercised had jurisdiction under jurisdictional prerequisites substantially in accordance with the Uniform Child Custody Jurisdiction Act or had declined to assume jurisdiction to modify the decree. . . . This determination, which must be made by the Wyoming court, is to be made not at the commencement of the Wyoming action, but rather at the time of the hearing on the matter in light of the evidence presented. . . . Other courts which have construed this Uniform Child Custody Jurisdiction Act generally have applied a two-stage test in determining whether the local court had jurisdiction to modify a foreign custody determination. First the court must consider whether the court whose decree is sought to be modified no longer has jurisdiction under standards such as those set forth in § 20–5–104, W.S.1977 [U.C.C.J.A. § 4], and secondly it may consider whether the court whose decree is sought to be modified has declined jurisdiction to modify its prior judgment. If either of these tests is met, then the forum state must determine whether it has jurisdiction under its own laws. . . .

On the date that the Wyoming court held its hearing the Texas court no longer had jurisdiction under standards which substantially comply with the Uniform Child Custody Jurisdiction Act. This test having been met, the Wyoming court was not foreclosed from exercising jurisdiction by the provisions of § 20–5–115(a), W.S.1977. We justify this holding first by alluding to one of the general purposes of the Uniform Child Custody Jurisdiction Act set forth in § 20–5–102, W.S.1977 [U.C.C.J.A. § 1] as follows:

"(a) The general purposes of this act are:

. . .

"(iii) To assure that litigation concerning the custody of a child take place ordinarily in the state with which the child and his family have the closest connection and where significant evidence concerning his care, protection, training and personal relationships is most readily available, and that courts of this state decline the exercise of jurisdiction when the child and his family have a closer connection with another state;"

We find in this statement of policy an explicit recognition that the paramount consideration of the best interest of the child mandates that custody determinations be made in the forum having the best access to the relevant evidence. . . .

At the time that Wyoming exercised its jurisdiction in this matter it was the "home state" under the Uniform Child Custody Jurisdiction Act and § 20–5–104(a)(i), W.S.1977. . . . At the pertinent date the state which had the most significant connections with the child and her mother was Wyoming. In February of 1982 the daughter had been present in Wyoming nearly eighteen months. She was attending local schools and receiving weekly counseling in Jackson, Wyoming, from a professional psychologist. Evidence of the mother's parental fitness and her relationship with the daughter was most accessible in Wyoming. Most importantly, however, the child's presence in this state gave the district court the best opportunity to gather evidence concerning the daughter's emotional and personal development, as well as furnishing to it the opportunity for the child to testify directly with respect to her early allegations in the Texas habeas corpus proceeding of drug use and mistreatment at the hands of her mother. She had earlier recanted that testimony by a letter to the Texas judge, and the Wyoming court had the opportunity to evaluate personally with the daughter the two versions of her prior testimony. The evidence available in Wyoming was relevant and substantial with respect to the issue of the best interest of the child. Under these criteria the Wyoming court properly exercised jurisdiction in the matter and entered its decree modifying the custody provisions of the Texas decree. . . .

. . . the last argument of the father relates to the sufficiency of the evidence to justify the finding by the district court of a substantial change in circumstances. . . . He also urges the proposition that the brief period between the date of the modification order in Texas and the beginning of the Wyoming proceedings negates the possibility that a change of circumstances occurred in the interim.

Once vested with jurisdiction over the cause, it is the duty of the court to hear evidence to determine whether a substantial material

change in circumstances has occurred so that the welfare of the child
will be best served by a change in custody. . . . Although the
brief period of time between the entry of the order sought to be modified and the institution of new proceedings may indicate that circumstances have not changed, we cannot as a matter of law hold that the
movant, who bears the burden of proof, could not present such sufficient evidence. . . .

. . . The district court in this instance made detailed and explicit findings concerning the changes in the daughter's circumstances.
In addition, the record contains exhibits . . . including the deposi-
tions of the daughter and the psychologist, both of which support the
findings made by the district court. The evidence is sufficient to support a conclusion that the mother has established a stable home with
her new husband, and this has greatly aided the daughter's own emotional stability and maturity. The deposition of the psychologist details the advances the daughter has made since treatment was obtained. The daughter is happy and manifesting significant
improvement in her school work and social development under the
mother's care and supervision. She has established a strong parent-
child relationship with her stepfather. Other improvements in the
daughter and the mother's circumstances are detailed in the record.
The record in this case is adequate to support the action of the district court. . . .

The order of the trial court hereby is affirmed on the basis of the
conclusions reached in the foregoing opinion.

NOTES

(1) Among other things, the Parental Kidnaping Prevention Act makes
available the facilities of the Federal Parent Locator Service in aid of attempts to ascertain the whereabouts of a kidnaped child.

(2) The Parental Kidnaping Prevention Act is applicable only to sister
state custody decrees. On the other hand, the Uniform Child Custody Jurisdiction Act has been held to apply as well to custody decrees rendered in
foreign countries. See, e.g., Com. ex rel. Zaubi v. Zaubi, 492 Pa. 183, 423
A.2d 333 (1981), discussed in Note, 20 Duq.L.Rev. 43 (1981).

(3) For discussion of the relationship between the Parental Kidnaping
Prevention Act and the Uniform Child Custody Jurisdiction Act, see Katz,
Child Snatching (1981); Bruch, Interstate Child Custody Law and Eicke, 16
Fam.L.Q. 277 (1982); Coombs, Custody Conflicts in the Courts, 16 Fam.L.Q.
251 (1982); Coombs, Interstate Child Custody: Jurisdiction, Recognition, and
Enforcement, 66 Minn.L.Rev. 711 (1982); Foster, Child Custody Jurisdiction:
UCCJA and PKPA, 27 N.Y.L.Sch.L.Rev. 297 (1981); Note, The Effect of the
Parental Kidnaping Prevention Act of 1980 on Child Snatching, 17 N.Eng.L.
Rev. 499 (1982); Note, The Parental Kidnaping Prevention Act, 27 N.Y.L.
Rev. 553 (1982).

(4) Articles on the Uniform Child Custody Jurisdiction Act by Professor
Brigitte Bodenheimer, its principal draftsman, include Bodenheimer, Interstate Custody: Initial Jurisdiction and Continuing Jurisdiction Under the

UCCJA, 14 Fam.L.Q. 203 (1981); Bodenheimer, Progress Under the Uniform Child Custody Jurisdiction Act and Remaining Problems: Punitive Decrees, Joint Custody, and Excessive Modifications, 65 Calif.L.Rev. 978 (1977); Bodenheimer, The Rights of Children and The Crisis in Custody Litigation, 46 Colo.L.Rev. 495 (1975); Bodenheimer, The Uniform Child Custody Jurisdiction Act: A Legislative Remedy for Children Caught in the Conflict of Laws, 22 Vand.L.Rev. 1207 (1969).

(5) For a discussion and intensive examination of the Uniform Child Custody Jurisdiction Act, see Ratner, Procedural Due Process and Jurisdiction to Adjudicate, 75 Nw.L.Rev. 363 (1980); Note, The UCCJA Coming of Age, 34 Mercer L.Rev. 811 (1983).

SECTION 8. SUPPORT

A. ENFORCEMENT OF SUPPORT CLAIMS WITHOUT REGARD TO RECIPROCAL SUPPORT LEGISLATION

Introductory Note: If a claim for support arises against a husband who has abandoned his wife and children and fled to another state, what are the methods of enforcing the claim in the other state? What are the legal and practical difficulties in the way? How much better off are the wife and children if the claim for support has been reduced to judgment in the first state? These are some of the questions suggested by the cases incorporated below.

LYNDE v. LYNDE

Supreme Court of the United States, 1901.
181 U.S. 183, 21 S.Ct. 555, 45 L.Ed. 810.

[The case appears p. 231, supra.]

YARBOROUGH v. YARBOROUGH

Supreme Court of the United States, 1933.
290 U.S. 202, 54 S.Ct. 181, 78 L.Ed. 269, 90 A.L.R. 924.

[The case appears p. 260, supra.]

BARBER v. BARBER

Supreme Court of the United States, 1944.
323 U.S. 77, 65 S.Ct. 137, 89 L.Ed. 82.

[The case appears p. 293, supra.]

WORTHLEY v. WORTHLEY

Supreme Court of California, 1955.
44 Cal.2d 465, 283 P.2d 19.

[The case appears p. 296, supra.]

ESTIN v. ESTIN

Supreme Court of the United States, 1948.
334 U.S. 541, 68 S.Ct. 1213, 92 L.Ed. 1561, 1 A.L.R.2d 1412.

[The case appears p. 846, supra.]

THE LAW GOVERNING SUPPORT

Apart from the problem of enforcement of a foreign support order, there is the question of what law governs the duty of one person to support another. This has been said to be "anything but clear." [1] It is hard to understand why the question has not arisen more frequently, since, as stated in the Commissioners' Prefatory Note to the Uniform Reciprocal Enforcement of Support Act (1950),

". . . it is little realized how different are the duties [of support] existing in our . . . states. Some enforce a duty toward illegitimate children, others do not. Forty jurisdictions require children to support their parents, the others do not. A dozen states require support between brothers and sisters, the others do not. Seventeen states require a wife to support a husband under certain circumstances, the others do not. And even in the duty of a parent to support his child the several states require this support up to different ages, varying from 14 to 21 years."

A related problem concerns the question of what law to apply in the case where a third party seeks recovery for goods furnished a member of the family group.

STATE OF CALIFORNIA v. COPUS

Supreme Court of Texas, 1958.
158 Tex. 196, 309 S.W.2d 227.

[In 1936 Mrs. Copus, the mother of the defendant, Dale Copus was adjudged mentally ill in California and admitted to a California state institution where she had been a patient ever since. A California statute imposed a duty on a son to pay for the support of his incompetent mother in a state hospital. On July 16, 1951, the son

---

1. Ehrenzweig, Interstate Recognition of Support Duties, 42 Calif.L.Rev. 382, 384–385 (1954).

changed his domicile from California to Texas. On May 21, 1953, the State of California brought the present action in a Texas court against the son for the amounts accrued under the California statute during the four years preceding.

California had a four year statute of limitations for the enforcement of the obligation. Texas had a general statute of limitations setting a period of two years for such an obligation. The trial court gave a judgment for the plaintiff for the full amount sued for, $3,470, stating: ". . . the liability of the defendant . . . is a continuing one; and the removal of the defendant . . . does not discharge him from such continuing liability under the laws of the State of California, the defendant having been a resident of California at the time of the commencement of such continuing liability."]

CULVER, JUSTICE. . . . The general rule rather universally recognized is that the statutes of a state ex proprio vigore have no extraterritorial effect. It must be concluded, therefore, that the California statute could not create a legal obligation upon a citizen of Texas who was not a citizen of California when the obligation arose, that is, at the time the mother became institutionalized in California or at any time thereafter. We are aware of no rule of law that would make the obligation a continuing one after removal from California even though it attached to him while a resident of that state. Citizens of a state equally share the burdens and privileges of citizenship regardless of when or how that status is attained. To say that the support statute compelled liability for that period of time after the respondent moved to Texas would seem to deny to him equality with other citizens of the state. . . .

This cause of action in so far as it concerns the accruals after respondent's removal to Texas cannot be said to have arisen while respondent was under the legislative jurisdiction of California. . . . We hold, therefore, that respondent is not liable for any sums accrued after his removal to this state.

. . . we prefer to follow those decisions that would treat the [time] limitation in the California statute as substantive and not procedural. . . .

It cannot be said that the maintenance of this suit in Texas and the rendition of a judgment in California's favor for the amount accruing before the respondent became a citizen of Texas is against the public policy of this state. It is true that our Legislature has not seen fit to enact a statute to impose legal liability upon a son for the maintenance of a parent inmate in a state institution, although it does by statute obligate the husband or wife and the father or mother, if financially able, to bear the expense of maintaining a patient in a state hospital where the patient has not sufficient estate of his own. . . . And not only that, but our Probate Code, Sec. 423, requires that an incompetent person, having no estate of his own, shall be maintained by the husband or wife and by the father or mother and even by the children and grandchildren, if able to do so. . . .

This California statutory requirement of support does not run counter to good morals or natural justice or appear prejudicial in any way to the general interest of the citizens of Texas.

We, therefore, hold that the petitioner is entitled to judgment for the sum of money charged by the State of California for the support of his mother while the respondent was a citizen of that state that accrued within four years of the commencement of this suit and will be denied recovery for any sums that accrued after respondent's removal to this state.

GREENHILL, JUSTICE. I respectfully dissent. . . .

As I view it, the bare legal point here is: does the fact that Copus moved to Texas, standing alone, relieve him of his legal obligation to contribute thereafter to his mentally-ill mother's support? I think not. Texas should not become a haven for deserting providers who would ignore or repudiate their duty to support.

Viewed the other way, if Copus and his mother had been Texas citizens and he were obligated in Texas to contribute to her support, should he be able to shirk that responsibility by just moving out of the State?

There is no evidence before us that Copus is unable to support his mother, that other relatives should bear or share in the burden, or that she has forfeited any right to support from her son. . . .

The majority opinion correctly states that it is not against the public policy of Texas to enforce such an obligation. Our policy in that regard has been fixed in comparatively recent times by the enactment of our Uniform Support Act and the Texas Probate Code.

Section 423 of the Probate Code provides:

"Where an incompetent has no estate of his own, he shall be maintained: (a) By the husband or wife . . . if able to do so; or, if not, (b) By the father or mother . . . if able to do so; or, if not, (c) *By the children and grandchildren of such person*, respectively if able to do so; or, if not, (d) By the county . . . ."

The Legislature has thus determined that it is the policy of Texas that under the circumstances above set out, an incompetent person (such as the mother here) shall be supported by her children, if able. The mother here was incompetent. . . .

The Texas trial court found that "the liability of . . . Copus is a continuing one; and that the removal of the defendant [Copus] to Texas . . . does not discharge him from such continuing liability."

I would affirm the judgment of the trial court.

NOTES

(1) In a more recent case, the Supreme Court of Texas upheld the constitutionality of a Texas statute, no longer in effect, which called for the application of the law of the obligee's domicile to determine whether an obligor domiciled in Texas owed the obligee a duty of support. The court disavowed its suggestion in Copus that application of the law of the obligee's domicile would deny equal protection to the obligor. Bjorgo v. Bjorgo, 402 S.W.2d 143 (Tex.1966).

Compare Elkind v. Byck, 68 Cal.2d 453, 67 Cal.Rptr. 404, 439 P.2d 316 (1968) (p. 265, note 1, supra). Following a divorce in Georgia, the wife and children moved to New York and the husband moved to California. In New York the wife initiated support proceedings against the husband and the case was then transferred to a court in California for proceedings pursuant to the Uniform Reciprocal Enforcement of Support Act, which is discussed below. Held that pursuant to the Act the husband's duty of support should be determined under California law.

(2) Hardy v. Betz, 105 N.H. 169, 195 A.2d 582 (1963). The case involved an attempt under the Uniform Criminal Extradition Act to extradite to Massachusetts a New Hampshire man for failure to support what was alleged to be his illegitimate child. The mother had come to Massachusetts from New Hampshire shortly before the birth of the child; the man had remained at all times in New Hampshire. Held that extradition should be denied. "Since the [man] was never present in Massachusetts during the period for which support is sought, no obligation could arise under its laws, and he never became subject to its criminal laws." Two judges dissented.

(3) As to the enforcement in other states of a duty to pay for necessaries furnished to a husband, wife or minor child, see Mandell Bros. v. Fogg, 182 Mass. 582, 66 N.E. 198 (1903). Spouses domiciled in Massachusetts were present in Illinois when the husband purchased goods there. Seller sued the wife in Massachusetts for the price, basing its claim on an Illinois statute under which the wife was liable for such purchases. In denying recovery, the court said: ". . . it may be doubted whether [the statute] was intended to apply to citizens of other states 'temporarily' within [Illinois]. If it was intended to apply to such citizens, it is not a liability which will be enforced by the courts of other states."

B. RECIPROCAL SUPPORT LEGISLATION

Originally, attempts to recover support from one who has left the state where his dependents live faced almost insuperable difficulties. Where a support judgment had been obtained against the deserter prior to his flight, it was frequently not enforced by the state of his refuge on the ground that it was modifiable in the state of rendition. In this situation two suits, as well as delay, became inevitable. First, it was necessary to wait until installments under the support decree had had time to accrue. Next, the claimant was forced to recover judgment for the accrued installments in the first state and then sue to enforce this judgment in the second state. In the absence of statute, the entire process would have to be repeated after still further installments had become due, unless, as in Worthley v. Worthley, p. 296, supra, the second court were to prove willing to order the defendant to pay future installments of alimony as they accrued.

If no judgment for support had been obtained before the defendant left the state, the plight of the dependent might be hopeless. At least in the absence of a modern long-arm statute (see pp. 121–124, supra), presumably no judgment could be obtained against the defendant in the first state for lack of jurisdiction or competence unless he had left property there. An action to recover support brought against the defendant in the state of his refuge, might involve traveling and legal expenses beyond the means of the dependent. Moreover, the action might be dismissed in the latter state on the ground that no duty of support was there recognized except with respect to dependents who were residing within the state at the time the claim arose.

To ameliorate the situation, every state in this country, except New York, has adopted some form of the Uniform Reciprocal Enforcement of Support Act.[1] Apart from any provision made for the extradition of the defendant, the Act operates as follows:

The proceeding opens with the filing of a petition in a court of what will usually be the state where petitioner resides. This court, called the "initiating court," examines the petition to decide whether it "sets forth facts from which it may be determined that the defendant owes a duty of support and that a court of the responding state may obtain jurisdiction of the defendant or his property. . . ."[2] If the court answers these two questions in the affirmative, it will send copies of the petition to an appropriate court of the responding state. The latter court then takes the necessary steps to obtain jurisdiction over the defendant or his property. If the defendant appears and presents a defense, further hearings will be held, but the Act does not specify the procedure to be followed. In some states, the denials are transmitted to the initiating court which will hear the evidence of the petitioner. A transcript of this hearing is transmitted to the responding court, which will give the defendant opportunity to intro-

1. The Uniform Reciprocal Enforcement of Support Act was approved by the Commissioners on Uniform State Laws in 1950 and amended in 1952 and 1958. A revised Act was approved in 1968. The Commissioners' Prefatory Note to the 1968 Act states that by 1957 the Act (or a substantially similar act) had been enacted in all States, the District of Columbia, Puerto Rico, and most of the other areas subject to the jurisdiction of the United States.

New York has an essentially similar statute, the Uniform Support of Dependents Law, which provides for reciprocal enforcement of support actions with states having the Uniform Act. N.Y. Dom.Rel.Law §§ 30–43.

2. Uniform Reciprocal Enforcement of Support Act § 13.

duce proof and to cross-examine the petitioner and the petitioner's witnesses by written interrogatories.[3] In the alternative, it has been suggested that the testimony of the petitioner be taken by deposition or commission in the initiating state and then mailed to the responding state. The defendant will be permitted, if he so desires, to conduct his cross-examination in the initiating state by attorney.[4]

After all the evidence is in, the responding court, if satisfied of the petitioner's need for support and of defendant's liability, will enter an order requiring the defendant to make support payments, which will be forwarded to the initiating court and by it delivered to petitioner. To enforce compliance with its orders, the responding court may require the defendant to furnish bond or to make periodic payments or, in case of refusal may punish him for contempt. Both the initiating and responding courts may, in a proper case, request a designated legal officer of the state to represent petitioner without fee.

The Uniform Reciprocal Enforcement of Support Act makes provision for the enforcement either of a previously granted support order or of an original claim for support. Suit to enforce an original claim for support raises the problem of what law determines whether the alleged obligor owes any such duty and, if so, what is its extent. The 1952, 1958 and 1968 versions of the Act provide:

"§ 7. Choice of Law. Duties of support applicable under this law [act] are those imposed or imposable under the laws of any state where the obligor was present during the period for which support is sought. The obligor is presumed to have been present in the responding state during the period for which support is sought until otherwise shown." [5]

The 1968 Act and earlier 1958 amendment to the Act[6] provide for the registration and enforcement of modifiable support orders rendered under the Act in sister states.

The Uniform Civil Liability for Support Act was approved in 1954 by the National Conference of Commissioners on Uniform State Laws.[7] This act is designed to supplement the Uniform Reciprocal

3. Duncan v. Smith, 262 S.W.2d 373 (Ky.1953); Allain v. Allain, 24 Ill.App.2d 400, 164 N.E.2d 611 (1960).

4. Brockelbank, Interstate Enforcement of Family Support (The Runaway Pappy Act) 52–55 (1960).

5. The draftsmen of the Act deliberately employed "presence" rather than "domicile" in § 7 to avoid the technicalities and difficulty of proof which they felt would be engendered by use of the latter term. Brockelbank, The Problem of Family Support: A New Uniform Act Offers a Solution, 37 A.B.A.J. 93 (1951).

Section 7 deals with the case where claimant seeks support for a period that has already passed, since it provides that the law to be applied is that of any state where the obligor was present during the period for which support is sought.

6. §§ 34–38.

7. The Uniform Civil Liability for Support Act has been adopted by four states: California, Maine, New Hampshire, and Utah.

Enforcement of Support Act. It is intended to make uniform the law
of support and, by putting it in statutory form, to make the duties of
support owed under the law of a particular state readily ascertainable. Among other things, the Uniform Civil Liability for Support Act
states the various persons to whom a man or woman may owe a duty
of support and lists various factors such as the standard of living and
situation of the parties, which the court shall consider in determining
the amount of support that a given obligor shall be ordered to pay.

NOTES

(1) For a case applying the current version of Section 7 of the Act and
determining the duty of support in accordance with the law of the state
where the obligor was present during the critical time, see Engelson v. Mal-
lea, 180 N.W.2d 127 (Iowa 1970).

(2) In the 1950 version of the Act, Section 7 read as follows: "Duties of
support applicable under this law [act] are those imposed or imposable under
the laws of any state where the obligor was present during the period for
which support is sought, or where the obligee was present when the failure
to support commenced, at the election of the obligee." Was this provision
constitutional insofar as it called for application of the law of the state where
the obligee was present? In Commonwealth ex rel. Department of Public
Assistance v. Mong, 160 Ohio St. 455, 117 N.E.2d 32 (1954), a father living in
Pennsylvania sought support from his son living in Ohio. The father chose
the law of Pennsylvania under which he would have recovered, whereas under Ohio law the son owed no duty of support. Held, no recovery. To apply
Pennsylvania law would be a violation of the son's right to equal protection
of the laws. But compare Bjorgo v. Bjorgo, 402 S.W.2d 143 (Tex.1966), discussed at p. 885, note 1, supra.

(3) For a general discussion of the Uniform Reciprocal Enforcement of
Support Act, see Brockelbank, Interstate Enforcement of Family Support (2d
ed. Infausto 1971); Note, Interstate Enforcement of Support Obligations
Through Long-Arm Statutes and URESA, 18 J.Fam.L. 537 (1980).

(4) The reciprocal support legislation has survived many constitutional attacks. Among the claims of invalidity that have been urged are those asserting that this legislation confers "extraterritorial jurisdiction" on the initiating court, and that it denies defendant the opportunity to confront and
cross-examine the petitioner and his witnesses. The former objection has
been overruled on the ground that jurisdiction over the respondent is acquired by the responding court by operation of its own statute rather than
by that of the initiating state. See Duncan v. Smith, 262 S.W.2d 373 (Ky.
1953). With respect to the latter objection, cross-examination by deposition
has been held sufficient. See Smith v. Smith, 125 Cal.App.2d 154, 270 P.2d
613 (1954). See also Brockelbank, Is the Uniform Reciprocal Enforcement of
Support Act Constitutional?, 17 Mo.L.Rev. 1 (1952).

(5) It has been held that under the Reciprocal Enforcement of Support
Act the responding state can modify a decree previously handed down
against the defendant in a third state if the decree is also subject to modification in the third state. Moore v. Moore, 252 Iowa 404, 107 N.W.2d 97 (1961).

(6) The Uniform Support of Dependents Law, in force in New York, does not contain a choice of law provision comparable to § 7 of the Uniform Reciprocal Enforcement of Support Act. On the other hand, it sets forth those relationships which give rise to a duty of support. As a result, the New York courts have construed the New York statute to preclude their acting as either initiating or responding court unless petitioner and respondent are within one of the enumerated relationships. See Ross v. Ross, 206 Misc. 1073, 136 N.Y.S.2d 23 (Children's Ct.1954); Vincenza v. Vincenza, 197 Misc. 1027, 98 N.Y.S.2d 470 (N.Y.Dom.Rel.Ct.1950); 30 St. John's L.Rev. 309 (1956).

(7) The reciprocal support legislation involves planned and directed cooperation between courts of different states of the Union in hearing and deciding a single controversy and in enforcing the judgment. Are there areas other than support in which such cooperation is needed, and in which it should be established, either through legislation or on the initiative of the courts? What are these areas? How should the cooperation be carried out?

(8) For a discussion of the enforcement of support obligations in international settings, see Cavers, International Enforcement of Family Support, 81 Colum.L.Rev. 994 (1981).

SECTION 9.   MARITAL PROPERTY *

Introductory Note. "Marital property" may be defined as the interests which one spouse acquires, solely by reason of the marital relation, in the property, whether movable or immovable, of the other spouse, apart from the bare expectancy of inheriting upon the death of the other intestate. Two marital property systems are in effect in the United States. The common law system prevails in more than forty states and the District of Columbia, while community property is to be found in Arizona, California, Idaho, Louisiana, Nevada, New Mexico, Texas and Washington. There have been many drastic statutory modifications, and marked divergencies are to be found between states having the same general system.

There is no need to discuss these two systems in detail or to describe the form they originally took. They protect a spouse's economic interests in different ways. In common law states, a spouse is entitled to a fraction of all the property owned by the other spouse at the time of death. This interest is contingent upon surviving the other, but cannot be affected by any testamentary disposition the other spouse makes. Under community property systems, a spouse has a

---

* Restatement, Second, Conflict of Laws §§ 233–234, 257–259.

one-half interest in that part of the other's property which falls into the community. This is a present and vested interest which is not dependent upon surviving the other. Upon the dissolution of the marriage by death or divorce, the community property is divided equally among the spouses or their estates. Some property, however, does not fall into the community. A spouse retains full ownership to (and the other spouse has no marital interest in) property which belonged to him or her at the time of marriage or which he or she acquires thereafter by gift, will or descent. All other acquisitions, except in some states income derived from a spouse's separate property, belong to the community. Originally, the husbund had exclusive control over the community property during the existence of the marriage, but this rule has been extensively modified by statute.

Marital property is in this country a fertile field for conflict of laws problems. This is not only because of the differences between common law and community property systems but also on account of the frequent divergencies in the laws of states belonging to the same general system.

NOTES

(1) In no state of the United States at the present time does a spouse acquire a marital property interest in property owned by the other spouse at the time of marriage. Hence the question of what law governs the effect of marriage on existing interests in movables has little practical importance. The majority of cases held, at a time when under the law of some states marriage did affect existing interests in movables, that the governing law is that of the state where the husband was domiciled at the time of marriage. See, e.g., Jaffrey v. McGough, 83 Ala. 202, 3 So. 594 (1888); Mason v. Homer, 105 Mass. 116 (1870). The most recent case, however, held that the governing law is that of the state of the domicile at the time of marriage of the spouse who owned the movables involved. Locke v. McPherson, 163 Mo. 493, 63 S.W. 726 (1901). The rule of this latter case is followed in § 257 of the Restatement, Second.

The question may still arise in cases where the law of a foreign country is involved. An example is Harral v. Harral, 39 N.J.Eq. 279 (1884). There H (an American citizen) and W were married in France where both were domiciled. After H's death, W asserted a community property interest in movables located in New Jersey and owned by H at the time of marriage. The New Jersey courts found for W on the ground that under French law a spouse obtained a community property interest in the movables possessed by the other spouse on the day of marriage.

(2) In DeNicols v. Curlier, [1900] A.C. 21, the House of Lords treated a marriage in France between French citizens as creating by tacit contract an agreement that French community property law was to govern acquisition of personal property in England after the parties had become domiciled there. In DeNicols v. Curlier, [1900] 2 Ch. 410, the same rule was applied to real property acquired in England.

The rule of the Curlier cases is not followed in the United States. Saul v. His Creditors, 5 Mart., N.S., 569 (La.1827).

(3) As to express ante-nuptial contracts, see Harding, Matrimonial Domicil and Marital Rights in Movables, 30 Mich.L.Rev. 859, 873–875 (1932). Americans do not frequently enter ante-nuptial contracts and there appear to be few cases in this country on the subject.

ROZAN v. ROZAN

Supreme Court of California, 1957.
49 Cal.2d 322, 317 P.2d 11.

TRAYNOR, JUSTICE.   Plaintiff brought this action against her husband, Maxwell M. Rozan, for divorce, support, custody of their minor child, and division of their community property. . . .

The trial court granted plaintiff an interlocutory judgment of divorce on the ground of extreme cruelty, awarded her the custody of the minor child, ordered defendant to pay $75 per month for child support, $250 per month for plaintiff's support, and $12,500 for attorney's fees.   The court adjudged that the parties became domiciled in California . . . in any event not later than July 1948 and that the property thereafter acquired was community property . . . .

Although defendant "does not challenge the lower Court for granting the divorce" . . . he contends . . . that certain oil properties outside of California adjudged to be community property were his separate property . . . .

The first finding essential to the division of the property is that plaintiff and defendant "established their residence and domicile in California . . . in any event not later than July, 1948" and "that ever since they have been and still are residents of and domiciled in the State of California."   A determination of the domicile is essential, for marital interests in movables acquired during coverture are governed by the law of the domicile at the time of their acquisition. . . .   Moreover, the interests of the spouses in movables do not change even though the movables are taken into another state or are used to purchase land in another state. . . .

. . . The . . . evidence amply supports the trial court's finding of domicile not later than July, 1948. . . .

The last finding on which the division of property depends is that the North Dakota properties "were acquired with community property and community property money."   It is undisputed that these properties were acquired after 1949 . . . . It . . . appears that the purchase money for the North Dakota properties was acquired by the efforts and skill of defendant as an oil operator subsequent to the establishment of the California domicile and was therefore community property. . . .   Moreover there is a presumption that in the absence of evidence of gift, bequest, devise or descent, all property acquired by the husband after marriage is community property. . . . There is no evidence that the purchase money was acquired by gift, bequest, devise, or descent. There is, therefore, substantial evidence to sustain the trial court's finding that the North Dakota properties were purchased with community property funds. . . .

After acquiring the real property in North Dakota, defendant divested himself of title thereto by means of various conveyances, and title was eventually put in the name of Eugene Rosen, defendant's nephew, either individually or as trustee of a purported trust for the minor child. . . . there is abundant evidence to support the trial court's findings that these transactions were fraudulent as to plaintiff.

Defendant contends finally that the judgment directly affects the title to land in another state and therefore exceeded the court's jurisdiction. A court of one state cannot directly affect or determine the title to land in another. Fall v. Eastin, 215 U.S. 1 . . . It is well settled, however, that a court, with the parties before it, can compel the execution of a conveyance in the form required by the law of the situs and that such a conveyance will be recognized there. . . . Currie, Full Faith and Credit to Foreign Land Decrees, 21 U. of Chi. L.Rev. 620, 628–629. If the court has entered a decree of specific performance, but the conveyance has not been executed, the majority of states, including California, will give effect to the decree. . . . Thus in Redwood Investment Co. of Stithton, Ky. v. Exley, 64 Cal. App. 455, 459, 221 P. 973, 975, the court stated with reference to a Kentucky decree of specific performance to land in California: "It may be pleaded as a basis or cause of action or defense in the courts of the state where the land is situated, and is entitled in such a court to the force and effect of record evidence of the equities therein determined, unless it be impeached for fraud." There is no sound reason for denying a decree of a court of equity the same full faith and credit accorded any other kind of judgment. "Without exception, the courts recognize the validity of a deed executed under the compulsion of a foreign decree. But if the decree did not deal rightfully and constitutionally with the title to the land it would be voidable for duress. Recognition of the deed necessarily involves acceptance of the decree. Whatever intrusion on the state's exclusive control is implied in the recognition of the decree is accomplished through the recognition of the deed. A policy so easily evaded, so dependent on the success of the defendant in eluding the enforcement process of the foreign court, is a formal, lifeless thing, and the truth must be that foreign judicial proceedings of this type pose no real threat to the legitimate interest of the situs state." (Currie, supra, 21 U. of Chi.L. Rev. 620, 628–629.) Thus in the majority of states, such decrees are given effect as a res judicata declaration of the rights and equities of the parties. . . . Fall v. Eastin, 215 U.S. 1, on which defendant relies did not hold otherwise. In that case the Washington decree directly affected title to land in Nebraska. A commissioner of the Washington court had executed a deed to that land and Mrs. Fall attempted to use this deed as a muniment of title in her action to quiet title against a grantee of the husband.

In the light of the foregoing principles the judgment in the present case is res judicata and entitled to full faith and credit in North Dakota to the extent that it determines the rights and equities of the parties with respect to the land in question. An action on that judgment in North Dakota, however, is necessary to effect any change in the title to the land there. Thus, the judgment must be affirmed to the extent that it declares the rights of the parties before the court and modified to the extent that it purports to affect the title to the land.

Neither Eugene Rosen, who holds record title, nor the minor child, who is the beneficiary of the purported trust, were parties to this action and the judgment is therefore not binding on them. . . .

In several respects the judgment purports to affect title to the land and must therefore be modified. Thus, paragraph . . . 21 . . . awards 65 per cent of the North Dakota properties and the past, present, and future rents, issues and profits therefrom to plaintiff as her sole and separate property and awards 35 per cent thereof to Rozan subject to a lien for alimony, child support, and attorney's fees. This paragraph . . . is therefore modified to read as follows: "21. It Is Further Ordered and Adjudged, that each and every one of the aforementioned North Dakota properties . . . were acquired with community property funds of plaintiff and Rozan; . . . that plaintiff is entitled to 65% of the aforementioned properties and of the rents, issues and profits thereof as against Rozan; that Rozan is entitled to 35% of the aforementioned properties and of the rents, issues and profits thereof as against plaintiff; and," . . .

The judgment is affirmed as modified. Defendant shall bear the costs on appeal.

NOTES

(1) Following the decision in the principal case, the wife instituted an action in North Dakota to enforce the California decree. The North Dakota court awarded the wife judgment for the sums accrued under the California decree. It also gave res judicata effect to the California finding that the North Dakota real property had been purchased with community funds and accordingly held that the wife was entitled to a one-half interest in this property. On the other hand, the court held that it would not recognize the California decree insofar as it purported to award the wife a 65% interest in this property. This was because the decree (a) did not order the husband to convey such an interest to his wife and (b) did not have to be recognized under

full faith and credit since it directly affected title to North Dakota real property. Rozan v. Rozan, 129 N.W.2d 694 (N.Dak.1964).

(2) Estate of Warner, 167 Cal. 686, 140 Pac. 583 (1914). H and W made their home in Illinois, a common law state. During the marriage, H sent from Illinois certain funds which were used to purchase land in California. After H's death W renounced her rights under H's will and claimed a community property interest in the California land. W's claim was, however, rejected by the California courts on the ground that "it is well settled that separate personal property, enjoyed under the law of the domicile by one of the spouses at the time it was acquired is not lost by its investment in real property in another jurisdiction where a different law is in force."

(3) For a discussion of the converse situation, where persons move from a community property state to a common law property state, see Lay, Community Property in Common Law States, 41 Temp.L.Q. 1 (1967); Leflar, From Community to Common Law State; Estate Problems of Citizens Moving from One to Other, 99 Trusts & Estates 882 (1960).

(4) Depas v. Mayo, 11 Mo. 314 (1848). While domiciled in Louisiana, a community property state, husband and wife accumulated considerable assets. They then moved to Missouri, where the husband used part of the assets accumulated in Louisiana to purchase in his own name a lot in the city of St. Louis. Thereafter the parties resumed their Louisiana domicile and ultimately were divorced. Action was brought by the wife for determination that she was entitled to a one-half interest in the St. Louis property. Held for the wife. Missouri law must decide "all questions" concerning title to the land in St. Louis. ". . . according to the law in this state, if A purchases land with the money of B, and takes legal title to himself, a court of equity will regard him as a trustee. . . . " The husband purchased the land with assets in which his wife had a one-half interest. She is therefore entitled to one-half interest in the land. It makes no difference that prior to the purchase the parties had changed their domicile to Missouri.

(5) Restatement, Second, Conflict of Laws § 258, Comment *c.* ". . . When the spouses have separate domicils at the time of the acquisition of the movable, the local law of the state where the spouse who acquired the movable was domiciled will usually be held to determine the extent of the other spouse's marital interest therein."

(6) Restatement, Second, Conflict of Laws § 166, Comment *b.* ". . . [At times] one spouse is injured either through the negligence of the other spouse or through the joint negligence of the other spouse and of a third person. Then, if the injured spouse brings suit against the employer or insurer of the other spouse or against the third person, he may be met with the argument that relief should be denied because the negligent spouse would share in any recovery that might be obtained. It might be thought that the law [selected to determine related issues of tort law] should be applied to determine whether the negligence of one person should be imputed to another if the negligent person would share in any recovery that the other might obtain. On the other hand, it might be thought that the local law of the state of the spouses' domicil should be applied to determine whether any recovery would be community property and thus would be shared by the negligent spouse . . . In the majority of the few cases in point, the plain-

tiff spouse has been permitted to recover. . . . " See also Marsh, Marital Property in Conflict of Laws 193–194 (1952).

WYATT v. FULRATH

Court of Appeals of New York, 1965.
16 N.Y.2d 169, 264 N.Y.S.2d 233, 211 N.E.2d 637.

BERGAN, JUDGE. The Duke and Duchess of Arion were nationals and domiciliaries of Spain. Neither of them had ever been in New York, but through a long period of political uncertainty in Spain, from 1919 to the end of the [Spanish] Civil War, they sent cash and securities to New York for safekeeping and investment.

Under the law of Spain this was the community property of the spouses. Substantial parts of it were placed with the New York custodians in joint accounts. In establishing or in continuing these accounts, the husband and wife either expressly agreed in writing that the New York law of survivorship would apply or agreed to a written form of survivorship account conformable to New York law.

The husband died in November, 1957; the wife in March, 1959. After the husband's death the wife took control of the property in New York and undertook to dispose of it by a will executed according to New York law and affecting property in New York. . . . Some additional property in joint account in England was transferred by the wife to New York after the husband's death which had not been placed by either spouse in New York during the husband's life.

This action is by plaintiff as an ancillary administrator in New York of the husband against defendant as executor of the wife's will to establish a claim of title to one half of the property which at the time of the husband's death was held in custody accounts under sole or joint names of the spouses by banks in New York and London.

The total value of the property in New York is about $2,275,000, of which about $370,000 was transferred by the wife after the husband's death from the London accounts to New York. . . .

The main issue in the case is whether the law of Spain should be applied to the property placed in New York during the lives of the spouses, in which event only half of the property would have gone to the wife at her husband's death, or the law of New York, in which event all of such jointly held property would have gone to her as survivor. . . .

The controversy here is . . . . to be governed by the legal capacity of the husband and wife, as citizens and domiciliaries of Spain, to make an agreement as to their community property inconsistent with Spanish law.

The agreements giving full title to the survivor in the joint accounts were executed either in Spain, or if not there at least not in New York, and were, in any event, executed by persons who were domiciliaries and citizens of Spain. Usually rights flowing from this kind of legal act are governed by the law of the domiciliary jurisdiction . . . .

Dispositions of property in violation of this prohibition are shown to be void according to Spanish law. . . .

But New York has the right to say as a matter of public policy whether it will apply its own rules to property in New York of foreigners who choose to place it here for custody or investment, and to honor or not the formal agreements or suggestions of such owners by which New York law would apply to the property they place here. (Cf. Decedent Estate Law, § 47; Personal Property Law, Consol. Laws, c. 41, § 12–a.)

It seems preferable that as to property which foreign owners are able to get here physically, and concerning which they request New York law to apply to their respective rights, when it actually gets here, that we should recognize their physical and legal submission of the property to our laws, even though under the laws of their own country a different method of fixing such rights would be pursued.

Thus we would at once honor their intentional resort to the protection of our laws and their recognition of the general stability of our Government which may well be deemed inter-related things. . . .

The Special Term in the case before us found for the defendant . . . . We agree that this disposition is the correct one as to property placed in New York during the husband's lifetime.

This effect would include, too, those accounts which had formerly been joint accounts but which during the lifetime of the husband were transferred to the wife's sole name. . . .

The assent of the husband to arrangements in respect of joint property transferred to the sole account of the wife with the legal consequence of sole ownership to be anticipated from the effect of New York law would lead us to treat the property as the property of the wife and to be controlled by the same principle applicable to joint accounts. . . .

We would treat the wife's own separate property similarly where, during the lifetime of her husband and apparently with his recognition and assent, she was able to transfer the separate property to New York and keep it here in her own name.

But the property in the value of about $370,000 transferred from London to New York by the wife after the husband's death raises a somewhat different question. Adjudication of its title requires further factual exploration. At the time of the husband's death this property and other property were held in three-name custody ac-

counts by London depositories. The accounts were in the names of
the husband, the wife and their daughter Hilda, who had no proprietary interest. . . .

The reasons grounded on New York policy and affected by the
physical transfer of the property to New York during the lifetime of
the spouses and by their directions relating to it do not necessarily
apply to property of Spanish nationals placed in a third country during their lifetime.

If the local law of the third country would deem title to have
passed to the wife on the death of the husband, we would treat this
property as we now treat that placed in New York during their lives.

But if the third country would have applied the Spanish community property law or, if it is not demonstrated what rule would be applied by the third country and the subject is open or equivocal, we
would, under general principles, feel bound to apply the law of Spain
to the title of property owned by these Spanish nationals.

. . .

The order should be modified to direct the remission to Special
Term to determine the rights of parties in respect of the property
transferred by the wife from London to New York after the husband's death in accordance with this opinion and, as modified, affirmed, without costs.

DESMOND, CHIEF JUDGE (dissenting). Resolution of the dispute as
to this property (or any part of it) by any law other than that of
Spain, the matrimonial domicile, is utterly incompatible with historic
and settled conflict of laws principles and is not justifiable on any
ground. No policy ground exists for upsetting the uniform rules and
no precedent commands such a result. . . .

The majority of this court is throwing overboard not one but three
of the oldest and strongest conflict rules: first, that with exceptions
not pertinent here the law of the domicile of the owner governs as to
the devolution of personal property . . .; second, that the law of
the matrimonial domicile controls as to the property and contract
rights of husband and wife *inter sese* . . .; and, third, that whether such personalty is separate or community property is determined
by the law of the matrimonial domicile. . . .

. . . The Duke and Duchess of Arion were Spanish nationals,
were married in Spain and always had their domicile there as had
their ancestors for generations or centuries. Neither was ever in
New York. New York State's only contact with this property was
that for purposes of convenience or safety the husband and wife left
valuable property in the custody of New York banks for safekeeping
only. The banks were mere bailees without other title or interest.
To say that setting up of joint accounts of personalty in New York
subjected that personalty to New York law rather than to the law of

the matrimonial domicile is to refuse to follow one of the most basic of Conflict of Laws rules. . . .

. . . The signing by the Duke and Duchess in Spain of routine joint-account-for-custody agreements on forms supplied by the New York banks is not substantial proof that these people (who had no apparent reason for so doing) were attempting to abrogate as to these items of property the ancient community laws of their country. There is no other proof of such an intent to substitute New York law and a much more reasonable explanation of the documents exacted by the banks is that they operated and were intended merely to release the banks on payment to one spouse or the other. . . .

MATTER OF CRICHTON, 20 N.Y.2d 124, 228 N.E.2d 799 (1967): Crichton died domiciled in New York, where he had moved early in life, owning movables in Louisiana. His will made no provision for his wife, from whom he had been separated for twenty-seven years, and the question was whether she had a community property interest in the Louisiana movables or whether her rights were limited to a forced share under New York law. A Louisiana statute provided that all property acquired in the state by a nonresident should be treated as community property. It was held that the wife's rights in the Louisiana movables were limited to a forced share under New York law. Speaking for the court, JUDGE KEATING said: . . .

The choice of law problem here should be resolved by an examination of the contacts which Louisiana and New York have with this controversy for the purpose of determining which of those jurisdictions has the paramount interest in the application of its law. . . .

The issue in this case is whether the community property laws of Louisiana should be applied to govern the property rights of New York domiciliaries in intangible personal property acquired during coverture. . . . it is clear that the community property system is designed to regulate the property rights of married persons and, in particular, to protect the interest of each spouse in the property accumulated during marriage. . . . For reasons which become obvious merely in stating the purpose of the rule, Louisiana has no such interest in protecting and regulating the rights of married persons residing and domiciled in New York.

The State of New York which has such an interest has not adopted a community property system. Instead it has sought to protect a *surviving* spouse by giving her a right to take one third of the entire estate of the deceased as against a testamentary disposition by which the deceased has attempted to exclude her from a share of the estate. (Decedent Estate Law, § 18.) And, depending upon the nature of the property in the estate, a surviving spouse under New York law might well be entitled to receive a greater portion of the over-all estate than under the community property system.

By affording the surviving spouse such a right in the estate of the deceased spouse, the Legislature has sought to preserve the right of the testator to distribute his property as he desires, while at the same time to provide protection for the surviving spouse. New York, as the domicile of Martha and Powell Crichton, has not only the dominant interest in the application of its law and policy but the only interest. . . .

It is urged by the appellant that the Louisiana contacts with this case give it the paramount interest in the application of its law. Among the contacts which are urged as being significant are the facts the deceased was born in Louisiana, that, although he was domiciled in New York, the bulk of his fortune was made in Louisiana, and that the documentary evidences of his intangible property are located in that jurisdiction. Exactly how these contacts are related to the policies sought to be vindicated by Louisiana's community property laws is not made clear. The reason, no doubt, is that they have no relation whatever.[8] . . .

. . . this case is distinguishable from Hutchison v. Ross, 262 N.Y. 381, 187 N.E. 65, 89 A.L.R. 1007, supra, and Wyatt v. Fulrath, 16 N.Y.2d 169, 264 N.Y.S.2d 233, 211 N.E.2d 637, supra, relied upon by the appellant in support of her argument for the application of Louisiana law.

In the latter case . . . [r]elying upon sections 12–a of the Personal Property Law, Consol.Laws, c. 41, and 47 of the Decedent Estate Law, which are designed to encourage investment of funds in this State by permitting a nondomiciliary to designate New York law as applicable to determine questions of law relating to testamentary dispositions of personal property located here as well as *inter vivos* trusts having a situs in this State, we held that New York law and not the Spanish community property laws would govern. In so doing, we cited the earlier case of Hutchison v. Ross (supra) in which the court, speaking through Judge Lehman, relying upon section 12–a of the Personal Property Law, held that it was the policy of this State to

8. Contacts obtain significance only to the extent that they relate to the policies and purposes sought to be vindicated by the conflicting laws. Once these contacts are discovered and analyzed they will indicate (1) that there exists no true conflict of laws, as in the case at bar and as in most choice of law cases, or (2) that a true conflict exists, i.e., both jurisdictions have an interest in the application of their law. In the former case, of course, the law of the jurisdiction having the only real interest in the litigation will be applied. . . . (Oltarsh v. Aetna Ins. Co., 15 N.Y.2d 111, 256 N.Y.S.2d 577, 204 N.E.2d 622.) In the case of a true conflict, while our decisions have normally resulted in application of forum law (Wyatt v. Fulrath, 16 N.Y.2d 169, 264 N.Y.S.2d 233, 211 N.E.2d 637, supra), we are not as yet prepared to formulate what may be deemed a rule of general application but prefer rather to give further consideration to the question as the cases arise. (See Currie, The Disinterested Third State, 28 Law & Contemp.Prob., 754, 756–764.)

permit out-of-State settlors of trusts to designate that rights in that property be determined by New York law.

In both these cases we were giving effect to New York's policy and governmental interest. . . .

NOTES

(1) Subsequent to the New York decision in the principal case, the Louisiana court held in Mrs. Crichton's action against her husband's estate that the New York courts had misinterpreted Louisiana law and that under that law Mrs. Crichton was entitled to a one half interest in the movable property left by Mr. Crichton in Louisiana. The court found for the estate, however, for the reason that it felt required by full faith and credit to give res judicata effect to the New York judgment. Crichton v. Succession of Crichton, 232 So.2d 109 (La.App.2d Cir. 1970), writ ref'd result correct, 256 La. 274, 236 So. 2d 39 (1970).

(2) Is Judge Keating's approach in Crichton a sound one? Is marital property an area where there is real need for actual rules of choice of law?

(3) Granted that in Wyatt v. Fulrath New York had an interest in applying its law, can it convincingly be urged that New York, rather than Spain, was the state of paramount interest? If not, what is the status of the Wyatt holding in the light of Matter of Crichton? Can the Wyatt decision be justified on other grounds? Does it bear an analogy to the power of the parties to select the law governing their contract? See pp. 376–596, supra.

(4) For a fine article comparing the American, French and English approaches to marital property in conflict of laws, see Juenger, Marital Property and the Conflict of Laws: A Tale of Two Countries, 81 Colum.L.Rev. 1061 (1981).

(5) See generally Clausnitzen, Property Rights of Surviving Spouse and the Conflict of Laws, 18 J.Fam.L. 471 (1980).

ESTATE OF O'CONNOR

Supreme Court of California, 1933.
218 Cal. 518, 23 P.2d 1031, 88 A.L.R. 856.

[Plaintiff and defendant were married in Indiana, where both were domiciled at the time. Shortly after the marriage, defendant deserted plaintiff and went to California, where he died leaving a will in which he bequeathed his property to a third person. At the time of the marriage, defendant owned some $200,000 worth of stocks and bonds, and these, or property acquired in exchange therefor, were in his estate at the time of his death. In the California administration proceedings, plaintiff claimed one-third of the estate relying upon the Indiana law which permits a widow to take this amount against the will of her deceased husband. The plaintiff is now appealing from the action of the trial court in sustaining the executor's demurrer to her petition.]

THE COURT.   We have re-examined the questions involved in this appeal and find ourselves in entire accord with the conclusion and opinion of the District Court of Appeal, Division One of the First Appellate District, and we hereby adopt that opinion as the opinion of this court in this cause, as follows:

"Appellant contends that she is entitled to the portion of decedent's personal estate which she could have claimed under the laws of Indiana notwithstanding his attempted disposal thereof by his will. . . .

"The community system does not prevail in Indiana, and appellant admits that prior to 1891 there was no statute of that state giving to a surviving widow an interest in her deceased husband's personal estate akin to the common-law right of dower and not subject to be defeated by will. . . .   She claims, however, that the act of March 9, 1891 (Acts 1891, p. 404) (Burns' Annotated Indiana Statutes 1926, sec. 3343 (3025)), gives such right. [The statute, which gives the widow the right to elect, is omitted.] . . .

". . . no statute or decision from that state has been called to our attention which provides or holds that the wife enjoys any ordinary rights of ownership in her husband's personal property during his lifetime, or has a more complete interest therein than that of an expectancy as heir if she survives him.

"Appellant concedes that the property in question if governed by the California law would be the separate property of decedent and subject to his testamentary disposition; also that as a general rule the descent of personal property is governed by the laws of the state where decedent was domiciled at the time of his death, but she insists that the contract of marriage in relation to property rights should be governed, as other contracts, by the laws of the jurisdiction where it was to be carried out—in this instance by the laws of Indiana.

"This doctrine has been recognized and applied in instances where rights in the property of one spouse were held to have vested at the time of the marriage. The rule is stated in Wharton on Conflict of Laws, section 193a, as follows: 'While . . . it is undoubtedly true that the intestacy laws of the last domicile of the deceased govern the distribution of the personal estate of either husband or wife in case of intestacy, a distinction is to be observed between the mere inchoate rights of either spouse to share in the distribution of the other's estate at his death and a vested right which attaches at the time of marriage though its enjoyment may be postponed until the death of the other spouse.' The author says further that the latter right is not divested by a change of domicile, but that a mere statute of distribution of the original matrimonial domicile, or any domicile other than the last, by which either spouse is to share in the other's personal estate upon the latter's death creates no vested right, and therefore offers no obstacle to the application of the statute of distribution of the last domicile. . . .

"The mere fact that under the Indiana laws, above cited, the power of the husband to dispose of his personal property by will was subject to the right of his wife at her election to claim a third thereof gave her no more than an expectancy in this portion of his estate. As was held in Spreckels v. Spreckels, 116 Cal. 339 (48 P. 228, 58 Am. St.Rep. 170, 36 L.R.A. 497), such a limitation of the husband's right would give the wife no interest in his property during his lifetime. We are satisfied that appellant had no present fixed right or interest in decedent's personal estate, or more than a mere expectancy, which depended upon survivorship to become a vested right. This being true, and he having established his domicile in California, as he might do (Civ.Code, sec. 129), the property was subject to the law of this state, which governs its disposition and distribution whether he died testate or intestate."

The order appealed from is affirmed.

NOTES

(1) It will be noted that in the principal case the plaintiff wife was denied the economic protection accorded a spouse by either the California or Indiana law. Could the court have properly reached a different result? If so, by what reasoning?

(2) A pervasive problem is whether a given issue should be characterized as one of marital property or of succession. Questions of marital property are governed by the rules set forth in this Section, while those involving succession are determined by the law of the situs in the case of land and by that of the state where the decedent died domiciled in the case of movables. Whether a spouse has a community property interest in the other's property is considered a problem of marital property. On the other hand, whether a spouse has a nonbarrable interest in the property owned by the other spouse at the time of death is considered a question of succession.

Should application of a given rule of foreign law depend upon the way in which it is characterized by the forum or by the courts of the foreign state? For example, was the court in the principal case correct in refusing to apply the Indiana rule on the ground that it was one of succession rather than of marital property?

ADDISON v. ADDISON

Supreme Court of California, 1965.
62 Cal.2d 558, 43 Cal.Rptr. 97, 399 P.2d 897.

PETERS, JUSTICE. Plaintiff Leona Addison (hereafter referred to as Leona) was granted an interlocutory decree of divorce from defendant Morton Addison (hereafter referred to as Morton) on the ground of his adultery. . . .

At the time of their marriage in Illinois in 1939, Morton, having previously engaged in the used car business, had a net worth which he estimated as being between $15,000 and $20,000. Leona, however, testified that her husband's net worth was almost nothing at the time of their marriage. In 1949 the Addisons moved to California bringing with them cash and other personal property valued at $143,000 which had been accumulated as a result of Morton's various Illinois business enterprises. Since that time Morton has participated in several California businesses.

On February 20, 1961, Leona filed for divorce and requested an equitable division of the marital property. On trial, Leona . . . attempted to apply the recently enacted quasi-community property legislation[3] by contending that the property presently held in Morton's name was acquired by the use of property brought from Illinois and that the property would have been community property had it been originally acquired while the parties were domiciled in California.

The trial court . . . held the quasi-community property legislation to be unconstitutional.

The trial court . . . did find the household furniture and furnishings to be community property and, pursuant to Civil Code section 146, awarded them to Leona. In addition, the court found that the residence of the parties was held in joint tenancy and thus each owned an undivided one-half separate interest therein. Finally, all other property which had been in Morton's name alone was found to be his sole and separate property.

3. The key sections of the 1961 legislation which are involved in the instant case are as follows:

Civil Code section 140.5: "As used in Sections 140.7, 141, 142, 143, 146, 148, 149 and 176 of this code, 'quasi-community property' means all personal property wherever situated and all real property situated in this State heretofore or hereafter acquired:

"(a) By either spouse while domiciled elsewhere which would have been community property of the husband and wife had the spouse acquiring the property been domiciled in this State at the time of its acquisition; or

"(b) In exchange for real or personal property, wherever situated, acquired other than by gift, devise, bequest or descent by either spouse during the marriage while domiciled elsewhere.

"For the purposes of this section, personal property does not include and real property does include leasehold interests in real property."

Civil Code section 146 provides in part: "In case of the dissolution of the marriage by decree of a court of competent jurisdiction or in the case of judgment or decree for separate maintenance of the husband or the wife without dissolution of the marriage, the court shall make an order for disposition of the community property and the quasi-community property and for the assignment of the homestead as follows:

"(a) If the decree is rendered on the ground of adultery, incurable insanity or extreme cruelty, the community property and quasi-community property shall be assigned to the respective parties in such proportions as the court, from all the fact of the case, and the condition of the parties, may deem just.

"(b) If the decree be rendered on any other ground than that of adultery, incurable insanity or extreme cruelty, the community property and quasi-community property shall be equally divided between the parties."

The sociological problem to which the quasi-community property legislation addresses itself has been an area of considerable legislative and judicial activity in this state. One commentator has expressed this thought as follows: "Among the perennial problems in the field of community property in California, the status of marital personal property acquired while domiciled in another State has been particularly troublesome. Attempts of the Legislature to designate such personalty as community property uniformly have been thwarted by court decisions." (Comment (1935) 8 So.Cal.L.Rev. 221, 222).

The problem arises as a result of California's attempts to apply community property concepts to the foreign, and radically different (in hypotheses) common-law theory of matrimonial rights. In fitting the common-law system into our community property scheme the process is of two steps. First, property acquired by a spouse while domiciled in a common-law state is characterized as separate property. (Estate of O'Connor, 218 Cal. 518, 23 P.2d 1031, 88 A.L.R. 856.) Second, the rule of tracing is invoked so that all property later acquired in exchange for the common-law separate property is likewise deemed separate property. . . . Thus, the original property, and all property subsequently acquired through use of the original property is classified as the separate property of the acquiring spouse.

One attempt to solve the problem was the 1917 amendment to Civil Code section 164 which had the effect of classifying all personal property wherever situated and all real property located in California into California community property if that property would not have been the separate property of one of the spouses had that property been acquired while the parties were domiciled in California. Insofar as the amendment attempted to affect personal property brought to California which was the separate property of one of the spouses while domiciled outside this state Estate of Thornton, 1 Cal.2d 1, 33 P.2d 1, 92 A.L.R. 1343, held the section was unconstitutional. The amendment's effect upon real property located in California was never tested but generally was considered to be a dead letter as the section was never again invoked on the appellate level.

Another major attempt to alter the rights in property acquired prior to California domicile was the passage of Probate Code section 201.5. This section gave to the surviving spouse one half of all the personal property wherever situated and the real property located in California which would not have been the separate property of the acquiring spouse had it been acquired while domiciled in California. As a succession statute, its constitutionality was upheld on the theory that the state of domicile of the decedent at the time of his death has full power to control rights of succession. (In re Miller, 31 Cal.2d 191, 196, 187 P.2d 722). In other words, no one has a vested right to succeed to another's property rights, and no one has a vested right in the distribution of his estate upon his death. Hence succession rights may be constitutionally altered. This theory was a basis of the dissent in Thornton.

In the present case it is contended that Estate of Thornton, supra, 1 Cal.2d 1, 33 P.2d 1, is controlling and that the current legislation, by authority of Thornton, must be held to be unconstitutional. Thornton involved a situation of a husband and wife moving to California and bringing with them property acquired during their former domicile in Montana. Upon the husband's death, his widow sought to establish her community property rights in his estate as provided by the then recent amendment to Civil Code section 164. The majority held the section unconstitutional on the theory that upon acquisition of the property the husband obtained vested rights which could not be altered without violation of his privileges and immunities as a citizen and also that "to take the property of A and transfer it to B because of his citizenship and domicile, is also to take his property without due process of law. This is true regardless of the place of acquisition or the state of his residence." (Estate of Thornton, supra, 1 Cal.2d 1, 5, 33 P.2d 1, 3, 92 A.L.R. 1343.)

The underlying rationale of the majority was the same in Thornton as it had been since Spreckels v. Spreckels, 116 Cal. 339, 48 P. 228, 36 L.R.A. 497, which established, by a concession of counsel, that changes in the community property system which affected "vested interests" could not constitutionally be applied retroactively but must be limited to prospective application.

Langdon, J., in his dissent in Thornton, conceded the correctness of the vested right theory but argued that the statute was merely definitional, giving no rights to anyone except as provided by other legislation. Therefore, the widow would only be acquiring rights pursuant to a right of succession as granted by statute. As to the constitutionality of this application of amended Civil Code section 164 he declared: "It is a rule of almost universal acceptance that the rights of testamentary disposition and of succession are wholly subject to statutory control, and may be enlarged, limited, or abolished without infringing upon the constitutional guaranty of due process of law." (Estate of Thornton, supra, 1 Cal.2d 1, 7, 33 P.2d 1, 3.) The majority refused to construe amended Civil Code section 164 in this limited fashion.

The constitutional doctrine announced in Estate of Thornton, supra, has been questioned. Justice (now Chief Justice) Traynor in his concurring opinion in Boyd v. Oser, 23 Cal.2d 613, at p. 623, 145 P.2d 312, at page 318, had the following to say: "The decisions that existing statutes changing the rights of husbands and wives in community property can have no retroactive application have become a rule of property in this state and should not now be overruled. It is my opinion, however, that the constitutional theory on which they are based is unsound. [Citations.] That theory has not become a rule of property and should not invalidate future legislation in this field intended by the Legislature to operate retroactively." . . .

Thus, the correctness of the rule of Thornton is open to challenge. But even if the rule of that case be accepted as sound, it is not here controlling. This is so because former section 164 of the Civil Code has an entirely different impact from the legislation presently before us. The legislation under discussion, unlike old section 164, makes no attempt to alter property rights merely upon crossing the boundary into California. It does not purport to disturb vested rights "of a citizen of another state, who chances to transfer his domicile to this state, bringing his property with him . . . ." (Estate of Thornton, supra, 1 Cal.2d 1, at p. 5, 33 P.2d 1, at p. 3.) Instead, the concept of quasi-community property is applicable only if a divorce or separate maintenance action is filed here after the parties have become domiciled in California. Thus, the concept is applicable only if, after acquisition of domicile in this state, certain acts or events occur which give rise to an action for divorce or separate maintenance. These acts or events are not necessarily connected with a change of domicile at all. . . .

Clearly the interest of the state of the current domicile in the matrimonial property of the parties is substantial upon the dissolution of the marriage relationship. . . .

In recognition of much the same interest as that advanced by the quasi-community property legislation, many common-law jurisdictions have provided for the division of the separate property of the respective spouses in a manner which is "just and reasonable" and none of these statutes have been overturned on a constitutional basis.

In the case at bar it was Leona who was granted a divorce from Morton on the ground of the latter's adultery and hence it is the spouse guilty of the marital infidelity from whom the otherwise separate property is sought by the operation of the quasi-community property legislation. We are of the opinion that where the innocent party would otherwise be left unprotected the state has a very substantial interest and one sufficient to provide for a fair and equitable distribution of the marital property without running afoul of the due process clause of the Fourteenth Amendment. . . .

Morton also asserts that there is an abridgment of the privileges and immunities clause of the Fourteenth Amendment citing Estate of Thornton, supra . . . Aside from the due process clause, already held not to be applicable, Thornton may be read as holding that the legislation there in question impinged upon the right of a citizen of the United States to maintain a domicile in any state of his choosing without the loss of valuable property rights. As to this contention, the distinction we have already noted between former Civil Code section 164 and quasi-community property legislation is relevant. Unlike the legislation in Thornton, the quasi-community property legislation does not cause a loss of valuable rights through change of domicile. The concept is applicable only in case of a decree of divorce or separate maintenance.   .   .   .

The judgment is affirmed insofar as it decrees divorce and custody of the minor child.   In all other respects the judgment is reversed .   .   .   .

NOTES

(1) The facts of In re Thornton's Estate are stated in the principal case. The statute declared unconstitutional in Thornton provided in effect that all movables originally owned by a spouse as separate property, but which would be community property under California rules, would be converted into community property as soon as the spouse acquired a domicile in California.   It should be noted that Mrs. Thornton had a nonbarrable interest in her husband's movables under Montana law.   The decision in effect held that Mrs. Thornton lost this interest in her husband's movables as soon as she and he acquired a domicile in California.   This was the result the California statute sought to avoid.

(2) The California Probate Code, as amended in 1957, contains the following sections:

Section 201.5 provides that the surviving spouse of a decedent who dies domiciled in California is entitled to half of his California real estate and to half of all his personal property wherever situated if, (a) "acquired by the decedent while domiciled elsewhere which would have been the community property of the decedent and the surviving spouse had the decedent been domiciled in this State at the time of its acquisition" or (b) "acquired in exchange for real or personal property wherever situated which would have been the community property of the decedent and the surviving spouse if the decedent had been domiciled in this state at the time the property so exchanged was acquired."   This Section further provides that the remaining half of the decedent's property shall also go to the surviving spouse if not willed to a third person.

Section 201.7 provides that if the decedent has provided in his will for the surviving spouse, that spouse must elect whether to take under the will or against the will under Section 201.5 unless the will makes clear that the testator intended that the surviving spouse should take both under the will and against it.

Section 201.8 provides that, upon electing to take against the will of a deceased spouse who died domiciled in California, the surviving spouse may require restoration to the estate of one-half of any property transferred by the deceased spouse without substantial consideration if (a) the surviving spouse had an expectancy in this property under § 201.5 and (b) the deceased spouse "had a substantial quantum of ownership or control of the property at death."

(3) In 1961 the California statutes were further amended to provide for "quasi community property" interests in the event of a divorce.   These provisions are set forth in footnote 3 to the Addison opinion.

(4) The California legislation is discussed in Note, Marital Property and
the Conflict of Laws, 54 Calif.L.Rev. 252 (1966); Schreter, "Quasi-Community Property" in Conflict of Laws, 50 Calif.L.Rev. 206 (1962); compare Buch-
schacher, Rights of a Surviving Spouse in Texas in Marital Property Acquired While Domiciled Elsewhere, 45 Tex.L.Rev. 321 (1966).

(5) A basic book in the area is Marsh, Marital Property in Conflict of
Laws (1952). For other discussions of marital property, see the articles by
Professor Lay, Migrants from Community Property States—Filling the Leg-
islative Gap, 53 Corn.L.Rev. 832 (1968); Marital Property Rights of the Non-
Native in a Community Property State, 18 Hast.L.J. 295 (1967); The Role of
the Matrimonial Domicile in Marital Property Rights, 4 Fam.L.Q. 61 (1970).

Chapter 13

ADMINISTRATION OF ESTATES

SECTION 1. DECEDENTS' ESTATES*

Introductory Note. The casebook has dealt in earlier chapters with the substantive law applicable to succession to a decedent's property. This section is concerned with the machinery for the transfer of wealth from generation to generation. In the United States the method of transfer is through the personal representative, who is either an executor or administrator and who has been confirmed or appointed by a competent court.

The first stage is the determination in a judicial proceeding that the alleged decedent is dead and that he died either testate or intestate in a certain domicile. These determinations are followed by the appointment or qualification of the personal representative to administer the estate. At this stage there are problems of jurisdiction of courts, the nature of an administration proceeding, whether in rem or in personam, and the effect of foreign judgments.

The second stage is administration of the estate by the personal representative. His functions are essentially three: to collect and protect the property of the decedent, whether by voluntary payment or delivery or by suit; to pay creditors either voluntarily or after suit; and to distribute the net proceeds.

The last stage is the termination of the administration through a report to the court and its discharge of the personal representative.

The second stage presents the greatest difficulties. The central question is whether a personal representative appointed in one state may act and sue or be sued in another state, or whether he is confined to the state of his appointment. In support of wider powers are practical considerations: "An estate is for practical purposes a single thing, whether the items of property which compose it are all within the borders of one State or are scattered among several. . . . It is difficult to administer an estate as a unit, if that portion of it in each State is to be treated as a completely separate affair." (Restatement, Second, Conflict of Laws, Chap. 14, Topic 1, Introductory Note.) The principal support of the narrower view is the traditional conception of a personal representative as an artificial legal person

---

* See Restatement, Second, Conflict of
Laws §§ 314–366.

who by the nature of his being is confined to the territory of the sovereign that created him.   There are further complicating elements: the desire to protect local creditors out of local assets and the nature of the property involved, whether it is immovable or movable, tangible or intangible, or represented by a specialty.

Matters of probate and administration, as well as of the substantive validity of wills, are frequently affected by statutes, some of which are designed to simplify the handling of estates with assets in two or more states.   An example is the Uniform Probate Code, some provisions of which will be referred to at various places in this chapter.   A number of other uniform acts are in effect in some states. Several of these acts are discussed in Atkinson, The Uniform Ancillary Administration and Probate Acts, 67 Harv.L.Rev. 619 (1954).

MILMOE v. TOOMEY

United States Court of Appeals, District of Columbia Circuit, 1966.
123 U.S.App.D.C. 40, 356 F.2d 793.

McGowan, Circuit Judge.   This appeal challenges the jurisdiction of the District Court . . .   to appoint an ancillary administrator by reason of an asset in the District of Columbia consisting solely of the protection against liability afforded by an automobile insurance policy.   . . .

The decedent was a girl who, for some time prior to June 6, 1964, had been residing in Washington while working for the Peace Corps. On the morning of that day, in company with a fellow employe, she rented a Hertz car and set out for her family home in New York State.   In Lebanon County, Pennsylvania, during the early afternoon, the rented car was in a collision, and both of its occupants were killed.   Also dying in the crash were a married couple from Illinois who were in the other car; and a minor child with them was seriously injured.

The rental agreement executed by the decedent with Hertz recites her "local address" in Washington to be 3336 P Street.   An affidavit submitted in the District Court by her father asserts, however, that before leaving Washington the decedent had resigned from the Peace Corps and given up her P Street apartment; and that her purpose was to return to the family home in New York to live.   Execution of the rental agreement with Hertz operated to bring the decedent directly within the coverage of a liability policy issued to Hertz by Royal Indemnity Company.   Although not District of Columbia corporations, both Hertz and Royal Indemnity are doing business in the District so as to be subject to suit here.

Appellee O'Keefe is the Illinois administrator of the estate of the deceased Illinois couple.   He filed a petition in the District Court reciting the rental agreement and the accompanying insurance coverage, and asked that letters of administration issue to a disinterested attorney in order that suit might be brought against such appointee in the District on behalf of the deceased Illinois couple and their surviving minor child. Appellee Toomey is the ancillary administrator appointed in response to this petition.

Appellant, the decedent's father, appeared in the District Court to oppose the appointment. It was urged by him that the decedent was, at the time of her death, domiciled in New York, and that any relationship of significance between her and the District of Columbia had ended before her death. As the administrator of his daughter's estate duly appointed in New York, appellant represented that he could be sued in New York or in Pennsylvania, as could Hertz and the estate of the decedent's companion on the fatal journey. He further asserted that the insurance policy running to Hertz and its customers was nation-wide in character, and that its benefits could be claimed in both New York and Pennsylvania.

At the hearing before the District Court it appeared that a suit had in fact been filed in Pennsylvania; and, promptly after the appointment of the ancillary administrator in the District of Columbia, suit was brought against him in the District Court. So far as we are aware, these actions remain pending before trial.

The immediately relevant statute is Title 20 D.C.Code § 201, which provides as follows:

"On the death of any person leaving real or personal estate in the District, letters of administration on his estate may be granted, on the application of any person interested, on proof satisfactory to the probate court, that the decedent died intestate."

The District Judge conceived that the controversy before him was to be resolved by a scrupulous attention to the terms of this statute; and that, accordingly, the question before him was whether the decedent was an intestate person "leaving . . . personal estate in the District" within the contemplation of the statute. He did not find it necessary to choose explicitly and finally between the conflicting contentions as to whether the decedent was a resident of the District at her death. He thought that the decedent's interest in the insurance policy was "personal estate," and that the circumstances surrounding the creation of that interest gave it a *locus* "in the District," within the scope of those phrases as used in the statute. Thus, he considered the conditions of the statute to be met, and that the appointment by him of an ancillary administrator was in order.

We agree with this concept of the issue presented, and see no occasion to disturb the resolution made of it. With respect to the narrow question of whether coverage under an insurance policy constitutes a personal property interest supporting administration, we think the answer is as clear in reason as it is settled in authority.
. . . And, whatever may be the precise outer limits of the relationship of such an interest to the District of Columbia contemplated by

Congress as warranting administration here, we agree with the District Judge that they were not exceeded in this case. The decedent was certainly not an ordinary transient in her relationship with the District of Columbia at the time she entered into the Hertz contract which created her insurance rights. Those rights came into being here; and we think that, on this record, they continue to constitute a "personal estate in the District" within the statutory prescription.

Appellant's claim of an absence of jurisdictional power to make the appointment is largely cast . . . in terms of the lack of necessity for bringing the tort action here and of the greater appropriateness of other forums for its trial. This argument essentially is that, since the District Court should decline jurisdiction over the tort action from *forum non conveniens* considerations, it must be taken to have lacked jurisdiction to appoint the ancillary administrator. But the logic of this, if such there be, is not to be discovered from the language of the governing statute. Section 201 does not address itself generally to the purposes for which administration is sought, and, in particular, it prescribes nothing with respect to which lawsuits may be appropriately brought in the District of Columbia against the administrator, and which may not. Its concern appears to be mainly, if not exclusively, with the designation of a legal custodian of an asset in the District of an intestate decedent.

The District Judge . . . looking only to Section 201, refused to be drawn into the question of whether the tort claim should be tried here or in Pennsylvania. In this he was . . . wholly right. He regarded that question as one reserved to the judge before whom the tort suit comes . . . There may or may not be persuasive reasons why the issue of liability in negligence should be tried elsewhere than in the District of Columbia . . . But that is a matter for exploration and resolution in the tort action itself, and not in [this] proceeding.

The judgment appealed from is Affirmed.

NOTES

(1) The circumstances in which a will may be probated, and an executor or administrator appointed, are usually regulated by statute. The District of Columbia statute involved in the principal case is similar to statutes commonly found among the states. The statutes do not usually require that a representative be appointed, but authorize the making of such an appointment in the court's discretion—e.g., if the appointment would be in the best interests of the estate and is required for the protection of local creditors. Restatement, Second, Conflict of Laws §§ 314–315.

(2) Local ancillary administrators have frequently been appointed in the circumstances involved in the principal case. See e.g., Gordon v. Shea, 300 Mass. 95, 14 N.E.2d 105 (1938); Estate of Riggle, 11 N.Y.2d 73, 181 N.E.2d 436 (1962). One reason for the appointment of local ancillary administrators in these circumstances is the perceived difficulty involved in bringing suit against a foreign domiciliary administrator. See pp. 928–930, infra.

(3) The Shea and Riggle cases were relied upon by the New York Court of Appeals as authority for the proposition that the obligation owed by a liability insurer to the insured is subject to garnishment in a state where the insurer does business. Seider v. Roth, p. 159, supra. Do these cases support such a proposition?

(4) On the privileges and functions of a consul in dealing with the estate of a national of his country, see Boyd, Consular Functions in Connection with Decedents' Estates, 47 Iowa L.Rev. 823 (1962); Boyd, Constitutional, Treaty, and Statutory Requirement of Probate Notice to Consuls and Aliens, 47 Iowa L.Rev. 29 (1961).

(5) On the administration of estates in which aliens have an interest, see Boyd, The Administration in the United States of Alien Connected Decedents' Estates, 2 Int.Law 601 (1968).

IN RE FISCHER'S ESTATE

Prerogative Court of New Jersey, 1935.
118 N.J.Eq. 599, 180 A. 633.

Petition by George Platto for revocation of letters of administration in the estate of Mae P. Fischer, deceased, issued to Milton Mermelstein, and for issuance of letters to petitioner instead.

Petition granted.

BUCHANAN, VICE ORDINARY. Mrs. Mae Platto Fischer died at Denville (Indian Lake), Morris county, N. J., on August 21, 1933. She left no descendants, but was survived by her husband, Frederick G. Fischer, and by one brother, George Platto, but by no other brother or sister or representative thereof. No will being found, her husband applied to this court for letters of administration, and letters of general administration were issued to him on September 12, 1933.

These letters were issued on Fischer's allegation that decedent was a resident of ("late of") New Jersey, and without notice to the brother, Platto. It is the law of the state of domicile of an intestate decedent, which governs and determines the rights of intestate succession. Under the law of New Jersey, if the decedent had been domiciled here at her death, the husband would have had the sole right to succeed to all the decedent's personal property, and the sole right to letters of administration, and no notice was required to be given to Platto or any one else.

If the decedent, however, were domiciled in New York at the time of her death, the New York law would control, and under that law the brother, Platto, would succeed to a substantial share in the estate.

On October 20, 1933, the brother, Platto, filed petition for administration of Mrs. Fischer's estate, in the Surrogate's Court in New York, alleging her to have been a resident of New York at her death; and process was issued and served on the husband, Fischer.

Fischer had become mentally deranged, and on November 8, 1933, the letters of administration which had been issued to him by this court were revoked on that ground and letters issued in their stead to one Milton Mermelstein. . . .

Mermelstein, as substituted administrator of Mrs. Fischer's estate, appointed by this court, entered appearance and answer in the New York proceeding above mentioned. He also himself filed a petition in the New York court for the issuance of ancillary letters to himself, on the basis of the allegation that Mrs. Fischer had been domiciled in New Jersey and that original letters of administration had been issued to him here. Under the New York law it is a requisite to the grant of ancillary letters that it be shown that original letters have been issued in the state of decedent's domicile. To this petition Platto answered, denying that Mrs. Fischer's residence was in New Jersey, and alleging such residence to have been in New York.

Both proceedings in New York therefore involved the issue as to whether Mrs. Fischer had been domiciled in New York or New Jersey. Both proceedings were consolidated and duly tried in New York, and . . . Mr. Fischer also appeared as a party, and contended that the domicile of Mrs. Fischer was not New York but New Jersey. The determination of the issue in and by the New York court was that Mrs. Fischer had been domiciled in New York, and original letters of administration were issued to Platto. In re Fischer's Estate, 151 Misc. 74, 271 N.Y.S. 101. . . .

Following the determination aforesaid in the New York Surrogate's Court, Platto, as general administrator appointed by the New York court, commenced the present proceeding in this court, being a petition for the revocation of the letters issued by this court to Mermelstein and for the issuance of letters to him (Platto), in the place and stead thereof. The basis of this petition is the allegation that Mrs. Fischer was not a resident of New Jersey but of New York; that hence New Jersey had not the right to issue letters of general or original administration on her estate; that although New Jersey had the right to issue letters of administration for the administration of such assets of the estate as were in this state, such letters (on Fischer's becoming incompetent) should have been issued to Platto and not to Mermelstein; that the issuance of the letters to Mermelstein was the result of mistake and misrepresentation, to wit, the mistake of this court in believing that Mrs. Fischer's residence had been in this state, which mistake was caused by the misrepresentation to that effect made to this court by Fischer in his original petition . . . that Platto, not having been brought in to the proceedings in this court nor given notice thereof, had had no opportunity to raise or be heard on the issue as to the domicile of Mrs. Fischer, in this court.

. . . .

. . . .

Platto contends that under the "full faith and credit clause" of the Federal Constitution (article 4, section 1) the adjudication of the New York court on this issue of domicile is conclusive upon, and must be given effect to by, this court in this proceeding. It seems unnecessary to decide this particular question since in any event the well-established principles of comity and the doctrine of res adjudicata and estoppel by record lead to the same result. . . .

It clearly appears herein that precisely the same issue involved herein, as to whether Mrs. Fischer was domiciled at the time of her death in New York or in New Jersey, was before the New York court; that the New York court was a court of competent jurisdiction (having general probate jurisdiction) to determine that issue; that it did determine it; that such determination was a final decree or judgment; and that the parties to the present proceeding were parties to that New York proceeding. The contest there, as here, was between Platto on the one side, and Frederick Fischer . . . on the other. The present administrator Mermelstein, was also a party to the New York proceeding and took an active part therein on the same side as the Fischer interest; he is also a party to the present proceeding, although he has taken no active part herein. . . .

If the original grant of letters by this court is deemed an adjudication that decedent was domiciled in New Jersey (this court would have the right to grant letters for administration of the assets in this state even though decedent were not domiciled here), Platto is not bound thereby in the present proceeding, for he was not a party to the prior proceeding in this court and had no notice or opportunity to be heard therein.

On the other hand, Fischer . . . and the New Jersey substituted administrator, are all bound by the determination in the New York proceeding, because they were all parties to that proceeding, and not only had the opportunity to be heard therein, but therein actively litigated, against Platto, the same issue now sought by them to be relitigated against him herein. . . .

. . . By section 29 of our Orphans' Court Act, 3 Comp.St.1910, p. 3823, [N.J.S.A. 3:7–10] the general or domiciliary administrator has the prior right to the letters of ancillary administration in this state. . . . In September, 1933, no domiciliary administrator had been appointed in New York, so that the ancillary letters here could not be issued to such domiciliary administrator, and might well have been issued to Fischer; he being the husband, and entitled to the larger share of the net estate under the statute of distribution of the domiciliary state, New York. But the letters issued to him would have been ancillary not general; and the finding or recital as to the decedent's domicile would have been New York and not New Jersey, had it not been for Fischer's representation [that the decedent had died domiciled in New Jersey] . . .

Reopening the action and finding of this court of 1933, and according to Platto, now, the opportunity to be heard on the question of the right to letters of ancillary administration, results in the revocation of Mermelstein's letters and the grant of ancillary letters to Platto. . . .

———

RILEY v. NEW YORK TRUST CO.

Supreme Court of the United States, 1941.
315 U.S. 343, 62 S.Ct. 608, 86 L.Ed 885.

[The case appears p. 244, supra.]

———

RESTATEMENT, SECOND, CONFLICT OF LAWS:*

§ 317.　Effect Given in Other States to Judgments in Administration Proceedings

(1) A judgment in administration proceedings by a competent court in the state where the decedent was domiciled at the time of his death will usually be followed by the forum with respect to local movables insofar as the judgment deals with questions of succession that under the choice-of-law rules of the forum are governed by the law that would be applied by the courts of the state of the decedent's domicil.

(2) A judgment in administration proceedings by a competent court in the state where the decedent was domiciled at the time of his death will not of itself invalidate a prior inconsistent judgment by a court in another state in administering the estate of the same decedent in that state.

(3) A judgment in administration proceedings by a competent court of any state will be held conclusive in other states as to the issues determined upon all persons who were subject to the jurisdiction of the original court if the judgment is conclusive upon such persons in the state of rendition.

(4) If an issue as to the state in which a decedent was domiciled at the time of his death is raised by a person not precluded from raising this issue under Subsection (3), a court will not regard itself as concluded by a prior finding made in another state as to the place of the decedent's domicil.

NOTES

(1) In order to facilitate solution of these problems, the Uniform Probate Code provides:

_____

* Quoted with the permission of the copyright owner, The American Law Institute.

In § 3–202, that when probate or appointment proceedings are pending at the same time in the state of the forum and in one or more other states, "[t]he determination of domicile in the proceeding first commenced must be accepted as determinative in the proceeding in this state." The Comment explains that the "section is designed to reduce the possibility that conflicting findings of domicile in two or more states may result in inconsistent administration and distribution of parts of the same estate," and that "the local suitor always will have a chance to contest the question of domicile in the other state."

In § 3–203, that, in the absence of a contrary provision in the decedent's will, the domiciliary administrator "has priority over all other persons" for appointment as ancillary administrator of local assets.

In § 3–408, that a previous determination by a court of another state of testacy or of the validity or construction of a will must be accepted as conclusive by the local courts provided the previous determination was rendered after proper notice and opportunity to be heard and included "a finding that the decedent was domiciled in the state where the [previous determination] was made." The Comment makes clear that the section applies to cases where parties before the local court were not subject to the personal jurisdiction of the foreign court.

(2) See Hopkins, The Extraterritorial Effect of Probate Decrees, 53 Yale L.J. 221 (1944); Simes, The Administration of a Decedent's Estate as a Proceeding in Rem, 43 Mich.L.Rev. 675 (1945).

(3) The statutes of many states provide that the will of a non-resident may be admitted to probate upon proof of its probate in the state of his residence.

WILKINS v. ELLETT, ADM'R

Supreme Court of the United States, 1883.
108 U.S. 256, 2 S.Ct. 641, 27 L.Ed. 718.

GRAY, J.   This is an action of *assumpsit* on the common counts, brought in the circuit court of the United States for the western district of Tennessee. The plaintiff is a citizen of Virginia, and sues as administrator, appointed in Tennessee, of the estate of Thomas N. Quarles. The defendant is a citizen of Tennessee and surviving partner of the firm of F. H. Clark & Co. The answer sets up that Quarles was a citizen of Alabama at the time of his death; that the sum sued for has been paid to William Goodloe, appointed his administrator in that state, and has been inventoried and accounted for by him upon a final settlement of his administration; and that there are no creditors of Quarles in Tennessee. The undisputed facts, appearing by the bill of exceptions, are as follows:

Quarles was born at Richmond, Virginia, in 1835. In 1839 his mother, a widow, removed with him, her only child, to Courtland, Alabama. They lived there together until 1856, and she made her home there until her death, in 1864. In 1856, he went to Memphis, Tennessee, and there entered the employment of F. H. Clark & Co., and continued in their employment as a clerk, making no investments himself, but leaving the surplus earnings on interest in their hands until January, 1866, when he went to the house of a cousin in Courtland, Alabama, and while there died by an accident, leaving personal estate in Alabama. On the twenty-seventh of January, 1866, Goodloe took out letters of administration in Alabama, and in February, 1866, went to Memphis, and there, upon exhibiting his letters of administration, received from defendant the sum of money due to Quarles, amounting to $3,455.22 (which is the same for which this suit is brought,) and included it in his inventory and in his final account, which was allowed by the probate court in Alabama. There were no other debts due from Quarles in Tennessee. All his next of kin resided in Virginia or in Alabama; and no administration was taken out on his estate in Tennessee until June, 1866, when letters of administration were there issued to the plaintiff.

. . . we are of opinion that the court erred in instructing the jury that if the domicile was in Tennessee they must find for the plaintiff; and in refusing to instruct them, as requested by the defendant, that the payment to the Alabama administrator before the appointment of one in Tennessee, and there being no Tennessee creditors, was a valid discharge of the defendant, without reference to the domicile.

There is no doubt that the succession to the personal estate of a deceased person is governed by the law of his domicile at the time of his death; that the proper place for the principal administration of his estate is that domicile; that administration may also be taken out in any place in which he leaves personal property; and that no suit for the recovery of a debt, due to him at the time of his death, can be brought by an administrator as such in any state in which he has not taken out administration. But the reason for this last rule is the protection of the rights of citizens of the state in which the suit is brought; and the objection does not rest upon any defect of the administrator's title in the property, but upon his personal incapacity to sue as administrator beyond the jurisdiction which appointed him.

If a debtor, residing in another state, comes into the state in which the administrator has been appointed, and there pays him, the payment is a valid discharge everywhere. If the debtor, being in that state, is there sued by the administrator, and judgment recovered against him, the administrator may bring suit in his own name upon that judgment in the state where the debtor resides. Talmage v. Chapel, 16 Mass. 71.

The administrator, by virtue of his appointment and authority as such, obtains the title in promissory notes or other written evidences of debt, held by the intestate at the time of his death, and coming to the possession of the administrator; and may sell, transfer, and indorse the same; and the purchasers or indorsees may maintain actions in their own names against the debtors in another state, if the debts are negotiable promissory notes, or if the law of the state in which the action is brought permits the assignee of a chose in action to sue in his own name. . . .

In accordance with these views, it was held by this court, when this case was before it after a former trial, at which the domicile of the intestate appeared to have been in Alabama, that the payment in Tennessee to the Alabama administrator was good as against the administrator afterwards appointed in Tennessee. Wilkins v. Ellett, 9 Wall. 740.

The fact that the domicile of the intestate has now been found by the jury to be in Tennessee does not appear to us to make any difference. There are neither creditors nor next of kin in Tennessee. The Alabama administrator has inventoried and accounted for the amount of this debt in Alabama. The distribution among the next of kin, whether made in Alabama or in Tennessee, must be according to the law of the domicile; and it has not been suggested that there is any difference between the laws of the two states in that regard.

The judgment must, therefore, be reversed, and the case remanded with directions to set aside the verdict and to order a new trial.

NOTES

(1) Why should not the state where the decedent died domiciled have power to appoint a universal successor whose title to the decedent's assets in other states would have to be recognized under full faith and credit and who could sue everywhere as of right to collect these assets? Obviously, the existence of such a successor would vastly simplify the handling of a multi-state estate. So far as is known, only one court has attempted to appoint such a universal successor, and this appointment was vacated on appeal on the ground that no jurisdiction could be exercised over assets in other states. In re De Lano's Estate, 181 Kan. 729, 315 P.2d 611 (1957); cf. Hanson v. Denckla, p. 75, supra. On the other hand, universal succession has been achieved in the area of debtors' estates through the appointment of a statutory successor. See pp. 941–946, infra and Cheatham, The Statutory Successor, the Receiver and the Executor in Conflict of Laws, 44 Colum.L.Rev. 549 (1944). Why should what is possible in the area of debtors' estates not likewise be possible in decedents' estates? See D. Currie, The Multiple Personality of the Dead: Executors, Administrators, and the Conflict of Laws, 33 U.Chi.L.Rev. 429, 435–438 (1966).

(2) The Uniform Probate Code provides in §§ 4–201 to 4–203 that, unless he has been given notice not to do so by a resident creditor, a debtor may without danger of double liability pay a debt owed a nonresident decedent to a foreign domiciliary representative upon the latter's affidavit stating, among other things that "no local administration, or application or petition therefore, is pending in this state." Also under §§ 4–204 to 4–205, that a foreign domiciliary representative, upon filing copies of his appointment and giving bond, "may exercise as to assets in this state all powers of a local personal representative," including the bringing of suit, if no local representative has been appointed and no petition for such an appointment is pending.

(3) "Most of the difficulty found in the reported decisions has concerned the effect of a voluntary payment made to an administrator outside the state of his appointment. The results are conflicting and reflect the divergent theoretical conceptions, heretofore discussed, of territorial restriction upon the legal personality of an administrator. . . . [T]he great majority of decisions have upheld such payments, at least where no local representative has been appointed at the time of payment." Hopkins, Conflict of Laws in Administration of Decedents' Intangibles, 28 Iowa L.Rev. 422, 435, 437 (1943).

(4) In over half of the states statutes in one form or another authorize the payment of debts or the delivery of personal property to a foreign personal representative. See McDowell, Foreign Personal Representatives 163–166 (1957).

(5) The personal representative in possession of a negotiable instrument belonging to the estate is the appropriate representative to collect the claim embodied in the instrument. Smith v. Normart, 51 Ariz. 134, 75 P.2d 38 (1938).

(6) Most case authority holds that a domiciliary administrator may assign, and the assignee may enforce, a claim which is not represented by a negotiable instrument and which is owed the decedent by a person who is not subject to suit in a state where an ancillary administrator has been appointed. Petersen v. Chemical Bank, 32 N.Y. 21 (1865); Restatement, Second, Conflict of Laws § 333; Scoles and Hay, Conflict of Laws 851–852 (1983); McDowell, Foreign Personal Representatives 63–66 (1957).

(7) Would it be effective and desirable to include in a will a provision directed to the collection of assets? The provision might authorize and direct any debtor of the estate or anyone holding property of the estate to pay the debt or turn the property over to a personal representative qualified in any state, and it might specify further that the payment or delivery wherever made would be a satisfaction of the obligation to the estate and a defense against a claim made by any other personal representative. See generally Alford, Collecting a Decedent's Assets without Ancillary Administration, 18 Sw.L.J. 329 (1964).

ADMINISTRATION OF LAND

Land owned by a decedent is subject to administration as part of his estate only when and to the extent that a statute of the state of the situs so provides. When assets within State X where the land is are insufficient to satisfy claims proved and allowed in X, the land will be ordered sold even though there may be other assets in State Y. The land will also be ordered sold to satisfy claims proved and allowed in State Y when the assets in State Y are insufficient to satisfy creditors. When a will confers upon an executor the power to sell land, he need not receive an appointment from the court of the state where the land is in order to exercise the power to sell. This is because he is said to be acting in an individual and not in a representative capacity. Bacharach v. Spriggs, 173 Ark. 250, 292 S.W. 150 (1927).

Unless authorized by an X statute, an executor or administrator appointed in State Y may not foreclose a mortgage on land in State X. Under certain circumstances, however, his assignee will be permitted to do so. See Restatement, Second, Conflict of Laws §§ 339–340.

ESTATE OF HANREDDY

Supreme Court of Wisconsin, 1922.
176 Wis. 570, 186 N.W. 744.

One Joseph Hanreddy, a resident citizen of Chicago, Illinois, died there testate April 8, 1918. On June 25, 1918, his widow, Margaret Hanreddy, was duly appointed, qualified, and ever since has acted and is still acting as executrix of his estate in the probate court of Cook county, Illinois. Claims were therein filed aggregating more than $50,000. The available assets subject to that jurisdiction do not exceed $4,000.

In August, 1918, in the county court of Milwaukee county, Wisconsin, the will of said Joseph Hanreddy was duly probated and the said Margaret Hanreddy appointed executrix in ancillary proceedings, there being assets aggregating over $50,000 belonging to said estate as well as resident creditors within the state of Wisconsin. Claims have been filed therein by both resident and nonresident creditors in amounts in excess of the assets. Some creditors have filed their respective claims in both jurisdictions.

In August, 1919, the said executrix filed a petition in the county court of Milwaukee county reciting the probate proceedings in Illinois and in this state; the claims filed in the respective proceedings and their respective assets substantially as above set forth; the fact that the assets of the said estate are insufficient to pay all of the debts of the said estate and that the said estate is insolvent; that if all the claims filed were allowed there would be assets in the Wisconsin jurisdiction sufficient to pay the claims filed in that jurisdiction to approximately ninety per cent. thereof, and that as to the claims in the Illinois jurisdiction the assets there would not be sufficient to pay more than a ten per cent. dividend thereon . . . . She asked that no payment be made upon the claims filed in the Wisconsin jurisdiction until after final adjudication in both states upon all the claims and a determination had of the pro rata percentage that could properly be paid from the entire assets in both jurisdictions upon the respective claims in the several jurisdictions and that after such ascertainment and payment upon such pro rata percentage of the claims filed and allowed in the Wisconsin jurisdiction the surplus should be turned over to her as executrix in the jurisdiction of Illinois, to be there likewise applied.

.   .   .   After a hearing the court made his findings of fact reciting substantially as above stated and his conclusions of law as follows:

"I.   That the assets in said ancillary administration constitute a fund out of which the claims of creditors residing in Wisconsin, and who have duly filed their claims, be paid in full.   .   .   .

"III.   That this court has no jurisdiction to consider or allow claims of foreign creditors   .   .   .

"IV.   That any residue in the possession of the ancillary administrator after the payment of the claims of Wisconsin creditors duly allowed, and after the payment of the costs and expenses of the ancillary administration, are hereby ordered to be paid and delivered by said ancillary administrator to the executrix of the domiciliary estate."

An appeal was taken from the judgment or order entered in conformity with said conclusions of law.   .   .   .

ESCHWEILER, J.   .   .   .

Where the assets of a deceased, though found in several jurisdictions, are sufficient to pay the debts allowed against his estate in the several jurisdictions, ordinarily each of the separate jurisdictions proceeds to adjust claims and provide for their payment out of the assets in their control, each independently of the other; but where, as here, the entire assets of the deceased are insufficient to pay all his just obligations, there is such an interdependence between the various jurisdictions as to require the application of the old maxim that "Equality is equity"; and the several courts administering the affairs of the deceased, each being apprised of that situation, must no longer consider the assets within their respective controls as separate and distinct funds for distribution to the creditors within such jurisdictions, but as one entire fund in which all creditors of the deceased having just claims of equal standing shall share pro rata.   It makes no material difference by whom or how the situation is brought to the knowledge of the court.   In this case the petition of the executrix alone was sufficient.   It is the fact of insolvency that raises the equity.   It then becomes the duty of the court itself, administering the assets, to subordinate the demands of the local creditors to be paid in full or to the exhaustion of the assets to the broader rights of the creditors as a whole to share on an equal footing in the assets as a whole.   .   .   .

.   .   .   [This] is but the application in another form of the rule that is applied in the distribution of the assets of an insolvent corporation foreign to the disturbing jurisdiction, where resident and non-resident creditors must share pro rata.   Blake v. McClung, 172 U.S. 239, 19 S.Ct. 165, 43 L.Ed. 432;   .   .   .

It is of course proper that sufficient of the assets belonging to the estate and found in Wisconsin should be held here so that when the proper percentage is ultimately determined in the two jurisdictions the creditors whose claims are filed and allowed in this jurisdiction shall be here paid their proper percentage.

. . . [I]t is clear that, there being assets of the deceased and resident creditors within the state of Wisconsin, the county court of Milwaukee county had . . . the duty . . . to receive, examine, and adjust the claims and demands of all persons against the deceased . . .

Under [the Wisconsin] statute as well as under the general principles governing such matters, no distinction can be made between ancillary administration and domiciliary administration as to the rights of nonresident creditors to file, in accordance with the established practice of this state, their claims against such an estate for adjustment and allowance. . . .

BY THE COURT. Judgment reversed, and the cause remanded with directions to enter judgment in accordance with this opinion.

NOTES

(1) Sister state creditors of an insolvent decedent's estate are undoubtedly entitled to the same constitutional protection that is given to the creditors of an insolvent corporation. See Blake v. McClung, p. 933, infra, which is cited in the principal case.

(2) Although the law of the domicile provides that claims not presented against the estate there within the period of limitations shall be forever barred, a claim may be presented in any other state where there is an administration and whose period of limitations has not yet run. Restatement, Second, Conflict of Laws § 345.

(3) In support of treating the estate as a unit even though it is composed of assets located in different states or nations, see Scoles and Hay, Conflict of Laws, 867–869 (1982); Scoles, Conflict of Laws and Creditors' Rights in Decedents' Estates, 42 Iowa L.Rev. 341 (1957). See also Nadelmann, Insolvent Decedents' Estates, 49 Mich.L.Rev. 1129 (1951). In the latter article, the author shows the relation of the problems of insolvent decedents' estates to those of debtors' estates, which are discussed in the next section.

LENN v. RICHE

Supreme Judicial Court of Massachusetts, 1954.
331 Mass. 104, 117 N.E.2d 129.

[During his life, Paul Bonn made a gift to plaintiff of a valuable painting. The gift was made in Germany. Later in France plaintiff loaned the painting to Bonn so that he could exhibit and preserve it. Bonn died in France and by his will duly "allowed" there named his wife as "universal legatee." After she refused to return the painting to plaintiff, plaintiff brought this suit against the ancillary administrator of Bonn's Massachusetts estate. Plaintiff recovered in the court below and defendant excepted.]

QUA, CHIEF JUSTICE. . . . the defendant insists that this action cannot be maintained against the administrator of Bonn's estate in Massachusetts because Bonn left a will duly established in France, in which he made his wife . . . his universal legatee, and because under French law, the universal legatee, who takes all the property of the deceased, becomes personally chargeable with his obligations. The argument is that if suit had been brought in France it must have been brought against [his wife] personally. This may be true. . . . But it is not controlling over the law governing the administration of estates in this Commonwealth. Here the administrator is liable to suit upon obligations of the deceased, and creditors resident here, of whom the plaintiff is one, are entitled to secure payment of their claims out of Massachusetts assets in the manner provided by Massachusetts law. At the moment of Bonn's death he owed to the plaintiff an obligation which had arisen under French law to return her property to her upon request. This obligation was chargeable against his Massachusetts assets. It was like a promissory note owed but not yet due. Even though at Bonn's death there was as yet no breach of his obligation, there was a breach when the plaintiff made her request to the universal legatee for a return of her property. We think the request, if any was necessary, was properly made to the universal legatee in France. She was the general representative of the succession and of the personalty of the deceased at the domicil of the deceased. The defendant had not at that time been appointed administrator here. A request to the defendant after his appointment would have been a barren gesture. There was no reason to suppose that the plaintiff's property was in this Commonwealth or in the control of the administrator appointed here in his capacity as ancillary administrator. The plaintiff can maintain her action here. She was not obliged to see Massachusetts assets swept away and then go to France to assert her rights. . . .

Exceptions overruled.

NOTES

(1) The principal case is in line with authority. But was the result reached a desirable one? The administration of a multistate estate would obviously be facilitated by requiring all creditors to file their claims in the court of domiciliary administration. But would the advantages that such a rule would bring to estate administration be outweighed by the hardship that it would visit upon out-of-state creditors? Compare D. Currie, The Multiple Personality of the Dead: Executors, Administrators and the Conflict of Laws, 33 U.Chi.L.Rev. 429, 453–462 (1966).

(2) On the different methods in the civil law and the common law for the determination of death and the administration of the property of a decedent and the coordination of the two methods, see Ehrenzweig, Conflict of Laws 180–182 (1962). In Wren, Problems in Probating Foreign Wills and Using

Foreign Personal Representatives, 17 Sw.L.J. 55 (1963), special attention is given to differences in the laws of Mexico and Texas.

GHILAIN v. COUTURE

Supreme Court of New Hampshire, 1929.
84 N.H. 48, 146 A. 395, 65 A.L.R. 553.

SNOW, J. This action was brought by the plaintiff as administratrix by appointment in Massachusetts, the domicile of the deceased, against defendants resident in this state, to recover for death from an injury received here.

In claims for death the nature of the right of action, and the party in whom it is vested, are fixed by the lex loci delicti. . . . The plaintiff's right of action, if any, is therefore determined by the law of this state. At the time of the accident the sole basis for such a right was P.S., c. 191, ss. 10–13. Poff v. New England Tel. & Teleg. Company, 72 N.H. 164, 55 A. 891. This statute authorized an action to recover damages for death caused by wrongful physical injury to the person, for the benefit of the widow or widower and the children, if any, otherwise for the benefit of the heirs at law of the deceased; said action to be brought at any time within two years after the death of the injured party and not afterwards. Though not expressed in so many words, the statute clearly contemplated that actions to enforce the right should be brought by the "administrator of the deceased party." P.S. c. 191, s. 12; Cogswell v. Concord & M. Railroad, 68 N.H. 192, 194, 44 A. 293. See Laws 1887, c. 71, s. 1. The interpretation of the quoted words is the principal and the controlling issue presented.

The contentions of the defendants are that the plaintiff, domiciliary administratrix, was not an "administrator of the deceased party" within the meaning of the statute, and that she was, therefore, wholly without authority to bring the suit; that her attempted action was a mere nullity; and that, the limitation having run, the plaintiff's writ is incapable of amendment by substitution of herself as the ancillary administratrix so as to relate back and cure her defective suit.*

In support of their contention of the plaintiff's want of authority the defendants cite the general rule that an administrator cannot sue outside of the state of his appointment, . . .

While the rule presupposes that an administrator has no claim to recognition *as a matter of right*, beyond the bounds of the state of his appointment . . . such want of *legal right* is not the reason for the rule. The rule does not arise from any want of inherent au-

---

* The decedent, a resident of Massachusetts, was killed in New Hampshire on May 13, 1924. The present action was brought on May 12, 1926. The plaintiff was appointed administratrix in New Hampshire in 1928. (Editors' note.)

thority in the court to accord such recognition. . . . No statute or
. . . principle of the common law forbids it. . . .

. . . in a larger sense, the so-called rule that executors and administrators will not ordinarily be granted extra-territorial recognition, and therefore will not generally be permitted to bring actions in
the courts of foreign jurisdictions . . . is but an exception to the
broader doctrine that the acts of foreign representatives or fiduciaries, as a matter of practice, convenience and expediency, will be giv-
en effect through the exercise of a liberal comity. . . . An exception is made whenever such a course would conflict with any principle
of public policy. It is in such a conflict with state policy that the
denial of the right of action generally to foreign administrators, without first taking out letters here, finds a sufficient, and its only, justification. Upon whatever ground the rule calling for such denial may
formerly have been thought to rest it is now generally recognized
that it is based solely upon the policy of the courts of each state to
protect resident creditors of the decedent against the withdrawal into
another state of assets on which they may equitably rely for the payment of the debts that may be due them. . . .

The damages recoverable under the statute by its terms (s. 13)
"shall belong and be distributed" to the designated beneficiaries.
They are not assets of the estate within the ordinary meaning of the
word. . . . As no creditor of the deceased can be either benefited
or burdened by any action brought under the statute or have "the
slightest . . . interest in the recovery sought" . . . it is clear
that the legislature, in designating the person who shall bring the
action, could not have been influenced by a rule which had as its sole
justification the protection of local creditors. In interpreting the statute the rule relied upon by the defendants may, therefore, be laid out
of the case.

Nor is it perceived that the recognition of a domiciliary administrator as the plaintiff in actions under our death statute offends any
state policy so as to require his exclusion under the broader principles
of comity. . . . To assume otherwise would be in effect saying
that it would be impolitic to extend the courtesy of our courts to a
Massachusetts representative for fear that the courts of that commonwealth would not hold its own appointee accountable for his special trust according to its definitive terms. The acceptance of such a
postulate would be to impugn the mutual confidence possessed by the
courts of the respective states in each other so essential to the very
existence of the doctrine of comity. . . .

We therefore come to the interpretation of the statute un-
hampered by any rules or questions of state policy peculiar to the
ordinary administration of intestate property to which it has no relation, except as it utilizes the personal representative of the decedent,
ex officio, as the instrument of enforcement of the right of action
which it provides. . . .

While it may fairly be assumed that the legislature had in mind the domestic administrator if there be one, there is nothing in the language showing an intention to restrict the court in the exercise of its powers, under the principles of comity, to recognize the domiciliary administrator in the absence of a local representative. It is our conclusion that the legislature used the words "the administrator of the deceased party" as inclusive of any representative who, by comity or otherwise, may be admitted to sue in this forum without infringing any principle of state policy. . . .

. . . The suggestion in argument that the defendant would not be protected by a judgment in the suit as instituted is without merit. It seems to be well settled that a judgment for damages for the wrongful death of a person is a bar to an action in another state to recover damages of the same character and for the same death, where the real parties in interest are the same, even though the nominal parties are different. . . .

. . . There was no error in the ruling that the plaintiff was not precluded by law on the record from maintaining the suit for her beneficiaries under the statute.

Exceptions overruled.

NOTES

(1) The common law rule that a foreign personal representative lacks capacity to maintain an action outside the state of his appointment has been deeply eroded. The principal exception has been created by statutes which are to be found in many states. These are discussed in McDowell, Foreign Personal Representatives 67–75 (1957). One way to overcome the ban, where it persists, is for the foreign representative to be appointed ancillary representative in the second state.

(2) Courts have created several exceptions to the rule: (a) The defendant waives the defense of incapacity of the representative by failing to plead it promptly. (b) When the representative has "title" in himself personally, he may sue, as when he makes a contract or recovers a judgment after the death of the decedent, or holds negotiable paper. This result may be wise, though the form of expression can scarcely be justified since the personal representative does not hold these assets for himself but must account for them as representative. (c) An action for the death of a decedent may be maintained, at least if the proceeds will go to the members of the family rather than to the general estate, so creditors are not concerned. (d) An action may be maintained by a foreign personal representative when this would be for the best interests of the estate and would not prejudice the interests of local creditors. The states vary in their recognition of the exceptions mentioned. The cases and statutes are considered in McDowell, Foreign Personal Representatives Chap. II (1957). See also Restatement, Second, Conflict of Laws § 354.

EUBANK HEIGHTS APARTMENTS, LIMITED v. LEBOW

United States Court of Appeals, First Circuit, 1980.
615 F.2d 571.

ALDRICH, SENIOR CIRCUIT JUDGE.

On September 28, 1972, Saul L. Lebow executed in Massachusetts a limited partnership agreement and, in connection therewith, six promissory notes. . . . The payee was the partnership, Eubank Heights Apartments, Ltd. The partnership was created under Texas law, with its general partners and its principal office in Texas. Lebow, a resident of Massachusetts, died on March 12, 1973. His wife, Estelle, was appointed executrix on May 22, 1973. Apparently not until March, 1974, did the partnership, hereinafter plaintiff, learn of Lebow's death and of the probate proceedings. On April 3, 1974, plaintiff exercised its right to make the notes payable in Texas by notifying defendant. On December 13, 1974, plaintiff brought suit on the notes in the state court of Texas, naming as defendant the Estate of Saul L. Lebow. Service was made on the Secretary of State, and notice was sent to, and received by, the executrix. She made no response, and on May 16, 1975, a default judgment for the amounts of the notes, interest, and attorney's fees was entered, naming the Estate as the judgment debtor. There is, of course, no such entity; at least none such is recognized in Massachusetts. . . . Nor were there any assets, to be denominated an estate, in Texas.

Action was brought on the judgment in the district court for the District of Massachusetts on February 12, 1976, naming as defendant Estelle I. Lebow, Executrix of the Estate of Saul L. Lebow. The above facts having been made to appear by affidavits, plaintiff moved for summary judgment . . . .. The court granted the motion . . . and defendant appeals.

The first defense asserted is that decedent did not have sufficient connection with Texas to give that state jurisdiction over him under its longarm statute, Tex.Rev.Civ.Stat.Ann. art. 2031b, §§ 3, 4. This is a conventional statute, whose reach is restricted only by the Constitution. . . . Although the partnership was created to deal with New Mexico land, it was a Texas-run enterprise, by the terms of the agreement governed by Texas law, and had cumulatively such Texas connections that we see no merit in defendant's attack on the Texas court's in personam jurisdiction so far as the decedent was concerned.

. . . .

This, however, is only one step. However labeled, this was not an action against the decedent—he no longer existed. The suit was, in effect, against his former assets; obviously defendant would not be liable individually. The fact that Texas would have had in personam jurisdiction over him does not mean that it had jurisdiction in rem, or quasi in rem. Indeed, he died before there even was a claim against his assets. What happens to a person's intangible assets after death is determined by the state of domicile. . . . We must look, accordingly, to the law of Massachusetts to determine whether plaintiff took adequate steps to secure an interest chargeable against the assets. . . .

. . . In the district court defendant did not claim that the Estate of Saul L. Lebow was a nonentity, but asserted that it was "a different party . . . than the defendant in this action." We think defendant's present claim, that there was no party at all, hypertechnical. Identification was clear, and statutory service was made on the executrix. We would not hold this judgment a worthless piece of paper simply because defendant's name as estate representative was not included thereon. Rather, we take the issue to be whether plaintiff could obtain a judgment in Texas valid against estate assets in Massachusetts by suing the executrix in Texas. . . .

A long held view is that a court-appointed estate representative cannot represent the estate for purposes of suit, whether as plaintiff or defendant, beyond the state borders. It would have advanced consideration of this case substantially if plaintiff had called our attention to Saporita v. Litner, 1976, 371 Mass. 607, 358 N.E.2d 809. It is not our primary obligation to be acquainted with Massachusetts law; counsel owe a duty to the court.[3]

In *Saporita* a Massachusetts creditor succeeded in obtaining a judgment in Massachusetts against an executor of a Connecticut estate. The court, after extensive discussion of the old cases, held that such procedure was in accord with the times. We cannot think that Massachusetts would decline to take the reciprocal view, and refuse to recognize a Texas judgment against a Massachusetts executor. It is true that plaintiff Saporita obtained service in hand on the foreign executor in Massachusetts, whereas defendant here received only substituted service by mail, but we do not think that a significant difference. If the Texas long arm would have reached the decedent, we do not believe it withered on his death. . . . We hold the judgment valid.

. . .

NOTES

(1) Most of the modern long-arm statutes provide that in the event of the defendant's death suit may be brought against his personal representative. For a good discussion of the problem, see D. Currie, The Multiple Personality of the Dead: Executors, Administrators, and the Conflict of Laws, 33 U.Chi. L.Rev. 429 (1966).

(2) Section 4–302 of the Uniform Probate Code provides that "a foreign personal representative is subject to the jurisdiction of the courts of this

---

3. We are also critical of defendant, who either shared plaintiff's negligence in not discovering *Saporita*, or else was disingenuous in arguing that defendant "had no standing to be subject to an action in Texas" without mentioning it.

state to the same extent that his decedent was subject to jurisdiction immediately prior to death."

(3) Restatement, Second, Conflict of Laws:*

§ 358. Suit Against Foreign Executor or Administrator

An action may be maintained against an executor or administrator outside the state of his appointment upon a claim against the decedent when the local law of the forum authorizes suit against the executor or administrator and

(a) suit could have been maintained within the state against the decedent during his lifetime because of the existence of a basis of jurisdiction, other than mere physical presence . . ., or

(b) the executor or administrator has done an act in the state in his official capacity.

———

INGERSOLL v. CORAM, 211 U.S. 335 (1908). [An action was brought in a state court of Montana by the Montana ancillary administrator of a New York lawyer against the lawyer's clients for a large fee alleged to have been earned in Montana. On motion of the defendants the complaint was dismissed for failure to state a cause of action. The present action was then brought in the federal court in Massachusetts by the New York domiciliary administratrix, who had also been appointed ancillary administratrix in Massachusetts, of the lawyer to recover the fee. The defense was that the judgment in the Montana proceeding was a bar. The Supreme Court of the United States held, two justices dissenting without opinion, that it was not a bar.]

MR. JUSTICE McKENNA . . . Respondents assert the identity of the action in Montana with the present suit, and upon that identity they urge that such action constitutes *res judicata*. Petitioner denies the identity of the actions, and urges besides that there is no such privity between the parties as to make the Montana action *res judicata* of the pending case. In support of the latter contention petitioner urges that an ancillary administrator in one jurisdiction is not in privity with an ancillary administrator in another jurisdiction, and that therefore a judgment against one is not a bar to a suit by the other. . . .

We shall assume that there is identity of subject-matter between the Montana action and that at bar, but the question remains, Was there identity of parties? An extended discussion of the question is made unnecessary by the case of Brown v. Fletcher, 210 U.S. 82 . . . The latter case [Stacy v. Thrasher, 6 How. 42] was quoted from as follows: "Where administrations are granted to different persons in different states, they are so far deemed independent of

* Quoted with the permission of the copyright owner, The American Law Institute.

each other that a judgment obtained against one will furnish no right of action against the other, to affect assets received by the latter in virtue of his own administration; for, in contemplation of law, there is no privity between him and the other administrator." . . . That there is a certain amount of artificiality in the doctrine was pointed out in Stacy v. Thrasher, and that it leads to the inconvenience and burdensome result of retrying controversies and repeating litigations. The doctrine, however, was vindicated as a necessary consequence of the different sources from which the different administrators received their powers, and the absence of privity between them, and that the imputations against it were not greater than could be made against other "logical conclusions upon admitted legal principles." It is not necessary, therefore, to review in detail the argument of respondents.

[The Supreme Court reversing the Circuit Court of Appeals, held the Montana judgment was not binding in the later proceeding in the federal court in Massachusetts and allowed recovery of the fee.]

NOTES

(1) The Supreme Court of the United States has held that if the same person is executor in two states a judgment rendered against him in one state will be recognized as binding him in the other state.

It seems likely that if the issue were to arise today the Supreme Court would overrule Ingersoll v. Coram and hold that a judgment involving one administrator is binding on administrators appointed in other states. See Scoles and Hay, Conflict of Laws 860–867 (1982).

(2) Nash v. Benari, 117 Me. 491, 105 A. 107 (1918). The decedent died domiciled in Massachusetts and Benari was appointed the domiciliary administrator in Massachusets and the ancillary administrator in Maine. The plaintiff recovered judgment in Masachusetts against Benari, as domiciliary administrator, on an alleged debt owed her by the decedent. This judgment being largely unsatisfied, the plaintiff brought action on the original claim against Benari, as ancillary administrator, in Maine. He claimed by way of defense that this claim had been merged in the Massachusetts judgment. Held for the plaintiff. There is no privity between administrators for the same decedent appointed in different states. ". . . the fact that one and the same person is administrator in both states does not alter the doctrine."

(3) According to the majority rule, when a claimant brings suit against an administrator to recover on an alleged debt owed him by the decedent and loses, he will thereafter be precluded from bringing an action on the same claim against another administrator in a second state. Restatement, Second, Conflict of Laws § 357.

(4) Section 4–401 of the Uniform Probate Code provides that "An adjudication rendered in any jurisdiction in favor of or against any personal representative of the estate is as binding on the local personal representative as if he were a party to the adjudication."

DISTRIBUTION, TAXES, AND PLANNING

Distribution. The domiciliary representative distributes the net estate in his hands after payment of debts and expenses to those entitled to it. The ancillary representative may, subject to the order of the court, transmit the net estate in his hands to the domiciliary representative, or he may turn the net proceeds over to the distributees directly when this is the fair and economical thing to do. The distribution may be made more complex by the assertion of nonbarrable interests or the necessity of election. See Scoles, Conflict of Laws and Elections in Administration of Decedents' Estates, 30 Ind.L.J. 293 (1955); Scoles, Conflict of Laws and Nonbarrable Interests in Administration of Decedents' Estates, 8 U.Fla.L.Rev. 151 (1955).

Taxes. Problems of disputed domicile in relation to state succession taxes are discussed at pp. 14–17, supra. There are problems on the apportionment of the burden of the federal estate tax. See Uniform Estate Tax Apportionent Act; Scoles, Apportionment of Federal Estate Taxes and Conflict of Laws, 55 Colum.L.Rev. 261 (1955); Scoles and Stephens, Proposed Uniform Estate Tax Apportionment, 43 Minn.L.Rev. 907 (1959).

Estate Planning. Estate planning with attention to conflict of laws is considered in Casner, Estate Planning ch. 16 (4th ed. 1980); Ester and Scoles, Estate Planning and Conflict of Laws, 24 Ohio S.L.J. 270 (1963); Scoles and Rheinstein, Conflict Avoidance in Succession Planning, 21 Law and Contemp.Prob. 427 (1956).

See generally Scoles and Hay, Conflict of Laws 870–876 (1982).

SECTION 2.   DEBTORS' ESTATES *

Introductory Note. The Federal Bankruptcy Act with its national reach has, for the most part, supplanted the old system of administration of insolvent estates through state court receiverships and so has obliterated interstate conflicts problems. The Act does not apply to municipal, insurance or banking corporations and building and loan associations. As to them the old problems of interstate conflicts continue and are similar, in large part, to those arising in decedents' estates. Often the liquidator is elevated from the position of a receiver to that of a "statutory successor" and given the enlarged rights in other states that cases in this section reveal. The section is directed principally to the rights of foreign creditors and of foreign liquida-

---

* See Restatement, Second, Conflict of
Laws §§ 367–423.

tors, especially statutory successors. To the last, the full faith and credit clause gives important protection.

BLAKE v. McCLUNG

Supreme Court of the United States, 1898.
172 U.S. 239, 19 S.Ct. 165, 43 L.Ed. 432.

[The Embreeville Company, a British corporation, qualified to do business in Tennessee under a statute of the state which contained this provision:

". . . creditors who may be residents of this State shall have a priority in the distribution of assets . . . over all simple contract creditors, being residents of any other country or countries, . . ." The corporation acquired property in Tennessee. In a proceeding in a court of the state it was alleged that the corporation was insolvent and a receiver of its property in the state was appointed. Several classes of creditors filed claims against the corporation in the receivership proceedings. They included British creditors, Ohio individual creditors, a Virginia corporation, and residents of Tennessee. The state court applied the statute quoted above so as to give the Tennessee creditors priority over all the others. The state court judgment was appealed to the Supreme Court of the United States.]

MR. JUSTICE HARLAN delivered the opinion of the court. . . .

The plaintiffs in error contend that the judgment of the state court, based upon the statute, denies to them rights secured by the second section of the Fourth Article of the Constitution of the United States providing that "the citizens of each State shall be entitled to all privileges and immunities of citizens in the several States," as well as by the first section of the Fourteenth Amendment, declaring that no State shall "deprive any person of life, liberty or property without due process of law," nor "deny to any person within its jurisdiction the equal protection of the laws." . . .

The suggestion is made that as the statute refers only to "residents," there is no occasion to consider whether it is repugnant to the provision of the National Constitution relating to citizens. We cannot accede to this view. . . . The State did not intend to place creditors, citizens of other States, upon an equality with creditors, citizens of Tennessee, and to give priority only to Tennessee creditors over creditors who resided in, but were not citizens of, other States. The manifest purpose was to give to all Tennessee creditors priority over all creditors residing out of that State, whether the latter were citizens or only residents of some other State or country. . . .

We hold such discrimination against citizens of other States to be repugnant to the second section of the Fourth Article of the Constitution of the United States, although, generally speaking, the State has the power to prescribe the conditions upon which foreign corporations may enter its territory for purposes of business. Such a power cannot be exerted with the effect of defeating or impairing rights secured to citizens of the several States by the supreme law of the land. . . .

It may be appropriate to observe that the objections to the statute of Tennessee do not necessarily embrace enactments that are found in some of the States requiring foreign insurance corporations, as a condition of their coming into the State for purposes of business, to deposit with the state treasurer funds sufficient to secure policy holders in its midst. Legislation of that character does not present any question of discrimination against citizens forbidden by the Constitution. Insurance funds set apart in advance for the benefit of home policy holders of a foreign insurance company doing business in the State are a trust fund of a specific kind to be administered for the exclusive benefit of certain persons. . . .

As to the plaintiff in error, the Hull Coal & Coke Company of Virginia, different considerations must govern our decision. It has long been settled that, for purposes of suit by or against it in the courts of the United States, the members of a corporation are to be conclusively presumed to be citizens of the state creating such corporation . . .; and therefore it has been said that a corporation is to be deemed, for such purposes, a citizen of the state under whose laws it was organized. But it is equally well settled, and we now hold, that a corporation is not a citizen within the meaning of the constitutional provision that "the citizens of each state shall be entitled to all privileges and immunities of citizens in the several states". . . . The Virginia corporation, therefore, cannot invoke that provision for protection against the decree of the state court denying its right to participate upon terms of equality with Tennessee creditors in the distribution of the assets of the British corporation in the hands of the Tennessee court.

Since, however, a corporation is a "person," within the meaning of the fourteenth amendment . . . may not the Virginia corporation invoke for its protection the clause of the amendment declaring that no state shall deprive any person of property without due process, nor deny to any person within its jurisdiction the equal protection of the laws?

. . . this question must receive a negative answer. . . . this court has adjudged that the prohibitions of the fourteenth amendment refer to all the instrumentalities of the state, to its legislative, executive, and judicial authorities . . . [But the] corporation was not, in any legal sense, deprived of its claim, nor was its right to reach the assets of the British corporation in other states or countries disputed. It was only denied the right to participate upon terms of equality with Tennessee creditors in the distribution of par-

ticular assets of another corporation doing business in that state.
. . .

It is equally clear that the Virginia corporation cannot rely upon
the clause declaring that no state shall "deny to any person within its
jurisdiction the equal protection of the laws." That prohibition manifestly relates only to the denial by the state of equal protection to
persons "within its jurisdiction." . . . Without attempting to
state what is the full import of the words, "within its jurisdiction," it
is safe to say that a corporation not created by Tennessee, nor doing
business there under conditions that subjected it to process issuing
from the courts of Tennessee at the instance of suitors, is not, under
the above clause of the fourteenth amendment, within the jurisdiction
of that state. . . . Nor do we think it came within the jurisdiction
of Tennessee, within the meaning of the amendment, simply by
presenting its claim in the state court, and thereby becoming a party
to this cause. . . .

What may be the effect of the judgment of this court in the present case upon the rights of creditors not residing in the United States
it is not necessary to decide. Those creditors are not before the court
on this writ of error. The final judgment of the supreme court of
Tennessee must be affirmed as to the Hull Coal & Coke Company
. . . Rev.St. § 709. As to the other plaintiffs in error, citizens of
Ohio, the judgment must be reversed, and the cause remanded for
further proceedings not inconsistent with this opinion. It is so ordered.

MR. JUSTICE BREWER, with whom MR. CHIEF JUSTICE FULLER concurred, dissenting. . . .

NOTES

(1) On the rights of a corporate creditor under the equal protection of the
laws clause, see Kentucky Finance Corp. v. Paramount Auto Exchange
Corp., 262 U.S. 544 (1923), p. 979, infra.

(2) A 1952 amendment to the Federal Bankruptcy Act (11 U.S.C.A.
§ 105(d)) deals with international aspects and seeks to advance the policy of
effectuating equal distribution between foreign and domestic creditors. On
equality in distribution, compare Estate of Hanreddy, p. 921, supra, dealing
with an insolvent decedent's estate.

(3) "Both in Canada and the United States, the federal legislature has
power to pass national bankruptcy legislation . . . Internally, creditors
are prevented from obtaining more than their equal share in the distribution
of the assets of the insolvent debtors. Matters can work out differently on
the so-called international level [through a local creditor attaching local as-
sets] . . . This need not be so, however. Under the American Bankruptcy Act a nonresident debtor may be adjudged a bankrupt in the United
States courts if he has assets in the United States, and this notwithstanding
a bankruptcy declared abroad. An attachment or garnishment obtained
within the four months preceding the American bankruptcy may be voided
. . . . if the attaching or garnishing creditor does not relinquish his prefer-

ence, an adjudication in bankruptcy in the United States becomes necessary. The result is concurrent bankruptcies in Canada and the United States . . . . In such a case, under an amendment to the American Bankruptcy Act, in force since September 25, 1963, the bankruptcy court has power to suspend the exercise of its jurisdiction in view of the bankruptcy pending abroad. A finding that the local creditors will obtain their equal share in the foreign bankruptcy may lead to a suspension of the proceedings after the local assets have been turned over to the foreign trustee in bankruptcy." Nadelmann, Bankruptcy in Canada: Assets in New York, 11 Am.J.Comp.L. 628, 629–630 (1962); see also Nadelmann, The American Bankruptcy Act and Conflicting Administrations, 12 Int. & Comp.L.Q. 684 (1963).

MORRIS v. JONES

Supreme Court of the United States, 1946.
329 U.S. 545, 67 S.Ct. 451, 91 L.Ed. 488, 168 A.L.R. 656.

Certiorari to the Supreme Court of Illinois.

MR. JUSTICE DOUGLAS delivered the opinion of the Court.

This case presents a substantial question under the Full Faith and Credit Clause (Art. IV, § 1) of the Constitution.

Chicago Lloyds, an unincorporated association, was authorized by Illinois to transact an insurance business in Illinois and other States. It qualified to do business in Missouri. In 1934 petitioner sued Chicago Lloyds in a Missouri court for malicious prosecution and false arrest. In 1938, before judgment was obtained in Missouri, respondent's predecessor was appointed by an Illinois court as statutory liquidator for Chicago Lloyds. The Illinois court fixed a time for the filing of claims against Chicago Lloyds and issued an order staying suits against it. Petitioner had notice of the stay order but nevertheless continued to prosecute the Missouri suit. At the instance of the liquidator, however, counsel for Chicago Lloyds withdrew from the suit and did not defend it, stating to the Missouri court that the Illinois liquidation proceedings had vested all the property of Chicago Lloyds in the liquidator. Thereafter petitioner obtained a judgment in the Missouri court and filed an exemplified copy of it as proof of his claim in the Illinois proceedings. An order disallowing the claim was sustained by the Illinois Supreme Court against the contention that its allowance was required by the Full Faith and Credit Clause. People ex rel. Jones v. Chicago Lloyds, 391 Ill. 492, 63 N.E.2d 479.

. . .

First. We can put to one side, as irrelevant to the problem at hand, several arguments which have been pressed upon us. We are not dealing here with any question of priority of claims against the property of the debtor. For in this proceeding petitioner is not seeking, nor is respondent denying him, anything other than the right to prove his claim in judgment form. No question of parity of treatment of creditors, or the lack thereof (see Blake v. McClung, 172 U.S

239), is in issue. Nor is there involved in this case any challenge to the Illinois rule, which follows Relfe v. Rundle, 103 U.S. 222, that title to all the property of Chicago Lloyds, wherever located, vested in the liquidator. Nor do we have here a challenge to the possession of the liquidator either through an attempt to obtain a lien on the property or otherwise. As pointed out in Riehle v. Margolies, 279 U.S. 218, 224, the distribution of assets of a debtor among creditors ordinarily has a "two-fold aspect." It deals "directly with the property" when it fixes the time and manner of distribution. No one can obtain part of the assets or enforce a right to specific property in the possession of the liquidation court except upon application to it. But proof and allowance of claims are matters distinct from distribution. They do not "deal directly with any of the property." "The latter function, which is spoken of as the liquidation of a claim is strictly a proceeding in personam." Id., p. 224. The establishment of the existence and amount of a claim against the debtor in no way disturbs the possession of the liquidation court, in no way affects title to the property, and does not necessarily involve a determination of what priority the claim should have. . . .

Moreover, we do not have here a situation like that involved in Pendleton v. Russell, 144 U.S. 640, where it was sought to prove in a New York receivership of a dissolved corporation a judgment obtained in Tennessee after dissolution. The proof was disallowed, dissolution having operated, like death, as an abatement of the suit. No such infirmity appears to be present in the Missouri judgment; and the Illinois Supreme Court did not hold that the appointment of a liquidator for Chicago Lloyds operated as an abatement of the suit. . . . The Missouri judgment represents a liability for acts committed by Chicago Lloyds, not for those of the liquidator. The claims for which the Illinois assets are being administered are claims against Chicago Lloyds. The Missouri judgment represents one of them. There is no more reason for discharging a liquidator from the responsibility for defending pending actions than there is for relieving a receiver of that task. Riehle v. Margolies, supra.

Second. "A judgment of a court having jurisdiction of the parties and of the subject matter operates as res judicata, in the absence of fraud or collusion, even if obtained upon a default." Riehle v. Margolies, supra, p. 225. . . . The full faith and credit to which a judgment is entitled is the credit which it has in the State from which it is taken, not the credit that under other circumstances and conditions it might have had. Moreover, the question whether a judgment is entitled to full faith and credit does not depend on the presence of reciprocal engagements between the States. . . .

As to respondent's contention that the Illinois decree, of which petitioner had notice, should have been given full faith and credit by the Missouri court, only a word need be said. Roche v. McDonald [p. 309, supra], makes plain that the place to raise that defense was in the

Missouri proceedings. And see Treinies v. Sunshine Mining Co., [p. 289, supra]. And whatever might have been the ruling on the question, the rights of the parties could have been preserved by a resort to this Court which is the final arbiter of questions arising under the Full Faith and Credit Clause. Williams v. State of North Carolina, [p. 830, supra]. In any event the Missouri judgment is res judicata as to the nature and amount of petitioner's claim as against all defenses which could have been raised. . . .

It is finally suggested that since the Federal Bankruptcy Act provides for exclusive adjudication of claims by the bankruptcy court and excepts insurance companies from the Act (§ 4, 52 Stat. 840, 845, 11 U.S.C. § 22; . . .), the state liquidators of insolvent insurance companies should have the same control over the determination of claims as the bankruptcy court has. This is to argue that by reason of its police power a State may determine the method and manner of proving claims against property which is in its jurisdiction and which is being administered by its courts or administrative agencies. We have no doubt that it may do so except as such procedure collides with the federal Constitution or an Act of Congress. . . . There is such a collision here. When we look to the general statute which Congress has enacted pursuant to the Full Faith and Credit Clause, we find no exception in case of liquidations of insolvent insurance companies. The command is to give full faith and credit to every judgment of a sister State. And where there is no jurisdictional infirmity, exceptions have rarely, if ever, been read into the constitutional provision or the Act of Congress in cases involving money judgments rendered in civil suits. . . .

The function of the Full Faith and Credit Clause is to resolve controversies where state policies differ. Its need might not be so greatly felt in situations where there was no clash of interests between the States. The argument of convenience in administration is at best only another illustration of how the enforcement of a judgment of one State in another State may run counter to the latter's policies. But the answer given by Fauntleroy v. Lum [p. 306, supra], is conclusive. If full faith and credit is not given in that situation, the Clause and the statute fail where their need is the greatest. The argument of convenience, moreover, proves too much. In the first place, it would often be equally appealing to individuals or corporations engaging in multistate activities which might well prefer to defend law suits at home. In the second place, against the convenience of the administration of assets in Illinois is the hardship on the Missouri creditor if he were forced to drop his Missouri litigation, bring his witnesses to Illinois, and start all over again. But full faith and credit is a more inexorable command; its applicability does not turn on a balance of convenience as between litigants. If this were a situation where Missouri's policy would result in the dismemberment of the Illinois estate so that Illinois creditors would go begging, Illinois would have such a large interest at stake as to prevent it. See Clark v. Williard [p. 942, infra]. But, as we have said, proof and allowance of claims are matters distinct from distribution of assets.

The single point of our decision is that the nature and amount of petitioner's claim has been conclusively determined by the Missouri judgment and may not be relitigated in the Illinois proceedings, it not appearing that the Missouri court lacked jurisdiction over either the parties or the subject matter. . . . Reversed.

MR. JUSTICE FRANKFURTER, with whom concur MR. JUSTICE BLACK and MR. JUSTICE RUTLEDGE, dissenting.

. . . the real issue is this. May Illinois provide that when an insurance concern to which Illinois has given life can, in the judgment of the State courts, no longer be allowed to conduct the insurance business in Illinois, the State may take over the local assets of such an insurance concern for fair distribution among all who have claims against the defunct concern? May the State, pursuant to such a policy, announce in advance, as a rule of fairness, that all claims not previously reduced to valid judgment, no matter how or where they arose, if they are to be paid out of assets thus administered by the State, must be proven on their merits to the satisfaction of Illinois? And may the State specify that this mode of proof apply also to out-of-State creditors so as to require such creditors to prove the merit of their claims against the Illinois assets in liquidation as though they were Illinois creditors, and preclude them from basing their claims merely on a judgment against the insurance concern, obtained after it had legally ceased to be, and after its Illinois assets had by appropriate proceedings passed into ownership of an Illinois liquidator?

. . . The Full Faith and Credit Clause does not eat up the powers reserved to the States by the Constitution. That clause does not embody an absolutist conception of mechanical applicability. As is so often true of constitutional problems, an accommodation must be struck between different provisions of the Constitution. When rights are asserted in one State on the basis of a judgment procured in another, it frequently becomes necessary, as it does here, to define the duty of the courts of the former State in view of that State's power to regulate its own affairs. . . . Surely, the Full Faith and Credit Clause does not require a State to give an advantage to persons dwelling without, when State policy may justifiably restrict its own citizens to a particular procedure in proving claims against a State fund. . . .

Precedent and policy sustain the right of Illinois to have each claimant prove his fair share to the assets in Illinois by the same procedure. . . . Of course Missouri has a right to provide for its methods of administration, in case of default, as to Missouri assets. But we are not here concerned with an attempt to enforce the Missouri judgment against Missouri assets. . . .

. . . The precise relation of the liquidator's legal position to the Missouri judgment, on the basis of which Morris asserts a claim against the liquidator's assets, reinforces the more general considerations. Morris had no judgment against the company when by Illinois law title to Lloyds' assets passed to the liquidator. . . . The liquidator, as trustee for the creditors of the extinct Illinois company, represented interests that were not the same as those represented by the extinct company when it conducted its own business. In short, the Illinois liquidator was thus a stranger to the Missouri judgment and it cannot be invoked against him in Illinois. . . . Indeed, to subject the assets of the Illinois liquidator to the claim of a judgment obtained against Lloyds in Missouri subsequent to the passage of those assets to the liquidator may well raise constitutional questions. Riley v. New York Trust Co. [p. 244, supra].

. . . Against the claim of out-of-State creditors must be set not merely the interests of Illinois creditors, but also the importance of a unified liquidation administration, the burden to the liquidator of defending suits anywhere in the United States, and the resulting hazards to a fair distribution of the estate. . . . The resolution of this conflict so that the out-of-State creditor must take his place with the Illinois creditors is another instance of a price to be paid for our federalism . . .

This is not to say that the Missouri judgment is invalid. Whether recovery may be based on this judgment in Missouri, or in any other State except Illinois or even in Illinois should the assets go out of the State's hands and return to a reanimated Chicago Lloyds, are questions that do not now call for consideration.

The judgment should be affirmed.

NOTES

(1) Can Pendleton v. Russell, discussed by Justice Douglas in his opinion, satisfactorily be distinguished from Morris v. Jones?

(2) Restatement, Second, Conflict of Laws:*

§ 299. Termination or Suspension of Corporate Existence

(1) Whether the existence of a corporation has been terminated or suspended is determined by the local law of the state of incorporation.

(2) The termination or suspension of a corporation's existence by the state of incorporation will be recognized for most purposes by other states.

Comment . . .

e. *Statute of state of incorporation extending life of corporation.* To facilitate collection by the corporation of its assets, and the assertion of creditors' claims against it, statutes commonly provide that for a period of time after the termination or suspension of the corporate existence, suits may be

* Quoted with the permission of the copyright owner, The American Law Institute.

brought by or against the corporation. Likewise, such statutes usually permit the corporation to settle and discharge claims, to transfer its assets, and to do other acts incidental to the winding-up of its affairs.

A corporation whose existence has been terminated or suspended will usually be permitted to exercise in another state such powers as are accorded it by the state of incorporation even though the other state does not give similar powers to domestic corporations. . . .

f. Statute of other state making corporation subject to suit after termination or suspension of existence. Primarily for the purpose of saving local creditors from the inconvenience of having to present their claims in the state of incorporation, statutes sometimes provide that foreign corporations which own things or do business in the state can sue, and remain subject to suit, in the corporate name for a period after their existence has been terminated or suspended. Even if there is no similar statute in the state of incorporation, such a statute will permit suit to be brought in the state of enactment to wind up the corporation's business in that state or to proceed against corporate property located there. . . .

Reporter's Note: . . .

Whether full faith and credit should require extraterritorial enforcement of a judgment rendered against a dissolved foreign corporation under a statute of a State where the corporation did business depends upon which of two considerations is the weightier. The first is the desirability of having a unified winding-up of the corporation's affairs. This can best be achieved by limiting the effect of such statutes to property located within the particular State so as to permit the state of incorporation to insist that, in general, claims against the corporation must be proved before its courts. The second consideration is the convenience of the corporation's creditors who would usually prefer to prove their claims at home and might find it a serious hardship to be compelled to do so in the state of incorporation. . . .

MARTYNE V. AMERICAN UNION FIRE INSURANCE CO., 216 N.Y. 183, 110 N.E. 502 (1915): [The American Union Fire Insurance Company was a Pennsylvania corporation, authorized to carry on business in New York. In 1913, it was ordered dissolved in a court proceeding in Pennsylvania, and its liquidation was directed to be made by the insurance commissioner of that state. There was in force in Pennsylvania a statute which provided that on the dissolution of such a corporation, the insurance commissioner of the state "shall be vested by operation of law with title to all the property, contracts and rights of action of such corporation as of the date of the order so directing him to liquidate." As a result of the dissolution, the policies of fire insurance issued by the corporation became void. After the dissolution, the present action was instituted in New York for the return of unearned premiums under some of the canceled policies, and an alleged indebtedness to the corporation or to the insurance commissioner was attached. A few days later, the New York superintendent of insurance was appointed liquidator of the corporation under the insurance law of New York.

The Pennsylvania insurance commissioner appeared specially in the New York action and moved to have the garnishment and all other proceedings in the action set aside. The trial court granted the motion, and the order was affirmed by the Appellate Division. Appeal, with certain questions of law certified.]

CHASE, J. This action is brought against a corporation that has ceased to exist as such. . . .

The insurance commissioner of Pennsylvania is a statutory liquidator and as such took the title to all of the corporate property of the dissolved corporation. The title of foreign statutory assignees is recognized and enforced where it can be without injustice. (Matter of Waite, 99 N.Y. 433, 2 N.E. 440; Relfe v. Rundle, 103 U.S. 222. See 237 U.S. 531.) . . .

. . . The rule in this state seems to be so thoroughly established that the title of an assignee or receiver under involuntary or bankruptcy proceedings in a foreign state will not be upheld as against an attachment obtained and served by a resident of this state, that perhaps it should not be changed except by an act of the legislature.

To hold, however, in this case that the title which vested by the Statutes of Pennsylvania in the insurance superintendent of that state as a statutory liquidator does not extend to property in this state as against an attaching creditor here, would be to extend the rule which permits a local creditor to ignore the laws of a foreign state. We are of the opinion that the plaintiff and those from whom he received assignments of claims against the dissolved corporation have no equity that should prevent enforcing the general rule of comity in this case. . . .

The order should be affirmed, with costs. . . .

————

CLARK V. WILLIARD, 292 U.S. 112, 54 S.Ct. 615, 78 L.Ed. 1160 (1934): [An Iowa insurance company was adjudged insolvent and ordered dissolved in a state court proceeding in Iowa, and pursuant to a statute of Iowa the state commissioner of insurance was adjudged "the successor to said corporation" and as such to hold "title to all property owned by [the corporation] at the time it so ceased to exist." The Iowa insurance company had been authorized to do business in Montana under a statute providing in effect that the dissolution of a domestic or foreign corporation did not impair any remedy against the corporation for a liability previously incurred. Two creditors had brought an action in a Montana state court against the Iowa corporation prior to its dissolution and recovered a judgment by default after the dissolution.

Another creditor then brought a suit in a Montana state court against the corporation and the Iowa liquidator in which he prayed for an ancillary receivership and a receiver was appointed. The judgment creditors mentioned above then filed a petition for leave to satisfy their judgment out of Montana assets, and the Iowa liquidator filed a cross-petition asserting his title as statutory successor to the dissolved corporation and urging that his title should be recognized under the full faith and credit clause. The Montana Supreme Court held that the Iowa liquidator was only an equity receiver, and that as against such a liquidator the Montana creditors were entitled to satisfy their claims out of Montana assets. On certiorari, the Supreme Court of the United States vacated the state court decree and remanded the cause to the Supreme Court of Montana for further proceedings not inconsistent with its opinion.]

MR. JUSTICE CARDOZO. . . . The question is whether full faith and credit has been given by the courts of Montana to the statutes and judicial proceedings of the state of Iowa. . . .

We assume in accordance with the decision of the Montana court that the respondents' action against the surety company did not abate on dissolution, but was lawfully pursued to judgment. . . . But this . . . is only a partial statement of the problem. To ascertain the procedure by which the [judgment] is to be enforced, whether by the levy of execution or by a ratable division, other considerations must be weighed. In particular, it must be known whether superior interests or titles have developed between the summons and the judgment, and whether the quality or operation of those interests affects the method of distribution. Something did intervene here, the appointment of a liquidator under the statutes of the domicile. That much is undisputed. Did the Supreme Court of Montana misjudge the quality and operation of this intervening interest, and in so doing did it deny to the statutes and decrees of Iowa the faith and credit owing to them under the Constitution of the United States?

In our judgment, the statutes of Iowa have made the official liquidator the successor to the corporation, and not a mere receiver. . . . His title is not the consequence of a decree of a court whereby a corporation still in being has made a compulsory assignment of its assets with a view to liquidation. . . . His title is the consequence of a succession established for the corporation by the law of its creation. . . . So the lawmakers have plainly said. So the Iowa court adjudged in decreeing dissolution.

We think the Supreme Court of Montana denied full faith and credit to the statutes and judicial proceedings of Iowa in holding, as it did, that the petitioner was a receiver deriving title through a judicial proceeding, and not through the charter of its being and the succession there prescribed. . . .

In thus holding we do not say that there is an invariable rule by which the title of a statutory liquidator must prevail over executions and attachments outside of the state of his appointment. The subject is involved in confusion, with decisions pro and con. . . .

Whether there is in Montana a local policy, expressed in statute or decision, whereby judgments and attachments have a preference over the title of a charter liquidator, is a question as to which the Supreme Court of that state will speak with ultimate authority.

NOTES

(1) When the cause was remanded to the Supreme Court of Montana, that court by a divided vote again held the judgment creditors had priority over the Iowa statutory liquidator because Montana's law permitted attachments on property in Montana of insolvent corporations, both domestic and foreign, for which a statutory liquidator had been appointed. Mieyr v. Federal Surety Co., 97 Mont. 503, 34 P.2d 982 (1934). The Supreme Court of the United States affirmed this decision. "Iowa may say that one who is a liquidator with title, appointed by her statutes, shall be so recognized in Montana with whatever rights and privileges accompany such recognition according to Montana law . . . Iowa may not say . . . that a liquidator with title who goes into Montana may set at naught Montana law as to the distribution of Montana assets, and carry over into another state the rule of distribution prescribed by the statutes of the domicile." Clark v. Williard, 294 U.S. 211 (1935).

(2) In Relfe v. Rundle, 103 U.S. 222 (1880), a Missouri insurance company had been dissolved under the law of Missouri and its property vested in the Missouri State Superintendent of Insurance. The Missouri Superintendent of Insurance had himself made a party defendant to a suit which had been instituted in Louisiana against this insurance company. Held, this is proper, and the Superintendent can remove the suit to the federal court in Louisiana on the ground of diversity of citizenship. "Relfe is not an officer of the Missouri state court. . . . He was the statutory successor of the Corporation for the purpose of winding up its affairs. . . . He is an officer of the State, and as such represents the State in its sovereignty while performing its public duties connected with the winding up of the affairs of one of its insolvent and dissolved corporations."

CONVERSE v. HAMILTON

Supreme Court of the United States, 1912.
224 U.S. 243, 32 S.Ct. 415, 56 L.Ed. 749, Ann.Cas.1913D, 1292.

[A creditor of a Minnesota corporation brought a suit in a Minnesota state court against the corporation for the sequestration of its property and the appointment of a receiver. The court found the corporation was insolvent, appointed a receiver, and ascertained it was necessary to resort to the double liability of the stockholders imposed by Minnesota law for the payment of the creditors. The court then levied upon the corporation's stockholders assessments amounting to 100 per cent. of the par value of their shares, and directed the receiver to prosecute such actions within or without the state as were necessary to enforce the assessment.

The present actions were brought by the Minnesota receiver in Wisconsin against Wisconsin stockholders of the corporation to recover the assessments. The Wisconsin stockholders had not been made parties to the Minnesota suit and were not notified, otherwise than by publication or by mail, of the application for the orders levying the assessments. The Wisconsin court refused to enforce the assessments because they were contrary to Wisconsin policy. The receiver sued out writs of error to the Supreme Court of the United States.]

MR. JUSTICE VAN DEVANTER delivered the opinion of the court. . . . This liability is not to the corporation but to the creditors collectively, is not penal but contractual, is not joint but several, and the mode and means of its enforcement are subject to legislative regulation. . . .

The proceedings in the sequestration suit, looking to the enforcement of this liability, were had under chapter 272, Laws of 1899, and sections 3184–3190, Revised Laws of 1905, the latter being a continuation of the former with changes not here material. . . . It expressly prescribed the mode of enforcement pursued in the present instance; that is to say, it made provision for bringing all the creditors into the sequestration suit, for the presentation and adjudication of their claims, for ascertaining the relation of the corporate debts and the expenses of the receivership to the available assets, and whether and to what extent it was necessary to resort to the stockholders' double liability for levying such assessments upon the stockholders according to their respective holdings as should be necessary to pay the debts, and for investing the receiver with authority to collect the assessments on behalf of the creditors. . . .

Under this statute, as interpreted by the Supreme Court of the State, as also by this court, the receiver is not an ordinary chancery receiver or arm of the court appointing him, but a quasi-assignee and representative of the creditors, and when the order levying the assessment is made he becomes invested with the creditors' rights of action against the stockholders and with full authority to enforce the same in any court of competent jurisdiction in the State or elsewhere.

The constitutional validity of chapter 272 has been sustained by the Supreme Court of the State, as also by this court; and this because (1) the statute is but a reasonable regulation of the mode and means of enforcing the double liability assumed by those who become stockholders in a Minnesota corporation; (2) while the order levying the assessment is made conclusive, as against all stockholders, of all matters relating to the amount and propriety of the assessment and the necessity therefor, one against whom it is sought to be enforced is not precluded from showing that he is not a stockholder, or is not the holder of as many shares as is alleged, or has a claim against the corporation which in law or equity he is entitled to set off against the assessment, or has any other defense personal to himself, and (3) while the order is made conclusive as against a stockholder, even although he may not have been a party to the suit in which it was made and may not have been notified that an assessment was contemplated, this is not a tenable objection, for the order is not in the nature of a personal judgment against the stockholder and as to him is amply sustained by the presence in that suit of the corporation, considering his relation to it and his contractual obligation in respect of its debts. . . .

This statement of the nature of the liability in question, of the laws of Minnesota bearing upon its enforcement, and of the effect which judicial proceedings under those laws have in that State, discloses, as we think, that in the cases now before us the Supreme Court of Wisconsin failed to give full faith and credit to those laws and to the proceedings thereunder, upon which the receiver's right to sue was grounded. It is true that an ordinary chancery receiver is a mere arm of the court appointing him, is invested with no estate in the property committed to his charge, and is clothed with no power to exercise his official duties in other jurisdictions. . . . But here the receiver was not merely an ordinary chancery receiver, but much more. By the proceedings in the sequestration suit, had conformably to the laws of Minnesota, he became a quasi-assignee and representative of the creditors, was invested with their rights of action against the stockholders, and was charged with the enforcement of those rights in the courts of that State and elsewhere. So when he invoked the aid of the Wisconsin court the case presented was, in substance, that of a trustee, clothed with adequate title for the occasion, seeking to enforce, for the benefit of his cestuis que trustent, a right of action, transitory, in character, against one who was liable contractually and severally, if at all. . . .

In these circumstances we think the conclusion is unavoidable that the laws of Minnesota and the judicial proceedings in that State, upon which the receiver's title, authority and right to relief were grounded, and by which the stockholders were bound, were not accorded that faith and credit to which they were entitled under the Constitution and laws of the United States.

The judgments are accordingly reversed, and the cases are remanded for further proceedings not inconsistent with this opinion.

Reversed.

NOTE

(1) On the law determining whether policyholders of a mutual insurance company are members of the company and hence are liable to pay assessments, see Pink v. A.A.A. Highway Express, Inc., 314 U.S. 201, 62 S.Ct. 241 (1941).

BRODERICK v. ROSNER

Supreme Court of the United States, 1935.
294 U.S. 629, 55 S.Ct. 589, 79 L.Ed. 1100, 100 A.L.R. 1133.

MR. JUSTICE BRANDEIS delivered the opinion of the Court.

Pursuant to article 8, section 7, of the Constitution of New York, its Banking Law (Consol.Laws, c. 2) provides, section 120: "The stockholders of every bank will be individually responsible, equally and ratably and not one for another, for all contracts, debts and engagements of the bank, to the extent of the amount of their stock therein, at the par value thereof, in addition to the amount invested in such shares."

The Bank of the United States is a corporation organized under the Banking Law of New York and had its places of business in New York City. Its outstanding capital stock is $25,250,000 represented by 1,010,000 shares of $25 par value. On November 17, 1933, Joseph A. Broderick, as Superintendent of Banks of the State of New York, brought, in the Supreme Court of New Jersey, this action against 557 of its stockholders who are residents of New Jersey, to recover unpaid assessments levied by him upon them pursuant to law.

The defendant moved to strike out the complaint on the ground, among others, that, by reason of section 94b of the Corporation Act of New Jersey (2 Comp.St.1910, p. 1656), it failed to set out a cause of action enforceable in any court of that State. The section, first enacted March 30, 1897, provides: "No action or proceeding shall be maintained in any court of law in this state against any stockholder, officer or director of any domestic or foreign corporation by or on behalf of any creditor of such corporation to enforce any statutory personal liability of such stockholder, officer or director for or upon any debt, default or obligation of such corporation, whether such statutory personal liability be deemed penal or contractual, if such statutory personal liability be created by or arise from the statutes or laws of any other state or foreign country, and no pending or future action or proceeding to enforce such statutory personal liability shall be maintained in any court of this state other than in the nature of an equitable accounting for the proportionate benefit of all parties interested, to which such corporation and its legal representatives, if any, and all of its creditors and all of it stockholders shall be necessary parties."

Broderick seasonably claimed that to sustain the asserted bar of the statute would violate article 4, section 1, of the Federal Constitution, which provides that, "Full Faith and Credit shall be given in each State to the public Acts, Records and judicial Proceedings of every other State," and the legislation of Congress enacted pursuant thereto. The trial court sustained the motion to strike out the complaint, Broderick v. Abrams, 112 N.J.L. 309, 170 A. 214, on the ground that the statute of the State constituted a bar to the action.

Judgment against the plaintiff, with costs, was entered in favor of each of the defendants, and the judgment was affirmed by the Court of Errors and Appeals "for the reasons expressed in the opinion" of the trial court. 113 N.J.L. 305, 174 A. 507. An appeal to this Court was allowed. Broderick v. Rosner, 293 U.S. 613.

First. The conditions imposed by section 94b of the New Jersey statute upon the bringing of suits to enforce such assessments, as here applied, deny to the Superintendent the right to resort to the courts of the State to enforce the assessment of liability upon the stockholders there resident. The requirement that the proceeding be by bill in equity, instead of by an action at law, would, if standing alone, be no obstacle. But by withholding jurisdiction unless the proceeding be a suit for an equitable accounting to which the "corporation and its legal representatives, if any, and all of its creditors and all of its stockholders shall be necessary parties," it imposes a condition which, as here applied, is legally impossible of fulfillment. For it is not denied that according to the decisions of the New Jersey courts "necessary parties" means those whose presence in a suit is essential as a jurisdictional prerequisite to the entry of judgment, so that no decree can be made respecting the subject-matter of litigation until they are before the court . . . and that to secure jurisdiction personally over those who are not residents of New Jersey, or engaged in business there, is impossible. . . . The corporation has no place of business in New Jersey; only a few of the many stockholders and creditors have either residence or place of business there.

Moreover, even if it were legally possible to satisfy the statutory condition by making substituted service by publication upon non-resident stockholders and creditors . . ., the cost would be prohibitive. The number of the stockholders is 20,843; the number of depositors and other creditors exceeds 400,000; and the amounts assessed against the individual defendants are relatively small—against some only $50. The aggregate of sheriff's fees alone as to the nonresident defendants, aside from expenses of publication and mailing, would exceed the aggregate amount due from the New Jersey stockholders. The suggestion, in the opinion of the Supreme Court, that leave might be granted to file a bill in equity is, therefore, without legal significance.

Second. But for the statute, the action would have been entertained. . . . The plaintiff is not, as in Booth v. Clark, 17 How. 322, 15 L.Ed. 164, a foreign receiver. He sues as an independent executive in whom has been vested by statute the cause of action sued on. Converse v. Hamilton, 224 U.S. 243, 257. . . .

Third. The power of a State to determine the limits of the jurisdiction of its courts and the character of the controversies which shall be heard therein is subject to the limitations imposed by the Federal Constitution. . . . A "State cannot escape its constitutional obligations [under the full faith and credit clause] by the simple device of

denying jurisdiction in such cases to courts otherwise competent."
Kenney v. Supreme Lodge, [p. 314, supra] [3] . . . it may not, under the guise of merely affecting the remedy, deny the enforcement of claims otherwise within the protection of the full faith and credit clause, when its courts have general jurisdiction of the subject-matter and the parties. . . . For the States of the Union, the constitutional limitation imposed by the full faith and credit clause abolished, in large measure, the general principle of international law by which local policy is permitted to dominate rules of comity.

Here the nature of the cause of action brings it within the scope of the full faith and credit clause. The statutory liability sought to be enforced is contractual in character. The assessment is an incident of the incorporation. Thus the subject-matter is peculiarly within the regulatory power of New York, as the State of incorporation. . . . In respect to the determination of liability for an assessment, the New Jersey stockholders submitted themselves to the jurisdiction of New York. . . . Obviously recognition could not be accorded to a local policy of New Jersey, if there really were one, of enabling all residents of the State to escape from the performance of a voluntarily assumed statutory obligation, consistent with morality, to contribute to the payment of the depositors of a bank of another State of which they were stockholders.

Fourth. The fact that the assessment here in question was made under statutory direction by an administrative officer does not preclude the application of the full faith and credit clause. If the assessment had been made in a liquidation proceeding conducted by a court, New Jersey would have been obliged to enforce it, although the stockholders sued had not been made parties to the proceedings, and, being nonresidents, could not have been personally served with process. Converse v. Hamilton [p. 944, supra]. The reason why in that case the full faith and credit clause was held to require Wisconsin courts to enforce the assessment made in Minnesota was not because the determination was embodied in a judgment. Against the nonresident stockholders there had been no judgment in Minnesota. Wisconsin was required to enforce the Minnesota assessment because statutes are "public acts" within the meaning of the clause, Bradford Electric Light Co. v. Clapper, 286 U.S. 145, 155 [p. 351,]; Alaska Packers Association v. Industrial Accident Commission [294 U.S. 532 (1934)]; and because the residents of Wisconsin had, by becoming stockholders of a Minnesota corporation, submitted themselves to that extent, to the jurisdiction and laws of the latter State. Where a State has had jurisdiction of the subject-matter and the parties, obligations validly imposed upon them by statute must, within the limitations above stated, be given full faith and credit by all the other states. . . .

3. Chambers v. Baltimore & Ohio R. Co., 207 U.S. 142, is not to the contrary; there no claim was made under the full faith and credit clause. [Footnote by the Court.]

Fifth. The Superintendent contends that his assessment is a "public act" within the meaning of the full faith and credit clause, and is entitled to receive in every other State of the Union, the same recognition accorded to it by the laws of New York. He insists that, while under the law of New York defenses personal to individual stockholders are open to them whenever and wherever sued, Selig v. Hamilton, 234 U.S. 652, 662, 663, his determinations as to the propriety and amount of the assessment, in so far as they involve merely the exercise of judgment, are conclusive; and are not subject to review by any court, except on grounds for which equity commonly affords relief against administrative orders. . . . Whether this contention is sound, we have no occasion to consider now. . . . It is sufficient to decide that, since the New Jersey courts possess general jurisdiction of the subject-matter and the parties, and the subject-matter is not one as to which the alleged public policy of New Jersey could be controlling, the full faith and credit clause requires that this suit be entertained.

Reversed.

MR. JUSTICE CARDOZO is of the opinion that the judgment should be affirmed.

NOTE

See generally Cheatham, The Statutory Successor, The Receiver and the Executor in Conflict of Laws, 44 Colum.L.Rev. 549 (1944).

Chapter 14

AGENCY, PARTNERSHIPS AND ASSOCIATIONS

Introductory Note. A relationship of agency or of partnership may give rise to several choice-of-law problems: what law governs the rights and duties (a) of the principal and agent, or of the partners, as between themselves, (b) of the principal, or of the partnership and partners, on the one hand, and of some third person on the other, on account of one or more acts done on behalf of the principal or partnership by an agent, who in the case of a partnership will frequently be a partner, and (c) as between the agent and the third person on account of an act done by the agent. The second of these questions is the one primarily dealt with in this chapter. The third question is not considered, since the law governing a person's individual liability for an act is the same irrespective of whether he was acting for himself or for another.

Young v. Masci, 289 U.S. 253 (1933): Action brought by a New Yorker in a New Jersey court to recover for injuries suffered in an automobile accident in New York. The defendant, a New Jersey resident, had loaned his automobile in that state "without restriction upon its use" to one Balbino who drove the automobile into New York and there negligently injured the plaintiff. The New Jersey courts gave judgment to the plaintiff by application of a New York statute which made the "owner of a motor vehicle" liable for injuries caused by the negligence of any person operating the same with the "permission, express or implied, of such owner." The defendant appealed to the Supreme Court of the United States, contending that application of the New York statute under the circumstances violated due process. Affirmed. "When Young [the defendant] gave permission to drive his car to New York, he subjected himself to the legal consequences imposed by that state upon Balbino's negligent driving as fully as if he had stood in the relation of master to servant. A person who sets in motion in one state the means by which injury is inflicted in another may, consistently with the due process clause, be made liable for that injury whether the means employed be a responsible agent or an irresponsible instrument. . . . The power of the state to protect itself and its inhabitants is not limited by the scope of the doctrine of principal and agent. . . . No good reason is suggested why, when there is permission to take the automobile into a state for use upon its highways, personal liability should not be im-

951

posed upon the owner in case of injury inflicted there by the driver's negligence. . . ."

———

Agency relationships are usually created by contract but they can arise otherwise. For example, one person may act at another's direction without any express agreement between them but the law may raise the existence of an agency or there may be a ratification by the principal of the alleged agent's acts. The obligations between principal and agent are determined, according to Restatement, Second, Conflict of Laws § 291, "by the local law of the state which, with respect to the particular issue, has the most significant relationship to the parties and the transaction under the principles stated in § 6." The law is selected by applying the rules set forth in Sections 187–188 with regard to contracts. Comment *f* to Section 291 states that "the state where performance by the agent is to take place will usually be given the greatest weight, in the absence of an effective choice of law by the parties (see § 187), in determining what law governs the rights and duties owed by the principal and agent to each other."

———

MERCIER v. JOHN HANCOCK MUTUAL LIFE INSURANCE CO.

Supreme Court of Maine, 1945.
141 Me. 376, 44 A.2d 372.

MANSER, JUSTICE. [Action to recover on a life insurance policy, the application for which had been written in Maine. From a jury verdict in favor of the plaintiff, the insurance company appealed.]

The defendant Company contested payment upon the ground that [the insured] made false representations to the effect that no albumin or sugar had ever been found in his urine, and that he had never been told that he had symptoms of diabetes, when in truth he had been diabetic for ten years and had used the insulin treatment therefor. Also that he stated his brother was in good health, when he was at the time a patient in a tuberculosis sanitarium, and died soon thereafter. . . .

. . .

The issues presented to the jury were whether there were, in fact, any material misrepresentations or concealments by or on behalf of the [insured]; whether the agent knew or was informed of the diabetes and took the responsibility of assuring the [insured] that it made no difference and need not be mentioned in the application; and again whether the agent failed to ask the question as to the health of the brother of the [insured], and instead assumed the responsibility of inserting a favorable answer.

The testimony was flatly contradictory. The instructions by the presiding Justice were clear and lucid upon the factual issues. It was for the jury to determine as to the credibility of witnesses and the weight of the evidence. The record would not warrant a ruling by this Court that the verdict was manifestly wrong.

This brings us to a consideration of the exceptions. [The defendant complained of the refusal of the trial judge to charge that the Maine statute, which provided that an insurance company could not rely as a defense on misrepresentations known to the agent, was not applicable because the insurance contract was a "Massachusetts contract".]

The question of whether the policy was, technically, a Maine or a Massachusetts contract was not passed upon by the presiding Justice or the jury. It did not need to be.

The situation presented here is simply whether the defendant Company is responsible for the acts of a duly authorized agent, licensed in the State of Maine, in connection with an application for insurance which he procured in Maine from a citizen thereof, when our statute says that such agent stands in the place of the Company with regard to all insurance effected by him.

In the Restatement of the Law upon the title Conflict of Laws, § 345, the rule is succinctly stated us follows:

"The law of the state in which an agent or a partner is authorized or apparently authorized to act for the principal or other partners determines whether an act done on account of the principal or other partners imposes a contractual duty upon the principal or other partners."

Then under the Comment, after discussing the effect of an agent's acts, we find the definite statement:

"But whether or not a particular act of the agent or partner is authorized, the law of the state where the act is done determines whether the principal is bound by a contract with a third person."

. . .

Exceptions overruled.

RESTATEMENT, SECOND, CONFLICT OF LAWS:*

§ 292. Contractual Liability of Principal to Third Person

(1) Whether a principal is bound by action taken on his behalf by an agent in dealing with a third person is determined by the local law of the state which, with respect to the particular issue, has the most

significant relationship to the parties and the transaction under the principles stated in § 6.

(2) The principal will be held bound by the agent's action if he would so be bound under the local law of the state where the agent dealt with the third person, provided at least that the principal had authorized the agent to act on his behalf in that state or had led the third person reasonably to believe that the agent had such authority.

NOTES

(1) See generally Reese and Flesch, Agency and Vicarious Liability in Conflict of Laws, 60 Colum.L.Rev. 764 (1960); Hay and Müller-Freienfels, Agency in the Conflict of Laws and the 1978 Hague Convention, 27 Am.J. Comp.L. 1 (1979).

(2) For a case applying the principles of the Restatement (Second) to determine the law governing the liability of an undisclosed principal to the person with whom the agent dealt, see Shasta Livestock Auction Yard, Inc. v. Bill Evans Cattle Management Corp., 375 F.Supp. 1027 (D. Idaho 1974).

(3) In state X, P authorizes A to manage P's farm in State X and to use the livestock on it as required. A drives the livestock to state Y and sells them to T, remitting the proceeds to P. By what law will it be determined whether A is liable to P for having exceeded the terms of his authority? By what law will it be determined whether T obtained title to the livestock? See Restatement, Second, Conflict of Laws §§ 291–292.

(4) The law governing the agent's contract with the third person will usually be applied to determine whether the principal is bound by the contract and entitled to its benefits.

Maspons Y Hermano v. Mildred, L.R. 9 Q.B.D. 531 (1882). Defendants, a London firm, entered into an agreement with Demestre & Co. whereby defendants were to receive a cargo of tobacco for purposes of resale and were also to insure the cargo for the benefit of all concerned. Defendants realized that Demestre & Co. were acting in the capacity of agents but did not know the names of their principals, who in fact were the present plaintiffs, a Spanish firm carrying on business in Havana. The ship carrying the tobacco sank and plaintiffs brought suit for the proceeds of the insurance which had been paid to the defendants. The defense was that under Spanish law an undisclosed principal was not entitled to sue the person with whom his agent had contracted. Held, for the plaintiffs. Spanish law is material only for the purpose of determining the nature and extent of the authority given by plaintiffs to their agent. "The contract between Demestre & Co. and the defendants is governed by English law, not Spanish, and the persons who can sue and be sued on that contract in England must also be determined by our law, and not by the law of Spain."

(5) In the case of land, the law of the situs governs questions relating to the validity and effect of the deed executed by the agent. Clark v. Graham, 6 Wheat. (U.S.) 577 (1821); Restatement, Second, Conflict of Laws § 223. On the other hand, since a contract whereby a broker is authorized to buy or sell land does not create an interest in the land, the obligations owed by the principal and broker to each other under the contract are determined by the law governing the contract. This law may or may not be that of the state

where the land is. Frankel v. Allied Mills, Inc., 369 Ill. 578, 17 N.E.2d 570 (1938); Johnson v. Allen, 108 Utah 148, 158 P.2d 134 (1945).

Ratification. A ratification by the principal of the agent's act will usually bind the principal if the ratification would be effective under the law of either (a) the state where the agent dealt with the third person or (b) the state whose law governs the principal-agent relationship. Restatement, Second, Conflict of Laws § 293. This is an example of an alternative reference rule seeking validation of the contract.

RESTATEMENT, SECOND, CONFLICT OF LAWS:*

§ 294.   Relationship of Partners Inter Se

The rights and duties owed by partners to each other are determined by the local law of the state which, with respect to the particular issue, has the most significant relationship to the partners and the transaction under the principles stated in § 6. This law is selected by application of the rules of §§ 187–188.

NOTES

(1) The paucity of conflict-of-laws cases involving the rights and duties owed by partners to each other is perhaps due in part to the nearly universal adoption of the Uniform Partnership Act.

(2) Among the legal issues that arise between partners are questions as to the share of each partner in the control and profits of the business, the extent of their liabilities to one another, and the effect of death or withdrawal of a partner on continuation of the firm. Usually, the partnership will conduct its business in the state where it was organized. If so, the law of this state will be applied. If the partnership has little or no contact with the state of its organization, the courts have held that the applicable law is that of another state having a closer relationship to the partnership. See, e.g., Teas v. Kimball, 257 F.2d 817 (5th Cir. 1958); Wright v. Armwood, 107 A.2d 702 (D.C.Cir.1954).

RESTATEMENT, SECOND, CONFLICT OF LAWS:*

§ 295.   Contractual Liability of Partnership, Partners and Third Person

(1) Whether a partnership is bound by action taken on its behalf by an agent in dealing with a third person is determined by the local law of the state selected by application of the rule of § 292.

* Quoted with the permission of the copyright owner, The American Law Institute.

(2) Whether a general partner is bound by action taken on behalf of the partnership by an agent in dealing with a third person is determined by the local law of the state selected by application of the rule of § 292.

(3) The liability of a limited partner for action taken on behalf of the partnership by an agent in dealing with a third person is determined by the local law of the state selected by application of the rule of § 294 [the law governing the relationship of partners inter se], unless the limited partner has taken a significant part in the control of the partnership business or has led the third person reasonably to believe that he was a general partner. In either of these latter events, the liability of the limited partner will be determined by application of the local law of the state selected by application of the rule of § 292.

WAVERLY NATIONAL BANK v. HALL

Supreme Court of Pennsylvania, 1892.
150 Pa. 466, 24 A. 665, 30 Am.St.Rep. 823.

[Action against Hall and others on promissory notes signed by Crandall. The defendants and Crandall made in Pennsylvania a contract, with the following provisions: Crandall agreed to establish and operate under his sole control a toy factory in New York; the defendants agreed to furnish the necessary working capital, not to exceed three thousand dollars; the defendants were to receive 6 per cent per annum on all sums so furnished, and in addition 40 per cent of the net profits of the business; Crandall was to have the privilege to repay in installments the money so advanced and as the money was repaid the share of the net profits going to the defendants would be correspondingly reduced; the defendants should have a mortgage lien on the machinery and fixtures of the business to secure the repayment of the money advanced; and "nothing in this writing shall be construed to create a partnership between the respective parties except with respect to the net profits as herein provided." The notes sued upon were made by Crandall to a New York bank, apparently in New York, in connection with the operation of the business in that state.]

Opinion by MR. JUSTICE HEYDRICK . . .

The plaintiff sues upon notes made by C.M. Crandall, one of the defendants, in his own name, and seeks to charge the other defendants as partners of Crandall in a business in which the proceeds of certain other notes, of which these were renewals, were used. . . .

[The court here outlined the agreement between Crandall and the defendants.] These provisions are all consistent with the relation of borrower and lender, and some of them are inconsistent with any other relation. It is therefore manifest that that relation was intended to be established; and the next question is whether, in spite of the intention of the parties, the community of interest in the profits constituted them a partnership as to creditors.

[The court held that this question should be determined by the law which governed the agreement between Crandall and the defendants and that this law was that of New York, the state where the toy factory was to be established. The court found that under the law of New York the agreement did not create a partnership as to third persons, and the judgment for the defendants was affirmed.]

BARROWS v. DOWNS & CO.

Supreme Court of Rhode Island, 1870.
9 R.I. 446, 11 Am.Rep. 283.

These were two actions of assumpsit, one brought by Henry F. Barrows against the defendants, to recover the sum of $8,494.39 alleged to be due on book account for goods sold and delivered, and the other by the Meriden Britannia Company, upon a promissory note for $8,467.82, made by the said J.F. Downs & Co., and also to recover the sum of $1,142.09, alleged to be due on book account for goods sold and delivered.

Service of the writ in each of these cases was made solely upon William C. Downs, described therein as one of the co-partners of the firm of Joseph F. Downs & Co., the said Joseph F. Downs not being found within the state. . . .

POTTER, J. . . .

The plaintiffs rely on evidence that said William, while on a visit to this country, held himself out as a partner, and a general partner, in the firm.

The defendant denies these representations, and contends that he was only a special partner in the Havana firm, and under the Spanish law not liable as a general partner.

He testifies to a special partnership existing between him and Joseph for several years previous to 1866, the terms of which were, however, not reduced to writing until April, 1866, a copy of which he produces, and he also offers the evidence of A. F. Bramoso, a Spanish lawyer formerly of Havana, but now of New York, that said verbal special partnership was valid there. . . .

Being satisfied, . . . that the partnership in Havana was a special one and authorized by Spanish law, the next inquiry is, what is the liability of William C. Downs, the special partner in this case.

The orders for these goods were by the general partner, Joseph, by letter or personally. No goods were ever ordered by William except once,—some ear-drops from Mr. Barrows.

Now, if the parties had remained in Havana, and the general partner had made contracts abroad by letter or otherwise, there can be no doubt but that the extent to which he could bind his copartners and make them liable for his acts, would depend upon the law of the place of the partnership; the extent to which they had made him their agent with power to bind them, would be regulated by the law of Cuba. And if the general partner himself went abroad, (the special partners remaining at home,) his authority to bind them would still be regulated by the law of Cuba. . . .

But the plaintiffs offer evidence to show that the defendant, W.C. Downs, was in New York in the summer of 1865, and there represented himself as a partner, and, as they contend, a general partner in the firm. Of course, if he was actually a general partner, he would be liable for the whole amount.

And if he was not a general partner in fact, yet if he made such representations to these parties as to his interest in the concern, his responsibility, and his share in the profits, as to lead them to suppose he was a partner personally liable, and the goods or any portion of them were advanced on the strength of his representations, then he should be liable for all so advanced.

And this is the view we take from all the evidence in the case; that the defendant should be held liable for all the goods advanced after these representations made in the summer of 1865.

Judgment for plaintiffs for $2,054.61 and costs.

NOTES

(1) In King v. Sarria, 69 N.Y. 24 (1877), the action was against a special partner of limited liability in a Cuban partnership on a contract made in New York. Cuba was Sarria's domicile and it was found that he had neither participated in managing the business nor held himself out as a general partner. The limitation on his liability was upheld by application of Cuban law. See also Gilman Paint & Varnish Co. v. Legum, 197 Md. 665, 80 A.2d 906 (1951). Cf. Uniform Limited Partnership Act § 303 (1976).

(2) Section 901 of the Uniform Limited Partnership Act (1976) provides that "the laws of the state under which a foreign limited partnership is organized governs its organization and internal affairs and the liability of its limited partners."

(3) For discussion of the choice-of-law problems relating to limited partnerships, see Notes, 52 B.U.L.Rev. 64, 65–69 (1972).

GREENSPUN v. LINDLEY

New York Court of Appeals, 1975.
36 N.Y.2d 473, 369 N.Y.S.2d 123, 330 N.E.2d 79.

JONES, J. In the circumstances of this case we conclude that hold-ers of beneficial shares of interest in this real estate investment trust who desire to challenge investment decisions of the trustees and the payment by them of what are alleged to be excessive management fees must first make a demand on the trustees before commencing what is the equivalent of a shareholders' derivative action against the trustees individually.

Mony Mortgage Investors was organized as a business trust un-der the laws of the Commonwealth of Massachusetts to carry on busi-ness as a "real estate investment trust" as described in the REIT provisions of the Internal Revenue Code (§§ 856–858; US Code, tit 26, §§ 856–858). . . .

The declaration of trust, initially dated February 25, 1970, pro-vides that there shall be no less than 3 and no more than 15 trustees, to be elected by the shareholders, except that a majority of the trust-ees shall not be affiliated with the manager to be employed for the transaction of the business of the trust. On April 6, 1970, the trust-ees approved a management contract with the Mutual Life Insurance Company of New York. At the time of the institution of the present action there were 11 trustees, 5 of whom were officers of the insur-ance company and 6 of whom were unaffiliated. The 11 trustees, the insurance company and the investment trust were all named as de-fendants.

The gravamen of the complaint, pleaded in conclusory terms only, is that in consequence of the subservience of the trustees to domina-tion by the insurance company they are paying excessive manage-ment fees to the insurance company and make investment decisions only if the interest of the insurance company is thereby served, and that the investments so made are unsuitable for the purposes of the investment trust and inconsistent with its stated investment policy. Plaintiff seeks an accounting by defendants to the investment trust for damages sustained by the trust and for profits realized by defend-ants, together with counsel fees.

Defendants moved to dismiss the complaint, principally on the ground that plaintiff failed, prior to the commencement of the action, to make a demand on either the trustees or the other shareholders.
. . .

We hold, as did the Appellate Division, that the law of the Com-monwealth of Massachusetts governs the disposition of the present motions.

The investment trust is a business trust organized and existing under the laws of Massachusetts. The declaration of trust, with which the shareholders became associated only by voluntary choice on the part of each of them, expressly provides that the law of Massachusetts shall be the applicable law as to the rights of all parties. Thus, prima facie Massachusetts law is applicable. . . .

We conclude . . . in the circumstances of this case that reference must be made to the authorities in the Commonwealth of Massachusetts to determine the rights of the parties in this litigation. In so holding we incidentally note the pragmatic as well as the theoretical advantages which would appear to flow from a conclusion that the rights of all shareholders of this real estate investment trust in comparable situations should be determined on a trust-wide basis rather than in consequence of the litigants' choice of forum or the assessment by several courts as to which State it is where the investment trust may be said to be present.

In deciding this case as we do, however, we expressly leave open what law we might apply were there proof from which it could properly be found, in consequence of significant contacts with New York State, that this investment trust, although a Massachusetts business trust, was nonetheless so "present" in our State as perhaps to call for the application of New York law. In that sense we reject any automatic application of the so-called "internal affairs" choice-of-law rule, under which the relationship between shareholders and trustees of a business trust by strict analogy to the relationship between shareholders and directors of a business corporation would be governed by the law of the State in which the business entity was formed.

Similarly we do not reach the question of what significance we would accord the explicit agreement of the parties that their rights are to be governed by Massachusetts law, were we disposed, entirely without reference to that provision of the declaration of trust, to apply the law of New York or the law of some State other than Massachusetts.

Turning then to the law of Massachusetts, we conclude . . . that the courts of that Commonwealth would treat the shareholders of a Massachusetts business trust the same as they would the shareholders of a Massachusetts business corporation in enforcing conditions precedent to the institution of a shareholders' derivative action. There is no question that the shareholders of a Massachusetts corporation are required to make a demand on the corporate directors prior to bringing a derivative action. . . . We conclude that a parallel rule would be applied by the Massachusetts courts to a business trust. . . .

Order affirmed . . .

———

NOTES

(1) Hemphill v. Orloff, 277 U.S. 537 (1928). Action on a promissory note that had been executed in Michigan and made payable to the Commercial Investment Trust. The Supreme Court upheld the Michigan courts' ruling that the Trust, which had been organized in Massachusetts, was a foreign corporation within the meaning of the Michigan statutes providing that a foreign corporation could not make a valid contract in Michigan unless it had previously obtained a certificate of authority to do business in that state. The Trust had not obtained such a certificate and hence the judgment was for the defendant. "Clothed with the ordinary functions and attributes of a corporation, [the Trust] is subject to similar treatment . . . ."

(2) For discussion of the situations where liability imposed by the state of organization of a business trust will be recognized or rejected in other states, see Comment, Limited Liability of Shareholders in Real Estate Investment Trusts and the Conflict of Laws, 50 Calif.L.Rev. 696 (1962).

(3) What law determines the legal power of an unincorporated association to engage in a particular activity? For material dealing with the analogous problem of the powers of a foreign corporation, see pp. 980–990, infra.

(4) Should the same law be used to govern all of the following problems: (a) the capacity of an association to take legal or equitable title to property; (b) the liabilities of the members of an association to third parties; (c) the liabilities of the members of an association inter se; (d) the liabilities of the members of an association to an agent of the association?

(5) On the power of a state to impose upon foreign partnerships that wish to do business in its territory essentially the same qualification requirements that are imposed upon foreign corporations, see Note, 52 Corn.L.Q. 157 (1966).

Chapter 15

CORPORATIONS

Introductory Note

This chapter deals principally with the questions which arise when a corporation acts through agents in a state other than the one in which it was incorporated. This is but one segment of a far broader problem; namely, what are the various methods by which a corporation can extend its activities into another state or nation? It may be helpful at this point to list briefly some of these methods.

To put a concrete case, let us suppose that a corporation, incorporated in X, a state of the United States, wishes to extend its market into a sister state, Y, and seeks legal advice as to how to proceed. There are four principal methods which the lawyer would consider. The first is that the corporation remain as it is and sell only for cash against shipping documents f.o.b. its own plant or port. The second is for the corporation actively to solicit would-be customers in Y, but only by mail or by some other advertising medium, and then fill orders received from them by freight or parcel post. The third possibility is for the corporation to do business in state Y through a subsidiary corporation, incorporated either in Y or elsewhere. By this procedure, the subsidiary would be subject to the control of state Y, but the parent corporation itself might escape entanglement either with the Y law or the Y courts [1] and also might avoid being held responsible for any liabilities which the subsidiary might incur. The last method—the one with which we are here concerned—is for the corporation to enter state Y itself.

The needs of the individual case will, of course, determine which of these four methods should be selected. Much will depend upon the type of activity which the corporation wishes to pursue in state Y. An isolated business transaction, for example, would almost certainly be carried out by the corporation itself, while extensive manufacturing operations might well most feasibly be conducted by a subsidiary. The applicable provisions of X and Y law, including those relating to taxation, would be of crucial importance.

What has been said above with respect to the interstate area is also generally true of the international. By and large, the same

---

1. The activities of the subsidiary in state Y might be held to subject the parent both to Y law and to the jurisdiction of the Y courts if either the parent had acted in disregard of the subsidiary's separate corporate existence or the subsidiary were found to be an agent of the parent. See pp. 127–129, supra.

choice of procedures is available to a corporation which wishes to do business in foreign nations. But a variety of reasons will lead in a given case to the choice of a different procedure. Sometimes, for example, the law of the nation involved may not permit the activity in question to be conducted by foreign corporations; here, of course, the creation of a subsidiary incorporated under that nation's law is mandatory. The danger of discriminatory legislation or of unfair treatment at the hands of a foreign court may make an American corporation loathe to subject its American assets to possible liability for its operations conducted abroad; this fact also makes desirable the insulation provided by the subsidiary device. The same is true in the case of those nations which do not permit foreign corporations to do business within their borders except upon payment of a registration fee based upon the corporation's entire capitalization or upon minute disclosures relating to the details of the corporation's business.

One obvious word of warning should be added at this point. Corporation law is by no means uniform among the nations of the world, and frequently the law of a particular nation will differ markedly in this regard from that prevailing in this country. And, to make matters worse, sometimes the foreign law will contain a concept (e.g., doing business) familiar to American lawyers but used in quite a different sense. The moral is clear: the legal adviser to a corporation which conducts, or is contemplating conducting, even isolated transactions in foreign nations must take pains to know, and to understand, the law of the nations involved.

SECTION 1.   CORPORATE PERSONALITY AND CONFLICT OF LAWS

"The proper function of a juristic theory is to make for certainty and foreseeability of judicial decision, for simplicity and harmony of legal technique. A legal theory approaches perfection according as it achieves these results and yet steers as close as may be to the dominant conceptions of policy and public interest."[1] The purpose of this section is: first, to set forth the classic theory of American law relating to foreign corporations; second, to ascertain whether this theory is in accord with the results reached by the actual decisions; and third, to determine whether the theory is in accord with modern "conceptions of policy and public interest."

---

1. Henderson, The Position of Foreign Corporations in American Constitutional Law 164 (1918).

A. THE BASIC LEGAL THEORY AND PRINCIPLES

American legal theory on the subject of foreign corporations was based largely upon four principles embodied in Chief Justice Taney's opinion in Bank of Augusta v. Earle, 13 Pet. (38 U.S.) 519 (1839).

They are:

(1) A corporation, being a creature of law, cannot exist outside the boundaries of the state of incorporation.

(2) Being a creature of law, a corporation can nowhere exercise powers not granted it either by its charter or by the general laws of the state of incorporation.

(3) A state is under no obligation to adhere to the doctrine of comity and hence has the power not only to refuse recognition to the foreign corporation but also to prevent the corporation from acting within its territory.

This principle was reaffirmed by the Supreme Court in Paul v. Virginia, 8 Wall. 168 (1868), where Justice Field, in a frequently quoted extract, stated: " . . . Having no absolute right of recognition in other States, but depending for such recognition and the enforcement of its contracts upon their assent, it follows, as a matter of course, that such assent may be granted upon such terms and conditions as those States may think proper to impose. They may exclude the foreign corporation entirely; they may restrict its business to particular localities, or they may exact such security for the performance of its contracts with their citizens as in their judgment will best promote the public interest. The whole matter rests in their discretion."

(4) The fourth principle, largely complementary of the third, is that a state is under no obligation to accord a foreign corporation the privileges which are enjoyed by its individual citizens.

In Paul v. Virginia, the Supreme Court held that a corporation is not a "citizen" within the meaning of the privileges and immunities clause (Art. IV, § 2) and refused to look through the corporation to the stockholders, because " . . . the privileges and immunities secured to citizens of each State in the several States, by the provision in question, are those privileges and immunities which are common to the citizens in the latter States under their constitution and laws by virtue of their being citizens. Special privileges enjoyed by citizens in their own States are not secured in other States by this provision. . . . Now a grant of corporate existence is a grant of special privileges to the corporators, enabling them to act for certain designated purposes as a single individual, and exempting them (unless otherwise specially provided) from individual liability. . . ."

"If the right asserted of the foreign corporation, when composed of citizens of one State, to transact business in other States were even restricted to such business as corporations of those States were authorized to transact, it would still follow that those States would be unable to limit the number of corporations doing business therein. They could not charter a company for any purpose, however restricted, without at once opening the door to a flood of corporations from other States to engage in the same pursuits. They could not repel an intruding corporation, except on the condition of refusing incorporation for a similar purpose to their own citizens; and yet it might be of the highest public interest that the number of corporations in the State should be limited; that they should be required to give publicity to their transactions; to submit their affairs to proper examination; to be subject to forfeiture of their corporate rights in case of mismanagement, and that their officers should be held to a strict accountability for the manner in which the business of the corporations is managed, and be liable to summary removal."

B.　THE BASIC PRINCIPLES IN THE LIGHT OF THE CASES

Do the conclusions reached by these four principles follow logically from the stated premises and do these principles adequately explain the results reached by the actual decisions? Consider the following:

1.　In the course of his opinion in Bank of Augusta v. Earle, Chief Justice Taney stated that ". . . it has been decided in many of the state courts, we believe in all of them where the question has arisen, that a corporation of one state may sue in the courts of another." Can these decisions be reconciled with the principle that a corporation has "no existence" outside of the state of incorporation? Is consistency attained by the Chief Justice's suggestion that a corporation can act through agents in other states? How can there be an agent in a state which does not recognize the existence of the principal?

Can this principle of "non-existence" be squared with the present rule that a corporation subjects itself to the judicial jursidiction of a foreign state by "doing business" within the latter's territory or, as stated by the Supreme Court in International Shoe Co. v. State of Washington, p. 66, supra, when the corporation's contacts with the forum "make it reasonable, in the context of our federal system of government, to require the corporation to defend the particular suit which is brought there"?

Does it follow that because a corporation is "a creature of law," it cannot exist outside the state of incorporation? Does the fact that corporations owe their legal existence to the laws of the incorporating state adequately serve to distinguish them from individuals for the purpose at hand?   The problem of legal personality extends throughout the field of conflict laws.   An individual's "legal personality"—i.e., his particular bundle of rights, duties, privileges and powers—is the creation of law.   As such, would it not follow that if a New York corporation has no existence in other states, neither would a man and woman who were legally married in New York be considered married elsewhere because their marriage status (like the status of incorporation) is a creation of New York law which is without force in other states?

The problem of legal personality has caused the courts least trouble in the case of individuals, presumably, at least in large part, because the need was always apparent of recognizing rights and duties acquired by them under the law of other states.   With respect to corporations, a similar need became apparent as soon as significant numbers of them began to spread their activities through two or more states.   As a result, the courts have tended more and more to by-pass questions of corporate personality and to concentrate instead upon practical problems.   In other areas, particularly in the case of foreign administrators, executors and receivers, the difficulties posed by the concept of legal personality have not yet been overcome.   See pp. 925–931, supra.

2.   The validity of the second principle should be considered in the light of the material contained in Section 3(A), infra.   If the first principle is incorrect, must not the same also be true of the second principle?

Since an individual's rights and powers are as much "creations of law" as those of a corporation, it could as logically be contended that an individual can exercise no powers in a foreign state that were not granted by the state of his domicile.   Such, however, is not the law. See, for example, Milliken v. Pratt, p. 446, supra.

3.   The third principle—that a state has the absolute power to prevent foreign corporations from entering its territory—is frequently repeated in the opinions.   See, e. g., Wheeling Steel Corp. v. Glander, 337 U.S. 562, 571 (1949); Asbury Hospital v. Cass County, 326 U.S. 207, 211 (1945).   Nevertheless, it cannot be accepted without reservations.

The states had no desire to exclude foreign corporations altogether, but they did wish to regulate and place conditions upon the activities of such corporations within their borders.   As such, the third principle has been employed primarily as the basis for regulation rather than for outright exclusion.   The conditions commonly imposed upon foreign corporations as the price of entry within a state are briefly discussed at pp. 60–62, supra and in Section 2(A), of this Chapter, pp. 970–979, infra.[2]

It will be recalled that in Paul v. Virginia, Justice Field reasoned that, since a state has power to exclude a foreign corporation, it is privileged, as a matter of course, to impose any terms it may desire as the price of admission. This conclusion follows logically from the stated premise and has frequently been reiterated in later decisions. See, e.g., Doyle v. Continental Insurance Co., 94 U.S. 535 (1877); Security Mutual Life Insurance Co. v. Prewitt, 202 U.S. 246 (1906). The development of constitutional law, however, has placed limitations upon premise and conclusion alike.

The commerce clause provides one source of limitation. A state cannot forbid corporations from carrying on business in foreign or interstate commerce within its borders (Pensacola Telegraph Co. v. Western Union Telegraph Co., 96 U.S. 1 (1877)) and cannot attach conditions upon their entrance which amount to an undue burden on interstate commerce. Thus, for example, the states do not have unfettered power to tax such corporations or to make them amenable to suit in the local courts (Davis v. Farmers Co-op. Equity Co., p. 219, supra); nor can they place unreasonable conditions upon access by such corporations to the local courts. Eli Lilly & Co. v. Sav-on-Drugs, p. 972, infra; Sioux Remedy Co. v. Cope, p. 218, supra. On the other hand, reasonable taxation and reasonable regulation is permissible. International Shoe Co. v. State of Washington, p. 66, supra; Union Brokerage Co. v. Jensen, p. 977, infra.

Corporations are also "persons" within the due process and equal protection clauses of the Fourteenth Amendment. Thus, a state, once it has permitted a foreign corporation to enter its territory and acquire property therein, cannot subject the corporation to unduly burdensome legislation or discriminate against it unreasonably in favor of domestic corporations. WHYY, Inc. v. Borough of Glassboro, 393 U.S. 117 (1968); Wheeling Steel Corp. v. Glander, 337 U.S. 562 (1949).

The Supreme Court has also developed the doctrine of "unconstitutional conditions" which, in effect, prohibits the states from demanding the surrender of constitutional rights either as the price of admission or to avoid the penalty of expulsion. A state cannot, for example, require foreign corporations to refrain from invoking the jurisdiction of the federal courts. Terral v. Burke Construction Co.,

2. Sometimes the conditions imposed verge on total exclusion. See, for example, Railway Express Agency v. Virginia, 282 U.S. 440 (1931) where the Supreme Court upheld the constitutionality of an order of the Corporation Commission of Virginia denying the plaintiff, a Delaware corporation, a certificate of authority to do intrastate business in Virginia. This order was based upon a provision of the Virginia constitution which denied foreign corporations the privilege of carrying on a public service business intrastate. Here, in other words, the price of entry was actual reincorporation within the state.

257 U.S. 529 (1922). See French, Unconstitutional Conditions, 50 Geo.
L.J. 234 (1961).

Subject to these limitations, it is still true that a state can prohibit
a foreign corporation from doing business within its borders and can
exclude it once it has obtained admission. Asbury Hospital v. Cass
County, 326 U.S. 207 (1945).

4. A state, of course, need not accord to foreign corporations
privileges which under its law can be enjoyed only by its citizens in
their individual capacity. Situations of this sort, however, are unlikely to arise today. General incorporation laws are now common, and
these permit the formation of corporations to engage in a great variety of activities. Incorporation, in other words, is no longer a special
privilege as it was at the time of Bank of Augusta v. Earle.

Nevertheless, it is still firmly established that a corporation is not
a "citizen" within the meaning of the privileges and immunities
clauses of Article IV, Sec. 2 of the Constitution and of the Fourteenth
Amendment. Asbury Hospital v. Cass County, 326 U.S. 207 (1945).
Apart from the doctrine of Blake v. McClung, p. 933, supra, what is
the precise effect of this rule? Is the rule necessary to permit the
states to exercise adequate control over foreign corporations within
their borders? Note in this regard the control that the states may
constitutionally exercise over individuals, partnerships and unincorporated associations which transact business or do certain acts within
their borders. Hess v. Pawloski, p. 62, supra; Doherty & Co. v.
Goodman, p. 62, supra. Yet individuals and partnerships, at least,
are included within the protection of the privileges and immunities
clauses. Flexner v. Farson, p. 62, supra.

Now that the privilege of incorporation is considered no more special or peculiar than that of forming a partnership, is there any reason why corporations should receive less constitutional protection
than partnerships?

NOTES

(1) What law determines whether a given association is a corporation for
the purpose at hand? In Liverpool & L. Life & Fire Insurance Co. v. Massachusetts, 10 Wall. (77 U.S.) 566 (1870), the Supreme Court affirmed a determination by the Massachusetts courts that a joint-stock association, formed
under a British statute which expressly declared an intention not to incorporate, was properly taxed as a corporation under a Massachusetts tax statute.

See also Greenspun v. Lindley, p. 959, supra.

(2) State v. United Royalty Co., 188 Kan. 443, 363 P.2d 397 (1961), involved a "Massachusetts trust," organized in Oklahoma and doing business
in Kansas. As a trust, United Royalty was unincorporated, but its organization and powers were very similar to those of a corporation. In a suit in quo
warranto, the Kansas Supreme Court held that the trust was in effect an
unlicensed forign corporation, and was subject to penalties for doing corporate type business without a permit. The court enjoined United Royalty

from doing any business in Kansas until it had complied with the Kansas corporation laws. See Note, Limited Liability of Shareholders in Real Estate and Investment Trusts, and the Conflict of Laws, 50 Calif.L.Rev. 696 (1962).

(3) For discussions of the history of the corporation and the development of the theories of corporate personality, see Henn, Law of Corporations 11–25, 107–130 (2d ed. 1970).

(4) On the subject of unconstitutional conditions, see Hale, Unconstitutional Conditions and Constitutional Rights, 35 Colum.L.Rev. 321 (1935); Note, "Doing Business": Defining State Control of Foreign Corporations, 32 Vand.L.Rev. 1105 (1979).

C. THE PUBLIC ATTITUDE TOWARDS CORPORATIONS: PAST AND PRESENT

The reason for the inconsistency between legal theory and actual decisions may be found in the following passages:

HENDERSON, POSITION OF FOREIGN CORPORATIONS IN AMERICAN CONSTITUTIONAL LAW 19–21, 66–67 (1918). The identification of incorporation with the grant of special and exclusive privileges or monopolies, and the fear that the corporation would infringe on the "natural rights" of citizens, was the chief source of early opposition to corporations. . . . Among persons who thus identified incorporation with monopoly and exclusive franchise the law of foreign corporations must have been most simple. It hardly needed argument that one sovereign could not give a monopoly in the territory of another sovereign. And as long as these corporate monopolies were looked upon with such a jealous eye—the power rigidly confined to what the charter expressed, and its language strictly construed against them—international comity could hardly expect the courts of the foreign sovereign to admit them without express legislative mandate. . . .

. . . We have seen how deeply ingrained in the history of American corporation law was this conception, how Jefferson identified incorporation with the grant of patents and copyrights, how Marshall regarded the exercise of every corporate franchise as a "restriction of individual rights," how a corporation was denounced as a "monopoly on the great charter of mankind." This conception dominated the corporation law of the eighteenth and early nineteenth centuries, determined its phraseology and shaped its definitions. It is not surprising that judges who learnt their law in the period in which this theory was in accord with the facts, should carry over its terminology and conceptions into an era in which the facts had changed. . . . To corporations in general, even at that time [of Paul v. Virginia], the language of the court was inapplicable, for the era of freedom of incorporation had already definitely arrived.

NOTES

(1) A corporation is often said to have its domicile in the state of incorporation. Bergner & Engel Brewing Co. v. Dreyfus, p. 23, supra. Can the concept of domicile, developed in the law of individuals and based on the idea of home, appropriately be applied to corporations? Consider what is said in Section 11 of the Restatement, Second, Conflict of Laws:

l. . . . No useful purpose is served by assigning a domicil to a corporation. Most of the uses . . . which the concept of domicil serves for individuals . . . are inapplicable to corporations, which do not, for example, vote, marry, become divorced, beget or bear children and bequeath property. Certain problems, such as judicial jurisdiction and the power to tax and to regulate, are common both to individuals and corporations. But unlike an individual, a corporation has a state of incorporation. This state may tax the corporation, exercise judicial jurisdiction over it and regulate its corporate activities. It is both inaccurate and unnecessary to explain the existence of these powers on the ground that the corporation has its domicil in the state of incorporation. . . .*

(2) A corporation is generally said to be a national of the state of incorporation regardless of the nationality of its stockholders. Practical exigencies, particularly those arising in times of war, may demand a departure from the ordinary rule and on occasion the courts are specifically directed by statute to look through the corporation to the individual stockholder. See Corcoran, The Trading with the Enemy Act and the Controlled Canadian Corporation, 14 McGill L.J. 174 (1968). On corporate nationality in other legal systems, see The 'Nationality' of International Corporations under Civil Law and Treaty, 74 Harv.L.Rev. 1429 (1961).

(3) For purposes of diversity of citizenship, a corporation is deemed a citizen both of the state of incorporation and of the state where it has its principal place of business, 28 U.S.C.A. § 1332(c).

SECTION 2.   CORPORATE ACTIVITY

A.   "DOING BUSINESS" AND QUALIFICATION STATUTES

The term "doing business" is found in three general types of statutes. The first type is directed to the amenability of foreign corporations to service of process in the state, on the basis of their "doing business" in the state.[1] The second type of statute is concerned with the taxing of foreign corporations for the privilege of "doing business" in the state. The third type involves statutes which declare

---

* Quoted with the permission of the copyright owner, The American Law Institute.

1. See pp. 60–62, supra.

that a foreign corporation which desires to carry on activities constituting "doing business" in the state must "qualify," that is, comply with certain prerequsites such as the payment of a fee, the submission of information on the organization and the financial condition of the corporation, and the appointment of an agent for the service of a process. The usual penalty imposed for failure to comply with a qualification statute is to deny the corporation the right to bring suit in the state courts. Another penalty frequently imposed is a fine on the corporation, and sometimes upon its officers, directors and agents as well. A few statutes make the officers and directors individually liable on corporate obligations incurred in the state during the period in which the corporation was doing business there without having qualified or declare void contracts made by the corporation in the state during the period of noncompliance. See Henn, Law of Corporations 166–170 (2d ed. 1970).

Thus, the term "doing business" is used in three distinct situations. But "doing business" for one purpose may not satisfy the requirements of "doing business" for another purpose.

"The least degree [of doing business] is that which will permit service of process in a suit against a foreign corporation. . . . A higher degree is necessary to subject such a corporation to a tax on its activity, namely continued efforts in the pursuit of profit and gain, and such activities as are essential to these purposes. A still higher degree is the standard for the application of statutes requiring qualification in the state . . ." [2]

NOTES

(1) The Model Business Corporation Act provides in § 106 (1979):

. . . Without excluding other activities which may not constitute transacting business in this State, a foreign corporation shall not be considered to be transacting business in this State [in the qualification sense] by reason of carrying on in this State any one or more of the following activities:

(a) Maintaining or defending any action or suit or any administrative or arbitration proceeding, or effecting the settlement thereof or the settlement of claims or disputes.

(b) Holding meetings of the directors or shareholders or carrying on other activities concerning its internal affairs.

(c) Maintaining bank accounts.

(d) Maintaining offices or agencies for the transfer, exchange and registration of its securities, or appointing and maintaining trustees or depositaries with relation to its securities.

(e) Effecting sales through independent contractors.

2. Isaacs, An Analysis of Doing Business, 25 Colum.L.Rev. 1018, 1024 (1925). To the same general effect, see Huntington, "Doing Business" in Utah, 4 Utah L.Rev. 518 (1955).

(f) Soliciting or procuring orders, whether by mail or through employees or agents or otherwise, where such orders require acceptance without this State before becoming binding contracts.

(g) Creating as borrower or lender, or acquiring indebtedness or mortgages or other security interests in real or personal property.

(h) Securing or collecting debts or enforcing any rights in property securing the same.

(i) Transacting any business in interstate commerce.

(j) Conducting an isolated transaction completed within a period of thirty days and not in the course of a number of repeated transactions of like nature.

See also Restatement, Second, Conflict of Laws § 311.

(2) Suppose that on the facts of International Shoe Co. v. State of Washington, p. 66, supra, a Washington retailer had failed to pay for a consignment of shoes. Could the International Shoe Co. have maintained an action in a Washington court to recover the price, assuming that (a) the company had not qualified to do business in that state and (b) the Washington courts were closed by statute to foreign corporations which did business there without having so qualified?

(3) For a detailed discussion of the various statutory penalties for failure to qualify, see Note, Sanctions for Failure to Comply with Corporate Qualification Statutes: An Evaluation, 63 Colum.L.Rev. 117 (1963).

(4) See Okilski, Foreign Corporations: What Constitutes "Doing Business" under New York's Qualification Statute?, 44 Ford.L.Rev. 1042 (1976).

ELI LILLY & CO. v. SAV–ON–DRUGS, INC.

Supreme Court of the United States, 1960.
366 U.S. 276, 81 S.Ct. 1316, 6 L.Ed.2d 288.

Mr. Justice Black delivered the opinion of the Court.

The appellant Eli Lilly and Company, an Indiana corporation dealing in pharmaceutical products, brought this action in a New Jersey state court to enjoin the appellee Sav-On-Drugs, Inc., a New Jersey corporation, from selling Lilly's products in New Jersey at prices lower than those fixed in minimum retail price contracts into which Lilly had entered with a number of New Jersey drug retailers. . . . Sav-On moved to dismiss this complaint under a New Jersey statute that denies a foreign corporation transacting business in the State the right to bring any action in New Jersey upon any contract made there unless and until it files with the New Jersey Secretary of State a copy of its charter together with a limited amount of information about its operations [1] and obtains from him a certificate authorizing it to do business in the State.

---

1. The information required is: (1) the amount of the corporation's authorized capital stock; (2) the amount of stock actually issued by the corporation; (3) the character of the business which the corporation intends to transact in New Jersey; (4) the principal office of the corporation in New Jersey; and (5) the name

Lilly opposed the motion to dismiss, urging that its business in New Jersey was entirely in interstate commerce and arguing, upon that ground, that the attempt to require it to file the necessary information and obtain a certificate for its New Jersey business was forbidden by the Commerce Clause of the Federal Constitution. . . . the trial court . . . granted Sav-On's motion to dismiss . . . The State Supreme Court . . . affirmed . . .

The record shows that the New Jersey trade in Lilly's pharmaceutical products is carried on through both interstate and intrastate channels. Lilly manufactures these products and sells them in interstate commerce to certain selected New Jersey wholesalers. These wholesalers then sell the products in intrastate commerce to New Jersey hospitals, physicians and retail drug stores, and these retail stores in turn sell them, again in intrastate commerce, to the general public. It is well established that New Jersey cannot require Lilly to get a certificate of authority to do business in the State if its participation in this trade is limited to its wholly interstate sales to New Jersey wholesalers. Under the authority of the so-called "drummer" cases . . . Lilly is free to send salesmen into New Jersey to promote this interstate trade without interference from regulations imposed by the State. On the other hand, it is equally well settled that if Lilly is engaged in intrastate as well as interstate aspects of the New Jersey drug business, the State can require it to get a certificate of authority to do business. In such a situation, Lilly could not escape state regulation merely because it is also engaged in interstate commerce. . . .

We agree with the trial court that "[t]o hold . . . that plaintiff [Lilly] is not doing business in New Jersey is to completely ignore reality." Eighteen "detailmen," working out of a big office in Newark, New Jersey, with Lilly's name on the door and in the lobby of the building, and with Lilly's district manager and secretary in charge, have been regularly engaged in work for Lilly which relates directly to the intrastate aspects of the sale of Lilly's products. These eighteen "detailmen" have been traveling throughout the State of New Jersey promoting the sales of Lilly's products, not to the wholesalers, Lilly's interstate customers, but to the physicians, hospitals and retailers who buy those products in intrastate commerce from the wholesalers. To this end, they have provided these hospitals, physicians and retailers with up-to-date knowledge of Lilly's products and with free advertising and promotional material designed to encourage the general public to make more intrastate purchases of Lilly's products. And they sometimes even directly participate in the intrastate sales themselves by transmitting orders from the hospitals, physicians and drugstores they service to the New Jersey wholesalers. . . .

and place of abode of an agent upon whom process against the corporation may be served. N.J.Rev.Stat. 14:15–3. [Footnote by the Court.]

Lilly also contends that even if it is engaged in intrastate commerce in New Jersey and can by virtue of that fact be required to get a license to do business in that State, New Jersey cannot properly deny it access to the courts in this case because the suit is one arising out of the interstate aspects of its business. . . . We do not think that . . . the present suit is . . . of that kind. Here, Lilly is suing upon a contract entirely separable from any particular interstate sale . . .

Affirmed.

MR. JUSTICE HARLAN, concurring. . . .

It is clear that sending "drummers" into New Jersey seeking customers to whom Lilly's goods may be sold and shipped . . . and suing in the state courts to enforce contracts for sales from an out-of-state store of goods . . . are both so intimately connected with Lilly's right to access to the local market, free of local controls, that they cannot be separated off as "local business" even if they are conducted wholly within New Jersey. However, I do not think that the systematic promotion of Lilly's products among local retailers and consumers who, as Lilly conducts its affairs, can only purchase them from a New Jersey wholesaler bears the same close relationship to the necessities of keeping the channels of interstate commerce state-unburdened. I believe that New Jersey can treat as "local business" such promotional activities, which are pointed at and result initially in local sales by Lilly's customers, and not in direct sales from its own out-of-state store of goods. . . .

. . . The only aspect of the present case that resembles the "drummer" cases is the fact that Lilly's promotion of local sales ultimately serves to increase its interstate sales. To treat this factor as bringing the present situation within the drummer cases would, in my view, be substantially to extend the reach of those cases. . . .

MR. JUSTICE DOUGLAS, with whom MR. JUSTICE FRANKFURTER, MR. JUSTICE WHITTAKER and MR. JUSTICE STEWART concur, dissenting. . . .

(1) If New Jersey sought to collect from appellant a tax apportioned to some local business activity which it carries on in *that State*, I would see no constitutional objection to it. . . .

(2) If appellant were sued in New Jersey, I think its connections with that State have been sufficient to make it subject to the jurisdiction of the state courts . . . at least as to suits which reveal a "substantial connection" with the State. . . .

(3) The present case falls in neither of those two categories. New Jersey demands that appellant obtain from it a certificate authorizing it to do business in the State, absent which she denies appellant access to her courts. The case thus presents the strikingly different issue—whether an interstate business can be subjected to a licensing system. . . .

In this case, appellant's employees within the State were engaged solely in the "drumming up" of appellant's interstate trade. They did this, not by direct solicitation of the interstate buyers, but by contacts with the customers of the buyers. . . . The Court finds these activities to be separable from appellant's interstate business; appellant is "inducing" sales, not "soliciting" them. It is not a distinction I can accept. . . .

ALLENBERG COTTON COMPANY, INC. v. PITTMAN, 419 U.S. 20 (1974): [Action for breach of a contract under which the defendant of Mississippi agreed to sell cotton to the plaintiff, a Tennessee corporation. Plaintiff had no office in Mississippi, did not own or operate a warehouse there and had no employees soliciting business in the state on a regular basis. It did employ an independent broker to identify farmers in the state who would be prepared to sell cotton to the plaintiff. The actual contracts were prepared by the plaintiff in Tennessee and signed by it there; they were then forwarded to the individual farmers in Mississippi for their signatures. The contracts provided that the farmer was to be paid for the cotton upon its delivery to a local warehouse in Mississippi. After delivery to the warehouse, the plaintiff would sort and classify the cotton preliminary to its shipment to mills in other states. The defendant failed to deliver the cotton he had contracted to sell the plaintiff and, when suit was brought against him in a Mississippi state court, claimed that the Mississippi courts were not open to the plaintiff since it was doing business in the state without having obtained the requisite certificate. The defendant was successful in having the suit dismissed by the state courts, but the Supreme Court reversed on the ground that the plaintiff was doing business in interstate commerce.]

MR. JUSTICE DOUGLAS delivered the opinion of the Court.

. . .

Appellant's arrangements with Pittman and the broker, Covington, are representative of a course of dealing with many farmers whose cotton, once sold to appellant, enters a long interstate pipeline. That pipeline ultimately terminates at mills across the country or indeed around the world, after a complex sorting and matching process designed to provide each mill with the particular grade of cotton which the mill is equipped to process.

Due to differences in soil, time of planting, harvesting, weather and the like, each bale of cotton, even though produced on the same farm, may have a different quality. Traders or merchants like appellant, with the assistance of the Department of Agriculture, must sample each bale and classify it according to grade, staple length, and color. Similar bales, whether from different farms or even from different collection points, are then grouped in multiples of 100 into "even-running lots" which are uniform as to all measurable characteristics. This grouping process typically takes place in card files in the merchant's office; when enough bales have been pooled to make an even-running lot, the entire lot can be targeted for a mill equipped to handle cotton of that particular quality, and the individual bales in the lot will then be shipped to the mill from their respective collection points. It is true that title often formally passes to the merchant upon delivery of the cotton at the warehouse, and that the cotton may rest at the warehouse pending completion of the classification and grouping processes; but as the description above indicates, these fleeting events are an integral first step in a vast system of distribution of cotton in interstate commerce. . . .

We deal here with a species of control over an intricate interstate marketing mechanism. . . . Delivery of the cotton to a warehouse, taken in isolation, is an intrastate transaction. But that delivery is also essential for the completion of the interstate transaction, for sorting and classification in the warehouse are essential before the precise interstate destination of the cotton, whether in this country or abroad, is determined. The determination of the precise market cannot indeed be made until the classification is made. The cotton in this Mississippi sale . . . though temporarily in a warehouse, was still in the stream in interstate commerce. . . .

Much reliance is placed on Eli Lilly & Co. v. Sav-On-Drugs, Inc. [p. 972, supra], for sustaining Mississippi's action. The case is not in point. There the Court found that the foreign corporation had an office and salesmen in New Jersey selling drugs intrastate. Since it was engaged in an intrastate business it could be required to obtain a license even though it also did an interstate business. . . .

In short, appellant's contacts with Mississippi do not exhibit the sort of localization or intrastate character which we have required in situations where a state seeks to require a foreign corporation to qualify to do business. Whether there were local tax incidents of those contacts which could be reached is a different question on which we express no opinion. Whether the course of dealing would subject appellant to suits in Mississippi is likewise a different question on which we express no view. We hold only that Mississippi's refusal to honor and enforce contracts made for interstate or foreign commerce is repugnant to the Commerce Clause. . . .

MR. JUSTICE REHNQUIST, dissenting.

. . . .

But even if I were able to agree with the Court that Allenberg's activities in Mississippi were purely "interstate," I do not believe that our cases, properly understood, prevent Mississippi from exacting qualification from a foreign corporation as a condition for use of the Mississippi courts. . . .

Mississippi's qualifications statute is concededly not discriminatory. Domestic corporations organized under her laws must submit themselves to her taxing jurisdiction, to service of process within the State, and to a number of other incidents of corporate existence which state law may impose. . . . qualifications statutes [aid] in the collection of state taxes by identifying foreign corporations operating within the State and in the protection of citizens within the State through insuring ready susceptibility to service of process of the corporation. The qualification statute also serves an important informational function making available to citizens of the State who may deal with the foreign corporation details of its financing and control. Although the result of Allenberg's failure to comply with the qualification statute is a drastic one, our decisions hold that the burden imposed on interstate commerce by such statutes is to be judged with reference to the measures required to comply with such legislation, and not to the sanctions imposed for violation of it. . . . The steps necessary in order to comply with this statute are not unreasonably burdensome.

SIOUX REMEDY CO. v. COPE

Supreme Court of the United States, 1914.
235 U.S. 197, 35 S.Ct. 57, 59 L.Ed. 193.

[The case appears, p. 218, supra.]

UNION BROKERAGE CO. v. JENSEN

Supreme Court of the United States, 1943.
322 U.S. 202, 64 S.Ct. 967, 88 L.Ed. 1227, 152 A.L.R. 1072.

[Plaintiff, a North Dakota corporation, which was licensed under federal statute to do business in Minnesota as a custom house broker, brought suit in the Minnesota courts against two former employees for breach of fiduciary obligations. Suit was dismissed by the state courts under a Minnesota statute which denied access to the local courts to all foreign corporations doing business in the state unless they had previously obtained a certificate of authority. The requirements for obtaining such a certificate included (1) the payment of a license fee of $50.00, (2) the filing of a statement containing the name of the corporation, the names and addresses of its directors and officers, the aggregate number of its authorized shares and kindred information and (3) the filing of a consent by the corporation to service of process upon it and appointment of an agent upon whom service of process could be made. Plaintiff appealed to the Supreme Court of the United States contending that, as applied to it, the Minnesota statute was unconstitutional since it placed an undue burden upon a federal instrumentality engaged in foreign commerce.]

MR. JUSTICE FRANKFURTER delivered the opinion of the Court.

. . . In a situation like the present, where an enterprise touches different and not common interests between Nation and State, our task is that of harmonizing these interests without sacrificing either. . . . The Tariff Act of 1930 . . . confers upon licensees certain privileges, and secures to the Federal Government by means of these licensing provisions a measure of control over those engaged in the customhouse brokerage business. But such circumscribed control by the Federal Government does not imply immunity from control by the State within the sphere of its special interests. . . . The state and federal regulations here applicable have their separate spheres of operation. . . . Minnesota is legitimately concerned with safeguarding the interests of its own people in business dealings with corporations not of its own chartering but who do business within its borders. . . . To safeguard responsibility in all such dealings . . . Minnesota has made the same exactions of Union as of every other foreign corporation engaged in similar transactions.

. . . we have not here a case of a foreign corporation merely coming into Minnesota to contribute to or to conclude a unitary interstate transaction . . . nor of the State's withholding "the right to sue even in a single instance until the corporation renders itself amenable to suit in all the courts of the state by whosoever chooses to sue it there." Sioux Remedy Co. v. Cope, 235 U.S. 197, 205. The business of Union, we have seen, is localized in Minnesota, and Minnesota, in the requirement before us, merely seeks to regularize its conduct. . . . In the absence of applicable federal regulation, a State may impose non-discriminatory regulations on those engaged in foreign commerce. . . .

The Commerce Clause . . . does not imply relief to those engaged in interstate or foreign commerce from the duty of paying an appropriate share for the maintenance of the various state governments. Nor does it preclude a State from giving needful protection to its citizens in the course of their contacts with businesses conducted by outsiders when the legislation by which this is accomplished is general in its scope, is not aimed at interstate or foreign commerce, and involves merely burdens incident to effective administration. . . .

Judgment affirmed.

NOTES

(1) A corporation which has failed to comply with a state qualification statute and is thereby barred from suing in the state courts on a contract made in the state is also precluded from bringing suit on the same claim in a local federal court. Woods v. Interstate Realty Co., 337 U.S. 535 (1949). It has been held, however, that the federal courts remain open to the corporation when the issue involves a federal question. Lisle Mills, Inc. v. Arkay Infants Wear, Inc., 90 F.Supp. 676 (E.D.N.Y.1950) (validity of a patent).

(2) Fed.R.Civ.P. 17(b) provides in part that " . . . The capacity of a corporation to sue or be sued shall be determined by the law under which it was organized . . .". For cases applying this rule to a dissolved foreign corporation, see Johnson v. Helicopter & Airplane Services Corp., 404 F.Supp. 726 (D.Md.1975); Stone v. Gibson Refrigerator Sales Corp., 366 F.Supp. 733 (E.D.Pa.1973).

———

KENTUCKY FINANCE CORP. v. PARAMOUNT AUTO EXCHANGE, 262 U.S. 544 (1923): [A Kentucky corporation brought an action of replevin in a Wisconsin State court against a Wisconsin corporation to recover an automobile which the plaintiff alleged had been stolen from it in Kentucky and turned over in Wisconsin to the defendant. Except for the present suit, the plaintiff had engaged in no business activities of any kind in Wisconsin. On the defendant's motion under a Wisconsin statute (applicable only to foreign corporations), the court ordered the plaintiff to send its secretary from Louisville, Kentucky, to Milwaukee, Wisconsin, for an examination before trial. Upon the plaintiff's refusal to comply with the order, the court made a further order that the complaint be dismissed. The plaintiff appealed to the state supreme court, contending that the statute under which both orders were made violated the equal protection clause of the Fourteenth Amendment. The Supreme Court of Wisconsin affirmed the lower court and the plaintiff appealed to the Supreme Court of the United States. Held, reversed.]

VAM DEVANTER, J. "The State court whose aid it [the plaintiff] invoked was one whose jurisdiction was general and adequate for the purpose. . . . when the plaintiff went into Wisconsin, as it did, for the obviously lawful purpose of repossessing itself, by a permissible action in her courts, of specific personal property unlawfully taken out of its possession elsewhere and fraudulently carried into that state, it was, in our opinion, within her jurisdiction for all the purposes of that undertaking. . . . And we think there is no tenable ground for regarding it as any less entitled to the equal protection of the laws in that state than an individual would have been in the same circumstances; . . . The discrimination was essentially arbitrary."

MR. JUSTICE BRANDEIS, with whom MR. JUSTICE HOLMES concurred, dissented. "To sustain the contention that the statute denies to plaintiff equal protection of the laws would seem to require the court to overrule Blake v. McClung [p. 933, supra] . . . and many other cases."

———

SECTION 3. THE LAW GOVERNING
CORPORATE ACTIVITIES *

It will be recalled that one of the principles announced by Chief Justice Taney in Bank of Augusta v. Earle, 13 Pet. (38 U.S.) 519 (1839) was that a corporation, being a creature of law, can nowhere exercise powers not granted it either by its charter or by the general laws of the state of incorporation. This principle, although frequently voiced in earlier opinions, has been either evaded or disregarded in practice. For an opinion relying on many of the potential escape devices, see E. C. Warren Co. v. W. B. Foshay, 57 F.2d 656 (8th Cir. 1932). On the other hand, it is accepted law that a corporation cannot rely on the law of the state of its incorporation to validate action not permitted by the law of the state in which the action is taken. So a corporation which is permitted to own land in the state of its incorporation cannot validly acquire land in a state where such acquisition is forbidden to corporations.

Few cases have dealt with the question whether a corporation can validly exercise in other states powers that have not been granted it by the state of its incorporation. This may be due to the fact that usually corporation laws and corporate charters are drafted broadly to permit corporations to engage in a wide variety of activities and rarely will a corporation seek to act in a manner not authorized by the law of the state of its incorporation.

RESTATEMENT, SECOND, CONFLICT OF LAWS: **

§ 301. Rights Against and Liabilities to Third Person

The rights and liabilities of a corporation with respect to a third person that arise from a corporate act of a sort that can likewise be done by an individual are determined by the same choice-of-law principles as are applicable to noncorporate parties.

NOTES

(1) Stone v. Southern Illinois & Mo. Bridge Co., 206 U.S. 267 (1907). Suit by the plaintiff bridge company, an Illinois corporation, to condemn a strip of Missouri land which was to form one of the approaches to a bridge which the plaintiff was about to construct over the Mississippi river. The Missouri courts found for the plaintiff and the defendant landowners appealed to the Supreme Court of the United States on the ground, among others, that the plaintiff did not have the power of eminent domain under the law of Illinois, the state of its incorporation, and that "a corporation of Illinois can only exercise in Missouri such powers as are conferred upon it by the State of its creation." Held for the plaintiff. The question involved ". . . the pow-

* Restatement, Second, Conflict of Laws §§ 301–313.

** Quoted with the permission of the copyright owner, The American Law Institute.

ers of corporations under the laws of Missouri . . . no federal right was taken from the [defendants] by the action complained of under the state laws as interpreted by the Supreme Court of the State of Missouri. . . ."

(2) Warren v. First Nat. Bank of Columbus, 149 Ill. 9, 38 N.E. 122 (1893). Suit to declare void as in contemplation of insolvency an assignment, executed in Ohio by a New York corporation, of a fund in Illinois. Such a transfer was prohibited by New York law. Held, upholding the validity of the transfer, "We are aware of no decision in this state, . . . which holds that the local statutes of another state, regulating the mode in which corporate powers shall be exercised, or determining the validity of corporate acts performed in the exercise of such powers, are to be given any extraterritorial effect."

(3) See generally Reese and Kaufman, The Law Governing Corporate Affairs: Choice of Law and the Impact of Full Faith and Credit, 58 Colum.L. Rev. 1118 (1958); Hawkland, Control of Foreign Corporate Activity by the State of Incorporation, 6 Miami L.Q. 41 (1951).

RESTATEMENT, SECOND, CONFLICT OF LAWS: *

§ 302.   Other Issues with Respect to Powers and Liabilities of a Corporation

(1) Issues involving the rights and liabilities of a corporation, other than those dealt with in § 301, are determined by the local law of the state which, with respect to the particular issue, has the most significant relationship to the occurrence and the parties under the principles stated in § 6.

(2) The local law of the state of incorporation will be applied to determine such issues, except in the unusual case where, with respect to the particular issue, some other state has a more significant relationship to the occurrence and the parties, in which event the local law of the other state will be applied.

Comment:

a.   *Scope of section.*   The rule of this Section is to be contrasted with that of § 301. The rule of this Section is concerned with issues involving matters that are peculiar to corporations and other associations, whereas the rule of § 301 is concerned with issues arising from corporate acts of a sort that can also be done by individuals. Many of the matters that fall within the scope of the rule of this Section involve the "internal affairs" of a corporation—that is the relations *inter se* of the corporation, its shareholders, directors, officers or agents . . . . Other such matters affect the interests of the corporation's creditors.

Matters falling within the scope of the rule of this Section and which involve primarily a corporation's relationship to its shareholders include steps taken in the course of the original incorporation, the election or appointment of directors and officers, the adoption of by-laws, the issuance of corporate shares, preemptive rights, the holding of directors' and shareholders' meetings, methods of voting including any requirement for cumulative voting, shareholders' rights to examine corporate records, charter and by-law amendments, mergers, consolidations and reorganizations and the reclassification of shares. Matters which may also affect the interests of the corporation's creditors include the issuance of bonds, the declaration and payment of dividends, loans by the corporation to directors, officers and shareholders, and the purchase and redemption by the corporation of outstanding shares of its own stock.

The rule of this Section will be applied in the absence of a local statute that is explicitly applicable to the situation at hand.   All States of the United States have statutes which regulate in various ways the affairs of foreign corporations within their territory.   Blue sky laws and statutes regulating the activities of public utilities are typical examples.   .   .   .

   e.   Rationale.   Application of the local law of the state of incorporation will usually be supported by those choice-of-law factors favoring the needs of the interstate and international systems, certainty, predictability and uniformity of result, protection of the justified expectations of the parties and ease in the application of the law to be applied.   Usually, application of this law will also be supported by the factor looking toward implementation of the relevant policies of the state with the dominant interest in the decision of the particular issue.

Uniform treatment of directors, officers and shareholders is an important objective which can only be attained by having the rights and liabilities of those persons with respect to the corporation governed by a single law.   .   .   .

In addition, many matters involving a corporation cannot practicably be determined differently in different states.   Examples of such matters, most of which have already been mentioned in Comment *a*, include steps taken in the course of the original incorporation, the election or appointment of directors and officers, the adoption of by-laws, the issuance of corporate shares   .   .   ., the holding of directors' and shareholders' meetings, methods of voting including any requirement for cumulative voting, the declaration and payment of dividends and other distributions, charter amendments, mergers, consolidations, and reorganizations, the reclassification of shares and the purchase and redemption by the corporation of outstanding shares of its own stock.

Matters such as these must be contrasted with the acts dealt with in § 301, which include, for example, the making of contracts, the commission of torts and the transfer of property.   There is no reason why corporate acts of the latter sort should not be governed by the local law of different states. There is no reason, for example, why an issue involving one corporate contract should not be governed by the local law of state X while an issue involving another corporation contract is governed by the local law of state Y. On the other hand, it would be impractical to have matters of the sort mentioned in the previous paragraph, which involve a corporation's organic structure or internal administration, governed by different laws. It would be impractical, for example, if an election of directors, an issuance of shares, a payment of dividends, a charter amendment, or a consolidation or reorganization were to be held valid in one state and invalid in another. Possible alternatives would be either to have matters of this sort governed by the local law of a particular state or else to hold applicable the local law of any state having a reasonable relationship to the corporation which imposed the strictest requirement. . . .

It should be added that certain issues which are peculiar to corporations or to other organizations do not affect matters of organic structure or internal administration and need not, as a practical matter, be governed by a single law. An example is the transfer of individual shares of a share issue. There is no practical reason, for example, why a corporation incorporated in state X should not comply with the requirements of state Y when it seeks to sell its shares in the latter state. Even as to such matters, however, the local law of the state of incorporation has usually been applied in the absence of an explicitly applicable local statute. . . .

The "Internal Affairs" Rule. At one time American courts took the position that they would not entertain actions involving the internal organization, management, capitalization, issuance of dividends, etc., of foreign corporations. This view has given way in more recent times to the thought that this is but one aspect of the forum non conveniens principle. See Chapter 4, p. 198, supra. "A court will exercise jurisdiction over an action involving the internal affairs of a foreign corporation unless it is an inappropriate or an inconvenient forum for the trial of the action." Restatement, Second, Conflict of Laws § 313.*

NOTES

(1) Hausman v. Buckley, 299 F.2d 696 (2d Cir. 1962), cert. denied 369 U.S. 885 (1962). This was a derivative action brought by minority stockholders on behalf of the Pantepec Oil Company against its officers and directors to recover damages for what was alleged to be the unlawful sale of the corporation's assets. The Pantepec Company was incorporated in Venezuela, its shareholders' meetings were held there, and it had substantial assets in that country. On the other hand, Pantepec was an American financed and Ameri-

* Quoted with the permission of the copyright owner, The American Law Institute.

can controlled corporation, and all the parties to the action were American citizens. The defendants moved to dismiss the complaint on the ground that under Venezuelan law actions on behalf of a corporation cannot be brought by minority stockholders but only by persons appointed at a stockholders' meeting. Held for the defendants. The law of the state of incorporation determines the right of a shareholder to object to action taken by the directors and officers in behalf of the corporation. Whether a derivative action can be brought is a substantive, rather than a procedural, question and the Venezuelan law is not contrary to the public policy of New York. Mansfield Hardwood Lumber Co. v. Johnson (Note 2, infra) was distinguished on the ground that Pantepec is not a "paper" corporation of Venezuela.

(2) Mansfield Hardwood Lumber Co. v. Johnson, 268 F.2d 317 (5th Cir. 1959). Suit in a federal court in Louisiana by minority shareholders against the officers and majority shareholders of a Delaware corporation complaining that the defendants had breached their fiduciary obligations to the plaintiffs in purchasing the plaintiffs' stock. The corporation did all of its business in Louisiana. Held for the plaintiffs. Under Delaware law there was no breach of fiduciary obligation, but the rule calling for application of the law of the state of incorporation should not be applied to determine the internal affairs of a corporation "where the only contact point with the incorporating state is the naked fact of incorporation and where all other contact points . . . are found" in the state of the forum.

(3) In European and other civil law countries, the basic law governing a corporation's internal affairs and the liability of its officers, directors and shareholders is the law of the corporation's "social seat" which can generally be described as the main office or executive headquarters of the corporation. Latty, Pseudo-Foreign Corporations, 65 Yale L.J. 137, 166–173 (1955); 2 Rabel, Conflict of Laws 33 et seq. (2d ed. 1958).

GERMAN–AMERICAN COFFEE CO. v. DIEHL

Court of Appeals of New York, 1915.
216 N.Y. 57, 109 N.E. 875.

[Action brought under a former New York statute by a New Jersey corporation against one of its directors to recover damages for the declaration of a dividend that was illegal under a New York statute. The dividend was also illegal under New Jersey law but under that law an action against the directors could only be brought by the stockholders. The plaintiff corporation has "maintained in New York its main business office; has held in New York the regular and most of the special meetings of its directors; and in New York has 'generally,' to follow the words of the complaint, 'managed, directed and conducted its business.'" Held that the statute was intended to apply to this situation and could constitutionally be so applied.]

CARDOZO, J. . . . We come, then, to the question of power. On that question the argument has taken a wide range, yet the decision, when confined to the facts of the case at hand, is brought within a narrow compass. As long as a foreign corporation keeps away

from this state, it is not for us to say what it may do or not do. But
when it comes into this state, and transacts its business here, it must
yield obedience to our laws . . .. This statute makes no attempt
to regulate foreign corporations while they keep within their domicile.
A prohibition which lasts while business within the state continues,
and may be escaped when business within the state is stopped, is, in
effect, a condition imposed on the right to do business, and nothing
more. . . .

———

Is the problem of local regulation of the affairs of a foreign corporation as simple as Judge Cardozo apparently conceived it to be in his
opinion in the *Diehl* case? Does the fact that a corporation does
some business in a state give that state power to regulate all aspects
of the corporation's internal affairs?

As seen from the preceding material in this Section, the courts
will not hesitate to apply their local law to a corporate act, such as
the making of a contract or the commission of a tort, which is of the
sort that can likewise be done by an individual. Restatement, Second, Conflict of Laws § 301. On the other hand, the courts will rarely, in the absence of an explicit statute, apply their local law to matters that are peculiar to corporations. Restatement, Second, Conflict
of Laws § 302.

Matters that are peculiar to corporations can be grouped into two
categories: those that practicably can be regulated differently in different states and those where this cannot be done. Examples of matters falling within the first category are individual sales of a corporation's stock and the power of shareholders to inspect the corporate
books. Many states have statutes, such as blue sky laws, that regulate matters falling within this category.

Examples of matters falling within the second category are the
declaration and payment of dividends, cumulative voting and the issuance of stock. Other matters falling within this category are set
forth in Comment *e* of § 302 of the Restatement, Second, which is set
forth above. Relatively few statutes are directed to foreign corporations with regard to matters in this second category. Presumably, a
state, which is not that of incorporation, can appropriately apply its
law to such matters if the foreign corporation involved does all, or
nearly all, of its business within the territory of that state and if all,
or nearly all, of the corporation's shareholders reside there. On the
other hand, there are undoubtedly constitutional limitations upon the
power of a state to apply its law in circumstances where its contacts
with the foreign corporation are of lesser extent.

———

WESTERN AIRLINES, INC. v. SOBIESKI

California District Court of Appeal, 1961.
191 Cal.App.2d 399, 12 Cal.Rptr. 719.

[Western Airlines, a Delaware corporation, had originally been formed for the purpose of acquiring the assets of a California corporation. Western did substantial business in California and in several other states. It did no business in Delaware. Residents of California held 30% of its stock; 55% of its passenger traffic started or ended in that state; 60% of its wages were paid there; and there were other substantial contacts.

The Board of Directors of Western wished to eliminate cumulative voting on its stock, and, in accordance with Delaware law, started to seek shareholders' approval when the California Commissioner of Corporations intervened. He ruled that this would be a "sale" of stock in California within the meaning of Section 25009(a) of the California Corporations Code which defines "sale" to include "any change in the rights, preferences, privileges, or restrictions on outstanding securities."

The Commissioner granted a permit to proceed with the shareholder vote on condition that the amendment of the articles should not be filed with the Secretary of State of Delaware until a hearing had been held in California on the "fairness" of the proposal, pursuant to the California Corporation Code. At that hearing, the Commissioner found that the plan was "unfair" and disallowed it. The Commissioner noted a strong public policy in favor of cumulative voting which is required for all California corporations. He also treated Western as a "pseudo-foreign corporation," saying that "the fiction of Delaware residence should yield to the totality of California contacts so as to require, in addition to compliance with the Delaware law, the approval of the California Corporations Commissioner as a condition to eliminating the right of cumulative voting by the shareholders."

The ruling of the Commissioner was upheld by the California District Court of Appeal. The court relied, among other things, on the fact that Western had originally been a California corporation and that, when it applied to the California Corporations Commissioner for permission to exchange its shares for those of its California predecessor, it represented to the Commissioner that the shareholders of the California corporation would not be hurt in any way by the exchange.

The Court also said:]

It would appear that the provisions of the Corporate Securities Act here before us are a proper exercise of legislative discretion in requiring that corporate dealings with residents of this state be authorized by the Commissioner of Corporations, particularly where such corporation does a substantial amount of business within the state, and the act is not violative of the constitutional clauses of equal protection, contract, due process and full faith and credit if such legislative enactments operate equally upon such foreign corporations and domestic corporations in this state. . . .

When we consider the complexity of present-day corporate structure and operation, and the far-flung area of corporate activities where transportation or nation-wide distribution of products may be involved, we are persuaded that the commissioner has this discretion. To hold otherwise, and to follow the argument of Western to its conclusion, would be to say that the commissioner might have the power in the first instance to require certain rights to be guaranteed to shareholders before he would permit the sale or issuance of a foreign corporation's stock in this state, but that immediately thereafter, by the device of amending the charter of such corporation in another state, the entire structure of that corporation, even to substantial changes in the rights of shareholders in California, might be legally effected.   Such a holding would enable a foreign corporation to destroy the rights which the State of California has deemed worthy of protection by the enactment of the Corporate Securities Act.

This position is not without support in other jurisdictions.   The mere fact that the last act here necessary to effectuate the change in the voting rights of the numerous California residents who are shareholders of Western will take place in Delaware does not of itself necessitate a finding that the commissioner for that reason was without jurisdiction in this matter. . . .

NOTES

(1) The problem of this case is discussed in Reese and Kaufman, The Law Governing Corporate Affairs: Choice of Law and the Impact of Full Faith and Credit, 58 Colum.L.Rev. 1118 (1958).

(2) UNIFORM COMMERCIAL CODE

Section 8–106.   Applicability.

The validity of a security and the rights and duties of the issuer with respect to registration of transfer are governed by the law (including the conflict of laws rules) of the jurisdiction of organization of the issuer.

(3) In State of Iowa ex rel. Weede v. Bechtel, 239 Iowa 1298, 31 N.W.2d 853 (1948), cert. denied 337 U.S. 918 (1949), Iowa law was held determinative of the validity of a stock issue made by a corporation incorporated in Delaware, but which had nearly all of its assets and transacted nearly all of its business in Iowa.   Should the result have been different if the corporation's business had been more equally divided between Delaware and Iowa?   What law should govern in a case where an X corporation does substantial business in state X and in several other states as well?   See Latty, Pseudo-Foreign Corporations, 65 Yale L.J. 137 (1955);   Annotation, 8 A.L.R.2d 1185 (1949).

(4) See generally Loss and Cowett, Blue Sky Law (1958), especially Chapter V, Conflict of Laws: The Blue Sky Laws in Interstate Contexts; Loss, The Conflict of Laws and the Blue Sky Laws, 71 Harv.L.Rev. 209 (1957).

California (in 1976)[1] and New York (in 1962)[2] enacted statutes which provide for application of their law in certain circumstances to foreign corporations with which they have a substantial relationship. Both statutes are expressly made inapplicable to corporations whose shares are listed on a national securities exchange. Hence, in the nature of things, they will rarely affect corporations that do a substantial multistate business. The California statute only becomes operative if two additional tests are met. "[T]he average of the property factor, the payroll factor and the sales factor" (all factors being a proportion of the corporation's California activity to its total activity) must exceed 50 percent during the corporation's "latest full income year." Also, "more than one-half of [the corporation's] outstanding voting securities [must be] held of record by persons having addresses" in California. Once these conditions are met, California law is made applicable to a variety of issues, including the election of directors, the liability and indemnification of directors and the payment of dividends. It seems apparent that California law would not have been applied if this statute had been in effect at the time that Western Airlines, Inc. v. Sobieski was decided.

The New York statute only becomes applicable if the shares of the foreign corporation are not listed on a national securities exchange and if at least half of the corporation's "business income for the preceding three fiscal years . . . was allocable to this state for franchise tax purposes under the tax law." In contrast to the California statute, the New York statute does not apply to shareholders' voting rights.

To date, only the California statute appears to have given rise to litigation. Its application to require cumulative voting by the shareholders of a Utah corporation was upheld in Wilson v. Louisiana-Pacific Resources, Inc., 138 Cal.App.2d 216, 187 Cal.Rptr. 852 (1982). The corporation in question "had initially no business connection with Utah and had maintained" its principal place of business in California since at least 1975. In addition, the meetings of its shareholders and directors were held in California and all of its employees and bank accounts were located in that state. Utah law provides for straight voting in an election of directors, but permits cumulative voting if the articles of incorporation so provide. The court held that application of the California statute was not prohibited by any provision of the Constitution, saying:

1. West's Ann.Cal.Corp.Code § 2115.   2. N.Y.Bus.Corp.Law § 1320.

. . .   California's present law requiring cumulative voting by shareholders continues in effect a policy which has existed in this state since the Constitution of 1879. . . .

Utah, on the other hand, has no interests which are offended by cumulative voting; and, whatever interest it might have in maintaining a *laissez faire* policy on that score would seem to be clearly outweighed by the interests of California, in which a majority of shareholders and the corporation's business activity is located. . . .

There is no suggestion, or evidence, that section 2115 was adopted for the purpose of deterring foreign corporations from doing business in this state; nor is there any direct evidence that it has had or will have such an effect. On the contrary, what evidence there is in the record on this point consists of testimony by appellant's president that he knew of no adverse effect on appellant's business which would be caused by cumulative voting.

Appellant argues that adverse consequences are predictable from "potentially conflicting claims of shareholders as to which state [law] governs" the method of voting by shareholders, and from the "transient nature of the applicability of the California statute." . . .

The potential for conflict and resulting uncertainty from California's statute is substantially minimized by the nature of the criteria specified in section 2115. A corporation can do a majority of its business in only one state at a time; and it can have a majority of its shareholders resident in only one state at a time. If a corporation meets those requirements in this state, no other state is in a position to regulate the method of voting by shareholders on the basis of the same or similar criteria. It might also be said that no other state could claim as great an interest in doing so. In any event, it does not appear that any other state has attempted to do so. If California's statute were replicated in all states, no conflict would result. We conclude that the potential for conflict is, on this record, speculative and without substance.

What appellant refers to as the "transient nature" of the statute's applicability, i.e., its application from year to year based upon the prior year's activity, could conceivably be a problem for a corporation whose business activity within the state fluctuated widely, but the "worst-case" scenario—that such a corporation might find it necessary to adopt cumulative voting as a means of assuring compliance on a continuing basis—does not appear to be so burdensome as to result in a significant restraint upon commerce among the states. . . .

NOTES

(1) Application of the California statute to require cumulative voting and the annual election of directors of a publicly owned Delaware corporation was held unconstitutional in Louart Corp. v. Arden-Mayfair, Inc., No. c192091 (Sup.Ct.Cal., Aug. 5, 1977) (an unreported opinion). The court noted that there was an irreconcilable conflict between California and Delaware

law and that the corporation might have the requisite contacts with California in some years but not in others. It concluded that application of the California statute would impose an improper burden on interstate commerce because of the uncertainty that would result from the corporation's being subject in different years to different state laws.

(2) The choice-of-law problems dealt with here would be mitigated if, pursuant to Professor Cary's suggestion, Congress were to prescribe minimum standards for corporations doing business in interstate commerce. Such a statute would permit corporations to incorporate in the state of their choosing, but would remove many of the present incentives for incorporating in states, such as Delaware, which have lenient corporation laws. See Cary, Federalism and Corporate Law: Reflections upon Delaware, 83 Yale L.J. 663 (1974).

(3) Articles on the general subject include Oldham, Regulating the Regulators: Limitations upon a State's Ability to Regulate Corporations with Multi-State Contacts, 57 Denver L.Rev. 345 (1980); Ratner and Schwartz, The Impact of Shaffer v. Heitner on the Substantive Law of Corporations, 45 Brooklyn L.Rev. 641 (1979); Halloran and Hammer, Section 2115 of the New California General Corporation Law, 23 U.C.L.A.L.Rev. 1282 (1976); Kaplan, Foreign Corporations and Local Corporate Policy, 21 Vand.L.Rev. 433 (1968); Coleman, Corporate Dividends and the Conflict of Laws, 63 Harv.L.Rev. 433 (1950).

EDGAR v. MITE CORP.

Supreme Court of the United States, 1982.
457 U.S. 624, 102 S.Ct. 2629, 73 L.Ed.2d 269.

Justice WHITE delivered . . . the opinion of the Court.
. . .

Appellee MITE Corporation and its wholly-owned subsidiary, MITE Holdings, Inc., are corporations organized under the laws of Delaware with their principal executive offices in Connecticut. Appellant James Edgar is the Secretary of State of Illinois and is charged with the administration and enforcement of the Illinois Act. Under the Illinois Act any takeover offer for the shares of a target company must be registered with the Secretary of State. Ill.Rev. Stat., ch. 121½, ¶ 137.54.A (1979). A target company is defined as a corporation or other issuer of securities of which shareholders located in Illinois own 10% of the class of equity securities subject to the offer, or for which any two of the following three conditions are met: the corporation has its principal executive office in Illinois, is organized under the laws of Illinois, or has at least 10% of its stated capital and paid-in surplus represented within the state. Id., at ¶ 137.52–10. An offer becomes registered 20 days after a registration statement is filed with the Secretary unless the Secretary calls a hearing. Id., at ¶ 137.54.E. The Secretary may call a hearing at any time during the 20-day waiting period to adjudicate the substantive fairness of the offer if he believes it is necessary to protect the shareholders of the target company, and a hearing must be held if requested by a majority of a target company's outside directors or by Illinois shareholders who own 10% of the class of securities subject to the offer. Id., at ¶ 137.57.A. If the Secretary does hold a hearing, he is directed by the statute to deny registration to a tender offer if he finds that it "fails to provide full and fair disclosure to the offerees of all material information concerning the take-over offer, or that the take-over offer is inequitable or would work or tend to work a fraud or deceit upon the offerees. . . ." Id., at ¶ 137.57.E.

On January 19, 1979, MITE initiated a cash tender offer for all outstanding shares of Chicago Rivet and Machine Co., a publicly held Illinois corporation, by filing a Schedule 14D–1 with the Securities and Exchange Commission in order to comply with the Williams Act.[2] . . . MITE did not comply with the Illinois Act, however, and commenced this litigation on the same day by filing an action in the United States District Court for the Northern District of Illinois. The complaint asked for a declaratory judgment that the Illinois Act was preempted by the Williams Act and violated the Commerce Clause. In addition, MITE sought a temporary restraining order and preliminary and permanent injunctions prohibiting the Illinois Secretary of State from enforcing the Illinois Act. . . .

[In the first part of his opinion, Justice White held that the Illinois Act was preempted by the Williams Act. This part of the opinion did not gain the support of a majority of the Court.]

The Illinois Act is . . . unconstitutional under the test of Pike v. Bruce Church, Inc., 397 U.S., at 142, 90 S.Ct., at 847, for even when a state statute regulates interstate commerce indirectly, the burden imposed on that commerce must not be excessive in relation to the local interests served by the statute. The most obvious burden the Illinois Act imposes on interstate commerce arises from the statute's previously-described nationwide reach which purports to give Illinois the power to determine whether a tender offer may proceed anywhere.

The effects of allowing the Illinois Secretary of State to block a nationwide tender offer are substantial. Shareholders are deprived of the opportunity to sell their shares at a premium. The reallocation of economic resources to their highest-valued use, a process which

2. The Williams Act, 82 Stat. 454, et seq., codified at 15 U.S.C. §§ 78m(d)–(e) and 78n(d)–(f), added new sections 13(d), 13(e) and 14(d)–(f) to the Securities Exchange Act of 1934. Section 14(d)(1) of the Securities Exchange Act requires an offeror seeking to acquire more than five percent of any class of equity security by means of a tender offer to first file a Schedule 14D–1 with the Securities and Exchange Commission. The Schedule requires disclosure of the source of funds used to purchase the target shares, past transactions with the target company, and other material financial information about the offeror. In addition, the offeror must disclose any antitrust or other legal problems which might result from the success of the offer. 17 CFR § 240.14d–100 (1981). Section 14(d)(1) requires the offeror to publish or send a statement of the relevant facts contained in the Schedule 14D–1 to the shareholders of the target company. . . .

can improve efficiency and competition, is hindered. The incentive the tender offer mechanism provides incumbent management to perform well so that stock prices remain high is reduced. . . .

Appellant claims the Illinois Act furthers two legitimate local interests. He argues that Illinois seeks to protect resident security holders and that the Act merely regulates the internal affairs of companies incorporated under Illinois law. We agree with the Court of Appeals that these asserted interests are insufficient to outweigh the burdens Illinois imposes on interstate commerce.

While protecting local investors is plainly a legitimate state objective, the state has no legitimate interest in protecting non-resident shareholders. Insofar as the Illinois law burdens out-of-state transactions, there is nothing to be weighed in the balance to sustain the law. . . .

We are also unconvinced that the Illinois Act substantially enhances the shareholders' position. The Illinois Act seeks to protect shareholders of a company subject to a tender offer by requiring disclosures regarding the offer, assuring that shareholders have adequate time to decide whether to tender their shares, and according shareholders withdrawal, proration and equal consideration rights. However, the Williams Act provides these same substantive protections . . . [T]he Court of Appeals . . . also was of the view that the possible benefits of the potential delays required by the Act may be outweighed by the increased risk that the tender offer will fail due to defensive tactics employed by incumbent management. We are unprepared to disagree with the Court of Appeals in these respects, and conclude that the protections the Illinois Act affords resident security holders are, for the most part, speculative.

Appellant also contends that Illinois has an interest in regulating the internal affairs of a corporation incorporated under its laws. The internal affairs doctrine is a conflict of laws principle which recognizes that only one state should have the authority to regulate a corporation's internal affairs—matters peculiar to the relationships among or between the corporation and its current officers, directors, and shareholders—because otherwise a corporation could be faced with conflicting demands. See Restatement (Second) of Conflict of Laws, § 302, Comment b at 307–308 (1971). That doctrine is of little use to the state in this context. Tender offers contemplate transfers of stock by stockholders to a third party and do not themselves implicate the internal affairs of the target company. . . . Furthermore, the proposed justification is somewhat incredible since the Illinois Act applies to tender offers for any corporation for which 10% of the outstanding shares are held by Illinois residents, . . . The Act thus applies to corporations that are not incorporated in Illinois and have their principal place of business in other states. Illinois has no interest in regulating the internal affairs of foreign corporations.

We conclude with the Court of Appeals that the Illinois Act imposes a substantial burden on interstate commerce which outweighs its putative local benefits. It is accordingly invalid under the Commerce Clause.

The judgment of the Court of Appeals is

Affirmed.

[The concurring opinions of Justices Powell, O'Connor and Stevens are omitted. Justices Marshall and Rehnquist dissented on the ground that the case was moot.]

NOTES

(1) Could not the rationale employed by Justice White in the MITE case be used as a basis for imposing constitutional limitations upon the power of a state to apply its law to affect the internal affairs of a foreign corporation?

(2) Some 36 states have recently enacted statutes regulating tender offers. Many of these statutes have been found unconstitutional by the federal courts either because they conflicted with the Supremacy Clause (on preemption grounds) or with the Commerce Clause. Coffee, Preview of United States Supreme Court Cases, October 1981 Term (No. 4, December 24, 1981).

(3) In Martin-Marietta Corp. v. Bendix Corp., 690 F.2d 558 (6th Cir. 1982), the court held the Michigan tender offer statute to be unconstitutional despite a previous ruling by a Michigan judge that, properly interpreted, the application of the statute was limited to Michigan shareholders. The court reasoned that, nevertheless, the statute "still impermissibly burdens interstate commerce. It prevents Michigan shareholders from participating in the nationwide tender offer . . . This is an indirect burden on interstate commerce in that it has the effect of defeating the tender offers of residents from other states where the tendered shares owned by Michigan residents are needed to provide sufficient tendered shares to satisfy the tender offer."

(4) For a suggestion that a state's tender offer statute can constitutionally be applied in situations where the target company has a majority of its contacts with the state, see Oldham, Regulating the Regulators: Limitations upon a State's Ability to Regulate Corporations with Multi-State Contacts, 57 Denver L.Rev. 345, 370–388 (1980).

*

INDEX

References are to Pages

995

MOTORISTS
Non-resident, jurisdiction over, 62–65, 121–127.

MOVABLES
See Property.

NATIONALITY
Compared with domicile, 12–13.
Jurisdiction of courts, 50–51.

NEGLIGENCE
  See also Contributory Negligence; Torts.
Comparative or contributory, 416–417, 480–481.

NEGOTIABILITY
See Bills and Notes.

NO FAULT, 567–572

NO–ACTION CLAUSE, 352–354

NON–RESIDENT
  See also Direct Action Against Insurer; Jurisdiction of Courts.
Local actions or effects as a basis of jurisdiction, 60–131.
Motorists, jurisdiction over, 62–65, 121–127.

NOTICE
Requisite for jurisdiction, 35–36, 173–182.

PARENT AND CHILD
  See also Infants.
Adoption, 864–867.
Custody of Children, 867–881.
Decree for support, 260–265, 882–889.
Legitimation, 862–864.

PAROL EVIDENCE RULE
See Procedure.

PARTNERSHIPS, 955–961
Jurisdiction over, 130–131.

PENAL LAWS, 384–388, 711–713
Enforcement of judgment based on, 301–305, 311–313.
Wrongful death statutes, 384–388.

PERFORMANCE
See Contracts.

PHYSICAL INJURY
See Torts.

POLYGAMY
See Marriage.

POWERS OF APPOINTMENT
Choice of law, rules as to, 788–793.

PRESENCE
As basis of jurisdiction of courts, 46–47, 148–157.

PRESUMPTIONS, 414–418

PRINCIPAL AND AGENT
See Agency.

PRIVILEGES AND IMMUNITIES
See Constitutional Law.

PROCEDURE
  See also Direct Action Against Insurer.
Administration of justice issue, 407–409.
Burden of proof, 414–418, 703–704.
Characterization, 329–334, 407–414, 441, 455–457.
Damages, 464–467, 704–706.
Discovery, 418–425.
Erie v. Tompkins, 681–691, 703–704.
Evidence, 418–425.
Federal and state law, 681–703, 720–733.
Federal rules of civil procedure, 682–683, 696–703.
Formalities, 460, 602–613.
Limitations, statute of, 425–434.
Parol evidence rule, 606–607.
Presumptions, 414–418.
Privilege, 418–425.
Reasons for using local law, 407–409.
Statute of frauds, 602–613.

PROCESS
Service of, see Jurisdiction of Courts.

PROOF
  See also Procedure.
Burden of proof, 414–418, 703–704.
Of facts, 414–418, 703–704.
Of laws, 399–406.

PROPERTY
  See also Intangibles; Land; Movables.
Characterization, 757–773.
Chattel mortgages, 777–788.
Conditional sales, 777–788.
Conveyances and contracts, land, 761–773.
Equitable conversion, 757–758.
Future interests and trusts, 788–798.
Intangibles, government seizure, 373–383.
  Jurisdiction of courts, 141–169.
Inter vivos transactions, movables, 776–788.
Interpretation and construction of documents, 798–801.
Jurisdiction of courts over things, 133–169.
Jurisdiction to tax, 66–72.
Marital property, 889–907.
Security transactions,
  Land, 626–628, 759–761.
  Movables, 777–788.

†